THE BROTHERS KARAMAZOV

THE CONSTANCE GARNETT TRANSLATION
REVISED BY RALPH E. MATLAW
BACKGROUNDS AND SOURCES
ESSAYS IN CRITICISM

A NORTON CRITICAL EDITION

FYODOR DOSTOEVSKY

THE BROTHERS KARAMAZOV

THE CONSTANCE GARNETT TRANSLATION
REVISED BY RALPH E. MATLAW
BACKGROUNDS AND SOURCES
ESSAYS IN CRITICISM

Edited by

RALPH E. MATLAW

LATE OF
UNIVERSITY OF CHICAGO

W · W · NORTON & COMPANY

New York · London

W. W. Norton & Company, Inc., 500 Fifth Avenue, New York, N.Y. 10110

Copright © 1976 by W. W. Norton & Company, Inc.

Library of Congress Cataloging in Publication Data

Dostoevskiĭ, Fedor Mikhaĭlovich, 1821–1881.
  The Brothers Karamazov.
  (A Norton critical edition)
  Translation of Brat'ĭa Karamazovy.
  Bibliograhy: p.
  I. Garnett, Constance Black, 1862–1946.
II. Matlaw, Ralph E.   III. Title.
PZ3.D742Br53   [PG3326]   891.7'3'3   75-37792

7 8 9 0

ISBN 0-393-04426-2
ISBN 0-393-09214-3 pbk.

Contents

Essays in Criticism

Preface

The Brothers Karamazov was written almost a hundred years ago. Some of its details are necessarily those of a different age, a different society, and a different culture. Nevertheless, it becomes accessible to the reader almost immediately if it can be presented in an accurate and readable version. The *Afterword* to the text discusses the revision of Mrs. Garnett's translation which performs this function and seeks to resolve many formidable problems that the complexity of the novel and the multiplicity of its styles ultimately make insurmountable.

The *Background* materials present some of the impulses toward the writing of the novel, in Dostoevsky's own experiences, in current events, and in reflections on the transformations of life and society at a particular epoch. Letters dealing with the novel are quoted extensively: they reflect the evolution of the novel, the development of its structure during the process of composition, and Dostoevsky's concern with projecting his vision adequately both in its main lines and in the minutest details of the text. They present a fascinating picture of an artist's involvement with his work, apart from their importance to a study of the novel itself. They also call attention to the extraordinary importance of purely literary problems in a novel that has all too frequently been used only as the basis for apocalyptic generalizations on existence, Dostoevsky, man, religion, and so on.

The *Essays in Criticism* run the gamut from such generalizations to concern with specific words. The first essay, one of the best chapters in Mochulsky's book on Dostoevsky—probably the best single volume of all the many that have dealt with Dostoevsky—is a splendid introduction to the novel. It is followed by a seminal essay on Dostoevsky's art and thought by Professor Tschižewskij, parts of which, concerned too extensively with Schiller for the purposes of this volume, have had to be omitted. They would have further emphasized Dostoevsky's extraordinary concern with the use of literature, the possibilities of characterization and deepening of portraits by the citation of other literary works, a technical innovation of Dostoevsky's which has not yet been sufficiently investigated, but which is at least in part suggested by the footnotes to the text itself. I have attempted to arrange the rest of the essays, regardless of approach, so that they might correspond to the progression of the novel, but this has not always been possible. Many approaches to the work are suggested: structural, thematic, theological, stylistic, mythological, psychoanalytic. Several views are given of the "Grand Inquisitor" episode, including one that quite properly seeks to reintegrate it into the novel rather than treat it as an independent text or basis for a sermon, as has been done by all too many commentators. It is, indeed, an advantage to have most of the interpretations urge a closer, more extensive, and more integrated look at the text. For by force of argument and literary skill Dostoevsky has made all too inviting the discussion of what Ivan Karamazov calls "the eternal questions" without reference to their novelistic context.

RALPH E. MATLAW

Post-script:

Since the publication of this volume in 1976, a detailed introduction and an extensive running commentary on the style, implications, and shades of meaning, keyed to the Norton edition, was written by Victor Terras, A *Karamazov Companion: Commentary on the Genesis, Language, and Style of Dostoevsky's Novel*, Madison, the University of Wisconsin Press, 1981. I have incorporated several of his emendations and corrections, and further identifications made possible by the appearance of the long awaited Russian Academy of Sciences edition and commentary of this novel in the *Complete Works* of Dostoevsky.

I would like to express my thanks and admiration for Professor Terras's excellent volume and to urge the reader to consult it for specific elaborations of problems (some of which are discussed in my *Afterword* [p. 736]), especially those of biblical overtones, slang, stylistic levels, and Dostoevsky's repetition of key words and concepts, particularly "devil" and "beauty," which I felt could not always be rendered in English by the same word. "Damnation!," "Damn it!" and "Hell!" involve the "devil," at least by implication. And that is the lot of the translator.

RALPH E. MATLAW

Thanksgiving, 1981

The Text of
The Brothers Karamazov

Pronunciation of the
Main Characters' Names

(Note: the second name is a patronymic—"son of" or "daughter of." In almost all patronymics Russians drop the syllable "ov" or "ev" in all but the most formal occasions. "*Fyodorovich*" would therefore normally sound "*Fyodorich*"; "*Ivanovna*," "*Ivanna*."

Karamazov, Fyodor Pavlovich
        Ivan Fyodorovich (Vanechka, Vanka)
        Dmitri Fyodorovich (Mitya, Mitenka)
        Alexey Fyodorovich (Alyosha)
Smerdyakov, Pavel Fyodorovich
Katerina Ivanovna Verkhovtsev (Katya)
Grushenka (Grusha, Agrafena Alexandrovna Svetlov)
Khokhlakov, Lisa (Lise—when given French pronounciation)
Rakitin, Mikhail, (Misha)
Zosima
Fetyukovich
Snegiryov, Ilyusha, (Ilyushechka)
Krasotkin, Kolya
Kalganov, Pyotr Fomich
Miusov, Pyotr Alexandrovich
Perkhotin, Pyotr Ilich

Skotoprigonevsk—the locale
Mokroe—location of the inn where Mitya carouses
Chermashnya—the town where Fyodor Pavlovich has land and a forest

Dedicated to
Anna Grigorievna Dostoevsky*

"*Verily, verily, I say unto you, except a corn of wheat fall into the ground and die, it abideth alone: but if it die, it bringeth forth much fruit.*"

John 12:24

* Dostoevsky's wife.

Contents of *The Brothers Karamazov*

EPILOGUE

From the Author

In beginning the life story of my hero, Alexey Fyodorovich Karamazov, I find myself in somewhat of a quandary. Namely, although I call Alexey Fyodorovich my hero, I myself know that he is by no means a great man, and hence I foresee such unavoidable questions as these: "What is so remarkable about your Alexey Fyodorovich, that you have chosen him as your hero? What has he accomplished? What is he known for, and by whom? Why should I, the reader, waste time learning the facts of his life?"

The last question is the most fateful, for to it I can only answer: "Perhaps you will see for yourself from the novel." Well, suppose you read the novel, and fail to see, and so do not agree that my Alexey Fyodorovich is remarkable? I say this because unhappily I anticipate it. For me he is remarkable, but I doubt strongly whether I shall succeed in proving this to the reader. The fact is, if you please, that he is a protagonist, but a vague and undefined protagonist. And, in truth, in times such as ours it would be strange to require clarity of people. One thing, I dare say, is fairly certain: this man is odd, even eccentric. But oddness and eccentricity interfere rather than help, especially when everyone is trying to put the particulars together and to find some sort of common meaning in the general confusion. In most cases the eccentric is a particularity, a separate element. Isn't that so?

Now, if you do not agree with this last thesis, and answer, "It isn't so," or "It isn't always so," then I, if you please, might become encouraged about the significance of my hero, Alexey Fyodorovich. For not only is an eccentric "not always" a particularity and a separate element, but, on the contrary, it happens sometimes that such a person, I dare say, carries within himself the very heart of the whole, and the rest of the men of his epoch have for some reason been temporarily torn from it, as if by a gust of wind . . .

Still, I should not have plunged into these quite uninteresting and confused explanations and should have begun quite simply, without introduction: "If they like it, they will read it"; but the trouble is that I have two novels and only one life story.[1] The main novel is the second—it is the action of my hero in our day, at the very present time. The first novel takes place thirteen years ago, and it is hardly even a novel, but only one moment in my hero's early youth. I cannot do without this first novel, because much in the second novel would be unintelligible without it. But in this way my original difficulty is rendered still more complicated: if I, that is, the biographer himself, find that even one novel might perhaps be

---

1. According to Dostoevsky's wife, he had planned to start writing the second part in 1882. It was to take place in the 1880s. Dmitri returns from prison, and Alyosha has lived through a complex drama with Lisa.

superfluous for such a modest and undefined hero, how ever can I appear with two, and how from my point of view can I justify such presumption?

Finding myself lost in the solution of these questions, I decide to bypass them with no solution at all. Of course, the astute reader has long since guessed that from the very first I was leading up to this, and was vexed with me for wasting fruitless words and precious time. To this, I shall answer explicitly: I was spending fruitless words and precious time, first, out of courtesy, and second, out of shrewdness: "Still," the reader might say, "he has forewarned us of something." Indeed, I am actually glad that my novel has of itself split into two narratives, "with essential unity of the whole": having become acquainted with the first tale, the reader will then decide for himself whether it is worth his while to attempt the second. Of course, one is not bound by anything—the book can be abandoned at the second page of the first tale, never to be opened again. But then, you know, there are those considerate readers who absolutely must read to the end, so as not to be mistaken in their impartial judgment; such, for example, are all the Russian critics. It is before this type of person that my heart somehow becomes lighter: despite all their careful exactness and conscientiousness, I nevertheless give them a perfectly legitimate pretext to abandon the tale at the novel's first episode. Well, there is the whole foreword. I completely agree that it is superfluous, but since it has already been written, let it stand.

And now to the matter at hand.

Part One

Book One

THE HISTORY OF A CERTAIN FAMILY

Chapter I

Fyodor Pavlovich Karamazov

Alexey Fyodorovich Karamazov was the third son of Fyodor Pavlovich Karamazov, a landowner well known in our district in his own day (and still remembered among us) owing to his tragic and obscure death, which happened exactly thirteen years ago, and which I shall describe in its proper place. For the present I will only say that this "landowner"—for so we used to call him, although he hardly lived on his own estate at all—was a strange type, yet one pretty frequently to be met with, a trashy and depraved type and, in addition, senseless. But he was one of those senseless persons who are very well capable of looking after their worldly affairs, and, apparently, after nothing else. Fyodor Pavlovich, for instance, began with next to nothing; his estate was of the smallest; he ran to dine at other men's tables, and fastened on them as a toady, yet at his death it appeared that he had a hundred thousand rubles[1] in hard cash. At the same time, he was all his life one of the most senseless madcaps in the whole district. I repeat, it was not stupidity—the majority of these foolish fellows are shrewd and intelligent enough—but just senselessness, and a peculiar and national form of it.

He was married twice, and had three sons, the eldest, Dmitri, by his first wife, and two, Ivan and Alexey, by his second. Fyodor Pavlovich's first wife, Adelaïda Ivanovna, belonged to a fairly rich and distinguished noble family, also landowners in our district, the Miüsovs. How it came to pass that an heiress, who was also a beauty, and moreover one of those vigorous, intelligent girls not at all uncommon in this generation, but sometimes also to be found in the last, could have married such an insignificant "puny fellow," as we all called him, I won't attempt to explain. I knew a young lady of the "romantic" generation before the last who after some years of an enigmatic passion for a gentleman, whom she might quite easily have married at any moment, invented insuperable obstacles to their union, and ended by throwing herself one stormy night into

---

1. The ruble was then worth about half a dollar.

2

a rather deep and rapid river from a high bank, almost a precipice, and so perished, entirely to satisfy her own caprice, and to be like Shakespeare's Ophelia. Indeed, if this precipice, a chosen and favorite spot of hers, had been less picturesque, if there had been a prosaic flat bank in its place, most likely the suicide would never have taken place. This is a fact, and probably there have been not a few similar instances in the last two or three generations of our Russian life. Adelaïda Ivanovna Miüsov's action was similarly, no doubt, an echo of foreign ideas,[2] and was also due to the irritation caused by lack of mental freedom. Perhaps she wanted to show feminine independence, to override class-distinctions and the despotism of her family and birth, and we must suppose a pliable imagination persuaded her for a brief moment that Fyodor Pavlovich, in spite of his parasitic position, was one of the bold and ironical spirits of that progressive epoch, though he was in fact an ill-natured buffoon and nothing more. What gave the marriage piquancy was that it was preceded by an elopement, and this greatly flattered Adelaïda Ivanovna. Fyodor Pavlovich's position at the time made him especially eager for any such enterprise, for he was passionately anxious to make a career in one way or another. To attach himself to a good family and obtain a dowry was an alluring prospect. As for mutual love it did not exist at all apparently, either in the bride or in him, in spite of Adelaïda Ivanovna's beauty. This was, perhaps, a unique case of the kind in the life of Fyodor Pavlovich, who was always of a voluptuous temper, and ready to run after any petticoat on the slightest encouragement. She seems to have been the only woman who made no particular appeal to his sensuality.

Immediately after the elopement Adelaïda Ivanovna discerned in a flash that she had no feeling for her husband but contempt. The marriage accordingly showed itself in its true colors with extraordinary rapidity. Although the family accepted the event pretty quickly and apportioned the runaway bride her dowry, the husband and wife began to lead a most disorderly life, and there were everlasting scenes between them. It was said that the young wife showed incomparably more nobility and dignity than Fyodor Pavlovich, who, as is now known, got hold of all her money, some twenty-five thousand rubles, as soon as she received it, so that those thousands were lost to her for ever. The little village and the rather fine town house which formed part of her dowry he did his utmost for a long time to transfer to his name, by means of some deed of conveyance. He would probably have succeeded, merely from her emotional fatigue and desire to get rid of him, and from the contempt and loathing he aroused by his persistent and shameless

2. Dostoevsky uses a line from Lermontov's poem "Do Not Believe in Yourself" (1839) without quotation marks.

extortion and importunity. But, fortunately, Adelaïda Ivanovna's family intervened and circumvented the swindler. It is known for a fact that frequent fights took place between the husband and wife, but rumor had it that Fyodor Pavlovich did not beat his wife but was beaten by her, for she was a hot-tempered, bold, dark-browed, impatient woman, possessed of remarkable physical strength. Finally, she left the house and ran away from Fyodor Pavlovich with a destitute divinity student, leaving Mitya, a child of three years old, in her husband's hands. Immediately Fyodor Pavlovich introduced a regular harem into the house, and abandoned himself to orgies of drunkenness. In the intervals he used to drive all over the province, complaining tearfully to each and all of Adelaïda Ivanovna's having left him, going into details too disgraceful for a husband to mention in regard to his own married life. What seemed to gratify and flatter him most was to play the ridiculous part of the injured husband, and to parade his woes with embellishments.

"One would think that you'd got a promotion, Fyodor Pavlovich, you seem so pleased in spite of your sorrow," scoffers said to him. Many even added that he was glad of a new comic part in which to play the buffoon, and that it was simply to make it funnier that he pretended to be unaware of his ludicrous position. But who knows, it may have been simplicity. At last he succeeded in getting on the track of his runaway wife. The poor woman turned out to be in Petersburg, where she had gone with her divinity student, and where she had thrown herself into a life of complete emancipation. Fyodor Pavlovich at once began bustling about, making preparations to go to Petersburg, with what object he could not himself have said. He would perhaps have really gone; but having determined to do so he felt at once entitled to fortify himself for the journey by another bout of reckless drinking. And just at that time his wife's family received the news of her death in Petersburg. She had died quite suddenly in a garret, according to one story, of typhus, or as another version had it, of starvation. Fyodor Pavlovich was drunk when he heard of his wife's death, and the story is that he ran out into the street and began shouting with joy, raising his hands to Heaven: "Lord, now lettest Thou Thy servant depart in peace," but others say he wept without restraint like a little child, so much so that people were sorry for him, in spite of the repulsion he inspired. It is quite possible that both versions were true, that he rejoiced at his release, and at the same time wept for her who released him. As a general rule, people, even the wicked, are much more naïve and simple-hearted than we suppose. And we ourselves are, too.

Chapter II

He Gets Rid of His Eldest Son

You can easily imagine what a father such a man would be and how he would bring up his children. His behavior as a father was exactly what might be expected. He completely abandoned the child of his marriage with Adelaïda Ivanovna, not from malice, nor because of his matrimonial grievances, but simply because he forgot him. While he was wearying every one with his tears and complaints, and turning his house into a sink of debauchery, a faithful servant of the family, Grigory, took the three-year-old Mitya into his care. If he hadn't looked after him there would have been no one even to change the child's little shirt.

It happened moreover that the child's relations on his mother's side forgot him too at first. His grandfather, that is, Mr. Miüsov himself, Adelaïda Ivanovna's father, was no longer living, his widow, Mitya's grandmother, had moved to Moscow, and was seriously ill, while his daughters were married, so that Mitya remained for almost a whole year in old Grigory's charge and lived with him in the servant's cottage. But if his father had remembered him (he could not, indeed, have been altogether unaware of his existence) he would have sent him back to the cottage, as the child would only have been in the way of his debaucheries. But a cousin of the late Adelaïda Ivanovna, Pyotr Alexandrovich Miüsov, happened to return from Paris. Afterwards he lived abroad for many years, but he was at that time still quite a young man, and distinguished among the Miüsovs as a man of enlightened ideas and of European culture, who had been in the capitals and abroad. Towards the end of his life he became a Liberal of the type common in the forties and fifties. In the course of his career he had come into contact with many of the most Liberal men of his epoch, both in Russia and abroad. He had known Proudhon and Bakunin[3] personally, and in his declining years was very fond of describing the three days of the Paris Revolution of February, 1848, hinting that he himself had almost taken part in the fighting on the barricades. This was one of the most comforting recollections of his youth. He had an independent property of about a thousand souls, to reckon in the old style. His splendid estate lay on the outskirts of our little town and bordered on the lands of our famous monastery, with which Pyotr Alexandrovich began an endless lawsuit, almost as soon as he came into the estate, concerning the rights of fishing in the river or woodcutting in the forest, I don't know exactly which.

3. P. J. Proudhon (1809–1865) was a French socialist. M. A. Bakunin (1814– 1876) was a renowned Russian anarchist.

He regarded it as his duty as a citizen and a man of culture to open an attack upon the "clericals." Hearing all about Adelaïda Ivanovna, whom he, of course, remembered, and in whom he had at one time been interested, and learning of the existence of Mitya, he intervened, in spite of all his youthful indignation and contempt for Fyodor Pavlovich. He made the latter's acquaintance for the first time, and told him directly that he wished to undertake the child's education. He used long afterwards to tell as a characteristic touch, that when he began to speak of Mitya, Fyodor Pavlovich looked for some time as though he did not understand what child he was talking about, and even as though he was surprised to hear that he had a little son in the house. The story may have been exaggerated, yet it must have been something like the truth.

But Fyodor Pavlovich really was all his life fond of acting, of suddenly playing an unexpected part, and particularly sometimes without any motive for doing so, and even to his own direct disadvantage, as for instance in the present case. This habit, however, is characteristic of a very great number of people, some of them very clever ones, not like Fyodor Pavlovich. Pyotr Alexandrovich carried the business through vigorously, and was appointed, with Fyodor Pavlovich, joint guardian of the child, who had a small property, a house and land, left him by his mother. Mitya did, in fact, pass into this cousin's keeping, but as the latter had no family of his own, and after securing the revenues of his estates was in haste to return at once to Paris, he left the boy in charge of one of his aunts once removed, a lady living in Moscow. It came to pass that, settling permanently in Paris he, too, forgot the child, especially when the revolution of February broke out making an impression on his mind that he remembered all the rest of his life. The Moscow lady died, and Mitya passed into the care of one of her married daughters. I believe he changed his home a fourth time later on. I won't enlarge upon that now, as I shall have much to tell later of Fyodor Pavlovich's firstborn, and must confine myself now to the most essential facts about him, without which I could not begin my story.

In the first place, this Dmitri Fyodorovich was the only one of Fyodor Pavlovich's three sons who grew up in the belief that he had property, and that he would be independent on coming of age. He spent an irregular boyhood and youth. He did not finish his studies at the gymnasium, he got into a military school, then went to the Caucasus, was promoted, fought a duel, and was degraded to the ranks, earned promotion again, led a wild life, and spent a good deal of money. He did not begin to receive any income from Fyodor Pavlovich until he came of age, and until then got into debt. He saw and knew his father, Fyodor Pavlovich, for the first time on coming of age, when he visited our neighborhood on purpose to settle with him about his property. He seems not to have liked his father. He did not stay long with him, and made haste to get away, having only succeeded in obtaining a sum of money, and entering into an agreement for future payments from the estate, of the revenues or value of which he was unable (a fact worthy of note) upon this occasion to get a statement from his father. Fyodor Pavlovich remarked for the first time then (this, too, should be noted) that Mitya had a false and exaggerated idea of his property. Fyodor Pavlovich was very well satisfied with this, as it fell in with his own designs. He gathered only that the young man was frivolous, unruly, of violent passions, impatient, and dissipated, and that if he could only obtain ready money he would be satisfied, although only, of course, for a short time. So Fyodor Pavlovich began to take advantage of this fact, sending him from time to time small doles, installments. In the end, when four years later Mitya, losing patience, came a second time to our little town to settle up once for all with his father, it turned out to his great amazement that he had nothing, that it was difficult to get an account even, that he had received the whole value of his property in sums of money from Fyodor Pavlovich, and was perhaps even in debt to him, that by various agreements into which he had of his own desire entered at various previous dates, he had no right to expect anything more, and so on, and so on. The young man was overwhelmed, suspected deceit and cheating, and was almost beside himself. And, indeed, this circumstance led to the catastrophe, the account of which forms the subject of my first introductory novel, or rather the external side of it. But before I pass to that novel I must say a little of Fyodor Pavlovich's other two sons, and of their origin.

Chapter III

The Second Marriage and the Second Family

Very shortly after getting his four-year-old Mitya off his hands Fyodor Pavlovich married a second time. His second marriage lasted eight years. He took this second wife, Sofya Ivanovna, also a very young girl, from another province, where he had gone upon some small piece of business in company with a Jew. Though Fyodor Pavlovich caroused, drank and went on debauches he never neglected investing his capital, and managed his business affairs very successfully, though, of course, always unscrupulously. Sofya Ivanovna was the daughter of an obscure deacon, and was left from childhood an orphan without relations. She grew up in the house of the widow of General Vorokhov, a wealthy old lady of good position, who was at once her benefactress, educator, and tormentor. I do not know the details, but I have only heard that the orphan girl, a mild, meek, and gentle creature, was once cut down from a halter in which she was hanging from a nail in the loft, so terrible were her sufferings from the caprice and everlasting nagging of this old woman, who was apparently not bad-hearted but had become an insufferable tyrant through idleness.

Fyodor Pavlovich made her an offer; inquiries were made about him and he was kicked out. But again, as in his first marriage, he proposed an elopement to the orphan girl. There is very little doubt that she would not on any account have married him if she had known a little more about him in time. But she lived in another province; besides, what could a little girl of sixteen know about it, except that she would be better at the bottom of the river than remaining with her benefactress. So the poor child exchanged a benefactress for a benefactor. Fyodor Pavlovich did not get a penny this time, for the general's widow was furious. She gave them nothing and cursed them both. But he had not reckoned on a dowry; what allured him was the remarkable beauty of the innocent girl, above all her innocent appearance, which had a peculiar attraction for a sensualist and hitherto depraved admirer of only the coarser types of feminine beauty.

"Those innocent eyes slit my soul up like a razor," he used to say afterwards, with his loathsome snigger. In a man so depraved this, of course, could only mean sensual attraction. As he had received no dowry with his wife, and had so to speak taken her "from the halter," he did not stand on ceremony with her. Making her feel that she had "wronged" him, he took advantage of her phenomenal meekness and submissiveness to trample on the elementary decencies of marriage. He gathered loose women into his house, and carried on orgies of debauchery in his wife's presence. As a characteristic trait, I may mention that Grigory, the gloomy, stupid, obstinate, argumentative servant, who had always hated his first mistress, Adelaïda Ivanovna, took the side of his new mistress. He championed her cause, abusing Fyodor Pavlovich in a manner little befitting a servant, and, on one occasion even broke up the revels and drove all the disorderly women out of the house. In the end this unhappy young woman, kept in terror from her childhood, fell into that kind of nervous disease which is most frequently found in peasant women who are said to be "possessed by devils." At times after terrible fits of hysterics she even lost her reason. Yet she bore Fyodor Pavlovich two sons, Ivan and Alexey, the eldest in the first year of marriage and the second three years later. When she died, little Alexey was in his fourth year, and, strange as it seems, I know that he remembered his mother all his life, like a dream, of course. At her death almost exactly the same thing happened to the two little boys as to their elder brother, Mitya. They were completely forgotten and abandoned by their father. They were looked after by the same Grigory and lived in his cottage, where they were found by the tyrannical old lady who had brought up their mother. She was still alive, and had not, all those eight years, forgotten the insult done her. All that time she was obtaining exact information as to her "Sofie's" manner of life, and hearing of her illness and hideous surroundings she declared aloud two or three times to her retainers:

"It serves her right. God has punished her for her ingratitude."

Exactly three months after Sofya Ivanovna's death the general's widow suddenly appeared in our town, and went straight to Fyodor Pavlovich's house. She spent only half an hour in the town but she did a great deal. It was evening. Fyodor Pavlovich, whom she had not seen for those eight years, came in to her drunk. The story is that instantly upon seeing him, without any sort of explanation, she gave him two good, resounding slaps on the face, seized him by a tuft of hair, and shook him three times up and down. Then, without a word, she went straight to the cottage to the two boys. Seeing at the first glance that they were unwashed and in dirty linen, she promptly gave Grigory too a box on the ear, and announcing that she would carry off both the children she wrapped them just as they were in a rug, put them in the carriage, and drove off to her own town. Grigory accepted the blow like a devoted slave, without a word, and when he escorted the old lady to her carriage he made her a low bow and pronounced impressively that "God would repay her for the orphans." "You are a blockhead all the same," the old lady shouted to him as she drove away.

Fyodor Pavlovich, thinking it over, decided that it was a good thing, and did not refuse the general's widow his formal consent to any proposition in regard to his children's education. As for the slaps she had given him, he drove all over the town telling the story.

It happened that the old lady died soon after this, but she left the boys in her will a thousand rubles each "for their instruction, and so that all be spent on them exclusively, with the condition that it be so portioned out as to last till they are twenty-one, for it is more than adequate provision for such children. If other people think fit to throw away their money, let them, etc., etc." I have not read the will myself, but I heard there was something queer of the sort, very whimsically expressed. The principal heir, Yefim Petrovich Polyonov, the Marshal of Nobility[4] of the province, turned out, however, to be an honest man. Writing to Fyodor Pavlovich, and discerning at once that he could extract nothing from him for his children's education (though the latter never directly refused but only procrastinated as he always did in such cases, and was indeed at times

---

4. The highest elective office in an administrative region. The governor and other administrative officers were appointed.

effusively sentimental), Yefim Petrovich took a personal interest in the orphans. He became especially fond of the younger, Alexey, who lived for a long while as one of his family. I beg the reader to note this from the beginning. And to Yefim Petrovich, a man of a generosity and humanity rarely to be met with, the young people were more indebted for their education and bringing up than to any one. He kept the two thousand rubles left to them by the general's widow intact, so that by the time they came of age their portions had been doubled by the accumulation of interest. He educated them both at his own expense, and certainly spent far more than a thousand rubles upon each of them. I won't enter into a detailed account of their boyhood and youth for the time being, but will only mention a few of the most important events. Of the elder, Ivan, I will only say that he grew into a somewhat morose and reserved, though far from timid boy. At ten years old he had realized that they were living not in their own home but on other people's charity, and that their father was a man of whom it was disgraceful to speak, etc., etc. This boy began very early, almost in his infancy (so they say at least), to show a brilliant and unusual aptitude for learning. I don't know precisely why, but he left the family of Yefim Petrovich when he was hardly thirteen, entering a Moscow gymnasium, and boarding with an experienced and celebrated teacher, an old friend of Yefim Petrovich. Ivan used to declare afterwards that this was all due to the "ardor for good works" of Yefim Petrovich, who was captivated by the idea that the boy's genius should be trained by a teacher of genius. But neither Yefim Petrovich nor this teacher was living when the young man finished at the gymnasium and entered the university. As Yefim Petrovich had made no provision for the payment of the tyrannical old lady's legacy, which had grown from one thousand to two, it was delayed, owing to formalities inevitable in Russia, and the young man was in great straits for the first two years at the university, as he was forced to keep himself all the time he was studying. It must be noted that he did not even attempt to communicate with his father, perhaps from pride, from contempt for him, or perhaps from his cool common sense, which told him that from such a father he would get no real assistance. However that may have been, the young man was by no means despondent and succeeded in getting work, at first giving sixpenny lessons and afterwards getting paragraphs on street incidents into the newspapers under the signature of "Eye-Witness." These paragraphs, it was said, were so interesting and piquant that they soon became popular. This alone showed the young man's practical and intellectual superiority over the masses of needy and unfortunate students of both sexes who hang about the offices of the newspapers and journals, unable to think of anything better than everlasting entreaties for copying and translations from the French. Having once got in touch with the editors, Ivan Fyodorovich always kept up his connection with them, and in his last years at the university he published brilliant reviews of books upon various special subjects, so that he became well known in literary circles. But only in his last year he suddenly succeeded in attracting the attention of a far wider circle of readers, so that a great many people noticed and remembered him. It was rather a curious incident. When he had just left the university and was preparing to go abroad upon his two thousand rubles, Ivan Fyodorovich published in one of the more important journals a strange article, which attracted general notice, on a subject of which he might have been supposed to know nothing, as he was a student of natural science. The article dealt with a subject which was being debated everywhere at the time—the position of the ecclesiastical courts.[5] After discussing several opinions on the subject he went on to explain his own view. What was most striking about the article was its tone, and its remarkably unexpected conclusion. Many of the Church party regarded him unquestioningly as on their side. And yet not only the secularists but even atheists joined them in their applause. Finally some sagacious persons opined that the article was nothing but an impudent farce and a mockery. I mention this incident particularly because this article in time penetrated into the famous monastery in our neighborhood, where the inmates, being particularly interested in the question of the ecclesiastical courts, were completely bewildered by it. Learning the author's name, they were also interested in his being a native of the town and the son of "that Fyodor Pavlovich." And just then it was that the author himself made his appearance among us.

Why Ivan Fyodorovich had come amongst us I remember asking myself with a certain uneasiness even then. This fateful visit, which was the first step leading to so many consequences, I never fully explained to myself. It seemed strange on the face of it that a young man so learned, so proud, and apparently so cautious, should suddenly visit such an infamous house and a father who had ignored him all his life, hardly knew him, never thought of him, and would not under any circumstances have given him money, though he was always afraid that his sons Ivan and Alexey would also come to ask him for it. And here the young man was staying in the house of such a father, had been living with him for two months, and they were on the best possible terms. This last fact was a special cause of wonder to many others as well as to me. Pyotr Alexandrovich Miüsov, of whom we have spoken already, the cousin of Fyodor Pavlovich's first wife, happened to be in the neighborhood again on a visit to his estate. He had come from

5. The judicial reform act of 1864 necessarily initiated a review of ecclesiastical courts.

Paris, which was his permanent home. I remember that he was more surprised than anyone when he made the acquaintance of the young man, who interested him extremely, and with whom he sometimes, not without an inner pang, had intellectual altercations. "He is proud," he used to say, "he will never be in want of money; he has money enough to go abroad now. What does he want here? Every one can see that he hasn't come for money, for his father would never give him any. He has no taste for drink and dissipation, and yet his father can't do without him. They get on so well together!" That was the truth; the young man had an unmistakable influence over his father, who positively appeared to be behaving more decently and even seemed at times ready to obey his son, though often extremely and even spitefully perverse.

It was only later that we learned that Ivan Fyodorovich had come partly at the request of, and in the interests of, his elder brother, Dmitri Fyodorovich, whom he saw for the first time on this very visit, though he had before leaving Moscow been in correspondence with him about an important matter of more concern to Dmitri Fyodorovich than himself. What that business was the reader will learn fully in due time. Yet even when I did know of this special circumstance I still felt Ivan Fyodorovich to be an enigmatic figure, and still thought his visit inexplicable.

I may add that Ivan Fyodorovich appeared at the time in the light of a conciliator and mediator between his father and his elder brother Dmitri Fyodorovich, who was in open quarrel with his father and even planning to bring an action against him.

The family, I repeat, was now united for the first time, and some of its members met for the first time in their lives. The younger brother, Alexey Fyodorovich, had been a year already among us, having been the first of the three to arrive. It is of that brother Alexey I find it most difficult to speak in this introduction, before bringing him on the scene in the novel. Yet I must give some preliminary account of him, if only to explain one queer fact, which is that I have to introduce the future hero of the novel to the reader wearing the cassock of a novice. Yes, he had been for the last year in our monastery, and seemed willing to be cloistered there for the rest of his life.

Chapter IV

The Third Son, Alyosha

He was only twenty, his brother Ivan was in his twenty-fourth year at the time, while their elder brother Dmitri was twenty-seven. First of all, I must explain that this young man, Alyosha, was not a fanatic, and, in my opinion, at least, was not even a mystic. I may as well give my full opinion from the beginning. He was simply an early lover of humanity, and that he adopted the monastic life was simply because at that time it struck him, so to speak, as the ideal escape for his soul struggling from the darkness of worldly wickedness to the light of love. And the reason this life struck him that way was that he found in it at that time, as he thought, an extraordinary being, our celebrated elder, Zosima, to whom he became attached with all the warm first love of his insatiable heart. But I do not dispute that he was very strange even at that time, and had been so indeed from his cradle. I have mentioned already, by the way, that though he lost his mother in his fourth year he remembered her all his life—her face, her caresses, "as though she stood living before me." Such memories may persist, as every one knows, from an even earlier age, even from two years old, but scarcely standing out through a whole lifetime like spots of light out of darkness, like a corner torn out of a huge picture, which was all faded and disappeared except that fragment. That is how it was with him. He remembered one still summer evening, an open window, the slanting rays of the setting sun (he recalled the slanting rays most vividly of all); in a corner of the room the holy image, before it a lighted lamp, and on her knees before the image his mother, sobbing hysterically with cries and shrieks, snatching him up in both arms, squeezing him close till it hurt, and praying for him to the Mother of God, holding him out in both arms to the image as though to put him under the Mother's protection . . . and suddenly a nurse runs in and snatches him from her in terror. That was the picture! And Alyosha remembered his mother's face at that minute. He used to say that it was frenzied but beautiful, judging by what he could remember. But he rarely cared to entrust this memory to anyone. In his childhood and youth he was by no means expansive, and indeed, talked little, but not from shyness or a sullen unsociability; quite the contrary, from something different, from a sort of inner preoccupation entirely personal and unconcerned with other people, but so important to him that he seemed, as it were, to forget others on account of it. But he was fond of people: he seemed throughout his life to put implicit trust in people: yet no one ever looked on him as a simpleton or naïve person. There was something about him which made one feel at once (and it was so all his life afterwards) that he did not care to be a judge of others—that he would never take it upon himself to censure and would never condemn anyone for anything. He seemed, indeed, to accept everything without the least condemnation though often grieving bitterly; and this was so much so that no one could surprise or frighten him even in his earliest youth. Coming at twenty to his father's house, which was a very sink of filthy debauchery, he, chaste and pure as he was, simply withdrew in silence when to look on was unbearable, but without the slightest sign of contempt or condemnation. His father, who had once been a toady and so was sensitive and ready to take offense, met him at first with distrust and sullenness. "He does not say much," he used to say, "and thinks the more." But soon, within a fortnight indeed, he took to embracing him and kissing him terribly often, to be sure with drunken tears, with sottish sentimentality, yet he evidently felt a real and deep affection for him, such as he had never been capable of feeling for anyone before.

Everyone, indeed, loved this young man wherever he went, and it was so from his earliest childhood. When he entered the household of his patron and benefactor, Yefim Petrovich Polyonov, he gained the hearts of all the family, so that they looked on him quite as their own child. Yet he entered the house at such a tender age that he could not have acted from design nor artfulness in winning affection. So that the gift of making himself loved directly and unconsciously was inherent in him, in his very nature so to speak. It was the same at school, though he seemed to be just one of those children who are distrusted, sometimes ridiculed, and even hated by their schoolfellows. He was dreamy, for instance, and rather solitary. From his earliest childhood he was fond of going off to a corner to read, and yet his schoolmates liked him so much that he was decidedly a favorite all the while he was at school. He was rarely playful or merry, but anyone could see at the first glance that this was not from any sullenness. On the contrary he was bright and good-tempered. He never tried to show off among his schoolfellows. Perhaps because of this, he was never afraid of anyone, yet the boys immediately understood that he was not proud of his fearlessness and seemed to be unaware that he was bold and courageous. He never resented an insult. It would happen that an hour after the offense he would address the offender or answer some question with as trustful and candid an expression as though nothing had happened between them. And it was not that he seemed to have forgotten or intentionally forgiven the affront, but simply that he did not regard it as an affront, and this completely conquered and captivated the boys. He had one characteristic which made all his schoolfellows from the bottom class to the top want to mock at him, not from malice but because it amused them. This characteristic was a wild fanatical modesty and chastity. He could not bear to hear certain words and certain conversations about women. There are "certain" words and conversations unhappily impossible to eradicate in schools. Boys pure in mind and heart, almost children, are fond of talking in school among themselves, and even aloud, of things, pictures, and images of which even soldiers would sometimes hesitate to speak. More than that, much that soldiers have no knowledge or conception of is familiar to quite young children of our intellectual and higher classes. There is as yet no moral depravity, no real corrupt inner cynicism in it, but there is the appearance of it, and it is often looked upon among them as something refined, subtle, daring, and worthy of imitation. Seeing that "Alyoshka Karamazov" put his fingers in his ears when they talked of "that," they used sometimes to crowd round him, pull his hands away, and shout nastiness into both ears, while he struggled, slipped to the floor, tried to hide himself without uttering one word of abuse, enduring their insults in silence. But at last they left him alone and gave up taunting him with being a "regular girl," and what's more they looked upon it with compassion as a weakness. He was always one of the best in the class but was never first.

At the time of Yefim Petrovich's death Alyosha had two more years to complete at the provincial gymnasium. The inconsolable widow went almost immediately after his death for a long visit to Italy with her whole family, which consisted only of women and girls. Alyosha went to live in the house of two distant relations of Yefim Petrovich, ladies whom he had never seen before. On what terms he lived with them he did not know himself. It was very characteristic of him, indeed, that he never cared at whose expense he was living. In that respect he was a striking contrast to his elder brother Ivan Fyodorovich, who struggled with poverty for his first two years in the university, maintained himself by his own efforts, and had from childhood been bitterly conscious of living at the expense of his benefactor. But this strange trait in Alyosha's character must not, I think, be criticised too severely, for at the slightest acquaintance with him anyone would have perceived that Alyosha was one of those youths, almost of the type of religious eccentric, who, if they were suddenly to come into possession of a large fortune would not hesitate to give it away for the asking, either for good works or perhaps to a clever rogue. In general he seemed scarcely to know the value of money, not, of course, in a literal sense. When he was given pocket money, which he never asked for, he was either terribly careless of it so that it was gone in a moment or he kept it for weeks together, not knowing what to do with it.

Pyotr Alexandrovich Miüsov, a man very sensitive on the score of money and bourgeois honesty, later pronounced the following aphorism, after getting to know Alyosha: "Here is perhaps the one man in the world whom you might leave alone without a penny, in the center of a strange city of a million inhabitants, and he would not come to harm, he would not die of cold and hunger, for he would be fed and sheltered at once; and if he were not, he would find a shelter for himself, and it would cost him no effort or humiliation, and to shelter him would be no burden, but, on the contrary, would probably be looked on as a pleasure."

He did not finish his studies at the gymnasium. A year before the end of the course he suddenly announced to the ladies that he was going to see his father about a plan which had occurred to him. They were sorry and unwilling to let him go. The journey was not an expensive one, and the ladies would not let him pawn his watch, a parting present from his benefactor's family when they went abroad. They provided him liberally with money and even fitted him out with new clothes and linen. But he returned half the money they gave him, saying that he intended to go third class. On his arrival in the town he made no answer to his father's first inquiry why he had come before completing his studies, and seemed, so they say, unusually thoughtful. It soon became apparent that he was looking for his mother's tomb. He practically acknowledged at the time that that was the only object of his visit. But it can hardly have been the whole reason of it. It is more probable that he himself did not understand and could not explain what had suddenly arisen in his soul, and drawn him irresistibly into a new, unknown, but inevitable path. Fyodor Pavlovich could not show him where his second wife was buried, for he had never visited her grave since he had thrown earth upon her coffin, and in the course of years had entirely forgotten where she was buried.

Fyodor Pavlovich, by the way, had for some time previously not been living in our town. Three or four years after his wife's death he had gone to the south of Russia and finally turned up in Odessa, where he spent several years. He made the acquaintance at first, in his own words, "of a lot of low Jews, Jewesses, and Jewkins," and ended by being received by "Jews high and low alike." It may be presumed that at this period he developed a peculiar faculty for making and hoarding money. He finally returned to our town only three years before Alyosha's arrival. His former acquaintances found him looking terribly aged, although he was by no means an old man. He behaved not exactly with more dignity but with more effrontery. The former buffoon showed an insolent propensity for making buffoons of others. His depravity with women was not simply what it used to be, but even more revolting. In a short time he opened a great number of new taverns in the district. It was evident that he had perhaps a hundred thousand rubles or not much less. Many of the inhabitants of the town and district were soon in his debt, and, of course, had given good security. Of late, too, he looked somehow bloated and seemed more irresponsible, more uneven, had sunk into a sort of incoherence, used to begin one thing and go on with another, as though he were letting himself go altogether. He was more and more frequently drunk. And, if it had not been for the same servant Grigory, who by that time had aged considerably too, and used to look after him sometimes almost like a tutor, Fyodor Pavlovich might have got into terrible scrapes. Alyosha's arrival seemed to affect even his moral side, as though something had awakened in this prematurely old man which had long been dead in his soul.

"Do you know," he used often to say, looking at Alyosha, "that you are like her, 'the possessed woman' "—that was what he used to call his dead wife, Alyosha's mother. Grigory it was who pointed out the "possessed woman's" grave to Alyosha. He took him to our town cemetery and showed him in a remote corner a cast-iron tombstone, cheap but decently kept, on which were inscribed the name and age of the deceased and the date of her death, and below a four-line verse, such as are commonly used on old-fashioned middle-class tombs. To Alyosha's amazement this tomb turned out to be Grigory's doing. He had put it up on the poor "possessed woman's" grave at his own expense, after Fyodor Pavlovich, whom he had often pestered about the grave, had gone to Odessa, abandoning the grave and all his memories. Alyosha showed no particular emotion at the sight of his mother's grave. He only listened to Grigory's reasoned and solemn account of the erection of the tomb; he stood with bowed head and walked away without uttering a word. After that, perhaps the whole year, he did not visit the cemetery again. But this little episode was not without an influence upon Fyodor Pavlovich—and a very original one. He suddenly took a thousand rubles to our monastery to pay for requiems for the soul of his wife; but not for the second, Alyosha's mother, the "possessed woman," but for the first, Adelaïda Ivanovna, who used to thrash him. In the evening of the same day he got drunk and abused the monks to Alyosha. He himself was far from being religious; he had probably never put a penny candle before the image of a saint. Strange impulses of sudden feeling and sudden thought are common in such subjects.

I have mentioned already that he looked bloated. His countenance at this time bore traces of something that testified unmistakably to the life he had led. Besides the long fleshy bags under his little, always insolent, suspicious, and ironical eyes; besides the multitude of deep wrinkles in his little fat face, the Adam's apple hung below his sharp chin like a great, fleshy goiter, which gave him a peculiar, repulsive, sensual appearance; add to that a long rapacious mouth with puffy lips, between which could be seen little stumps of black decayed teeth. He slobbered every time he began to speak. He was fond indeed of making fun of his own face, though, I believe, he was well satisfied with it. He used particularly to point to his nose, which was not very large, but very delicate and conspicuously aquiline. "A regular Roman nose," he used to say, "with my goiter I've quite the countenance of an ancient Roman patrician of the decadent period." He seemed proud of it.

Not long after visiting his mother's grave Alyosha suddenly announced that he wanted to enter the monastery, and that the monks were willing to receive him as a novice. He explained that this was his strong desire, and that he was solemnly asking his consent as his father. The old man knew that the elder Zosima, who was living in the monastery hermitage, had made a special impression upon his "gentle boy."

"That is the most honest monk among them, of course," he observed, after listening in thoughtful silence to Alyosha, and seeming scarcely surprised at his request. "Hmm! . . . So that's where you want to be, my gentle boy?" He was half drunk, and suddenly he grinned his slow half-drunken grin, which was not without a certain cunning and tipsy slyness. "H'm! . . . I had a presentiment that you would end in something like this. Would you believe it? You were making straight for it. Well, to be sure you have your own two thousand. That's a dowry for you. And I'll never desert you, my angel. And I'll pay what's wanted for you there, if they ask for it. But, of course, if they don't ask, why should we worry them? What do you say? You know, you spend money like a canary, two grains a week. Hmm . . . Do you know that near one monastery there's a place outside the town where every baby knows there are none but 'the monks' wives' living, as they are called. Thirty women, I believe. I have been there myself. You know, it's interesting in its own way, of course, as a variety. The worst of it is it's awfully Russian. There are no French women there. Of course they could get them fast enough, they have plenty of money. If they get to hear of it they'll come along. Well, there's nothing of that sort here, no 'monks' wives,' and two hundred monks. They're honest. They keep the fasts. I admit it. . . . Hmm . . . So you want to be a monk? And do you know I'm sorry to lose you, Alyosha; would you believe it, I've really grown fond of you? Well, it's a good opportunity. You'll pray for us sinners; we have sinned too much here. I've always been thinking who would pray for me, and whether there's anyone in the world to do it. My dear boy, I'm awfully stupid about that. You wouldn't believe it. Awfully. You see, however stupid I am about it, I keep thinking, I keep thinking —from time to time, of course, not all the while. It's impossible, I think, for the devils to forget to drag me down to hell with their hooks when I die. Then I wonder—hooks? Where would they get them? What of? Iron hooks? Where do they forge them? Have they a foundry there of some sort? The monks in the monastery probably believe that there's a ceiling in hell, for instance. Now I'm ready to believe in hell, but without a ceiling. It makes it more refined, more enlightened, more Lutheran that is. And, after all, what does it matter whether it has a ceiling or hasn't? But, do you know, there's a damnable question involved in it? If there's no ceiling there can be no hooks, and if there are no hooks it all breaks down, which is unlikely again, for then there would be none to drag me down to hell, and if they don't drag me down what justice is there in the world? *Il faudrait les inventer,*[6] those hooks, on purpose for me alone, for, if you only knew, Alyosha, what a blackguard I am."

"But there are no hooks there," said Alyosha, looking gently and seriously at his father.

"Yes, yes, only the shadows of hooks. I know, I know. That's how a Frenchman described hell. *'J'ai vu l'ombre d'un cocher qui avec l'ombre d'une brosse frottait l'ombre d'une carosse.'*[7] How do you know there are no hooks, darling? When you've lived with the monks you'll sing a different tune. But go and get at the truth there, and then come and tell me. Anyway it's easier going to the other world if one knows what there is there. Besides, it will be more seemly for you with the monks than here with me, with a drunken old man and young harlots . . . though you're like an angel, nothing touches you. And I daresay nothing will touch you there. That's why I let you go, because I hope for that. You've got all your wits about you. You will burn and you will burn out; you will be healed and come back again. And I will wait for you. I feel that you're the only creature in the world who has not condemned me. My dear boy, I feel it, you know. I can't help feeling it."

And he even began blubbering. He was sentimental. He was wicked and sentimental.

Chapter V

Elders

Some of my readers may imagine that my young man was a sickly, ecstatic, poorly developed creature, a pale, thin, consumptive dreamer. On the contrary, Alyosha was at this time a well-grown, red-cheeked, clear-eyed lad of nineteen, radiant with health. He was very handsome, too, graceful, moderately tall, with hair of a dark brown, with a regular, rather long, oval-shaped face, and wide-set dark gray, shining eyes; he was very thoughtful, and apparently very serene. I shall be told, perhaps, that red cheeks are not incompatible with fanaticism and mysticism; but I fancy that Alyosha was more of a realist than any one. Oh, no doubt, in the monastery he fully believed in miracles, but, to my thinking, miracles are never a stumbling-block to the realist. It is not miracles that dispose realists to belief. The genuine realist, if he is an unbeliever, will always find strength and ability to disbelieve in the miraculous, and if he is confronted with a miracle as an irrefutable

6. "They would have to be invented."
7. "I saw the shade of a coachman, who scrubbed the shade of a coach with the shade of a brush." From Charles Perrault's *Eneïde travesti* (*Aeneid* travestied).

fact he would rather disbelieve his own senses than admit the fact. Even if he admits it, he admits it as a fact of nature till then unrecognized by him. Faith does not, in the realist, spring from the miracle but the miracle from faith. If the realist once believes, then he is bound by his very realism to admit the miraculous also. The Apostle Thomas said that he would not believe till he saw, but when he did see he said, "My Lord and my God!" Was it the miracle forced him to believe? Most likely not, but he believed solely because he desired to believe and possibly he fully believed in his secret heart even when he said, "I shall not believe except I see."

I shall be told, perhaps, that Alyosha was stupid, undeveloped, had not finished his studies, and so on. That he did not finish his studies is true, but to say that he was stupid or dull would be a great injustice. I'll simply repeat what I have said above. He entered upon this path only because, at that time, it alone struck his imagination and presented itself to him as offering an ideal means of escape for his soul from darkness to light. Add to that that he was to some extent a youth of our last epoch—that is, honest in nature, desiring the truth, seeking for it and believing in it, and seeking to serve it at once with all the strength of his soul, seeking for immediate action, and ready to sacrifice everything, life itself, for it. Though these young men unfortunately fail to understand that the sacrifice of life is, perhaps, the easiest of all sacrifices, and that to sacrifice, for instance, five or six years of their seething youth to hard and tedious study, if only to multiply tenfold their powers of serving the truth and the cause they have set before them as their goal—such a sacrifice is utterly beyond the strength of many of them. The path Alyosha chose was a path going in the opposite direction, but he chose it with the same thirst for swift achievement. As soon as he reflected seriously he was convinced of the existence of God and immortality, and at once he instinctively said to himself: "I want to live for immortality, and I will accept no compromise." In the same way, if he had decided that God and immortality did not exist, he would at once have become an atheist and a socialist (for socialism is not merely the labor question or the so-called fourth estate, it is before all things the atheistic question, the question of the form taken by atheism today, the question of the tower of Babel built without God, not to mount to Heaven from earth but to set up Heaven on earth). Alyosha even found it strange and impossible to go on living as before. It is written: "Give all that thou hast to the poor and follow Me, if thou wouldst be perfect." Alyosha said to himself: "I can't give two rubles instead of 'all,' and only go to mass instead of 'following Him.'" Perhaps his memories of childhood brought back our monastery, to which his mother may have taken him to mass. Perhaps the slanting rays of the setting sun and the holy image to which his poor "possessed" mother had held him up still acted upon his imagination. Brooding on these things he may have come to us perhaps only to see whether here he could sacrifice all or only "two rubles," and in the monastery he met this elder.

This elder, as I have already mentioned, was the elder Zosima. I must digress to explain what an "elder" is in Russian monasteries, and I am sorry that I do not feel very sure and competent to do so. I will try, however, to give a superficial account of it in a few words. Authorities on the subject assert that the institution of "elders" is of recent date, not more than a hundred years old in our monasteries, though in the orthodox East, especially in Sinai and Athos, it has existed over a thousand years. It is maintained that it existed in ancient times in Russia also, but through the calamities which overtook Russia—the Tartars, civil war, the interruption of relations with the East after the destruction of Constantinople[8]— this institution fell into oblivion. It was revived among us towards the end of last century by one of the great "ascetics," as they called him, Païssy Velichkovsky,[9] and his disciples. But to this day, even after a century, it exists in only a few monasteries, and has sometimes been almost persecuted as an innovation in Russia. It flourished especially in the celebrated Kozelskaya Optina Monastery. When and how it was introduced into our monastery I cannot say. There had already been three such elders and Zosima was the last of them. But he was almost dying of weakness and disease, and they had no one to take his place. The question was an important one for our monastery, for it had not been distinguished by anything in particular till then: it had neither relics of saints, nor wonder-working icons, nor even glorious traditions connected with our history, it had no historical exploits or services to the Fatherland. It had flourished and been glorious all over Russia through its elders, to see and hear whom pilgrims had flocked for thousands of miles from all parts.

What was such an elder? An elder was one who took your soul, your will, into his soul and his will. When you choose an elder, you renounce your own will and yield it to him in complete submission, complete self-abnegation. This novitiate, this terrible school of abnegation, is undertaken voluntarily, in the hope of self-conquest, of self-mastery, in order, after a life of obedience, to attain perfect freedom, that is, from self; to escape the lot of those who have lived their whole life without finding their true selves in themselves. This institution of elders is not founded on theory, but was established in the East from the practice of a thousand years. The obligations due to an elder are not the ordinary "obedience" which has always existed in our Russian monasteries. The obligation in-

8. Constantinople was taken by the Turks in 1453.

9. Velichkovsky (1722–1794) was at Mt. Athos and other places.

volves confession to the elder by all who have submitted themselves to him, and to the indissoluble bond between him and them.

The story is told, for instance, that in the early days of Christianity one such novice, failing to fulfill some command laid upon him by his elder, left his monastery in Syria and went to Egypt. There, after great exploits he was found worthy at last to suffer torture and a martyr's death for the faith. When the Church, regarding him as a saint, was burying him, suddenly, at the deacon's exhortation, "Depart all ye unbaptized," the coffin containing the martyr's body left its place and was cast forth from the church, and this took place three times. And only at last they learned that this holy man had broken his vow of obedience and left his elder, and, therefore, could not be forgiven without the elder's absolution in spite of his great deeds. Only after this could the funeral take place. This, of course, is only an old legend. But here is a recent instance.

A monk was suddenly commanded by his elder to quit Athos, which he loved as a sacred place and a haven of refuge, and to go, first to Jerusalem to do homage to the Holy Places and then to the north to Siberia: "There is the place for thee and not here." The monk, overwhelmed with sorrow, went to the Ecumenical Patriarch at Constantinople and besought him to release him from his obedience. But the Patriarch replied that not only was he unable to release him, but there was not and could not be on earth a power which could release him except the elder who had himself laid that duty upon him. In this way the elders are endowed in certain cases with unbounded and inexplicable authority. That is why in many of our monasteries the institution was at first resisted almost to persecution. Meantime the elders immediately began to be highly esteemed among the people. Masses of the ignorant people as well as men of distinction flocked, for instance, to the elders of our monastery to confess their doubts, their sins, and their sufferings, and ask for counsel and admonition. Seeing this, the opponents of the elders declared, among other objections, that the sacrament of confession was being arbitrarily and frivolously degraded, though the continual opening of the heart to the elder by the monk or the layman had nothing of the character of the sacrament. In the end, however, the institution of elders has been retained and is becoming established in Russian monasteries. It is true, perhaps, that this instrument which had stood the test of a thousand years for the moral regeneration of a man from slavery to freedom and to moral perfectibility may be a two-edged weapon and it may lead some not to humility and complete self-control but to the most Satanic pride, that is, to bondage and not to freedom.

The elder Zosima was sixty-five. He came of a family of landowners, had been in the army in early youth, and served in the Caucasus as an officer. He had, no doubt, impressed Alyosha by some peculiar quality of his soul. Alyosha lived in the cell of the elder, who was very fond of him and let him wait upon him. It must be noted that Alyosha, who lived in the monastery at that time, was bound by no obligation and could go where he pleased and be absent for whole days. Though he wore the monastic dress it was voluntarily, not to be different from others. No doubt he liked to do so. Possibly his youthful imagination was deeply stirred by the power and fame of his elder. It was said that so many people had for years past come to confess their sins to Father Zosima and to entreat him for words of advice and healing, that he had taken into his heart so many disclosures, afflictions, admissions, that Father Zosima had acquired the keenest intuition and could tell from an unknown face what a newcomer wanted, and what was the suffering on his conscience. He sometimes astounded and almost alarmed his visitors by his knowledge of their secrets before they had spoken a word.

Alyosha almost always noticed that many, almost all, went in to the elder for the first time with apprehension and uneasiness, but almost always came out with bright and happy faces, and the gloomiest face turned into a happy one. Alyosha was particularly struck by the fact that Father Zosima was not at all stern. On the contrary, he was always almost gay. The monks used to say that he was more drawn to those who were more sinful, and the greater the sinner the more he loved him. There were, no doubt, up to the end of his life, among the monks some who hated and envied him, but they were few in number and they were silent, though among them were some of great dignity in the monastery, one, for instance, of the older monks distinguished for his strict keeping of fasts and vows of silence. But the majority were on Father Zosima's side and very many of them loved him with all their hearts, warmly and sincerely. Some were almost fanatically devoted to him, and declared, though not quite aloud, that he was a saint, that there could be no doubt of it, and, seeing that his end was near, they anticipated miracles and great glory to the monastery in the immediate future from his relics. Alyosha had unquestioning faith in the miraculous power of the elder, just as he had unquestioning faith in the story of the coffin that flew out of the church. He saw many who came with sick children or relatives and besought the elder to lay hands on them and to pray over them, return shortly after— some of the next day—and, falling in tears at the elder's feet, thank him for healing their sick.

Whether they had really been healed or were simply better in the natural course of the disease was a question which did not exist for Alyosha, for he fully believed in the spiritual power of his teacher and rejoiced in his fame, in his glory, as though it were his own triumph. His heart throbbed, and he beamed, as it were, all over when the elder came out to the gates of the hermitage into the waiting crowd of pilgrims of the humbler class who had flocked from all parts of Russia on purpose to see the elder and obtain his blessing. They fell down before him, wept, kissed his feet, kissed the earth on which he stood, and wailed, while the women held up their children to him and brought him the sick "possessed with devils." The elder spoke to them, read a brief prayer over them, blessed them, and dismissed them. Of late he had become so weak through attacks of illness that he was sometimes unable to leave his cell, and the pilgrims waited for him to come out for several days. Alyosha did not wonder why they loved him so, why they fell down before him and wept with emotion merely at seeing his face. Oh! he understood that for the humble soul of the Russian plebeian, worn out by grief and toil, and still more by the everlasting injustice and everlasting sin, his own and the world's, it was the greatest need and comfort to find some one or something holy to fall down before and worship.

"Among us there is sin, injustice, and temptation, but yet, somewhere on earth there is someone holy and exalted. He has the truth; he knows the truth; so it is not dead upon the earth; so it will come one day to us, too, and rule over all the earth according to the promise."

Alyosha knew that this was just how the people felt and even reasoned. He understood it, but that the elder Zosima was the saint and custodian of God's truth—of that he had no more doubt than the weeping peasants and the sick women who held out their children to the elder. The conviction that after his death the elder would bring extraordinary glory to the monastery was even stronger in Alyosha than in anyone there, and of late a kind of deep flame of inner ecstasy burnt more and more strongly in his heart. He was not at all troubled at this elder's standing as a solitary example before him.

"No matter. He is holy. He carries in his heart the secret of renewal for all: that power which will, at last, establish truth on the earth, and all men will be holy and love one another, and there will be no more rich nor poor, no exalted nor humbled, but all will be as the children of God, and the true Kingdom of Christ will come." That was the dream in Alyosha's heart.

The arrival of his two brothers, whom he had not known till then, seemed to make a great impression on Alyosha. He more quickly made friends with his half-brother Dmitri Fyodorovich (though he arrived later) than with his own brother Ivan Fyodorovich. He was extremely interested in his brother Ivan, but when the latter had been two months in the town, though they had met fairly often, they were still not intimate. Alyosha was naturally silent, and he seemed to be expecting something, ashamed about something, while his brother Ivan, though Alyosha noticed at first that he looked long and curiously at him, seemed soon to have left off thinking of him. Alyosha noticed it with some embarrassment. He ascribed his brother's indifference at first to the disparity in their ages and particularly in their education. But he also wondered whether the absence of curiosity and sympathy in Ivan might be due to some other cause entirely unknown to him. He kept fancying that Ivan was absorbed in something—something inward and important—that he was striving towards some goal, perhaps very hard to attain, and that that was the only reason why he had no thought for him. Alyosha wondered, too, whether there was not some contempt on the part of the learned atheist for him—a foolish novice. He knew for certain that his brother was an atheist. He could not take offense at this contempt, if it existed; yet, with an uneasy embarrassment which he did not himself understand, he waited for his brother to come nearer to him. His brother Dmitri Fyodorovich used to speak of Ivan with the deepest respect and with a peculiar earnestness. From him Alyosha learned all the details of the important affair which had of late formed such a close and remarkable bond between the two elder brothers. Dmitri's enthusiastic references to Ivan were the more striking in Alyosha's eyes since Dmitri was, compared with Ivan, almost uneducated, and the two brothers were such a contrast in personality and character that it would be difficult to find two men more unlike.

It was at this time that the meeting, or rather gathering, of the members of this inharmonious family took place in the cell of the elder who had such an extraordinary influence on Alyosha. The pretext for this gathering was a false one. It was at this time that the discord between Dmitri Fyodorovich and his father seemed at its acutest stage and their relations had become insufferably strained. Fyodor Pavlovich seems to have been the first to suggest, apparently in jest, that they should all meet in Father Zosima's cell, and that, without appealing to his direct intervention, they might more decently come to an understanding under the conciliating influence of the elder's presence. Dmitri Fyodorovich, who had never seen the elder, naturally supposed that his father was trying to intimidate him, but, as he secretly blamed himself for his outbursts of temper with his father on several recent occasions, he accepted the challenge. It must be noted that he was not, like Ivan Fyodorovich, staying with his father, but living apart at the other end of the town. It happened that Pyotr Alexandrovich Miüsov, who was staying in the district at the time, caught eagerly at the idea. A Liberal of the forties and fifties, a freethinker and atheist, he may have been led on by boredom or the hope of frivolous diversion. He was suddenly seized with the desire to see the monastery and the "holy man." As his lawsuit with the monastery about boundaries, woodcutting rights, river fishing, and so on still dragged on, he made it the pretext for seeing the Superior, in order to attempt to settle it amicably. A visitor coming with such laudable intentions might be received with more attention and consideration than if he came from simple curiosity. Influences from within the monastery were brought to bear on the elder, who of late had scarcely left his cell, and had been forced by illness to deny even his ordinary visitors. In the end he consented to see them, and the day was fixed.

"Who has made me a judge over them?" was all he said, smilingly, to Alyosha.

Alyosha was much perturbed when he heard of the proposed visit. Of all the wrangling, quarrelsome party, his brother Dmitri was the only one who could regard the interview seriously. All the others would come from frivolous motives, perhaps insulting to the elder. Alyosha was well aware of that. His brother Ivan and Miüsov would come from curiosity, perhaps of the coarsest kind, while his father might be contemplating some piece of acting and buffoonery. Oh, though he said nothing, Alyosha thoroughly understood his father. The boy, I repeat, was far from being so simple as everyone thought him. He awaited the day with a heavy heart. No doubt he was always secretly pondering in his heart how the family discord could be ended. But his chief anxiety concerned the elder. He trembled for him, for his glory, and dreaded any affront to him, especially the refined, courteous irony of Miüsov and the supercilious half-utterances of the highly educated Ivan. That is how he imagined all that. He even wanted to venture on warning the elder, telling him something about them, but, on second thoughts, said nothing. He only sent word the day before, through a friend, to his brother Dmitri, that he loved him and expected him to keep his promise. Dmitri wondered, for he could not remember what he had promised, but he answered by letter that he would do his utmost not to let himself be provoked "by vileness," but that, although he had a deep respect for the elder and for his brother Ivan, he was convinced that the meeting was either a trap for him or an unworthy farce.

"Nevertheless I would rather bite out my tongue than be lacking in respect to the sainted man whom you reverence so highly," he wrote in conclusion. Alyosha was not greatly cheered by the letter.

Book Two

AN UNFORTUNATE GATHERING

Chapter I

They Arrive at the Monastery

It was a splendid, warm, bright day at the end of August. The interview with the elder had been fixed for half-past eleven in the morning, immediately after late mass. Our visitors did not take part in the service, but arrived just as it was over. First an elegant open carriage, drawn by two valuable horses, drove up with Miüsov and a distant relative of his, a very young man of twenty, called Pyotr Fomich Kalganov. This young man was preparing to enter the university. Miüsov, with whom he was staying for the time, was trying to persuade him to go abroad to the university of Zurich or Jena. The young man was still undecided. He was thoughtful and absent-minded. He was nice-looking, strongly built, and rather tall. There was a strange fixity in his gaze at times. Like all very absent-minded people he would sometimes stare at a person for some time without seeing him. He was silent and rather awkward, but sometimes, when he was alone with anyone he became talkative and effusive, and would laugh at anything or nothing. But his animation vanished as quickly as it appeared. He was always well and even elegantly dressed; he already had some independent fortune and expectations of much more. He was a friend of Alyosha's.

In an ancient, jolting, but roomy hired carriage, with a pair of old pinkish-gray horses, a long way behind Miüsov's carriage, came Fyodor Pavlovich, with his son Ivan Fyodorovich. Dmitri Fyodorovich was late, though he had been informed of the time the evening before. The visitors left their carriage at the hotel, outside the precincts, and went to the gates of the monastery on foot. Except Fyodor Pavlovich, none of the party had ever seen the monastery, and Miüsov had probably not even been to church for thirty years. He looked about him with some curiosity, together with assumed ease. But, except the church and the domestic buildings, though these too were ordinary enough, there was nothing of interest to his observant mind in the interior of the monastery. The last of the worshippers were coming out of the church, bareheaded and crossing themselves. Among the humbler people were a few of higher rank—two or three ladies and a very old general. They were all staying at the hotel. Our visitors were at once surrounded by beggars, but none of them gave them anything, except young Kalganov, who took a ten-kopeck piece out of his purse, and, nervous and embarrassed—God knows why!—hurriedly gave it to an old woman, quickly saying: "Divide it equally." None of his companions made any remark upon it, so that he had no reason to be embarrassed; but, perceiving this, he was even more overcome.

It was strange that their arrival did not seem expected, and that they were not received with special honor, though one of them had recently made a donation of a thousand rubles, while another was a very wealthy and highly cultured landowner, upon whom all in the monastery were in a sense dependent, as a decision of the lawsuit might at any moment put their fishing rights in his hands. Yet no official personage met them.

Miüsov looked absent-mindedly at the tombstones round the church, and was on the point of saying that the dead buried here must have paid a pretty penny for the right of lying in this "holy place," but refrained. His liberal irony was rapidly changing almost into anger.

"Who the devil is there to ask in this imbecile place? We must find out, for time is passing," he observed suddenly, as though speaking to himself.

All at once there came up a bald-headed, elderly man with ingratiating little eyes, wearing a broad summer overcoat. Lifting his hat, he introduced himself with a honeyed lisp as Maximov, a landowner of Tula. He at once entered into our visitors' difficulty.

"Father Zosima lives in the hermitage, apart, four hundred paces from the monastery, the other side of the copse."

"I know it's the other side of the copse," observed Fyodor Pavlovich, "but we don't remember the way. It is a long time since we've been here."

"This way, by this gate, and straight across the copse . . . the copse. Come with me, won't you? I'll show you. I have to go . . . I am going myself. This way, this way."

They came out of the gate and turned towards the copse. Maximov, a man of sixty, ran rather than walked, turning sideways to stare at them all, with an incredible degree of nervous curiosity. His eyes seemed to start out of his head.

"You see, we have come to the elder upon business of our own," observed Miüsov severely. "That personage has granted us an audience so to speak, and so, though we thank you for showing us the way, we cannot ask you to accompany us."

"I've been there. I've been already; *un chevalier parfait*,"[1] and Maximov snapped his fingers in the air.

---

1. "A perfect cavalier."

"Who is a *chevalier?*" asked Miüsov.

"The elder, the splendid elder, the elder! The honor and glory of the monastery, Zosima. Such an elder!"

But his incoherent talk was cut short by a very pale, wan-looking monk of medium height, wearing a monk's cap, who overtook them. Fyodor Pavlovich and Miüsov stopped.

The monk, with an extremely courteous, profound bow, announced:

"The Father Superior invites all of you gentlemen to dine with him after your visit to the hermitage. At one o'clock, not later. And you also," he added, addressing Maximov.

"That I certainly will, without fail," cried Fyodor Pavlovich, hugely delighted at the invitation. "And, believe me, we've all given our word to behave properly here. . . . And you, Pyotr Alexandrovich, will you go, too?"

"Yes, of course. What have I come for but to study all the customs here? The only obstacle to me is your company. . . ."

"Yes, Dmitri Fyodorovich is still not here."

"It would be a capital thing if he didn't turn up. Do you suppose I like all this business, and in your company, too? So we will come to dinner. Thank the Father Superior," he said to the monk.

"No, it is my duty now to conduct you to the elder," answered the monk.

"If so I'll go straight to the Father Superior—to the Father Superior," babbled Maximov.

"The Father Superior is engaged just now. But as you please——" the monk hesitated.

"Impertinent old man!" Miüsov observed aloud, while Maximov ran back to the monastery.

"He's like von Sohn,"[2] Fyodor Pavlovich said suddenly.

"Is that all you can think of? . . . In what way is he like von Sohn? Have you ever seen von Sohn?"

"I've seen his portrait. It's not the features, but something indefinable. He's a second von Sohn. I can always tell from the physiognomy."

"Ah, I dare say you are a connoisseur in that. But, look here, Fyodor Pavlovich, you said just now that we had given our word to behave properly. Remember it. I advise you to control yourself. But, if you begin to play the fool I don't intend to be associated with you here. . . . You see what a man he is"—he turned to the monk—"I'm afraid to go among decent people with him." A fine smile, not without a certain slyness, came on to the pale, bloodless lips of the monk, but he made no reply, and was evidently silent from a sense of his own dignity. Miüsov frowned more than ever.

"Oh, devil take them all! An outer show elaborated through

2. See page 77.

centuries, and nothing but charlatanism and nonsense underneath," flashed through Miüsov's mind.

"Here's the hermitage. We've arrived," cried Fyodor Pavlovich. "The gates are shut."

And he repeatedly made the sign of the cross to the saints painted above and on the sides of the gates.

"When in Rome, do as the Romans do. Here in this hermitage there are twenty-five saints being saved. They look at one another, and eat cabbage. And not one woman goes in at this gate. That's what is especially remarkable. And that really is so. But I did hear that the elder receives ladies," he remarked suddenly to the monk.

"Women of the people are here too now, lying near the portico there waiting. But for ladies of higher rank two rooms have been built adjoining the portico, but outside the precincts—you can see the windows—and the elder goes out to them by an inner passage when he is well enough. They are always outside the precincts. There is a Kharkov lady, Madame Khokhlakov, waiting there now with her sick daughter. Probably he has promised to come out to her, though of late he has been so weak that he has hardly shown himself even to the people."

"So then there are loopholes, after all, to creep out of the hermitage to the ladies. Don't suppose, holy father, that I mean any harm. But do you know that at Athos not only the visits of women are not allowed, but no creature of the female sex—no hens, nor turkey-hens, nor cows. . . ."

"Fyodor Pavlovich, I warn you I shall go back and leave you here. They'll turn you out when I'm gone."

"But I'm not interfering with you, Pyotr Alexandrovich. Look," he cried suddenly, stepping within the precincts, "what a vale of roses they live in!"

Though there were no roses now, there were numbers of rare and beautiful autumn flowers growing wherever there was space for them, and evidently tended by a skillful hand; there were flower-beds round the church, and between the tombs; and the one-storied wooden house where the elder lived was also surrounded with flowers.

"And was it like this in the time of the last elder, Varsonofy? He didn't care for such elegance. They say he used to jump up and thrash even ladies with a stick," observed Fyodor Pavlovich, as he went up the steps.

"The elder Varsonofy did sometimes seem rather strange, but a great deal that's told is foolishness. He never thrashed anyone," answered the monk. "Now, gentlemen, if you will wait a minute I will announce you."

"Fyodor Pavlovich, for the last time, your compact, do you hear? Behave properly or you'll get it!" Miüsov had time to mutter again.

"I can't think why you are so agitated," Fyodor Pavlovich observed sarcastically. "Are you uneasy about your sins? They say he can tell by one's eyes what one has come about. And what a lot you think of their opinion! you, a Parisian, and so advanced. I'm surprised at you."

But Miüsov had no time to reply to this sarcasm. They were asked to come in. He walked in, somewhat irritated.

"Now, I know myself, I am annoyed, I shall lose my temper and begin to quarrel—and lower myself and my ideas," he reflected.

Chapter II

The Old Buffoon

They entered the room almost at the same moment that the elder came in from his bedroom. There were already in the cell, awaiting the elder, two monks of the hermitage, one the Father Librarian, and the other Father Païssy, a very learned man, so they said, in delicate health, though not old. There was also a tall young lad, who looked about twenty-two, standing in the corner throughout the interview. He was quite tall, had a broad, fresh face, and clever, observant, narrow brown eyes, and was wearing ordinary dress. He was a divinity student and a future cleric, for some reason living under the protection of the monastery and the brethren. His expression was one of unquestioning, but self-respecting, reverence. Being in a subordinate and dependent position, and so not on an equal level with the guests, he did not greet them with a bow.

Father Zosima was accompanied by a novice, and by Alyosha. The two monks rose and greeted him with a very deep bow, touching the ground with their fingers; then they crossed themselves and kissed his hand. Blessing them, the elder replied with as deep a reverence to them, and touching the ground with his fingers, asked each for his blessing. The whole ceremony was performed very seriously and with an appearance of feeling, not like an everyday rite. But Miüsov fancied that it was all done with intentional impressiveness. He stood in front of the other visitors. He ought—he had reflected upon it the evening before—despite whatever ideas he held, from simple politeness, since it was the custom here, to have gone up to receive the elder's blessing, even if he did not kiss his hand. But when he saw all this bowing and kissing on the part of the monks he instantly changed his mind. With dignified gravity he made a rather deep, conventional bow, and moved away to a chair. Fyodor Pavlovich did the same, mimicking Miüsov like an ape. Ivan Fyodorovich bowed with great dignity and courtesy, but he too kept his hands at his sides, while Kalganov was so confused that he did not bow at all. The elder let fall the hand raised to bless them, and bowing to them again, asked them all to sit down. The blood rushed to Alyosha's cheeks. He was ashamed. His forebodings were coming true.

Father Zosima sat down on a very old-fashioned mahogany sofa, covered with leather, and made his visitors sit down in a row along the opposite wall on four mahogany chairs, covered with shabby black leather. The monks sat, one at the door and the other at the window. The divinity student, the novice, and Alyosha remained standing. The cell was not very large and had a faded look. It contained nothing but the most necessary furniture, of coarse and poor quality. There were two pots of flowers in the window, and many holy pictures in the corner. Before one huge, very ancient icon of the Virgin a lamp was burning. Near it were two other holy pictures in shining settings, and, next them, carved cherubims, china eggs, a Catholic cross of ivory, with a Mater Dolorosa embracing it, and several foreign engravings from the great Italian artists of past centuries. Next to these costly and artistic engravings were several of the roughest Russian prints of saints, martyrs, prelates and so on, such as are sold for a few farthings at all the fairs. On the other walls were portraits of Russian bishops, past and present.

Miüsov took a cursory glance at all these "conventional" surroundings and bent an intent look upon the elder. He had a high opinion of his own insight, a weakness excusable in him as he was fifty, an age in which a clever man of the world of established position can hardly help taking himself rather seriously. From the first moment he did not like Zosima. There was, indeed, something in the elder's face which many people besides Miüsov might not have liked. He was a short, bent, little man, with very weak legs, and though he was only sixty-five, illness made him look at least ten years older. His face was very thin and covered with a network of fine wrinkles, particularly numerous about his eyes, which were small, light-colored, quick, and shining like two bright points. He had a sprinkling of gray hair left around his temples. His pointed beard was small and scanty, and his lips, which smiled frequently, were as thin as two threads. His nose was not long, but sharp, like a bird's beak.

"To all appearances a malicious soul, full of petty pride," thought Miüsov. He felt altogether dissatisfied with his position.

A cheap little clock on the wall struck twelve hurriedly, and served to begin the conversation.

"Precisely to our time," cried Fyodor Pavlovich, "but no sign of my son, Dmitri Fyodorovich. I apologize for him, sacred elder!" (Alyosha shuddered all over at "sacred elder.") "I am always punctual myself, minute for minute, remembering that punctuality is the courtesy of kings . . ."

"But you are not a king, anyway," Miüsov muttered, losing his self-restraint at once.

"Yes; that's true. I'm not a king, and, would you believe it, Pyotr Alexandrovich, I was aware of that myself. But, there! I always say the wrong thing. Your reverence," he cried, with sudden pathos, "you behold before you a real buffoon! I introduce myself as such. It's an old habit, alas! And if I sometimes talk nonsense out of place it's with an object, with the object of amusing people and making myself agreeable. One must be agreeable, mustn't one? I was seven years ago in a little town where I had business, and I made friends with some merchants there. We went to the captain of police because we had to see him about something, and to ask him to dine with us. He was a tall, fat, fair, sulky man, the most dangerous type in such cases. It's their liver. I went straight up to him, and with the ease of a man of the world, you know, 'Mr. Ispravnik,'[3] said I, 'be our Napravnik.' 'What do you mean by Napravnik?' said he. I saw, at the first half-second, that it had missed fire. He stood there so glum. 'I wanted to make a joke,' said I, 'for the general diversion, as Mr. Napravnik is our well-known Russian orchestra conductor and what we need for the harmony of our undertaking is someone of that sort.' And I explained my comparison very reasonably, didn't I? 'Excuse me,' said he, 'I am an Ispravnik, and I do not allow puns to be made on my calling.' He turned and walked away. I followed him, shouting, 'Yes, yes, you are an Ispravnik, not a Napravnik.' 'No,' he said, 'since you called me a Napravnik I am one.' And would you believe it, it ruined our business! And I'm always like that, always like that. Always injuring myself with my politeness. Once, many years ago, I said to an influential person: 'Your wife is a ticklish lady,' in an honorable sense, of the moral qualities, so to speak. But he asked me, 'Why, have you tickled her?' I thought I'd be polite, so I couldn't help saying 'Yes,' and he gave me a fine tickling on the spot. Only that happened long ago, so I'm not ashamed to tell the story. I'm always injuring myself like that."

"You're doing it now," muttered Miüsov, with disgust.

Father Zosima scrutinized them both in silence.

"Am I? Would you believe it, I was aware of that, too, Pyotr Alexandrovich, and let me tell you, indeed, I foresaw I should as soon as I began to speak. And do you know I foresaw, too, that you'd be the first to remark on it. The minute I see my joke isn't coming off, your reverence, both my cheeks feel as though they

---

3. An *ispravnik* is a captain of police. The pun is elaborate because the conductor's name actually suggests "conductor" or "director" while *ispravnik* suggests "rectifier" or "corrector." E. F. Napravnik (1839–1916) conducted at the Marinsky Opera in Petersburg.

were drawn down to the lower jaw and there is almost a spasm in them. That's been so since I was young, when I had to make jokes for my living in noblemen's families. I am an inveterate buffoon, and have been from my birth up, your reverence, it's as though it were a madness in me. I daresay it's a devil within me. But only a little one. A more serious one would have chosen another lodging. But not your soul, Pyotr Alexandrovich; you're not a lodging worth having either. But I do believe—I believe in God, though I have had doubts of late. But now I sit and await words of wisdom. I'm like the philosopher, Diderot,[4] your reverence. Did you ever hear, most Holy Father, how Diderot went to see the Metropolitan Platon, in the time of the Empress Catherine. He went in and said straight out, 'There is no God.' To which the great Bishop lifted up his finger and answered, 'The fool has said in his heart there is no God.' And he fell down at his feet on the spot. 'I believe,' he cried, 'and will be christened.' And so he was. Princess Dashkov[5] was his godmother, and Potyomkin his godfather."

"Fyodor Pavlovich, this is unbearable! You know you're telling lies and that that stupid anecdote isn't true. Why are you playing the fool?" cried Miüsov in a shaking voice.

"I suspected all my life that it wasn't true," Fyodor Pavlovich cried with conviction. "But I'll tell you the whole truth, gentlemen. Great Elder! Forgive me, the last thing about Diderot's christening I made up just now. I never thought of it before. I made it up to add piquancy. I play the fool, Pyotr Alexandrovich, to make myself agreeable. Though I really don't know myself, sometimes, what I do it for. And as for Diderot, I heard as far as 'the fool hath said in his heart' twenty times from the gentry about here when I was young. I heard your aunt, Pyotr Alexandrovich, tell the story. They all believe to this day that the infidel Diderot came to dispute about God with the Metropolitan Platon. . . ."

Miüsov got up, forgetting himself in his impatience. He was furious, and conscious of being ridiculous.

What was taking place in the cell was really incredible. For forty or fifty years past, from the times of former elders, no visitors had entered that cell without feelings of the profoundest veneration. Almost everyone admitted to the cell felt that a great favor was being shown him. Many remained kneeling during the whole visit. Of those visitors, many had been men of high rank and learning, even some freethinkers, attracted by curiosity, or for other reasons, but all without exception had shown the profoundest reverence and

4. Denis Diderot (1713–1784), one of the French *encyclopédistes*, visited Russia for five months in 1773. Empress Catherine II was one of his patrons.
5. Princess Dashkov (1743–1810), a brilliant writer and a supporter of Catherine, became president of the Russian Academy. Potyomkin was the most famous of Catherine's favorites and, from 1774 to his death in 1791, the major force in Russian affairs.

delicacy, for here there was no question of money, but only on the one side love and kindness, and on the other penitence and eager desire to decide some difficult spiritual problem or crisis. So that the buffoonery shown by Fyodor Pavlovich, the lack of reverence for the place he was in, amazed and bewildered the spectators, or at least some of them. The monks, with unchanged countenances, waited, with earnest attention, to hear what the elder would say, but seemed on the point of standing up, like Miüsov. Alyosha stood, with hanging head, on the verge of tears. What seemed to him strangest of all was that his brother Ivan Fyodorovich, on whom alone he had rested his hopes, and who alone had such influence on his father that he could have stopped him, sat now quite unmoved, with downcast eyes, apparently waiting with curious interest to see how it would end, as though he had nothing to do with it. Alyosha did not dare to look at Rakitin, the divinity student, whom he knew almost intimately. He knew his thoughts (though he alone in the monastery knew Rakitin's thoughts).

"Forgive me," began Miüsov, addressing Father Zosima, "for perhaps I seem to be taking part in this shameful foolery. I made a mistake in believing that even a man like Fyodor Pavlovich would understand what was due on a visit to so honored a personage. I did not suppose I should have to apologize simply for having come with him...."

Pyotr Alexandrovich could say no more, and was about to leave the room, overwhelmed with confusion.

"Don't distress yourself, I beg." The elder got onto his feeble legs and taking Pyotr Alexandrovich by both hands, made him sit down again. "I beg you not to disturb yourself. I particularly beg you to be my guest." And with a bow he went back and sat down again on his little sofa.

"Great elder, speak! Do I annoy you by my vivacity?" Fyodor Pavlovich cried suddenly, clutching the arms of his chair in both hands, as though ready to leap up from it if the answer was unfavorable.

"I earnestly beg you, too, not to disturb yourself, and not to be uneasy," the elder said impressively. "Do not trouble. Make yourself quite at home. And, above all, do not be so ashamed of yourself, for that is at the root of it all.'

"Quite at home? To be my natural self? Oh, that is much too much, but I accept it with grateful joy. Do you know, blessed father, you'd better not invite me to be my natural self. Don't risk it.... I will not go so far as that myself. I warn you for your own sake. Well, the rest is still plunged in the mists of uncertainty, though there are people who'd be pleased to describe me for you. I mean that for you, Pyotr Alexandrovich. But as for you, holy being, let me tell you, I am brimming over with ecstasy."

He got up, and throwing up his hands, declaimed, "Blessed be the womb that bare thee, and the paps that gave thee suck—the paps especially. When you said just now, 'Don't be so ashamed of yourself for that is at the root of it all,' you pierced right through me by that remark, and read me to the core. Indeed, I always feel when I meet people that I am lower than all, and that they all take me for a buffoon. So I say, 'Let me really play the buffoon. I am not afraid of your opinion, for you are every one of you worse than I am.' That is why I am a buffoon. It is from shame, great elder, from shame; it's simply over-sensitiveness that makes me rowdy. If I had only been sure that everyone would accept me as the kindest and wisest of men, oh, Lord, what a good man I should have been then! Teacher!" he fell suddenly on his knees, "what must I do to gain eternal life?" It was difficult even now to decide whether he was joking or really moved.

Father Zosima, lifting his eyes, looked at him, and said with a smile:

"You have known for a long time what you must do. You have sense enough: don't give way to drunkenness and incontinence of speech; don't give way to sensual lust; and, above all, to the love of money. And close your taverns. If you can't close all, at least two or three. And, above all—don't lie."

"You mean about Diderot?"

"No, not about Diderot. Above all, don't lie to yourself. The man who lies to himself and listens to his own lie comes to such a pass that he cannot distinguish the truth within him, or around him, and so loses all respect for himself and for others. And having no respect he ceases to love, and in order to occupy and distract himself without love he gives way to passions and coarse pleasures, and sinks to bestiality in his vices, all from continual lying to other men and to himself. The man who lies to himself can be more easily offended than anyone. You know it is sometimes very pleasant to take offense, isn't it? A man may know that nobody has insulted him, but that he has invented the insult for himself, has lied and exaggerated to make it picturesque, has caught at a word and made a mountain out of a molehill—he knows that himself, yet he will be the first to take offense, and will revel in his resentment till he feels great pleasure in it, and so pass to genuine vindictiveness. But get up, sit down, I beg you. All this, too, is deceitful posturing..."

"Blessed man! Give me your hand to kiss."

Fyodor Pavlovich skipped up, and imprinted a rapid kiss on the elder's thin hand. "It is, it is pleasant to take offense. You said that so well, as I never heard it before. Yes, I have been all my life taking offense, to please myself, taking offense on esthetic grounds, for it is not so much pleasant as distinguished sometimes to be insulted—that you had forgotten, great elder, it is distinguished! I shall make a note of that. But I have been lying, lying positively my whole life long, every day and hour of it. Of a truth, I am a lie, and the father of lies. Though I believe I am not the father of lies. I am getting mixed in my texts. Say, the son of lies, and that will be enough. Only . . . my angel . . . I may sometimes talk about Diderot! Diderot will do no harm, though sometimes a word will do harm. Great elder, by the way, I was forgetting, though I had been meaning for the last two years to come here on purpose to ask and to find out something. Only do tell Pyotr Alexandrovich not to interrupt me. Here is my question: Is it true, great Father, that the story is told somewhere in the *Lives of the Saints* of a holy saint martyred for his faith who, when his head was cut off at last, stood up, picked up his head, and, 'courteously kissing it,' walked a long way, carrying it in his hands. Is that true or not, honored Father?"

"No, it is untrue," said the elder.

"There is nothing of the kind in all the lives of the saints. What saint do you say the story is told of?" asked the Father Librarian.

"I do not know what saint. I do not know, and can't tell. I was deceived. I was told the story. I had heard it, and do you know who told it? Pyotr Alexandrovich Miüsov here, who was so angry just now about Diderot. He it was who told the story."

"I have never told it to you. I never speak to you at all."

"It is true you did not tell me, but you told it when I was present. It was three years ago. I mentioned it because by that ridiculous story you shook my faith, Pyotr Alexandrovich. You knew nothing of it, but I went home with my faith shaken, and I have been getting more and more shaken ever since. Yes, Pyotr Alexandrovich, you were the cause of a great fall. That was not a Diderot!"

Fyodor Pavlovich got excited and pathetic, though it was perfectly clear to everyone by now that he was playing a part again. Yet Miüsov was stung by his words.

"What nonsense, and it is all nonsense," he muttered. "I may really have told it, sometime or other . . . but not to you. I was told it myself. I heard it in Paris from a Frenchman. He told me it was read at our mass from the *Lives of the Saints* . . . he was a very learned man who had made a special study of Russian statistics and had lived a long time in Russia. . . . I have not read the *Lives of the Saints* myself, and I am not going to read them . . . all sorts of things are said at dinner—we were dining then."

"Yes, you were dining then, and so I lost my faith!" said Fyodor Pavlovich, mimicking him.

"What do I care for your faith?" Miüsov was on the point of shouting, but he suddenly checked himself, and said with contempt, "You defile everything you touch."

The elder suddenly rose from his seat. "Excuse me, gentlemen, for leaving you a few minutes," he said, addressing all his guests. "I have visitors awaiting me who arrived before you. But don't you tell lies all the same," he added, turning to Fyodor Pavlovich with a good-humored face. He went out of the cell. Alyosha and the novice flew to escort him down the steps. Alyosha was breathless: he was glad to get away, but he was glad, too, that the elder was good-humored and not offended. Father Zosima was going towards the portico to bless the people waiting for him there. But Fyodor Pavlovich persisted in stopping him at the door of the cell.

"Blessed man!" he cried, with feeling. "Allow me to kiss your hand once more. Yes, with you I could still talk, I could still get on. Do you think I always lie and play the fool like this? Believe me, I have been acting like this all the time on purpose to try you. I have been testing you all the time to see whether I could get on with you. Is there room for my humility beside your pride? I am ready to give you a testimonial that one can get on with you! But now, I'll be quiet; I will keep quiet all the time. I'll sit in a chair and hold my tongue. Now it is for you to speak, Pyotr Alexandrovich. You are the principal person left now—for ten minutes."

Chapter III

Peasant Women Who Have Faith

Near the wooden portico below, built onto the outer wall of the precinct, there was a crowd of about twenty peasant women. They had been told that the elder was at last coming out, and they had gathered together in anticipation. Two ladies, Madame Khokhlakov and her daughter, had also come out into the portico to wait for the elder, but in a separate part of it set aside for women of rank.

Madame Khokhlakov was a wealthy lady, still young and attractive, and always dressed with taste. She was rather pale, and had lively black eyes. She was not more than thirty-three, and had been five years a widow. Her daughter, a girl of fourteen, was partially paralyzed. The poor child had not been able to walk for the last six months, and was wheeled about in a long reclining chair. She had a charming little face, rather thin from illness, but full of gaiety. There was a gleam of mischief in her big dark eyes with their long lashes. Her mother had been intending to take her abroad ever since the spring, but they had been detained all the summer by business connected with their estate. They had been staying a week in our town, where they had come more for purposes of business than devotion, but had visited Father Zosima once already, three days before. Though they knew that the elder scarcely saw anyone, they had now suddenly turned up again, and urgently entreated "the happiness of looking once again on the great healer."

The mother was sitting on a chair by the side of her daughter's invalid carriage, and two paces from her stood an old monk, not one of our monastery, but a visitor from an obscure monastery in the far north. He too sought the elder's blessing.

But Father Zosima, on entering the portico, went first straight to the peasants who were crowded at the foot of the three steps that led up into the portico. Father Zosima stood on the top step, put on his stole, and began blessing the women who thronged about him. One possessed woman was led up to him. As soon as she caught sight of the elder she began shrieking and writhing as though in the pains of childbirth. Laying the stole on her forehead, he read a short prayer over her, and she was at once soothed and quieted.

I do not know how it may be now, but in my childhood I often happened to see and hear these "possessed" women in the villages and monasteries. They used to be brought to mass; they would squeal or bark like a dog so that they were heard all over the church. But when the sacrament was carried in and they were led up to it, at once the "possession" ceased, and the sick women were always soothed for a time. I was greatly impressed and amazed at this as a child; but then I heard from country neighbors and from my town teachers that the whole illness was simulated to avoid work, and that it could always be cured by suitable severity; various anecdotes were told to confirm this. But later on I learned with astonishment from medical specialists that there is no pretense about it, that it is a terrible illness to which women are subject, specially prevalent among us in Russia, and that it is due to the hard lot of the peasant women. It is a disease, I was told, arising from exhausting toil too soon after hard, abnormal and unassisted labor in childbirth, and from the hopeless misery, from beatings, and so on, which some women were not able to endure like others. The strange and instant healing of the frantic and struggling woman as soon as she was led up to the holy sacrament, which had been explained to me as pretense and even trickery on the part of the "clericals," arose probably in the most natural manner. Both the women who supported her and the invalid herself fully believed as a truth beyond question that the evil spirit in possession of her could not hold out if the sick woman were brought to the sacrament and made to bow down before it. And so, with a nervous and psychically deranged woman, a sort of convulsion of the whole organism always took place, and was bound to take place, at the moment of bowing down to the sacrament, aroused by the expectation of the miracle of healing and the implicit belief that it would come to pass; and it did come to pass, though only for a moment. It was exactly the same now as soon as the elder touched the sick woman with the stole.

Many of the women in the crowd were moved to tears of emotional ecstasy by the effect of the moment; some strove to kiss the hem of his garment, others cried out in singsong voices. He blessed them all and talked with some of them. The "possessed" woman he knew already. She came from a village only four miles from the monastery, and had been brought to him before.

"But here is one from afar." He pointed to a woman by no means old but very thin and wasted, with a face not merely sunburned but almost blackened by exposure. She was kneeling and gazing with a fixed stare at the elder; there was something almost frenzied in her eyes.

"From afar off, Father, from afar off! From two hundred miles from here. From afar off, Father, from afar off!" the woman began in a singsong voice as though she were chanting a dirge, swaying her head from side to side with her cheek resting in her hand.

There is silent and long-suffering sorrow to be met with among the peasantry. It withdraws into itself and is still. But there is also a grief that breaks out, and from that minute it bursts into tears and finds vent in wailing. This is particularly common with women. But it is no lighter a grief than the silent. Lamentations comfort only by lacerating the heart still more. Such grief does not desire consolation. It feeds on the sense of its hopelessness. Lamentations spring only from the constant craving to reopen the wound.

"You are of the tradesman class?" said Father Zosima, looking curiously at her.

"Townfolk we are, Father, townfolk. Yet we are peasants though we live in the town. I have come to see you, oh Father! We heard of you, Father, we heard of you. I have buried my little son, and I have come on a pilgrimage. I have been in three monasteries, but they told me, 'Go, Nastasya, go to them'—that is to you, my dear. I have come; I was yesterday at the service, and today I have come to you."

"What are you weeping for?"

"It's my little son I'm grieving for, Father. He was three years old—three years all but three months. I grieve for my little boy, Father, for my little boy. I'm in anguish for my little boy. He was the last one left. We had four, my Nikita and I, and now we've no children, our dear ones have all gone. I buried the first three without grieving overmuch, and now I have buried the last I can't forget him. He seems always standing before me. He never leaves me. He has withered my heart. I look at his little clothes, his little shirt, his little boots, and I wail. I lay out all that is left of him, all his little things. I look at them and wail. I say to Nikita, my husband, let me go on a pilgrimage, master. He is a driver. We're not poor people, Father, not poor; he drives our own horse. It's all our own, the horse and the carriage. And what good is it all to us now? My Nikita has begun drinking while I am away. He's sure to. It used to be so before. As soon as I turn my back he gives way to it. But now I don't think about him. It's three months since I left home. I've forgotten him. I've forgotten everything. I don't want to remember. And what would our life be now together? I've done with him, I've done. I've done with them all. I don't care to look upon my house and my goods. I don't care to see anything at all!"

"Listen, mother," said the elder. "Once in olden times a holy saint saw in the Temple a mother like you weeping for her little one, her only one, whom God had taken. 'Knowest thou not,' said the saint to her, 'how bold these little ones are before the throne of God? Verily there are none bolder than they in the Kingdom of Heaven. "Thou didst give us life, oh Lord," they say, "and scarcely had we looked upon it when Thou didst take it back again." And so boldly they ask and ask again that God gives them at once the rank of angels. Therefore,' said the saint, 'thou too, oh mother, rejoice and weep not, for thy little one is with the Lord in the fellowship of the angels.' That's what the saint said to the weeping mother of old. He was a great saint and he could not have spoken falsely. Therefore you too, mother, know that your little one is surely before the throne of God, is rejoicing and happy, and praying to God for you, and therefore weep, but rejoice."

The woman listened to him, looking down with her cheek in her hand. She sighed deeply.

"My Nikita tried to comfort me with the same words as you. 'Foolish one,' he said, 'why weep? Our son is no doubt singing with the angels before God.' He says that to me, but he weeps himself. I see that he cries like me. 'I know, Nikita,' said I. 'Where could he be if not with the Lord God? Only, here with us now he is not as he used to sit beside us before.' And if only I could look upon him one little time, if only I could peep at him one little time, without going up to him, without speaking, if I could be hidden in a corner and only see him for one little minute, hear him playing in the yard, calling in his little voice, 'Mummy, where are you?' If only I could hear him pattering with his little feet about the room just once, only once; for so often, so often I remember how he used to run to me and shout and laugh, if only I could hear his little feet I should know him! But he's gone, Father, he's gone, and I shall never hear him again. Here's his little sash, but him I shall never see or hear now."

She drew out of her bosom her boy's little embroidered sash, and as soon as she looked at it she began shaking with sobs, hiding her eyes with her fingers through which the tears flowed in a sudden stream.

"It is 'Rachel of old,' " said the elder, " 'weeping for her children, and will not be comforted because they are not.' Such is the lot set on earth for you mothers. Be not comforted. Consolation is not what you need. Weep and be not consoled, but weep. Only every time that you weep be sure to remember that your little son is one of the angels of God, that he looks down from there at you and sees you, and rejoices at your tears, and points at them to the Lord God; and a long while yet you will keep that great mother's grief. But it will turn in the end into quiet joy, and your bitter tears will be only tears of tender sorrow that purifies the heart and delivers it from sin. And I shall pray for the peace of your child's soul. What was his name?"

"Alexey, Father."

"A sweet name. After Alexey, the man of God?"[6]

"The man of God, Father, the man of God, Alexey, the man of God."

"What a saint he was! I will remember him, mother, and your grief in my prayers, and I will pray for your husband's health. It is a sin for you to leave him. Your little one will see from heaven that you have forsaken his father, and will weep over you. Why do you trouble his happiness? He is living, for the soul lives forever, and though he is not in the house, he is near you, unseen. How can he go into the house when you say that the house is hateful to you? To whom is he to go if he finds you not together, his father and mother? He comes to you in dreams now, and you grieve. But then he will send you gentle dreams. Go to your husband, mother; go this very day."

"I will go, Father, at your word. I will go. You've gone straight to my heart. My Nikita, my Nikita, you are waiting for me, my dear," the woman began in a singsong voice; but the elder had already turned away to a very old woman, dressed like a dweller in the town, not like a pilgrim. Her eyes showed that she had come with an object, and in order to say something. She said she was the widow of a noncommissioned officer, and lived close by in the town. Her son Vasenka was in the commissariat service, and had gone to Irkutsk in Siberia. He had written twice from there, but now a year had passed since he had written. She did inquire about him, but she did not know the proper place to inquire.

"Only the other day Stepanida Ilyinishna—she's a rich merchant's wife—said to me, 'You go, Prokhorovna, and put your son's name down for prayer in the church, and pray for the peace of his soul as though he were dead. His soul will be troubled,' she said, 'and he will write you a letter.' And Stepanida Ilyinishna told me it was a certain thing which had been many times tried. Only I am in doubt. . . . Oh, you light of ours! Is it true or false, and would it be right?"

"Don't think of it. It's shameful to ask the question. How is it

6. Alexey was a saint whose popular early as the twelfth century. "Life" was translated from Greek as

possible to pray for the peace of a living soul? And his own mother too! It's a great sin, akin to sorcery. Only for your ignorance it is forgiven you. Better pray to the Queen of Heaven, our swift defense and help, for his good health, and that she may forgive you for your error. And another thing I will tell you, Prokhorovna. Either he will soon come back to you, your son, or he will be sure to send a letter. Go, and henceforward be in peace. Your son is alive, I tell you."

"Dear Father, God reward you, our benefactor, who prays for all of us and for our sins!"

But the elder had already noticed in the crowd two glowing eyes fixed upon him. An exhausted, consumptive-looking, though young peasant woman was gazing at him in silence. Her eyes besought him, but she seemed afraid to approach.

"What is it, my child?"

"Absolve my soul, Father," she articulated softly and slowly, sank on her knees and bowed down at his feet. "I have sinned, Father. I am afraid of my sin."

The elder sat down on the lower step. The woman crept closer to him, still on her knees.

"I am a widow these three years," she began in a half-whisper, with a sort of shudder. "I had a hard life with my husband. He was an old man. He used to beat me cruelly. He lay ill; I thought, looking at him, if he were to get well, if he were to get up again, what then? And then the thought came to me—"

"Stay!" said the elder, and he put his ear close to her lips. The woman went on in a low whisper, so that it was almost impossible to catch anything. She had soon done.

"Three years ago?" asked the elder.

"Three years. At first I didn't think about it, but now I've begun to be ill, and the thought never leaves me."

"Have you come from far?"

"Over three hundred miles away."

"Have you told it in confession?"

"I have confessed it. Twice I have confessed it."

"Have you been admitted to Communion?"

"Yes. I am afraid. I am afraid to die."

"Fear nothing and never be afraid; and don't fret. If only your penitence fail not, God will forgive all. There is no sin, and there can be no sin on all the earth, which the Lord will not forgive to the truly repentant! Man cannot commit a sin so great as to exhaust the infinite love of God. Can there be a sin which could exceed the love of God? Think only of repentance, continual repentance, but dismiss fear altogether. Believe that God loves you as you cannot conceive; that He loves you with your sin, in your sin. It has been said of old that over one repentant sinner there is more joy in heaven than over ten righteous men. Go, and fear not. Be not bitter against men. Be not angry if you are wronged. Forgive the dead man in your heart what wrong he did you. Be reconciled with him in truth. If you are penitent, you love. And if you love you are of God. All things are atoned for, all things are saved by love. If I, a sinner, even as you are, am tender with you and have pity on you, how much more will God. Love is such a priceless treasure that you can redeem the whole world by it, and expiate not only your own sins but the sins of others. Go, and be not afraid."

He signed her three times with the cross, took from his own neck a little icon and put it upon her. She bowed down to the earth without speaking. He got up and looked cheerfully at a healthy peasant woman with a tiny baby in her arms.

"From Vyshegorye, dear Father."

"Four miles you have dragged yourself with the baby. What do you want?"

"I've come to look at you. I have been to you before—or have you forgotten? You've no great memory if you've forgotten me. They told us you were ill. Thinks I, I'll go and see him for myself. Now I see you, and you're not ill. You'll live another twenty years. God bless you! There are plenty to pray for you; how should you be ill?"

"I thank you for all, daughter."

"By the way, I have a thing to ask, not a great one. Here are sixty kopecks. Give them, dear Father, to some one poorer than me. I thought as I came along, better give through him. He'll know whom to give to."

"Thanks, my dear, thanks! You are a good woman. I love you. I will do so certainly. Is that your little girl?"

"My little girl, Father, Lizaveta."

"May the Lord bless you both, you and your babe Lizaveta! You have gladdened my heart, mother. Farewell, dear children, farewell, dear ones."

He blessed them all and bowed low to them.

Chapter IV

A Lady of Little Faith

The visiting wealthy lady, looking on the scene of his conversation with the peasants and his blessing them, shed silent tears and wiped them away with her handkerchief. She was a sentimental society lady of genuinely good disposition in many respects. When the elder went up to her at last she met him ecstatically.

"Ah, I have borne so much, so much, looking on at this touching scene! . . ." She could not go on for emotion. "Oh, I understand the people's love for you. I love the people myself. I want to love them. And who could help loving them, our splendid Russian people, so simple in their greatness!"

"How is your daughter's health? You wanted to talk to me again?"

"Oh, I have been urgently begging for it, I have prayed for it! I was ready to fall on my knees and kneel for three days at your windows until you let me in. We have come, great healer, to express our ecstatic gratitude. You have helped my Lise,[7] healed her completely, merely by praying over her last Thursday and laying your hands upon her. We have hastened here to kiss those hands, to pour out our feelings and our homage."

"What do you mean by healed? Isn't she still lying down in her chair?"

"But her night fevers have stopped completely, for two days now, ever since Thursday," said the lady with nervous haste. "And that's not all. Her legs are stronger. This morning she got up well; she had slept all night. Look at her rosy cheeks, her bright eyes! She used to be always crying, but now she laughs and is gay and happy. This morning she insisted on my letting her stand up, and she stood up for a whole minute without any support. She wagers that in a fortnight she'll be dancing a quadrille. I've called in the local doctor, Herzenstube. He shrugged his shoulders and said, 'I am amazed; I can make nothing of it.' And would you have us not come here to disturb you, not fly here to thank you? Lise, thank him—thank him!"

Lise's pretty little laughing face became suddenly serious. She rose in her chair as far as she could and, looking at the elder, clasped her hands before him, but could not restrain herself and broke into laughter.

"It's at him, at him," she said, pointing to Alyosha, with childish vexation at herself for not being able to repress her mirth.

If anyone had looked at Alyosha standing a step behind the elder, he could have caught a quick flush crimsoning his cheeks in an instant. His eyes shone and he looked down.

"She has a message for you, Alexey Fyodorovich. How are you?" the mother went on, holding out her exquisitely gloved hand to Alyosha. The elder turned round and all at once looked attentively at Alyosha. The latter went nearer to Lise and, smiling in a strangely awkward way, held out his hand to her too. Lise assumed an important air.

"Katerina Ivanovna has sent you this through me." She handed him a little note. "She particularly begs you to go and see her as

7. The name is given the French pro-
nunciation by the mother and occasion- ally by others. Alyosha usually gives the Russian version, Lisa.

soon as possible; that you will not fail her, but will be sure to come."

"She asks me to go and see her? Me? What for?" Alyosha muttered in great astonishment. His face at once looked anxious.

"Oh, it's all to do with Dmitri Fyodorovich and—what has happened lately," the mother explained hurriedly. "Katerina Ivanovna has made a certain decision, but she must see you about it. . . . Why, of course, I can't say. But she wants to see you at once. And you will go to her, of course. It is a Christian duty."

"I have only seen her once," Alyosha protested with the same perplexity.

"Oh, she is such a lofty, incomparable creature! If only for her suffering . . . Think what she has gone through, what she is enduring now! Think what awaits her! It's all terrible, terrible!"

"Very well, I will come," Alyosha decided, after rapidly scanning the brief, enigmatic note, which consisted of an urgent entreaty that he would come, without any sort of explanation.

"Oh, how sweet and magnificent that would be of you!" cried Lise with sudden animation. "I told mamma you'd be sure not to go. I said you were saving your soul. How splendid you are! I've always thought you were splendid. How glad I am to tell you so!"

"Lise!" said her mother significantly, though she smiled after she had said it.

"You have quite forgotten us, Alexey Fyodorovich," she said; "you never come to see us. Yet Lise has told me twice that she is never happy except with you." Alyosha raised his downcast eyes and again flushed, and again smiled without knowing why. But the elder was no longer watching him. He had begun talking to a monk who, as mentioned before, had been awaiting his entrance by Lise's chair. He was evidently a monk of the humblest, that is of the peasant, class, of a narrow unshakable outlook, but a true believer, and, in his own way, a stubborn one. He announced that he had come from the far north, from Obdorsk, from Saint Sylvester, and was a member of a poor monastery, consisting of only nine monks. The elder gave him his blessing and invited him to come to his cell whenever he liked.

"How can you presume to do such deeds?" the monk asked suddenly, pointing solemnly and significantly at Lise. He was referring to her "healing."

"It's too early, of course, to speak of that. Relief is not complete cure, and may proceed from different causes. But if there has been any healing, it is by no power but God's will. It's all from God. Visit me, Father," he added to the monk. "It's not often I can see visitors. I am ill, and I know that my days are numbered."

"Oh, no, no! God will not take you from us. You will live a long,

long time yet," cried the lady. "And in what way are you ill? You look so well, so gay and happy."

"I am extraordinarily better today. But I know that it's only for a moment. I understand my disease now thoroughly. If I seem so happy to you, you could never say anything that would please me so much. For men are made for happiness, and anyone who is completely happy has a right to say to himself, 'I am doing God's will on earth.' All the righteous, all the saints, all the holy martyrs were happy."

"Oh, how you speak! What bold and lofty words!" cried the lady. "You seem to pierce with your words. And yet—happiness, happiness—where is it? Who can say of himself that he is happy? Oh, since you have been so good as to let us see you once more today, let me tell you what I could not utter last time, what I dared not say, all I am suffering and have been for so long, for so long! I am suffering! Forgive me! I am suffering!" And in a rush of fervent feeling she clasped her hands before him.

"From what specially?"

"I suffer . . . from lack of faith."

"Lack of faith in God?"

"Oh, no, no! I dare not even think of that. But the future life—it is such an enigma! And no one, no one can solve it. Listen! You are a healer, you are deeply versed in the human soul, and of course I dare not expect you to believe me entirely, but I assure you on my word of honor that I am not speaking lightly now. The thought of the life beyond the grave distracts me to anguish, to terror and to fear. And I don't know to whom to appeal, and have not dared to all my life. And now I am so bold as to ask you. Oh, God! What will you think of me now?" She clasped her hands.

"Don't distress yourself about my opinion of you," said the elder. "I quite believe in the sincerity of your suffering."

"Oh, how thankful I am to you! You see, I shut my eyes and ask myself if everyone has faith, where did it come from? And then they do say that it all comes from terror at the menacing phenomena of nature, and that none of it's real. And I say to myself, 'What if I've been believing all my life, and when I come to die, there's nothing but the "burdocks growing on my grave?" '[7a] as I read in some author. It's awful! How—how can I get back my faith? But I only believed when I was a little child, mechanically, without thinking of anything. How, how is one to prove it? I have come now to lay my soul before you and to ask you about it. If I let this chance slip, no one all my life will answer me. How can I prove it? How can I convince myself? Oh, how unhappy I am! I stand and look about me and see that scarcely anyone else cares; no one troubles

---

7a. Bazarov's remark in Turgenev's *Fathers and Sons*, 1862.

his head about it now, and I'm the only one who can't stand it. It's deadly—deadly!"

"No doubt, deadly. But there's no proving it, though you can be convinced of it."

"How?"

"By the experience of active love. Strive to love your neighbor actively and indefatigably. Insofar as you advance in love you will grow surer of the reality of God and of the immortality of your soul. If you attain to perfect self-forgetfulness in the love of your neighbor, then you will believe without doubt, and no doubt can possibly enter your soul. This has been tried. This is certain."

"In active love? There's another question—and such a question! You see, I so love humanity that—would you believe it?—I often dream of forsaking all that I have, leaving Lise, and becoming a sister of mercy. I close my eyes and think and dream, and at that moment I feel full of strength to overcome all obstacles. No wounds, no festering sores could at that moment frighten me. I would bind them up and wash them with my own hands. I would nurse the afflicted. I would be ready to kiss such wounds."

"It is much, and well that your mind is full of such dreams and not others. Sometime, unawares, you may do a good deed in reality."

"Yes. But could I endure such a life for long?" the lady went on fervently, almost frantically. "That's the chief question—that's my most agonizing question. I shut my eyes and ask myself, 'Would you persevere long on that path? And if the patient whose wounds you are washing did not meet you with gratitude, but worried you with his whims, without valuing or remarking your charitable services, began abusing you and rudely commanding you, and complaining to the superior authorities of you (which often happens when people are in great suffering)—what then? Would you persevere in your love, or not?' And do you know, I came with horror to the conclusion that, if anything could dissipate my active love to humanity, it would be ingratitude. In short, I am a hired servant, I expect my payment at once—that is, praise, and the repayment of love with love. Otherwise I am incapable of loving anyone."

She was in a very paroxysm of self-castigation, and, concluding, she looked with defiant resolution at the elder.

"It's just the same story a doctor once told me," observed the elder. "He was a man getting on in years, and undoubtedly clever. He spoke as frankly as you, though in jest, in bitter jest. 'I love humanity,' he said, 'but I wonder at myself. The more I love humanity in general, the less I love man in particular, that is, separately, as single individuals. In my dreams,' he said, 'I have often come to making enthusiastic schemes for the service of humanity, and perhaps I might actually have faced crucifixion if it had been suddenly necessary; and yet I am incapable of living in the same room with anyone for two days together, as I know by experience. As soon as anyone is near me, his personality disturbs my self-esteem and restricts my freedom. In twenty-four hours I begin to hate even the best of men: one because he's too long over his dinner; another because he has a cold and keeps on blowing his nose. I become hostile to people the moment they come close to me. But it has always happened that the more I detest men individually the more ardent becomes my love for humanity.' "

"But what's to be done? What can one do in such a case? Must one despair?"

"No. It is enough that you are distressed at it. Do what you can, and it will be reckoned unto you. Much is done already in you since you can so deeply and sincerely know yourself. If you have been talking to me so sincerely, simply to gain approbation for your frankness, as you did from me just now, then of course you will not attain to anything in the achievement of real love; it will all get no further than dreams, and your whole life will slip away like a phantom. In that case you will naturally cease to think of the future life too, and will of yourself grow calmer after a fashion in the end."

"You have crushed me! Only now, as you speak, I understand that I was really only seeking your approbation for my sincerity when I told you I could not endure ingratitude. You have revealed me to myself. You have seen through me and explained me to myself!"

"Are you speaking the truth? Well, now, after such an admission, I believe that you are sincere and good at heart. If you do not attain happiness, always remember that you are on the right road, and try not to leave it. Above all, avoid falsehood, every kind of falsehood, especially falseness to yourself. Watch over your own deceitfulness and look into it every hour, every minute. Avoid being scornful, both to others and to yourself. What seems to you bad within you will grow purer from the very fact of your observing it in yourself. Avoid fear, too, though fear is only the consequence of every sort of falsehood. Never be frightened at your own faint-heartedness in attaining love. Don't be frightened overmuch even at your evil actions. I am sorry I can say nothing more consoling to you, for love in action is a harsh and dreadful thing compared with love in dreams. Love in dreams is greedy for immediate action, rapidly performed and in the sight of all. Men will even give their lives if only the ordeal does not last long but is soon over, with all looking on and applauding as though on the stage. But active love is labor and fortitude, and for some people too, perhaps, a complete science. But I predict that just when you see with horror that in spite of all your efforts you are getting further from your goal instead of nearer to it—at that very moment I predict that you will reach it and behold clearly the miraculous power of the Lord who has been all the time loving and mysteriously guiding you. Forgive me for not being able to stay longer with you. They are waiting for me. Good-bye."

The lady was weeping.

"Lise, Lise! Bless her—bless her!" she cried, starting up suddenly.

"She does not deserve to be loved. I have seen her naughtiness all along," the elder said jestingly. "Why have you been laughing at Alexey?"

Lise had in fact been occupied in mocking at him all the time. She had noticed before that Alyosha was shy and tried not to look at her, and she found this extremely amusing. She waited intently to catch his eye. Alyosha, unable to endure her persistent stare, was irresistibly and suddenly drawn to glance at her, and at once she smiled triumphantly in his face. Alyosha was even more disconcerted and vexed. At last he turned away from her altogether and hid behind the elder's back. After a few minutes, drawn by the same irresistible force, he turned again to see whether he was being looked at or not, and found Lise almost hanging out of her chair to peep sideways at him, eagerly waiting for him to look. Catching his eye, she laughed so that the elder could not help saying, "Why do you make fun of him like that, naughty girl?"

Lise suddenly and quite unexpectedly blushed. Her eyes flashed and her face became terribly serious. She began speaking quickly and nervously, with a resentful, heated complaint:

"Why has he forgotten everything, then? He used to carry me about when I was little. We used to play together. He used to come to teach me to read, do you know. Two years ago, when he went away, he said that he would never forget me, that we were friends forever, forever, forever! And now he's afraid of me all at once. Am I going to eat him? Why doesn't he want to come near me? Why doesn't he talk? Why won't he come and see us? It's not that you won't let him. We know that he goes everywhere. It's not good manners for me to invite him. He ought to have thought of it first, if he hasn't forgotten me. No, now he's saving his soul! Why have you put that long gown on him? If he runs he'll fall."

And suddenly, no longer able to contain herself, she hid her face in her hand and went off into irresistible, prolonged, nervous, inaudible laughter. The elder listened to her with a smile, and blessed her tenderly. As she kissed his hand she suddenly pressed it to her eyes and began crying.

"Don't be angry with me. I'm silly and good for nothing . . . and perhaps Alyosha's right, quite right, in not wanting to come and see such a ridiculous girl."

"I will certainly send him," said the elder.

Chapter V

So Be It! So Be It!

The elder's absence from his cell had lasted for about twenty-five minutes. It was more than half-past twelve, but Dmitri Fyodorovich, on whose account they had all met there, had still not appeared. But he seemed almost to be forgotten, and when the elder entered the cell again, he found his guests engaged in eager conversation. Ivan Fyodorovich and the two monks took the leading share in it. Miüsov, too, was trying to take a part, and apparently very eagerly, in the conversation. But he was unsuccessful in this also. He was evidently in the background, and his remarks were treated with neglect, so that this new circumstance only increased his irritability. He had had intellectual encounters with Ivan Fyodorovich before and he could not endure a certain carelessness Ivan showed him. "Hitherto at least I have stood in the front ranks of all that is progressive in Europe, and here the new generation positively ignores us," he thought.

Fyodor Pavlovich, who had given his word to sit still and be quiet, had actually been quiet for some time, but he watched his neighbor Miüsov with an ironical little smile, obviously enjoying his discomfiture. He had been waiting for some time to pay off old scores, and now he could not let the opportunity slip. Bending over to his neighbor's shoulder he began teasing him again in a whisper.

"Why didn't you go away just now, after the 'courteously kissing'? Why did you consent to remain in such unseemly company? It was because you felt insulted and aggrieved, and you remained to vindicate your self by showing off your intelligence. Now you won't go till you've displayed your intellect to them."

"You again? . . . On the contrary, I'm just going."

"You'll be the last, the last of all to go!" Fyodor Pavlovich delivered him another thrust, almost at the moment of Father Zosima's return.

The discussion died down for a moment, but the elder, seating himself in his former place, looked at them all as though cordially inviting them to go on. Alyosha, who knew every expression of his face, saw that he was fearfully exhausted and making a great effort. Of late he had been liable to fainting fits from exhaustion. His face had the pallor that was common before such attacks, and his lips were white. But he evidently did not want to break up the gathering. He seemed to have some special object of his own in keeping them. What object? Alyosha watched him intently.

"We are discussing this gentleman's most interesting article," said Father Iosif, the librarian, addressing the elder, and indicating Ivan Fyodorovich. "He brings forward much that is new, but I think the

argument cuts both ways. It is an article written in answer to a
book by an ecclesiastical authority on the question of the ecclesiastical court, and the scope of its jurisdiction."

"I'm sorry I have not read your article, but I've heard of it," said
the elder, looking keenly and intently at Ivan Fyodorovich.

"He takes up a most interesting position," continued the Father
Librarian. "As far as Church jurisdiction is concerned he is apparently quite opposed to the separation of Church from State."

"That's interesting. But in what sense?" Father Zosima asked
Ivan Fyodorovich.

The latter, at last, answered him, not condescendingly, as Alyosha had feared, but with modesty and reserve, with evident
goodwill and apparently without the slightest ulterior purpose.

"I start from the position that this merging of elements, that is,
of the essential principles of Church and State taken separately,
will, of course, go on for ever, in spite of the fact that it is impossible, and can never lead to any consistent or even normal results, for
there is falsity at the very foundation of it. Compromise between
the Church and State in such questions as, for instance, jurisdiction, is, to my thinking, impossible in any real sense. My clerical
opponent maintained that the Church holds a precise and defined
position in the State. I maintain, on the contrary, that the Church
ought to include the whole State, and not simply to occupy a
corner in it, and, if this is, for some reason, impossible at present,
then it ought, in reality, to be set up as the direct and chief aim of
the future development of Christian society!"

"Perfectly true," Father Païssy, the silent and learned monk,
assented with fervor and decision.

"The purest Ultramontanism!"[8] cried Miüsov impatiently, crossing and recrossing his legs.

"Oh, well, we have no mountains," cried Father Iosif, and turning to the elder he continued, "observe the answer he makes to the
following 'fundamental and essential' propositions of his opponent,
who is, you must note, an ecclesiastic. First, that 'no social organization can or ought to arrogate to itself power to dispose of the
civic and political rights of its members.' Secondly, that 'criminal
and civil jurisdiction ought not to belong to the Church, and is
inconsistent with its nature, both as a divine institution and as an
organization of men for religious purposes,' and, finally, in the
third place, 'the Church is a kingdom not of this world.' "

"A most unworthy play upon words for an ecclesiastic!" Father
Païssy could not refrain from breaking in again. "I have read the
book which you have answered," he added, addressing Ivan Fyodorovich, "and was astounded at the words 'the Church is a king-

8. The movement to give the Pope supreme power in the state as well as in the
church.

dom not of this world.' If it is not of this world, then it cannot exist
on earth at all. In the Gospel, the words 'not of this world' are not
used in that sense. To play with such words is indefensible. Our
Lord Jesus Christ came to set up the Church upon earth. The
Kingdom of Heaven, of course, is not of this world, but in Heaven;
but it is only entered through the Church which has been founded
and established upon earth. And so a frivolous play upon words in
such a connection is unpardonable and improper. The Church is, in
truth, a kingdom and ordained to rule, and in the end must undoubtedly become the kingdom ruling over all the earth. For that
we have the divine promise."

He ceased speaking suddenly, as though checking himself. After
listening attentively and respectfully Ivan Fyodorovich went on,
addressing the elder with perfect composure and as before with
ready cordiality:

"The whole point of my article lies in the fact that during the
first three centuries Christianity only existed on earth in the Church
and was nothing but the Church. When the pagan Roman Empire
desired to become Christian, it inevitably happened that, by becoming Christian, it included the Church but remained a pagan State in
very many of its departments. In reality this was bound to happen.
But Rome as a State retained too much of the pagan civilization
and culture, as, for example, in the very objects and fundamental
principles of the State. The Christian Church entering into the State
could, of course, surrender no part of its fundamental principles—
the rock on which it stands—and could pursue no other aims than
those which have been ordained and revealed by God Himself, and
among them that of drawing the whole world and, therefore the
ancient pagan State itself, into the Church. In that way (that is,
with a view to the future) it is not the Church that should seek a
definite position in the State, like 'every social organization' or as
'an organization of men for religious purposes' (as my opponent
calls the Church) but, on the contrary, every earthly State should
be, in the end, completely transformed into the Church and should
become nothing else but a Church, rejecting every purpose incongruous with the aims of the Church. All this will not degrade it in
any way or take from its honor and glory as a great State, nor from
the glory of its rulers, but will only turn it from a false, still pagan,
and mistaken path to the true and rightful path, which alone leads
to the eternal goal. This is why the author of the book *On the
Foundations of Church Jurisdiction* would have judged correctly if,
in seeking and laying down those foundations, he had looked upon
them as only a temporary compromise inevitable in our sinful and
imperfect days. But as soon as the author ventures to declare that
the foundations which he predicates now, part of which Father
Iosif just enumerated, are the permanent, essential, and eternal

foundations, he is going directly against the Church and its sacred and eternal vocation. That is the gist of my article."

"That is, in brief," Father Païssy began again, laying stress on each word, "according to certain theories only too clearly formulated in the nineteenth century, the Church ought to be transformed into the State, as though this would be an advance from a lower to a higher form, so as to disappear into it, making way for science, for the spirit of the age, and civilization. And if the Church resists and is unwilling, some corner will be set apart for her in the State, and even that under control—and this will be so everywhere in all modern European countries. But Russian hopes and conceptions demand not that the Church should pass as from a lower into a higher type into the State, but, on the contrary, that the State should end by being worthy to become only the Church and nothing else. So be it! So be it!"

"Well, I confess you've reassured me somewhat," Miüsov said smiling, again crossing his legs. "So far as I understand then, the realization of such an ideal is infinitely remote, at the second coming of Christ. That's as you please. It's a beautiful utopian dream of the abolition of war, diplomacy, banks, and so on—something after the fashion of socialism, indeed. But I imagined that it was all meant seriously, and that the Church might be *now* going to try criminals, and sentence them to beating, prison, and even death."

"But if there were none but the ecclesiastical court, the Church would not even now sentence a criminal to prison or to death. Crime and the way of regarding it would inevitably change, not all at once of course, but fairly soon," Ivan Fyodorovich replied calmly, without flinching.

"Are you serious?" Miüsov glanced keenly at him.

"If everything became the Church, the Church would exclude all the criminal and disobedient, and would not cut off their heads," Ivan Fyodorovich went on. "I ask you, what would become of the excluded? He would be cut off then not only from men, as now, but from Christ. By his crime he would have transgressed not only against men but against the Church of Christ. This is so even now, of course, strictly speaking, but it is not clearly enunciated, and very, very often the criminal of today compromises with his conscience: 'I steal,' he says, 'but I don't go against the Church. I'm not an enemy of Christ.' That's what the criminal of today is continually saying to himself, but when the Church takes the place of the State it will be difficult for him, in opposition to the Church all over the world, to say: 'All men are mistaken, all in error, all mankind are the false Church. I, a thief and murderer, am the only true Christian Church.' It will be very difficult to say this to himself; it requires a rare combination of unusual circumstances. Now, on the other side, take the Church's own view of crime: is it not bound to renounce the present almost pagan attitude, and to transform itself from a mechanical cutting off of its tainted member for the preservation of society, as at present, into completely and honestly adopting the idea of the regeneration of the man, of his reformation and salvation?"

"What do you mean? I fail to understand again," Miüsov interrupted. "Some sort of dream again. Something shapeless and even incomprehensible. What is excommunication? What sort of exclusion? I suspect you are simply amusing yourself, Ivan Fyodorovich."

"Yes, but you know, in reality it is so now," said the elder suddenly, and all turned to him at once. "If it were not for the Church of Christ there would be nothing to restrain the criminal from evildoing, no real chastisement for it afterwards; none, that is, but the mechanical chastisement spoken of just now, which in the majority of cases only embitters the heart; and not the real chastisement, the only effectual one, the only deterrent and softening one, which lies in the recognition of sin by conscience."

"How is that, may one inquire?" asked Miüsov, with lively curiosity.

"Why," began the elder, "all these sentences to exile with hard labor, and formerly with flogging also, reform no one, and what's more, deter hardly a single criminal, and the number of crimes does not diminish but is continually on the increase. You must admit that. Consequently the security of society is not preserved, for, although the harmful member is mechanically cut off and sent far away out of sight, another criminal always comes to take his place at once, and often two of them. If anything does preserve society, even in our time, and does regenerate and transform the criminal, it is only the law of Christ speaking in his conscience. It is only by recognizing his wrongdoing as a son of a Christian society—that is, of the Church—that he recognizes his sin against society—that is, against the Church. So that it is only against the Church, and not against the State, that the criminal of today can recognize that he has sinned. If society, as a Church, had jurisdiction then it would know whom to bring back from exclusion and to reunite to itself. Now the Church having no real jurisdiction, but only the power of moral condemnation, withdraws of her own accord from chastising the criminal actively. She does not excommunicate him but simply persists in fatherly exhortation of him. What is more, the Church even tries to preserve all Christian communion with the criminal. She admits him to church services, to the holy sacrament, gives him alms, and treats him more as a captive than as a convict. And what would become of the criminal, O Lord, if even the Christian society—that is, the Church—were to reject him even as the civil law rejects him and cuts him off? What would become of him if the

Church chastised him with her excommunication as the direct consequence of the secular law? There could be no more terrible despair, at least for a Russian criminal, for Russian criminals still
have faith. Though, who knows, perhaps then a fearful thing would
happen, perhaps the despairing heart of the criminal would lose its
faith and then what would become of him? But the Church, like a
tender, loving mother, holds aloof from active chastisement herself,
as the sinner is too severely punished already by the civil law, and
there must be at least some one to have pity on him. The Church
holds aloof, above all, because her judgment is the only one that
contains the truth, and therefore cannot practically and morally be
united to any other judgment even as a temporary compromise. She
can enter into no compact about that. The foreign criminal, they
say, rarely repents, for the very doctrines of today confirm him in
the idea that his crime is not a crime, but only a reaction against an
unjustly oppressive force. Society cuts him off completely by a
force that triumphs over him mechanically and (so at least they say
of themselves in Europe) accompanies this exclusion with hatred,
forgetfulness, and the most profound indifference as to the ultimate
fate of the erring brother. In this way, it all takes place without the
compassionate intervention of the Church, for in many cases there
are no churches there at all, for though ecclesiastics and splendid
church buildings remain, the churches themselves have long ago
striven to pass from the lower form, as Church, into the higher
form, as State and to disappear in it completely. So it seems at least
in Lutheran countries. As for Rome, it was proclaimed a State
instead of a Church a thousand years ago. And so the criminal is
no longer conscious of being a member of the Church and sinks
into despair. If he returns to society, often it is with such hatred
that society itself cuts him off. You can judge for yourself how it
must end. In many cases it would seem to be the same with us, but
the difference is that besides the established law courts we have the
Church too, which always keeps up relations with the criminal as a
dear and still precious son. And besides that, there is still preserved,
though only in thought, the judgment of the Church, which though
no longer existing in practice is still living as a dream for the
future, and is, no doubt, instinctively recognized by the criminal in
his soul. What was said here just now is true too, that is, that if the
jurisdiction of the Church were introduced in practice in its full
force, that is, if the whole of the society were changed into the
Church, not only would the judgment of the Church have influence
on the reformation of the criminal such as it never has now, but
possibly also the crimes themselves would be incredibly diminished.
And there can be no doubt that the Church would look upon the
criminal and the crime of the future in many cases quite differently
and would succeed in restoring the excluded, in restraining those

who plan evil, and in regenerating the fallen. It is true," said Father Zosima, with a smile, "the Christian society now is not ready and is only resting on some seven righteous men, but as they are never lacking, it will continue still unshaken in expectation of its complete transformation from a society almost heathen in character into a single universal and all-powerful Church. So be it, so be it! even though at the end of the ages, for it is ordained to come to pass! And there is no need to be troubled about times and seasons, for the secret of the times and seasons is in the wisdom of God, in His foresight, and His love. And what in human reckoning seems still afar off, may by the Divine ordinance be close at hand, on the eve of its appearance. And so be it, so be it!"

"So be it, so be it!" Father Païssy repeated austerely and reverently.

"Strange, extremely strange!" Miüsov pronounced, not so much with heat as with latent indignation.

"What strikes you as so strange?" Father Iosif inquired cautiously.

"Why it's beyond anything!" cried Miüsov, suddenly breaking out, "the State is eliminated and the Church is raised to the position of the State. It's not simply Ultramontanism, it's arch-ultramontanism! It's beyond the dreams of Pope Gregory the Seventh!"[9]

"You completely misunderstand it," said Father Païssy sternly. "Understand the Church is not to be transformed into the State. That is Rome and its dream. That is the third temptation of the devil. On the contrary, the State is transformed into the Church, will ascend and become a Church over the whole world—which is the complete opposite of Ultramontanism and Rome, and your interpretation, and is only the glorious destiny ordained for the Orthodox Church. This star will arise in the east!"

Miüsov was significantly silent. His whole figure expressed extraordinary personal dignity. A supercilious and condescending smile played on his lips. Alyosha watched it all with a throbbing heart. The whole conversation stirred him profoundly. He glanced casually at Rakitin, who was standing immovable in his place by the door listening and watching intently through with downcast eyes. But from the color in his cheeks Alyosha guessed that Rakitin was probably no less excited, and he knew what caused his excitement.

"Allow me to tell you one little anecdote, gentlemen," Miüsov said impressively, with a peculiarly majestic air. "Some years ago, soon after the coup d'état of December,[1] I happened to be calling in Paris on an extremely influential personage in the Government,

9. Pope Gregory VII (1073–85) was a defender of the idea that the Pope controlled the secular as well as the spiritual rule of mankind.

1. On December 2, 1851, Louis Napoleon overthrew the French government. He became emperor the following year.

and I met a very interesting man in his house. This individual was not precisely a detective but was a sort of superintendent of a whole regiment of political detectives—a rather powerful position in its own way. I was prompted by curiosity to seize the opportunity of conversation with him. And as he had not come as a visitor but as a subordinate official bringing a special report, and as he saw the reception given me by his chief he deigned to speak with some openness, to a certain extent only, of course. He was rather courteous than open, as Frenchmen know how to be courteous, especially to a foreigner. But I thoroughly understood him. The subject was the socialist revolutionaries who were at that time persecuted. Skipping the gist of the conversation, I will quote only one most curious remark dropped by this person. 'We are not particularly afraid,' said he, 'of all these socialists, anarchists, atheists, and revolutionists; we keep watch on them and know all their goings on. But there are a few peculiar men among them who believe in God and are Christians, but at the same time are socialists. Those are the people we are most afraid of. They are dreadful people! The socialist who is a Christian is more to be dreaded than a socialist who is an atheist.' The words struck me at the time, and now they have suddenly come back to me here, gentlemen."

"You apply them to us, and look upon us as socialists?" Father Païssy asked directly, without beating about the bush. But before Pyotr Alexandrovich could think what to answer, the door opened, and the guest so long expected, Dmitri Fyodorovich, came in. They had, in fact, given up expecting him, and his sudden appearance caused some surprise for a moment.

Chapter VI

Why Is Such a Man Alive?

Dmitri Fyodorovich, a young man of twenty-eight, of medium height and agreeable countenance, looked much older than his years. He was muscular, and showed signs of considerable physical strength. Yet there was something not healthy in his face. It was rather thin, his cheeks were hollow, and there was an unhealthy sallowness in their color. His rather large, prominent dark eyes had an expression of firm determination, and yet there was a vague look in them, too. Even when he was excited and talking irritably, his eyes somehow did not follow his mood, but betrayed something else, sometimes quite incongruous with what was passing. "It's hard to tell what he's thinking," those who talked to him sometimes declared. People who saw something pensive and sullen in his eyes were startled by his sudden laugh, which bore witness to mirthful and light-hearted thoughts at the very time when his eyes were so gloomy. Moreover, a certain strained look in his face was easy to understand at this moment. Everyone knew or had heard of the extremely restless and "dissipated" life which he had been leading of late, as well as of the violent anger to which he had been roused in his quarrels with his father about the disputed money. There were several stories current in the town about it. It is true that he was irascible by nature, "of an unstable and unbalanced mind," as our justice of the peace, Kachalnikov, characteristically described him at one gathering.

He was stylishly and irreproachably dressed in a carefully buttoned frock coat. He wore black gloves and carried a top hat. Having only lately left the army, he still had moustaches and no beard. His dark brown hair was cropped short, and combed forward on his temples. He had the long determined stride of a military man. He stood still for a moment on the threshold, and glancing at the whole party went straight up to the elder, guessing him to be their host. He made him a low bow, and asked his blessing. Father Zosima, rising in his chair, blessed him. Dmitri Fyodorovich kissed his hand respectfully, and with intense feeling, almost anger, he said:

"Be so generous as to forgive me for having kept you waiting so long, but Smerdyakov, the servant sent me by my father, in reply to my insistent inquiries, told me twice over in the most assured tone that the appointment was for one. Now I suddenly learn——"

"Don't disturb yourself," interposed the elder. "No matter. You are a little late. It's of no consequence. . . ."

"I'm extremely obliged to you, and expected no less from your goodness." Saying this abruptly Dmitri Fyodorovich bowed once more. Then, turning suddenly towards his father, he made him, too, a similarly low and respectful bow. He had evidently considered it beforehand, and made this bow in all seriousness, thinking it his duty to show his respect and good intentions. Although Fyodor Pavlovich was taken unaware, he was equal to the occasion. In response to Dmitri Fyodorovich's bow he jumped up from his chair and made his son a bow as low in return. His face was suddenly solemn and impressive, which gave him a positively malignant look. Dmitri Fyodorovich bowed generally to all present, and without a word walked to the window with his long, resolute stride, sat down on the only empty chair, near Father Païssy, and, bending forward, prepared to listen to the conversation he had interrupted.

Dmitri Fyodorovich's entrance had taken no more than two minutes, and the conversation was resumed. But this time Miüsov thought it unnecessary to reply to Father Païssy's persistent and almost irritable question.

"Allow me to withdraw from this discussion," he observed with a certain well-bred nonchalance. "It's a subtle question, too. Here

Ivan Fyodorovich is smiling at us. He must have something interesting to say about that also. Ask him."

"Nothing special, except one little remark," Ivan Fyodorovich replied at once. "European Liberals in general, and even our liberal dilettantes, often mix up the final results of socialism with those of Christianity. This wild conclusion is, of course, a characteristic feature. But it's not only Liberals and dilettantes who mix up socialism and Christianity, but, in many cases, it appears, the police —the foreign police, of course—do the same. Your Paris anecdote is rather to the point, Pyotr Alexandrovich."

"I ask your permission to drop this subject altogether," Miüsov repeated. "I will tell you instead, gentlemen, another interesting and rather characteristic anecdote of Ivan Fyodorovich himself. Only five days ago, in a gathering here, principally of ladies, he solemnly declared in argument that there was nothing in the whole world to make men love their neighbors. That there was no law of nature that man should love mankind, and that, if there had been any love on earth hitherto, it was not owing to a natural law, but simply because men have believed in immortality. Ivan Fyodorovich added in parenthesis that the whole natural law lies in that faith, and that if you were to destroy in mankind the belief in immortality, not only love but every living force maintaining the life of the world would at once be dried up. Moreover, nothing then would be immoral, everything would be lawful, even cannibalism. That's not all. He ended by asserting that for every individual, like ourselves, who does not believe in God or immortality, the moral law of nature must immediately be changed into the exact contrary of the former religious law, and that egoism, even unto crime, must become, not only lawful but even recognized as the inevitable, the most rational, even honorable outcome of his position. From this paradox, gentlemen, you can judge of the rest of our eccentric and paradoxical friend Ivan Fyodorovich's theories."

"Excuse me," Dmitri Fyodorovich cried suddenly, "If I've heard aright: crime must not only be permitted but even recognized as the inevitable and the most rational outcome of his position for every atheist! Is that so or not?"

"Quite so," said Father Païssy.

"I'll remember it."

Having uttered these words Dmitri Fyodorovich ceased speaking as suddenly as he had begun. Everyone looked at him with curiosity.

"Is that really your conviction as to the consequences of the disappearance of the faith in immortality?" the elder asked Ivan Fyodorovich suddenly.

"Yes. That was my contention. There is no virtue if there is no immortality."

"You are blessed in believing that, or else most unhappy."

"Why unhappy?" Ivan Fyodorovich asked smiling.

"Because, in all probability you don't believe yourself in the immortality of your soul, nor in what you have written yourself in your article on Church jurisdiction."

"Perhaps you are right! . . . But I wasn't altogether joking," Ivan Fyodorovich suddenly and strangely confessed, flushing quickly.

"You were not altogether joking. That's true. The question is still fretting your heart, and not answered. But the martyr likes sometimes to divert himself with his despair, as it were driven to it by despair itself. Meanwhile, in your despair, you, too, divert yourself with magazine articles, and discussions in society, though you don't believe your own arguments, and with an aching heart mock at them inwardly. . . . That question you have not answered, and it is your great grief, for it clamors for an answer."

"But can it be answered by me? Answered in the affirmative?" Ivan Fyodorovich went on asking strangely, still looking at the elder with the same inexplicable smile.

"If it can't be decided in the affirmative, it will never be decided in the negative. You know that that is the peculiarity of your heart, and all its suffering is due to it. But thank the Creator who had given you a lofty heart capable of such suffering; of thinking and seeking higher things, for our dwelling is in the heavens. God grant that your heart will attain the answer on earth, and may God bless your path."

The elder raised his hand and would have made the sign of the cross over Ivan Fyodorovich from where he stood. But the latter rose from his seat, went up to him, received his blessing, kissed his hand, and went back to his place in silence. His face looked firm and earnest. This action and all the preceding conversation, which was so surprising from Ivan Fyodorovich, impressed everyone by its strangeness and a certain solemnity, so that all were silent for a moment, and there was a look almost of fear in Alyosha's face. But Miüsov suddenly shrugged his shoulders. And at the same moment Fyodor Pavlovich jumped up from his seat.

"Most pious and holy elder," he cried pointing to Ivan Fyodorovich, "that is my son, flesh of my flesh, the dearest of my flesh! He is my most dutiful Karl Moor, so to speak, while this son who has just come in, Dmitri Fyodorovich, against whom I am seeking justice from you, is the undutiful Franz Moor—they are both out of Schiller's *Robbers*, and so I am the *regierender* Graf von Moor![2] Judge and save us! We need not only your prayers but your prophecies!"

"Speak without buffoonery, and don't begin by insulting the

---

2. "The reigning Count Moor." (See *The Brothers Karamazov*.")
Tschizewskij's essay on "Schiller and

members of your family," answered the elder, in a faint, exhausted voice. He was obviously getting more and more fatigued, and his strength was failing.

"An unseemly farce which I foresaw when I came here!" cried Dmitri Fyodorovich indignantly. He too leaped up. "Forgive it, reverend Father," he added, addressing the elder. "I am not a cultivated man, and I don't even know how to address you properly, but you have been deceived and you have been too good-natured in letting us meet here. All my father wants is a scandal. Why he wants it only he can tell. He always has some motive. But I believe I know why——"

"They all blame me, all of them!" cried Fyodor Pavlovich in his turn. "Pyotr Alexandrovich here blames me too. You have been blaming me, Pyotr Alexandrovich, you have!" he turned suddenly to Miüsov, although the latter was not dreaming of interrupting him. "They all accuse me of having hidden the children's money in my boots, and cheated them, but isn't there a court of law? There they will reckon out for you, Dmitri Fyodorovich, from your notes, your letters, and your agreements, how much money you had, how much you have spent, and how much you have left. Why does Pyotr Alexandrovich refuse to pass judgment? Dmitri Fyodorovich is not a stranger to him. Because they are all against me, while Dmitri Fyodorovich is in debt to me, and not a little, but some thousands, of which I have documentary proof. The whole town shakes and echoes with his debaucheries. And where he was stationed before, he several times spent a thousand or two for the seduction of some respectable girl; we know all about that, Dmitri Fyodorovich, sir, in its most secret details. I'll prove it, sir . . . Would you believe it, holy Father, he has captivated the heart of the most honorable of young ladies of good family and fortune, daughter of a gallant colonel, formerly his superior officer, who had received many honors and had the Anna Order on his breast. He compromised the girl by his promise of marriage, now she is an orphan and here; she is betrothed to him, yet before her very eyes he is dancing attendance on a certain enchantress. And although this enchantress has lived in, so to speak, civil marriage with a respectable man, yet she is of an independent character, an unapproachable fortress for everybody, just like a legal wife—for she is virtuous, yes, holy Father, she is virtuous. Dmitri Fyodorovich wants to open this fortress with a golden key, and that's why he is insolent to me now, trying to get money from me, though he had wasted thousands on this enchantress already. He's continually borrowing money for the purpose. From whom do you think? Shall I say, Mitya?"

"Be silent! cried Dmitri Fyodorovich, "wait till I'm gone. Don't dare in my presence to asperse the good name of an honorable girl!

That you should utter a word about her is an outrage, and I won't permit it!"

He was breathless.

"Mitya! Mitya!" cried Fyodor Pavlovich hysterically, squeezing out a tear. "And is your father's blessing nothing to you? If I curse you, what then?"

"Shameless hypocrite!" exclaimed Dmitri Fyodorovich furiously.

"He says that to his father! his father! What would he be with others? Gentlemen, only fancy; there's a poor but honorable man living here, burdened with a numerous family, a captain who got into trouble and was discharged from the army, but not publicly, not by court-martial, with no slur on his honor. And three weeks ago, our Dmitri Fyodorovich seized him by the beard in a tavern, dragged him out into the street by that very beard, and beat him publicly, and all because he is an agent in a little business of mine."

"It's all a lie! Outwardly it's the truth, but inwardly, a lie!" Dmitri Fyodorovich was trembling with rage. "Father, I don't justify my action. Yes, I confess it publicly, I behaved like a brute to that captain, and I regret it now, and I'm disgusted with myself for my brutal rage. But this captain, this agent of yours, went to that lady whom you call an enchantress, and suggested to her from you, that she should take IOUs of mine which were in your possession, and should sue me for the money so as to get me into prison by means of them, if I persisted in claiming an account from you of my property. Now you reproach me for having a weakness for that lady when you yourself incited her to captivate me! She told me so to my face. She told me the story and laughed at you! You wanted to put me in prison because you are jealous of me with her, because you'd begun to force your attentions upon her; and I know all about that, too; she laughed at you for that as well—you hear—she laughed at you as she described it. So here you have this man, holy men, this father who reproaches his profligate son! Gentlemen, forgive my anger, but I foresaw that this crafty old man had only brought you together to create a scandal. I had come to forgive him if he held out his hand; to forgive him, and ask forgiveness! But as he has just this minute insulted not only me, but an honorable young lady for whom I feel such reverence that I dare not take her name in vain, I have made up my mind to show up his game, though he is my father! . . ."

He could not go on. His eyes were glittering and he breathed with difficulty. But everyone in the cell was stirred. All except Father Zosima got up from their seats uneasily. The monks looked severe but waited for guidance from the elder. He sat still, pale, not from excitement but from the weakness of illness. An imploring smile played on his lips; from time to time he raised his hand, as though to check the storm, and, of course, a gesture from him would have been enough to end the scene; but he seemed to be waiting for something and watched them intently as though trying to make out something which was not perfectly clear to him. At last Miüsov felt completely humiliated and disgraced.

"We are all to blame for this scandalous scene," he said hotly. "But I did not foresee it when I came, though I knew with whom I had to deal. This must be stopped at once! Believe me, your reverence, I had no precise knowledge of the details that have just come to light, I was unwilling to believe them, and I learn for the first time. . . . A father is jealous of his son's relations with a woman of loose behavior and intrigues with the creature to get his son into prison! This is the company in which I have been forced to be present! I was deceived. I declare to you all that I was as much deceived as any one."

"Dmitri Fyodorovich," yelled Fyodor Pavlovich suddenly, in an unnatural voice, "if you were not my son I would challenge you this instant to a duel . . . with pistols, at three paces! . . . across a handkerchief,"[3] he ended, stamping with both feet.

With old liars who have been acting all their lives there are moments when they enter so completely into their part that they tremble or shed tears of emotion in earnest, although at that very moment, or a second later, they are able to whisper to themselves, "You know you are lying, you shameless old sinner! You're acting now, in spite of your 'holy' wrath and your 'holy' moment of wrath."

Dmitri Fyodorovich frowned painfully, and looked with unutterable contempt at his father.

"I thought . . . I thought," he said, in a soft and, as it were, controlled voice, "that I was coming to my native place with the angel of my heart, my betrothed, to cherish his old age, and I find nothing but a depraved sensualist, a despicable clown!"

"A duel!" yelled the old wretch again, breathless and spluttering at each syllable. "And you, Pyotr Alexandrovich Miüsov, let me tell you, sir, that there has never been in all your family a loftier, and more honest—you hear—more honest woman than this 'creature,' as you have dared to call her! And you, Dmitri Fyodorovich, have abandoned your betrothed for that 'creature,' so you must yourself have thought that your betrothed couldn't hold a candle to her. That's the woman called a 'creature'!"

"Shameful!" broke suddenly from Father Iosif.

"Shameful and disgraceful!" Kalganov, flushing crimson, cried in his adolescent voice, trembling with emotion. He had been silent till that moment.

---

3. An echo of Schiller's *Kabale und Liebe* (Intrigue and love) (1783).

"Why is such a man alive?" Dmitri Fyodorovich, beside himself with rage, growling in a hollow voice, hunching up his shoulders till he looked almost deformed. "Tell me, can he be allowed to go on defiling the earth?" He looked round at everyone and pointed at the old man. He spoke evenly and deliberately.

"Listen, listen, monks, to the parricide!" cried Fyodor Pavlovich, rushing up to Father Iosif. "That's the answer to your 'shameful!' What is shameful? That 'creature,' that 'woman of loose behavior' is perhaps holier than you are yourselves, you monks who are seeking salvation! She fell perhaps in her youth, ruined by her environment. But she loved much, and Christ himself forgave the woman 'who loved much.' "

"It was not for such love Christ forgave her," broke impatiently from the gentle Father Iosif.

"Yes, it was for such, monks, it was! You save your souls here, eating cabbage, and think you are the righteous. You eat a gudgeon a day, and you think you bribe God with gudgeon."

"This is unendurable!" was heard on all sides in the cell.

But this unseemly scene was cut short in a most unexpected way. Father Zosima rose suddenly from his seat. Almost distracted with anxiety for the elder and everyone else, Alyosha succeeded, however, in supporting him by the arm. Father Zosima moved towards Dmitri Fyodorovich and reaching him sank on his knees before him. Alyosha thought that he had fallen from weakness, but this was not so. The elder distinctly and deliberately bowed down at Dmitri Fyodorovich's feet till his forehead touched the floor. Alyosha was so astounded that he failed to assist him when he got up again. There was a faint smile on his lips.

"Good-bye! Forgive me, all of you!" he said, bowing on all sides to his guests.

Dmitri Fyodorovich stood for a few moments in amazement. Bowing down to him—what did it mean? Suddenly he cried aloud, "Oh God!" hid his face in his hands, and rushed out of the room. All the guests flocked out after him, in their confusion not saying good-bye, or bowing to their host. Only the monks went up to him again for a blessing.

"What did it mean, falling at his feet like that? Was it symbolic or what?" said Fyodor Pavlovich, suddenly quieted and trying to reopen conversation without venturing to address anybody in particular. They were all passing out of the precincts of the hermitage at the moment.

"I can't answer for a madhouse and for madmen," Miüsov answered at once ill-humoredly, "but I will spare myself your company, Fyodor Pavlovich, and, trust me, forever. Where's that monk?"

"That monk," that is, the monk who had invited them to dine

with the Superior, did not keep them waiting. He met them as soon as they came down the steps from the elder's cell, as though he had been waiting for them all the time.

"Reverend Father, kindly do me a favor. Convey my deepest respect to the Father Superior, apologize for me, personally, Miüsov, to his reverence, telling him that I deeply regret that owing to unforeseen circumstances I am unable to have the honor of being present at his table, greatly as I should desire to do so," Miüsov said irritably to the monk.

"And that unforeseen circumstance, of course, is myself," Fyodor Pavlovich cut in immediately. "Do you hear, Father; this gentleman doesn't want to remain in my company or else he'd come at once. And you shall go, Pyotr Alexandrovich, pray go to the Father Superior and good appetite to you. I will decline, and not you. Home, home, I'll eat at home, I don't feel equal to it here, Pyotr Alexandrovich, my amiable relative."

"I am not your relative and never have been, you contemptible man!"

"I said it on purpose to madden you, because you always disclaim the relationship, though you really are a relation in spite of your shuffling. I'll prove it by the church calendar. As for you, Ivan Fyodorovich, stay if you like. I'll send the horses for you later. Propriety requires you to go to the Father Superior, Pyotr Alexandrovich, to apologize for the disturbance we've been making. . . ."

"Is it true that you are going home? Aren't you lying?"

"Pyotr Alexandrovich! How could I dare after what's happened! Forgive me, gentlemen, I was carried away! And upset besides! And, indeed, I am ashamed. Gentlemen, one man has the heart of Alexander the Great and another the heart of the little dog Fido. Mine is that of the little dog Fido. I am abashed! After such an escapade how can I go to dinner, to gobble up the monastery's sauces. I am ashamed, I can't. You must excuse me!"

"The devil only knows, what if he deceives us," thought Miüsov, still hesitating, and watching the retreating buffoon with distrustful eyes. The latter turned round, and noticing that Miüsov was watching him, waved him a kiss.

"Well, are you coming to the Superior?" Miüsov asked Ivan Fyodorovich abruptly.

"Why not? I was especially invited by the Superior yesterday."

"Unfortunately I feel myself almost compelled to go to this confounded dinner," said Miüsov with the same bitter irritability, regardless of the fact that the monk was listening. "We ought, at least, to apologize for the disturbance, and explain that it was not our doing. What do you think?"

"Yes, we must explain that it wasn't our doing. Besides, father won't be there," observed Ivan Fyodorovich.

"Well, I should hope not! Confound this dinner!"

They all walked on, however. The monk listened in silence. On the road through the copse he made one observation however—that the Father Superior had been waiting a long time, and that they were more than half an hour late. He received no answer. Miüsov looked with hatred at Ivan Fyodorovich.

"Here he is, going to the dinner as though nothing had happened," he thought. "A brazen face, and the conscience of a Karamazov!"

Chapter VII

A Seminarian Bent on a Career

Alyosha helped Father Zosima to his bedroom and seated him on his bed. It was a little room furnished with the bare necessities. There was a narrow iron bedstead, with a strip of felt for a mattress. In the corner, under the icons, was a lectern with a cross and the Gospel lying on it. The elder sank exhausted on the bed. His eyes glittered and he breathed hard. He looked intently at Alyosha, as though considering something.

"Go, my dear boy, go. Porfiry is enough for me. Make haste, you are needed there, go and wait at the Father Superior's table."

"Let me stay here," Alyosha entreated.

"You are more needed there. There is no peace there. You will wait, and be of use. If evil spirits rise up, repeat a prayer. And remember, my son"—the elder liked to call him that—"this is not the place for you in the future. Remember that, young man. When it is God's will to call me, leave the monastery. Go away for good."

Alyosha started.

"What is it? This is not your place for the time. I bless you for great service in the world. Yours will be a long pilgrimage. And you will have to take a wife, too, you will have to. You will have to bear all before you come back. There will be much to do. But I don't doubt of you, and so I send you forth. Christ is with you. Do not abandon Him and He will not abandon you. You will see great sorrow, and in that sorrow you will be happy. This is my last message to you: in sorrow seek happiness. Work, work unceasingly. Remember my words henceforth, for although I shall talk with you again, not only my days but my hours are numbered."

Alyosha's face again betrayed strong emotion. The corners of his mouth quivered.

"What is it again?" Father Zosima asked, smiling gently. "The worldly may follow the dead with tears, but here we rejoice over the father who is departing. We rejoice and pray for him. Leave me, I must pray. Go, and make haste. Be near your brothers. And not near one only, but near both."

Father Zosima raised his hand to bless him. Alyosha could make no protest, though he had a great longing to remain. He longed, moreover, to ask the significance of his bowing to his brother Dmitri, the question was on the tip of his tongue, but he dared not ask it. He knew that the elder would have explained it unasked if he had thought fit. But evidently it was not his will. That action had made a terrible impression on Alyosha; he believed blindly in its mysterious significance. Mysterious, and perhaps awful.

As he hastened out of the hermitage precincts to reach the monastery in time to serve at the Father Superior's dinner, he felt a sudden pang at his heart, and stopped short. He seemed to hear again Father Zosima's words, foretelling his approaching end. What he had foretold so exactly must infallibly come to pass. Alyosha believed that implicitly. But how could he be left without him? How could he live without seeing and hearing him? Where should he go? He had told him not to weep, and to leave the monastery. Good God! It was long since Alyosha had known such anguish. He hurried through the copse that divided the monastery from the hermitage, and unable to bear the burden of his thoughts, he gazed at the ancient pines beside the path. He had not far to go—about five hundred paces. He expected to meet no one at that hour, but at the first turn of the path he noticed Rakitin. He was waiting for someone.

"Are you waiting for me?" asked Alyosha, overtaking him.

"Yes, you in particular," grinned Rakitin. "You are hurrying to the Father Superior, I know; he has a banquet. There's not been such a banquet since the Superior entertained the Bishop and General Pakhatov, do you remember? I won't be there, but you go and hand the sauces. Tell me one thing, Alexey, what does that vision mean? That's what I want to ask you."

"What vision?"

"That bowing to your brother, Dmitri Fyodorovich. And didn't he tap the ground with his forehead, too!"

"You speak of Father Zosima?"

"Yes, of Father Zosima."

"Tapped the ground?"

"Ah, an irreverent expression! Well, what of it? Anyway, what does that vision mean?"

"I don't know what it means, Misha."

"I knew he wouldn't explain it to you! There's nothing wonderful about it, of course, only the usual holy mummery. But there was an object in the performance. All the pious people in the town will talk about it and spread the story through the province, wondering what it meant. To my thinking the old man really has a keen nose; he sniffed a crime. Your house stinks of it."

"What crime?"

Rakitin evidently had something he was eager to speak of.

"It'll be in your family, this crime. Between your brothers and your rich old father. So Father Zosima tapped the ground to be ready for what may turn up. If something happens later on, it'll be: 'Ah, the holy man foresaw it, prophesied it!' though it's a poor sort of prophecy, tapping the ground like that. 'Ah, but it was symbolic,' they'll say, 'an allegory,' and the devil knows what all! It'll be remembered to his glory: 'He predicted the crime and marked the criminal!' That's always the way with these crazy fanatics; they cross themselves at the tavern and throw stones at the temple. Like your elder, he takes a stick to a just man and falls at the feet of a murderer."

"What crime? What murderer? What do you mean?"

Alyosha stopped dead. Rakitin stopped, too.

"What murderer? As though you didn't know! I'll bet you've thought of it before. That's interesting, too, by the way. Listen, Alyosha, you always speak the truth, though you're always between two stools. Have you thought of it or not? Answer."

"I have," answered Alyosha in a low voice. Even Rakitin was taken aback.

"What? Have you really?" he cried.

"I . . . I've not exactly thought it," muttered Alyosha, "but directly you began speaking so strangely, I fancied I had thought of it myself."

"You see? (And how well you expressed it!) You see? Looking at your father and your brother Mitenka today you thought of a crime. Then I'm not mistaken?"

"But wait, wait a minute," Alyosha broke in uneasily, "What has led you to see all this? Why does it interest you? That's the first question."

"Two questions, disconnected, but natural. I'll deal with them separately. What led me to see it? I wouldn't have seen it, if I hadn't suddenly understood your brother Dmitri Fyodorovich, seen right into the very heart of him all at once. I caught the whole man from one trait. These very honest but passionate people have a line which mustn't be crossed. If it were, he'd run at your father with a knife. But your father's a drunken and abandoned old sinner, who can never draw the line—if they both let themselves go, they'll both come to grief."

"No, Misha, no. If that's all, you've reassured me! It won't come to that."

"But why are you trembling? Let me tell you; he may be honest —your Mitenka (he is stupid, but honest) but he's—a sensualist. That's the very definition and inner essence of him. It's your father who has handed him on his low sensuality. Do you know, I simply wonder at you, Alyosha, how you can have kept your chastity.

You're a Karamazov too, you know! In your family sensuality is carried to a disease. But now, these three sensualists are watching one another, with their knives in their belts. The three of them are knocking their heads together, and you may be the fourth."

"You are mistaken about that woman. Dmitri—despises her," said Alyosha, with a sort of shudder.

"Grushenka? No, brother, he doesn't despise her. Since he has openly abandoned his betrothed for her, he doesn't despise her. There's something here, my dear boy, that you don't understand yet. A man will fall in love with some beauty, with a woman's bódy, or even with a part of a woman's body (a sensualist can understand that) and he'll abandon his own children for her, sell his father and mother, and his country, Russia, too. If he's honest, he'll steal; if he's humane, he'll murder; if he's faithful, he'll deceive. Pushkin, the poet of women's feet,[4] sung of their feet in his verse. Others don't sing their praises, but they can't look at feet without a thrill—and it's not only feet. Contempt's no help here, brother, even if he did despise Grushenka. Even if he does, he can't tear himself away."

"I understand that," Alyosha jerked out suddenly.

"Really? Well, I daresay you do understand, since you blurt it out at the first word," said Rakitin, malignantly. "That escaped you unawares, and the admission is the more precious. So it's a familiar subject; you've thought about it already, about sensuality, I mean! Oh, you chaste one! You're a quiet one, Alyosha, you're a saint, I know, but the devil only knows what you've thought about, and what you know already! You are pure, but you've been down into the depths. . . . I've been watching you a long time. You're a Karamazov yourself; you're a thorough Karamazov—no doubt birth and selection have something to answer for. You're a sensualist from your father, a crazy saint from your mother. Why do you tremble? Is it true, then? Do you know, Grushenka has been begging me to bring you along. 'I'll pull off his cassock,' she says. You can't think how she keeps begging me to bring you. I wondered why she took such an interest in you. Do you know, she's an extraordinary woman, too!"

"Thank her and say I'm not coming," said Alyosha, with a strained smile. "Finish what you were saying, Michael. I'll tell you my idea after."

"There's nothing to finish. It's all clear. It's the same old tune, brother. If even you are a sensualist at heart what of your brother, Ivan, your full brother? He's a Karamazov, too. What is at the root of all you Karamazovs is that you're all sensual, grasping and crazy! Your brother Ivan writes theological articles in jest, for some

4. See note to page 544.

idiotic, unknown motive of his own, though he's an atheist, and he admits that vileness himself—that's your brother Ivan. Moreover, he is trying to get Mitya's betrothed for himself, and I fancy he'll succeed, too. And what's more it's with Mitenka's consent. For Mitenka will surrender his betrothed to him to be rid of her, and escape to Grushenka. And he's ready to do that in spite of all his nobility and disinterestedness. Observe that. Those are the most fatal people! Who the devil can make you out? He recognizes his vileness and goes on with it! Let me tell you, too, the old man, your father, is standing in Mitenka's way now. He has suddenly gone crazy over Grushenka. His mouth waters at the sight of her. It's simply on her account he made that scene in the cell just now, simply because Miüsov called her an 'abandoned creature.' He's worse than a tomcat in love. At first she was only employed by him in connection with his taverns and in some other shady business, but now he has suddenly realized all she is and has gone wild about her. He keeps pestering her with his offers, not honorable ones, of course. And they'll come into collision, the precious father and son, on that path! But Grushenka favors neither of them, she's still playing with them, and teasing them both, considering which she can get most out of. For though she could filch a lot of money from the papa he wouldn't marry her, and maybe he'll turn stingy in the end, and keep his purse shut. That's where Mitenka's value comes in, he has no money, but he's ready to marry her. Yes, ready to marry her! to abandon his betrothed, a rare beauty, Katerina Ivanovna, who's rich, and the daughter of a colonel, and to marry Grushenka, who has been the mistress of a dissolute old merchant, Samsonov, a coarse, uneducated, provincial mayor. Some murderous conflict may well come to pass from all this, and that's what your brother Ivan is waiting for. It would suit him down to the ground. He'll carry off Katerina Ivanovna, for whom he is languishing, and pocket her dowry of sixty thousand. That's very alluring to start with, for a man of no consequence and a beggar. And, take note, he won't be wronging Mitya, but doing him the greatest service. For I know as a fact that Mitya only last week, when he was with some gypsy girls drunk in a tavern, cried out aloud that he was unworthy of his betrothed, Katya, but that his brother Ivan, he was the man who deserved her. And Katerina Ivanovna will not in the end refuse such a fascinating man as Ivan Fyodorovich. She's hesitating between the two of them already. And how has that Ivan won you all, so that you all worship him? He is laughing at you, and enjoying himself at your expense."

"How do you know? How can you speak so confidently?" Alyosha asked sharply, frowning.

"Why do you ask, and are frightened at my answer? It shows that you know I'm speaking the truth."

"You don't like Ivan. Ivan wouldn't be tempted by money."

"Really? And the beauty of Katerina Ivanovna? It's not only the money, though a fortune of sixty thousand is an attraction."

"Ivan is above that. He wouldn't make up to anyone for thousands. It is not money, it's not comfort Ivan is seeking. Perhaps he is seeking suffering."

"What wild dream now? Oh, you—aristocrats!"

"Ah, Misha, he has a stormy spirit. His mind is in bondage. He is haunted by a great, unsolved doubt. He is one of those who don't want millions, but an answer to their questions."

"That's plagiarism, Alyosha. You're quoting your elder's phrases. Ah, Ivan has set you a problem!" cried Rakitin, with undisguised malice. His face changed, and his lips twitched. "And the problem's a stupid one. It is no good guessing it. Rack your brains—you'll understand it. His article is absurd and ridiculous. And did you hear his stupid theory just now: if there's no immortality of the soul, then there's no virtue, and everything is lawful. (And by the way, do you remember how your brother Mitenka cried out: 'I will remember!') An attractive theory for scoundrels!—(I'm being abusive, that's stupid.) Not for scoundrels, but for pedantic poseurs, 'haunted by profound, unsolved doubts.' He's showing off, and what it all comes to is, 'on the one hand we cannot but admit' and 'on the other it must be confessed!' His whole theory is vileness! Humanity will find in itself the power to live for virtue even without believing in immortality. It will find it in love for freedom, for equality, for fraternity."

Rakitin could hardly restrain himself in his heat, but, suddenly, as though remembering something, he stopped short.

"Well, that's enough," he said, with a still more crooked smile. "Why are you laughing? Do you think I'm a vulgar fool?"

"No, I never dreamed of thinking you a vulgar fool. You are clever but . . . never mind, I was silly to smile. I understand your getting hot about it, Misha. I guess from your warmth that you are not indifferent to Katerina Ivanovna yourself; I've suspected that for a long time, brother, that's why you don't like my brother Ivan. Are you jealous of him?"

"And jealous of her money, too? Won't you add that?"

"I'll say nothing about money. I am not going to insult you."

"I believe it, since you say so, but confound you, and your brother Ivan with you. Don't you understand that one might very well dislike him, apart from Katerina Ivanovna? And why the devil should I like him? He condescends to abuse me, you know. Why haven't I a right to abuse him?"

"I never heard of his saying anything about you, good or bad. He doesn't speak of you at all."

"But I heard that the day before yesterday at Katerina Ivanovna's he was abusing me for all he was worth—you see what an interest he takes in your humble servant. And which is the jealous one after that, brother, I can't say. He was so good as to express the opinion that, if I don't go in for the career of an archimandrite in the immediate future and don't become a monk, I shall be sure to go to Petersburg and get on to some solid magazine as a reviewer, that I shall write for the next ten years, and in the end become the owner of the magazine, and bring it out on the liberal and atheistic side, with a socialistic tinge, with a tiny gloss of socialism, but keeping a sharp lookout all the time, that is, keeping in with both sides and hoodwinking the fools. According to your brother's account, the tinge of socialism won't hinder me from laying by the proceeds and investing them under the guidance of some Jew, till at the end of my career I build a great house in Petersburg and move my publishing offices to it, and let out the upper stories to lodgers. He has even chosen the place for it, near the new stone bridge across the Neva, which they say is to be built in Petersburg."

"Ah, Misha, that's just what will really happen, every word of it," cried Alyosha, unable to restrain a good-humored smile.

"You are pleased to be sarcastic, too, Alexey Fyodorovich."

"No, no, I'm joking, forgive me. I've something quite different in my mind. But, excuse me, who can have told you all this? You can't have been at Katerina Ivanovna's yourself when he was talking about you?"

"I wasn't there, but Dmitri Fyodorovich was; and I heard him tell it with my own ears; if you want to know, he didn't tell me, but I overheard him, unintentionally, of course, for I was sitting in Grushenka's bedroom and I couldn't go away because Dmitri Fyodorovich was in the next room."

"Oh yes, I'd forgotten she was a relation of yours."

"A relation! That Grushenka a relation of mine!" cried Rakitin, turning crimson. "Are you mad? You're out of your mind!"

"Why, isn't she a relation of yours? I heard so."

"Where can you have heard it? You Karamazovs brag of being an ancient, noble family, though your father used to run about playing the buffoon at other men's tables, and was only admitted to the kitchen as a favor. I may be only a priest's son, and dirt in the eyes of noblemen like you, but don't insult me so lightly and wantonly. I have a sense of honor, too, Alexey Fyodorovich, I couldn't be a relation of Grushenka, a common harlot. I beg you to understand that, sir!"

Rakitin was intensely irritated.

"Forgive me, for goodness' sake, I had no idea . . . besides . . . how can you call her a harlot? Is she . . . that sort of woman?" Alyosha flushed suddenly. "I tell you again, I heard that she was a relation of yours. You often go to see her, and you told me yourself you're not her lover. I never dreamed that you of all people had such contempt for her! Does she really deserve it?"

"I may have reasons of my own for visiting her. That's not your business. But as for relationship, your brother, or even your father is more likely to make her yours, than mine. Well, here we are. You'd better go to the kitchen. Hullo! what's wrong, what is it? Are we late? They can't have finished dinner so soon! Have the Karamazovs been making trouble again? No doubt they have. Here's your father and your Ivan Fyodorovich after him. They've broken out from the Father Superior's. And look, Father Isidor's shouting out something after them from the steps. And your father's shouting and waving his arms. I expect he's swearing. Bah, and there goes Miüsov driving away in his carriage. You see, he's going. And there's old Maximov running!—there must have been a row. There can't have been any dinner. Surely they've not been beating the Father Superior! Or have they, perhaps, been beaten? It would serve them right!"

There was reason for Rakitin's exclamations. There had been a scandalous, an unprecedented scene. It had all come from the "impulse of a moment."

Chapter VIII

A Scandalous Scene

Miüsov, as a man of breeding and delicacy, could not but feel some inward qualms, when he reached the Father Superior's with Ivan Fyodorovich: he felt ashamed of having lost his temper. He felt that he ought to have disdained that despicable wretch, Fyodor Pavlovich, too much to have been upset by him in Father Zosima's cell, and so to have forgotten himself. "The monks were not to blame, in any case," he reflected, on the steps. "And if they're decent people here (and the Father Superior, Nikolay, I understand, is a nobleman) why not be pleasant, friendly, and courteous with them? I won't argue, I'll fall in with everything, I'll win them by politeness, and . . . and . . . show them that I've nothing to do with that Aesop,[5] that buffoon, that Pierrot, and have merely been taken in over this affair, just as they have."

He determined to drop his litigation with the monastery, and relinquish his claims to the woodcutting and fishery rights at once. He was the more ready to do this because the rights had become much less valuable, and he had indeed the vaguest idea where the wood and river in question were.

5. Author of the *Fables* (sixth century B.C.). Pierrot was the clown in traditional comedy.

These excellent intentions were strengthened when he entered the Father Superior's dining room, though, strictly speaking, it was not a dining room, for the Father Superior had only two rooms altogether; they were, however, much larger and more comfortable than Father Zosima's. But there was no great luxury about the furnishing of these rooms either. The furniture was of mahogany, covered with leather, in the old-fashioned style of 1820; the floor was not even stained, but everything was shining with cleanliness, and there were many choice flowers in the windows; the most sumptuous thing in the room at the moment was, of course, the beautifully decorated table, here too comparatively speaking. The cloth was clean, the service shone; there were three kinds of well-baked bread, two bottles of wine, two of excellent mead, and a large glass jug of kvass[6]—both the latter made in the monastery, and famous in the neighborhood. There was no vodka. Rakitin related afterwards that there were five dishes: fish soup made of sterlets, served with little fish patties; then boiled fish served in a very special way; then salmon cutlets, ices and compote, and finally, blancmange. Rakitin found out about all these good things, for he could not resist peeping into the kitchen, where he already had a footing. He had a footing everywhere, and got information about everything. He was of an uneasy and envious temper. He was well aware of his own considerable abilities, and nervously exaggerated them in his self-conceit. He knew he would play a prominent part of some sort, but Alyosha, who was attached to him, was distressed to see that his friend Rakitin was dishonorable, and quite unconscious of being so himself, considering, on the contrary, that because he would not steal money left on the table he was a man of the highest integrity. Neither Alyosha nor anyone else could have influenced him in that.

Rakitin, of course, was a person of too little consequence to be invited to the dinner, to which Father Iosif, Father Païssy, and one other monk were the only inmates of the monastery invited. They were already waiting when Miüsov, Kalganov, and Ivan Fyodorovich arrived. The other guest, Maximov, stood a little aside, waiting also. The Father Superior stepped into the middle of the room to receive his guests. He was a tall, thin, but still vigorous old man, with black hair streaked with grey, and a long, grave, ascetic face. He bowed to his guests in silence. But this time they approached to receive his blessing. Miüsov even tried to kiss his hand, but the Father Superior drew it back in time to avoid the salute. But Ivan Fyodorovich and Kalganov went through the ceremony in the most simple-hearted and complete manner, kissing his hand as peasants do.

6. Common Russian beverage made by fermenting bread.

"We must apologize most humbly, your reverence," began Miüsov, simpering affably, and speaking in a dignified and respectful tone. "Pardon us for having come alone without the gentleman you invited, Fyodor Pavlovich. He felt obliged to decline the honor of your hospitality, and not without reason. In the reverend Father Zosima's cell he was carried away by the unhappy dissension with his son, and let fall words which were quite out of keeping . . . in fact, quite unseemly . . . as"—he glanced at the monks—"your reverence is, no doubt, already aware. And therefore, recognizing that he had been to blame, he felt sincere regret and shame, and begged me, and his son Ivan Fyodorovich, to convey to you his apologies and regrets. In brief, he hopes and desires to make amends later. He asks your blessing, and begs you to forget what has taken place."

As he uttered the last word of his tirade, Miüsov completely recovered his self-complacency, and all traces of his former irritation disappeared. He fully and sincerely loved humanity again.

The Father Superior listened to him with dignity, and, with a slight bend of the head, replied:

"I sincerely deplore his absence. Perhaps at our table he might have learned to like us, and we him. Pray be seated, gentlemen."

He stood before the holy image, and began to say grace, aloud. All bent their heads reverently, and Maximov clasped his hands before him, with peculiar fervor.

It was at this moment that Fyodor Pavlovich played his last prank. It must be noted that he really had meant to go home, and really had felt the impossibility of going to dine with the Father Superior as though nothing had happened, after his disgraceful behavior in the elder's cell. Not that he was so very much ashamed of himself—quite the contrary perhaps. But still he felt it would be unseemly to go to dinner. Yet his creaking carriage had hardly been brought to the steps of the hotel, and he had hardly got into it, when he suddenly stopped short. He remembered his own words at the elder's: "I always feel when I meet people that I am lower than all, and that they all take me for a buffoon; so I say let me play the buffoon, for you are, every one of you, stupider and lower than I." He longed to revenge himself on everyone for his own unseemliness. He suddenly recalled how he had once in the past been asked, "Why do you hate so and so, so much?" And he had answered them, in an access of his buffoonish impudence, "I'll tell you. He had done me no harm. But I played him a dirty trick, and ever since I have hated him."

Remembering that now, he smiled, quietly and malignantly, hesitating for a moment. His eyes gleamed, and his lips positively quivered. "Well, since I have begun, I may as well go on," he decided. His predominant sensation at that moment might be expressed in the following words, "Well, there is no rehabilitating myself now. So let me shame them for all I am worth. I will show them I don't care what they think—that's all!"

He told the coachman to wait, while with rapid steps he returned to the monastery and straight to the Father Superior's. He had no clear idea what he would do, but he knew that he could not control himself, and that a touch might drive him to the utmost limits of obscenity, but only to obscenity, to nothing criminal, nothing for which he could be legally punished. In the last resort, he could always restrain himself, and had indeed marveled at himself sometimes on that score. He appeared in the Father Superior's dining room, at the moment when the prayer was over, and all were moving to the table. Standing in the doorway, he scanned the company, and laughing his prolonged, impudent, malicious chuckle, looked them all boldly in the face. "They thought I had gone, and here I am again," he cried to the whole room.

For one moment everyone stared at him without a word; and at once everyone felt that something revolting, grotesque, positively scandalous, was about to happen. Miüsov passed immediately from the most benevolent frame of mind to the most savage. All the feelings that had subsided and died down in his heart revived instantly.

"No! this I cannot endure!" he cried. "I absolutely cannot! and . . . I certainly cannot!"

The blood rushed to his head. He positively stammered; but he was beyond thinking of style, and he seized his hat.

"What is it he cannot?" cried Fyodor Pavlovich, "that he absolutely cannot and certainly cannot? Your reverence, am I to come in or not? Will you receive me as your guest?"

"You are welcome with all my heart," answered the Superior. "Gentlemen!" he added, "I venture to beg you most earnestly to lay aside your dissensions, and to be united in love and family harmony—with prayer to the Lord at our humble table."

"No, no, it is impossible!" cried Miüsov, beside himself.

"Well, if it is impossible for Pyotr Alexandrovich, it is imposible for me, and I won't stop. That is why I came. I will keep with Pyotr Alexandrovich everywhere now. If you will go away, Pyotr Alexandrovich, I will go away too, if you remain, I will remain. You stung him by what you said about family harmony, Father Superior, he does not admit he is my relation. That's right, isn't it, von Sohn? Here's von Sohn. How are you, von Sohn?"

"Do you mean me?" muttered Maximov, puzzled.

"Of course I mean you," cried Fyodor Pavlovich, "Who else? The Father Superior could not be von Sohn."

"But I am not von Sohn either. I am Maximov."

"No, you are von Sohn. Your reverence, do you know who von Sohn was? It was a famous murder case. He was killed in a house

of harlotry. I believe that is what such places are called among
you—he was killed and robbed, and in spite of his venerable age,
he was nailed up in a box and sent from Petersburg to Moscow in
the luggage van, and while they were nailing him up, the harlots
sang songs and played the harp, that is to say, the piano. So this is
that very von Sohn. He has risen from the dead, hasn't he, von
Sohn?"

"What is happening? What's this?" voices were heard in the
group of monks.

"Let us go," cried Miüsov, addressing Kalganov.

"No, excuse me," Fyodor Pavlovich broke in shrilly, taking another step into the room. "Allow me to finish. There in the cell you
blamed me for behaving disrespectfully just because I spoke of
eating gudgeon, Pyotr Alexandrovich. Miüsov, my relation, prefers
to have *plus de noblesse que de sincerité* in his words, but I prefer
in mine *plus de sincerité que de noblesse*,[7] and—damn the noblesse!
That's right, isn't it, von Sohn? Allow me, Father Superior, though
I am a buffoon and play the buffoon, yet I am the soul of honor,
and I want to speak my mind. Yes, I am the soul of honor, while in
Pyotr Alexandrovich there is wounded vanity and nothing else. I
came here perhaps to have a look and speak my mind. My son,
Alexey, is here, being saved. I am his father; I care for his welfare,
and it is my duty to care. While I've been playing the fool, I have
been listening and having a look on the sly; and now I want to give
you the last act of the performance. You know how things are with
us? As a thing falls, so it lies. As a thing once has fallen, so it must
lie for ever. Not a bit of it! I want to get up again. Holy Father, I
am indignant with you. Confession is a great sacrament, before
which I am ready to bow down reverently; but there in the cell,
they all kneel down and confess aloud. Can it be right to confess
aloud? It was ordained by the holy fathers to confess in secret: then
only your confession will be a mystery, and so it was of old. But
how can I explain to him before everyone that I did this and
that . . . well, you understand what—sometimes it would not be
proper to talk about it—so it is really a scandal! No, fathers, one
might be carried along with you to the Flagellants,[8] I dare say . . .
at the first opportunity I shall write to the Synod, and I shall take
my son, Alexey, home."

We must note here that Fyodor Pavlovich knew where to look
for the weak spot. There had been at one time malicious rumors
which had even reached the Archbishop (not only regarding our
monastery, but in others where the institution of elders existed)
that too much respect was paid to the elders, even to the detriment
of the authority of the Superior, that the elders abused the sacra-

---

7. "more nobility than sincerity" . . .
"more sincerity than nobility."

8. A religious sect whose ritual included
flagellation.

ment of confession and so on and so on—absurd charges which had died away of themselves everywhere. But the spirit of folly, which had caught up Fyodor Pavlovich, and was bearing him on the current of his own nerves into lower and lower depths of ignominy, prompted him with this old slander. Fyodor Pavlovich did not understand a word of it, and he could not even put it sensibly, for on this occasion no one had been kneeling and confessing aloud in the elder's cell, so that he could not have seen anything of the kind. He was only speaking from confused memory of old slanders. But as soon as he had uttered his foolish tirade, he felt he had been talking absurd nonsense, and at once longed to prove to his audience and above all to himself, that he had not been talking nonsense. And, though he knew perfectly well that with each word he would be adding more and more absurdity, he could not restrain himself, and plunged forward blindly.

"How disgraceful!" cried Pyotr Alexandrovich.

"Pardon me!" said the Father Superior. "It was said of old, 'Many have begun to speak against me and have uttered evil sayings about me. And hearing it I have said to myself: it is the correction of the Lord and He has sent it to heal my vain soul.' And so we humbly thank you, honored guest!" and he made Fyodor Pavlovich a low bow.

"Tut-tut-tut—sanctimoniousness and stock phrases! Old phrases and old gestures. The old lies and formal prostrations. We know all about them. 'A kiss on the lips and a dagger in the heart,' as in Schiller's *Robbers*. I don't like falsehood, fathers, I want the truth. But the truth is not to be found in eating gudgeon and that I proclaim aloud! Father monks, why do you fast? Why do you expect reward in heaven for that? Why, for reward like that I will come and fast too! No, saintly monk, you try being virtuous in the world, do good to society, without shutting yourself up in a monastery at other people's expense, and without expecting a reward up aloft for it—you'll find that a bit harder. I can talk sense, too, Father Superior. What have they got here?" He went up to the table. "Old port wine, médoc from the Eliseyev Brothers.[9] Fie, fie, fathers! That is something beyond gudgeon. Look at the bottles the fathers have brought out, he! he! he! And who has provided it all? The Russian peasant, the laborer, brings here the farthing earned by his horny hand, wringing it from his family and the tax gatherer! You bleed the people, you know, holy fathers."

"This is too disgraceful!" said Father Iosif.

Father Païssy kept obstinately silent. Miüsov rushed from the room, and Kalganov after him.

"Well, Father, I will follow Pyotr Alexandrovich! I am not com-

9. Petersburg's fanciest provisioner.

ing to see you again. You may beg me on your knees, I shan't come. I sent you a thousand rubles, so you have more. I am taking my revenge for my youth, for all the humiliation I endured." He thumped the table with his first in a paroxysm of simulated feeling. "This monastery has played a great part in my life! It has cost me many bitter tears. You used to set my wife, the crazy one, against me. You cursed me with bell and book, you spread stories about me all over the place. Enough, fathers! This is the age of Liberalism, the age of steamers and railways. Neither a thousand, nor a hundred rubles, no, nor a hundred farthings will you get out of me!"

It must also be noted that our monastery never had played any great part in his life, and he never had shed a bitter tear owing to it. But he was so carried away by his simulated emotion, that for one moment he almost believed it himself. He was so touched he almost wept. But at that very instant, he felt that it was time to draw back.

The Father Superior bowed his head at his malicious lie, and again spoke impressively:

"It is written again, 'Bear circumspectly and gladly dishonor that cometh upon thee by no act of thine own, be not confounded and hate not him who hath dishonored thee.' And so will we."

"Tut-tut-tut! Bethinking thyself and the rest of the rigmarole. Bethink yourselves, fathers, I will go. But I will take my son, Alexey, away from here forever, on my parental authority. Ivan Fyodorovich, my most dutiful son, permit me to order you to follow me. Von Sohn, what have you to stay for? Come and see me now in the town. It is fun there. It is only one short mile. Instead of lenten oil, I will give you sucking pig and kasha. We will have dinner with some brandy and liqueur to it. . . . I've cloudberry wine. Hey, von Sohn, don't lose your chance." He went out, shouting and gesticulating.

It was at that moment Rakitin saw him and pointed him out to Alyosha.

"Alexey!" his father shouted, from far off, catching sight of him. "You come home to me today, for good, and bring your pillow and mattress, and leave no trace behind."

Alyosha stood rooted to the spot, watching the scene in silence. Meanwhile, Fyodor Pavlovich had got into the carriage, and Ivan Fyodorovich was about to follow him in grim silence without even turning to say good-bye to Alyosha. But at this point another almost incredible scene of grotesque buffoonery gave the finishing touch to the episode. Maximov suddenly appeared by the side of the carriage. He ran up, panting, afraid of being too late, Rakitin and Alyosha saw him running. He was in such a hurry that in his impatience he put his foot on the step on which Ivan Fyodorovich's left foot was still resting, and clutching the carriage he kept trying to jump in. "I am going with you!" he kept shouting, laughing a thin mirthful laugh with a look of reckless glee in his face. "Take me, too."

"There!" cried Fyodor Pavlovich, delighted. "Did I not say he was von Sohn. It is von Sohn himself, risen from the dead. Why, how did you tear yourself away? What did you vonsohn there? And how could you get away from the dinner? You must be a brazen-faced fellow! I am that myself, but I am surprised at you, brother! Jump in, jump in! Let him pass, Vanya. It will be fun. He can lie somewhere at our feet. Will you lie at our feet, von Sohn? Or perch on the box with the coachman. Skip onto the box, von Sohn!"

But Ivan Fyodorovich, who had by now taken his seat, without a word gave Maximov a violent punch in the breast and sent him flying. It was quite by chance he did not fall.

"Drive on!" Ivan Fyodorovich shouted angrily to the coachman.

"Why, what are you doing, what are you about? Why did you do that?" Fyodor Pavlovich protested.

But the carriage had already driven away. Ivan Fyodorovich made no reply.

"Well, you are a fellow," Fyodor Pavlovich said again.

After a pause of two minutes, looking askance at his son, "Why, it was you got up all this monastery business. You urged it, you approved of it. Why are you angry now?"

"You've talked rot enough. You might rest a bit now," Ivan Fyodorovich snapped sullenly.

Fyodor Pavlovich was silent again for two minutes.

"A drop of brandy would be nice now," he observed sententiously, but Ivan Fyodorovich made no response.

"You shall have some, too, when we get home."

Ivan Fyodorovich was silent.

Fyodor Pavlovich was silent again for two minutes.

"But I shall take Alyosha away from the monastery just the same, no matter how unpleasant that will be for you, most respectful Karl von Moor."

Ivan Fyodorovich shrugged his shoulders contemptuously, and turning away stared at the road. And they did not speak again all the way home.

Book Three

THE SENSUALISTS

Chapter I

In the Servants' Quarters

The Karamazovs' house was far from being in the center of the town, but it was not quite outside it. It was a pleasant-looking old one-story house with an attic, painted gray, with a red iron roof. It was roomy and snug, and might still last many years. There were all sorts of unexpected little cupboards and closets and staircases. There were rats in it, but Fyodor Pavlovich did not altogether dislike them. "One doesn't feel so solitary when one's left alone in the evening," he used to say. It was his habit to send the servants away to the lodge for the night and to lock himself up alone. The lodge was a roomy and solid building in the yard. Fyodor Pavlovich used to have the cooking done there, although there was a kitchen in the house; he did not like the smell of cooking, and, winter and summer alike, the dishes were carried in across the courtyard. The house was built for a large family; there was room for five times as many, with their servants. But at the time of our story there was no one living in the house but Fyodor Pavlovich and his son Ivan Fyodorovich. And in the lodge there were only three servants: old Grigory, and his old wife Martha, and a young man called Smerdyakov. Of these three we must say a few words. Of old Grigory Vasilyevich Kutuzov we have said something already. He was firm and determined and went blindly and obstinately for his object, if once he had been brought by any reasons (and they were often very illogical ones) to believe that it was immutably right. He was honest and incorruptible. His wife, Martha Ignatyevna, had obeyed her husband's will implicitly all her life, yet she had pestered him terribly after the emancipation of the serfs.[1] She was set on leaving Fyodor Pavlovich and opening a little shop in Moscow with their small savings. But Grigory decided then, once for all, that "the woman's talking nonsense, for every woman is dishonest," and that they ought not to leave their old master, whatever he might be, for "that was now their duty."

---

1. The serfs (slaves) were emancipated on February 19, 1861.

"Do you understand what duty is?" he asked Martha Ignatyevna.

"I understand what duty means, Grigory Vasilyevich, but why it's our duty to stay here I never shall understand," Martha Ignatyevna answered firmly.

"Well, don't understand then. But so it shall be. And you hold your tongue."

And so it was. They did not go away, and Fyodor Pavlovich promised them a small sum for wages, and paid it regularly. Grigory knew, too, that he had an indisputable influence over his master. It was true, and he was aware of it. Fyodor Pavlovich was an obstinate and cunning buffoon, yet, though his will was strong enough "in some of the affairs of life," as he expressed it, he found himself, to his surprise, extremely feeble in facing certain other emergencies. He knew his weaknesses and was afraid of them. There are positions in which one has to keep a sharp lookout. And that's not easy without a trustworthy man, and Grigory was a most trustworthy man. Many times in the course of his life Fyodor Pavlovich had only just escaped a sound thrashing through Grigory's intervention, and on each occasion the old servant gave him a good lecture. But it wasn't only thrashings that Fyodor Pavlovich was afraid of. There were graver occasions, and very subtle and complicated ones, when Fyodor Pavlovich could not have explained the extraordinary craving for someone faithful and devoted, which sometimes unaccountably came upon him all in a moment. It was almost a morbid condition. Corrupt and often cruel in his lust, like some noxious insect, Fyodor Pavlovich was sometimes, in moments of drunkenness, overcome by superstitious terror and a moral convulsion which took an almost physical form. "My soul simply quakes in my throat at those times," he used to say. At such moments he liked to feel that there was near at hand, in the lodge if not in the room, a strong, faithful man, virtuous and unlike himself, who had seen all his debauchery and knew all his secrets, but was ready in his devotion to overlook all that, not to oppose him, above all, not to reproach him or threaten him with anything, either in this world or in the next, and, in case of need, to defend him—from whom? From somebody unknown, but terrible and dangerous. What he needed was to feel that there was *another* man, an old and tried friend, that he might call him in his sick moments merely to look at his face, or, perhaps, exchange some quite irrelevant words with him. And if the old servant were not angry, he felt comforted, and if he were angry, he was more dejected. It happened even (very rarely however) that Fyodor Pavlovich went at night to the lodge to wake Grigory and fetch him for a moment. When the old man came, Fyodor Pavlovich would begin talking about the most trivial matters, and would soon let him go again, sometimes even with a jest. And after he had gone, Fyodor Pavlo-

vich would get into bed with a curse and sleep the sleep of the just.
Something of the same sort had happened to Fyodor Pavlovich on
Alyosha's arrival. Alyosha "pierced his heart" by "living with him,
seeing everything and blaming nothing." Moreover, Alyosha
brought with him something his father had never known before: a
complete absence of contempt for him and an invariable kindness,
a perfectly natural unaffected devotion to the old man who deserved it so little. All this was a complete surprise to the old
profligate, who had dropped all family ties. It was a new and
surprising experience for him, who had till then loved nothing but
"evil." When Alyosha had left him, he confessed to himself that he
had learned something he had not till then been willing to learn.

I have mentioned already that Grigory had detested Adelaïda
Ivanovna, the first wife of Fyodor Pavlovich and the mother of
Dmitri Fyodorovich, and that he had, on the contrary, protected
Sofya Ivanovna, the poor "possessed woman," against his master
and anyone who chanced to speak ill or lightly of her. His sympathy for the unhappy wife had become something sacred to him,
so that even twenty years after, he could not bear a slighting
allusion to her from anyone, and would at once check the offender.
Externally, Grigory was cold, dignified and taciturn, and spoke,
weighing his words, without frivolity. It was impossible to tell at
first sight whether he loved his meek, obedient wife; but he really
did love her, and she knew it.

Martha Ignatyevna was by no means foolish: she was probably,
indeed, cleverer than her husband, or, at least, more prudent than
he in worldly affairs, and yet she had given in to him in everything
without question or complaint ever since her marriage, and respected him for his spiritual superiority. It was remarkable how
little they spoke to one another in the course of their lives, and only
of the most necessary daily affairs. The grave and dignified Grigory
thought over all his cares and duties alone, so that Martha Ignatyevna had long grown used to knowing that he did not need her
advice. She felt that her husband respected her silence, and took it
as a sign of her good sense. He had never beaten her but once, and
then only slightly. Once during the year after Fyodor Pavlovich's
marriage with Adelaïda Ivanovna, the village girls and women—at
that time serfs—were called together before the house to sing and
dance. They were beginning "In the Green Meadows," when Martha, at that time a young woman, skipped forward and danced "the
Russian Dance," not in the village fashion, but as she had danced it
when she was a servant in the service of the rich Miüsov family, in
their private theater, where the actors were taught to dance by a
dancing master from Moscow. Grigory saw how his wife danced,
and, an hour later, at home in their cottage he gave her a lesson,
pulling her hair a little. But there it ended: the beating was never
repeated, and Martha Ignatyevna gave up dancing.

God had not blessed them with children. One child was born but it died. Grigory was fond of children, didn't hide it, that is, he was not ashamed of showing it. When Adelaïda Ivanovna had run away, Grigory took Dmitri Fyodorovich, then a child of three, combed his hair and washed him in a tub with his own hands, and looked after him for almost a year. Afterwards he had looked after Ivan Fyodorovich and Alyosha, for which the general's widow had rewarded him with a slap in the face; but I have already related all that. The only happiness his own child had brought him had been in the anticipation of its birth. When it was born, he was over-whelmed with grief and horror. The baby had six fingers. Grigory was so crushed by this, that he was not only silent till the day of the christening, but kept away in the garden. It was spring, and he spent three days digging the kitchen garden. The third day was fixed for christening the boy: meantime Grigory had reached a conclusion. Going into the cottage where the clergy were assembled and the visitors had arrived, including Fyodor Pavlovich, who was to stand godfather, he suddenly announced that the baby "ought not to be christened at all." He announced this quietly, briefly, forcing out his words and gazing with dull intentness at the priest, and did not elaborate further.

"Why not?" asked the priest with good-humored surprise.

"Because it's a dragon," muttered Grigory.

"A dragon? What dragon?"

Grigory did not speak for some time. "It's a confusion of nature," he muttered vaguely, but firmly, and obviously unwilling to say more.

They laughed, and of course christened the poor baby. Grigory prayed earnestly at the font, but his opinion of the newborn child remained unchanged. Yet he did not interfere in any way. As long as the sickly infant lived he scarcely looked at it, tried indeed not to notice it, and for the most part kept out of the cottage. But when, at the end of a fortnight, the baby died of thrush, he himself laid the child in its little coffin, looked at it in profound grief, and when they were filling up the shallow little grave he fell on his knees and bowed down to the earth. He did not for years afterwards mention his child, nor did Martha speak of the baby before him, and, even if Grigory were not present, she never spoke of it above a whisper. Martha observed that, from the day of the burial, he devoted him-self to "religion," and took to reading the *Lives of the Saints*, for the most part sitting alone and in silence, and always putting on his big, round, silver-rimmed spectacles. He rarely read aloud, only perhaps in Lent. He was fond of the book of Job, and had some-how got hold of a copy of the sayings and sermons of "the God-fearing Father Isaac the Syrian,"[2] which he read persistently for

2. A seventh-century hermit. Dostoevsky owned a copy of the book mentioned here (Moscow, 1858).

years together, understanding very little of it, but perhaps prizing and loving it the more for that. Of late he had begun to listen to the doctrines of the sect of Flagellants settled in the neighborhood. He was evidently shaken by them, but judged it unfitting to go over to the new faith. His habit of theological reading gave him an expression of still greater gravity.

He was perhaps predisposed to mysticism. And the birth of his deformed child, and its death, had, as though by special design, been accompanied by another strange and marvelous event, which, as he said later, had left a "stamp" upon his soul. It happened that, on the very night after the burial of his child, Martha was awakened by the wail of a newborn baby. She was frightened and woke up her husband. He listened and said he thought it was more like someone groaning, "it might be a woman." He got up and dressed. It was a rather warm night in May. As he went down the steps, he distinctly heard groans coming from the garden. But the gate from the yard into the garden was locked at night, and there was no other way of entering it, for it was enclosed all round by a strong, high fence. Going back into the house, Grigory lighted a lantern, took the garden key, and taking no notice of the hysterical fears of his wife, who was still persuaded that she heard a child crying, and that it was her own baby crying and calling for her, went into the garden in silence. There he heard at once that the groans came from the bathhouse that stood near the garden gate, and that they were groans of a woman. Opening the door of the bathhouse, he saw a sight which petrified him. An idiot girl, who wandered about the streets and was known to the whole town by the nickname of Lizaveta Smerdyaschaya (Stinking Lizaveta), had got into the bathhouse and had just given birth to a child. She lay dying with the baby beside her. She said nothing, for she had never been able to speak. But her story needs a chapter to itself.

Chapter II

Stinking Lizaveta

There was one circumstance which struck Grigory particularly, and confirmed a very unpleasant and revolting suspicion. This Lizaveta was a dwarfish creature, "not five foot within a wee bit," as many of the pious old women said pathetically about her, after her death. She was twenty years old. Her broad, healthy, red face had a look of blank idiocy and the fixed stare in her eyes was unpleasant, in spite of their meek expression. She wandered about, summer and winter alike, barefooted, wearing nothing but a hempen smock. Her coarse, almost black hair curled like lamb's wool, and formed a sort of huge cap on her head. It was always crusted with mud, and had leaves, bits of sticks, and shavings clinging to it, as she always slept on the ground and in the dirt. Her father, a homeless, sickly drunkard, called Ilya, had lost everything and lived many years as a workman with some well-to-do trades-people. Her mother had long been dead. Ill and spiteful, Ilya used to beat Lizaveta inhumanly whenever she returned to him. But she rarely did so, for everyone in the town was ready to look after her as being an idiot, and so specially dear to God. Ilya's employers, and Ilya himself, and many others in the town, especially of the tradespeople, tried to clothe her better, and always rigged her out with boots and a sheepskin coat for the winter. But, although she allowed them to dress her up without resisting, she usually went away, preferably to the cathedral porch, and taking off all that had been given her—kerchief, sheepskin, skirt or boots—she left them there and walked away barefoot in her smock as before. It hap-pened on one occasion that a new governor of the province, making a tour of inspection in our town, saw Lizaveta, and was wounded in his tenderest sensibilities. And though he was told she was an idiot, he pronounced that for a young woman of twenty to wander about in nothing but a smock was a breach of the proprieties, and must not occur again. But the governor went his way, and Lizaveta was left as she was. At last her father died, which made her even more acceptable in the eyes of the religious persons of the town, as an orphan. In fact, everyone seemed to like her; even the boys did not tease her, and the boys of our town, especially the schoolboys, are a mischievous lot. She would walk into strange houses, and no one drove her away. Everyone was kind to her and gave her something. If she were given a copper, she would take it, and at once drop it in the poor box of the church or prison. If she were given a roll or bun in the market, she would hand it to the first child she met. Sometimes she would stop one of the richest ladies in the town and give it to her, and the lady would be pleased to take it. She herself never tasted anything but black bread and water. If she went into an expensive shop, where there were costly goods or money lying about, no one kept watch on her, for they knew that if she saw thousands of rubles overlooked by them, she would not have touch-ing a farthing. She scarcely ever went to church. She slept either in the church porch or climbed over a wattle-fence (there are many wattle-fences instead of regular fences in our town to this very day) into a kitchen garden. She used at least once a week to turn up "at home," that is at the house of her father's former employers, and in the winter went there every night, and slept either in the passage or the cowshed. People were amazed that she could stand such a life, but she was accustomed to it, and, although she was so tiny, she was of a robust constitution. Some of the townspeople declared that she did all this only from pride, but that is hardly credible. She could hardly speak, and only from time to time uttered an inarticulate grunt. How could she have been proud?

It happened one clear, warm, moonlight night in September (many years ago) that a band of five or six of our gentlemen, drunken revelers were returning from the club at a very late hour, according to our provincial notions. They passed through the "backway," which led between the back gardens of the houses, with wattle-fences on either side. This way leads out onto the bridge over the long, stinking pool which we were accustomed to call a river. Among the nettles and burdocks under the hurdle our revelers saw Lizaveta asleep. They stopped to look at her, laughing, and began jesting with unbridled licentiousness. It occurred to one young gentleman to make the whimsical inquiry whether any one could possibly look upon such an animal as a woman, and so forth. . . . They all pronounced with lofty repugnance that it was impossible. But Fyodor Pavlovich, who was among them, sprang forward at once and declared that it was by no means impossible, and that, indeed, there was a certain piquancy about it, and so on. . . . It is true that at that time he was overdoing his part as a buffoon. He liked to put himself foward and entertain the company, ostensibly on equal terms, of course, though in reality he was on a servile footing with them. It was just at the time when he had received the news of his first wife's death in Petersburg, and, with crepe upon his hat, was drinking and behaving so shamelessly that even the most reckless among us were shocked at the sight of him. The revelers, of course, laughed at this unexpected opinion; and one of them even began challenging him to act upon it. The others repelled the idea even more emphatically, although still with the utmost hilarity, and at last they went on their way. Later on, Fyodor Pavlovich swore that he had gone with them, and perhaps it was so, no one knows for certain, and no one ever knew. But five or six months later, all the town was talking, with intense and sincere indignation, of Lizaveta's pregnancy, and trying to find out who was the miscreant who had wronged her. Then suddenly a terrible rumor was all over the town that this miscreant was no other than Fyodor Pavlovich. Who set the rumor going? Of that drunken band five had left the town and the only one still among us was an elderly and much respected civil councilor,[3] the father of grownup daughters, who could hardly have spread the tale, even if there had been any foundation for it. But rumor pointed straight at Fyodor Pavlovich, and persisted in pointing at him. Of course this was no great grievance to him: he would not have troubled to contradict a set of tradespeople. In those days he was proud, and did not condescend to talk

3. A high rank in the civil service.

except in his own circle of the officials and nobles, whom he entertained so well.

At the time, Grigory stood up for his master vigorously. He provoked quarrels and altercations in defense of him and succeeded in bringing some people round to his side. "It's the wench's own fault," he asserted, and the culprit was Karp, a dangerous convict, who had escaped from prison and whose name was well known to us, as he had hidden in our town. This conjecture sounded plausible, for it was remembered that Karp had been in the neighborhood just at that time in the autumn, and had robbed three people. But this affair and all the talk about it did not estrange popular sympathy from the poor idiot. She was better looked after than ever. A well-to-do merchant's widow named Kondratyev arranged to take her into her house at the end of April, meaning not to let her go out until after the confinement. They kept a constant watch over her, but in spite of their vigilance she escaped on the very last day, and made her way into Fyodor Pavlovich's garden. How, in her condition, she managed to climb over the high, strong fence remained a mystery. Some maintained that she must have been lifted over by somebody; others hinted at something more uncanny. The most likely explanation is that it happened naturally—that Lizaveta, accustomed to clambering over hurdles to sleep in gardens, had somehow managed to climb Fyodor Pavlovich's fence, in spite of her condition, and had leaped down, injuring herself.

Grigory rushed to Martha and sent her to Lizaveta, while he ran to fetch an old midwife who lived close by. They saved the baby, but Lizaveta died at dawn. Grigory took the baby, brought it home, and making his wife sit down, put it on her lap. "A child of God—an orphan is akin to all," he said, "and to us above others. Our little lost one has sent us this, who has come from the devil's son and a holy innocent. Nurse him and weep no more."

So Martha brought up the child. He was christened Pavel, to which people were not slow in adding Fyodorovich (son of Fyodor). Fyodor Pavlovich did not object to any of this, and thought it amusing, though he persisted vigorously in denying his responsibility. The townspeople were pleased at his adopting the foundling. Later on, Fyodor Pavlovich invented a surname for the child, calling him Smerdyakov, after his mother's nickname.

So this Smerdyakov became Fyodor Pavlovich's second servant, and was living in the lodge with Grigory and Martha at the time our story begins. He was employed as cook. I ought to say something of this Smerdyakov, but I am ashamed of keeping my readers' attention so long occupied with these common menials, and I will go back to my story, hoping to say more of Smerdyakov in the course of it.

Chapter III

The Confession of an Ardent Heart—in Verse

Alyosha remained irresolute for some time after hearing the command his father shouted to him from the carriage. But in spite of his uneasiness he did not stand still. That was not his way. He went at once to the kitchen to find out what his father had been doing above. Then he set off, trusting that on the way he would find some answer to the doubt tormenting him. I hasten to add that his father's shouts, commanding him to return home "with his mattress and pillow," did not frighten him in the least. He understood perfectly that those peremptory shouts were merely "a flourish" to produce an effect. In the same way a tradesman in our town who was celebrating his name day with a party of friends, getting angry at being refused more vodka, smashed up his own crockery and furniture and tore his own and his wife's clothes, and finally broke his windows, all for the sake of effect. Next day, of course, when he was sober, he regretted the broken cups and saucers. Alyosha knew that his father would let him go back to the monastery next day, possibly even that evening. Moreover he was fully persuaded that his father might hurt anyone else, but would not hurt him. Alyosha was certain that no one in the whole world ever would want to hurt him, and, what is more, he knew that no one could hurt him. This was for him an axiom, assumed once for all without question, and he went his way without hesitation, relying on it.

But at that moment an anxiety of a different sort disturbed him, and worried him the more because he could not formulate it. It was the fear of a woman, of Katerina Ivanovna, who had so urgently entreated him in the note handed to him by Madame Khokhlakov to come and see her about something. This request and the necessity of going had at once aroused an uneasy feeling in his heart, and this feeling had grown more and more painful all the morning in spite of all the scenes and events at the hermitage and at the Father Superior's. He was not uneasy because he did not know what she would speak of and what he must answer. And he was not afraid of her simply as a woman. Though he knew little of women, he had spent his life, from early childhood till he entered the monastery, entirely with women. He was afraid of that woman, Katerina Ivanovna. He had been afraid of her from the first time he saw her. He had only seen her two or three times, and had only chanced to say a few words to her. He thought of her as a beautiful, proud, imperious girl. It was not her beauty which troubled him, but something else. And the vagueness of his apprehension increased the apprehension itself. The girl's aims were of the noblest, he knew that. She was trying to save his brother Dmitri simply through generosity, though he had already behaved badly to her. Yet, although Alyosha recognized and did justice to all these fine and generous sentiments, a shiver began to run down his back as soon as he drew near her house.

He reflected that he would not find Ivan Fyodorovich, who was so intimate a friend, with her, for Ivan was certainly now with his father. Dmitri he was even more certain not to find there, and he had a foreboding of the reason. And so his conversation would be with her alone. He had a great longing to run and see his brother Dmitri before that fateful interview. Without showing him the letter, he could talk to him about it. But Dmitri lived a long way off, and he was sure to be away from home too. Standing still for a minute, he reached a final decision. Crossing himself with a rapid and accustomed gesture, and at once smiling, he turned resolutely in the direction of his terrible lady.

He knew her house. If he went by Main Street and then across the marketplace, it was a long way round. Though our town is small, it is scattered, and the houses are far apart. And meanwhile his father was expecting him, and perhaps had not yet forgotten his command. He might be unreasonable, and so he had to make haste to get there and back. So he decided to take a short cut by the back-way, for he knew every inch of the ground. This meant skirting fences, climbing over wattle-fences, and crossing other people's backyards, where everyone he met knew him and greeted him. In this way he could reach Main Street in half the time.

He had to pass the garden ajoining his father's and belonging to a little tumbledown house with four windows. The owner of this house, as Alyosha knew, was a bedridden old woman, living with her daughter, who had been a genteel maidservant in generals' families in Petersburg. Now she had been at home a year, looking after her sick mother. She always dressed up in fine clothes, though her old mother and she had sunk into such poverty that they went every day to Fyodor Pavlovich's kitchen for soup and bread, which Martha gave readily. Yet, though the young woman came up for soup, she had never sold any of her dresses, and one of these even had a long train—a fact which Alyosha had learned quite accidentally, of course, from Rakitin, who always knew everything that was going on in the town. He had forgotten it as soon as he heard it, but now, on reaching the garden, he remembered the dress with the train, raised his head, which had been bowed in thought, and came upon something quite unexpected.

Over the hurdle in the garden, his brother Dmitri Fyodorovich, mounted on something, was leaning forward, gesticulating violently, beckoning to him, obviously afraid to utter a word for fear of being overheard. Alyosha ran up to the hurdle.

"It's a good thing you looked up. I was nearly going to shout to you," Dmitri Fyodorovich said in a joyful, hurried whisper. "Climb in here quickly! How splendid that you've come! I was just thinking of you!"

Alyosha was delighted too, but he did not know how to get over the hurdle. But "Mitya" put his powerful hand under his elbow to help him jump. Tucking up his cassock, Alyosha leaped over the hurdle with the agility of a bare-legged street urchin.

"Well done! Now come along," said Mitya in an enthusiastic whisper.

"Where?" whispered Alyosha, looking about him and finding himself in a deserted garden with no one near but themselves. The garden was small, but the house was at least fifty paces away.

"There's no one here. Why do you whisper?" asked Alyosha.

"Why do I whisper? Devil take it!" cried Dmitri Fyodorovich at the top of his voice. "You see what silly tricks nature plays on one. I am here in secret, and I am guarding a secret. I'll explain later on, but, knowing it's a secret, I began to speak secretly and to whisper like a fool, when there's no need. Let us go. Over there. Till then be quiet. I want to kiss you.

> Glory to God in the world,
> Glory to God in me . . .[4]

I was just repeating that, sitting here, before you came."

The garden was about three acres in extent, and planted with trees only along the fence at the four sides. There were apple trees, maples, limes and birch trees. The middle of the garden was an empty grass space, from which several hundredweight of hay were carried in the summer. The garden was let out for a few rubles for the summer. There were also plantations of raspberries and currants and gooseberries laid out along the sides; a kitchen garden had been planted lately near the house.

Dmitri Fyodorovich led his brother to the most secluded corner of the garden. There, in a thicket of lime trees and old bushes of black currant, elder, snowball tree, and lilac, there stood a tumbledown green gazebo, blackened with age. Its walls were of lattice-work, but there was still a roof which could give shelter. God knows when this gazebo was built. There was a tradition that it had been put up some fifty years before by a retired colonel called von Schmidt, who owned the house at that time. It was all in decay, the floor was rotting, the planks were loose, the woodwork smelled musty. In the gazebo there was a green wooden table fixed in the ground, and round it were some green benches upon which it was still possible to sit. Alyosha had at once observed his brother's

---

4. Apparently Dmitri's own composition.

exhilarated condition, and on entering the arbor he saw half a bottle of brandy and a wineglass on the table.

"That's brandy," Mitya laughed. "I see your look: 'He's drinking again!' Distrust the apparition.

> Distrust the worthless, lying crowd,
> And lay aside thy doubts.[5]

I'm not drinking, I'm only 'indulging,' as that pig, your Rakitin, says. He'll be a civil councilor one day, but he'll always talk about 'indulging.' Sit down. I could take you in my arms, Alyosha, and press you to my bosom till I crush you, for in the whole world—in reality—in re-al-i-ty—(can you take it in?) I love no one but you!"

He uttered the last words in a sort of exaltation.

"No one but you and one 'jade' I have fallen in love with, to my ruin. But being in love doesn't mean loving. You may be in love with a woman and yet hate her. Remember that! I can talk about it gaily still. Sit down here by the table and I'll sit beside you and look at you, and go on talking. You shall keep quiet and I'll go on talking, for the time has come. But on reflection, you know, I'd better speak quietly, for here—here—you can never tell what ears are listening. I will explain everything, as they say, 'the story will be continued.' Why have I been longing for you? Why have I been thirsting for you all these days, and just now? (It's five days since I've cast anchor here.) Because it's only to you I can tell everything; because I must, because I need you, because tomorrow I shall fly from the clouds, because tomorrow life will end and begin. Have you ever felt, have you ever dreamt of falling down a precipice into a pit? That's just how I'm falling, but not in a dream. And I'm not afraid, and don't you be afraid. At least, I am afraid, but I enjoy it. It's not enjoyment though, but ecstasy. Damn it all, whatever it is! A strong spirit, a weak spirit, a womanish spirit—whatever it is! Let us praise nature: you see what sunshine, how clear the sky is, the leaves are all green, it's still summer; three o'clock in the afternoon and the stillness! Where were you going?"

"I was going to father's, but I meant to go to Katerina Ivanovna's first."

"To her, and to father! Oo! What a coincidence! Why was I waiting for you? Hungering and thirsting for you in every cranny of my soul and even in my ribs? Why, to send you to father from me and to her, Katerina Ivanovna, so as to have done with her and with father. To send an angel. I might have sent anyone, but I had

---

5. From Nekrasov's "When from the Gloom of Corruption" (1846), a famous poem about a redeemed prostitute, cited also in Dostoevsky's *Notes from Underground*.

to send an angel. And here you are on your way to see father and her."

"Did you really mean to send me?" cried Alyosha with a distressed expression.

"Stay! You knew it! And I see you understand it all at once. But be quiet, be quiet for a time. Don't be sorry, and don't cry."

Dmitri Fyodorovich stood up, thought a moment, and put his finger to his forehead.

"She's asked you, written to you a letter or something, that's why you're going to her? You wouldn't be going except for that?"

"Here is her note." Alyosha took it out of his pocket. Mitya looked through it quickly.

"And you were going the back-way! Oh, gods, I thank you for sending him by the back-way, and he came to me like the golden fish to the silly old fisherman in the fairy tale![6] Listen, Alyosha, listen, brother! Now I mean to tell you everything, for I must tell someone. An angel in heaven I've told already; but I want to tell an angel on earth. You are an angel on earth. You will hear and judge and forgive. And that's what I need, that someone above me should forgive. Listen! If two people break away from everything on earth and fly off into the unknown, or at least one of them, and before flying off or going to ruin he comes to someone else and says, 'Do this for me'—some favor never asked before that could only be asked on one's deathbed—would that other refuse, if he were a friend or a brother?"

"I will do it, but tell me what it is, and make haste," said Alyosha.

"Make haste! Hmm! . . . Don't be in a hurry, Alyosha, you hurry and worry yourself. There's no need to hurry now. Now the world has taken a new turning. Ah, Alyosha, what a pity you can't understand ecstasy. But what am I saying to him? As though you didn't understand it. What an ass I am, what am I saying: 'Be noble, oh, man!' Whose verse is that?"[7]

Alyosha made up his mind to wait. He felt that, perhaps, indeed, his work lay here. Mitya sank into thought for a moment, with his elbow on the table and his head in his hand. Both were silent.

"Lyosha," said Mitya, "you're the only one who won't laugh. I should like to begin—my confession—with Schiller's 'Hymn to Joy,' *An die Freude*! I don't know German, I only know it's called that. Don't think I'm talking nonsense because I'm drunk. I'm not a bit drunk. Brandy's all very well, but I need two bottles to make me drunk:

---

6. In Pushkin's verse "Tale of the Fisherman and the Fish" (1833), the fish grants the fisherman any wish if he will release him. The fisherman's wife as her last wish foolishly asks to rule the seas and have the fish as her servant, at which point all the material wealth she had gotten disappears.

7. Goethe, "Das Göttliche" (The divine).

> Silenus with his rosy phiz
> Upon his stumbling ass.[8]

But I've not drunk a quarter of a bottle, and I'm not Silenus. I'm not Silenus, though I am strong,[9] for I've made a decision once for all. Forgive me the pun; you'll have to forgive me a lot more than puns today. Don't be uneasy. I'm not spinning it out. I'm talking sense, and I'll come to the point in a minute. I won't keep you in suspense. Wait, how does it go?"

He raised his head, thought a minute, and began with enthusiasm:

> Wild and fearful in his cavern
> Hid the naked troglodyte,
> And the homeless nomad wandered
> Laying waste the fertile plain.
> Menacing with spear and arrow
> In the woods the hunter strayed. . . .
> Woe to all poor wretches stranded
> On those cruel and hostile shores!
>
> From the peak of high Olympus
> Came the mother Ceres[1] down,
>
> Seeking in those savage regions
> Her lost daughter Proserpine.
> But the Goddess found no refuge,
> Found no kindly welcome there,
> And no temple bearing witness
> To the worship of the gods.
>
> From the fields and from the vineyards
> Came no fruits to deck the feasts,
> Only flesh of blood-stained victims
> Smouldered on the altar-fires,
> And where'er the grieving goddess
> Turns her melancholy gaze,
> Man in deepest degradation
> Ceres beholds everywhere.[2]

Mitya broke into sobs and seized Alyosha's hand.

"My dear, my dear, in degradation, in degradation now, too. There's a terrible amount of suffering for man on earth, a terrible lot of trouble. Don't think I'm only a brute in an officer's uniform, who drinks vodka and leads a dissolute life. I hardly think of anything but of that degraded man—if only I'm not lying. I pray God I'm not lying now and showing off. I think about that man because I am that man myself.

8. Silenus was the eldest of the satyrs, the companion of Bacchus. From "Bas-relief" (1842) by A. N. Maykov.
9. In Russian, *silen*.
1. Ceres is the Roman name for Demeter.

2. Dmitri actually quotes, in Zhukovsky's translations, "The Eleusinian Festival" (stanzas 2–4 and the beginning of stanza 6) and then later the "Hymn to Joy" (stanzas 4 and 3).

> Would he purge his soul from vileness
> And attain to light and worth,
> He must turn and cling forever
> To his ancient Mother Earth.

But the difficulty is how am I to cling forever to Mother Earth. I don't kiss her. I don't cleave her bosom. Am I to become a peasant or a shepherd? I go on and I don't know whether I'm going to shame or to light and joy. That's the trouble, for everything in the world is a riddle! And whenever I've happened to sink into the vilest degradation (and it's always been happening) I always read that poem about Ceres and man. Has it reformed me? Never! For I'm a Karamazov. For when I do leap into the abyss, I go headlong with my heels up, and am pleased to be falling in that degrading attitude, and consider it something beautiful. And in the very depths of that degradation I begin a hymn of praise. Let me be accused. Let me be vile and base, only let me kiss the hem of the veil in which my God is shrouded. Though I may be following the devil, I am Thy son, O Lord, and I love Thee, and I feel the joy without which the world cannot stand.

> Joy everlasting fostereth
> The soul of God's creation,
> Her secret force of ferment fires
> The cup of life with flame.
> Enticed each blade towards the light
> And solar systems evolved
> From chaos and dark night,
> Filling the realms of boundless space
> Beyond the stargazer's sight.

> At bounteous nature's breast,
> All things that breathe drink Joy,
> All creatures, all nations,
> She draws in her wake.
> Her gifts to man are friends in need,
> The wreath, the foaming must,
> To angels—vision of God's throne,
> To insects—sensual lust.

But enough poetry! I am in tears; let me cry. It may be foolishness that everyone would laugh at. But you won't laugh. Your eyes are shining, too. Enough poetry. I want to tell you now about the insects to whom God gave 'sensual lust.'

> To insects—sensual lust.

I am that insect, brother, and it is said of me especially. All we Karamazovs are such insects, and, angel as you are, that insect lives in you, too, and will stir up a tempest in your blood. Tempests, because sensual lust is a tempest—worse than a tempest! Beauty is a terrible and awful thing! It is terrible because it has not been defined and is undefinable, for God sets us nothing but riddles. Here the two banks of the river meet and all contradictions exist side by side. I am not a cultivated man, brother, but I've thought a lot about this. It's terrible what mysteries there are! Too many riddles weigh men down on earth. We must solve them as we can, and try to keep a dry skin in the water. Beauty! I can't endure the thought that a man of lofty mind and heart begins with the ideal of the Madonna and ends with the ideal of Sodom. What's still more awful is that a man with the ideal of Sodom in his soul does not renounce the ideal of the Madonna, and his heart may be on fire with that ideal, genuinely on fire, just as in his days of youth and innocence. Yes, man is broad, too broad, indeed. I'd have him narrower. The devil only knows what to make of it! What to the mind is shameful is beauty and nothing else to the heart. Is there beauty in Sodom? Believe me, that for the immense mass of mankind beauty is found in Sodom. Did you know that secret? The awful thing is that beauty is mysterious as well as terrible. God and the devil are fighting there and the battlefield is the heart of man. But a man always talks of his own ache. Listen, now to come to facts."

Chapter IV

The Confession of an Ardent Heart—in Anecdote

"I was leading a wild life then. Father said just now that I spent several thousand rubles in seducing young girls. That's a swinish invention, and there was nothing of the sort. And if there was, I didn't need money simply for *that*. With me money is an accessory, the overflow of my heart, the framework. Today she would be my lady, tomorrow a wench out of the streets in her place. I entertained them both. I threw away money by the handful on music, rioting, and gypsies. Sometimes I gave it to the ladies, too, for they'll take it greedily, that must be admitted, and be pleased and thankful for it. Ladies used to be fond of me: not all of them, but it happened, it happened. But I always liked side paths, little dark back alleys behind the main road—there one finds adventures and surprises, and precious metal in the dirt. I am speaking figuratively, brother. In the town I was in, there were no such back alleys in the literal sense, but morally there were. If you were like me, you'd know what that means. I loved vice, I loved the ignominy of vice. I loved cruelty; am I not a bug, am I not a noxious insect? In fact a Karamazov! Once we went, a whole lot of us, for a picnic, in seven sleighs. It was dark, it was winter, and I began squeezing a girl's hand, and forced her to kiss me. She was the daughter of an official, a sweet, gentle, submissive creature. She allowed me, she allowed me much in the dark. She thought, poor thing, that I should come next day to make her an offer (I was looked upon as a good match, too). But I didn't say a word to her for five months. I used to see her in a corner at dances (we were always having dances), her eyes watching me. I saw how they glowed with fire—a fire of gentle indignation. This game only tickled that insect lust I cherished in my soul. Five months later she married an official and left the town, still angry, and still, perhaps, in love with me. Now they live happily. Observe that I told no one. I didn't boast of it. Though I'm full of low desires, and love what's low, I'm not dishonorable. You're blushing; your eyes flashed. Enough of this filth with you. And all this was nothing much—wayside blossoms à la Paul de Kock[3]—though the cruel insect had already grown strong in my soul. I've a perfect album of reminiscences, brother. God bless them, the darlings. I always tried to break it off without quarreling. And I never gave them away. I never bragged of one of them. But that's enough. You can't suppose I brought you here simply to talk of such nonsense. No, I'm going to tell you something more curious; and don't be surprised that I'm glad to tell you, instead of being ashamed."

"You say that because I blushed," Alyosha said suddenly. "I wasn't blushing at what you were saying or at what you've done. I blushed because I am the same as you are."

"You? Come, that's going a little too far!"

"No, it's not too far," said Alyosha warmly (obviously the idea was not a new one). "The ladder's the same. I'm at the bottom step, and you're above, somewhere about the thirteenth. That's how I see it. But it's all the same. Absolutely the same in kind. Anyone on the bottom step is bound to go up to the top one."

"Then one ought not to step on at all."

"Anyone who can help it had better not."

"But can you?"

"I think not."

"Hush, Alyosha, hush, darling! I could kiss your hand, you touch me so. That rogue Grushenka has an eye for men. She told me once that she'd devour you one day. There, there, I won't! From this field of corruption fouled by flies, let's pass to my tragedy, also befouled by flies, that is by every sort of vileness. Although the old man told lies about my seducing innocence, there really was something of the sort in my tragedy, though it was only once, and then it did not come off. The old man who has reproached me with what never happened does not even know of this

3. Paul de Kock (1794–1871) was an immensely popular writer of humorous   trashy romances.

fact; I never told anyone about it. You're the first, except Ivan, of course—Ivan knows everything. He knew about it long before you. But Ivan's a tomb."

"Ivan's a tomb?"

"Yes."

Alyosha listened with great attention.

"I was lieutenant in a line regiment, but still I was under supervision, like a kind of exile. Yet I was awfully well received in the little town. I spent money right and left. I was thought to be rich; I thought so myself. But I must have pleased them in other ways as well. Although they shook their heads over me, they liked me. My colonel, who was an old man, took a sudden dislike to me. He was always down upon me, but I had powerful friends, and, moreover, all the town was on my side, so he couldn't do me much harm. I was at fault myself for refusing to treat him with proper respect. I was proud. This obstinate fellow, who was really a very good sort, kind-hearted and hospitable, had had two wives, both now dead. His first wife, who was of a humble family, left a daughter as unpretentious as herself. She was a young woman of twenty-four when I was there, and was living with her father and an aunt, her mother's sister. The aunt was simple and illiterate; the niece was simple but lively. I like to say nice things about people. I never knew a woman of more charming character than Agatha—fancy, her name was Agatha Ivanovna! And she wasn't bad looking either, in the Russian style: tall, stout, with a full figure, and beautiful eyes, though a rather coarse face. She had not married, although she had had two suitors. She refused them, but was as cheerful as ever. I was intimate with her, not in 'that' way, it was pure friendship. I have often been friendly with women quite innocently. I used to talk to her with shocking frankness, and she only laughed. Many women like such freedom, and she was a maiden too, which made it very amusing. Another thing, one could never think of her as a young lady. She and her aunt lived in her father's house with a sort of voluntary humility, not putting themselves on an equality with other people. She was a general favorite, and of use to everyone, for she was a clever dressmaker. She had a talent for it. She gave her services freely without asking for payment, but if anyone offered her payment, she didn't refuse. The colonel, of course, was a very different matter. He was one of the chief personages in the district. He kept open house, entertained the whole town, gave suppers and dances. At the time I arrived and joined the battalion, all the town was talking of the expected return of the colonel's second daughter, a great beauty, who had just left a fashionable school in the capital. This second daughter was Katerina Ivanovna, and she was the child of the second wife, who belonged to a distinguished general's family; although, as I learned on good authority, she too brought the colonel no money. She had connections, and that was all. There may have been expectations, but they had come to nothing

"Yet, when the young lady came from boarding school on a visit, not to settle in, the whole town revived. Our most distinguished ladies—two 'Excellencies' and a colonel's wife—and all the rest following their lead, at once took her up and gave entertainments in her honor. She was the belle of the balls and picnics, and they got up charades in aid of distressed governesses. I took no notice, I went on as wildly as before, and one of my exploits at the time set all the town talking. I saw her eyes taking my measure one evening at the battery commander's, but I didn't go up to her, as though I disdained her acquaintance. I did go up and speak to her at an evening party not long after. She scarcely looked at me, and compressed her lips scornfully. 'Wait a bit. I'll have my revenge,' thought I. I behaved like an awful fool on many occasions at that time, and I was conscious of it myself. What made it worse was that I felt that 'Katenka' was not an innocent boarding-school miss, but a person of character, proud and really high-principled; above all, she had education and intellect, and I had neither. You think I meant to make her an offer? No, I simply wanted to revenge myself, because I was such a hero and she didn't seem to feel it.

"Meanwhile, I spent my time in drink and riot, till the lieutenant colonel put me under arrest for three days. Just at that time father sent me six thousand rubles in return for my sending him a deed giving up all claims upon him—settling our accounts, so to speak, and saying that I wouldn't expect anything more. I didn't understand a word of it at the time. Until I came here, Alyosha, till the last few days, indeed, perhaps even now, I haven't been able to make head or tail of my money affairs with father. But never mind that, we'll talk of it later.

"Just as I received the money, I got a letter from a friend telling me something that interested me immensely. The authorities, I learned, were dissatisfied with our lieutenant colonel. He was suspected of irregularities; in fact, his enemies were preparing a surprise for him. And then the commander of the division arrived, and kicked up a hell of a row. Shortly afterwards he was ordered to retire. I won't tell you how it all happened. He had enemies certainly. Suddenly there was a marked coolness in the town towards him and all his family. His friends all turned their backs on him. Then I took my first step. I met Agatha Ivanovna, with whom I'd always kept up a friendship, and said, 'Do you know there's a deficit of forty-five hundred rubles of government money in your father's accounts?'

" 'What do you mean? What makes you say so? The general was here not long ago, and everything was all right.'

" 'Then it was, but now it isn't.'

"She was terribly scared.

" 'Don't frighten me!' she said. 'Who told you so?'

" 'Don't be uneasy,' I said, 'I won't tell anyone. You know I'm as silent as the tomb. I only wanted, in view of "possibilities," to add, that when they demand that forty-five hundred rubles from your father, and he can't produce it, he'll be tried, and made to serve as a common soldier in his old age, unless you like to send me your young lady secretly. I've just had money paid me. I'll give her four thousand, if you like, and keep the secret religiously.'

" 'Ah, you scoundrel!' that's what she said. 'You wicked scoundrel! How dare you!'

"She went away furiously indignant, while I shouted after her once more that the secret would be kept sacred. Those two simple creatures, Agatha and her aunt, I may as well say at once, behaved like perfect angels all through this business. They genuinely adored their sister, the proud one, Katya, thought her far above them, and waited on her, hand and foot. But Agatha told her of our conversation. I found that out afterwards. She didn't keep it back, and of course that was all I wanted.

"Suddenly the new major arrived to take command of the battalion. The old lieutenant colonel was taken ill at once, couldn't leave his room for two days, and didn't hand over the government money. Dr. Kravchenko declared that he really was ill. But I knew for a fact, and had known for a long time, that for the last four years the money had never been in his hands except when the Commander made his visits of inspection. He used to lend it to a trustworthy person, a merchant of our town called Trifonov, an old widower, with a big beard and gold-rimmed spectacles. He used to go to the fair, do a profitable business with the money, and return the whole sum to the colonel, bringing with it a present from the fair, as well as interest on the loan. But this time (I heard all about it quite by chance from Trifonov's son and heir, a driveling youth and one of the most vicious in the world)—this time, I say, Trifonov brought nothing back from the fair. The lieutenant colonel flew to him. 'I've never received any money from you, and couldn't possibly have received any.' That was all the answer he got. So now our lieutenant colonel is confined to the house, with a towel round his head, while they're all three busy putting ice on it. All at once an orderly arrives on the scene with the book and the order to 'hand over the battalion money immediately, within two hours.' He signed the book (I saw the signature in the book afterwards), stood up, saying he would put on his uniform, ran to his bedroom, loaded his double-barreled gun, took the boot off his right foot, fixed the gun against his chest, and began feeling for the trigger with his foot. But Agatha, remembering what I had told her, had her suspicions. She stole up and peeped into the room just in time. She rushed in, flung herself upon him from behind, threw her arms round him, and the gun went off, hit the ceiling, but hurt no one. The others ran in, took away the gun, and held him by the arms. I heard all about this afterwards in detail. I was at home, it was getting dusk, and I was just preparing to go out. I had dressed, brushed my hair, scented my handkerchief, and taken up my cap, when suddenly the door opened, and facing me in the room stood Katerina Ivanovna.

"It's strange how things happen sometimes. No one had seen her in the street, so that no one knew of it in the town. I lodged with two decrepit old ladies, who looked after me. They were most obliging old things, ready to do anything for me, and at my request were as silent afterwards as two cast-iron posts. Of course I grasped the position at once. She walked in and looked straight at me, her dark eyes determined, even defiant, but on her lips and round her mouth I saw uncertainty.

" 'My sister told me,' she began, 'that you would give me four thousand rubles if I came to you for it—myself. I have come . . . give me the money!'

"She couldn't keep it up. She was breathless, frightened, her voice failed her, and the corners of her mouth and the lines round it quivered. Alyosha, are you listening, or are you asleep?"

"Mitya, I know you will tell the whole truth," said Alyosha in agitation.

"I am telling it. If I tell the whole truth just as it happened I shan't spare myself. My first idea was a—Karamazov one. Once I was bitten by a spider, brother, and laid up a fortnight with fever from it. Well, I felt a spider biting at my heart then—a noxious insect, you understand? I looked her up and down. You've seen her? She's a beauty. But she was beautiful in another way then. At that moment she was beautiful because she was noble, and I was a scoundrel; she in all the grandeur of her generosity and sacrifice for her father, and I—a bug! And, bug and scoundrel as I was, she was *completely* at my mercy, body and soul. She was hemmed in. I tell you frankly, that thought, that venomous thought, so possessed my heart that it almost swooned with suspense. It seemed as if there could be no resisting it; as though I should act like a bug, like a venomous spider, without a spark of pity. I could scarcely breathe. Understand, I should have gone next day to ask for her hand, so that it might end honorably, so to speak, and that nobody would or could know. For though I'm a man of base desires, I'm honest. And at that very second some voice seemed to whisper in my ear, 'But when you come tomorrow to make your proposal, that girl won't even see you; she'll order her coachman to kick you out of the yard. "Publish it through all the town," she would say, "I'm not afraid of you.'" I looked at the young lady, my voice had not deceived me. That is how it would be, not a doubt of it. I could see from her face now that I should be turned out of the house. My spite was roused. I longed to play her the nastiest swinish cad's trick: to look at her with a sneer, and on the spot where she stood before me to stun her with a tone of voice that only a shopman could use.

"'Four thousand! What do you mean? I was joking. You've been counting your chickens too easily, madam. Two hundred, if you like, with all my heart. But four thousand is not a sum to throw away on such frivolity. You've put yourself out to no purpose.'

"I should have lost the game, of course. She'd have run away. But it would have been an infernal revenge. It would have been worth it all. I'd have howled with regret all the rest of my life, only to have played that trick. Would you believe it, it has never happened to me with any other woman, not one, to look at her at such a moment with hatred. But, on my oath, I looked at that one for three seconds, or five perhaps, with fearful hatred—that hate which is only a hairsbreadth from love, from the maddest love!

"I went to the window, put my forehead against the frozen pane, and I remember the ice burned my forehead like fire. I did not keep her long, don't be afraid. I turned round, went up to the table, opened the drawer and took out a banknote for five thousand rubles (it was lying in a French dictionary). Then I showed it to her in silence, folded it, handed it to her, opened the door into the passage, and, stepping back, made her a deep bow, a most respectful, a most impressive bow, believe me! She shuddered all over, gazed at me for a second, turned horribly pale—white as a sheet, in fact—and all at once, not impetuously but softly, gently, bowed down to my feet—not a boarding-school curtsey, but a Russian bow, with her forehead to the floor. She jumped up and ran away. I was wearing my sword. I drew it and nearly stabbed myself with it on the spot; why, I don't know. It would have been frightfully stupid, of course. I suppose it was from delight. Can you understand that one might kill oneself from delight? But I didn't stab myself. I only kissed my sword and put it back in the scabbard—which there was no need to have told you, by the way. And I fancy that in telling you about my inner conflict I have laid it on rather thick to glorify myself. But let it pass, and to hell with all who pry into the human heart! Well, so much for that 'adventure' with Katerina Ivanovna. So now brother Ivan knows of it, and you—no one else."

Dmitri Fyodorovich got up, took a step or two in his excitement, pulled out his handkerchief and mopped his forehead, then sat down again, not in the same place as before, but on the opposite side, so that Alyosha had to turn quite round to face him.

Chapter V

The Confession of an Ardent Heart—"Heels Up"

"Now," said Alyosha, "I understand the first half."

"You understand the first half. That half is a drama, and it was played out there. The second half is a tragedy, and it is being acted here."

"And I understand nothing of that second half so far," said Alyosha.

"And I? Do you suppose I understand it?"

"Stop, Dmitri. There's one important question. Tell me, you were betrothed, you are betrothed still?"

"We weren't betrothed at once, not for three months after that adventure. The next day I told myself that the incident was closed, concluded, that there would be no sequel. It seemed to me caddish to make her an offer. On her side she gave no sign of life for the six weeks that she remained in the town; except, indeed, for one action. The day after her visit the maidservant slipped round with an envelope addressed to me. I tore it open; it contained the change out of the banknote. Only forty-five hundred was needed, but there was a discount of two hundred and something on changing it. She only sent me about two hundred sixty rubles, I don't remember exactly, but not a note, not a word of explanation. I searched the packet for a pencil mark—n-nothing! Well, I spent the rest of the money on such an orgy that the new major was obliged to reprimand me.

"Well, the lieutenant colonel produced the battalion money, to the astonishment of everyone, for nobody believed that he had the money untouched. He'd no sooner paid it than he fell ill, took to his bed, and, three weeks later, softening of the brain set in, and he died five days afterwards. He was buried with military honors, for he had not had time to receive his discharge. Ten days after his funeral, Katerina Ivanovna, with her aunt and sister, went to Moscow. And, behold, on the very day they went away (I hadn't seen them, didn't see them off) I received a tiny note, a sheet of thin blue paper, and on it only one line in pencil: 'I will write to you. Wait. K.' And that was all.

"I'll explain the rest now, in two words. In Moscow their fortunes changed with the swiftness of lightning and the unexpectedness of an Arabian fairy tale. That general's widow, their nearest relation, suddenly lost the two nieces who were her heiresses and next of kin—both died in the same week of smallpox. The old lady, prostrated with grief, welcomed Katya as a daughter, as her one hope, clutched at her, altered her will in Katya's favor. But that concerned the future. Meanwhile she gave her, for present use, eighty thousand rubles, as a marriage portion, to do what she liked with. She was an hysterical woman. I saw something of her in Moscow, later.

"Well, suddenly I received by post forty-five hundred rubles. I was speechless with surprise, as you may suppose. Three days later came the promised letter. I have it with me now. I always keep it, and shall keep it till I die. Shall I show you? You must read it. She offers to be my wife, offers herself to me. 'I love you madly,' she says, 'even if you don't love me, never mind. Be my husband. Don't be afraid. I won't hamper you in any way. I will be your chattel. I will be the carpet under your feet. I want to love you forever. I want to save you from yourself.' Alyosha, I am not worthy to repeat those lines in my vulgar words and in my vulgar tone, my everlastingly vulgar tone, that I can never cure myself of. That letter stabs me even now. Do you think I don't mind—that I don't mind still? I wrote her an answer at once, as it was impossible for me to go to Moscow. I wrote to her with tears. One thing I shall be ashamed of forever. I referred to her being rich and having a dowry while I was only a stuck-up beggar! I mentioned money! I ought to have borne it in silence, but it slipped from my pen. Then I wrote at once to Ivan, and told him all I could about it in a letter of six pages, and sent him to her. Why do you look like that? Why are you staring at me? Yes, Ivan fell in love with her; he's in love with her still. I know that. I did a stupid thing, in the world's opinion; but perhaps that one stupid thing may be the saving of us all now. Oo! Don't you see what a lot she thinks of Ivan, how she respects him? When she compares us, do you suppose she can love a man like me, especially after all that has happened here?"

"But I'm convinced that she does love a man like you, and not a man like him."

"She loves her own virtue, not me." The words broke involuntarily, and almost malignantly, from Dmitri. He laughed, but a minute later his eyes gleamed, he flushed crimson and struck the table violently with his fist.

"I swear, Alyosha," he cried, with intense and genuine anger at himself; "you may not believe me, but as God is holy, and as Christ is God, I swear that though I smiled at her lofty sentiments just now, I know that I am a million times baser in soul than she, and that these lofty sentiments of hers are as sincere as a heavenly angel's. That's the tragedy of it—that I know that for certain. What if anyone does show off a bit? Don't I do it myself? And yet I'm sincere, I'm sincere. As for Ivan, I can understand how he must be cursing nature now—with his intellect, too! To see the preference given—to whom, to what? To a monster who, though he is betrothed and all eyes are fixed on him, can't restrain his debaucheries—and before the very eyes of his betrothed! And a man like me is preferred, while he is rejected. And why? Because a girl wants to sacrifice her life and destiny out of gratitude. It's ridiculous! I've never said a word of this to Ivan, and Ivan of course has never dropped a hint of the sort to me. But destiny will be accomplished, and the best man will hold his ground while the undeserving one will vanish into his back alley forever—his filthy back alley, his beloved back alley, where he is at home and where he will sink in filth and stench at his own free will and with enjoyment. I've been talking foolishly. I've no words left. I use them at random, but it will be as I have said. I shall drown in the back alley, and she will marry Ivan."

"Stop, Dmitri," Alyosha interrupted again with great anxiety. "There's one thing you haven't made clear yet: you are still betrothed all the same, aren't you? How can you break off the engagement if she, your betrothed, doesn't want to?"

"Yes, formally and solemnly betrothed. It was all done on my arrival in Moscow, with great ceremony, with icons, all in fine style. The general's wife blessed us, and—would you believe it?—congratulated Katya. 'You've made a good choice, she said, 'I see right through him.' And, would you believe it, she didn't like Ivan, and hardly greeted him? I had a lot of talk with Katya in Moscow. I told her about myself—sincerely, honorably. She listened to everything.

> There was sweet confusion,
> There were tender words.[4]

Though there were proud words, too. She wrung out of me a mighty promise to reform. I gave my promise, and here——"

"What?"

"Why, I called to you and brought you out here today, this very day—remember it—to send you—this very day again—to Katerina Ivanovna, and——"

"What?"

"To tell her that I shall never come to see her again. Say 'He bows to you.' "

"But is that possible?"

"That's just the reason I'm sending you, in my place, because it's impossible. And, how could I tell her myself?"

"And where are you going?"

"To the back alley."

"To Grushenka then!" Alyosha exclaimed mournfully, clasping his hands. "Can Rakitin really have told the truth? I thought that you had just visited her, and that was all."

"Can a betrothed man pay such visits? Is such a thing possible

4. The lines have not been identified.

and with such a betrothed, and before the eyes of all the world? Confound it, I have some honor! As soon as I began visiting Grushenka, I ceased to be betrothed, and to be an honest man. I understand that. Why do you look at me? You see, I went in the first place to beat her. I had heard, and I know for a fact now, that that captain, father's agent, had given Grushenka an IOU of mine for her to sue me for payment, so as to put an end to me. They wanted to scare me. I went to beat her. I had had a glimpse of her before. She doesn't strike one at first sight. I knew about her old merchant, who's lying ill now, paralyzed; but he's leaving her a decent little sum. I knew, too, that she was fond of money, that she hoarded it, and lent it at a wicked rate of interest, that she's a merciless cheat and rogue. I went to beat her, and I stayed. The storm broke—it struck me down like the plague. I'm plague-stricken still, and I know that everything is over, that there will never be anything more for me. The cycle of the ages is accomplished. That's my position. And though I'm a beggar, as fate would have it, I had three thousand just then in my pocket. I drove with Grushenka to Mokroe, a place fifteen miles from here. I got gypsies there and champagne and made all the peasants there drunk on it, and all the women and girls. I sent the thousands flying. In three days' time I was stripped bare, but a hero. Do you suppose the hero had gained his end? Not a sign of it from her. I tell you that rogue, Grushenka, has a supple curve all over her body. You can see it in her little foot, even in her little toe. I saw it, and kissed it, but that was all I swear! 'I'll marry you if you like,' she said, 'you're a beggar you know. Say that you won't beat me, and will let me do anything I choose, and perhaps I will marry you.' She laughed, and she's laughing still!"

Dmitri Fyodorovich leaped up with a sort of fury. He seemed all at once as though he were drunk. His eyes became suddenly bloodshot.

"And do you really mean to marry her?"

"At once, if she will. And if she won't, I shall stay all the same. I'll be the porter at her gate. Alyosha!" he cried. He stopped short before him, and taking him by the shoulders began shaking him violently, "Do you know, you innocent boy, that this is all delirium, senseless delirium, for there's a tragedy here. Let me tell you, Alexey, that I may be a low man, with low and degraded passions, but a thief and a pickpocket Dmitri Karamazov never can be. Well, then; let me tell you that I am a thief and a pickpocket. That very morning, just before I went to beat Grushenka, Katerina Ivanovna sent for me, and in strict secrecy (why I don't know, I suppose she had some reason) asked me to go to the chief town of the province and to post three thousand rubles to Agatha Ivanovna in Moscow, so that nothing should be known of it in the town here. So I had that three thousand rubles in my pocket when I went to see Grushenka, and it was that money we spent at Mokroe. Afterwards I pretended I had been to the town, but did not show her the post office receipt. I said I had sent the money and would bring the receipt, and so far I haven't brought it. I've forgotten it. Now what do you think you're going to her today to say? 'He bows to you,' and she'll ask you, 'What about the money?' You might still have said to her, 'He's a degraded sensualist, and a low creature, with uncontrolled passions. He didn't send your money then, but wasted it, because, like a low brute, he couldn't control himself.' But still you might have added, 'He isn't a thief though. Here is your three thousand; he sends it back. Send it yourself to Agatha Ivanovna. But he told me to say "he bows to you." ' But, as it is, she will ask, 'But where is the money?' "

"Mitya, you are unhappy, yes! But not as unhappy as you think. Don't worry yourself to death with despair."

"What, do you suppose I'd shoot myself because I can't get three thousand to pay back? That's just it. I won't shoot myself. I haven't the strength now. Afterwards, perhaps. But now I'm going to Grushenka. I don't care what happens."

"And what then?"

"I'll be her husband if she deigns to have me, and when lovers come, I'll go into the next room. I'll clean her friends' galoshes, heat up their samovar, run their errands."

"Katerina Ivanovna will understand it all," Alyosha said solemnly. "She'll understand how great this trouble is and will forgive. She has a lofty mind, and no one could be more unhappy than you. She'll see that for herself."

"She won't forgive everything," said Mitya, with a grin. "There's something in it, brother, that no woman could forgive. Do you know what would be the best thing to do?"

"What?"

"Pay back the three thousand."

"Where can we get it from? I say, I have two thousand. Ivan will give you another thousand—that makes three. Take it and pay it back."

"And when would you get it, your three thousand? You're not of age, besides, and you must—you absolutely must—bow me out to her today, with the money or without it, for I can't drag on any longer, things have come to such a pass. Tomorrow is too late. I shall send you to father."

"To father?"

"Yes, to father first. Ask him for three thousand."

"But, Mitya, he won't give it."

"As though he would! I know he won't. Do you know the meaning of despair, Alexey?"

"Yes."

"Listen. Legally he owes me nothing. I've had it all from him, I know that. But morally he owes me something, doesn't he? You know he started with twenty-eight thousand of my mother's money and made a hundred thousand with it. Let him give me back only three out of the twenty-eight thousand, and he'll draw my soul out of hell, and it will atone for many of his sins. For that three thousand—I give you my solemn word—I'll make an end of everything, and he shall hear nothing more of me. For the last time I give him the chance to be a father. Tell him God Himself sends him this chance."

"Mitya, he won't give it for anything."

"I know he won't. I know it perfectly well. Now, especially. That's not all. I know something more. Now, only a few days ago, perhaps only yesterday he found out for the first time *in earnest* (underline *in earnest*) that Grushenka is really perhaps not joking, and really means to marry me. He knows her nature; he knows the cat. And do you suppose he's going to give me money to help to bring that about when he's crazy about her himself? And that's not all, either. I can tell you more than that. I know that for the last five days he has had three thousand drawn out of the bank, changed into notes of a hundred rubles, packed into a large envelope, sealed with five seals, and tied across with red tape. You see how well I know all about it! On the envelope is written: 'To my angel, Grushenka, when she will come to me.' He scrawled it himself in silence and in secret, and no one knows that the money's there except the valet, Smerdyakov, whom he trusts like himself. So now he has been expecting Grushenka for the last three or four days; he hopes she'll come for the money. He has sent her word of it, and she has sent him word that perhaps she'll come. And if she does go to the old man, can I marry her after that? You understand now why I'm here in secret and what I'm on the watch for."

"For her?"

"Yes, for her. Thomas has a room in the house of these sluts here. Thomas comes from our parts; he was a soldier in our regiment. He does jobs for them. He's watchman at night and goes grouse shooting in the daytime; and that's how he lives. I've established myself in his room. Neither he nor the women of the house know the secret—that is, that I am on the watch here."

"No one but Smerdyakov knows, then?"

"No one else. He will let me know if she goes to the old man."

"It was he who told you about the money, then?"

"Yes. It's top secret. Even Ivan doesn't know about the money, or anything. The old man is sending Ivan to Chermashnya on a two or three days' journey. A purchaser has turned up for the copse: he'll give eight thousand for the timber. So the old man keeps asking Ivan to help him by going to arrange it. It will take him two or three days. That's what the old man wants, so that Grushenka can come while he's away."

"Then he's expecting Grushenka today?"

"No, she won't come today; there are signs. She's certain not to come," cried Mitya suddenly. "Smerdyakov thinks so, too. Father's drinking now. He's sitting at a table with brother Ivan. Go to him, Alyosha, and ask for the three thousand."

"Mitya, dear, what's the matter with you?" cried Alyosha, jumping up from his place, and looking keenly at his brother's frenzied face. For one moment the thought struck him that Dmitri Fyodorovich was mad.

"What is it? I'm not insane," said Dmitri Fyodorovich, looking intently and earnestly at him. "No fear. I am sending you to father, and I know what I'm saying. I believe in miracles."

"In miracles?"

"In a miracle of Divine Providence. God knows my heart. He sees my despair. He sees the whole picture. Surely He won't let something awful happen. Alyosha, I believe in miracles. Go!"

"I am going. Tell me, will you wait for me here?"

"Yes. I know it will take some time. You can't go at him point blank. He's drunk now. I'll wait three hours—four, five, six, seven. Only remember you must go to Katerina Ivanovna today, if it has to be at midnight, *with the money or without the money*, and say, 'He bows to you.' I want you to say that verse to her: 'He bows to you.'"

"Mitya! And what if Grushenka comes today—if not today, tomorrow, or the next day?"

"Grushenka? I shall see her. I shall rush out and prevent it."

"And if——?"

"If there's an if, it will be murder. I couldn't endure it."

"Who will be murdered?"

"The old man. I won't kill her."

"Brother, what are you saying?"

"Oh, I don't know.... I don't know. Perhaps I won't kill him, and perhaps I shall. I'm afraid that he will suddenly become so loathsome to me with his face at that moment. I hate his ugly throat, his nose, his eyes, his shameless snigger. I feel a physical repulsion. That's what I'm afraid of. That's what may be too much for me."

"I'll go, Mitya. I believe that God will order things for the best, that nothing awful may happen."

"And I will sit and wait for the miracle. And if it doesn't come to pass——"

Alyosha went towards his father's house in deep thought.

Chapter VI

Smerdyakov

He did in fact find his father still at table. Though there was a dining room in the house, the table was laid as usual in the drawing room, which was the largest room, and furnished with old-fashioned ostentation. The furniture was white and very old, upholstered in old, red, silky material. In the spaces between the windows there were mirrors in elaborate white and gilt frames, of old-fashioned carving. On the walls, covered with white paper, which was torn in many places, there hung two large portraits—one of some prince who had been governor of the district thirty years before, and the other of some bishop, also long since dead. In the corner opposite the door there were several icons, before which a lamp was lighted at nightfall . . . not so much for devotional purposes as to light the room. Fyodor Pavlovich used to go to bed very late, at three or four o'clock in the morning, and would wander about the room at night or sit in an armchair, thinking. This had become a habit with him. He often slept quite alone in the house, sending his servants to the lodge; but usually Smerdyakov remained, sleeping on a bench in the hall.

When Alyosha came in, dinner was over, but coffee and preserves had been served. Fyodor Pavlovich liked sweet things with brandy after dinner. Ivan Fyodorovich was also at table, sipping coffee. The servants, Grigory and Smerdyakov, were standing by. Both the gentlemen and the servants seemed in singularly good spirits. Fyodor Pavlovich was roaring with laughter. Before he entered the room, Alyosha heard the shrill laugh he knew so well, and could tell from the sound of it that his father had only reached the good-humored stage, and was far from being completely drunk.

"Here he is! Here he is!" yelled Fyodor Pavlovich, highly delighted at seeing Alyosha. "Join us. Sit down. Coffee is a lenten dish, but it's hot and good. I don't offer you brandy, you're keeping the fast. But would you like some? No; I'd better give you some of our famous liqueur. Smerdyakov, go to the cupboard, the second shelf on the right. Here are the keys. Look sharp!"

Alyosha began refusing the liqueur.

"Never mind. If you won't have it, we will," said Fyodor Pavlovich, beaming. "But stay—have you dined?"

"Yes," answered Alyosha, who had in truth only eaten a piece of bread and drunk a glass of kvass in the Father Superior's kitchen. "Though I would very much like to have some hot coffee."

"Bravo, my darling! He'll have some coffee. Does it want warming? No, it's boiling. It's capital coffee: Smerdyakov's making. My

Smerdyakov's an artist at coffee and at fish patties, and at fish soup, too. You must come one day and have some fish soup. Let me know beforehand. . . . But, stay; didn't I tell you this morning to come home with your mattress and pillow and all? Have you brought your mattress? He, he, he!"

"No, I haven't," said Alyosha, smiling, too.

"Ah, but you were frightened, you were frightened this morning, weren't you? There, my darling, I couldn't do anything to vex you. Do you know, Ivan, I can't resist the way he looks one straight in the face and laughs? It makes me laugh all over. I'm so fond of him. Alyosha, let me give you my blessing—a father's blessing."

Alyosha rose, but Fyodor Pavlovich had already changed his mind.

"No, no," he said, "I'll just make the sign of the cross over you, for now. Sit still. Now we've a treat for you, in your own line, too. It'll make you laugh. Balaam's ass[5] has begun talking to us here— and how he talks! How he talks!"

Balaam's ass, it appeared, was the lackey, Smerdyakov. He was still a young man of about twenty-four, remarkably unsociable and taciturn. Not that he was shy or bashful. On the contrary, he was conceited and seemed to despise everybody. But we must pause to say a few words about him now. He was brought up by Grigory and Martha, but the boy grew up "with no sense of gratitude," as Grigory expressed it; he was an unfriendly boy, and seemed to look at the world mistrustfully. In his childhood he was very fond of hanging cats, and burying them with great ceremony. He used to dress up in a sheet as though it were a surplice, and sing, and wave some object over the dead cat as though it were a censer. All this he did on the sly, with the greatest secrecy. Grigory caught him once at this diversion and gave him a sound beating. He shrank into a corner and sulked there for a week. "He doesn't care for you or me, the monster," Grigory used to say to Martha, "and he doesn't care for anyone. Are you a human being?" he said, addressing the boy directly. "You're not a human being. You grew from the mildew in the bathhouse.[6] That's what you are." Smerdyakov, it appeared afterwards, could never forgive him those words. Grigory taught him to read and write, and when he was twelve years old, began teaching him the Scriptures. But this teaching came to nothing. At the second or third lesson the boy suddenly grinned.

"What's that for?" asked Grigory, looking at him threateningly from under his spectacles.

"Oh, nothing. God created light on the first day, and the sun, moon, and stars on the fourth day. Where did the light come from on the first day?"

---

5. Num. 22: 21–34. The ass finally speaks so that the angel of the Lord might spare its master.

6. A proverbial expression in Russian ("You sprang from nowhere").

Grigory was thunderstruck. The boy looked sarcastically at his teacher. There was something positively condescending in his expression. Grigory could not restrain himself. "I'll show you where!" he cried, and gave the boy a violent slap on the cheek. The boy took the slap without a word, but withdrew into his corner again for some days. A week later he had his first attack of the disease to which he was subject all the rest of his life—epilepsy. When Fyodor Pavlovich heard of it, his attitude to the boy seemed to change at once. Till then he had taken no notice of him, though he never scolded him, and always gave him a kopeck when he met him. Sometimes, when he was in good humor, he would send the boy something sweet from his table. But as soon as he heard of his illness, he showed an active interest in him, sent for a doctor, and tried remedies, but the disease turned out to be incurable. The fits occurred, on an average, once a month, but at various intervals. The fits varied, too, in violence: some were light and some were very severe. Fyodor Pavlovich strictly forbade Grigory to use corporal punishment on the boy, and began allowing him to come upstairs to him. He forbade him to be taught anything whatever for a time, too. One day when the boy was about fifteen, Fyodor Pavlovich noticed him lingering by the bookcase, and reading the titles through the glass. Fyodor Pavlovich had a fair number of books—over a hundred—but no one ever saw him reading. He at once gave Smerdyakov the key of the bookcase. "Come, read. You shall be my librarian. You'll be better sitting reading than hanging about the courtyard. Come, read this," and Fyodor Pavlovich gave him *Evenings on a Farm near Dikanka*.[7]

He read it, but didn't like it. He did not smile once, and finished it frowning.

"What? Isn't it funny?" asked Fyodor Pavlovich.

Smerdyakov did not speak.

"Answer, stupid!"

"It's all untrue," mumbled the boy, with a grin.

"Then go to the devil! You have the soul of a lackey. Stay, here's Smaragdov's *Universal History*. That's all true. Read that."

But Smerdyakov did not get through ten pages of Smaragdov. He thought it dull. So the bookcase was closed again.

Shortly afterwards Martha and Grigory reported to Fyodor Pavlovich that Smerdyakov was gradually beginning to show an extraordinary fastidiousness. He would sit before his soup, take up his spoon and look into the soup, bend over it, examine it, take a spoonful and hold it to the light.

"What is it? A cockroach?" Grigory would ask.

"A fly, perhaps," observed Martha.

The squeamish youth never answered, but he did the same with

7. The first collection of stories by the great Russian comic genius N. V. Gogol (1809–1852).

his bread, his meat, and everything he ate. He would hold a piece on his fork to the light, scrutinize it microscopically, and only after long deliberation decide to put it in his mouth.

"Ach! What fine gentleman's airs!" Grigory muttered, looking at him.

When Fyodor Pavlovich heard of his development in Smerdyakov he immediately determined to make him his cook, and sent him to Moscow to be trained. He spent some years there and came back remarkably changed in appearance. He looked extraordinarily old for his age. His face had grown wrinkled, yellow, and strangely emasculate. In character he seemed almost exactly the same as before he went away. He was just as unsociable, and showed not the slightest inclination for any companionship. In Moscow, too, it was later reported, he had always been silent. Moscow itself had little interest for him; he saw very little there, and took scarcely any notice of anything. He went once to the theater, but returned silent and displeased with it. On the other hand, he came back to us from Moscow well dressed, in a clean coat and clean linen. He invariably brushed his clothes most scrupulously twice a day, and was very fond of cleaning his smart calf boots with a special English polish, so that they shone like mirrors. He turned out a first-rate cook. Fyodor Pavlovich paid him a salary, almost the whole of which Smerdyakov spent on clothes, pomade, perfumes, and such things. But he seemed to have as much contempt for the female sex as for men; he was aloof, almost unapproachable, with them. Fyodor Pavlovich began to regard him rather differently. His fits were becoming more frequent, and on the days he was ill Martha cooked, which did not suit Fyodor Pavlovich at all.

"Why are your fits getting worse?" asked Fyodor Pavlovich, looking askance at his new cook. "Would you like to get married? Shall I find you a wife?"

But Smerdyakov turned pale with anger, and made no reply. Fyodor Pavlovich left him, giving it all up. The great thing was that he had absolute confidence in his honesty. It happened once, when Fyodor Pavlovich was drunk, that he dropped in the muddy courtyard three hundred-ruble notes which he had only just received. He only missed them next day, and was just hastening to search his pockets when he saw the notes lying on the table. Where had they come from? Smerdyakov had picked them up and brought them in the day before.

"Well, my lad, I've never met anyone like you," Fyodor Pavlovich snapped out, and gave him ten rubles. We may add that he not only believed in his honesty, but had, for some reason, a liking for him, although the young man looked as morosely at him as at everyone and was always silent. He rarely spoke. If it had occurred to any one to wonder at the time what the young man was interested in, and what was in his mind, it would have been impossible to tell by looking at him. Yet he used sometimes to stop suddenly in the house, or even in the yard or street, and would stand still for ten minutes, lost in thought. A physiognomist studying his face would have said that there was no thought in it, no reflection, but only a sort of contemplation. There is a remarkable picture by the painter Kramskoy,[8] called "Contemplation." There is a forest in winter, and on a roadway through the forest, in absolute solitude, stands a wandering peasant in a torn caftan and bark shoes. He stands, as it were, lost in thought. Yet he is not thinking; he is "contemplating." If any one touched him he would start and look at one as though awakening and bewildered. It's true he would come to himself immediately; but if he were asked what he had been thinking about, he would remember nothing. Yet probably he has hidden within himself, the impression which had dominated him during the period of contemplation. Those impressions are dear to him and no doubt he hoards them imperceptibly, and even unconsciously. How and why, of course, he does not know either. He may suddenly, after hoarding impressions for many years, abandon everything and go off to Jerusalem on a pilgrimage for his soul's salvation, or perhaps he will suddenly set fire to his native village, and perhaps do both. There are a good many "contemplatives" among the peasantry. Well, Smerdyakov was probably one of them, and he probably was greedily hoarding up his impressions, hardly knowing why.

Chapter VII

The Controversy

But Balaam's ass had suddenly spoken. The subject was a strange one. Grigory had gone in the morning to make purchases, and had heard from the shopkeeper Lukyanov the story of a Russian soldier which had appeared in the newspaper of that day. This soldier had been taken prisoner in some remote part of Asia, and was threatened with an immediate agonizing death if he did not renounce Christianity and follow Islam. He refused to deny his faith, and was tortured, flayed alive, and died, praising and glorifying Christ. Grigory had related the story at table. Fyodor Pavlovich always liked, over the dessert after dinner, to laugh and talk, if only with Grigory. This afternoon he was in a particularly good-humored and expansive mood. Sipping his brandy and listening to the story, he observed that they ought to make a saint of a soldier like that, and to take his skin to some monastery. "That would make the people flock, and bring the money in."

8. I. N. Kramskoy (1837–1887) was a Russian portraitist and painter.

Grigory frowned, seeing that Fyodor Pavlovich was by no means touched, but, as usual, was beginning to scoff. At that moment, Smerdyakov, who was standing by the door, smiled. Smerdyakov often waited at table towards the end of dinner, and since Ivan's arrival in our town he had done so every day.

"What are you grinning at?" asked Fyodor Pavlovich, catching the smile instantly, and knowing that it referred to Grigory.

"Well, my opinion is, sir," Smerdyakov began suddenly and unexpectedly in a loud voice, "that if that laudable soldier's exploit was so very great, sir, there would have been, to my thinking, no sin in it if he had on such an emergency renounced, so to speak, the name of Christ and his own christening, to save by that same his life, for good deeds, by which, in the course of years, to expiate his cowardice."

"How could it not be a sin? You're talking nonsense. For that you'll go straight to hell and be roasted there like mutton," put in Fyodor Pavlovich.

It was at this point that Alyosha came in, and Fyodor Pavlovich, as we have seen, was highly delighted at his appearance.

"We're on your subject, your subject," he chuckled gleefully, making Alyosha sit down to listen.

"As for mutton, that's not so, sir, and there'll be nothing there for this, and there shouldn't be either, sir, if it's according to justice," Smerdyakov maintained stoutly.

"How do you mean 'according to justice'?" Fyodor Pavlovich cried still more gaily, nudging Alyosha with his knee.

"He's a scoundrel, that's what he is!" burst from Grigory. He looked Smerdyakov wrathfully in the face.

"As for being a scoundrel, wait a little, Grigory Vasilyevich," answered Smerdyakov with perfect composure. "You'd better consider yourself that, once I am taken prisoner by the enemies of the Christian race, and they demand from me to curse the name of God and to renounce my holy christening, I am fully entitled to act by my own reason, since there would be no sin in it."

"But you've said that before. Don't waste words. Prove it," cried Fyodor Pavlovich.

"Soup maker!" muttered Grigory contemptuously.

"As for being a soup maker, wait a bit, too, and consider for yourself, Grigory Vasilyevich, without abusing me. For as soon as I say to those tormentors, 'No, I'm not a Christian, and I curse my true God,' then at once, by God's high judgment, I become immediately and specially anathema accursed, and I am cut off from the Holy Church, exactly as though I were a heathen, so that at that very instant, not only when I say it aloud, but when I think of saying it, before a quarter of a second has passed, I am cut off. Is that so or not, Grigory Vasilyevich?"

He addressed Grigory with obvious satisfaction, though he was really answering Fyodor Pavlovich's questions, and was well aware of it, and intentionally pretending that Grigory had asked the questions.

"Ivan," cried Fyodor Pavlovich suddenly, "stoop down for me to whisper. He's got this all up for your benefit. He wants you to praise him. Praise him."

Ivan Fyodorovich listened with perfect seriousness to his father's excited whisper.

"Wait, Smerdyakov, be quiet a minute," cried Fyodor Pavlovich once more. "Ivan, your ear again."

Ivan Fyodorovich bent down again with a perfectly grave face.

"I love you as I do Alyosha. Don't think I don't love you. Some brandy?"

"Yes." "But you're rather drunk yourself," thought Ivan Fyodorovich, looking steadily at his father. He was watching Smerdyakov with great curiosity.

"You're anathema accursed, as it is," Grigory suddenly burst out, "and how dare you argue, you scoundrel, after that, if . . ."

"Don't scold him, Grigory, don't scold him," Fyodor Pavlovich cut him short.

"You should wait, Grigory Vasilyevich, if only a short time, and listen, for I haven't finished all I had to say. For at the very moment I become accursed, sir, at that same highest moment, sir, I become exactly like a heathen, and my christening is taken off me and becomes of no avail. Isn't that so, sir?"

"Make haste and finish, my boy," Fyodor Pavlovich urged him, sipping from his wineglass with relish.

"And if I've ceased to be a Christian, then I told no lie to the enemy when they asked whether I was a Christian or not a Christian, seeing I had already been relieved by God Himself of my Christianity by reason of the thought alone, before I had time to utter a word to the enemy. And if I have already been discharged, in what manner and with what sort of justice can I be held responsible as a Christian in the other world for having denied Christ, when, through the very thought alone, before denying Him I had been relieved from my christening? If I'm no longer a Christian, then I can't renounce Christ, for I've nothing then to renounce. Who will hold a heathen Tatar responsible, Grigory Vasilyevich, even in heaven, for not having been born a Christian? And who would punish him for that, considering that you can't take two skins off one ox? For God Almighty Himself, even if He did make the Tatar responsible, when he dies would give him the smallest possible punishment, I imagine (since he must be punished), judging that he is not to blame if he has come into the world an unclean heathen, from heathen parents. The Lord God can't surely take a

Tatar and say he was a Christian? That would mean that the Almighty would tell a real untruth. And can the Lord of Heaven and Earth tell a lie, even in one word?"

Grigory was thunderstruck and looked at the orator, his eyes nearly starting out of his head. Though he did not clearly understand what was said, he caught something in his rigmarole, and stood, looking like a man who has just hit his head against a wall. Fyodor Pavlovich emptied his glass and went off into his shrill laugh.

"Alyosha! Alyosha! What do you say to that! Ah, you casuist! He must have been with the Jesuits somewhere, Ivan. Oh, you stinking Jesuit, who taught you? But you're talking nonsense, you casuist, nonsense, nonsense, nonsense. Don't cry, Grigory, we'll reduce him to smoke and ashes in a moment. Tell me this, oh, ass; you may be right before your tormentors, but you have renounced your faith all the same in your own heart, and you say yourself that in that very hour you became anathema accursed. And if once you're anathema they won't pat you on the head for it in hell. What do you say to that, my fine Jesuit?"

"There is no doubt, sir, that I have renounced it in my own heart, but there was no special sin in that, sir. Or if there was sin, it was the most ordinary, sir."

"How's that the most ordinary, sir?"

"You lie, accursed one!" hissed Grigory.

"Consider yourself, Grigory Vasilyevich," Smerdyakov went on, staid and unruffled, conscious of his triumph, but, as it were, generous to the vanquished foe. "Consider yourself, Grigory Vasilyevich; it is said in the Scripture that if you have faith, even as a mustard seed, and bid a mountain move into the sea, it will move without the least delay at your bidding. Well, Grigory Vasilyevich, if I'm without faith and you have so great a faith that you are continually swearing at me, you try yourself telling this mountain, not to move into the sea for that's a long way off, sir, but even to our stinking little river which runs at the bottom of the garden. You'll see for yourself, sir, that it won't budge, but will remain just where it is however much you shout at it, and that shows, Grigory Vasilyevich, that you haven't faith in the proper manner, and only abuse others about it. Again, taking into consideration that no one in our day, not only you, sir, but actually no one, from the highest person to the lowest peasant, sir, can shove mountains into the sea—except perhaps some one man in the world, or, at most, two, and they most likely are saving their souls in secret somewhere in the Egyptian desert, so you wouldn't find them—if so it be, sir, if all the rest have no faith, will God curse all the rest? that is, the population of the whole earth, except a couple of hermits in the desert, and in His well-known mercy will He not forgive one of them? And so I'm persuaded that though I may once have doubted I shall be forgiven if I shed tears of repentance."

"Wait!" cried Fyodor Pavlovich, in a transport of delight. "So you do suppose there are two who can move mountains? Ivan, make a note of it, write it down. There you have the Russian all over!"

"You're quite right in saying it's characteristic of the people's faith," Ivan Fyodorovich assented, with an approving smile.

"You agree. Then it must be so, if you agree. It's true, isn't it, Alyoshka? That's the Russian faith all over, isn't it?"

"No, Smerdyakov has not the Russian faith at all," said Alyosha firmly and gravely.

"I'm not talking about his faith. I mean those two in the desert, only that idea. Surely that's Russian, isn't it?"

"Yes, that's purely Russian," said Alyosha smiling.

"Your words are worth a gold piece, oh, ass, and I'll give it to you today. But as to the rest you talk nonsense, nonsense, nonsense. Let me tell you, stupid, that we here are all of little faith, only from carelessness, because we haven't time; things are too much for us, and, in the second place, the Lord God has given us so little time, only twenty-four hours in the day, so that one hasn't even time to get sleep enough, much less to repent of one's sins. Whereas you have denied your faith to your tormentors when you had nothing else to think about but to show your faith! So I consider, brother, that it constitutes a sin."

"Constitute a sin it may, but consider yourself, Grigory Vasilyevich, that it only extenuates it, if it does constitute. If I had believed then in very truth, as I ought to have believed, then it really would have been sinful if I had not faced tortures for my faith, and had gone over to the pagan Mohammedan faith. But, of course, it wouldn't have come to torture then, because I should only have had to say at that instant to the mountain 'move and crush the tormentor,' and it would have moved and at the very instant have crushed him like a cockroach, and I should have walked away as though nothing had happened, praising and glorifying God. But, suppose at that very moment I had tried all that, and cried to that mountain, 'Crush these tormentors,' and it hadn't crushed them, how could I have helped doubting, pray, at such a time, and at such a dread hour of mortal terror? And apart from that, I should know already that I could not attain to the fullness of the Kingdom of Heaven (for since the mountain had not moved at my word, they could not think very much of my faith up aloft, and there could be no very great reward awaiting me in the world to come). So why should I let them flay the skin off me as well, and to no good purpose? For, even though they had flayed my skin half off my back, even then the mountain would not have moved at my word or at my cry. And at such a moment not only doubt might come over one but one might lose one's reason from fear, so that one would not be able to think at all. And, therefore, how should I be particularly to blame if not seeing my advantage or reward there or here, I should, at least, save my skin? And so trusting fully in the grace of the Lord I should cherish the hope that I might be altogether forgiven, sir."

Chapter VIII

Over the Brandy

The controversy was over. But strange to say, Fyodor Pavlovich, who had been so gay, suddenly began frowning. He frowned and gulped brandy, and it was already a glass too much.

"Get along with you, Jesuits!" he cried to the servants. "Go away, Smerdyakov. I'll send you the gold piece I promised you today, but be off! Don't cry, Grigory. Go to Martha. She'll comfort you and put you to bed. The rascals won't let us sit in peace after dinner," he snapped peevishly, as the servants promptly withdrew at his word.

"Smerdyakov always pokes himself in now, after dinner. It's you he's so interested in. What have you done to fascinate him?" he added to Ivan Fyodorovich.

"Nothing whatever," he answered. "He's pleased to have a high opinion of me; he's a lackey and a mean soul. A prime candidate, however, when the time comes."

"Prime?"

"There will be others and better ones. But there will be some like him as well. His kind will come first, and better ones after."

"And when will the time come?"

"The rocket will go off and fizzle out, perhaps. The peasants are not very fond of listening to these soup makers, so far."

"Ah, brother, but a Balaam's ass like that thinks and thinks, and the devil knows where he gets to."

"He's storing up ideas," said Ivan, smiling.

"You see, I know he can't bear me, nor anyone else, even you, though you fancy that he has a high opinion of you. Worse still with Alyosha, he despises Alyosha. But he doesn't steal, that's one thing, and he's not a gossip, he holds his tongue, and doesn't wash our dirty linen in public. He makes capital fish patties too. But, damn him, is he worth talking about so much?"

"Of course he isn't."

"And as for the ideas he may be hatching, the Russian peasant, generally speaking, needs thrashing. That I've always maintained. Our peasants are swindlers, and don't deserve to be pitied, and it's a good thing they're still flogged sometimes. Russia is rich in birches. If they destroyed the forests, it would be the ruin of Russia. I stand up for the clever people. We've left off thrashing the peasants, we've grown so clever, but they go on thrashing themselves. And a good thing too. 'For with what measure ye mete it shall be measured to you again,' or how does it go? Anyhow, it will be measured. But Russia's all swinishness. My dear, if you only knew how I hate Russia. . . . That is, not Russia, but all this vice! But maybe I mean Russia. *Tout cela c'est de la cochonnerie.*[9] . . . Do you know what I like? I like wit."

"You've had another glass. That's enough."

"Wait a bit. I'll have one more, and then another, and then I'll stop. No, wait, you interrupted me. At Mokroe I was talking to an old man, and he told me: 'There's nothing we like so much as sentencing girls to be thrashed, and we always give the lads the job of thrashing them. And the girl he has thrashed today, the young man will ask in marriage tomorrow. So it quite suits the girls, too,' he said. There's a set of Marquis de Sades[1] for you! But it's clever, anyway. Shall we go over and have a look at it, eh? Alyoshka, are you blushing? Don't be bashful, child. I'm sorry I didn't stay to dinner at the Superior's and tell the monks about the girls at Mokroe. Alyosha, don't be angry that I offended your Superior this morning. I lost my temper. If there is a God, if He exists, then, of course, I'm to blame, and I shall have to answer for it. But if there isn't a God at all, what do they deserve, your fathers? It's not enough to cut their heads off, for they keep back progress. Would you believe it, Ivan, that that tears at my feelings? No, you don't believe it as I see from your eyes. You believe what people say, that I'm nothing but a buffoon. Alyosha, do you believe that I'm nothing but a buffoon?"

"No, I don't believe it."

"And I believe you don't, and that you speak the truth. You look sincere and you speak sincerely. But not Ivan. Ivan's supercilious. . . . I'd make an end of your monks, though, all the same. I'd take all that mystic stuff and suppress it, once for all, all over Russia, so as to bring all the fools to reason. And the gold and the silver that would flow into the mint!"

"But why suppress it?" asked Ivan.

"That Truth may prevail. That's why."

"Well, if Truth were to prevail, you know, you'd be the first to be robbed and then . . . suppressed."

"Bah! I daresay you're right. Ah, I'm an ass!" burst out Fyodor Pavlovich, striking himself lightly on the forehead. "Well, your monastery may stand then, Alyoshka, if that's how it is. And we clever people will sit snug and enjoy our brandy. You know, Ivan, it must have been so ordained by the Almighty Himself. Ivan,

9. "That's all swinishness."
1. De Sade (1740–1814) was a French writer and thinker whose cruelty produced the word "sadism."

speak, is there a God or not? Stay, speak the truth, speak seriously. Why are you laughing again?"

"I'm laughing that you should have made a clever remark just now about Smerdyakov's belief in the existence of two saints who could move mountains."

"Why, am I like him now, then?"

"Very much."

"Well, that shows I'm a Russian, too, and I have a Russian characteristic. And you may be caught in the same way, though you are a philosopher. Shall I catch you? What do you bet that I'll catch you tomorrow. Speak, all the same, is there a God, or not? Only, be serious. I want you to be serious now."

"No, there is no God."

"Alyoshka, is there a God?"

"There is."

"Ivan, and is there immortality of some sort, just a little, just a tiny bit?"

"There is no immortality either."

"None at all?"

"None at all."

"There's absolute nothingness then. Perhaps there is just something? Anything is better than nothing!"

"Absolute nothingness."

"Alyoshka, is there immortality?"

"There is."

"God and immortality?"

"God and immortality. In God is immortality."

"Hmm! It's more likely Ivan's right. Good Lord! to think what faith, what force of all kinds, man has lavished for nothing, on that dream, and for how many thousand years. Who is it laughing at man? Ivan! For the last time, once for all, is there a God or not? I ask for the last time!"

"And for the last time there is not."

"Who is laughing at mankind, Ivan?"

"It must be the devil," said Ivan Fyodorovich, smiling.

"And the devil? Does he exist?"

"No, there's no devil either."

"It's a pity. Damn it all, what wouldn't I do to the man who first invented God! Hanging on a bitter aspen tree would be too good for him."

"There would have been no civilization if they hadn't invented God."

"Wouldn't there have been? Without God?"

"No. And there would have been no brandy, either. But I must take your brandy away from you, anyway."

"Stop, stop, stop, dear boy, one more little glass. I've hurt Alyosha's feelings. You're not angry with me, Alexey? My dear little Alexeychik!"

"No, I am not angry. I know your thoughts. Your heart is better than your head."

"My heart better than my head, is it? Oh, Lord! And that from you. Ivan, do you love Alyoshka?"

"Yes."

"You must love him" (Fyodor Pavlovich was by this time very drunk). "Listen, Alyosha, I was rude to your elder this morning. But I was excited. But there's wit in that elder, don't you think, Ivan?"

"Very likely."

"There is, there is. *Il y a du Piron là dedans.*[2] He's a Jesuit, a Russian one, that is. As he's an honorable person there's a hidden indignation boiling within him at having to pretend and affect holiness."

"But, of course, he believes in God."

"Not a bit of it. Didn't you know? Why, he tells everyone so, himself. That is, not everyone, but all the clever people who come to him. He said straight out to Governor Schultz not long ago: 'Credo, but I don't know in what.' "

"Really?"

"He really did. But I respect him. There's something of Mephistopheles[3] about him, or rather of *The Hero of Our Time*. . . . Arbenin, or what's his name?[4] . . . You see, he's a sensualist. He's such a sensualist that I should be afraid for my daughter or my wife if she went to confess to him. You know, when he begins telling stories. . . . The year before last he invited us to tea, tea with liqueur (the ladies send him liqueur) and began telling us about old times till we nearly split our sides. . . . Especially how he once cured a paralyzed woman. 'If my legs were not bad I know a dance I could dance you,' he said. What do you say to that? 'I've pulled off plenty of tricks in my time,' said he. He did Demidov, the merchant, out of sixty thousand."

"What, he stole it?"

"He brought him the money as a man he could trust, saying, 'Take care of it for me, friend, there'll be a police search at my place tomorrow.' And he kept it. 'You have given it to the Church,' he declared. I said to him: 'You're a scoundrel,' I said. 'No,' said he, 'I'm not a scoundrel, but I'm broad-natured.' But that wasn't he, that was someone else. I've muddled him with someone else . . . without noticing it. Come, another glass and that's enough. Take

2. "There's something of Piron in him." A. Piron (1689–1773) was a French wit, poet, and dramatist.
3. In Goethe's *Faust*.

4. The disenchanted hero of Lermontov's novel is called Pechorin. Arbenin is the rake in Lermontov's play *Masquerade*.

away the bottle, Ivan. I've been telling lies. Why didn't you stop
me, Ivan, and tell me I was lying?"

"I knew you'd stop of yourself."

"That's a lie. You did it from spite, from simple spite against me.
You despise me. You have come to me and despised me in my own
house."

"Well, I'm going away. You've had too much brandy."

"I've begged you for Christ's sake to go to Chermashnya for a
day or two, and you don't go."

"I'll go tomorrow if you're so set upon it."

"You won't go. You want to keep an eye on me. That's what you
want, spiteful fellow. That's why you won't go."

The old man persisted. He had reached that state of drunkenness
when the drunkard who has till then been inoffensive tries to pick a
quarrel and to assert himself.

"Why are you looking at me? Why do you look like that? Your
eyes look at me and say, 'You ugly drunkard!' Your eyes are
mistrustful. They're contemptuous. . . . You've come here with
some design. Alyoshka, here, looks at me and his eyes shine. Alyosha doesn't despise me. Alexey, you mustn't love Ivan."

"Don't be ill-tempered with my brother. Leave off attacking
him," Alyosha said emphatically. "Oh, all right. Ugh, my head
aches. Take away the brandy, Ivan. It's the third time I've told
you."

He mused, and suddenly a slow, cunning grin spread over his
face. "Don't be angry with a feeble old man, Ivan. I know you
don't love me, but don't be angry all the same. You've nothing to
love me for. You go to Chermashnya. I'll come to you myself and
bring you a present. I'll show you a little wench there. I've had my
eye on her a long time. She's still running about barefoot. Don't be
afraid of barefooted wenches—don't despise them—they're pearls!"

And he kissed his hand with a smack.

"To my thinking," he revived at once, seeming to grow sober the
instant he touched on his favorite topic. "To my thinking . . . Ah,
you boys! You children, little sucking pigs, to my thinking . . . I
never thought a woman ugly in my life—that's been my rule! Can
you understand that? How could you understand it? You've milk in
your veins, not blood. You're not out of your shells yet. My rule
has been that you can always find something devilishly interesting
in every woman that you wouldn't find in any other. Only, one
must know how to find it, that's the point! That's a talent! To my
mind there are no ugly women. The very fact that she is a woman
is half the battle . . . but how could you understand that? Even in
vieilles filles,[5] even in them you may discover something that

5. "Old maids."

makes you simply wonder that men have been such fools as to let
them grow old without noticing them. Barefooted girls or unattractive ones, you must take by surprise. Didn't you know that? You
must astound them till they're fascinated, upset, ashamed that such
a gentleman should fall in love with such a little sloven. It's a jolly
good thing that there always are and will be masters and slaves in
the world, so there always will be a little maid-of-all-work and her
master, and you know, that's all that's needed for happiness. Stay
. . . listen, Alyoshka, I always used to surprise your mother, but in
a different way. I paid no attention to her at all, but all at once,
when the minute came, I'd be all devotion to her, crawl on my
knees, kiss her feet, and I always, always—I remember it as though
it were today—reduced her to that tinkling, quiet, nervous, queer
little laugh. It was peculiar to her. I knew her attacks always used
to begin like that, the next day she would begin shrieking hysterically, and that this little laugh was not a sign of delight, but it made
a very good counterfeit. That's the great thing, to know how to take
everyone. Once Belyavsky—he was a handsome fellow, and rich—
used to like to come here and hang about her—suddenly gave me a
slap in the face in her presence. And she—such a mild sheep—
why, I thought she would have knocked me down for that blow.
How she set on me! 'You're beaten, beaten now,' she said, 'You've
taken a blow from him. You have been trying to sell me to him,'
she said. . . . 'And how dared he strike you in my presence! Don't
dare come near me again, never, never! Run at once, challenge him
to a duel!' . . . I took her to the monastery then to bring her to her
senses. The holy Fathers prayed her back to reason. But I swear, by
God, Alyosha, I never insulted the poor possessed girl! Only once,
perhaps, in the first year; then she was very fond of praying. She
used to keep the feasts of Our Lady particularly and used to turn
me out of her room then. I'll knock that mysticism out of her,
thought I! 'Here,' said I, 'you see your holy image. Here it is. Here
I take it down. You believe it's miraculous, but here, I'll spit on it
directly and nothing will happen to me for it!' . . . When she saw it,
good Lord! I thought she would kill me. But she only jumped up,
wrung her hands, then suddenly hid her face in them, began trembling all over and fell on the floor . . . fell all of a heap. Alyosha,
Alyosha, what's the matter?"

The old man jumped up in alarm. From the time he had begun
speaking about his mother, a change had gradually come over
Alyosha's face. He flushed crimson, his eyes glowed, his lips quivered. The old sot had gone spluttering on, noticing nothing, till the
moment when something very strange happened to Alyosha. Precisely what he was describing in the possessed woman was suddenly
repeated with Alyosha. He jumped up from the table exactly as his
mother was said to have done, wrung his hands, hid his face in

them, and fell back in his chair, shaking all over in an hysterical paroxysm of sudden violent, silent weeping. His extraordinary resemblance to his mother particularly impressed the old man.

"Ivan, Ivan! Water, quickly! It's like her, exactly as she used to be then, his mother. Spurt some water on him from your mouth, that's what I used to do to her. He's upset about his mother, his mother," he muttered to Ivan.

"But she was my mother, too, I believe, his mother. Was she not?" said Ivan, with uncontrolled anger and contempt. The old man shrank before his flashing eyes. But something very strange had happened, though only for a second; it seemed really to have escaped the old man's mind that Alyosha's mother actually was the mother of Ivan too.

"Your mother?" he muttered, not understanding. "What do you mean? What mother are you talking about? Was she? . . . Why, damn it! of course she was yours too! Damn it! My mind has never been so darkened before. Excuse me, why, I was thinking Ivan . . . He, he, he!" He stopped. A broad, drunken, half senseless grin overspread his face.

At that moment a fearful noise and clamor was heard in the hall, there were violent shouts, the door was flung open, and Dmitri Fyodorovich burst into the room. The old man rushed to Ivan in terror.

"He'll kill me! He'll kill me! Don't let him get at me!" he screamed, clinging to the skirt of Ivan's coat.

Chapter IX

The Sensualists

Grigory and Smerdyakov ran into the room after Dmitri Fyodorovich. They had been struggling with him in the hall, refusing to admit him, acting on instructions given them by Fyodor Pavlovich some days before. Taking advantage of the fact that Dmitri Fyodorovich stopped a moment on entering the room to look about him, Grigory ran round the table, closed the double doors on the opposite side of the room leading to the inner rooms, and stood before the closed doors, stretching wide his arms, prepared to defend the entrance, so to speak, with the last drop of his blood. Seeing this, Dmitri uttered a scream rather than a shout and rushed at Grigory.

"Then she's there! She's hidden there! Out of the way, scoundrel!"

He tried to pull Grigory away, but the old servant pushed him back. Beside himself with fury, Dmitri struck out, and hit Grigory with all his might. The old man fell like a log, and Dmitri, leaping over him, broke through the door. Smerdyakov remained pale and trembling at the other end of the room, huddling close to Fyodor Pavlovich.

"She's here!" shouted Dmitri Fyodorovich. "I saw her turn towards the house just now, but I couldn't catch her. Where is she? Where is she?"

That shout, "She's here!" produced an indescribable effect on Fyodor Pavlovich. All his terror left him.

"Hold him! Hold him!" he cried, and dashed after Dmitri Fyodorovich. Meanwhile Grigory had got up from the floor, but still seemed stunned. Ivan Fyodorovich and Alyosha ran after their father. In the third room something was heard to fall on the floor with a ringing crash: it was a large glass vase—not an expensive one—on a marble pedestal which Dmitri Fyodorovich had upset as he ran past it.

"At him!" shouted the old man. "Help!"

Ivan Fyodorovich and Alyosha caught the old man and forcibly brought him back.

"Why do you run after him? He'll murder you outright," Ivan Fyodorovich cried wrathfully at his father.

"Vanechka, Lyoshechka! She must be here. Grushenka's here. He said he saw her himself, running."

He was choking. He was not expecting Grushenka at the time, and the sudden news that she was here made him beside himself. He was trembling all over. He seemed frantic.

"But you've seen for yourself that she hasn't come," cried Ivan.

"But she may have come by that other entrance."

"You know that entrance is locked, and you have the key."

Dmitri suddenly reappeared in the drawing room. He had, of course, found the other entrance locked, and the key actually was in Fyodor Pavlovich's pocket. The windows of all the rooms were also closed so Grushenka could not have come in anywhere nor have run out anywhere.

"Hold him!" shrieked Fyodor Pavlovich, as soon as he saw Dmitri again. "He's been stealing money in my bedroom." And tearing himself from Ivan he rushed again at Dmitri. But Dmitri raised both hands and suddenly clutched the old man by the two tufts of hair that remained on his temples, tugged at them, and flung him with a crash on the floor. He kicked him two or three times with his heel in the face. The old man moaned shrilly. Ivan Fyodorovich, though not so strong as Dmitri, threw his arms round him, and with all his might pulled him away. Alyosha helped him with his meager strength, holding his brother in front.

"Madman! You've killed him!" cried Ivan.

"Serve him right!" shouted Dmitri breathlessly. "If I haven't killed him, I'll come again and kill him. You can't protect him!"

"Dmitri! Go away at once!" cried Alyosha commandingly.

"Alexey! You tell me. It's only you I can believe; was she here just now, or not? I saw her myself creeping this way by the fence from the lane. I shouted, she ran away."

"I swear she's not been here, and no one expected her."

"But I saw her. . . . So she must . . . I'll find out at once where she is. . . . Goodbye, Alexey! Not a word to Aesop about the money now. But go to Katerina Ivanovna at once and be sure to say, 'He bows to you!' Bows! Bows! Expressly bows and bows out! Describe the scene to her."

Meanwhile Ivan and Grigory had raised the old man and seated him in an armchair. His face was covered with blood, but he was conscious and listened greedily to Dmitri's cries. He still fancied that Grushenka really was somewhere in the house. Dmitri Fyodorovich looked at him with hatred as he went out.

"I don't repent shedding your blood!" he cried. "Beware, old man, beware of your dream, for I have my dream, too. I curse you, and disown you altogether."

He ran out of the room.

"She's here. She must be here. Smerdyakov! Smerdyakov!" the old man wheezed, scarcely audibly, beckoning to him with his finger.

"No, she's not here, you old lunatic!" Ivan shouted at him angrily. "Here, he's fainting! Water! A towel! Make haste, Smerdyakov!"

Smerdyakov ran for water. At last they got the old man undressed, and put him to bed. They wrapped a wet towel round his head. Exhausted by the brandy, by his violent emotion, and the blows he had received, he shut his eyes and fell asleep as soon as his head touched the pillow. Ivan Fyodorovich and Alyosha went back to the drawing room. Smerdyakov removed the fragments of the broken vase, while Grigory stood by the table looking gloomily at the floor.

"Shouldn't you put a wet bandage on your head and go to bed, too?" Alyosha said to him. "We'll look after him. My brother gave you a terrible blow—on the head."

"He's insulted me!" Grigory articulated gloomily and distinctly.

"He's 'insulted' his father, not only you," observed Ivan Fyodorovich with a forced smile.

"I used to wash him in his tub. He's insulted me," repeated Grigory.

"Damn it all, if I hadn't pulled him away perhaps he'd have murdered him. It wouldn't take much to do for Aesop, would it?" whispered Ivan Fyodorovich to Alyosha.

"God forbid!" cried Alyosha.

"Why should He forbid?" Ivan went on in the same whisper,

with a malignant grimace. "One viper will devour the other. And serve them both right, too."

Alyosha shuddered.

"Of course I won't let him be murdered as I didn't just now. Stay here, Alyosha, I'll go for a turn in the yard. My head's begun to ache."

Alyosha went to his father's bedroom and sat by his bedside behind the screen for about an hour. The old man suddenly opened his eyes and gazed for a long while at Alyosha, evidently remembering and meditating. All at once his face betrayed extraordinary excitement.

"Alyosha," he whispered apprehensively, "where's Ivan?"

"In the yard. He's got a headache. He's on the watch."

"Give me that mirror. It stands over there. Give it to me."

Alyosha gave him a little round folding mirror which stood on the chest of drawers. The old man looked at himself in it; his nose was considerably swollen, and on the left side of his forehead there was a rather large crimson bruise.

"What does Ivan say? Alyosha, my dear, my only son, I'm afraid of Ivan. I'm more afraid of Ivan than the other. You're the only one I'm not afraid of. . . ."

"Don't be afraid of Ivan either. He is angry, but he'll defend you."

"Alyosha, and what of the other? He's run to Grushenka. My angel, tell me the truth, was she here just now or not?"

"No one has seen her. It was a mistake. She has not been here."

"You know Mitka wants to marry her, to marry her."

"She won't marry him."

"She won't. She won't. She won't. She won't on any account!"

The old man fairly fluttered with joy, as though nothing more comforting could have been said to him. In his delight he seized Alyosha's hand and pressed it warmly to his heart. Tears positively glittered in his eyes.

"That image of the Mother of God of which I was telling you just now," he said. "Take it home and keep it for yourself. And I'll let you go back to the monastery. . . . I was joking this morning, don't be angry with me. My head aches, Alyosha. . . . Alyosha, comfort my heart. Be an angel and tell me the truth!"

"You're still asking whether she has been here or not?" Alyosha said sorrowfully.

"No, no, no. I believe you. I'll tell you what it is: you go to Grushenka yourself, or see her somehow; make haste and ask her; see for yourself, which she means to choose, him or me? Eh? What? Can you?"

"If I see her I'll ask her," Alyosha muttered embarrassed.

"No, she won't tell you," the old man interrupted, "she's a

rogue. She'll begin kissing you and say that it's you she wants. She's a deceitful, shameless hussy. You mustn't go to her, you mustn't."

"No, father, and it wouldn't be suitable, it wouldn't be right at all."

"Where was he sending you just now? He shouted 'Go' as he ran away."

"To Katerina Ivanovna."

"For money? To ask her for money?"

"No. Not for money."

"He has no money; not a farthing. I'll settle down for the night, and think things over, and you can go. Perhaps you'll meet her. . . . Only be sure to come to me tomorrow in the morning. Be sure to. I have something to say to you tomorrow. Will you come?"

"Yes."

"When you come, pretend you've come of your own accord to ask after me. Don't tell any one I told you to. Don't say a word to Ivan."

"Very well."

"Goodbye, my angel. You stood up for me, just now. I shall never forget it. I've a word to say to you tomorrow—but I must think about it."

"And how do you feel now?"

"I shall get up tomorrow and go out, perfectly well, perfectly well, perfectly well!"

Crossing the yard Alyosha found his brother Ivan sitting on the bench at the gateway. He was sitting writing something in pencil in his notebook. Alyosha told Ivan that their father had woken up, was conscious, and had let him go back to sleep at the monastery.

"Alyosha, I would be very glad to meet you tomorrow morning," said Ivan cordially, standing up. His cordiality was a complete surprise to Alyosha.

"I shall be at the Khokhlakovs' tomorrow," answered Alyosha, "I may be at Katerina Ivanovna's, too, if I don't find her now."

"But you're going to her now, anyway? For that 'bows and bows out,' " said Ivan smiling. Alyosha was disconcerted.

"I think I quite understand his exclamations just now, and part of what went before. Dmitri has asked you to go to her and say that he—well, in fact—bows out?"

"Brother, how will all this horror end between father and Dmitri?" exclaimed Alyosha.

"One can't tell for certain. Perhaps in nothing: it may all fizzle out. That woman is a beast. In any case we must keep the old man indoors and not let Dmitri in the house."

"Brother, let me ask one thing more: has any man a right to look at other men and decide which is worthy to live?"

"Why bring in the question of worth? The matter is most often decided in men's hearts on other grounds much more natural. And as for rights—who has not the right to wish?"

"Not for another man's death?"

"What even if for another man's death? Why lie to oneself since all men live so and perhaps cannot help living so? Are you referring to what I said just now—that 'the two vipers will devour each other'? In that case let me ask you, do you think me like Dmitri capable of shedding Aesop's blood, murdering him, eh?"

"What are you saying, Ivan? Such an idea never crossed my mind. I don't think Dmitri is capable of it, either."

"Thanks, if only for that," smiled Ivan. "Be sure, I shall always defend him. But in my wishes I reserve myself full latitude in this case. Goodbye till tomorrow. Don't condemn me, and don't look on me as a villain," he added with smile.

They shook hands warmly as they had never done before. Alyosha felt that his brother had taken the first step towards him, and that he had certainly done this with some definite motive.

Chapter X

Both Together

Alyosha left his father's house feeling even more exhausted and dejected in spirit than when he had entered it. His mind too seemed shattered and unhinged, while he felt that he was afraid to put together the disjointed fragments and form a general idea from all the agonizing and conflicting experiences of the day. He felt something bordering upon despair, which he had never known till then. Towering like a mountain above all the rest stood the fatal insoluble question: How would things end between his father and his brother Dmitri with this terrible woman? Now he had himself been a witness of it, he had been present and seen them face to face. Yet only his brother Dmitri could be made unhappy, terribly, completely unhappy: there was trouble awaiting him. It appeared too that there were other people concerned, far more so than Alyosha could have supposed before. There was something positively mysterious in it, too. His brother Ivan had made a step towards him, which was what Alyosha had been long desiring. Yet now he felt for some reason that he was frightened at it. And these women? Strange to say, earlier he had set out for Katerina Ivanovna's in the greatest embarrassment; now he felt nothing of the kind. On the contrary, he was hastening there as though expecting to find guidance from her. Yet to give her this message was obviously more difficult than before. The matter of the three thousand was decided irrevocably, and Dmitri, feeling himself dishonored and losing his last hope, might sink to any depth. He had, moreover, told him to describe to Katerina Ivanovna the scene which had just taken place with his father.

It was by now seven o'clock, and it was getting dark as Alyosha entered the very spacious and convenient house on Main Street occupied by Katerina Ivanovna. Alyosha knew that she lived with two aunts. One of them, a woman of little education, was that aunt of her half-sister Agatha Ivanovna who had looked after her in her father's house when she came from boarding school. The other aunt was a Moscow lady of style and consequence, though in straitened circumstances. It was said that they both gave way in everything to Katerina Ivanovna, and that she only kept them with her as chaperones. Katerina Ivanovna herself gave way to no one but her benefactress, the general's widow, who had been kept by illness in Moscow, and to whom she was obliged to write twice a week a full account of all her doings.

When Alyosha entered the hall and asked the maid who opened the door to him to take his name up, it was evident that they were already aware of his arrival. Possibly he had been noticed from the window. At least, Alyosha heard a noise, caught the sound of flying footsteps and rustling skirts. Two or three women perhaps had run out of the room.

Alyosha thought it strange that his arrival should cause such excitement. He was conducted however to the drawing room at once. It was a large room, elegantly and amply furnished, not at all in provincial style. There were many sofas, lounges, settees, big and little tables. There were pictures on the walls, vases and lamps on the tables, masses of flowers, and even an aquarium in the window. It was twilight and rather dark. Alyosha made out a silk mantle thrown down on the sofa, where people had evidently just been sitting; and on a table in front of the sofa were two unfinished cups of chocolate, cakes, a crystal dish with Malaga raisins, and another with sweets. Alyosha saw that he had interrupted visitors, and frowned. But at that instant the portière was raised, and with rapid, hurrying footsteps Katerina Ivanovna came in, holding out both hands to Alyosha with a radiant smile of delight. At the same instant a servant brought in two lighted candles and set them on the table.

"Thank God! At last you have come too! I've been simply praying for you all day! Sit down."

Alyosha had been struck by Katerina Ivanovna's beauty when, three weeks before, his brother Dmitri had first brought him, at Katerina Ivanovna's special request, to be introduced to her. There had been no conversation between them at that interview, however. Supposing Alyosha to be very shy, Katerina Ivanovna had talked all the time to Dmitri Fyodorovich to spare him. Alyosha had been silent, but he had seen a great deal very clearly. He was struck by

the imperiousness, proud ease, and self-confidence, of the haughty
girl. And all that was certain, Alyosha felt that he was not exaggerating it. He thought her great glowing black eyes were very fine,
especially with her pale, even rather sallow, longish face. But in
those eyes and in the lines of her exquisite lips there was something
with which his brother might well be passionately in love, but
which perhaps could not be loved for long. He expressed this
thought almost plainly to Dmitri when, after the visit, his brother
besought and insisted that he should not conceal his impressions on
seeing his betrothed.

"You'll be happy with her, but perhaps—not tranquilly happy."

"Quite so, brother. Such people remain always the same. They
don't yield to fate. So you think I won't love her forever."

"No, perhaps you will love her forever. But perhaps you won't
always be happy with her."

Alyosha had given his opinion at the time, blushing, and angry
with himself for having yielded to his brother's entreaties and put
such "foolish" ideas into words. For his opinion had struck him as
awfully foolish immediately after he had uttered it. He felt ashamed
too of having given so confident an opinion about a woman. It was
with the more amazement that he felt now, at the first glance at
Katerina Ivanovna as she ran in to him, that he had perhaps been
utterly mistaken. This time her face was beaming with spontaneous
good-natured kindliness, and direct warm-hearted sincerity. The
"pride and haughtiness," which had struck Alyosha so much before, was only betrayed now in a frank, generous energy and a sort
of clear strong faith in herself. Alyosha realized at the first glance,
at the first word, that all the tragedy of her position in relation to
the man she loved so dearly was no secret to her; that she perhaps
already knew everything, positively everything. And yet, in spite of
that, there was such brightness in her face, such faith in the future.
Alyosha felt at once that he had gravely wronged her in his
thoughts. He was conquered and captivated immediately. Besides
all this, he noticed at her first words that she was very excited, an
excitement perhaps quite exceptional and almost approaching
ecstasy.

"I was so eager to see you, because I can learn from you the
whole truth—from you and no one else."

"I have come," muttered Alyosha confusedly, "I—he sent me."

"Ah, he sent you! I foresaw that. Now I know everything—
everything!" cried Katerina Ivanovna, her eyes flashing. "Wait a
moment, Alexey Fyodorovich, I'll tell you why I've been so longing
to see you. You see, I know perhaps far more than you do yourself,
and there's no need for you to tell me anything. I'll tell you what I
want from you. I want to know your own last impression of him. I
want you to tell me most directly, plainly, coarsely even (oh, as

coarsely as you like!), what you thought of him just now and of his position after your meeting with him today. That will perhaps be better than if I had a personal explanation with him, as he does not want to come to me. Do you understand what I want from you? Now, tell me simply, tell me every word of the message he sent you with (I knew he would send you)."

"He told me to bow to you—and to say that he would never come again—but to bow to you."

"To bow? Was that what he said—his own expression?"

"Yes."

"Accidentally perhaps he made a mistake in the word, perhaps he did not use the right word?"

"No; he told me precisely to repeat that word, 'bows.' He begged me two or three times not to forget to say so."

Katerina Ivanovna flushed hotly.

"Help me now, Alexey Fyodorovich. Now I really need your help. I'll tell you what I think, and you must simply say whether it's right or not. Listen! If he had said to bow to me in passing, without insisting on your repeating the words, without emphasizing them, that would be the end of everything! But if he particularly insisted on those words, if he particularly told you not to forget to repeat that *bow* to me, then perhaps he was excited, beside himself. He had made his decision and was frightened at it. He wasn't walking away from me with a resolute step, but leaping headlong. The emphasis on that phrase may have been simply bravado."

"Yes, yes!" cried Alyosha warmly. "I believe that is it."

"And, if so, he's not altogether lost. He is only in despair, but now I can still save him. Stay! Did he not tell you anything about money—about three thousand rubles?"

"He did speak about it, and it's that more than anything that's crushing him. He said he had lost his honor and that nothing matters now," Alyosha answered warmly, feeling a rush of hope in his heart and believing that there really might be a way of escape and salvation for his brother. "But do you know about the money?" he added, and suddenly broke off.

"I've known of it a long time; I telegraphed to Moscow to inquire, and heard long ago that the money had not arrived. He hadn't sent the money, but I said nothing. Last week I learnt that he was still in need of money. My only object in all this was that he should know to whom to turn, and who was his true friend. No, he won't recognize that I am his truest friend; he won't know me, and looks on me merely as a woman. I've been tormented all week, trying to think how to prevent him from being ashamed to face me because he spent that three thousand. Let him feel ashamed of himself, let him be ashamed of other people's knowing, but not of my knowing. He can tell God everything without shame.

Why is it he still does not understand how much I am ready to bear for his sake? Why, why doesn't he know me? How dare he not know me after all that has happened? I want to save him forever. Let him forget me as his betrothed. And here he fears that he is dishonored in my eyes. Why, he wasn't afraid to be open with you, Alexey Fyodorovich. How is it that I don't deserve the same?"

The last words she uttered in tears. Tears gushed from her eyes.

"I must tell you," Alyosha began, his voice trembling too, "what happened just now between him and my father." And he described the whole scene, how Dmitri had sent him to get the money, how he had broken in, knocked his father down, and after that had again specially and emphatically begged him to "bow to her and bow out." "He went to that woman," Alyosha added softly.

"And do you suppose that I can't put up with that woman? Does he think I can't? But he won't marry her," she suddenly laughed nervously. "Could such a passion last forever in a Karamazov? It's passion, not love. He won't marry her because she won't marry him." Again Katerina Ivanovna laughed strangely.

"He may marry her," said Alyosha mournfully, looking down.

"He won't marry her, I tell you. That girl is an angel. Do you know that? Do you know that?" Katerina Ivanovna exclaimed suddenly with extraordinary warmth. "She is one of the most fantastic of fantastic creatures. I know how bewitching she is, but I know too that she is kind, firm and noble. Why do you look at me like that, Alexey Fyodorovich? Perhaps you are wondering at my words, perhaps you don't believe me? Agrafena Alexandrovna, my angel!" she cried suddenly to someone, peeping into the next room, "come in to us. This is a friend. This is Alyosha. He knows all about our affairs. Show yourself to him."

"I've only been waiting behind the curtain for you to call me," said a soft, one might even say sugary, feminine voice.

The portière was raised and Grushenka herself, smiling and beaming, came up to the table. Alyosha seemed to flinch. He fixed his eyes on her and could not take them off. Here she was, that awful woman, the "beast," as his brother Ivan had called her half an hour before. And yet one would have thought the creature standing before him most simple and ordinary, a good-natured, kind woman, handsome certainly, but so like other handsome "ordinary" women! It is true she was very, very good looking with that Russian beauty so passionately loved by many men. She was a rather tall woman, though a little shorter than Katerina Ivanovna, who was exceptionally tall. She had a full figure, with soft, as it were, noiseless, movements, softened to a peculiar over-sweetness, like her voice. She moved, not like Katerina Ivanovna, with a vigorous, bold step, but noiselessly. Her feet made absolutely no sound on the floor. She sank softly into a low chair, softly rustling her sumptuous black silk dress, and delicately nestling her milk-white neck and broad shoulders in a costly black cashmere shawl. She was twenty-two years old, and her face looked exactly that age. She was very white in the face, with a pale pink tint on her cheeks. The modeling of her face might be said to be too broad, and the lower jaw was set a trifle forward. Her upper lip was thin, but the slightly prominent lower lip was at least twice as full, and looked swollen somehow. But her magnificent, abundant dark brown hair, her sable-colored eyebrows and charming gray-blue eyes with their long lashes would have made the most indifferent person, meeting her casually in a crowd in the street, stop at the sight of her face and remember it long after. What struck Alyosha most in that face was its expression of childlike good nature. There was a childlike look in her eyes, a look of childish delight. She came up to the table, beaming with delight and seeming to expect something with childish, impatient, and confiding curiosity. The light in her eyes gladdened the soul—Alyosha felt that. There was something else in her which he could not understand, or would not have been able to define, and which yet perhaps unconsciously affected him. It was that softness, that delicacy of her bodily movements, that catlike noiselessness. Yet it was a vigorous, ample body. Under the shawl could be seen full broad shoulders, a high, still quite girlish bosom. Her figure suggested the lines of the Venus de Milo, though already in somewhat exaggerated proportions. That could be divined. Connoisseurs of Russian beauty could have foretold with certainty that this fresh, still youthful, beauty would lose its harmony by the age of thirty, would "spread"; that the face would become puffy, and that wrinkles would very soon appear upon her forehead and round the eyes; the complexion would grow coarse and red perhaps—in fact, that it was the beauty of the moment, the fleeting beauty which is so often met with in Russian women. Alyosha, of course, did not think of this; but though he was fascinated, yet he wondered with an unpleasant sensation, and as it were regretfully, why she drawled in that way and could not speak naturally. She did so evidently feeling there was a charm in the exaggerated, honeyed modulation of the syllables. It was, of course, only a bad habit of bad taste that showed poor education and a false idea of good manners. And yet this intonation and manner of speaking impressed Alyosha as almost incredibly incongruous with the childishly simple and happy expression of her face, the soft, babyish joy in her eyes! Katerina Ivanovna at once made her sit down in an armchair facing Alyosha, and ecstatically kissed her several times on her smiling lips. She seemed quite in love with her.

"This is the first time we've met, Alexey Fyodorovich," she said rapturously. "I wanted to know her, to see her. I wanted to go to her, but I'd no sooner expressed the wish than she came to me. I knew we should settle everything together—everything! My heart told me so—I was begged not to take the step, but I foresaw it would be a way out of the difficulty, and I was not mistaken. Grushenka has explained everything to me, told me all she means to do. She flew here like an angel of goodness and brought us peace and joy."

"You did not disdain me, sweet, excellent young lady," drawled Grushenka in her singsong voice, still with the same charming smile of delight.

"Don't dare to speak to me like that, you sorceress, you witch! Disdain you! Here I must kiss your lower lip once more. It looks as though it were swollen, and now it will be more so, and more and more. Look how she laughs, Alexey Fyodorovich! It does one's heart good to see the angel."

Alyosha flushed, and faint, imperceptible shivers kept running down him.

"You make so much of me, dear young lady, and perhaps I am not at all worthy of your kindness."

"Not worthy! She's not worthy of it!" Katerina Ivanovna cried again with the same warmth. "You know, Alexey Fyodorovich, we're fanciful, we're self-willed, but proudest of the proud in our little heart. We're noble, we're generous, Alexey Fyodorovich, let me tell you. We have only been unfortunate. We were too ready to make every sacrifice for an unworthy, perhaps, or fickle man. There was one man—one, an officer too, we loved him, we sacrificed everything to him. That was long ago, five years ago, and he has forgotten us, he has married. Now he is a widower, he has written, he is coming here, and do you know, we've loved him, none but him, all this time, and we've loved him all our life! He will come, and Grushenka will be happy again. For the last five years she's been wretched. But who can reproach her, who can boast of her favor? Only that bedridden old merchant, but he is more like our father, our friend, our protector. He found us then in despair, in agony, deserted by the man we loved. She was ready to drown herself then, but the old merchant saved her—saved her!"

"You defend me very kindly, dear young lady. You are in a great hurry about everything," Grushenka drawled again.

"Defend you! Is it for me to defend you? Should I dare to defend you? Grushenka, angel, give me your hand. Look at that charming soft little hand, Alexey Fyodorovich! Look at it! It has brought me happiness and has lifted me up, and I'm going to kiss it, outside and inside, here, here, here!"

And three times she kissed the certainly charming, though rather fat, hand of Grushenka in a sort of rapture. She held out her hand with a charming musical, nervous little laugh, watched the "sweet young lady," and obviously liked having her hand kissed.

"Perhaps there's rather too much ecstasy," thought Alyosha. He blushed. He felt a peculiar uneasiness at heart the whole time.

"You won't make me blush, dear young lady, kissing my hand like this before Alexey Fyodorovich."

"Do you think I meant to make you blush?" said Katerina Ivanovna, somewhat surprised. "Ah, my dear, how little you understand me!"

"Yes, and you too perhaps quite misunderstand me, dear young lady. Maybe I'm not so good as I seem to you. I've a bad heart; I will have my own way. I fascinated poor Dmitri Fyodorovich that day simply for fun."

"But now you'll save him. You've given me your word. You'll explain it all to him. You'll break it to him that you have long loved another man, who is now offering you his hand."

"Oh, no! I didn't give you my word to do that. It was you kept talking about that. I didn't give you my word."

"Then I didn't quite understand you," said Katerina Ivanovna slowly, turning a little pale. "You promised . . ."

"Oh no, angel lady, I've promised nothing." Grushenka interrupted softly and evenly, still with the same gay and simple expression. "You see at once, dear young lady, what a willful wretch I am compared with you. If I want to do a thing I do it. I may have made you some promise just now. But now again I'm thinking: I may take to Mitya again. I liked him very much once—liked him for almost a whole hour. Now maybe I shall go and tell him to stay with me from this day forward. You see, I'm so changeable."

"Just now you said—something quite different," Katerina Ivanovna whispered faintly.

"Ah, just now! But, you know, I'm such a soft-hearted, silly creature. Only think what he's gone through on my account! What if when I go home I feel sorry for him? What then?"

"I never expected——"

"Ah, young lady, how good and generous you are compared with me! Now perhaps you won't care for a silly creature like me, now you know my character. Give me your sweet little hand, angelic lady," she said tenderly, and with a sort of reverence took Katerina Ivanovna's hand.

"Here, dear young lady, I'll take your hand and kiss it as you did mine. You kissed mine three times, but I ought to kiss yours three hundred times to be even with you. Well, but let that pass. And then it shall be as God wills. Perhaps I shall be your slave entirely and want to do your bidding like a slave. Let it be as God wills, without any agreements and promises. What a sweet hand—what a sweet hand you have! You sweet young lady, you incredible beauty!"

She slowly raised the hands to her lips, with the strange object indeed of "being even" with her in kisses. Katerina Ivanovna did not take her hand away. She listened with timid hope to the last words, though Grushenka's promise to do her bidding like a slave was very strangely expressed. She looked intently into her eyes; she still saw in those eyes the same simple-hearted, confiding expression, the same bright gaiety. "She's perhaps too naïve," thought Katerina Ivanovna, with a gleam of hope. Grushenka meanwhile seemed enthusiastic over the "sweet hand." She raised it deliberately to her lips. But she held it for two or three moments near her lips, as though reconsidering something.

"Do you know, angel lady," she suddenly drawled in an even more soft and sugary voice, "do you know, after all, I think I won't kiss your hand?" And she laughed a little merry laugh.

"As you please. What's the matter with you?" said Katerina Ivanovna, starting suddenly.

"So that you may be left to remember that you kissed my hand, but I didn't kiss yours." There was a sudden gleam in her eyes. She looked with awful intentness at Katerina Ivanovna.

"Insolent creature!" cried Katerina Ivanovna, as though suddenly grasping something. She flushed all over and leaped up from her seat. Grushenka too got up, but without haste.

"So I shall tell Mitya how you kissed my hand, but I didn't kiss yours at all. And how he will laugh!"

"Slut! Go away!"

"Ah, for shame, young lady! Ah, for shame! That's unbecoming for you, dear young lady, a word like that."

"Go away! You're a creature for sale!" screamed Katerina Ivanovna. Every feature was working in her utterly distorted face.

"For sale indeed! You used to visit gentlemen in the dusk for money once; you brought your beauty for sale. You see, I know."

Katerina Ivanovna shrieked, and would have rushed at her, but Alyosha held her with all his strength.

"Not a step, not a word! Don't speak, don't answer her. She'll go away—she'll go at once."

At that instant Katerina Ivanovna's two aunts ran in at her cry, and with them a maidservant. All hurried to her.

"I will go away," said Grushenka, taking up her mantle from the sofa. "Alyosha, darling, see me home!"

"Go away—go away, make haste!" cried Alyosha, clasping his hands imploringly.

"Dear little Alyoshenka, see me home! I've got a pretty little story to tell you on the way. I got up this scene for your benefit, Alyoshenka. See me home, dear, you'll be glad of it afterwards."

Alyosha turned away, wringing his hands. Grushenka ran out of the house, laughing musically.

Katerina Ivanovna went into a fit of hysterics. She sobbed, and was shaken with convulsions. Everyone fussed round her.

"I warned you," said the elder of her aunts. "I tried to prevent your doing this. You're too impulsive. How could you do such a thing? You don't know these creatures, and they say she's worse than any of them. You are too self-willed."

"She's a tigress!" yelled Katerina Ivanovna. "Why did you hold me, Alexey Fyodorovich! I'd have beaten her—beaten her!"

She could not control herself before Alyosha; perhaps she did not care to, indeed.

"She ought to be flogged in public on a scaffold!"

Alyosha withdrew towards the door.

"But, my God!" cried Katerina Ivanovna, clasping her hands. "He! He! He could be so dishonorable, so inhuman! Why, he told that creature what happened on that fatal, accursed day! 'You brought your beauty for sale, dear young lady.' She knows it! Your brother's a scoundrel, Alexey Fyodorovich."

Alyosha wanted to say something, but he couldn't find a word. His heart ached.

"Go away, Alexey Fyodorovich! It's shameful, it's awful for me! Tomorrow, I beg you on my knees, come tomorrow. Don't condemn me. Forgive me. I don't know what I shall do with myself now!"

Alyosha walked out into the street reeling. He could have wept as she did. Suddenly he was overtaken by the maid.

"The young lady forgot to give you this letter from Madame Khokhlakov; it's been left with us since dinnertime."

Alyosha took the little pink envelope mechanically and put it, almost unconsciously, into his pocket.

Chapter XI

Another Reputation Ruined

It was not much more than half a mile from the town to the monastery. Alyosha walked quickly along the road, at that hour deserted. It was almost night, and too dark to see anything clearly thirty paces ahead. There was a crossroad half way. A figure came into sight under a solitary willow at the crossroad. As soon as Alyosha reached the crossroad the figure moved out and rushed at him, shouting savagely:

"Your money or your life!"

"So it's you, Mitya," cried Alyosha, in surprise, violently startled however.

"Ha, ha, ha! You didn't expect me? I wondered where to wait for you. By her house? There are three ways from it, and I might have missed you. At last I thought of waiting here, for you had to pass here, there's no other way to the monastery. Come, tell me the truth. Crush me like a cockroach. But what's the matter?"

"Nothing, brother—it's the fright you gave me. Oh, Dmitri! Father's blood just now." Alyosha began to cry, he had been on the verge of tears for a long time, and now something seemed to snap in his soul. "You almost killed him—cursed him—and now—here —you're making jokes—Your money or your life!"

"Well, what of that? It's not seemly—is that it? Not suitable in my position?"

"No—I only——"

"Stay. Look at the night. You see what a gloomy night, what clouds, what a wind has risen. I hid here under the willow waiting for you. And as God's above, I suddenly thought, why go on in misery any longer, what is there to wait for? Here I have a willow, a handkerchief, a shirt, I can twist them into a rope in a minute, and suspenders besides, and why go on burdening the earth, dishonoring it with my vile presence. And then I heard you coming— Heavens, it was as though something flew down to me suddenly. So there is a man, then, whom I love. Here he is, that man, my dear little brother, whom I love more than anyone in the world, the only one I love in the world. And I loved you so much, so much at that moment that I thought, 'I'll fall on his neck at once.' Then a stupid idea struck me, to have a joke with you and scare you. I shouted, like a fool, 'your money!' Forgive my foolery—it was only nonsense, and there's nothing unseemly in my soul. . . . Damn it all, tell me what's happened. What did she say? Strike me, crush, me, don't spare me! Was she furious?"

"No, not that. . . . There was nothing like that, Mitya. There—I found them both there."

"Both? Whom?"

"Grushenka at Katerina Ivanovna's."

Dmitri Fyodorovich was struck dumb.

"Impossible!" he cried. "You're raving! Grushenka with her?"

Alyosha described all that had happened from the moment he went into Katerina Ivanovna's. He was ten minutes telling his story. He can't be said to have told it fluently and consecutively, but he seemed to make it clear, not omitting any word or action of significance, and vividly describing, often in one word, his own sensations. His brother Dmitri listened in silence, gazing at him with a terrible fixed stare, but it was clear to Alyosha that he understood it all, and had grasped every point. But as the story went on, his face became not merely gloomy, but menacing. He scowled, he clenched his teeth, and his fixed stare became still more rigid, more concentrated, more terrible, when suddenly, with incredible rapidity, his wrathful, savage face changed, his tightly compressed lips parted, and Dmitri Fyodorovich broke into uncontrolled, spontaneous laughter. He literally shook with laughter. For a long time he could not speak.

"So she wouldn't kiss her hand! So she didn't kiss it; so she ran away!" he kept exclaiming with hysterical delight; insolent delight it might have been called, if it had not been so spontaneous. "So the other one called her tigress! And a tigress she is! So she ought to be flogged on a scaffold! Yes, yes, so she ought. That's just what I think; she ought to have been long ago. It's like this, brother, let her be punished, but I must get better first. I understand the queen of impudence. That's her all over! You saw her all over in that hand-kissing, the infernal woman! She's the queen of all infernal women you can imagine in the world! She's magnificent in her own line! So she ran home? I'll go—ah—I'll run to her! Alyosha, don't blame me, I agree that hanging is too good for her."

"But Katerina Ivanovna!" exclaimed Alyosha sorrowfully.

"I see her, too! I see right through her, as I've never done before! It's a regular discovery of the four continents of the world, that is, of the five! What a thing to do! That's just like Katenka, the young lady from the Institute, who was not afraid to face a coarse, un-mannerly officer and risk a deadly insult on a generous impulse to save her father! But the pride, the recklessness, the defiance of fate, the unbounded defiance! You say that aunt tried to stop her? That aunt, you know, is overbearing, herself. She's the sister of the general's widow in Moscow, and even more stuck-up than she. But her husband was caught stealing government money. He lost every-thing, his estate and all, and the proud wife had to lower her colors, and hasn't raised them since. So she tried to prevent Katya, but she wouldn't listen to her! She thinks she can overcome everything, that everything will give way to her. She thought she could bewitch Grushenka if she liked, and she believed it herself; she plays a part to herself, and whose fault is it? Do you think she kissed Grushen-ka's hand first, on purpose, with a motive? No, she really was fascinated by Grushenka, that's to say, not by Grushenka, but by her own dream, her own delusion—because it was *her* dream, *her* delusion! Alyosha, darling, how did you escape from them, those women? Did you pick up your cassock and run? Ha, ha, ha!"

"Brother, you don't seem to have noticed how you've insulted Katerina Ivanovna by telling Grushenka about that day. And she flung it in her face just now that she had gone to gentlemen in secret to sell her beauty! Brother, what could be worse than that insult?"

What worried Alyosha more than anything was that his brother appeared pleased at Katerina Ivanovna's humiliation, though, of course, it could not be so.

"Bah!" Dmitri Fyodorovich frowned fiercely, and struck his forehead with his hand. He only now realized it, though Alyosha had just told him of the insult, and Katerina Ivanovna's cry: "Your brother is a scoundrel!"

"Yes, perhaps, I really did tell Grushenka about that 'fatal day,' as Katya calls it. Yes, I did tell her, I remember! It was that time at

Mokroe. I was drunk, the gypsies were singing. . . . But I was sobbing. I was sobbing then, kneeling and praying to Katya's image,
and Grushenka understood it. She understood it all then. I remember, she cried herself. . . . Damn it all! But it's bound to be so
now. . . . Then she cried, but now 'the dagger in the heart'! That's
how women are."

He looked down and sank into thought.

"Yes, I am a scoundrel, a thorough scoundrel!" he said suddenly, in a gloomy voice. "It doesn't matter whether I cried or not,
I'm a scoundrel! Tell her I accept the name, if that's any comfort.
Come, that's enough. Good-bye. It's no use talking! It's not amusing. You go your way and I mine. And I don't want to see you
again except as a last resource. Good-bye, Alexey!" He warmly
pressed Alyosha's hand, and still looking down, without raising his
head, as though tearing himself away, turned rapidly towards the
town. Alyosha looked after him, unable to believe he would go
away so abruptly.

"Stay, Alexey, one more admission to you alone!" cried Dmitri
Fyodorovich, suddenly turning back. "Look at me. Look at me
well. You see here, here—there's terrible disgrace in store for me."
(As he said "here," Dmitri Fyodorovich struck his chest with
his fist with a strange air, as though the dishonor lay precisely on
his chest, in some spot, in a pocket, perhaps, or hanging round his
neck.) "You know me now, a scoundrel, an avowed scoundrel, but
let me tell you that I've never done anything before and never shall
again, anything that can compare in baseness with the dishonor
which I bear now at this very minute on my breast, here, here,
which will come to pass, though I'm perfectly free to stop it. I can
stop it or carry it through, note that. Well, let me tell you, I shall
carry it through. I shall not stop it. I told you everything just now,
but I didn't tell you this, because even I am not brazen enough for
it. I can still stop; if I do, I can give back the full half of my lost
honor tomorrow. But I won't stop. I will carry out my base plan,
and you can bear witness that I told you so beforehand. Darkness
and destruction! No need to explain. You'll find out in due time.
The filthy back alley and the infernal woman. Good-bye. Don't pray
for me, I'm not worth it. And there's no need, no need at all . . . I
don't need it! Away!"

And he suddenly retreated, this time finally. Alyosha went towards the monastery. "What? I shall never see him again! What is
he saying?" he wondered wildly. "Why, I shall certainly see him
tomorrow. I shall look him up. I shall make a point of it. What
does he mean?"

He went round the monastery, and crossed the pine wood to the
hermitage. The door was opened to him, though no one was admit-

ted at that hour. There was a tremor in his heart as he went into Father Zosima's cell. "Why, why, had he gone forth? Why had he sent him into the world? Here was peace. Here was holiness. But there there was confusion, there was gloom in which one lost one's way and went astray at once. . . ."

In the cell he found the novice Porfiry and Father Païssy, who came every hour to inquire after Father Zosima. Alyosha learned with alarm that he was getting worse and worse. Even his usual discourse with the brothers could not take place that day. As a rule every evening after service the monks flocked into Father Zosima's cell, and all confessed aloud their sins of the day, their sinful thoughts and temptations, even their disputes, if there had been any. Some confessed kneeling. The elder absolved, reconciled, exhorted, imposed penance, blessed, and dismissed them. It was against this general "confession" that the opponents of "elders" protested, maintaining that it was a profanation of the sacrament of confession, almost a sacrilege, though this was quite a different thing. They even represented to the diocesan authorities that such confessions attained no good object, but actually to a large extent led to sin and temptation. Many of the brothers disliked going to the elder, and went against their own will because everyone went, and for fear they should be accused of pride and rebellious ideas. People said that some of the monks agreed beforehand, saying, "I'll confess I lost my temper with you this morning, and you confirm it," simply in order to have something to say. Alyosha knew that this actually happened sometimes. He knew, too, that there were among the monks some who deeply resented the fact that letters from relations were habitually taken to the elder, to be opened and read by him before those to whom they were addressed.

It was assumed, of course, that all this was done freely, and in good faith, by way of voluntary submission and salutary guidance. But, in fact, there was sometimes no little insincerity, and much that was false and strained in this practice. Yet the older and more experienced of the monks adhered to their opinion, arguing that "for those who have come within these walls sincerely seeking salvation, such obedience and sacrifice will certainly be salutary and of great benefit; those, on the other hand, who find it irksome, and repine, are no true monks, and have made a mistake in entering the monastery—their proper place is in the world. Even in the temple one cannot be safe from sin and the devil. So it was no good taking it too much into account."

"He is weaker, a drowsiness has come over him," Father Païssy whispered to Alyosha, as he blessed him. "It's difficult to rouse him. And he must not be roused. He woke up for five minutes, sent his blessing to the brothers, and begged their prayers for him at night. He intends to take the sacrament again in the morning. He remembered you, Alexey. He asked whether you had gone away, and was told that you were in the town. 'I blessed him for that work,' he said, 'his place is there, not here, for awhile.' Those were his words about you. He remembered you lovingly, with anxiety; do you understand how he honored you? But how is it that he has decided that you shall spend some time in the world? He must have foreseen something in your destiny! Understand, Alexey, that if you return to the world, it must be to do the duty laid upon you by your elder, and not for frivolous vanity and worldly pleasures."

Father Païssy went out. Alyosha had no doubt that Father Zosima was dying, though he might live another day or two. Alyosha firmly and ardently resolved that in spite of his promises to his father, the Khokhlakovs, and Katerina Ivanovna, he would not leave the monastery next day, but would remain with his elder to the end. His heart glowed with love, and he reproached himself bitterly for having been able for one instant to forget him whom he had left in the monastery on his deathbed, and whom he honored above everyone in the world. He went into Father Zosima's bedroom, knelt down, and bowed to the ground before the elder, who slept quietly without stirring, with regular, hardly audible breathing and a peaceful face.

Alyosha returned to the other room, where Father Zosima had received his guests in the morning. Taking off only his boots, he lay down on the hard, narrow, leather sofa, which he had long used as a bed, bringing nothing but a pillow. The mattress, about which his father had shouted to him that morning, he had long forgotten to lay on. He took off his cassock, which he used as a blanket. But before going to bed, he fell on his knees and prayed a long time. In his fervent prayer he did not beseech God to lighten his darkness but only thirsted for the joyous emotion which always visited his soul after the praise and adoration of which his evening prayer usually consisted. That joy always brought him light untroubled sleep. As he was praying, he suddenly felt in his pocket the little pink note the servant had handed him as he left Katerina Ivanovna's. He was disturbed, but finished his prayer. Then, after some hesitation, he opened the envelope. In it was a letter to him, signed by Lise, the young daughter of Madame Khokhlakov, who had laughed at him before the elder in the morning.

"Alexey Fyodorovich," she wrote, "I am writing to you without anyone's knowledge, even mamma's, and I know how wrong it is. But I cannot live without telling you the feeling that has sprung up in my heart, and this no one but us two must know for a time. But how am I to say what I want so much to tell you? Paper, they say, does not blush, but I assure you it's not true and that it's blushing just as I am now, all over. Dear Alyosha, I love you, I've loved you from my childhood, since our Moscow days, when you were very different from what you are now, and I shall love you all my life. My heart has chosen you, to unite our lives, and pass them together till our old age. Of course, on condition that you will leave the monastery. As for our age we will wait for the time fixed by the law. By that time I shall certainly be quite strong, I shall be walking and dancing. There can be no doubt of that.

"You see how I've thought of everything. There's only one thing I can't imagine: what you'll think of me when you read this? I'm always laughing and being naughty. I made you angry this morning, but I assure you before I took up my pen, I prayed before the image of the Mother of God, and now I'm praying, and almost crying.

"My secret is in your hands. When you come tomorrow, I don't know how I shall look at you. Ah, Alexey Fyodorovich, what if I can't restrain myself like a silly and laugh when I look at you as I did today? You'll think I'm a nasty girl making fun of you, and you won't believe my letter. And so I beg you, dear one, if you've any pity for me, when you come tomorrow, don't look me straight in the face, for if I meet your eyes, it will be sure to make me laugh, especially, as you'll be in that long gown. I feel cold all over when I think of it, so when you come, don't look at me at all for a time, look at mamma or at the window. . . .

"Here I've written you a love letter. Oh, dear, what have I done? Alyosha, don't despise me, and if I've done something very horrid and wounded you, forgive me. Now the secret of my reputation, ruined perhaps forever, is in your hands.

"I shall certainly cry today. Good-bye till our meeting, our *awful* meeting.—LISE

"P.S.—Alyosha! You must, must, must come!—LISE."

Alyosha read the note in amazement, read it through twice, thought a little, and suddenly laughed a soft, sweet laugh. He started. That laugh seemed to him sinful. But a minute later he laughed again just as softly and happily. He slowly replaced the note in the envelope, crossed himself and lay down. The agitation in his heart passed at once. "God have mercy upon all of them, have all these unhappy and turbulent souls in Thy keeping, and set them in the right path. All ways are Thine. Save them according to Thy wisdom. Thou art love. Thou wilt send joy to all!" Alyosha murmured, crossing himself, and falling into peaceful sleep.

Part Two

Book Four

LACERATIONS

Chapter I

Father Ferapont

Alyosha was roused early, before daybreak. Father Zosima woke up feeling very weak, though he wanted to get out of bed and sit up in a chair. His mind was quite clear; his face looked very tired, yet bright and almost joyful. It wore an expression of gaiety, kindness and cordiality. "Maybe I shall not live through the coming day," he said to Alyosha. Then he desired to confess and take the communion at once. He always confessed to Father Païssy. After the two sacraments, the service of extreme unction followed. The monks assembled and the cell was gradually filled up by the inmates of the hermitage. Meantime it was daylight. People began coming from the monastery. After the service was over the elder desired to kiss and take leave of everyone. As the cell was so small the earlier visitors withdrew to make room for others. Alyosha stood beside the elder, who was seated again in his armchair. He talked as much as he could. Though his voice was weak, it was fairly steady. "I've been teaching you so many years, and therefore I've been talking aloud so many years, that I've got into the habit of talking, and so much so that it's almost more difficult for me to hold my tongue than to talk, even now, in spite of my weakness, dear fathers and brothers," he jested, looking with emotion at the group round him.

Alyosha remembered afterwards something of what he said to them. But though he spoke out distinctly and his voice was fairly steady, his speech was somewhat disconnected. He spoke of many things, he seemed anxious before the moment of death to say everything he had not said in his life, and not simply for the sake of instructing them, but as though thirsting to share with all men and all creation his joy and ecstasy, and once more in his life to open his whole heart.

"Love one another, Fathers," said Father Zosima, as far as Alyosha could remember afterwards. "Love God's people. Because we have come here and shut ourselves within these walls, we are no holier than those that are outside, but on the contrary, from the very fact of coming here, each of us has confessed to himself that he is worse than others, than all men on earth. . . . And the longer the monk lives in his seclusion, the more keenly he must recognize that. Else he would have had no reason to come here. When he realizes that he is not only worse than others, but that he is responsible to all men for all and everything, for all human sins, general and individual, only then the aim of our seclusion is attained. For know, dear ones, that every one of us is undoubtedly responsible for all men and everything on earth, not merely through the general sinfulness of creation, but each one personally for all mankind and every individual man. This knowledge is the crown of life for the monk and for every man. For monks are not a special sort of men, but only what all men ought to be. Only through that knowledge, our heart grows soft with infinite, universal, inexhaustible love. Then every one of you will have the power to win over the whole world by love and to wash away the sins of the world with your tears. . . . Each of you keep watch over your heart and confess your sins to yourself unceasingly. Be not afraid of your sins, even when perceiving them, if only there be penitence, but make no conditions with God. Again I say, be not proud. Be proud neither to the little nor to the great. Hate not those who reject you, who insult you, who abuse and slander you. Hate not the atheists, the teachers of evil, the materialists—and I mean not only the good ones—for there are many good ones among them, especially in our day—hate not even the wicked ones. Remember them in your prayers thus: Save, O Lord, all those who have none to pray for them, save too all those who will not pray. And add: it is not in pride that I make this prayer, O Lord, for I am lower than all men. . . . Love God's people, let not strangers draw away the flock, for if you slumber in your slothfulness and disdainful pride, or worse still, in covetousness, they will come from all sides and draw away your flock. Expound the Gospel to the people unceasingly . . . be not extortionate. . . . Do not love gold and silver, do not hoard them. . . . Have faith. Cling to the banner and raise it on high."

But the elder spoke more disconnectedly than Alyosha reported his words afterwards. Sometimes he broke off altogether, as though to take breath and recover his strength, but he was in a sort of ecstasy. They heard him with emotion, though many wondered at his words and found them obscure. . . . Afterwards all remembered those words.

When Alyosha happened for a moment to leave the cell, he was struck by the general excitement and suspense in the monks who were crowding about it. This anticipation showed itself in some by anxiety, in others by devout solemnity. All were expecting that something great would happen immediately after the elder's death. Their suspense was, from one point of view, almost frivolous, but even the most austere of the monks were affected by it. Father Païssy's face looked the gravest of all. Alyosha was secetly summoned by a monk to see Rakitin, who had arrived from town with a singular letter for him from Madame Khokhlakov. In it she informed Alyosha of a strange and very opportune incident. It appeared that among the women who had come on the previous day to receive Father Zosima's blessing, there had been an old woman from the town, a sergeant's widow, called Prokhorovna. She had inquired whether she might pray for the rest of the soul of her son, Vasenka, who had gone to Irkutsk, and had sent her no news for over a year. To which Father Zosima had answered sternly, forbidding her to do so, and saying that to pray for the living as though they were dead was a kind of sorcery. He afterwards forgave her on account of her ignorance, and added "as though reading the book of the future" (this was Madame Khokhlakov's expression) words of comfort: "that her son Vasya was certainly alive and he would either come himself very shortly or send a letter, and that she was to go home and expect him." And "would you believe it," exclaimed Madame Khokhlakov enthusiastically, "the prophecy has been fulfilled literally indeed, and more than that." Scarcely had the old woman reached home when they gave her a letter from Siberia which had been awaiting her. But that was not all; in the letter written on the road from Ekaterinburg, Vasya informed his mother that he was returning to Russia with an official, and that three weeks after her receiving the letter he hoped "to embrace his mother."

Madame Khokhlakov warmly entreated Alyosha to report this new "miracle of prediction" to the Superior and all the brotherhood. "All, all, ought to know of it!" she exclaimed in conclusion. The letter had been written in haste, the excitement of the writer was apparent in every line of it. But Alyosha had no need to tell the monks, for all knew of it already. Rakitin had commissioned the monk who brought his message "to inform most respectully his reverence Father Païssy, that he, Rakitin, has a matter to speak of with him, of such gravity that he dare not defer it for a moment, and humbly begs forgiveness for his presumption." As the monk had given the message to Father Païssy before that to Alyosha, the latter found after reading the letter that there was nothing left for him to do but to hand it to Father Païssy in confirmation of the story. And even that austere and cautious man, though he frowned as he read the news of the "miracle," could not completely restrain some inner emotion. His eyes gleamed, and a grave and solemn smile came into his lips.

"We shall see greater things!" broke from him.

"We shall see greater things, greater things yet!" the monks around repeated.

But Father Païssy, frowning again, begged all of them at least for a time not to speak of the matter "till it be more fully confirmed, seeing there is so much credulity among those of this world, and indeed this might well have chanced naturally," he added, prudently, as it were to satisfy his conscience, though scarcely believing his own disavowal, a fact his listeners very clearly perceived.

Within the hour the "miracle" was of course known to the whole monastery, and many visitors who had come for the mass. No one seemed more impressed by it than the monk who had come the day before from St. Sylvester, from the little monastery of Obdorsk in the far north. It was he who had been standing near Madame Khokhlakov the previous day and had asked Father Zosima earnestly, referring to the "healing" of the lady's daughter, "How can you presume to do such things?"

He was now somewhat puzzled and did not know whom to believe. The evening before he had visited Father Ferapont in his cell apart, behind the apiary, and had been greatly impressed and overawed by the visit. This Father Ferapont was that aged monk so devout in fasting and observing silence who had been mentioned already, as antagonistic to Father Zosima and the whole institution of "elders," which he regarded as a pernicious and frivolous innovation. He was a very formidable opponent, although from his practice of silence he scarcely spoke a word to anyone. What made him formidable was that a number of monks fully shared his feeling, and many of the visitors looked upon him as a great saint and ascetic, although they had no doubt that he was crazy. But it was just his craziness that attracted them.

Father Ferapont never went to see the elder. Though he lived in the hermitage they did not worry him to keep its regulations, and this too because he behaved as though he were crazy. He was seventy-five or more, and he lived in a corner beyond the apiary in an old decaying wooden cell which had been built long ago for another great ascetic, Father Iona, who had lived to be a hundred and five, and of whose saintly doings many curious stories were still extant in the monastery and the neighborhood.

Father Ferapont had succeeded in getting himself installed in this same solitary cell seven years previously. It was simply a peasant's hut, though it looked like a chapel, for it contained an extraordinary number of icons with lamps perpetually burning before them —which men brought to the monastery as offerings to God. Father Ferapont had been appointed to look after them and keep the lamps burning. It was said (and indeed it was true) that he ate only two pounds of bread in three days. The beekeeper, who lived close by the apiary, used to bring him the bread every three days, and even to this man who waited upon him, Father Ferapont rarely uttered a word. The four pounds of bread, together with the sacrament bread, regularly sent him on Sundays after the late mass by the Father Superior, made up his weekly rations. The water in his jug was changed every day. He rarely appeared at mass. Visitors who came to do him homage saw him sometimes kneeling all day long at prayer without looking round. If he addressed them, he was brief, abrupt, strange, and almost always rude. On very rare occasions, however, he would talk to visitors, but for the most part he would utter some one strange saying which was a complete riddle, and no entreaties would induce him to pronounce a word in explanation. He was not a priest, but a simple monk. There was a strange belief, chiefly however among the most ignorant, that Father Ferapont had communication with heavenly spirits and would only converse with them, and so was silent with men.

The monk from Obdorsk, having been directed to the apiary by the beekeeper, who was also a very silent and surly monk, went to the corner where Father Ferapont's cell stood. "Maybe he will speak as you are a stranger and maybe you'll get nothing out of him," the beekeeper had warned him. The monk, as he related afterwards, approached in the utmost apprehension. It was rather late in the evening. Father Ferapont was sitting at the door of his cell on a low bench. A huge old elm was lightly rustling overhead. There was an evening freshness in the air. The monk from Obdorsk bowed down before the saint and asked his blessing.

"Do you want me to bow down to you, monk?" said Father Ferapont. "Get up."

The monk got up.

"Blessing, be blessed! Sit beside me. Where have you come from?"

What most struck the poor monk was the fact that in spite of his strict fasting and great age, Father Ferapont still appeared to be a vigorous old man. He was tall, held himself erect, and had a thin but fresh and healthy face. There was no doubt he still had considerable strength. He was of athletic build. In spite of his great age he was not even quite gray, and still had very thick hair and a full beard, both of which had once been black. His eyes were gray, large and luminous, but strikingly prominent. He spoke with a broad accent. He was dressed in a long reddish coat of coarse convict cloth (as it used to be called) and had a stout rope round his waist. His throat and chest were bare. Beneath his coat, his shirt of the coarsest linen showed almost black with dirt, not having been changed for months. They said that he wore irons weighing thirty pounds under his coat. His stockingless feet were thrust in old shoes almost dropping to pieces.

"From the little Obdorsk monastery, from St. Sylvester," the monk answered humbly, while his keen and inquisitive, but rather frightened little eyes kept watch on the hermit.

"I have been at your Sylvester's. I used to stay there. Is Sylvester well?"

The monk hesitated.

"You are a senseless lot! How do you keep the fasts?"

"Our dietary is according to the ancient conventional rules. During Lent there are no meals provided for Monday, Wednesday, and Friday. For Tuesday and Thursday we have white bread, stewed fruit with honey, wild berries, or salt cabbage and wholemeal stirabout. On Saturday white cabbage soup, noodles with peas, kasha, all with hemp oil. On weekdays we have dried fish and kasha with the cabbage soup. From Monday till Saturday evening, six whole days in Holy Week, nothing is cooked, and we have only bread and water, and that sparingly; if possible not taking food every day, just the same as is ordered for first week in Lent. On Good Friday nothing is eaten. In the same way on the Saturday we have to fast till three o'clock, and then take a little bread and water and drink a single cup of wine. On Holy Thursday we drink wine and have something cooked without oil or not cooked at all. Inasmuch as the Laodicean council lays down for Holy Thursday: 'it is unseemly by remitting the fast on the Holy Thursday to dishonor the whole of Lent!' This is how we keep the fast. But what is that compared with you, holy Father," added the monk, growing more confident, "for all the year round, even at Easter, you take nothing but bread and water, and what we should eat in two days lasts you full seven. It's truly marvelous—your great abstinence."

"And mushrooms?" asked Father Ferapont, suddenly.

"Mushrooms?" repeated the surprised monk.

"Yes. I can give up their bread, not needing it at all, and go away into the forest and live there on the mushrooms or the berries, but they can't give up their bread here, wherefore they are in bondage to the devil. Nowadays the unclean deny that there is need of such fasting. Haughty and unclean is their judgment."

"Och, true," sighed the monk.

"And have you seen devils among them?" asked Father Ferapont.

"Among them? Among whom?" asked the monk, timidly.

"I went to the Father Superior on Trinity Sunday last year, I haven't been since. I saw a devil sitting on one man's chest hiding under his cassock, only his horns poked out; another had one peeping out of his pocket with such sharp eyes, he was afraid of me; another settled in the unclean belly of one, right in the guts, another was hanging round a man' neck, and he was carrying him about without seeing him."

"You—can see spirits?" the monk inquired.

"I tell you I can see, I can see through them. When I was coming out from the Superior's I saw one hiding from me behind the door, and a big one, a yard and a half or more high, with a thick long gray tail, and the tip of his tail was in the crack of the door and I was quick and slammed the door, pinching his tail in it. He squealed and began to struggle, and I made the sign of the cross over him three times. And he died on the spot like a crushed spider. He must have rotted there in the corner and be stinking, but they don't see, they don't smell it. It's a year since I have been there. I reveal it to you, as you are a stranger."

"Your words are terrible! But, holy and blessed Father," said the monk, growing bolder and bolder, "is it true, as they noise abroad even to distant lands about you, that you are in continual communication with the Holy Ghost?"

"He does fly down at times."

"How does he fly down? In what form?"

"As a bird."

"The Holy Ghost in the form of a Dove?"

"There's the Holy Ghost and there's the Holy Spirit. The Holy Spirit can appear as other birds—sometimes as a swallow, sometimes a goldfinch and sometimes as a blue tit."

"How do you know him from an ordinary tit?"

"He speaks."

"How does he speak, in what language?"

"Human language."

"And what does he tell you?"

"Why, today he told me that a fool would visit me and would ask me unseemly questions. You want to know too much, monk."

"Terrible are your words, most holy and blessed Father," the monk shook his head. But there was a doubtful look in his frightened little eyes.

"Do you see this tree?" asked Father Ferapont, after a pause.

"I do, blessed Father."

"You think it's an elm, but for me it has another shape."

"What sort of shape?" inquired the monk, after a pause of vain expectation.

"It happens at night. You see those two branches? In the night it is Christ holding out His arms to me and seeking me with those arms, I see it clearly and tremble. It's terrible, terrible!"

"What is there terrible if it's Christ Himself?"

"Why, He'll snatch me up and carry me away."

"Alive?"

"In the spirit and glory of Elijah, haven't you heard? He will take me in His arms and bear me away."

Though the monk returned to the cell he was sharing with one of the brothers, in considerable perplexity of mind, he still cherished at heart a greater reverence for Father Ferapont than for Father Zosima. He was strongly in favor of fasting, and it was not strange that one who kept so rigid a fast as Father Ferapont should "see marvels." His words certainly seemed queer, but God only could tell what was hidden in those words, and were not worse words and acts commonly seen in those who have sacrificed their intellects for the glory of God? The pinching of the devil's tail he was ready and eager to believe, and not only in the figurative sense. Besides he had, before visiting the monastery, a strong prejudice against the institution of "elders," which he only knew of by hearsay and believed to be a pernicious innovation. Before he had been long at the monastery, he had detected the secret murmurings of some shallow brothers who disliked the institution. He was, besides, a meddlesome, inquisitive man, who poked his nose into everything. This was why the news of the fresh "miracle" performed by Father Zosima reduced him to extreme perplexity. Alyosha remembered afterwards how their inquisitive guest from Obdorsk had been continually flitting to and fro from one group to another, listening and asking questions among the monks who were crowding within and without the elder's cell. But he did not pay much attention to him at the time, and only recollected it afterwards. He had no thought to spare for it indeed, for when Father Zosima, feeling tired again, had gone back to bed, he thought of Aloysha as he was closing his eyes, and sent for him. Alyosha ran at once. There was no one else in the cell but Father Païssy, Father Iosif, and the novice Porfiry. The elder, opening his weary eyes and looking intently at Alyosha, asked him suddenly:

"Are your people expecting you, my son?"

Alyosha hesitated.

"Haven't they need of you? Didn't you promise someone yesterday to see them today?"

"I did promise—to my father—my brothers—others too."

"You see, you must go. Don't grieve. Be sure I shall not die without your being by to hear my last word. To you I will say that word, my son, it will be my last gift to you. To you, dear son, because you love me. But now go to keep your promise."

Alyosha immediately obeyed, though it was hard to go. But the promise that he should hear his last word on earth, that it should be the last gift to him, Alyosha, sent a thrill of rapture through his soul. He made haste that he might finish what he had to do in the town and return quickly. Father Païssy, too, uttered some words of exhortation which moved and surprised him greatly. He spoke as they left the cell together.

"Remember, young man, unceasingly," Father Païssy began, without preface, "that the science of this world, which has become a great power, has, especially in the last century, analyzed everything divine handed down to us in the holy books. After this cruel analysis the learned of this world have nothing left of all that was sacred of old. But they have only analyzed the parts and overlooked the whole, and indeed their blindness is marvelous. Yet the whole still stands steadfast before their eyes, and the gates of hell shall not prevail against it. Has it not lasted nineteen centuries, is it not still a living, a moving power in the individual soul and in the masses of people? It is still as strong and living even in the souls of atheists, who have destroyed everything! For even those who have renounced Christianity and attack it, in their inmost being still follow the Christian idea, for hitherto neither their subtlety nor the ardor of their hearts has been able to create a higher ideal of man and of virtue than the ideal given by Christ of old. When it has been attempted, the result has been only grotesque. Remember this especially, young man, since you are being sent into the world by your departing elder. Maybe, remembering this great day, you will not forget my words, uttered from the heart for your guidance, seeing you are young, and the temptations of the world are great and beyond your strength to endure. Well, now go, my orphan."

With these words Father Païssy blessed him. As Alyosha left the monastery and thought them over, he suddenly realized that he had met a new and unexpected friend, a warmly loving teacher, in this austere monk who had hitherto treated him sternly. It was as though Father Zosima had bequeathed him to him at his death, and "perhaps that's just what had passed between them," Alyosha thought suddenly. The philosophic reflections he had just heard so unexpectedly testified to the warmth of Father Païssy's heart. He was in haste to arm the boy's mind for conflict with temptation and to guard the young soul left in his charge with the strongest defense he could imagine.

Chapter II

At His Father's

First of all, Alyosha went to his father. On the way he remembered that his father had insisted the day before that he should come without his brother Ivan seeing him. "Why so?" Alyosha wondered suddenly. "Even if my father has something to say to me alone, why should I go in unseen? Most likely in his excitement yesterday he meant to say something different," he decided. Yet he was very glad when Martha Ignatyevna, who opened the garden gate to him (Grigory, it appeared, was ill in bed in the lodge), told him in answer to his question that Ivan Fyodorovich had gone out two hours ago.

"And my father?"

"He is up, taking his coffee," Martha answered somewhat drily.

Alyosha went in. The old man was sitting alone at the table, wearing slippers and a little old overcoat. He was amusing himself by looking through some accounts, rather inattentively however. He was quite alone in the house, for Smerdyakov too had gone out marketing. Though he had got up early and was trying to put a bold face on it, he looked tired and weak. His forehead, upon which huge purple bruises had come out during the night, was bandaged with a red handkerchief; his nose too had swollen terribly in the night, and some smaller bruises covered it in patches, giving his whole face a peculiarly spiteful and irritable look. The old man was aware of this, and turned a hostile glance on Alyosha as he came in.

"The coffee is cold," he cried harshly; "I won't offer you any. I've ordered nothing but a Lenten fish soup today, and I don't invite anyone to share it. Why have you come?"

"To find out how you are," said Alyosha.

"Yes. Besides, I told you to come yesterday. It's all of no consequence. You need not have troubled. But I knew you'd come poking in directly."

He said this with almost hostile feeling. At the same time he got up and looked anxiously in the mirror (perhaps for the fortieth time that morning) at his nose. He began, too, binding his red handkerchief more becomingly on his forehead.

"Red's better. It's just like the hospital in a white one," he observed sententiously. "Well, how are things over there? How is your elder?"

"He is very bad; he may die today," answered Alyosha. But his father had not listened, and had forgotten his own question at once.

"Ivan's gone out," he said suddenly. "He is doing his utmost to carry off Mitka's betrothed. That's what he is staying here for," he added maliciously, and, twisting his mouth, looked at Alyosha.

"Surely he did not tell you so himself?" asked Alyosha.

"Yes, he did, long ago. Would you believe it, he told me three weeks ago? You don't suppose he too came to murder me, do you? He must have had some object in coming."

"What do you mean? Why do you say such things?" said Alyosha, troubled.

"He doesn't ask for money, it's true, but yet he won't get a farthing from me. I intend living as long as possible, you may as well know, my dear Alexey Fyodorovich, and so I need every farthing, and the longer I live, the more I shall need it," he continued, pacing from one corner of the room to the other, keeping his hands in the pockets of his loose greasy overcoat made of yellow cotton material. "I can still pass for a man at fifty-five, but I want to pass for one for another twenty years. As I get older, you know, I won't be a pretty object. The wenches won't come to me of their own accord, so I shall want my money. So I am saving up more and more, simply for myself, my dear son Alexey Fyodorovich. You may as well know. For I mean to go on in my sins to the end, let me tell you. For sin is sweet; all abuse it, but all men live in it, only others do it on the sly, and I openly. And so all the other sinners fall upon me for being so simple. And your paradise, Alexey Fyodorovich, is not to my taste, let me tell you that; and it's not the proper place for a gentleman, your paradise, even if it exists. I believe that I fall asleep and don't wake up again, and that's all. You can pray for my soul if you like. And if you don't want to, don't, damn you! That's my philosophy. Ivan talked well here yesterday, though we were all drunk. Ivan is a conceited coxcomb, but he has no particular learning . . . nor education either. He sits silent and smiles at one without speaking—that's what pulls him through."

Alyosha listened to him in silence.

"Why won't he talk to me? If he does speak, he gives himself airs. Your Ivan is a scoundrel! And I'll marry Grushka in a minute if I want to. For if you've money, Alexey Fyodorovich, you have only to want a thing and you can have it. That's what Ivan is afraid of, he is on the watch to prevent my getting married and that's why he is egging on Mitka to marry Grushka himself. He hopes to keep me from Grushka by that (as though I should leave him my money if I don't marry her!). Besides if Mitka marries Grushka, Ivan will carry off his rich betrothed, that's what he's reckoning on! He's a scoundrel, your Ivan!"

"How cross you are. It's because of yesterday; you had better lie down," said Alyosha.

"There! you say that," the old man observed suddenly, as though it had struck him for the first time, "and I am not angry with you. But if Ivan said it, I would be angry with him. It is only with you I have good moments, else you know I am a spiteful man."

"You are not spiteful, but twisted," said Alyosha with a smile.

"Listen. I meant this morning to get that ruffian Mitya locked up and I don't know now what I shall decide about it. Of course in these fashionable days fathers and mothers are looked upon as a prejudice, but even now the law does not allow you to drag your old father about by the hair, to kick him in the face in his own house, and brag of murdering him outright—all in the presence of witnesses. If I liked, I could crush him and could have him locked up at once for what he did yesterday."

"Then you don't mean to take proceedings?"

"Ivan has dissuaded me. I don't care about Ivan, but there's another thing."

And bending down to Alyosha, he went on in a confidential half-whisper.

"If I send the scoundrel to prison, she'll hear of it and run to see him at once. But if she hears that he has beaten me, a weak old man, within an inch of my life, she may give him up and come to me. . . . For that's her way, everything by contraries. I know her through and through! Won't you have a drop of brandy? Take some cold coffee and I'll pour a quarter of a glass of brandy into it, it's delicious, my boy."

"No, thank you. I'll take that roll with me if I may," said Alyosha, and taking a halfpenny French roll he put it in the pocket of his cassock. "And you'd better not have brandy, either," he suggested apprehensively, looking into the old man's face.

"You are quite right, it irritates my nerves instead of soothing them. Only one little glass. I'll get it out of the cupboard." He unlocked the cupboard, poured out a glass, drank it, then locked the cupboard and put the key back in his pocket.

"That's enough. One glass won't kill me."

"You see you are in a better humor now," said Alyosha smiling.

"Um! I love you even without the brandy, but with scoundrels I am a scoundrel. Vanka is not going to Chermashnya—why is that? He wants to spy on how much I give Grushenka if she comes. They are all scoundrels! But I don't recognize Ivan, I don't know him at all. Where does he come from? He is not one of us in soul. As though I'd leave him anything! I won't leave a will at all, you may as well know. And I'll crush Mitya like a cockroach. I squash cockroaches at night with my slipper; they squelch when you tread on them. And your Mitka will squelch too. *Your* Mitka, for you love him. Yes, you love him and I am not afraid of your loving him. But if Ivan loved him I would be afraid for myself at his loving him. But Ivan loves nobody. Ivan is not one of us. People like Ivan are not our sort, my boy. They are like a cloud of dust. When the wind blows, the dust will be gone. . . . I had a silly idea in my head when I told you to come today; I wanted to find out from you about Mitka. If I were to hand him over a thousand or maybe two now, would the beggarly wretch agree to take himself off altogether for five years or, better still, thirty-five, and without Grushka, and give her up once for all, eh?"

"I—I'll ask him," muttered Alyosha. "If you would give him three thousand, perhaps he——"

"That's nonsense! You needn't ask him now, no need! I've changed my mind. It was a nonsensical idea of mine. I won't give him anything, not a penny, I want my money myself," cried the old man, waving his hand. "I'll crush him like a cockroach without it. Don't say anything to him or else he will begin hoping. There's nothing for you to do here, either, you needn't stay. Is that betrothed of his, Katerina Ivanovna, whom he has kept so carefully hidden from me all this time, going to marry him or not? You went to see her yesterday, I believe?"

"Nothing will induce her to abandon him."

"There you see how dearly these fine young ladies love a rake and a scoundrel. They are trash I tell you, those pale young ladies, very different from . . . Ah, if I had his youth and the looks I had then (for I was better-looking than he at twenty-eight) I'd have been a conquering hero just as he is. He is a low cad! But he will not have Grushenka, sir, anyway, he will not, sir! I'll crush him!"

His anger had returned with the last words.

"You can go. There's nothing for you to do here today," he snapped harshly.

Alyosha went up to say good-bye to him, and kissed him on the shoulder.

"What's that for?" the old man was a little surprised. "We will see each other again, or do you think we won't?"

"Not at all, I didn't mean anything."

"Nor did I, I did not mean anything," said the old man, looking at him. "Listen, listen," he shouted after him, "make haste and come again and I'll have a fish soup for you, a fine one, not like today. Be sure to come! Come tomorrow, do you hear, tomorrow!"

And as soon as Alyosha had gone out of the door, he went to the cupboard again and poured out another half glass.

"I won't have more!" he muttered, clearing his throat, and again he locked the cupboard and put the key in his pocket. Then he went into his bedroom, lay down on the bed, exhausted, and in one minute he was asleep.

Chapter III

A Meeting with the Schoolboys

"Thank goodness he did not ask me about Grushenka," thought Alyosha, as he left his father's house and turned towards Madame Khokhlakov's, "or I might have to tell him of my meeting with Grushenka yesterday."

Alyosha felt painfully that since yesterday both combatants had renewed their energies, and that their hearts had grown hard again. "Father is spiteful and angry, he's made some plan and will stick to it. And what of Dmitri? He too will be harder than yesterday, he too must be spiteful and angry, and he too, no doubt, has made some plan. Oh, I must succeed in finding him today, whatever happens."

But Alyosha had not long to meditate. An incident occurred on the road, which, though apparently of little consequence, made a great impression on him. Just after he had crossed the square and turned the corner coming out into Mikhailovsky Street, which is divided by a small ditch from Main Street (our whole town is intersected by ditches), he saw at the bridge a group of schoolboys, all young children, between the ages of nine and twelve, no older. They were going home from school, some with their bags on their shoulders, others with leather satchels slung across them, some in short jackets, others in little overcoats. Some even had those high boots with creases round the ankles, such as little boys spoiled by rich fathers love to wear. The whole group was talking eagerly about something, apparently holding a council. Alyosha had never from his Moscow days been able to pass children without taking notice of them, and although he was particularly fond of children of three or thereabout, he liked schoolboys of ten and eleven too. And so, anxious as he was today, he wanted at once to turn aside to talk to them. He looked into their excited rosy faces, and noticed at once that all the boys had stones in their hands. Beyond the ditch some thirty paces away, there was another schoolboy standing by a fence. He too had a satchel at his side. He was about ten years old, no older, if anything, younger, pale, delicate-looking and with sparkling black eyes. He kept an attentive and anxious watch on the other six, obviously his schoolfellows with whom he had just come out of school, but with whom he had evidently had a feud. Alyosha went up and addressing a fair, curly-headed, rosy boy in a black jacket observed:

"When I used to wear a satchel like yours, I always used to carry it on my left side, so as to have my right hand free, but you've got yours on your right side. So it will be awkward for you to get at it."

Alyosha had no art or premeditation in beginning with this practical remark. But it is the only way for a grown-up person to get at once into confidential relations with a child, or still more with a group of children. One must begin in a serious businesslike way so as to be on a perfectly equal footing. Alyosha understood it by instinct.

"But he is left-handed," another, a fine healthy-looking boy of eleven, answered promptly. All the others stared at Alyosha.

"He even throws stones with his left hand," observed a third. At that instant a stone flew into the group, but only just grazed the left-handed boy, though it was well and vigorously thrown by the boy standing on the other side of the ditch.

"Give it to him, hit him back, Smurov," they all shouted. But Smurov, the left-handed boy, needed no telling, and at once revenged himself; he threw a stone, but it missed the boy and hit the ground. The boy on the other side of the ditch, the pocket of whose coat was, at thirty paces, visibly bulging with stones, flung another stone at the group; this time it flew straight at Alyosha and hit him painfully on the shoulder.

"He aimed it at you, he meant it for you. You are Karamazov,

Karamazov!" the boys shouted laughing, "Come, all throw at him at once!" and six stones flew at the boy. One struck the boy on the head and he fell down, but at once leaped up and began ferociously returning their fire. Both sides threw stones incessantly. Many of the group had their pockets full too.

"What are you about! Aren't you ashamed, gentlemen? Six against one! Why, you'll kill him," cried Alyosha.

He ran forward and met the flying stones to screen the solitary boy. Three or four ceased throwing for a minute.

"He began first!" cried a boy in a red shirt in an angry childish voice. "He is a scoundrel, he stabbed Krasotkin in class the other day with a penknife. It bled. Krasotkin wouldn't tell tales, but he must be thrashed."

"But what for? I suppose you tease him."

"There, he sent a stone in your back again, he knows you," cried the children. "It's you he is throwing at now, not us. Come, all of you, at him again, don't miss, Smurov!" and again a fire of stones, and a very vicious one, began. The boy on the other side of the ditch was hit in the chest; he screamed, began to cry and ran away uphill towards Mikhailovsky Street. They all shouted: "Aha, quitter, he is running away. Wisp of tow!"

"You don't know what a beast he is, Karamazov, killing is too good for him," said the boy in the jacket, with flashing eyes. He seemed to be the eldest.

"What's wrong with him?" asked Alyosha. "Is he a tattletale or what?"

The boys looked at one another as though derisively.

"Are you going that way, to Mikhailovsky?" the same boy went on. "Catch up with him. . . . You see he's stopped again, he is waiting and looking at you."

"He is looking at you," the other boys chimed in.

"You ask him, does he like a disheveled bathhouse wisp of tow. Do you hear, ask him that!"

There was a general burst of laughter. Alyosha looked at them, and they at him.

"Don't go near him, he'll hurt you," cried Smurov in a warning voice.

"I won't ask him about the wisp of tow, for I expect you tease him with that question somehow. But I'll find out from him why you hate him so."

"Find out then, find out," cried the boys, laughing.

Alyosha crossed the bridge and walked uphill by the fence, straight towards the boy.

"You'd better look out," the boys called after him; "he won't be afraid of you. He will stab you in a minute, on the sly, as he did Krasotkin."

The boy waited for him without budging. Coming up to him, Alyosha saw facing him a child no older than nine. He was an undersized weakly boy with a thin long pale face, with large dark eyes that gazed at him vindictively. He was dressed in a rather shabby old overcoat, which he had monstrously outgrown. His bare arms stuck out beyond his sleeves. There was a large patch on the right knee of his trousers, and in his right boot just at the toe there was a big hole in the leather, carefully blackened with ink. Both pockets of his overcoat were weighed down with stones. Alyosha stopped two steps in front of him, looking inquiringly at him. The boy, seeing at once from Alyosha's eyes that he wouldn't beat him, became less defiant, and addressed him first.

"I am alone, and there are six of them. I'll beat them all, alone!" he said suddenly, with flashing eyes.

"I think one of the stones must have hurt you badly," observed Alyosha.

"But I hit Smurov on the head!" cried the boy.

"They told me that you know me, and that you threw a stone at me on purpose," said Alyosha.

The boy looked darkly at him.

"I don't know you. Do you know me?" Alyosha continued.

"Let me alone!" the boy cried irritably, but he did not move, as though he were expecting something, and again there was a vindictive light in his eyes.

"Very well, I am going," said Alyosha; "only I don't know you and I don't tease you. They told me how they tease you, but I don't want to tease you. Goodbye!"

"Monk in silk trousers!" cried the boy, following Alyosha with the same vindictive and defiant expression, and he threw himself into an attitude of defense, feeling sure that now Alyosha would fall upon him; but Alyosha turned, looked at him, and walked away. He had not gone three steps before the biggest stone the boy had in his pocket hit him a painful blow in the back.

"So you'll hit a man from behind! They tell the truth, then, when they say that you attack on the sly," said Alyosha, turning round again. This time the boy threw a stone savagely right into Alyosha's face; but Alyosha just had time to guard himself, and the stone struck him on the elbow.

"Aren't you ashamed? What have I done to you?" he cried.

The boy waited in silent defiance, certain that now Alyosha would attack him. Seeing that even now he would not, his rage was like a little wild beast's; he flew at Alyosha himself, and before Alyosha had time to move, the spiteful child had seized his left hand with both of his and bit his middle finger. He fixed his teeth in it and it was ten seconds before he let go. Alyosha cried out with pain and pulled his finger away with all his might. The child let go at last and retreated to his former distance. Alyosha's finger had been badly bitten to the bone, close to the nail; it began to bleed. Alyosha took out his handkerchief and bound it tightly round his injured hand. He was a full minute bandaging it. The boy stood waiting all the time. At last Alyosha raised his gentle eyes and looked at him.

"Very well," he said, "you see how badly you've bitten me. That's enough, isn't it? Now tell me, what have I done to you?"

The boy stared in amazement.

"Though I don't know you and it's the first time I've seen you," Alyosha went on with the same serenity, "yet I must have done something to you—you wouldn't have hurt me like this for nothing. So what have I done? How have I wronged you, tell me?"

Instead of answering, the boy broke into a loud tearful wail and ran away. Alyosha walked slowly after him towards Mikhailovsky Street, and for a long time he saw the child running in the distance as fast as ever, not turning his head, and no doubt still keeping up his tearful wail. He made up his mind to find him out as soon as he had time, and to solve this mystery. Just now he had not the time.

Chapter IV

At the Khokhlakovs'

Alyosha soon reached Madame Khokhlakov's house, a handsome stone house of two stories, one of the finest in our town. Though Madame Khokhlakov spent most of her time in another province where she had an estate, or in Moscow, where she had a house of her own, yet she had a house in our town, too, inherited from her forefathers. The estate in our district was the largest of her three estates, yet she had been very little in our province before this time. She ran out to Alyosha in the hall.

"Did you get my letter about the new miracle?" She spoke rapidly and nervously.

"Yes."

"Did you show it to everyone? He restored the son to his mother!"

"He will die today," said Alyosha.

"I have heard, I know, oh, how I long to talk to you, to you, or someone, about all this. No, to you, to you! And how sorry I am I can't see him! The whole town is in excitement, they are all suspense. But now—do you know Katerina Ivanovna is here now?"

"Ah, that's lucky," cried Alyosha. "Then I shall see her here. She told me yesterday to be sure to come and see her today."

"I know, I know all. I've heard exactly what happened yesterday —and the atrocious behavior of that—creature. *C'est tragique,*[1] and if I'd been in her place I don't know what I would have done. And your brother Dmitri Fyodorovich, what do you think of him? —my goodness! Alexey Fyodorovich, I am forgetting, only fancy; your brother is in there with her, not that dreadful brother who was so shocking yesterday, but the other, Ivan Fyodorovich, he is sitting with her talking; they are having a solemn conversation. If you could only imagine what's passing between them now—it's awful, I tell you it's lacerating, it's like some incredible tale of horror. They are ruining their lives for no reason anyone can see. They both recognize it and revel in it. I've been watching for you! I've been thirsting for you! It's too much for me, that's the worst of it. I'll tell you all about it presently, but now I must speak of something else, the most important thing—I had quite forgotten what's most important. Tell me, why has Lise been in hysterics? As soon as she heard you were here, she began to be hysterical!"

"*Maman,* it's you who are hysterical now, not I." Lise's voice caroled through a tiny crack of the door at the side. Her voice sounded strained as though she wanted to laugh, but was doing her utmost to control it. Alyosha at once noticed the crack, and no doubt Lise was peeping through it from her chair, but that he could not see.

"And no wonder, Lise, no wonder . . . your caprices will make me hysterical too. But she is so ill, Alexey Fyodorovich, she has been so ill all night, feverish and moaning! I could hardly wait for the morning and for Herzenstube to come. He says that he can make nothing of it, that we must wait. Herzenstube always comes and says that he can make nothing of it. As soon as you approached the house, she screamed, fell into hysterics, and insisted on being wheeled back into this room here."

"Mamma, I didn't know he had come. It wasn't on his account I wanted to be wheeled into this room."

"That's not true, Lise, Yulia ran to tell you that Alexey Fyodorovich was coming. She was on the lookout for you."

"My darling mamma, it's not at all clever of you. But if you want to make up for it and say something very clever, dear mamma, you'd better tell our honored visitor, Alexey Fyodorovich, that he has shown his want of wit by venturing to us after what happened yesterday and although everyone is laughing at him."

"Lise, you go too far. I declare I shall have to be severe. Who laughs at him? I am so glad he has come, I need him, I can't do without him. Oh, Alexey Fyodorovich, I am exceedingly unhappy!"

"But what's the matter with you, mamma, darling?"

1. "It is tragic."

"Ah, your caprices, Lise, your fidgetiness, your illness, that awful night of fever, that awful everlasting Herzenstube, everlasting, everlasting, that's the worst of it! Everything, in fact, everything. . . . even that miracle, too! Oh, how it has upset me, how it has shattered me, that miracle, dear Alexey Fyodorovich! And that tragedy in the drawing room, it's more than I can bear, I warn you. I can't bear it. A comedy, perhaps, not a tragedy. Tell me, will Father Zosima live till tomorrow, will he? Oh, my God! What is happening to me? Every minute I close my eyes and see that it's all nonsense, all nonsense."

"I should be very grateful," Alyosha interrupted suddenly, "if you could give me a clean rag to bind up my finger with. I have hurt it, and it's very painful."

Alyosha unbound his bitten finger. The handkerchief was soaked with blood. Madame Khokhlakov screamed and shut her eyes.

"God heavens, what a wound, how awful!"

But as soon as Lise saw Alyosha's finger through the crack, she flung the door wide open.

"Come, come here," she cried, imperiously. "No nonsense now! Good heavens, why did you stand there saying nothing about it all this time? He might have bled to death, mamma! How did you do it? Water, water! You must wash it first of all, simply hold it in cold water to stop the pain, and keep it there, keep it there. . . . Make haste, mamma, some water in a basin. But do make haste," she finished nervously. She was quite frightened at the sight of Alyosha's wound.

"Shouldn't we send for Herzenstube?" cried Madame Khokhlakov.

"Mamma, you'll be the death of me. Your Herzenstube will come and say that he can make nothing of it! Water, water! Mamma, for goodness' sake go yourself and hurry Yulia, she is such a slowpoke and never can come quickly! Make haste, mamma, or I shall die."

"Why, it's nothing much," cried Alyosha, frightened at this alarm.

Yulia ran in with water and Alyosha put his finger in it.

"Some lint, mamma, for mercy's sake, bring some lint and that muddy caustic lotion for wounds, what's it called? We have some, we have some, we have some. You know where the bottle is, mamma; it's in your bedroom in the right-hand cupboard, there's a big bottle of it there with the lint."

"I'll bring everything in a minute, Lise, only don't scream and don't fuss. You see how bravely Alexey Fyodorovich bears it. Where did you get such a dreadful wound, Alexey Fyodorovich?"

Madame Khokhlakov hastened away. This was all Lise was waiting for.

"First of all, answer the question, where did you get hurt like this?" she asked Alyosha, quickly. "And then I'll talk to you about something quite different. Well?"

Instinctively feeling that the time of her mother's absence was precious for her, Alyosha hastened to tell her of his enigmatic meeting with the schoolboys in the fewest words possible. Lise clasped her hands at his story.

"How can you, and in that dress too, associate with schoolboys!" she cried angrily, as though she had a right to control him. "You are nothing but a boy yourself if you can do that, a perfect boy! But you must find out for me about that horrid boy and tell me all about it, for there's some mystery in it. Now for the second thing, but first a question: does the pain prevent you, Alexey Fyodorovich, talking about utterly unimportant things, but talking sensibly?"

"Of course not, and I don't feel much pain now."

"That's because your finger is in the water. It must be changed directly for it will get warm in a minute. Yulia, bring some ice from the cellar and another basin of water. Now she is gone, I can speak; will you give me the letter I sent you yesterday, dear Alexey Fyodorovich—be quick for mamma will be back in a minute and I don't want——"

"I haven't got the letter."

"That's not true, you have. I knew you would say that. You've got it in that pocket. I've been regretting that joke all night. Give me back the letter at once, give it to me."

"I've left it at home."

"But you can't consider me as a child, a little girl, after that silly joke! I beg your pardon for that silliness, but you must bring me the letter, if you really haven't got it—bring it today, you must, you must."

"Today, I can't possibly, for I am going back to the monastery and I won't come and see you for the next two days—three or four perhaps—for Father Zosima——"

"Four days, what nonsense! Listen. Did you laugh at me very much?"

"I didn't laugh at all."

"Why not?"

"Because I believed all you said."

"You are insulting me!"

"Not at all. As soon as I read it, I thought that all that would come to pass, for as soon as Father Zosima dies, I am to leave the monastery. Then I shall go back and finish my studies, and when you reach the legal age we will be married. I will love you. Though I haven't had time to think about it, I believe I couldn't find a better wife than you, and Father Zosima tells me I must marry."

"But I am a cripple, wheeled about in a chair," laughed Lisa, flushing crimson.

"I'll wheel you about myself, but I'm sure you'll get well by then."

"But you are mad," said Lisa, nervously, "to make all this nonsense out of a joke! Here's mamma, just in time, perhaps. Mamma, how slow you always are, how can you be so long! And here's Yulia with the ice."

"Oh, Lise, don't scream, above all things don't scream. That scream drives me ... How can I help it when you put the lint in another place. I've been hunting and hunting—I do believe you did it on purpose."

"But I couldn't tell that he would come with a bad finger, or else perhaps I might have done it on purpose. My darling mamma, you begin to say really witty things."

"Never mind my being witty, but I must say you show nice feeling for Alexey Fyodorovich's sufferings. Oh, my dear Alexey Fyodorovich, what's killing me is no one thing in particular, not Herzenstube, but everything together, that's what is too much for me."

"That's enough, mamma, enough about Herzenstube," Lisa laughed gaily. "Make haste with the lint and the lotion, mamma. That's simply Goulard's water, Alexey Fyodorovich, I remember the name now, but it's a splendid lotion. Would you believe it, mamma, on the way here he had a fight with the boys in the street, and it was a boy bit his finger, isn't he a child, a child himself? Is he fit to be married after that? For only fancy, he wants to be married, mamma. Just think of him married, wouldn't it be funny, wouldn't it be awful?"

And Lise kept laughing her thin hysterical giggle, looking slyly at Alyosha.

"But why married, Lise? What makes you talk of such a thing? It's quite out of place—and perhaps the boy was rabid."

"Why, mamma! As though there were rabid boys!"

"Why not, Lise, as though I had said something stupid! Your boy might have been bitten by a mad dog and he would become mad and bite anyone near him. How well she has bandaged it, Alexey Fyodorovich, I couldn't have done it. Do you still feel the pain?"

"It's nothing much now."

"You don't feel afraid of water?" asked Lise.

"Come, that's enough, Lise, perhaps I really was rather too quick talking of the boy being rabid, and you pounced upon it at once. Katerina Ivanovna has only just heard that you are here, Alexey Fyodorovich, she simply rushed at me, she's dying to see you, dying!"

"Ach, mamma, go to them yourself. He can't go just now, he is in too much pain."

"Not at all, I can go quite well," said Alyosha.

"What! You are going away? Is that what you say?"

"Well, when I've seen them, I'll come back here and we can talk as much as you like. But I should like to see Katerina Ivanovna at once, for I am very anxious to be back at the monastery as soon as I can."

"Mamma, take him away quickly. Alexey Fyodorovich, don't trouble to come and see me afterwards, but go straight back to your monastery and good riddance. I want to sleep, I didn't sleep all night."

"Ah, Lise, you are only making fun, but how I wish you would sleep!" cried Madame Khokhlakov.

"I don't know what I've done. . . . I'll stay another three minutes, five if you like," muttered Alyosha.

"Even five! Do take him away quickly, mamma, he is a monster."

"Lise, you've gone mad. Let us go, Alexey Fyodorovich, she is too capricious today. I am afraid to cross her. Oh, the trouble one has with nervous girls! Perhaps she really will be able to sleep after seeing you. How quickly you have made her sleepy, and how fortunate it is."

"Ah, mamma, how sweetly you talk. I must kiss you for it, mamma."

"And I kiss you too, Lise. Listen, Alexey Fyodorovich," Madame Khokhlakov began mysteriously and importantly, speaking in a rapid whisper. "I don't want to suggest anything, I don't want to lift the veil, you will see for yourself what's going on. It's appalling. It's the most fantastic farce. She loves your brother, Ivan Fyodorovich, and she is doing her utmost to persuade herself she loves your brother, Dmitri Fyodorovich. It's appalling! I'll go in with you, and if they don't turn me out, I'll stay to the end."

Chapter V

A Laceration in the Drawing Room

But in the drawing room the conversation was already over. Katerina Ivanovna was greatly excited, though she looked resolute. At the moment Alyosha and Madame Khokhlakov entered, Ivan Fyodorovich stood up to take leave. His face was rather pale, and Alyosha looked at him anxiously. For this moment was to solve a doubt, a harassing enigma which had for some time haunted Alyosha. During the preceding month it had been several times suggested to him that his brother Ivan was in love with Katerina Ivanovna, and, what was more, that he meant "to carry her off" from Mitya. Until quite lately the idea seemed to Alyosha monstrous, though it worried him extremely. He loved both his brothers, and dreaded such rivalry between them. Meantime, Dmitri Fyodorovich had said outright on the previous day that he was glad that his brother Ivan was his rival, and that it was a great assistance to him, Dmitri. In what way did it assist him? To marry Grushenka? But that Alyosha considered the worst thing possible. Besides all this, Alyosha had till the evening before implicitly believed that Katerina Ivanovna had a steadfast and passionate love for his brother Dmitri; but he had only believed it till the evening before. He had fancied, too, that she was incapable of loving a man like Ivan, and that she did love his brother Dmitri, and loved him just as he was, in spite of all the strangeness of such a passion.

But during yesterday's scene with Grushenka another idea had struck him. The word "lacerating," which Madame Khokhlakov had just uttered, almost made him start, because half waking up towards daybreak that night he had cried out. "Laceration, laceration," probably applying it to his dream. He had been dreaming all night of the previous day's scene at Katerina Ivanovna's. Now Alyosha was impressed by Madame Khokhlakov's blunt and persistent assertion that Katerina Ivanovna was in love with his brother Ivan, and only deceived herself through some sort of pose, from "laceration," and tortured herself by her pretended love for Dmitri from some fancied duty of gratitude. "Yes," he thought, "perhaps the whole truth lies in those words." But in that case what was his brother Ivan's position? Alyosha felt instinctively that a character like Katerina Ivanovna's must dominate, and she could only dominate someone like Dmitri, and never a man like Ivan. For Dmitri might at last submit to her domination "to his own happiness" (which was what Alyosha would have desired), but Ivan—no, Ivan could not submit to her, and such submission would not give him happiness. Alyosha could not help believing that of Ivan. And now all these doubts and reflections flitted through his mind as he entered the drawing room. Another idea, too, forced itself upon him: "What if she loved neither of them—neither Ivan nor Dmitri?"

It must be noted that Alyosha felt as it were ashamed of his own thoughts and blamed himself when they kept recurring to him during the last month. "What do I know about love and women and how can I decide such questions?" he thought reproachfully, after such doubts and surmises. And yet it was impossible not to think about it. He felt instinctively that this rivalry was of immense importance in his brothers' lives and that a great deal depended upon it.

"One reptile will devour the other," his brother Ivan had pronounced the day before, speaking in anger of his father and his brother Dmitri. So Ivan looked upon his brother Dmitri as a reptile, and perhaps had long done so. Was it perhaps since he had known Katerina Ivanovna? That phrase had, of course, escaped Ivan unawares yesterday, but that only made it more important. If he felt like that, what chance was there of peace? Were there not, on the contrary, new grounds for hatred and hostility in their family? And with which of them was Alyosha to sympathize? And what was he to wish for each of them? He loved them both, but what could he desire for each in the midst of these conflicting interests? He might go quite astray in this maze, and Alyosha's heart could not endure uncertainty, because his love was always of an active character. He was incapable of passive love. If he loved anyone, he set to work at once to help him. And to do so he must know what he was aiming at; he must know for certain what was best for each, and having ascertained this it was natural for him to help them both. But instead of a definite aim, he found nothing but uncertainty and perplexity on all sides. "It was lacerating," as was said just now. But what could he understand even in this "laceration"? He did not understand the first word in this perplexing maze.

Seeing Alyosha, Katerina Ivanovna said quickly and joyfully to Ivan Fyodorovich, who had already got up to go, "A minute! Stay another minute! I want to hear the opinion of this person here whom I trust absolutely. Don't go away," she added, addressing Madame Khokhlakov. She made Alyosha sit down beside her, and Madame Khokhlakov sat opposite, by Ivan Fyodorovich.

"You are all my friends here, all I have in the world, my dear friends," she began warmly, in a voice which quivered with genuine tears of suffering, and Alyosha's heart warmed to her at once. "You, Alexey Fyodorovich, were witness yesterday to that abominable scene, and saw what I was like. You did not see it, Ivan Fyodorovich, he did. What he thought of me yesterday I don't know. I only know one thing, that if it were repeated today, this minute, I would express the same feelings again as yesterday—the same feelings, the same words, the same actions. You remember my actions, Alexey Fyodorovich; you checked me in one of them" . . . (as she said that, she flushed and her eyes shone). "I must tell you that I can't get over it. Listen, Alexey Fyodorovich. I don't even know whether I still love *him*. I feel *pity* for him, and that is a poor sign of love. If I loved him, if I still loved him, perhaps I wouldn't be sorry for him now, but would hate him."

Her voice quivered, and tears glittered on her eyelashes. Alyosha shuddered inwardly. "That girl is truthful and sincere," he thought, "and she does not love Dmitri any more."

"That's true, that's true," Madame Khokhlakov started to cry out.

"Wait, Katerina Osipovna, dear. I haven't told you the chief, the final decision I came to during the night. I feel that perhaps my decision is a terrible one—for me, but I foresee that nothing will induce me to change it—nothing. It will be so all my life. My dear, kind, ever-faithful and generous adviser, the one friend I have in the world, Ivan Fyodorovich, and with his deep insight into the heart, approves and commends my decision. He knows it."

"Yes, I approve of it," Ivan Fyodorovich assented, in a subdued but firm voice.

"But I should like Alyosha, too (Ah! Alexey Fyodorovich, forgive my calling you simply Alyosha), I should like Alexey Fyodorovich, too, to tell me before my two friends whether I am right. I feel instinctively that you, Alyosha, my dear brother (for you are a dear brother to me)," she said again ecstatically, taking his cold hand in her hot one, "I foresee that your decision, your approval, will bring me peace, in spite of all my sufferings, for, after your words, I shall be calm and submit—I feel that."

"I don't know what you are asking me," said Alyosha, flushing. "I only know that I love you and at this moment wish for your happiness more than my own! . . . But I know nothing about such affairs," something impelled him to add hurriedly.

"In such affairs, Alexey Fyodorovich, in such affairs, the chief thing is honor and duty and something higher—I don't know what —but higher perhaps even than duty. I am conscious of this irresistible feeling in my heart, and it compels me irresistibly. But it may all be put in two words. I've already decided, even if he marries that—creature," she began solemnly, "whom I never, never can forgive, *even then I will not abandon him.* Henceforward I will never, never abandon him!" she cried, with an outburst of a sort of pale, tormented ecstasy. "Not that I would run after him continually, get in his way and worry him. Oh, no! I will go away to another town—where you like—but I will watch over him all my life—I will watch over him all my life unceasingly. When he becomes unhappy with that woman, and that is bound to happen quite soon, let him come to me and he will find a friend, a sister. . . . Only a sister, of course, and so forever; but he will learn at least that that sister is really his sister, who loves him and has sacrificed all her life to him. I will gain my point. I will insist on his knowing me and confiding entirely in me, without reserve," she cried, in a sort of frenzy. "I will be a god to whom he can pray—and that, at least, he owes me for his treachery and for what I suffered yesterday through him. And let him see that all my life I will be true to him and the promise I gave him, in spite of his being untrue and betraying me. I will—I will become nothing but a means for his happiness, or—how shall I say?—an instrument, a machine for his happiness, and that for my whole life, my whole life, and that he

may see that all his life! That's my decision. Ivan Fyodorovich fully
approves me."

She was breathless. She had perhaps intended to express her idea
with more dignity, art and naturalness, but her speech was too
hurried and crude. It was full of youthful impulsiveness, it betrayed
that she was still smarting from yesterday's insult, and that her
pride craved satisfaction. She felt this herself. Her face suddenly
darkened, an unpleasant look came into her eyes. Alyosha at once
saw it and felt a pang of sympathy. His brother Ivan made it worse
by adding:

"I've only expressed my own view," he said. "From anyone else,
this would have been affected and overstrained, but from you—no.
Any other woman would have been wrong, but you are right. I
don't know how to explain it, but I see that you are absolutely
genuine and, therefore, you are right."

"But that's only for the moment. And what does this moment
stand for? Nothing but yesterday's insult." Madame Khokhlakov
obviously had not intended to interfere, but she could not refrain
from this very just comment.

"Quite so, quite so," interrupted Ivan, with peculiar eagerness,
obviously annoyed at being interrupted, "in anyone else this moment would be only due to yesterday's impression and would be
only a moment. But with Katerina Ivanovna's character, that moment will last all her life. What for anyone else would be only a
promise is for her an everlasting, burdensome, grim perhaps, but
unflagging duty. And she will be sustained by the feeling of this
duty being fulfilled. Your life, Katerina Ivanovna, will henceforth
be spent in painful brooding over your own feelings, your own
heroism, and your own suffering; but in the end that suffering will
be softened and will pass into sweet contemplation of the fulfill-
ment of a bold and proud design. Yes, proud it certainly is, and
desperate in any case, but a triumph for you. And the consciousness of it will at last be a source of complete satisfaction and will
make you resigned to everything else."

This was unmistakably said with some malice and obviously with
intention; even perhaps with no desire to conceal that he spoke
ironically and with intention.

"Oh, dear, how mistaken it all is!" Madame Khokhlakov cried
again.

"Alexey Fyodorovich, you speak. I want dreadfully to know
what you will say!" cried Katerina Ivanovna, and burst into tears.
Alyosha got up from the sofa.

"It's nothing, nothing!" she went on through her tears. "I'm
upset, I didn't sleep last night. But by the side of two such friends
as you and your brother I still feel strong—for I know—you two
will never desert me."

"Unluckily I am obliged to return to Moscow—perhaps to-morrow—and to leave you for a long time—And, unluckily, it's unavoidable," Ivan Fyodorovich said suddenly.

"Tomorrow—to Moscow!" her face was suddenly contorted; "but—but, dear me, how fortunate," she cried in a voice suddenly changed. In one instant there was no trace left of her tears. She underwent an instantaneous transformation, which amazed Alyosha. Instead of a poor, insulted girl, weeping in a sort of laceration, he saw a woman completely self-possessed and even exceedingly pleased, as though something agreeable had just happened.

"Oh, not fortunate that I am losing you, of course not," she corrected herself suddenly, with a charming society smile. "Such a friend as you are could not suppose that. I am only too unhappy at losing you." She rushed impulsively at Ivan Fyodorovich and seizing both his hands, pressed them warmly. "But what is fortunate is that you will be able in Moscow to see auntie and Agatha and to tell them all the horror of my present position. You can speak with complete frankness to Agatha, but spare dear auntie. You will know how to do that. You can't think how wretched I was yesterday and this morning, wondering how I could write them that dreadful letter—for one can never tell such things in a letter. . . . Now it will be easy for me to write, for you will see them and explain everything. Oh, how glad I am! But I am only glad of that, believe me. Of course, no one can take your place. . . . I will run at once to write the letter," she finished suddenly, and took a step as though to go out of the room.

"And what about Alyosha? Alexey Fyodorovich and his opinion, which you were so desperately anxious to hear?" cried Madame Khokhlakov. There was a sarcastic, angry note in her voice.

"I had not forgotten that," cried Katerina Ivanovna, coming to a sudden standstill, "and why are you so antagonistic at such a moment, Katerina Osipovna?" she added, with hot and bitter reproachfulness. "What I said, I repeat. I must have his opinion. More than that, I must have his decision! As he says, so it shall be. You see how anxious I am for your words, Alexey Fyodorovich. . . . But what's the matter?"

"I couldn't have believed it. I can't understand it!" Alyosha cried suddenly in distress.

"What? what?"

"He is going to Moscow, and you cry out that you are glad. You cried it out on purpose! And you begin explaining that you are not glad of that but sorry to be—losing a friend. But that was acting, too—you were playing a part—as in a theater!"

"In a theater? What? What do you mean?" exclaimed Katerina Ivanovna, profoundly astonished, flushing crimson, and frowning.

"Though you assure him you are sorry to lose a friend in him,

you persist in telling him to his face that it's fortunate he is going,"
said Alyosha breathlessly. He was standing at the table and did not
sit down.

"What are you talking about? I don't understand."

"I don't understand myself. . . . I seemed to see in a flash . . . I
know I am not saying it properly but I'll say it all the same,"
Alyosha went on in the same shaking and broken voice. "What I
see is that perhaps you don't love my brother Dmitri at all . . . and
never have, from the beginning. . . . And Dmitri, too, perhaps, has
never loved you . . . and only esteems you. . . . I really don't know
how I dare to say all this, but somebody must tell the truth . . . for
nobody here will tell the truth."

"What truth?" cried Katerina Ivanovna, and there was an hysterical ring in her voice.

"I'll tell you," Alyosha went on with desperate haste, as though
he were jumping from the top of a house. "Call Dmitri at once—I
will fetch him—and let him come here and take your hand and
take my brother Ivan's and join your hands. For you're torturing
Ivan, simply because you love him—and torturing him, because
you love Dmitri through 'laceration'—with an unreal love—
because you've persuaded yourself."

Alyosha broke off and was silent.

"You . . . you . . . you are a little religious idiot—that's what you
are!" Katerina Ivanovna snapped. Her face was white and her lips
were moving with anger. Ivan Fyodorovich suddenly laughed and
got up. His hat was in his hand.

"You are mistaken, my good Alyosha," he said, with an expression Alyosha had never seen in his face before—an expression of
youthful sincerity and strong, irresistibly frank feeling. "Katerina
Ivanovna has never loved me! She has known all the time that I
loved her—though I never said a word of my love to her—she
knew, but she didn't love me. I have never been her friend either,
not for one moment; she is too proud to need my friendship. She
kept me at her side as a means of revenge. She revenged with me
and on me all the insults which she has been continually receiving
from Dmitri ever since their first meeting. For even that first meeting has rankled in her heart as an insult—that's what her heart is
like! She has talked to me of nothing but her love for him. I am
going now; but, believe me, Katerina Ivanovna, you really love
only him. And the more he insults you, the more you love him—
that's your 'laceration.' You love him just as he is; you love him for
insulting you. If he reformed, you'd give him up at once and cease
to love him. But you need him so as to contemplate continually
your heroic fidelity and to reproach him for infidelity. And it all
comes from your pride. Oh, there's a great deal of humiliation and
self-abasement about it, but it all comes from pride. . . . I am too

young and I've loved you too much. I know that I ought not to say this, that it would be more dignified on my part simply to leave you, and it would be less offensive for you. But I am going far away, and shall never come back. . . . It is forever. I don't want to sit beside a 'laceration.' . . . But I no longer know how to speak. I've said everything. . . . Goodbye, Katerina Ivanovna; you can't be angry with me, for I am a hundred times more severely punished than you, if only by the fact that I shall never see you again. Goodbye! I don't want your hand. You have tortured me too deliberately for me to be able to forgive you at this moment. I shall forgive you later, but now I don't want your hand. '*Den Dank, Dame, begehr ich nicht,*' "[2] he added, with a forced smile, showing completely unexpectedly, however, that he, too, could read Schiller, and read him till he knew him by heart—which Alyosha would never have believed. He went out of the room without saying good-bye even to his hostess, Madame Khokhlakov. Alyosha clasped his hands.

"Ivan!" he cried desperately after him. "Come back, Ivan! No, no, nothing will induce him to come back now!" he cried again, regretfully realizing it; "but it's my fault, my fault. I began it! Ivan spoke angrily, wrongly. Unjustly and angrily," Alyosha kept exclaiming frantically.

Katerina Ivanovna went suddenly into the next room.

"You have done no harm. You behaved beautifully, like an angel," Madame Khokhlakov whispered rapidly and ecstatically to Alyosha. "I will do my utmost to prevent Ivan Fyodorovich from going."

Her face beamed with delight, to the great distress of Alyosha, but Katerina Ivanovna suddenly returned. She had two hundred-ruble bills in her hand.

"I have a great favor to ask of you, Alexey Fyodorovich," she began, addressing Alyosha with an apparently calm and even voice, as though nothing had happened. "A week—yes, I think it was a week ago—Dmitri Fyodorovich was guilty of a hasty and unjust action—a very ugly action. There is a low tavern here and in it he met that discharged officer, that captain, whom your father used to employ in some business. Dmitri Fyodorovich somehow lost his temper with this captain, seized him by the beard and dragged him out into the street and for some distance along it, in that insulting fashion. And I am told that his son, a boy, quite a child, who is at the school here, saw it and ran beside them crying and begging for his father, appealing to everyone to defend him, while everyone laughed. You must forgive me, Alexey Fyodorovich, I cannot think without indignation of that disgraceful action of *his* . . . one of those actions of which only Dmitri Fyodorovich would be capable

2. **"This reward, my lady, I do not crave."** From Schiller's poem "Der Handschuh" (The glove).

in his anger . . . and in his passions! I can't describe it even. . . . I can't find my words. I've made inquiries about his victim, and find he is quite a poor man. His name is Snegiryov. He did something wrong in the army and was discharged. I can't tell you what. And now he has sunk into terrible destitution, with his family—an unhappy family of sick children, and, I believe, an insane wife. He has been living here a long time; he used to work as a copying clerk, but now he is getting nothing. I thought if you . . . that is I thought . . . I don't know. I am so confused. You see, I wanted to ask you, my dear Alexey Fyodorovich, to go to him, to find some excuse to go to them—I mean to that captain—oh, goodness, how badly I explain it!—and delicately, carefully, as only you know how to"—Alyosha blushed—"manage to give him this assistance, these two hundred rubles. He will be sure to take it. . . . I mean, persuade him to take it. . . . Or, rather, what do I mean? You see it's not by way of compensation to prevent him from taking proceedings (for I believe he meant to), but simply a token of sympathy, of a desire to assist him from me, Dmitri Fyodorovich's betrothed, not from himself. . . . But you know. . . . I would go myself, but you'll know how to do it ever so much better. He lives on Lake Street, in the house of a woman called Kalmiykov. . . . For God's sake, Alexey Fyodorovich, do it for me, and now . . . now I am rather . . . tired. Goodbye!"

She turned so quickly and disappeared behind the portière that Alyosha had not time to utter a word, though he wanted to speak. He longed to beg her pardon, to blame himself, to say something, for his heart was full and he could not bear to go out of the room without it. But Madame Khokhlakov took him by the hand and drew him along with her. In the hall she stopped him again as before.

"She is proud, she is struggling with herself; but kind, charming, generous," she exclaimed, in a half-whisper. "Oh, how I love her, especially sometimes, and how glad I am again of everything! Dear Alexey Fyodorovich, you didn't know, but I must tell you, that we all, all—both her aunts, I and all of us, Lise, even—have been hoping and praying for nothing for the last month but that she may give up your favorite Dmitri Fyodorovich, who takes no notice of her and does not love her, and may marry Ivan Fyodorovich—such an excellent and cultivated young man, who loves her more than anything in the world. We are in a regular plot to bring it about, and I am even staying on here perhaps on that account."

"But she has been crying—she has been wounded again," cried Alyosha.

"Never trust a woman's tears, Alexey Fyodorovich. I am never for the woman in such cases. I am always on the side of the man."

"Mamma, you are spoiling and ruining him," Lise's little voice cried from behind the door.

"No, it was all my fault. I am horribly to blame," Alyosha repeated unconsoled, hiding his face in his hands in an agony of remorse for his indiscretion.

"Quite the contrary; you behaved like an angel, like an angel. I am ready to say so a thousand times over."

"Mamma, how has he behaved like an angel?" Lise's voice was heard again.

"I somehow fancied all at once," Alyosha went on as though he had not heard Lisa, "that she loved Ivan, and so I said that stupid thing. . . . What will happen now?"

"To whom, to whom?" cried Lise. "Mamma, you really want to be the death of me. I ask you and you don't answer."

At the moment the maid ran in.

"Katerina Ivanovna is ill. . . . She is crying, struggling . . . hysterics."

"What is the matter?" cried Lise, in a tone of real anxiety. "Mamma, I shall be having hysterics, and not she!"

"Lise, for mercy's sake, don't scream, don't persecute me. At your age one can't know everything that grown-up people know. I'll come and tell you everything you ought to know. Oh, mercy on us! I am coming, I am coming. . . . Hysterics are a good sign, Alexey Fyodorovich; it's an excellent thing that she is hysterical. That's just as it ought to be. In such cases I am always against the woman, against all these feminine tears and hysterics. Run and say, Yulia, that I'll fly to her. As for Ivan Fyodorovich's going away like that, it's her own fault. But he won't go away. Lise, for mercy's sake, don't scream! Oh, yes; you are not screaming. It's I am screaming. Forgive your mamma; but I am delighted, delighted, delighted! Did you notice, Alexey Fyodorovich, how young, how young Ivan Fyodorovich was just now when he went out, when he said all that and went out? I thought he was so learned, such an academician, and all of a sudden he behaved so warmly, openly, and youthfully, with such youthful inexperience and it was all so fine, like you. . . . And the way he repeated that German verse, it was just like you! But I must fly, I must fly! Alexey Fyodorovich, make haste to carry out her commission, and then make haste back. Lise, do you want anything now? For mercy's sake, don't keep Alexey Fyodorovich a minute. He will come back to you at once."

Madame Khokhlakov at last ran off. Before leaving, Alyosha would have opened the door to see Lise.

"On no account," cried Lise. "On no account now. Speak through the door. How have you come to be an angel? That's the only thing I want to know."

"For an awful piece of stupidity, Lise! Good-bye!"

"Don't dare to go away like that!" Lise was beginning.

"Lise, I have a real grief! I'll be back directly, but I have a great, great grief!"

And he ran out of the room.

Chapter VI

A Laceration in a Hut

He certainly was really grieved in a way he had seldom been before. He had rushed in like a fool, and meddled in what? In a love affair. "But what do I know about it? What can I tell about such things?" he repeated to himself for the hundredth time, flushing crimson. "Oh, being ashamed would be nothing; shame is only the punishment I deserve. The trouble is I shall certainly have caused more unhappiness. . . . And Father Zosima sent me to reconcile and bring them together. Is that the way to bring them together?" Then he suddenly remembered how he had tried to join their hands, and he felt fearfully ashamed again. "Though I acted quite sincerely, I must be more sensible in the future," he concluded suddenly, and did not even smile at his conclusion.

Katerina Ivanovna's commission took him to Lake Street, and his brother Dmitri lived close by, in a turning out of Lake Street. Alyosha decided to go to him in any case before going to the captain, though he had a presentiment that he would not find his brother. He suspected that he would intentionally keep out of his way now, but he must find him anyhow. Time was passing: the thought of his dying elder had not left Alyosha for one minute from the time he set off from the monastery.

There was one point which interested him particularly about Katerina Ivanovna's commission; when she had mentioned the captain's son, the little schoolboy who had run beside his father crying, the idea had at once struck Alyosha that this must be the schoolboy who had bitten his finger when he, Alyosha, asked him what he had done to hurt him. Now Alyosha felt practically certain of this, though he could not have said why. Thinking of another subject was a relief, and he resolved to think no more about the "mischief" he had done, and not to torture himself with remorse, but to do what he had to do, let come what would. At that thought he was completely comforted. Turning onto the street where his brother Dmitri lodged, he felt hungry, and taking out of his pocket the roll he had brought from his father's, he ate it. It made him feel stronger.

Dmitri was not at home. The people of the house, an old cabinetmaker, his son, and his old wife, looked with positive suspicion at Alyosha. "He hasn't slept here for the last three nights. Maybe he has gone away," the old man said in answer to Alyosha's persistent inquiries. Alyosha saw that he was answering in accordance with instructions. When he asked whether he were not at Grushenka's or in hiding at Thomas's (Alyosha spoke so freely on purpose), all three looked at him in alarm. "They are fond of him, they are doing their best for him," thought Alyosha. "That's good."

At last he found Mrs. Kalmykov's house on Lake Street. It was a decrepit little house, sunk on one side, with three windows looking into the street, and with a muddy yard, in the middle of which stood a solitary cow. He crossed the yard and found the door opening into the hall. On the left of the hall lived the old woman of the house with her old daughter. Both seemed to be deaf. In answer to his repeated inquiry for the captain, one of them at last understood that he was asking for their lodgers, and pointed across the hall at a door to the living room. The captain's lodging actually turned out to be an ordinary hut. Alyosha had his hand on the iron latch to open the door, when he was struck by the strange hush within. Yet he knew from Katerina Ivanovna's words that the man had a family. "Either they are all asleep or perhaps they have heard me coming and are waiting for me to open the door. I'd better knock first," and he knocked. An answer came, but not at once, after an interval of perhaps ten seconds.

"Who's there?" shouted someone in a loud and very angry voice.

Then Alyosha opened the door and crossed the threshold. He found himself in a hut. Though it was large, it was cluttered up with domestic belongings of all sorts, and there were several people in it. On the left was a large Russian stove. From the stove to the window on the left was a string running across the room, and on it rags were hanging. There was a bedstead against the wall on each side, right and left, covered with knitted quilts. On the one on the left was a pyramid of four print-covered pillows, each smaller than the one beneath. On the other there was only one very small pillow. The opposite corner was screened off by a curtain or a sheet hung on a string. Behind this curtain could be seen a bed made up on a bench and a chair set against it. The rough square table of plain wood had been moved from the foreroom to the middle window. The three windows, which consisted each of four tiny greenish mildewy panes, gave little light, and were close shut, so that the room was not very light and rather stuffy. On the table was a frying pan with the remains of some fried eggs, a half-eaten piece of bread, and a small bottle with a few drops of vodka remaining on the bottom.

A woman of genteel appearance, wearing a cotton gown, was sitting on a chair by the bed on the left. Her face was thin and yellow, and her sunken cheeks betrayed at the first glance that she was ill. But what struck Alyosha most was the expression in the poor woman's eyes—a look of surprised inquiry and yet of haughty pride. And while he was talking to her husband, her big brown eyes moved from one speaker to the other with the same haughty and questioning expression. Beside her at the window stood a young girl, rather plain, with scanty reddish hair, poorly but very neatly dressed. She looked disdainfully at Alyosha as he came in. Beside the other bed was sitting another female figure. She was a very sad sight, a young girl of about twenty, but hunchback and crippled "with withered legs," as Alyosha was told afterwards. Her crutches stood close by in the corner, between the bed and the wall. The strikingly beautiful and gentle eyes of this poor girl looked with mild serenity at Alyosha. A man of forty-five was sitting at the table, finishing the fried eggs. He was spare, small and weakly built. He had reddish hair and a scanty light-colored beard, very much like a wisp of tow (this comparison and the phrase "a wisp of tow" flashed at once into Alyosha's mind for some reason; he remembered it afterwards). It was obviously this gentleman who had shouted to him, as there was no other man in the room. But when Alyosha went in, he leaped up from the bench on which he was sitting, and, hastily wiping his mouth with a ragged napkin, darted up to Alyosha.

"It's a monk come to beg for the monastery. A nice place to come to!" the girl standing in the left corner said aloud. The man spun round instantly towards her and answered her in an excited and breaking voice.

"No, ma'am, Barbara Nikolavna, that's not it, ma'am, you are wrong, ma'am. Allow me to ask in turn, sir," he turned again to Alyosha, "what has brought you, sir, to—our retreat?"

Alyosha looked attentively at him. It was the first time he had seen him. There was something angular, flurried and irritable about him. Though he had obviously just been drinking, he was not drunk. There was extraordinary impudence in his expression, and yet, strange to say, at the same time there was fear. He looked like a man who had long been kept in subjection and had submitted to it, and now had suddenly turned and was trying to assert himself. Or, better still, like a man who wants dreadfully to hit you but is horribly afraid you will hit him. In his words and in the intonation of his shrill voice there was a sort of crazy humor, at times spiteful and at times cringing, and continually shifting from one tone to another. The question about "our retreat" he had asked as it were quivering all over, rolling his eyes, and skipping up so close to Alyosha that he instinctively drew back a step. He was dressed in a very shabby dark cotton coat, patched and spotted. He wore checked trousers of an extremely light color, long out of fashion, and of very thin material. They were so crumpled and so short that he looked as though he had grown out of them like a boy.

"I am Alexey Karamazov," Alyosha began in reply.

"I quite understand that, sir," the gentleman snapped out at once to assure him that he knew who he was already. "I, sir, in turn am Captain Snegiryov, sir, but I am still desirous to know precisely what has led you, sir——"

"Oh, I've come for nothing special. I wanted to have a word with you—if only you allow me."

"In that case, here is a chair, sir; kindly be seated, sir. That's what they used to say in the old comedies, 'kindly be seated,' " and with a rapid gesture he seized an empty chair (it was a rough wooden chair, not upholstered) and set it for him almost in the middle of the room; then, taking another similar chair for himself, he sat down facing Alyosha, so close to him that their knees almost touched.

"Nikolay Ilyich Snegiryov, sir, formerly a captain in the Russian infantry, sir, put to shame for his vices, but still a captain. Though I should say Captain Yessirov rather than Snegiryov; for the last half of my life I've learned to say 'sir.' It's a word you use when you've come down in the world."

"That's very true," smiled Alyosha. "But is it used involuntarily or on purpose?"

"As God's above, it's involuntary, and I didn't use it before! I didn't use the word 'sir' all my life, but as soon as I sank into low water I began to say 'sir.' It's the work of a higher power. I see you are interested in contemporary questions, but how can I have excited your curiosity, living as I do in surroundings impossible for the exercise of hospitality?"

"I've come—about that business."

"About what business?" the captain interrupted impatiently.

"About your meeting with my brother Dmitri Fyodorovich," Alyosha blurted out awkwardly.

"What meeting, sir? You don't mean that meeting, sir? About my wisp of tow, then, my bathhouse wisp of tow?" He moved closer so that his knees positively knocked against Alyosha. His lips were strangely compressed like a thread.

"What wisp of tow?" muttered Alyosha.

"He is come to complain of me, daddy!" cried a voice familiar to Alyosha—the voice of the schoolboy—from behind the curtain. "I bit his finger just now." The curtain was pulled, and Alyosha saw his assailant lying on a little bed made up on the bench and the chair in the corner under the icons. The boy lay covered by his coat and an old wadded quilt. He was evidently unwell, and, judging by his glittering eyes, he was in a fever. He looked at Alyosha without fear, as though he felt he was at home and could not be touched.

"What! Did he bite your finger?" The captain jumped up from his chair. "Was it your finger he bit, sir?"

"Yes. He was throwing stones with other schoolboys. There were six of them against him alone, I went up to him, and he threw a stone at me and then another at my head. I asked him what I had done to him. And then he rushed at me and bit my finger badly, I don't know why."

"I'll thrash him, sir, at once—this minute!" The captain jumped up from his seat.

"But I am not complaining at all, I am simply telling you . . . I don't want him to be thrashed. Besides, he seems to be ill."

"And do you suppose I'd thrash him, sir? That I'd take my Ilyushechka and thrash him before you for your satisfaction? Would you like it done at once, sir?" said the captain, suddenly turning to Alyosha, as though he were going to attack him. "I am sorry about your finger sir; but instead of thrashing Ilyushechka, would you like me to chop off my four fingers with this knife here before your eyes to satisfy your just wrath? I should think four fingers would be enough to satisfy your thirst for vengeance, sir. You won't ask for the fifth one too?" He stopped short with a catch in his throat. Every feature in his face was twitching and working; he looked extremely defiant. He was in a sort of frenzy.

"I think I understand it all now," said Alyosha gently and sorrowfully, still keeping his seat. "So your boy is a good boy, he loves his father, and he attacked me as the brother of your assailant. . . . Now I understand it," he repeated thoughtfully. "But my brother Dmitri Fyodorovich regrets his action, I know that, and if only it is possible for him to come to you, or better still, to meet you in that same place, he will ask your forgiveness before everyone—if you wish it."

"After pulling out my beard, you mean, he will ask my forgiveness? And he thinks that will be a satisfactory finish, does he, sir?"

"Oh, no! On the contrary, he will do anything you like and in any way you like."

"So if I were to ask his highness to go down on his knees, sir, before me in that very tavern—'The Metropolis' it's called—or in the marketplace, he would do it?"

"Yes, he would even go down on his knees."

"You've pierced me to the heart, sir. Touched me to tears and pierced me to the heart, sir! I am only too sensible of your brother's generosity. Allow me to introduce my family, my two daughters and my son—my litter, sir. If I die, who will care for them, and while I live who but they will care for a wretch like me? That's a great thing the Lord has ordained for every man of my sort, sir. For there must be someone able to love even a man like me, sir."

"Ah, that's perfectly true!" exclaimed Alyosha.

"Oh, do leave off playing the fool! Some fool comes in, and you put us to shame!" cried the girl by the window, suddenly turning to her father with a disdainful and contemptuous air.

"Wait a little, Barbara Nikolavna! Permit me to maintain the tenor," cried her father, speaking peremptorily but looking at her quite approvingly. "That's her character, sir," he said, addressing Alyosha again.

> And in all nature there was nothing
> He wished to bless[3]

or rather in the feminine: that she wished to bless. But now, sir, let me present you to my wife, Arina Petrovna. She is crippled, she is forty-three; she can move, but very little. She is of humble origin. Arina Petrovna, compose your countenance. This is Alexey Fyodorovich Karamazov. Get up, Alexey Fyodorovich." He took him by the hand and with unexpected force pulled him up. "You must stand up to be introduced to a lady, sir. It's not the Karamazov, mamma, who . . . hmm . . . etcetera, but his brother, radiant with modest virtues. Come Arina Petrovna, come, mamma, but first permit me to kiss your hand."

And he kissed his wife's hand respectfully and even tenderly. The girl at the window turned her back indignantly on the scene; an expression of extraordinary cordiality came over the haughtily inquiring face of the woman.

"Hello! Sit down, Mr. Chernomazov[4]," she said.

"Karamazov, mamma, Karamazov (we are of humble origin, sir)," he whispered again.

"Well, Karamazov, or whatever it is, but I always think of Chernomazov. . . . Sit down. Why has he pulled you up? He calls me crippled but I am not, only my legs are swollen like barrels, and I am shriveled up myself. Once I used to be so fat, but now it's as though I had swallowed a needle."

"We are of humble origin, sir, humble origin, sir," the captain muttered again.

"Oh, father, father!" the hunchback girl, who had till then been silent on her chair, said suddenly, and she hid her eyes in her handkerchief.

"Buffoon!" blurted out the girl at the window.

"Have you heard our news?" said the mother, pointing at her daughters. "It's like clouds coming over; the clouds pass and we have music again. When we were with the army, we used to have many such guests. I don't mean to make any comparisons; everyone to his taste. The deacon's wife used to come then and say, 'Alexandr Alexandrovich is a man of the noblest heart, but Nastasya Petrovna,' she would say, 'is of the brood of hell.' 'Well,' I said,

---

3. From Pushkin's poem "The Demon."
4. Arina Petrovna substitutes the Russian

form of "black" for the Turkic derived "Kara" (*black*).

'that's a matter of taste; but you are a little spitfire.' 'And you want keeping in your place,' says she. 'You black sword,' said I, 'who asked you to teach me?' 'But my breath,' says she, 'is clean, and yours is unclean.' 'You ask all the officers whether my breath is unclean.' And ever since then I had it in my mind. Not long ago I was sitting here as I am now, when I saw that very general come in who came here for Easter, and I asked him: 'Your Excellency,' said I, 'can a lady's breath be unpleasant?' 'Yes,' he answered; 'you ought to open a window or open the door, for the air is not fresh here.' And they all go on like that! And what is my breath to them? The dead smell worse still! 'I won't spoil the air,' said I, 'I'll order some slippers and go away.' My darlings, don't blame your own mother! Nikolay Ilyich, how is it I can't please you? There's only Ilyushechka who comes home from school and loves me. Yesterday he brought me an apple. Forgive your own mother— forgive a poor lonely creature! Why has my breath become unpleasant to you?"

And the poor mad woman broke into sobs, and tears streamed down her cheeks. The captain rushed up to her.

"Mamma, mamma, my dear, stop! You are not lonely. Everyone loves you, everyone adores you." He began kissing both her hands again and tenderly stroking her face; taking the dinner napkin, he began wiping away her tears. Alyosha fancied that he too had tears in his eyes. "There, sir, you see, sir, you hear?" he turned with a sort of fury to Alyosha, pointing to the poor imbecile.

"I see and hear," muttered Alyosha.

"Father, father, how can you—with him! Let him alone!" cried the boy, sitting up in his bed and gazing at his father with glowing eyes.

"Do give over fooling, showing off your silly antics which never lead to anything!" shouted Barabara Nikolaevna, stamping her foot with passion.

"Your anger is quite just this time, Barbara Nikolavna, and I'll make haste to satisfy you. Come, put on your cap, Alexey Fyodorovich, and I'll put on mine. We will go out. I have a word to say to you in earnest, sir, but not within these walls. This girl sitting here is my daughter Nina Nikolaevna, sir. I forgot to introduce her to you, sir. She is a heavenly angel incarnate . . . who has flown down to us mortals, . . . if you can understand."

"There he is shaking all over, as though he is in convulsions!" Barabara Nikolaevna went on indignantly.

"And she there stamping her foot at me and calling me a fool just now, she is a heavenly angel incarnate too, and she has good reason to call me so. Come along, Alexey Fyodorovich, we must make an end, sir."

And, snatching Alyosha's hand, he drew him out of the room into the street.

Chapter VII

And in the Open Air

"The air is fresh, sir, but in my mansion it is not so in any sense of the word. Let us walk slowly, my good sir. I should be glad of your kind interest."

"I too have something important to say to you," observed Alyosha, "only I don't know how to begin."

"To be sure you must have business with me, sir. You would never have come to see me without some object. Unless you come simply to complain of the boy, and that's hardly likely, sir. And, by the way, about the boy, sir: I could not explain to you in there, but here I will describe that scene to you. My tow was thicker a week ago—I mean my beard, sir. That's the nickname they give to my beard, the schoolboys most of all. Well, your brother Dmitri Fyodorovich was pulling me by my beard, I'd done nothing, he was in a towering rage and happened to come upon me. He dragged me out of the tavern into the marketplace; at that moment the boys were coming out of school, and with them Ilyusha. As soon as he saw me in such a state, sir, he rushed up to me. 'Dad,' he cried, 'dad!' He caught hold of me, hugged me, tried to pull me away, crying to my assailant, 'Let go, let go, it's my dad, forgive him!'— yes, he actually cried 'forgive him.' He clutched at that hand, that very hand, in his little hands and kissed it, sir. . . . I remember his little face at that moment. I haven't forgotten it, sir, and I never shall!"

"I swear," cried Alyosha, "that my brother will express his most deep and sincere regret, even if he has to go down on his knees in that same marketplace. . . . I'll make him or he is no brother of mine!"

"Aha, then it's only a draft project! And it does not come from him but simply from the generosity of your own warm heart, sir. You should have said so, sir. No, in that case allow me to tell you of your brother's highly chivalrous soldierly generosity, for he did give expression to it at the time, sir. He stopped dragging me by my beard and released me: 'You are an officer,' he said, 'and I am an officer, if you can find a decent man to be your second send me your challenge. I will give you satisfaction, though you are a scoundrel.' That's what he said, sir. A chivalrous spirit indeed! I retired with Ilyusha, and that scene is a family record imprinted forever on Ilyusha's soul. No, it's not for us to claim the privileges of noblemen. Judge for yourself, sir. You've just been in our mansion, sir, what did you see there? Three ladies, one a cripple and weak-minded, another a cripple and hunchback and the third not crippled but far too clever. She is a student, sir, dying to get back to Petersburg, to work for the emancipation of the Russian woman on the banks of the Neva. I won't speak of Ilyusha, sir, he is only nine. I am alone in the world, and if I die, what will become of all of them, I simply ask you that, sir. And if I challenge him and he kills me on the spot, what then? What will become of them? And worse still, if he doesn't kill me but only cripples me: I couldn't work, but I should still be a mouth to feed. Who would feed it and who would feed them all? Must I take Ilyusha from school and send him to beg in the streets? That's what it means for me to challenge him to a duel, sir. It's silly talk, sir, and nothing else, sir."

"He will beg your forgiveness, he will bow down at your feet in the middle of the marketplace," cried Alyosha again, with glowing eyes.

"I did think of prosecuting him," the captain went on, "but look in our code, could I get much compensation for a personal injury? And then Agrafena Alexandrovna[5] sent for me and shouted at me: 'Don't dare to dream of it! If you proceed against him, I'll publish it to all the world that he beat you for your dishonesty, and then you will be prosecuted.' I call God to witness, sir, whose was the dishonesty and by whose commands I acted, wasn't it by her own and Fyodor Pavlovich's? 'And what's more,' she went on, 'I'll dismiss you for good and you'll never earn another penny from me. I'll speak to my merchant too'—that's what she calls her old man—'and he will dismiss you!' And if he dismisses me, what can I earn then from anyone? Those two are all I have to look to, for your Fyodor Pavlovich has not only stopped employing me, for another reason, sir, but he means to make use of papers I've signed to go to law against me. And so I kept quiet, sir, and you have seen our retreat. But now let me ask you: did Ilyusha hurt your finger much? I didn't like to go into it in our mansion before him."

"Yes, very much, and he was in a great fury. He was avenging you on me as a Karamazov, I see that now. But if only you had seen how he was throwing stones at his schoolfellows! It's very dangerous. They might kill him. They are children and stupid. A stone may be thrown and break somebody's head."

"That's just what has happened, sir. He has been bruised by a stone today. Not on the head but on the chest, sir, just above the heart. He came home crying and groaning and now he is ill."

"And you know he attacks them first. He is bitter against them on your account. They say he stabbed a boy called Krasotkin with a penknife not long ago."

"I've heard about that too, it's dangerous, sir. Krasotkin is an official here, we may hear more about it, sir."

5. Grushenka.

"I would advise you," Alyosha went on warmly, "not to send him to school at all for a time till he is calmer . . . and his anger is passed."

"Anger!" the captain repeated, "that's just what it is, sir. He is a little creature, sir, but it's a mighty anger. You don't know all, sir. Permit me to explain that story to you in detail. Since that incident all the boys have been teasing him about the 'wisp of tow.' School-boys are a merciless race, individually they are angels of God, but together, especially in schools, they are often merciless. Their teasing has stirred up a gallant spirit in Ilyusha. An ordinary boy, a weak son, would have submitted, have felt ashamed of his father, sir, but he stood up for his father against them all. For his father and for truth and justice, sir. For what he suffered when he kissed your brother's hand and cried to him 'forgive daddy, forgive daddy,'—that only God knows—and I, sir, his father. For our children—that is, not your children, but ours—the children of the poor gentlemen looked down upon by everyone—know what justice means, sir, even at the age of nine. How should the rich know? They don't explore such depths once in their lives. But at that moment in the square when he kissed his hand, at that moment my Ilyushka had grasped all that justice means, sir. That truth entered into him and crushed him forever, sir," the captain said hotly again with a sort of frenzy, and he struck his right fist against his left palm as though he wanted to show how "the truth" crushed Ilyusha. "That very day, sir, he fell ill with fever and was delirious all night. All that day he hardly said a word to me, sir, but I noticed he kept watching me from the corner, though he turned to the window and pretended to be learning his lessons. But I could see his mind was not on his lessons. Next day I got drunk to forget my troubles, sinful man as I am, sir, and I don't remember much. Mamma began crying, too—I am very fond of mamma, sir—well, I spent my last penny drowning my troubles. Don't despise me for that, sir, in Russia men who drink are the best. The best men among us are the greatest drunkards. I lay down and I don't remember about Ilyusha, though all that day the boys had been jeering at him at school, sir, 'Wisp of tow,' they shouted, 'your father was pulled out of the tavern by his wisp of tow, you ran by and begged forgiveness.'

"On the third day when he came back from school, I saw he looked pale and wretched. 'What is it?' I asked. He wouldn't answer. Well, there's no talking in our mansion without mamma and the girls taking part in it. What's more the girls had heard about it the very first day. Barbara Nikolavna had begun snarling. 'You fools and buffoons, can you ever do anything rational?' 'Quite so,' I said, 'can we ever do anything rational?' For the time I turned it off like that, sir. So in the evening I took the boy out for a walk, for you must know we go for a walk every evening, always the same way, along which we are going now—from our gate to that great stone which lies alone in the road under the hurdle, which marks the beginning of the town pasture. A beautiful and lonely spot, sir. Ilyusha and I walked along hand in hand as usual. He has a little hand, his fingers are thin and cold—he suffers with his chest, you know. 'Dad,' said he, 'dad!' 'Well?' said I. I saw his eyes flashing. 'Dad, how he treated you then!' 'It can't be helped, Ilyusha,' I said. 'Don't forgive him, dad, don't forgive him! At school they say that he has paid you ten rubles for it.' 'No, Ilyusha,' said I, 'I would not take money from him for anything.' Then he began trembling all over, took my hand in both his and kissed it again. 'Dad,' he said, 'dad, challenge him to a duel, at school they say you are a coward and won't challenge him, and that you'll accept ten rubles from him.' 'I can't challenge him to a duel, Ilyusha,' I answered. And I told briefly what I've just told you. He listened. 'Dad,' he said, 'anyway don't forgive it. When I grow up I'll call him out myself and kill him.' His eyes shone and glowed. And of course I am his father, and I had to put in a word: 'It's a sin to kill,' I said, 'even in a duel,' 'Dad,' he said, 'when I grow up, I'll knock him down, knock the sword out of his hand, I'll fall on him, wave my sword over him and say: "I could kill you, but I forgive you, so there!" ' You see what the workings of his little mind have been during these two days; he must have been planning that vengeance all day, and raving about it at night, sir.

"But he began to come home from school badly beaten, I found out about it the day before yesterday, and you are right, sir. I won't send him to that school any more. I heard that he was standing up against all the class alone and defying them all, that his heart was full of resentment, of bitterness—I was alarmed about him. We went for another walk. 'Dad,' he asked, 'are the rich people stronger than any one else on earth?' 'Yes, Ilyusha,' I said, 'there are no people on earth stronger than the rich.' 'Dad,' he said, 'I will get rich, I will become an officer and conquer everybody. The Tsar will reward me, I will come back here and then no one will dare.' . . . Then he was silent and his lips still kept trembling, 'Dad,' he said, 'what a horrid town this is.' 'Yes, Ilyushechka,' I said, 'it isn't a very nice town.' 'Dad, let us move into another town, a nice one,' he said, 'where people don't know about us.' 'We will move, we will, Ilyusha,' said I, 'only I must save up for it.' I was glad to be able to turn his mind from painful thoughts, and we began to dream of how we would move to another town, how we would buy a horse and cart. 'We will put mamma and your sisters inside, we will cover them up and we'll walk, you shall have a lift now and then, and I'll walk beside, for we must take care of our horse, we can't all ride. That's how we'll go.' He was enchanted at that, most of all at the thought of having a horse and driving him. For of course a Russian boy is born among horses. We chattered a long while. Thank God, I thought, I have diverted his mind and comforted him.

"That was the day before yesterday, in the evening, but last night everything was changed. He had gone to school in the morning, he came back depressed, terribly depressed. In the evening I took him by the hand and we went for a walk; he would not talk. There was a wind blowing and no sun, and a feeling of autumn; twilight was coming on. We walked along, both of us depressed. 'Well, my boy,' said I, 'how about our setting off on our travels?' I thought I might bring him back to our talk of the day before. He didn't answer, but I felt his fingers trembling in my hand. Ah, I thought, it's a bad job; there's something new. We had reached the stone where we are now. I sat down on the stone. And in the air there were lots of kites flapping and whirling. There were as many as thirty in sight. Of course, it's just the season for the kites, sir. 'Look, Ilyusha,' said I, 'it's time we got out our last year's kite again. I'll mend it, where have you put it away?' My boy made no answer. He looked away and turned sideways to me. And then a gust of wind blew up the sand. He suddenly fell on me, threw both his little arms round my neck and held me tight. You know, when children are silent and proud, and try to keep back their tears when they are in great trouble and suddenly break down, their tears fall in streams, sir. With those warm streams of tears, sir, he suddenly wetted my face. He sobbed and shook as though he were in convulsions, and squeezed me up against him as I sat on the stone. 'Daddy,' he kept crying, 'Daddy, darling daddy, how he insulted you!' And I sobbed too, sir. We sat shaking in each other's arms. 'Daddy,' he said, 'daddy.' 'Ilyusha,' I said to him, 'Ilyusha darling.' No one saw us then, sir. God alone saw us, I hope he will enter it on my service record, sir. You must thank your brother, sir, Alexey Fyodorovich. No, sir, I won't thrash my boy for your satisfaction, sir."

He had gone back to his original tone of resentful buffoonery. Alyosha felt though that he trusted him, and that if there had been someone else in his, Alyosha's place, the man would not have spoken so openly and would not have told what he had just told. This encouraged Alyosha, whose soul was trembling on the verge of tears.

"Ah, how I would like to make friends with your boy!" he cried, "If you could arrange it——"

"Certainly, sir," muttered the captain.

"But now listen to something quite different!" Alyosha went on. "I have a message for you. That same brother of mine, Dmitri, has insulted his betrothed, too, a noble-hearted girl of whom you have probably heard. I have a right to tell you of her wrong; I ought to do so, in fact, for hearing of the insult done to you and learning all about your unfortunate position, she commissioned me at once——

just now—to bring you this help from her—but only from her alone, not from Dmitri, who has abandoned her. Nor from me, his brother, nor from anyone else, but from her, only from her! She entreats you to accept her help. . . . You have both been insulted by the same man. She thought of you only when she had just received a similar insult from him—similar in its cruelty, I mean. She comes like a sister to help a brother in misfortune. . . . She told me to persuade you to take these two hundred rubles from her, as from a sister, knowing that you are in such need. No one will know if it, it can give rise to no unjust slander. There are the two hundred rubles, and I swear you must take them unless—unless all men are to be enemies on earth! But there are brothers even on earth. . . . You have a generous heart, . . . you must see that, you must."

And Alyosha held out two new rainbow-colored hundred-ruble bills. They were both standing at the time by the great stone close to the fence, and there was no one near. The bills seemed to produce a tremendous impression on the captain. He started, but at first only from astonishment. Such an outcome of their conversation was the last thing he expected. Nothing could have been further from his dreams than help from any one—and such a sum! He took the bills, and for a minute he was almost unable to answer, quite a new expression came into his face.

"That for me? So much money—two hundred rubles! Good heavens! Why, I haven't seen so much money for the last four years! Mercy on us! And she says she is a sister . . . And is that the truth?"

"I swear that all I told you is the truth," cried Alyosha. The captain flushed red.

"Listen, sir, my dear, listen, sir, if I take it, won't I be behaving like a scoundrel? In your eyes, Alexey Fyodorovich, won't I be a scoundrel? No, Alexey Fyodorovich, listen, sir, listen," he hurried, touching Alyosha with both his hands. "You are persuading me to take it, saying that it's a sister sends it, but inwardly, in your heart won't you feel contempt for me if I take it, sir, eh?"

"No, no, on my salvation I swear I won't! And no one will ever know but me—I, you and she, and one other lady, her great friend."

"Never mind the lady! Listen, Alexey Fyodorovich, at a moment like this you must listen, sir, for you can't understand what these two hundred rubles mean to me now." The poor fellow went on rising gradually into a sort of incoherent, almost wild enthusiasm. He was thrown off his balance and talked extremely fast, as though afraid he would not be allowed to say all he had to say.

"Besides its being honestly acquired from a 'sister,' so highly respected and revered, do you know that now I can look after mamma and Nina, my hunchback angel daughter? Doctor Herzenstube came to me in the kindness of his heart and was examin-

ing them both for a whole hour. 'I can make nothing of it,' said he,
but he prescribed a mineral water which is kept at a chemist's here.
He said it would be sure to do her good, and he ordered baths, too,
with some medicine in them. The mineral water costs thirty kopecks, and she'd need to drink forty bottles perhaps; so I took the
prescription and laid it on the shelf under the icons, and there it
lies. And he ordered hot baths for Nina with something dissolved in
them, morning and evening. But how can we carry out such a cure
in our mansion, sir, without servants, without help, without a bath,
and without water? Nina is rheumatic all over, I don't think I told
you that. All her right side aches at night, she is in agony, and,
would you believe it, the angel bears it without groaning for fear of
waking us. We eat what we can get, and she'll only take the leavings,
what you'd scarcely give to a dog. 'I am not worth it, I am taking it
from you, I am a burden on you,' that's what her angel eyes try to
express. We wait on her, but she doesn't like it. 'I am a useless
cripple, no good to anyone.' As though she were not worth it, sir,
when she is the saving of all of us with her angelic sweetness.
Without her, without her gentle word it would be hell among us!
She softens even Barbara. And don't judge Barbara Nikolavna
harshly either, she is an angel too, she, too, has suffered wrong. She
came to us for the summer, and she brought sixteen rubles she had
earned by lessons and saved up, to go back with to Petersburg in
September, that is now. But we took her money and lived on it, so
now she has nothing to go back with, sir. Though indeed she
couldn't go back, for she has to work for us like a slave. She is like
an overdriven horse with all of us on her back. She waits on us all,
mends and washes, sweeps the floor, puts mamma to bed. And
mamma is capricious and tearful and insane, sir! And now I can
get a servant, sir, with this money, you understand, Alexey Fyodorovich, I can get medicines for the dear creatures, I can send my
student to Petersburg, sir, I can buy beef, I can feed them properly.
Good Lord, but it's a dream!"

Alyosha was delighted that he had brought him such happiness
and that the poor fellow had consented to be made happy.

"Wait, Alexey Fyodorovich, wait," the captain began to talk with
frenzied rapidity carried away by a new daydream. "Do you know
that Ilyusha and I will perhaps really carry out our dream. We will
buy a horse and cart, a black horse, he insists on its being black,
and we will set off as we pretended the other day. I have an old
friend, a lawyer in K—— province, sir, and I heard through a
trustworthy man that if I were to go he'd give me a place as clerk in
his office, so, who knows, maybe he would. So I'd just put mamma
and Nina in the cart, and Ilyushechka could drive, and I'd walk, I'd
walk. . . . Why, if I only succeed in getting one debt paid that's
owing me, I would have perhaps enough for that too!"

"There would be enough!" cried Alyosha. "Katerina Ivanovna will send you as much more as you need, and you know, I have money too, take what you want, as you would from a brother, from a friend, you can give it back later. . . . (You'll get rich, you'll get rich!) And you know you couldn't have a better idea than to move to another province! It would be the saving of you, especially of your boy—and you ought to go quickly, before the winter, before the cold. You must write to us when you are there, and we will always be brothers. . . . No, it's not a dream!"

Alyosha could have hugged him, he was so pleased. But glancing at him he stopped short. The man was standing with his neck outstretched and his lips protruding, with a pale and frenzied face. His lips were moving as though trying to articulate something; no sound came, but still his lips moved. It was uncanny.

"What is it?" asked Alyosha, startled.

"Alexey Fyodorovich . . . I . . . you," muttered the captain, faltering, looking at him with a strange, wild, fixed stare, and an air of desperate resolution. At the same time there was a sort of grin on his lips. "I, sir . . . you, sir . . . wouldn't you like me to show you a little trick I know, sir?" he murmured, suddenly, in a firm rapid whisper, his voice no longer faltering.

"What trick?"

"A pretty trick," whispered the captain. His mouth was twisted on the left side, his left eye was screwed up. He still stared at Alyosha.

"What is the matter, what trick?" Alyosha cried, now thoroughly alarmed.

"Why, look," squealed the captain suddenly, and showing him the two bills, which he had been holding by one corner between his thumb and forefinger during the conversation, he crumpled them up savagely and squeezed them tight in his right hand.

"Do you see, sir, do you see, sir?" he shrieked, pale and infuriated. And suddenly flinging up his hand, he threw the crumpled bills on the sand. "Do you see, sir?" he shrieked again, pointing to them. "Look there!"

And with wild fury he began trampling them under his heel, gasping and exclaiming as he did so:

"So much for your money, sir! So much for your money, sir! So much for your money, sir! So much for your money, sir!"

Suddenly he darted back and drew himself up before Alyosha, and his whole figure expressed unutterable pride.

"Tell those who sent you that the wisp of tow does not sell his honor, sir," he cried, raising his arm in the air. Then he turned quickly and began to run; but he had not run five steps before he turned completely round and kissed his hand to Alyosha. He ran another five paces and then turned round for the last time. This time his face was not contorted with laughter, but quivering all over with tears. In a tearful, faltering, sobbing voice he cried:

"What should I say to my boy if I took money from you for our shame?"

And then he ran on without turning. Alyosha looked after him, inexpressibly grieved. Oh, he saw that till the very last moment the man had not known he would crumple up and fling away the bills. He did not turn back. Alyosha knew he would not. He would not follow him and call him back, he knew why. When he was out of sight, Alyosha picked up the two bills. They were very much crushed and crumpled, and had been pressed into the sand, but were uninjured and even rustled like new ones when Alyosha unfolded them and smoothed them out. After smoothing them out, he folded them up, put them in his pocket and went to Katerina Ivanovna to report on the success of her commission.

Book Five

PRO AND CONTRA

Chapter I

An Engagement

Madame Khokhlakov was again the first to meet Alyosha. She was flustered; something important had happened. Katerina Ivanovna's hysterics had ended in a fainting fit, and then "a terrible, awful weakness had followed, she lay with her eyes turned up and was delirious. Now she was in a fever. They had sent for Herzenstube; they had sent for the aunts. The aunts were already here, but Herzenstube had not yet come. They were all sitting in her room, waiting. She was unconscious now, and what if it turned to brain fever!"

Madame Khokhlakov looked gravely alarmed. "This is serious, serious," she added at every word, as though nothing that had happened to her before had been serious. Alyosha listened with distress, and was beginning to describe his adventures, but she interrupted him at the first words. She had not time to listen. She begged him to sit with Lise and wait for her there.

"Lise," she whispered almost in his ear, "Lise has greatly surprised me just now, dear Alexey Fyodorovich. She touched me, too, and so my heart forgives her everything. Only fancy, as soon as you had gone, she began to be truly remorseful for having laughed at you today and yesterday, though she was not laughing at you, but only joking. But she was seriously sorry for it, almost ready to cry, so that I was quite surprised. She has never been really sorry for laughing at me, but has only made a joke of it. And you know she laughs at me all the time. But this time she was in earnest. She thinks a great deal of your opinion, Alexey Fyodorovich, and don't take offense or be wounded by her if you can help it. I am never hard upon her, for she's such a clever little thing—would you believe it? She said just now that you were a friend of her childhood, 'the greatest friend of her childhood'—just think of that— 'greatest friend'—and what about me? She has very strong feelings and memories, and, what's more, she uses these phrases, most unexpected words, which come out all of a sudden when you least expect them. She spoke lately about a pine tree, for instance: there used to be a pine tree standing in our garden in her early childhood.

195

Very likely it's standing there still; so there's no need to speak in the past tense. Pine trees are not like people, Alexey Fyodorovich, they don't change quickly. 'Mamma,' she said, 'I remember this pine tree and pine for it,' that is, pine tree and pine for it, she must have expressed it differently because there is something wrong there, 'pine' is a stupid word, only she said something so original about it that I can't repeat it. Besides, I've forgotten it. Well, good-bye! I am so worried I feel I shall go out of my mind. Ah! Alexey Fyodorovich, I've been out of my mind twice in my life. Go to Lise, cheer her up, as you always can so charmingly. Lise," she cried, going to her door, "here I've brought you Alexey Fyodorovich, whom you insulted so. He is not at all angry, I assure you; on the contrary, he is surprised that you could suppose so."

"*Merci, maman.* Come in, Alexey Fyodorovich."

Alyosha went in. Lise looked rather embarrassed, and at once flushed crimson. She was evidently ashamed of something, and, as people always do in such cases, she began immediately talking of other things, as though they were of absorbing interest to her at the moment.

"Mamma has just told me all about the two hundred rubles, Alexey Fyodorovich, and your taking them to that poor officer . . . and she told me all the awful story of how he had been insulted . . . and you know, although mamma muddles things . . . she always rushes from one thing to another . . . I cried when I heard. Well, did you give him the money and how is that poor man getting on?"

"The fact is I didn't give it to him, and it's a long story," answered Alyosha, as though he, too, could think of nothing but his regret at having failed, yet Lise saw perfectly well that he, too, looked away, and that he, too, was trying to talk of other things. Alyosha sat down to the table and began to tell his story, but at the first words he lost his embarrassment and gained the whole of Lise's attention as well. He spoke with deep feeling, under the influence of the strong impression he had just received, and he succeeded in telling his story well and circumstantially. In old days in Moscow he had been fond of coming to Lise and describing to her what had just happened to him, and what he had read, or what he remembered of his childhood. Sometimes they had made daydreams and woven whole romances together—generally cheerful and amusing ones. Now they both felt suddenly transported to the old days in Moscow, two years before. Lise was extremely touched by his story. Alyosha described "Ilyushechka" with warm feeling. When he finished describing how the luckless man trampled on the money, Lise could not help clasping her hands and crying out:

"So you didn't give him the money! So you let him run away! Oh, dear, you ought to have run after him!"

"No, Lise; it's better I didn't run after him," said Alyosha, getting up from his chair and walking thoughtfully across the room.

"How so? How is it better? Now they are without food and their case is hopeless."

"Not hopeless, for the two hundred rubles will still come to them. He'll take the money tomorrow. Tomorrow he will be sure to take it," said Alyosha, pacing up and down, pondering. "You see, Lise," he went on, stopping suddenly before her, "I made one blunder, but that, even that, is all for the best."

"What blunder, and why is it for the best?"

"I'll tell you. He is a man of weak and timorous character; he has suffered so much and is very good-natured. I keep wondering why he took offense so suddenly, for I assure you, up to the last minute, he did not know that he was going to trample on the bills. And I think now that there was a great deal to offend him . . . and it could not have been otherwise in his position. . . . To begin with, he was offended at having been so glad of the money in my presence and not having concealed it from me. If he had been pleased, but not so much; if he had not shown it; if he had begun affecting scruples and difficulties, as other people do when they take money, he might still endure to take it. But he was too genuinely delighted, and that was mortifying. Ah, Lise, he is a good and truthful man— that's the worst of the whole business. All the while he talked, his voice was so weak, so broken, he talked so fast, so fast, he kept laughing such a laugh, or perhaps he was crying—yes, I am sure he was crying, he was so delighted—and he talked about his daughters —and about the situation he could get in another town. . . . And when he had poured out his heart, he felt ashamed at having shown me his inmost soul like that. So he began to hate me at once. He is one of those awfully sensitive poor people. What had made him feel most ashamed was that he had given in too soon and accepted me as a friend, you see. At first he almost flew at me and tried to intimidate me, but as soon as he saw the money he had begun embracing me; he kept touching me with his hands. This must have been how he came to feel it all so humiliating, and then I made that blunder, a very important one. I suddenly said to him that if he had not money enough to move to another town, we would give it to him, and, indeed, I myself would give him as much as he wanted out of my own money. That struck him all at once. Why, he thought, did I put myself forward to help him? You know, Lise, it's awfully hard for a man who has been injured, when other people look at him as though they were his benefactors. . . . I've heard that; Father Zosima told me so. I don't know how to put it, but I have often seen it myself. And I feel like that myself, too. And the worst of it was that though he did not know, up to the very last minute, that he would trample on the bills, he had a kind of presentiment of it, I am sure of that. That's just what made him so ecstatic, that he had that presentiment.... And though it's so dreadful, it's all for the best. In fact, I believe nothing better could have happened."

"Why, why could nothing better have happened?" cried Lise, looking with great surprise at Alyosha.

"Because if he had taken the money, in an hour after getting home, he would be crying with mortification, that's just what would have happened. And most likely he would have come to me early tomorrow, and perhaps have flung the bills at me and trampled upon them as he did just now. But now he has gone home awfully proud and triumphant, though he knows he has 'ruined himself.' So now nothing could be easier than to make him accept the two hundred rubles by tomorrow, for he has already vindicated his honor, tossed away the money, and trampled it under foot.... He couldn't know when he did it that I would bring it to him again tomorrow, and yet he is in terrible need of that money. Though he is proud of himself now, yet even today he'll be thinking what a help he has lost. He will think of it more than ever at night, will dream of it, and by tomorrow morning he may be ready to run to me to ask forgiveness. It's just then that I'll appear. 'Here, you are a proud man,' I shall say: 'you have shown it; but now take the money and forgive us!' And then he will take it!"

Alyosha was carried away with joy as he uttered the last words. "And then he will take it!" Lise clapped her hands.

"Ah, that's true! I understand that perfectly now. Ah, Alyosha, how do you know all this? So young and yet he knows what's in the heart.... I should never have worked it out."

"The great thing now is to persuade him that he is on an equal footing with us, in spite of his taking money from us," Alyosha went on in his excitement, "and not only on an equal, but even on a higher footing."

" 'On a higher footing' is splendid, Alexey Fyodorovich; but go on, go on!"

"You mean there isn't such an expression as 'on a higher footing'; but that doesn't matter because——"

"Oh, no, no, of course it doesn't matter. Forgive me, Alyosha, dear.... You know, I scarcely respected you till now—that is I respected you but on an equal footing; but now I shall begin to respect you on a higher footing. Don't be angry, dear, at my joking," she put in at once, with strong feeling. "I am absurd and small, but you, you! Listen, Alexey Fyodorovich. Isn't there in all our analysis—I mean your analysis ... no, better call it ours— aren't we showing contempt for him, for that poor man—in analyzing his soul like this, as it were, from above, eh? In deciding so certainly that he will take the money?"

"No, Lise, it's not contempt," Alyosha answered, as though he had prepared himself for the question. "I was thinking of that on the way here. How can it be contempt when we are all like him, when we are all just the same as he is? For you know we are just the same, no better. If we are better, we should have been just the same in his place. . . . I don't know about you, Lise, but I consider that I have a sordid soul in many ways, and his soul is not sordid; on the contrary, full of fine feeling. . . . No, Lise, I have no contempt for him. Do you know, Lise, my elder told me once to care for most people exactly as one would for children, and for some of them as one would for the sick in hospitals."

"Ah, Alexey Fyodorovich, dear, let us care for people as we would for the sick!"

"Let us, Lise; I am ready. Though I am not altogether ready in myself. I am sometimes very impatient and at other times I don't see things. It's different with you."

"Ah, I don't believe it! Alexey Fyodorovich, how happy I am."

"I am so glad you say so, Lise."

"Alexey Fyodorovich, you are wonderfully good, but you are sometimes sort of formal. . . . And yet you are not a bit formal really. Go to the door, open it gently, and see whether mamma is listening," said Lise, in a nervous, hurried whisper.

Alyosha went, opened the door, and reported that no one was listening.

"Come here, Alexey Fyodorovich," Lise went on, flushing redder and redder. "Give me your hand—that's right. I have to make a great confession, I didn't write to you yesterday in joke, but in earnest," and she hid her eyes with her hand. It was evident that she was greatly ashamed of the confession.

Suddenly she snatched his hand and impulsively kissed it three times.

"Ah, Lise, what a good thing!" cried Alyosha joyfully. "You know, I was perfectly sure you were in earnest."

"Sure? Upon my word!" she put aside his hand, but did not leave go of it, blushing hotly, and laughing a little happy laugh. "I kiss his hand and he says, 'What a good thing.' "

But her reproach was undeserved; Alyosha, too, was greatly overcome.

"I should like to please you always, Lise, but I don't know how to do it," he muttered, blushing too.

"Alyosha, dear, you are cold and rude. Do you see? He has chosen me as his wife and is quite settled about it. He is sure I was in earnest. What a thing to say! Why, that's impertinence—that's what it is."

"Why, was it wrong of me to feel sure?" Alyosha asked, laughing suddenly.

"Ah, Alyosha, on the contrary, it was delightfully right," cried Lise, looking tenderly and happily at him. Alyosha stood still, holding her hand in his. Suddenly he stooped down and kissed her right on her lips.

"Oh, what are you doing?" cried Lise. Alyosha was terribly abashed.

"Oh, forgive me if I shouldn't. . . . Perhaps I'm awfully stupid. . . . You said I was cold, so I kissed you. . . . But I see it was stupid."

Lise laughed, and hid her face in her hands. "And in that dress!" she ejaculated in the midst of her mirth. But she suddenly ceased laughing and became serious, almost stern.

"Alyosha, we must put off kissing. We are not ready for that yet, and we shall have a long time to wait," she ended suddenly. "Tell me rather why you who are so clever, so intellectual, so observant, choose a little fool, an invalid like me? Ah, Alyosha, I am awfully happy for I don't deserve you a bit."

"You do, Lise. I shall be leaving the monastery altogether in a few days. If I go into the world, I must marry. I know that. *He* told me to marry, too. Whom could I marry better than you—and who would have me except you? I have been thinking it over. In the first place, you've known me since childhood and you've a great many qualities I haven't. You are more light-hearted than I am; above all, you are more innocent than I am. I have been brought into contact with many, many things already. . . . Ah, you don't know, but I, too, am a Karamazov. What does it matter if you do laugh and make jokes, and at me, too? Go on laughing. I am so glad you do. You laugh like a little child, but you think like a martyr."

"Like a martyr? How?"

"Yes, Lise, your question just now: whether we weren't showing contempt for that poor man by dissecting his soul—that was the question of a sufferer. . . . You see, I don't know how to express it, but anyone who thinks of such questions is capable of suffering. Sitting in your invalid chair you must have thought over many things already."

"Alyosha, give me your hand. Why are you taking it away?" murmured Lise in a failing voice, weak with happiness. "Listen, Alyosha. What will you wear when you come out of the monastery? What sort of suit? Don't laugh, don't be angry, it's very, very important to me."

"I haven't thought about the suit, Lise; but I'll wear whatever you like."

"I should like you to have a dark blue velvet coat, a white piqué waistcoat, and a soft gray felt hat. . . . Tell me, did you believe that I didn't care for you when I said I didn't mean what I wrote?"

"No, I didn't believe it."

"Oh, you insupportable person, you are incorrigible."

"You see, I knew that you—seemed to care for me, but I pretended to believe that you didn't care for me to make it—easier for you."

"That makes it worse! Worse and better than all! Alyosha, I love you terribly. Just before you came this morning, I tried my fortune. I decided I would ask you for my letter, and if you brought it out calmly and gave it to me (as might have been expected from you) it would mean that you did not love me at all, that you felt nothing, and were simply a stupid boy, good for nothing, and that I am ruined. But you left the letter at home and that cheered me. You left it behind on purpose, so as not to give it back, because you knew I would ask for it? That was it, wasn't it?"

"Ah, Lise, it was not so a bit. The letter is with me now, and it was this morning, in this pocket. Here it is."

Alyosha pulled the letter out laughing, and showed it to her at a distance.

"But I am not going to give it to you. Look at it from here."

"Why, then you told a lie? You, a monk, told a lie!"

"I told a lie if you like," Alyosha laughed, too. "I told a lie so as not to give you back the letter. It's very precious to me," he added suddenly, with strong feeling, and again he flushed. "It always will be, and I won't give it up to anyone!"

Lise looked at him joyfully. "Alyosha," she murmured again, "look at the door. Isn't mamma listening?"

"Very well, Lise, I'll look; but wouldn't it be better not to look? Why suspect your mother of such meanness?"

"What meanness? As for her spying on her daughter, it's her right, it's not meanness!" cried Lise, firing up. "You may be sure, Alexey Fyodorovich, that when I am a mother, if I have a daughter like myself I shall certainly spy on her!"

"Really, Lise? That's not right."

"Oh, my goodness! What has meanness to do with it? If she were listening to some ordinary worldly conversation, it would be meanness, but when her own daughter is shut up with a young man . . . Listen, Alyosha, do you know I shall spy upon you as soon as we are married, and let me tell you I shall open all your letters and read them, so you may as well be prepared."

"Yes, of course, if so—" muttered Alyosha, "only it's not right."

"Ah, how contemptuous! Alyosha, dear, we don't quarrel the very first day. I'd better tell you the whole truth. Of course, it's very wrong to spy on people, and, of course, I am not right and you are, only I shall spy on you all the same."

"Do, then; you won't find out anything," laughed Alyosha.

"And Alyosha, will you give in to me? We must decide that too."

"I shall be delighted to, Lise, and certain to, only not in the most important things. Even if you don't agree with me, I shall do my duty in the most important things."

"That's right; but let me tell you I am ready to give in to you not only in the most important matters, but in everything. And I am ready to vow to do so now—in everything, and for all my life!" cried Lise fervently, "and I'll do it gladly, gladly! What's more I'll swear never to spy on you, never once, never to read one of your letters. For you are right and I am not. And though I shall be awfully tempted to spy, I know that I won't do it since you consider it dishonorable. You are my conscience now. . . . Listen, Alexey Fyodorovich, why have you been so sad lately—both yesterday and today? I know you have a lot of anxiety and trouble, but I see you have some special grief besides, some secret one, perhaps?"

"Yes, Lise, I have a secret one, too," answered Alyosha mournfully. "I see you love me, since you guessed that."

"What grief? What about? Can you tell me?" asked Lise with timid entreaty.

"I'll tell you later, Lise—afterwards," said Alyosha, confused. "Now you wouldn't understand it perhaps—and perhaps I couldn't explain it."

"I know your brothers and your father are worrying you, too?"

"Yes, my brothers too," murmured Alyosha, pondering.

"I don't like your brother Ivan Fyodorovich, Alyosha," said Lise suddenly.

He noticed this remark with some surprise, but did not answer it.

"My brothers are destroying themselves," he went on, "my father, too. And they are destroying others with them. It's 'the primitive force of the Karamazovs,' as Father Païssy said the other day, a crude, unbridled, earthly force. Does the spirit of God move above that force? Even that I don't know. I only know that I, too, am a Karamazov. . . . Me a monk, a monk! Am I a monk, Lise? You said just now that I was."

"Yes, I did."

"And perhaps I don't even believe in God."

"You don't believe? What is the matter?" said Lise quietly and gently. But Alyosha did not answer. There was something too mysterious, too subjective in these last words of his, perhaps obscure to himself, but yet torturing him.

"And now on the top of it all, my friend, the best man in the world is going, is leaving the earth! If you knew, Lise, how bound up in soul I am with him! And then I shall be left alone. . . . I shall come to you, Lise. . . . For the future we will be together."

"Yes, together, together! Henceforward we shall be always together, all our lives! Listen, kiss me, I permit you to."

Alyosha kissed her.

"Well, now go. Christ be with you!" and she made the sign of the cross over him. "Make haste back to *him* while he is alive. I see I've kept you cruelly. I'll pray today for him and you. Alyosha, we shall be happy! Shall we be happy, shall we?"

"I believe we shall, Lise."

Alyosha thought it better not to go in to Madame Khokhlakov and was going out of the house without saying goodbye to her. But no sooner had he opened the door than he found Madame Khokhlakov standing before him. From the first word Alyosha guessed that she had been waiting on purpose to meet him.

"Alexey Fyodorovich, this is awful. This is all childish nonsense and ridiculous. I trust you won't dream . . . It's foolishness, foolishness, nothing but foolishness!" she said, attacking him at once.

"Only don't tell her that," said Alyosha, "or she will be upset, and that's bad for her now."

"Sensible advice from a sensible young man. Am I to understand that you only agreed with her from compassion for her invalid state, because you didn't want to irritate her by contradiction?"

"Oh, no, not at all. I was quite serious in what I said," Alyosha declared stoutly.

"To be serious about it is impossible, unthinkable, and in the first place I shall never be at home to you again, and I shall take her away, you may be sure of that."

"But why?" asked Alyosha. "It's all so far off. We may have to wait another year and a half."

"Ah, Alexey Fyodorovich, that's true, of course, and you'll have time to quarrel and separate a thousand times in a year and a half. But I am so unhappy, so unhappy! Though it's such nonsense, it's a great blow to me. I feel like Famusov in the last scene of *Woe from Wit*.[1] You are Chatsky and she is Sofya, and, only fancy, I've run down to meet you on the stairs, and in the play the fatal scene takes place on the staircase. I heard it all; I almost dropped. So this is the explanation of her dreadful night and her hysterics of late! It means love to the daughter but death to the mother. I might as well be in my grave at once. And a more serious matter still, what is this letter she has written? Show it me at once, at once!"

"No, there's no need. Tell me, how is Katerina Ivanovna now? I must know."

"She still lies in delirium; she has not regained consciousness. Her aunts are here; but they do nothing but sigh and give themselves airs. Herzenstube came, and he was so alarmed that I didn't know what to do for him. I nearly sent for a doctor to look after him. He was driven home in my carriage. And on top of it all, you and this letter! It's true nothing can happen for a year and half. In

1. A famous comedy by A. S. Griboedov (1823).

the name of all that's holy, in the name of your dying elder, show me that letter, Alexey Fyodorovich. I'm her mother. Hold it in your hand, if you like, and I will read it so."

"No, I won't show it to you, Katerina Osipovna. Even if she sanctioned it, I wouldn't. I am coming tomorrow, and if you like, we can talk over many things, but now goodbye!"

And Alyosha ran downstairs and into the street.

Chapter II

Smerdyakov with a Guitar

He had no time to lose indeed. Even while he was saying goodbye to Lise, the thought had struck him that he must attempt some stratagem to find his brother Dmitri, who was evidently keeping out of his way. It was getting late, nearly three o'clock. Alyosha's whole soul turned to the monastery, to his dying elder, but the necessity of seeing Dmitri outweighed everything. The conviction that a great inevitable catastrophe was about to happen grew stronger in Alyosha's mind with every hour. What that catastrophe was, and what he would say at that moment to his brother, he could perhaps not have said definitely. "Even if my benefactor must die without me, anyway I won't have to reproach myself all my life with the thought that I might have saved something and did not, but passed by and hastened home. If I do as I intend, I shall be following his great precept."

His plan was to catch his brother Dmitri unawares, to climb over the fence, as he had the day before, get into the garden and sit in the gazebo. If Dmitri were not there, thought Alyosha, he would not announce himself to Thomas or the women of the house, but would remain hidden in the gazebo, even if he had to wait there till evening. If, as before, Dmitri were lying in wait for Grushenka to come, he would be very likely to come to the gazebo. Alyosha did not, however, give much thought to the details of his plan, but resolved to act upon it, even if it meant not getting back to the monastery that day.

Everything happened without hindrance; he climbed over the hurdle almost in the same spot as the day before, and stole into the gazebo unseen. He did not want to be noticed. The women of the house and Thomas too, if he were here, might be loyal to his brother and obey his instructions, and so refuse to let Alyosha come into the garden, or might warn Dmitri that he was being sought and inquired for.

There was no one in the gazebo. Alyosha sat down and began to wait. He looked round the gazebo, which somehow struck him as a great deal more ancient than before. Though the day was just as fine as yesterday, it seemed a wretched little place this time. There was a circle on the table, left no doubt from the glass of brandy having been spilt the day before. Foolish and irrelevant ideas strayed about his mind, as they always do in a time of tedious waiting. He wondered, for instance, why he had sat down precisely in the same place as before, why not in the other seat. At last he felt very depressed—depressed by suspense and uncertainty. But he had not sat there more than a quarter of an hour, when he suddenly heard the strumming of a guitar somewhere quite close. People were sitting, or had only just sat down, somewhere in the bushes not more than twenty paces away. Alyosha suddenly recollected that on coming out of the gazebo the day before, he had caught a glimpse of an old green low garden seat among the bushes on the left, by the fence. The people must be sitting on it now. Who were they?

A young man's voice suddenly began singing in a sugary falsetto, accompanying himself on the guitar:

> With invincible force
> I am bound to my dear.
> Oh, Lord, have mercy
> On her and on me!
> On her and on me!
> On her and on me![2]

The voice ceased. It was a lackey's tenor and a lackey's song. Another voice, a woman's, suddenly asked insinuatingly and bashfully, though with mincing affectation:

"Why haven't you been to see us for so long, Pavel Fyodorovich? Why do you always look down upon us?"

"Not at all, ma'am," answered a man's voice politely, but with emphatic dignity. It was clear that the man had the best of the position, and that the woman was making advances. "I believe the man must be Smerdyakov," thought Alyosha, "from his voice. And the lady must be the daughter of the house here, who has come from Moscow, the one who wears the dress with a train and goes to Martha for soup."

"I am awfully fond of verses of all kinds, if they rhyme," the woman's voice continued. "Why don't you go on?"

The man sang again:

> What do I care for royal wealth
> If but my dear one be in health?
> Lord have mercy
> On her and on me!
> On her and on me!
> On her and on me!

2. See Dostoevsky's letter to Lyubimov, May 10, 1879.

"It was even better last time," observed the woman's voice. "You sang 'If my darling be in health'; it sounded more tender. I suppose you've forgotten today."

"Poetry is rubbish, ma'am!" said Smerdyakov curtly.

"Oh, no! I am very fond of poetry."

"So far as it's poetry, it's essential rubbish, ma'am. Consider yourself, who ever talks in rhyme? And if we were all to talk in rhyme, even though it were decreed by government, we shouldn't say much, ma'am, should we? Poetry is no good, Marya Kondratyevna."

"How clever you are! How is it you've gone so deep into everything?" The woman's voice was more and more insinuating.

"I could have done better than that, ma'am. I could have known more than that, if it had not been for my destiny from my childhood up. I would have shot a man in a duel if he called me names because I am descended from the stinking one and have no father. And they used to throw it in my teeth in Moscow. It had reached them from here, thanks to Grigory Vasilyevich, ma'am. Grigory Vasilyevich blames me for rebelling against my birth, 'You rent her womb,' he says, but I would have sanctioned their killing me before I was born that I might not have come into the world at all, ma'am. They used to say in the market, and your mamma too, with great lack of delicacy, set off telling me that her hair was like a mat on her head, and that she was short of five foot by '*a wee bit*.' Why talk of '*a wee bit*' while she might have said 'a little bit,' like everyone else? She wanted to make it touching, like a peasant's tear, ma'am, so to speak, a regular peasant's feeling. Can a Russian peasant be said to feel, in comparison with an educated man? He can't be said to have feeling at all, in his ignorance. From my childhood up when I hear 'a wee bit,' I am ready to burst with rage. I hate all Russia, Marya Kondratyevna."

"If you'd been a cadet in the army, or a young hussar, you wouldn't have talked like that, but would have drawn your saber to defend all Russia."

"I don't want to be a hussar, Marya Kondratyevna, and, what's more, I should like to abolish all soldiers."

"And when an enemy comes, who is going to defend us?"

"There's no need of defense. In 1812 there was a great invasion of Russia by Napoleon, first Emperor of the French, father of the present one,[3] and it would have been a good thing if they had conquered us. A clever nation would have conquered a very stupid one and annexed it, ma'am. We should have had quite different institutions, ma'am."

"Are they so much better in their own country than we are? I

3. Napolean III was the nephew of Napoleon I.

wouldn't change a dandy I know of for three young Englishmen," observed Marya Kondratyevna tenderly, doubtless accompanying her words with a most languishing glance.

"That's as one prefers, ma'am."

"But you are just like a foreigner—just like a most gentlemanly foreigner. I tell you that, though it makes me bashful."

"If you care to know, the folks there and ours here are just alike in their vice. They are swindlers, ma'am, only there the scoundrel wears polished boots and here he stinks in filth and sees no harm in it. The Russian people want thrashing, ma'am, as Fyodor Pavlovich said very truly yesterday, though he is mad, and all his children."

"You said yourself you had such a respect for Ivan Fyodorovich."

"But he said I was a stinking lackey. He thinks that I might revolt. He is mistaken there. If I had a certain sum in my pocket, I would have left here long ago. Dmitri Fyodorovich is lower than any lackey in his behavior, in his mind, and in his poverty, ma'am. He doesn't know how to do anything, and yet he is respected by everyone. I may be only a soup maker, but with luck I could open a café restaurant on the Petrovka, in Moscow, for my cookery is something special, and there's no one in Moscow, except the foreigners, whose cookery is anything special. Dmitri Fyodorovich is a beggar, but if he were to challenge the son of the first count in the country, he'd fight him, ma'am. Though in what way is he better than I am? For he is ever so much stupider than I am. Look at the money he has wasted without any need!"

"It must be lovely, a duel," Marya Kondratyevna observed suddenly.

"How so, ma'am?"

"It must be so dreadful and so brave, especially when young officers with pistols in their hands pop at one another for the sake of some lady. A perfect picture! Ah, if only girls were allowed to look on, I'd give anything to see one!"

"It's all very well when you are firing at someone, but when he is firing straight in your mug, you must feel pretty silly. You'd be glad to run away, Marya Kondratyevna."

"You don't mean you would run away?"

But Smerdyakov did not deign to reply. After a moment's silence the guitar sounded again, and he sang again in the same falsetto:

> Whatever you may say,
> I shall go far away.
> Life will be bright and gay
> In the city far away.
> I shall not grieve,
> I shall not grieve at all,
> I don't intend to grieve at all.

Then something unexpected happened. Alyosha suddenly sneezed. They were silent. Alyosha got up and walked towards them. He found Smerdyakov dressed up and wearing polished boots, his hair pomaded, and perhaps curled. The guitar lay on the garden seat. His companion was the daughter of the house, wearing a light blue dress with a train two yards long. She was young and would not have been bad-looking, but that her face was so round and terribly freckled.

"Will my brother Dmitri soon be back?" asked Alyosha with as much composure as he could.

Smerdyakov got up slowly; Marya Kondratyevna rose too.

"How am I to know about Dmitri Fyodorovich? It's not as if I were his keeper," answered Smerdyakov quietly, distinctly, and superciliously.

"But I simply asked whether you do know?" Alyosha explained.

"I know nothing of his whereabouts and don't want to, sir."

"But my brother told me that you let him know all that goes on in the house, and promised to let him know when Agrafena Alexandrovna comes."

Smerdyakov turned a deliberate, unmoved glance upon him.

"And how did you get in this time, since the gate was bolted an hour ago?" he asked, looking at Alyosha.

"I came in from the back alley, over the fence, and went straight to the gazebo. I hope you'll forgive me," he added, addressing Marya Kondratyevna. "I was in a hurry to find my brother."

"Ach, as though we could take it amiss in you!" drawled Marya Kondratyevna, flattered by Alyosha's apology. "For Dmitri Fyodorovich often goes to the gazebo in that way. We don't know he is here and he is sitting in the gazebo."

"I am very anxious to find him or to learn from you where he is now. Believe me, it's on business of great importance to him."

"He never tells us," lisped Marya Kondratyevna.

"Though I used to come here as a friend," Smerdyakov began again, "Dmitri Fyodorovich has pestered me in a merciless way even here by his incessant questions about the master. 'What news?' he'll ask. 'What's going on in there now? Who's coming and going?' and can't I tell him something more. Twice already he's threatened me with death."

"With death?" Alyosha exclaimed in surprise.

"Do you suppose he'd think much of that, with his temper, which you had a chance of observing yourself yesterday? He says if I let Agrafena Alexandrovna in and she passes the night there, I'll be the first to suffer for it. I am terribly afraid of him, sir, and if I were not even more afraid of doing so, I ought to let the police know. God only knows what he might not do, sir!"

"His honor said to him the other day, 'I'll pound you in a mortar!' " added Marya Kondratyevna.

"Oh, if it's pounding in a mortar, it may be only talk," observed Alyosha. "If I could meet him, I might speak to him about that too."

"Well, the only thing I can tell you is this," said Smerdyakov, as though thinking better of it; "I am here as an old friend and neighbor, and it would be odd if I didn't come. On the other hand, Ivan Fyodorovich sent me first thing this morning to your brother's lodging on Lake Street, without a letter, sir, but with a message to Dmitri Fyodorovich to go to dine with him at the restaurant here, in the marketplace. I went, sir, but didn't find Dmitri Fyodorovich at home, though it was eight o'clock. 'He's been here, but he is quite gone,' those were the very words of his landlady. It's as though there was an understanding between them, sir. Perhaps at this moment he is in the restaurant with Ivan Fyodorovich, for Ivan Fyodorovich has not been home to dinner and Fyodor Pavlovich dined alone an hour ago, and has gone to lie down. But I beg you most particularly not to speak of me and of what I have told you, for he'd kill me for nothing at all, sir."

"Brother Ivan invited Dmitri to the restaurant today?" repeated Alyosha quicky.

"Just so, sir."

"The Metropolis tavern in the marketplace?"

"The very same, sir."

"That's quite likely," cried Alyosha, much excited. "Thank you, Smerdyakov; that's important. I'll go there at once."

"Don't betray me, sir," Smerdyakov called after him.

"Oh, no, I'll go to the tavern as though by chance. Don't be anxious."

"But wait a minute, I'll open the gate to you," cried Marya Kondratyevna.

"No; it's a short cut, I'll get over the fence again."

What he had heard threw Alyosha into great agitation. He ran to the tavern. It was impossible for him to go into the tavern in his monastic dress, but he could inquire at the entrance for his brothers and call them down. But just as he reached the tavern, a window was flung open, and his brother Ivan called down to him from it.

"Alyosha, can you come up here to me now or not? I would be awfully grateful."

"To be sure I can, only I don't quite know whether in this dress . . ."

"But I am in a room apart. Come up the steps; I'll run down to meet you."

A minute later Alyosha was sitting beside his brother. Ivan was alone, dining.

Chapter III

The Brothers Get Acquainted

Ivan was not, however, in a separate room, but only in a place shut off by a screen, so that it was unseen by other people in the room. It was the first room from the entrance with a buffet along the wall. Waiters were continually darting to and fro in it. The only customer in the room was an old retired military man drinking tea in a corner. But there was the usual bustle going on in the other rooms of the tavern; there were shouts for the waiters, the sound of bottles being opened, the click of billiard balls, the drone of the organ. Alyosha knew that Ivan did not usually visit this tavern and disliked taverns in general. So he must have come here, he reflected, simply to meet his brother Dmitri by arrangement. Yet Dmitri was not there.

"Shall I order you fish soup, or anything? You don't live by tea alone, I suppose," cried Ivan, apparently delighted at having got hold of Alyosha. He had finished dinner and was drinking tea.

"Let me have fish soup, and tea afterwards; I am hungry," said Alyosha gaily.

"And cherry jam? They have it here. You remember how you used to love cherry jam at the Polyonovs' when you were little?"

"You remember that? Let me have jam too; I like it still."

Ivan called for the waiter and ordered fish soup, jam and tea.

"I remember everything, Alyosha; I remember you till you were eleven, I was nearly fifteen. There's such a difference between fifteen and eleven that brothers are never friends at those ages. I don't know whether I was fond of you even. When I went away to Moscow for the first few years I never thought of you at all. Then, when you came to Moscow yourself, we only met once somewhere, I believe. And now I've been here more than three months, and so far we have scarcely said a word to each other. Tomorrow I am going away, and I was just thinking as I sat here how I could see you to say good-bye and just then you passed."

"Were you very anxious to see me then?"

"Very, I want to get to know you once for all, and I want you to know me. And then to say goodbye. I believe it's always best to get to know people just before leaving them. I've noticed how you've been looking at me these three months. There has been a continual look of expectation in your eyes, and I can't endure that. That's how it is I've kept away from you. But in the end I have learned to respect you. The little man stands firm, I thought. Though I am laughing, I am serious. You do stand firm, don't you? I like people who are firm like that whatever it is they stand by, even if they are such little fellows as you. Your expectant eyes ceased to annoy me, I grew fond of them in the end, those expectant eyes. You seem to love me for some reason, Alyosha?"

"I do love you, Ivan. Brother Dmitri says of you—Ivan is a tomb! I say of you, Ivan is a riddle. You are a riddle to me even now. But I understand something in you, and I did not understand it till this morning."

"What's that?" laughed Ivan.

"You won't be angry?" Alyosha laughed too.

"Well?"

"That you are just as young as other young men of twenty-three, that you are just a young and fresh and nice boy, green in fact! Now, have I insulted you dreadfully?"

"On the contrary, I am struck by a coincidence," cried Ivan, warmly and good-humoredly. "Would you believe it that ever since that scene with her, I have thought of nothing else but my youthful greenness, and just as though you guessed that, you begin about it. Do you know I've been sitting here thinking to myself: that if I didn't believe in life, if I lost faith in the woman I love, lost faith in the order of things, were convinced in fact that everything is a disorderly, damnable, and perhaps devil-ridden chaos, if I were struck by every horror of man's disillusionment—still I should want to live and, having once tasted of the cup, I would not turn away from it till I had drained it! At thirty, though, I shall be sure to fling down the cup, even if I've not emptied it, and turn away—where I don't know. But till I am thirty, I know that my youth will triumph over everything—every disillusionment, every disgust with life. I've asked myself many times whether there is in the world any despair that would overcome this frantic and perhaps unseemly thirst for life in me, and I've come to the conclusion that there isn't, that is till I am thirty, and then I shall lose it of myself, I fancy. Some driveling consumptive moralists—and poets especially—often call that thirst for life base. It's a feature of the Karamazovs it's true, that thirst for life regardless of everything; you have it no doubt too, but why is it base? The centripetal force on our planet is still fearfully strong, Alyosha. I have a longing for life, and I go on living in spite of logic. Though I may not believe in the order of the universe, yet I love the sticky little leaves as they open in spring.[4] I love the blue sky, I love some people, whom one loves you know sometimes without knowing why. I love some great deeds done by men, though I've long ceased perhaps to have faith in them, yet from old habit one's heart prizes them. Here they have brought the soup for you, eat it, it will do you good. It's first-rate soup, they know how to make it here. I want to travel in Europe, Alyosha, I

---

4. The expression occurs in Pushkin's poem "Chill Winds Still Blow" (1828).

shall set off from here. And yet I know that I am only going to a graveyard, but it's a most precious graveyard, that's what it is! Precious are the dead that lie there, every stone over them speaks of such burning life in the past, of such passionate faith in their work, their truth, their struggle and their science, that I know I shall fall on the ground and kiss those stones and weep over them; though I'm convinced in my heart that it's long been nothing but a graveyard. And I shall not weep from despair, but simply because I shall be happy in my tears, I shall steep my soul in my emotion. I love the sticky leaves in spring, the blue sky—that's all it is. It's not a matter of intellect or logic, it's loving with one's inside, with one's guts. One loves the first strength of one's youth. Do you understand anything of my tirade, Alyosha?" Ivan laughed suddenly.

"I understand too well, Ivan. One longs to love with one's inside, with one's guts. You said that so well and I am awfully glad that you have such a longing for life," cried Alyosha. "I think every one should love life above everything in the world."

"Love life more than the meaning of it?"

"Certainly, love it, regardless of logic as you say, it must be regardless of logic, and it's only then one will understand the meaning of it. I have thought so a long time. Half your work has been done and has been acquired, Ivan, you love life, now you've only to try to do the second half and you are saved."

"You are trying to save me, but perhaps I am not lost! And what does your second half mean?"

"Why, one has to raise up your dead, who perhaps have not died after all. Come, let me have tea. I am so glad of our talk, Ivan."

"I see you are feeling inspired. I am awfully fond of such *professions de foi*[5] from such—novices. You are a steadfast person, Alexey. Is it true that you mean to leave the monastery?"

"Yes, my elder sends me out into the world."

"We shall see each other then in the world. We shall meet before I am thirty, when I shall begin to turn aside from the cup. Father doesn't want to turn aside from his cup till he is seventy, he dreams of hanging on to eighty in fact, so he says. He means it only too seriously, though he is a buffoon. He stands on a firm rock, too, he stands on his sensuality—though after we are thirty, indeed, there may be nothing else to stand on. . . . But to hang on to seventy is nasty, better only to thirty; one might retain 'a shadow of nobility' by deceiving oneself. Have you seen Dmitri today?"

"No, but I saw Smerdyakov," and Alyosha rapidly, though minutely, described his meeting with Smerdyakov. Ivan began listening anxiously and questioned him.

"But he begged me not to tell brother Dmitri that he had told me about him," added Alyosha. Ivan frowned and pondered.

5. Professions of faith.

"Are you frowning on Smerdyakov's account?" asked Alyosha.

"Yes, on his account. Damn him, I certainly did want to see Dmitri, but now there's no need," said Ivan reluctantly.

"But are you really going so soon, brother?"

"Yes."

"What of Dmitri and father? how will it end?" asked Alyosha anxiously.

"You are always harping upon it! What have I to do with it? Am I my brother Dmitri's keeper?" Ivan snapped irritably, but then he suddenly smiled bitterly. "Cain's answer to God, about his murdered brother, wasn't it? Perhaps that's what you're thinking at this moment? Well, damn it all, I can't stay here to be their keeper, can I? I've finished what I had to do, and I am going. Do you imagine I am jealous of Dmitri, that I've been trying to steal his beautiful Katerina Ivanovna for the last three months? Oh, hell, I had business of my own. I finished it. I am going. I finished it just now, you were witness."

"At Katerina Ivanovna's?"

"Yes, and I've released myself once for all. And after all, what have I to do with Dmitri? Dmitri doesn't come in. I had my own business to settle with Katerina Ivanovna. You know, on the contrary, that Dmitri behaved as though there was an understanding between us. I didn't ask him to do it, but he solemnly handed her over to me and gave us his blessing. It's all too funny. Ah, Alyosha, if you only knew how light my heart is now! Would you believe it, I sat here eating my dinner and almost ordered champagne to celebrate my first hour of freedom. Whew! It's been going on nearly six months, and all at once I've thrown it off. I could never have guessed even yesterday, how easy it would be to put an end to it if I wanted."

"You are speaking of your love, Ivan?"

"Of my love, if you like. I fell in love with the young lady, with the girl from the Institute, I tormented myself over her and she tormented me. I sat watching over her ... and all at once it's collapsed! I spoke this morning with inspiration, but I went away and roared with laughter. Would you believe it? Yes, it's the literal truth."

"You seem very merry about it now," observed Alyosha, looking into his face, which had suddenly grown brighter.

"But how could I tell that I didn't care for her a bit! He-he! It appears after all I didn't. And yet how she attracted me! How attractive she was just now when I made my speech! And do you know she attracts me awfully even now, yet how easy it is to leave her. Do you think I am boasting?"

"No, only perhaps it wasn't love."

"Alyoshka," laughed Ivan, "don't make reflections about love, it's unseemly for you. How you rushed into the discussion this morning! I've forgotten to kiss you for it. . . . But how she tormented me! It certainly was sitting by a 'laceration.' Ah, she knew how I loved her! She loved me and not Dmitri," Ivan insisted gaily. "Her feeling for Dmitri was simply a laceration. All I told her just now was perfectly true, but the worst of it is, it may take her fifteen or twenty years to find out that she doesn't care for Dmitri, and loves me whom she torments, and perhaps she may never find it out at all, in spite of her lesson today. Well, it's better so; I can simply go away for good. By the way, how is she now? What happened after I departed?"

Alyosha told him she had been hysterical, and that she was now, he heard, unconscious and delirious.

"Isn't Madame Khokhlakov laying it on?"

"I think not."

"I must find out. Nobody ever dies of hysterics though. They don't matter. God gave woman hysterics as a relief. I won't go to her at all. Why push myself forward again?"

"But you told her that she had never cared for you."

"I did that on purpose. Alyoshka, shall I call for some champagne? Let us drink to my freedom. Ah, if only you knew how glad I am!"

"No, brother, we had better not drink," said Alyosha suddenly. "Besides I feel somehow depressed."

"Yes, you've been depressed a long time, I've noticed it."

"Have you settled to go tomorrow morning then?"

"Morning? I didn't say I would go in the morning. . . . But perhaps it may be the morning. Would you believe it, I dined here today only to avoid dining with the old man, I loathe him so. I should have left long ago, so far as he is concerned. But why are you so worried about my going away? We've plenty of time before I go, an eternity!"

"If you are going away tomorrow, what do you mean by an eternity?"

"But what does it matter to us?" laughed Ivan. "We've time enough for our talk, for what brought us here. Why do you look so surprised? Answer: why have we met here? To talk of my love for Katerina Ivanovna? of the old man and Dmitri? of foreign travel? of the fatal position of Russia? of the Emperor Napoleon? Is that it?"

"No."

"Then you know what for. It's different for other people; but we in our green youth have to settle the eternal questions first of all. That's what we care about. The young in Russia talk of nothing but the eternal questions now. Just when the old folks are all taken up with practical questions. Why have you been looking at me in expectation for the last three months? To ask me 'what do you believe, or don't you believe at all?' That's what your eyes have been meaning for these three months, haven't they?"

"Perhaps so," smiled Alyosha. "You are not laughing at me, now, Ivan?"

"Me laughing! I don't want to wound my little brother who has been watching me with such expectation for three months. Alyosha, look straight at me! Of course I am just such a little boy as you are, only not a novice. And what have Russian boys been doing up till now, some of them, I mean? In this stinking tavern, for instance, here, they meet and sit down in a corner. They've never met in their lives before and, when they go out of the tavern, they won't meet again for forty years. And what do they talk about in that momentary halt in the tavern? Of the eternal questions, of the existence of God and immortality. And those who do not believe in God talk of socialism or anarchism, of the transformation of all humanity on a new pattern, so that it all comes to the same, they're the same questions turned inside out. And masses, masses of the most original Russian boys do nothing but talk of the eternal questions! Isn't it so?"

"Yes, for real Russians the questions of God's existence and of immortality, or, as you say, the same question turned inside out, come first and foremost, of course, and so they should," said Alyosha, still watching his brother with the same gentle and inquiring smile.

"Well, Alyosha, it's sometimes very unwise to be a Russian at all, but anything stupider than the way Russian boys spend their time one can hardly imagine. But there's one Russian boy called Alyosha I am awfully fond of."

"How nicely you put that in!" Alyosha laughed suddenly.

"Well, tell me where to begin, give your orders. The existence of God, eh?"

"Begin where you like, even 'turned inside out.' You declared yesterday at father's that there was no God." Alyosha looked searchingly at his brother.

"I said that yesterday at dinner on purpose to tease you and I saw your eyes glow. But now I've no objection to discussing it with you, and I say so very seriously. I want to be friends with you, Alyosha, for I have no friends and want to try it. Well, only fancy, perhaps I too accept God," laughed Ivan, "that's a surprise for you, isn't it?"

"Yes, of course, if you are not joking now."

"Joking? I was told at the elder's yesterday that I was joking. You know, dear boy, there was an old sinner in the eighteenth century who declared that, if there were no God, he would have to be invented. *S'il n'existait pas Dieu, il faudrait l'inventer.*[6] And

6. "If God did not exist, he would have to be invented." From an Epistle of Voltaire, 1769.

man has actually invented God. And what's strange, what would be marvelous, is not that God should really exist; the marvel is that such an idea, the idea of the necessity of God, could enter the head of such a savage, vicious beast as man. So holy it is, so touching, so wise and so great a credit it does to man. As for me, I've long resolved not to think whether man created God or God man. And I won't go through all the axioms laid down by Russian boys on that subject, all derived from European hypotheses; for what's a hypothesis there, is an axiom with the Russian boy, and not only with the boys but with their professors too, for our Russian professors are often just the same boys themselves. And so I omit all the hypotheses. For what are we aiming at now? I am trying to explain as quickly as possible my essential nature, that is what manner of man I am, what I believe in, and for what I hope, that's it, isn't it? And therefore I tell you that I accept God outright simply. But you must note this: if God exists and if He really did create the world, then, as we all know, He created it according to the geometry of Euclid and the human mind with the conception of only three dimensions in space. Yet there have been and still are geometricians and philosophers, and even some of the most distinguished, who doubt whether the whole universe, or to speak more widely the whole of being, was only created in Euclid's geometry; they even dare to dream that two parallel lines, which according to Euclid can never meet on earth, may meet somewhere in infinity.[7] I have come to the conclusion that, since I can't understand even that, I can't expect to understand about God. I acknowledge humbly that I have no faculty for settling such questions, I have a Euclidean earthly mind, and how could I solve problems that are not of this world? And I advise you never to think about it either, my dear Alyosha, especially about God, whether He exists or not. All such questions are utterly inappropriate for a mind created with an idea of only three dimensions. And so I accept God and am glad to, and what's more I accept His wisdom, His purpose—which are utterly beyond our ken; I believe in the underlying order and the meaning of life; I believe in the eternal harmony in which they say we shall one day be blended. I believe in the Word to Which the universe is striving, and Which Itself was 'with God,' and Which Itself is God and so on, and so on, to infinity. There are all sorts of phrases for it. I seem to be on the right path, don't I? Yet would you believe it, in the final result I don't accept this world of God's, and, although I know it exists, I don't accept it at all. It's not that I don't accept God, you must understand, it's the world created by Him I don't and cannot accept. Let me make it plain. I believe like a child that suffering will be healed and made up for, that all the humiliating

7. N. I. Lobachevsky first published his non-Euclidean geometry in 1826. The notion became more generally known after Lobachevsky's death in 1856.

absurdity of human contradictions will vanish like a pitiful mirage, like the despicable fabrication of the impotent and infinitely small Euclidean mind of man, that in the world's finale, at the moment of eternal harmony, something so precious will come to pass that it will suffice for all hearts, for the comforting of all resentments, for the atonement of all the crimes of humanity, of all the blood they've shed; that it will make it not only possible to forgive but to justify all that has happened with men—but though all that may come to pass, I don't accept it. I won't accept it. Even if parallel lines do meet and I see it myself, I shall see it and say that they've met, but still I won't accept it. That's what's at the root of me, Alyosha; that's my thesis. I am in earnest in what I say. I began our talk as stupidly as I could on purpose, but I've led up to my confession, for that's all you want. You didn't want to hear about God, but only to know what the brother you love lives by. And so I've told you."

Ivan concluded his long tirade with marked and unexpected feeling.

"And why did you begin 'as stupidly as you could'?" asked Alyosha, looking pensively at him.

"To begin with, for the sake of being Russian. Russian conversations on such subjects are always carried on inconceivably stupidly. And secondly, besides, the stupider, the closer to reality. The stupider, the clearer. Stupidity is brief and artless, while intelligence wriggles and hides itself. Intelligence is a scoundrel, but stupidity is honest and straightforward. I've led the conversation to my despair, and the more stupidly I have presented it, the better for me."

"Will you explain why you don't accept the world?" said Alyosha.

"To be sure I will, it's not a secret, that's what I've been leading up to. Dear little brother, I don't want to corrupt you or to turn you from your stronghold, perhaps I want to be healed by you." Ivan smiled suddenly quite like a little gentle child. Alyosha had never seen such a smile on his face before.

Chapter IV

Rebellion

"I must admit one thing to you," Ivan began. "I could never understand how one can love one's neighbors. It's just one's neighbors, to my mind, that one can't love, though one might love those at a distance. I once read somewhere of "John the Merciful,"[8] a

8. Flaubert's *The Legend of St. Julian the Hospitaler* was published in a translation by Turgenev in 1877, a dozen years after the purported time of the novel. Ivan changes the name to Ioann—that is, John (Ivan).

saint, that when a hungry, frozen beggar came to him, and asked him to warm him up, he took him into his bed, held him in his arms, and began breathing into his mouth, which was putrid and loathsome from some awful disease. I am convinced that he did that from the laceration of falsity, for the sake of the love imposed by duty, as a penance laid on him. For anyone to love a man, he must be hidden, for as soon as he shows his face, love is gone."

"Father Zosima has talked of that more than once," observed Alyosha; "he, too, said that the face of a man often hinders many people not practised in love, from loving him. But yet there's a great deal of love in mankind, and almost Christ-like love. I know that myself, Ivan."

"Well, I know nothing of it so far, and can't understand it, and the innumerable mass of mankind are with me there. The question is, whether that's due to men's bad qualities or whether it's inherent in their nature. To my thinking, Christ-like love for men is a miracle impossible on earth. He was God. But we are not gods. Suppose I, for instance, suffer intensely. Another can never know how much I suffer, because he is another and not I. And what's more, a man is rarely ready to admit another's suffering (as though it were a distinction). Why won't he admit it, do you think? Because I smell unpleasant, because I have a stupid face, because I once trod on his foot. Besides there is suffering and suffering; degrading, humiliating suffering such as humbles me—hunger, for instance—my benefactor will perhaps allow me; but when you come to higher suffering—for an idea, for instance—he will very rarely admit that, perhaps because my face strikes him not at all as what he fancies a man should have who suffers for an idea. And so he deprives me instantly of his favor, and not at all from badness of heart. Beggars, especially genteel beggars, ought never to show themselves, but to ask for charity through the newspapers. One can love one's neighbors in the abstract, or even at a distance, but at close quarters it's almost impossible. If it were as on the stage, in the ballet, where if beggars come in, they wear silken rags and tattered lace and beg for alms dancing gracefully, then one might like looking at them. But even then we would not love them. But enough of that. I simply wanted to show you my point of view. I meant to speak of the suffering of mankind generally, but we had better confine ourselves to the sufferings of the children. That reduces the scope of my argument to a tenth of what it would be. Still we'd better keep to the children, though it does weaken my case. But, in the first place, children can be loved even at close quarters, even when they are dirty, even when they are ugly (I fancy, though, children never are ugly). The second reason why I won't speak of grown-up people is that, besides being disgusting and unworthy of love, they have retribution—they've eaten the apple and know good and evil, and they have become 'like God.' They go on eating it still. But the children haven't eaten anything, and are so far innocent. Are you fond of children, Alyosha? I know you are, and you will understand why I prefer to speak of them. If they, too, suffer horribly on earth, they must suffer for their fathers, they must be punished for their fathers, who have eaten the apple; but that reasoning is of the other world and is incomprehensible for the heart of man here on earth. The innocent must not suffer for another's sins, and especially such innocents! You may be surprised at me, Alyosha, but I am awfully fond of children, too. And observe, cruel people, the violent, the rapacious, the Karamazovs are sometimes very fond of children. Children while they are quite little—up to seven, for instance—are so remote from grownup people; they are different creatures, as it were, of a different species. I knew a criminal in prison who had, in the course of his career as a burglar, murdered whole families, including several children.[9] But when he was in prison, he had a strange affection for them. He spent all his time at his window, watching the children playing in the prison yard. He trained one little boy to come up to his window and made great friends with him. . . . You don't know why I am telling you all this, Alyosha? My head aches and I am sad."

"You speak with a strange air," observed Alyosha uneasily, "as though you were not quite yourself."

"By the way, a Bulgarian I met lately in Moscow," Ivan went on, seeming not to hear his brother's words, "told me about the crimes committed by Turks and Circassians in all parts of Bulgaria through fear of a general rising of the Slavs. They burn villages, murder, rape women and children, they nail their prisoners to the fences by the ears, leave them so till morning, and in the morning they hang them—all sorts of things you can't imagine. People talk sometimes of bestial cruelty, but that's a great injustice and insult to the beast; a beast can never be so cruel as a man, so artistically, so artfully cruel. The tiger only tears and gnaws, that's all he can do. He would never think of nailing people by the ears, even if he were able to do it. These Turks took a pleasure in torturing children, too; cutting the unborn child from the mother's womb, and tossing babies up in the air and catching them on the points of their bayonets before their mother's eyes. Doing it before the mother's eyes was what gave zest to the amusement. Here is another scene that I thought very interesting. Imagine a trembling mother with her baby in her arms, a circle of invading Turks around her. They've planned a diversion; they pet the baby, laugh to make it laugh. They succeed, the baby laughs. At that moment a Turk

9. Dostoevsky relates such things in his fictionalized autobiography *Notes from*   *a Dead House.* Ivan was never in prison.

points a pistol four inches from the baby's face. The baby laughs with glee, holds out its little hands to the pistol, and he pulls the trigger in the baby's face and blows out its brains. Artistic, wasn't it? By the way, Turks are particularly fond of sweet things, they say."

"Brother, what are you driving at?" asked Alyosha.

"I think if the devil doesn't exist, but man has created him, he has created him in his own image and likeness."

"Just as he did God, then?" observed Alyosha.

"It's wonderful how you can turn words, as Polonius says in *Hamlet*," laughed Ivan. "You turn my words against me. Well, I am glad. Yours must be a fine God, if man created Him in His image and likeness. You asked just now what I was driving at. You see, I am fond of collecting certain little facts, and, would you believe, I even copy anecdotes of a certain sort from newspapers and stories, and I've already got a fine collection. The Turks, of course, have gone into it, but they are foreigners. I have specimens from home that are even better than the Turks. You know we prefer beating—rods and scourges—that's our national institution. Nailing ears is unthinkable for us, for we are, after all, Europeans. But the rod and the scourge we have always with us and they cannot be taken from us. Abroad now they scarcely do any beating. Perhaps manners are more humane, or laws have been passed, so that they don't dare to flog men now. But they make up for it in another way just as national as ours. And so national that it would be practically impossible among us, though I believe we are being inoculated with it, since the religious movement began in our aristocracy. I have a charming pamphlet, translated from the French, describing how, quite recently, five years ago, a murderer, Richard, was executed—a young man, of twenty-three, I believe, who repented and was converted to the Christian faith at the very scaffold. This Richard was an illegitimate child who was *given* as a child of six by his parents to some shepherds on the Swiss mountains. They brought him up to work for them. He grew up like a little wild beast among them. The shepherds taught him nothing, and scarcely fed or clothed him, but sent him out at age seven to herd the flock in cold and wet, and no one hesitated or scrupled to treat him so. Quite the contrary, they thought they had every right, for Richard had been given to them as a chattel, and they did not even see the necessity of feeding him. Richard himself describes how in those years, like the Prodigal Son in the Gospel, he longed to eat of the mash given to the pigs, which were fattened for sale. But they wouldn't even give him that, and beat him when he stole from the pigs. And that was how he spent all his childhood and his youth, till he grew up and was strong enough to go away and be a thief. The savage began to earn his living as a day laborer in

Geneva. He drank what he earned, he lived like a monster, and finished by killing and robbing an old man. He was caught, tried, and condemned to death. They are not sentimentalists there. And in prison he was immediately surrounded by pastors, members of Christian brotherhoods, philanthropic ladies, and the like. They taught him to read and write in prison, and expounded the Gospel to him. They exhorted him, worked upon him, drummed at him incessantly, till at last he solemnly confessed his crime. He was converted. He wrote to the court himself that he was a monster, but that in the end God had vouchsafed him light and shown grace. All Geneva was in excitement about him—all philanthropic and religious Geneva. All the aristocratic and well-bred society of the town rushed to the prison, kissed Richard and embraced him; 'You are our brother, you have found grace.' And Richard does nothing but weep with emotion, 'Yes, I've found grace! All my youth and childhood I was glad of pigs' food, but now even I have found grace. I am dying in the Lord.' 'Yes, Richard, die in the Lord; you have shed blood and must die in the Lord. Though it's not your fault that you knew not the Lord, when you coveted the pig's food and were beaten for stealing it (which was very wrong of you, for stealing is forbidden); but you've shed blood and you must die.' And on the last day, Richard, perfectly limp, did nothing but cry and repeat every minute 'This is my happiest day. I am going to the Lord.' 'Yes,' cry the pastors and the judges and philanthropic ladies. 'This is the happiest day of your life, for you are going to the Lord!' They all walk or drive to the scaffold in procession behind the prison van. At the scaffold they call to Richard: 'Die, brother, die in the Lord, for even thou hast found grace!' And so, covered with his brothers' kisses, Richard is dragged on to the scaffold, and led to the guillotine. And they chopped off his head in brotherly fashion, because he had found grace. Yes, that's characteristic. That pamphlet is translated into Russian by some Russian philanthropists of aristocratic rank and evangelical aspirations, and has been distributed gratis for the enlightenment of the people. The case of Richard is interesting because it's national. Though to us it's absurd to cut off a man's head, because he has become our brother and has found grace, yet we have our own speciality, which is all but worse. Our historical pastime is the direct satisfaction of inflicting pain. There are lines in Nekrasov describing how a peasant lashes a horse on the eyes, 'on its meek eyes,' everyone must have seen it.[10] It's peculiarly Russian. He describes how a feeble little nag had foundered under too heavy a load and cannot move. The peasant beats it, beats it savagely, beats it at last not knowing what he is doing in the intoxication of cruelty, thrashes it mercilessly

10. In *Till Twilight* (1859). Dostoevsky had earlier used the scene in *Crime and Punishment* (1866).

over and over again. 'However weak you are, you must pull, if you die for it.' The nag strains, and then he begins lashing the poor defenseless creature on its weeping, on its 'meek eyes.' The frantic beast tugs and draws the load, trembling all over, gasping for breath, moving sideways, with a sort of unnatural spasmodic action —it's awful in Nekrasov. But that's only a horse, and God has given horses to be beaten. So the Tatars have taught us, and they left us the knout as a remembrance of it. But men, too, can be beaten. A well-educated, cultured gentleman and his wife beat their own child with a birch rod; a girl of seven. I have an exact account of it. The papa was glad that the birch was covered with twigs. 'It stings more,' said he, and so he began stinging his daughter. I know for a fact there are people who at every blow are worked up to sensuality, to literal sensuality, which increases progressively at every blow they inflict. They beat for a minute, for five minutes, for ten minutes, more often and more savagely. The child screams. At last the child cannot scream, it gasps, 'Daddy! daddy!' By some diabolical unseemly chance the case was brought into court. A lawyer is engaged. The Russian people have long called a lawyer 'a conscience for hire.' The lawyer protests in his client's defense. 'It's such a simple thing,' he says, 'an everyday domestic event. A father corrects his child. To our shame be it said, it is brought into court.' The jury, convinced by him, gives a favorable verdict.[1] The public roars with delight that the torturer is acquitted. Ah, pity I wasn't there! I would have proposed to raise a subscription in his honor! . . . Charming pictures.

"But I've still better things about children. I've collected a great, great deal about Russian children, Alyosha. There was a little girl of five who was hated by her father and mother, 'most worthy and respectable people, of good education and breeding.' You see, I must repeat again, it is a peculiar characteristic of many people, this love of torturing children, and children only. To all other types of humanity these torturers behave mildly and benevolently, like cultivated and humane Europeans; but they are very fond of tormenting children, even fond of children themselves in that sense. It's just their defenselessness that tempts the tormentor, just the angelic confidence of the child who has no refuge and no appeal, that sets his vile blood on fire. In every man, of course, a beast lies hidden—the beast of rage, the beast of lustful heat at the screams of the tortured victim, the beast of lawlessness let off the chain, the beast of diseases that follow on vice, gout, kidney disease, and so on.

"This poor girl of five was subjected to every possible torture by those cultivated parents. They beat her, thrashed her, kicked her for

1. See Dostoevsky's article from *The Writer's Diary*, 1876.

no reason till her body was one bruise. Then, they went to greater
refinements of cruelty—shut her up all night in the cold and frost
in a privy, and because she didn't ask to be taken up at night (as
though a child of five sleeping its angelic, sound sleep could be
trained to wake and ask), they smeared her face and made her eat
that excrement, and it was her mother, her mother did this. And
that mother could sleep, hearing the poor child's groans locked up
in that vile place! Can you understand why a little creature, who
can't even understand what's done to her, should beat her little
tormented breast with her tiny fist in that vile place, in the dark and
the cold, and weep her sanguine meek, unresentful tears to dear, kind
God to protect her? Do you understand that infamy, my friend and
my brother, my pious and humble novice? Do you understand why
this rigmarole must be and is permitted? Without it, I am told, man
could not have existed on earth, for he could not have known good
and evil. Why should he know that diabolical good and evil when it
costs so much? Why, the whole world of knowledge is not worth
that child's prayer to 'dear, kind God'! I say nothing of the sufferings of grown-up people, they have eaten the apple, damn them,
and the devil take them all! But these little ones! I am making you
suffer, Alyoshka, you are not yourself. I'll leave off if you like."

"Never mind, I want to suffer too," muttered Alyosha.

"One picture, only one more, because it's so curious, so characteristic, and I have only just read it in some collection of Russian
antiquities in the *Archive*, or the *Past*. I've forgotten the name. I
must look it up. It was in the darkest days of serfdom at the
beginning of the century, and long live the Liberator of the People!
There was in those days a general of aristocratic connections, the
owner of great estates, one of those men—somewhat exceptional, I
believe, even then—who, retiring from the service into a life of
leisure, are convinced that they've earned the power of life and
death over their subjects. There were such men then. So our general, settled on his property of two thousand souls, lives in pomp,
and domineers over his poor neighbors as though they were dependents and buffoons. He has kennels of hundreds of hounds and
nearly a hundred dog-boys—all mounted, and in uniform. One day
a serf boy, a little child of eight, threw a stone in play and hurt the
paw of the general's favorite hound. 'Why is my favorite dog lame?'
He is told that the boy threw a stone that hurt the dog's paw. 'So
you did it.' The general looked the child up and down. 'Take him.'
He was taken—taken from his mother and kept shut up all night.
Early that morning the general comes out in full pomp, mounts his
horse with the hounds, his dependents, dog-boys, and the hunts-
men, all mounted around him. The servants are summoned for
their edification, and in front of them all stands the mother of the
child. The child is brought from the lockup. It's a gloomy cold,

foggy autumn day, a capital day for hunting. The general orders the child to be undressed; the child is stripped naked. He shivers, numb with terror, not daring to cry.... 'Make him run,' commands the general. 'Run! run!' shout the dog-boys. The boy runs.... 'At him!' yells the general, and he sets the whole pack of hounds on the child. The hounds catch him, and tear him to pieces before his mother's eyes!... I believe the general was afterwards declared incapable of administering his estates. Well—what did he deserve? To be shot? To be shot for the satisfaction of our moral feelings? Speak, Alyoshka!"

"To be shot," murmured Alyosha, lifting his eyes to Ivan with a pale, twisted smile.

"Bravo!" shouted Ivan delighted. "If even you say so, it means ... You're a pretty monk! So there is a little devil sitting in your heart, Alyoshka Karamazov!"

"What I said was absurd, but——"

"That's just the point, that 'but'!" cried Ivan. "Let me tell you, novice, that the absurd is only too necessary on earth. The world stands on absurdities, and perhaps nothing would have come to pass in it without them. We know what we know!"

"What do you know?"

"I understand nothing," Ivan went on, as though in delirium. "I don't want to understand anything now. I want to stick to the fact. I made up my mind long ago not to understand. If I try to understand anything, I shall be false to the fact and I have determined to stick to the fact."

"Why are you trying me?" Alyosha cried out with a tormented outburst. "Will you say what you mean at last?"

"Of course, I will; that's what I've been leading up to. You are dear to me, I don't want to let you go, and I won't give you up to your Zosima."

Ivan for a minute was silent, his face became all at once very sad.

"Listen! I took the case of children only to make my case clearer. Of the other tears of humanity with which the earth is soaked from its crust to its center, I will say nothing. I have narrowed my subject on purpose. I am a bug, and I recognize in all humility that I cannot understand why the world is arranged as it is. Men are themselves to blame, I suppose; they were given paradise, they wanted freedom, and stole fire from heaven, though they knew they would become unhappy, so there is no need to pity them. With my pitiful, earthly, Euclidean understanding, all I know is that there is suffering and that there are none guilty; that cause follows effect, simply and directly; that everything flows and finds its level—but that's only Euclidean nonsense, I know that, and I can't consent to live by it! What comfort is it to me that there are none guilty and that cause follows effect simply and directly, and that I know it—I must have retribution, or I will destroy myself. And not retribution in some remote infinite time and space, but here on earth, and that I could see myself. I have believed in it. I want to see it, and if I am dead by then, let me rise again, for if it all happens without me, it will be too unfair. Surely I haven't suffered, simply that I, my crimes and my sufferings, may manure the soil of the future harmony for somebody else. I want to see with my own eyes the hind lie down with the lion and the victim rise up and embrace his murderer. I want to be there when everyone suddenly understands what it has all been for. All the religions of the world are built on this longing, and I am a believer. But then there are the children, and what am I to do about them? That's a question I can't answer. For the hundredth time I repeat, there are numbers of questions, but I've only taken the children, because in their case what I mean is so unanswerably clear. Listen! If all must suffer to pay for the eternal harmony, what have children to do with it, tell me, please? It's beyond all comprehension why they should suffer, and why they should pay for the harmony. Why should they, too, furnish material to enrich the soil for the harmony of the future? I understand solidarity in sin among men. I understand solidarity in retribution, too; but there can be no such solidarity in sin with children. And if it is really true that they must share responsibility for all their fathers' crimes, such a truth is not of this world and is beyond my comprehension. Some jester will say, perhaps, that the child would have grown up and have sinned, but you see he didn't grow up, he was torn to pieces by the dogs, at eight years old. Oh, Alyosha, I am not blaspheming! I understand, of course, what an upheaval of the universe it will be, when everything in heaven and earth blends in one hymn of praise and everything that lives and has lived cries aloud: 'Thou art just, O Lord, for Thy ways are revealed.' When the mother embraces the fiend who threw her child to the dogs, and all three cry aloud with tears, 'Thou art just, O Lord!' then, of course, the crown of knowledge will be reached and all will be made clear. But what pulls me up here is that I can't accept that harmony. And while I am on earth, I make haste to take my own measures. You see, Alyosha, perhaps it really may happen that if I live to that moment, or rise again to see it, I, too, perhaps, may cry aloud with the rest, looking at the mother embracing the child's torturer, 'Thou art just, O Lord!' but I don't want to cry aloud then. While there is still time, I hasten to protect myself and so I renounce the higher harmony altogether. It's not worth the tears of that one tortured child who beat itself on the breast with its little fist and prayed in its stinking outhouse, with its unexpiated tears to 'dear, kind God'! It's not worth it, because those tears are unatoned for. They must be atoned for, or there can be no harmony. But

how? How are you going to atone for them? Is it possible? By their
being avenged? But what do I care for avenging them? What do I
care for a hell for oppressors? What good can hell do, since those
children have already been tortured? And what becomes of harmony, if there is hell? I want to forgive. I want to embrace. I don't
want more suffering. And if the sufferings of children go to swell
the sum of sufferings which was necessary to pay for truth, then I
protest that the truth is not worth such a price. I don't want the
mother to embrace the oppressor who threw her son to the dogs!
She dare not forgive him! Let her forgive him for herself, if she
will, let her forgive the torturer for the immeasurable suffering of
her mother's heart. But the sufferings of her tortured child she has
no right to forgive; she dare not forgive the torturer, even if the
child were to forgive him! And if that is so, if they dare not forgive,
what becomes of harmony? Is there in the whole world a being who
would have the right to forgive and could forgive? I don't want
harmony. From love for humanity I don't want it. I would rather
be left with the unavenged suffering. I would rather remain with my
unavenged suffering and unsatisfied indignation, *even if I were
wrong*. Besides, too high a price is asked for harmony; it's beyond
our means to pay so much to enter on it. And so I hasten to give
back my entrance ticket,[2] and if I am an honest man I am bound
to give it back as soon as possible. And that I am doing. It's not
God that I don't accept, Alyosha, only I most respectfully return
Him the ticket."

"That's rebellion," murmured Alyosha, looking down.

"Rebellion? I am sorry you call it that," said Ivan earnestly.
"One can hardly live in rebellion, and I want to live. Tell me
yourself, I challenge you—answer. Imagine that you are creating a
fabric of human destiny with the object of making men happy in
the end, giving them peace and rest at last, but that it was essential
and inevitable to torture to death only one tiny creature—that little
child beating its breast with its fist, for instance—and to found that
edifice on its unavenged tears, would you consent to be the architect on those conditions? Tell me, and tell the truth."

"No, I wouldn't consent," said Alyosha softly.

"And can you admit the idea that men for whom you are building it would agree to accept their happiness on the foundation of
the unexpiated blood of a little victim? And accepting it would
remain happy forever?"

"No, I can't admit it. Brother," said Alyosha suddenly, with
flashing eyes, "you said just now, is there a being in the whole
world who would have the right to forgive and could forgive? But
there is a Being and He can forgive everything, all *and for all*,

---

2. A reference to Schiller's poem "Resignation." (See Tschizewskij's essay.)

because He gave His innocent blood for all and everything. You have forgotten Him, and on Him is built the edifice, and it is to Him they cry aloud, 'Thou art just, O Lord, for Thy ways are revealed!' "

"Ah! the One without sin and His blood! No, I have not forgotten Him; on the contrary I've been wondering all the time how it was you did not bring Him in before, for usually all arguments on your side put Him in the foreground. Do you know, Alyosha—don't laugh! I composed a poem about a year ago. If you can waste another ten minutes on me, I'll tell it to you."

"You wrote a poem?"

"Oh, no, I didn't write it," laughed Ivan, "and I've never written two lines of poetry in my life. But I composed up this poem in prose and I remembered it. I was carried away when I composed it. You will be my first reader—that is, listener. Why should an author forego even one listener?" smiled Ivan. "Shall I tell it to you?"

"I am all attention," said Alyosha.

"My poem is called 'The Grand Inquisitor'; it's a ridiculous thing, but I want to tell it to you."

Chapter V

The Grand Inquisitor

"But even this must have a preface—that is, a literary preface, whew," laughed Ivan, "and I am a poor hand at making one. You see, my action takes place in the sixteenth century, and at that time, as you probably learned at school, it was customary in poetry to bring down heavenly powers to earth. Not to speak of Dante, in France, clerks, as well as the monks in the monasteries, used to give regular performances in which the Madonna, the saints, the angels, Christ, and God Himself were brought on the stage. In those days it was done in all simplicity. In Victor Hugo's *Notre Dame de Paris* an edifying and gratuitous spectacle was provided for the people in the town hall of Paris in the reign of Louis XI, in honor of the birth of the dauphin. It was called *Le bon jugement de la très sainte et gracieuse Vierge Marie*,[3] and she appears herself on the stage and pronounces her *bon jugement*. Similar plays, chiefly from the Old Testament, were occasionally performed in Moscow too, up to the time of Peter the Great. But besides plays there were all sorts of legends and "verses" scattered about the world, in which the saints and angels and all the powers of Heaven took part when required. In our monasteries the monks busied themselves in translating, copying, and even composing such poems—and think when

---

3. "The compassionate judgment of the very holy and gracious Virgin Mary."

—under the Tatars. There is, for instance, one such poem (of course, from the Greek), 'The Wanderings of Our Lady through Hell,'⁴ with descriptions as bold as Dante's. Our Lady visits Hell, and the Archangel Michael leads her through the torments. She sees the sinners and their punishment. There she sees among others one most entertaining set of sinners in a burning lake; some of them sink to the bottom of the lake so that they can't swim out, and 'these God forgets'—an expression of extraordinary depth and force. And so Our Lady, shocked and weeping, falls before the throne of God and begs for mercy for all in Hell—for all she has seen there, indiscriminately. Her conversation with God is immensely interesting. She beseeches Him, she will not desist, and when God points to the hands and feet of her Son, nailed to the Cross, and asks, 'How can I forgive His tormentors?' she bids all the saints, all the martyrs, all the angels and archangels to fall down with her and pray for mercy on all without distinction. It ends by her winning from God a respite of suffering every year from Good Friday till Trinity day, and the sinners at once raise a cry of thankfulness from Hell, chanting, 'Thou art just, O Lord, in this judgment.' Well, my poem would have been of that kind of it had appeared at that time. He comes on the scene in my poem, but He says nothing, only appears and passes on. Fifteen centuries have passed since He promised to come in His glory, fifteen centuries since His prophet wrote, 'Behold, I come quickly'; 'Of that day and that hour knoweth no man, neither the Son, but the Father,' as He Himself predicted on earth. But humanity awaits him with the same faith and with the same love. Oh, with greater faith, for it is fifteen centuries since man has ceased to see signs from Heaven.

> Have faith in the heart's prompting
> For the heavens give no pledge.⁵

There was nothing left but faith in what the heart prompts. It is true there were many miracles in those days. There were saints who performed miraculous cures; some holy people, according to their biographies, were visited by the Queen of Heaven herself. But the devil did not slumber, and doubts were already arising among men of the truth of these miracles. And just then there appeared in the north of Germany a terrible new heresy. A huge star 'burning as it were a lamp' (that is, to a church) 'fell on the sources of the waters and they were made bitter.'⁶ These heretics began blasphemously denying miracles. But those who remained faithful were all the more ardent in their faith. The tears of humanity rose up to Him as before, awaited His coming, loved Him, hoped for him, yearned to

4. A twelfth-century apocryphal tale, translated from a Byzantine source.
5. From Schiller's poem "Sehnsucht" [Longing].
6. Rev. 8:10–11.

suffer and die for Him as before. And so many ages mankind had prayed with faith and fervor, 'O Lord our God, hasten Thy coming,' so many ages called upon Him, that in His infinite mercy He deigned to come down to His servants. Before that day He had come down, too, He had visited some holy men, martyrs and hermits, as is written in their 'Lives.' Among us, Tyutchev, with absolute faith in the truth of his words, bore witness that

> Burdened with bearing the cross,
> The Heavenly King in slave's form
> Went throughout all of you, you,
> Native land, with his blessings.[7]

And that certainly was so, I assure you. And behold, He deigned to appear for a moment to the people, to the tortured, suffering people, sunk in inquity, but loving Him like children. My story is laid in Spain, in Seville, in the most terrible time of the Inquisition, when fires were lighted every day to the glory of God, and

> In the splendid *auto da fé*
> The wicked heretics were burnt.[8]

Oh, of course, this was not the coming in which He will appear according to His promise at the end of time in all His heavenly glory, and which will be sudden 'as lightning flashing from east to west.' No, He visited His children only for a moment, and there where the flames were crackling round the heretics. In His infinite mercy He came once more among men in that human shape in which He walked among men for three years fifteen centuries ago. He came down to the 'hot pavement' of the southern town in which on the day before almost a hundred heretics had, *ad majorem gloriam Dei*,[9] been burned by the cardinal, the Grand Inquisitor, in a magnificent *auto da fé*, in the presence of the king, the court, the knights, the cardinals, the most charming ladies of the court, and the whole population of Seville.

"He came softly, unobserved, and yet, strange to say, everyone recognized Him. That might be one of the best passages in the poem. I mean, why they recognized Him. The people are irresistibly drawn to Him, they surround Him, they flock about Him, follow Him. He moves silently in their midst with a gentle smile of infinite compassion. The sun of love burns in His heart. Light, enlightenment, and power shine from His eyes, and their radiance, shed on the people, stirs their hearts with responsive love. He holds out His hands to them, blesses them, and a healing virtue comes from contact with Him, even with His garments. An old man in the

---

7. From the lyric "These Poor Villages" by F. I. Tyutchev (1803–1873).
8. From a poem, "Corialanus," (1834)

by A. I. Polezhaev.
9. "For the greater glory of God"—motto of the Society of Jesus.

crowd, blind from childhood, cries out, 'O Lord, heal me and I shall see Thee!' and, as it were, scales fall from his eyes and the blind man sees Him. The crowd weeps and kisses the earth under His feet. Children throw flowers before Him, sing, and cry 'Hosannah.' 'It is He—it is He!' all repeat. 'It must be He, it can be no one but Him!' He stops at the steps of the Seville cathedral at the moment when the weeping mourners are bringing in a little open white coffin. In it lies a child of seven, the only daughter of a prominent citizen. The dead child lies hidden in flowers. 'He will raise your child,' the crowd shouts to the weeping mother. The priest, coming to meet the coffin, looks perplexed, and frowns, but the mother of the dead child throws herself at His feet with a wail. 'If it is Thou, raise my child!' she cries, holding out her hands to Him. The procession halts, the coffin is laid on the steps at His feet. He looks with compassion, and His lips once more softly pronounce, 'Maiden, arise!' and the maiden arises. The little girl sits up in the coffin and looks round, smiling with wide-open wondering eyes, holding a bunch of white roses they had put in her hand.

"There are cries, sobs, confusion among the people, and at that moment the cardinal himself, the Grand Inquisitor, passes by the cathedral. He is an old man, almost ninety, tall and erect, with a withered face and sunken eyes, in which there is still a gleam of light, like a fiery spark. He is not dressed in his gorgeous cardinal's robes, as he was the day before, when he was burning the enemies of the Roman Church—at that moment he was wearing his coarse, old, monk's cassock. At a distance behind him come his gloomy assistants and slaves and the 'holy guard.' He stops at the sight of the crowd and watches it from a distance. He sees everything; he sees them set the coffin down at His feet, sees the child rise up, and his face darkens. He knits his thick gray brows and his eyes gleam with a sinister fire. He holds out his finger and bids the guards take Him. And such is his power, so completely are the people cowed into submission and trembling obedience to him, that the crowd immediately make way for the guards, and in the midst of deathlike silence they lay hands on Him and lead Him away. The crowd instantly bows down to the earth, like one man, before the old inquisitor. He blesses the people in silence and passes on. The guards lead their prisoner to the close, gloomy vaulted prison in the ancient palace of the Holy Inquisition and shut Him in it. The day passes and is followed by the dark, burning 'breathless' night of Seville. The air is 'fragrant with laurel and lemon.'[1] In the pitch darkness the iron door of the prison is suddenly opened and the Grand Inquisitor himself comes in with a light in his hand. He is alone; the door is closed at once behind him. He stands in the

---

1. From Pushkin's play *The Stone Guest (Don Juan)*.

doorway and for a long time, for a minute or two, gazes into His face. At last he goes up slowly, sets the light on the table and speaks.

" 'Is it Thou? Thou?' but receiving no answer, he adds at once, 'Don't answer, be silent. What canst Thou say, indeed? I know too well what Thou wouldst say. And Thou hast no right to add anything to what Thou hadst said of old. Why, then, art Thou come to hinder us? For Thou hast come to hinder us, and Thou knowest that. But dost Thou know what will be tomorrow? I know not who Thou art and care not to know whether it is Thou or only a semblance of Him, but tomorrow I shall condemn Thee and burn Thee at the stake as the worst of heretics. And the very people who have today kissed Thy feet, tomorrow at the faintest sign from me will rush to heap up the embers of Thy fire. Knowest Thou that? Yes, maybe Thou knowest it,' he added with thoughtful penetration, never for a moment taking his eyes off the Prisoner."

"I don't quite understand, Ivan. What does it mean?" Alyosha, who had been listening in silence, said with a smile. "Is it simply a wild fantasy, or a mistake on the part of the old man—some impossible *qui pro quo?*"[2]

"Take it as the last," said Ivan, laughing, "if you are so corrupted by modern realism and can't stand anything fantastic. If you like it to be a case of *qui pro quo*, let it be so. It is true," he went on, laughing, "the old man was ninety, and he might well be crazy over his set idea. He might have been struck by the appearance of the Prisoner. It might, in fact, be simply his ravings, the delusion of an old man of ninety, approaching his death, overexcited by the *auto da fé* of a hundred heretics the day before. But does it matter to us after all whether it was a *qui pro quo* or a wild fantasy? All that matters is that the old man should speak out, should speak openly of what he has thought in silence for ninety years."

"And the Prisoner too is silent? Does He look at him and not say a word?"

"That's inevitable in any case," Ivan laughed again. "The old man has told Him He hasn't the right to add anything to what He has said of old. One may say it is the most fundamental feature of Roman Catholicism, in my opinion at least. 'All has been given by Thee to the Pope,' they say, 'and all, therefore, is still in the Pope's hands, and there is no need for Thee to come now at all. Thou must not meddle for the time, at least.' That's how they speak and write too—the Jesuits, at any rate. I have read it myself in the works of their theologians. 'Hast Thou the right to reveal to us one of the mysteries of that world from which Thou hast come?' my old man asks Him, and answers the question for Him. 'No, Thou hast

2. "One for the other," a mix-up, mistaken identity.

not; that Thou mayest not add to what has been said of old, and mayest not take from men the freedom which Thou didst exalt when Thou wast on earth. Whatsoever Thou revealest anew will encroach on men's freedom of faith; for it will be manifest as a miracle, and the freedom of their faith was dearer to Thee than anything in those days fifteen hundred years ago. Didst Thou not often say then, "I will make you free"? But now Thou hast seen these "free" men,' the old man adds suddenly, with a pensive smile. 'Yes, we've paid dearly for it,' he goes on, looking sternly at Him, 'but at last we have completed that work in Thy name. For fifteen centuries we have been wrestling with Thy freedom, but now it is ended and over for good. Dost Thou not believe that it's over for good? Thou lookest meekly at me and deignest not even to be wroth with me. But let me tell Thee that now, today, people are more persuaded than ever that they have perfect freedom, yet they have brought their freedom to us and laid it humbly at our feet. But that has been our doing. Was this what Thou didst? Was this Thy freedom?' "

"I don't understand again," Alyosha broke in. "Is he ironical, is he jesting?"

"Not a bit of it! He claims it as a merit for himself and his Church that at last they have vanquished freedom and have done so to make men happy. 'For now' (he is speaking of the Inquisition, of course) 'for the first time it has become possible to think of the happiness of men. Man was created a rebel; and how can rebels be happy? Thou wast warned,' he says to Him. 'Thou hast had no lack of admonitions and warnings, but Thou didst not listen to those warnings; Thou didst reject the only way by which men might be made happy. But, fortunately, departing Thou didst hand on the work to us. Thou hast promised, Thou hast established by Thy word, Thou hast given to us the right to bind and to unbind, and now, of course, Thou canst not think of taking it away. Why, then, hast Thou come to hinder us?' "

"And what's the meaning of 'no lack of admonitions and warnings'?" asked Alyosha.

"Why, that's the chief part of what the old man must say."

" 'The wise and dread spirit, the spirit of self-destruction and nonexistence,' the old man goes on, 'the great spirit talked with Thee in the wilderness, and we are told in the books that he "tempted" Thee. Is that so? And could anything truer be said than what he revealed to Thee in three questions and what Thou didst reject, and what in the books is called "the temptation"? And yet if there has ever been on earth a real stupendous miracle, it took place on that day, on the day of the three temptations. The statement of those three questions was itself the miracle. If it were possible to imagine simply for the sake of argument that those three questions of the dread spirit had perished utterly from the books, and that we had to restore them and to invent them anew, and to do so had gathered together all the wise men of the earth—rulers, chief priests, learned men, philosophers, poets—and had set them the task to invent three questions, such as would not only fit the occasion, but express in three words, three human phrases, the whole future history of the world and of humanity—dost Thou believe that all the wisdom of the earth united could have invented anything in depth and force equal to the three questions which were actually put to Thee then by the wise and mighty spirit in the wilderness? From those questions alone, from the miracle of their statement, we can see that we have here to do not with the fleeting human intelligence, but with the absolute and eternal. For in those three questions the whole subsequent history of mankind is, as it were, brought together into one whole, and foretold, and in them are united all the unsolved historical contradictions of human nature. At the time it could not be so clear, since the future was unknown; but now that fifteen hundred years have passed, we see that everything in those three questions was so justly grasped and foretold, and has been so truly fulfilled, that nothing can be added to them or taken from them.

" 'Judge Thyself who was right—Thou or he who questioned Thee then? Remember the first question; its meaning, though not the exact words, was this: "Thou wouldst go into the world, and art going with empty hands, with some promise of freedom which men in their simplicity and their natural unruliness cannot even understand, which they fear and dread—for nothing has ever been more insupportable for a man and a human society than freedom. But seest Thou these stones in this parched and barren wilderness? Turn them into bread, and mankind will run after Thee like a flock, grateful and obedient, though forever trembling, lest Thou withdraw Thy hand and deny them Thy bread." But Thou wouldst not deprive man of freedom and didst reject the offer, thinking, what is that freedom worth, if obedience is bought with bread? Thou didst reply that man lives not by bread alone. But dost Thou know that for the sake of that earthly bread the spirit of the earth will rise up against Thee and will strive with Thee and overcome Thee, and all will follow him, crying, "Who can compare with this beast? He has given us fire from heaven!" Dost Thou know that the ages will pass, and humanity will proclaim by the lips of their sages that there is no crime, and therefore no sin; there is only hunger? "Feed men, and then ask of them virtue!" that's what they'll write on the banner, which they will raise against Thee, and with which they will destroy Thy temple. Where Thy temple stood will rise a new building; the terrible tower of Babel will be built again, and though, like the one of old, it will not be finished, yet Thou mightest have prevented that new tower and have cut short the sufferings of men for a thousand years; for they will come back to us after a thousand years of agony with their tower. They will seek us again, hidden underground in the catacombs, for we shall again be persecuted and tortured. They will find us and cry to us, "Feed us, for those who have promised us fire from heaven haven't given it!" And then we shall finish building their tower, for he finishes the building who feeds them. And we alone shall feed them in Thy name, declaring falsely that it is in Thy name. Oh, never, never can they feed themselves without us! No science will give them bread so long as they remain free. In the end they will lay their freedom at our feet, and say to us, "Make us your slaves, but feed us." They will understand themselves, at last, that freedom and bread enough for all are inconceivable together, for never, never will they be able to share between them! They will be convinced, too, that they can never be free, for they are weak, vicious, worthless and rebellious. Thou didst promise them the bread of Heaven, but, I repeat again, can it compare with earthly bread in the eyes of the weak, ever sinful and ignoble race of man? And if for the sake of the bread of Heaven thousands and tens of thousands shall follow Thee, what is to become of the millions and tens of thousands of millions of creatures who will not have the strength to forego the earthly bread for the sake of the heavenly? Or dost Thou care only for the tens of thousands of the great and strong, while the millions, numerous as the sands of the sea, who are weak but love Thee, must exist only for the sake of the great and strong? No, we care for the weak too. They are sinful and rebellious, but in the end they too will become obedient. They will marvel at us and look on us as gods, because we are ready to endure the freedom which they have found so dreadful and to rule over them—so awful it will seem to them to be free. But we shall tell them that we are Thy servants and rule them in Thy name. We shall deceive them again, for we will not let Thee come to us again. That deception will be our suffering, for we shall be forced to lie. This is the significance of the first question in the wilderness, and this is what Thou hast rejected for the sake of that freedom which Thou hast exalted above everything. Yet in this question lies hid the great secret of this world. Choosing "bread," Thou wouldst have satisfied the universal and everlasting craving of humanity individually and together as one—to find someone to worship. So long as man remains free he strives for nothing so incessantly and so painfully as to find someone to worship. But man seeks to worship what is established beyond dispute, so that all men would agree at once to worship it. For these pitiful creatures are concerned not only to find what one or the other can worship, but to find something that all would believe in and worship; what is essential is that all may be *together* in it. This craving for com-

munity of worship is the chief misery of every man individually and of all humanity from the beginning of time. For the sake of common worship they've slain each other with the sword. They have set up gods and challenged one another, "Put away your gods and come and worship ours, or we will kill you and your gods!" And so it will be to the end of the world, even when gods disappear from the earth; they will fall down before idols just the same. Thou didst know, Thou couldst not but have known, this fundamental secret of human nature, but Thou didst reject the one infallible banner which was offered Thee to make all men bow down to Thee alone—the banner of earthly bread; and Thou hast rejected it for the sake of freedom and the bread of Heaven. Behold what Thou didst further. And all again in the name of freedom! I tell Thee that man is tormented by no greater anxiety than to find someone quickly to whom he can hand over that gift of freedom with which the ill-fated creature is born. But only one who can appease their conscience can take over their freedom. In bread there was offered Thee an invincible banner; give bread, and man will worship Thee, for nothing is more certain than bread. But if someone else gains possession of his conscience—oh! then he will cast away Thy bread and follow after him who has ensnared his conscience. In that Thou wast right. For the secret of man's being is not only to live but to have something to live for. Without a stable conception of the object of life, man would not consent to go on living, and would rather destroy himself than remain on earth, though he had bread in abundance. That is true. But what happened? Instead of taking men's freedom from them, Thou didst make it greater than ever! Didst Thou forget that man prefers peace, and even death, to freedom of choice in the knowledge of good and evil? Nothing is more seductive for man than his freedom of conscience, but nothing is a greater cause of suffering. And behold, instead of giving a firm foundation for setting the conscience of man at rest forever, Thou didst choose all that is exceptional, vague and enigmatic; Thou didst choose what was utterly beyond the strength of men, acting as though Thou didst not love them at all—Thou who didst come to give Thy life for them! Instead of taking possession of men's freedom, Thou didst increase it, and burdened the spiritual kingdom of mankind with its sufferings forever. Thou didst desire man's free love, that he should follow Thee freely, enticed and taken captive by Thee. In place of the rigid ancient law, man must hereafter with free heart decide for himself what is good and what is evil, having only Thy image before him as his guide. But didst Thou not know he would at last reject even Thy image and Thy truth, if he is weighed down with the fearful burden of free choice? They will cry aloud at last that the truth is not in Thee, for they could not have been left in greater confusion and suffering than

Thou hast caused, laying upon them so many cares and unanswerable problems.

" 'So that, in truth, Thou didst Thyself lay the foundation for the destruction of Thy kingdom, and no one is more to blame for it. Yet what was offered Thee? There are three powers, three powers alone, able to conquer and to hold captive forever the conscience of these impotent rebels for their happiness—those forces are miracle, mystery and authority. Thou hast rejected all three and hast set the example for doing so. When the wise and dread spirit set Thee on the pinnacle of the temple and said to Thee, "If Thou wouldst know whether Thou art the Son of God then cast Thyself down, for it is written: the angels shall hold him up lest he fall and bruise himself, and Thou shalt know then whether Thou art the Son of God and shalt prove then how great is Thy faith in Thy Father." But Thou didst refuse and wouldst not cast Thyself down. Oh! of course, Thou didst proudly and well, like God; but the weak, rebellious race of men, are they gods? Oh, Thou didst know then that in taking one step, in making one movement to cast Thyself down, Thou wouldst be tempting God and have lost all Thy faith in Him, and wouldst have been dashed to pieces against that earth which Thou didst come to save. And the wise spirit that tempted Thee would have rejoiced. But I ask again, are there many like Thee? And couldst Thou believe for one moment that men, too, could face such a temptation? Is the nature of men such, that they can reject miracle, and at the great moments of their life, the moments of their deepest, most agonizing spiritual difficulties, cling only to the free verdict of the heart? Oh, Thou didst know that Thy deed would be recorded in books, would be handed down to remote times and the utmost ends of the earth, and Thou didst hope that man, following Thee, would cling to God and not ask for a miracle. But Thou didst not know that when man rejects miracle he rejects God too; for man seeks not so much God as the miraculous. And as man cannot bear to be without the miraculous, he will create new miracles of his own for himself, and will worship deeds of sorcery and witchcraft, though he might be a hundred times over a rebel, heretic and infidel. Thou didst not come down from the Cross when they shouted to Thee, mocking and reviling Thee, "Come down from the cross and we will believe that Thou art He." Thou didst not come down, for again Thou wouldst not enslave man by a miracle, and didst crave faith given freely, not based on miracle. Thou didst crave for free love and not the base raptures the slave before the might that has overawed him forever. But Thou didst think too highly of men therein, for they are slaves, of course, though rebellious by nature. Look round and judge; fifteen centuries have passed, look upon them. Whom hast Thou raised up to Thyself? I swear, man is weaker and baser by nature than Thou hast believed him! Can he, can he do what Thou didst? By showing him so much respect, Thou didst, as it were, cease to feel for him, for Thou didst ask far too much from him—Thou who hast loved him more than Thyself! Respecting him less, Thou wouldst have asked less of him. That would have been more like love, for his burden would have been lighter. He is weak and vile. What though he is everywhere now rebelling against our power, and proud of his rebellion? It is the pride of a child and a schoolboy. They are little children rioting and barring out the teacher at school. But their childish delight will end; it will cost them dear. They will cast down temples and drench the earth with blood. But they will see at last, the foolish children, that, though they are rebels, they are impotent rebels, unable to keep up their own rebellion. Bathed in their foolish tears, they will recognize at last that He who created them rebels must have meant to mock at them. They will say this in despair, and their utterance will be a blasphemy which will make them more unhappy still, for man's nature cannot bear blasphemy, and in the end always avenges it on itself. And so unrest, confusion and unhappiness—that is the present lot of man after Thou didst bear so much for their freedom! Thy great prophet tells in vision and in image, that he saw all those who took part in the first resurrection and that there were of each tribe twelve thousand.[3] But if there were so many of them, they must have been not men but gods. They had borne Thy cross, they had endured scores of years in the barren, hungry wilderness, living upon locusts and roots—and Thou mayest indeed point with pride at those children of freedom, of free love, of free and splendid sacrifice for Thy name. But remember that they were only some thousands, and gods at that; and what of the rest? And how are the other weak ones to blame, because they could not endure what the strong have endured? How is the weak soul to blame that it is unable to receive such terrible gifts? Canst Thou really have come only to the elect and for the elect? But if so, it is a mystery and we cannot understand it. And if it is a mystery, we too have a right to preach a mystery, and to teach them that it's not the free judgment of their hearts, not love that matters, but a mystery which they must follow blindly, even against their conscience. So we have done. We have corrected Thy work and have founded it upon *miracle, mystery* and *authority.* And men rejoiced that they were again led like sheep, and that the terrible gift that had brought them such suffering, was, at last, lifted from their hearts. Were we right teaching them this? Speak! Did we not love mankind, so meekly acknowledging their feebleness, lovingly lightening their burden, and permitting their weak nature even sin with our sanction? Why

3. Rev. 8.

hast Thou come now to hinder us? And why dost Thou look
silently and searchingly at me with Thy mild eyes? Be angry. I
don't want Thy love, for I love Thee not. And what use is it for me
to hide anything from Thee? Don't I know to Whom I am speaking? All that I can say is known to Thee already. I can see it in
Thine eyes. And is it for me to conceal from Thee our mystery?
Perhaps it is Thy will to hear it from my lips. Listen, then. We are
not working with Thee, but with *him*—that is our mystery. It's
long—eight centuries—since we have been on *his* side and not on
Thine. Just eight centuries ago, we took from him what Thou didst
reject with scorn, that last gift he offered Thee, showing Thee all
the kingdoms of the earth. We took from him Rome and the sword
of Caesar, and proclaimed ourselves sole rulers of the earth, though
hitherto we have not been able to complete our work.[4] But whose
fault is that? Oh, the work is only beginning, but it has begun. It
has long to await completion and the earth has yet much to suffer,
but we shall triumph and shall be Caesars, and then we shall plan
the universal happiness of man. But Thou mightest have taken even
then the sword of Caesar. Why didst Thou reject that last gift?
Hadst Thou accepted that last counsel of the mighty spirit, Thou
wouldst have accomplished all that man seeks on earth—that is,
someone to worship, someone to keep his conscience, and some
means of uniting all in one unanimous and harmonious anthill, for
the craving for universal unity is the third and last anguish of men.
Mankind as a whole has always strived to organize a universal
state. There have been many great nations with great histories, but
the more highly they were developed the more unhappy they were,
for they felt more acutely than other people the craving for world-
wide union. The great conquerors, Tamerlane[5] and Genghis
Khan,[6] whirled like hurricanes over the face of the earth striving to
subdue its people, and they too were but the unconscious expression of the same craving for universal unity. Hadst Thou taken the
world and Caesar's purple, Thou wouldst have founded the universal state and have given universal peace. For who can rule men if
not he who holds their conscience and their bread in his hands? We
have taken the sword of Caesar, and in taking it, of course, have
rejected Thee and followed *him*. Oh, ages are yet to come of the
confusion of free thought, of their science and cannibalism. For
having begun to build their tower of Babel without us, they will
end, of course, with cannibalism. But then the beast will crawl to
us and lick our feet and spatter them with tears of blood. And we
shall sit upon the beast and raise the cup, and on it will be written,
"Mystery." But then, and only then, the reign of peace and happi-

4. Pepin the Short, king of the Franks, granted Ravenna to Pope Stephen III in 756; this was the origin of the pope's temporal power.

5. Tamerlane (1336–1406), Tartar conqueror.
6. Genghis Khan (1155–1227), Mongolian conqueror.

ness will come for men. Thou art proud of Thine elect, but Thou hast only the elect, while we give rest to all. And besides, how many of those elect, those mighty ones who could become elect, have grown weary waiting for Thee, and have transferred and will transfer the powers of their spirit and the warmth of their heart to the other camp, and end by raising their *free* banner against Thee. Thou didst Thyself lift up that banner. But with us all will be happy and will no more rebel nor destroy one another as under Thy freedom. Oh, we shall persuade them that they will only become free when they renounce their freedom to us and submit to us. And shall we be right or shall we be lying? They will be convinced that we are right, for they will remember the horrors of slavery and confusion to which Thy freedom brought them. Freedom, free thought and science, will lead them into such straits and will bring them face to face with such marvels and insoluble mysteries, that some of them, the fierce and rebellious, will destroy themselves, others, rebellious but weak, will destroy one another, while the rest, weak and unhappy, will crawl fawning to our feet and whine to us: "Yes, you were right, you alone possess His mystery, and we come back to you, save us from ourselves!" Receiving bread from us, they will of course see clearly that we take the bread made by their hands from them, to give it to them, without any miracle. They will see that we do not change the stones to bread, but in truth they will be more thankful for taking it from our hands than for the bread itself! For they will remember only too well that in the old days, without our help, even the bread they made turned to stones in their hands, while since they have come back to us, the very stones have turned to bread in their hands. Too, too well they know the value of complete submission! And until men know that, they will be unhappy. Who is most to blame for their not knowing it, speak? Who scattered the flock and sent it astray on unknown paths? But the flock will come together again and will submit once more, and then it will be once for all. Then we shall give them the quiet humble happiness of weak creatures such as they are by nature. Oh, we shall persuade them at last not to be proud, for Thou didst lift them up and thereby taught them to be proud. We shall show them that they are weak, that they are only pitiful children, but that childlike happiness is the sweetest of all. They will become timid and will look to us and huddle close to us in fear, as chicks to the hen. They will marvel at us and will be awestricken before us, and will be proud at our being so powerful and clever, that we have been able to subdue such a turbulent flock of thousands of millions. They will tremble impotently before our wrath, their minds will grow fearful, they will be quick to shed tears like women and children, but they will be just as ready at a sign from us to pass to laughter and rejoicing, to happy mirth and childish song. Yes, we shall set them to work, but in their leisure hours we shall make their life like a child's game, with children's songs and innocent dance. Oh, we shall allow them even sin, they are weak and help-less, and they will love us like children because we allow them to sin. We shall tell them that every sin will be expiated, if it is done with our permission, that we allow them to sin because we love them, and the punishment for these sins we take upon ourselves. And we shall take it upon ourselves, and they will adore us as their saviors who have taken on themselves their sins before God. And they will have no secrets from us. We shall allow or forbid them to live with their wives and mistresses, to have or not to have children—according to whether they have been obedient or dis-obedient—and they will submit to us gladly and cheerfully. The, most painful secrets of their conscience, all, all they will bring to us, and we shall have an answer for all. And they will be glad to believe our answer, for it will save them from the great anxiety and terrible agony they endure at present in making a free decision for themselves. And all will be happy, all the millions of creatures except the hundred thousand who rule over them. For only we, we who guard the mystery, shall be unhappy. There will be thousands of millions of happy babes, and a hundred thousand sufferers who have taken upon themselves the curse of the knowledge of good and evil. Peacefully they will die, peacefully they will expire in Thy name, and beyond the grave they will find nothing but death. But we shall keep the secret, and for their happiness we shall entice them with the reward of heaven and eternity. Though if there were anything in the other world, it certainly would not be for such as they. It is prophesied that Thou wilt come again in victory, Thou wilt come with Thy chosen, the proud and strong, but we will say that they have only saved themselves, but we have saved all. We are told that the harlot who sits upon the beast, and holds in her hands the *mystery*, shall be put to shame, that the weak will rise up again, and will rend her royal purple and will strip naked her 'loathsome' body.[7] But then I will stand up and point out to Thee the thousand millions of happy children who have known no sin. And we who have taken their sins upon us for their happiness will stand up before Thee and say: "Judge us if Thou canst and darest." Know that I fear Thee not. Know that I too have been in the wilderness, I too have lived on roots and locusts, I too prized the freedom with which Thou hast blessed men, and I too was striving to stand among Thy elect, among the strong and powerful, thirsting "to make up the number." But I awakened and would not serve mad-ness. I turned back and joined the ranks of those *who have cor-rected Thy work*. I left the proud and went back to the humble, for

7. Rev. 17.

the happiness of the humble. What I say to Thee will come to pass, and our dominion will be built up. I repeat, tomorrow Thou shalt see that obedient flock who at a sign from me will hasten to heap up the hot cinders about the pile on which I shall burn Thee for coming to hinder us. For if anyone has ever deserved our fires, it is Thou. Tomorrow I shall burn Thee. *Dixi*.' "[8]

Ivan stopped. He was carried away as he talked and spoke with excitement; when he had finished, he suddenly smiled.

Alyosha had listened in silence; towards the end he was greatly moved and seemed several times on the point of interrupting, but restrained himself. Now his words came with a rush.

"But . . . that's absurd!" he cried, flushing. "Your poem is in praise of Jesus, not in blame of Him—as you meant it to be. And who will believe you about freedom? Is that the way to understand it? That's not the idea of it in the Orthodox Church . . . That's Rome, and not even the whole of Rome, it's false—those are the worst of the Catholics, the Inquisitors, the Jesuits! . . . And there could not be such a fantastic creature as your Inquisitor. What are these sins of mankind they take on themselves? Who are these keepers of the mystery who have taken some curse upon themselves for the happiness of mankind? When have they been seen? We know the Jesuits, they are spoken ill of, but surely they are not what you describe? They are not that at all, not at all. . . . They are simply the Romish army for the earthly sovereignty of the world in the future, with the Pontiff of Rome for Emperor . . . that's their ideal, but there's no sort of mystery or lofty sorrow about it. . . . It's simple lust for power, for filthy earthly gain, for domination—something like a universal serfdom with them as masters—that's all they stand for. They don't even believe in God perhaps. Your suffering inquisitor is a mere fantasy."

"Wait, wait," laughed Ivan, "how excited you are! A fantasy you say, let it be so! Of course it's a fantasy. But allow me to say: do you really think that the Roman Catholic movement of the last centuries is actually nothing but the lust for power, for filthy earthly gain? Is that Father Païssy's teaching?"

"No, no, on the contrary, Father Païssy did once say something rather the same as you . . . but of course it's not the same, not a bit the same," Alyosha hastily corrected himself.

"A precious bit of information, in spite of your 'not a bit the same.' I ask you why your Jesuits and Inquisitors have united simply for vile material gain? Why can there not be among them one martyr oppressed by great sorrow and loving humanity? You see, only suppose that there was one such man among all those who desire nothing but filthy material gain—if there's only one like my

8. "I have spoken (finished)."

old inquisitor, who had himself eaten roots in the desert and made frenzied efforts to subdue his flesh to make himself free and perfect. But yet all his life he loved humanity, and suddenly his eyes were opened, and he saw that it is no great moral blessedness to attain perfection and freedom, if at the same time one gains the conviction that millions of God's creatures have been created as a mockery, that they will never be capable of using their freedom, that these poor rebels can never turn into giants to complete the tower, that it was not for such geese that the great idealist dreamt his dream of harmony. Seeing all that he turned back and joined—the clever people. Surely that could have happened?"

"Joined whom, what clever people?" cried Alyosha, completely carried away. "They have no such great cleverness and no mysteries and secrets. . . . Perhaps nothing but Atheism, that's all their secret. Your inquisitor does not believe in God, that's his secret!"

"What if it is so! At last you have guessed it. It's perfectly true that that's the whole secret, but isn't that suffering, at least for a man like that, who has wasted his whole life in the desert and yet could not shake off his incurable love of humanity? In his old age he reached the clear conviction that nothing but the advice of the great dread spirit could build up any tolerable sort of life for the feeble, unruly, 'incomplete, specimen creatures created in jest.' And so, convinced of this, he sees that he must follow the counsel of the wise spirit, the dread spirit of death and destruction, and therefore accept lying and deception, and lead men consciously to death and destruction, and yet deceive them all the way so that they may not notice where they are being led, that the poor blind creatures may at least on the way think themselves happy. And note, the deception is in the name of Him in Whose ideal the old man had so fervently believed all his life long. Is not that tragic? And if only one such stood at the head of the whole army 'filled with the lust for power only for the sake of filthy gain'—would not one such be enough to make a tragedy? More than that, one such standing at the head is enough to create the actual leading idea of the Roman Church with all its armies and Jesuits, its highest idea. I tell you frankly that I firmly believe that there has always been such a man among those who stood at the head of the movement. Who knows, there may have been some such even among the Roman popes. Who knows, perhaps the spirit of that accursed old man who loves mankind so obstinately in his own way, is to be found even now in a whole multitude of such old men, existing not by chance but by agreement, as a secret league formed long ago for the guarding of the mystery, to guard it from the weak and the unhappy, so as to make them happy. No doubt it is so, and so it must be indeed. I fancy that even among the Masons there's something of the same mystery at the bottom, and that that's why the Catholics so detest the

Masons as their rivals breaking up the unity of the idea, while it is so essential that there should be one flock and one shepherd. . . . But from the way I defend my idea I might be an author impatient of your criticism. Enough of it."

"You are perhaps a Mason yourself!" broke suddenly from Alyosha. "You don't believe in God," he added, speaking this time very sorrowfully. He fancied besides that his brother was looking at him ironically. "How does your poem end?" he asked, suddenly looking down. "Or was it the end?"

"I meant to end it like this. When the Inquisitor ceased speaking he waited some time for his Prisoner to answer him. His silence weighed down upon him. He saw that the Prisoner had listened intently and quietly all the time, looking gently in his face and evidently not wishing to reply. The old man longed for Him to say something, however bitter and terrible. But He suddenly approached the old man in silence and softly kissed him on his bloodless aged lips. That was all his answer. The old man shuddered. His lips moved. He went to the door, opened it, and said to Him: 'Go, and come no more. . . . come not at all, never, never!' And he let Him out into the dark squares of the town. The Prisoner went away."

"And the old man?"

"The kiss glows in his heart, but the old man adheres to his idea."

"And you with him, you too?" cried Alyosha, mournfully. Ivan laughed.

"Why, it's all nonsense, Alyosha. It's only a senseless poem of a senseless student, who could never write two lines of verse. Why do you take it so seriously? Surely you don't suppose I am going straight off to the Jesuits, to join the swarm of men who are correcting His work? Good Lord, it's no business of mine. I told you, all I want is to live on to thirty, and then . . . dash the cup to the ground!"

"But the little sticky leaves, and the precious tombs, and the blue sky, and the woman you love! How will you live, how will you love them?" Alyosha cried sorrowfully. "With such a hell in your heart and your head, how can you? No, that's just what you are going away for, to join them . . . if not, you will kill yourself, you can't endure it!"

"There is a strength to endure everything," Ivan said with a cold smile.

"What strength?"

"The strength of the Karamazov—the strength of the Karamazov baseness."

"To sink into debauchery, to stifle your soul with corruption, yes?"

"Possibly even that . . . only perhaps till I am thirty I shall escape it, and then."

"How will you escape it? By what will you escape it? That's impossible with your ideas."

"In the Karamazov way, again."

" 'Everything is lawful,' you mean? Everything is lawful, is that it?"

Ivan scowled, and all at once turned strangely pale.

"Ah, you've caught up yesterday's phrase, which so offended Miüsov—and which brother Dmitri pounced upon so naïvely and paraphrased!" he smiled queerly. "Yes, if you like, 'everything is lawful' since the word has been said. I won't deny it. And Mitenka's version isn't bad."

Alyosha looked at him in silence.

"I thought, brother, that going away from here I have you at least,'" Ivan said suddenly, with unexpected feeling; "but now I see that there is no place for me even in your heart, my dear hermit. The formula, 'all is lawful,' I won't renounce—will you renounce me for that, yes?"

Alyosha got up, went to him and softly kissed him on the lips.

"That's plagiarism," cried Ivan, highly delighted. "You stole that from my poem. Thank you though. Get up, Alyosha, it's time we were going, both of us."

They went out, but stopped when they reached the entrance of the restaurant.

"Listen, Alyosha," Ivan began in a resolute voice, "if I am really able to care for the sticky little leaves I shall only love them, remembering you. It's enough for me that you are somewhere here, and I shan't lose my desire for life yet. Is that enough for you? Take it as a declaration of love if you like. And now you go to the right and I to the left. And it's enough, do you hear, enough. I mean even if I don't go away tomorrow (I think I certainly shall go) and we meet again, don't say a word more on these subjects. I beg that particularly. And about brother Dmitri too, I ask you specially never speak to me again," he added, with sudden irritation; "it's all exhausted, it has all been said over and over again, hasn't it? And I'll make you one promise in return for it. When at thirty, I want to 'dash the cup to the ground,' wherever I may be I'll come to have one more talk with you, even though it were from America, you may be sure of that. I'll come on purpose. It will be very interesting to have a look at you, to see what you'll be by that time. It's rather a solemn promise, you see. And we really may be parting for seven years or ten. Come, go now to your *Pater Seraphicus*,[9] he is dying. If he dies without you, you will be angry with

---

9. "Angelic father"; from Goethe's *Faust*, II.

me for having kept you. Goodbye, kiss me once more; that's right, now go."

Ivan turned suddenly and went his way without looking back. It was just as brother Dmitri had left Alyosha the day before, though the parting had been very different. The strange resemblance flashed like an arrow through Alyosha's mind in the distress and dejection of that moment. He waited a little, looking after his brother. He suddenly noticed that Ivan swayed as he walked and that his right shoulder looked lower than his left. He had never noticed it before. But all at once he turned too, and almost ran to the monastery. It was nearly dark, and he felt almost frightened; something new was growing up in him for which he could not account. The wind had risen again as on the previous evening, and the ancient pines murmured gloomily about him when he entered the hermitage copse. He almost ran. "*Pater Seraphicus*—he got that name from somewhere—where from?" Alyosha wondered. "Ivan, poor Ivan, and when shall I see you again? . . . Here is the hermitage. Yes, yes, that he is, Pater Seraphicus, he will save me—from him and forever!"

Several times afterwards he wondered how he could on leaving Ivan so completely forget his brother Dmitri, though he had that morning, only a few hours before, so firmly resolved to find him and not to give up doing so, even should he be unable to return to the monastery that night.

Chapter VI

For a While a Very Obscure One

And Ivan Fyodorovich, on parting from Alyosha, went home to Fyodor Pavlovich's house. But, strange to say, he was overcome by insufferable depression, which grew greater at every step he took towards the house. There was nothing strange in his being depressed; what was strange was that Ivan Fyodorovich could not have said what was the cause of it. He had often been depressed before, and there was nothing surprising at his feeling so at such a moment, when he had broken off with everything that had brought him here, and was preparing that day to make a new start and enter upon a new, unknown future. He would again be as solitary as ever, and though he had great hopes, and great—too great—expectations from life, he could not have given any definite account of his hopes, his expectations, or even his desires.

Yet at that moment, though the apprehension of the new and unknown certainly found place in his heart, what was worrying him was something quite different. "Is it loathing for my father's house?" he wondered. "Quite likely; I am so sick of it; and though it's the last time I shall cross its hateful threshold, still I loathe it. . . . No, it's not that either. Is it the parting with Alyosha and the conversation I had with him? For so many years I've been silent with the whole world and not deigned to speak, and all of a sudden I reel off a rigmarole like that." It certainly might have been the youthful vexation of youthful inexperience and vanity, vexation at having failed to express himself, especially with such a being as Alyosha, on whom his heart had certainly been reckoning. No doubt that came in, that vexation, it must have done indeed; but yet that was not it, that was not it either. "I feel sick with depression and yet I can't tell what I want. Better not think, perhaps."

Ivan Fyodorovich tried "not to think," but that, too, was no use. What made his depression so vexatious and irritating was that it had a kind of casual, external character—he felt that. Some person or thing seemed to be standing out somewhere, just as something will sometimes obtrude itself upon the eye, and though one may be so busy with work or conversation that for a long time one does not notice it, yet it irritates and almost torments one till at last one realizes, and removes the offending object, often quite a trifling and ridiculous one—some article left about in the wrong place, a handkerchief on the floor, a book not replaced on the shelf, and so on. At last, feeling very cross and ill-humored, Ivan Fyodorovich arrived home, and suddenly, about fifteen paces from the garden gate, he guessed what was fretting and worrying him.

On a bench in the gateway the lackey Smerdyakov was sitting, enjoying the coolness of the evening, and at the first glance at him Ivan Fyodorovich knew that the lackey Smerdyakov was on his mind, and that it was this man that his soul loathed. It all dawned upon him suddenly and became clear. Just before, when Alyosha had been telling him of his meeting with Smerdyakov, he had felt a sudden twinge of gloom and loathing, which had immediately stirred responsive anger in his heart. Afterwards, as he talked, Smerdyakov had been forgotten for the time; but still he had been in his mind, and as soon as Ivan Fyodorovich parted from Alyosha and was walking home, the forgotten sensation began to obtrude itself again. "Is it possible that a miserable, contemptible creature like that can worry me so much?" he wondered, with insufferable irritation.

It was true that Ivan Fyodorovich had come of late to feel an intense dislike for the man, especially during the last few days. He had even begun to notice in himself a growing feeling that was almost of hatred for the creature. Perhaps this hatred was accentuated by the fact that when Ivan Fyodorovich first came to the neighborhood he had felt quite differently. Then he had taken a marked interest in Smerdyakov, and had even thought him very original. He had encouraged him to talk to him, although he had always wondered at a certain incoherence, or rather restlessness in his mind, and could not understand what it was that so continually and insistently worked upon the brain of "the contemplative." They discussed philosophical questions and even how there could have been light on the first day when the sun, moon, and stars were only created on the fourth day, and how that was to be understood. But Ivan Fyodorovich soon saw that, though the sun, moon, and stars might be an interesting subject, yet that it was quite secondary to Smerdyakov, and that he was looking for something altogether different. In one way and another, he began to betray a boundless vanity, and a wounded vanity, too, and that Ivan Fyodorovich disliked. It had first given rise to his aversion. Later on, there had been trouble in the house. Grushenka had come on the scene, and there had been the scandals with his brother Dmitri—they discussed that, too. But though Smerdyakov always talked of that with great excitement, it was impossible to discover what he desired to come of it. There was, in fact, something surprising in the illogicality and incoherence of some of his desires, accidentally betrayed and always vaguely expressed. Smerdyakov was always inquiring, putting certain indirect but obviously premeditated questions, but what his object was he did not explain, and usually at the most important moment he would break off and relapse into silence or pass to another subject. But what finally irritated Ivan Fyodorovich most and confirmed his dislike for him was the peculiar revolting familiarity which Smerdyakov began to show more and more markedly. Not that he forgot himself and was rude; on the contrary, he always spoke very respectfully, yet he had obviously begun to consider—goodness knows why!—that there was some sort of understanding between him and Ivan Fyodorovich. He always spoke in a tone that suggested that those two had some kind of compact, some secret between them, that had at some time been expressed on both sides, only known to them and beyond the comprehension of those mortals bustling around them. But for a long while Ivan Fyodorovich did not recognize the real cause of his growing dislike and he had only lately realized what was at the root of it. With a feeling of disgust and irritation he tried to pass in at the gate without speaking or looking at Smerdyakov. But Smerdyakov rose from the bench, and from that action alone, Ivan Fyodorovich knew instantly that he wanted particularly to talk to him. Ivan Fyodorovich looked at him and stopped, and the fact that he did stop, instead of passing by, as he meant to the minute before, drove him to fury. With anger and repulsion he looked at Smerdyakov's emasculate, sickly face, with the little curls combed forward on his forehead. His left eye winked and grinned as though to say, "Where are you going? You won't pass by; you see that we two clever people have something to say to each other."

Ivan Fyodorovich shuddered. "Get away, you wretch. What have

I to do with you, fool?" was on the tip of his tongue, but to his profound astonishment he heard himself say, "Is my father still asleep, or has he woken up?"

He asked the question softly and meekly, to his own surprise, and at once, again to his own surprise, sat down on the bench. For an instant he felt almost frightened; he remembered it afterwards. Smerdyakov stood facing him, his hands behind his back, looking at him with assurance and almost severity.

"His honor is still asleep," he articulated deliberately ("You were the first to speak, not I," he seemed to say). "I am surprised at you, sir," he added, after a pause, dropping his eyes affectedly, setting his right foot forward, and playing with the tip of his polished boot.

"Why are you surprised at me?" Ivan asked abruptly and sullenly, doing his utmost to restrain himself, and suddenly realizing, with disgust, that he felt intense curiosity and would not, on any account, have gone away without satisfying it.

"Why don't you go to Chermashnya, sir?" Smerdyakov suddenly raised his eyes and smiled familiarly. "Why I smile you must understand of yourself, if you are a clever man," his screwed-up left eye seemed to say.

"Why should I go to Chermashnya?" Ivan asked in surprise.

Smerdyakov was silent again.

"Fyodor Pavlovich himself has so begged you to, sir," he said at last, slowly and apparently attaching no significance to his answer. "I put you off with a secondary reason," he seemed to suggest, "simply to say something."

"Damn you! Speak out what you want!" Ivan Fyodorovich cried angrily at last, passing from meekness to violence.

Smerdyakov drew his right foot up to his left, pulled himself up, but still looked at him with the same serenity and the same little smile.

"Substantially nothing, sir—but just by way of conversation."

Another silence followed. They did not speak for nearly a minute. Ivan Fyodorovich knew that he ought to get up and show anger, and Smerdyakov stood before him and seemed to be waiting as though to see whether he would be angry or not. So at least it seemed to Ivan Fyodorovich. At last he moved to get up. Smerdyakov seemed to seize the moment.

"I'm in an awful position, Ivan Fyodorovich. I don't know how to help myself," he said resolutely and distinctly, and at his last word he sighed. Ivan Fyodorovich sat down again.

"They are both utterly crazy, sir, they are no better than little children, sir," Smerdyakov went on. "I am speaking of your parent and your brother Dmitri Fyodorovich. Here Fyodor Pavlovich will get up directly and begin worrying me every minute, 'Has she come? Why hasn't she come?' and so on up til midnight and even after midnight. And if Agrafena Alexandrovna doesn't come (for very likely she does not mean to come at all) then he will be at me again tomorrow morning, 'Why hasn't she come? When will she come?'—as though I were to blame for it. On the other side it's no better, sir. As soon as it gets dark, or even before, your brother will appear with his weapon in his hands: 'Look out, you rogue, you soup-maker. If you miss her and don't let me know she's been—I'll kill you before anyone.' When the night's over, in the morning, he, too, like Fyodor Pavlovich, begins worrying me to death. 'Why hasn't she come? Will she come soon?' And he, too, thinks me to blame because his lady hasn't come. And every day and every hour they get angrier and angrier, so that I sometimes think I shall kill myself in a fright, sir. I can't depend upon them, sir."

"And why have you meddled? Why did you begin to spy for Dmitri Fyodorovich?" said Ivan Fyodorovich irritably.

"How could I help meddling, sir? Though, indeed, I haven't meddled at all, if you want to know the truth of the matter. I kept quiet from the very beginning, not daring to answer; but he picked on me to be his servant Licharda.[1] He has had only one thing to say since: 'I'll kill you, you scoundrel, if you miss her.' I feel certain, sir, that I shall have a long fit tomorrow."

"What do you mean by 'a long fit'?"

"A long fit, lasting a long time, sir—several hours, or perhaps a day or two, sir. Once it went on for three days. I fell from the garret that time. The struggling ceased and then began again, and for three days I couldn't come back to my senses. Fyodor Pavlovich sent for Herzenstube, the doctor here, and he put ice on my head and tried another remedy, too. . . . I might have died, sir."

"But they say one can't tell with epilepsy when a fit is coming. What makes you say you will have one tomorrow?" Ivan Fyodorovich inquired, with a peculiar, irritable curiosity.

"That's just so. You can't tell beforehand, sir."

"Besides you fell from the garret then."

"I climb up to the garret every day. I might fall from the garret again tomorrow. And, if not, I might fall down the cellar steps, sir. I have to go into the cellar every day, too, sir."

Ivan Fyodorovich took a long look at him.

"You are talking nonsense, I see, and I don't quite understand you," he said softly, but with a sort of menace. "Do you mean to pretend to be ill tomorrow for three days, eh?"

Smerdyakov, who was looking at the ground again, and playing with the toe of his right foot, set the foot down, moved the left one forward, and, grinning, articulated:

1. Servant used as a tool in the murder of his master in the *Tale of Bova*, a seventeenth-century Russian adaptation of *Bevis of Hampton*.

"If I were able to play such a trick, sir, that is, pretend to have a fit, sir—and it would not be difficult for a man accustomed to them—I would have a perfect right to use such a means to save my life from death, sir. For even if Agrafena Alexandrovna comes to see his father while I am ill, his honor can't blame a sick man for not telling him. He'd be ashamed to."

"Damn it all!" Ivan Fyodorovich cried, his face working with anger, "Why are you always in such a funk for your life? All my brother Dmitri's threats are only hasty words and mean nothing. He won't kill you; it's not you he'll kill!"

"He'd kill me first of all, sir, like a fly. But even more than that, I am afraid I shall be taken for an accomplice of his when he does something crazy to his father."

"Why should you be taken for an accomplice?"

"They'll think I am an accomplice, because I let him know the signals as a great secret, sir."

"What signals? Whom did you tell? Confound you, speak more plainly."

"I'm bound to admit the fact," Smerdyakov drawled with pedantic composure, "that I have a secret with Fyodor Pavlovich in this business. As you know yourself (if only you do know it) he has for several days past locked himself in as soon as night or evening comes on. Of late you've been going upstairs to your room early every evening, and yesterday you did not come down at all, sir, and so perhaps you don't know how carefully he has begun to lock himself in at night, and even if Grigory Vasilyevich comes to the door he won't open to him till he hears his voice. But Grigory Vasilyevich does not come, because I wait upon him alone in his room now, sir. That's the arrangement he made himself ever since this to-do with Agrafena Alexandrovna began. But at night, by his orders, I go away to the lodge so that I don't get to sleep till midnight, but am on the watch, getting up and walking about the yard, waiting for Agrafena Alexandrovna to come. For the last few days he's been perfectly frantic expecting her. What he argues is, sir, she is afraid of him, Dmitri Fyodorovich (Mitka, as he calls him) 'and so,' says he, 'she'll come the back-way, late at night, to me. You look out for her,' says he, 'till midnight and later; and if she does come, you run up and knock at my door or at the window from the garden. Knock at first twice, rather gently, like this, one, two, and then three times more quickly, tap-tap-tap, then,' says he, 'I shall understand at once that she has come, and will open the door to you quietly.' Another signal he gave me in case anything unexpected happens. At first, two quick knocks, one, two, and then, after an interval, another much louder. Then he will understand that something has happened suddenly and that I must see him, and he will open to me so that I can go and speak to him. That's all in case Agrafena Alexandrovna can't come herself, but sends a message. Besides, Dmitri Fyodorovich might come, too, so I must let him know he is near. His honor is awfully afraid of Dmitri Fyodorovich, so that even if Agrafena Alexandrovna had come and were locked in with him, and Dmitri Fyodorovich were to turn up anywhere near at the time, I should be bound to let him know at once, knocking three times. So that the first signal of five knocks means Agrafena Alexandrovna has come, while the second signal of three knocks means 'something important to tell you.' His honor has shown me them several times and explained them. And as in the whole universe no one knows of these signals but myself and his honor, sir, so he'd open the door without the slightest hesitation and without calling out (he is awfully afraid of calling out aloud). Well, those signals are known to Dmitri Fyodorovich too, now."

"How are they known? Did you tell him? How dared you tell him?"

"It was through fright I did it, sir. How could I dare to keep it back from him? Dmitri Fyodorovich kept persisting every day, 'You are deceiving me, you are hiding something from me! I'll break both your legs for you.' So I told him those secret signals that he might see my slavish devotion, and might be satisfied that I was not deceiving him, but was telling him all I could."

"If you think that he'll make use of those signals and try to get in, don't let him in."

"But if I should be laid up with a fit, sir, how could I prevent his coming in then, sir, even if I dared prevent him, knowing how desperate he is?"

"Damn it! How can you be so sure you are going to have a fit, confound you? Are you laughing at me?"

"How could I dare laugh at you, and am I in a mood for laughing with this fear on me? I feel I am going to have a fit. I have a presentiment. Fright alone will bring it on."

"Confound it! If you are laid up, Grigory will be on the watch. Let Grigory know beforehand; he will be sure not to let him in."

"I would never dare to tell Grigory Vasilyevich about the signals without orders from my master. And as for Grigory Vasilyevich's hearing him and not admitting him, he has been ill ever since yesterday, and Martha Ignatyevna intends to give him medicine tomorrow. They've just arranged it. It's a very strange remedy of hers. Martha Ignatyevna knows of a preparation and always keeps it, sir. It's a strong thing made from some herb. She has the secret of it, sir, and she always gives it to Grigory Vasilyevich three times a year, sir, when his lumbago's so bad he is almost paralyzed by it. Then she takes a towel, wets it with the stuff, and rubs his whole back for half an hour till it's quite red and swollen, and what's left in the bottle she gives him to drink with a special prayer, sir; but not quite all, for on such occasions she leaves some for herself, and drinks it herself. And as they never take strong drink, sir, I assure you they both fall asleep at once and sleep sound a very long time. And when Grigory Vasilyevich wakes up he is perfectly well after it, but Martha Ignatyevna always has a headache from it, sir. So, if Martha Ignatyevna carries out her intention tomorrow, they won't hear anything and hinder Dmitri Fyodorovich. They'll be asleep, sir."

"What a rigmarole! And it all seems to happen at once, as though it were planned. You'll have a fit and they'll both be unconscious," cried Ivan Fyodorovich. "But aren't you trying to arrange it so?" broke from him suddenly, and he frowned threateningly.

"How could I, sir? . . . And why should I, when it all depends on Dmitri Fyodorovich and his plans? . . . If he means to do anything, he'll do it; but if not, I won't be thrusting him upon his father."

"And why should he go to father, especially on the sly, if, as you say yourself, Agrafena Alexandrovna won't come at all?" Ivan Fyodorovich went on, turning white with anger. "You say that yourself, and all the while I've been here, I've felt sure it was all the old man's fancy, and the creature won't come to him. Why should Dmitri break in on him if she doesn't come? Speak, I want to know what you are thinking!"

"You know yourself why he'll come, sir. What's the use of what I think? His honor will come simply because he is in a rage or suspicious on account of my illness perhaps, and he'll dash in, as he did yesterday through impatience to search the rooms, to see whether she hasn't escaped him on the sly. He is perfectly well aware, too, that Fyodor Pavlovich has a big envelope with three thousand rubles in it, tied up with ribbon and sealed with three seals. On it is written in his own hand, 'To my angel Grushenka, if she will come,' to which he added three days later, 'for my little chicken.' There's no knowing what that might do, sir."

"Nonsense!" shouted Ivan Fyodorovich, almost beside himself. "Dmitri won't come to steal money and kill my father to do it. He might have killed him yesterday on account of Grushenka, like the frantic, savage fool he is, but he won't steal."

"He is in very great need of money now—the greatest need, Ivan Fyodorovich. You don't know in what need he is," Smerdyakov explained, with perfect composure and remarkable distinctness. "He looks on that three thousand as his own, too. He said so to me himself. 'My father still owes me just three thousand,' he said. And besides that, consider, Ivan Fyodorovich, there is something else perfectly true, sir. It's as good as certain, so to say, that Agrafena Alexandrovna will force him, if only she cares to, to marry her—the master himself, I mean Fyodor Pavlovich, sir—if only she cares to, and of course she may care to. All I've said is that she won't come, but maybe she's looking for more than that, sir—I mean, to be mistress here. I know myself that Samsonov, her merchant, was laughing with her about it, telling her quite openly that it would not be at all a stupid thing to do. And she's got plenty of sense, sir. She wouldn't marry a beggar like Dmitri Fyodorovich. So, taking that into consideration, Ivan Fyodorovich, reflect that then neither Dmitri Fyodorovich nor yourself and your brother, Alexey Fyodorovich, would have anything after the master's death, not a ruble, for Agrafena Alexandrovna would marry him simply to get hold of the whole, all the money there is. But if your father were to die now, there'd be some forty thousand for sure, even for Dmitri Fyodorovich whom he hates so, for he's made no will. . . . Dmitri Fyodorovich knows all that very well."

A sort of shudder passed over Ivan Fyodorovich's face. He suddenly flushed.

"Then why on earth," he suddenly interrupted Smerdyakov, "do you advise me to go to Chermashnya? What did you mean by that? If I go away, you see what will happen here." Ivan Fyodorovich drew his breath with difficulty.

"Precisely so, sir," said Smerdyakov, softly and reasonably, watching Ivan Fyodorovich intently, however.

"What do you mean by 'precisely so'?" Ivan Fyodorovich questioned him, with a menacing light in his eyes, restraining himself with difficulty.

"I spoke because I felt sorry for you. If I were in your place I should simply throw it all up . . . rather than stay on in such a position, sir," answered Smerdyakov, with the most candid air looking at Ivan Fyodorovich's flashing eyes. They were both silent.

"You seem to be a perfect idiot, and what's more . . . an awful scoundrel, too." Ivan Fyodorovich rose suddenly from the bench. He was about to pass straight through the gate, but he stopped short and turned to Smerdyakov. Something strange followed. Ivan Fyodorovich, in a sudden paroxysm, bit his lip, clenched his fists, and, in another minute, would have flung himself on Smerdyakov. The latter, anyway, noticed it at the same moment, started, and shrank back. But the moment passed without mischief to Smerdyakov, and Ivan Fyodorovich turned in silence, as it seemed in perplexity, to the gate.

"I am going away to Moscow tomorrow, if you care to know— early tomorrow morning. That's all!" he suddenly said angrily, loudly, and clearly, and wondered himself afterwards what need there was to say this then to Smerdyakov.

"That's the best thing you can do, sir," he responded, as though he had expected to hear it; "except that you can always be telegraphed for from Moscow, sir, if anything should happen here."

Ivan stopped again, and again turned quickly to Smerdyakov. But a change had passed over him, too. All his familarity and carelessness had completely disappeared. His face expressed attention and expectation, intent but timid and cringing.

"Haven't you something more to say—something to add?" could be read in the intent gaze he fixed on Ivan Fyodorovich.

"And couldn't I be sent for from Chermashnya, too—in case anything happened?" Ivan Fyodorovich shouted suddenly, for some unknown reason raising his voice terribly.

"From Chermashnya, too . . . you could be sent for, sir," Smerdyakov muttered, almost in a whisper, looking disconcerted, but gazing intently into Ivan Fyodorovich's eyes.

"Only Moscow is further and Chermashnya is nearer. Is it to save my spending money on the fare, or to save my going so far out of my way, that you insist on Chermashnya?"

"Precisely so, sir . . ." muttered Smerdyakov, with a breaking voice. He looked at Ivan Fyodorovich with a revolting smile, and again made ready to draw back. But to his astonishment Ivan Fyodorovich broke into a laugh, and went through the gate still laughing. Anyone who had seen his face at that moment would have known that he was not laughing from lightness of heart, and he could not have explained himself what he was feeling at that instant. He moved and walked as though in a nervous frenzy.

Chapter VII

"It's Always Worthwhile Speaking to a Clever Man"

And in the same nervous frenzy, too, he spoke. Meeting Fyodor Pavlovich in the drawing room as soon as he went in, he shouted to him, waving his hands, "I am going upstairs to my room, not in to you. Goodbye!" and passed by, trying not even to look at his father. Very possibly the old man was too hateful to him at that moment; but such an unceremonious display of hostility was a surprise even to Fyodor Pavlovich. And the old man evidently wanted to tell him something at once and had come to meet him in the drawing room on purpose. Receiving this amiable greeting, he stood still in silence and with an ironical air watched his son going upstairs, till he passed out of sight.

"What's the matter with him?" he promptly asked Smerdyakov, who had followed Ivan Fyodorovich.

"Angry about something, sir. Who can tell?" he muttered evasively.

"Confound him! Let him be angry then. Bring in the samovar, and get along with you. Look sharp! No news?"

Then followed a series of questions such as Smerdyakov had just complained of to Ivan Fyodorovich, all relating to his expected visitor, and these questions we will omit. Half an hour later the house was locked, and the crazy old man was wandering alone through the rooms in excited expectation of hearing every minute the five knocks agreed upon. Now and then he peered out into the darkness, seeing nothing.

It was very late, but Ivan Fyodorovich was still awake and reflecting. He sat up late that night, till two o'clock. But we will not give an account of his thoughts, and this is not the place to look into that soul—its turn will come. And even if one tried, it would be very hard to give an account of them, for there were no thoughts in his brain, but something very vague, and, above all, intense excitement. He felt himself that he had lost his bearings. He was fretted, too, by all sorts of strange and almost surprising desires; for instance, after midnight he suddenly had an intense irresistible inclination to go down, open the door, go to the lodge and beat Smerdyakov. But if he had been asked why, he could not have given any exact reason, except perhaps that he loathed the lackey as one who had insulted him more gravely than anyone in the world. On the other hand, he was more than once that night overcome by a sort of inexplicable humiliating terror, which he felt positively paralyzed his physical powers. His head ached and he was giddy. A feeling of hatred was rankling in his heart, as though he meant to avenge himself on someone. He even hated Alyosha, recalling the conversation he had just had with him. At moments he hated himself intensely. Of Katerina Ivanovna he almost forgot to think, and wondered greatly at this afterwards, especially as he remembered perfectly that when he had protested so valiantly to Katerina Ivanovna that he would go away next day to Moscow, something had whispered in his heart, "That's nonsense, you are not going, and it won't be so easy to tear yourself away as you are boasting now."

Remembering that night long afterwards, Ivan recalled with peculiar repulsion how he had suddenly got up from the sofa and stealthily, as though he were afraid of being watched, had opened the door, gone out on the staircase and listened to Fyodor Pavlovich stirring down below, had listened a long while—some five minutes—with a sort of strange curiosity, holding his breath while his heart throbbed. And why he had done all this, why he was listening, he could not have said. That "action" all his life afterwards he called "infamous," and at the bottom of his heart, he thought of it as the basest action of his life. For Fyodor Pavlovich himself he felt no hatred at that moment, but was simply intensely curious to know how he was walking down there below and what he must be doing now. He wondered and imagined how he must be peeping out of the dark windows and stopping in the middle of the

room, listening, listening—for someone to knock. Ivan Fyodorovich went out onto the stairs twice to listen like this.

About two o'clock when everything was quiet, and even Fyodor
Pavlovich had gone to bed, Ivan Fyodorovich had got into bed,
firmly resolved to fall asleep at once, as he felt fearfully exhausted.
And he did fall asleep at once, and slept soundly without dreams,
but waked early, at seven o'clock, when it was broad daylight.
Opening his eyes, he was surprised to feel himself extraordinarily
vigorous. He jumped up at once and dressed quickly; then dragged
out his trunk and began packing immediately. His linen had come
back from the laundress the previous morning. Ivan Fyodorovich
positively smiled at the thought that everything was helping his
sudden departure. And his departure certainly was sudden. Though
Ivan Fyodorovich had said the day before (to Katerina Ivanovna,
Alyosha, and Smerdyakov) that he was leaving next day, yet he
remembered that he had no thought of departure when he went to
bed, or, at least, had not dreamed that his first act in the morning
would be to pack his trunk. At last his trunk and bag were ready. It
was about nine o'clock when Martha Ignatyevna came in with her
usual inquiry, "Where will your honor take your tea, in your own
room or downstairs?" He looked almost cheerful, but there was
about him, about his words and gestures, something hurried and
scattered. Greeting his father affably, and even inquiring specially
after his health, though he did not wait to hear his answer to the
end, he announced that he was starting off in an hour to return to
Moscow for good, and begged him to send for the horses. His
father heard this announcement with no sign of surprise, and forgot
in an unmannerly way to show regret at losing him. Instead of
doing so, he flew into a great flutter at the recollection of some
important business of his own.

"What a fellow you are! Not to tell me yesterday! Never mind;
we'll manage it all the same. Do me a great service, my dear boy.
Go to Chermashnya on the way. It's only to turn to the left from
the station at Volovya, only another eight little miles and you come
to Chermashyna."

"I'm sorry, I can't. It's fifty miles to the railway and the train
starts for Moscow at seven o'clock tonight. I can only just catch
it."

"You'll catch it tomorrow or the day after, but today turn off to
Chermashnya. It won't put you out much to humor your father! If
I hadn't had something to keep me here, I would have run over
myself long ago, for I have some important and pressing business
there. But here I . . . it's not the time for me to go now . . . You see,
I've two pieces of copse land there, in two sections, one in Begichev
and one in Dyachkino, lying fallow. The Maslovs, an old merchant
and his son, will give only eight thousand for the timber. But last

year I just missed a purchaser who would have given twelve, but
he's not from around here, that's the trouble. There's no getting
anyone around here to buy it. The Maslovs have it all their own
way. One has to take what they'll give, because no one here dares
bid against them. The priest at Ilyinskoe wrote to me last Thursday
that a merchant called Gorstkin, a man I know, had turned up.
What makes him valuable is that he is not from these parts, but
from Pogryobov, so he is not afraid of the Maslovs. He says he will
give me eleven thousand for the copse. Do you hear? But he'll only
be here, the priest writes, for a week altogether, so you must go at
once and make a bargain with him."

"Well, you write to the priest; he'll make the bargain."

"He can't do it. He has no eye for business. He is a perfect
treasure, I'd give him twenty thousand to take care of for me
without a receipt; but he has no eye for business, he is a perfect
child, a crow could deceive him. And yet he is a learned man,
would you believe it? This Gorstkin looks like a peasant, he wears a
blue caftan, but as for character, he's an out and out scoundrel.
That's the common complaint. He is a liar, that's the trouble.
Sometimes he tells such lies that you wonder why he is doing it. He
told me the year before last that his wife was dead and that he had
married another, and would you believe it, there was not a word of
truth in it? His wife has never died at all, she is alive to this day
and gives him a beating twice a week. So what you have to find out
is whether he is lying or speaking the truth, when he says he wants
to buy it and would give eleven thousand."

"I shall be no use in such a business. I have no eye either."

"Stay, wait a bit! You will be of use, for I will tell you the signs
by which you can judge about Gorstkin. I've done business with
him a long time. You see, you must watch his beard; he has a
nasty, thin, red beard. If his beard shakes when he talks and he gets
cross, it's all right, he is saying what he means, he wants to do
business. But if he strokes his beard with his left hand and grins—
he is trying to cheat you. Don't watch his eyes, you won't find out
anything from his eyes, he is a deep one, a rogue—but watch his
beard! I'll give you a note and you show it to him. He's called
Gorstkin, though his real name is Lyagavy;[2] but don't call him so,
he will be offended. If you come to an understanding with him, and
see it's all right, write here at once. You need only write: 'He's not
lying.' Stand out for eleven thousand; one thousand you can knock
off, but not more. Just think! there's a difference between eight
thousand and eleven thousand. It's as good as picking up three
thousand; it's not so easy to find a purchaser, and I'm in desperate
need of money. Only let me know it's serious, and I'll run over and

2. I.e., setter dog.

fix it up. I'll snatch the time somehow. But what's the good of my galloping over, if it's all a notion of the priest's? Come, will you go?"

"Oh, I can't spare the time. You must excuse me."

"Come, you might oblige your father. I won't forget it. You've no heart, any of you—that's what it is! What's a day or two to you? Where are you going now—to Venice? Your Venice will keep another two days. I would have sent Alyosha, but what use is Alyosha in a thing like that? I send you just because you are a clever man. Do you suppose I don't see that? You know nothing about timber, but you've got an eye. All that is wanted is to see whether the man is in earnest. I tell you, watch his beard—if his beard shakes you know he is in earnest."

"You force me to go to that damned Chermashnya yourself, then?" cried Ivan Fyodorovich, with a malignant smile.

Fyodor Pavlovich did not catch, or would not catch, the malignancy, but he caught the smile.

"Then you'll go, you'll go? I'll scribble the note for you at once."

"I don't know whether I shall go. I don't know. I'll decide on the way."

"Nonsense! Decide at once. My dear fellow, decide! If you settle the matter, write me a line; give it to the priest and he'll send it on to me at once. And I won't delay you more than that. You can go to Venice. The priest will give you horses back to Volovya station."

The old man was quite delighted. He wrote the note, and sent for the horses. A light lunch was brought in, with brandy. When Fyodor Pavlovich was pleased, he usually became expansive, but today he seemed to restrain himself. Of Dmitri Fyodorovich, for instance, he did not say a word. He was quite unmoved by the parting, and seemed, in fact, at a loss for something to say. Ivan Fyodorovich noticed this particularly. "He must be bored with me," he thought. Only when accompanying his son out on to the steps, the old man began to fuss about. He would have kissed him, but Ivan Fyodorovich made haste to hold out his hand, obviously avoiding the kiss. His father saw it at once, and instantly pulled himself up.

"Well, good luck to you, good luck to you!" he repeated from the steps. "You'll come again some time or other? Mind you do come. I shall always be glad to see you. Well, Christ be with you!"

Ivan Fyodorovich got into the carriage.

"Good-bye, Ivan! Don't be too hard on me!" the father called for the last time.

The whole household came out to take leave—Smerdyakov, Martha and Grigory. Ivan gave them ten rubles each. When he had seated himself in the carriage, Smerdyakov jumped up to arrange the rug.

"You see . . . I am going to Chermashnya," broke suddenly from Ivan Fyodorovich. Again, as the day before, the words seemed to drop of themselves, and he laughed, too, a peculiar, nervous laugh. He remembered it long after.

"It's a true saying then, that 'it's always worthwhile speaking to a clever man,' " answered Smerdyakov firmly, looking significantly at Ivan Fyodorovich.

The carriage rolled away. Nothing was clear in the traveler's soul, but he looked eagerly around him at the fields, at the hills, at the trees, at a flock of geese flying high overhead in the bright sky. And all of a sudden he felt very happy. He tried to talk to the driver, and he felt intensely interested in an answer the peasant made him; but a minute later he realized that he was not catching anything, and that he had not really even taken in the peasant's answer. He was silent, and it was pleasant even so. The air was fresh, pure and cool, the sky bright. The images of Alyosha and Katerina Ivanovna floated into his mind. But he softly smiled, blew softly on the friendly phantoms, and they flew away. "There's plenty of time for them," he thought. They reached the station quickly, changed horses, and galloped to Volovya. "Why is it worthwhile speaking to a clever man? What did he mean by that?" The thought seemed suddenly to clutch at his breathing. "And why did I tell him I was going to Chermashnya?" They reached Volovya Station. Ivan Fyodorovich got out of the carriage, and the drivers stood round him bargaining over the journey of eight miles to Chermashnya. He told them to harness the horses. He went into the station house, looked round, glanced at the overseer's wife, and suddenly went back to the entrance.

"I won't go to Chermashnya. Am I too late to reach the railway by seven, brothers?"

"We shall just do it. Shall we get the carriage out?"

"At once. Will any one of you be going to the town tomorrow?"

"To be sure. Mitri here will."

"Can you do me a service, Mitri? Go to my father's, to Fyodor Pavlovich Karamazov, and tell him I haven't gone to Chermashnya. Can you?"

"Of course I can. I've known Fyodor Pavlovich a long time."

"And here's something for you, for I daresay he won't give you anything," said Ivan Fyodorovich, laughing gaily.

"You may depend on it he won't." Mitri laughed too. "Thank you, sir. I'll be sure to do it."

At seven o'clock Ivan Fyodorovich got into the train and set off for Moscow. "Away with the past. I've done with the old world forever, and may I have no news, no echo, from it. To a new life, new places, and no looking back!" But instead of delight his soul was filled with such gloom, and his heart ached with such anguish, as he had never known in his life before. He was thinking all the night. The train flew on, and only at daybreak, when he was approaching Moscow, he suddenly roused himself from his meditation.

"I am a scoundrel," he whispered to himself.

Meanwhile Fyodor Pavlovich remained well satisfied at having seen his son off. For two hours afterwards he felt almost happy, and sat drinking brandy. But suddenly something happened which was very annoying and unpleasant for everyone in the house, and completely upset Fyodor Pavlovich's equanimity at once. Smerdyakov went to the cellar for something and fell down from the top of the steps. Fortunately, Martha Ignatyevna was in the yard and heard him in time. She did not see the fall, but heard his scream—the strange, peculiar scream, long familiar to her—the scream of the epileptic falling in a fit. They could not tell whether the fit had come on him at the moment he was descending the steps, so that he must have fallen unconscious, or whether it was the fall and the shock that had caused the fit in Smerdyakov, who was known to be liable to them. They found him at the bottom of the cellar steps, writhing in convulsions and foaming at the mouth. It was thought at first that he must have broken something—an arm or a leg—and hurt himself, but "God had preserved him," as Martha Ignatyevna expressed it—nothing of the kind had happened. But it was difficult to get him out of the cellar, into God's light. They asked the neighbors to help and managed it somehow. Fyodor Pavlovich himself was present at the whole ceremony. He helped, evidently alarmed and upset. The sick man did not regain consciousness; the convulsions ceased for a time, but then began again, and everyone concluded that the same thing would happen as had happened a year before, when he accidentally fell from the garret. They remembered that ice had been put on his head then. There was still ice in the cellar, and Martha Ignatyevna had some brought up. In the evening, Fyodor Pavlovich sent for Doctor Herzenstube, who arrived at once. He was a most estimable old man, and the most careful and conscientious doctor in the province. After careful examination, he concluded that the fit was a very violent one and might have serious consequences; that meanwhile he, Herzenstube, did not fully understand it, but that by tomorrow morning, if the present remedies were unavailing, he would venture to try something else. The invalid was taken to the lodge, to a room next to Grigory's and Martha Ignatyevoa's.

Then Fyodor Pavlovich had one misfortune after another to put up with that day. Martha Ignatyevna cooked the dinner, and the soup, compared with Smerdyakov's, was no "better than dishwater," and the fowl was so dried up that it was impossible even to chew it. To her master's bitter, though deserved, reproaches, Martha Ignatyevna replied that the fowl was a very old one to begin with, and that she had never been trained as a cook. In the evening there was another trouble in store for Fyodor Pavlovich; he was informed that Grigory, who had not been well for the last three days, was completely laid up by his lumbago. Fyodor Pavlovich finished his tea as early as possible and locked himself up alone in the house. He was in terrible excitement and suspense. That evening he reckoned on Grushenka's coming almost as a certainty. He had received from Smerdyakov that morning an assurance "that she had promised to come without fail." The incorrigible old man's heart throbbed with excitement; he paced up and down his empty rooms listening. He had to be on the alert. Dmitri Fyodorovich might be on the watch for her somewhere, and when she knocked on the window (Smerdyakov had informed him two days before that he had told her where and how to knock) the door must be opened at once. She must not be a second in the passage, for fear—which God forbid!—that she should be frightened and run away. Fyodor Pavlovich had much to think of, but never had his heart been steeped in such voluptuous hopes. This time he could say almost certainly that she would come!

Book Six

THE RUSSIAN MONK

Chapter I

Father Zosima and His Visitors

When with an anxious and aching heart Alyosha went into his elder's cell, he stood still almost astonished. Instead of a sick man at his last gasp, perhaps unconscious, as he had feared to find him, he saw him sitting up in his chair and, though weak and exhausted, his face was bright and cheerful, he was surrounded by visitors and engaged in a quiet and joyful conversation. But he had only got up from his bed a quarter of an hour before Alyosha's arrival; his visitors had gathered together in his cell earlier, waiting for him to wake, having received a most confident assurance from Father Païssy that "the teacher would get up, and as he had himself promised in the morning, converse once more with those dear to his heart." This promise and indeed every word of the dying elder's Father Païssy put implicit trust in. If he had seen him unconscious, if he had seen him breathe his last, and yet had his promise that he would rise up and say goodbye to him, he would not have believed perhaps even in death, but would still have expected the dead man to recover and fulfill his promise. In the morning as he lay down to sleep, Father Zosima had told him positively: "I shall not die without the delight of another conversation with you, beloved of my heart. I shall look once more on your dear faces and pour out my heart to you once again." The monks, who had gathered for this probably last conversation with Father Zosima, had all been his devoted friends for many years. There were four of them; Father Iosif and Father Païssy, Father Mikhail, the warden of the hermitage, a man not very old and far from being learned. He was of humble origin, of strong will and steadfast faith, of austere appearance, but of deep tenderness, though he obviously concealed it as though he were almost ashamed of it. The fourth, Father Anfim, was a very old and humble little monk of the poorest peasant class. He was almost illiterate, and very quiet, scarcely speaking to anyone. He was the humblest of the humble, and looked as though he had been frightened by something great and awful beyond the scope of his intelligence. Father Zosima had a great affection for this timorous man, and always treated him with marked respect, though perhaps there was no one he had known to whom he had said less, in spite of the fact that he had spent years wandering about holy Russia with him. That was very long ago, forty years before, when Father Zosima first began his life as a monk in a poor and little monastery at Kostroma, and when, shortly after, he had accompanied Father Anfim on his pilgrimage to collect alms for their poor monastery. The whole party were in the bedroom which, as we mentioned before, was very small, so that there was scarcely room for the four of them (in addition to Porfiry, the novice, who stood) to sit round Father Zosima on chairs brought from the sitting room. It was already beginning to get dark, the room was lighted up by the lamps and the candles before the icons. Seeing Alyosha standing embarrassed in the doorway, Father Zosima smiled at him joyfully and held out his hand.

"Welcome, my quiet one, welcome, my dear, here you are too. I knew you would come."

Alyosha went up to him, bowed down before him to the ground and wept. Something surged up from his heart, his soul was quivering, he wanted to sob.

"Come, don't weep over me yet," Father Zosima smiled, laying his right hand on his head. "You see I am sitting up talking; maybe I shall live another twenty years yet, as that dear good woman from Vishegorye, with her little Lizaveta in her arms, wished me yesterday. God bless the mother and the little girl Lizaveta," he crossed himself. "Porfiry, did you take her offering where I told you?"

He meant the sixty kopecks brought him the day before by the good-humored woman to be given "to someone poorer than me." Such offerings, always of money gained by personal toil, are made by way of penance voluntarily undertaken. The elder had sent Porfiry the evening before to a widow, whose house had been burned down lately, and who after the fire had gone with her children begging alms. Porfiry hastened "to reply that he had given the money, as he had been instructed, from an unknown benefactress."

"Get up, my dear boy," the elder went on to Alyosha. "Let me look at you. Have you been home and seen your brother?" It seemed strange to Alyosha that he asked so confidently and precisely, about one of his brothers only—but which one? Then perhaps he had sent him out both yesterday and today for the sake of that brother.

"I have seen one of my brothers," answered Alyosha.

"I mean the elder one, to whom I bowed down."

"I only saw him yesterday and could not find him today," said Alyosha.

"Make haste to find him, go again tomorrow and make haste, leave everything and make haste. Perhaps you may still have time to prevent something terrible. I bowed down yesterday to the great suffering in store for him."

He was suddenly silent and seemed to be pondering. The words were strange. Father Iosif, who had witnessed the scene yesterday, exchanged glances with Father Païssy. Alyosha could not resist asking:

"Father and teacher," he began with extreme emotion, "your words are too obscure. . . . What is this suffering in store for him?"

"Don't inquire. I seemed to see something terrible yesterday . . . as though his whole future were expressed in his eyes. A look came into his eyes—so that I was instantly horror-stricken at what that man is preparing for himself. Once or twice in my life I've seen such a look in a man's face . . . reflecting as it were his future fate, and that fate, alas, came to pass. I sent you to him, Alexey, for I thought your brotherly face would help him. But everything and all our fates are from the Lord. 'Except a corn of wheat fall into the ground and die, it abideth alone; but if it die, it bringeth forth much fruit.' Remember that. You, Alexey, I've many times silently blessed for your face, know that," added the elder with a gentle smile. "This is what I think of you, you will go forth from these walls, but will live like a monk in the world. You will have many enemies, but even your foes will love you. Life will bring you many misfortunes, but you will find your happiness in them, and will bless life and will make others bless it—which is what matters most. Well, that is your character. Fathers and teachers," he addressed his friends with a tender smile, "I have never till today told even him why the face of his youth is so dear to me. Now I will tell you. His face has been as it were a remembrance and a prophecy for me. At the dawn of my life when I was a child I had an elder brother who died before my eyes at seventeen. And later on in the course of my life I gradually became convinced that that brother had been for a guidance and a sign from on high for me. For had he not come into my life, I should never perhaps, so I fancy at least, have become a monk and entered on this precious path. He appeared first to me in my childhood and here at the end of my pilgrimage, he seems to have come to me over again. It is marvelous, fathers and teachers, that Alexey, who has some, though not a great, resemblance in face, seems to me so like him spiritually, that many times I have taken him for that young man, my brother, mysteriously come back to me at the end of my pilgrimage, as a reminder and an inspiration. So that I positively wondered at so strange a dream in myself. Do you hear this, Porfiry?" he turned to the novice who waited on him. "Many times I've seen in your face as it were a look of mortification that I love Alexey more than you.

Now you know why that was so, but I love you too, know that, and many times I grieved at your mortification. I should like to tell you, dear friends, of that youth, my brother, for there has been no presence in my life more precious, more significant and touching. My heart is full of tenderness, and I look at my whole life at this moment as though living through it again."

Here I must observe that this last conversation of Father Zosima with the friends who visited him on the last day of his life had been partly preserved in writing. Alexey Fyodorovich Karamazov wrote it down from memory, some time after his elder's death. But whether this was only the conversation that took place then, or whether he added to it his notes of parts of former conversations with his teacher, I cannot determine. In his account, Father Zosima's talk goes on without interruption, as though he told his life to his friends in the form of a story, though there is no doubt, from other accounts of it, that the conversation that evening was general. Though the guests did not interrupt Father Zosima much, yet they too talked, perhaps even told something themselves. Besides, Father Zosima could not have carried on an uninterrupted narrative, for he was sometimes gasping for breath, his voice failed him, and he even lay down to rest on his bed, though he did not fall asleep and his visitors did not leave their seats. Once or twice the conversation was interrupted by Father Païssy's reading the Gospel. It is worthy of note, too, that no one of them supposed that he would die that night, for on that evening of his life after his deep sleep in the day he seemed suddenly to have found new strength, which kept him up through this long conversation. It was like a last effort of love which gave him incredible energy; only for a little time, however, for his life was cut short immediately ... But of that later. I will only add now that I have preferred to confine myself to the account given by Alexey Fyodorovich Karamazov, without going into the details of the conversation. It will be shorter and not so fatiguing, though of course, as I must repeat, Alyosha took a great deal from previous conversations and added them to it.

Chapter II

Notes of the Life in God[1] of the Deceased Priest and Monk, the Elder Zosima, Taken from His Own Words by Alexey Fyodorovich Karamazov

Biographical Notes

(a) FATHER ZOSIMA'S BROTHER

Beloved fathers and teachers, I was born in a distant province in the north, in the town of V——. My father was a nobleman by birth, but of no great distinction or position. He died when I was only two years old, and I don't remember him at all. He left my mother a small house built of wood, and some capital, not much, but sufficient to keep her and her children in comfort. There were two of us, my elder brother Markel and I, Zinovy. He was eight years older than I was, of hasty irritable temperament, but kind-hearted and not sarcastic. He was remarkably silent, especially at home with me, his mother, and the servants. He did well at school, but did not get on with his schoolfellows, though he never quarreled, at least so my mother has told me. Six months before his death, when he was seventeen, he made friends with a political exile who had been banished from Moscow to our town for freethinking, and led a solitary existence there. He was a good scholar who had gained distinction in philosophy in the university. Something made him take a fancy to Markel, and he used to ask him to see him. The young man would spend whole evenings with him during that winter, till the exile was summoned to Petersburg to take up his post again at his own request, as he had powerful friends.

It was the beginning of Lent, and Markel would not fast, he was rude and laughed at it. "That's all silly twaddle and there is no God," he said, horrifying my mother, the servants, and me too. For though I was only nine, I too was aghast at hearing such words. We had four servants, all serfs, bought in the name of a landowner who was a friend of ours. I remember my mother selling one of the four, the cook Afimya, who was lame and elderly, for sixty paper rubles, and hiring a free servant to take her place.

In the sixth week in Lent, my brother, who was never strong and had a tendency to consumption, was taken ill. He was tall but thin and delicate-looking, and of very pleasing countenance. I suppose he caught cold; anyway the doctor, who came, soon whispered to my mother that it was galloping consumption, that he would not live through the spring. My mother began weeping, and careful not

---

1. The Russian word used for "life"—*zhitie*—is a genre heading: "Saint's Life."

to alarm my brother she entreated him to go to church, to confess and take the sacrament, as he was still able to move about. This made him angry, and he said something profane about the church. He grew thoughtful, however; he guessed at once that he was seriously ill, and that that was why his mother was begging him to confess and take the sacrament. He had been aware, indeed, for a long time past, that he was far from well, and had a year before coolly observed at dinner to our mother and me, "My life won't be long among you, I may not live another year," which seemed now like a prophecy.

Three days passed and Holy Week had come. And on Tuesday morning my brother began going to church. "I am doing this simply for your sake, mother, to please and comfort you," he said. My mother wept with joy and grief, "his end must be near," she thought, "if there's such a change in him." But he was not able to go to church long, he took to his bed, so he had to confess and take the sacraments at home.

It was a late Easter, and the days were bright, fine, and full of fragrance. I remember he used to cough all night and sleep badly, but in the morning he dressed and tried to sit up in an armchair. That's how I remember him sitting, quiet and gentle, smiling, his face bright and joyous, in spite of his illness. A marvelous change passed over him, his spirit seemed transformed. The old nurse would come in and say, "Let me light the lamp before the holy image, my dear." And formerly he would not have allowed it and would have blown it out.

"Light it, light it, dear, I was a wretch to have prevented your doing it. You are praying when you light the lamp, and I am praying when I rejoice seeing you. So we are praying to the same God."

Those words seemed strange to us, and mother would go to her room and weep, but when she went in to him she wiped her eyes and looked cheerful. "Mother, don't weep, darling," he would say, "I've long to live yet, long to rejoice with you, and life is glad and joyful."

"Ah, dear boy, how can you talk of joy when you lie feverish at night, coughing as though you would tear yourself to pieces."

"Don't cry, mother," he would answer, "life is paradise, and we are all in paradise, but we won't see it, if we would, we should have heaven on earth the next day."

Everyone wondered at his words, he spoke so strangely and positively; we were all touched and wept. Friends came to see us. "Dear ones," he would say to them, "what have I done that you should love me so, how can you love anyone like me, and how was it I did not know, I did not appreciate it before?"

When the servants came in to him he would say continually,

"Dear, kind people, why are you doing so much for me, do I deserve to be waited on? If it were God's will for me to live, I would wait on you, for all men should wait on one another." Mother shook her head as she listened. "My darling, it's your illness makes you talk like that."

"Mother, my joy," he would say, "there must be servants and masters, but if so I will be the servant of my servants, the same as they are to me. And another thing, mother, every one of us has sinned against all men, and I more than any."

Mother positively smiled at that, smiled through her tears. "Why, how could you have sinned against all men, more than all? Robbers and murderers have done that, but what sin have you committed yet, that you hold yourself more guilty than all?"

"Mother, little heart of mine," he said (he had begun using such strange caressing words at that time), "little heart of mine, my joy, believe me, everyone is really responsible to all men for all men and for everything. I don't know how to explain it to you, but I feel it is so, painfully even. And how is it we went on then living, getting angry and not knowing?" So he would get up every day, more and more sweet and joyous and full of love. When the doctor, an old German called Eisenschmidt, came:

"Well, doctor, have I another day in this world?" he would ask, joking.

"You'll live many days yet," the doctor would answer, "and months and years too."

"Months and years!" he would exclaim. "Why reckon the days? One day is enough for a man to know all happiness. My dear ones, why do we quarrel, try to outshine each other and keep grudges against each other? Let's go straight into the garden, walk and play there, love, appreciate, and kiss each other, and glorify life."

"Your son cannot last long," the doctor told my mother, as she accompanied him to the door. "The disease is affecting his brain."

The windows of his room looked out into the garden, and our garden was a shady one, with old trees in it which were coming into bud. The first birds of spring were flitting in the branches, chirruping and singing at the windows. And looking at them and admiring them, he began suddenly begging their forgiveness too, "Birds of heaven, happy birds, forgive me, for I have sinned against you too." None of us could understand that at the time, but he shed tears of joy. "Yes," he said, "there was such a glory of God all about me; birds, trees, meadows, sky, only I lived in shame and dishonored it all and did not notice the beauty and glory."

"You take too many sins on yourself," mother used to say, weeping.

"Mother, my joy, it's for joy, not for grief I am crying. Though I can't explain it to you, I like to humble myself before them, for I don't know how to love them enough. If I have sinned against everyone, yet all forgive me, too, and that's heaven. Am I not in heaven now?"

And there was a great deal more I don't remember. I remember I went once into his room when there was no one else there. It was a bright evening, the sun was setting, and a slanting ray lit up the whole room. He beckoned me, and I went up to him. He put his hands on my shoulders and looked into my face tenderly, lovingly; he said nothing for a minute, only looked at me like that. "Well," he said, "run and play now, enjoy life for me too."

I went out then and ran to play. And many times in my life afterwards I remembered with tears how he told me to enjoy life for him too. There were many other marvelous and beautiful sayings of his, though we did not understand them at the time. He died the third week after Easter. He was fully conscious though he could not talk; up to his last hour he did not change. He looked happy, his eyes beamed and sought us, he smiled at us, beckoned us. There was a great deal of talk even in the town about his death. I was impressed by all this at the time, but not too much so, though I cried a great deal at his funeral. I was young then, a child, but a lasting impression, a hidden feeling of it all, remained in my heart, ready to rise up and respond when the time came. So indeed it happened.

(b)   OF THE HOLY SCRIPTURES IN THE LIFE OF FATHER ZOSIMA

I was left alone with my mother. Her friends began advising her to send me to Petersburg as other parents did. "You have only one son now," they said, "and have a fair income, and perhaps you will be depriving him of a brilliant career if you keep him here." They suggested I should be sent to Petersburg to the Cadet Corps, that I might afterwards enter the Imperial Guard. My mother hesitated for a long time, it was awful to part with her only child, but she made up her mind to it at last, though not without many tears, believing she was acting for my happiness. She brought me to Petersburg and put me into the Cadet Corps, and I never saw her again. For she too died three years afterwards. She spent those three years mourning and grieving for both of us.

From the house of my childhood I have brought nothing but precious memories, for there are no memories more precious than those of early childhood in one's first home. And that is almost always so if there is any love and harmony in the family at all. Indeed, precious memories may remain even of a bad home, if only the heart knows how to find what is precious. With my memories of home I count, too, my memories of the Bible, which, child as I was, I was very eager to read at home. I had a book of Scripture history then with excellent pictures, called *A Hundred and Four Stories from the Old and New Testament*, and I learned to read from it. I have it lying on my shelf now, I keep it as a precious relic of the past. But even before I learned to read, I remember first being moved to devotional feeling at eight years old. My mother took me alone to the house of the Lord, to mass (I don't remember where my brother was at the time) on the Monday before Easter. It was a fine day, and I remember today, as though I saw it now, how the incense rose from the censer and softly floated upwards and, overhead in the cupola, mingled in rising waves with the sunlight that streamed in at the little window. I was stirred by the sight, and for the first time in my life I consciously received the seed of God's word in my heart. A youth came out into the middle of the church carrying a big book, so large that at the time I fancied he could scarcely carry it. He laid it on the lectern, opened it, and began reading, and suddenly for the first time I understood something read in the church of God. In the land of Uz, there lived a man, righteous and God-fearing, and he had great wealth, so many camels, so many sheep and asses, and his children feasted, and he loved them very much and prayed for them. "It may be that my sons have sinned in their feasting." Now the devil came before the Lord together with the sons of God, and said to the Lord that he had gone up and down the earth and under the earth. "And hast thou considered my servant Job?" God asked of him. And god boasted to the devil, pointing to his great and holy servant. And the devil laughed at God's words. "Give him over to me and Thou wilt see that Thy servant will murmur against Thee and curse Thy name." And God gave up the just man He loved so, to the devil. And the devil smote his children and his cattle and scattered his wealth, all of a sudden like a thunderbolt from heaven. And Job rent his mantle and fell down upon the ground and cried aloud, "Naked came I out of my mother's womb, and naked shall I return into the earth; the Lord gave and the Lord has taken away. Blessed be the name of the Lord forever and ever."

Fathers and teachers, forgive my tears now, for all my childhood rises up again before me, and I breathe now as I breathed then, with the breast of a little child of eight, and I feel as I did then, awe and wonder and gladness. The camels at that time caught my imagination, and Satan, who talked like that with God, and God who gave His servant up to destruction, and His servant crying out: "Blessed be Thy name although Thou dost punish me," and then the soft and sweet singing in the church: "Let my prayer rise up before Thee," and again incense from the priest's censer and the kneeling and the prayer. Ever since then—only yesterday I took it up—I've never been able to read that sacred tale without tears. And how much that is great, mysterious and unfathomable there is in it!

Afterwards I heard the words of mockery and blame, proud words, "How could God give up the most loved of His saints for the diversion of the devil, take from him his children, smite him with sore boils so that he cleansed the corruption from his sores with a potsherd—and for no object except to boast to the devil? 'See what My saint can suffer for My sake.' " But the greatness of it lies just in the fact that it is a mystery—that the passing earthly show and the eternal verity are brought together in it. In the face of the earthly truth, the eternal truth is accomplished. The Creator, just as on the first days of creation He ended each day with praise: "that is good that I have created," looks upon Job and again praises His creation. And Job praising the Lord, serves not only Him but all His creation for generations and generations, and forever and ever, since for that he was ordained. Good heavens, what a book it is, and what lessons there are in it! What a book the Bible is, what a miracle, what strength is given with it to man. It is like a mold cast of the world and man and human nature, everything is there, and a law for everything for all the ages. And what mysteries are solved and revealed; God raises Job again, gives him wealth again. Many years pass by, and he has other children and loves them. But how could he love those new ones when those first children are no more, when he has lost them? Remembering them, how could he be fully happy with those new ones, however dear the new ones might be? But he could, he could. It's the great mystery of human life that old grief passes gradually into quiet tender joy. The mild serenity of age takes the place of the riotous blood of youth. I bless the rising sun each day, and, as before, my heart sings to meet it, but now I love even more its setting, its long slanting rays and the soft tender gentle memories that come with them, the dear images from the whole of my long happy life—and over all the Divine Truth, softening, reconciling, forgiving! My life is ending, I know that well, but every day that is left me I feel how my earthly life is in touch with a new infinite, unknown, but approaching life, the nearness of which sets my soul quivering with rapture, my mind glowing and my heart weeping with joy.

Friends and teachers, I have heard more than once, and of late one may hear it more often, that the priests, and above all the village priests, are complaining on all sides of their miserable income and their humiliating lot. They plainly state, even in print—I've read it myself—that they are unable to teach the Scriptures to the people because of the smallness of their means, and if Lutherans and heretics come and lead the flock astray, they let them lead them astray because they have so little to live upon. May the Lord increase the sustenance that is so precious to them, for their complaint is just, too. But of a truth I say, if anyone is to blame in the matter, half the fault is ours. For he may be short of time, he may

say truly that he is overwhelmed all the while with work and
services, but still it's not all the time, even he has an hour a week to
remember God. And he does not work the whole year round. Let
him gather round him once a week, some hour in the evening, if
only the children at first—the fathers will hear of it and they too
will begin to come. There's no need to build halls for this, let him
take them into his own cottage. They won't spoil his cottage, they
would only be there one hour. Let him open that book and begin
reading it without grand words or superciliousness, without condescension to them, but gently and kindly, being glad that he is
reading to them and that they are listening with attention, loving
the words himself, only stopping from time to time to explain
words that are not understood by the peasants. Don't be anxious,
they will understand everything, the orthodox heart will understand
all! Let him read them about Abraham and Sarah, about Isaac and
Rebecca, of how Jacob went to Laban and wrestled with the Lord
in his dream and said, "This place is holy"—and he will impress the
devout mind of the peasant. Let him read, especially to the children, how the brothers sold Joseph, the tender boy, the dreamer
and prophet, into bondage, and told their father that a wild beast
had devoured him, and showed him his blood-stained clothes. Let
him read them how the brothers afterwards journeyed into Egypt
for corn, and Joseph, already a great ruler, unrecognized by them,
tormented them, accused them, kept his brother Benjamin, and all
through love: "I love you, and loving you I torment you." For he
remembered all his life how they had sold him to the merchants in
the burning desert by the well, and how, wringing his hands, he had
wept and besought his brothers not to sell him as a slave in a
strange land. And how, seeing them again after many years, he
loved them beyond measure, but he harassed and tormented them
in love. He left them at last not able to bear the suffering of his
heart, flung himself on his bed and wept. Then, wiping his tears
away he went out to them joyful and told them, "Brothers, I am
your brother Joseph!" Let him read them further how happy old
Jacob was on learning that his darling boy was still alive, and how
he went to Egypt leaving his own country, and died in a foreign
land, bequeathing his great prophecy that had lain mysteriously
hidden in his meek and timid heart all his life, that from his
offspring, from Judah, will come the great hope of the world, the
Messiah and Savior.

Fathers and teachers, forgive me and don't be angry, that like a
little child I've been babbling of what you know long ago, and can
teach me a hundred times more skillfully. I only speak from rapture, and forgive my tears, for I love the Bible. Let him too weep,
the priest of God, and be sure that the hearts of his listeners will
throb in response. Only a little tiny seed is needed—drop it into the

heart of the peasant and it won't die, it will live in his soul all his life, it will be hidden in the midst of his darkness, in the midst of the foulness of his sin, like a bright spot, like a great reminder. And there's no need of much teaching or explanation, he will understand it all simply. Do you suppose that the peasants don't understand? Try reading them the touching story of the fair Esther and the haughty Vashti; or the miraculous story of Jonah in the whale. Don't forget either the parables of Our Lord, choose especially from the Gospel of St. Luke (that is what I did) and then from the Acts of the Apostles the conversion of St. Paul (that you mustn't leave out on any account), and from the *Lives of the Saints,* for instance, the life of Alexey, the man of God and, greatest of all, the happy martyr and the seer of God, Mary of Egypt—and you will penetrate their hearts with these simple tales. Give one hour a week to it in spite of your poverty, only one little hour. And you will see for yourself that our people are benevolent and grateful, and will repay you a hundredfold. Mindful of the kindness of their priest and the moving words they have heard from him, they will of their own accord help him in his fields and in his house, and will treat him with more respect than before—so that it will even increase his worldly well-being too. The thing is so simple that sometimes one is even afraid to put it into words, for fear of being laughed at, and yet how true it is! One who does not believe in God will not believe in God's people. He who believes in God's people will see His Holiness too, even though he had not believed in it till then. Only the people and their future spiritual power will convert our atheists, who have torn themselves away from their native soil.

And what is the use of Christ's words, unless we set an example? The people are lost without the word of God, for their soul is athirst for the Word and for all that is good.

In my youth, long ago, nearly forty years ago, I traveled all over Russia with Father Anfim, collecting funds for our monastery, and we stayed one night on the bank of a great navigable river with some fishermen. A good-looking peasant lad, about eighteen, joined us; he had to hurry back next morning to pull a merchant's barge along the bank. I noticed him looking straight before him with clear and tender eyes. It was a bright, warm, still, July night, a cool mist rose from the broad river, we could hear the splash of a fish, the birds were still, all was hushed and beautiful, everything praying to God. Only we two were not sleeping, the lad and I, and we talked of the beauty of this world of God's and of the great mystery of it. Every blade of grass, every insect, ant, and golden bee, all so amazingly know their path, though they have not intelligence, they bear witness to the mystery of God and continually accomplish it themselves. I saw the dear lad's heart was moved. He told me that he loved the forest and the forest birds. He was a bird-catcher, knew the note of each of them, could call each bird. "I know nothing better than to be in the forest," said he, "though all things are good."

"Truly," I answered him, "all things are good and fair, because all is truth. Look," said I, "at the horse, that great beast that is so near to man; or the lowly, pensive ox, which feeds him and works for him; look at their faces, what meekness, what devotion to man, who often beats them mercilessly. What gentleness, what confidence and what beauty in their faces! It's touching to know that there's no sin in them, for all, all except man, is sinless, and Christ has been with them before us."

"Why," asked the boy, "is Christ with them too?"

"It cannot but be so," said I, "since the Word is for all. All creation and all creatures, every leaf is striving to the Word, singing glory to God, weeping to Christ, unconsciously accomplishing this by the mystery of their sinless life. Yonder," said I, "in the forest wanders the dreadful bear, fierce and menacing, and yet innocent in it." And I told him how once a bear came to a great saint who had taken refuge in a tiny cell in the wood. And the great saint pitied him, went up to him without fear and gave him a piece of bread. "Go along," said he, "Christ be with you," and the savage beast walked away meekly and obediently, doing no harm. And the lad was delighted that the bear had walked away without hurting the saint, and that Christ was with him too. "Ah," said he, "how good that is, how good and beautiful is all God's work!" He sat musing softly and sweetly. I saw he understood. And he slept beside me a light and sinless sleep. May God bless youth! And I prayed for him as I went to sleep. Lord, send peace and light to Thy people!

(c) RECOLLECTIONS OF FATHER ZOSIMA'S YOUTH BEFORE HE BECAME A MONK. THE DUEL

I spent a long time, almost eight years, in the military cadet school at Petersburg, and with my new education there, many of my childish impressions grew dimmer, though I forgot nothing. I picked up so many new habits and opinions that I was transformed into a cruel, absurd, almost savage creature. A surface polish of courtesy and society manners I did acquire together with the French language. But we all, myself included, looked upon the soldiers in our service as cattle. I was perhaps worse than the rest in that respect, for I was so much more impressionable than my companions. By the time we left the school as officers, we were ready to shed our blood for the honor of the regiment, but no one of us had any knowledge of the real meaning of honor, and if anyone had known it, he would have been the first to ridicule it. Drunkenness, debauchery and devilry were what we almost prided ourselves on. I don't say that we were bad by nature, all these young men were good fellows, but they behaved badly, and I worst of all. What made it worse for me was that I had come into my own money, and so I flung myself into a life of pleasure, and plunged headlong into all the recklessness of youth. I was fond of reading, yet strange to say, the Bible was the one book I never opened at that time, though I always carried it about with me, and I was never separated from it; in very truth I was keeping that book "for the day and the hour, for the month and the year," though I knew it not.

After four years of this life, I chanced to be in the town of K—— where our regiment was stationed at the time. We found the people of the town hospitable, rich and fond of entertainments. I met with a cordial reception everywhere, as I was of a lively temperament and was known to be well off, which always goes a long way in the world. And then a circumstance happened which was the beginning of it all. I formed an attachment to a beautiful and intelligent young girl of noble and lofty character, the daughter of people much respected. They were well-to-do people of influence and position. They always gave me a cordial and friendly reception. I fancied that the young lady looked on me with favor and my heart was aflame at such an idea. Later on I saw and fully realized that I perhaps was not so passionately in love with her at all, but only recognised the elevation of her mind and character, which I could not indeed have helped doing. I was prevented, however, from making her an offer at the time by my selfishness, I was loth to part with the allurements of my free and licentious bachelor life in the heyday of my youth, and with my pockets full of money. I did drop some hint as to my feelings, however, though I put off taking any decisive step for a time. Then, all of a sudden, we were ordered off for two months to another district.

On my return two months later, I found the young lady already married to a rich neighboring landowner, a very amiable man, still young though older than I was, connected with the best Petersburg society, which I was not, and of excellent education, which I also was not. I was so overwhelmed at this unexpected circumstance that my mind was positively clouded. The worst of it all was that, as I learned then, the young landowner had been a long while betrothed to her, and I had indeed met him many times in her house, but blinded by my conceit I had noticed nothing. And this particularly mortified me; almost everybody had known all about it, while I knew nothing. I was filled with sudden irrepressible fury. With flushed face I began recalling how often I had been on the point of declaring my love to her, and as she had not attempted to stop me or to warn me, she must, I concluded, have been laughing at me all the time. Later on, of course, I reflected and remembered that she had been very far from laughing at me; on the contrary, she used to turn off any courting on my part with a jest and begin talking of other subjects; but at that moment I was incapable of reflecting and was all eagerness for revenge. I am surprised to remember that my wrath and revengeful feelings were extremely oppressive and repugnant to my own nature, for being of an easy temper, I found it difficult to be angry with anyone for long, and so I had to work myself up artificially and became at last revolting and absurd.

I waited for an opportunity and succeeded in insulting my "rival" in the presence of a large company. I insulted him on a perfectly extraneous pretext, jeering at his opinion upon an important event —it was in the year 1826[2]—and my jeer was, so people said, clever and effective. Then I forced him to ask for an explanation, and behaved so rudely that he accepted my challenge in spite of the vast inequality between us, as I was younger, a person of no consequence, and of inferior rank. I learned afterwards for a fact that it was from a jealous feeling on his side also that my challenge was accepted; he had been rather jealous of me on his wife's account before their marriage; he fancied now that if he submitted to be insulted by me and refused to accept any challenge, and if she heard of it, she might begin to despise him and waver in her love for him. I soon found a second in a comrade, an ensign of our regiment. In those days though duels were severely punished, yet dueling was a kind of fashion among the officers—so strong and deeply rooted will a brutal prejudice sometimes be.

It was the end of June, and our meeting was to take place at seven o'clock the next day on the outskirts of the town—and then something happened that in very truth was the turning point of my life. In the evening, returning home in a savage and brutal humor, I flew into a rage with my orderly Afanasy, and gave him two blows in the face with all my might, so that it was covered with blood. He had not long been in my service and I had struck him before, but never with such ferocious cruelty. And, believe me, though it's forty years ago, I recall it now with shame and pain. I went to bed and slept for about three hours; when I woke up the day was breaking. I got up—I did not want to sleep any more—I went to the window—opened it, it looked out upon the garden; I saw the sun rising; it was warm and beautiful, the birds were singing. What's the meaning of it, I thought, I feel in my heart as it were something vile and shameful? Is it because I am going to shed blood? No, I thought, I feel it's not that. Can it be that I am afraid of death, afraid of being killed? No, that's not it, that's not it at all. . . . And all at once I knew what it was; it was because I had beaten

2. Probably the abortive Decembrist revolt in 1825.

Afanasy the evening before! It all rose before my mind, it all was as it were repeated over again; he stood before me and I was beating him straight on the face and he was holding his arms stiffly down, his head erect, his eyes fixed upon me as though on parade. He staggered at each blow and did not even dare to raise his hands to protect himself. That is what a man has been brought to, and that was a man beating a fellow creature! What a crime! It was as though a sharp dagger had pierced me right through. I stood as if I were struck dumb, while the sun was shining, the leaves were rejoicing and sparkling and the birds were trilling the praise of God. . . . I hid my face in my hands, fell on my bed and broke into a storm of tears. And then I remembered my brother Markel and what he said on his deathbed to his servants: "My dear ones, why do you wait on me, why do you love me, am I worth your waiting on me?" Yes, am I worth it? flashed through my mind. After all what am I worth, that another man, a fellow creature, made in the likeness and image of God, should serve me? For the first time in my life this question forced itself upon me. He had said, "Mother, my little heart, in truth we are each responsible to all for all, it's only that men don't know this. If they knew it, the world would be a paradise at once."

"God, can that too be false?" I thought as I wept. "In truth, perhaps, I am more than all others responsible for all, a greater sinner than all men in the world." And all at once the whole truth in its full light appeared to me: what was I going to do? I was going to kill a good, clever, noble man, who had done me no wrong, and by depriving his wife of happiness for the rest of her life, I should be torturing and killing her too. I lay thus in my bed with my face in the pillow, heedless how the time was passing. Suddenly my second, the ensign, came in with the pistols to fetch me.

"Ah," said he, "it's a good thing you are up already, it's time we were off, come along!" I did not know what to do and hurried to and fro undecided; we went out to the carriage, however. "Wait here a minute," I said to him. "I'll be back directly, I have forgotten my purse." And I ran back alone, straight to Afanasy's little room. "Afanasy," I said, "I gave you two blows on the face yesterday, forgive me," I said.

He started as though he were frightened, and looked at me; and I saw that it was not enough, and on the spot, in my full officer's uniform, I dropped at his feet and bowed my head to the ground. "Forgive me," I said.

Then he was completely aghast.

"Your honor . . . sir, what are you doing? Am I worth it?" And he burst out crying as I had done before, hid his face in his hands, turned to the window and shook all over with his sobs. I flew out to my comrade and jumped into the carriage.

"Ready," I cried. "Have you ever seen a conqueror?" I asked him. "Here is one before you." I was in ecstasy, laughing and talking all the way, I don't remember what about. He looked at me. "Well, brother, you are a plucky fellow, you'll keep up the honor of the uniform, I can see."

So we reached the place and found them there, waiting us. We were placed twelve paces apart; he had the first shot. I stood gaily, looking him full in the face; I did not twitch an eyelash, I looked lovingly at him, for I knew what I would do. His shot just grazed my cheek and ear. "Thank God," I cried, "no man has been killed," and I seized my pistol, turned back and flung it far away into the wood.

"That's the place for you," I cried.

I turned to my adversary. "Forgive me, young fool that I am, sir," I said, "for my unprovoked insult to you and for forcing you to fire at me. I am ten times worse than you and more, maybe. Tell that to the person whom you hold dearest in the world."

I had no sooner said this than they all three shouted at me.

"Upon my word," cried my adversary, in great anger, "if you did not want to fight, why did not you let me alone?"

"Yesterday I was a fool, today I know better," I answered him gaily.

"As to yesterday, I believe you, but as for today, it is difficult to agree with your opinion," said he.

"Bravo," I cried, clapping my hands. "I agree with you there too, I have deserved it!"

"Will you shoot, sir, or not?"

"No, I won't," I said, "if you like, fire at me again, but it would be better for you not to fire."

The seconds, especially mine, were shouting too: "Can you disgrace the regiment like this, facing your antagonist and begging his forgiveness! If I'd only known this!"

I stood facing them all, not laughing now. "Gentlemen," I said, "is it really so wonderful in these days to find a man who can repent of his stupidity and publicly confess his wrongdoing?"

"But not in a duel," cried my second again.

"That's what's so strange," I said. "For I ought to have owned my fault as soon as I got here, before he had fired a shot, before leading him into a great and mortal sin; but we have made our life so grotesque, that to act in that way would have been almost impossible, for only after I have faced his shot at the distance of twelve paces could my words have any significance for him, and if I had spoken before, he would have said 'he is a coward, the sight of the pistols had frightened him, no use to listen to him.' Gentlemen," I cried suddenly, speaking straight from my heart, "look around you at the gifts of God, the clear sky, the pure air, the tender grass, the birds; nature is beautiful and sinless, and we, only we, are godless and foolish, and we don't understand that life is a paradise, for we have only to understand that and it will at once be fulfilled in all its beauty, we shall embrace each other and weep."

I would have said more but I could not; my voice broke with the sweetness and youthful gladness of it, and there was such bliss in my heart as I had never known before in my life.

"All this is rational and edifying," said my antagonist, "and in any case you are an original person."

"You may laugh," I said to him, laughing too, "but afterwards you will approve of me."

"Oh, I am ready to approve of you now," said he; "will you shake hands, for I believe you are genuinely sincere."

"No," I said, "not now, later on when I have grown worthier and deserve your esteem, then shake hands and you will do well."

We went home, my second upbraiding me all the way, while I kissed him. All my comrades heard of the affair at once and gathered together to pass judgment on me the same day.

"He has disgraced the uniform," they said; "let him resign his commission."

Some stood up for me: "He faced the shot," they said.

"Yes, but he was afraid of his other shot and begged for forgiveness."

"If he had been afraid of being shot, he would have shot his own pistol first before asking forgiveness, while he flung it loaded into the forest. No, there's something else in this, something original."

I enjoyed listening and looking at them. "My dear friends and comrades," said I, "don't worry about my resigning my commission, for I have done so already. I have sent in my papers this morning and as soon as I get my discharge I shall go into a monastery—it's with that object I am leaving the regiment."

When I had said this every one of them burst out laughing.

"You should have told us of that first, that explains everything, we can't judge a monk."

They laughed and could not stop themselves, and not scornfully, but kindly and merrily. They all felt friendly to me at once, even those who had been sternest in their censure, and all the following month, before my discharge came, they could not make enough of me. "Ah, you monk," they would say. And everyone said something kind to me, they began trying to dissuade me, even to pity me: "What are you doing to yourself?"

"No," they would say, "he is a brave fellow, he faced fire and could have fired his own pistol too, but he had a dream the night before that he should become a monk, that's why he did it."

It was the same thing with the society of the town. Till then I had been kindly received, but had not been the object of special attention, and now all came to know me at once and invited me; they laughed at me, but they loved me. I may mention that although everybody talked openly of our duel, the authorities took no notice of it, because my antagonist was a near relation of our general, and as there had been no bloodshed and no serious consequences, and as I resigned my commission, they turned it into a joke. And I began then to speak aloud and fearlessly, regardless of their laughter, for it was always kindly and not spiteful laughter. These conversations mostly took place in the evenings, in the company of ladies; women particularly liked listening to me then and they made the men listen.

"But how can I possibly be responsible for all?" everyone would laugh in my face. "Can I, for instance, be responsible for you?"

"You may well not know it," I would answer, "since the whole world has long been going on a different line, since we consider the veriest lies as truth and demand the same lies from others. Here I have for once in my life acted sincerely and, well, you all look upon me as a madman. Though you are friendly to me, yet, you see, you all laugh at me."

"But how can we help being friendly to you?" said my hostess, laughing. The room was full of people. All of a sudden rose the young lady on whose account the duel had been fought and whom only lately I had intended to be my future wife. I had not noticed her coming into the room. She got up, came to me and held out her hand.

"Let me tell you," she said, "that I am the first not to laugh at you, but on the contrary I thank you with tears and express my respect for you and for your action then."

Her husband too came up and then they all approached me and almost kissed me. My heart was filled with joy, but my attention was especially caught by a middle-aged man who came up to me with the others. I knew him by name already, but had never made his acquaintance nor exchanged a word with him till that evening.

(d) THE MYSTERIOUS VISITOR

He had long been an official in the town; he was in a prominent position, respected by all, rich and had a reputation for benevolence. He subscribed considerable sums to the almshouse and the orphan asylum; he was very charitable, too, in secret, a fact which only became known after his death. He was a man of about fifty, almost stern in appearance and not much given to conversation. He had been married some ten years and his wife, who was still young, had borne him three children. Well, I was sitting alone in my room the following evening, when my door suddenly opened and this gentleman walked in.

I must mention, by the way, that I was no longer living in my former quarters. As soon as I resigned my commission, I took rooms with an old lady, the widow of a government clerk. My landlady's servant waited upon me, for I had moved into her rooms simply because on my return from the duel I had sent Afanasy back to the regiment, as I felt ashamed to look him in the face after my last interview with him. So prone is the man of the world to be ashamed of any righteous action.

"I have," said my visitor, "with great interest listened to you speaking in different houses the last few days and I wanted at last to make your personal acquaintance, so as to talk to you more intimately. Can you, dear sir, grant me this great service?"

"I can, with the greatest pleasure and I shall look upon it as an honor." I said this, though I felt almost dismayed, so greatly was I impressed from the first moment by the appearance of this man. For though other people had listened to me with interest and attention, no one had come to me before with such a serious, stern and concentrated expression. And now he had come to see me in my rooms. He sat down.

"You are, I see, a man of great strength of character," he said; "as you have dared to serve the truth, even when by doing so you risked incurring the contempt of all."

"Your praise is, perhaps, excessive," I replied.

"No, it's not excessive," he answered; "believe me, such a course of action is far more difficult than you think. It is that which has impressed me, and it is only on that account that I have come to you," he continued. "Tell me, please, that is if you are not annoyed by my perhaps unseemly curiosity, what were your exact sensations, if you can recall them, at the moment when you made up your mind to ask forgiveness at the duel? Do not think my question frivolous; on the contrary, I have in asking the question a secret motive of my own, which I will perhaps explain to you later on, if it is God's will that we should become more intimately acquainted."

All the while he was speaking, I looked him straight in the face and I felt all at once a complete trust in him and great curiosity on my side also, for I felt that there was some strange secret in his soul.

"You ask what were my exact sensations at the moment when I asked my opponent's forgiveness," I answered; "but I had better tell you from the beginning what I have not yet told anyone else." And I described all that had passed between Afanasy and me, and how I had bowed down to the ground at his feet. "From that you can see for yourself," I concluded, "that at the time of the duel it was easier for me, for I had made a beginning already at home, and when once I had started on the road, to go further along it was far from being difficult, but became a source of joy and happiness."

I liked the way he looked at me as he listened. "All that," he said, "is exceedingly interesting. I will come to see you again and again." And from that time forth he came to see me nearly every evening. And we should have become greater friends, if only he had ever talked of himself. But about himself he scarcely ever said a word, yet continually asked me about myself. In spite of that I became very fond of him and spoke with perfect frankness to him about all my feelings; for, thought I, what need have I to know his secrets, since I can see without that that he is a good man. Moreover, though he is such a serious man and my senior, he comes to see a youngster like me and treats me as his equal. And I learned a great deal that was profitable from him, for he was a man of lofty mind.

"That life is a paradise," he said to me suddenly, "that I have long been thinking about"; and all at once he added, "I think of nothing else indeed." He looked at me and smiled. "I am more convinced of it than you are, I will tell you later why."

I listened to him and thought that he evidently wanted to tell me something.

"Paradise" he went on, "lies hidden within all of us—here it lies hidden in me now, and if I will it, it will be revealed to me tomorrow and for all time."

I looked at him; he was speaking with great emotion and gazing mysteriously at me, as if he were questioning me.

"And that we are all responsible to all for all, apart from our own sins, you were quite right in thinking that, and it is wonderful how you could comprehend it in all its significance at once. And in very truth, so soon as men understand that, the Kingdom of Heaven will be for them not a dream, but a living reality."

"And when," I cried out to him bitterly, "when will that come to pass? and will it ever come to pass? Is not it simply a dream of ours?"

"What then, you don't believe it," he said. "You preach it and don't believe it yourself. Believe me, this dream, as you call it, will come to pass without doubt; it will come, but not now, for every process has its law. It's a spiritual, psychological process. To transform the world, to recreate it afresh, men must turn into another path psychologically. Until you have become really, in actual fact, a brother to everyone, brotherhood will not come to pass. No sort of scientific teaching, no kind of common interest, will ever teach men to share property and privileges with equal consideration for all. Everyone will think his share too small and they will always envy, complain, and attack one another. You ask when it will come to pass; it will come to pass, but first we have to go through the period of *isolation*."

"What do you mean by isolation?" I asked him.

"Why, the isolation that prevails everywhere, above all in our age—it has not fully developed, it has not reached its limit yet. For everyone strives to keep his individuality as apart as possible, wishes to secure the greatest possible fullness of life for himself; but meantime all his efforts result not in attaining fullness of life but self-destruction, for instead of self-realization he ends by arriving at complete isolation. All mankind in our age have split up into units, they all keep apart, each in his own groove; each one holds aloof, hides himself and hides what he has, from the rest, and he ends by being repelled by others and repelling them. He heaps up riches by himself and thinks, 'how strong I am now and how secure,' and in his madness he does not understand that the more he heaps up, the more he sinks into self-destructive impotence. For he is accustomed to rely upon himself alone and to cut himself off from the whole; he has trained himself not to believe in the help of others, in men and in humanity, and only trembles for fear he should lose his money and the privileges that he has won for himself. Everywhere in these days men have, in their mockery, ceased to understand that the true security is to be found in social solidarity rather than in isolated individual effort. But this terrible individualism must inevitably have an end, and all will suddenly understand how unnaturally they are separated from one another. It will be the spirit of the time, and people will marvel that they have sat so long in darkness without seeing the light. And then the sign of the Son of Man will be seen in the heavens. . . . But, until then, we must keep the banner flying. Sometimes even if he has to do it alone, and his conduct seems to be crazy, a man must set an example, and so draw men's souls out of their solitude, and spur them to some act of brotherly love even if he seems crazy, so that the great idea may not die."

Our evenings, one after another, were spent in such stirring and fervent talk. I gave up society and visited my neighbors much less frequently. Besides, my vogue was somewhat over. I say this, not as blame, for they still loved me and treated me good-humoredly, but there's no denying that fashion is a great power in society. I began to regard my mysterious visitor with admiration, for besides enjoying his intelligence, I began to perceive that he was brooding over some plan in his heart, and was perhaps preparing himself for a great deed. Perhaps he liked my not showing curiosity about his secret, not seeking to discover it by direct question nor by insinuation. But I noticed at last that he seemed to show signs of wanting to tell me something. This had become quite evident, indeed, about a month after he first began to visit me.

"Do you know," he said to me once, "that people are very inquisitive about us in the town and wonder why I come to see you so often. But let them wonder, for *soon all will be explained.*"

Sometimes an extraordinary agitation would come over him, and almost always on such occasions he would get up and go away. Sometimes he would fix a long piercing look upon me, and I thought "he will say something directly now." But he would suddenly begin talking of something ordinary and familiar. He often complained of headache too. One day, quite unexpectedly indeed, after he had been talking with great fervor a long time, I saw him suddenly turn pale, and his face worked convulsively, while he stared persistently at me.

"What's the matter?" I said: "do you feel ill?"—he had just been complaining of headache.

"I . . . do you know . . . I murdered someone."

He said this and smiled with a face as white as chalk. "Why is it he is smiling?" The thought flashed through my mind before I realized anything else. I too turned pale.

"What are you saying?" I cried.

"You see," he said, with a pale smile, "how much it has cost me to say the first word. Now I have said it, I feel I've taken the first step and shall go on."

For a long while I could not believe him, and I did not believe him at that time, but only after he had been to see me three days running and told me all about it. I thought he was mad, but ended by being convinced, to my great grief and amazement. His crime was a great and terrible one.

Fourteen years before, he had murdered the widow of a landowner, a wealthy and handsome young woman who had a house in our town. He fell passionately in love with her, declared his feeling and tried to persuade her to marry him. But she had already given her heart to another man, an officer of noble birth and high rank in the service, who was at that time away at the front, though she was expecting him soon to return. She refused his offer and begged him not to come and see her. After he had ceased to visit her, he took advantage of his knowledge of the house to enter at night through the garden by the roof, at great risk of discovery. But as often happens, a crime committed with extraordinary audacity is more successful than others.

Entering the garret through the skylight, he went down the ladder, knowing that the door at the bottom of it was sometimes, through the negligence of the servants, left unlocked. He hoped to find it so, and so it was. He made his way in the dark to her bedroom, where a light was burning. As though on purpose, both her maids had gone off to a birthday party in the same street, without asking leave. The other servants slept in the servants' quarters or in the kitchen on the ground floor. His passion flamed up at the sight of her asleep, and then vindictive, jealous anger took possession of his heart, and like a drunken man, beside himself, he thrust a knife into her heart, so that she did not even cry out. Then with devilish and criminal cunning he contrived that suspicion should fall on the servants. He was so base as to take her purse, to open her chest with keys from under her pillow, and to take some things from it, doing it all as it might have been done by an ignorant servant, leaving valuable papers and taking only money. He took some of the larger gold things, but left smaller articles that were ten times as valuable. He took with him, too, some things for himself as remembrances, but of that later. Having done this awful deed, he returned by the way he had come.

Neither the next day, when the alarm was raised, nor at any time after in his life, did anyone dream of suspecting that he was the criminal! Indeed no one knew of his love for her, for he was always reserved and silent and had no friend to whom he would have opened his heart. He was looked upon simply as an acquaintance, and not a very intimate one, of the murdered woman, as for the previous fortnight he had not even visited her. A serf of hers called Pyotr was at once suspected, and every circumstance confirmed the suspicion. The man knew—indeed his mistress did not conceal the fact—that having to send one of her serfs as a recruit she had decided to send him, as he had no relations and his conduct was unsatisfactory. People had heard him angrily threatening to murder her when he was drunk in a tavern. Two days before her death, he had run away, staying no one knew where in the town. The day after the murder, he was found on the road leading out of the town, dead drunk, with a knife in his pocket and his right hand happened to be stained with blood. He declared that his nose had been bleeding, but no one believed him. The maids confessed that they had gone to a party and that the street door had been left open till they returned. And a number of similar details came to light, throwing suspicion on the innocent servant. They arrested him, and he was tried for the murder; but a week after the arrest, the prisoner fell sick of a fever and died unconscious in the hospital. There the matter ended, left to God's will, and the judges and the authorities and everyone in the town remained convinced that the crime had been committed by no one but the servant who had died in the hospital. And after that the punishment began.

My mysterious visitor, now my friend, told me that at first he was not in the least troubled by pangs of conscience. He was miserable a long time, but not for that reason; only from regret that he had killed the woman he loved, that she was no more, that in killing her he had killed his love, while the fire of passion was still in his veins. But of the innocent blood he had shed, of the murder of a fellow creature, he scarcely thought. The thought that his victim might have become the wife of another man was insupportable to him, and so, for a long time, he was convinced in his conscience that he could not have acted otherwise.

At first he was troubled at the arrest of the servant, but his illness and death soon set his mind at rest, for the man's death was apparently (so he reflected at the time) not owing to his arrest or his fright, but a chill he had taken on the day he ran away, when he had lain all night dead drunk on the damp ground. The theft of the money and other things troubled him little, for he argued that the theft had not been committed for gain but to avert suspicion. The sum stolen was small, and he shortly afterwards subscribed the whole of it, and much more, towards the funds for maintaining an almshouse in the town. He did this on purpose to set his conscience at rest about the theft, and it's a remarkable fact that for a long time he really was at peace—he told me this himself. He entered then upon a career of great activity in the service, volunteered for a difficult and laborious duty, which occupied him two years, and being a man of strong will almost forgot the past. Whenever he recalled it, he tried not to think of it at all. He became active in philanthropy too, founded and helped to maintain many institutions in the town, did a good deal in the two capitals, and in both Moscow and Petersburg was elected a member of philanthropic societies. At last, however, he began brooding over the past, and the strain of it was too much for him. Then he was attracted by a fine and intelligent girl and soon after married her, hoping that marriage would dispel his lonely depression, and that by entering on a new life and scrupulously doing his duty to his wife and children, he would escape from old memories altogether. But the very opposite of what he expected happened. He began, even in the first month of his marriage, to be continually fretted by the thought, "My wife loves me—but what if she knew?" When she first told him that she would soon bear him a child, he was troubled. "I am giving life, but I have taken life." Children came. "How dare I love them, teach and educate them, how can I talk to them of virtue? I have shed blood." They were splendid children, he longed to caress them; "and I can't look at their innocent candid faces, I am unworthy."

At last he began to be bitterly and ominously haunted by the blood of his murdered victim, by the young life he had destroyed, by the blood that cried out for vengeance. He had begun to have awful dreams. But, being a man of fortitude, he bore his suffering a long time, thinking: "I shall expiate everything by this secret agony." But that hope too, was vain; the longer it went on, the more intense was his suffering.

He was respected in society for his active benevolence, though everyone was overawed by his stern and gloomy character. But the more he was respected, the more intolerable it was for him. He confessed to me that he had thoughts of killing himself. But he began to be haunted by another idea—an idea which he had at first regarded as impossible and unthinkable, though at last it got such a hold on his heart that he could not shake it off. He dreamed of rising up, going out and confessing in the face of all men that he had committed murder. For three years this dream had pursued him, haunting him in different forms. At last he believed with his whole heart that if he confessed his crime, he would heal his soul and would be at peace forever. But this belief filled his heart with terror, for how could he carry it out? And then came what happened at my duel. "Looking at you, I have made up my mind." I looked at him.

"Is it possible," I cried, clasping my hands, "that such a trivial incident could give rise to such a resolution in you?"

"My resolution has been growing for the last three years," he answered, "and your story only gave the last touch to it. Looking at you, I reproached myself and envied you," he said this to me almost sullenly.

"But you won't be believed," I observed; "it's fourteen years ago."

"I have proofs, great proofs. I shall show them."

Then I cried and kissed him.

"Tell me one thing, one thing," he said (as though it all depended upon me), "my wife, my children! My wife may die of grief, and though my children won't lose their rank and property, they'll be a convict's children and forever! And what a memory, what a memory of me I shall leave in their hearts!"

I said nothing.

"And to part from them, to leave them forever? It's forever, you know, forever!"

I sat still and repeated a silent prayer. I got up at last, I felt afraid.

"Well?" He looked at me.

"Go!" said I, "proclaim it to the world. Everything passes, only the truth remains. Your children will understand, when they grow up, the nobility of your resolution."

He left me that time as though he had made up his mind. Yet for more than a fortnight afterwards, he came to me every evening, still preparing himself, still unable to bring himself to the point. He made my heart ache. One day he would come determined and say fervently:

"I know it will be heaven for me, heaven, the moment I confess. Fourteen years I've been in hell. I want to suffer. I will take my punishment and begin to live. You can pass through the world doing wrong, but there's no turning back. Now I dare not love my neighbor nor even my own children. Good God, my children will understand, perhaps, what my punishment has cost me and will not condemn me! God is not in strength but in truth."

"All will understand your great deed," I said to him, "if not at once, they will understand later; for you have served truth, the higher truth, not the earthly one."

And he would go away seeming comforted, but next day he would come again, bitter, pale, sarcastic.

"Every time I come to you, you look at me so inquisitively as though to say, 'He has still not proclaimed it!' Wait a bit, don't depise me too much. It's not such an easy thing to do, as you would think. Perhaps I shall not do it at all. You won't go and inform against me then, will you?"

And far from looking at him with indiscreet curiosity, I was afraid to look at him at all. I was quite ill from anxiety, and my soul was full of tears. I could not sleep at night.

"I have just come from my wife," he went on. "Do you understand what the word 'wife' means? When I went out, the children called to me, 'Goodbye, daddy, make haste back to read *The Children's Magazine* with us.' No, you don't understand that! No one is wise from another man's woe."

His eyes were glittering, his lips were twitching. Suddenly he struck the table with his fist so that everything on it danced—it was the first time he had done such a thing, he was such a mild man.

"But need I?" he exclaimed, "must I! No one has been condemned, no one has been sent to Siberia in my place, the man died of fever. And I've been punished by my sufferings for the blood I shed. And they won't believe me, they won't believe my proofs. Need I confess, need I? I am ready to go on suffering all my life for the blood I have shed, if only my wife and children may be spared. Will it be just to ruin them with me? Aren't we making a mistake? What is right in this case? And will people recognize it, will they appreciate it, will they respect it?"

"Good Lord!" I thought to myself, "he is thinking of other people's respect at such a moment!" And I felt so sorry for him then, that I believe I would have shared his fate if it could have comforted him. I saw he was beside himself. I was aghast, realizing with my heart as well as my mind what such a resolution meant.

"Decide my fate!" he exclaimed again.

"Go and proclaim," I whispered to him. My voice failed me, but I whispered it firmly. I took up the New Testament from the table, the Russian translation, and showed him the Gospel of St. John, chapter xii, verse 24:

"Verily, verily, I say unto you, except a corn of wheat fall into the ground and die, it abideth alone: but if it die, it bringeth forth much fruit."

I had just been reading that verse when he came in. He read it.

"That's true," he said, but he smiled bitterly. "It's terrible the things you find in those books," he said, after a pause. "It's easy enough to thrust them upon one. And who wrote them? Can they have been written by men?"

"The Holy Spirit wrote them," said I.

"It's easy for you to prate," he smiled again, this time almost with hatred. I took the book again, opened it in another place and showed him the Epistle to the Hebrews, chapter x, verse 31. He read:

"It is a fearful thing to fall into the hands of the living God."

He read it and simply flung down the book. He was trembling all over.

"An awful text," he said. "There's no denying you've picked out fitting ones." He rose from the chair. "Well!" he said, "Goodbye, perhaps I won't come again . . . we shall meet in heaven. So I have been for fourteen years 'in the hands of the living God,' that's how one must think of those fourteen years. Tomorrow I will beseech those hands to let me go."

I wanted to take him in my arms and kiss him, but I did not dare—his face was contorted and somber. He went away. "Good God," I thought, "what has he gone to face!" I fell on my knees before the icon and wept for him before the Holy Mother of God, our swift defender and helper. I was half an hour praying in tears, and it was late, about midnight. Suddenly I saw the door open and he came in again. I was surprised.

"Where have you been?" I asked him.

"I think," he said, "I've forgotten something . . . my handkerchief, I think. . . . Well, even if I've not forgotten anything, let me stay a little."

He sat down. I stood over him. "You sit down, too," said he. I sat down. We sat still for two minutes; he looked intently at me and suddenly smiled—I remembered that—then he got up, embraced me warmly and kissed me.

"Remember," he said, "how I came to you a second time. Dost thou hear, remember it!"

For the first time he addressed me with the familiar pronoun. And he went out. "Tomorrow," I thought.

And so it was. I did not know that evening that the next day was his birthday. I had not been out for the last few days so I had no chance of hearing it from anyone. On that day he always had a great gathering, everyone in the town went to it. It was the same this time. After dinner he walked into the middle of the room, with a paper in his hand—a formal declaration to the chief of his department who was present. This declaration he read aloud to the whole assembly. It contained a full account of the crime, in every detail. "I cast myself out from men as a monster. God has visited me," he said in conclusion. "I want to suffer for my sin!"

Then he brought out and laid on the table all the things he had been keeping for fourteen years, that he thought would prove his crime, the jewels belonging to the murdered woman which he had stolen to divert suspicion, a cross and a locket taken from her neck with a portrait of her betrothed in the locket, her notebook and two letters; one from her betrothed, telling her that he would soon be with her, and her unfinished answer left on the table to be sent off next day. He carried off these two letters—what for? Why had he kept them for fourteen years afterwards instead of destroying them as evidence against him?

And this is what happened: everyone was amazed and horrified, everyone refused to believe it and thought that he was deranged, though all listened with intense curiosity. A few days later it was fully decided and agreed in every house that the unhappy man was mad. The legal authorities could not refuse to take the case up, but they too dropped it. Though the trinkets and letters made them ponder, they decided that even if they did turn out to be authentic, no charge could be based on those alone. Besides, she might have given him those things as a friend, or asked him to take care of them for her. I heard afterwards, however, that the genuineness of the things was proved by the friends and relations of the murdered woman, and that there was no doubt about them. Yet nothing was destined to come of it, after all.

Five days later, all had heard that he was ill and that his life was in danger. The nature of his illness I can't explain, they said it was an affection of the heartbeat. But it became known that the doctors had been induced by his wife to investigate his mental condition also, and had come to the conclusion that it was a case of insanity. I betrayed nothing, though people ran to question me. But when I wanted to visit him, I was for a long while forbidden to do so, above all by his wife.

"It's you who have caused his illness," she said to me; "he was always gloomy, but for the last year people noticed that he was peculiarly excited and did strange things, and now you have been the ruin of him. Your preaching has brought him to this; for the last month he was always with you." Indeed, not only his wife but the whole town was down on me and blamed me. "It's all your doing," they said. I was silent and indeed rejoiced at heart, for I saw plainly God's mercy to the man who had turned against himself and punished himself. I could not believe in his insanity. They let me see him at last, he insisted upon saying goodbye to me. I went in to him and saw at once that not only his days but his hours were numbered. He was weak, yellow, his hands trembled, he gasped for breath, but his face was full of tender and happy feeling.

"It is done!" he said. "I've long been yearning to see you, why didn't you come?"

I did not tell him that they would not let me see him.

"God has had pity on me and is calling me to Himself. I know I am dying, but I feel joy and peace for the first time after so many years. There was heaven in my heart from the moment I had done what I had to do. Now I dare to love my children and to kiss them. Neither my wife nor the judges, nor anyone has believed it. My children will never believe it either. I see in that God's mercy to them. I shall die, and my name will be without a stain for them. And now I feel God near, my heart rejoices as in Heaven. . . . I have done my duty."

He could not speak, he gasped for breath, he pressed my hand warmly, looking fervently at me. We did not talk for long, his wife kept peeping in at us. But he had time to whisper to me:

"Do you remember how I came back to you that second time, at midnight? I told you to remember it. You know what I came back for? I came to kill you!"

I started.

"I went out from you then into the darkness, I wandered about the streets, struggling with myself. And suddenly I hated you so that I could hardly bear it. Now, I thought, he is all that binds me, and he is my judge. I can't refuse to face my punishment tomorrow, for he knows all. It was not that I was afraid you would betray me (I never even thought of that) but I thought, 'How can I look him in the face if I don't proclaim my crime?' And if you had been at the other end of the earth, but alive, it would have been all the same, the thought was unendurable that you were alive knowing everything and condemning me. I hated you as though you were the cause, as though you were to blame for everything. I came back to you then, remembering that you had a dagger lying on your table. I sat down and asked you to sit down, and for a whole minute I pondered. If I had killed you, I should have been ruined by that murder even if I had not confessed the other. But I didn't think about that at all, and I didn't want to think of it at that moment. I only hated you and longed to revenge myself on you for everything. The Lord vanquished the devil in my heart. But let me tell you, you were never nearer death."

A week later he died. The whole town followed him to the grave. The chief priest made a speech full of feeling. All lamented the terrible illness that had cut short his days. But all the town was up in arms against me after the funeral, and people even refused to see me. Some, at first a few and afterwards more, began indeed to believe in the truth of his story, and they visited me and questioned me with great interest and eagerness, for man loves to see the downfall and disgrace of the righteous. But I held my tongue, and very shortly after, I left the town, and five months later by God's grace I entered upon the safe and blessed path, praising the unseen finger which had guided me so clearly to it. But every day, to this very day, I remember in my prayer to this day, the servant of God, Mikhail, who suffered so greatly.

Chapter III

Conversations and Exhortations of Father Zosima

(e)   THE RUSSIAN MONK AND HIS POSSIBLE SIGNIFICANCE

Fathers and teachers, what is the monk? In the cultivated world the word is nowadays pronounced by some people with a jeer, and by others it is used as a term of abuse, and this contempt for the monk is growing. It is true, alas, it is true, that there are many sluggards, gluttons, profligates and insolent beggars among monks. Educated people point to these: "You are idlers, useless members of society, you live on the labor of others, you are shameless beggars." And yet how many meek and humble monks there are, yearning for solitude and fervent prayer in peace. These are less noticed, or passed over in silence. And how surprised men would be if I were to say that from these meek monks, who yearn for solitary prayer, the salvation of Russia will come perhaps once more. For they are in truth made ready in peace and quiet "for the day and the hour, the month and the year." Meanwhile, in their solitude, they keep the image of Christ fair and undefiled, in the purity of God's truth, from the times of the Fathers of old, the Apostles and the martyrs. And when the time comes they will show it to the tottering creeds of the world. That is a great thought. That star will rise out of the East.

That is my view of the monk, and is it false? is it too proud? Look at the worldly and all who set themselves up above the people of God, has not God's image and His truth been distorted in them? They have science; but in science there is nothing but what is the object of sense. The spiritual world, the higher part of man's being is rejected altogether, dismissed with a sort of triumph, even with hatred. The world has proclaimed the reign of freedom, especially of late, but what do we see in this freedom of theirs? Nothing but slavery and self-destruction! For the world says:

"You have desires and so satisfy them, for you have the same rights as the most rich and powerful. Don't be afraid of satisfying them and even multiplying your desires." That is the modern doctrine of the world. In that they see freedom. And what follows from this right of multiplication of desires? In the rich, *isolation* and spiritual suicide; in the poor, envy and murder; for they have been given rights, but have not been shown the means of satisfying their wants. They maintain that the world is getting more and more united, more and more bound together in brotherly community, as it overcomes distance and sets thoughts flying through the air. Alas, put no faith in such a bond of union. Interpreting freedom as the multiplication and rapid satisfaction of desires, men distort their own nature, for many senseless and foolish desires and habits and ridiculous fancies are fostered in them. They live only for mutual envy, for gluttony and ostentation. To have dinners, visits, carriages, rank and slaves to wait on one is looked upon as a necessity, for which life, honor and human feeling are sacrificed, and men even commit suicide if they are unable to satisfy it. We see the same thing among those who are not rich, while the poor drown their unsatisfied need and their envy in drunkenness. But soon they will drink blood instead of wine, they are being led on to it. I ask you is such a man free? I knew one "champion of freedom" who told me himself that, when he was deprived of tobacco in prison, he was so wretched at the privation that he almost went and betrayed his cause for the sake of getting tobacco again! And such a man says, "I am fighting for the cause of humanity." How can such a one fight, what is he fit for? He is capable perhaps of some action quickly over, but he cannot hold out long. And it's no wonder that instead of gaining freedom they have sunk into slavery, and instead of serving the cause of brotherly love and the union of humanity have fallen, on the contrary, into separation and isolation, as my mysterious visitor and teacher said to me in my youth. And therefore the idea of the service of humanity, of brotherly love and the solidarity of mankind, is more and more dying out in the world, and indeed this idea is sometimes treated with derision. For how can a man shake off his habits, what can become of him if he is in such bondage to the habit of satisfying the innumerable desires he has created for himself? He is isolated, and what concern has he with the rest of humanity? They have succeeded in accumulating a greater mass of objects, but the joy in the world has grown less.

The monastic way is very different. Obedience, fasting and prayer are laughed at, yet only through them lies the way to real, true freedom. I cut off my superfluous and unnecessary desires, I subdue my proud and wanton will and chastise it with obedience, and with God's help I attain freedom of spirit and with it spiritual joy. Who is more capable of conceiving a great idea and serving it—the rich man in his isolation or the man who has *freed himself* from the tyranny of material things and habits? The monk is reproached for his solitude, "You have secluded yourself within the walls of the monastery for your own salvation, and have forgotten the brotherly service of humanity!" But we shall see which will be most zealous in the cause of brotherly love. For it is not we, but they, who are in isolation, though they don't see that. Of old, leaders of the people came from among us, and why should they not again? The same meek and humble ascetics will rise up and go out to work for the great cause. The salvation of Russia comes from the people. And the Russian monk has always been on the side of the people. We are isolated only if the people are isolated. The people believe as we do, and an unbelieving reformer will never do anything in Russia, even if he is sincere in heart and a genius. Remember that! The people will meet the atheist and overcome him, and Russia will be one and orthodox. Take care of the people and guard their hearts. Go on educating them quietly. That's your duty as monks, for this is a godbearing people.

(f) OF MASTERS AND SERVANTS, AND OF WHETHER IT IS POSSIBLE FOR THEM TO BE BROTHERS IN THE SPIRIT

Of course, I don't deny that there is sin in the peasants too. And the fire of corruption is spreading visibly, hourly, working from above downwards. The spirit of isolation is coming upon the people too. Moneylenders and devourers of the commune are rising up. Already the merchant grows more and more eager for rank, and strives to show himself cultured though he has not a trace of culture, and to this end meanly despises his old traditions, and is even ashamed of the faith of his fathers. He visits princes, though he is only a peasant corrupted. The peasants are rotting in drunkenness and cannot shake off the habit. And what cruelty to their wives, to their children even! All from drunkenness! I've seen in the factories children of ten, frail, rickety, bent and already depraved. The stuffy workshop, the din of machinery, work all day long, the vile language and the drink, the drink—is that what a little child's heart needs? He needs sunshine, childish play, good examples all about him, and at least a little love. There must be no more of this, monks, nor more torturing of children, rise up and preach that, make haste, make haste! But God will save Russia, for though the peasants are corrupted and cannot renounce their filthy sin, yet they know it is cursed by God and that they do wrong in sinning. So that our people still believe in righteousness, have faith in God and weep tears of devotion.

It is different with the upper classes. They, following science, want to base justice on reason alone, but not with Christ, as before, and they have already proclaimed that there is no crime, that there is no sin. And that's consistent, for if you have no God what is the meaning of crime? In Europe the people are already rising up against the rich with violence, and the leaders of the people are everywhere leading them to bloodshed, and teaching them that their wrath is righteous. But their "wrath is accursed, for it is cruel." But God will save Russia as He has saved her many times. Salvation will come from the people, from their faith and their meekness.

Fathers and teachers, watch over the people's faith and this will not be a dream. I've been struck all my life in our great people by their dignity, their true and seemly dignity. I've seen it myself, I can testify to it, I've seen it and marveled at it, I've seen it in spite of the degraded sins and poverty-stricken appearance of our peasantry. They are not servile, and even after two centuries of serfdom, they are free in manner and bearing, yet without insolence, and not revengeful and not envious. "You are rich and noble, you are clever and talented, well be so, God bless you. I respect you, but I know that I too am a man. By the very fact that I respect you without envy I prove my dignity as a man."

In truth if they don't say this (for they don't know how to say this yet) that is how they *act*. I have seen it myself, I have known it myself, and, would you believe it, the poorer our Russian peasant is, the more noticeable is that serene goodness, for the rich among them are for the most part corrupted already, and much of that is due to our carelessness and indifference. But God will save His people, for Russia is great in her humility. I dream of seeing, and seem to see clearly already, our future. It will come to pass, that even the most corrupt of our rich will end by being ashamed of his riches before the poor, and the poor, seeing his humility, will understand and give way before him, will respond joyfully and kindly to his honorable shame. Believe me that it will end in that; things are moving to that. Equality is to be found only in the spiritual dignity of man, and that will only be understood among us. If we were brothers, there would be fraternity, but before that, they will never agree about the division of wealth. We preserve the image of Christ, and it will shine forth like a precious diamond to the whole world. So may it be, so may it be!

Fathers and teachers, a touching incident befell me once. In my wanderings I met in the town of K—— my old orderly, Afanasy. It was eight years since I had parted from him. He chanced to see me in the marketplace, recognized me, ran up to me, and how delighted he was, he simply pounced on me: "Master dear, is it you? is it really you I see?" He took me home with him. He was no longer in the army, he was married and already had two little children. He and his wife earned their living hawking wares in the marketplace. His room was poor, but bright and clean. He made me sit down, set the samovar, sent for his wife, as though my appearance were a festival for them. He brought me his children: "Bless them, father."

"Is it for me to bless them? I am only a humble monk. I will pray for them. And for you, Afanasy Pavlovich, I have prayed every day since that day, for it all came from you," said I. And I explained that to him as well as I could. And what do you think? The man kept gazing at me and could not believe that I, his former master, an officer, was now before him in such a guise and position; it even made him shed tears.

"Why are you weeping?" said I, "better rejoice over me, dear friend, whom I can never forget, for my path is a glad and joyful one."

He did not say much, but kept sighing and shaking his head over me tenderly.

"What has become of your fortune?" he asked.

"I gave it to the monastery," I answered; "we live in common."

After tea I began saying goodbye, and suddenly he brought out half a ruble as an offering to the monastery, and another half-ruble I saw him thrusting hurriedly into my hand: "That's for you in your wanderings, it may be of use to you, father."

I took his half-ruble, bowed to him and his wife, and went out rejoicing. And on my way I thought: "Here we are both now, he at home and I on the road, sighing and shaking our heads, no doubt, and yet smiling joyfully in the gladness of our hearts, remembering how God brought about our meeting." I have never seen him again since then. I had been his master and he my servant, but now when we exchanged a loving kiss with softened hearts, there was a great human bond between us. I have thought a great deal about that, and now what I think is this: is it so inconceivable that that grand and simple-hearted unity might in due time become universal among the Russian people? I believe that it will come to pass and that the time is at hand.

And of the servants I will add this, in old days when I was young I was often angry with servants; "the cook had served something too hot, the orderly had not brushed my clothes." But what taught me better then was a thought of my dear brother's, which I had heard from him in childhood: "Am I worth it, that another should serve me and be ordered about by me in his poverty and ignorance?" And I wondered at the time that such simple and self-evident ideas should be so slow to occur to our minds. It is impossible that there should be no servants in the world, but act so that your servant may be freer in spirit than if he were not a servant. And why cannot I be a servant to my servant and even let him see it, and that without any pride on my part or any mistrust on his? Why should not my servant be like my own kindred, so that I may take him into my family and rejoice in doing so? Even now this can be done, but it will lead to the grand unity of men in the future, when a man will not seek servants for himself, or desire to turn his fellow creatures into servants as he does now, but on the contrary, will long with his whole heart to be the servant of all, as the Gospel teaches.

And can it be a dream, that in the end man will find his joy only in deeds of light and mercy, and not in cruel pleasures as now, in gluttony, fornication, ostentation, boasting and envious rivalry of one with the other? I firmly believe that it is not and that the time is at hand. People laugh and ask: "When will that time come and does it look as if it is coming?" I believe that with Christ's help we shall accomplish this great thing. And how many ideas there have been on earth in the history of man which were unthinkable ten years before they appeared? Yet when their destined hour had come, they came forth and spread over the whole earth. So it will be with us, and our people will shine forth in the world, and all men will say: "The stone which the builders rejected has become the cornerstone of the building."

And we may ask the scornful themselves: if our hope is a dream, when will you build up your edifice and order things justly by your intellect alone, without Christ? If they declare that it is they who are advancing towards unity, only the most simple-hearted among them believe it, so that one may positively marvel at such simplicity. Of a truth, they have more fantastic dreams than we. They aim at justice, but, denying Christ, they will end by flooding the earth with blood, for blood cries out for blood, and he that taketh up the sword shall perish by the sword. And if it were not for Christ's covenant, they would slaughter one another down to the last two men on earth. And those two last men would not be able to restrain each other in their pride, and the one would slay the other and then himself. And that would come to pass, were it not for the promise of Christ that for the sake of the humble and meek the days shall be shortened.

While I was still wearing an officer's uniform after my duel, I talked about servants in general society, and I remember everyone was amazed at me: "What!" they asked, "are we to make our servants sit down on the sofa and offer them tea?" And I answered them: "Why not, sometimes at least." Everyone laughed. Their question was frivolous and my answer was not clear; but the thought in it was to some extent right.

(g)   OF PRAYER, OF LOVE, AND OF CONTACT WITH OTHER WORLDS

Young man, be not forgetful of prayer. Every time you pray, if your prayer is sincere, there will be new feeling and new meaning in it, which will give you fresh courage, and you will understand that prayer is an education. Remember too, every day, and whenever you can, repeat to yourself, "Lord, have mercy on all who appear before Thee today." For every hour and every moment thousands of men leave life on this earth, and their souls appear before God. And how many of them depart in solitude, unknown, sad, dejected, that no one mourns for them or even knows whether they have lived or not. And behold, from the other end of the earth perhaps, your prayer for their rest will rise up to God though you knew them not nor they you. How touching it must be to a soul standing in dread before the Lord to feel at that instant that, for him too, there is one to pray, that there is a fellow creature left on earth to love him too. And God will look on you both more graciously, for if you have had so much pity on him, how much more will He have pity Who is infinitely more loving and merciful than you. And He will forgive him for your sake.

Brothers, have no fear of men's sin. Love a man even in his sin, for that is the semblance of Divine Love and is the highest love on earth. Love all God's creation, the whole and every grain of sand in it. Love every leaf, every ray of God's light. Love the animals, love the plants, love everything. If you love everything, you will perceive the divine mystery in things. Once you perceive it, you will begin to comprehend it better every day. And you will come at last to love the whole world with an all-embracing love. Love the animals: God has given them the rudiments of thought and joy untroubled. Do not trouble it, don't harass them, don't deprive them of their happiness, don't work against God's intent. Man, do not pride yourself on superiority to the animals; they are without sin, and you, with your greatness, defile the earth by your appearance on it, and leave the traces of your foulness after you—alas, it is true of almost every one of us! Love children especially, for they too are sinless like the angels; they live to soften and purify our hearts and as it were to guide us. Woe to him who offends a child! Father Anfim taught me to love children. The kind, silent man used often on our wanderings to spend the pennies given us on sweets and cakes for the children. He could not pass by a child without emotion, that's the nature of the man.

At some thoughts one stands perplexed, especially at the sight of men's sin, and wonders whether one should use force or humble love. Always decide to use humble love. If you resolve on that once for all, you may subdue the whole world. Loving humility is marvelously strong, the strongest of all things and there is nothing else like it.

Every day and every hour, every minute, walk round yourself and watch yourself, and see that your image is a seemly one. You pass by a little child, you pass by, spiteful, with ugly words, with wrathful heart; you may not have noticed the child, but he has seen you, and your image, unseemly and ignoble, may remain in his defenseless heart. You don't know it, but you may have sown an evil seed in him and it may grow, and all because you were not careful before the child, because you did not foster in yourself a careful, actively benevolent love. Brothers, love is a teacher; but one must know how to acquire it, for it is hard to acquire, it is dearly bought, it is won slowly by long labor. For we must love not only occasionally, for a moment, but forever. Everyone can love occasionally, even the wicked can.

My brother asked the birds to forgive him; that sounds senseless, but it is right; for all is like an ocean, all is flowing and blending; a touch in one place sets up movement at the other end of the earth. It may be senseless to beg forgiveness of the birds, but birds would be happier at your side—a little happier, anyway—and children and all animals, if you yourself were nobler than you are now. It's all like an ocean, I tell you. Then you would pray to the birds too, consumed by an all-embracing love, in a sort of transport, and pray that they too will forgive you your sin. Treasure this ecstasy, however senseless it may seem to men.

My friends, pray to God for gladness. Be glad as children, as the birds of heaven. And let not the sin of men confound you in your doings. Fear not that it will wear away your work and hinder its being accomplished. Do not say, "Sin is mighty, wickedness is mighty, evil environment is mighty, and we are lonely and helpless, and evil environment is wearing us away and hindering our good work from being done." Fly from that dejection, children! There is only one means of salvation, then take yourself and make yourself responsible for all men's sins, that is the truth, you know, friends, for as soon as you sincerely make yourself responsible for everything and for all men, you will see at once that it is really so, and that you are to blame for everyone and for all things. But throwing your own indolence and impotence on others you will end by sharing the pride of Satan and murmuring against God.

Of the pride of Satan what I think is this: it is hard for us on earth to comprehend it, and therefore it is so easy to fall into error and to share it, even imagining that we are doing something grand and fine. Indeed many of the strongest feelings and movements of our nature we cannot comprehend on earth. Let not that be a stumbling block, and think not that it may serve as a justification to you for anything. For the Eternal Judge asks of you what you can comprehend and not what you cannot. You will know that yourself hereafter, for you will behold all things truly then and will not dispute them. On earth, indeed, we are as it were astray, and if it were not for the precious image of Christ before us, we should be undone and altogether lost, as was the human race before the flood. Much on earth is hidden from us, but to make up for that we have been given a precious mystic sense of our living bond with the other world, with the higher heavenly world, and the roots of our thoughts and feelings are not here but in other worlds. That is why the philosophers say that we cannot apprehend the reality of things on earth.

God took seeds from different worlds and sowed them on this earth, and His garden grew up and everything came up that could come up, but what grows lives and is alive only through the feeling of its contact with other mysterious worlds. If that feeling grows weak or is destroyed in you, the heavenly growth will die away in you. Then you will be indifferent to life and even grow to hate it. That's what I think.

(h) CAN A MAN JUDGE HIS FELLOW CREATURES? FAITH TO THE END

Remember particularly that you cannot be a judge of anyone. For no one can judge a criminal, until he recognizes that he is just such a criminal as the man standing before him, and that he perhaps is more than all men to blame for that crime. When he understands that, he will be able to be a judge. Though that sounds absurd, it is true. If I had been righteous myself, perhaps there would have been no criminal standing before me. If you can take upon yourself the crime of the criminal your heart is judging, take it at once, suffer for him yourself, and let him go without reproach. And even if the law itself makes you his judge, act in the same spirit so far as possible, for he will go away and condemn himself more bitterly than you have done. If, after your kiss, he goes away untouched, mocking at you, do not let that be a stumbling block to you. It shows his time has not yet come, but it will come in due course. And if it come not, no matter; if not he, then another in his place will understand and suffer, and judge and condemn himself, and the truth will be fulfilled. Believe that, believe it without doubt; for in that lies all the hope and faith of the saints.

Work without ceasing. If you remember in the night as you go to sleep, "I have not done what I ought to have done," rise up at once and do it. If the people around you are spiteful and callous and will not hear you, fall down before them and beg their forgiveness; for in truth you are to blame for their not wanting to hear you. And if you cannot speak to them in their bitterness, serve them in silence and in humility, never losing hope. If all men abandon you and even drive you away by force, then when you are left alone fall on the earth and kiss it, water it with your tears and it will bring forth fruit even though no one has seen or heard you in your solitude. Believe to the end, even if all men went astray and you were left the only one faithful; bring your offering even then and praise God in your loneliness. And if two of you are gathered together—then there is a whole world, a world of living love. Embrace each other tenderly and praise God, for if only in you two His truth has been fulfilled.

If you sin yourself and grieve even unto death for your sins or for your sudden sin, then rejoice for others, rejoice for the righteous man, rejoice that if you have sinned, he is righteous and has not sinned.

If the evildoing of men moves you to indignation and overwhelming distress, even to a desire for vengeance on the evildoers, shun above all things that feeling. Go at once and seek suffering for yourself, as though you were yourself guilty of that wrong. Accept that suffering and bear it and your heart will find comfort, and you will understand that you too are guilty, for you might have been a light to the evildoers, even as the one man sinless, and you were not a light to them. If you had been a light, you would have lightened the path for others too, and the evildoer might perhaps have been saved by your light from his sin. And even though your light was shining, yet you see men were not saved by it, hold firm and doubt not the power of the heavenly light. Believe that if they were not saved, they will be saved hereafter. And if they are not saved hereafter, then their sons will be saved, for your light will not die even when you are dead. The righteous man departs, but his light remains. Men are always saved after the death of the deliverer. Men reject their prophets and slay them, but they love their martyrs and honor those whom they have slain. You are working for the whole, you are acting for the future. Seek no reward, for great is your reward on this earth: the spiritual joy which is only vouch-safed to the righteous man. Fear not the great nor the mighty, but be wise and ever serene. Know measure, know the proper time, study that. When you are left alone, pray. Love to throw yourself on the earth and kiss it. Kiss the earth and love it with an unceas-ing, consuming love. Love all men, love everything. Seek that rap-ture and ecstasy. Water the earth with the tears of your joy and love those tears. Don't be ashamed of that ecstasy, prize it, for it is a gift of God and a great one; it is not given to many but only to the elect. (pride of the righteous)

(i) OF HELL AND HELLFIRE, A MYSTIC REFLECTION

Fathers and teachers, I ponder "What is hell?" I maintain that it is the suffering of no longer being able to love. Once in infinite existence, immeasurable in time and space, a spiritual creature was given on his coming to earth, the power of saying, "I am and I love." Once, only once, there was given him a moment of active *living* love and for that was earthly life given him, and with it times and seasons. And that happy creature rejected the priceless gift, prized it and loved it not, scorned it and remained callous. Such a one, having left the earth, sees Abraham's bosom and talks with Abraham as we are told in the parable of the rich man and Lazarus, and beholds heaven and can go up to the Lord. But that is just his torment, to rise up to the Lord without ever having loved, to be brought close to those who have loved when he has despised their love. For he sees clearly and says to himself, "Now I have under-standing and though I now thirst to love, there will be nothing great, no sacrifice in my love, for my earthly life is over, and Abraham will not come even with a drop of living water (that is the gift of earthly, active life) to cool the fiery thirst of spiritual love which burns in me now, though I despised it on earth; there is no more life for me and there will be no more time! Even though I would gladly give my life for others, it can never be, for that life is passed which can be sacrificed for love, and now there is a gulf fixed between that life and this existence."

They talk of hellfire in the material sense. I don't go into that mystery and I shun it. But I think if there were fire in material sense they would be glad of it, for, I imagine, that in material agony, their still greater spiritual agony would be forgotten for a moment. Moreover, that spiritual agony cannot be taken from them, for that suffering is not external but within them. And if it could be taken from them, I think it would be bitterer still for the unhappy creatures. For even if the righteous in Paradise forgave them, beholding their torments, and called them up to heaven in their infinite love, they would only multiply their torments, for they would arouse in them still more keenly a flaming thirst for responsive, active and grateful love which is now impossible. In the timidity of my heart I imagine, however, that the very recognition of this impossibility would serve at last to console them. For accepting the love of the righteous together with the impossibility of repaying it, by this submissiveness and the effect of this humility, they will attain at last, as it were, to a certain semblance of that active love which they scorned in life, to something like its outward expression. . . . I am sorry, friends and brothers, that I cannot express this clearly.

But woe to those who have slain themselves on earth, woe to the suicides! I believe that there can be none more miserable than they. They tell us that it is a sin to pray to God for them and outwardly the Church, as it were, renounces them, but in my secret heart I believe that we may pray even for them. Love can never be an offense to Christ. For such as those I have prayed inwardly all my life, I confess it, fathers and teachers, and even now I pray for them every day.

Oh, there are some who remain proud and fierce even in hell, in spite of their certain knowledge and contemplation of the absolute truth; there are some fearful ones who have given themselves over to Satan and his proud spirit entirely. For such, hell is voluntary and ever consuming; they are tortured by their own choice. For they have cursed themselves, cursing God and life. They live upon their vindictive pride like a starving man in the desert sucking blood out of his own body. But they are never satisfied, and they refuse forgiveness, they curse God Who calls them. They cannot behold the living God without hatred, and they cry out that the God of life should be annihilated, that God should destroy Himself and His own creation. And they will burn in the fire of their own wrath for ever and yearn for death and annihilation. But they will not attain to death. . . .

Here Alexey Fyodorovich Karamazov's manuscript ends. I repeat, it is incomplete and fragmentary. Biographical details, for instance, cover only Father Zosima's earliest youth. Of his teaching and opinions we find brought together sayings evidently uttered at different times and in response to various situations. His utterances during the last few hours have not been kept separate from the rest, but their general character can be gathered from what we have in Alexey Fyodorovich's manuscript.

The elder's death came in the end quite unexpectedly. For although those who were gathered about him that last evening realized that his death was approaching, yet it was difficult to imagine that it would come so suddenly. On the contrary, his friends, as I observed already, seeing him that night apparently so cheerful and talkative, were convinced that there was at least a temporary change for the better in his condition. Even five minutes before his death, they said afterwards wonderingly, it was impossible to foresee it. He seemed suddenly to feel an acute pain in his chest, he turned pale and pressed his hands to his heart. All rose from their seats and hastened to him. But though suffering, he still looked at them with a smile, sank slowly from his chair on his knees, then bowed his face to the ground, stretched out his arms and as though in joyful ecstasy, praying and kissing the earth (as he taught), quietly and joyfully gave up his soul to God.

The news of his death spread at once through the hermitage and reached the monastery. The nearest friends of the deceased and those whose duty it was from their position began to lay out the corpse according to the ancient ritual, and all the monks gathered together in the church. And before dawn the news of the death reached the town. By the morning all the town was talking of the event, and crowds were flocking from the town to the monastery. But this subject will be treated in the next book; I will only add here that before a day had passed something happened so unexpected, so strange, upsetting, and bewildering in its effect on the monks and the townspeople, that after all these years, that day of general suspense is still vividly remembered in the town.

Part Three

Book Seven

ALYOSHA

Chapter I

The Odor of Corruption

The body of Father Zosima was prepared for burial according to the established ritual. As is well known, the bodies of dead monks and hermits are not washed. In the words of the Church Ritual: "If any one of the monks depart in the Lord, the monk designated (that is, whose office it is) shall wipe the body with warm water, making first the sign of the cross with a sponge on the forehead of the deceased, on the breast, on the hands and feet and on the knees, and that is enough." All this was done by Father Païssy, who then clothed the deceased in his monastic garb and wrapped him in his cloak, which was, according to custom, somewhat slit to allow of its being folded about him in the form of a cross. On his head he put a hood with an eight-cornered cross. The hood was left open and the dead man's face was covered with black gauze. In his hand was put an icon of the Savior. Towards morning he was put in the coffin which had been made ready long before. It was decided to leave the coffin all day in the cell, in the larger room in which the elder used to receive his visitors and fellow monks. As the deceased was a priest and monk of the strictest rule, the Gospel, not the Psalter, had to be read over his body by monks in holy orders. The reading was begun by Father Iosif immediately after the requiem service. Father Païssy desired later on to read the Gospel all day and night over his dead friend, but for the present he, as well as the Father Superintendent of the hermitage, was very busy and occupied, for something extraordinary, and unheard of, even "unseemly" excitement and impatient expectation began to be apparent in the monks, and the visitors from the monastery hostels, and the crowds of people flocking from the town. And as time went on, this grew more and more marked. Both the Superintendent and Father Païssy did their utmost to calm the general bustle and agitation.

When it was fully daylight, some people began bringing their sick, in most cases children, with them from the town—as though they had been waiting expressly for this moment to do so, evidently persuaded that the dead elder's remains had a power of healing, which would be immediately made manifest in accordance with their faith. It was only then apparent how unquestionably everyone in our town had accepted Father Zosima during his lifetime as a great saint. And those who came were far from being all of the humbler classes. This intense expectation on the part of believers displayed with such haste, such openness, even with impatience and almost insistence, Father Païssy considered an evil temptation. Though he had long foreseen something of the sort, the actual manifestation of the feeling was beyond anything he had looked for. When he came across any of the monks who displayed this excitement, Father Païssy began to reprove them. "Such immediate expectation of something extraordinary," he said, "shows a levity, possible to worldly people but unseemly in us."

But little attention was paid him and Father Païssy noticed it uneasily. Yet he himself (if the whole truth must be told) secretly, at the bottom of his heart, cherished almost the same hopes and could not but be aware of it, though he was indignant at the too impatient expectation around him, and saw in it light-mindedness and vanity. Nevertheless, it was particularly unpleasant to him to meet certain persons, whose presence aroused in him great misgivings. In the crowd in the dead man's cell he noticed with inward aversion (for which he immediately reproached himself) the presence of Rakitin, for example, and of the monk from Obdorsk, who was still staying in the monastery. Of both of them Father Païssy felt for some reason suddenly suspicious—though, indeed, he might well have felt the same about others.

The monk from Obdorsk was conspicuous as the most fussy in the excited crowd. He was to be seen everywhere; everywhere he asked questions, everywhere he listened, on all sides he whispered with a peculiar, mysterious air. His expression showed the greatest impatience and even a sort of irritation.

As for Rakitin, he, as appeared later, had come so early to the hermitage at the special request of Madame Khokhlakov. As soon as that good-hearted but weak-minded woman, who could not herself have been admitted to the hermitage, woke and heard of the death of Father Zosima, she was overtaken with such intense curiosity that she promptly despatched Rakitin to the hermitage, to keep a careful lookout and report to her by letter every half hour or so *"everything that takes place."* She regarded Rakitin as a most religious and devout young man. He was particularly clever in getting round people and assuming whatever part he thought most to their taste, if he detected the slightest advantage to himself from doing so.

It was a bright, clear day and many of the visitors were thronging about the tombs, which were particularly numerous round church and scattered here and there about the hermitage walked round the hermitage, Father Païssy suddenly remembered Alyosha and that he had not seen him for some time, not since the night. And he had no sooner thought of him than he at once noticed him in the furthest corner of the hermitage garden, sitting on the tombstone of a monk who had been famous long ago for his saintliness. He sat with his back to the hermitage and his face to the wall, and seemed to be hiding behind the tombstone. Going up to him, Father Païssy saw that he was weeping quietly but bitterly, with his face hidden in his hands and that his whole frame was shaking with sobs. Father Païssy stood over him for a little.

"Enough, dear son, enough, dear," he pronounced with feeling at last. "Why do you weep? Rejoice and weep not. Don't you know that this is the greatest of *his* days? Think only where he is now, at this moment!"

Alyosha glanced at him, uncovering his face, which was swollen with crying like a child's, but turned away at once without uttering a word and hid his face in his hands again.

"Maybe it is well," said Father Païssy thoughtfully: "weep if you must, Christ has sent you those tears."

"Your touching tears are but a relief to your spirit and will serve to gladden your dear heart," he added to himself, walking away from Alyosha, and thinking lovingly of him. He moved away quickly, however, for he felt that he too might weep looking at him. Meanwhile the time was passing; the monastery services and the requiems for the dead followed in their due course. Father Païssy again took Father Iosif's place by the coffin and began reading the Gospel. But before three o'clock in the afternoon that something took place to which I alluded at the end of the last book, something so unexpected by all of us and so contrary to the general hope, that, I repeat, this trivial incident has been minutely remembered to this day in our town and all the surrounding neighborhood. I may add here, for myself personally, that I feel it almost repulsive to recall that event which caused such frivolous agitation and was such a stumbling block to many, though in reality it was the most natural and trivial matter. I would, of course, have omitted all mention of it in my story, if it had not exerted a very strong influence on the heart and soul of the chief, *though future*, hero of my story, Alyosha, forming a crisis and turning point in his spiritual development, giving a shock to his intellect, which finally strengthened it for the rest of his life and gave it a definite aim.

And so, to return to our story. When before dawn they laid Father Zosima's body in the coffin and brought it into the front room, the question of opening the windows was raised among those who were around the coffin. But this suggestion made casually by someone was unanswered and almost unnoticed. Some of those present may perhaps have inwardly noticed it, only to reflect that the anticipation of decay and the odor of corruption from the body of such a saint was an actual absurdity, calling for compassion (if not a smile) for the lack of faith and the frivolity it implied. For they expected something quite different.

And, behold, soon after midday there were signs of something, at first only observed in silence by those who came in and out and were evidently each afraid to communicate the thought in his mind. But by three o'clock those signs had become so clear and unmistakable, that the news swiftly reached all the monks and visitors in the hermitage, promptly penetrated to the monastery, throwing all the monks into amazement, and finally, in the shortest possible time, spread to the town, exciting everyone in it, believers, and unbelievers alike. The unbelievers rejoiced, and as for the believers some of them rejoiced even more than the unbelievers, for "men love the downfall and disgrace of the righteous," as the deceased elder had said in one of his exhortations.

The fact is that an odor of corruption began to come from the coffin, growing gradually more marked, and by three o'clock it was quite unmistakable. In all the past history of our monastery, no such scandal could be recalled, and in no other circumstances could such a scandal have been possible, as showed itself in unseemly disorder immediately after this discovery among the very monks themselves. Afterwards, even many years afterwards, some sensible monks were amazed and horrified, when they recalled that day, that the scandal could have reached such proportions. For in the past, monks of very holy life had died, God-fearing old men, whose saintliness was acknowledged by all, yet from their humble coffins, too, the odor of corruption had come, naturally, as from all dead bodies, but that had caused no scandal nor even the slightest excitement. Of course there had been, in former times, saints in the monastery whose memory was carefully preserved and whose relics, according to tradition, showed no signs of corruption. This fact was regarded by the monks as touching and mysterious, and the tradition of it was cherished as something blessed and miraculous, and as a promise, by God's grace, of still greater glory from their tombs in the future.

One such, whose memory was particularly cherished, was an old monk, Job, who had died seventy years before at the age of a hundred and five. He had been a celebrated ascetic, rigid in fasting and silence, had died long ago, in the second decade of this century, and his tomb was pointed out to all visitors on their arrival with peculiar respect and mysterious hints of great hopes connected with it. (That was the very tomb on which Father Païssy had found Alyosha sitting in the morning.) Another memory cherished in the monastery was that of the famous Father Varsonofy, who preceded Father Zosima in the eldership. He was revered d·

lifetime as a crazy saint by all the pilgrims to the monastery. There was a tradition that both of these had laid in their coffins as though alive, that they had shown no signs of decomposition when they were buried and that there had been a holy light in their faces. And some people even insisted that a sweet fragrance came from their bodies.

Yet, in spite of these edifying memories, it would be difficult to explain the frivolity, absurdity and malice that were manifested beside the coffin of Father Zosima. It is my private opinion that several different causes were simultaneously at work, one of which was the deeply rooted hostility to the institution of elders as a pernicious innovation, an antipathy hidden deep in the hearts of many of the monks. Even more powerful was jealousy of the dead man's saintliness, so firmly established during his lifetime that it was almost a forbidden thing to question it. For though the late elder had won over many hearts, more by love than by miracles, and had gathered round him a mass of loving adherents, nonetheless, in fact, rather the more on that account he had awakened jealousy and so had come to have bitter enemies, secret and open, not only in the monastery but in the world outside it. He did no one any harm, but "Why do they think him so saintly?" And that question alone gradually repeated gave rise at last to an intense, insatiable hatred of him. That I believe was why many people were extremely delighted at the smell of decomposition which came so quickly, for not a day had passed since his death. At the same time there were some among those who had been hitherto reverently devoted to the elder, who were almost mortified and personally affronted by this incident. This was how the thing happened.

As soon as signs of decomposition had begun to appear, the whole aspect of the monks betrayed their secret motives in entering the cell. They went in, stayed a little while and hastened out to confirm the news to the crowd of other monks waiting outside. Some of the latter shook their heads mournfully, but others did not even care to conceal the delight, which gleamed unmistakably in their malignant eyes. And now no one reproached them for it, no one raised his voice in protest, which was strange, for the majority of the monks had been devoted to the dead elder. But it seemed as though God had in this case let the minority get the upper hand for a time.

Visitors from outside, particularly of the educated class, soon went into the cell, too, with the same spying intent. Of the peasantry few went into the cell, though there were crowds of them at the gates of the hermitage. After three o'clock the rush of worldly visitors was greatly increased and this was no doubt owing to the shocking news. People were attracted who would not otherwise have come on that day and had not intended to come, and among them were some personages of high standing. But external decorum was still preserved and Father Païssy, with a stern face, continued firmly and distinctly reading aloud the Gospel, apparently not noticing what was taking place around him, though he had, in fact, observed something unusual long before. But at last the murmurs, first subdued but gradually louder and more confident, reached even him. "It shows God's judgment is not as man's," Father Païssy heard suddenly. The first to give utterance to this sentiment was a layman, an elderly official from the town, known to be a man of great piety. But he only repeated aloud what the monks had long been whispering. They had long before formulated this damning conclusion, and the worst of it was that a sort of triumphant satisfaction at that conclusion became more and more apparent every moment. Soon they began to lay aside even external decorum and almost seemed to feel they had a sort of right to discard it.

"And for what reason can *this* have happened," some of the monks said, at first with a show of regret; "he had a small frame and his flesh was dried up on his bones, what was there to decay?"

"It must be a sign from heaven," others hastened to add, and their opinion was adopted at once without protest. For it was pointed out, too, that if the odor had been natural, as in the case of every dead sinner, it would have been apparent later, after a lapse of at least twenty-four hours, but this hasty prematureness of corruption "was in excess of nature," and so the finger of God was evident. It was meant for a sign. This conclusion seemed irresistible.

Gentle Father Iosif, the librarian, a great favorite of the dead man's, tried to reply to some of the evil speakers that "this is not held everywhere alike," and that the incorruptibility of the bodies of the just was not a dogma of the Orthodox Church, but only an opinion, and that even in the most Orthodox regions, at Athos for instance, they were not greatly confounded by the odor of corruption, and there the chief sign of the glorification of the saved was not bodily incorruptibility, but the color of the bones when the bodies have lain many years in the earth and have decayed in it. "And if the bones are yellow as wax, that is the great sign that the Lord has glorified the dead saint, if they are not yellow but black, it shows that God has not deemed him worthy of such glory—that is the belief in Athos, a great place, where the Orthodox doctrine has been preserved from of old, unbroken and in its greatest purity," said Father Iosif in conclusion.

But the meek father's words had little effect and even provoked a mocking retort. "That's all pedantry and innovation, no use listening to it," the monks decided. "We stick to the old doctrine, ther~ are all sorts of innovations nowadays, are we to follow them ~" added others.

"We have had as many holy fathers as they had. There they are among the Turks, they have forgotten everything. Their doctrine has long been impure and they have no bells even," the most sneering added.

Father Iosif walked away grieving the more since he had put forward his own opinion with little confidence as though scarcely believing in it himself. He foresaw with distress that something very unseemly was beginning and that there were positive signs of disobedience. Little by little, all the sensible monks were reduced to silence like Father Iosif. And so it came to pass that all who loved the elder and had accepted with devout obedience the institution of the eldership were all at once terribly cast down and glanced timidly in one another's faces, when they met. Those who were hostile to the institution of elders, as a novelty, held up their heads proudly. "There was no odor of corruption from the late elder Varsonofy, but a sweet fragrance," they recalled malignantly. "But he gained that glory not because he was an elder, but because he was a holy man." And this was followed by a shower of criticism and even blame of Father Zosima. "His teaching was false; he taught that life is a great joy and not a vale of tears," said some of the more unreasonable. "He followed the fashionable belief, he did not recognize material fire in hell," others, still more unreasonable, added. "He was not strict in fasting, allowed himself sweet things, ate cherry jam with his tea, ladies used to send it to him. Is it for a monk of strict rule to drink tea?" could be heard among some of the envious. "He sat in pride," the most malignant declared vindictively; "he considered himself a saint and he took it as his due when people knelt before him." "He abused the sacrament of confession," the fiercest opponents of the institution of elders added in a malicious whisper. And among these were some of the oldest monks, strictest in their devotion, genuine ascetics, who had kept silent during the life of the deceased elder, but now suddenly unsealed their lips. And this was terrible, for their words had great influence on your monks who were not yet firm in their convictions. The monk from Obdorsk heard all this attentively, heaving deep sighs and nodding his head. "Yes, clearly Father Ferapont was right in his judgment yesterday," and at that moment Father Ferapont himself made his appearance, as though on purpose to increase the confusion.

I have mentioned already that he rarely left his wooden cell by the apiary. He was seldom even seen at church and they overlooked this neglect on the ground of his craziness, and did not keep him to the rules binding on all the rest. But if the whole truth is to be told, they hardly had a choice about it. For it would have been discreditable to insist on burdening with the common regulations so great an ascetic and hermit, who prayed day and night (he even dropped asleep on his knees). If they had insisted, the monks would have said "he is holier than all of us and he follows a rule harder than ours. And if he does not go to church, it's because he knows when he ought to; he has his own rule." It was to avoid the chance of these sinful murmurs Father Ferapont was left in peace. As everyone was aware, Father Ferapont particularly disliked Father Zosima. And now the news had reached him in his hut that "God's judgment is not the same as man's," and that something had happened which was "in excess of nature." It may well be supposed that among the first to run to him with the news was the monk from Obdorsk, who had visited him the evening before and left his cell terror-stricken.

I have mentioned above, that though Father Païssy, standing firm and immovable reading the Gospel over the coffin, could not hear nor see what was passing outside the cell, he gauged most of it correctly in his heart, for he knew the men surrounding him well. He was not shaken by it, but awaited what would come next without fear, watching with penetration and insight for the outcome of the general excitement.

Suddenly an extraordinary uproar in the passage in open defiance of decorum burst on his ears. The door was flung open and Father Ferapont appeared in the doorway. Behind him there could be seen accompanying him a crowd of monks, together with many people from the town. They did not, however, enter the cell, but stood at the bottom of the steps, waiting to see what Father Ferapont would say or do. For they felt with a certain awe, in spite of their audacity, that he had not come for nothing. Standing in the doorway, Father Ferapont raised his arms, and under his right arm the keen inquisitive little eyes of the monk from Obdorsk peeped in. He alone, in his intense curiosity, could not resist running up the steps after Father Ferapont. The others, on the contrary, pressed further back in sudden alarm when the door was noisily flung open. Holding his hands aloft, Father Ferapont suddenly roared:

"Casting out I cast out!" and, turning in all directions, he began at once making the sign of the cross at each of the four walls and four corners of the cell in succession. All who accompanied Father Ferapont immediately understood his action. For they knew he always did this wherever he went, and that he would not sit down or say a word, till he had driven out the evil spirits.

"Satan, go hence! Satan, go hence!" he repeated at each sign of the cross. "Casting out I cast out," he roared again. He was wearing his coarse gown girt with a rope. His bare chest, covered with gray hair, could be seen under his hempen shirt. His feet were bare. As soon as he began waving his arms, the cruel irons he wore under his gown could be heard clanking. Father Païssy paused in reading, stepped forward and stood before him waiting.

"What have you come for, worthy Father? Why do you offend against good order? Why do you disturb the peace of the flock?" he said at last, looking sternly at him.

"What have I come for? You ask why? What is your faith?" shouted Father Ferapont crazily. "I've come here to drive out your visitors, the unclean devils. I've come to see how many have gathered here while I have been away. I want to sweep them out with a birch broom."

"You cast out the evil spirit, but perhaps you are serving him yourself," Father Païssy went on fearlessly. "And who can say of himself 'I am holy.' Can you, Father?"

"I am unclean, not holy. I would not sit in an armchair and would not have them bow down to me as an idol," thundered Father Ferapont. "Nowadays folks destroy the true faith. The dead man, your saint," he turned to the crowd, pointing with his finger to the coffin, "did not believe in devils. He gave purgatives to keep off the devils. And so they have become as common as spiders in the corners. And now he has begun to stink himself. In that we see a great sign from God."

The incident he referred to was this. One of the monks was haunted in his dreams and, later on, in waking moments, by visions of evil spirits. When in the utmost terror he confided this to Father Zosima, the elder had advised continual prayer and rigid fasting. But when that was of no use, he advised him, while persisting in prayer and fasting, to take a special medicine. Many persons were shocked at the time and wagged their heads as they talked over it—and most of all Father Ferapont, to whom some of the censorious had hastened to report this "extraordinary" counsel on the part of the elder.

"Go away, Father!" said Father Païssy, in a commanding voice, "it's not for man to judge but for God. Perhaps we see here a 'sign' which neither you, nor I, nor any one of us is able to comprehend. Go, Father, and do not trouble the flock!" he repeated impressively.

"He did not keep the fasts according to the rule and therefore the sign has come. That is clear and it's a sin to hide it," the fanatic, carried away by a zeal that outstripped his reason, would not be quieted. "He was seduced by sweets, ladies brought them to him in their pockets, he sipped tea, he worshipped his belly, filling it with sweet things and his mind with haughty thought. . . . And for this he is put to shame. . . ."

"You speak lightly, Father." Father Païssy too raised his voice. "I admire your fasting and severities, but you speak lightly like some frivolous youth, fickle and childish. Go away, Father, I command you!" Father Païssy thundered in conclusion.

"I will go," said Ferapont, seeming somewhat taken aback, but still as bitter. "You learned men! You are so clever you look down upon my humbleness. I came hither with little learning and here I have forgotten what I did know, God himself has preserved me in my weakness from your subtlety."

Father Païssy stood over him, waiting resolutely. Father Ferapont paused and, suddenly leaning his cheek on his hand despondently, pronounced in a singsong voice, looking at the coffin of the dead elder:

"Tomorrow they will sing over him 'Our Helper and Defender'— a splendid anthem—and over me when I die all they'll sing will be 'What earthly joy'—a little canticle,"[1] he added with tearful regret. "You are proud and puffed up, this is a vain place!" he shouted suddenly like a madman, and with a wave of his hand he turned quickly and quickly descended the steps. The crowd awaiting him below wavered; some followed him at once and some lingered, for the cell was still open, and Father Païssy, following Father Ferapont on to the steps, stood watching him. But the excited old fanatic was not completely silenced. Walking twenty steps away, he suddenly turned towards the setting sun, raised both his arms and, as though someone had cut him down, fell to the ground with a loud scream.

"My God has conquered! Christ has conquered with the setting sun!" he shouted frantically, stretching up his hands to the sun, and falling face downwards on the ground, he sobbed like a little child, shaken by his tears and spreading out his arms on the ground. Then all rushed up to him; there were exclamations and sympathetic sobs . . . a kind of frenzy seemed to take possession of them all.

"This is the one who is a saint! This is the one who is a holy man!" some cried aloud, losing their fear. "This is he who should be an elder," others added malignantly.

"He wouldn't be an elder . . . he would refuse . . . he wouldn't serve a cursed innovation . . . he wouldn't imitate their foolery," other voices chimed in at once. And it is hard to say how far they might have gone, but at that moment the bell rang summoning them to service. All began crossing themselves at once. Father Ferapont, too, got up and crossing himself went back to his cell without looking round, still uttering exclamations which were utterly incoherent. A few followed him, but the greater number dispersed, hastening to service. Father Païssy let Father Iosif read in his place and went down. The frantic outcries of bigots could not shake him, but his heart was suddenly filled with melancholy for some special reason and he felt that. He stood still and suddenly wondered, "Why am I sad even to dejection?" and immediately grasped with surprise that his sudden sadness was due to a very

1. When a monk's body is carried out from the cell to the church and from the church to the graveyard, the canticle "What earthly joy . . ." is sung. If the deceased was a priest as well as a monk the canticle "Our Helper and Defender" is sung instead. [Dostoevsky's note.]

small and special cause. In the crowd thronging at the entrance to the cell, he had noticed Alyosha and he remembered that he had felt at once a pang at heart on seeing him. "Can that boy mean so much to my heart now?" he asked himself, wondering. At that moment Alyosha passed him, hurrying away, but not in the direction of the church. Their eyes met. Alyosha quickly turned away his eyes and dropped them to the ground, and from the boy's look alone, Father Païssy guessed what a great change was taking place in him at that moment.

"Have you, too, fallen into temptation?" cried Father Païssy. "Can you be with those of little faith?" he added mournfully.

Alyosha stood still and gazed vaguely at Father Païssy, but quickly turned his eyes away again and again looked on the ground. He stood sideways and did not turn his face to Father Païssy, who watched his attentively.

"Where are you hastening? The bell calls to service," he asked again, but again Alyosha gave no answer.

"Are you leaving the hermitage? What, without asking leave, without asking a blessing?"

Alyosha suddenly gave a wry smile, cast a strange, very strange, look at the father to whom his former guide, the former sovereign of his heart and mind, his beloved elder, had confided him as he lay dying. And suddenly, still without speaking, waved his hand, as though not caring even to be respectful, and with rapid steps walked towards the gates away from the hermitage.

"You will come back again!" murmured Father Païssy, looking after him with sorrowful surprise.

Chapter II

A Critical Moment

Father Païssy, of course, was not wrong when he decided that his "dear boy" would come back again. Perhaps indeed, to some extent, he penetrated with insight into the true meaning of Alyosha's spiritual condition. Yet I must frankly own that it would be very difficult for me to give a clear account of that strange, vague moment in the life of the hero of my tale whom I love so much and who was still so young. To Father Païssy's sorrowful question, "Are you too with those of little faith?" I could of course confidently answer for Alyosha no, he is not with those of little faith. Quite the contrary. Indeed, all his trouble came from the fact that he was of great faith. But still the trouble was there and was so agonizing that even long afterwards Alyosha thought of that sorrowful day as one of the bitterest and most fatal days of his life. If the question is asked: "Could all his grief and disturbance have been only due to the fact that his elder's body had shown signs of premature decomposition instead of at once performing miracles?" I must answer without beating about the bush, "Yes, it certainly was." I would only beg the reader not to be in too great a hurry to laugh at my young hero's pure heart. I am far from intending to apologize for him or to justify his innocent faith on the ground of his youth, or the little progress he had made in his studies, or any such reason. I must declare, on the contrary, that I have genuine respect for the qualities of his heart. No doubt a youth who received impressions cautiously, whose love was lukewarm, and whose mind was too prudent for his age and so of little value, such a young man might, I admit, have avoided what happened to my hero. But in some cases it is really more creditable to be carried away by an emotion, however unreasonable, which springs from a great love, than to be unmoved. And this is even truer in youth, for a young man who is always sensible is to be suspected and is of little worth—that's my opinion! "But," reasonable people will exclaim perhaps, "every young man cannot believe in such a superstition and your hero is no model for others." To this I reply again, yes! my hero had faith, a faith holy and steadfast, but still I am not going to apologize for him.

Don't you see, though I declared above, and perhaps too hastily, that I would not explain, apologize for, or justify my hero, I see that some explanation is necessary for the understanding of the rest of my story. Let me say then, it was not a question of miracles. There was no frivolous and impatient expectation of miracles in his mind. And Alyosha needed no miracles at the time, for the triumph of some preconceived idea—oh, no, not at all—what he saw before all was one figure—the figure of his beloved elder, the figure of that holy man whom he revered with such adoration. The fact is that all the love that lay concealed in his pure young heart for "everyone and everything" had, for the past year, been concentrated—and perhaps wrongly so—primarily on one being, at least in the strongest impulses of his heart, his beloved elder, now dead. It is true that being had for so long been accepted by him as his ideal, that all his young strength and energy could not but turn towards that ideal, even to the forgetting at the moment "of everyone and everything." He remembered afterwards how, on that terrible day, he had entirely forgotten his brother Dmitri, about whom he had been so anxious and troubled the day before; he had forgotten too to take the two hundred rubles to Ilyusha's father, though he had so warmly intended to do so the preceding evening. But again it was not miracles he needed but only "the higher justice" which had been in his belief outraged by the blow that had so suddenly and cruelly wounded his heart. And what does it signify that this "justice" looked for by Alyosha inevitably took the shape of miracles to be wrought immediately by the ashes of his adored teacher? Why, everyone in the monastery cherished the same thought and the same hope, even those whose intellects Alyosha revered, Father Païssy himself, for instance. And so Alyosha, untroubled by doubts, clothed his dreams too in the same form as all the rest. And a whole year of life in the monastery had formed the habit of this expectation in his heart. But it was justice, justice, he thirsted for, not simply miracles.

And now the man who should, he believed, have been exalted above everyone in the whole world, that man, instead of receiving the glory that was his due, was suddenly degraded and dishonored! What for? Who had judged him? Who could have decreed this? Those were the questions that wrung his inexperienced and virginal heart. He could not endure without mortification, without resentment even, that the holiest of holy men should have been exposed to the jeering and spiteful mockery of the frivolous crowd so inferior to him. Even had there been no miracles, had there been nothing marvelous to justify his hopes, why this indignity, why this humiliation, why this premature decay, "in excess of nature," as the spiteful monks said? Why this "sign from heaven," which they so triumphantly acclaimed in company with Father Ferapont, and why did they believe they had gained the right to acclaim it? Where is the finger of Providence? Why did Providence hide its face "at the most critical moment" (so Alyosha thought it), as though voluntarily submitting to the blind, dumb, pitiless laws of nature?

That was why Alyosha's heart was breaking, and, of course, as I have said already, the sting of it all was that the man he loved above everything on earth should be put to shame and humiliated! This murmuring may have been shallow and unreasonable in my hero, but I repeat again for the third time—and am prepared to admit that it, too, might be shallow—I am glad that my hero showed himself not too reasonable at that moment, for any man of sense will always come back to reason in time, but, if love does not gain the upper hand in a boy's heart at such an exceptional moment, when will it? I will not, however, omit to mention something strange, which came for a time to the surface of Alyosha's mind at this fatal and obscure moment. This new *something* was the harassing impression left by the conversation with his brother Ivan, which now persistently haunted Alyosha's mind. At this moment it haunted him. Oh, it was not that something of the fundamental, elemental, so to speak, faith of his soul had been shaken. He loved his God and believed in Him steadfastly, though he was suddenly murmuring against Him. Yet a vague but tormenting and evil impression left by his conversation with his brother Ivan the day before, suddenly revived again now in his soul and seemed forcing its way to the surface.

It had begun to get dusk when Rakitin, crossing the pine copse from the hermitage to the monastery, suddenly noticed Alyosha, lying face downwards on the ground under a tree, not moving and apparently asleep. He went up and called him by his name.

"You here, Alexey? Can you have . . ." he began wondering but broke off. He had meant to say, "Can you have *come to this?*" Alyosha did not look at him, but from a slight movement Rakitin at once saw that he heard and understood him.

"What's the matter?" he went on; but the surprise in his face gradually passed into a smile that became more and more ironical.

"Listen, I've been looking for you for the last two hours. You suddenly disappeared. What are you about? What foolery is this? You might just look at me . . ."

Alyosha raised his head, sat up and leaned his back against the tree. He was not crying, but there was a look of suffering and irritability in his face. He did not look at Rakitin, however, but looked away to one side of him.

"Do you know your face is quite changed? There's none of your famous mildness to be seen in it. Are you angry with someone? Have they been ill-treating you?"

"Let me alone," said Alyosha suddenly, with a weary gesture of his hand, still looking away from him.

"Oho! So that's how we are feeling! So you can shout at people like other mortals. That is a comedown from the angels. I say, Aloyshka, you have surprised me, do you hear? I mean it. It's long since I've been surprised at anything here. I always took you for an educated man . . ."

Alyosha at last looked at him, but vaguely, as though scarcely understanding what he said.

"Can you really be so upset simply because your old man has begun to stink? You don't mean to say you seriously believed that he was going to work miracles?" exclaimed Rakitin, genuinely surprised again.

"I believe, I believe, I want to believe, and I will believe, what more do you want?" cried Alyosha irritably.

"Nothing at all, my boy. Damn it all, why no schoolboy of thirteen believes in that now. But there . . . So now you are in a temper with your God, you are rebelling against Him; He didn't promote him. He hasn't bestowed the order of merit! Eh, what a bunch!"

Alyosha gazed a long while with his eyes half closed at Rakitin, and there was a sudden gleam in his eyes . . . but not of anger with Rakitin.

"I am not rebelling against my God; I simply 'don't accept His world.' " Alyosha suddenly smiled a forced smile.

"How do you mean, you don't accept the world?" Rakitin thought a moment over his answer. "What idiocy is this?"

Alyosha did not answer.

"Come, enough nonsense, now to business. Have you had anything to eat today?"

"I don't remember . . . I think I have."

"You ought to have something, to judge by your face. It makes one sorry to look at you. You didn't sleep all night either, I hear, you had a meeting in there. And then all this fuss and bother afterwards. Most likely you've had nothing to eat but a mouthful of holy bread. I've got some sausage in my pocket; I've brought it from the town in case of need, only you won't eat sausage. . . ."

"Give me some."

"Well! You really are going all out! Why, it's a regular mutiny, with barricades! Well, my boy, we must make the most of it. Come to my place . . . I wouldn't mind a drop of vodka myself, I am tired to death. Vodka is going too far for you, I suppose . . . or would you like some?"

"Give me some vodka too."

"Well, now! You surprise me, brother!" Rakitin looked at him in amazement. "Well, one way or another, vodka or sausage, this is a jolly fine chance and mustn't be missed. Come along."

Alyosha got up in silence and followed Rakitin.

"If your brother Vanechka could see this—wouldn't he be surprised! By the way, your brother Ivan Fyodorovich set off to Moscow this morning, did you know?"

"Yes," answered Alyosha listlessly, and suddenly the image of his brother Dmitri rose before his mind. But only for a minute, and though it reminded him of something that must not be put off for a moment, some duty, some terrible obligation, even that reminder made no impression on him, did not reach his heart and instantly faded out of his mind and was forgotten. But, a long while afterwards, Alyosha remembered this.

"Your brother Vanechka once declared that I was a 'liberal nonentity without any talent.' Once you, too, could not resist letting me know I was 'dishonorable.' Well! I would like to see what your talents and sense of honor will do for you now." This phrase Rakitin finished to himself in a whisper. "Ha, listen!" he said aloud, "let's go by the path beyond the monastery straight to the town. Hmm! I ought to go to Madame Khokhlakov's by the way. Just think, I've written to tell her everything that happened, and would you believe it, she answered me instantly in pencil (the lady has a passion for writing notes) that she would never have expected '*such conduct* from a man of such a reverend character as Father Zosima.' That was her very word: 'conduct.' She is angry too. Eh, you are a bunch! Wait!" he cried suddenly again. He suddenly stopped and taking Alyosha by the shoulder made him stop too.

"Do you know, Alyoshka," he peeped inquisitively in his eyes, absorbed in a sudden new thought which had dawned on him, and though he was laughing outwardly he was evidently afraid to utter that new idea aloud, so difficult he still found it to believe in the strange and unexpected mood in which he now saw Alyosha. "Alyoshka, do you know where we had better go?" he brought out at last timidly, and insinuatingly.

"I don't care . . . where you like."

"Let's go to Grushenka, eh? Will you come?" pronounced Rakitin at last, trembling with timid suspense.

"Let's go to Grushenka," Alyosha answered calmly, at once, and this prompt and calm agreement was such a surprise to Rakitin that he almost started back.

"Well! Really!" he cried in amazement, but seizing Alyosha firmly by the arm he led him along the path still dreading that he would change his mind. They walked along in silence, Rakitin was positively afraid to talk.

"And how glad she will be, how delighted," he muttered, but lapsed into silence again. And indeed it was not to please Grushenka he was taking Alyosha to see her. He was a practical person and never undertook anything without a prospect of gain for himself. His object in this case was twofold, first a revengeful desire to see "the downfall of the righteous," and Alyosha's fall "from the saints to the sinners," over which he was already gloating in his imagination, and in the second place he had in view a certain material gain for himself, of which more will be said later.

"So the moment has come," he thought to himself with spiteful glee, "and we shall catch it on the fly, for it's just what we want."

Chapter III

An Onion

Grushenka lived in the busiest part of town, near the cathedral square, in a small wooden lodge in the courtyard belonging to the house of the widow Morozov. The house was a large stone building of two stories, old and very ugly. The widow led a secluded life with her two nieces, who were also elderly spinsters. She had no need to let her lodge, but everyone knew that she had taken in Grushenka as a lodger, four years before, solely to please her kinsman, the merchant Samsonov, who was known to be the girl's protector. It was said that the jealous old man's object in placing his "favorite" with the widow Morozov was that the old woman should keep a sharp eye on her new lodger's conduct. But this sharp eye soon proved to be unnecessary, and in the end the widow Morozov seldom met Grushenka and did not worry her by looking after her in any way. It is true that four years had passed since the old man had brought the slim, delicate, shy, timid, dreamy, and sad girl of eighteen from the chief town of the province, and much had happened since then. Little was known of the girl's history in the town and that little was vague. Nothing more had been learned during the last four years, even after many persons had become interested in the "extraordinary beauty" into whom Agrafena Alexandrovna had meanwhile developed. There were rumors that she had been betrayed by someone at seventeen, some sort of officer, and immediately afterwards abandoned by him. The officer had gone away and afterwards married, while Grushenka had been left in poverty and disgrace. It was said, however, that though Grushenka had been raised from destitution by the old man, Samsonov, she came of a respectable family belonging to the clerical class, that she was the daughter of a deacon or something of the sort.

And now after four years the sensitive, injured and pathetic little orphan had become a plump, rosy beauty of the Russian type, a woman of bold and determined character, proud and insolent. She had a good head for business, was acquisitive, saving and careful, and by fair means or foul had succeeded, it was said, in amassing a little fortune. There was only one point on which all were agreed. Grushenka was not easily to be approached and except her aged protector there had not been one man who could boast of her favors during those four years. It was a positive fact, for there had been a good many, especially during the last two years, who had attempted to obtain those favors. But all their efforts had been in vain and some of these suitors had been forced to beat an undignified and even comic retreat, owing to the firm and ironical resistance they met from the strong-willed young person. It was known too that the young person had, especially of late, been given to what is called "speculation," and that she had shown marked abilities in that direction, so that many people began to say that she was no better than a Jew. It was not that she lent money on interest, but it was known, for instance, that she had for some time past, in partnership with old Karamazov, actually invested in the purchase of bad debts for a trifle, a tenth of their nominal value, and afterwards had made out of them ten times their value.

The ailing old widower Samsonov, a man of large fortune, was stingy and merciless. He tyrannized over his grown-up sons, but, for the last year during which he had lost the use of his swollen legs, he had fallen greatly under the influence of his protégée, whom he had at first kept strictly and in humble surroundings "on Lenten fare" as the wits said at the time. But Grushenka had succeeded in emanicipating herself, while she established in him a boundless belief in her fidelity. The old man, now long since dead, had had a large business in his day and was also a noteworthy character, miserly and hard as flint. Though Grushenka's hold upon him was so strong that he could not live without her (it had been so especially for the last two years), he did not settle any considerable fortune on her and would not have been moved to do so, if she had threatened to leave him. But he had presented her with a small sum, and even that was a surprise to everyone when it became known. "You are a wench with brains," he said to her, when he gave her eight thousand rubles, "and you must look after yourself, but let me tell you that except your yearly allowance as before, you'll get nothing more from me to the day of my death, and I'll leave you nothing in my will either." And he kept his word; he died and left everything to his sons, whom, with their wives and children, he had treated all his life as servants. Grushenka was not even mentioned in his will. All this became known afterwards. He helped Grushenka with his advice to increase her capital and put business in her way.

When Fyodor Pavlovich, who first came into contact with Grushenka over a piece of speculation, ended to his own surprise by falling madly in love with her, old Samsonov, gravely ill as he was, was immensely amused. It is remarkable that throughout their whole acquaintance Grushenka was absolutely and spontaneously open with the old man, and he seems to have been the only person in the world with whom she was so. Of late, when Dmitri Fyodorovich too had come on the scene with his love, the old man stopped laughing. On the contrary, he once gave Grushenka a stern and earnest piece of advice.

"If you have to choose between the two, father or son, you'd better choose the old man, if only you make sure the old scoundrel will marry you and settle some fortune on you beforehand. But don't keep on with the captain, you'll get no good out of that." These were the very words of the old profligate, who felt already that his death was not far off and who actually died five months later.

I will note, too, in passing, that although many in our town knew of the grotesque and monstrous rivalry of the Karamazovs, father and son, the object of which was Grushenka, scarcely anyone understood what really underlay her attitude to both of them. Even Grushenka's two servants (after the catastrophe of which we will speak later) testified in court that she received Dmitri Fyodorovich simply from fear because "he threatened to murder her." These servants were an old cook, ailing and almost deaf, who came from Grushenka's old home, and her granddaughter, a smart young girl of twenty, who performed the duties of a maid. Grushenka lived very economically and her surroundings were anything but luxurious. Her lodge consisted of three rooms furnished with old ma-

hogany furniture in the fashion of 1820, belonging to her landlady.
It was quite dark when Rakitin and Alyosha entered her rooms,
yet they were not lighted up. Grushenka was lying down in her
drawing room on the big, hard, clumsy sofa, with a mahogany
back. The sofa was covered with shabby and ragged leather. Under
her head she had two white down pillows taken from her bed. She
was lying stretched out motionless on her back with her hands
behind her head. She was dressed as though expecting someone, in
a black silk dress, with a dainty lace fichu on her head, which was
very becoming. Over her shoulders was thrown a lace shawl pinned
with a massive gold brooch. She certainly was expecting someone.
She lay as though impatient and weary, her face rather pale and her
lips and eyes hot, restlessly tapping the arm of the sofa with the tip
of her right foot. The appearance of Rakitin and Alyosha caused a
slight excitement. From the hall they could hear Grushenka leap up
from the sofa and cry out in a frightened voice, "Who's there?" But
the maid met the visitors and at once called back to her mistress.

"It's not him, ma'am, it's nothing, only other visitors."

"What can be the matter?" muttered Rakitin leading Alyosha
into the drawing room. Grushenka was standing by the sofa as
though still alarmed. A thick coil of her dark brown hair escaped
from its lace covering and fell on her right shoulder, but she did
not notice it and did not put it back till she had gazed at her visitors
and recognized them.

"Ah, it's you, Rakitka? You quite frightened me. Whom have
you brought? Who is this with you? Good heavens, you have
brought him!" she exclaimed, recognizing Alyosha.

"Do send for candles!" said Rakitin, with the free-and-easy air of
a most intimate friend, who is privileged to give orders in the
house.

"Candles . . . of course, candles . . . Fenya, fetch him a candle . . .
Well, you have chosen a moment to bring him!" she exclaimed
again, nodding towards Alyosha, and turning to the mirror she
began quickly fastening up her hair with both hands. She seemed
displeased.

"Haven't I managed to please you?" asked Rakitin, instantly
almost offended.

"You frightened me, Rakitka, that's what it is." Grushenka
turned with a smile to Alyosha. "Don't be afraid of me, my dear
Alyosha, you can't think how glad I am to see you, my unexpected
visitor. But you frightened me, Rakitka, I thought it was Mitya
breaking in. You see, I deceived him just now, I made him promise
to believe me and I told him a lie. I told him that I was going to
spend the evening with my old man, Kuzma Kuzmich, and should
be there till late counting up his money. I always spend one whole
evening a week with him making up his accounts. We lock our-

selves in and he counts on the reckoning beads while I sit and put things down in the book. I am the only person he trusts. Mitya believes that I am there, but I came back and have been sitting locked in here, expecting some news. How was it Fenya let you in? Fenya, Fenya, run out to the gate, open it and look about whether the captain is to be seen! Perhaps he is hiding and spying, I am dreadfully frightened."

"There's no one there, Agrafena Alexandrovna, I've just looked out, I keep running to peep through the crack, I am in fear and trembling myself."

"Are the shutters fastened, Fenya? And we must draw the curtains—that's better!" She drew the heavy curtains herself. "He'd rush in at once if he saw a light. I am afraid of your brother Mitya today, Alyosha." Grushenka spoke loudly and, though she was alarmed, she seemed almost in some sort of frenzy.

"Why are you so afraid of Mitenka today?" inquired Rakitin. "I would have thought you were not timid with him, you'd twist him round your little finger."

"I tell you, I am expecting news, priceless news, so I don't want Mitenka at all. And he didn't believe, I feel he didn't, that I would stay at Kuzma Kuzmich's. He must be in his ambush now, behind Fyodor Pavlovich's, in the garden, watching for me. And if he's there, he won't come here, so much the better! But I really have been to Kuzma Kuzmich's, Mitya escorted me there. I told him I should stay there till midnight, and I asked him to be sure to come at midnight to fetch me home. He went away and I sat ten minutes with Kuzma Kuzmich and came back here again. Ugh, I was afraid, I ran for fear of meeting him."

"And why are you so dressed up? What a curious cap you've got on!"

"How curious you are yourself, Rakitin! I tell you, I am expecting a message. If the message comes, I shall fly, I shall gallop away and you will see no more of me. That's why I am dressed up, so as to be ready."

"And where are you flying to?"

"If you know too much, you'll get old too soon."

"Upon my word! You are highly delighted . . . I've never seen you like this before. You are dressed up as if you were going to a ball." Rakitin looked her up and down.

"Much you know about balls."

"And do you know much about them?"

"I have seen a ball. The year before last, Kuzma Kuzmich's son was married and I looked on from the gallery. Do you suppose I want to be talking to you, Rakitka, while a prince like this is standing here. Such a visitor! Alyosha, my dear boy, I gaze at you and can't believe my eyes. Good heavens, can you have come here to see me! To tell you the truth I never had a thought of seeing you and I didn't think that you would ever come and see me. Though this is not the moment now, I am awfully glad to see you. Sit down on the sofa, here, that's right, my bright young moon. I really can't take it in even now. . . . Eh, Rakitka, if only you had brought him yesterday or the day before! But I am glad as it is! Perhaps it's better he has come now, at such a moment, and not the day before yesterday."

She gaily sat down beside Alyosha on the sofa, looking at him with positive delight. And she really was glad, she was not lying when she said so. Her eyes glowed, her lips laughed, but it was a good-natured merry laugh. Alyosha had not expected to see such a kind expression on her face. . . . He had hardly met her till the day before, he had formed an alarming idea of her, and had been horribly struck the day before by the spiteful and treacherous trick she had played on Katerina Ivanovna. He was greatly surprised to find her now altogether different from what he had expected. And, crushed as he was by his own sorrow, his eyes involuntarily rested on her with attention. Her whole manner seemed changed for the better since yesterday, there was scarcely any trace of that mawkish sweetness in her speech, of that voluptuous softness in her movements. Everything was simple and good-natured, her gestures were rapid, direct, confiding, but she was greatly excited.

"Dear me, how everything comes together today," she chattered on again. "And why I am so glad to see you, Alyosha, I couldn't say myself! If you ask me, I couldn't tell you."

"Come, don't you know why you're glad?" said Rakitin, grinning. "You always used to pester me to bring him, you'd some object, I suppose."

"I had a different object once, but now that's over, this is not the moment. I want you to have something nice, that's what! I am so good-natured now. You sit down, too, Rakitka, why are you standing? You've sat down already? There's no fear of Rakitushka's forgetting to look after himself. Look, Alyosha, he's sitting there opposite us, so offended that I didn't ask him to sit down before you. Ugh, Rakitka is such a one to take offense!" laughed Grushenka. "Don't be angry, Rakitka, I'm kind today. Why are you so depressed, Alyoshechka, are you afraid of me?" she peeped into his eyes with merry mockery.

"He's sad. The promotion has not been given," boomed Rakitin.

"What promotion?"

"His elder stinks."

"What do you mean, 'stinks'? You are talking some nonsense, you want to say something nasty. Be quiet, stupid! Let me sit on your knee, Alyosha, like this." She suddenly skipped forward and jumped, laughing, on his knee, like a nestling kitten, with her right arm about his neck. "I'll cheer you up, my pious boy. Yes, really, will you let me sit on your knee, you won't be angry? If you tell me, I'll get off."

Alyosha did not speak. He sat afraid to move, he heard her words, "If you tell me, I'll get off," but he did not answer, he seemed numb. But there was nothing in his heart such as Rakitin, for instance, watching him malignantly from his corner, might have expected or fancied. The great grief in his heart swallowed up every sensation that might have been aroused, and, if only he could have thought clearly at that moment, he would have realised that he had now the strongest armor to protect him from every lust and temptation. Yet in spite of the vague irresponsiveness of his spiritual condition and the sorrow that overwhelmed him, he could not help wondering at a new and strange sensation in his heart. This woman, this "dreadful" woman, had no terror for him now, none of that terror that had stirred in his soul at any passing thought of woman, if such thoughts occurred to him at all. On the contrary, this woman, dreaded above all women, sitting now on his knee, holding him in her arms, aroused in him now a quite different, unexpected, peculiar feeling, a feeling of the intensest and purest interest without a trace of fear, of his former terror. That was what instinctively surprised him.

"You've talked nonsense enough," cried Rakitin, "you'd much better give us some champagne. You owe it me, you know you do!"

"Yes, I really do. Do you know, Alyosha, I promised him champagne on the top of everything, if he'd bring you? I'll have some too! Fenya, Fenya, bring us the bottle Mitya left! Look sharp! Though I am so stingy, I'll stand a bottle, not for you, Rakitka, you're a toadstool, but he is a prince! And though my heart is full of something very different, so be it, I'll drink with you. I long for some dissipation."

"But what is the matter with you? And what is this message may I ask, or is it a secret?" Rakitin put in inquisitively, doing his best to pretend not to notice the snubs that were being continually aimed at him.

"Ech, it's not a secret, and you know it, too," Grushenka said, in a voice suddenly anxious, turning her head towards Rakitin, and drawing a little away from Alyosha, though she still sat on his knee with her arm round his neck. "My officer is coming, Rakitin, my officer is coming."

"I heard he was coming, but is he so near?"

"He is at Mokroe now, he'll send a messenger from there, so he wrote, I got a letter from him today. I am expecting the messenger every minute."

"You don't say so! Why at Mokroe?"

"That's a long story, I've told you enough."

"That Mitenka will really be up to something now—you bet! Does he know or doesn't he?"

"He know! Of course he doesn't. If he knew, there would be murder. But I am not afraid of that now, I am not afraid of his knife. Be quiet, Rakitka, don't remind me of Dmitri Fyodorovich, he has bruised my heart. And I don't want to think of that at this moment. I can think of Alyoshechka here, I can look at Alyoshechka . . . smile at me dear, cheer up, smile at my foolishness, at my pleasure. . . . Ah, he's smiling, he's smiling! How kindly he looks at me! And you know, Alyosha, I've been thinking all this time you were angry with me, because of the day before yesterday, because of that young lady. I was a cur, that's what. . . . But it's a good thing it happened so. It was a horrid thing, but a good thing too." Grushenka smiled dreamily and a little cruel line showed in her smile. "Mitya told me that she screamed out that I 'ought to be flogged.' I did insult her dreadfully. She sent for me, she wanted to make a conquest of me, to win me over with her chocolate. . . . No, it's a good thing it did end like that." She smiled again. "But I am still afraid of your being angry."

"Yes, that's really true," Rakitin put in suddenly with genuine surprise. "Alyosha, she is really afraid of a chicken like you."

"He is a chicken to you, Rakitka, that's what . . . because you've no conscience, that's what! You see, I love him with all my soul, that's what! Alyosha, do you believe I love you with all my soul?"

"Ah, you shameless woman! She is making you a declaration, Alexey!"

"Well, what of it, I love him!"

"And what about your officer? And the priceless message from Mokroe?"

"That is quite different."

"That's a woman's way of looking at it!"

"Don't you make me angry, Rakitka." Grushenka caught him up hotly. "This is quite different. I love Alyosha in a different way. It's true, Alyosha, I had sly designs on you before. For I am a horrid, violent creature. But at other times I've looked upon you, Alyosha, as my conscience. I've kept thinking 'how anyone like that must despise a nasty thing like me.' I thought that the day before yesterday, as I ran home from the young lady's. I have thought of you a long time in that way, Alyosha, and Mitya knows, I've talked to him about it. Mitya understands. Would you believe it, I sometimes look at you and feel ashamed, utterly ashamed of myself. . . . And how, and since when, I began to think about you like that, I can't say, I don't remember . . ."

Fenya came in and put a tray with an uncorked bottle and three glasses of champagne on the table.

"Here's the champagne!" cried Rakitin. "You're excited, Agrafena Alexandrovna, and not yourself. When you've had a glass of champagne, you'll be ready to dance. Eh, they can't even do that properly," he added, looking at the bottle. "The old woman's poured it out in the kitchen and the bottle's been brought in warm and without a cork. Well, let me have some, anyway."

He went up to the table, took a glass, emptied it at one gulp and poured himself out another.

"One doesn't often stumble upon champagne," he said, licking his lips. "Now, Alyosha, take a glass, show what you can do! What shall we drink to? The gates of paradise? Take a glass, Grushka, you drink to the gates of paradise, too."

"What gates of paradise?"

She took a glass, Alyosha took his, tasted it and put it back.

"No, I'd better not," he smiled gently.

"And you bragged!" cried Rakitin.

"Well, if so, I won't either," chimed in Grushenka, "I really don't want any. You can drink the whole bottle alone, Rakitka. If Alyosha has some, I will."

"What touching sentimentality!" said Rakitin tauntingly, "and she's sitting on his knee, too! He's got something to grieve over, but what's the matter with you? He is rebelling against his God and ready to eat sausage . . ."

"How so?"

"His elder died today, Father Zosima, the saint."

"So Father Zosima is dead," cried Grushenka. "Good God, I did not know!" She crossed herself devoutly. "Goodness, what have I been doing, sitting on his knee like this at such a moment!" She started up as though in dismay, instantly slipped off his knee and sat down on the sofa. Alyosha fixed a long wondering look upon her and a light seemed to dawn in his face.

"Rakitin," he said suddenly, in a firm and loud voice; "don't taunt me with having rebelled against God. I don't want to feel angry with you, so you must be kinder, too. I've lost a treasure such as you have never had, and you cannot judge me now. You had much better look at her—do you see how she has pity on me? I came here to find a wicked soul—I felt drawn to evil because I was base and evil myself, and I've found a true sister, I have found a treasure—a loving heart. She had pity on me just now. . . . Agrafena Alexandrovna, I am speaking of you. You've raised my soul from the depths."

Alyosha's lips were quivering and he caught his breath.

"She has saved you, it seems," laughed Rakitin spitefully. "And she meant to get you in her clutches, do you realize that?"

"Wait, Rakitka." Grushenka jumped up. "Hush, both of you.

Now I'll tell you all about it. Hush, Alyosha, your words make me ashamed, for I am bad and not good—that's what I am. And you hush, Rakitka, because you are telling lies. I had the low idea of trying to get him in my clutches, but now you are lying, now it's all different. And don't let me hear anything more from you, Rakitka." All this Grushenka said with extreme emotion.

"They are both crazy," said Rakitin, looking at them with amazement. "I feel as though I were in a madhouse. They're both getting so feeble they'll begin crying in a minute."

"I shall begin to cry, I shall," repeated Grushenka. "He called me his sister and I shall never forget that. Only let me tell you, Rakitka, though I am bad, I did give away an onion."

"An onion? Oh, hell, you really are crazy."

Rakitin wondered at their exaltation. He was aggrieved and annoyed, though he might have reflected that each of them was just passing through a spiritual crisis such as does not come often in a lifetime. But though Rakitin was very sensitive about everything that concerned himself, he was very obtuse as regards the feelings and sensations of others—partly from his youth and inexperience, partly from his intense egoism.

"You see, Alyoshechka," Grushenka turned to him with a nervous laugh. "I was boasting when I told Rakitin I had given away an onion, but it's not to boast I tell you about it. It's only a story, but it's a nice story. I used to hear it when I was a child from Matryona, my cook, who is still with me. It's like this. Once upon a time there was a peasant woman and a very wicked woman she was. And she died and did not leave a single good deed behind. The devils caught her and plunged her into the lake of fire. So her guardian angel stood and wondered what good deed of hers he could remember to tell to God; 'she once pulled up an onion in her garden,' said he, 'and gave it to a beggar woman.' And God answered: 'You take that onion then, hold it out to her in the lake, and let her take hold and be pulled out. And if you can pull her out of the lake, let her come to Paradise, but if the onion breaks, then the woman must stay where she is.' The angel ran to the woman and held out the onion to her; 'Come,' said he, 'catch hold and I'll pull you out.' And he began cautiously pulling her out. He had just pulled her right out, when the other sinners in the lake, seeing she was being drawn out, began catching hold of her so as to be pulled out with her. But she was a very wicked woman and she began kicking them. 'I'm to be pulled out, not you. It's my onion, not yours.' As soon as she said that, the onion broke. And the woman fell into the lake and she is burning there to this day. So the angel wept and went away. So that's the story, Alyosha; I know it, by heart, for I am that wicked woman myself. I boasted to Rakitka that I had given away an onion, but to you I'll say: 'I've done nothing but give away *one* onion all my life, that's the only good deed I've done.' So don't praise me, Alyosha, don't think me good, I am bad, I'm a wicked woman and you make me ashamed if you praise me. Eh, I must confess everything. Listen, Alyosha. I was so anxious to get hold of you that I promised Rakitin twenty-five rubles if he would bring you to me. Stop, Rakitin, wait!" She went with rapid steps to the table, opened a drawer, pulled out a purse and took from it a twenty-five ruble bill.

"What nonsense! What nonsense!" cried Rakitin, disconcerted.

"Take it. Rakitka, I owe it you, there's no fear of your refusing it, you asked for it yourself." And she threw the bill to him.

"As if I'd refuse it," boomed Rakitin, obviously abashed, but carrying off his confusion with a swagger. "That will come in very handy; fools are made for wise men's profit."

"And now hold your tongue, Rakitka, what I am going to say now is not for your ears. Sit down in that corner and keep quiet. You don't like us, so hold your tongue."

"What should I like you for?" Rakitin snarled, not concealing his ill-humor. He put the twenty-five ruble bill in his pocket and he felt ashamed at Alyosha's seeing it. He had reckoned on receiving his payment later, without Alyosha's knowing of it, and now, feeling ashamed, he lost his temper. Till that moment he had thought it discreet not to contradict Grushenka too flatly in spite of her snubbing, since he had something to get out of her. But now he, too, was angry:

"One loves people for some reason, but what have either of you done for me?"

"You should love people without a reason, as Alyosha does."

"How does he love you? How has he shown it, that you make such a fuss about it?"

Grushenka was standing in the middle of the room; she spoke with heat and there were hysterical notes in her voice.

"Hush, Rakitka, you know nothing about us! And don't dare to speak to me like that again. How dare you be so familiar? Sit in that corner and be quiet, as though you were my lackey! And now, Alyosha, I'll tell you the whole truth, that you may see what a wretch I am! I am not talking to Rakitka, but to you. I wanted to ruin you, Alyosha, that's the holy truth; I quite meant to. I wanted to so much, that I bribed Rakitka to bring you. And why did I want to do such a thing? You knew nothing about it, Alyosha, you turned away from me, if you passed me, you dropped your eyes. And I've looked at you a hundred times before today, I began asking everyone about you. Your face haunted my heart. 'He despises me,' I thought, 'he won't even look at me.' And I felt it so much at last that I wondered at myself for being so frightened of a boy. I'll get him in my clutches and laugh at him. I was full of spite and anger. Would you believe it, nobody here dares talk or think of coming to Agrafena Alexandrovna with any evil purpose. Old Kuzma is the only man I have anything to do with here, I was bound and sold to him, Satan brought us together, but there has been no one else. But looking at you, I thought, I'll get him in my clutches and laugh at him. You see what a spiteful cur I am, and you called me your sister! And now that man who wronged me has come; I sit here waiting for a message from him. And do you know what that man has been to me? Five years ago, when Kuzma brought me here, I used to shut myself up, that no one might have sight or sound of me. I was a silly slip of a girl; I used to sit here sobbing, I used to lie awake all night, thinking: 'Where is he now, the man who wronged me? He is laughing at me with another woman, most likely. If only I could see him, if I could meet him again, I'd pay him back, I'd pay him back!' At night I used to lie sobbing into my pillow in the dark, and I used to brood over it, I used to tear my heart on purpose and gloat over my anger. 'I'll pay him back, I'll pay him back!' That's what I used to cry out in the dark. And when I suddenly thought that I could really do nothing to him, and that he was laughing at me then, or perhaps had utterly forgotten me, I would fling myself on the floor, melt into helpless tears, and lie there shaking till dawn. In the morning I would get up more spiteful than a dog, ready to tear the whole world to pieces. And then what do you think? I began saving money, I became hard-hearted, grew stout—grew wiser, would you say? No, no one in the whole world sees it, no one knows it, but when the night darkness comes on, I sometimes lie as I did five years ago, when I was a silly girl, clenching my teeth and crying all night, thinking: 'I'll pay him back, I'll pay him back!' Do you hear? Well then, now you understand me. A month ago a letter came to me—he was coming, he was a widower, he wanted to see me. It took my breath away, then I suddenly thought: 'If he comes and whistles to call me, I shall creep back to him like a beaten dog.' I couldn't believe myself. Am I so abject? Shall I run to him or not? And I've been in such a rage with myself all this month that I am worse than I was five years ago. Do you see now, Alyosha, what a violent, vindictive creature I am? I have shown you the whole truth! I played with Mitya to keep me from running to that other. Hush, Rakitka, it's not for you to judge me, I am not speaking to you. Before you came in, I was lying here waiting, brooding, deciding my whole future life, and you can never know what was in my heart. Yes, Alyosha, tell your young lady not to be angry with me for what happened the day before yesterday. . . . Nobody in the whole world knows what I am going through now, and no one ever can know. . . . For perhaps I shall take a knife with me today. I can't make up my mind . . ."

And at this "tragic" phrase Grushenka broke down, hid her face in her hands, flung herself on the sofa pillows, and sobbed like a little child. Alyosha got up and went to Rakitin.

"Misha," he said, "don't be angry. She wounded you, but don't be angry. You heard what she said just now? You mustn't ask too much of a human soul, one must be merciful."

Alyosha said this at the instinctive prompting of his heart. He felt obliged to speak and he turned to Rakitin. If Rakitin had not been there, he would have spoken to the air. But Rakitin looked at him ironically and Alyosha stopped short.

"You were so primed up with your elder's teaching last night that now you have to let it off on me, Alyoshechka, man of God!" said Rakitin, with a smile of hatred.

"Don't laugh, Rakitin, don't smile, don't talk of the dead—he was better than anyone in the world!" cried Alyosha, with tears in his voice. "I didn't speak to you as a judge but as the lowest of the judged. What am I beside her? I came here seeking my ruin, and said to myself, 'What does it matter?' in my cowardliness, but she after five years in torment, as soon as anyone says a word from the heart to her—it makes her forget everything, forgive everything, in her tears! The man who has wronged her has come back, he sends for her and she forgives him everything, and hastens joyfully to meet him and she won't take a knife with her. She won't! No, I am not like that. I don't know whether you are, Misha, but I am not like that. It's a lesson to me . . . She is more loving than we. . . . Have you heard her speak before of what she has just told us? No, you haven't; if you had, you'd have understood her long ago . . . and the person insulted the day before yesterday must forgive her, too! She will, when she knows . . . and she shall know. . . . This soul is not yet at peace with itself, one must be tender with it . . . there may be a treasure in that soul . . ."

Alyosha stopped, because he was out of breath. In spite of his ill-humor, Rakitin looked at him with astonishment. He had never expected such a tirade from the gentle Alyosha.

"She's found someone to plead her cause! Why, are you in love with her? Agrafena Alexandrovna, our monk's really in love with you, you've made a conquest!" he cried, with a coarse laugh.

Grushenka lifted her head from the pillow and looked at Alyosha with a tender smile shining on her face, which seemed somehow puffed up from her recent tears.

"Let him alone, Alyosha, my cherub, you see what he is, he is not a person for you to speak to. Mikhail Ospovich," she turned to Rakitin, "I meant to beg your pardon for being rude to you, but now I don't want to. Alyosha, come to me, sit down here." She beckoned to him with a happy smile. "That's right, sit here. Tell me," she took him by the hand and looked into his face, smiling, "tell me, do I love that man or not? the man who wronged me, do I love him or not? Before you came, I lay here in the dark, asking my heart whether I loved him. Decide for me, Alyosha, the time has come, it shall be as you say. Am I to forgive him or not?"

"But you have forgiven him already," said Alyosha, smiling.

"Yes, I really have forgiven him," Grushenka murmured thoughtfully. "What an abject heart! To my abject heart!" She snatched up a glass from the table, emptied it at a gulp, lifted it in the air and flung it on the floor. The glass broke with a crash. A little cruel line came into her smile.

"Perhaps I haven't forgiven him, though," she said, with a sort of menace in her voice, and she dropped her eyes to the ground as though she were talking to herself. "Perhaps my heart is only getting ready to forgive, I shall struggle with my heart. You see, Alyosha, I've grown to love my tears in these five years. . . . Perhaps I only love my resentment, not him . . ."

"Well, I wouldn't care to be in his shoes," hissed Rakitin.

"Well, you won't be, Rakitka, you'll never be in his shoes. You will shine my shoes, Rakitka, that's the place you are fit for. You'll never get a woman like me . . . and he won't either, perhaps . . ."

"Won't he? Then why are you dressed up like that?" said Rakitin, with a venomous sneer.

"Don't taunt me with dressing up, Rakitka, you don't know all that is in my heart! If I choose to tear off my finery, I'll tear it off at once, this minute," she cried in a resonant voice. "You don't know what that finery is for, Rakitka! Perhaps I shall see him and say: 'Have you ever seen me look like this before?' He left me a thin, consumptive crybaby of seventeen. I'll sit by him, fascinate him and work him up. 'Do you see what I am like now?' I'll say to him; 'well, and that's enough for you, my dear sir, there's many a slip twixt the cup and the lip!' That may be what the finery is for, Rakitka." Grushenka finished with a malicious laugh. "I'm violent and resentful, Alyosha, I'll tear off my finery, I'll destroy my beauty, I'll scorch my face, slash it with a knife, and turn beggar. If I choose, I won't go anywhere now to see anyone. If I choose, I'll send Kuzma back all he has ever given me, tomorrow, and all his money and I'll go out slaving as a charwoman for the rest of my life. You think I wouldn't do it, Rakitka, that I would not dare to do it? I would, I would, I could do it directly, only don't exasperate me . . . and I'll send him about his business. I'll snap my fingers in his face, he shall never see me again!"

She uttered the last words in an hysterical scream, but broke down again, hid her face in her hands, buried it in the pillow and shook with sobs. Rakitin got up.

"It's time we were off," he said "it's late, we shall be shut out of the monastery."

Grushenka leapt up from her place.

"Surely you don't want to go, Alyosha!" she cried, in mournful surprise. "What are you doing to me? You've stirred up my feeling, tortured me, and now you'll leave me to face this night alone!"

"He can hardly spend the night with you! Though if he wants to, let him! I'll go alone," Rakitin scoffed jeeringly.

"Hush, evil tongue!" Grushenka cried angrily at him; "you never said such words to me as he has come to say."

"What has he said to you so special?" asked Rakitin irritably.

"I can't say, I don't know. I don't know what he said to me, it went straight to my heart; he has wrung my heart. . . . He is the first, the only one who has pitied me, that's what it is. Why did you not come before, you cherub?" She fell on her knees before him as though in a sudden frenzy. "I've been waiting all my life for someone like you, I knew that someone like you would come and forgive me. I believed that nasty as I am, someone would really love me, not only with a shameful love!"

"What have I done to you?" answered Alyosha bending over her with a tender smile, and gently taking her by the hands; "I only gave you an onion, nothing but a tiny little onion, that's all, that's all!"

He started to cry himself as he said it. At that moment there was a sudden noise in the passage, someone came into the hall. Grushenka jumped up seeming greatly alarmed. Fenya ran noisily into the room, crying out:

"Mistress, mistress darling, a messenger has galloped up," she cried, breathless and joyful. "A carriage from Mokroe for you, Timothy the driver, with three horses, they are just putting in fresh horses. . . . A letter, here's the letter, mistress."

A letter was in her hand and she waved it in the air all the while she talked. Grushenka snatched the letter from her and carried it to the candle. It was only a note, a few lines. She read it in one instant.

"He has sent for me," she cried, her face white and distorted, with a wan smile; "he whistles! Crawl back, little dog!"

But only for one instant she stood as though hesitating; suddenly the blood rushed to her head and sent a glow to her cheeks.

"I will go," she cried; "five years of my life! Good-bye! Good-bye, Alyosha, my fate is sealed. Go, go, leave me all of you, don't let me see you again! Grushenka is flying to a new life. . . . Don't you remember evil against me either, Rakitka. I may be going to my death! Ugh! I feel as though I were drunk!"

She suddenly left them and ran into her bedroom.

"Well, she has no thoughts for us now!" grumbled Rakitin. "Let's go, or we may hear that feminine shriek again. I am sick of all these tears and cries."

Alyosha mechanically let himself be led out. In the yard stood a covered cart. Horses were being taken out of the shafts, men were running to and fro with a lantern. Three fresh horses were being led in at the open gate. But when Alyosha and Rakitin reached the bottom of the steps, Grushenka's bedroom window was suddenly opened and she called in a ringing voice after Alyosha:

"Alyoshechka, give my greetings to your brother Mitenka and tell him not to remember evil against me, though I have brought him misery. And tell him too in my words: 'Grushenka has fallen to a scoundrel, and not to you, noble heart.' And add, too, that Grushenka loved him only one hour, only one short hour she loved him—so let him remember that hour all his life—say, 'Grushenka tells you to!' "

She ended in a voice full of sobs. The window was shut with a slam.

"Hmm, hmm!" growled Rakitin, laughing, "she ruins your brother Mitya and then tells him to remember it all his life! What ferocity!"

Alyosha made no reply, he seemed not to have heard. He walked fast beside Rakitin as though in a terrible hurry. He was lost in thought and moved mechanically. Rakitin felt a sudden twinge as though he had been touched on an open wound. He had expected something quite different by bringing Grushenka and Alyosha together. Something very different from what he had hoped for had happened.

"He is a Pole, that officer of hers," he began again, restraining himself; "and indeed he is not an officer at all now. He served in the customs in Siberia, somewhere on the Chinese frontier, some puny little beggar of a Pole, I expect. Lost his job, they say. He's heard now that Grushenka's saved a little money, so he's turned up again—that's the explanation of the mystery."

Again Alyosha seemed not to hear. Rakitin could not control himself.

"Well, so you've saved the sinner?" he laughed spitefully. "Have you turned the Magdalene onto the true path? Driven out the seven devils, eh? So you see the miracles you were looking out for just now have come to pass!"

"Stop, Rakitin," Alyosha answered, with an aching heart.

"So you despise me now for those twenty-five rubles? I've sold my friend, you think. But you are not Christ, you know, and I am not Judas."

"Oh, Rakitin, I assure you I'd forgotten about it," cried Alyosha, "you remind me of it yourself . . ."

But this was the last straw for Rakitin.

"Damnation take you all and each of you!" he cried suddenly, "why the devil did I take you up? I don't want to know you from this time forward. Go alone, there's your road!"

And he turned abruptly into another street, leaving Alyosha alone in the dark. Alyosha came out of the town and walked across the fields to the monastery.

Chapter IV

Cana of Galilee

It was very late, by monastery rules, when Alyosha returned to the hermitage; the doorkeeper let him in by a special entrance. It had struck nine o'clock—the hour of rest and repose after a day of such agitation for all. Alyosha timidly opened the door and went into the elder's cell where his coffin was now standing. There was no one in the cell but Father Païssy, reading the Gospel in solitude over the coffin, and the young novice Porfiry, who, exhausted by the previous night's conversation and the disturbing incidents of the day, was sleeping the deep sound sleep of youth on the floor of the other room. Though Father Païssy heard Alyosha come in, he did not even look in his direction. Alyosha turned to the right from the door to the corner, fell on his knees and began to pray.

His soul was overflowing but with mingled feelings; no single sensation stood out distinctly, on the contrary, one drove out another in a slow, continual rotation. But there was a sweetness in his heart and, strange to say, Alyosha was not surprised at it. Again he saw that coffin before him, the hidden dead figure so precious to him, but the weeping and poignant grief of the morning was no longer aching in his soul. As soon as he came in, he fell down before the coffin as before a holy shrine, but joy, joy was glowing in his mind and in his heart. The one window of the cell was open, the air was fresh and cool. "So the odor must have become stronger, if they opened the window," thought Alyosha. But even this thought of the odor of corruption, which had seemed to him so awful and humiliating a few hours before, no longer made him feel miserable or indignant. He began quietly praying, but he soon felt that he was praying almost mechanically. Fragments of thought floated through his soul, flashed like stars and went out again at once, to be succeeded by others. But yet there was reigning in his soul a sense of the wholeness of things—something steadfast and comforting—and he was aware of it himself. Sometimes he began praying ardently, he longed to pour out his thankfulness and love. . . . But when he had begun to pray, he passed suddenly to something else, and sank into thought, forgetting both the prayer and what had interrupted it. He began listening to what Father Païssy was reading, but worn out with exhaustion he gradually began to doze.

"And the third day there was a marriage in Cana of Galilee," read Father Païssy. "And the mother of Jesus was there; And both Jesus was called, and his disciples, to the marriage."

"Marriage? What's that. . . . A marriage!" floated whirling through Alyosha's mind. "There is happiness for her, too. . . . She has gone to the feast. . . . No, she has not taken the knife. . . . That was only a "tragic" phrase. . . . Well . . . tragic phrases should be forgiven, they must be. Tragic phrases comfort the heart. . . . Without them, sorrow would be too heavy for men to bear. Rakitin has gone off to the back alley. As long as Rakitin broods over his wrongs, he will always go off to the back alley. . . . But the high road. . . . The road is wide and straight and bright as crystal, and the sun is at the end of it. . . . Ah! . . . What's being read?" . . .

"And when they wanted wine, the mother of Jesus saith unto him; 'They have no wine' " . . . Alyosha heard.

"Ah, yes, I was missing that, and I didn't want to miss it, I love that passage; it's Cana of Galilee, the first miracle. . . . Ah, that miracle! Ah, that sweet miracle! It was not men's grief, but their joy Christ visited, He worked His first miracle to help men's gladness . . . 'He who loves men loves their gladness, too.' . . . *He* was always repeating that, it was one of his leading ideas. . . . 'There's no living without joy,' Mitya says. . . . Yes, Mitya. . . . 'Everything that is true and good is always full of forgiveness,' he used to say that, too" . . .

"Jesus saith unto her, Woman, what has it to do with thee or me? Mine hour is not yet come.

"His mother saith unto the servants: Whatsoever he saith unto you, do it" . . .

"Do it. . . . Gladness, the gladness of some poor, very poor, people. . . . Of course they were poor, since they hadn't wine enough even at a wedding. . . . The historians write that, in those days, the people living about the Lake of Gennesaret were the poorest that can possibly be imagined . . . and another great heart, that other great being, His Mother, knew that He had come not only to make His great terrible sacrifice. She knew that His heart was open even to the simple, artless merrymaking of some obscure and unlearned people, who had warmly bidden Him to their poor wedding. 'Mine hour is not yet come,' He said, with a soft smile (He must have smiled gently to her). And indeed was it to make wine abundant at poor weddings He had come down to earth? And yet He went and did as she asked Him. . . . Ah, he is reading again" . . .

"Jesus saith unto them, Fill the waterpots with water. And they filled them up to the brim.

"And he saith unto them, Draw out now and bear unto the governor of the feast. And they bare it.

"When the ruler of the feast had tasted the water that was made wine, and knew not whence it was; [but the servants which drew the water knew] the governor of the feast called the bridegroom,

"And saith unto him: Every man at the beginning doth set forth good wine; and when men have well drunk, that which is worse; but thou hast kept the good wine until now."

"But what's this, what's this? Why is the room growing wider? . . . Ah, yes . . . It's the marriage, the wedding . . . yes, of course. Here are the guests, here are the young couple sitting, and the merry crowd and . . . Where is the wise governor of the feast? But who is this? Who? Again the walls are receding. . . . Who is getting up there from the great table? What! . . . He here, too? But he's in the coffin . . . but he's here, too. He has stood up, he sees me, he is coming here. . . . God!" . . .

Yes, he came up to him, to him, he, the little, thin old man, with tiny wrinkles on his face, joyful and laughing softly. There was no coffin now, and he was in the same dress as he had worn yesterday sitting with them, when the visitors had gathered about him. His face was uncovered, his eyes were shining. How was this then, he, too, had been called to the feast. He, too, at the marriage of Cana in Galilee. . . .

"Yes, my dear, I am called, too, called and bidden," he heard a soft voice saying over him. "Why have you hidden yourself here, out of sight? You come and join us too."

It was his voice, the voice of Father Zosima. And it must be he, since he called him! The elder raised Alyosha by the hand and he rose from his knees.

"We are rejoicing," the little, thin old man went on. "We are drinking the new wine, the wine of new, great gladness; do you see how many guests? Here are the bride and bridegroom, here is the wise governor of the feast, he is tasting the new wine. Why do you wonder at me? I gave an onion to a beggar, so I, too, am here. And many here have given only an onion each—only one little onion. . . . What are all our deeds? And you, my gentle one, you, my kind boy, you too have known how to give a famished woman an onion today. Begin your work, dear one, begin it, gentle one! . . . Do you see our Sun, do you see Him?"

"I am afraid . . . I dare not look," whispered Alyosha.

"Do not fear Him. He is terrible in His greatness, awful in His sublimity, but infinitely merciful. He has made Himself like unto us from love and rejoices with us. He is changing the water into wine that the gladness of the guests may not be cut short. He is expecting new guests, He is calling new ones unceasingly forever and ever. . . . There they are bringing new wine. Do you see they are bringing the vessels . . ."

Something glowed in Alyosha's heart, something filled it till it ached, tears of rapture rose from his soul. . . . He stretched out his hands, uttered a cry and woke up.

Again the coffin, the open window, and the soft, solemn, distinct reading of the Gospel. But Alyosha did not listen to the reading. It was strange, he had fallen asleep on his knees, but now he was on his feet, and suddenly, as though thrown forward, with three firm rapid steps he went right up to the coffin. His shoulder brushed against Father Païssy without his noticing it. Father Païssy raised his eyes for an instant from his book, but looked away again at once, seeing that something strange was happening to the youth. Alyosha gazed for half a minute at the coffin, at the covered, motionless dead man that lay in the coffin, with the icon on his breast and the peaked hood with the octangular cross, on his head. He had only just been hearing his voice, and that voice was still ringing in his ears. He was listening, still expecting other words, but suddenly he turned sharply and went out of the cell.

He did not stop on the steps either, but went quickly down; his soul, overflowing with rapture, yearned for freedom, space, openness. The vault of heaven, full of soft, shining stars, stretched vast and fathomless above him. The Milky Way ran in two pale streams from the zenith to the horizon. The fresh, motionless, still night enfolded the earth. The white towers and golden domes of the cathedral gleamed out against the sapphire sky. The gorgeous autumn flowers, in the beds round the house, were slumbering till morning. The silence of earth seemed to melt into the silence of the heavens. The mystery of earth was one with the mystery of the stars. . . . Alyosha stood, gazed, and suddenly threw himself down on the earth.

He did not know why he embraced it. He could not have told why he longed so irresistibly to kiss it, to kiss it all. But he kissed it weeping, sobbing and watering it with his tears, and vowed passionately to love it, to love it forever and ever. "Water the earth with the tears of your joy and love those tears," echoed in his soul. What was he weeping over? Oh! in his rapture he was weeping even over those stars, which were shining to him from the abyss of space, and "he was not ashamed of that ecstasy." There seemed to be threads from all those innumerable worlds of God, linking his soul to them, and it was trembling all over "in contact with other worlds." He longed to forgive everyone and for everything, and to beg forgiveness. Oh, not for himself, but for all men, for all and for everything. "And others are praying for me too," echoed again in his soul. But with every instant he felt clearly and, as it were, tangibly, that something firm and unshakable as that vault of heaven had entered into his soul. It was as though some idea had seized the sovereignty of his mind—and it was for all his life and forever and ever. He had fallen on the earth a weak youth, but he rose up a resolute champion, and he knew and felt it suddenly at the very moment of his ecstasy. And never, never, all his life long, could Alyosha forget that minute. "Someone visited my soul in that hour," he used to say afterwards, with implicit faith in his words.

Within three days he left the monastery in accordance with the words of his elder, who had bidden him to "sojourn in the world."

Book Eight

MITYA

Chapter I

Kuzma Samsonov

But Dmitri Fyodorovich, to whom Grushenka, flying away to a new life, had left her last greetings, "ordering" him to remember the hour of her love forever, knew nothing of what had happened to her, and was at that moment in a condition of feverish agitation and activity. For the last two days he had been in such an inconceivable state of mind that he might easily have fallen ill with brain fever, as he said himself afterwards. Alyosha had not been able to find him the morning before, and brother Ivan had not succeeded in meeting him at the tavern on the same day. The people at his lodgings, by his orders, concealed his movements. He had spent those two days literally rushing in all directions, "struggling with his destiny and trying to save himself," as he expressed it himself afterwards, and for some hours he even made a dash out of the town on urgent business, terrible as it was to him to lose sight of Grushenka for a moment. All this was explained afterwards in detail, and confirmed by documentary evidence; but for the present we will only note the most essential incidents of those two terrible days immediately preceding the awful catastrophe that broke so suddenly upon him.

Though Grushenka had, it is true, loved him for an hour, genuinely and sincerely, yet she tortured him sometimes cruelly and mercilessly. The worst of it was that he could never tell what she meant to do. To prevail upon her by force or kindness was also impossible: she would yield to nothing. She would only have become angry and turned away from him altogether, he knew that well already. He suspected, quite correctly, that she, too, was passing through an inward struggle, and was in a state of extraordinary indecision, that she was making up her mind to something, and unable to determine upon it. And so, not without good reason, he divined, with a sinking heart, that at moments she must simply hate him and his passion. And so, perhaps, it was, but what was distressing Grushenka he did not understand. For him the whole tormenting question lay between him and Fyodor Pavlovich.

Here, we must note, by the way, one certain fact: he was firmly persuaded that Fyodor Pavlovich would offer, or perhaps had offered, Grushenka lawful wedlock, and did not for a moment believe that the old voluptuary hoped to gain his object for three thousand rubles. Mitya had reached this conclusion from his knowledge of Grushenka and her character. That was how it was that he could believe at times that all Grushenka's uneasiness rose from not knowing which of them to choose, which was more to her advantage.

Strange to say, during those days it never occurred to him to think of the approaching return of the "officer," that is, of the man who had been such a fatal influence in Grushenka's life, and whose arrival she was expecting with such emotion and dread. It is true that of late Grushenka had been very silent about it. Yet he was perfectly aware of a letter she had received a month ago from her seducer, and had heard of it from her own lips. He partly knew, too, what the letter contained. In a moment of spite Grushenka had shown him that letter, but to her astonishment he attached hardly any consequence to it. It would be hard to say why this was. Perhaps, weighed down by all the hideous horror of his struggle with his own father for this woman, he was incapable of imagining any danger more terrible, at any rate for the time. He simply did not believe in a suitor who suddenly turned up again after five years' disappearance, still less in his speedy arrival. Moreover, in the "officer's" first letter which had been shown to Mitenka, the possibility of his new rival's visit was very vaguely suggested. The letter was very indefinite, high-flown, and full of sentimentality. It must be noted that Grushenka had concealed from him the last lines of the letter, in which his return was alluded to more definitely. He had, besides, noticed at that moment, he remembered afterwards, a certain involuntary proud contempt for this missive from Siberia on Grushenka's face. Grushenka told him nothing of what had passed later between her and this rival; so that by degrees he had completely forgotten the officer's existence. He felt that whatever might come later, whatever turn things might take, his final conflict with Fyodor Pavlovich was close upon him, and must be decided before anything else. With a sinking heart he was expecting every moment Grushenka's decision, always believing that it would come suddenly, on the impulse of the moment. All of a sudden she would say to him: "Take me, I'm yours forever," and it would all be over. He would seize her and bear her away at once to the ends of the earth. Oh, then he would bear her away at once, as far, far away as possible; to the furthest end of Russia, if not of the earth, then he would marry her, and settle down with her *incognito*, so that no one would know anything about them, there, here, or anywhere. Then, oh, then, a new life would begin at once! Of this different, reformed and "virtuous" life ("it must, it must be virtuous") he dreamed feverishly at every moment. He thirsted for that resurrection and renewal. The filthy morass, in which he had sunk of his own free will, was too revolting to him, and, like very many men in such cases, he put faith above all in change of place. If only it were not for these people, if only it were not for these circumstances, if only he could fly away from this accursed place— he would be altogether regenerated, would enter on a new path. That was what he believed in, and for what he was yearning.

But all this could only be on condition of the first, the *happy* solution of the question. There was another possibility, a different and awful ending. Suddenly she might say to him; "Go away. I have just come to terms with Fyodor Pavlovich. I am going to marry him and don't want you"—and then . . . but then. . . . But Mitya did not know what would happen then. Up to the last hour he didn't know. That must be said to his credit. He had no definite intentions, had planned no crime. He was simply watching and spying in agony, while he prepared himself for the first, happy solution of his destiny. He drove away any other idea, in fact. But for that ending a quite different anxiety arose, a new, incidental, but yet fatal and insoluble difficulty presented itself.

If she were to say to him: "I'm yours; take me away," how could he take her away? Where had he the means, the money to do it? It was just at this time that all sources of revenue from Fyodor Pavlovich, doles which had gone on without interruption for so many years, ceased. Grushenka had money, of course, but with regard to this Mitya suddenly evinced extraordinary pride; he wanted to carry her away and begin the new life with her himself, at his own expense, not at hers. He could not conceive of taking her money, and the very idea caused him a pang of intense repulsion. I won't enlarge on this fact or analyze it here, but confine myself to remarking that this was his attitude at the moment. All this may have arisen indirectly and unconsciously from the secret stings of his conscience for the money of Katerina Ivanovna that he had dishonestly appropriated. "I've been a scoundrel to one of them, and I shall be a scoundrel again to the other directly," with his feeling then, as he explained after: "and when Grushenka knows, she won't care for such a scoundrel." Where then was he to get the means, where was he to get the fateful money? Without it, all would be lost and nothing could be done, "and only because I hadn't the money. Oh, the shame of it!"

To anticipate things: he did, perhaps, know where to get the money, knew, perhaps, where it lay at that moment. I will say no more of this here, as it will all be clear later. But his chief trouble, I must explain however obscurely, lay in the fact that to have the sum he knew of, to *have the right* to take it, he must first restore

Katerina Ivanovna's three thousand—if not, "I'm a common pick-pocket, I'm a scoundrel, and I don't want to begin a new life as a scoundrel," Mitya decided. And so he made up his mind to move heaven and earth to return Katerina Ivanovna that three thousand, and that *first of all*. The final stage of this decision, so to say, had been reached only during the last hours, that is, after his last interview with Alyosha, two days before, on the highway, on the evening when Grushenka had insulted Katerina Ivanovna, and Mitya, after hearing Alyosha's account of it, had admitted that he was a scoundrel, and told him to tell Katerina Ivanovna so, "if it could be any comfort to her." After parting from his brother on that night, he had felt in his frenzy that it would be better "to murder and rob someone than fail to pay my debt to Katya. I'd rather everyone thought me a robber and a murderer, I'd rather go to Siberia than that Katya should have the right to say that I deceived her and stole her money, and used her money to run away with Grushenka and begin a virtuous new life! That I can't do!" So Mitya decided, grinding his teeth, and he might well fancy at times that his brain would give way. But meanwhile he went on struggling. . . .

Strange to say, though one would have supposed there was nothing left for him but despair—for what chance had he, with nothing in the world, to raise such a sum?—yet to the very end he persisted in hoping that he would get that three thousand, that the money would somehow come to him, of itself, as though it might drop from heaven. That is just how it is with people who, like Dmitri Fyodorovich, have never had anything to do with money, except to squander what had come to them by inheritance without any effort of their own, and have no notion how money is obtained. A whirl of the most fantastic notions took possession of his brain immediately after he had parted with Alyosha two days before, and threw his thoughts into a tangle of confusion. This is how it was he first hit upon a perfectly wild enterprise. And perhaps to men of that kind in such circumstances the most impossible, fantastic schemes occur first, and seem most practical.

He suddenly determined to go to Samsonov, the merchant who was Grushenka's protector, and to propose a "scheme" to him, and by means of it to obtain from him at once the whole of the sum required. Of the commercial value of his scheme he had no doubt, not the slightest, and was only uncertain how Samsonov would look upon his scheme, supposing he were to consider it from any but the commercial point of view. Though Mitya knew the merchant by sight, he was not acquainted with him and had never spoken a word to him. But for some unknown reason he had long entertained the conviction that the old reprobate, who was lying at death's door, would perhaps not at all object now to Grushenka's securing a respectable position, and marrying a man "to be depended upon." And he believed not only that he would not object, but that this was what he desired, and, if opportunity arose, that he would be ready to help. From some rumor, or perhaps from some stray words of Grushenka's, he had gathered further that the old man would perhaps prefer him to Fyodor Pavlovich for Grushenka.

Possibly many of the readers of my novel will feel that in reckoning on such assistance, and being ready to take his bride, so to speak, from the hands of her protector, Dmitri Fyodorovich showed great coarseness and want of delicacy. I will only observe that Mitya looked upon Grushenka's past as something completely over. He looked on that past with infinite compassion and resolved with all the fervor of his passion that when once Grushenka told him she loved him and would marry him, it would mean the beginning of a new Grushenka and a new Dmitri Fyodorovich, free from every vice, and containing only virtue. They would forgive one another and would begin their lives afresh. As for Kuzma Samsonov, Dmitri looked upon him as a man who had exercised a fateful influence in that remote past of Grushenka's, though she had never loved him, and who was now himself "a thing of the past," completely done with, and, so to speak, nonexistent. Besides, Mitya hardly looked upon him as a man at all, for it was known to everyone in the town that he was only a shattered wreck, whose relations with Grushenka had changed their character and were now simply paternal, so to speak, and that this had been so for a long time.

In any case there was much simplicity on Mitya's part in all this, for, in spite of all his vices, he was a very simple-hearted man. It was an instance of this simplicity that Mitya was seriously persuaded that, being on the eve of his departure for the next world, old Kuzma must sincerely repent of his past relations with Grushenka, and that she had no more devoted friend and protector in the world than this, now harmless, old man.

After his conversation with Alyosha, at the crossroads, he hardly slept all night, and, at ten o'clock next morning, he was at the house of Samsonov and telling the servant to announce him. It was a very large and gloomy old house, of two stories with a lodge and wings. In the lower story lived Samsonov's two married sons with their families, his old sister, and his unmarried daughter. In the lodge lived two of his clerks, one of whom also had a large family. Both the lodge and the lower story were overcrowded, but the old man kept the upper floor to himself, and would not even let the daughter live there with him, though she waited upon him, and in spite of her asthma was obliged at certain fixed hours, and at any time he might call her, to run upstairs to him from below.

This upper floor contained a number of large rooms kept purely for show, furnished in the old-fashioned merchant style, with long, monotonous rows of clumsy mahogany chairs along the walls, with glass chandeliers under shades, and gloomy mirrors on the walls. All these rooms were entirely empty and unused, for the old man kept to one room, a small, remote bedroom, where he was waited upon by an old servant with a kerchief on her head, and by a lad, who used to sit on the locker in the passage. Owing to his swollen legs, the old man could hardly walk at all, and was only rarely lifted from his leather armchair, when the old woman supporting him led up and down the room once or twice. He was morose and taciturn even with this old woman.

When he was informed of the arrival of the "captain," he at once refused to see him. But Mitya persisted and sent his name up again. Samsonov questioned the lad minutely: What he looked like? Whether he was drunk? Was he going to make a row? The answer he received was that he was sober, but wouldn't go away. The old man again refused to see him. Then Mitya, who had foreseen this, and purposely brought pencil and paper with him, wrote clearly on the piece of paper the words: "On most important business closely concerning Agrafena Alexandrovna," and sent it up, to the old man.

After thinking a little Samsonov told the lad to take the visitor to the drawing room, and sent the old woman downstairs with a summons to his younger son to come upstairs to him at once. The younger son, a man over six foot and of exceptional physical strength, who was closely shaven and dressed in the European style, though his father still wore a caftan and a beard, came at once without a comment. All the family trembled before the father. The old man had sent for this giant, not because he was afraid of the "captain" (he was by no means of a timorous temper), but in order to have a witness in case of an emergency. Supported by his son and the servant lad, he swept at last into the drawing room. It may be assumed that he felt considerable curiosity. The drawing room in which Mitya was awaiting him was a vast, dreary room that laid a weight of depression on the heart. It had a double row of windows, a gallery, marbled walls, and three immense chandeliers with glass lusters covered with shades.

Mitya was sitting on a little chair at the entrance, awaiting his fate with nervous impatience. When the old man appeared at the opposite door, seventy feet away, Mitya jumped up at once, and with his long, military stride walked to meet him. Mitya was well dressed, in a frock coat, buttoned up, with a round hat and black gloves in his hands, just as he had been three days before at the elder's, at the family meeting with his father and brothers. The old man waited for him, standing dignified and unbending, and Mitya felt at once that he had looked him through and through as he advanced. Mitya was greatly impressed, too, with Samsonov's immensely swollen face. His lower lip, which had always been thick, hung down now, looking like a bun. He bowed to his guest in dignified silence, motioned him to an armchair by the sofa, and leaning on his son's arm he began lowering himself on to the sofa facing Mitya, groaning painfully, so that Mitya, seeing his painful exertions, immediately felt remorseful and sensitively conscious of his insignificance in the presence of the dignified person he had ventured to disturb.

"What is it you want of me, sir?" said the old man, deliberately, distinctly, severely, but courteously, when he was at last seated.

Mitya started, leaped up, but sat down again. Then he began at once speaking with loud, nervous haste, gesticulating, and in a positive frenzy. He was unmistakably a man driven into a corner, on the brink of ruin, catching at the last straw, ready to sink if he failed. Old Samsonov probably grasped all this in an instant, though his face remained cold and immovable as a statue's.

"Most honored sir, Kuzma Kuzmich, you have no doubt heard, more than once, of my disputes with my father, Fyodor Pavlovich Karamazov, who robbed me of my inheritance from my mother . . . seeing the whole town is gossiping about it . . . for here everyone's gossiping of what they shouldn't . . . and besides, it might have reached you through Grushenka . . . I beg your pardon, through Agrafena Alexandrovna . . . Agrafena Alexandrovna, the lady for whom I have the highest respect and esteem . . ."

So Mitya began, and broke down at the first sentence. We will not reproduce his speech word for word, but will only summarize the gist of it. Three months ago, he said, he had of express intention (Mitya purposely used these words instead of "intentionally") consulted a lawyer in the chief town of the province, "a distinguished lawyer, Kuzma Kuzmich, Pavel Pavlovich Korneplodov. You have perhaps heard of him? A man of vast intellect, the mind of a statesman . . . he knows you, too . . . spoke of you in the highest terms . . ." Mitya broke down again. But these breaks did not deter him. He leaped instantly over the gaps, and struggled on and on.

This Korneplodov, after questioning him minutely, and inspecting the documents he was able to bring (Mitya alluded somewhat vaguely to these documents, and slurred over the subject with special haste), reported that they certainly might take proceedings concerning the village of Chermashnya, which ought, he said, to have come to him, Mitya, from his mother, and so stun the old villain, his father . . . "because every door was not closed and justice might still find a loophole." In fact, he might reckon on an additional sum of six or even seven thousand rubles from Fyodor Pavlovich, as Chermashnya was worth, at least, twenty-five thousand, he might say twenty-eight thousand, in fact, "thirty, thirty, Kuzma Kuzmich, and, would you believe it, I didn't get seventeen from that heartless man!" So he, Mitya, had thrown the business up, for the time, knowing nothing about the law, but on coming here was struck dumb by a cross claim made upon him (here Mitya went adrift again, and again took a flying leap forward), "so will not you, excellent and honored Kuzma Kuzmich, be willing to take up all my claims against that unnatural monster, and pay me a sum of only three thousand? . . . You see, you cannot, in any case, lose over it. On my honor, my honor, I swear that. Quite the contrary, you may make six or seven thousand instead of three" . . . Above all, he wanted this concluded "that very day."

"I'll do the business with you at a notary's, or whatever it is . . . in fact, I'm ready to do anything. . . . I'll hand over all the deeds . . . whatever you want, sign anything . . . and we could draw up the agreement at once . . . and if it were possible, if it were only possible, that very morning. . . . You could pay me that three thousand, for there isn't a capitalist in this town to compare with you, and so would save me from . . . would save me, in fact . . . for a good, I might say an honorable, action. . . . For I cherish the most honorable feelings for a certain person, whom you know well, and care for as a father. I would not have come, indeed, if it had not been as a father. And, indeed, it's a struggle of three in this business, for it's fate—that's a fearful thing, Kuzma Kuzmich! Real life, Kuzma Kuzmich, real life, Kuzma Kuzmich, real life! And as you've dropped out long ago, it's a tug-of-war between two. I'm expressing it awkwardly, ·perhaps, but I'm not a literary man. You see, I'm on the one side, and that monster on the other. So you must choose. It's either I or the monster. It all lies in your hands—the fate of three lives, and the happiness of two. . . . Excuse me, I'm making a mess of it, but you understand . . . I see from your venerable eyes that you understand . . . and if you don't understand, I'm done for . . . so you see!"

Mitya broke off his clumsy speech with that "so you see!" and jumping up from his seat, awaited the answer to his foolish proposal. At the last phrase he had suddenly become hopelessly aware that it had fallen flat, above all, that he had been talking utter nonsense.

"How strange it is! On the way here it seemed all right, and now it's nothing but nonsense." The idea suddenly dawned on his despairing mind. All the while he had been talking, the old man sat motionless, watching him with an icy expression in his eyes. After keeping him for a moment in suspense, Kuzma Kuzmich pronounced at last, in the most positive and chilling tone:

"Excuse me, we don't undertake such business."

Mitya suddenly felt his legs growing weak under him.

"What am I to do now, Kuzma Kuzmich?" he muttered, with a

pale smile. "I suppose it's all up with me—what do you think?"

"Excuse me, sir . . ."

Mitya remained standing, staring motionless. He suddenly noticed a movement in the old man's face. He started.

"You see, sir, business of that sort's not in our line," said the old man slowly. "There's the court, and the lawyers—it's a perfect misery. But if you like, there is a man here you might apply to."

"God heavens! Who is it? You're my salvation, Kuzma Kuzmich," faltered Mitya.

"He doesn't live here, and he's not here just now. He is a peasant, he does business in timber. His name is Lyagavy. He's been haggling with Fyodor Pavlovich for the last year, over your copse at Chermashnya. They can't agree on the price, maybe you've heard? Now he's come back again and is staying with the priest at Ilyinskoe, about eight miles from the Volovya station. He wrote to me, too, about the business of the copse asking my advice. Fyodor Pavlovich means to go and see him, himself. So if you were to be before Fyodor Pavlovich and to make Lyagavy the offer you've made me, he might possibly . . ."

"A brilliant idea!" Mitya interrupted ecstatically. "He's the very man, it would just suit him. He's haggling with him for it, being asked too much, and here he would have all the documents entitling him to the property itself. Ha-ha-ha!"

And Mitya suddenly went off into his short, wooden laugh, startling Samsonov.

"How can I thank you, Kuzma Kuzmich?" cried Mitya effusively.

"Don't mention it," said Samsonov, inclining his head.

"But you don't know, you've saved me. Oh, it was a true presentiment brought me to you. . . . so now to this priest!"

"No need of thanks, sir."

"I'll make haste and fly there. I'm afraid I've overtaxed your strength. I shall never forget it. It's a Russian says that, Kuzma Kuzmich, a R-r-russian!"

"To be sure!"

Mitya seized his hand to press it, but there was a malignant gleam in the old man's eye. Mitya drew back his hand, but at once blamed himself for his mistrustfulness. "It's because he's tired," he thought.

"For her sake! For her sake, Kuzma Kuzmich! You understand that it's for her," he roared, his voice ringing through the room. He bowed, turned sharply round, and with the same long stride walked to the door without looking back. He was trembling with delight.

"Everything was on the verge of ruin and my guardian angel saved me," was the thought in his mind. And if such a businessman as Samsonov (a most worthy old man, and what dignity!) had suggested this course, then . . . then success was assured. He would fly off immediately. "I will be back before night, I shall be back at night and the thing is done. Could the old man have been laughing at me?" exclaimed Mitya, as he strode towards his lodging. He could, of course, imagine nothing, but that the advice was practical "from such a businessman" with an understanding of the business, with an understanding of this Lyagavy (curious surname!). Or— the old man was laughing at him.

Alas! the second alternative was the correct one. Long after-wards, when the catastrophe had happened, old Samsonov himself confessed, laughing, that he had made a fool of the "captain." He was a cold, spiteful and sarcastic man, liable to violent antipathies. Whether it was the "captain's" excited face, or the foolish convic-tion of the "rake and spendthrift," that he, Samsonov, could be taken in by such a cock-and-bull story as his scheme, or jealousy over Grushenka, in whose name this "scapegrace" had rushed in on him with such a tale to get money—which worked on the old man I can't tell. But, at the instant when Mitya stood before him, feeling his legs grow weak under him, and frantically exclaiming that he was ruined, at that moment the old man looked at him with intense spite, and resolved to make a laughingstock of him. When Mitya had gone, Kuzma Kuzmich, white with rage, turned to his son and bade him see to it that that beggar never be seen again, and never admitted even into the yard, or else he'd . . .

He did not utter his threat. But even his son, who often saw him enraged, trembled with fear. For a whole hour afterwards, the old man was shaking with anger, and by evening he was worse, and sent for the doctor.

Chapter II

Lyagavy

So he must drive at full speed, and he had not the money for horses. He had forty kopecks, and that was all, all that was left after so many years of prosperity! But he had at home an old silver watch which had long ceased to go. He snatched it up and carried it to a Jewish watchmaker who had a shop in the marketplace. The Jew gave him six rubles for it. "And I didn't expect that," cried Mitya, ecstatically. (He was still in a state of ecstasy.) He seized his six rubles and ran home. At home he borrowed three rubles from the people of the house, who loved him so much that they were pleased to give it him, though it was all they had. Mitya in his excitement told them on the spot that his fate would be decided that day, and he described, in desperate haste, the whole "scheme" he had put before Samsonov, the latter's decision, his own hopes for the future, and so on. These people had been told many of their lodger's secrets before, and so looked upon him as a gentleman who was not at all proud, and almost one of *themselves*. Having thus collected nine rubles Mitya sent for posting horses to take him to the Volovya station. This was how the fact came to be remembered and established that "at midday, on the day before the event, Mitya had not a farthing, and that he had sold his watch to get money and had borrowed three rubles from his landlords, all in the presence of witnesses."

I note this fact; later on it will be apparent why I do so.

Though he was radiant with the joyful anticipation that he would at last solve "all his difficulties," yet, as he drew near Volovya station, he trembled at the thought of what Grushenka might be doing in his absence. What if she made up her mind today to go to Fyodor Pavlovich? This was why he had gone off without telling her and why he left orders with his landlady not to let out where he had gone, if anyone came to inquire for him. "I must, I must get back tonight," he repeated, as he was jolted along in the cart, "and I daresay I shall have to bring this Lyagavy back here . . . to draw up the deed." So mused Mitya, with a throbbing heart, but alas! his dreams were not fated to be carried out.

To begin with, he was late, taking a short cut from Volovya station which turned out to be twelve miles instead of eight. Secondly, he did not find the priest at home at Ilyinskoe; he had gone off to a neighboring village. While Mitya, setting off there with the same exhausted horses, was looking for him, it was almost dark.

The priest, a shy and amiable looking little man, informed him at once that, though Lyagavy had been staying with him at first, he was now at Sukhoy Possyolok, that he was staying the night in the forester's cottage, as he was buying timber there too. At Mitya's urgent request that he would take him to Lyagavy at once, and by so doing "save him, so to speak," the priest agreed, after some demur, to conduct him to Sukhoy Possyolok; his curiosity was obviously aroused. But, unluckily, he advised their going on foot, as it would not be "much over" a half mile or so. Mitya, of course, agreed, and marched off with his yard-long strides, so that the poor priest almost ran after him. He was a very cautious man, though not old. Mitya at once began talking to him, too, of his plans, nervously and excitedly asking advice in regard to Lyagavy, and talking all the way. He turned off Mitya's questions with: "I don't know. Ah, I can't say. How can I tell?" and so on. When Mitya began to speak of his quarrel with his father over his inheritance, the priest was positively alarmed, as he was in some way dependent on Fyodor Pavlovich. He inquired, however, with surprise, why he called the peasant trader Gorstkin, Lyagavy, and obligingly explained to Mitya that, though the man's name really was Lyagavy, he was never called so, as he would be grievously offended at the name, and that he must be sure to call him Gorstkin, "or you'll do nothing with him; he won't even listen to you," said the priest in conclusion.

Mitya was somewhat surprised for a moment, and explained that that was what Samsonov had called him. On hearing this fact, the priest dropped the subject, though he would have done well to put into words his doubt whether, if Samsonov had sent him to that peasant, calling him Lyagavy, there was not something wrong about it, and he was exposing him to ridicule. But Mitya had no time to pause "over such trifles." He hurried, striding along, and only when he reached Sukhoy Possyolok he realized that they had come not a half mile, nor one and one-half, but at least two. This annoyed him, but he controlled himself.

They went into the hut. The forester, the priest's friend, lived in one half of the hut, and Gorstkin was lodging in the other, the better room the other side of the passage. They went into that room and lighted a tallow candle. The hut was extremely overheated. On the pine table there was a samovar that had gone out, a tray with cups, an empty rum bottle, a bottle of vodka partly full, and some half-eaten crusts of wheat bread. The visitor himself lay stretched at full length on the bench, with his coat crushed up under his head for a pillow, snoring heavily. Mitya stood in perplexity.

"Of course I must wake him. My business is too important. I've come in such haste. I'm in a hurry to get back today," he said in great agitation. But the priest and the forester stood in silence, not giving their opinion. Mitya went up and began trying to wake him himself; he tried vigorously, but the sleeper did not wake. "He's drunk," Mitya decided. "Good Lord! What am I to do? What am I to do?" And, terribly impatient, he began pulling him by the arms, by the legs, shaking his head, lifting him up and making him sit on the bench. Yet, after prolonged exertions, he could only succeed in getting the drunken man to utter absurd grunts, and violent but inarticulate oaths.

"No, you'd better wait a little," the priest pronounced at last, "for he's obviously not in a fit state."

"He's been drinking the whole day," the forester chimed in.

"Good heavens!" cried Mitya. "If only you knew how important it is to me and how desperate I am!"

"No, you'd better wait till morning," the priest repeated.

"Till morning? Mercy! that's impossible!"

And in his despair he was on the point of attacking the sleeping man again, but stopped short at once, realizing the uselessness of his efforts. The priest said nothing, the sleepy forester looked gloomy.

"What terrible tragedies real life contrives for people," said Mitya, in complete despair. The perspiration was streaming down his face. The priest seized the moment to put before him, very reasonably, that even if he succeeded in wakening the man, he would still be drunk and incapable of conversation. "And your business is important," he said, "so you'd certainly better put it off till morning." With a gesture of despair Mitya agreed.

"Father, I will stay here with a light, and seize the favorable moment. As soon as he wakes I'll begin. I'll pay you for the light," he said to the forester, "for the night's lodging, too; you'll remember Dmitri Karamazov. Only, Father, I don't know what we're to do with you. Where will you sleep?"

"No, I'm going home. I'll take his horse and get home," he said, indicating the forester. "And now I'll say goodbye. I wish you all success."

So it was settled. The priest rode off on the forester's horse, delighted to escape, though he shook his head uneasily, wondering whether he ought not next day to inform his benefactor Fyodor Pavlovich of this curious incident, "or he may in an unlucky hour hear of it, be angry, and withdraw his favor." The forester, scratching himself, went back to his room without a word, and Mitya sat on the bench to "catch the favorable moment," as he expressed it. Profound dejection clung about his soul like a heavy mist. A profound, intense dejection! He sat thinking, but could reach no conclusion. The candle burned dimly, a cricket chirped; it became insufferably close in the overheated room. He suddenly pictured the garden, the path behind the garden, the door of his father's house mysteriously opening and Grushenka running in. He leaped up from the bench.

"It's a tragedy!" he said, grinding his teeth. Mechanically he went up to the sleeping man and looked in his face. He was a lean, middle-aged peasant, with a very long face, dark blond curls, and a long, thin, reddish beard, wearing a blue cotton shirt and a black waistcoat, from the pocket of which peeped the chain of a silver watch. Mitya looked at his face with intense hatred, and for some unknown reason his curly hair particularly irritated him. What was insufferably humiliating was, that, after leaving things of such importance and making such sacrifices, he, Mitya, utterly worn out, should with business of such urgency be standing over this dolt on whom his whole fate depended, while he snored as though there were nothing the matter, as though he'd dropped from another planet. "Oh, the irony of fate!" cried Mitya, and, quite losing his head, he fell again to rousing the tipsy peasant. He roused him with a sort of ferocity, pulled him, pushed him, even beat him; but after five minutes of vain exertions, he returned to his bench in helpless despair, and sat down.

"Stupid! Stupid!" cried Mitya. "And how dishonorable it all is!" something made him add. His head began to ache horribly. "Should he give it up and go away altogether?" he wondered. "No, wait till tomorrow now. I'll stay on purpose. What else did I come for? Besides, I've no means of going. How am I to get away from here now? Oh, the idiocy of it!"

But his head ached more and more. He sat without moving, and unconsciously dozed off and fell asleep as he sat. He seemed to have slept two hours or more. He was awakened by his head aching so unbearably that he could have screamed. There was a hammering in his temples, and the top of his head ached. It was a long time before he could wake up fully and understand what had happened to him.

At last he realized that the room was full of charcoal fumes from the stove, and that he might die of suffocation. And the drunken peasant still lay snoring. The candle guttered and was about to go out. Mitya cried out, and ran staggering across the passage into the forester's room. The forester woke up at once, but hearing that the other room was full of fumes, to Mitya's surprise and annoyance, accepted the fact with strange unconcern, though he did go to see to it.

"But he's dead, he's dead! and ... what am I to do then?" cried Mitya frantically.

They threw open the doors, opened a window and the chimney. Mitya brought a pail of water from the passage. First he wet his own head, then, finding a rag of some sort, dipped it into the water, and put it on Lyagavy's head. The forester still treated the matter contemptuously, and when he opened the window said grumpily: "It'll be all right, now." He went back to sleep, leaving Mitya a lighted lantern. Mitya fussed about the drunken peasant for half an hour, wetting his head, and gravely resolved not to sleep all night. But he was so worn out that when he sat down for a moment to take a breath, he closed his eyes, unconsciously stretched himself full length on the bench and slept like the dead.

It was dreadfully late when he awoke. It was somewhere about nine o'clock. The sun was shining brightly in the two little windows of the hut. The curly-headed peasant was sitting on the bench and had his coat on. He had another samovar and another bottle in front of him. Yesterday's bottle had already been finished, and the new one was more than half empty. Mitya jumped up and saw at once that the cursed peasant was drunk again, hopelessly and incurably. He stared at him for a moment with wide-open eyes. The peasant was silently and slyly watching him, with insulting composure, and even a sort of contemptuous condescension, so Mitya fancied. He rushed up to him.

"Excuse me, you see.... I ... you've most likely heard from the forester here in the hut. I'm Lieutenant Dmitri Karamazov, the son of the old Karamazov whose copse you are buying."

"That's a lie!" said the peasant, calmly and confidently.

"A lie? You know Fyodor Pavlovich?"

"I don't know any of your Fyodor Pavloviches," said the peasant, speaking thickly.

"You're bargaining with him for the copse, for the copse. Do wake up, and collect yourself. Father Pavel of Ilyinskoe brought me here. You wrote to Samsonov, and he has sent me to you," Mitya gasped breathlessly.

"You're l—lying!" Lyagavy blurted out again. Mitya's legs went cold.

"For mercy's sake! It isn't a joke! You're a little high, perhaps. Yet you can speak and understand . . . or else . . . I understand nothing!"

"You're a painter!"

"For mercy's sake! I'm Karamazov, Dmitri Karamazov. I have an offer to make you, an advantageous offer . . . very advantageous offer, concerning the copse!"

The peasant stroked his beard importantly.

"No, you've contracted for the job and turned out a scamp. You're a scoundrel!"

"I assure you you're mistaken," cried Mitya, wringing his hands in despair. The peasant still stroked his beard, and suddenly screwed up his eyes cunningly.

"No, you show me this: you tell me the law that allows roguery. D'you hear? You're a scoundrel! Do you understand that?"

Mitya stepped back gloomily, and suddenly "something seemed to hit him on the head," as he said afterwards. In an instant a light seemed to dawn in his mind, "a light was kindled and I grasped it all." He stood, stupefied, wondering how he, after all a man of intelligence, could have yielded to such folly, have been led into such an adventure, and have kept it up for almost twenty-four hours, fussing round this Lyagavy, wetting his head.

"Why, the man's drunk, dead drunk, and he'll go on drinking now for a week; what's the use of waiting here? And what if Samsonov sent me here on purpose? What if she? . . . Oh, God, what have I done?"

The peasant sat watching him and grinning. Another time Mitya might have killed the fool in a fury, but now he felt as weak as a child. He went quietly to the bench, took up his overcoat, put it on without a word, and went out of the hut. He did not find the forester in the next room; there was no one there. He took fifty kopecks in small change out of his pocket and put them on the table for his night's lodging, the candle, and the trouble he had given. Coming out of the hut he saw nothing but forest all round.

He walked haphazardly, not knowing which way to turn out of the hut, to the right or to the left. Hurrying there the evening before with the priest, he had not noticed the road. He had no revengeful feeling for anybody, even for Samsonov, in his heart. He strode along a narrow forest path, dazed, lost, with his "lost idea," without heeding where he was going. A child could have knocked him down, so weak was he in body and soul. He got out of the forest somehow, however, and a vista of fields, bare after the harvest, stretched as far as the eye could see. "What despair! What death all round!" he repeated striding on and on.

He was saved by meeting an old merchant who was being driven across country in a hired carriage. When he overtook him, Mitya asked the way, and it turned out that the old merchant, too, was going to Volovya. After some discussion Mitya got into the trap. Three hours later they arrived. At Volovya, Mitya at once ordered posting horses to drive to the town, and suddenly realized that he was appallingly hungry. While the horses were being harnessed, an omelette was prepared for him. He ate it all in an instant, ate a huge hunk of bread, ate a sausage, and swallowed three glasses of vodka. After eating, his spirits and his heart grew lighter. He flew towards the town, urged on the driver, and suddenly made a new and "unalterable" plan to procure that "accursed money" before evening. "And to think, only to think that a man's life should be ruined for the sake of that paltry three thousand!" he cried, contemptuously. "I'll settle it today." And if it had not been for the thought of Grushenka and of what might have happened to her, which never left him, he would perhaps have become quite cheerful again. . . . But the thought of her was stabbing him to the heart every moment, like a sharp knife.

At last they arrived, and Mitya at once ran to Grushenka.

Chapter III

Gold Mines

This was the visit of Mitya of which Grushenka had spoken to Rakitin with such horror. She was just then expecting the "message," and was much relieved that Mitya had not been to see her that day or the day before. She hoped that "please God he won't come till I'm gone away," and he suddenly burst in on her. The rest we know already. To get him off her hands she suggested at once that he should walk with her to Samsonov's, where she said she absolutely must go "to settle his accounts," and when Mitya accompanied her at once, she said good-bye to him at the gate, making him promise to come at twelve o'clock to take her home again. Mitya, too, was delighted at this arrangement. If she was sitting at Samsonov's she could not be going to Fyodor Pavlovich's, "if only she's not lying," he added at once. But he thought she was not lying from what he saw.

He was that sort of jealous man who, in the absence of the beloved woman, at once invents all sorts of awful fancies of what may be happening to her, and how she may be "betraying" him, but, when shaken, heartbroken, convinced of her faithlessness, he runs back to her; at the first glance at her face, her gay, laughing, affectionate face, he revives at once, lays aside all suspicion and with joyful shame abuses himself for his jealousy. After leaving Grushenka at the gate he rushed home. Oh, he had so much still to do that day! But a load had been lifted from his heart, anyway. "Now I must only make haste and find out from Smerdyakov whether anything happened there last night, whether, by any chance, she went to Fyodor Pavlovich; ugh!" floated through his mind. Before he had time to reach his lodging, jealously had surged up again in his restless heart.

Jealousy! "Othello was not jealous, he was trustful," observed Pushkin. And that remark alone is enough to show the deep insight of our great poet. Othello's soul was shattered and his whole outlook clouded simply because *his ideal was destroyed.* But Othello did not begin hiding, spying, peeping. He was trustful. On the contrary, he had to be led on, pushed on, excited with great difficulty before he could entertain the idea of deceit. The truly jealous man is not like that. It is impossible to picture to oneself the shame and moral degradation to which the jealous man can descend without a qualm of conscience. And yet it's not as though the jealous were all vulgar and base souls. On the contrary, a man of lofty feelings, whose love is pure and full of self-sacrifice, may yet hide under tables, bribe the vilest people, and be familiar with the lowest ignominy of spying and eavesdropping.

Othello was incapable of reconciling himself to faithlessness—not incapable of forgiving it, but of reconciling himself to it—though his soul was as innocent and free from malice as a babe's. It is not so with the really jealous man. It is hard to imagine what a jealous man can reconcile himself to and overlook, and what he can forgive! The jealous are the readiest of all to forgive, and all women know it. The jealous man can forgive extraordinarily quickly (though, of course, after a violent scene), and he is able to forgive infidelity almost conclusively proved, the very kisses and embraces he has seen, if only he can somehow be convinced that it has all been "for the last time," and that his rival will vanish from that day forward, will depart to the ends of the earth, or that he himself will carry her away somewhere, where that dreaded rival will not get near her. Of course the reconciliation is only for an hour. For, even if the rival did disappear next day, he would invent another one and would be jealous of him. And one might wonder what there was in a love that had to be so watched over, what a love could be worth that needed such strenuous guarding. But that the jealous will never understand. And yet among them are men of noble hearts. It is remarkable, too, that those very men of noble hearts, standing hidden in some cupboard, listening and spying, never feel the stings of conscience at that moment, anyway, though they understand clearly enough with their "noble hearts" the shameful depths to which they have voluntarily sunk.

At the sight of Grushenka, Mitya's jealousy vanished, and for an instant he became trustful and generous, and positively despised himself for his evil feelings. But that only proved that, in his love for that woman, there was an element of something far higher than he himself imagined, that it was not only a sensual passion, not only the "curve of her body," of which he had talked to Alyosha. But, as soon as Grushenka had gone, Mitya began to suspect her of all the low cunning of faithlessness, and he felt no sting of conscience at it.

And so jealousy surged up in him again. He had, in any case, to make haste. The first thing to be done was to get hold of at least a small, temporary loan of money. The nine rubles had almost all gone on his expedition. And, as we all know, one can't take a step without money. But he had thought over in the cart where he could get a loan. He had a brace of fine dueling pistols in a case, which he had not pawned till then because he prized them above all his possessions.

In the Metropolis tavern he had some time ago made acquaintance with a young official and had learned that this very opulent bachelor was passionately fond of weapons. He used to buy pistols, revolvers, daggers, hang them on his wall and show them to acquaintances. He prided himself on them, and was quite a specialist on the mechanism of revolvers, how to load them, how to shoot them, and so on. Mitya, without stopping to think, went straight to him, and offered to pawn his pistols to him for ten rubles. The official, delighted, began trying to persuade him to sell them outright. But Mitya would not consent, so the young man gave him ten rubles, protesting that nothing would induce him to take interest. They parted friends. Mitya was in haste; he rushed towards Fyodor Pavlovich's by the back way, to his gazebo, to get hold of Smerdyakov as soon as possible. In this way the fact was established that three or four hours before a certain event, of which I shall speak later on, Mitya had not a farthing, and pawned for ten rubles a possession he valued, though, three hours later, he was in possession of thousands. . . . But I am anticipating.

From Marya Kondratyevna (the woman living near Fyodor Pavlovich's) he learned the very disturbing fact of Smerdyakov's illness. He heard the story of his fall in the cellar, his fit, the doctor's visit, Fyodor Pavlovich's anxiety; he heard with interest, too, that his brother Ivan Fyodorovich had set off that morning for Moscow. "Then he must have driven through Volovya before me," thought Dmitri Fyodorovich but he was terribly distressed about Smerdyakov. "What will happen now? Who'll keep watch for me? Who'll bring me word?" he thought. He began greedily questioning the women whether they had seen anything the evening before. They quite understood what he was trying to find out, and completely reassured him. No one had been there. Ivan Fyodorovich had been there through the night; "everything had been in perfect order." Mitya grew thoughtful. He would certainly have to keep watch today, but where? Here or at Samsonov's gate? He decided that he must be on the lookout both here and there, and meanwhile . . . meanwhile . . . The difficulty was that he had to carry out the new plan that he had made on the journey back. He was sure of its success, but he must not delay acting upon it. Mitya resolved to sacrifice an hour to it: "in an hour I shall know everything, I shall settle everything, and then, then, first of all to Samsonov's. I'll inquire whether Grushenka's there and instantly be back here again, stay till eleven, and then to Samsonov's again to bring her home." This is what he decided.

He flew home, washed, combed his hair, brushed his clothes, dressed, and went to Madame Khokhlakov's. Alas! he had built his hopes on her. He had resolved to borrow three thousand from that lady. And what was more, he felt suddenly convinced that she would not refuse to lend it to him. It may be wondered why, if he felt so certain, he had not gone to her at first, one of his own sort, so to speak, instead of to Samsonov, a man he did not know, who was not of his own class, and to whom he hardly knew how to speak. But the fact was that he had never known Madame Khokhlakov well, and had seen nothing of her for the last month, and that he knew she could not endure him. She had detested him from the first because he was engaged to Katerina Ivanovna, while she had, for some reason, suddenly conceived the desire that Katerina Ivanovna should throw him over, and marry the "charming, chivalrously educated Ivan Fyodorovich, who had such excellent manners." Mitya's manners she detested. Mitya positively laughed at her, and had once said about her that she was just as lively and at her ease as she was uncultivated. But that morning in the cart a brilliant idea had struck him: "If she is so anxious I should not marry Katerina Ivanovna"—and he knew she was positively hysterical upon the subject—"why should she refuse me now that three thousand, just to enable me to leave Katya and get away from her forever? These spoiled fine ladies, if they set their hearts on anything will spare no expense to satisfy their caprice. Besides, she's so rich," Mitya argued.

As for his "plan" it was just the same as before; it consisted of the offer of his rights to Chermashnya—but not with a commercial object, as it had been with Samsonov, not trying to lure the lady with the possibility of making a profit of six or seven thousand— but simply as a noble security for the debt. As he worked out this new idea, Mitya was enchanted with it, but so it always was with him in all his undertakings, in all his sudden decisions. He gave himself up to every new idea with passionate enthusiasm. Yet, when he mounted the steps of Madam Khokhlakov's house he felt a shiver of fear run down his spine. At that moment he saw fully, as a mathematical certainty, that this was his last hope, that if this broke down, nothing else was left him in the world but to "rob and murder someone for the three thousand." It was half past seven when he rang at the bell.

At first fortune seemed to smile upon him. As soon as he was announced he was received with extraordinary rapidity. "As though she were waiting for me," thought Mitya, and as soon as he had been led to the drawing room, the lady of the house herself ran in, and declared at once that she was expecting him.

"I was expecting you! I was expecting you! Though I'd no reason to suppose you would come to see me, as you will admit yourself. Yet, I did expect you. You may marvel at my instinct, Dmitri Fyodorovich, but I was convinced all the morning that you would come."

"That is certainly wonderful, Madame," observed Mitya, sitting down limply, "but I have come to you on a matter of great importance.... On a matter of supreme importance for me that is, Madame ... for me alone ... and I hasten ..."

"I know you've come on most important business, Dmitri Fyodorovich; it's not a case of presentiment, no reactionary harking back to the miraculous (have you heard about Father Zosima?). This is a case of mathematics: you couldn't help coming, after all that has passed with Katerina Ivanovna; you couldn't, you couldn't, that's a mathematical certainty."

"The realism of actual life, Madame, that's what it is. But allow me to explain ..."

"Realism indeed, Dmitri Fyodorovich. I'm all for realism now. I've seen too much of miracles. You've heard that Father Zosima is dead?"

"No, Madame, it's the first time I've heard of it." Mitya was a little surprised. The image of Alyosha rose to his mind.

"Last night, and only imagine ..."

"Madame," interrupted Mitya, "I can imagine nothing except that I'm in a desperate position, and that if you don't help me, everything will come to grief, and I first of all. Excuse me, for the triviality of the expression, but I'm in a fever ..."

"I know, I know that you're in a fever. You could hardly fail to be, and whatever you may say to me, I know beforehand. I have long been thinking over your destiny, Dmitri Fyodorovich, I am watching over it and studying it. . . . Oh, believe me, I'm an experienced doctor of the soul, Dmitri Fyodorovich."

"Madame, if you are an experienced doctor, I'm certainly an experienced patient," said Mitya, with an effort to be polite, "and I feel that if you are watching over my destiny in this way, you will come to my help in my ruin, and so allow me, at least to explain to you the plan with which I have ventured to come to you . . . and what I am hoping of you. . . . I have come, Madame . . ."

"Don't explain it. It's of secondary importance. But as for help, you're not the first I have helped, Dmitri Fyodorovich. You have most likely heard of my cousin, Madame Belmesov. Her husband was ruined, 'had come to grief,' as you characteristically express it, Dmitri Fyodorovich. I recommended him to take to horse breeding, and now he's doing well. Have you any idea of horse breeding, Dmitri Fyodorovich?"

"Not the faintest, Madame; ah, Madame, not the faintest!" cried Mitya, in nervous impatience, positively starting from his seat. "I simply implore you, Madame, to listen to me. Only give me two minutes of free speech that I may just explain to you everything, the whole plan with which I have come. Besides I am short of time. I'm in a fearful hurry," Mitya cried hysterically, feeling that she was just going to begin talking again, and hoping to cut her short. "I have come in despair . . . in the last gasp of despair, to beg you to lend me the sum of three thousand, a loan, but on safe, most safe security, madame, with the most trustworthy guarantees! Only let me explain . . ."

"You must tell me all that afterwards, afterwards!" Madame Khokhlakov with a gesture demanded silence in her turn, "and whatever you may tell me, I know it all beforehand; I've told you so already. You ask for a certain sum, for three thousand, but I can give you more, immeasurably more, I will save you, Dmitri Fyodorovich, but you must listen to me."

Mitya started from his seat again.

"Madame, will you really be so good!" he cried, with a strong feeling. "Good God, you've saved me! You have saved a man from a violent death, from a bullet. . . . My eternal gratitude . . ."

"I will give you more, infinitely more than three thousand!" cried Madame Khokhlakov, looking with a radiant smile at Mitya's ecstasy.

"Infinitely? But I don't need so much. I only need that fatal three thousand, and on my part I can give security for that sum with infinite gratitude, and I propose a plan which . . ."

"Enough, Dmitri Fyodorovich, it's said and done." Madame

Khokhlakov cut him short, with the modest triumph of beeficence: "I have promised to save you, and I will save you. I will save you as I did Belmesov. What do you think of gold mines, Dmitri Fyodorovich?"

"Of the gold mines, Madame? I have never thought anything about them."

"But I have thought of them for you. Thought of them over and over again. I have been watching you for the last month. I've watched you a hundred times as you've walked past, saying to myself: that's a man of energy who ought to go to the gold mines. I've studied your gait and come to the conclusion: that's a man who would find mines."

"From my gait, Madame?" said Mitya, smiling.

"Yes, from your gait. You surely don't deny that character can be told from the gait, Dmitri Fyodorovich? Science supports the idea. I'm all for science and realism now. After all this business with Father Zosima, which has so upset me, from this very day I'm a realist and I want to devote myself to practical usefulness. I'm cured. 'Enough!' as Turgenev says."[1]

"But, Madame, the three thousand you so generously promised to lend me . . ."

"It is yours, Dmitri Fyodorovich," Madame Khokhlakov cut in at once. "The money is as good as in your pocket, not three thousand, but three million, Dmitri Fyodorovich, in less than no time. I'll make you a present of the idea: you shall find gold mines, make millions, return and become a leader, and wake us up and lead us to better things. Are we to leave it all to the Jews? You will found institutions and enterprises of all sorts. You will help the poor, and they will bless you. This is the age of railways, Dmitri Fyodorovich. You'll become famous and indispensable to the Department of Finance, which is so badly off at present. The depreciation of the ruble keeps me awake at night, Dmitri Fyodorovich; people don't know that side of me . . ."

"Madame, Madame!" Dmitri Fyodorovich interrupted with an uneasy presentiment. "I shall indeed, perhaps, follow your advice, your wise advice, Madame. . . . I shall perhaps set off . . . to the gold mines. . . . I'll come and see you again about it . . . many times, indeed . . . but now, that three thousand you so generously . . . oh, that would set me free, and if you could today . . . you see, I haven't a minute, a minute to lose today . . ."

"Enough, Dmitri Fyodorovich, enough!" Madame Khokhlakov interupted emphatically. "The question is, will you go to the gold mines or not; have you quite made up your mind? Answer mathematically."

---

1. The title of Turgenev's "farewell" to literature (1862). Turgenev continued writing till his death (1883).

"I will go, Madame, afterwards. . . . I'll go wherever you like . . . but now . . ."

"Wait!" cried Madame Khokhlakov. And jumping up and running to a handsome bureau with numerous little drawers, she began pulling out one drawer after another, looking for something with desperate haste.

"The three thousand," thought Mitya, his heart almost stopping, "and at once . . . without any papers or formalities . . . that's doing things in gentlemanly style! She's a splendid woman, if only she didn't talk so much!"

"Here!" cried Madame Khokhlakov, running back joyfully to Mitya, "here is what I was looking for!"

It was a tiny silver icon on a cord, such as is sometimes worn next to the skin with a cross.

"This is from Kiev, Dmitri Fyodorovich," she went on reverently, "from the relics of the Holy martyr, Barbara. Let me put it on your neck myself, and with it dedicate you to a new life, to a new career."

And she actually put the cord round his neck, and began arranging it. In extreme embarrassment, Mitya bent down and helped her, and at last he got it under his necktie and collar through his shirt to his chest.

"Now you can set off," Madame Khokhlakov pronounced, sitting down triumphantly in her place again.

"Madame, I am so touched. I don't know how to thank you, indeed . . . for such kindness, but . . . if only you knew how precious time is to me. . . . That sum of money, for which I shall be indebted to your generosity. . . . Oh, Madame, since you are so kind, so touchingly generous to me" (Mitya exclaimed impulsively) "then let me reveal to you . . . though, of course, you've known it a long time . . . that I love somebody here. . . . I have been false to Katya . . . Katerina Ivanovna I should say. . . . Oh, I've behaved inhumanly, dishonorably to her, but I fell in love here with another woman . . . a woman whom you, Madame, perhaps, despise, for you know everything already, but whom I cannot leave on any account, and therefore that three thousand now . . ."

"Leave everything, Dmitri Fyodorovich," Madame Khokhlakov interrupted in the most decisive tone. "Leave everything, especially women. Mines are your goal, and there's no place for women there. Afterwards, when you come back rich and famous, you will find the girl of your heart in the highest society. That will be a modern girl, a girl of education and advanced ideas. By that time the dawning woman question will have gained ground, and the new woman will have appeared."

"Madame, that's not the point, not at all. . . ." Mitya clasped his hands in entreaty.

"Yes, it is, Dmitri Fyodorovich, just what you need; the very thing you're yearning for, though you don't realize it yourself. I am not at all opposed to the present woman movement, Dmitri Fyodorovich. The development of woman, and even the political emancipation of woman in the near future—that's my ideal. I've a daughter myself, Dmitri Fyodorovich, people don't know that side of me. I wrote a letter to the author, Shchedrin,[2] on that subject. That author has taught me so much, so much about the vocation of woman. So last year I sent him an anonymous letter of two lines: 'I kiss and embrace you, my author, for the modern woman. Persevere.' And I signed myself, 'a Mother.' I thought of signing myself 'a contemporary Mother,' and hesitated, but I stuck to the simple 'Mother'; there's more moral beauty in that, Dmitri Fyodorovich. And the word 'contemporary' might have reminded him of *The Contemporary*—a painful recollection owing to the censorship. . . . Good Heavens, what is the matter!"

"Madame!" cried Mitya, jumping up at last, clasping his hands before her in helpless entreaty. "You will make me weep if you delay what you have so generously . . ."

"Oh, do weep, Dmitri Fyodorovich, do weep! That's a noble feeling . . . such a path lies open before you! Tears will ease your heart, and later on you will return rejoicing. You will hasten to me from Siberia on purpose to share your joy with me . . ."

"But allow me, too!" Mitya cried suddenly. "For the last time I entreat you, tell me, can I have the sum you promised me today, if not, when may I come for it?"

"What sum, Dmitri Fyodorovich?"

"The three thousand you promised me . . . that you so generously . . ."

"Three thousand? Rubles? Oh, no, I haven't got three thousand," Madame Khokhlakov announced with serene amazement. Mitya was stupefied.

"Why, you said just now . . . you said . . . you said it was as good as in my hands . . ."

"Oh, no, you misunderstood me, Dmitri Fyodorovich. In that case you misunderstood me. I was talking of the gold mines. It's true I promised you more, infinitely more than three thousand, I remember it all now, but I was referring to the mines."

"But the money? The three thousand?" Dmitri Fyodorovich exclaimed, stupidly.

"Oh, if you meant money, I haven't any. I haven't a penny, Dmitri Fyodorovich. I'm quarreling with my steward about it, and

2. M. E. Saltykov-Shchedrin (1826–1889) was a Russian satirist, publicist, spokesman for liberals, and publisher of the journal *The Contemporary*, which was closed by the censors in 1866. This was a blow to Saltykov. Later he edited *Notes of the Fatherland*, where he published a "Letter to Khokhlakov" in reply to Dostoevsky. There are extensive and bitter polemics between the two writers.

I've just borrowed five hundred rubles from Miüsov, myself. No, no, I've no money. And, do you know, Dmitri Fyodorovich, if I had, I wouldn't give it to you. In the first place I never lend money. Lending money means losing friends. And I wouldn't give it to you particularly. I wouldn't give it you, because I like you and want to save you, for all you need is the gold mines, the gold mines, the gold mines!"

"Oh, go to hell!" roared Mitya, and with all his might brought his fist down on the table.

"Aie! Aie!" cried Madame Khokhlakov, alarmed, and she flew to the other end of the drawing room.

Mitya spat on the floor, and strode rapidly out of the room, out of the house, into the street, into the darkness! He walked like one possessed, and beating himself on the breast, on the spot where he had struck himself two days previously, before Alyosha, the last time he saw him in the dark, on the road. What those blows upon his breast signified, *on that spot,* and what he meant by it—that was, for the time, a secret which was known to no one in the world, and had not been told even to Alyosha. But that secret meant for him more than disgrace; it meant ruin, suicide. So he had determined, if he did not get hold of the three thousand that would pay his debt to Katerina Ivanovna, and so remove from his breast, from *that spot on his breast,* the shame he carried upon it, that weighed on his conscience. All this will be fully explained to the reader later on, but now that his last hope had vanished, this man, so strong in appearance, burst out crying like a little child a few steps from the Khokhlakovs' house. He walked on, and not knowing what he was doing, wiped away his tears with his fist. In this way he reached the square, and suddenly became aware that he had stumbled against something. He heard a piercing wail from an old woman whom he had almost knocked down.

"Good Lord, you've nearly killed me! Why don't you look where you're going, rascal?"

"Why, it's you!" cried Mitya, recognizing the old woman in the dark. It was the old servant who waited on Samsonov, whom Mitya had particularly noticed the day before.

"And who are you, my good sir?" said the old woman in quite a different voice. "I don't know you in the dark."

"You live at Kuzma Kuzmich's. You're the servant there?"

"Just so, sir, I was only running out to Prokhorich's . . . But I don't know you now."

"Tell me, my good woman, is Agrafena Alexandrovna there now?" said Mitya, beside himself with suspense. "I saw her to the house some time ago."

"She has been there, sir. She stayed a little while, and went off again."

"What? Went away?" cried Mitya. "When did she go?"

"Why, as soon as she came. She only stayed a minute. She only told Kuzma Kuzmich a tale that made him laugh, and then she ran away."

"You're lying, damn you!" roared Mitya.

"Aie! Aie!" shrieked the old woman, but Mitya had vanished.

He ran with all his might to the house where Grushenka lived. At the moment he reached it, Grushenka was on her way to Mokroe. It was not more than a quarter of an hour after her departure. Fenya was sitting with her grandmother, the old cook, Matryona, in the kitchen when "the captain" ran in. Fenya uttered a piercing shriek on seeing him.

"You scream?" roared Mitya, "where is she?" But without giving the terror-stricken Fenya time to utter a word, he fell all of a heap at her feet.

"Fenya, for Christ's sake, tell me, where is she?"

"I don't know. Dmitri Fyodorovich, my dear, I don't know. You may kill me but I can't tell you." Fenya swore and protested. "You went out with her yourself not long ago . . ."

"She came back!"

"Indeed she didn't. By God I swear she didn't come back."

"You're lying!" shouted Mitya. "From your terror I know where she is."

He rushed away. Fenya in her fright was glad she had got off so easily. But she knew very well that it was only that he was in such haste, or she might not have fared so well. But as he ran, he surprised both Fenya and old Matryona by an unexpected action. On the table stood a brass mortar, with a pestle in it, a small brass pestle, not much more than six inches long. Mitya already had opened the door with one hand when, with the other, he snatched up the pestle, and thrust it in his side pocket and was off.

"Oh Lord! He's going to murder someone!" cried Fenya, flinging up her hands.

Chapter IV

In the Dark

Where was he running? Obviously, "where could she be except at Fyodor Pavlovich's? She must have run straight to him from Samsonov's, that was clear now. The whole intrigue, the whole deceit was evident." . . . It all rushed whirling through his mind. He did not run to Marya Kondratyevna's. "There was no need to go there . . . not the slightest need . . . he must raise no alarm . . . they would run and tell directly. . . . Marya Kondratyevna was clearly in the plot, Smerdyakov too, he too, all had been bought over!"

He formed another plan of action: he ran a long way round Fyodor Pavlovich's house, crossing the lane, running down Dmitrovsky Street, then over the little bridge, and so came straight to the deserted alley at the back, which was empty and uninhabited, with, on one side the hurdle fence of a neighbor's kitchen garden, on the other, the strong high fence that ran all round Fyodor Pavlovich's garden. Here he chose a spot, apparently the very place, where, according to the tradition, he knew Stinking Lizaveta had once climbed over it: "If she could climb over it," the thought, God knows why, occurred to him, "surely I can." He did in fact jump up, and instantly contrived to catch hold of the top of the fence. Then he vigorously pulled himself up and sat astride on it. Close by, in the garden, stood the bathhouse, but from the fence he could see the lighted window of the house too. "Yes, the old man's bedroom is lit up. She's there!" and he leaped from the fence into the garden. Though he knew Grigory was ill and very likely Smerdyakov, too, and that there was no one to hear him, he instinctively hid himself, stood still, and began to listen. But there was dead silence on all sides and, as though by design, complete stillness, not the slightest breath of wind.

"And nought but the whispering silence,"[3] the line for some reason rose to his mind. "If only no one heard me jump over the fence! I think not." After standing still for a minute, he walked softly over the grass in the garden, avoiding the trees and shrubs. He walked slowly, creeping stealthily at every step, listening to his own footsteps. It took him five minutes to reach the lighted window. He remembered that just under the window there were several thick and high bushes of elder and white hazel. The door from the house into the garden, on the left-hand side, was shut; he had carefully looked purposely to see, in passing. At last he reached the bushes and hid behind them. He held his breath. "I must wait now," he thought, "to reassure them, in case they heard my footsteps and are listening. . . . If only I don't cough or sneeze."

He waited two minutes. His heart was beating violently, and, at moments, he could scarcely breathe. "No, this throbbing at my heart won't stop," he thought. "I can't wait any longer." He was standing behind a bush in the shadow. The light of the window fell on the front part of the bush. "How red the white hazel berries are!"[4] he murmured, not knowing why. Softly and noiselessly, step by step, he approached the window, and raised himself on tiptoe. All Fyodor Pavlovich's bedroom lay open before him. It was not a

---

3. The quotation is a slightly inexact rendering of Book II, line 419 from Pushkin's jocular and mildly erotic narrative poem *Ruslan and Lyudmila* (1820). Though the context is very different, the text is worth quoting: "[She] does not sleep, redoubles attention,/Motionless looks into the darkness . . . /All is obscure, deathly silence!/(She) only hears the heart's throbbing . . . /And thinks . . . the silence whispers."

4. The lines have not yet been identified.

large room, and was divided in two parts by a red screen, "Chinese," as Fyodor Pavlovich used to call it. The word "Chinese" flashed into Mitya's mind, "and behind the screen, is Grushenka," thought Mitya. He began watching Fyodor Pavlovich, who was wearing his new striped-silk dressing gown, which Mitya had never seen, and a silk cord with tassels round the waist. A clean, dandified shirt of fine linen with gold studs peeped out under the collar of the dressing gown. On his head Fyodor Pavlovich had the same red bandage which Alyosha had seen.

"He has got himself up," thought Mitya. His father was standing near the window, apparently lost in thought. Suddenly he jerked up his head, listened a moment, and, hearing nothing, went up to the table, poured out half a glass of brandy from a decanter, and drank it off. Then he uttered a deep sigh, again stood still a moment, walked distractedly up to the mirror on the wall, with his right hand raised the red bandage on his forehead a little, and began examining his bruises and scars, which had not yet disappeared. "He's alone," thought Mitya, "in all probability he's alone." Fyodor Pavlovich moved away from the mirror, turned suddenly to the window and looked out. Mitya instantly slipped away into the shadow.

"She may be there behind the screen. Perhaps she's asleep by now," he thought, with a pang at his heart. Fyodor Pavlovich moved away from the window. "He's looking for her out of the window, so she'd not there. Why should he stare out into the dark? He's wild with impatience." . . . Mitya slipped back at once, and fell to gazing in at the window again. The old man was sitting down at the table, apparently disappointed. At last he put his elbow on the table, and laid his right cheek against his hand. Mitya watched him eagerly.

"He's alone, he's alone!" he repeated again. "If she were here, his face would be different." Strange to say, a queer, irrational vexation rose up in his heart that she was not here. "It's not that she's not here," he explained to himself, immediately, "but that I can't tell for certain whether she is or not." Mitya remembered afterwards that his mind was, at that moment, exceptionally clear, that he took in everything to the slightest detail, and missed no point. But a feeling of misery, the misery of uncertainty and indecision was growing in his heart with every instant. "Is she here or not?" The angry doubt filled his heart, and suddenly, making up his mind, he put out his hand and softly knocked on the window frame. He knocked the signal the old man had agreed upon with Smerdyakov, twice slowly and then three times more quickly, tap-tap-tap, the signal that meant "Grushenka is here!" The old man started, jerked up his head, and, jumping up quickly, ran to the window. Mitya slipped away into the shadow. Fyodor Pavlovich opened the window and thrust his whole head out.

"Grushenka, is it you? Is it you?" he said, in a sort of trembling half-whisper. "Where are you, my angel, where are you?" He was fearfully agitated and breathless.

"He's alone," Mitya decided.

"Where are you?" cried the old man again; and he thrust his head out further, thrust it out to the shoulders, gazing in all directions, right and left. "Come here, I've a little present for you. Come, I'll show you . . ."

"He means the three thousand," thought Mitya.

"But where are you? Are you at the door? I'll open it directly."

And the old man almost climbed out of the window, peering out to the right, where there was a door into the garden, trying to see into the darkness. In another second he would certainly have run out to open the door without waiting for Grushenka's answer. Mitya looked at him from the side without stirring. The old man's profile that he loathed so, his pendant Adam's apple, his hooked nose, his lips that smiled in greedy expectation, were all brightly lit up by the slanting lamplight falling on the left from the room. A horrible fury of hatred suddenly surged up in Mitya's heart, "There he was, his rival, the man who had tormented him, had ruined his life!" It was a rush of that sudden, furious, revengeful anger of which he had spoken, as though foreseeing it, to Alyosha, four days ago in the gazebo, in answer to Alyosha's question, "How can you say you'll kill our father?"

"I don't know, I don't know," he had said then. "Perhaps I shall not kill him, perhaps I shall. I'm afraid he'll suddenly be so loathsome to me *at that moment, with that face of his*. I hate his Adam's apple, his nose, his eyes, his shameless grin. I feel a personal repulsion. That's what I'm afraid of, that's what may be too much for me . . ."

This personal repulsion was growing unendurable. Mitya was beside himself. He suddenly pulled the brass pestle out of his pocket.

. . . . .

"God was watching over me then," Mitya himself said afterwards. At that very moment Grigory woke up on his bed of sickness. Earlier in the evening he had undergone the treatment which Smerdyakov had described to Ivan Fyodorovich. He had rubbed himself all over with vodka mixed with a secret very strong decoction, had drunk what was left of the mixture while his wife repeated a "certain prayer" over him, after which he had gone to bed. Martha Ignatyevna had tasted the stuff, too, and, being unused to strong drink, slept like the dead beside her husband.

But Grigory woke up in the night, quite suddenly, and, after a moment's reflection, though he immediately felt a sharp pain in his back, he sat up in bed. Then he deliberated again, got up and dressed hurriedly. Perhaps his conscience was uneasy at the thought of sleeping while the house was unguarded "in such perilous times." Smerdyakov, exhausted by his fit, lay motionless in the next room. Martha Ignatyevna did not stir. "The stuff's been too much for the woman," Grigory thought, glancing at her, and groaning, he went out on the steps. No doubt he only intended to look out from the steps, for he was hardly able to walk, the pain in his back and his right leg was intolerable. But he suddenly remembered that he had not locked the little gate into the garden that evening. He was the most punctual and precise of men, a man who adhered to an unchangeable routine, and habits that lasted for years. Limping and writhing with pain he went down the steps and towards the garden. Yes, the gate stood wide open. Mechanically he stepped into the garden. Perhaps he fancied something, perhaps caught some sound, and, glancing to the left he saw his master's window open. No one was looking out of it then.

"What's it open for? It's not summer now," thought Grigory, and suddenly, at that very instant he caught a glimpse of something extraordinary before him in the garden. Forty paces in front of him a man seemed to be running in the dark, a sort of shadow was moving very fast. "Good Lord!" cried Grigory beside himself, and forgetting the pain in his back, he hurried to intercept the running figure. He took a short cut, evidently he knew the garden better; the flying figure went towards the bathhouse, ran behind it and rushed to the garden fence. Grigory followed, not losing sight of him, and ran, forgetting everything. He reached the fence at the very moment the man was climbing over it. Grigory cried out, beside himself, pounced on him, and clutched his leg in his two hands.

Yes, his foreboding had not deceived him. He recognized him, it was he, the "monster," the "parricide."

"Parricide!" the old man shouted so that the whole neighborhod could hear, but he had not time to shout more, he fell at once, as though struck by lightning. Mitya jumped back into the garden and bent over the fallen man. In Mitya's hands was a brass pestle, and he flung it mechanically in the grass. The pestle fell two paces from Grigory, not in the grass but on the path, in a most conspicuous place. For some seconds he examined the prostrate figure before him. The old man's head was covered with blood. Mitya put out his hand and began feeling it. He remembered afterwards clearly, that he had been awfully anxious "to make sure" whether he had broken the old man's skull, or simply "stunned" him with the pestle. But the blood was flowing horribly; and in a moment Mitya's fingers were drenched with the hot stream. He remembered taking out of his pocket the clean white handkerchief with which he had provided himself for his visit to Madame Khokhlakov, and putting it to the old man's head, senselessly trying to wipe the blood from his face and temples. But the handkerchief was instantly soaked with blood.

"Good heavens! what am I doing it for?" thought Mitya, suddenly pulling himself together. "If I have broken his skull, how can I find out now? And what difference does it make now?" he added, hopelessly. "If I've killed him, I've killed him . . . you've come to grief, old man, so there you must lie!" he said aloud. And suddenly, turning to the fence, he vaulted over it into the lane and fell to running—the handkerchief soaked with blood he held, crushed up, in his right fist, and, as he ran, he thrust it into the back pocket of his coat. He ran headlong, and the few passersby who met him in the dark, in the streets, remembered afterwards that they had met a man running that night. He flew back again to the widow Morozov's house.

Immediately after he had left it, that evening, Fenya had rushed to the chief porter, Nazar Ivanovich, and begged him, for Christ's sake, "not to let the captain in again today or tomorrow." Nazar Ivanovich promised, but went upstairs to his mistress who had suddenly sent for him, and meeting his nephew, a boy of twenty, who had recently come from the country, on the way up told him to take his place, but forgot to mention "the captain." Mitya, running up to the gate, knocked. The lad instantly recognized him, for Mitya had more than once tipped him. Opening the gate at once, he let him in, and hastened to inform him with a good-humored smile that "Agrafena Alexandrovna is not at home now, you know."

"Where is she then, Prokhor?" asked Mitya, stopping short.

"She set off this evening, some two hours ago, with Timothy, to Mokroe."

"What for?" cried Mitya.

"That I can't say. To see some officer. Someone invited her and horses were sent to fetch her."

Mitya left him, and ran like a madman to Fenya.

Chapter V

A Sudden Resolution

She was sitting in the kitchen with her grandmother; they were both just going to bed. Relying on Nazar Ivanovich, they had not locked themselves in. Mitya ran in, pounced on Fenya and seized her by the throat.

"Speak at once! Where is she? With whom is she now, at Mok-roe?" he roared furiously.

Both the women squealed.

"Aie! I'll tell you. Aie, Dmitri Fyodorovich, darling, I'll tell you everything directly, I won't hide anything," gabbled Fenya, frightened to death; "she's gone to Mokroe, to her officer."

"What officer?" roared Mitya.

"To her officer, the same one she used to know, the one who threw her over five years ago," cackled Fenya, as fast as she could speak.

Mitya withdrew the hands with which he was squeezing her throat. He stood facing her, pale as death, unable to utter a word, but his eyes showed that he realized it all, all, from the first word, and guessed the whole position. Poor Fenya was not in a condition at that moment to observe whether he understood or not. She remained sitting on the trunk as she had been when he ran into the room, trembling all over, holding her hands out before her as though trying to defend herself. She seemed to have grown rigid in that position. Her wide-open, scared eyes were fixed immovably upon him. And to make matters worse, both his hands were smeared with blood. On the way, as he ran, he must have touched his forehead with them, wiping off the perspiration, so that on his forehead and his right cheek were bloodstained patches. Fenya was on the verge of hysterics. The old cook had jumped up and was staring at him like a madwoman, almost unconscious with terror.

Mitya stood for a moment, then mechanically sank on to a chair next to Fenya. He sat, not reflecting but, as it were, terror-stricken, benumbed. Yet everything was clear as day: that officer, he knew about him, he knew everything perfectly, he had known it from Grushenka herself, had known that a letter had come from him a month before. So that for a month, for a whole month this had been going on in secret from him, till the very arrival of this new man, and he had never thought of him! But how could he, how could he not have thought of him? Why was it he had forgotten this officer, like that, forgotten him as soon as he heard of him? That was the question that faced him like some monstrous thing. And he looked at this monstrous thing with horror, growing cold with horror.

But suddenly, as gently and mildly as a gentle and affectionate child, he began speaking to Fenya as though he had utterly forgotten how he had scared and hurt her just now. He fell to questioning Fenya with an extreme preciseness, astonishing in his position, and though the girl looked wildly at his bloodstained hands, she, too, with wonderful readiness and rapidity, answered every question as though eager to put the whole truth and nothing but the truth before him. Little by little, even with a sort of enjoyment, she began

'I don't understand' [margin annotation]

explaining every detail, not wanting to torment him, but, as it were, eager to be of the utmost service to him. She described the whole of that day, in great detail, the visit of Rakitin and Alyosha, how she, Fenya, had stood on the watch, how the mistress had set off, and how she had called out of the window to Alyosha to give him, Mitya, her greetings, and to tell him "to remember forever how she had loved him for an hour." Hearing of the message, Mitya suddenly smiled, and there was a flush of color on his pale cheeks. At the same moment Fenya said to him, not a bit afraid now to be inquisitive:

"Look at your hands, Dmitri Fyodorovich. They're all over blood!"

"Yes," answered Mitya mechanically. He looked carelessly at his hands and at once forgot them and Fenya's question. He sank into silence again. Twenty minutes had passed since he had run in. His first horror was over, but evidently some new fixed determination had taken possession of him. He suddenly stood up, smiling dreamily.

"What has happened to you, sir?" said Fenya, pointing to his hands again. She spoke compassionately, as though she felt very near to him now in his grief. Mitya looked at his hands again.

"'That's blood, Fenya," he said, looking at her with a strange expression. "That's human blood, and, my God! why was it shed? But ... Fenya ... there's a fence here" (he looked at her as though setting her a riddle) "a high fence, and terrible to look at. But, at dawn tomorrow, when the sun rises, Mitya will leap over that fence. ... You don't understand what fence, Fenya, and never mind. ... You'll hear tomorrow and understand ... and now, goodbye. I won't stand in her way. I'll step aside, I know how to step aside. Live, my joy. . . . You loved me for an hour, remember Mitenka Karamazov so forever. ... She always used to call me Mitenka, do you remember?"

And with those words he went suddenly out of the kitchen. Fenya was almost more frightened at this sudden departure than she had been when he ran in and attacked her.

Just ten minutes later Dmitri Fyodorovich went in to Pyotr Ilyich Perkhotin, the young official with whom he had pawned his pistols. It was by now half past eight, and Pyotr Ilyich had finished his evening tea, and had just put his coat on again to go to the Metropolis to play billiards. Mitya caught him coming out. Seeing him with his face all smeared with blood, the young man uttered a cry of surprise.

"Good heavens! What is the matter?"

"I've come for my pistols," said Mitya quickly, "and brought you the money. And thanks very much. I'm in a hurry, Pyotr Ilyich, please make haste."

Pyotr Ilyich grew more and more surprised; he suddenly caught sight of a bundle of bills in Mitya's hand, and what was more, he had walked in holding the bills as no one walks in and no one carries money: he had them in his right hand, and held them outstretched as if to show them. Perkhotin's servant boy, who met Mitya in the passage, said afterwards that he walked into the passage in the same way, with the money outstretched in his hand, so he must have been carrying them like that even in the street. They were all rainbow-colored hundred-ruble bills, and the fingers holding them were covered with blood. When Pyotr Ilyich was questioned later on as to the sum of money, he said that it was difficult to judge at a glance, but that it might have been two thousand, or perhaps three, but it was a big, "fat" bundle. "Dmitri Fyodorovich," so he testified afterwards, "seemed unlike himself, too; not drunk, but, as it were, exalted, lost to everything, but at the same time, as it were, absorbed, as though pondering and searching for something and unable to come to a decision. He was in great haste, answered abruptly and very strangely, and at moments seemed not at all dejected but quite cheerful."

"But what *is* the matter with you? What's wrong?" cried Pyotr Ilyich, looking wildly at his guest. "How is it that you're all covered with blood? Have you had a fall? Look at yourself!"

He took him by the elbow and led him to the glass.

Seeing his bloodstained face, Mitya started and scowled wrathfully.

"Damnation! That's the last straw," he muttered angrily, hurriedly changing the bills from his right hand to the left, and impulsively jerked the handkerchief out of his pocket. But the handkerchief turned out to be soaked with blood, too (it was the handkerchief he had used to wipe Grigory's face). There was scarcely a white spot on it, and it had not merely begun to dry, but had stiffened into a crumpled ball and could not be pulled apart. Mitya threw it angrily on the floor.

"Oh, damn it!" he said. "Haven't you a rag of some sort . . . to wipe my face?"

"So you're only stained, not wounded? You'd better wash," said Pyotr Ilyich. "Here's a washstand. I'll pour you out some water."

"A washstand? That's all right . . . but where am I to put this?" With the strangest perplexity he indicated his bundle of hundred-ruble bills, looking inquiringly at Pyotr Ilyich as though it were for him to decide what he, Mitya, was to do with his own money.

"In your pocket, or on the table here. They won't be lost."

"In my pocket? Yes, in my pocket. All right. . . . But, I say, that's all nonsense," he cried, as though suddenly coming out of his absorption. "Look here, let's first settle that business of the pistols. Give them back to me. Here's your money . . . because I am in great need of them . . . and I haven't a minute, a minute to spare."

And taking the topmost bill from the bundle he held it out to Pyotr Ilyich.

"But I don't have enough change. Don't you have anything smaller?"

"No," said Mitya, looking again at the bundle, and as though not trusting his own words he turned over two or three of the topmost ones. "No, they're all alike," he added, and again he looked inquiringly at Pyotr Ilyich.

"How have you grown so rich?" the latter asked. "Wait, I'll send my boy to Plotnikov's, they close late—to see if they won't change it. Here, Misha!" he called into the passage.

"To Plotnikov's shop—first rate!" cried Mitya, as though struck by an idea. "Misha," he turned to the boy as he came in, "look here, run to Plotnikov's and tell them that Dmitri Fyodorovich sends his greetings, and will be there directly. . . . But listen, listen, tell them to have champagne, three cases ready before I come, and packed as it was to take to Mokroe. I took four cases with me then," he added (suddenly addressing Pyotr Ilyich); "they know all about it, don't you trouble, Misha," he turned again to the boy. "Stay, listen; tell them to put in cheese, Strasbourg pâté, smoked fish, ham, caviar, and everything, everything they've got, up to a hundred rubles, or a hundred and twenty as before. . . . But wait: don't let them forget dessert, sweets, pears, watermelons, two or three or four—no, one melon's enough, and chocolate, candy, toffee, fondants; in fact, everything I took to Mokroe before, three hundred rubles' worth with the champagne . . . let it be just the same again. And remember, Misha, if you are called Misha. . . . His name is Misha, isn't it?" He turned to Pyotr Ilyich again.

"Wait a minute," Pyotr Ilyich intervened, listening and watching him uneasily, "you'd better go yourself and tell them. He'll muddle it."

"He will, I see he will! Eh, Misha! Why, I was going to kiss you for the commission. . . . If you don't make a mistake, there's ten rubles for you, run along, make haste. . . . Champagne's the chief thing, let them bring up champagne. And brandy, too, and red and white wine, and all I had then. . . . They know what I had then."

"But listen!" Pyotr Ilyich interrupted with some impatience. "I say, let him simply run and change the money and tell them not to close, and you go and tell them. . . . Give him your bill. Be off, Misha! Put your best leg forward!" Pyotr Ilyich seemed to hurry Misha off on purpose, because the boy remained standing with his mouth and eyes wide open, apparently understanding little of Mitya's orders, gazing up with amazement and terror at his bloodstained face and the trembling bloodstained fingers that held the bills.

"Well, now come and wash," said Pyotr Ilyich, sternly. "Put the money on the table or else in your pocket. . . . That's right, come along. But take off your coat."

And beginning to help him off his coat, he cried out again:

"Look, your coat's covered with blood, too!"

"That . . . it's not the coat. It's only a little here on the sleeve. . . . And that's only here where the handkerchief lay. It must have soaked through. I must have sat on the handkerchief at Fenya's, and the blood's come through," Mitya explained at once with astounding ingenuousness. Pyotr Ilyich listened, frowning.

"Well, you must have been up to something; you must have been fighting with someone," he muttered.

They began to wash. Pyotr Ilyich held the jug and poured out the water. Mitya, in desperate haste, scarcely soaped his hands (they were trembling, and Pyotr Ilyich remembered it afterwards). But the young official insisted on his soaping them thoroughly and rubbing them more. He seemed to exercise more and more sway over Mitya, as time went on. It may be noted in passing that he was a young man of sturdy character.

"Look, you haven't got your nails clean. Now rub your face; here, on your temples, by your ear. . . . Will you go in that shirt? Where are you going? Look, all the cuff of your right sleeve is covered with blood."

"Yes, it's all bloody," observed Mitya, looking at the cuff of his shirt.

"Then change your shirt."

"I don't have time. You see I'll . . ." Mitya went on with the same confiding ingenuousness, drying his face and hands on the towel, and putting on his coat. "I'll turn it up at the wrist. It won't be seen under the coat. . . . You see!"

"Tell me now, what game have you been up to? Have you been fighting with someone? In the tavern again, as before? Have you been beating that captain again?" Pyotr Ilyich asked him reproachfully. "Whom have you been beating now . . . or killing, perhaps?"

"Nonsense!" said Mitya.

"Why 'nonsense'?"

"Don't worry," said Mitya, and he suddenly laughed. "I smashed an old woman in the marketplace just now."

"Smashed? An old woman?"

"An old man!" cried Mitya, looking Pyotr Ilyich straight in the face, laughing, and shouting at him as though he were deaf.

"Confound it! An old woman, an old man. . . . Have you killed someone?"

"We made it up. We had a row—and made it up. In a place I know of. We parted friends. A fool. . . . He's forgiven me. . . . He's sure to have forgiven me by now . . . if he had got up, he wouldn't have forgiven me"—Mitya suddenly winked—"only, damn him, you know, I say, Pyotr Ilyich, damn him! Don't worry about him! I don't want to just now!" Mitya snapped out, resolutely.

"Whatever do you want to go picking quarrels with everyone for? . . . Just as you did with that captain over some nonsense. . . .

You've been fighting and now you're rushing off on the spree—that's you all over! Three cases of champagne—what do you want all that for?"

"Bravo! Now give me the pistols. Upon my honor I've no time now. I should like to have a chat with you, my dear boy, but I haven't the time. And there's no need, it's too late for talking. Where's my money? Where have I put it?" he cried, thrusting his hands into his pockets.

"You put it on the table . . . yourself. . . . Here it is. Had you forgotten? Money's like dirt or water to you, it seems. Here are your pistols. It's an odd thing, at six o'clock you pledged them for ten rubles, and now you've got thousands. Two or three I should say."

"Three, you bet," laughed Mitya, stuffing the notes into the side pocket of his trousers.

"You'll lose it like that. Have you found a gold mine?"

"The mines? The gold mines?" Mitya shouted at the top of his voice and went off in a roar of laughter. "Would you like to go to the mines, Perkhotin? There's a lady here who'll stump up three thousand for you, if only you'll go. She did it for me, she's so awfully fond of gold mines. Do you know Madame Khokhlakov?"

"I don't know her, but I've heard of her and seen her. Did she really give you three thousand? Did she really?" said Pyotr Ilyich, eyeing him dubiously.

"As soon as the sun rises tomorrow, as soon as Phoebus, ever young, flies upwards, praising and glorifying God, you go to her, this Madame Khokhlakov, and ask her whether she did stump up that three thousand or not. Try and find out."

"I don't know on what terms you are . . . since you say it so positively, I suppose she did give it to you. You've got the money in your paw, but instead of going to Siberia you're spending it all. . . . Where are you really off to now, eh?"

"To Mokroe."

"To Mokroe? But it's night!"

"Once the lad had all, now the lad has nought," cried Mitya suddenly.

"How 'nought'? You say that with all those thousands!"

"I'm not talking about thousands. Damn thousands! I'm talking of the female character.

> Fickle is the heart of woman
> Treacherous and full of vice;[5]

I agree with Ulysses.[6] That's what he says."

---

5. From Tyutchev's translation of Schiller's "Das Siegesfest" (Victory celebration).

6. Homer's *Odyssey* was also translated by Zhukovsky.

"I don't understand you!"

"Am I drunk?"

"Not drunk, but worse."

"I'm drunk in spirit, Pyotr Ilyich, drunk in spirit! But that's enough!"

"What are you doing, loading the pistol?"

"I'm loading the pistol."

Unfastening the pistol case, Mitya actually opened the powder horn, and carefully sprinkled and rammed in the charge. Then he took the bullet and before inserting it, held it in two fingers in front of the candle.

"Why are you looking at the bullet?" asked Pyotr Ilyich, watching him with uneasy curiosity.

"Oh, a fancy. Why, if you meant to put that bullet in your brain, would you look at it or not?"

"Why look at it?"

"It's going into my brain, so it's interesting to look and see what it's like. But that's foolishness, a moment's foolishness. Now that's done," he added, putting in the bullet and driving it home with the ramrod. "Pyotr Ilyich, my dear fellow, that's nonsense, all nonsense, and if only you knew what nonsense! Give me a little piece of paper now."

"Here's some paper."

"No, a clean new piece, writing paper. That's right."

And taking a pen from the table, Mitya rapidly wrote two lines, folded the paper in four, and thrust it in his waistcoat pocket. He put the pistols in the case, locked it up, and kept it in his hand. Then he looked at Pyotr Ilyich with a slow, thoughtful smile.

"Now, let's go," he said.

"Where are we going? No, wait a minute. . . . Are you thinking of putting that bullet in your brain, perhaps?" Pyotr Ilyich asked uneasily.

"I was fooling about the bullet! I want to live. I love life! You may be sure of that. I love golden-haired Phoebus and his warm light. . . . Dear Pyotr Ilyich, do you know how to step aside?"

"What do you mean by 'stepping aside'?"

"Making way. Making way for a dear creature, and for one I hate. And to let the one I hate become dear—that's what making way means! And to say to them: God bless you, go your way, pass on, while I . . ."

"While you?"

"That's enough, let's go."

"Upon my word. I'll tell someone to prevent your going there," said Pyotr Ilyich, looking at him. "What are you going to Mokroe for, now?"

"There's a woman there, a woman. That's enough for you. You shut up."

"Listen, though you're such a savage I've always liked you. . . . I feel anxious."

"Thanks, old fellow. I'm a savage you say. Savages, savages! That's what I am always saying. Savages! Why, here's Misha! I was forgetting him."

Misha ran in, post haste, with a handful of bills in change, and reported that everyone was in a bustle at the Plotnikovs'; "They're carrying down the bottles, and the fish, and the tea; it will all be ready directly." Mitya seized ten rubles and handed it to Pyotr Ilyich, then tossed another ten-ruble note to Misha.

"Don't dare to do such a thing!" cried Pyotr Ilyich. "I won't have it in my house, it's a bad, demoralizing habit. Put your money away. Here, put it here, why waste it? It would come in handy tomorrow, and I daresay you'll be coming to me to borrow ten rubles again. Why do you keep putting the bills in your side pocket? Ah, you'll lose them!"

"I say, my dear fellow, let's go to Mokroe together."

"What should I go for?"

"I say, let's open a bottle at once, and drink to life! I want to drink, and especially to drink with you. I've never drunk with you, have I?"

"Very well, we can go the Metropolis. I was just going there."

"I haven't time for that. Let's drink at the Plotnikovs', in the back room. Shall I ask you a riddle?"

"Ask away."

Mitya took the piece of paper out of his waistcoat pocket, unfolded it and showed it. In a large, distinct hand was written:

"I punish myself for my whole life, my whole life I punish!"

"I certainly will speak to someone. I'll go at once," said Pyotr Ilyich, after reading the paper.

"You won't have time, dear boy, come and have a drink. March!"

Plotnikov's shop was at the corner of the street next door but one to Pyotr Ilyich's. It was the largest grocery shop in our town, and by no means a bad one, belonging to some rich merchants. They kept everything that could be got in a Petersburg shop, grocery of all sorts, wines "bottled by the brothers Eliseyev," fruits, cigars, tea, coffee, sugar, and so on. There were three shop assistants and two errand boys always employed. Though our part of the country had grown poorer, the landowners had gone away, and trade had got worse, yet the grocery stores flourished as before, every year with increasing prosperity; there were plenty of purchasers for their goods. They were awaiting Mitya with impatience in the shop. They had vivid recollections of how he had bought, three or four weeks ago, wine and goods of all sorts to the value of several hundred rubles, paid for in cash (they would never have let him have anything on credit, of course). They remembered that then, as now, he had had a bundle of hundred-ruble bills in his hand, and had scattered them at random, without bargaining, without reflecting, or caring to reflect what use so much wine and provisions would be to him. The story was told all over the town that driving off then with Grushenka to Mokroe he had "spent three thousand in one night and the following day, and had come back from the spree without a penny, cleaned out." He had picked up a whole troop of gypsies (encamped in our neighborhood at the time), who for two days got money without stint out of him while he was drunk, and drank expensive wine without stint. People used to tell, laughing at Mitya, how he had given champagne to grimy-handed peasants, and feasted the village women and girls on sweets and Strasbourg pâté. Though to laugh at Mitya to his face was rather a risky proceeding, there was much laughter behind his back, especially in the tavern, at his own ingenuous public avowal that all he had got out of Grushenka by this "escapade" was "permission to kiss her foot, and that was the utmost she had allowed him."

By the time Mitya and Pyotr Ilyich reached the shop, they found a cart with three horses harnessed abreast with bells, and with Andrey, the driver, ready waiting for Mitya at the entrance. In the shop they had almost entirely finished packing one box of provisions, and were only waiting for Mitya's arrival to nail it down and put it in the cart. Pyotr Ilyich was astounded.

"Where did this cart come from in such a hurry?" he asked Mitya.

"I met Andrey as I ran to you, and told him to drive straight here to the shop. There's no time to lose. Last time I drove with Timothy, but Timothy now has gone on before me with a certain enchantress. Shall we be very late, Andrey?"

"They'll only get there an hour at most before us, not even that maybe. I got Timothy ready to start. I know how he'll go. Their pace won't be ours, Dmitri Fyodorovich. How could it be? They won't get there an hour earlier!" Andrey, a lanky, red-haired, middle-aged driver, wearing a full-skirted coat, and with a caftan on his arm, replied warmly.

"Fifty rubles for vodka if we're only an hour behind them."

"I'll guarantee the time, Dmitri Fyodorovich. Ech, they won't be half an hour before us, let alone an hour."

Though Mitya bustled about seeing after things, he gave his orders strangely, as it were disconnectedly, and inconsecutively. He began a sentence and forgot the end of it. Pyotr Ilyich found himself obliged to come to the rescue.

"Four hundred rubles' worth, not less than four hundred rubles' worth, just as it was then," commanded Mitya. "Four cases of champagne, not a bottle less."

"What do you want with so much? What's it for? Wait!" cried Pyotr Ilyich. "What's this box? What's in it? Surely there isn't four hundred rubles' worth here?"

The officious shopmen began explaining with oily politeness that the first box contained only half a case of champagne, and only "the most indispensable articles" such as appetizers, sweets, toffee, and so on. But the main part of the "comestibles" ordered would be packed and sent off, as on the previous occasion, in a special cart, also with three horses, traveling at full speed, so that it would arrive not more than an hour later than Dmitri Fyodorovich himself.

"Not more than an hour! Not more than an hour! And put in more toffee and fondants. The girls there are so fond of it," Mitya insisted hotly.

"The fondants are all right. But what do you want with four cases of champagne? One would be enough," said Pyotr Ilyich, almost angry. He began bargaining, asking for a bill of the goods, and refused to be satisfied. But he only succeeded in saving a hundred rubles. In the end it was agreed that only three hundred rubles' worth should be sent.

"Well, you may go to the devil!" said Pyotr Ilyich, on second thought. "What's it to do with me? Throw away your money, since it's cost you nothing."

"This way, my economist, this way, don't be angry." Mitya drew him into a room at the back of the shop. "They'll give us a bottle here directly. We'll taste it. Ech, Pyotr Ilyich, come along with me, for you're a nice fellow, the sort I like."

Mitya sat down on a wicker chair, before a little table, covered with a filthy dinner napkin. Pyotr Ilyich sat down opposite, and the champagne soon appeared, and oysters were suggested to the gentlemen. "First class oysters, the last lot in."

"To hell with the oysters. I don't eat them. And we don't need anything," cried Pyotr Ilyich, almost angrily.

"There's no time for oysters," said Mitya. "And I'm not hungry. Do you know, friend," he said suddenly, with feeling, "I have never liked all this disorder."

"Who does like it? Three cases of champagne for peasants, upon my word, that's enough to make anyone angry!"

"That's not what I mean. I'm talking of a higher order. There's no order in me, no higher order. But . . . that's all over. There's no need to grieve about it. It's too late, damn it! My whole life has been disorder, and one must set it in order. Is that a pun, eh?"

"You're raving, not making puns!"

"Glory be to God in Heaven,
Glory be to God in me . . .

That verse came from my heart once, it's not a verse, but a tear. . . . I wrote it myself . . . not while I was pulling the captain's beard, though . . ."

"Why do you bring him in all of a sudden?"

"Why do I bring him in? Foolery! All things come to an end; all things are made equal. That's the long and short of it."

"You know, I keep thinking of your pistols."

"That's all foolery, too! Drink, and don't be fanciful. I love life. I've loved life too much, shamefully much. Enough! Let's drink to life, dear boy, I propose the toast. Why am I pleased with myself? I'm a scoundrel, but I'm satisfied with myself. And yet I'm tortured by the thought that I'm a scoundrel, but satisfied with myself. I bless creation. I'm ready to bless God and His creation directly, but . . . I must kill one noxious insect for fear it should crawl and spoil life for others. . . . Let us drink to life, dear brother. What can be more precious than life? Nothing, nothing! To life, and to one queen of queens."

"Let's drink to life and to your queen, too, if you like."

They drank a glass each. Although Mitya was excited and expansive, yet he was melancholy, too. It was as though some heavy, overwhelming anxiety were weighing upon him.

"Misha . . . here's your Misha come! Misha, come here, my boy, drink this glass to Phoebus, the golden-haired, of tomorrow morn . . ."

"What are you giving it to him for?" cried Pyotr Ilyich, irritably.

"Yes, yes, yes, let me! I want to!"

"E—ech!"

Misha emptied the glass, bowed, and ran out.

"He'll remember it afterwards," Mitya remarked. "Woman, I love woman! What is woman? The queen of creation! My heart is sad, my heart is sad, Pyotr Ilyich. Do you remember Hamlet? 'I am very sorry, good Horatio! Alas, poor Yorick!' Perhaps that's me, Yorick? Yes, I'm Yorick now, and a skull afterwards."

Pyotr Ilyich listened in silence. Mitya, too, was silent for awhile.

"What dog's that you've got here?" he asked the shopman, casually, noticing a pretty little lapdog with dark eyes, sitting in the corner.

"It belongs to Barbara Alexyeevna, the mistress," answered the clerk. "She brought it and forgot it here. It must be taken back to her."

"I saw one like it . . . in the regiment . . ." murmured Mitya dreamily, "only that one had its hind leg broken. . . . By the way,

Pyotr Ilyich, I wanted to ask you: have you ever stolen anything in your life?"

"What a question!"

"Oh, I didn't mean anything. From somebody's pocket, you know. I don't mean government money, everyone steals that, and no doubt you do, too . . ."

"You go to the devil."

"I'm talking of other people's money. Stealing straight out of a pocket? Out of a purse, eh?"

"I stole twenty kopecks from my mother when I was nine years old. I took it off the table on the sly, and held it tight in my hand."

"Well, and what happened?"

"Oh, nothing. I kept it three days, then I felt ashamed, confessed and gave it back."

"And what then?"

"Naturally I was whipped. But why do you ask? Have you stolen something?"

"I have," said Mitya, winking slyly.

"What have you stolen?" inquired Pyotr Ilyich curiously.

"I stole twenty kopecks from my mother when I was nine years old, and gave it back three days later." After he said this, Mitya suddenly got up.

"Dmitri Fyodorovich, won't you come now?" called Andrey from the door of the shop.

"Are you ready? We'll come!" Mitya started. "A few more last words and . . . Andrey, a glass of vodka as we leave. Give him some brandy as well! That box" (the one with the pistols) "put under my seat. Goodbye, Pyotr Ilyich, think kindly of me."

"But you're coming back tomorrow?"

"Of course."

"Will you settle the little bill now?" cried the clerk, springing forward.

"Oh yes, the bill. Of course."

He pulled the bundle of bills out of his pocket again, picked out three hundred rubles, threw them on the counter, and ran hurriedly out of the shop. Everyone followed him out, bowing and wishing him good luck. Andrey, coughing from the brandy he had just swallowed, jumped up on the box. But Mitya was only just taking his seat when suddenly, to his surprise, he saw Fenya before him. She ran up panting, clasped her hands before him with a cry, and plumped down at his feet.

"Dmitri Fyodorovich, dear good Dmitri Fyodorovich don't harm my mistress. And it was I who told you all about it. . . . And don't murder him, he came first, he's hers! He'll marry Agrafena Alexandrovna now. That's why he's come back from Siberia.

Dmitri Fyodorovich, dear, don't take a fellow creature's life!"

"Tut—tut—tut! That's it, is it? So you're off there to make trouble!" muttered Pyotr Ilyich. "Now, it's all clear, as clear as daylight. Dmitri Fyodorovich, give me your pistols at once if you mean to behave like a man," he shouted aloud to Mitya. "Do you hear, Dmitri?"

"The pistols? Wait a bit, brother, I'll throw them into the pool on the road," answered Mitya. "Fenya, get up, don't kneel to me. Mitya won't hurt anyone, the silly fool won't hurt anyone again. But I say, Fenya," he shouted, after having taken his seat. "I hurt you just now, so forgive me and have pity on me, forgive a scoundrel. . . . But it doesn't matter if you don't. It's all the same now. Now then, Andrey, look alive, fly along full speed!"

Andrey whipped up the horses, and the bells began ringing.

"Goodbye, Pyotr Ilyich! My last tear is for you! . . ."

"He's not drunk, but he keeps babbling like a lunatic," Pyotr Ilyich thought as he watched him go. He had half a mind to stay and see the cart packed with the remaining wines and provisions, knowing that they would deceive and defraud Mitya. But, suddenly feeling vexed with himself, he turned away with a curse and went to the tavern to play billiards.

"He's a fool, though he's a good fellow," he muttered as he went. "I've heard of that officer, Grushenka's former flame. Well, if he has turned up. . . . Ech, those pistols! Damn it all! I'm not his nurse! Let them do what they like! Besides, it'll all come to nothing. They're a set of brawlers, that's all. They'll drink and fight, fight and make friends again. They are not men who do anything real. What does he mean by 'I'm stepping aside, I'm punishing myself'? It'll come to nothing! He's shouted such phrases a thousand times, drunk, in the taverns. But now he's not drunk. 'Drunk in spirit'— they're fond of fine phrases, the villains. Am I his nurse? He must have been fighting, his whole mug was bloody. With whom? I shall find out at the Metropolis. And his handkerchief was soaked in blood. . . . Fooh, damn it, it's still lying on my floor. . . . The hell with it!"

He reached the tavern in a bad humor and at once made up a game. The game cheered him. He played a second game, and suddenly began telling one of his partners that Dmitri Karamazov had come in for some cash again—something like three thousand rubles, and had gone to Mokroe again to spend it with Grushenka. . . . This news aroused singular interest in his listeners. They all spoke of it, not laughing, but with a strange gravity. They stopped playing.

"Three thousand? But where can he have got three thousand?"

Questions were asked. The story of Madame Khokhlakov's present was received with scepticism.

"Hasn't he robbed his old father, that's the question?"

"Three thousand! There's something odd about it."

"He boasted aloud that he would kill his father; we all heard him, here. And it was three thousand he talked about . . ."

Pyotr Ilyich listened. All at once he became short and dry in his answers. He said not a word about the blood on Mitya's face and hands, though he had meant to speak of it at first.

They began a third game, and by degrees the talk about Mitya died away. But by the end of the third game, Pyotr Ilyich felt no more desire for billiards; he laid down the cue, and without having supper as he had intended, he walked out of the tavern. When he reached the marketplace he stood still in perplexity, wondering at himself. He realized that what he wanted was to go to Fyodor Pavlovich's and find out if anything had happened there, "On account of some stupid nonsense—as it's sure to turn out—am I going to wake up the household and make a scandal? Fooh! damn it, is it my business to look after them?"

In a very bad humor he went straight home, and suddenly remembered Fenya. "Damn it all! I ought to have questioned her just now," he thought with vexation, "I should have heard everything." And the desire to speak to her, and so find out, became so pressing and importunate that when he was halfway home he turned abruptly and went towards the house where Grushenka lodged. Going up to the gate he knocked. The sound of the knock in the silence of the night sobered him and made him feel annoyed. And no one answered him; everyone in the house was asleep. "And I shall be making a fuss!" he thought, with a feeling of positive discomfort. But instead of going away altogether, he fell to knocking again with all his might, filling the street with clamor. "Not coming? Well, I will wake them up, I will!" he muttered at each knock, fuming at himself, but at the same time he redoubled his knocks on the gate.

Chapter VI

"I Am Coming, Too!"

But Dmitri Fyodorovich was speeding along the road. It was a little more than twelve miles to Mokroe, but Andrey's three horses galloped at such a pace that the distance might be covered in an hour and a quarter. The swift motion revived Mitya. The air was fresh and cool, there were big stars shining in the sky. It was the very night, and perhaps the very hour, in which Alyosha fell on the earth, and rapturously swore "to love it forever and ever." But all was confusion, confusion, in Mitya's soul, and although many things were goading his heart, at that moment his whole being was yearning for her, his queen, to whom he was flying to look on her for the last time. One thing I can say for certain; his heart did not waver for one instant. I shall perhaps not be believed when I say that this jealous lover felt not the slightest jealousy of this new man, new rival, this officer, who seemed to have sprung out of the earth. If any other had appeared on the scene, he would have been jealous at once, and would perhaps have stained his terrible hands with blood again. But as he flew through the night, he felt no envy, no hostility even, for the man who had been her first lover. . . . It is true he had not yet seen him. "Here there was no room for dispute; it was her right and his; this was her first love which, after five years, she had not forgotten; so she had loved him only for those five years, and I, how do I come in? What right have I? Step aside, Mitya, and make way! What am I now? Now everything is over apart from the officer—even if he had not appeared, everything would be over . . ."

These words would roughly have expressed his feelings, if he had been capable of reasoning. But he could not reason at that moment. His present plan of action had arisen without reasoning. At Fenya's first words, it had sprung from feeling, and been adopted in a flash, with all its consequences. And yet, in spite of his resolution, there was confusion in his soul, an agonizing confusion: his resolution did not give him peace. There was so much behind that tortured him. And it seemed strange to him, at moments, to think that he had written his own sentence of death with pen and paper: "I punish myself," and the paper was lying there in his pocket, ready; the pistol was loaded; he had already resolved how, next morning, he would meet the first warm ray of "golden-haired Phoebus." And yet he could not be rid of the past, of all that he had left behind and that tortured him. He felt that miserably, and the thought of it sank into his heart with despair. There was one moment when he felt an impulse to stop Andrey, to jump out of the cart, to pull out his loaded pistol, and to make an end of everything without waiting for the dawn. But that moment flew by like a spark. The horses galloped on, "devouring space," and as he drew near his goal, again the thought of her, of her alone, took more and more complete possession of his soul, chasing away the fearful images that had been haunting it. Oh, how he longed to look upon her, if only for a moment, if only from a distance! "She's now with *him*," he thought, "now I shall see what she looks like with him, her first love, and that's all I want." Never had this woman, who was such a fateful influence in his life, aroused such love in his breast, such new and unknown feeling, surprising even to himself, a feeling tender to devoutness, to self-effacement before her! "I will efface myself!" he said, in a rush of almost hysterical ecstasy.

They had been galloping nearly an hour. Mitya was silent, and though Andrey was, as a rule, a talkative peasant, he did not utter a word, either. He seemed afraid to talk, he only whipped up smartly his three lean, but mettlesome, bay horses. Suddenly Mitya cried out in horrible anxiety:

"Andrey! What if they're asleep?"

This thought fell upon him like a blow. It had not occurred to him before.

"It may well be that they're gone to bed, by now, Dmitri Fyodorovich."

Mitya frowned as though in pain. Yes, indeed . . . he was rushing there . . . with such feelings . . . while they were asleep . . . she was asleep, perhaps, there too. . . . And angry feeling surged up in his heart.

"Drive on, Andrey! Whip them up! Look alive!" he cried, beside himself.

"But maybe they're not in bed!" Andrey reconsidered after a pause. "Timothy said there were a lot of them there . . ."

"At the station?"

"Not at the posting station, but at Plastunov's, at the inn, where they let out horses, too."

"I know. So you say there are a lot of them? How's that? Who are they?" cried Mitya, greatly dismayed at this unexpected news.

"Well, Timothy was saying they're all gentlefolk. Two from our town—who they are I can't say—and there are two others, strangers, maybe more besides. I didn't ask particularly. They've set to playing cards, so Timothy said."

"Cards?"

"So, maybe they're not in bed if they're at cards. It's most likely not more than eleven."

"Quicker, Andrey! Quicker!" Mitya cried again, nervously.

"May I ask you something, sir?" said Andrey, after a pause. "Only I'm afraid of angering you, sir."

"What is it?"

"Why, Fenya threw herself at your feet just now, and begged you not to harm her mistress, and someone else, too . . . so you see, sir . . . It's I am taking you there . . . forgive me, sir, it's my conscience . . . maybe it's stupid of me to speak of it . . ."

Mitya suddenly seized him by the shoulders from behind.

"Are you a driver? A driver?" he asked frantically.

"Yes, sir . . ."

"Then you know that one has to make way. What would you say to a driver who wouldn't make way for anyone, but would just drive on and crush people? No, a driver mustn't run over people. One can't run over a man. One can't spoil people's lives. And if you have spoiled a life—punish yourself. . . . If you've spoiled a life, if only you've ruined any one's life—punish yourself and go away."

These phrases burst from Mitya almost hysterically. Though Andrey was surprised at him, he kept up the conversation.

"That's right, Dmitri Fyodorovich, you're quite right, one mustn't crush or torment a man, or any kind of creature, for every creature is created by God. Take a horse, for instance, for some folks, even among us drivers, drive anyhow. Nothing will restrain them, they just force it along."

"To hell?" Mitya interrupted, and went off into his abrupt, short laugh. "Andrey, simple soul," he seized him by the shoulders again, "tell me, will Dmitri Fyodorovich Karamazov go to hell, or not, what do you think?"

"I don't know, dear man, it depends on you, for you are . . . you see, sir, when the Son of God was nailed on the Cross and died, He went straight down to hell from the Cross, and set free all sinners that were in agony. And the devil groaned, because he thought that he would get no more sinners in hell. And God said to him, then, 'Don't groan, for you shall have all the mighty of the earth, the rulers, the chief judges, and the rich men, and shall be filled up as you have been in all the ages till I come again.' Those were His very words . . ."

"A peasant legend! Capital! Whip up the left, Andrey!"

"So you see, sir, who it is hell's for," said Andrey, whipping up the left horse, "but you're like a little child . . . that's how we look on you . . . and though you're hasty-tempered, sir, yet God will forgive you for your kind heart."

"And you, do you forgive me, Andrey?"

"What should I forgive you for, sir? You've never done me any harm."

"No, for everyone, for everyone, you here alone, on the road, will you forgive me for everyone? Speak, simple peasant heart!"

"Oh, sir! I feel afraid of driving you, your talk is so strange."

But Mitya did not hear. He was frantically praying and muttering to himself.

"Lord, receive me, with all my lawlessness, and do not condemn me. Let me pass by Thy judgment . . . do not condemn me, for I have condemned myself, do not condemn me, for I love Thee, O Lord. I am a wretch, but I love Thee. If Thou sendest me to hell, I shall love Thee there, and from there I shall cry out that I love Thee forever and ever. . . . But let me love to the end. . . . Here and now for just five hours . . . till the first ardent ray of Thy day . . . for I love the queen of my soul . . . I love her and I cannot help loving her. Thou seest my whole heart. . . . I shall gallop up, I shall fall before her and say, 'You are right to pass on and leave me. Farewell and forget your victim . . . never fret yourself about me!' "

"Mokroe!" cried Andrey, pointing ahead with his whip.

Through the pale darkness of the night loomed a solid black

mass of buildings, flung down, as it were, on the vast plain. The village of Mokroe numbered two thousand inhabitants, but at that hour all were asleep, and only here and there a few lights still twinkled.

"Drive on, Andrey, I am coming!" Mitya exclaimed, feverishly.

"They're not asleep," said Andrey again, pointing with his whip to the Plastunovs' inn, which was at the entrance to the village. The six windows, looking on the street, were all brightly lit up.

"They're not asleep," Mitya repeated, joyously. "Quicker, Andrey! Gallop! Drive up with a dash! Set the bells ringing! Let all know that I have come. I'm coming! I'm coming, too!"

Andrey lashed his exhausted team into a gallop, drove with a dash and pulled up his steaming, panting horses at the high flight of steps. Mitya jumped out of the cart just as the innkeeper, on his way to bed, peered out from the steps curious to see who had arrived.

"Trifon Borisich, is that you?"

The innkeeper bent down, looked intently, ran down the steps, and rushed up to the guest with obsequious delight.

"Dmitri Fyodorovich, your honor! Do I see you again?"

Trifon Borisich was a thickset, healthy peasant, of middle height, with a rather fat face. His expression was severe and uncompromising, especially with the peasants of Mokroe, but he had the power of assuming the most obsequious countenance, when he had an inkling that it was in his interest. He dressed in Russian style, with a shirt buttoning down on one side, and a full-skirted coat. He had saved a good sum of money, but was forever dreaming of improving his position. More than half the peasants were in his clutches, everyone in the neighborhood was in debt to him. From the neighboring landowners he bought and rented lands which were worked by the peasants, in payment of debts which they could never shake off. He was a widower, with four grown-up daughters. One of them was already a widow and lived in the inn with her two children, his grandchildren, and worked for him like a charwoman. Another of his daughters was married to a petty official and in one of the rooms of the inn, on the wall could be seen among the family photographs a miniature photograph of this official in uniform and official epaulettes. The two younger daughters used to wear fashionable blue or green dresses, fitting tight at the back, and with trains a yard long, on Church holidays or when they went to pay visits. But next morning they would get up at dawn, as usual, sweep out the rooms with a birch broom, empty the slops, and clean up after lodgers. In spite of the thousands of rubles he had saved, Trifon Borisich was very fond of emptying the pockets of a drunken guest, and, remembering that not a month ago he had, in twenty-four hours, made two if not three hundred rubles out of

Dmitri, when he had come on his escapade with Grushenka, he met him now with an eager welcome, scenting his prey the moment Mitya drove up to the steps.

"Dmitri Fyodorovich, dear sir, we see you once more!"

"Wait, Trifon Borisich," began Mitya, "first and foremost, where is she?"

"Agrafena Alexandrovna?" The innkeeper understood at once, looking sharply into Mitya's face. "She's here, too . . ."

"With whom? With whom?"

"Some strangers. One is an official gentleman, a Pole, to judge from his speech. He sent the horses for her from here; and there's another with him, a friend of his, or a fellow traveler, there's no telling. He's dressed like a civilian."

"Well, are they feasting? Have they money?"

"Poor sort of a feast! Nothing to boast of, Dmitri Fyodorovich."

"Nothing to boast of? And who are the others?"

"They're two gentlemen from the town. . . . They've come back from Cherny, and are putting up here. One's quite a young gentleman, a relative of Mr. Miüsov, he must be, but I've forgotten his name . . . and I expect you know the other, too, a gentleman called Maximov. He's been on a pilgrimage, so he says, to the monastery in the town. He's traveling with this young relation of Mr. Miüsov."

"Is that all?"

"Yes."

"Wait, listen, Trifon Borisich. Tell me the chief thing: What of her? How is she?"

"Oh, she's only just come. She's sitting with them."

"Is she cheerful? Is she laughing?"

"No. I think she's not laughing much. She's sitting quite bored. She's combing the young gentleman's hair."

"The Pole—the officer?"

"He's not young, and he's not an officer, either. Not him, sir. It's the young gentleman that's Mr. Miüsov's relation . . . I've forgotten his name."

"Kalganov?"

"That's it, Kalganov!"

"All right. I'll see for myself. Are they playing cards?"

"They have been playing, but they've stopped. They've been drinking tea, the official gentleman asked for liqueurs."

"Wait, Trifon Borisich, wait, my good soul, I'll see for myself. Now answer one more question: are the gypsies here?"

"You can't have the gypsies now, Dmitri Fyodorovich. The authorities have sent them away. But we've Jews that play the cymbals and the fiddle in the village, so one might send for them. They'd come."

"Send for them. Certainly send for them!" cried Mitya. "And

you can get the girls together as you did then. Marya especially, Stepanida, too, and Arina. Two hundred rubles for a chorus!"

"Oh, for a sum like that I can get all the village together, though by now they're asleep. Are the peasants here worth such kindness, Dmitri Fyodorovich, or the girls either? To spend a sum like that on such coarseness and rudeness! What's the good of giving a peasant a cigar to smoke, the stinking ruffian! And the girls are all lousy. Besides, I'll get my daughters up for nothing, let alone a sum like that. They've only just gone to bed, I'll give them a kick and set them singing for you. You gave the peasants champagne to drink the other time, e-ech!"

For all his pretended compassion for Mitya, Trifon Borisich had hidden half a case of champagne on the last occasion, and had picked up a hundred-ruble bill under the table, and it had remained in his clutches.

"Trifon Borisich, I sent more than one thousand flying last time I was here. Do you remember?"

"You did send it flying. I may well remember. You must have left three thousand behind you."

"Well, I've come to do the same again, do you see?"

And he pulled out his roll of bills, and held them up before the innkeeper's nose.

"Now, listen and remember. In an hour's time the wine will arrive, appetizers, pies, and sweets—bring them all up at once. That box Andrey has is to be brought up at once, too. Open it, and serve champagne immediately. And the girls, we must have the girls, Marya especially."

He turned to the cart and pulled out the box of pistols.

"Here, Andrey, let's settle. Here's fifteen rubles for the drive, and fifty for vodka . . . for your readiness, for your love. . . . Remember Karamazov!"

"I'm afraid, your honor," faltered Andrey. "Give me five rubles extra, but more I won't take. Trifon Borisich, bear witness. Forgive my foolish words . . ."

"What are you afraid of?" asked Mitya, scanning him. "Well, go to the devil, if that's it!" he cried, fling him five rubles. "Now, Trifon Borisich, take me up quietly and let me first get a look at them, so that they don't see me. Where are they? In the blue room?"

Trifon Borisich looked apprehensively at Mitya, but at once obediently did his bidding. Leading him into the hall, he went himself into the first large room, adjoining that in which the visitors were sitting, and took the light away. Then he stealthily led Mitya in, and put him in a corner in the dark, whence he could freely watch the company without being seen. But Mitya did not look long, and, indeed, he could not see them, he saw her, his heart throbbed violently, and all was dark before his eyes. She was sitting sideways to the table in a low chair, and beside her, on the sofa, was the pretty youth, Kalganov. She was holding his hand and seemed to be laughing, while he, seeming vexed and not looking at her, was saying something in a loud voice to Maximov, who sat on the other side of the table, facing Grushenka. Maximov was laughing violently at something. On the sofa sat *he*, and on a chair by the sofa there was another stranger. The one on the sofa was lolling backwards, smoking a pipe, and Mitya had an impression of a stoutish broad-faced short little man, who was apparently angry about something. His friend, the other stranger, struck Mitya as extraordinarily tall, but he could make out nothing more. He caught his breath. He could not bear it for a minute, he put the pistol case on a chest, and with a throbbing heart he walked, growing numb and faint of heart, straight into the blue room to face the company.

"Aie!" shrieked Grushenka, the first to notice him.

Chapter VII

The First and Rightful Lover

With his long, rapid strides, Mitya walked straight up to the table.

"Gentlemen," he said in a loud voice, almost shouting, yet stammering at every word, "I . . . I'm all right! Don't be afraid!" he exclaimed, "I—there's nothing the matter," he turned suddenly to Grushenka, who had shrunk back in her chair towards Kalganov, and clasped his hand tightly. "I . . . I'm coming, too. I'm here till morning. Gentlemen, may a passing traveler . . . stay with you till morning? Only till morning, for the last time, in this same room?"

So he finished, turning to the fat little man, with the pipe, sitting on the sofa. The latter removed his pipe from his lips with dignity and observed severely:

"*Panie*,[7] we're here in private. There are other rooms."

"Why, it's you, Dmitri Fyodorovich! What do you mean?" answered Kalganov suddenly. "Sit down with us. How are you?"

"Delighted to see you, dear . . . and precious fellow, I always thought a lot of you." Mitya responded, joyfully and eagerly, at once holding out his hand across the table.

"Aie! How tight you squeeze! You've quite broken my fingers," laughed Kalganov.

"He always squeezes like that, always," Grushenka put in gaily, with a timid smile, seeming suddenly convinced from Mitya's face that he was not going to make a scene. She was watching him with

7. "Sir" (a polite form of address in Polish)—plural, "panovie"; "pan" (Mr.) and "pani" (Miss, Mrs.) are used later.

intense curiosity and still some uneasiness. She was impressed by something about him, and indeed the last thing she expected of him was that he would come in and speak like this at such a moment.

"Good evening," Maximov ventured mawkishly, on the left. Mitya rushed up to him, too.

"Good evening. You're here too! How glad I am to find you here, too! Gentlemen, gentlemen, I . . ." (He addressed the Polish gentleman with the pipe again, evidently taking him for the most important person present.) "I flew here. . . . I wanted to spend my last day, my last hour in this room, in this very room . . . where I, too, adored . . . my queen. . . . Forgive me, *panie*," he cried wildly, "I flew here and vowed. . . . Oh, don't be afraid, it's my last night! Let's drink to our good understanding. They'll bring the wine at once. . . . I brought this with me." (Something made him pull out his bundle of bills.) "Allow me, *panie*! I want to have music, singing, a revel, as we had before. But the worm, the unnecessary worm, will crawl away, and there'll be no more of him. I will commemorate my day of joy and my last night."

He was almost choking. There was so much, so much he wanted to say, but strange exclamations were all that came from his lips. The Pole gazed fixedly at him, at the bundle of bills in his hand; looked at Grushenka, and was in evident perplexity.

"If my suverin lady is permitting . . ." he began.

"What does 'suverin' mean? 'Sovereign,' I suppose?" interrupted Grushenka. "I can't help laughing at you, the way you talk. Sit down, Mitya, what are you talking about? Don't frighten us, please. You won't frighten us, will you? If you won't, I am glad to see you . . ."

"Me, me frighten you?" cried Mitya, flinging up his hands. "Oh, pass me by, go your way, I won't hinder you!" And suddenly he surprised them all, and no doubt himself as well, by flinging himself on a chair, and bursting into tears, turning his head away to the opposite wall, while his arms clasped the back of the chair tight, as though embracing it.

"Come, come, what a fellow you are!" cried Grushenka reproachfully. "That's just how he comes to see me—he begins talking, and I can't make out what he means. He cried like that once before, and now he's crying again! It's shameful! Why are you crying? *As though you had anything to cry for!*" she added enigmatically, emphasizing each word with some irritability.

". . . I'm not crying. . . . Well, good evening!" he instantly turned round in his chair, and suddenly laughed, not his abrupt, wooden laugh but a long, quivering, inaudible nervous laugh.

"Well, there you are again. . . . Come, cheer up, cheer up." Grushenka said to him persuasively. "I'm very glad you've come, very glad, Mitya, do you hear, I'm very glad! I want him to stay here with us," she said peremptorily, addressing the whole company, though her words were obviously meant for the man sitting on the sofa. "I wish it, I wish it! And if he goes away I shall go, too!" she added with flashing eyes.

"What my queen commands is law!" pronounced the Pole, gallantly kissing Grushenka's hand. "I beg you, *panie*, to join our company," he added politely, addressing Mitya.

Mitya was jumping up with the obvious intention of delivering another tirade, but the words did not come.

"Let's drink, *panie*," he blurted out instead of making a speech. Everyone laughed.

"Good heavens! I thought he was going to begin again!" Grushenka exclaimed nervously. "Do you hear, Mitya," she went on insistently, "don't prance about, but it's nice you've brought the champagne. I want some myself, and I can't bear liqueurs. And best of all, you've come yourself. We were fearfully dull here. . . . You've come for a spree again, I suppose? But put your money in your pocket. Where did you get such a lot?"

Mitya had been, all this time, holding in his hand the crumpled bundle of bills on which the eyes of all, especially of the Poles, were fixed. In confusion he thrust them hurriedly into his pocket. He flushed. At that moment the innkeeper brought in an uncorked bottle of champagne, and glasses on a tray. Mitya snatched up the bottle, but he was so bewildered that he did not know what to do with it. Kalganov took it from him and poured out the champagne.

"Another! Another bottle!" Mitya cried to the innkeeper, and, forgetting to clink glasses with the Pole whom he had so solemnly invited to drink to their good understanding, he drank off his glass without waiting for anyone else. His whole countenance suddenly changed. The solemn and tragic expression with which he had entered vanished completely, and a look of something childlike came into his face. He seemed to have become suddenly gentle and subdued. He looked shyly and happily at everyone, with a continual nervous little laugh, and the blissful expression of a dog who had done wrong, been punished, and forgiven. He seemed to have forgotten everything, and was looking round at everyone with a childlike smile of delight. He looked at Grushenka, laughing, continually, and bringing his chair close up to her. By degrees he had gained some idea of the two Poles, though he had formed no definite conception of them yet.

The Pole on the sofa struck him by his dignified demeanor and his Polish accent; and, above all, by his pipe. "Well, what of it? It's a good thing he's smoking a pipe," he reflected. The Pole's puffy, middle-aged face, with its tiny nose and very thin, pointed, dyed and impudent looking mustache, had not so far roused the faintest doubts in Mitya. He was not even particularly struck by the Pole's absurd wig made in Siberia, with lovelocks foolishly combed forward over the temples. "I suppose it's all right since he wears a wig," he went on, musing blissfully. The other, younger Pole, who was staring insolently and defiantly at the company and listening to the conversation with silent contempt, still only impressed Mitya by his great height, which was terribly disproportionate to that of the Pole on the sofa. "If he stood up he'd be six foot three." The thought flitted through Mitya's mind. It occurred to him, too, that this Pole must be the friend of the other, as it were, a "bodyguard," and no doubt the big Pole was at the disposal of the little Pole with the pipe. But this all seemed to Mitya perfectly right and not to be questioned. In his mood of doglike submissiveness all feeling of rivalry had died away. Grushenka's mood and the enigmatic tone of some of her words he completely failed to grasp. All he understood, with thrilling heart, was that she was kind to him, that she had forgiven him, and made him sit by her. He was beside himself with delight, watching her sip her glass of champagne. The silence of the company seemed somehow to strike him, however, and he looked round at everyone with expectant eyes. "Why are we sitting here though, gentlemen? Why don't you begin doing something?" his smiling eyes seemed to ask.

"He keeps talking nonsense, and we were all laughing," Kalganov began suddenly, as though divining his thoughts, and pointing to Maximov.

Mitya immediately stared at Kalganov and then at Maximov.

"He's talking nonsense?" he laughed his short, wooden laugh, seemingly suddenly delighted at something—"ha, ha!"

"Yes. Would you believe it, he will have it that all our cavalry officers in the twenties married Polish women. That's awful rot, isn't it?"

"Polish women?" repeated Mitya, perfectly ecstatic.

Kalganov was well aware of Mitya's attitude to Grushenka, and he guessed about the Pole, too, but that did not much interest him, perhaps did not interest him at all; what he was interested in was Maximov. He had come here with Maximov by chance, and he met the Poles here at the inn for the first time in his life. Grushenka he knew before, and had once been with someone to see her; but she had not taken to him. But here she looked at him very affectionately: before Mitya's arrival, she had been making much of him, but he seemed somehow to be unmoved by it. He was a young man, not over twenty, dressed like a dandy, with a very charming fair-skinned face, and splendid thick, fair hair. From his fair face looked out beautiful pale blue eyes, with an intelligent and sometimes even deep expression, beyond his age indeed, although the young man sometimes looked and talked quite like a child, and was not at all ashamed of it, even when he was aware of it himself. As a rule he was very odd, even capricious, though always friendly. Sometimes there was something fixed and obstinate in his expression. He would look at you and listen, seeming all the while to be persistently dreaming over something else. Often he was listless and lazy, at other times he would grow excited, sometimes, apparently, over the most trivial matters.

"Only imagine, I've been taking him about with me for the last four days," he went on, indolently drawling his words, quite naturally though, without the slightest affectation. "Ever since your brother, do you remember, shoved him off the carriage and sent him flying. That made me take an interest in him at the time, and I took him into the country, but he keeps talking such rot I'm ashamed to be with him. I'm taking him back."

"The gentleman has not seen Polish ladies, and says what is impossible," the Pole with the pipe observed to Maximov.

He spoke Russian fairly well, much better, anyway, than he pretended. If he used Russian words, he always distorted them into a Polish form.

"But I was married to a Polish lady myself," tittered Maximov.

"But did you serve in the cavalry? You were talking about the cavalry. Were you a cavalry officer?" put in Kalganov at once.

"Was he a cavalry officer indeed? Ha, ha!" cried Mitya, listening eagerly, and turning his inquiring eyes to each as he spoke, as though there were no knowing what he might hear from each.

"No, no, sir, you see, sir," Maximov turned to him. "What I mean is that those pretty Polish ladies, sir . . . when they danced the mazurka with our Uhlans . . . when one of them dances a mazurka with a Uhlan she immediately jumps on his knee like a kitten, sir . . . a little white one . . . and the pan-father and pan-mother look on and allow it. . . . They allow it . . . and next day the Uhlan comes and offers her his hand. . . . That's how it is, sir . . . offers her his hand, he-he!" Maximov ended, tittering.

"The *pan* is a *lajdak!*"[8] The tall Pole on the chair growled suddenly and crossed one leg over the other. Mitya's eye was caught by his huge greased boot, with its thick, dirty sole. The dress of both the Poles looked rather greasy.

"Well, now it's *lajdak*! What's he scolding about?" said Grushenka, suddenly vexed.

"*Pani* Agrippina, what the gentleman saw in Poland were servant girls, and not ladies of good birth," the Pole with the pipe observed to Grushenka.

"You can bet on that," the tall Pole snapped contemptuously.

"What next! Let him talk! People talk, why hinder them? It makes it cheerful," Grushenka said crossly.

8. "Scoundrel."

"I'm not hindering them, *pani*," said the Pole in the wig significantly, with a long look at Grushenka, and relapsing into dignified silence he sucked his pipe again.

"No, no. The Polish gentleman spoke the truth." Kalganov got excited again, as though it were a question of vast import. "He's never been in Poland, so how can he talk about it? I suppose you weren't married in Poland, were you?"

"No, sir, in the province of Smolensk, sir. Only, a Uhlan had brought her to Russia before that, my future wife, that is, sir, with her pan-mamma and her aunt, and another female relation with a grown-up son. He brought her straight from Poland and . . . gave her up to me. He was a lieutenant in our regiment, a very nice young man. At first he meant to marry her himself. But he didn't marry her, because she turned out to be lame."

"So you married a lame woman?" cried Kalganov.

"Yes, sir. They both deceived me a little bit at the time, and concealed it. I thought she was hopping; she kept hopping . . . I thought it was for fun."

"So pleased she was going to marry you!" yelled Kalganov, in a ringing, childish voice.

"Yes, sir, so pleased. But it turned out to be quite a different cause. Afterwards, when we were married, after the wedding, that very evening, she confessed, and very touchingly asked forgiveness. 'I once jumped over a puddle when I was a child,' she said, 'and injured my leg,' he, he!"

Kalganov went off into the most childish laughter, almost falling on the sofa. Grushenka, too, laughed. Mitya was at the pinnacle of happiness.

"Do you know, that's the truth, he's not lying now," exclaimed Kalganov, turning to Mitya; "and do you know, he's been married twice; it's his first wife he's talking about. But his second wife, do you know, ran away, and is alive now."

"Is it possible?" said Mitya, turning quickly to Maximov with an expression of the utmost astonishment.

"Yes, sir. She did run away, sir. I've had that unpleasant experience," Maximov modestly assented, "with a monsieur, sir. And what was worse, she'd had all my little property transferred to her beforehand. 'You're an educated man,' she said to me. 'You can always make your living.' She settled my business with that. A venerable bishop once said to me: 'One of your wives was lame, but the other was too lightfooted,' he-he!"

"Listen, listen!" cried Kalganov, bubbling over, "if he's telling lies—and he often is—he's only doing it to amuse us all. There's no harm in that, is there? You know, I sometimes like him. He's awfully low, but it's natural to him, eh? Don't you think so? Some people are low from self-interest, but he's simply so, from nature.

Only fancy, he claims (he was arguing about it all the way yesterday) that Gogol wrote *Dead Souls*[9] about him. Do you remember, there's a landowner called Maximov in it, whom Nozdryov thrashed. He was charged, do you remember, 'for inflicting bodily injury with rods on the landowner Maximov in a drunken condition.' Would you believe it, he claims that he was that Maximov and that he was beaten! Now can it be so? Chichikov made his journey, at the very latest, at the beginning of the twenties, so that the dates don't fit. He couldn't have been thrashed then, he couldn't, could he?"

It was difficult to imagine what Kalganov was excited about, but his excitement was genuine. Mitya followed his lead without protest.

"Well, but if they did thrash him!" he cried, laughing.

"It's not that they thrashed me exactly, sir, but just so . . ." put in Maximov.

"What do you mean 'just so'? Either they thrashed you or they didn't."

"What time is it, *panie?*" the Pole, with the pipe, asked his tall friend in Polish, with a bored expression. The other shrugged his shoulders in reply. Neither of them had a watch.

"Why not talk? Let other people talk. Must other people not talk because you're bored?" Grushenka flew at him with evident intention of finding fault. Something seemed to flash upon Mitya's mind for the first time. This time the Pole answered with unmistakable irritability.

"*Pani,* I didn't oppose it. I didn't say anything."

"All right then. Come, tell us your story," Grushenka cried to Maximov. "Why are you all silent?"

"There's nothing to tell, it's all so foolish, ma'am," answered Maximov at once, with evident satisfaction, mincing a little. "Besides, all that's by way of allegory in Gogol, for he's made all the names have a meaning. Nozdryov was really called Nosov, and Kuvshinikov had quite a different name, he was called Shkvornev. Fenardi really was called Fenardi, only he wasn't an Italian but a Russian, Petrov, gentlemen, and Mam'selle Fenardi was a pretty girl with her pretty little legs in tights, and she had a little short skirt with spangles, gentlemen, and she kept turning round and round, only not for four hours but for four minutes only, gentlemen, and she bewitched everyone . . ."

"But what were you beaten for, why were you beaten?" cried Kalganov.

"For Piron!" answered Maximov.

"What Piron?" cried Mitya.

9. Gogol's comic masterpiece (1842).

"The famous French writer, Piron. We were all drinking then, a big party of us, in a tavern at that very fair. They'd invited me, and first of all I began quoting epigrams. 'Is that you, Boileau?[1] What a funny get-up!' and Boileau answers that he's going to a masquerade, that is to the baths, he-he! And they took it to themselves, so I made haste to repeat another, very sarcastic, well known to all educated people:

> Yes, Sappho and Phaon are we!
> But one grief is weighing on me.
> You don't know your way to the sea![2]

They were still more offended and began abusing me in the most unseemly way for it. And as luck would have it, to set things right, I began telling a very cultivated anecdote about Piron, how he was not accepted into the French Academy, and to revenge himself wrote his own epitaph:

> *Ci-gît Piron qui ne fut rien*
> *Pas même académicien.*[3]

They seized me and thrashed me."

"But what for? What for?"

"For my education. People can thrash a man for anything," Maximov concluded, briefly and sententiously.

"Eh, that's enough! That's all stupid, I don't want to listen. I thought it would be amusing," Grushenka cut them short, suddenly. Mitya started, and at once stopped laughing. The tall Pole rose upon his feet and, with the haughty air of a man bored and out of his element, began pacing from corner to corner of the room, his hands behind his back.

"Ah, he can't sit still," said Grushenka, looking at him contemptuously. Mitya began to feel anxious. He noticed besides that the Pole on the sofa was looking at him with an irritable expression.

"*Panie!*" cried Mitya, "let's drink! and the other *pan*, too! Let us drink."

In a flash he had pulled three glasses towards him, and filled them with champagne.

"To Poland, *panovie*, I drink to your Poland!" cried Mitya.

"I shall be delighted, *panie*," said the Pole on the sofa, with dignity and affable condescension, and he took his glass.

"And the other *pan*, what's his name? Drink, most illustrious, take your glass!" Mitya urged.

1. An epigram by fabulist and dramatist I. A. Krylov on a very bad translation of Boileau's *L'Art poétique* (The art of poetry) (1674).
2. K. Batyushkov's epigram (1809) on the woman poet A. P. Bunin, "Madrigal to a New Sappho."
3. "Here lies Piron, who was nothing/ Not even a member of the Academy."

"Pan Vrublevsky," put in the Pole on the sofa.

Pan Vrublevsky came up to the table, swaying as he walked.

"To Poland, *panovie!*" cried Mitya, raising his glass. "Hurrah!"

All three drank. Mitya seized the bottle and again poured out three glasses.

"Now to Russia, *panovie*, and let us be brothers!"

"Pour out some for us," said Grushenka; "I'll drink to Russia, too!"

"So will I," said Kalganov.

"And I would, too . . . to Russia, the old grandmother!" tittered Maximov.

"All! All!" cried Mitya. "Landlord, some more bottles!"

The other three bottles Mitya had brought with him were put on the table. Mitya filled the glasses.

"To Russia! Hurrah!" he shouted again. All drank the toast except the Poles, and Grushenka tossed off her whole glass at once. The Poles did not touch theirs.

"How's this, *panovie?*" cried Mitya, "won't you drink it?"

Pan Vrublevsky took the glass, raised it, and said with a resonant voice:

"To Russia as she was before 1772."[4]

"Come, that's better!" cried the other Pole in Polish, and they both emptied their glasses at once.

"You're fools, you *panovie*," broke suddenly from Mitya.

"*Panie!*" shouted both the Poles, menacingly, setting on Mitya like a couple of cocks. Pan Vrublevsky was specially furious.

"Can one help loving one's own country?" he shouted in Polish.

"Be silent! Don't quarrel! I won't have any quarreling!" cried Grushenka imperiously, and she stamped her foot on the floor. Her face glowed, her eyes were shining. The effects of the glass she had just drunk were apparent. Mitya was terribly alarmed.

"*Panovie*, forgive me! It was my fault, I'm sorry. Vrublevsky, *panie* Vrublevsky, I'm sorry."

"Hold your tongue, you, anyway! Sit down, you stupid!" Grushenka scolded with angry annoyance.

Everyone sat down, all were silent, looking at one another.

"Gentlemen, I was the cause of it all," Mitya began again, unable to make anything of Grushenka's words. "Come, why are we sitting here? What shall we do . . . to amuse ourselves again?"

"Ach, it's certainly anything but amusing!" Kalganov mumbled lazily.

"Let's play faro again, sir, as we did just now," Maximov tittered suddenly.

"Faro? Splendid!" cried Mitya. "If only the *panovie* . . .'

4. The partition of Poland among Russia, Austria, and Prussia in 1772 ended the monarchy.

"It's lite, *panovie*," the Pole on the sofa responded, as it were unwillingly.

"That's true," assented Pan Vrublevsky.

"Lite? What do you mean by 'lite'?" asked Grushenka.

"Late, *pani*, 'a late hour,' I mean," the Pole on the sofa explained.

"It's always late with them. They can never do anything!" Grushenka almost shrieked in her anger. "They're dull themselves, so they want others to be dull. Before you came, Mitya, they were just as silent and kept turning up their noses at me."

"My goddess!" cried the Pole on the sofa in Polish, "I see you're not well-disposed to me, that's why I'm gloomy. I'm ready, *panie*," added he, addressing Mitya.

"Begin, *panie*," Mitya assented, pulling his money out of his pocket, and laying two hundred-ruble bills on the table. "I want to lose a lot to you. Take your cards. Make the bank."

"We'll get cards from the landlord, *panie*," said the little Pole, gravely and emphatically.

"That's much the best way," chimed in Pan Vrublevsky in Polish.

"From the landlord? Very good, I understand, let's get them from him, that's clever of you, *panovie*. Cards!" Mitya shouted to the landlord.

The landlord brought in a new, unopened pack, and informed Mitya that the girls were getting ready, and that the Jews with the cymbals would most likely be here soon; but the cart with the provisions had not yet arrived. Mitya jumped up from the table and ran into the next room to give orders, but only three girls had arrived, and Marya was not there yet. And he did not know himself what orders to give and why he had run out. He only told them to take out of the box the presents for the girls, the sweets, the toffee and the fondants. "And vodka for Andrey, vodka for Andrey!" he cried in haste. "I was rude to Andrey!"

Suddenly Maximov, who had followed him out, touched him on the shoulder.

"Give me five rubles," he whispered to Mitya. "I'll stake something at faro, too, he-he!"

"Capital! Splendid! Take ten, here!"

Again he took all the bills out of his pocket and picked out one for ten rubles. "And if you lose that, come again, come again."

"Very good, sir," Maximov whispered joyfully, and he ran back again. Mitya too, returned, apologizing for having kept them waiting. The Poles had already sat down, and opened the pack. They looked much more amiable, almost cordial. The Pole on the sofa had lit another pipe and was preparing to deal. He wore an air of solemnity.

"To your plices, *panovie*!" cried Pan Vrublevsky.

"No, I'm not going to play any more," observed Kalganov, "I've lost fifty rubles to them just now."

"The *pan* had no luck, perhaps he'll be lucky this time," the Pole on the sofa observed in his direction.

"How much in the bank? To cover?" asked Mitya.

"That depends, *panie*, maybe a hundred, maybe two hundred, as much as you will stake."

"A million!" laughed Mitya.

"The *Pan* Captain has heard of *Pan* Podvysotsky, perhaps?"

"What Podvysotsky?"

"In Warsaw there was a bank and anyone comes and stakes against it. Podvysotsky comes, sees a thousand gold pieces, stakes against the bank. The banker says, '*Panie* Podvysotsky, are you laying down the gold, or must we trust to your honor?' 'To my honor, *panie*,' says Podvysotsky. 'So much the better.' The banker deals. Podvysotsky wins. 'Take it, *panie*,' says the banker, and pulling out the drawer he gives him a million. 'Take it, *panie*, this is your gain.' There was a million in the bank. 'I didn't know that,' says Podvysotsky, '*Panie* Podvysotsky,' said the banker, 'you pledged your honor and we pledged ours.' Podvysotsky took the million."

"That's not true," said Kalganov.

"*Panie* Kalganov, in gentlemanly society one doesn't say such things."

"As if a Polish gambler would give away a million!" cried Mitya, but checked himself at once. "Forgive me, *panie*, it's my fault again, he would, he would give away a million, for honor, for Polish honor. You see how I talk Polish, ha-ha! Here, I stake ten rubles, on the jack."

"And I put a ruble on the queen, the queen of hearts, the pretty little *panienochka*, he-he!" laughed Maximov, pulling out his queen, and, as though trying to conceal it from everyone, he moved right up and crossed himself hurriedly under the table. Mitya won. The ruble won, too.

"Press it!" cried Mitya.

"I'll bet another ruble, a single stake," Maximov muttered gleefully, hugely delighted at having won a ruble.

"Lost!" shouted Mitya. "Double on the seven!"

The seven too lost.

"Stop!" cried Kalganov suddenly.

"Double! Double!" Mitya doubled his stakes, and each time he doubled the stake, the card he doubled lost. The ruble stakes kept winning.

"Double!" shouted Mitya, furiously.

"You've lost two hundred, *panie*. Will you take another hundred?" the Pole on the sofa inquired.

"What? Lost two hundred already? Then another two hundred! All doubles!"

And pulling his money out of his pocket, Mitya was about to fling two hundred rubles on the queen, but Kalganov covered it with his hand.

"That's enough!" he shouted in his ringing voice.

"What's the matter?" Mitya stared at him.

"That's enough! I don't want you to play any more. Don't!"

"Why?"

"Because I don't. Hang it, come away. That's why. I won't let you go on playing."

Mitya gazed at him in astonishment.

"Give it up, Mitya. He may be right. You've lost a lot as it is," said Grushenka, with a curious note in her voice. Both the Poles rose from their seats with a deeply offended air.

"Are you joking, *panie?*" said the short man, looking severely at Kalganov.

"How dare you!" Pan Vrublevsky, too, growled at Kalganov.

"Don't dare to shout like that," cried Grushenka. "Ah, you turkey cocks!"

Mitya looked at each of them in turn. But something in Grushenka's face suddenly struck him, and at the same instant something new flashed into his mind—a strange new thought!

"*Pani* Agrippina," the little Pole was beginning, crimson with anger, when Mitya suddenly went up to him and slapped him on the shoulder.

"Most illustrious one, two words with you."

"What do you want?"

"In the next room, I've two words to say to you, something pleasant, very pleasant. You'll be glad to hear it."

The little *pan* was taken aback and looked apprehensively at Mitya. He agreed at once, however, on condition that Pan Vrublevsky went with them.

"The bodyguard? Let him come, and I want him, too. I must have him!" cried Mitya. "March, *panovie!*"

"Where are you going?" asked Grushenka, anxiously.

"We'll be back in one moment," answered Mitya.

There was a sort of boldness, a sudden confidence shining in his eyes. His face had looked very different when he entered the room an hour before. He led the Poles, not into the large room where the chorus of girls was assembling and the table was being set, but into the bedroom on the right, where the trunks and packages were kept, and there were two large beds, with pyramids of cotton pillows on each. There was a lighted candle on a small wooden table in the corner. The Pole and Mitya sat down to this table, facing each other, while the huge Vrublevsky stood beside them, his hands behind his back. The Poles looked severe but were evidently inquisitive.

"What can I do for you, *panie?*" lisped the little Pole.

"Well, look here, *panie*, I won't keep you long. There's money for you," he pulled out his bills. "Would you like three thousand? Take it and go your way."

The Pole gazed, open-eyed at Mitya, with a searching look.

"Three thousand, *panie?*" He exchanged glances with Vrublevsky.

"Three, *panovie*, three! Listen, *panie*, I see you're a sensible man. Take three thousand and go to the devil, and Vrublevsky with you—d'you hear? But, at once, this very minute, and forever. You understand that, *panie*, forever. Here's the door, you go out of it. What have you got there, an overcoat, a fur coat? I'll bring it out to you. They'll get the horses out directly, and then—good-bye, *panie!*"

Mitya awaited an answer with assurance. He had no doubts. An expression of extraordinary resolution passed over the Pole's face.

"And the money, *panie?*"

"The money, *panie?* Five hundred rubles I'll give you this moment for the journey, and as a first installment, and twenty-five hundred tomorrow, in the town—I swear on my honor, I'll get it, I'll get it at any cost!" cried Mitya.

The Poles exchanged glances again. The short man's face looked more forbidding.

"Seven hundred, seven hundred, not five hundred, at once, this minute, cash down!" Mitya added, feeling something wrong. "What's the matter, *panie?* Don't you trust me? I can't give you the whole three thousand right away. If I give it to you now, you may come back to her tomorrow.... Besides, I haven't got the three thousand with me. I've got it at home in town," faltered Mitya, his spirit sinking at every word he uttered. "Upon my word, the money's there, hidden."

In an instant an extraordinary sense of personal dignity showed itself in the little Pole's face.

"What next?" he asked ironically. "For shame!" and he spat on the floor. Pan Vrublevsky spat too.

"You do that, *panie*," said Mitya, recognizing with despair that all was over, "because you hope to make more out of Grushenka? You're a couple of capons, that's what you are!"

"This is a mortal insult!" The little Pole turned as red as a crab, and he went out of the room, briskly, as though unwilling to hear another word. Vrublevsky swung out after him, and Mitya followed, confused and crestfallen. He was afraid of Grushenka, afraid that the *pan* would at once raise an outcry. And so indeed he did. The Pole walked into the room and threw himself in a theatrical attitude before Grushenka.

"*Pani* Agrippina, I have received a mortal insult!" he exclaimed in Polish. But Grushenka suddenly lost all patience, as though they had wounded her in the tenderest spot.

"Speak Russian! Speak Russian!" she cried, "not another word of Polish! You used to talk Russian. You can't have forgotten it in five years." She flushed with anger.

"*Pani* Agrippina . . ."

"My name's Agrafena, Grushenka, speak Russian or I won't listen!" The Pole gasped with offended dignity, and quickly and pompously delivered himself in broken Russian:

"*Pani* Agrafena, I came here to forget the past and forgive it, to forget all that has happened till today . . ."

"Forgive? Come here to forgive me?" Grushenka cut him short, jumping up from her seat.

"Just so, *pani*, I'm not pusillanimous, I'm magnanimous. But I was astounded when I saw your lovers. Pan Mitya offered me three thousand, in the other room, to depart. I spat in the *pan's* face."

"What? He offered you money for me?" cried Grushenka, hysterically. "Is it true, Mitya? How dare you? Am I for sale?"

"*Panie, panie!*" yelled Mitya, "she's pure and shining, and I have never been her lover! That's a lie . . ."

"How dare you defend me to him?" shrieked Grushenka. "It wasn't virtue kept me pure, and it wasn't that I was afraid of Kuzma, but that I might hold up my head when I met him, and tell him he's a scoundrel. And did he actually refuse the money?"

"He took it! He took it!" cried Mitya; "only he wanted to get the whole three thousand at once, and I could only give him seven hundred right away."

"I see: he heard I had money, and came here to marry me!"

"*Pani* Agrippina!" cried the little Pole. "I'm—a knight, I'm—a nobleman, and not a *lajdak*. I came here to make you my wife and I find you a different woman, perverse and shameless."

"Oh, go back where you came from! I'll tell them to turn you out and you'll be turned out," cried Grushenka, furious. "I've been a fool, a fool, to have been miserable these five years! And it wasn't for his sake, it was my anger made me miserable. And this isn't he at all! Was he like this? It might be his father! Where did you get your wig from? He was a falcon, but this is a gander. He used to laugh and sing to me. . . . And I've been crying for five years, damned fool that I am, base, shameless fool!"

She sank back in her low chair and hid her face in her hands. At that instant the chorus of Mokroe girls began singing in the room on the left—a rollicking dance song.

"A regular Sodom!" Vrublevsky roared suddenly. "Landlord, send the shameless hussies away!"

The landlord, who had been for some time past inquisitively

peeping in at the door, hearing shouts and guessing that his guests were quarreling, at once entered the room.

"What are you shouting for? D'you want to split your throat?" he said, addressing Vrublevsky, with surprising rudeness.

"Animal!" bellowed Pan Vrublevsky.

"Animal? And what sort of cards were you playing with just now? I gave you a pack and you hid it. You played with marked cards! I could send you to Siberia for playing with false cards, d'you know that, for it's just the same as counterfeit bills . . ." And going up to the sofa he thrust his fingers between the sofa back and the cushion, and pulled out an unopened pack of cards.

"Here's my pack unopened!" He held it up and showed it to all in the room. "From where I stood I saw him slip my pack away, and put his in place of it—you're a cheat and not a gentleman!"

"And I twice saw the *pan* change a card!" cried Kalganov.

"How shameful! How shameful!" exclaimed Grushenka, clasping her hands, and blushing for genuine shame. "Good Lord, he's come to that!"

"I thought so, too!" said Mitya. But before he had uttered the words, Vrublevsky, with a confused and infuriated face, shook his fist at Grushenka, shouting:

"You low harlot!"

Mitya flew at him at once, clutched him in both hands, lifted him in the air, and in one instant had carried him into the room on the right, from which they had just come.

"I've laid him on the floor, there," he announced, returning at once, gasping with excitement. "He's struggling, the scoundrel! But he won't come back, no fear of that! . . ." He closed one half of the folding doors, and holding the other ajar called out to the little Pole:

"Most illustrious excellence, will you be pleased to retire as well?"

"My dear Dmitri Fyodorovich," said Trifon Borisich, "make them give you back the money you lost. It's as good as stolen from you."

"I don't want my fifty rubles back," Kalganov declared suddenly.

"I don't want my two hundred, either," cried Mitya, "I wouldn't take it for anything! Let him keep it as a consolation."

"Bravo, Mitya! You're a brick, Mitya!" cried Grushenka, and there was a note of fierce anger in the exclamation. The little *pan*, crimson with fury, but still mindful of his dignity, was making for the door, but he stopped short and said suddenly, addressing Grushenka:

"*Pani*, if you want to come with me, come. If not, goodbye."

And swelling with indignation and importance he went to the door. This was a man of character: he had so good an opinion of himself that after all that had passed, he still expected that she would follow him. Mitya slammed the door after him.

"Lock it," said Kalganov. But the key clicked on the other side, they had locked it from within.

"That's capital!" exclaimed Grushenka relentlessly. "Capital! Serves them right!"

Chapter VIII

Delirium

What followed was almost an orgy, a feast to which all were welcome. Grushenka was the first to call for wine. "I want to drink. I want to be quite drunk, as we were before. Do you remember, Mitya, do you remember how we made friends here last time!" Mitya himself was almost delirious, feeling that his happiness was at hand. But Grushenka was continually sending him away from her: "Go and enjoy yourself. Tell them to dance, to make merry, 'let the stove and cottage dance'; as we had it last time," she kept exclaiming. She was tremendously excited. And Mitya hastened to obey her. The chorus were in the next room. The room in which they had been sitting till that moment was too small, and was divided in two by cotton curtains, behind which was a huge bed with a puffy feather mattress and a pyramid of cotton pillows. In all four rooms for visitors there were beds. Grushenka settled herself just at the door. Mitya set an easy chair for her. She had sat in the same place to watch the dancing and singing "the time before," when they had their spree there. All the girls who had come had been there then; the Jewish band with fiddles and zithers had come, too, and at last the long-expected cart had arrived with the wines and provisions.

Mitya bustled about. All sorts of people began coming into the room to look on, peasants and their women, who had been roused from sleep and attracted by the hopes of another marvelous entertainment such as they had enjoyed a month before. Mitya remembered their faces, greeting and embracing everyone he knew. He uncorked bottles and poured out wine for everyone who presented himself. Only the girls were very eager for the champagne. The men preferred rum, brandy, and, above all, hot punch. Mitya had chocolate made for all the girls, and ordered that three samovars should be kept going all night to provide tea and punch for everyone to help himself. In short, an absurd chaotic confusion followed, but Mitya was in his natural element, and the more foolish it became, the more his spirits rose. If the peasants had asked him for money at that moment, he would have pulled out his bills and given them away right and left. This was probably why the landlord,

Trifon Borisich, kept hovering about Mitya to protect him. He seemed to have given up all idea of going to bed that night, though he drank little, only one glass of punch, and kept a sharp lookout on Mitya's interests after his own fashion. He intervened in the nick of time, civilly and obsequiously persuading Mitya not to give away "cigars and Rhine wine," and, above all, money to the peasants as he had done before. He was very indignant, too, at the peasant girls drinking liqueurs, and eating sweets. "They're a lousy lot, Dmitri Fyodorovich," he said. "I'd give them a kick, every one of them, and they'd take it as an honor—that's all they're worth!"

Mitya remembered Andrey again, and ordered punch to be sent out to him. "I was rude to him just now," he repeated with a sinking, softened voice. Kalganov did not want to drink, and at first did not care for the girls' singing; but after he had drunk a couple of glasses of champagne he became extraordinarily lively, strolling about the room, laughing and praising the music and the songs, admiring everyone and everything. Maximov, blissfully drunk, never left his side. Grushenka, too, was beginning to get drunk. Pointing to Kalganov, she said to Mitya: "What a dear, charming boy he is!" And Mitya, delighted, ran to kiss Kalganov and Maximov. Oh, great were his hopes! She had said nothing yet, and seemed, indeed, purposely to refrain from speaking. But she looked at him from time to time with caressing and ardent eyes. At last she suddenly gripped his hand and drew him vigorously to her. She was sitting at the moment in the low chair by the door.

"How was it you came just now, eh? How you walked in! . . . I was so frightened. So you wanted to give me up to him, did you? Did you really want to?"

"I didn't want to spoil your happiness!" Mitya faltered blissfully. But she did not need his answer.

"Well, go and enjoy yourself . . ." she sent him away once more. "Don't cry, I'll call you back again."

He ran off, and she listened to the singing and looked at the dancing, though her eyes followed him wherever he went. But in another quarter of an hour she called him once more and again he ran back to her.

"Come, sit beside me, tell me, how did you hear about me, and my coming here yesterday? From whom did you first hear it?

And Mitya began telling her all about it, disconnectedly, incoherently, feverishly. He spoke strangely, often frowning, and stopping abruptly.

"What are you frowning at?" she asked.

"Nothing. . . . I left a man ill there. I'd give ten years of my life for him to get well, to know he was all right!"

"Well, never mind him, if he's ill. So you meant to shoot yourself tomorrow! What a silly boy! What for? I like such reckless fellows as you," she lisped, her speech beginning to get thick. "So you would go any length for me, eh? Did you really mean to shoot yourself tomorrow, you stupid? No, wait a little. Tomorrow I may have something to say to you. . . . I won't say it today, but tomorrow. You'd like it to be today? No, I don't want to today. Well, go along now, go and amuse yourself."

Once, however, she called him, as it were, puzzled and uneasy.

"Why are you sad? I see you're sad. . . . Yes, I see it," she added, looking intently into his eyes. "Though you keep kissing the peasants and shouting, I see something. No, be merry. I'm merry; you be merry, too. . . . I love somebody here. Guess who it is. Ah, look, my boy has fallen asleep, poor dear, he's drunk."

She meant Kalganov. He was, in fact, drunk, and had dropped asleep for a moment, sitting on the sofa. But he was not merely drowsy from drink; he felt suddenly dejected, or, as he said, "bored." He was intensely depressed by the girls' songs, which, as the drinking went on, gradually became coarse and more reckless. And the dances were as bad. Two girls dressed up as bears, and a lively girl, called Stepanida, with a stick in her hand, acted the part of keeper, and began to "show them." "Look alive, Marya, or you'll get the stick!" The bears rolled on the ground at last in the most unseemly fashion, amid roars of laughter from the closely packed crowd of men and women. "Well, let them! Let them!" said Grushenka sententiously, with an ecstatic expression on her face. "When they do get a day to enjoy themselves, why shouldn't folks be happy?"

But Kalganov looked as though he had been besmirched with dirt. "It's swinish, all this peasant foolery," he murmured, moving away; "it's the games they play when it's light all night in summer." He particularly disliked one "new" song to a jaunty dance tune. It described how a gentleman came and tried his luck with the girls, to see whether they would love him:

> The master came to try the girls:
> Would they love him, would they not?

But the girls could not love the master:

> He would beat me cruelly
> And such love won't do for me.

Then a gypsy comes along and he, too, tries:

> The gypsy came to try the girls:
> Would they love him, would they not?

But they couldn't love the gypsy either:

> He would be a thief, I fear,
> And would cause me many a tear.

And many more men come to try their luck, among them a soldier:

> The soldier came to try the girls:
> Would they love him, would they not?

But the soldier is rejected with contempt:

> The soldier he would strap his pack
> And after him I . . .

here followed an indecent line, sung with absolute frankness and causing a sensation in the audience. The song ends with a merchant:

> The merchant came to try the girls:
> Would they love him, would they not?

And it appears that he wins their love because:

> The merchant will make gold for me
> And his queen I will gladly be.

Kalganov was positively indignant:

"That's just a song of yesterday," he said aloud. "Who writes such things for them? They might just as well have had a railway man or a Jew come to try his luck with the girls; they'd have carried all before them." And, almost as though it were a personal affront, he declared, on the spot, that he was bored, sat down on the sofa and immediately fell asleep. His pretty little face looked rather pale, as it fell back on the sofa cushion.

"Look how pretty he is," said Grushenka, taking Mitya up to him. "I was combing his hair just now; his hair's like flax, and so thick . . ."

And, bending over him tenderly, she kissed his forehead. Kalganov instantly opened his eyes, looked at her, stood up, and with the most anxious air inquired where was Maximov?

"So that's who it is you want." Grushenka laughed. "Stay with me a minute. Mitya, run and find his Maximov."

Maximov, it appeared, could not tear himself away from the girls, only running away from time to time to pour himself out a glass of liqueur. He had drunk two cups of chocolate. His face was red, and his nose was crimson; his eyes were moist, and mawkishly sweet. He ran up and announced that he was going to dance the "sabotière."

"They taught me all those well-bred, aristocratic dances when I was little . . ."

"Go, go with him, Mitya, and I'll watch from here how he dances," said Grushenka.

"No, no, I'm coming to look on, too," exclaimed Kalganov, brushing aside in the most naïve way Grushenka's offer to sit with him. They all went to look on. Maximov danced his dance. But it roused no great admiration in anyone but Mitya. It consisted of nothing but skipping and hopping, kicking up the feet, and at every skip Maximov slapped the upturned sole of his foot. Kalganov did not like it all, but Mitya kissed the dancer.

"Thanks. You're tired perhaps? What are you looking for here? Would you like some sweets? A cigar, perhaps?"

"A cigarette, sir."

"Don't you want a drink?"

"I'll just have a liqueur, sir . . . Have you any chocolates?"

"Yes, there's a heap of them on the table there. Choose one, my dear soul!"

"I like one with vanilla, sir . . . for old people. He-he!"

"No, brother, we've none of that special sort."

"I say," the old man bent down to whisper in Mitya's ear. "That girl there, little Marya, he-he! How would it be if you were to help me make friends with her?"

"So that's what you're after! No, brother, that won't do!"

"I'd do no harm to anyone," Maximov muttered disconsolately.

"Oh, all right, all right. They only come here to dance and sing, you know, brother. But damn it all, wait a bit! . . . Eat and drink and be merry, meanwhile. Don't you want money?"

"Later on perhaps," smiled Maximov.

"All right, all right . . ."

Mitya's head was burning. He went outside to the wooden balcony which ran round the whole building on the inner side, overlooking the courtyard. The fresh air revived him. He stood alone in the dark, in a corner, and suddenly clutched his head in both hands. His scattered thoughts came together; his sensations blended into a whole and threw a sudden light into his mind. A fearful and terrible light! "If I'm to shoot myself, why not now?" passed through his mind. "Why not go for the pistols, bring them here, and here, in this dark, dirty corner, make an end?" Almost a minute he stood, undecided. A few hours earlier, when he had been dashing here, he was pursued by disgrace, by the theft he had committed, and that blood, that blood! . . . But yet it was easier for him then. Then everything was over: he had lost her, given her up. She was gone for him—oh, then his death sentence had been easier for him; at least it had seemed necessary, inevitable, for what had he to stay on earth for? But now? Was it the same as then? Now one phantom, one terror at least was at an end: that first, rightful lover, that fateful figure had vanished, leaving no trace. The terrible phantom had turned into something so small, so comic; it had been carried into the bedroom and locked in. It would never return. She was ashamed, and from her eyes he could see now whom she loved. Now he had everything to make life happy . . . but he could not go on living, he could not; oh, damnation! "Oh, God! restore to life the man I knocked down at the fence! Let this fearful cup pass from me! Lord, thou hast wrought miracles for such sinners as me! But what, what if the old man's alive? Oh, then the shame of the other disgrace I would wipe away. I would restore the stolen money. I'd give it back; I'd get it somehow. . . . No trace of that shame will remain except in my heart forever! But no, no; oh, impossible cowardly dreams! Oh, damnation!"

Yet a ray of bright hope shone to him in his darkness. He jumped up and ran back to the room—to her, to her, his queen forever! Was not one hour, one moment of her love worth all the rest of life, even in the agonies of disgrace? This wild question clutched at his heart. "To her, to her alone, to see her, to hear her, to think of nothing, to forget everything, if only for that night, for an hour, for a moment!" Just as he turned from the balcony into the passage, he came upon the landlord, Trifon Borisich. He thought he looked gloomy and worried, and fancied he had come to find him.

"What is it, Trifon Borisich? are you looking for me?"

"No, sir." The landlord seemed disconcerted. "Why should I be looking for you? Where have you been?"

"Why do you look so glum? You're not angry, are you? Wait a bit, you shall soon get to bed. . . . What's the time?"

"It'll be three o'clock. Past three, it must be."

"We'll stop soon. We'll stop."

"Don't mention it; it doesn't matter. Keep it up as long as you like . . ."

"What's the matter with him?" Mitya wondered for an instant, and he ran back to the room where the girls were dancing. But she was not there. She was not in the blue room either; there was no one but Kalganov asleep on the sofa. Mitya peeped behind the curtain—she was there. She was sitting in the corner, on a trunk. Bent forward, with her head and arms on the bed close by, she was crying bitterly, doing her utmost to stifle her sobs that she might not be heard. Seeing Mitya, she beckoned him to her, and when he ran to her, she grasped his hand tightly.

"Mitya, Mitya, I loved him, you know," she began in a whisper. "How I have loved him these five years, all that time! Did I love him or only my own anger? No, him, him! It's a lie that it was my anger I loved and not him. Mitya, I was only seventeen then; he was so kind to me, so merry; he used to sing to me. . . . Or so it seemed to a silly girl like me. . . . And now, O Lord, it's not the same man. Even his face is not the same; he's different altogether. I wouldn't have recognized him. I drove here with Timothy, and all the way I was thinking how would I meet him, what would I say to him, how would we look at one another. My soul was faint, and all of a sudden it was just as though he had emptied a pail of dirty water over me. He talked to me like a schoolmaster, all so grave and learned; he met me so solemnly that I was struck dumb. I couldn't get a word in. At first I thought he was ashamed to talk before his great big Pole. I sat staring at him and wondering why I couldn't say a word to him now. It must have been his wife that ruined him; you know he threw me up to get married. She must have changed him like that. Mitya, how shameful it is! Oh, Mitya, I'm ashamed, I'm ashamed for all my life. Curse it, curse it, curse those five years!" And again she burst into tears, but clung tight to Mitya's hand and did not let it go.

"Mitya, darling, stay, don't go away. I want to say one word to you," she whispered, and suddenly raised her face to him. "Listen, tell me who it is I love? I love one man here. Who is that man? That's what you must tell me." A smile lighted up her face that was swollen with weeping, and her eyes shone in the half darkness.

"A falcon flew in, and my heart sank. 'Fool! that's the man you love!' That was what my heart whispered to me at once. You came in and all grew bright. What's he afraid of? I wondered. For you were frightened; you couldn't speak. It's not them he's afraid of— could you be frightened of any one? It's me he's afraid of, I thought, only me. So Fenya told you, you little stupid, how I called to Alyosha out of the window that I'd loved Mitenka for one hour, and that I was going now to love . . . another. Mitya, Mitya, how could I be such a fool as to think I could love anyone after you? Do you forgive me, Mitya? Do you forgive me or not? Do you love me? Do you love me?"

She jumped up and held him with both hands on his shoulders. Mitya, dumb with rapture, gazed into her eyes, at her face, at her smile, and suddenly clasped her tightly in his arms and kissed her passionately.

"You will forgive me for having tormented you? It was through spite I tormented you all. It was for spite I drove the old man out of his mind. . . . Do you remember how you drank at my house one day and broke the wine glass? I remembered that and I broke a glass today and drank 'to my vile heart.' Mitya, my falcon, why don't you kiss me? He kissed me once, and now he draws back and looks and listens. Why listen to me? Kiss me, kiss me hard, that's right. If you love, well then love! I'll be your slave now, your slave for the rest of my life. It's sweet to be a slave. Kiss me! Beat me, ill-treat me, do what you will with me. . . . And I do deserve to suffer. Stop, wait, afterwards, I won't have that . . ." she suddenly thrust him away. "Go along, Mitya, I'll come and have some wine, I want to be drunk, I'm going to get drunk and dance; I must, I must!"

She tore herself away from him and disappeared behind the curtain. Mitya followed like a drunken man. "Yes, come what may—whatever may happen now, for one minute I'd give the whole world," he thought. Grushenka did, in fact, toss off a whole glass of champagne at one gulp, and became at once very tipsy. She sat down in the same chair as before, with a blissful smile on her face. Her cheeks were glowing, her lips were burning, her flashing eyes were moist; there was passionate appeal in her eyes. Even Kalganov felt a stir at the heart and went up to her.

"Did you feel how I kissed you when you were asleep just now?" she said thickly. "I'm drunk now, that's what it is. . . . And aren't you drunk? And why isn't Mitya drinking? Why don't you drink, Mitya? I'm drunk, and you don't drink . . ."

"I am drunk! I'm drunk as it is . . . drunk with you . . . and now I'll be drunk with wine, too."

He drank off another glass, and—he thought it strange himself—that glass made him completely drunk. He was suddenly drunk, although till that moment he had been quite sober, he remembered that. From that moment everything whirled about him, as though he were delirious. He walked, laughed, talked to everybody, without knowing what he was doing. Only one persistent burning sensation made itself felt continually, "like a red-hot coal in his heart," he said afterwards. He went up to her, sat beside her, gazed at her, listened to her. . . . She became very talkative, kept calling everyone to her, and beckoned to different girls out of the chorus. When the girl came up, she either kissed her, or made the sign of the cross over her. In another minute she might have cried. She was greatly amused by the "little old man," as she called Maximov. He ran up every minute to kiss her hands, "each little finger," and finally he danced another dance to an old song, which he sang himself. He danced with special vigor to the refrain:

> The little pig says—oink, oink, oink,
> The little calf says—moo, moo, moo,
> The little duck says—quack, quack, quack,
> The little goose says—ga, ga, ga.
> The hen goes strutting through the halls,
> Troo-roo-roo-roo-roo, she'll say,
> Troo-roo-roo-roo-roo, she'll say!

"Give him something, Mitya," said Grushenka. "Give him a present, he's poor, you know. Ah, the poor, the insulted. . . . Do you know, Mitya, I shall go into a nunnery. No, I really shall one day. Alyosha said something to me today that I shall remember all my life. . . . Yes. . . . But today let us dance. Tomorrow to the nunnery, but today we'll dance. I want to play today, good people, and what of it? God will forgive us. If I were God, I'd forgive everyone: 'My dear sinners, from this day forth I forgive you.' I'm going to beg forgiveness: 'Forgive me, good people, a silly wench.' I'm a beast, that's what I am. But I want to pray. I gave a little onion. Wicked as I've been, I want to pray. Mitya, let them dance, don't stop them. Everyone in the world is good. Everyone—even the worst of them. The world's a nice place. Though we're bad the world's all right. We're good and bad, good and bad. . . . Come, tell me, I've something to ask you; come here everyone, and I'll ask you: Why am I so good? You know I am good. I'm very good. . . . Come, why am I so good?" So Grushenka babbled on, getting more and more drunk. At last she announced that she was going to dance, too. She got up from her chair, staggering. "Mitya, don't give me any more wine—if I ask you, don't give it to me. Wine doesn't give peace. Everything's going round, the stove, and everything. I want to dance. Let everyone see how I dance . . . let them see how beautifully I dance . . ."

She really meant it. She pulled a white cambric handkerchief out of her pocket, and took it by one corner in her right hand, to wave it in the dance. Mitya ran to and fro, the girls were quiet, and got ready to break into a dancing song at the first signal. Maximov, hearing that Grushenka wanted to dance, squealed with delight, and ran skipping about in front of her, humming:

> With legs so slim and sides so trim
> And its little tail curled tight.

But Grushenka waved her handkerchief at him and drove him away.

"Shh! Mitya, why don't they come? Let everyone come . . . to look on. Call them in, too, that were locked in. . . . Why did you lock them in? Tell them I'm going to dance. Let them look on, too . . ."

Mitya walked with a drunken swagger to the locked door, and began knocking to the Poles with his fist.

"Hi, you . . . Podvysotskys! Come, she's going to dance. She calls you."

"*Lajdak!*" one of the Poles shouted in reply.

"You're a *lajdak* yourself! You're a petty Polish scoundrel, that's what you are."

"Stop laughing at Poland," said Kalganov sententiously. He too was drunk.

"Be quiet, boy! If I call him a scoundrel, it doesn't mean that I called all Poland so. One *lajdak* doesn't make a Poland. Be quiet, my pretty boy, have a candy."

"Ach, what fellows! As though they were not men. Why won't they make friends?" said Grushenka, and went forward to dance. The chorus broke into "Ah, my hall, my hall!" Grushenka flung back her head, half opened her lips, smiled, waved her handkerchief, and suddenly, with a violent lurch, stood still in the middle of the room, looking bewildered.

"I'm weak . . ." she said in an exhausted voice. "Forgive me. . . . I'm weak, I can't. . . . I'm sorry."

She bowed to the chorus, and then began bowing in all directions.

"I'm sorry. . . . Forgive me . . ."

"The lady's been drinking. The pretty lady has been drinking," voices were heard saying.

"The lady's drunk too much," Maximov explained to the girls, giggling.

"Mitya, lead me away . . . take me," said Grushenka helplessly. Mitya pounced on her, snatched her up in his arms, and carried the precious burden through the curtains. "Well, now I'll leave," thought Kalganov, and walking out of the blue room, he closed the two halves of the door after him. But the orgy in the larger room went on and grew louder and louder. Mitya laid Grushenka on the bed and kissed her on the lips.

"Don't touch me . . ." she faltered, in an imploring voice. "Don't touch me, till I'm yours. . . . I've told you I'm yours, but don't touch me . . . spare me. . . . With them here, with them close, you mustn't. He's here. It's nasty here . . ."

"I'll obey you! I won't think of it . . . I worship you!" muttered Mitya. "Yes, it's nasty here, it's abominable." And still holding her in his arms, he sank on his knees by the bedside.

"I know, though you're a brute, you're generous," Grushenka articulated with difficulty. "It must be honorable . . . it shall be honorable for the future . . . and let us be honest, let us be good, not brutes, but good . . . take me away, take me far away, do you hear? I don't want it to be here, but far, far away . . ."

"Oh, yes, yes, it must be!" said Mitya, pressing her in his arms. "I'll take you and we'll fly away. . . . Oh, I'd give my whole life for one year only to know about that blood!"

"What blood?" asked Grushenka, bewildered.

"Nothing," muttered Mitya, through his teeth. "Grusha, you wanted to be honest, but I'm a thief. But I've stolen money from Katya. . . . Disgrace, a disgrace!"

"From Katya, from that young lady? No, you didn't steal it. Give it back to her, take it from me. . . . Why make a fuss? Now everything of mine is yours. What does money matter? We shall waste it anyway. . . . Folks like us are bound to waste money. But we'd better go and work the land. I want to dig the earth with my own hands. We must work, do you hear? Alyosha said so. I won't be your mistress, I'll be faithful to you, I'll be your slave, I'll work for you. We'll go to the young lady and bow down to her together, so that she may forgive us, and then we'll go away. And if she won't forgive us, we'll go anyway. Take her her money and love me. . . . Don't love her. . . . Don't love her any more. If you love her, I shall strangle her. . . . I'll put out both her eyes with a needle . . ."

"I love you. I love only you. I'll love you in Siberia . . ."

"Why Siberia? Never mind, Siberia if you like. I don't care . . . we'll work . . . there's snow in Siberia. . . . I love driving in the snow . . . and must have bells. . . . Do you hear, there's a bell ringing? Where is that bell ringing? There are people coming. . . . Now it's stopped."

She closed her eyes, exhausted, and suddenly fell asleep for an instant. There had certainly been the sound of a bell in the distance, but the ringing had ceased. Mitya let his head sink on her breast. He did not notice that the bell had ceased ringing, nor did he notice that the songs had ceased, and that instead of singing and drunken clamor there was deathly silence in the house. Grushenka opened her eyes.

"What's the matter? Was I asleep? Yes . . . a bell . . . I've been asleep and dreamed I was driving over the snow with bells, and I dozed. I was with someone I loved, with you. And far, far away. I was holding you and kissing you, nestling close to you. I was cold, and the snow glistened. . . . You know how the snow glistens at night when the moon shines. It was as though I was not on earth. I woke up, and my dear one is close to me. How sweet that is . . ."

"Close to you," murmured Mitya, kissing her dress, her bosom, her hands. And suddenly he had a strange fancy: it seemed to him that she was looking straight before her, not at him, not into his face, but over his head, with an intent, almost uncanny fixity. An expression of wonder, almost of alarm, came suddenly into her face.

"Mitya, who is that looking at us?" she whispered suddenly. Mitya turned, and saw that someone had, in fact, parted the curtains and seemed to be watching them. And not one person alone, it seemed. He jumped up and walked quickly to the intruder.

"Here, come to us, come here," said a voice, speaking not loudly, but firmly and peremptorily.

Mitya passed to the other side of the curtain and stood stock still. The room was filled with people, but not those who had been there before. An instantaneous shiver ran down his back, and he shuddered. He recognized all those people instantly. That tall, stout old man in the overcoat and forage cap with a cockade—was the police captain, Mikhail Makarovich. And that "consumptive-looking" trim dandy, "who always has such polished boots"—that was the deputy prosecutor. "He has a chronometer worth four hundred rubles; he showed it to me." And that small young man in spectacles. . . . Mitya forgot his surname though he knew him, had seen him: he was the "district attorney" from the "Jurisprudence," who had only lately come to the town. And this man—the inspector of police, Mavriky Mavrikyevich, a man he knew well. And those fellows with the badges, why are they here? And those other two . . . peasants. . . . And there at the door Kalganov with Trifon Borisich. . . .

"Gentlemen! What's this for, gentlemen?" began Mitya, but suddenly, as though beside himself, not knowing what he was doing, he cried aloud, at the top of his voice:

"I un—der—stand!"

The young man in spectacles moved forward suddenly, and stepping up to Mitya, began with dignity, though hurriedly:

"We have to make . . . in brief, I beg you to come this way, this way to the sofa. . . . It is absolutely imperative that you should give an explanation."

"The old man!" cried Mitya frantically. "The old man and his blood! . . . I understand."

And he sank, almost fell, on a chair close by, as though he had been mown down by a scythe.

"You understand? He understands it! Monster and parricide! Your father's blood cries out against you!" the old captain of police roared suddenly, stepping up to Mitya. He was beside himself, crimson in the face and quivering all over.

"This is impossible!" cried the small young man. "Mikhail Makarovich, Mikhail Makarovich, this won't do! . . . I beg you'll allow me to speak. I should never have expected such behavior from you . . ."

"This is delirium, gentlemen, raving delirium," cried the captain of police; "look at him: drunk, at this time of night, in the company of a disreputable woman, with the blood of his father on his hands. . . . It's delirium! delirium!"

"I beg you most earnestly, dear Mikhail Makarovich, to restrain your feelings," the prosecutor said in a rapid whisper to the old police captain, "or I shall be forced to resort to . . ."

But the little attorney did not allow him to finish. He turned to Mitya, and delivered himself in a loud, firm, dignified voice:

"Ex-Lieutenant Karamazov, it is my duty to inform you that you are charged with the murder of your father, Fyodor Pavlovich Karamazov, perpetrated this night . . ."

He said something more, and the prosecutor, too, put in something, but though Mitya heard them he did not understand them. He stared at them all with wild eyes.

Book Nine

THE PRELIMINARY INVESTIGATION

Chapter I

The Beginning of Perkhotin's Official Career

Pyotr Ilyich Perkhotin, whom we left knocking as loud as he could at the strong locked gates of the widow Morozov's house, ended, of course, by making himself heard. Fenya, who was still excited by the fright she had had two hours before, and too much "upset" to go to bed, was almost frightened into hysterics on hearing the furious knocking at the gate. Though she had herself seen him drive away, she fancied that it must be Dmitri Fyodorovich knocking again, no one else could knock so "savagely." She ran to the house porter, who had already woken up and gone out to the gate, and began imploring him not to open it. But having questioned Pyotr Ilyich, and learned that he wanted to see Fenya on very "important business," the man made up his mind at last to let him in. Pyotr Ilyich was admitted into Fenya's kitchen but the girl begged him to allow the house porter to be present, "because of her misgivings." He began questioning her and at once learned the most vital fact, that is, that when Dmitri Fyodorovich had run out to look for Grushenka, he had snatched up a pestle from the mortar, and that when he returned, the pestle was not with him and his hands were smeared with blood.

"And the blood was simply flowing, dripping from him, dripping!" Fenya kept exclaiming. This horrible detail was simply the product of her disordered imagination. But although not "dripping," Pyotr Ilyich had himself seen those hands stained with blood, and had helped to wash them. Moreover, the question he had to decide was not how soon the blood had dried, but where Dmitri Fyodorovich had run with the pestle, or rather, whether it really was to Fyodor Pavlovich's, and what might be concluded from that. Pyotr Ilyich persisted in returning to this point, and though he found out nothing conclusive, yet he carried away a conviction that Dmitri Fyodorovich could have gone nowhere but to his father's house, and that therefore *something* must have happened there.

"And when he came back," Fenya added with excitement, "I told him the whole story, and then I began asking him, 'Why have you got blood on your hands, Dmitri Fyodorovich?' and he answered that that was human blood, and that he had just killed someone. He confessed it all to me, and suddenly ran off like a madman. I sat down and began thinking, where's he run off to now like a madman? He'll go to Mokroe, I thought, and kill my mistress there. I ran out to beg him not to kill her. I was running to his lodgings, but I looked at Plotnikov's shop, and saw him just setting off, and there was no blood on his hands then." (Fenya had noticed this and remembered it.) Fenya's old grandmother confirmed her evidence as far as she was capable. After asking some further questions, Pyotr Ilyich left the house, even more upset and uneasy than he had been when he entered it.

The most direct and the easiest thing for him to do would have been to go straight to Fyodor Pavlovich's, to find out whether anything had happened there, and if so, what; and only to go to the police captain, as Pyotr Ilyich firmly intended doing, when he had satisfied himself of the fact. But the night was dark, Fyodor Pavlovich's gates were strong, and he would have to knock again. His acquaintance with Fyodor Pavlovich was of the slightest, and what if, after he had been knocking, they opened to him, and nothing had happened, and Fyodor Pavlovich in his jeering way would go telling the story all over the town, how a stranger, called Perkhotin, had broken in upon him at midnight to ask if anyone had killed him. It would make a scandal. And scandal was what Pyotr Ilyich dreaded more than anything in the world. Yet the feeling that possessed him was so strong, that though he stamped his foot angrily and swore at himself, he set off again, not to Fyodor Pavlovich's but to Madame Khokhlakov's. He decided that if she denied having just given Dmitri Fyodorovich three thousand rubles, he would go straight to the police captain, but if she admitted having given him the money, he would go home and let the matter rest till next morning.

It is, of course, perfectly evident that there was even more likelihood of causing scandal by going at eleven o'clock at night to a fashionable lady, a complete stranger, and perhaps rousing her from her bed to ask her an amazing question, than by going to Fyodor Pavlovich. But that is just how it is, sometimes, especially in cases like the present one, with the decisions of the most precise and phlegmatic people. Pyotr Ilyich was by no means phlegmatic at that moment. He remembered all his life how a haunting uneasiness gradually gained possession of him, growing more and more painful and driving him on, against his will. Yet he kept cursing himself, of course, all the way for going to this lady, but "I will get to the bottom of it, I will!" he repeated for the tenth time, grinding his teeth, and he carried out his intention.

It was exactly eleven o'clock when he entered Madame Khokhla-kov's house. He was admitted into the yard pretty quickly, but, in response to his inquiry whether the lady was still up, the porter could give no answer, except that she was usually in bed by that time. "Ask at the top of the stairs. If the lady wants to receive you, she'll receive you. If she won't, she won't."

Pyotr Ilyich went up, but did not find things so easy here. The lackey was unwilling to take in his name, but finally called a maid. Pyotr Ilyich politely but insistently begged her to inform her lady that an official, living in the town, called Perkhotin, had called on particular business, and that, if it were not of the greatest importance, he would not have ventured to come. "Tell her in those words, in those words exactly," he asked the girl.

She went away. He remained waiting in the entry. Madame Khokhlakov herself was already in her bedroom, though not yet asleep. She had felt upset ever since Mitya's visit, and had a presentiment that she would not get through the night without the migraine headache which always, with her, followed such excitement. She was surprised on hearing the announcement from the maid. She irritably declined to see him, however, though the unexpected visit at such an hour, of an "official living in the town," who was a total stranger, roused her feminine curiosity intensely. But this time Pyotr Ilyich was as obstinate as a mule. He begged the maid most earnestly to take another message "in these very words":

"That he had come on business of the greatest importance, and that Madame Khokhlakov might have cause to regret it later, if she refused to see him now."

"I plunged headlong," he described it afterwards. The maid, gazing at him in amazement, went to take his message again. Madame Khokhlakov was impressed. She thought a little, asked what he looked like, and learned that he was "very well dressed, young and so polite." We may note, parenthetically, that Pyotr Ilyich was a rather good-looking young man, and well aware of the fact. Madame Khokhlakov made up her mind to see him. She was in her dressing-gown and slippers, but she flung a black shawl over her shoulders. "The official" was asked to walk into the drawing room, the very room in which Mitya had been received shortly before. The lady came to meet her visitor, with a sternly inquiring countenance, and, without asking him to sit down, began at once with the question: "What do you want?"

"I have ventured to disturb you, Madame, on a matter concerning our common acquaintance, Dmitri Fyodorovich Karamazov," Perkhotin began. But he had hardly uttered the name, when the lady's face showed signs of acute irritation. She almost shrieked, and interrupted him in a fury:

"How much longer am I to be tormented by that awful man?"

she cried hysterically. "How dare you, sir, how could you venture to disturb a lady who is a stranger to you, in her own house at such an hour! . . . And to force yourself upon her to talk of a man who came here, to this very drawing room, only three hours ago, to murder me, and went stamping out of the room, as no one would go out of a decent house. Let me tell you, sir, that I shall lodge a complaint against you, that I will not let it pass. Kindly leave me at once . . . I am a mother. . . . I . . . I . . ."

"Murder! then he tried to murder you, too?"

"Why, has he killed somebody else?" Madame Khokhlakov asked impulsively.

"If you would kindly listen, Madame, for half a moment, I'll explain it all in a couple of words," answered Perkhotin, firmly. "At five o'clock this afternoon Dmitri Fyodorovich borrowed ten rubles from me, and I know for a fact he had no money. Yet at nine o'clock, he came to see me with a bundle of hundred-ruble bills in his hand, about two or three thousand rubles. His hands and face were all covered with blood, and he looked like a madman. When I asked him where he had got so much money, he answered that he had just received it from you, that you had given him a sum of three thousand to go to the gold mines . . ."

Madame Khokhlakov's face assumed an expression of intense and painful excitement.

"Good God! He must have killed his old father!" she cried, clasping her hands. "I never gave him any money, never! Oh, run, run! . . . Don't say another word! Save the old man . . . run to his father . . . run!"

"Excuse me, Madame, then you did not give him money? You remember for a fact that you did not give him any money?"

"No, I didn't, I didn't! I refused to give it to him, for he could not appreciate it. He ran out in a fury, stamping. He rushed at me, but I slipped away . . . And let me tell you, as I wish to hide nothing from you now, that he positively spat at me. Can you fancy that! But why are we standing? Ah, sit down. . . . Excuse me, I . . . or better run, run, you must run and save the poor old man from an awful death!"

"But if he has killed him already?"

"Ah, good heavens, yes! Then what are we to do now? What do you think we must do now?"

Meantime she had made Pyotr Ilyich sit down and sat down herself, facing him. Briefly, but fairly clearly, Pyotr Ilyich told her the history of the affair, that part of it at least which he had himself witnessed. He described, too, his visit to Fenya, and told her about the pestle. All these details produced an overwhelming effect on the distracted lady, who kept uttering shrieks, and covering her face with her hands. . . .

"Would you believe it, I foresaw all this! I have that special faculty, whatever I imagine comes to pass. And how often, how often, I've looked at that awful man and always thought, that man will end by murdering me. And now it's happened . . . that is, if he hasn't murdered me, but only his own father, it's only because the finger of God preserved me, and what's more, he was ashamed to murder me because, on this very place, I put the holy icon from the relics of the holy martyr, Saint Barbara, on his neck. . . . And to think how near I was to death at that minute, I went close up to him and he stretched out his neck to me! . . . Do you know, Pyotr Ilyich (I think you said your name was Pyotr Ilyich), I don't believe in miracles, but that icon and this unmistakable miracle with me now—that shakes me, and I'm ready to believe in anything you like. Have you heard about Father Zosima? . . . But I don't know what I'm saying . . . and only fancy, with the icon on his neck he spat at me. . . . He only spat, it's true, he didn't murder me and . . . he dashed away! But what shall we do, what must we do now? What do you think?"

Pyotr Ilyich got up, and announced that he was going straight to the police captain, to tell him all about it, and leave him to do what he thought fit.

"Oh, he's an excellent man, excellent! Mikhail Makarovich, I know him. Of course, he's the person to go to. How practical you are, Pyotr Ilyich! How well you've thought of everything! I should never have thought of it in your place!"

"Especially as I know the police captain very well, too," observed Pyotr Ilyich, who still continued to stand, and was obviously anxious to escape as quickly as possible from the impulsive lady, who would not let him say good-bye and go away.

"And be sure, be sure," she prattled on, "to come back and tell me what you see there, and what you find out . . . what comes to light . . . how they'll try him . . . and what he's condemned to . . . Tell me, we have no capital punishment, have we? But be sure to come, even if it's at three o'clock at night, at four, at half past four. . . . Tell them to wake me, to wake me, to shake me, if I don't get up. . . . But, good heavens, I shan't sleep! But wait, hadn't I better come with you?"

"No—no, madame. But if you would write three lines with your own hand, stating that you did not give Dmitri Fyodorovich money, it might, perhaps, be of use . . . in case it's needed . . ."

"To be sure!" Madame Khokhlakov skipped, delighted, to her bureau. "And you know I'm simply struck, amazed at your resourcefulness, your good sense in such affairs. Are you in government here? I'm delighted to think that you're in the service here!"

And still speaking, she scribbled on half a sheet of notepaper the following lines in a large hand:

"I've never in my life lent to that unhappy man, Dmitri Fyodorovich Karamazov (for, in spite of all, he is unhappy) three thousand rubles today. I've never given him money, never! That I swear by all that's holy in our world!"

"K. Khokhlakov."

"Here's the note!" she turned quickly to Pyotr Ilyich. "Go, save him. It's a noble deed on your part!"

And she made the sign of the cross three times over him. She ran out to accompany him to the passage.

"How grateful I am to you! You can't think how grateful I am to you for having come to me, first. How is it I haven't met you before? I shall feel flattered at seeing you at my house in the future. How delightful it is that you are in government service here! . . . Such precision! Such practical ability! . . . They must appreciate you, they must understand you. If there's anything I can do, believe me . . . oh, I love young people! I'm in love with young people! The younger generation are the one prop of our suffering Russia. Her one hope. . . . Oh, go, go!" . . .

But Pyotr Ilyich had already run away or she would not have let him go so soon. Yet Madame Khokhlakov had made a rather agreeable impression on him, which had somewhat softened his anxiety at being drawn into such an unpleasant affair. Tastes differ, as we all know. "She's by no means so elderly," he thought, feeling pleased, "on the contrary I should have taken her for her daughter."

As for Madame Khokhlakov, she was simply enchanted by the young man. "Such sense! such exactness! in so young a man! in our day! and all that with such manners and appearance! People say the young people of today are no good for anything, but here's an example!" etc., etc. So she simply forgot this "dreadful affair," and it was only as she was getting into bed, that, suddenly recalling "how near death she had been," she exclaimed: "Ah, it is awful, awful!" But she fell at once into a sound, sweet sleep.

I would not, however, have dwelt on such trivial and irrelevant details, if this eccentric meeting of the young official with the by no means elderly widow, had not subsequently turned out to be the foundation of the whole career of that practical and precise young man. His story is remembered to this day with amazement in our town, and I shall perhaps have something to say about it, when I have finished my long history of the Karamazov brothers.

Chapter II
The Alarm

Our police captain, Mikhail Makarovich Makarov, a retired lieutenant colonel, was a widower and an excellent man. He had only come to us three years previously, but had won general esteem, chiefly because he "knew how to keep society together." He was never without visitors, and could not have got along without them. Someone or other was always dining with him; without a couple of guests, or even just one, he would not sit down to table. He gave regular dinners, too, on all sorts of occasions, sometimes most surprising ones. Though the fare was not elegant, it was abundant. The fish pies were excellent, and the wine made up in quantity for what it lacked in quality.

The first room his guests entered was a well-appointed billiard room, with pictures of English racehorses, in black frames on the walls, an essential decoration, as we all know, for a bachelor's billiard room. There was card-playing every evening at his house, if only at one table. But at frequent intervals, all the society of our town, with the mammas and young ladies, assembled at his house to dance. Though Mikhail Makarovich was a widower, he did not live alone. His widowed daughter lived with him, with her two unmarried daughters, grown-up girls, who had finished their education. They were of pleasant appearance and lively character, and though everyone knew they would have no dowry, they attracted all the young men of fashion to their grandfather's house.

Mikhail Makarovich was by no means very efficient in his work, though he performed his duties no worse than many others. To speak plainly, he was a man of rather narrow education. His understanding of the limits of his administrative power could not always be relied upon. It was not so much that he failed to grasp certain reforms enacted during the present reign, as that he made conspicuous blunders in his interpretation of them. This was not from any special lack of intelligence, but from carelessness, for he was always in too great a hurry to go into the subject. "I have the heart of a soldier rather than of a civilian," he used to say of himself. He had not even formed a definite idea of the fundamental principles of the reforms connected with the emancipation of the serfs, and only picked it up, so to speak, from year to year, involuntarily increasing his knowledge by practice. And yet he was himself a landowner. Pyotr Ilyich knew for certain that he would meet some of Mikhail Makarovich's visitors there that evening, but he didn't know which. As it happened, at that moment the prosecutor, and Varvinsky, our district doctor, a young man, who had only just come to us from Petersburg after taking a brilliant degree at the Academy of Medicine, were playing whist at the police captain's. Ippolit Kirillovich, the prosecutor (he was really the deputy prosecutor, but we always called him the prosecutor), was rather a peculiar man, of about thirty-five, inclined to be consumptive, and married to a fat and childless woman. He was vain and irritable, though he had a good intellect, and even a kind heart. It seemed that all that was wrong with him was that he had a better opinion of himself than his ability warranted. And that made him seem constantly uneasy. He had, moreover, certain higher, even artistic, leanings, towards psychology, for instance, a special study of the human heart, a special knowledge of the criminal and his crime. He cherished a grievance on this ground, considering that he had been passed over in the service, and being firmly persuaded that in higher spheres he had not been properly appreciated, and had enemies. In gloomy moments he even threatened to give up his post, and practice as a lawyer in criminal cases. The unexpected Karamazov case agitated him profoundly: "It was a case that might well be talked about all over Russia." But I am anticipating.

Nikolay Parfenovich Nelyudov, the young district attorney, who had come from Petersburg only two months before, was sitting in the next room with the young ladies. People talked about it afterwards and wondered that all the gentlemen should, as though intentionally, on the evening of "the crime" have been gathered together at the house of the executive authority. Yet it was perfectly simple and happened quite naturally. Ippolit Kirillovich's wife had had toothache for the last two days, and he was obliged to go out to escape from her groans. The doctor, from the very nature of his being, could not spend an evening except at cards. Nikolay Parfenovich Nelyudov had been intending for the last three days to drop in that evening at Mikhail Makarovich's, so to speak casually, so as slyly to startle the elder granddaughter, Olga Mikhailovna, by showing that he knew her secret, that he knew it was her birthday, and that she was trying to conceal it on purpose, so as not to be obliged to give a dance. He anticipated a great deal of merriment, many playful jests about her age, and her being afraid to reveal it, about his knowing her secret and telling everybody, and so on. The charming young man was a great adept at such teasing; the ladies had christened him "the naughty man," and he seemed to be delighted at the name. He was extremely well bred, however, of good family, education and feelings, and, though leading a life of pleasure, his sallies were always innocent and in good taste. He was short and weak and delicate looking. On his white, slender, little fingers he always wore a number of big, glittering rings. When he was engaged in his official duties, he always became extraordinarily grave, as though realizing his position and the sanctity of the obligations laid upon him. He had a special gift for mystifying murderers and other criminals of the peasant class during interrogation, and if he did not win their respect, he certainly succeeded in arousing their wonder.

Pyotr Ilyich was simply dumbfounded when he went into the police captain's. He saw instantly that everyone knew. They had positively thrown down their cards, all were standing up and talking. Even Nikolay Parfenovich had left the young ladies and ran in, looking urgent and ready for action. Pyotr Ilyich was met with the astounding news that old Fyodor Pavlovich really and in fact had been murdered that evening in his own house, murdered and robbed. The news had only just reached them in the following manner.

Martha Ignatyevna, the wife of old Grigory, who had been knocked senseless near the fence, was sleeping soundly in her bed and might well have slept till morning after the draught she had taken. But, all of a sudden she woke up, no doubt roused by a fearful epileptic scream from Smerdyakov, who was lying in the next room unconscious. That scream always preceded his fits, and always terrified and upset Martha Ignatyevna. She could never get accustomed to it. She jumped up and ran half-awake to Smerdyakov's room. But it was dark there, and she could only hear the invalid beginning to gasp and struggle. Then Martha Ignatyevna herself screamed out and was going to call her husband, but suddenly realized that when she had got up, he was not beside her in bed. She ran back to the bedstead and began groping with her hands, but the bed was really empty. Then he must have gone out—where? She ran to the steps and timidly called him. She got no answer, of course, but she caught the sound of groans far away in the garden in the stillness of the night. She listened. The groans were repeated, and it was evident they came from the garden.

"Good Lord! Just as it was with Lizaveta Smerdyashchaya!" she thought distractedly. She went timidly down the steps and saw that the gate into the garden was open. "He must be out there, poor dear," she thought. She went up to the gate and all at once she distinctly heard Grigory calling her by name, "Martha! Martha!" in a weak, moaning, dreadful voice.

"Lord, preserve us from harm!" Martha Ignatyevna murmured, and ran towards the voice, and that was how she found Grigory. However, she found him not by the fence where he had been knocked down, but about twenty paces off. It appeared later that he had crawled away on coming to himself, and probably had been a long time getting so far, losing consciousness several times. She noticed at once that he was covered with blood, and screamed at the top of her voice. Grigory was muttering incoherently: "He has murdered . . . his father murdered. . . . Why scream, silly . . . run . . . fetch someone . . ."

But Martha continued screaming, and seeing that her master's window was open and that there was a candle alight in the window, she ran there and began calling Fyodor Pavlovich. But peeping in at the window, she saw a fearful sight. Her master was lying on his back, motionless, on the floor. His light-colored dressing gown and white shirt were soaked with blood. The candle on the table brightly lighted up the blood and the motionless dead face of Fyodor Pavlovich. Terror-stricken, Martha rushed away from the window, ran out of the garden, drew the bolt of the big gate, and ran headlong by the back way to the neighbor, Marya Kondratyevna. Both mother and daughter were asleep, but they woke up at Martha's desperate and persistent screaming and knocking at the shutter. Martha, shrieking and screaming incoherently, managed to tell them the main fact, and to beg for assistance. It happened that Thomas had come back from his wanderings and was staying the night with them. They got him up immediately and all three ran to the scene of the crime. On the way, Marya Kondratyevna remembered that at about eight o'clock she heard a dreadful scream from their garden, and this was no doubt Grigory's scream, "Parricide!" uttered when he caught hold of Mitya's leg.

"Some one person screamed out and then was silent," Marya Kondratyevna explained as she ran. Running to the place where Grigory lay, the two women with the help of Thomas carried him to the lodge. They lighted a candle and saw that Smerdyakov was no better, that he was writhing in convulsions, his eyes fixed in a squint, and that foam was flowing from his lips. They moistened Grigory's forehead with water mixed with vinegar, and the water revived him at once. He asked immediately: "Is the master murdered?" Then Thomas and both the women ran to the house and saw this time that not only the window, but also the door into the garden was wide open, though Fyodor Pavlovich had for the last week locked himself in every night and did not allow even Grigory to come in on any pretext. Seeing that door open, they were afraid to go in to Fyodor Pavlovich "for fear anything should happen afterwards." And when they returned to Grigory, the old man told them to go straight to the police captain. Marya Kondratyevna ran there and gave the alarm to the whole party at the police captain's. She arrived only five minutes before Pyotr Ilyich, so that his story came, not as his own surmise and theory, but as the direct confirmation, by a witness, of the theory held by all, as to the identity of the criminal (a theory he had in the bottom of his heart refused to believe till that moment).

It was resolved to act with energy. The deputy police inspector of the town was commissioned to take four witnesses, to enter Fyodor Pavlovich's house and there to open an inquiry on the spot, according to the regular forms, which I will not go into here. The district doctor, a zealous man, new to his work, almost insisted on accompanying the police captain, the prosecutor, and the district attorney.

I will note briefly that Fyodor Pavlovich was found to be quite dead, with his skull battered in. But with what? Most likely with the same weapon with which Grigory had been attacked later. And immediately that weapon was found, Grigory, to whom all possible medical assistance was at once given, described in a weak and breaking voice how he had been knocked down. They began looking with a lantern by the fence and found the brass pestle dropped in a most conspicuous place on the garden path. There were no signs of disturbance in the room where Fyodor Pavlovich was lying. But by the bed, behind the screen, they picked up from the floor a big and thick envelope with the inscription: "A present of three thousand rubles for my angel Grushenka, if she is willing to come." And below had been added by Fyodor Pavlovich, "For my little chicken." There were three seals of red sealing wax on the envelope, but it had been torn open and was empty; the money had been removed. They found also on the floor a piece of narrow pink ribbon, with which the envelope had been tied up.

One piece of Pyotr Ilyich's evidence made a great impression on the prosecutor and the district attorney, namely, his idea that Dmitri Fyodorovich would shoot himself before daybreak, that he had resolved to do so, had spoken of it to Pyotr Ilyich, had taken the pistols, loaded them before him, written a letter, put it in his pocket, etc. When Pyotr Ilyich, though still unwilling to believe in it, threatened to tell someone so as to prevent the suicide, Mitya had answered grinning: "You'll be too late." So they must make haste to Mokroe to find the criminal, before he really did shoot himself.

"That's clear, that's clear!" repeated the prosecutor in great excitement. "That's just the way with mad fellows like that: 'I shall kill myself tomorrow, so I'll make merry till I die!' "

The story of how he had bought the wine and provisions excited the prosecutor more than ever. "Do you remember the fellow that murdered a merchant called Olsufyev, gentlemen? He stole fifteen hundred, went at once to have his hair curled, and then, without even hiding the money, carrying it almost in his hand in the same way, he went off to the girls."

All were delayed, however, by the inquiry, the search, and the formalities, etc., in the house of Fyodor Pavlovich. It all took time and so, two hours before starting, they sent on ahead to Mokroe the officer of the rural police, Mavriky Mavrikyevich Shmertsov, who had arrived in the town the morning before to get his pay. He was instructed to avoid raising the alarm when he reached Mokroe, but to keep constant watch over the "criminal" till the arrival of the proper authorities, also to procure witnesses for the arrest, policemen and so on. Mavriky Mavrikyevich did as he was told, preserving his incognito, and giving no one but his old acquaintance, Trifon Borisovich, the slightest hint of his secret business. He had spoken to him just before Mitya met the landlord in the balcony, looking for him in the dark, and noticed at once a change in Trifon Borisovich's face and voice. So neither Mitya nor anyone else knew that he was being watched. The box with the pistols had been carried off by Trifon Borisovich and put in a suitable place. Not until after four o'clock, almost at sunrise, did all the officials, the police captain, the prosecutor, the district attorney, drive up in two carriages, each drawn by three horses. The doctor remained at Fyodor Pavlovich's to perform a post-mortem next day on the body. But he was particularly interested in the condition of the servant, Smerdyakov. "Such violent and protracted epileptic fits, recurring continually for two days, are rarely to be met with, and are of interest to science," he declared enthusiastically to his companions, and, as they left, they laughingly congratulated him on his find. The prosecutor and the district attorney distinctly remembered the doctor's saying that Smerdyakov could not outlive the night.

After these long, but, I think, necessary explanations, we will return to that moment of our tale at which we broke off.

Chapter III

The Torments of a Soul. The First Torment[1]

And so Mitya sat looking wildly at the people round him, not understanding what was said to him. Suddenly he got up, flung up his hands and shouted aloud:

"I'm not guilty! I'm not guilty of that blood! I'm not guilty of my father's blood. . . . I meant to kill him. But I'm not guilty. Not I."

But he had hardly said this, before Grushenka rushed from behind the curtain and flung herself at the police captain's feet.

"It was my fault, accursed I am! Mine! My wickedness!" she cried, in a heart-rending voice, bathed in tears, stretching out her clasped hands towards them. "He did it through me. I tortured him and drove him to it. I tortured that poor old man that's dead, too, in my wickedness, and brought him to this! It's my fault, mine first, mine most, my fault!"

"Yes, it's your fault! You're the chief criminal! You fury! You harlot! You're the most to blame!" shouted the police captain, threatening her with his hand. But he was quickly and resolutely suppressed. The prosecutor positively seized hold of him.

1. The title designates the period of forty days after death, after which the soul reaches its destination according to Russian Orthodoxy.

"This is absolutely irregular, Mikhail Makarovich!" he cried. "You are positively hindering the inquiry. . . . You're ruining the case . . ." he almost gasped.

"Follow the regular course! Follow the regular course!" cried Nikolay Parfenovich, fearfully excited too, "otherwise it's absolutely impossible! . . ."

"Judge us together!" Grushenka cried frantically, still kneeling. "Punish us together. I will go with him now, if it's to death!"

"Grusha, my life, my blood, my holy one!" Mitya fell on his knees beside her and held her tight in his arms. "Don't believe her," he cried, "she's not guilty of anything, of any blood, of anything!"

He remembered afterwards that he was forcibly dragged away from her by several men, and that she was led out, and that when he recovered himself he was sitting at the table. Beside him and behind him stood the men with badges. Facing him on the other side of the table sat Nikolay Parfenovich, the district attorney. He kept persuading him to drink a little water out of a glass that stood on the table. "That will refresh you, that will calm you. Be calm, don't be frightened," he added, extremely politely. Mitya (he remembered it afterwards) became suddenly intensely interested in his big rings, one with an amethyst, and another with a transparent bright yellow stone, of great brilliance. And long afterwards he remembered with wonder how those rings had riveted his attention through all those terrible hours of interrogation, so that he was utterly unable to tear himself away from them and dismiss them, as things that had nothing to do with his position. On Mitya's left side, in the place where Maximov had been sitting at the beginning of the evening, the prosecutor was now seated and on Mitya's right hand, where Grushenka had been, was a rosy-cheeked young man in a sort of shabby hunting jacket, with ink and paper before him. This was the secretary of the district attorney, who had brought him with him. The police captain was now standing by the window at the other end of the room, beside Kalganov, who was sitting there.

"Drink some water," said the district attorney softly, for the tenth time.

"I have drunk it, gentlemen, I have . . . but . . . come, gentlemen, crush me, punish me, decide my fate!" cried Mitya, staring with terribly fixed wide-open eyes at the district attorney.

"So you positively declare that you are not guilty of the death of your father, Fyodor Pavlovich?" asked the district attorney, softly but insistently.

"Not guilty. I am guilty of the blood of another old man, but not of my father's. And I weep for it! I killed, I killed the old man and knocked him down. . . . But it's hard to have to answer for that murder with another, a terrible murder of which I am not guilty. . . .

It's a terrible accusation, gentlemen, a knockout blow. But who has killed my father, who has killed him? Who can have killed him if I didn't? It's marvelous, extraordinary, impossible."

"Yes, who can have killed him?" the district attorney was beginning, but Ippolit Kirillovich, the assistant prosecutor, but for the sake of brevity we will call him the prosecutor, glancing at him, addressed Mitya.

"You need not worry yourself about the old servant, Grigory Vasilyevich. He is alive, he has recovered, and in spite of the terrible blows inflicted, according to his own and your evidence, by you, there seems no doubt that he will live, so the doctor says, at least."

"Alive? He's alive?" howled Mitya, flinging up his hands. His whole face beamed. "Lord, I thank Thee for the miracle Thou hast wrought for me, a sinner and evildoer. That's an answer to my prayer. I've been praying all night." And he crossed himself three times. He was almost breathless.

"So from this Grigory we have received such important evidence concerning you, that . . ." the prosecutor would have continued, but Mitya suddenly jumped up from his chair.

"One minute, gentlemen, for God's sake, one minute; I will run to her—"

"Excuse me, at this moment it's quite impossible," Nikolay Parfenovich almost shrieked. He, too, leaped to his feet. Mitya was seized by the men with the badges, but he sat down on his own accord. . . .

"Gentlemen, what a pity! I wanted to see her for one minute only; I wanted to tell her that it has been washed away, it has gone, that blood that was weighing on my heart all night, and that I am not a murderer now! Gentlemen, she is my betrothed!" he said ecstatically and reverently, looking round at them all. "Oh, thank you, gentlemen! Oh, in one minute you have given me new life, new heart! . . . That old man used to carry me in his arms, gentlemen. He used to wash me in the tub when I was a baby three years old, abandoned by everyone, he was like a father to me! . . ."

"And so you . . ." the district attorney began.

"Allow me, gentlemen, allow me one minute more," interposed Mitya, putting his elbows on the table and covering his face with his hands. "Let me have a moment to think, let me breathe, gentlemen. All this is horribly upsetting, horribly. A man is not a drum, gentlemen!"

"Drink a little more water," murmured Nikolay Parfenovich. Mitya took his hands from his face and laughed. His eyes were confident. He seemed completely transformed in a moment. His whole bearing was changed; he was once more the equal of these men, with all of whom he was acquainted, as though they had all met the day before, when nothing had happened, at some social gathering. We may note in passing that, on his first arrival, Mitya had been made very welcome at the police captain's, but later, during the last month especially, Mitya had hardly called at all, and when the police captain met him, in the street, for instance, Mitya noticed that he frowned and only bowed out of politeness. His acquaintance with the prosecutor was less intimate, though he sometimes paid his wife, a nervous and fanciful lady, polite visits, without quite knowing why, and she always received him graciously and had, for some reason, taken an interest in him up to the last. He had not had time to get to know the district attorney, though he had met him and talked to him twice, each time about the fair sex.

"You're a most skillful lawyer, I see, Nikolay Parfenovich," cried Mitya, laughing gaily, "but I can help you now. Oh, gentlemen, I feel like a new man, and don't be offended at my addressing you so simply and directly. I'm rather drunk, too, I'll tell you that frankly. I believe I've had the honor . . . the honor and pleasure of meeting you, Nikolay Parfenovich, at my kinsman Miüsov's. Gentlemen, gentlemen, I don't pretend to be on equal terms with you. I understand, of course, in what character I am sitting before you. Oh, of course, there's a horrible suspicion . . . hanging over me . . . if Grigory has given evidence. . . . A horrible suspicion! It's awful, awful, I understand that! But to business, gentlemen, I am ready, and we will make an end of it in one moment; for, listen, listen, gentlemen! Since I know I'm innocent, we can put an end to it in a minute. Can't we? Can't we?"

Mitya spoke much and quickly, nervously and effusively, as though he positively took his listeners to be his best friends.

"So, for the present, we will write that you absolutely deny the charge brought against you," said Nikolay Parfenovich, impressively, and bending down to the secretary he dictated to him in an undertone what to write.

"Write it down? You want to write that down? Well, write it; I consent, I give my full consent, gentlemen, only . . . do you see. . . . Stay, stay, write this. Of disorderly conduct I am guilty, of violence on a poor old man I am guilty. And there is something else at the bottom of my heart, of which I am guilty, too—but that you need not write down" (he turned suddenly to the secretary) "that's my personal life, gentlemen, that doesn't concern you, the bottom of my heart, that's to say. . . . But of the murder of my old father I'm not guilty. That's a wild idea. It's quite a wild idea! . . . I will prove you that and you'll be convinced directly. . . . You will laugh, gentlemen. You'll laugh yourself at your suspicion! . . ."

"Be calm, Dmitri Fyodorovich," said the district attorney, evidently trying to allay Mitya's excitement by his own composure.

"Before we go on with our inquiry, I should like, if you will consent to answer, to hear you confirm the statement that you disliked your father, Fyodor Pavlovich, that you were involved in continual disputes with him. Here at least, a quarter of an hour ago, you exclaimed that you wanted to kill him: 'I didn't kill him,' you said, 'but I wanted to kill him'?"

"Did I exclaim that? Ach, that may be so, gentlemen! Yes, unhappily, I did want to kill him . . . many times I wanted to . . . unhappily, unhappily!"

"You wanted to. Would you consent to explain what motives precisely led you to such a sentiment of hatred for your parent?"

"What is there to explain, gentlemen?" Mitya shrugged his shoulders sullenly, looking down. "I have never concealed my feelings. All the town knows about it—everyone knows in the tavern. Only lately I declared them in Father Zosima's cell. . . . And the very same day, in the evening I beat my father. I nearly killed him, and I swore I'd come again and kill him, before witnesses. . . . Oh, a thousand witnesses! I've been shouting it aloud for the last month, anyone can tell you that! . . . The fact stares you in the face, it speaks for itself, it cries aloud, but, feelings, gentlemen, feelings are another matter. You see, gentlemen" (Mitya frowned) "it seems to me that about feelings you've no right to question me. I know that you are bound by your office, I quite understand that, but that's my affair, my private, intimate affair, yet . . . since I haven't concealed my feelings in the past . . . in the tavern, for instance, I've talked to everyone, so . . . so I won't make a secret of it now. You see, I understand, gentlemen, that there are terrible facts against me in this business. I told everyone that I'd kill him, and now, all of a sudden, he's been killed. So it must have been me! Ha, ha! I can make allowances for you, gentlemen, I can quite make allowances. I'm shocked to the epidermis myself, for who can have murdered him, if not I? That's what it comes to, isn't it? If not I, who can it be, who? Gentlemen, I want to know, I insist on knowing!" he exclaimed suddenly. "Where was he murdered? How was he murdered? How, and with what? Tell me," he asked quickly, looking at the two lawyers.

"We found him in his study, lying on his back on the floor, with his head battered in," said the prosecutor.

"That's horrible!" Mitya shuddered and, putting his elbows on the table, hid his face in his right hand.

"We will continue," interposed Nikolay Parfenovich. "So what was it that impelled you to this sentiment of hatred? You have asserted in public, I believe, that it was based upon jealousy?"

"Well, yes, jealousy. And not only jealousy."

"Disputes about money?"

"Yes, about money, too."

"There was a dispute about three thousand rubles, I think, which you claimed as part of your inheritance?"

"Three thousand! More, more," cried Mitya hotly; "more than six thousand, more than ten, perhaps. I told everyone so, shouted it at them. But I made up my mind to let it go at three thousand. I was desperately in need of that three thousand ... so the bundle of bills for three thousand that I knew he kept under his pillow, ready for Grushenka, I considered as simply stolen from me. Yes, gentlemen, I looked upon it as mine, as my own property ..."

The prosecutor looked significantly at the district attorney, and had time to wink at him on the sly.

"We will return to that subject later," said the district attorney promptly. "You will allow us to note that point and write it down; that you looked upon that money as your own property?"

"Write it down, by all means. I know that's another fact that tells against me, but I'm not afraid of facts and I tell them against myself. Do you hear? Do you know, gentlemen, you take me for a different sort of man from what I am," he added, suddenly, gloomy and dejected. "You have to deal with a man of honor, a man of the highest honor; above all—don't lose sight of it—a man who's done a lot of nasty things, but has always been, and still is, honorable at bottom, in his inner being. I don't know how to express it. That's just what's made me wretched all my life, that I yearned to be honorable, that I was, so to speak, a martyr to a sense of honor, seeking for it with a lantern, with the lantern of Diogenes and yet, all my life I've been doing filthy things like all of us, gentlemen ... that is like me alone. That was a mistake, like me alone, me alone! ... Gentlemen, my head aches ..." His brows contracted with pain. "You see, gentlemen, I couldn't bear the look of him, there was something in him ignoble, impudent, trampling on everything sacred, something sneering and irreverent, loathsome, loathsome. But now that he's dead, I feel differently."

"How do you mean?"

"I don't feel differently, but I wish I hadn't hated him so."

"You feel penitent?"

"No, not penitent, don't write that. I'm not much good myself, I'm not very beautiful, so I had no right to consider him repulsive. That's what I mean. Write that down, if you like."

Saying this Mitya became very mournful. He had grown more and more gloomy as the inquiry continued. At that moment another unexpected scene followed. Though Grushenka had been removed, she had not been taken far away, only into the room next to the blue room, in which the examination was proceeding. It was a little room with one window, just beyond the large room in which they had danced and feasted so lavishly. She was sitting there with no one by her but Maximov, who was terribly depressed, terribly scared, and clung to her side, as though for security. At their door stood one of the peasants with a badge on his breast. Grushenka was crying, and suddenly her grief was too much for her, she jumped up, flung up her arms, and with a loud wail, "oh, sorrow, my sorrow," rushed out of the room to him, to her Mitya, and so unexpectedly that they had not time to stop her. Mitya, hearing her cry, trembled, jumped up, and with a yell rushed impetuously to meet her, not knowing what he was doing. But they were not allowed to come together, though they saw one another. He was seized by the arms. He struggled, and tried to tear himself away. It took three or four men to hold him. She was seized too, and he saw her stretching out her arms to him, crying aloud as they carried her away. When the scene was over, he came to himself again, sitting in the same place as before, opposite the district attorney, and crying out to them:

"What do you want with her? Why do you torment her? She's done nothing, nothing! . . ."

The attorneys tried to soothe him. About ten minutes passed like this. At last Mikhail Makarovich, who had been absent, came hurriedly into the room, and said in a loud and excited voice to the prosecutor:

"She's been removed, she's downstairs. Will you allow me to say one word to this unhappy man, gentlemen? In your presence, gentlemen, in your presence."

"By all means, Mikhail Makarovich," answered the district attorney. "In the present case we have nothing against it."

"Listen, Dmitri Fyodorovich, my dear fellow," began the police captain, and there was a look of warm, almost fatherly, feeling for the luckless prisoner on his excited face, "I took your Agrafena Alexandrovna downstairs myself, and confided her to the care of the landlord's daughters, and that old fellow Maximov is with her all the time. And I soothed her, do you hear? I soothed and calmed her. I impressed on her that you have to clear yourself, so she mustn't hinder you, must not depress you, or you may lose your head and say the wrong thing in your evidence. In fact, I talked to her and she understood. She's a sensible girl, my boy, a good-hearted girl, she would have kissed my old hands, begging help for you. She sent me herself, to tell you not to worry about her. And I must go, my dear fellow, I must go and tell her that you are calm and comforted about her. And so you must be calm, do you understand? I was unfair to her; she is a Christian soul, gentlemen, yes, I tell you, she's a gentle soul, and not to blame for anything. So what am I to tell her, Dmitri Fyodorovich, will you sit quiet or not?"

The good-natured police captain said a great deal that was irregular, but Grushenka's suffering, a fellow creature's suffering, touched his good-natured heart, and tears stood in his eyes. Mitya jumped up and rushed towards him.

"Forgive me, gentlemen, oh, allow me, allow me!" he cried. "You've the heart of an angel, an angel, Mikhail Makarovich, I thank you for her. I will, I will be calm, cheerful, in fact. Tell her, in the infinite kindness of your heart, that I am cheerful, quite cheerful, that I shall be laughing in a minute, knowing that she has a guardian angel like you. I shall be finished with all this directly, and as soon as I'm free, I'll be with her, she'll see, let her wait. Gentlemen," he said, turning to the two attorneys, "now I'll open my whole soul to you; I'll pour out everything. We'll finish this off directly, finish it off gaily. We shall laugh at it in the end, won't we? But, gentlemen, that woman is the queen of my heart. Oh, let me tell you that. That one thing I'll tell you now.... I see I'm with honorable men. She is my light, she is my holy one, and if only you knew! Did you hear her cry, 'I'll go to death with you'? And what have I, a penniless beggar, done for her? Why such love for me? How can a clumsy, ugly brute like me, with my ugly face, deserve such love, that she is ready to go to exile with me? And how she fell down at your feet for my sake, just now?... and yet she's proud and has done nothing! How can I help adoring her, how can I help crying out and rushing to her as I did just now? Gentlemen, forgive me! But now, now I am comforted."

And he sank back in his chair and covering his face with his hands, burst into tears. But they were happy tears. He recovered himself instantly. The old police captain seemed much pleased, and the jurists also. They felt that the examination was passing into a new phase. When the police captain went out, Mitya was positively gay.

"Now, gentlemen, I am at your disposal, entirely at your disposal. And if it were not for all these trivial details, we should understand one another in a minute. I'm at those details again. I'm at your disposal, gentlemen, but I declare that we must have mutual confidence, you in me and I in you, or there'll be no end to it. I speak in your interests. To business, gentlemen, to business, and don't rummage in my soul; don't tease me with trifles, but only ask me about facts and what matters, and I will satisfy you at once. And damn the details!"

So spoke Mitya. The interrogation began again.

Chapter IV

The Second Torment

"You don't know how you encourage us, Dmitri Fyodorovich, by your readiness to answer," said Nikolay Parfenovich, with an

animated air, and obvious satisfaction beaming in his very prominent, short-sighted, light gray eyes, from which he had removed his
spectacles a moment before. "And you have made a very just
remark about the mutual confidence, without which it is sometimes
positively impossible to get on in cases of such importance, if the
suspected party really hopes and desires to defend himself and is in
a position to do so. We, on our side, will do everything in our
power, and you can see for yourself how we are conducting the
case. You approve, Ippolit Kirillovich?" He turned to the prosecutor.

"Oh, undoubtedly," replied the prosecutor. His tone was somewhat cold, compared with Nikolay Parfenovich's impulsiveness.

I will note once for all that Nikolay Parfenovich, who had but
lately arrived among us, had from the first felt marked respect for
Ippolit Kirillovich, our prosecutor, and had become almost his
bosom friend. He was almost the only person who put implicit faith
in Ippolit Kirillovich's extraordinary talents as a psychologist and
orator and in the justice of his grievance. He had heard of him in
Petersburg. On the other hand, young Nikolay Parfenovich was the
only person in the whole world whom our "unappreciated" prosecutor genuinely liked. On their way to Mokroe they had time to
come to an understanding about the present case. And now as they
sat at the table, the sharp-witted junior caught and interpreted
every indication on his senior colleague's face, every glance, or
wink, or half a word.

"Gentlemen, only let me tell my own story and don't interrupt
me with trivial questions and I'll tell you everything in a moment,"
said Mitya excitedly.

"Excellent! Thank you. But before we proceed to listen to your
communication, will you allow me to inquire as to another little
fact of great interest to us. I mean the ten rubles you borrowed
yesterday at about five o'clock on the security of your pistols, from
your friend, Pyotr Ilyich Perkhotin."

"I pledged them, gentlemen. I pledged them for ten rubles. What
more? That's all about it. As soon as I got back to town I pledged
them."

"You got back to town? Then had you been out of town?"

"Yes, I went on a journey of twenty-five miles into the country.
Didn't you know?"

The prosecutor and Nikolay Parfenovich exchanged glances.

"Well, how would it be if you began your story with a systematic
description of all you did yesterday, from the morning onwards?
Allow us, for instance, to inquire why you were absent from the
town, and just when you left and when you came back—all those
facts."

"You should have asked me like that from the beginning," cried

Mitya, laughing aloud, "and if you like, we won't begin from yesterday, but from the morning of the day before; then you'll understand how, why, and where I went. I went the day before yesterday,
gentlemen, to a merchant of the town, called Samsonov, to borrow
three thousand rubles from him on safe security. It was a pressing
matter, gentlemen, it was a sudden necessity."

"Allow me to interrupt you," the prosecutor put in politely.
"Why were you in such pressing need for just that sum, three
thousand?"

"Oh, gentlemen, you needn't go into details, how, when and why,
and why just so much money, and not so much, and all that
rigmarole. Why, it'll run to three volumes, and then you'll want an
epilogue!"

Mitya said all this with the good-natured but impatient familiarity of a man who is anxious to tell the whole truth and is full of the
best intentions.

"Gentlemen!" he corrected himself hurriedly—"don't be vexed
with me for my restiveness, I beg you again. Believe me once more,
I feel the greatest respect for you and understand the true position
of affairs. Don't think I'm drunk. I'm quite sober now. And, besides, being drunk would be no hindrance. With me it's you know,
like the saying: 'When he is sober, he is a fool; when he is drunk,
he is a wise man.' Ha, ha! But I see, gentlemen, it's not the proper
thing to make jokes to you, till we've had our explanation, I mean.
And I've my own dignity to keep up, too. I quite understand the
difference for the moment. I am, after all, in the position of a
criminal, and so, far from being on equal terms with you. And it's
your business to watch me. I can't expect you to pat me on the
head for what I did to Grigory, for one can't break old men's heads
with impunity. I suppose you'll put me away for him for six
months, or a year perhaps, in a house of correction. I don't know
what the punishment is—but it will be without loss of the rights of
my rank, without loss of my rank, Mr. Prosecutor, won't it? So you
see, gentlemen, I understand the distinction between us. . . . But
you must see that you could puzzle God Himself with such questions. 'How did you step? Where did you step? When did you step?
And on what did you step?' I shall get mixed up, if you go on like
this, and you will put it all down against me. And what will that
lead to? To nothing! And even if it's nonsense I'm talking now, let
me finish, and you, gentlemen, being men of honor and refinement,
will forgive me! I'll finish by asking you, gentlemen, to drop that
conventional method of questioning. I mean, beginning from some
miserable trifle, how I got up, what I had for breakfast, how I spat,
and where I spat, and so distracting the attention of the criminal,
suddenly stun him with an overwhelming question, 'Whom did you
murder? Whom did you rob?' Ha, ha! That's your regulation

method, that's where all your cunning comes in. You can put peasants off their guard like that, but not me. I know the tricks. I've been in the service, too. Ha, ha, ha! You're not angry, gentlemen? You forgive my impertinence?" he cried, looking at them with a good nature that was almost surprising. "It's only Mitya Karamazov, you know, so you can overlook it. It would be inexcusable in a sensible man; but you can forgive it in Mitya. Ha, ha!"

Nikolay Parfenovich listened, and laughed, too. Though the prosecutor did not laugh, he kept his eyes fixed keenly on Mitya, as though anxious not to miss the least syllable, the slightest movement, the smallest twitch of any feature of his face.

"That's how we have treated you from the beginning," said Nikolay Parfenovich, still laughing. "We haven't tried to put you out by asking how you got up in the morning and what you had for breakfast. We began, indeed, with questions of the greatest importance."

"I understand. I saw it and appreciated it, and I appreciate still more your present kindness to me, an unprecedented kindness, worthy of your noble hearts. We three here are gentlemen, and let everything be on the footing of mutual confidence between educated, well-bred people, who have the common bond of noble birth and honor. In any case, allow me to look upon you as my best friends at this moment of my life, at this moment when my honor is assailed. That's no offense to you, gentlemen, is it?"

"On the contrary. You've expressed all that so well, Dmitri Fyodorovich," Nikolay Parfenovich answered with dignified approbation.

"And enough of those trivial questions, gentlemen, all those tricky questions!" cried Mitya enthusiastically. "Or there's simply no knowing where we shall get to! Is there?"

"I will follow your sensible advice entirely," the prosecutor interposed, addressing Mitya. "But I don't withdraw my question, however. It is now vitally important for us to know exactly why you needed that sum, I mean precisely three thousand."

"Why I needed it? . . . Oh, for one thing and another. . . . Well, it was to pay a debt."

"A debt to whom?"

"That I absolutely refuse to answer, gentlemen. Not because I couldn't, or because I wouldn't dare, or because it would be damaging, for it's all a paltry matter and absolutely trifling, but—I won't, because it's a matter of principle; that's my private life, and I won't allow any intrusion into my private life. That's my principle. Your question has no bearing on the case, and whatever has nothing to do with the case is my private affair. I wanted to pay a debt. I wanted to pay a debt of honor, but to whom I won't say."

"Allow me to make a note of that," said the prosecutor.

"By all means. Write down that I won't say, that I won't. Write that I would think it dishonorable to say. Ech! you can write it; you've nothing else to do with your time."

"Allow me to caution you, sir, and to remind you once more, if you are unaware of it," the prosecutor began, with a peculiar and stern impressiveness, "that you have a perfect right not to answer the questions put to you now, and we on our side, have no right to extort an answer from you, if you decline to give it for one reason or another. That is entirely a matter for your personal decision. But it is our duty, on the other hand, in such cases as the present, to explain and set before you the degree of injury you will be doing yourself by refusing to give this or that piece of evidence. After which I will beg you to continue."

"Gentlemen, I'm not angry . . . I . . ." Mitya muttered in a rather disconcerted tone. "Well, gentlemen, you see, that Samsonov to whom I went then . . ."

Of course, we will not reproduce his account of what is known to the reader already. Mitya was impatiently anxious not to omit the slightest detail. At the same time he was in a hurry to get it over. But as he gave his evidence it was written down, and therefore they continually had to stop him. Dimitri Fyodorovich disliked this, but submitted; got angry, though still good-humoredly. He did, it is true, exclaim, from time to time, "Gentlemen, that's enough to drive an angel out of patience!" Or, "Gentlemen, it's no good your irritating me."

But even though he exclaimed he still preserved for a time his genially expansive mood. So he told them how Samsonov had made a fool of him two days before. (He had completely realized by now that he had been fooled.) The sale of his watch for six rubles to obtain money for the journey was something new to the attorneys. They were at once greatly interested, and even, to Mitya's intense indignation, thought it necessary to write the fact down as a secondary confirmation of the circumstance that he had hardly a cent in his pocket at the time. Little by little Mitya began to grow surly. Then, after describing his journey to see Lyagavy, the night spent in the stifling hut, and so on, he came to his return to the town. Here he began, without being particularly urged, to give a minute account of the agonies of jealousy he endured on Grushenka's account.

He was heard with silent attention. They inquired particularly into the circumstance of his having an observation post in Marya Kondratyevna's house at the back of Fyodor Pavlovich's garden to keep watch on Grushenka, and of Smerdyakov's bringing him information. They laid particular stress on this, and noted it down. Of his jealousy he spoke warmly and at length, and though inwardly ashamed at exposing his most intimate feelings, so to speak, to "public ignominy," he evidently overcame his shame in order to tell the truth. The frigid severity with which the district attorney, and still more the prosecutor, stared intently at him as he told his story, disconcerted him at last considerably.

"That boy, Nikolay Parfenovich, to whom I was talking nonsense about women only a few days ago, and that sickly prosecutor are not worth my telling this to," he reflected mournfully. "It's ignominious. 'Be patient, humble, hold thy peace.' "[2] He wound up his reflections with that line. But he pulled himself together to go on again. When he came to telling of his visit to Madame Khokhlakov, he regained his spirits and even wished to tell a little anecdote of that lady which had nothing to do with the case. But the district attorney stopped him, and politely suggested that he should pass on to "more essential matters." At last, when he described his despair and told them how, when he left Madame Khokhlakov's, he thought that he'd "get three thousand if he had to murder someone to do it," they stopped him again and noted down that he had "meant to murder someone." Mitya let them write it without protest. At last he reached the point in his story when he learned that Grushenka had deceived him and had returned from Samsonov's as soon as he left her there, though she had said that she would stay there till midnight. "If I didn't kill Fenya then, gentlemen, it was only because I hadn't time," broke from him suddenly at that point in his story. That, too, was carefully written down. Mitya waited gloomily, and was beginning to tell how he ran into his father's garden when the district attorney suddenly stopped him, and opening the big portfolio that lay on the sofa beside him he brought out the brass pestle.

"Do you recognise this object?" he asked, showing it to Mitya.

"Oh, yes," he smiled gloomily. "Of course I recognize it. Let me have a look at it. . . . Damn it, never mind!"

"You have forgotten to mention it," observed the district attorney.

"Hang it all, I wouldn't have concealed it from you. Do you suppose I could have managed without it? It simply escaped my memory."

"Be so good as to tell us precisely how you came to arm yourself with it."

"Certainly I will be so good, gentlemen."

And Mitya described how he took the pestle and ran.

"But what object had you in view in arming yourself with such a weapon?"

"What object? No object. I just picked it up and ran off."

"What for, if you had no object?"

---

2. From Tyutchev's poem "Silentium" [Silence!], published in 1833.

Mitya's wrath flared up. He looked intently at "the boy" and smiled gloomily and malignantly. He was feeling more and more ashamed at having told "such people" the story of his jealousy so sincerely and spontaneously.

"To hell with the pestle!" broke from him suddenly.

"But still . . ."

"Oh, to keep off dogs. . . . Oh, because it was dark. . . . In case anything turned up."

"But have you ever on previous occasions taken a weapon with you when you went out, since you're so afraid of the dark?"

"Ugh! damn it all, gentlemen! There's positively no talking to you!" cried Mitya, exasperated beyond endurance, and turning to the secretary, crimson with anger, he said quickly, with a note of fury in his voice:

"Write down at once . . . at once . . . 'that I snatched up the pestle to go and kill my father . . . Fyodor Pavlovich . . . by hitting him on the head with it!' Well, now are you satisfied, gentlemen? Are your minds relieved?" he said, glaring defiantly at the attorneys.

"We quite understand that you made that statement just now through exasperation with us and the questions we put to you, which you consider trivial, though they are, in fact, essential," the prosecutor remarked drily in reply.

"Well, upon my word, gentlemen! Yes, I took the pestle. . . . What does one pick things up for at such moments? I don't know what for. I snatched it up and ran—that's all. It's shameful, gentlemen, *passons*, or I declare I won't tell you any more."

He sat with his elbows on the table and his head in his hand. He sat sideways to them and gazed at the wall, struggling against a feeling of nausea. He had, in fact, an awful inclination to get up and declare that he wouldn't say another word, "not if you hang me for it."

"You see, gentlemen," he said at last, with difficulty controlling himself, "you see. I listen to you and am haunted by a dream. . . . It's a dream I have sometimes, you know. . . . I often dream it—it's always the same . . . that someone is hunting me, someone I'm awfully afraid of . . . that he's hunting me in the dark, in the night . . . tracking me, and I hide somewhere from him, behind a door or cupboard, hide in a degrading way, and the worst of it is, he always knows where I am, but he pretends not to know where I am on purpose, to prolong my agony, to enjoy my terror. . . . That's just what you're doing now. It's just like that!"

"Is that the sort of thing you dream about?" inquired the prosecutor.

"Yes, it is. Don't you want to write it down?" said Mitya, with a distorted smile.

"No; no need to write it down. But still you do have curious dreams."

"It's not a question of dreams now, gentlemen—this is realism, this is real life! I'm a wolf and you're the hunters. Well, hunt him down!"

"You are wrong to make such comparisons . . ." began Nikolay Parfenovich, with extraordinary softness.

"No, I'm not wrong, not at all!" Mitya flared up again, though his outburst of wrath had obviously relieved his heart. He grew more good-humored at every word. "You may not trust a criminal or a man on trial tortured by your questions, but an honorable man, the honorable impulses of the heart (I say that boldly!)—no! That you must believe you have no right indeed . . . but—

> Be patient, humble, hold thy peace.
> Be silent, heart,

Well, shall I go on?" he broke off gloomily.

"If you'll be so kind," answered Nikolay Parfenovich.

Chapter V

The Third Torment

Though Mitya spoke sullenly, it was evident that he was trying more than ever not to forget or miss a single detail of his story. He told them how he had leaped over the fence into his father's garden; how he had gone up to the window; told them all that had passed under the window. Clearly, precisely, distinctly, he described the feelings that troubled him during those moments in the garden when he longed so terribly to know whether Grushenka was with his father or not. But, strange to say, both attorneys listened now with a sort of awful reserve, looked coldly at him, asked few questions. Mitya could gather nothing from their faces. "They're angry and offended," he thought. "Well, to hell with them!" When he described how he made up his mind at last to give the "signal" to his father that Grushenka had come, so that he would open the window, the lawyers paid no attention to the word "signal," as though they entirely failed to grasp the meaning of the word in this connection: so much so, that Mitya noticed it. Coming at last to the moment when, seeing his father peering out of the window, his hatred flared up and he pulled the pestle out of his pocket, he suddenly, as though of design, stopped short. He sat gazing at the wall and was aware that their eyes were fixed upon him.

"Well?" said the district attorney. "You pulled out the weapon and . . . and what happened then?"

"Then? Why, then I murdered him . . . hit him on the head and cracked his skull. . . . I suppose that's your story. That's it!" His eyes suddenly flashed. All his smothered wrath suddenly flamed up with extraordinary violence in his soul.

"Our story?" repeated Nikolay Parfenovich. "Well—and yours?"

Mitya dropped his eyes and was silent a long time.

"My story, gentlemen? Well, it was like this," he began softly. "Whether it was someone's tears, or my mother prayed to God, or a good angel kissed me at that instant, I don't know. But the devil was conquered. I rushed from the window and ran to the fence. My father was alarmed and, for the first time, he saw me then, cried out, and sprang back from the window. I remember that very well. I ran across the garden to the fence . . . and there Grigory caught me, when I was sitting on the fence."

At that point he raised his eyes at last and looked at his listeners. They seemed to be staring at him with perfectly unruffled attention. A sort of paroxysm of indignation seized on Mitya's soul.

"Why, you're laughing at me at this moment, gentlemen!" he broke off suddenly.

"What makes you think that?" observed Nikolay Parfenovich.

"You don't believe one word—that's why! I understand, of course, that I have come to the vital point. The old man's lying there now with his skull broken, while I—after dramatically describing how I wanted to kill him, and how I snatched up the pestle—I suddenly ran away from the window. A poem! In verse! As though one could believe a fellow on his word. Ha, ha! You are scoffers, gentlemen!"

And he swung his whole body round on his chair so that the chair creaked.

"And did you notice," asked the prosecutor suddenly, as though not observing Mitya's excitement, "did you notice when you ran away from the window, whether the door into the garden was open?"

"No, it was not open."

"It was not?"

"It was shut. And who could open it? Bah! the door. Wait a bit!" he seemed suddenly to bethink himself, and almost with a start:

"Why, did you find the door open?"

"Yes, it was open."

"Why, who could have opened it if you did not open it yourselves?" cried Mitya, greatly astonished.

"The door stood open, and your father's murderer undoubtedly went in at that door, and, having accomplished the crime, went out again by the same door," the prosecutor pronounced deliberately, as though chiseling out each word separately. "That is perfectly clear. The murder was committed in the room and *not through the window*; that is absolutely certain from the examination that has been made, from the position of the body, and everything. There can be no doubt of that circumstance."

Mitya was absolutely dumbfounded.

"But that's utterly impossible!" he cried, completely at a loss. "I ... I didn't go in.... I tell you positively, definitely, the door was shut the whole time I was in the garden, and when I ran out of the garden. I only stood at the window and saw him through the window. That's all, that's all.... I remember to the last minute. And if I didn't remember, it would be just the same. I know it, for no one knew the *signals* except Smerdyakov, and me, and the dead man. And he wouldn't have opened the door to anyone in the world without the signals."

"Signals? What signals?" asked the prosecutor, with greedy, almost hysterical, curiosity. He instantly lost all trace of his reserve and dignity. He asked the question with a sort of cringing timidity. He scented an important fact of which he had known nothing, and was already filled with dread that Mitya might be unwilling to disclose it.

"So you didn't know!" Mitya winked at him with a malicious and mocking smile. "What if I won't tell you? From whom could you find out? No one knew about the signals except my father, Smerdyakov, and me: that was all. Heaven knew, too, but it won't tell you. But it's an interesting fact. There's no knowing what you might build on it. Ha, ha! Take comfort, gentlemen, I'll reveal it. You've some foolish idea in your hearts. You don't know the man you have to deal with! You have to do with a prisoner who gives evidence against himself, to his own damage! Yes, for I'm a knight of honor and you—are not."

The prosecutor swallowed this without a murmur. He was trembling with impatience to hear the new fact. Minutely and exactly Mitya told them everything about the signals invented by Fyodor Pavlovich for Smerdyakov. He told them exactly what every tap on the window meant, tapped the signals on the table, and when Nikolay Parfenovich said that he supposed he, Mitya, had tapped the signal "Grushenka has come," when he tapped to his father, he answered precisely that he had tapped that signal, that "Grushenka had come."

"So now you can build up your tower," Mitya broke off, and again turned away from them contemptuously.

"So no one knew of the signals but your dead father, you, and the servant Smerdyakov? And no one else?" Nikolay Parfenovich inquired once more.

"Yes. The servant Smerdyakov, and heaven. Write down about heaven. That may be of use. Besides, you will need God yourselves."

And they had already, of course, begun writing it down. But

while they wrote, the prosecutor said suddenly, as though hitting on a new idea:

"But if Smerdyakov also knew of these signals and you absolutely deny all responsibility for the death of your father, was it not he, perhaps, who knocked the signal agreed upon, induced your father to open to him, and then . . . committed the crime?"

Mitya turned upon him a look of profound irony and intense hatred. His silent stare lasted so long that it made the prosecutor blink.

"You've caught the fox again," commented Mitya at last; "you've got the beast by the tail. Ha, ha! I see right through you, Mr. Prosecutor. You thought, of course, that I should jump at that, catch at your prompting, and shout with all my might, 'Aie, it's Smerdyakov; he's the murderer.' Admit that's what you thought. Admit it, and I'll go on."

But the prosecutor did not admit it. He held his tongue and waited.

"You're mistaken. I'm not going to shout 'it's Smerdyakov,' " said Mitya.

"And you don't even suspect him?"

"Why, do you suspect him?"

"He is suspected, too."

Mitya fixed his eyes on the floor.

"Joking apart," he brought out gloomily. "Listen. From the very beginning, almost from the moment when I ran out to you from behind the curtain, I've had the thought of Smerdyakov in my mind. I've been sitting here, shouting that I'm innocent and thinking all the time 'Smerdyakov!' I can't get Smerdyakov out of my head. In fact, I, too, thought of Smerdyakov just now; but only for a second. Almost at once I thought, 'No, it's not Smerdyakov.' It's not his doing, gentlemen."

"In that case is there anybody else you suspect?" Nikolay Parfenovich inquired cautiously.

"I don't know anyone it could be, whether it's the hand of Heaven or of Satan, but . . . not Smerdyakov," Mitya jerked out with decision.

"But what makes you affirm so confidently and emphatically that it's not he?"

"From my conviction—my impression. Because Smerdyakov is a man of the most abject character and a coward. He's not a coward, he's the epitome of all the cowardice in the world walking on two legs. He has the heart of a chicken. When he talked to me, he was always trembling for fear I would kill him, though I never raised my hand against him. He fell at my feet and blubbered; he has kissed these very boots, literally, beseeching me 'not to frighten him.' Do you hear? 'Not to frighten him.' What a thing to say!

Why, I offered him money. He's a puling chicken—sickly, epileptic, weak-minded—a child of eight could thrash him. He has no character worth talking about. It's not Smerdyakov, gentlemen. He doesn't care for money; he wouldn't take my presents. Besides, what motive had he for murdering the old man? Why, he's very likely his son, you know—his natural son. Do you know that?"

"We have heard that legend. But you are your father's son, too, you know; yet you yourself told everyone you meant to murder him."

"That's a thrust! And a nasty, mean one, too! I'm not afraid! Oh, gentlemen, isn't it too base of you to say that to my face? It's base, because I told you that myself. I not only wanted to murder him, but I might have done it. And, what's more, I went out of my way to tell you of my own accord that I nearly murdered him. But, you see, I didn't murder him, you see, my guardian angel saved me— that's what you have not taken into account. And that's why it's so base of you, so base! For I didn't kill him, I didn't kill him, I didn't kill him! Do you hear, I did not kill him."

He was almost choking. He had not been so moved before during the whole interrogation.

"And what has he told you, gentlemen—Smerdyakov, I mean?" he added suddenly, after a pause. "May I ask that question?"

"You may ask any question," the prosecutor replied with frigid severity, "any question relating to the facts of the case, and we are, I repeat, bound to answer every inquiry you make. We found the servant Smerdyakov, concerning whom you inquire, lying unconscious in his bed, in an epileptic fit of extreme severity, that had recurred, possibly, ten times. The doctor who was with us told us, after seeing him, that he may possibly not outlive the night."

"Well, if that's so, the devil must have killed my father," broke suddenly from Mitya, as though until that moment he had been asking himself: "Was it Smerdyakov or not?"

"We will come back to this later," Nikolay Parfenovich decided. "Now, wouldn't you like to continue your statement?"

Mitya asked for a rest. His request was courteously granted. After resting, he went on with his story. But he was evidently depressed. He was exhausted, mortified and morally shaken. To make things worse the prosecutor exasperated him, as though intentionally, by vexatious interruptions about "trifling points." Scarcely had Mitya described how, sitting on the wall, he had struck Grigory on the head with the pestle, while the old man had hold of his left leg, and how he had then jumped down to look at him, when the prosecutor stopped him to ask him to describe exactly how he was sitting on the wall. Mitya was surprised.

"Oh, I was sitting like this, astride, one leg on one side of the wall and one on the other."

"And the pestle?"

"The pestle was in my hand."

"Not in your pocket? Do you remember that precisely? Was it a violent blow you gave him?"

"It must have been a violent one. But why do you ask?"

"Would you mind sitting on the chair just as you sat on the wall then and showing us just how you moved your arm, and in what direction?"

"You're making fun of me, aren't you?" asked Mitya, looking haughtily at his interrogator; but the latter did not flinch. Mitya turned abruptly, sat astride on his chair, and swung his arm.

"This was how I struck him! That's how I killed him! What more do you want?"

"Thank you. May I trouble you now to explain why you jumped down, with what object, and what you had in view?"

"Oh, hang it! . . . I jumped down to look at the man I'd hurt . . . I don't know what for!"

"Though you were so excited and were running away?"

"Yes, though I was excited and running away."

"You wanted to help him?"

"Help! . . . Yes, perhaps I did want to help him. . . . I don't remember."

"You don't remember? Then you didn't quite know what you were doing?"

"Not at all. I remember everything—every detail. I jumped down to look at him, and wiped his face with my handkerchief."

"We have seen your handkerchief. Did you hope to restore him to consciousness?"

"I don't know whether I hoped it. I simply wanted to make sure whether he was alive or not."

"Ah! You wanted to be sure? Well, what then?"

"I'm not a doctor. I couldn't decide. I ran away thinking I'd killed him. And now he's recovered."

"Excellent," commented the prosecutor. "Thank you. That's all I wanted. Kindly proceed."

Alas! it never entered Mitya's head to tell them, though he remembered it, that he had jumped back from pity, and standing over the prostrate figure had even uttered some words of regret: "You've come to grief, old man—there's no help for it. Well, there you must lie." The prosecutor could only draw one conclusion: that the man had jumped back "at such a moment and in such excitement" simply with the object of ascertaining whether the *only* witness of his crime were dead; that he must therefore have been a man of great strength, coolness, decision and foresight even at such a moment," . . . and so on. The prosecutor was satisfied: "I've provoked the nervous fellow by 'trifles' and he has said more than he meant to."

With painful effort Mitya went on. But this time he was pulled up immediately by Nikolay Parfenovich.

"How came you ran to the servant, Fenya, with your hands so covered with blood, and, as it appears, your face too?"

"Why, I didn't notice the blood at all at the time," answered Mitya.

"That's quite likely. It does happen sometimes." The prosecutor exchanged glances with Nikolay Parfenovich.

"I simply didn't notice. You're quite right there, prosecutor," Mitya assented suddenly. Next came the account of Mitya's sudden determination to "step aside" and make way for their happiness. But he could not make up his mind to open his heart to them as before, and tell them about "the queen of his soul." He disliked speaking of her before these chilly persons "who were fastening on him like bugs." And so in response to their reiterated questions he answered briefly and abruptly:

"Well, I made up my mind to kill myself. What had I left to live for? That question stared me in the face. Her first rightful lover had come back, the man who wronged her but who'd hurried back to offer his love, after five years and atone for the wrong with marriage. . . . So I knew it was all over for me. . . . And behind me disgrace, and that blood—Grigory's. . . . What had I to live for? So I went to redeem the pistols I had pledged, to load them and put a bullet in my brain tomorrow."

"And a grand feast the night before?"

"Yes, a grand feast the night before. Damn it all, gentlemen! Do make haste and finish it. I meant to shoot myself not far from here, beyond the village, and I'd planned to do it at five o'clock in the morning. And I had a note in my pocket already. I wrote it at Perkhotin's when I loaded my pistols. Here's the letter. Read it! It's not for you I tell it," he added contemptuously. He took it from his waistcoat pocket and flung it on the table. The attorneys read it with curiosity, and, as is usual, added it to the papers connected with the case.

"And you didn't even think of washing your hands at Perkhotin's? You were not afraid then of arousing suspicion?"

"What suspicion? Suspicion or not, I should have galloped here just the same, and shot myself at five o'clock, and you wouldn't have been in time to do anything. If it hadn't been for what's happened to my father, you would have known nothing about it, and wouldn't have come here. Oh, it's the devil's doing. It was the devil murdered father, it was through the devil that you found it out so soon. How did you manage to get here so quick? It's marvelous, a dream!"

"Mr. Perkhotin informed us that when you come to him, you held in your hands . . . your blood-stained hands . . . your money . . . a lot of money . . . a bundle of hundred-ruble bills, and that his servant boy saw it too."

"That's true, gentlemen. I remember it was so."

"Now, there's one little point presents itself. Can you inform us," Nikolay Parfenovich began, with extreme gentleness, "where did you get so much money all of a sudden, when it appears from the facts, from the reckoning of time, that you had not been home?"

The prosecutor's brows contracted at the question being asked so plainly, but he did not interrupt Nikolay Parfenovich.

"No, I didn't go home," answered Mitya, apparently perfectly composed, but looking at the floor.

"Allow me then to repeat my question," Nikolay Parfenovich went on as though creeping up to the subject. "Where were you able to procure such a sum all at once, when, by your own confession, at five o'clock the same day you . . ."

"I was in want of ten rubles and pledged my pistols with Perkhotin, and then went to Madame Khokhlakov to borrow three thousand which she wouldn't give me, and so on, and all the rest of it," Mitya interrupted sharply. "Yes, gentlemen, I was in want of it, and suddenly thousands turned up, eh? Do you know, gentlemen, you're both afraid now 'what if he won't tell us where he got it?' That's just how it is. I'm not going to tell you, gentlemen. You've guessed right. You'll never know," said Mitya, chipping out each word with extraordinary determination. The attorneys were silent for a moment.

"You must understand, Mr. Karamazov, that it is of vital importance for us to know," said Nikolay Parfenovich, softly and suavely.

"I understand; but still I won't tell you."

The prosecutor, too, intervened, and again reminded him that the prisoner was at liberty to refuse to answer questions, if he thought it to his interest, and so on. But in view of the damage he might do himself by his silence, especially in a question of such importance as . . .

"And so on, gentlemen, and so on. Enough! I've heard that rigmarole before," Mitya interrupted again. "I can see for myself how important it is, and that this is the vital point, and still I won't say."

"What is it to us? It's not our business, but yours. You are doing yourself harm," observed Nikolay Parfenovich nervously.

"You see, gentlemen, joking apart"—Mitya lifted his eyes and looked firmly at them both—"I had an inkling from the first that we should come to loggerheads at this point. But at first when I began to give my evidence, it was all still far away and misty; it was all floating, and I was so simple that I began with the supposition of 'mutual confidence existing between us.' Now I can see for myself that such confidence is out of the question, for in my case we were bound to come to this cursed barrier. And now we've come to it! It's impossible and there's an end of it! But I don't blame you. You can't believe it all simply on my word. I understand that, of course."

He relapsed into gloomy silence.

"Couldn't you, without abandoning your resolution to be silent about the chief point, could you not, at the same time, give us some slight hint as to the nature of the motives which are strong enough to induce you to refuse to answer, at a point so full of danger to you?"

Mitya smiled mournfully, almost dreamily.

"I'm much more good-natured than you think, gentlemen. I'll tell you the reason why and give you that hint, though you don't deserve it. I won't speak of that, gentlemen, because it would be a stain on my honor. The answer to the question where I got the money would expose me to far greater disgrace than the murder and robbing of my father, if I had murdered and robbed him. That's why I can't tell you. I can't for fear of disgrace. What, gentlemen, are you going to write that down?"

"Yes, we'll write it down," lisped Nikolay Parfenovich.

"You ought not to write that down about 'disgrace.' I only told you that in the goodness of my heart. I needn't have told you. I made you a present of it, so to speak, and you pounce upon it at once. Oh, well, write—write what you like," he concluded, with scornful disgust. "I'm not afraid of you and I can still hold up my head before you."

"And can't you tell us the nature of that disgrace?" Nikolay Parfenovich hazarded.

The prosecutor frowned darkly.

"No, no, *c'est fini*,[3] don't trouble yourself. It's not worthwhile soiling one's hands. I have soiled myself enough through you as it is. You're not worth it—no one is . . . Enough, gentlemen. I'm not going on."

This was said too peremptorily. Nikolay Parfenovich did not insist further, but from Ippolit Kirillovich's eyes he saw that he had not given up hope.

"Can you not, at least, tell us what sum you had in your hands when you went into Mr. Perkhotin's—how many rubles exactly?"

"I can't tell you that."

"You spoke to Mr. Perkhotin, I believe, of having received three thousand from Madame Khokhlakov."

"Perhaps I did. Enough, gentlemen. I won't say how much I had."

3. "That's all."

"Will you be so good then as to tell us how you came here and what you have done since you arrived?"

"Oh! you might ask the people here about that. But I'll tell you if you like."

He proceeded to do so, but we won't repeat his story. He told it drily and curtly. Of the raptures of his love he said nothing, but told them that he abandoned his determination to shoot himself, owing to "new factors in the case." He told the story without going into motives or details. And this time the attorneys did not trouble him much. It was obvious that there was no essential point of interest to them here.

"We shall verify all that. We will come back to it during the examination of the witnesses, which will, of course, take place in your presence," said Nikolay Parfenovich in conclusion. "And now allow me to request you to lay on the table everything in your possession, especially all the money you still have with you."

"My money, gentlemen? Certainly. I understand that that is necessary. I'm surprised, indeed, that you haven't inquired about it before. It's true I couldn't get away anywhere. I'm sitting here where I can be seen. But here's my money—count it—take it. That's all, I think."

He turned it all out of his pockets; even the small change—two pieces of twenty kopecks—he pulled out of his waistcoat pocket. They counted the money, which amounted to eight hundred and thirty-six rubles, and forty kopecks.

"And is that all?" asked the district attorney.

"Yes."

"You stated just now in your evidence that you spent three hundred rubles at Plotnikov's. You gave Perkhotin ten, your driver twenty, here you lost two hundred, then . . ."

Nikolay Parfenovich reckoned it all up. Mitya helped him readily. They recollected every penny and included it in the reckoning. Nikolay Parfenovich hurriedly added up the total.

"With this eight hundred you must have had about fifteen hundred at first?"

"I suppose so," snapped Mitya.

"How is it they all assert there was much more?"

"Let them assert it."

"But you asserted it yourself."

"Yes, I did, too."

"We will compare all this with the evidence of other persons not yet examined. Don't be anxious about your money. It will be properly taken care of and be at your disposal at the conclusion of . . . what is beginning . . . if it appears, or, so to speak, is proved that you have undisputed right to it. Well, and now . . ."

Nikolay Parfenovich suddenly got up, and informed Mitya firmly that it was his duty and obligation to conduct a minute and thorough search "of your clothes and everything else . . ."

"By all means, gentlemen. I'll turn out all my pockets, if you like."

And he did, in fact, begin turning out his pockets.

"It will be necessary to take off your clothes, too."

"What! Undress! Ugh! Damn it. Won't you search me as I am? Can't you?"

"It's utterly impossible, Dmitri Fyodorovich. You must take off your clothes."

"As you like," Mitya submitted gloomily; "only, please, not here, but behind the curtains. Who will search them?"

"Behind the curtains, of course."

Nikolay Parfenovich bent his head in assent. His small face wore an expression of peculiar solemnity.

Chapter VI

The Prosecutor Catches Mitya

Something utterly unexpected and amazing to Mitya followed. He could never, even a minute before, have conceived that anyone could behave like that to him, Mitya Karamazov! What was worst of all, there was something humiliating in it, and on their side something "supercilious and scornful." It was nothing to take off his coat, but he was asked to undress further, or rather not asked but "commanded," he quite understood that. From pride and contempt he submitted without a word. Several peasants accompanied the attorneys and remained on the same side of the curtain. "To be ready if force is required," thought Mitya, "and perhaps for some other reason, too."

"Well, must I take off my shirt, too?" he asked sharply, but Nikolay Parfenovich did not answer. He was busily engaged with the prosecutor in examining the coat, the trousers, the waistcoat and the cap; and it was evident that they were both much interested in the scrutiny. "They make no bones about it," flashed through Mitya's mind, "they don't keep up the most elementary politeness."

"I ask you for the second time—need I take off my shirt or not?" he said, still more sharply and irritably.

"Don't trouble yourself. We will tell you what to do," Nikolay Parfenovich said, and his voice was positively peremptory, or so it seemed to Mitya.

Meantime a consultation was going on in undertones between the attorneys. There turned out to be on the coat, especially on the left side at the back, huge patches of blood, dry, hardened, and still stiff. There were bloodstains on the trousers, too. Nikolay Parfenovich, moreover, in the presence of the peasant witnesses, passed his fingers along the collar, the cuffs, and all the seams of the coat and trousers, obviously looking for something—money, of course. He didn't even hide from Mitya his suspicion that he was capable of sewing money up in his clothes. "He treats me not as an officer but as a thief," Mitya muttered to himself. They communicated their ideas to one another with amazing frankness. The secretary, for instance, who was also behind the curtain, fussing about and listening, called Nikolay Parfenovich's attention to the cap, which they were also fingering.

"You remember Gridyenko, the clerk," observed the secretary. "Last summer he received the wages of the whole office, and pretended to have lost the money when he was drunk. And where was it found? Why, in just such pipings in his cap. The hundred-ruble bills were screwed up in little rolls and sewed in the piping." Both attorneys remembered Gridyenko's case perfectly well, and so laid aside Mitya's cap, and decided that all his clothes must be more thoroughly examined later.

"Excuse me," cried Nikolay Parfenovich, suddenly, noticing that the right cuff of Mitya's shirt was turned in, and covered with blood, "excuse me, what's that, blood?"

"Yes," Mitya jerked out.

"That is, what blood . . . and why is the cuff turned in?"

Mitya told him how he had got the sleeve stained with blood looking after Grigory, and had turned it inside when he was washing his hands at Perkhotin's.

"You must take off your shirt, too. That's very important as material evidence."

Mitya flushed red and flew into a rage.

"What, am I to stay naked?" he shouted.

"Don't disturb yourself. We will arrange something. And meanwhile take off your socks."

"You're not joking? Is that really necessary?" Mitya's eyes flashed.

"We are in no mood for joking," answered Nikolay Parfenovich sternly.

"Well, if I must . . ." muttered Mitya, and sitting down on the bed, he took off his socks. He felt unbearably awkward. All were clothed, while he was naked, and strange to say, when he was undressed he felt somehow guilty in their presence, and was almost ready to believe himself that he was inferior to them, and that now they had a perfect right to despise him. "When all are undressed, one is somehow not ashamed, but when one's the only one undressed and everybody is looking, it's degrading," he kept repeating to himself, again and again. "It's like a dream, I've sometimes dreamed of being in such degrading positions." It was a misery to him to take off his socks. They were very dirty, and so were his underclothes, and now everyone could see it. And what was worse, he disliked his feet. All his life he had thought both his big toes hideous. He particularly loathed the coarse, flat, crooked nail on the right one, and now they would all see it. Feeling intolerably ashamed made him, at once and intentionally, coarser. He pulled off his shirt, himself.

"Would you like to look anywhere else if you're not ashamed to?"

"No, there's no need to, at present."

"Well, am I to stay naked like this?" he added savagely.

"Yes, that can't be helped for the time . . . Kindly sit down here for a while. You can wrap yourself in a quilt from the bed, and I . . . I'll see to all this."

All the things were shown to the witnesses. The report of the search was drawn up, and at last Nikolay Parfenovich went out, and the clothes were carried out after him. Ippolit Kirillovich went out, too. Mitya was left alone with the peasants, who stood in silence, never taking their eyes off him. Mitya wrapped himself up in the quilt. He felt cold. His bare feet stuck out, and he couldn't pull the quilt over so as to cover them. Nikolay Parfenovich seemed to be gone a long time, "an insufferable time." "He thinks of me as a puppy," thought Mitya, gnashing his teeth. "That rotten prosecutor has gone, too, contemptuous no doubt, it disgusts him to see me naked!" Mitya imagined, however, that his clothes would be examined and returned to him. But what was his indignation when Nikolay Parfenovich came back with quite different clothes, brought in behind him by a peasant.

"Here are clothes for you," he observed airily, seeming well satisfied with the success of his mission. "Mr. Kalganov has kindly provided these for this unusual emergency, as well as a clean shirt. Luckily he had them all in his trunk. You can keep your own socks and underclothes."

Mitya flew into a passion.

"I won't have other people's clothes!" he shouted menacingly, "give me my own!"

"It's impossible!"

"Give me my own. Damn Kalganov and his clothes, too!"

It was a long time before they could persuade him. But they succeeded somehow in quieting him down. They impressed upon him that, his clothes being stained with blood, must be "included with the other material evidence," and that they "had not even the right to let him have them now . . . taking into consideration the possible outcome of the case." Mitya at last understood this. He subsided into gloomy silence and hurriedly dressed himself. He merely observed, as he put them on, that the clothes were much better than his old ones, and that he disliked "gaining by the change." It was, besides, "ridiculously narrow. Am I to be dressed up like a fool . . . for your amusement?"

They urged upon him again that he was exaggerating, that Kalganov was only a little taller, so that only the trousers might be a little too long. But the coat turned out to be really tight in the shoulders.

"Damn it all! I can hardly button it," Mitya grumbled. "Be so good as to tell Mr. Kalganov from me that I didn't ask for his clothes, and it's not my doing that they've dressed me up like a clown."

"He quite understands that, and is sorry . . . I mean, not sorry to lend you his clothes, but sorry about all this business," mumbled Nikolay Parfenovich.

"Confound his sorrow! Well, where now, or am I to go on sitting here?"

He was asked to go back to the "other room." Mitya went in, scowling with anger, and trying to avoid looking at any one. Dressed in another man's clothes he felt himself disgraced, even in the eyes of the peasants, and of Trifon Borisovich, whose face appeared, for some reason, in the doorway, and vanished immediately. "He's come to look at me dressed up like a mummer," thought Mitya. He sat down on the same chair as before. He had an absurd nightmarish feeling, as though he were out of his mind.

"Well, what now? Are you going to flog me? That's all that's left for you," he said, clenching his teeth and addressing the prosecutor. He would not turn to Nikolay Parfenovich, as though he disdained to speak to him. "He looked too closely at my socks, and turned them inside out on purpose to show everyone how dirty my underclothes were—the scoundrel!"

"Well, now we must proceed to the examination of witnesses," observed Nikolay Parfenovich, as though in reply to Mitya's question.

"Yes," said the prosecutor thoughtfully, as though reflecting on something.

"We've done what we could in your interest, Dmitri Fyodorovich," Nikolay Parfenovich went on, "but having received from you such an uncompromising refusal to explain to us the source from which you obtained the money found upon you, we are, at the present moment . . ."

"What is the stone in your ring?" Mitya interrupted suddenly, as though awakening from a reverie. He pointed to one of the three large rings adorning Nikolay Parfenovich's right hand.

"Ring?" repeated Nikolay Parfenovich with surprise.

"Yes, that one . . . on your middle finger, with the little veins in it, what stone is that?" Mitya persisted, like a peevish child.

"That's a smoky topaz," said Nikolay Parfenovich, smiling. "Would you like to look at it? I'll take it off . . ."

"No, don't take it off," cried Mitya furiously, suddenly waking up, and angry with himself. "Don't take it off . . . there's no need. . . . Damn it. . . . Gentlemen, you've sullied my heart! Can you suppose that I would conceal it from you, if I really had killed my father, that I would shuffle, lie, and hide myself? No, that's not like Dmitri Karamazov, that he couldn't do, and if I were guilty, I swear I wouldn't have waited for your coming, or for the sunrise as I meant at first, but would have destroyed myself before this, without waiting for the dawn! I know that about myself now. I couldn't have learned so much in twenty years as I've found out in this accursed night! . . . And would I have been like this on this night, and at this moment, sitting with you, could I have talked like this, could I have moved like this, could I have looked at you and at the world like this, if I had really been the murderer of my father, when the very thought of having accidentally killed Grigory gave me no peace all night—not from fear—oh, not simply from fear of your punishment! The disgrace of it! And you expect me to be open with such scoffers as you, who see nothing and believe in nothing, blind moles and scoffers, and to tell you another nasty thing I've done, another disgrace, even if that would save me from your accusation! No, better Siberia! The man who opened the door to my father and went in at that door, he killed him, he robbed him. Who was he—I'm racking my brains and can't think who. But I can tell you it was not Dmitri Karamazov, and that's all I can tell you, and that's enough, enough, leave me alone. . . . Exile me, punish me, but don't bother me any more. I'll say no more. Call your witnesses!"

Mitya uttered his sudden monologue as though he were determined to be absolutely silent for the future. The prosecutor watched him the whole time and only when he had ceased speaking, observed, as though it were the most ordinary thing, with the most frigid and composed air:

"Oh, about the open door of which you spoke just now, we may as well inform you, by the way, now, of a very interesting piece of evidence of the greatest importance both to you and to us, that has been given us by Grigory, the old man you wounded. On his recovery, he clearly and emphatically stated, in reply to our questions, that when, on coming out to the steps, and hearing a noise in the garden, he made up his mind to go into it through the little gate which stood open, before he noticed you running, as you have told us already, in the dark from the open window where you saw your father, he, Grigory, glanced to the left, and, while noticing the open window, observed at the same time, much nearer to him, the door, standing wide open—that door which you have stated to have been shut the whole time you were in the garden. I will not conceal from you that Grigory himself confidently affirms and bears witness that you must have run from that door, though, of course, he did not see you do so with his own eyes, since he only noticed you first some distance away in the garden, running towards the fence."

Mitya had leapt up from his chair half way through this speech.

"Nonsense!" he yelled, in a sudden frenzy, "it's a bare-faced lie. He couldn't have seen the door open because it was shut. He's lying!"

"I consider it my duty to repeat that he is firm in his statement. He does not waver. He adheres to it. We've cross-examined him several times."

"Precisely. I have cross-examined him several times," Nikolay Parfenovich confirmed warmly.

"It's false, false! It's either an attempt to slander me, or the hallucination of a madman," Mitya still shouted. "He's simply raving, from loss of blood, from the wound. He must have fancied it when he came to. . . . He's raving."

"Yes, but he noticed the open door, not when he came to after his injuries, but before that, as soon as he went into the garden from the lodge."

"But it's false, it's false! It can't be so! He's slandering me from spite. . . . He couldn't have seen it . . . I didn't come from the door," gasped Mitya.

The prosecutor turned to Nikolay Parfenovich and said to him impressively:

"Confront him with it."

"Do you recognize this object?"

Nikolay Parfenovich laid upon the table a large and thick official envelope, on which three seals still remained intact. The envelope was empty, and slit open at one end. Mitya stared at it with open eyes.

"It . . . it must be that envelope of my father's, the envelope that contained the three thousand rubles . . . and if there's inscribed on it, allow me, 'For my little chicken' . . . yes—three thousand!" he shouted, "do you see, three thousand, do you see?"

"Of course, we see. But we didn't find the money in it. It was empty, and lying on the floor by the bed, behind the screen."

For some seconds Mitya stood as though thunderstruck.

"Gentlemen, it's Smerdyakov!" he shouted suddenly, at the top of his voice. "It's he who's murdered him! He's robbed him! No one else knew where the old man hid the envelope. It's Smerdyakov, that's clear, now!"

"But you, too, knew of the envelope and that it was under the pillow."

"I never knew it. I've never seen it. This is the first time I've looked at it. I've only heard of it from Smerdyakov. . . . He was the only one who knew where the old man kept it hidden, I didn't know . . ." Mitya was completely breathless.

"But you told us yourself that the envelope was under your deceased father's pillow. You especially stated that it was under the pillow, so you must have known it."

"We've got it written down," confirmed Nikolay Parfenovich.

"Nonsense! It's absurd! I'd no idea it was under the pillow. And perhaps it wasn't under the pillow at all. . . . It was just a chance guess that it was under the pillow. What does Smerdyakov say? Have you asked him where it was? What does Smerdyakov say? that's the chief point. . . . And I went out of my way to tell lies against myself. . . . I told you without thinking that it was under the pillow, and now you . . . Oh, you know how one says the wrong thing, without meaning it. No one knew but Smerdyakov, only Smerdyakov, and no one else. . . . He didn't even tell me where it was! But it's his doing, his doing; there's no doubt about it, he murdered him, that's as clear as daylight now," Mitya exclaimed more and more frantically, repeating himself incoherently, and growing more and more exasperated and excited. "You must understand that, and arrest him at once. . . . He must have killed him while I was running away and while Grigory was unconscious, that's clear now. . . . He gave the signal and father opened to him . . . for no one but he knew the signal, and without the signal father would never have opened the door. . . ."

"But you're again forgetting the circumstance," the prosecutor observed, still speaking with the same restraint, though with a note of triumph, "that there was no need to give the signal if the door already stood open when you were there, while you were in the garden . . ."

"The door, the door," muttered Mitya, and he stared speechless at the prosecutor. He sank back helpless in his chair. All were silent.

"Yes, the door! . . . It's a nightmare! God is against me!" he exclaimed, staring before him in complete stupefaction.

"Come, you see," the prosecutor went on with dignity, "and you can judge for yourself, Dmitri Fyodorovich. On the one hand we have the evidence of the open door from which you ran out, a fact which overwhelms you and us. On the other side your incomprehensible, persistent, and, so to speak, obdurate silence with regard to the source from which you obtained the money which was so suddenly seen in your hands, when only three hours earlier, on your own testimony, you pledged your pistols for the sake of ten rubles! In view of all these facts, judge for yourself. What are we to believe, and what can we depend upon? And don't accuse us of being 'frigid, cynical, scoffing people,' who are incapable of believing in the generous impulses of your heart. . . . Try to enter into our position . . ."

Mitya was indescribably agitated. He turned pale.

"Very well!" he exclaimed suddenly, "I will tell you my secret. I'll tell you where I got the money! . . . I'll reveal my shame, that I may not have to blame myself or you hereafter."

"And believe me, Dmitri Fyodorovich," put in Nikolay Parfenovich, in a voice of almost pathetic delight, "that every sincere and complete confession on your part at this moment may, later on, have an immense influence in your favor, and may, indeed, moreover . . ."

But the prosecutor gave him a slight shove under the table, and he checked himself in time. Mitya, it is true, had not heard him.

Chapter VII

Mitya's Great Secret. Received with Hisses

"Gentlemen," he began, still in the same agitation, "I want to make a full confession: that money was *my own.*"

The attorneys' faces lengthened. That was not at all what they expected.

"How do you mean?" faltered Nikolay Parfenovich, "when at five o'clock on the same day, by your own admission . . ."

"Damn five o'clock on the same day and my own admission. That's nothing to do with it now! That money was my own, my own, that is, stolen by me . . . not mine, I mean, but stolen by me, and it was fifteen hundred rubles, and I had it on me all the time, all the time . . ."

"But where did you get it?"

"I took it off my neck, gentlemen, off this very neck . . . it was here, round my neck, sewn up in a rag, and I'd had it round my neck a long time, it's a month since I put it round my neck . . . to my shame and disgrace!"

"And from whom did you . . . appropriate it?"

"You mean, 'steal it'? Speak out plainly now. Yes, I consider that I practically stole it, but, if you prefer, I 'appropriated it.' I consider I stole it. And last night I stole it finally."

"Last night? But you said that it's a month since you . . . obtained it? . . ."

"Yes. But not from my father. Not from my father, don't be uneasy. I didn't steal it from my father, but from her. Let me tell you without interrupting. It's hard to do, you know. You see, a month ago, I was sent for by Katerina Ivanovna Verkhovtsev, formerly my betrothed. Do you know her?"

"Yes, of course."

"I know you know her. She's a noble creature, noblest of the noble. But she has hated me ever so long, oh, ever so long . . . and hated me with good reason, good reason!"

"Katerina Ivanovna!" Nikolay Parfenovich exclaimed with amazement. The prosecutor, too, stared.

"Oh, don't take her name in vain! I'm a scoundrel to bring her into it. Yes, I've seen that she hated me . . . a long while. . . . From the very first, even that evening at my lodging . . . but enough, enough. You're unworthy even to know of that. No need of that at all. . . . I need only tell you that she sent for me a month ago, gave me three thousand rubles to send to her sister and another relation in Moscow (as though she couldn't have sent it off herself!), and I . . . it was just at that fatal moment in my life when I . . . Well, in fact, when I'd just come to love another, *her*, she's sitting down below now, Grushenka. I carried her off here to Mokroe then, and wasted here in two days half that damned three thousand, but the other half I kept on me. Well, I've kept that other half, that fifteen hundred like a locket round my neck, but yesterday I undid it, and spent it. What's left of it, eight hundred rubles, is it your hands now, Nikolay Parfenovich. That's what's left from the fifteen hundred I had yesterday."

"Excuse me. How's that? Why, when you were here a month ago you spent three thousand, not fifteen hundred, everybody knows that."

"Who knows it? Who counted the money? Did I let anyone count it?"

"Why, you told everyone yourself that you'd spent exactly three thousand."

"It's true, I did. I told the whole town so, and the whole town said so. And here, at Mokroe, too, everyone reckoned it was three thousand. Yet I didn't spend three thousand, but fifteen hundred. And the other fifteen hundred I sewed into a little bag. That's how it was, gentlemen. That's where I got that money yesterday . . ."

"This is almost miraculous," murmured Nikolay Parfenovich.

"Allow me to inquire," observed the prosecutor at last, "have you informed anyone whatever of this circumstance before, I mean that you had fifteen hundred left about you a month ago?"

"I told no one."

"That's strange. Do you mean absolutely no one?"

"Absolutely no one. No one and nobody."

"What was your reason for this reticence? What was your motive for making such a secret of it? To be more precise: You have told us at last your secret, in your words, so 'disgraceful,' though in reality—that is, of course, comparatively speaking—this action, that is, the appropriation of three thousand rubles belonging to someone else, and, of course, only for a time is, in my view at least, only an act of the greatest recklessness and not so disgraceful, when one takes into consideration your character. . . . Even admitting that it was an action in the highest degree discreditable, still, discreditable is not 'disgraceful.' . . . Many people have already guessed, during this last month, about the three thousand of Miss Verkhovtsev's that you have spent, and I had heard the legend myself, apart from your confession. . . . Mikhail Makarovich, for instance, had heard it, too, so that indeed, it was scarcely a legend, but the gossip of the whole town. There are indications, too, if I am not mistaken, that you confessed this yourself to someone, I mean that the money was from Miss Verkhovtsev and so, it's extremely surprising to me that hitherto, that is, up to the present moment, you have made such an extraordinary secret of the fifteen hundred you say you put by, apparently connecting a feeling of positive horror with that secret. . . . It's not easy to believe that it could cost you such distress to confess such a secret. . . . You cried out, just now, that Siberia would be better than confessing it . . ."

The prosecutor ceased speaking. He was provoked. He did not conceal his vexation, which was almost anger, and gave vent to all his accumulated spleen, without choosing words, disconnectedly and incoherently.

"It's not the fifteen hundred that's the disgrace, but that I put it apart from the rest of the three thousand," said Mitya firmly.

"Why," smiled the prosecutor irritably. "What is there disgraceful, to your thinking, in your having set aside half of the three thousand you had discreditably, if you prefer, 'disgracefully,' appropriated? Your taking the three thousand is more important than what you did with it. And by the way, why did you do that—why did you set apart that half, for what purpose, for what object did you do it? Can you explain that to us?"

"Oh, gentlemen, the purpose is the whole point!" cried Mitya. "I put it aside because I was vile, that is, because I was calculating, and to be calculating in such a case is vile . . . and that vileness has been going on a whole month."

"It's incomprehensible."

"I wonder at you. But I'll make it clearer. Perhaps it really is incomprehensible. You see, attend to what I say. I appropriate three thousand entrusted to my honor, I spent it on a spree, say I spend it all, and next morning I go to her and say, 'Katya, I've done wrong, I've squandered your three thousand,' well, is that right? No, it's not right—it's dishonest and cowardly, I'm a beast, with no more self-control than a beast, that's so, isn't it? But still I'm not a thief? Not a downright thief, you'll admit! I squandered it, but I didn't steal it. Now a second, rather more favorable alternative: follow me carefully, or I may get confused again—my head's going round—and so for the second alternative: I spend here only fifteen hundred out of the three thousand, that is, only half. Next day I go and take that half to her: 'Katya, take this fifteen hundred from me, I'm a low beast, and an untrustworthy scoundrel, for I've wasted half the money, and I shall waste this, too, so keep me from temptation!' Well, what of that alternative? I would be a beast and a scoundrel, and whatever you like; but not a thief, not altogether a thief, or I would not have brought back what was left, but have kept that, too. She would see at once that since I brought back half, I would pay back what I'd spent, that I would never give up trying to, that I would work to get it and pay it back. So in that case I would be a scoundrel, but not a thief, you may say what you like, not a thief!"

"I admit that there is a certain distinction," said the prosecutor, with a cold smile. "But it's strange that you see such a vital difference."

"Yes, I see a vital difference! Every man may be a scoundrel, and perhaps every man is a scoundrel, but not everyone can be a thief, it takes an arch-scoundrel to be that. Oh, of course, I don't know how to make these fine distinctions ... but a thief is lower than a scoundrel, that's my conviction. Listen, I carry the money about me a whole month, I may make up my mind to give it back tomorrow, and I'm a scoundrel no longer, but I cannot make up my mind, you see, though I make up my mind every day, and every day spur myself on to do it, and yet for a whole month I can't bring myself to it, you see. Is that right to your thinking, is that right?"

"Certainly, that's not right, that I can quite understand, and that I don't dispute," answered the prosecutor with reserve. "And let us give up all discussions of these subtleties and distinctions, and, if you will be so kind, get back to the point. And the point is, that you have still not told us, although we've asked you, why, in the first place, you halved the money, squandering one half and hiding the other? For what purpose exactly did you hide it, what did you mean to do with that fifteen hundred? I insist upon that question, Dmitri Fyodorovich."

"Yes, of course!" cried Mitya, striking himself on the forehead; "forgive me, I'm troubling you, and am not explaining the chief point, or you'd understand in a minute, for it's just the motive of it that's the disgrace! You see, it was all to do with the old man, my dead father. He was always pestering Agrafena Alexandrovna, and I was jealous; I thought then that she was hesitating between me and him. So I kept thinking every day, suppose she were to make up her mind all of a sudden, suppose she were to stop tormenting me, and were suddenly to say to me, 'I love you, not him; take me to the other end of the world.' And I'd only forty kopecks; how could I take her away, what could I do? Why, I'd be lost. You see,

I didn't know her then, I didn't understand her, I thought she wanted money, and that she wouldn't forgive my poverty. And so I fiendishly counted out the half of that three thousand, sewed it up, calculating on it, sewed it up before I was drunk, and after I had sewn it up, I went off to get drunk on the rest. Yes, that was base. Do you understand now?"

Both attorneys laughed aloud.

"I would have called it sensible and moral on your part not to have squandered it all," chuckled Nikolay Parfenovich, "for after all what does it amount to?"

"Why, that I stole it, that's what it amounts to! Oh, God, you horrify me by not understanding! Every day that I had that fifteen hundred sewn up round my neck, every day and every hour I said to myself, 'You're a thief! you're a thief!' Yes, that's why I've been so savage all this month, that's why I fought in the tavern, that's why I attacked my father, it was because I felt I was a thief. I couldn't make up my mind, I didn't dare even to tell Alyosha, my brother, about that fifteen hundred: I felt I was such a scoundrel and such a pickpocket. But, do you know, while I carried it I said to myself at the same time every hour: 'No, Dmitri Fyodorovich, you may yet not be a thief.' Why? Because I might go next day and pay back that fifteen hundred to Katya. And only yesterday I made up my mind to tear my amulet off my neck, on my way from Fenya's to Perkhotin. I hadn't been able till that moment to bring myself to it. And it was only when I tore it off that I became a downright thief, a thief and a dishonest man for the rest of my life. Why? Because, with that I destroyed, too, my dream of going to Katya and saying, 'I'm a scoundrel, but not a thief!' Do you understand now? Do you understand?"

"What was it made you decide to do it yesterday?" Nikolay Parfenovich interrupted.

"Why? It's absurd to ask. Because I had condemned myself to die at five o'clock this morning, here, at dawn. I thought it made no difference whether I died a thief or a man of honor. But I see it's not so, it turns out that it does make a difference. Believe me, gentlemen, what has tortured me most during this night has not been the thought that I'd killed the old servant, and that I was in danger of Siberia just when my love was being rewarded, and Heaven was open to me again. Oh, that did torture me, but not in the same way; not so much as the damned consciousness that I had torn that damned money off my breast at last and spent it, and had become a downright thief! Oh, gentlemen, I tell you again, with a bleeding heart, I have learned a great deal this night. I have learned that it's not only impossible to live a scoundrel, but impossible to die a scoundrel. . . . No, gentlemen, one must die honest . . ."

Mitya was pale. His face had a haggard and exhausted look, in spite of his being intensely excited.

"I am beginning to understand you, Dmitri Fyodorovich," the prosecutor said slowly, in a soft and almost compassionate tone. "But all this, if you'll excuse my saying so, is a matter of nerves, in my opinion . . . your overwrought nerves, that's what it is. And why, for instance, should you not have saved yourself such misery for almost a month, by going and returning that fifteen hundred to the lady who had entrusted it to you? And why could you not have explained things to her, and in view of your position, which you describe as being so awful, why could you not have had recourse to the plan which would so naturally have occurred to one's mind, that is, after honorably confessing your errors to her, why could you not have asked her to lend you the sum needed for your expenses, which, with her generous heart, she would certainly not have refused you in your distress, especially if it had been with some guarantee, or even on the security you offered to the merchant Samsonov, and to Madame Khokhlakov. I suppose you still regard that security as of value?"

Mitya suddenly crimsoned.

"Surely you don't think me such an out and out scoundrel as that? You can't be speaking in earnest?" he said, with indignation, looking the prosecutor straight in the face, and seeming unable to believe his ears.

"I assure you I'm in earnest. . . . Why do you imagine I'm not serious?" It was the prosecutor's turn to be surprised.

"Oh, how base that would have been! Gentlemen, do you know, you are torturing me! Let me tell you everything, so be it. I'll confess all my infernal wickedness, but to put you to shame, and you'll be surprised yourself at the depths of ignominy to which a medley of human passions can sink. You must know that I already had that plan myself, that plan you spoke of, just now, prosecutor! Yes, gentlemen, I, too, have had that thought in my mind all this current month, so that I was on the point of deciding to go to Katya—I was base enough for that. But to go to her, to tell her of my treachery, and for that very treachery, to carry it out, for the expenses of that treachery, to beg for money from her, Katya (to beg, do you hear, to beg), and to go straight from her to run away with the other, the rival, who hated and insulted her—to think of it! You must be mad, prosecutor!"

"Mad I am not, but I did speak in haste, without thinking . . . of that feminine jealousy . . . if there could be jealousy in this case, as you assert . . . yes, perhaps there is something of the kind," said the prosecutor, smiling.

"But that would have been so infamous!" Mitya brought his fist down on the table fiercely. "That would have been filthy beyond everything! Yes, do you know that she might have given me that money, yes, and she would have given it too; she'd have given it to satisfy her vengeance, to show her contempt for me, for hers is an infernal nature, too, and she's a woman of great wrath. I'd have taken the money, too, oh, I would have taken it; I would have taken it, and then, for the rest of my life . . . oh, God! Forgive me, gentlemen, I'm making such an outcry because I've had that thought in my mind so much lately, only the day before yesterday, that night when I was having all that bother with Lyagavy, and afterwards yesterday, all day yesterday, I remember, till that happened . . ."

"Till what happened?" put in Nikolay Parfenovich inquisitively, but Mitya did not hear it.

"I have made you an awful confession," Mitya said gloomily in conclusion. "You must appreciate it, and what's more, you must respect it, for if not, if that leaves your souls untouched, then you've simply no respect for me, gentlemen, I tell you that, and I shall die of shame at having confessed it to men like you! Oh, I shall shoot myself! Yes, I see, I see already that you don't believe me. What, you want to write that down, too?" he cried in dismay.

"Yes, what you said just now," said Nikolay Parfenovich, looking at him in surprise, "that is, that up to the last hour you were still contemplating going to Miss Verkhovtsev to beg that sum from her. . . . I assure you, that's a very important piece of evidence for us, Dmitri Fyodorovich, I mean for the whole case . . . and particularly for you, particularly important for you."

"Have mercy, gentlemen!" Mitya flung up his hands, "Don't write that, anyway; have some shame. Here I've torn my heart asunder before you, and you seize the opportunity and are rummaging in the wounds of both halves. . . . Oh, my God!"

In despair he hid his face in his hands.

"Don't worry yourself so, Dmitri Fyodorovich," observed the prosecutor, "everything that is written down will be read over to you afterwards, and what you don't agree to we'll alter as you like. But now I'll ask you one little question for the third time. Has no one, absolutely no one, heard from you of that money you sewed up? That, I must tell you, is almost impossible to believe."

"No one, no one, I told you so before, or you've not understood anything! Let me alone!"

"Very well, this matter is bound to be explained, and there's plenty of time for it, but meantime, consider; we have perhaps a dozen witnesses that you yourself spread it abroad, and even shouted almost everywhere about the three thousand you'd spent here; three thousand, not fifteen hundred. And now, too, when you got hold of the money you had yesterday, you gave many people to understand that you had brought three thousand with you."

"You've got not dozens, but hundreds of witnesses, two hundred witnesses, two hundred have heard it, thousands have heard it!" cried Mitya.

"Well, you see, all bear witness to it. And the word *all* means something."

"It means nothing. I talked rot, and everyone began repeating it."

"But what need have you to 'talk rot,' as you call it?"

"The devil knows. From bravado perhaps . . . at having wasted so much money. . . . To try and forget that money I had sewn up, perhaps . . . yes, that was why . . . damn it . . . how often will you ask me that question? Well, I told a fib, and that was the end of it, once I'd said it, I didn't care to correct it. What does a man tell lies for sometimes?"

"That's very difficult to decide, Dmitri Fyodorovich, what makes a man tell lies," observed the prosecutor impressively. "Tell me, though, was that 'amulet,' as you call it, on your neck, a big thing?"

"No, not big."

"How big, for instance?"

"If you fold a hundred-ruble bill in half, that would be the size."

"You'd better show us the remains of it. You must have them somewhere."

"Damnation, what nonsense! I don't know where they are."

"But excuse me: where and when did you take it off your neck? According to your own evidence you didn't go home."

"When I was going from Fenya's to Perkhotin's, on the way I tore it off my neck and took out the money."

"In the dark?"

"What should I want a light for? I did it with my fingers in one minute."

"Without scissors, in the street?"

"In the marketplace I think it was. Why scissors? It was an old rag. It was torn in a minute."

"Where did you put it afterwards?"

"I dropped it there."

"Where was it, exactly?"

"In the marketplace, in the marketplace! The devil knows whereabouts. What do you want to know for?"

"That's extremely important, Dmitri Fyodorovich. It would be material evidence in your favor. How is it you don't understand that? Who helped you to sew up in a month ago?"

"No one helped me. I did it myself."

"Can you sew?"

"A soldier has to know how to sew. No knowledge was needed to do that."

"Where did you get the material, that is, the rag in which you sewed the money?"

"Are you laughing at me?"

"Not at all. And we are in no mood for laughing, Dmitri Fyodorovich."

"I don't know where I got the rag from—somewhere, I suppose."

"I would have thought you couldn't have forgotten it?"

"Upon my word, I don't remember. I might have torn a bit off my linen."

"That's very interesting. We might find in your lodgings tomorrow the shirt or whatever it is from which you tore the rag. What sort of rag was it, cloth or linen?"

"Goodness only knows what it was. Wait a bit. . . . I believe I didn't tear it off anything. It was a bit of calico. . . . I believe I sewed it up in a cap of my landlady's."

"In your landlady's cap?"

"Yes. I took it from her."

"How did you get it?"

"You see, I remember once taking a cap for a rag, perhaps to wipe my pen on. I took it without asking, because it was a worthless rag. I tore it up, and I took the notes and sewed them up in it. I believe it was in that very rag I sewed it. An old piece of calico, washed a thousand times."

"And you remember that for certain now?"

"I don't know whether for certain. I think it was in the cap. But, hang it, what does it matter?"

"In that case your landlady will remember that the thing was lost?"

"No, she won't, she didn't miss it. It was an old rag, I tell you, an old rag not worth a cent."

"And where did you get the needle and thread?"

"I'll stop now. I won't say any more. Enough of it!" said Mitya, losing his temper at last.

"It's strange that you should have so completely forgotten where you threw the 'amulet' in the marketplace."

"Give orders for the marketplace to be swept tomorrow, and perhaps you'll find it," said Mitya sneering. "Enough, gentlemen, enough!" he decided, in an exhausted voice. "I see you don't believe me! Not for a moment! It's my fault, not yours. I ought not to have been so ready. Why, why did I degrade myself by confessing my secret to you? It's a joke to you. I see that from your eyes. You led me on to it, prosecutor! Sing a hymn of triumph if you can. . . . Damn you, you torturers!"

He bent his head, and hid his face in his hands. The attorneys were silent. A minute later he raised his head and looked at them almost vacantly. His face now expressed complete, hopeless despair, and he sat mute and passive as though hardly conscious of what was happening. In the meantime they had to finish what they were doing. They had to begin examining the witnesses immediately. It was by now eight o'clock in the morning. The lights had been extinguished long ago. Mikhail Makarovich and Kalganov, who had been continually in and out of the room all the while the interrogation had been going on, had now both gone out again. The attorneys, too, looked very tired. It was a wretched morning, the whole sky was overcast, and the rain streamed down in buckets. Mitya gazed blankly out of the window.

"May I look out of the window?" he asked Nikolay Parfenovich, suddenly.

"Oh, as much as you like," the latter replied.

Mitya got up and went to the window. The rain lashed against the little greenish panes of the window. He could see the muddy road just below the window, and further away, in the rainy mist, a row of poor, black, dismal huts, looking even blacker and poorer in the rain. Mitya thought of "Phoebus the golden-haired," and how he had meant to shoot himself at his first ray. "Perhaps it would be even better on a morning like this," he thought with a smile, and suddenly, flinging his hand downwards, he turned to his "torturers."

"Gentlemen," he cried, "I see that I am lost! But she? Tell me about her, I beseech you. Surely she need not be ruined with me? She's innocent, you know, she was out of her mind when she cried last night 'it's all my fault!' She's done nothing, nothing! I've been grieving over her all night as I sat with you. . . . Can't you, won't you tell me what you are going to do with her now?"

"You can set your mind quite at rest on that score, Dmitri Fyodorovich," the prosecutor answered at once, with evident alacrity. "We have, so far, no grounds for interfering with the lady in whom you are so interested. I trust that it may be the same in the later development of the case. . . . On the contrary, we'll do everything that lies in our power in that matter. Set your mind completely at rest."

"Gentlemen, I thank you. I knew that you were honest, straightforward people in spite of everything. You've taken a load off my heart. . . . Well, what are we to do now? I'm ready."

"Well, we ought to make haste. We must pass to examining the witnesses without delay. That must be done in your presence and therefore . . ."

"Shouldn't we have some tea first?" interposed Nikolay Parfenovich, "I think we've deserved it!"

They decided that if tea were ready downstairs (Mikhail Makarovich had, no doubt gone down to get some) they would have a glass and then "go on and on," putting off their proper breakfast until a more favorable opportunity. Tea really was ready below, and was soon brought up. Mitya at first refused the glass that Nikolay Parfenovich politely offered him, but afterwards he asked for it himself and drank it greedily. He looked surprisingly exhausted. It might have been supposed from his herculean strength that one night of carousing, even accompanied by the most violent emotions, could have had little effect on him. But he felt that he could hardly hold his head up, and from time to time all the objects about him seemed heaving and dancing before his eyes. "A little more and I shall begin raving," he said to himself.

Chapter VIII

The Evidence of the Witnesses. The Babe

The examination of the witnesses began. But we will not continue our story in such detail as before. And so we will not dwell on how Nikolay Parfenovich impressed on every witness called that he must give his evidence in accordance with truth and conscience, and that he would afterwards have to repeat his evidence on oath, how every witness was called upon to sign the protocol of his evidence, and so on. We will only note that the point principally insisted upon in the examination was the question of the three thousand rubles, that is, was the sum spent here, at Mokroe, by Dmitri Fyodorovich on the first occasion, a month before, three thousand or fifteen hundred? And again had he spent three thousand or fifteen hundred yesterday? Alas, all the evidence given by everyone turned out to be against Mitya. There was not one in his favor, and some witnesses introduced new, almost crushing facts, in contradiction of Mitya's story.

The first witness examined was Trifon Borisich. He was not in the least abashed as he stood before the attorneys. He had, on the contrary, an air of stern and severe indignation with the accused, which gave him an appearance of truthfulness and personal dignity. He spoke little, and with reserve, waited to be questioned, answered precisely and deliberately. Firmly and unhesitatingly he bore witness that the sum spent a month before could not have been less than three thousand, that all the peasants about here would testify that they had heard the sum of three thousand mentioned by Mitri Fyodorich himself. "What a lot of money he flung away on the gypsy girls alone. He wasted a thousand, I daresay, on them alone."

"I don't believe I gave them five hundred," was Mitya's gloomy comment on this. "It's a pity I didn't count the money at the time, but I was drunk . . ."

Mitya was sitting sideways with his back to the curtains. He listened gloomily, with a melancholy and exhausted air, as though he would say: "Oh, say what you like. It makes no difference now."

"More than a thousand went on them, Mitri Fyodorvich," retorted Trifon Borisovich firmly. "You flung it about at random and they picked it up. They were a rascally, thievish lot, horse stealers, they've been driven away from here, or maybe they'd bear witness themselves how much they got from you. I saw the sum in your hands, myself—count it I didn't, you didn't let me, that's true enough—but by the look of it I would say it was far more than fifteen hundred . . . fifteen hundred, indeed! We've seen money too. We can judge amounts . . ."

As for the sum spent yesterday he asserted that Dmitri Fyodorovich had told him, as soon as he arrived, that he had brought three thousand with him.

"Come now, is that so, Trifon Borisich?" replied Mitya. "Surely I didn't declare so positively that I'd brought three thousand?"

"You did say so, Mitri Fyodorovich. You said it before Andrey. Andrey himself is still here. Send for him. And in the hall, when you were treating the chorus, you shouted straight out that you would leave your sixth thousand here—that is with what you spent before, we must understand. Stepan and Semyon heard it, and Pyotr Fomich Kalganov, too, was standing beside you at the time. Maybe he'd remember it . . ."

The evidence as to the "sixth" thousand made an extraordinary impression on the two examiners. They were delighted with this new mode of reckoning, three and three made six, three thousand then and three now made six, that was clear.

They questioned all the peasants suggested by Trifon Borisovich, Stepan and Semyon, the driver Andrey, and Kalganov. The peasants and the driver hesitatingly confirmed Trifon Borisich's evidence. They noted down, with particular care, Andrey's account of the conversation he had had with Mitya on the road: " 'Where,' says he, 'am I, Dmitri Fyodorovich, going, to Heaven or to Hell, and shall I be forgiven in the next world or not?' " The "psychologist" Ippolit Kirillovich heard this with a subtle smile, and ended by recommending that these remarks as to where Dmitri Fyodorovich would go should be "included in the case."

Kalganov, when called, came in reluctantly, frowning and ill-humored, and he spoke to the attorneys as though he had never met them before in his life, though they were acquaintances whom he had been meeting every day for a long time past. He began by saying that "he knew nothing about it and didn't want to." But it appeared that he had heard of the "sixth" thousand, and he admitted that he had been standing close by at the moment. As far as he could see he "didn't know" how much money Mitya had in his hands. He affirmed that the Poles had cheated at cards. In reply to reiterated questions he stated that, after the Poles had been turned out, Mitya's position with Agrafena Alexandrovna had certainly improved, and that she had said that she loved him. He spoke of

Agrafena Alexandrovna with reserve and respect, as though she
had been a lady of the best society, and did not once allow himself
to call her Grushenka. In spite of the young man's obvious repugnance at giving evidence, Ippolit Kirillovich examined him at great
length, and only from him learned all the details of what made up
Mitya's "romance," so to speak, on that night. Mitya did not once
stop Kalganov. At last they let the young man go, and he left the
room with unconcealed indignation.

The Poles, too, were examined. Though they had gone to bed in
their room, they had not slept all night, and on the arrival of the
police officers they hastily dressed and got ready, realizing that they
would certainly be sent for. They gave their evidence with dignity,
though not without some fear. The little Pole turned out to be a
retired official of the twelfth class,[4] who had served in Siberia as a
veterinary surgeon. His name was Mussyalovich. Pan Vrublevsky
turned out to be an uncertified dentist. Although Nikolay Parfenovich asked him questions on entering the room they both addressed
their answers to Mikhail Makarovich, who was standing on one
side, taking him in their ignorance for the most important person
and in command, and addressed him at every word as "Panie
Colonel." Only after several reproofs from Mikhail Makarovich
himself, they grasped that they had to address their answers only to
Nikolay Parfenovich. It turned out that they could speak Russian
quite correctly except for their accent in some words. Of his
relations with Grushenka, past and present, Pan Mussyalovich
spoke proudly and warmly, so that Mitya was roused at once and
declared that he would not allow the "scoundrel" to speak like that
in his presence! Pan Mussyalovich at once called attention to the
word "scoundrel," and begged that it should be put down in the
deposition. Mitya fumed with rage.

"He's a scoundrel! A scoundrel! You can put that down. And put
down, too, that, in spite of the deposition I still declare that he's a
scoundrel!" he cried.

Though Nikolay Parfenovich did insert this in the deposition, he
showed the most praiseworthy tact and management. After sternly
reprimanding Mitya, he cut short all further inquiry into the romantic aspect of the case, and hastened to pass to what was essential. One piece of evidence given by the Poles roused special interest
in the attorneys: that was how, in that very room, Mitya had tried
to buy off Pan Mussyalovich, and had offered him three thousand
rubles to resign his claims, seven hundred rubles down, and the
remaining twenty-three hundred "to be paid next day in the town."
He had sworn at the time that he had not the whole sum with him
at Mokroe, but that his money was in the town. Mitya observed

4. The third lowest rank in the fourteen steps of the civil service.

hotly that he had not said that he would be sure to pay him the re-
mainder next day in the town. But Pan Vrublevsky confirmed the
statement, and Mitya, after thinking for a moment admitted, frowning, that it must have been as the Poles stated, that he had been
excited at the time, and might indeed have said so.

The prosecutor positively pounced on this piece of evidence. It
seemed to establish for the prosecution (and they did, in fact, base
this deduction on it) that half, or a part of, the three thousand that
had come into Mitya's hands might really have been left somewhere
hidden in the town, or even, perhaps, somewhere here, in Mokroe.
This would explain the circumstance, so baffling for the prosecution, that only eight hundred rubles were to be found in Mitya's
hands. This circumstance had been the one piece of evidence which,
insignificant as it was, had hitherto told, to some extent, in Mitya's favor. Now this one piece of evidence in his favor had broken
down. In answer to the prosecutor's inquiry, where he would have
got the remaining twenty-three hundred rubles, since he himself
had denied having more than fifteen hundred, Mitya confidently
replied that he had meant to offer the "little Pole," not money, but
a formal deed of conveyance of his rights to the village of Chermashnya, those rights which he had already offered to Samsonov and
Madame Khokhlakov. The prosecutor positively smiled at the "innocence of this subterfuge."

"And you imagine he would have accepted such a deed as a
substitute for twenty-three hundred rubles in cash?"

"He certainly would have accepted it," Mitya declared warmly.
"Why, look here, he might have grabbed not two thousand, but
four or six, for it. He would have put his shysters, Poles and Jews,
onto the job, and might have got, not three thousand, but the whole
property out of the old man."

The evidence of Pan Mussyalovich was, of course, entered into
the deposition in the fullest detail. Then they let the Poles go. The
incident of the cheating at cards was hardly touched upon. Nikolay
Parfenovich was too well pleased with them, as it was, and did not
want to worry them with trifles, moreover, it was nothing but a
foolish, drunken quarrel over cards. There had been drinking and
disorder enough, that night. . . . So the two hundred rubles remained in the pockets of the Poles.

Then old Maximov was summoned. He came in timidly, approached with little steps, looking very disheveled and depressed.
He had, all this time, taken refuge below with Grushenka, sitting
dumbly beside her, and "now and then he'd begin blubbering over
her and wiping his eyes with a blue check handkerchief," as Mikhail Makarovich described afterwards. So that she, herself, began
trying to pacify and comfort him. The old man at once confessed
that he had done wrong, that he had borrowed "ten rubles in my

poverty, sir," from Dmitri Fyodorovich, and that he was ready to pay it back. To Nikolay Parfenovich's direct question, had he noticed how much money Dmitri Fyodorovich held in his hand, as he must have been able to see the sum better than anyone when he took the note from him, Maximov, in the most positive manner, declared that there was twenty thousand.

"Have you ever seen so much as twenty thousand before, then?" inquired Nikolay Parfenovich, with a smile.

"To be sure I have, sir, not twenty, but seven, when my wife mortgaged my little property. She'd only let me look at it from a distance, boasting of it to me. It was a very thick bundle, all rainbow-colored bills. And Dmitri Fyodorovich's were all rainbow-colored . . ."

He was not kept long. At last it was Grushenka's turn. Nikolay Parfenovich was obviously apprehensive of the effect her appearance might have on Dmitri Fyodorovich, and he muttered a few words of admonition to him, but Mitya bowed his head in silence, giving him to understand "that he would not make a scene." Mikhail Makarovich, himself, led Grushenka in. She entered with a stern and gloomy face, that looked almost composed, and sat down quietly on the chair offered her by Nikolay Parfenovich. She was very pale, she seemed to be cold, and wrapped herself closely in her magnificent black shawl. She was suffering from a slight feverish chill—the first symptom of the long illness which followed that night. Her grave air, her direct earnest look and quiet manner made a very favorable impression on everyone. Nikolay Parfenovich was even a little bit "fascinated." He admitted himself, when talking about it afterwards, that only then had he seen "how handsome the woman was," for, though he had seen her several times before, he had always looked upon her as something of a "provincial hetaera." "She has the manners of the best society," he said enthusiastically, gossiping about her in a circle of ladies. But this was received with positive indignation by the ladies, who immediately called him a "naughty man," to his great satisfaction. As she entered the room, Grushenka only glanced for an instant at Mitya, who looked at her uneasily. But her face reassured him at once. After the first inevitable inquiries and warnings, Nikolay Parfenovich asked her, hesitating a little, but preserving the most courteous manner, on what terms she was with the retired lieutenant, Dmitri Fyodorovich Karamazov. To this Grushenka firmly and quietly replied:

"He was an acquaintance. He came to see me as an acquaintance during the past month."

To further inquisitive questions she answered plainly and with complete frankness, that, though "at times" she had thought him attractive, she had not loved him, but had won his heart as well as his old father's "in my nasty spite," that she had seen that Mitya was very jealous of Fyodor Pavlovich and everyone else; but that had only amused her. She had never meant to go to Fyodor Pavlovich, she had simply been laughing at him. "I had no thoughts for either of them all this last month, I was expecting another man who had wronged me. But I think," she said in conclusion, "that there's no need for you to inquire about that, nor for me to answer you, for that's my own affair."

Nikolay Parfenovich immediately acted upon this hint. He again dismissed the "romantic" aspect of the case and passed to the serious one, that is, to the question of most importance, concerning the three thousand rubles. Grushenka confirmed the statement that three thousand rubles had certainly been spent on the first carousal at Mokroe, and, though she had not counted the money herself, she had heard that it was three thousand from Dmitri Fyodorovich's own lips.

"Did he tell you that alone, or before someone else, or did you only hear him speak of it to others in your presence?" the prosecutor inquired immediately.

To which Grushenka replied that she had heard him say so before other people, and had heard him say so when they were alone.

"Did he say it to you alone once, or several times?" inquired the prosecutor, and learned that he had told Grushenka so several times.

Ippolit Kirillovich was very well satisfied with this piece of evidence. Further examination elicited that Grushenka knew, too, where that money had come from, and that "Dmitri Fyodorovich had got it from Katerina Ivanovna."

"And did you never, once, hear that the money spent a month ago was not three thousand, but less, and that Dmitri Fyodorivich had saved half that sum for his own use?"

"No, I never heard that," answered Grushenka.

It was explained further that Mitya had, on the contrary, often told her during that month that he didn't have a cent. "He was always expecting to get some from his father," said Grushenka in conclusion.

"Did he never say before you ... casually, or in a moment of irritation," Nikolay Parfenovich put in suddenly, "that he intended to make an attempt on his father's life?"

"Ach, he did say so," sighed Grushenka.

"Once or several times?"

"He mentioned it several times, always in anger."

"And did you believe he would do it?"

"No, I never believed it," she answered firmly. "I had faith in his noble heart."

"Gentlemen, allow me," cried Mitya suddenly, "allow me to say one word to Agrafena Alexandrovna, in your presence."

"You can speak," Nikolay Parfenovich assented.

"Agrafena Alexandrovna!" Mitya got up from his chair, "have faith in God and in me. I am not guilty of my father's murder!"

Having uttered these words Mitya sat down again on his chair. Grushenka stood up and crossed herself devoutly before the icon.

"Thanks be to Thee, O Lord," she said, in a voice thrilled with emotion, and still standing, she turned to Nikolay Parfenovich and added: "As he has spoken now, believe it! I know him. He'll say anything as a joke or from obstinacy, but he'll never deceive you against his conscience. He's telling the whole truth, you may believe it."

"Thanks, Agrafena Alexandrovna, you've given me fresh courage," Mitya responded in a quivering voice.

As to the money spent the previous day, she declared that she did not know what sum it was, but had heard him tell several people that he had three thousand with him. And to the question where he got the money, she said that he had told her that he had "stolen" it from Katerina Ivanovna, and that she had replied to that that he hadn't stolen it, and that he must pay the money back next day. On the prosecutor's asking her emphatically whether the money he said he had stolen from Katerina Ivanovna was what he had spent yesterday, or what he had squandered there a month ago, she declared that he meant the money spent a month ago, and that that was how she understood him.

Grushenka was at last released, and Nikolay Parfenovich informed her impulsively that she might at once return to the town and that if he could be of any assistance to her, with horses for example, or if she would care for an escort he . . . would be . . .

"I thank you sincerely,' said Grushenka, bowing to him, "I'm going with this old gentleman, I am driving him back to town with me, and meanwhile, if you'll allow me, I'll wait below to hear what you decide about Dmitri Fyodorovich."

She went out. Mitya was calm, and even looked more cheerful, but only for a moment. He felt more and more oppressed by a strange physical weakness. His eyes were closing with fatigue. The examination of the witness was, at last, over. They proceeded to a final revision of the deposition. Mitya got up, moved from his chair to the corner by the curtain, lay down on a large chest covered with a rug, and instantly fell asleep.

He had a strange dream, utterly out of keeping with the place and the time. He was driving somewhere in the steppes, where he had been stationed long ago, and a peasant was driving him in a cart with a pair of horses, through snow and sleet. He was cold, it was early in November, and the snow was falling in big wet flakes, melting as soon as it touched the earth. And the peasant drove him smartly, snapping his whip, he had a fair, long beard. He was not an old man, somewhere about fifty, and he had on a gray peasant's smock. And there, not far off was a village, he could see the very black huts, and half the huts were burned down, there were only the charred beams sticking up. And as they drove in, there were peasant women drawn up along the road, a lot of women, a whole row, all thin and wan, with their faces a sort of brownish color, especially one at the edge, a tall, bony woman, who looked forty, but might have been only twenty, with a long thin face. And in her arms was a little baby crying. And her breasts must have been so dried up that there was not a drop of milk in them. And the child cried and cried, and held out its little bare arms, with its little fists blue from cold.

"Why are they crying? Why are they crying?" Mitya asked, as they dashed briskly by.

"It's the babe," answered the driver, "the babe weeping."

And Mitya was struck by his saying, in his peasant way, "the babe," and he liked the peasant's calling it a "babe." There seemed more pity in it. "But why is it weeping?" Mitya persisted stupidly, "why are its little arms bare? Why don't they wrap it up?"

"The babe's cold, its little clothes are frozen and don't warm it."

"But why is it? Why?" foolish Mitya still persisted.

"Why, they're poor people, burned out. They've no bread. They're begging because they've been burned out."

"No, no," Mitya, as it were, still did not understand. "Tell me why it is those poor mothers stand there? Why are people poor? Why is the babe poor? Why is the steppe barren? Why don't they hug each other and kiss? Why don't they sing songs of joy? Why are they so dark from black misery? Why don't they feed the babe?"

And he felt that, though his questions were unreasonable and senseless, yet he wanted to ask just that, and he had to ask it just in that way. And he felt also that a passion of pity, such as he had never known before, was rising in his heart, and he wanted to cry, that he wanted to do something for them all, so that the babe should weep no more, so that the dark-faced, dried-up mother should not weep, that no one should shed tears again from that moment, and he wanted to do it at once, at once, regardless of all obstacles, with all the Karamazov recklessness.

"And I'm coming with you. I won't leave you now for the rest of my life, I'm coming with you," he heard close beside him Grushenka's tender voice, full of emotion. And his whole heart glowed, and he struggled forward towards the light, and he longed to live, to live, to go on and on, towards the new, beckoning light, and to hasten, hasten, now, at once!

"What! Where?" he exclaimed opening his eyes, and sitting up on the chest, as though he had revived from a swoon, smiling brightly. Nikolay Parfenovich was standing over him, suggesting that he should hear the deposition read aloud and sign it. Mitya guessed that he had been asleep an hour or more, but he did not hear Nikolay Parfenovich. He was suddenly struck by the fact that there was a pillow under his head, which hadn't been there when he had leaned back, exhausted, on the chest.

"Who put that pillow under my head? Who was so kind?" he cried, with a sort of ecstatic gratitude, and tears in his voice, as though some great kindness had been shown him. He never found out who this kind man was, perhaps one of the peasant witnesses, or Nikolay Parfenovich's little secretary, had compassionately thought to put a pillow under his head, but his whole soul was quivering with tears. He went to the table and said that he would sign whatever they liked.

"I've had a good dream, gentlemen," he said in a strange voice, with a new light, as of joy, in his face.

Chapter IX

They Carry Mitya Away

When the deposition had been signed, Nikolay Parfenovich turned solemnly to the prisoner and read him the indictment, setting forth, that in such a year, on such a day, in such a place, the district attorney of such-and-such a district court, having examined so-and-so (to wit, Mitya) accused of this and of that (all the charges were carefully written out) and having considered that the accused, not pleading guilty to the charges made against him, had brought forward nothing in his defense, while the witnesses, so-and-so, and so-and-so, and the circumstances such-and-such testify against him, acting in accordance with such-and-such articles of the Statutes, and so on, has ruled, that, in order to preclude such-and-such (Mitya) from all means of evading pursuit and judgment he be detained in such-and-such a prison, which he hereby notifies to the accused and communicates a copy of this same indictment to the deputy prosecutor, and so on, and so on. In brief, Mitya was informed that he was, from that moment, a prisoner, and that he would be driven at once to town, and there shut up in a very unpleasant place. Mitya listened attentively, and only shrugged his shoulders.

"Well, gentlemen, I don't blame you. I'm ready. . . . I understand that there's nothing else for you to do."

Nikolay Parfenovich informed him gently that he would be escorted at once by the rural police officer, Mavriky Mavrikyevich, who happened to be on the spot. . . .

"Wait," Mitya interrupted, suddenly, and impelled by uncontrollable feeling he pronounced, addressing all in the room: "Gentlemen, we're all cruel, we're all monsters, we all make men weep, and mothers, and babes at the breast, but of all, let it be settled here, now, of all I am the lowest reptile! I've sworn to amend every day of my life, beating my breast, and every day I've done the same filthy things. I understand now that such men as I need a blow, a blow of destiny to catch them as with a noose, and bind them by a force from without. Never, never should I have risen of myself! But the thunderbolt has fallen. I accept the torment of accusation, and my public shame, I want to suffer and by suffering I shall be purified. Perhaps I shall be purified, gentlemen, what? But listen, for the last time, I am not guilty of my father's blood. I accept my punishment, not because I killed him, but because I meant to kill him, and perhaps I really might have killed him. Still I mean to fight it out with you, I warn you of that. I'll fight it out with you to the end, and then God will decide. Good-bye, gentlemen, don't be vexed with me for having shouted at you during the examination. Oh, I was still such a fool then. . . . In another minute I shall be a prisoner, but now, for the last time, as a free man, Dmitri Karamazov offers you his hand. Saying goodbye to you, I say it to all men."

His voice quivered and he stretched out his hand, but Nikolay Parfenovich, who happened to stand nearest to him, with a sudden, almost nervous movement, hid his hands behind his back. Mitya instantly noticed this, and started. He let his outstretched hand fall at once.

"The preliminary inquiry is not yet over," Nikolay Parfenovich faltered, somewhat embarrassed. "We will continue it in town, and I, for my part, of course, am ready to wish you all success . . . in your defense. . . . As a matter of fact, Dmitri Fyodorovich, I've always been disposed to regard you as, so to speak, more unfortunate than guilty. All of us here, if I may make bold to speak for all, we are all ready to recognize that you are, at bottom, a young man of honor, but, alas, one who has been carried away by certain passions to a somewhat excessive degree . . ."

Nikolay Parfenovich's little figure was positively majestic by the time he had finished speaking. It struck Mitya that in another minute this "boy" would take his arm, lead him to another corner, and renew their conversation about "girls." But many quite irrelevant and inappropriate thoughts sometimes occur even to a prisoner when he is being led out to execution.

"Gentlemen, you are good, you are humane, may I see *her* to say 'goodbye' for the last time?" asked Mitya.

"Certainly, but considering . . . in fact, now it's impossible except in the presence of . . ."

"Be present, if you like!"

Grushenka was brought in, but the farewell was brief, and of few words, and did not at all satisfy Nikolay Parfenovich. Grushenka made a deep bow to Mitya.

"I have told you I am yours, and I will be yours. I will follow you forever, wherever they may send you. Farewell; you are guiltless, though you've been your own undoing."

Her lips quivered, tears flowed from her eyes.

"Forgive me, Grusha, for my love, for ruining you, too, with my love."

Mitya would have said something more, but he broke off and went out. He was at once surrounded by men who kept a constant watch on him. At the bottom of the steps to which he had driven up with such a dash the day before with Andrey's three horses, two carts stood in readiness. Mavriky Mavrikyevich, a sturdy, thickset man with a wrinkled face, was annoyed about something, some sudden irregularity. He was shouting angrily. He asked Mitya to get into the cart with somewhat excessive surliness. "When I stood him drinks in the tavern, the man had quite a different face," thought Mitya, as he got in. At the gates there was a crowd of people, peasants, women and drivers. Trifon Borisovich came down the steps too. All stared at Mitya.

"Forgive me at parting, good people!" Mitya shouted suddenly from the cart.

"Forgive us too!" he heard two or three voices.

"Goodbye to you, too, Trifon Borisich!"

But Trifon Borisich did not even turn round. He was, perhaps, too busy. He, too, was shouting and fussing about something. It appeared that everything was not yet ready in the second cart, in which two constables were to accompany Mavriky Mavrikyevich. The peasant who had been ordered to drive the second cart was pulling on his coat, stoutly maintaining that it was not his turn to go, but Akim's. But Akim was not to be seen. They ran to look for him. The peasant persisted and asked them to wait.

"You see what our peasants are, Mavriky Mavrikyevich. They have no shame!" exclaimed Trifon Borisich. "Akim gave you twenty-five kopecks the day before yesterday. You've drunk it all and now you cry out. I'm simply surprised at your good nature, with our low peasants, Mavriky Mavrikyevich, that's all I can say."

"But what do we want a second cart for?" Mitya put in. "Let's start with the one, Mavriky Mavrikyevich. I won't be unruly, I won't run away from you, old fellow. What do we want an escort for?"

"I'll trouble you, sir, to learn how to speak to me if you've never been taught. I'm not 'old fellow' to you, and you can keep your advice for another time!" Mavriky Mavrikyevich snapped out savagely, as though glad to vent his wrath.

Mitya was reduced to silence. He flushed all over. A moment

later he felt suddenly very cold. The rain had ceased, but the dull sky was still overcast with clouds, and a keen wind was blowing straight in his face. "I've caught a cold," thought Mitya, twitching his shoulders.

At last Mavriky Mavrikyevich, too, got into the cart, sat down heavily, and, as though without noticing it, squeezed Mitya into the corner. It is true that he was out of humor and greatly disliked the task that had been laid upon him.

"Goodbye, Trifon Borisich!" Mitya shouted again, and felt himself, that he had not called out this time from good nature, but involuntarily, from resentment.

But Trifon Borisich stood proudly, with both hands behind his back, and staring straight at Mitya with a stern and angry face, he made no reply.

"Goodbye, Dmitri Fyodorovich, goodbye!" he heard all at once the voice of Kalganov, who had suddenly darted out. Running up to the cart he held out his hand to Mitya. He had no cap on. Mitya had time to seize and press his hand.

"Goodbye, dear fellow! I won't forget your generosity," he cried warmly. But the cart moved and their hands parted. The bell began ringing and Mitya was driven off.

Kalganov ran back, sat down in a corner, bent his head, hid his face in his hands, and burst out crying. For a long while he sat like that, crying as though he were a little boy instead of a young man of twenty. Oh, he believed almost without doubt in Mitya's guilt. "What are these people? What can men be after this?" he exclaimed incoherently, in bitter despondency, almost despair. At that moment he had no desire to live. "Is it worth it? Is it worth it?" exclaimed the youth in his grief.

Part Four

Book Ten

BOYS

Chapter I

Kolya Krasotkin

It was the beginning of November. There had been a hard frost, the temperature had dropped to ten above, without snow, but a little dry snow had fallen on the frozen ground during the night, and a "dry and sharp" wind was lifting and blowing it along the dreary streets of our town, especially about the marketplace. It was a dull morning, but the snow had ceased.

Not far from the marketplace, close to Plotnikov's shop, there stood a small house, very clean both inside and out. It belonged to Mrs. Krasotkin, the widow of a former provincial secretary, who had died long ago, almost fourteen years ago. His widow, a lively still attractive woman of thirty,[1] was living in her neat little house on her "private means." She lived in respectable seclusion; she was of a soft but fairly cheerful disposition. She was about eighteen at the time of her husband's death; she had been married only a year and had just borne him a son. From the day of his death she had devoted herself heart and soul to the bringing up of her precious treasure, her boy Kolya. Though she had loved him passionately those fourteen years, he had caused her far more suffering than happiness. She trembled and fainted with terror almost every day, afraid he would fall ill, would catch cold, do something naughty, climb on a chair and fall off it, and so on and so on. When Kolya began going to school, the mother devoted herself to studying all the sciences with him so as to help him, and go through his lessons with him. She hastened to make the acquaintance of the teachers and their wives, even made up to Kolya's schoolfellows, and fawned upon them in the hope of thus saving Kolya from being teased, laughed at, or beaten by them. She went so far that the boys actually began to mock at him on her account, and taunt him with being a "mamma's boy."

But the boy could hold his own. He was a resolute boy, "tremendously strong," as was rumored in his class, and which soon proved

---

1. In adjusting Kolya's age (see letter no. 727), Dostoevsky neglected to adjust his mother's age.

to be the fact; he was agile, strong-willed, and of an audacious and enterprising temper. He was good at lessons, and there was a rumor in the school that he could beat the teacher, Dardanelov, at arithmetic and universal history. Though he looked down upon everyone, he was a good comrade and not supercilious. He accepted his schoolfellows' respect as his due, but was friendly with them. Above all, he knew where to draw the line. He could restrain himself on occasion, and in his relations with the teachers he never overstepped that last mystic limit beyond which a prank became disorder, rebellion, and lawlessness. But he was very, very fond of mischief on every possible occasion as much so as the smallest boy in school, and not so much for the sake of mischief as for creating a sensation, inventing something, doing something effective, flashy, and conspicuous. He was extremely vain. He knew how to make even his mother give way to him; he was almost despotic in his control of her. She gave way to him, oh, she had given way to him for years. The one thought unendurable to her was that her boy had no great love for her. She was always fancying Kolya was "unfeeling" to her, and at times, dissolving into hysterical tears, she used to reproach him with his coldness. The boy disliked this, and the more demonstrations of feeling were demanded of him the more he seemed intentionally to avoid them. Yet it was not intentional on his part but instinctive—it was his character. His mother was mistaken; he was very fond of her. He only disliked "sheepish sentimentality," as he expressed it in his schoolboy language.

There was a bookcase in the house containing a few books that had been his father's. Kolya was fond of reading, and had read several of them by himself. His mother did not mind that and only wondered sometimes at seeing the boy staying for hours by the bookcase poring over a book instead of going to play. And in that way Kolya read some things unsuitable for his age.

Though the boy, as a rule, knew where to draw the line in his mischief, he had of late begun to play pranks that caused his mother serious alarm. It is true there was nothing immoral in what he did, but a wild mad recklessness.

It happened that July, during the summer holidays, that the mother and son went to another district, forty-five miles away, to spend a week with a distant relation, whose husband was an official at the railway station (the very station, the nearest one to our town, from which a month later Ivan Fyodorovich Karamazov set off for Moscow). There Kolya began by carefully investigating every detail connected with the railway, knowing that he could impress his schoolfellows when he got home with his newly acquired knowledge. But there happened to be some other boys in the place with whom he soon made friends. Some of them lived at the station, others in the neighborhood; there were six or seven of them, all between twelve and fifteen, and two of them came from our town. The boys played together, and on the fourth or fifth day of Kolya's stay at the station, a mad bet was made by the foolish boys. Kolya, who was almost the youngest of the party and rather looked down upon by the others in consequence, was moved by vanity or by reckless bravado to bet them two rubles that he would lie down between the rails at night when the eleven o'clock train was due, and would lie there without moving while the train rolled over him at full speed. It is true they made a preliminary study, from which it appeared that it was possible to lie so flat between the rails that the train could pass over without touching, but to lie there was no joke! Kolya maintained stoutly that he would. At first they laughed at him, called him a little liar, a braggart, but that only egged him on. What piqued him most was that these boys of fifteen turned up their noses at him too superciliously, and were at first disposed to treat him as "a small boy," not fit to associate with them, and that was an unendurable insult.

And so it was resolved to go in the evening, half a mile from the station, so that the train might have time to get up full speed after leaving the station. The boys assembled. It was a pitch dark night without a moon. At the time fixed, Kolya lay down between the rails. The five others who had taken the bet waited among the bushes below the embankment, their hearts beating with suspense, which was followed by alarm and remorse. At last they heard in the distance the rumble of the train leaving the station. Two red lights gleamed out of the darkness; the monster roared as it approached.

"Run, run away from the rails," the boys cried to Kolya from the bushes, breathless with terror. But it was too late: the train darted up and flew past. The boys rushed to Kolya. He lay without moving. They began pulling at him, lifting him up. He suddenly got up from the roadbed and walked away without a word. Then he explained that he had lain there as though he were insensible to frighten them, but the fact was that he really had lost consciousness, as he confessed long after to his mother. In this way his reputation as "a desperate character" was established forever. He returned home to the station as white as a sheet. Next day he had a slight attack of nervous fever, but he was in high spirits and well pleased with himself. The incident did not become known at once, but when they came back to the town it penetrated to the school and even reached the ears of the masters. But then Kolya's mother hastened to entreat the masters on her boy's behalf, and in the end Dardanelov, a respected and influential teacher, exerted himself in his favor, and the affair was ignored.

Dardanelov was a middle-aged bachelor, who had been passionately in love with Mrs. Krasotkin for many years past, and had once already, about a year previously, ventured, trembling with fear and the delicacy of his sentiments, to offer her most respectfully his hand in marriage. But she refused him resolutely, feeling that to accept him would be an act of treachery to her son, though Dardanelov had, to judge from certain mysterious symptoms, reason for believing that he was not an object of aversion to the charming but too chaste and tenderhearted widow. Kolya's mad prank seemed to have broken the ice, and Dardanelov was rewarded for his intercession by a suggestion of hope. The suggestion, it is true, was a faint one, but then Dardanelov was such a paragon of purity and delicacy that it was enough for the time being to make him perfectly happy. He was fond of the boy, though he would have felt it beneath him to try and win him over, and was severe and strict with him in class. Kolya, too, kept him at a respectful distance. He learned his lessons perfectly; he was second in his class, was reserved with Dardanelov, and the whole class firmly believed that Kolya was so good at universal history that he could "beat" even Dardanelov. Kolya did indeed ask him the question, "Who founded Troy?" to which Dardanelov had made a very vague reply, referring to the movements and migrations of races, to the remoteness of the period, to the mythical legends. But the question, "Who had founded Troy?" that is, what individuals, he could not answer, and even for some reason regarded the question as idle and frivolous. But the boys remained convinced that Dardanelov did not know who founded Troy. Kolya had read of the founders of Troy in Smaragdov, whose history was among the books in his father's bookcase. In the end all the boys became interested in the question, who it was that had founded Troy, but Krasotkin would not tell his secret, and his reputation for knowledge remained unshaken.

After the incident on the railway a certain change came over Kolya's attitude to his mother. When Anna Fyodorovna (Mrs. Krasotkin) heard of her son's exploit, she almost went out of her mind with horror. She had such terrible attacks of hysterics, lasting with intervals for several days, that Kolya, seriously alarmed at last, promised on his honor that such pranks should never be repeated. He swore on his knees before the holy image, and swore by the memory of his father, at Mrs. Krasotkin's instance, and the "manly" Kolya burst into tears like a boy of six, from "feelings." And all that day the mother and son were constantly rushing into each other's arms sobbing. Next day Kolya woke up as "unfeeling" as before, but he had become more silent, more modest, sterner, and more thoughtful.

Six weeks later, it is true, he got into another scrape, which even brought his name to the ears of our justice of the peace, but it was a scrape of quite another kind, amusing, foolish, and he did not, as it turned out, take the leading part in it, but was only implicated in it. But of this later. His mother still fretted and trembled, but the more uneasy she became, the greater were the hopes of Dardanelov. It must be noted that Kolya understood and divined what was in Dardanelov's heart and, of course, despised him profoundly for his "feelings"; he had in the past been so tactless as to show this contempt before his mother, hinting vaguely that he knew what Dardanelov was after. But from the time of the railway incident his behavior in this respect also was changed; he did not allow himself the remotest allusion to the subject and began to speak more respectfully of Dardanelov before his mother, which the sensitive woman at once appreciated with boundless gratitude. But at the slightest mention of Dardanelov by a visitor in Kolya's presence, she would flush as pink as a rose from shame. At such moments Kolya would either stare out of the window scowling, or would investigate the state of his boots, or would shout angrily for "Perezvon," the big, shaggy, mangy dog, which he had picked up a month before, brought home, and kept for some reason secretly indoors, not showing him to any of his schoolfellows. He bullied him frightfully, teaching him all sorts of tricks, so that the poor dog howled for him whenever he was absent at school, and when he came in, whined with delight, rushed about as if he were crazy, begged, lay down on the ground pretending to be dead, and so on; in fact, showed all the tricks he had taught him, not at the word of command, but simply from the zeal of his excited and grateful heart.

I have forgotten, by the way, to mention that Kolya Krasotkin was the boy stabbed in the thigh with a penknife by the boy already known to the reader as the son of Captain Snegiryov. Ilyusha had been defending his father when the schoolboys jeered at him, shouting the nickname of "wisp of tow."

Chapter II

Children

And so on that frosty, snowy, and windy morning in November, the boy Kolya Krasotkin was sitting at home. It was Sunday and there was no school. It had just struck eleven, and he particularly wanted to go out "on very urgent business," but he was left alone in charge of the house, for it so happened that all its elder inmates were absent owing to a sudden and singular event. Mrs. Krasotkin had let two little rooms, separated from the rest of the house by a passage, to a doctor's wife with her two small children. This lady was the same age as Anna Fyodorovna, and a great friend of hers. Her husband, the doctor, had left a year before, going first to Orenburg and then to Tashkent, and for the last six months she had not heard a word from him. Had it not been for her friendship with Mrs. Krasotkin, which was some consolation to the forsaken lady, she would certainly have completely dissolved away in tears. And now, to add to her misfortunes, Katerina, her only servant, was suddenly moved the evening before to announce, to her mistress's amazement, that she proposed to bring a child into the world before morning. It seemed almost miraculous to everyone that no one had noticed the probability of it before. The astounded doctor's wife decided to move Katerina while there was still time to an establishment in the town kept by a midwife for such emergencies. As she set great store by her servant, she promptly carried out this plan and remained there looking after her. By the morning all Mrs. Krasotkin's friendly sympathy and energy were called upon to render assistance and appeal to someone for help in the case.

So both the ladies were absent from home, the Krasotkins' servant, Agatha, had gone out to the market, and Kolya was thus left for a time to protect and look after the "kids," that is, the son and daughter of the doctor's wife, who were left alone. Kolya was not afraid of taking care of the house, besides he had Perezvon, who had been told to lie down without moving, under the bench in the hall. Every time Kolya, walking to and fro through the rooms, came into the hall, the dog shook his head and gave two loud and insinuating taps on the floor with his tail, but alas! the whistle did not sound to release him. Kolya looked sternly at the luckless dog, who relapsed again into obedient rigidity. The one thing that troubled Kolya was "the kids." He looked, of course, with the utmost scorn on Katerina's unexpected adventure, but he was very fond of the bereaved "kiddies," and had already taken them a picture book. Nastya, the elder, a girl of eight, could read, and Kostya, the boy, aged seven, was very fond of being read to by her. Krasotkin could, of course, have provided more diverting entertainment for them. He could have made them stand side by side and played soldiers with them, or send them hiding all over the house. He had done so more than once before and was not above doing it, so much so that a report once spread at school that Krasotkin played horses with the little lodgers at home, prancing with his head on one side like a trace horse. But Krasotkin haughtily parried this thrust, pointing out that to play horses with boys of one's own age, boys of thirteen, would certainly be disgraceful "these days," but that he did it for the sake of "the kids" because he liked them, and no one had a right to call him to account for his feelings. The two "kids" adored him. But on this occasion he was in no mood for games. He had very important business of his own before him, something almost mysterious. Meanwhile time was passing and Agatha, with whom he could have left the children, would not come back from market. He had several times already crossed the hall, opened the door of the lodgers' room and looked anxiously at the kids who were sitting over the book, as he had bidden them. Every time he opened the door they grinned at him, hoping he would come in and would do something delightful and amusing. But Kolya was preoccupied and did not go in.

At last it struck eleven and he made up his mind, once for all, that if that "damned" Agatha did not come back within ten minutes he would go out without waiting for her, making the "kids" promise, of course, to be brave when he was away, not to be naughty, not to cry from fright. With this idea he put on his padded winter overcoat with its catskin fur collar, slung his satchel round his shoulder, and, regardless of his mother's constantly reiterated entreaties that he always put on galoshes in such cold weather, he looked at them contemptuously as he crossed the hall and went out with only his boots on. Perezvon, seeing him in his outdoor clothes, began tapping vigorously on the floor with his tail, nervously. Twitching all over, he even uttered a plaintive whine. But Kolya, seeing his dog's passionate excitement, decided that it was a breach of discipline, kept him for another minute under the bench, and only when he had opened the door into the hall did he whistle for him. The dog leaped up like a mad creature and rushed bounding before him rapturously.

Kolya opened the door to peep at the "kids." They were both sitting as before at the table, not reading but warmly disputing about something. The children often argued together about various exciting problems of life, and Nastya, being the elder, always got the best of it. If Kostya did not agree with her, he almost always appealed to Kolya Krasotkin, and his verdict was regarded as infallible by both of them. This time the kids' discussion rather interested Krasotkin, and he stood still in the hall to listen. The children saw he was listening and that made them dispute with even greater energy.

"I shall never, never believe," Nastya prattled, "that the old women find babies among the cabbages in the kitchen garden. It's winter now and there are no cabbages, and so the old woman couldn't have taken Katerina a daughter."

"Whew!" Kolya whistled to himself.

"Or perhaps they do bring babies from somewhere, but only to those who are married."

Kostya stared at Nastya and listened, pondering profoundly.

"Nastya, how silly you are," he said at last, firmly and calmly. "How can Katerina have a baby when she isn't married?"

Nastya was exasperated.

"You know nothing about it," she snapped irritably. "Perhaps she has a husband, only he is in prison, so now she's got a baby."

"But is her husband in prison?" the matter-of-fact Kostya inquired gravely.

"Or, I tell you what," Nastya interrupted impulsively, completely rejecting and forgetting her first hypothesis. "She has no husband, you are right there, but she wants to be married, and so she's been thinking of getting married, and thinking and thinking of it till now she's got it, that is, not a husband but a baby."

"Well, perhaps so," Kostya agreed, entirely vanquished. "But you didn't say so before. So how could I tell?"

"Come, kiddies," said Kolya, stepping into the room. "You're terrible people, I see."

"And Perezvon with you!" grinned Kostya, and began snapping his fingers and calling Perezvon.

"I am in a difficulty, kids," Krasotkin began solemnly, "and you must help me. Agatha must have broken her leg, since she has not turned up till now, that's certain. I must go out. Will you let me go?"

The children looked anxiously at one another. Their smiling faces showed signs of uneasiness, but they did not yet fully grasp what was expected of them.

"You won't be naughty while I am gone? You won't climb on the cupboard and break your legs? You won't be frightened alone and cry?"

A look of profound despondency came into the children's faces.

"And I could show you something as a reward, a little copper cannon which can be fired with real gunpowder."

The children's faces instantly brightened. "Show us the cannon," said Kostya, beaming all over.

Krasotkin put his hand in his satchel, and pulling out a little bronze cannon stood it on the table.

"Ah, you are bound to ask that! Look, it's on wheels." He rolled the toy along on the table. "And it can be fired off, too. It can be loaded with shot and fired off."

"And could it kill anyone?"

"It can kill anyone; you've only got to aim at anybody," and Krasotkin explained where the powder had to be put, where the shot should be rolled in, showed a tiny hole like a touch hole, and told them that it recoiled when it was fired. The children listened with intense interest. What particularly struck their imagination was that the cannon recoiled.

"And have you got any powder?" Nastya inquired.

"Yes."

"Show us the powder, too," she drawled with a smile of entreaty.

Krasotkin dived again into his satchel and pulled out a small flask containing a little real gunpowder. He had some shot, too, in a folded piece of paper. He even uncorked the flask and shook a little powder into the palm of his hand.

"One has to be careful there's no fire about, or it would blow up and kill us all,' Krasotkin warned them sensationally.

The children gazed at the powder with an awestricken alarm that only intensified their enjoyment. But Kostya liked the shot better.

"And does the shot burn?" he inquired.

"No, it doesn't."

"Give me a little shot," he asked in an imploring voice.

"I'll give you a little shot; here, take it, but don't show it to your mother till I come back, or she'll be sure to think it's gunpowder, and will die of fright and give you a thrashing."

"Mother never does whip us," Nastya observed at once.

"I know, I only said it for stylistic reasons. And don't you ever deceive your mother except just this once, until I come back. And so, kiddies, can I go out? You won't be frightened and cry when I'm gone?"

"We sha—all cry," drawled Kostya, on the verge of tears already.

"We shall cry, we shall be sure to cry," Nastya chimed in with timid haste.

"Oh, children, children, how fraught with peril are your years! There's no help for it, chickens, I shall have to stay with you I don't know how long. And time is passing, time is passing, oogh!"

"Tell Perezvon to pretend to be dead!" Kostya begged.

"There's no help for it, we must have recourse to Perezvon. *Ici*,[2] Perezvon." And Kolya began giving orders to the dog, who performed all his tricks. He was a rough-haired dog, of medium size, with a coat of a sort of lilac gray color. He was blind in his right eye, and his left ear was torn. He whined and jumped, stood and walked on his hind legs, lay on his back with his paws in the air, rigid as though he were dead. While this last performance was going on, the door was opened and Agatha, Mrs. Krasotkin's servant, a stout woman of forty, marked with smallpox, appeared in the doorway. She had come back from market and had a bag full of provisions in her hand. Holding up the bag of provisions in her left hand she stood still to watch the dog. Though Kolya had been so anxious for her return, he did not cut short the performance, and after keeping Perezvon dead for the appropriate time, at last he whistled to him. The dog jumped up and began bounding about in his joy at having done his duty.

"Only think, a dog!" Agatha observed sententiously.

"Why are you late, female?" asked Krasotkin sternly.

"Female, indeed! Go on with you, you brat."

"Brat?"

"Yes, a brat. What is it to you if I'm late; if I'm late, you may be sure I have good reason," muttered Agatha, busying herself about the stove, without a trace of anger or displeasure in her voice. She

2. "Here."

seemed quite pleased, in fact, to enjoy a skirmish with her merry young master.

"Listen, you frivolous old woman," Krasotkin began, getting up from the sofa, "can you swear by all you hold sacred in the world and something else besides, that you will watch vigilantly over the kids in my absence? I am going out."

"And what am I going to swear for?" laughed Agatha. "I shall look after them without that."

"No, you must swear on your eternal salvation. Else I won't go."

"Well, don't then. What does it matter to me? It's cold out; stay at home."

"Kids," Kolya turned to the children, "this woman will stay with you till I come back or till your mother comes, for she ought to have been back long ago. She will give you some lunch, too. You'll give them something, Agatha, won't you?"

"That I can do."

"Goodbye, chickens, I go with my heart at rest. And you, granny," he added gravely, in an undertone, as he passed Agatha, "I hope you'll spare their tender years and not tell them any of your old woman's nonsense about Katerina. *Ici*, Perezvon!"

"Get along with you!" retorted Agatha, really angry this time. "Ridiculous boy! You want a whipping for saying such things, that's what you want!"

Chapter III

The Schoolboy

But Kolya did not hear her. At last he could go out. As he went out at the gate he looked round him, shrugged up his shoulders, and saying "It is freezing," went straight along the street and turned off to the right towards the marketplace. When he reached the last house but one before the marketplace he stopped at the gate, pulled a whistle out of his pocket, and whistled with all his might as though giving a signal. He did not have to wait more than a minute before a rosy-cheeked boy of about eleven, wearing a warm, neat, and even stylish coat, darted out to meet him. This was Smurov, a boy in the preparatory class (two classes below Kolya Krasotkin), son of a well-to-do official. Apparently he was forbidden by his parents to associate with Krasotkin, who was well known to be a desperately naughty boy, so Smurov was obviously slipping out on the sly. He was—if the reader has not forgotten—one of the group of boys who two months before had thrown stones at Ilyusha. He was the one who told Alyosha Karamazov about Ilyusha.

"I've been waiting for you for the last hour, Krasotkin," said Smurov stolidly, and the boys strode towards the marketplace.

"I am late," answered Krasotkin. "I was detained by circumstances. You won't be thrashed for coming with me?"

"Well, really! I'm never thrashed! And you've got Perezvon with you?"

"Yes."

"You're taking him, too?"

"Yes."

"Ah! if it were only Zhuchka!"

"That's impossible. Zhuchka doesn't exist. Zhuchka is lost in the mists of obscurity."

"Ah! couldn't we do this?" Smurov suddenly stood still. "You see Ilyusha says that Zhuchka was a shaggy, grayish, smoky-looking dog like Perezvon. Couldn't you tell him this is Zhuchka, and he might believe you?"

"Boy, shun a lie, that's one thing; even with a good object—that's another. Above all, I hope you've not told them anything about my coming."

"Heaven forbid! I know what I am about. But you won't comfort him with Perezvon," said Smurov, with a sigh. "You know his father, the captain, 'the wisp of tow,' told us that he was going to bring him a real mastiff pup, with a black nose, today. He thinks that would comfort Ilyusha; but I doubt it."

"And how is Ilyusha?"

"Ah, he is bad, very bad! I believe he has consumption: he is quite conscious, but his breathing! His breathing's gone wrong. The other day he asked to have his boots on to be led round the room. He tried to walk, but he couldn't stand. 'Ah, I told you before, father,' he said, 'that those boots were no good. I could never walk properly in them.' He fancied it was his boots that made him stagger, but it was simply weakness, really. He won't live another week. Herzenstube is looking after him. Now they are rich again—they've got heaps of money."

"They are rogues."

"Who are rogues?"

"Doctors and the whole crew of quacks collectively, and also, of course, individually. I reject medicine. It's a useless institution. I mean to go into all that. But what's that sentimentality you've got up there? The whole class seems to be there every day?"

"Not the whole class: it's only about ten of us who go to see him every day. There's nothing in that."

"What I don't understand in all this is the part that Alexey Karamazov is taking in it. His brother's going to be tried tomorrow or next day for such a crime, and yet he has so much time to spend on sentimentality with boys."

"There's no sentimentality about it. You are going yourself now to make it up with Ilyusha."

"Make it up with him? What an absurd expression! But I allow no one to analyze my actions."

"And how pleased Ilyusha will be to see you! He has no idea that you are coming. Why was it, why was it you wouldn't come all this time?" Smurov cried with sudden warmth.

"My dear boy, that's my business, not yours. I am going on my own because I choose to, but you've all been hauled there by Alexey Karamazov—there's a difference, you know. And how do you know? I may not be going to make it up at all. It's a stupid expression."

"It's not Karamazov at all; it's not his doing. Our fellows began going there of themselves. Of course, they went with Karamazov at first. And there's been nothing of that sort—no silliness. First one went, and then another. His father was awfully pleased to see us. You know he will simply go out of his mind if Ilyusha dies. He sees that Ilyusha's dying. And he seems so glad we've made it up with Ilyusha. Ilyusha asked after you, that was all. He just asks and says no more. His father will go out of his mind or hang himself. He behaved like a madman before. You know he is a very decent man. We made a mistake then. It's all the fault of that murderer who beat him then."

"Karamazov's a riddle to me all the same. I might have made his acquaintance long ago, but I like to be aloof in some cases. Besides, I have a theory about him which I must work out and verify."

Kolya subsided into dignified silence. Smurov, too, was silent. Smurov, of course, worshipped Krasotkin and never dreamed of putting himself on a level with him. Now he was tremendously interested at Kolya's saying that he was "going of himself" to see Ilyusha. He felt that there must be some mystery in Kolya's suddenly taking it into his head to go to see him that day. They crossed the marketplace, in which at that hour were many loaded wagons from the country and a great number of live fowls. The market women were selling rolls, cottons and thread, etc., in their booths. These Sunday markets were naïvely called "fairs" in the town, and there were many such fairs during the year. Perezvon ran about in the wildest spirits, sniffing about first on one side, then the other. When he met other dogs they zealously smelled each other over according to the rules of canine etiquette.

"I like to watch such realistic scenes, Smurov," said Kolya suddenly. "Have you noticed how dogs sniff at one another when they meet? It seems to be a law of their nature."

"Yes; it's a funny habit."

"No, it's not funny; you are wrong there. There's nothing funny in nature, however funny it may seem to man with his prejudices.

If dogs could reason and criticize us they'd be sure to find just as much that would be funny to them, if not far more, in the social relations of men, their masters—far more, indeed. I repeat that, because I am convinced that there is far more foolishness among us. That's Rakitin's idea—a remarkable idea. I am a Socialist, Smurov."

"And what is a Socialist?" asked Smurov.

"That's when all are equal and all have property in common, there are no marriages, and everyone has any religion and laws he likes best, and all the rest of it. You are not old enough to understand yet. It's cold, though."

"Yes, eight above. Father looked at the thermometer just now."

"Have you noticed, Smurov, that in the middle of winter we don't feel so cold even when it's zero as we do now, in the beginning of winter, when there is a sudden cold wave, eight above, especially when there is not much snow. It's because people are not used to it. Everything is habit with men, everything even in their social and political relations. Habit is the great motive power. What a funny-looking peasant!"

Kolya pointed to a tall peasant, with a good-natured countenance, in a long sheepskin coat, who was standing by his wagon, clapping together his hands, in their shapeless leather gloves, to warm them. His long fair beard was all white with frost.

"That peasant's beard's frozen," Kolya cried in a loud provocative voice as he passed him.

"Lots of people's beards are frozen," the peasant replied, calmly and sententiously.

"Don't provoke him," observed Smurov.

"It's all right; he won't be cross; he's a nice fellow. Goodbye, Matvey."

"Goodbye."

"Is your name Matvey?"

"Yes. Didn't you know?"

"No, I didn't. It was a guess."

"You don't say so! You are a schoolboy, I suppose?"

"Yes."

"You get whipped, I expect?"

"Nothing to speak of—sometimes."

"Does it hurt?"

"Well, yes, it does."

"Ech, what a life!" The peasant heaved a sigh from the bottom of his heart.

"Goodbye, Matvey."

"Goodbye. You are a nice lad, that you are."

The boys went on.

"That was a nice peasant," Kolya observed to Smurov. "I like talking to the peasants, and am always glad to do them justice."

"Why did you tell a lie, pretending we are thrashed?" asked Smurov.

"I had to say that to please him."

"How do you mean?"

"You know, Smurov, I don't like being asked the same thing twice. I like people to understand at the first word. Some things can't be explained. According to a peasant's notions, schoolboys are whipped, and must be whipped. What would a schoolboy be, if he were not whipped? And if I were to tell him we are not, he'd be disappointed. But you don't understand that. One has to know how to talk to the peasants."

"Only don't tease them, please, or you'll get into another scrape as you did about that goose."

"So you're afraid?"

"Don't laugh, Kolya. Of course, I'm afraid. My father would be awfully cross. I am strictly forbidden to go out with you."

"Don't be uneasy, nothing will happen this time. Hullo, Natasha!" he shouted to a market woman in one of the booths.

"Call me Natasha! What next! My name is Marya," the middle-aged market woman shouted at him.

"I am so glad it's Marya. Goodbye!"

"Ah, you young rascal! A brat like you to carry on so!"

"I'm in a hurry. I can't stay now. You shall tell me next Sunday." Kolya waved his hand at her, as though she had attacked him and not he her.

"I've nothing to tell you next Sunday. You set upon me, you impudent thing. I didn't say anything," bawled Marya. "You want a whipping, that's what you want, you saucy jackanapes!"

There was a roar of laughter among the other market women round her. Suddenly a man in a violent rage darted out from the arcade of shops close by. He was a young man, not a native of the town, with dark, curly hair and a long, pale face, marked with smallpox. He wore a long blue coat and a peaked cap, and looked like a merchant's clerk. He was in a state of stupid excitement and brandished his fist at Kolya.

"I know you," he cried angrily, "I know you!"

Kolya stared at him. He could not recall when he could have had a row with the man. But he had been in so many rows on the street that he could hardly remember them all.

"Do you?" he asked sarcastically.

"I know you! I know you!" the man repeated idiotically.

"So much the better for you. Well, it's time I was going. Goodbye!"

"You are at your saucy pranks again?" cried the man. "You are at your saucy pranks again? I know, you are at it again!"

"It's not your business, brother, if I am at my saucy pranks again," said Kolya, standing still and scanning him.

"Not my business?"

"No; it's not your business."

"Whose then? Whose then? Whose then?"

"It's Trifon Nikitich's business now, not yours."

"What Trifon Nikitich?" asked the youth, staring with loutish amazement at Kolya, but still angry as ever.

"Have you been to the Church of the Ascension?" he suddenly asked him, with stern emphasis.

"What Church of Ascension? What for? No, I haven't," said the young man, somewhat taken aback.

"Do you know Sabaneyev?" Kolya went on even more emphatically and even more severely.

"What Sabaneyev? No, I don't know him."

"Well, then you can go to the devil," said Kolya, cutting short the conversation, and turning sharply to the right he strode quickly on his way as though he disdained further conversation with a dolt who did not even know Sabaneyev.

"Stop, hey! What Sabaneyev?" the young man recovered from his momentary stupefaction and was as excited as before. "What did he say?" He turned to the market women with a silly stare.

The women laughed.

"You can never tell what he's after," said one of them.

"What Sabaneyev is it he's talking about?" the young man repeated, still furious and brandishing his right arm.

"It must be a Sabeneyev who worked for the Kuzmichovs, that's who it must be," one of the women suggested.

The young man stared at her wildly.

"For the Kuzmichovs?" repeated another woman. "But his name wasn't Trifon. His name's Kuzma, not Trifon; but the boy said Trifon Nikitich, so it can't be the same."

"His name is not Trifon and not Sabaneyev, it's Chizhov," put in suddenly a third woman, who had hitherto been silent, listening gravely. "Alexey Ivanich is his name. Chizhov, Alexey Ivanich."

"Not a doubt about it, it's Chizhov," a fourth woman emphatically confirmed the statement.

The bewildered youth gazed from one to another.

"But what did he ask for, what did he ask for, good people?" he cried almost in desperation. "Do you know Sabeneyev?' says he. And who the devil's to know who is Sabeneyev?"

"You're a senseless fellow. I tell you it's not Sabaneyev, but Chizhov, Alexey Ivanich Chizhov, that's who it is!" one of the women shouted at him impressively.

"What Chizhov? Who is he? Tell me, if you know."

"That tall, sniveling fellow who used to sit in the market in the summer."

"And what's your Chizhov to do with me, good people, eh?"

"How can I tell what he's to do with you?" put in another. "You ought to know yourself what you want with him, if you make such a clamor about him. He spoke to you, he did not speak to us, you stupid. Don't you really know him?"

"Know whom?"

"Chizhov."

"The devil take Chizhov and you with him. I'll give him a hiding, that I will. He was laughing at me!"

"Will give Chizhov a hiding! More likely he will give you one. You are a fool, that's what you are!"

"Not Chizhov, not Chizhov, you spiteful, mischievous woman. I'll give the boy a hiding. Catch him, catch him, he was laughing at me!"

The women guffawed. But Kolya was by now a long a long way off, marching along with a triumphant air. Smurov walked beside him, looking round at the shouting group far behind. He, too, was in high spirits, though he was still afraid of getting into some scrape in Kolya's company.

"What Sabaneyev did you mean?" he asked Kolya, foreseeing what his answer would be.

"How do I know? Now there'll be a hubbub among them all day. I like to stir up fools in every class of society. There's another blockhead, that peasant there. You know, they say 'there's no one stupider than a stupid Frenchman,' but a stupid Russian shows it in his face just as much. Can't you see it all over his face that he is a fool, that peasant, eh?"

"Let him alone, Kolya. Let's go on."

"Nothing could stop me, now I am once off. Hey, good morning, peasant!"

A sturdy-looking peasant, with a round, simple face, and grizzled beard, who was walking by, raised his head and looked at the boy. He seemed not quite sober.

"Good morning, if you are not laughing at me," he said deliberately in reply.

"And if I am?" laughed Kolya.

"Well, a joke's a joke. Laugh away. I don't mind. There's no harm in a joke."

"I beg your pardon, brother, it was a joke."

"Well, God forgive you!"

"Do you forgive me, too?"

"I quite forgive you. Go along."

"I say, you seem a clever peasant."

"Cleverer than you," the peasant answered unexpectedly with the same gravity.

"I doubt it," said Kolya, somewhat taken aback.

"It's true though."

"Perhaps it is."

"It is, brother."

"Goodbye, peasant!"

"Goodbye!"

"There are all sorts of peasants," Kolya observed to Smurov, after a brief silence. "How could I tell I had hit on a clever one? I am always ready to recognize intelligence in the peasantry."

In the distance the cathedral clock struck half past eleven. The boys made haste and they walked as far as Captain Snegiryov's lodging, a considerable distance, quickly and almost in silence. Twenty paces from the house Kolya stopped and told Smurov to go on ahead and ask Karamazov to come out to him.

"One must sniff round a bit first," he observed to Smurov.

"Why ask him to come out?" Smurov protested. "You go in; they will be awfully glad to see you. What's the sense of getting acquainted in the frost out here?"

"I know why I want to see him out here in the frost," Kolya cut him short in the despotic tone he was fond of adopting with "small boys," and Smurov ran to do his bidding.

Chapter IV

The Lost Dog

Kolya leaned against the fence with an air of dignity, waiting for Alyosha to appear. Yes, he had long wanted to meet him. He had heard a great deal about him from the boys, but hitherto he had always maintained an appearance of disdainful indifference when he was mentioned, and he had even "criticized" what he heard about Alyosha. But secretly he had a great longing to make his acquaintance; there was something sympathetic and attractive in all he was told about Alyosha. So the present moment was important: to begin with, he had to show himself at his best, to show his independence. "Or, he'll think of me as thirteen and take me for a boy, like the rest of them. And what are these boys to him? I shall ask him when I get to know him. It's a pity I am so short, though. Tuzikov is younger than I am, yet he is half a head taller. But I have a clever face. I am not good-looking. I know I'm hideous, but I have a clever face. I mustn't talk too freely; if I fall into his arms all at once, he may think . . . Tfoo! how horrible if he should think . . . !"

Such were the thoughts that excited Kolya while he was doing his utmost to assume the most independent air. What distressed him most was his being so short; he did not mind so much his "hideous" face, as being so short. On the wall in a corner at home he had the year before made a pencil mark to show his height, and every two months since, he anxiously measured himself against it to see how much he had gained. But, alas! he grew very slowly, and this sometimes reduced him almost to despair. His face was in reality by no means "hideous"; on the contrary, it was rather attractive, with a fair, pale skin, freckled. His small, lively gray eyes had a fearless look, and often glowed with feeling. He had rather high cheek-bones; small, very red, but not very thick, lips; his nose was small and unmistakably turned up. "I've a regular pug nose, a regular pug nose," Kolya used to mutter to himself when he looked in the mirror, and he always left it with indignation. "But perhaps I haven't got a clever face?" he sometimes thought, doubtful even of that. But it must not be supposed that his mind was preoccupied with his face and his height. On the contrary, however bitter the moments before the mirror were to him, he quickly forgot them, and forgot them for a long time, "abandoning himself entirely to ideas and to real life," as he formulated his activities to himself.

Alyosha came out quickly and hastened up to Kolya. Before he reached him, Kolya could see that he looked delighted. "Can he be so glad to see me?" Kolya wondered, feeling pleased. We may note here, in passing, that Alyosha's appearance had undergone a complete change since we saw him last. He had abandoned his cassock and was now wearing a well-cut coat and a soft, round hat, and his hair had been cropped short. All this was very becoming to him, and he looked quite handsome. His charming face always had a good-humored expression; but there was a gentleness and serenity in his good humor. To Kolya's surprise, Alyosha came out to him just as he was, without an overcoat. He had evidently come in haste. He held out his hand to Kolya at once.

"Here you are at last! How anxious we've been to see you!"

"There were reasons which you shall know directly. Anyway, I am glad to make your acquaintance. I've long been hoping for an opportunity, and have heard a great deal about you," Kolya muttered, a little breathless.

"We should have met anyway. I've heard a great deal about you, too; but you've been a long time coming here."

"Tell me, how are things going?"

"Ilyusha is very ill. He is certainly dying."

"How awful! You must admit that medicine is a fraud, Karamazov," cried Kolya warmly.

"Ilyusha has mentioned you often, very often, even in his sleep, in delirium, you know. One can see that you used to be very, very dear to him . . . before the incident . . . with the knife. . . . Then there's another reason. . . . Tell me, is that your dog?"

"Yes, Perezvon."

"Not Zhuchka?" Alyosha looked at Kolya with eyes full of pity. "Is she lost forever?"

"I know you would all like it to be Zhuchka. I've heard all about it." Kolya smiled mysteriously. "Listen, Karamazov, I'll tell you all about it. That's what I came for; that's what I asked you to come out here for, to explain the whole episode to you before we go in," he began with animation. "You see, Karamazov, Ilyusha came into the preparatory class last spring. Well, you know what our prepara- tory class is—a lot of small boys. They began teasing Ilyusha at once. I am two classes higher up, and, of course, I only look on at them from a distance. I saw the boy was weak and small, but he wouldn't give in to them; he fought with them. I saw he was proud, and his eyes were full of fire. I like children like that. And they teased him all the more. The worst of it was he was horribly dressed at the time, his breeches were too small for him, and there were holes in his boots. They teased him about it; they jeered at him. That I can't stand. I stood up for him at once, and gave it to them hot. I beat them, but they adore me, do you know, Karama- zov?" Kolya boasted impulsively; "but I am always fond of chil- dren. I've two chickens on my hands at home now—that's what detained me today. So they stopped beating Ilyusha and I took him under my protection. I saw the boy was proud. I tell you that, the boy was proud; but in the end he became slavishly devoted to me: he did my slightest bidding, obeyed me as though I were God, tried to copy me. In the intervals between the classes he used to run to me at once, and I'd go about with him. On Sundays, too. They always laugh when an older boy makes friends with a younger one like that; but that's a prejudice. If it's my fancy, that's enough. I am teaching him, developing him. Why shouldn't I develop him if I like him? Here you, Karamazov, have taken up with all these nestlings. I see you want to influence the younger generation—to develop them, to be of use to them, and I assure you this trait in your character, which I knew by hearsay, attracted me more than any- thing. Let us get to the point, though. I noticed that there was a sort of softness and sentimentality coming over the boy, and you know I have a positive hatred of this sheepish sentimentality, and I have had it since birth. There were contradictions in him, too: he was proud, but he was slavishly devoted to me, and yet all at once his eyes would flash and he'd refuse to agree with me; he'd argue, fly into a rage. I used sometimes to propound certain ideas; I could see that it was not so much that he disagreed with the ideas, but that he was simply rebelling against me, because I was cool in responding to his endearments. And so, in order to train him prop- erly, the tenderer he was, the colder I became. I did it on purpose: that was my idea. My object was to form his character, to lick him into shape, to make a man of him . . . and besides . . . no doubt, you understand me at a word. Suddenly I noticed for three days in succession he was downcast and dejected, not because of my coldness, but for something else, something more important. I wondered what the tragedy was. I have pumped him and found out that he had somehow got to know Smerdyakov, who was lackey to your late father—it was before his death, of course—and he taught the little fool a silly trick—that is, a brutal, nasty trick. He told him to take a piece of bread, to stick a pin in it, and throw it to one of those hungry dogs who snap up anything without biting it, and then to watch and see what would happen. So they prepared a piece of bread like that and threw it to Zhuchka, that shaggy dog there's been such a fuss about. The people of the house it belonged to never fed it at all, though it barked all day. (Do you like that stupid barking, Karamazov? I can't stand it.) So it rushed at the bread, swallowed it, and began to squeal; it turned round and round and ran away, squealing as it ran out of sight. That was Ilyusha's own account of it. He confessed it to me, and cried bitterly. He hugged me, shaking all over. He kept on repeating 'He ran away squealing': the sight of that haunted him. He was tormented by remorse, I could see that. I took it seriously. I determined to give him a lesson for other things as well. So I must confess I wasn't quite straightforward, and pretended to be more indignant perhaps than I was. 'You've done a nasty thing,' I said, 'you are a scoundrel. I won't tell anyone, of course, but I shall have nothing more to do with you for awhile. I'll think it over and let you know through Smurov' (that's the boy who's just come with me; he's always ready to do anything for me) 'whether I will have anything to do with you in the future or whether I give you up for good as a scoundrel.' He was tremendously upset. I must confess I felt I'd gone too far as I spoke, but there was no help for it. I did what I thought best at the time. A day or two after, I sent Smurov to tell him that I would not speak to him again. That's what we call it when two schoolfellows refuse to have anything more to do with one another. Secretly I only meant to give him the silent treatment for a few days and then, if I saw signs of repentance, to hold out my hand to him again. That was my intention. But what do you think happened? He heard Smurov's message, his eyes flashed. "Tell Krasotkin from me,' he cried, 'that I will throw bread with pins to all the dogs—all—all of them!' 'So he's going in for a little temper. We must smoke it out of him.' And I began to treat him with contempt; whenever I met him I turned away or smiled sarcastically. And just then that affair with his father happened. You remember the 'wisp of tow'? You must realize that he was fearfully worked up by what had happened already. The boys, seeing I'd given him up, set on him and taunted him, shouting, 'Wisp of tow, wisp of tow!' And he had soon regular skirmishes with them, which I am very sorry for. They seem to have given him one very bad beating. One day he flew at them all as they were coming out of school. I stood a few yards off, looking on. And, I swear, I don't remember that I laughed; it was quite the other way, I felt awfully sorry for him, in another minute I would have run up to take his part. But he suddenly met my eyes. I don't know what he fancied; but he pulled out a penknife, rushed at me, and struck at my thigh, here in my right leg. I didn't move. I don't mind confessing I am plucky sometimes, Karamazov. I simply looked at him contemptuously, as though to say, 'this is how you repay all my kindness! Do it again, if you like, I'm at your service.' But he didn't stab me again; he broke down, he was frightened at what he had done, he threw away the knife, burst out crying, and ran away. I did not snitch on him, of course, and I made them all keep quiet, so it wouldn't come to the ears of the masters. I didn't even tell my mother till it had healed up. And the wound was a mere scratch. And then I heard that the same day he'd been throwing stones and had bitten your finger—but you understand now what a state he was in! Well, it can't be helped: it was stupid of me not to come and forgive him—that is, to make it up with him—when he was taken ill. I am sorry for it now. But I had a special reason. So now I've told you all about it . . . but I'm afraid it was stupid of me."

"Oh, what a pity," exclaimed Alyosha, with feeling, "that I didn't know before what terms you were on with him, or I'd have come to you long ago to beg you to go to him with me. Would you believe it, when he was feverish he talked about you in delirium. I didn't know how much you were to him! And you've really not succeeded in finding that dog? His father and the boys have been hunting all over the town for it. Would you believe it, since he's been ill, I've three times heard him repeat with tears, 'It's because I killed Zhuchka, dad, that I am ill now. God is punishing me for it.' He can't get that idea out of his head. And if the dog were found and proved to be alive, one might almost fancy the joy would cure him. We have all rested our hopes on you."

"Tell me, what made you hope that I would be the one to find him?" Kolya asked, with great curiosity. "Why did you reckon on me rather than anyone else?"

"There was a report that you were looking for the dog, and that you would bring it when you'd found it. Smurov said something of the sort. We've all been trying to persuade Ilyusha that the dog is alive, that it's been seen. The boys brought him a live hare: he just looked at it, with a faint smile, and asked them to set it free in the fields. And so we did. His father has just this moment come back, bringing him a mastiff pup, hoping to comfort him with that; but I think it only makes it worse."

"Tell me, Karamazov, what sort of man is the father? I know him, but what do you make of him—a mountebank, a buffoon?"

"Oh, no; there are people of deep feeling who have been somehow crushed. Buffoonery in them is a form of resentful irony against those to whom they daren't speak the truth, from having been for years humiliated and intimidated by them. Believe me, Krasotkin, that sort of buffoonery is sometimes tragic in the extreme. His whole life now is centered on Ilyusha, and if Ilyusha dies, he will either go mad with grief, or kill himself. I feel almost certain of that when I look at him now."

"I understand you, Karamazov. I see you understand human nature," Kolya added, with feeling.

"And as soon as I saw you with a dog, I thought it was Zhuchka you were bringing."

"Wait a bit, Karamazov, perhaps we shall find it yet; but this is Perezvon. I'll let him go in now and perhaps it will amuse Ilyusha more than the mastiff pup. Wait a bit, Karamazov, you will know something in a minute. But, I say, I am keeping you here!" Kolya cried suddenly. "You have no overcoat on in this bitter cold. You see what an egoist I am. Oh, we are all egoists, Karamazov!"

"Don't trouble; it is cold, but I don't often catch cold. Let us go in though, and, by the way, what is your name? I know you are called Kolya, but what else?"

"Nikolay—Nikolay Ivanovich Krasotkin, or, as they say in official documents 'Krasotkin son.' " Kolya laughed for some reason, but added suddenly. "Of course I hate my name Nikolay."

"Why so?"

"It's so trivial, so ordinary."

"You are thirteen?" asked Alyosha.

"No, fourteen—that is, I shall be fourteen very soon, in a couple of weeks. I'll confess one weakness of mine, Karamazov, just to you, since it's our first meeting, so that you may understand my character at once. I hate being asked my age, more than that . . . and in fact . . . there's a libelous story going around about me, that last week I played robbers with the preparatory boys. It's a fact that I did play with them, but it's a perfect libel to say I did it for my own amusement. I have reasons for believing that you've heard the story; but I wasn't playing for my own amusement, it was for the sake of the children, because they couldn't think of anything to do by themselves. But they've always got some silly tale. This is an awful town for gossip, I can tell you."

"But what if you had been playing for your own amusement, what's the harm?"

"Come, I say, for my own amusement! You don't play horsey, do you?"

"But you must look at it like this," said Alyosha, smiling. "Grown-up people go to the theater and there the adventures of all sorts of heroes are represented—sometimes there are robbers and battles, too—and isn't that just the same thing, in a different form, of course? And young people's games of soldiers or robbers in their playtime are also art in its first stage. You know, they spring from the growing artistic instincts of the young. And sometimes these games are much better than performances in the theater, the only difference is that people go there to look at actors, while in these games the young people are the actors themselves. But that's only natural."

"You think so? Is that your conviction?" Kolya looked at him intently. "Oh, you know, that's rather an interesting view. When I go home, I'll think it over. I'll admit I thought I might learn something from you. I've come to learn of you, Karamazov," Kolya concluded, in a voice full of spontaneous feeling.

"And I of you," said Alyosha, smiling and pressing his hand.

Kolya was much pleased with Alyosha. What struck him most was that he treated him exactly like an equal and that he talked to him just as if he were "quite grown up."

"I'll show you something directly, Karamazov; it's a theatrical performance, too," he said, laughing nervously. "That's why I've come."

"Let us go first to the people of the house, on the left. All the boys leave their coats in there, because the room is small and hot."

"Oh, I'm only coming in for a minute. I'll keep on my overcoat. Perezvon will stay here in the passage and be dead. *Ici*, Perezvon, lie down and be dead! You see how he's dead. I'll go in first and explore, then I'll whistle to him when I think fit, and you'll see, he'll dash in like mad. Only Smurov must not forget to open the door at the moment. I'll arrange it all and you'll see something."

Chapter V

At Ilyusha's Bedside

The room inhabited by the family of the retired captain Snegir-yov is already familiar to the reader. It was close and crowded at that moment with a number of visitors. Several boys were sitting with Ilyusha and, though all of them like Smurov were prepared to deny that it was Alyosha who had brought them and reconciled them with Ilyusha, it was really the fact. All the art he had used had been to take them, one by one, to Ilyusha, without "sheepish sentimentality," appearing to do so casually and without design. It was a great consolation to Ilyusha in his suffering. He was greatly touched by seeing the almost tender affection and sympathy shown him by these boys, who had been his enemies. Krasotkin was the only one missing and his absence was a heavy load on Ilyusha's

heart. Perhaps the bitterest of all his bitter memories was his stabbing Krasotkin, who had been his one friend and protector. Clever
little Smurov, who was the first to make up with Ilyusha, thought
it was so. But when Smurov hinted to Krasotkin that Alyosha
wanted to come and see him about something, the latter cut him
short, bidding Smurov tell "Karamazov" at once that he knew best
what to do, that he wanted no one's advice, and that, if he went to
see Ilyusha, he would choose his own time, for he had "his own
reasons."

That was two weeks before this Sunday. That was why Alyosha
had not been to see him, as he had meant to. But though he waited,
he sent Smurov to him twice again. Both times Krasotkin met him
with a curt, impatient refusal, sending Alyosha a message not to
bother him any more, that if he came himself, he, Krasotkin, would
not go to Ilyusha at all. Up to the very last day, Smurov did not
know that Kolya meant to go to Ilyusha that morning, and only the
evening before, as he parted from Smurov, Kolya abruptly told him
to wait at home for him next morning, for he would go with him to
the Snegiryovs', but warned him on no account to say he was
coming, as he wanted to drop in casually. Smurov obeyed.
Smurov's fancy that Kolya would bring back the lost dog was based
on the words Kolya had dropped that "they must be asses
not to find the dog, if it were alive." When Smurov, waiting for an
opportunity, timidly hinted at his guess about the dog, Krasotkin
flew into a violent rage. "I'm not such an ass as to go hunting about
the town for other people's dogs when I've got a dog of my own!
And how can you imagine a dog could be alive after swallowing a
pin? Sheepish sentimentality, that's what it is!"

For the last fortnight Ilyusha had not left his little bed under the
icons in the corner. He had not been to school since the day he met
Alyosha and bit his finger. He was taken ill the same day, though
for a month afterwards he was sometimes able to get up and walk
about the room and hall. But lately he had become so weak that he
could not move without help from his father. His father was terribly concerned about him. He even gave up drinking and was
almost crazy with terror that his boy would die. And often, especially after leading him round the room on his arm and putting him
back to bed, he would run to a dark corner in the hall and, leaning
his head against the wall, he would break into paroxysms of violent
weeping, stifling his sobs that they might not be heard by Ilyushechka.

Returning to the room, he would usually begin doing something
to amuse and comfort his precious boy, he would tell him stories,
funny anecdotes, or would mimic comic people he had happened to
meet, even imitate the howls and cries of animals. But Ilyusha
could not bear to see his father fooling and playing the buffoon.

Though the boy tried not to show how he disliked it, he saw with an aching heart that his father was an object of contempt, and he was continually haunted by the memory of the "wisp of tow" and that "terrible day."

Nina, Ilyusha's gentle, crippled sister, did not like her father's buffoonery either (Barbara Nikolaevna had been gone for some time past to Petersburg to study at the University). But the half-imbecile mother was greatly diverted and laughed heartily when her husband began capering about or performing something. It was the only way she could be amused; all the rest of the time she grumbled and complained that now everyone had forgotten her, that no one treated her with respect, that she was slighted, and so on. But during the last few days she had completely changed. She began looking constantly at Ilyusha's bed in the corner and seemed lost in thought. She was more silent, quieter, and, if she cried, she cried quietly so as not to be heard. The captain noticed the change in her with mournful perplexity. She did not like the boys' visits at first, but later on their merry shouts and stories began to divert her, and at last she liked them so much that, if the boys had given up coming, she would have felt dreary without them. When the children told some story or played a game, she laughed and clapped her hands. She called some of them to her and kissed them. She was particularly fond of Smurov.

As for the captain, the presence in his room of the children, who came to cheer up Ilyusha, filled his heart from the first with ecstatic joy. He even hoped that Ilyusha would now get over his depression, and that that would hasten his recovery. In spite of his alarm about Ilyusha, he had not, till lately, felt one minute's doubt of his boy's ultimate recovery. He met his little visitors with homage, waited upon them hand and foot, he was ready to be their horse and even began letting them ride on his back, but Ilyusha did not like the game and it was given up. He began buying little things for them, gingerbread and nuts, gave them tea and cut them sandwiches. It must be noted that all this time he had plenty of money. He had taken the two hundred rubles from Katerina Ivanovna just as Alyosha had predicted he would. And afterwards Katerina Ivanovna, learning more about their circumstances and Ilyusha's illness, visited them herself, made the acquaintance of the family and succeeded in fascinating the half-imbecile mother. Since then she had been lavish in helping them, and the captain, terror-stricken at the thought that his boy might be dying, forgot his pride and humbly accepted her assistance.

All this time Doctor Herzenstube, who was called in by Katerina Ivanovna, came punctually every other day, but little was gained by his visits and he dosed the invalid mercilessly. But on that Sunday morning a new doctor was expected, who had come from Moscow, where he had a great reputation. Katerina Ivanovna had sent for him from Moscow at great expense, not expressly for Ilyusha, but for another object of which more will be said in its place hereafter. But, as he had come, she had asked him to see Ilyusha as well, and the captain had been told to expect him. He hadn't the slightest idea that Kolya Krasotkin was coming, though he had long wished for a visit from the boy for whom Ilyusha was fretting.

At the moment when Krasotkin opened the door and came into the room, the captain and all the boys were round Ilyusha's bed, looking at a tiny mastiff pup, which had only been born the day before, though the captain had spoken for it a week ago to comfort and amuse Ilyushechka, who was still fretting over the lost and probably dead Zhuchka. Ilyusha, who had heard three days before that he was to be presented with a puppy, not an ordinary puppy, but a pedigreed mastiff (a very important point, of course), tried from delicacy of feeling to pretend that he was pleased. But his father and the boys could not help seeing that the puppy only served to recall to his little heart the thought of the unhappy dog he had killed. The puppy lay beside him feebly moving and he, smiling sadly, stroked it with his thin, pale, wasted hand. Clearly he liked the puppy, but . . . it wasn't Zhuchka; if he could have had Zhuchka and the puppy, too, then he would have been completely happy.

"Krasotkin!" cried one of the boys suddenly. He was the first to see him come in. Krasotkin's entrance made a general sensation; the boys moved away and stood on each side of the bed, so that he could get a full view of Ilyushechka. The captain ran eagerly to meet Kolya.

"Please come in . . . you are welcome!" he said hurriedly. "Ilyusha, Mr. Krasotkin has come to see you!"

But Krasotkin, shaking hands with him hurriedly, instantly showed his full knowledge of the manners of good society. He turned first to the captain's wife sitting in her armchair, who was very ill-humored at the moment, and was grumbling that the boys stood between her and Ilyusha's bed and did not let her see the new puppy. With the greatest courtesy he made her a bow, clicked his heels, and then turning to Nina, he made her, as the only other lady present, a similar bow. This polite behavior made an extremely favorable impression on the deranged lady.

"There, you can see at once he is a young man that has been well brought up," she commented aloud, throwing up her hands; "but as for our other visitors they come in one on the top of another."

"How do you mean, mamma, one on the top of another, how is that?" muttered the captain affectionately, though a little anxious on her account.

"That's how they ride in. They get on each other's shoulders in the hall and prance in like that on a respectable family. Strange sort of visitors!"

"But who's come in like that, mamma?"

"Why, that boy came in riding on that one's back and this one on that one's."

Kolya was already by Ilyusha's bedside. The sick boy turned visibly paler. He raised himself in the bed and looked intently at Kolya. Kolya had not seen his little friend for two months, and he was overwhelmed at the sight of him. He had never imagined that he would see such a wasted, yellow face, such enormous, feverishly glowing eyes and such thin little hands. He saw, with grieved surprise, Ilyusha's rapid, hard breathing and dry lips. He stepped close to him, held out his hand, and almost overwhelmed, he said:

"Well, old man . . . how are you?" But his voice failed him, he couldn't achieve an appearance of ease; his face suddenly twitched and the corners of his mouth quivered. Ilyusha smiled a pitiful little smile, still unable to utter a word. Something moved Kolya to raise his hand and pass it over Ilyusha's hair.

"Never mind!" he murmured softly to him to cheer him up, or perhaps not knowing why he said it. For a minute they were silent again.

"Hullo, so you've got a new puppy?" Kolya said suddenly, in a most callous voice.

"Ye-es," answered Ilyusha in a long whisper, gasping for breath.

"A black nose, that means he'll be fierce, a good house dog," Kolya observed gravely and stolidly, as if the only thing he cared about was the puppy and its black nose. But in reality he still had to do his utmost to control his feelings not to burst out crying like "a child," and do what he would he could not control it. "When it grows up, you'll have to keep it on the chain, I'm sure."

"He'll be a huge dog!" cried one of the boys.

"Of course he will," "a mastiff," "large," "like this," "as big as a calf," shouted several voices.

"As big as a calf, as a real calf," chimed in the captain. "I got one like that on purpose, one of the fiercest breed, and his parents are huge and very fierce, they stand as high as this from the floor. . . . Sit down here, on Ilyusha's bed, or here on the bench. You are welcome, we've been hoping to see you a long time . . . You were so kind as to come with Alexey Fyodorovich?"

Krasotkin sat on the edge of the bed, at Ilyusha's feet. Though he had perhaps prepared a free-and-easy opening for the conversation on his way, now he completely lost the thread of it.

"No . . . I came with Perezvon. I've got a dog now, called Perezvon.[3] A Slavonic name. He's out there . . . if I whistle, he'll run

3. "Chiming of bells."

in. I've brought a dog too," he said, addressing Ilyusha all at once. "Do you remember Zhuchka, old man?" he suddenly fired the question at him.

Ilyushechka's little face quivered. He looked with an agonized expression at Kolya. Alyosha, standing at the door, frowned and signed to Kolya not to speak of Zhuchka, but he did not or would not notice.

"Where . . . is Zhuchka?" Ilyusha asked in a broken voice.

"Oh, well, my boy, your Zhuchka's lost and done for!"

Ilyusha did not speak, but he fixed an intent gaze once more on Kolya. Alyosha, catching Kolya's eye, signed to him vigorously again, but he turned away his eyes pretending not to have noticed.

"It must have run away and died somewhere. It must have died after a meal like that," Kolya pronounced pitilessly, though he seemed a little breathless. "But I've got a dog, Perezvon . . . A Slavonic name. . . . I've brought him to show you."

"I don't want him!" said Ilyusha suddenly.

"No, no, you really must see him . . . it will amuse you. I brought him on purpose. . . . He's the same sort of shaggy dog. . . . You allow me to call in my dog, Madame?" he suddenly addressed Mrs. Snegiryov, with inexplicable excitement in his manner.

"I don't want him, I don't want him!" cried Ilyusha, with a mournful laceration in his voice. There was a reproachful light in his eyes.

"Perhaps, sir," the captain started up from the chest by the wall on which he had just sat down, "you'd better, sir . . . another time," he muttered, but Kolya could not be restrained. He hurriedly shouted to Smurov, "Open the door," and as soon as it was open, he blew his whistle. Perezvon dashed headlong into the room.

"Jump, Perezvon, beg! Beg!" shouted Kolya, jumping up, and the dog stood erect on his hind legs by Ilyusha's bedside. What followed was a surprise to everyone: Ilyusha started, lurched violently forward, bent over Perezvon and gazed at him, faint with suspense.

"It's . . . Zhuchka!" he cried suddenly, in a voice breaking with joy and suffering.

"And who did you think it was?" Krasotkin shouted with all his might, in a ringing, happy voice, and bending down he seized the dog and lifted him up to Ilyusha.

"Look, old man, you see, blind in one eye and the left ear is torn, just the marks you described to me. It was by that I found him. I found him directly. He did not belong to anyone!" he explained, turning quickly to the captain, to his wife, to Alyosha and then again to Ilyusha. "He used to live in the Fedotovs' back yard. Though he made his home there, they did not feed him. He was a stray dog that had run away from the village . . . I found him. . . .

You see, old man, he couldn't have swallowed what you gave him. If he had, he must have died, he must have! So he must have spat it out, since he is alive. You did not see him do it. But the pin pricked his tongue, that is why he squealed. He ran away squealing and you thought he'd swallowed it. He might well squeal, because the skin of dogs' mouths is so tender . . . tenderer than in men, much tenderer!" Kolya cried impetuously, his face glowing and radiant with delight.

Ilyusha could not speak. White as a sheet, he gazed open-mouthed at Kolya, with his great eyes almost popping out of his head. And if Krasotkin, who had no suspicion of it, had known what a disastrous and fatal effect such a moment might have on the sick child's health, nothing would have induced him to play such a trick on him. But Alyosha was perhaps the only person in the room who realized it. As for the captain he behaved like a small child.

"Zhuchka! It's Zhuchka!" he cried in a blissful voice. "Ilyusha, this is Zhuchka, your Zhuchka! Mamma, this is Zhuchka!" He was almost weeping.

"And I never guessed!" cried Smurov regretfully. "Bravo, Krasotkin, I said he'd find the dog and here he's found him."

"Here he's found him!" another boy repeated gleefully.

"Krasotkin's great!" cried a third voice.

"He's great, he's great!" cried the other boys, and they began clapping.

"Wait, wait," Krasotkin did his utmost to shout above them all. "I'll tell you how it happened, that's the whole point. I found him, I took him home and hid him at once. I kept him locked up at home and did not show him to anyone till today. Only Smurov had known for the last two weeks, but I assured him this dog was called Perezvon and he did not guess. And meanwhile I taught the dog all sorts of tricks. You should only see all the things he can do! I trained him so as to bring you a well-trained dog, in good condition, old man, so as to be able to say to you, 'See, old man, what a fine dog your Zhuchka is now!' Do you have a bit of meat, he'll show you a trick that will break you up laughing. A piece of meat, haven't you got any?"

The captain ran across the hall to the landlady, where their cooking was done. Not to lose precious time, Kolya, in desperate haste, shouted to Perezvon "dead!" And the dog immediately turned round and lay on its back with its four paws in the air. The boys laughed, Ilyusha looked on with the same suffering smile, but the person most delighted with the dog's performance was "mamma." She laughed at the dog and began snapping her fingers and calling it, "Perezvon, Perezvon!"

"Nothing will make him get up, nothing!" Kolya cried triumphantly, proud of his success. "He won't move for all the shouting

in the world, but if I call to him, he'll jump up in a minute. *Ici,*
Perezvon!"

The dog leaped up and bounded about, whining with delight. The
captain ran back with a piece of cooked beef.

"Is it hot?" Kolya inquired hurriedly, with a businesslike air,
taking the meat. "Dogs don't like hot things. No, it's all right.
Look, everybody, look, Ilyushechka, look, old man; why aren't you
looking? He does not look at him, now I've brought him."

The new trick consisted in making the dog stand motionless with
his nose out and putting a tempting morsel of meat just on his nose.
The luckless dog had to stand without moving, with the meat on his
nose, as long as his master chose to keep him, without a movement,
perhaps for half an hour. But he kept Perezvon only for a brief
moment.

"Paid for!" cried Kolya, and the meat passed in a flash from the
dog's nose to his mouth. The audience, of course, expressed enthusiasm and surprise.

"Can you really have put off coming all this time simply to train
the dog?" exclaimed Alyosha, with an involuntary note of reproach
in his voice.

"Simply for that!" answered Kolya, with perfect simplicity. "I
wanted to show him in all his glory."

"Perezvon! Perezvon," called Ilyusha suddenly, snapping his thin
fingers and beckoning to the dog.

"What is it? Let him jump up on the bed! *Ici,* Perezvon!" Kolya
slapped the bed and Perezvon darted up to Ilyusha. The boy threw
both arms round his head and Perezvon instantly licked his cheek.
Ilyusha crept close to him, stretched himself out in bed and hid
his face in the dog's shaggy coat.

"Dear, dear!" kept exclaiming the captain. Kolya sat down again
on the edge of the bed.

"Ilyusha, I can show you another trick. I've brought you a little
cannon. You remember, I told you about it before and you said
how much you'd like to see it. Well, here, I've brought it to you."

And Kolya hurriedly pulled out of his satchel the little bronze
cannon. He hurried, because he was happy himself. Another time
he would have waited till the sensation made by Perezvon had
passed off, now he hurried on regardless of all consideration. "You
are all happy now," he felt, "so here's something to make you
happier!" He was perfectly enchanted himself.

"I've been coveting this thing for a long while; it's for you, old
man, it's for you. It belonged to Morozov, it was no use to him, he
had it from his brother. I swopped a book from father's bookcase
for it, *A Kinsman of Mahomet or Salutary Folly,* a scandalous
book published in Moscow a hundred years ago, before they had

any censorship. And Morozov has a taste for such things. He was grateful to me, too . . ."

Kolya held the cannon in his hand so that all could see and admire it. Ilyusha raised himself, and, with his right arm still round the dog, he gazed enchanted at the toy. The sensation was even greater, when Kolya announced that he had gunpowder too, and that it could be fired off at once "if it won't alarm the ladies." "Mamma" immediately asked to look at the toy closer and her request was granted. She was much pleased with the little bronze cannon on wheels and began rolling it to and fro on her lap. She readily gave permission for the cannon to be fired, without any idea of what she had been asked. Kolya showed the powder and the shot. The captain, as a military man, undertook to load it, putting in a minute quantity of powder. He asked that the shot might be put off till another time. The cannon was put on the floor, aiming towards an empty part of the room, three grains of powder were thrust into the touch hole and a match was put to it. A magnificent explosion followed. Mamma was startled, but at once laughed with delight. The boys gazed in speechless triumph. But the captain, looking at Ilyusha, was more enchanted than any of them. Kolya picked up the cannon and immediately presented it to Ilyusha, together with the powder and the shot.

"I got it for you, for you! I've been keeping it for you a long time," he repeated once more in his delight.

"Oh, give it to me! No, give me the cannon!" Mamma began begging like a little child. Her face showed a piteous fear that she would not get it. Kolya was disconcerted. The captain fidgeted uneasily.

"Mamma, mamma," he ran to her, "the cannon's yours, of course, but let Ilyusha have it, because it's a present to him, but it's just as good as yours. Ilyusha will always let you play with it, it shall belong to both of you, both of you."

"No, I don't want it to belong to both of us, I want it to be mine altogether, not Ilyusha's," persisted mamma, on the point of tears.

"Take it, mother, here, keep it!" Ilyusha cried. "Krasotkin, may I give it to my mother?" he turned to Krasotkin with an imploring face, as though he were afraid he might be offended at his giving his present to someone else.

"Of course, you may," Krasotkin assented heartily, and, taking the cannon from Ilyusha, he handed it himself to mama with a polite bow. She was so touched that she cried.

"Ilyushechka, darling, he's the one who loves his mamma!" she said tenderly, and at once began wheeling the cannon to and fro on her lap again.

"Mamma, let me kiss your hand." The captain darted up to her at once and did so.

"And I never saw such a charming fellow as this nice boy," said the grateful lady, pointing to Krasotkin.

"And I'll bring you as much powder as you like, Ilyusha. We make the powder ourselves now. Borovikov found out how it's made—twenty-four parts of saltpeter, ten of sulphur and six of birchwood charcoal. It's all pounded together, mixed into a paste with water and rubbed through a sieve—that's how it's done."

"Smurov told me about your powder, only father says it's not real gunpowder," responded Ilyusha.

"Not real?" Kolya flushed. "It burns. I don't know, of course."

"No, sir, I didn't mean that," put in the captain with a guilty face. "I only said that real powder is not made like that, but that's nothing, it can be made that way, too."

"I don't know, you know best. We lighted some in a pomatum jar, it burned splendidly, it all burned away leaving only a tiny ash. But that was only the paste, and if you rub it through . . . but of course you know best, I don't know. . . . And Bulkin's father thrashed him on account of our powder, did you hear?" he turned to Ilyusha.

"Yes," answered Ilyusha. He listened to Kolya with immense interest and enjoyment.

"We had prepared a whole bottle of it and he used to keep it under his bed. His father saw it. He said it might explode, and thrashed him on the spot. He was going to make a complaint against me to the masters. He is not allowed to go about with me now, no one is allowed to go about with me now. Smurov is not allowed to either, I've got a bad name with everyone. They say I'm a 'desperate character,' " Kolya smiled scornfully. "It all began from what happened on the railway."

"Ah, we've heard of that exploit of yours, too," cried the captain. "How could you lie still on the line? It is possible you weren't the least afraid, lying there under the train? Weren't you frightened?"

The captain was abject in his flattery of Kolya.

"N-not particularly," answered Kolya carelessly. "What's blasted my reputation more than anything here was that cursed goose," he said, turning again to Ilyusha. But though he assumed an unconcerned air as he talked, he still could not control himself and was continually missing the note he tried to keep up.

"Ah! I heard about the goose!" Ilyusha laughed, beaming all over. "They told me, but I didn't understand. Did they really take you to the court?"

"The most stupid, trivial affair, they made a mountain out of a molehill as they always do," Kolya began carelessly. "I was walking through the marketplace here one day, just when they'd driven in the geese. I stopped and looked at them. All at once a fellow, who is an errand boy at Plotnikov's now, looked at me and said, 'What are you looking at the geese for?' I looked at him, he was a stupid, round-mugged fellow of twenty. I am always on the side of the peasantry, you know. I like talking to the peasants.... We've dropped behind the peasants—that's an axiom. I believe you are laughing, Karamazov?"

"No, heaven forbid, I am listening," said Alyosha with a most good-natured air, and the sensitive Kolya was immediately reassured.

"My theory, Karamazov, is clear and simple," he hurried on again, looking pleased. "I believe in the people and am always glad to give them their due, but I am not for spoiling them, that is a *sine qua non*[4] ... But I was telling you about the goose. So I turned to the fool and answered, 'I am wondering what the goose thinks about.' He looked at me quite stupidly, 'And what does the goose think about?' he asked. 'Do you see that cart full of oats?' I said. 'The oats are dropping out of the sack, and the goose has put its neck right under the wheel to gobble them up—do you see?' 'I see that quite well,' he said. 'Well,' said I, 'if that cart were to move on a little, would it break the goose's neck or not?' 'It'd be sure to break it,' and he grinned all over his face, highly delighted. 'Come on then,' said I, 'let's try.' 'Let's,' he said. And it did not take us long to arrange: he stood at the bridle without being noticed, and I stood on one side to direct the goose. And the owner wasn't looking, he was talking to someone, so I had nothing to do, the goose thrust its head in after the oats of itself, under the cart, just under the wheel. I winked at the lad, he tugged at the bridle, and crack! The goose's neck was broken in half. And, as luck would have it, all the peasants saw us at that moment and they kicked up a shindy at once. 'You did that on purpose!' 'No, not on purpose.' 'Yes, you did, on purpose!' Well, they shouted, 'Take him to the justice of the peace!' They took me, too. 'You were there, too,' they said, 'you helped, you're known all over the market!' And, for some reason, I really am known all over the market," Kolya added conceitedly. "We all went off to the justice's, they brought the goose, too. The fellow was crying in a great funk, simply blubbering like a woman. And the farmer kept shouting that you could kill any number of geese like that. Well, of course, there were witnesses. The justice of the peace settled it in a minute, that the farmer was to be paid a ruble for the goose, and the fellow to have the goose. And he was warned not to play such pranks again. And the fellow kept blubbering like a woman, 'It wasn't me,' he said, 'it was he who egged me on,' and he pointed to me. I answered with the utmost composure that I hadn't egged him on, that I simply stated the general proposition, had spoken hypothetically. The justice of the peace smiled and

---

4. "Basic requirement."

was vexed with himself at once for having smiled. 'I'll complain to your masters about you, so that in the future you won't waste your time on such general propositions, instead of sitting at your books and learning your lessons.' He didn't complain to the masters, that was a joke, but the matter was noised abroad and came to the ears of the masters. Their ears are long, you know! The classical master, Kolbasnikov, was particularly shocked about it, but Dardanelov got me off again. But Kolbasnikov is savage with everyone now like a green ass. Did you know, Ilyusha, he is just married, got a dowry of a thousand rubles, and his bride's a regular fright of the first rank and the last degree. The third class fellows wrote an epigram on it.

> Astounding news has reached the class,
> Kolbasnikov has been an ass.

And so on, awfully funny, I'll bring it to you later on. I say nothing against Dardanelov, he is a learned man, there's no doubt about it. I respect men like that and it's not because he stood up for me."

"But you took him down a peg about the founders of Troy!" Smurov put in suddenly, unmistakably proud of Krasotkin at such a moment. He was particularly pleased with the story of the goose.

"Did you really take him down a peg?" the captain inquired, in a flattering way. "On the question of who founded Troy, sir? We heard of it, Ilyusha told me about it at the time."

"He knows everything, dad, he knows more than any of us!" put in Ilyusha; "he only pretends to be like that, but really he is top in every subject . . ."

Ilyusha looked at Kolya with infinite happiness.

"Oh, that's all nonsense about Troy, a trivial matter. I consider this an unimportant question," said Kolya with haughty humility. He had by now completely recovered his dignity, though he was still a little uneasy. He felt that he was greatly excited and that he had talked about the goose, for instance, with too little reserve, while Alyosha had looked serious and had not said a word all the time. And the vain boy began by degrees to have a rankling fear that Alyosha was silent because he despised him, and thought he was showing off before him. If he dared to think anything like that Kolya would . . .

"I regard the question as quite a trivial one," he rapped out again, proudly.

"And I know who founded Troy," a boy, who had not spoken before, said suddenly, to the surprise of everyone. He was silent and seemed to be shy. He was a pretty boy of about eleven, called Kartashov. He was sitting near the door. Kolya looked at him with dignified amazement. The fact was that the identity of the founders of Troy had become a secret for the whole school, a secret which could only be discovered by reading Smaragdov, and no one had Smaragdov but Kolya. One day when Kolya's back was turned, Kartashov hastily opened Smaragdov, which lay among Kolya's books, and immediately lighted on the passage relating to the foundation of Troy. This was a good while ago, but he felt uneasy and could not bring himself to announce publicly that he, too, knew who had founded Troy, afraid of what might happen and of Krasotkin's somehow putting him to shame over it. But now he couldn't resist saying it. For weeks he had been longing to.

"Well, who did found it?" asked Kolya, turning to him with haughty superciliousness. He saw from his face that he really did know and at once made up his mind how to take it. There was, so to speak, a discordant note in the general harmony.

"Troy was founded by Teucer, Dardanus, Ilius and Tros," the boy rapped out at once, and in the same instant he blushed, blushed so, that it was painful to look at him. But the boys stared at him, stared at him for a whole minute, and then all the staring eyes turned at once and were fastened upon Kolya, who was still scanning the audacious boy with disdainful composure.

"In what sense did they found it?" he deigned to comment at last. "And what is meant by founding a city or a state? What did they do—did they go and each lay a brick, do you suppose?"

There was laughter. The offending boy turned from pink to crimson. He was silent and on the point of tears. Kolya held him so for a minute.

"Before you talk of a historical event like the foundation of a nationality, you must first understand what you mean by it," he admonished him in stern incisive tones. "But I attach no consequence to these old wives' tales and I don't think much of universal history in general," he added carelessly, addressing the company generally.

"Universal history, sir?" the captain inquired, looking almost scared.

"Yes, universal history! It's the study of the successive follies of mankind and nothing more.[5] The only subjects I respect are mathematics and natural science," said Kolya. He was showing off and he stole a glance at Alyosha; his was the only opinion he was afraid of there. But Alyosha was still silent and still serious as before. If Alyosha had said a word it would have stopped him, but Alyosha was silent and "it might be the silence of contempt" and that finally irritated Kolya.

"The classical languages, too . . . they are simply madness, nothing more. You seem to disagree with me again, Karamazov?"

"I don't agree," said Alyosha, with a faint smile.

5. Obviously a citation, probably from Voltaire. See next chapter.

"The study of the classics, if you ask my opinion, is simply a police measure, that's the only reason why it has been introduced into our schools." By degrees Kolya began to get breathless again. "Latin and Greek were introduced because they are a bore and because they stupefy the intellect. It was dull before, so what could they do to make things duller? It was senseless enough before, so what could they do to make it more senseless? So they thought of Greek and Latin. That's my entire opinion of them, I hope I shall never change it," Kolya finished abruptly. His cheeks were flushed.

"That's true," assented Smurov suddenly, in a ringing tone of conviction. He had listened attentively.

"And yet he is first in Latin himself," cried one of the group of boys suddenly.

"Yes, dad, he says that and yet he is first in Latin," echoed Ilyusha.

"What of it?" Kolya thought fit to defend himself, though the praise was very sweet to him. "I plug away at Latin, because I have to, because I promised my mother to pass my examination, and I think that whatever you do, it's worth doing it well. But in my soul I have a profound contempt for the classics and all that vileness. . . . You don't agree, Karamazov?"

"Why 'vileness'?" Alyosha smiled again.

"Well, all the classical authors have been translated into all languages, so it was not for the sake of studying the classics they introduced Latin, but solely as a police measure, to stupefy the intelligence. So what can one call it but vileness?"

"Why, who taught you all this?" cried Alyosha, surprised at last.

"In the first place I am capable of thinking for myself without being taught. Besides, what I said just now about the classics being translated our teacher Kolbasnikov has said to the whole of the third class."

"The doctor has come!" cried Nina, who had been silent till then.

A carriage belonging to Madame Khokhlakov drove up to the gate. The captain, who had been expecting the doctor all the morning, rushed headlong out to meet him. "Mamma" pulled herself together and assumed a dignified air. Alyosha went up to Ilyusha and began setting his pillows straight. Nina, from her invalid chair, anxiously watched him putting the bed tidy. The boys hurriedly took leave. Some of them promised to come again in the evening. Kolya called Perezvon and the dog jumped off the bed.

"I won't go away, I won't go away," Kolya said hastily to Ilyusha. "I'll wait in the passage and come back when the doctor's gone, I'll come back with Perezvon."

But by now the doctor had entered, an important-looking person with long, dark whiskers and a shiny, shaven chin, wearing a bear-skin coat. As he crossed the threshold he stopped, taken aback; he probably fancied he had come to the wrong place. "How is this? Where am I?" he muttered, not removing his coat nor his peaked sealskin cap. The crowd, the poverty of the room, the washing hanging on a line in the corner, puzzled him. The captain, bent double, was bowing low before him.

"It's here, sir, here, sir," he muttered cringingly; "it's here, you've come right, sir, you were coming to us . . ."

"Sne-gi-ryov?" the doctor said loudly and pompoudly. "Mr. Snegiryov—is that you?"

"That's me, sir!"

"Ah!"

The doctor looked round the room with a squeamish air once more and threw off his coat, displaying to all eyes the grand decoration of his neck. The captain caught the fur coat in the air, and the doctor took off his cap.

"Where is the patient?" he asked emphatically.

Chapter VI

Precocity

"What do you think the doctor will say to him?" Kolya asked quickly. "What a repulsive mug, though, hasn't he? I can't endure medicine!"

"Ilyusha will die. I think that's certain," answered Alyosha mournfully.

"They are frauds! Medicine's a fraud! I am glad to have made your acquaintance, though, Karamazov. I wanted to know you for a long time. I am only sorry we meet in such sad circumstances."

Kolya had a great inclination to say something even warmer and more demonstrative, but he felt ill at ease. Alyosha noticed this, smiled, and pressed his hand.

"I've long learned to respect you are a rare person," Kolya muttered again, faltering and uncertain. "I have heard you are a mystic and have been in the monastery. I know you are a mystic but . . . that hasn't put me off. Contact with real life will cure you. . . . It's always so with characters like yours."

"What do you mean by mystic? Cure me of what?" Alyosha was rather astonished.

"Oh, God, and all the rest of it."

"What, don't you believe in God?"

"Oh, I've nothing against God. Of course, God is only a hypothesis, but . . . I admit that He is needed . . . for the order of the universe and all that . . . and that if there were no God He would have to be invented," added Kolya, beginning to blush. He suddenly fancied that Alyosha might think he was trying to show off his knowledge and to prove that he was "grown up." "I haven't the slightest desire to show off my knowledge to him," Kolya thought indignantly. And all of a sudden he felt horribly annoyed.

"Frankly, I can't stand all these discussions," he said with a final air. "It's possible for one who doesn't believe in God to love mankind, don't you think so? Didn't Voltaire not believe in God and love mankind?" ("I am at it again," he thought to himself.)

"Voltaire believed in God, though not very much, I think, and I don't think he loved mankind very much either," said Alyosha quietly, gently, and quite naturally, as though he were talking to someone of his own age, or even older. Kolya was particularly struck by Alyosha's apparent diffidence about his opinion of Voltaire. He seemed to be leaving the question for him, little Kolya, to settle.

"Have you read Voltaire?" Alyosha finished.

"No, not to say read. . . . But I've read Candide[6] in the Russian translation . . . in an absurd, grotesque, old translation . . . (At it again! again!)"

"And did you understand it?"

"Oh, yes, everything. . . . That is . . . Why do you suppose I shouldn't understand it? There's a lot of nastiness in it, of course. . . . Of course I can understand that it's a philosophical novel and written to advocate an idea. . . ." Kolya was getting muddled by now. "I am a Socialist, Karamazov, I am an incurable Socialist," he announced suddenly, apropos of nothing.

"A Socialist?" smiled Alyosha. "But when have you had time to become one? Why, I thought you are only thirteen?"

Kolya winced.

"In the first place I am not thirteen, but fourteen, fourteen in a fortnight," he flushed angrily, "and in the second place I am at a complete loss to understand what my age has to do with it. The question is what are my convictions, not what is my age, isn't it?"

"When you are older, you'll understand for yourself the influence of age on convictions. I fancied, too, that you were not expressing your own ideas," Alyosha answered serenely and modestly, but Kolya interrupted him hotly:

"Come, you want obedience and mysticism. You must admit that the Christian religion, for instance, has only been of use to the rich and the powerful to keep the lower classes in slavery, that's so, isn't it?"

6. *Candide, or Optimism* (1759).

"Ah, I know where you read that, and I am sure someone told you so!" cried Alyosha.

"I say, what makes you think I read it? And certainly no one told me so. I can think for myself. . . . I am not opposed to Christ, if you like. He was a most humane person, and if He were alive today, He would be found in the ranks of the revolutionists, and would perhaps play a conspicuous part. . . . There's no doubt about that."

"Oh, where, where did you get that from? What fool have you made friends with?" exclaimed Alyosha.

"Come, the truth will out! It has so chanced that I have often talked to Mr. Rakitin, of course, but . . . old Belinsky[7] said that, too, so they say."

"Belinsky? I don't remember. He hasn't written that anywhere."

"If he didn't write it, they say he said it. I heard that from a . . . but never mind."

"And have you read Belinsky?"

"Well, no . . . I haven't read all of him, but . . . I read the passage about Tatyana, why she didn't go off with Onegin."[8]

"Didn't go off with Onegin? Surely, you don't . . . understand that already?"

"Why, you seem to take me for the child Smurov," said Kolya, with a grin of irritation. "But please don't suppose I am such a revolutionist. I often disagree with Mr. Rakitin. Though I mention Tatyana, I am not at all for the emancipation of women. I acknowledge that women are subservient creatures and must obey. *Les femmes tricottent*,[9] as Napoleon said." Kolya, for some reason, smiled. "And on that question at least I am quite of one mind with that pseudo-great man. I think, too, that to leave one's own country and fly to America is mean, worse than mean—silly. Why go to America when one may be of great service to humanity here? Now especially. There's a perfect mass of fruitful activity open to us. That's what I answered."

"What do you mean? Answered whom? Has someone suggested your going to America already?"

"I must confess, they've been at me to go, but I declined. That's between ourselves, of course, Karamazov; do you hear, not a word to anyone. I say this only to you. I am not at all anxious to fall into the clutches of the secret police and take lessons at the Chain bridge,

7. V. G. Belinsky (1811–1848), a leading Russian critic, heralded numerous new writers, including Dostoevsky. In *The Writer's Diary* for 1873, i.e., seven years after the purported action of the novel, Dostoevsky reports this conversation with Belinsky.
8. These characters appear in Pushkin's novel *Eugene Onegin* (1824–1830), discussed in Belinsky's ninth article on the works of Pushkin.
9. "Women knit."

Long will you remember
The house at the chain bridge.[1]

Do you remember? It's splendid. Why are you laughing? You don't
suppose I am fibbing, do you?" ("What if he should find out that I
have only that one number of *The Bell*[2] in father's bookcase, and
haven't read any more of it?" Kolya thought with a shudder.)

"Oh, no, I am not laughing and don't suppose for a moment that
you are lying. No, indeed, I can't suppose so, for all this alas! is
perfectly true. But tell me, have you read Pushkin, *Onegin*, for
instance? . . . You spoke just now of Tatyana."

"No, I haven't read it yet, but I want to read it. I have no
prejudices, Karamazov; I want to hear both sides. What makes you
ask?"

"Oh, nothing."

"Tell me, Karamazov, have you an awful contempt for me?"
Kolya rapped out suddenly and drew himself up before Alyosha, as
though he were on parade. "Be so kind as to tell me, without
beating about the bush."

"I have a contempt for you?" Alyosha looked at him wondering.
"What for? I am only sad that a charming nature such as yours
should be perverted by all this crude nonsense before you have
begun life."

"Don't be anxious about my nature," Kolya interrupted, not
without complacency. "But it's true that I am stupidly sensitive,
crudely sensitive. You smiled just now, and I fancied you seemed
to . . ."

"Oh, my smile meant something quite different. I'll tell you why
I smiled. Not long ago I read the criticism made by a German who
had lived in Russia, on our students and youth of today. 'Show a
Russian schoolboy,' he writes, 'a map of the stars, which he knows
nothing about, and he will give you back the map next day with
corrections on it.' No knowledge and unbounded conceit—that's
what the German meant to say about the Russian schoolboy."

"Yes, that's perfectly right," Kolya laughed suddenly, "truthis-
simo! exactly so! Bravo the German. But the Kraut did not see the
good side, what do you think? Conceit may be, that comes from
youth, that will be corrected if need be, but, on the other hand,
there is an independent spirit almost from childhood, boldness of
thought and conviction, and not the spirit of these sausage makers,
groveling before authority. . . . But the German was right all the
same. Bravo the German! But Germans want strangling all the

1. Kolya cites part of a satire by D. D.
Minaev on a venture in workers' educa-
tion. The headquarters of the Secret
Police were near the same bridge.

2. Alexander Herzen's newspaper, published in England and smuggled into Russia, where it was widely read. Minaev's
satire first appeared there.

same. Though they are so good at sciences and learning they must be strangled."

"Strangled, what for?" smiled Alyosha.

"Well, perhaps I am talking nonsense, I agree. I am awfully childish sometimes, and when I am pleased about anything I can't restrain myself and am ready to talk any nonsense. But, I say, we are chattering away here about nothing, and that doctor has been a long time in there. But perhaps he's examining the mamma and that poor crippled Nina. I like that Nina, you know. She whispered to me suddenly as I was coming away, 'Why didn't you come before?' And in such a voice, so reproachfully! I think she is awfully nice and pathetic."

"Yes, yes! Well, you'll be coming often, you will see what she is like. It would do you a great deal of good to know people like that, to learn to value a great deal which you will find out from knowing these people," Alyosha observed warmly. "That would have more effect on you than anything."

"Oh, how I regret and blame myself for not having come sooner!" Kolya exclaimed, with bitter feeling.

"Yes, it's a great pity. You saw for yourself how delighted the poor child was to see you. And how he fretted for you to come!"

"Don't tell me! You make it worse! But it serves me right. What kept me from coming was my conceit, my egoistic vanity, and the beastly willfulness, which I never can get rid of, though I've been struggling with it all my life. I see that now. I am a scoundrel in lots of ways, Karamazov!"

"No, you have a charming nature, though it's been distorted, and I quite understand why you have had such an influence on this generous, morbidly sensitive boy," Alyosha answered warmly.

"And you say that to me!" cried Kolya; "and would you believe it, I thought—I've thought several times since I've been here—that you despised me! If only you knew how I prize your opinion!"

"But are you really so sensitive? At your age! Would you believe it, just now, when you were telling your story, I thought, as I watched you, that you must be very sensitive!"

"You thought so? What an eye you've got, I say! I bet that was when I was talking about the goose. That was just when I fancied you had a great contempt for me for being in such a hurry to show off, and for a moment I quite hated you for it, and began talking like a fool. Then I fancied—just now, here—when I said that if there were no God He would have to be invented, that I was in too great a hurry to display my knowledge, especially as I got that phrase out of a book. But I swear I wasn't showing off out of vanity, though I really don't know why, because I was so pleased, yes, I believe it was because I was so pleased . . . though it's perfectly disgraceful for anyone to be gushing as soon as they are pleased, I know that. But I am convinced now that you don't despise me; it was all my imagination. Oh, Karamazov, I am profoundly unhappy. I sometimes fancy all sorts of things, that everyone is laughing at me, the whole world, and then I feel ready to overturn the whole order of things."

"And you torment everyone about you," smiled Alyosha.

"Yes, I torment everyone about me, especially my mother. Karamazov, tell me, am I very ridiculous now?"

"Don't think about that, don't think of it at all!" cried Alyosha. "And what does ridiculous mean? Isn't everyone constantly being or seeming ridiculous? Besides, nearly all clever people now are fearfully afraid of being ridiculous, and that makes them unhappy. All I am surprised at is that you should be feeling that so early, though I've observed it for some time past, and not only in you. Nowadays the very children have begun to suffer from it. It's almost a sort of insanity. The devil has taken the form of that vanity and entered into the whole generation; it's simply the devil," added Alyosha, without a trace of the smile that Kolya, staring at him, expected to see. "You are like everyone else," said Alyosha, in conclusion, "that is, like very many others. Only you must not be like everybody else, that's all."

"Even if everyone is like that?"

"Yes, even if everyone is like that. You be the only one not like it. You really are not like everyone else, here you are not ashamed to confess to something bad and even ridiculous. And who will admit so much in these days? No one. And people have even ceased to feel the impulse to self-criticism. Don't be like everyone else, even if you were the only one who is not like everyone else."

"Splendid! I was not mistaken in you. You know how to console one. Oh, how I have longed to know you, Karamazov. I've long been eager for this meeting. Can you really have thought about me, too? You said just now that you thought of me, too?"

"Yes, I'd heard of you and had thought of you, too . . . and if it's partly vanity that makes you ask, it doesn't matter."

"Do you know, Karamazov, our talk has been like a declaration of love," said Kolya, in a bashful and melting voice. "That's not ridiculous, is it?"

"Not at all ridiculous, and if it were ridiculous, it wouldn't matter, because it's been a good thing." Alyosha smiled brightly.

"But do you know, Karamazov, you must admit that you are a little ashamed yourself, now. . . . I see it by your eyes." Kolya smiled with a sort of sly happiness.

"Why ashamed?"

"Well, why are you blushing?"

"It was you made me blush," laughed Alyosha, and he really did blush. "Oh, well, I am a little ashamed, goodness knows why, I don't know . . ." he muttered almost embarrassed.

"Oh, how I love you and admire you at this moment just because you are rather ashamed! Because you are just like me," cried Kolya, in positive ecstasy. His cheeks glowed, his eyes beamed.

"You know, Kolya, you will be very unhappy in your life," something made Alyosha say suddenly.

"I know, I know. How you know it all beforehand!" Kolya agreed at once.

"But you will bless life on the whole, all the same."

"Just so, hurrah! You are a prophet. Oh, we shall get on together, Karamazov! Do you know, what delights me most, is that you treat me quite like an equal. But we are not equals, no, we are not, you are better! But we shall get on. Do you know, all this last month I've been saying to myself, 'either we shall be friends at once, forever, or we shall part enemies to the grave!' "

"And saying that, of course, you loved me," Alyosha laughed gaily.

"I did. I loved you awfully. I've been loving and dreaming of you. And how do you know it all beforehand? Ah, here's the doctor, Goodness! What will he tell us? Look at his face!"

Chapter VII

Ilyusha

The doctor came out of the room again, muffled in his fur coat and with his cap on his head. His face looked almost angry and disgusted, as though he were afraid of getting dirty. He cast a cursory glance round the hall, looking sternly at Alyosha and Kolya as he did so. Alyosha waved from the door to the coachman, and the carriage that had brought the doctor drove up. The captain darted out after the doctor, and, bowing, almost cringing, stopped him to get the final opinion. The poor fellow looked utterly crushed; there was a scared look in his eyes.

"Your Excellency, your Excellency . . . is it possible?" he began, but could not go on and clasped his hands in despair. Yet he still gazed imploringly at the doctor, as though a word from him might still change the poor boy's fate.

"I can't help it, I am not God!" the doctor answered offhand, though with the customary impressiveness.

"Doctor . . . your Excellency . . . and will it be soon, soon?"

"You must be prepared for anything," said the doctor incisively, emphasizing each syllable, and dropping his eyes he was about to step out to the coach.

"Your Excellency, for Christ's sake," the terror-stricken captain stopped him again. "Your Excellency! but can nothing, absolutely nothing save him now?"

"It's not in my hands now," said the doctor impatiently, "but hmm. . . ." he stopped suddenly. "If you could, for instance . . . send . . . your patient . . . at once, without delay" (the words "at once, without delay," the doctor uttered with an almost wrathful sternness that made the captain start) "to Sy-ra-cuse, the change to the new be-ne-ficial climatic conditions might possibly effect . . ."

"To Syracuse!" cried the captain, unable to grasp what was said.

"Syracuse is in Sicily," Kolya jerked out suddenly in explanation. The doctor looked at him.

"Sicily! your Excellency," faltered the captain, "but you've seen" —he spread out his hands, indicating his surroundings—"mamma and my family?"

"N-no, Sicily is not the place for the family, the family should go to Caucasus in the early spring . . . your daughter must go to the Caucasus, and your wife . . . after a course of the waters in the Caucasus for her rheumatism . . . must be sent straight to Paris to the psy-chi-a-trist Lepelletier; I could give you a note to him, and then . . . there might be a change . . ."

"Doctor, doctor! But you see!" The captain flung wide his hands again despairingly, indicating the bare wooden walls of the hall.

"Well, that's not my business," smiled the doctor. "I have only told you the answer of me-di-cal sci-ence to your question as to possible treatment. As for the rest, to my regret . . ."

"Don't be afraid, apothecary, my dog won't bite you," Kolya rapped out loudly, noticing the doctor's rather uneasy glance at Perezvon, who was standing in the doorway. There was a wrathful note in Kolya's voice. He used the word apothecary instead of doctor *on purpose*, and, as he explained afterwards, "I used it to insult him."

"What's that?" The doctor flung up his head, staring with surprise at Kolya. "Who's this?" he addressed Alyosha, as though asking him to explain.

"It's Perezvon's master, apothecary, don't worry about me," Kolya said incisively again.

"Perezvon," repeated the doctor, perplexed.

"He hears the bell, but where it is he cannot tell. Good-bye, apothecary, we shall meet in Syracuse."

"Who's this? Who's this?" The doctor flew into a terrible rage.

"He is a schoolboy, doctor, he is a mischievous boy; take no notice of him," said Alyosha, frowning and speaking quickly. "Kolya, hold your tongue!" he cried to Krasotkin. "Take no notice of him, doctor," he repeated, rather impatiently.

"He needs a thrashing, a good thrashing!" The doctor stamped in a perfect fury.

"And you know, apothecary, my Perezvon might bite!" said

Kolya, turning pale, with quivering voice and flashing eyes. "*Ici*, Perezvon!"

"Kolya, if you say another word, I'll have nothing more to do with you," Alyosha cried peremptorily.

"Apothecary, there is only one man in the world who can command Nikolay Krasotkin—this is the man" (Kolya pointed to Alyosha). "I obey him, goodbye!"

He stepped forward, opened the door, and quickly went into the inner room. Perezvon flew after him. The doctor stood still for five seconds in amazement, looking at Alyosha; then, with a curse, he went out quickly to the carriage, repeating aloud, "This is . . . this is . . . I don't know what it is!" The captain darted forward to help him into the carriage. Alyosha followed Kolya into the room. He was already by Ilyusha's bedside. The sick boy was holding his hand and calling for his father. A minute later the captain, too, came back.

"Father, father, come . . . we . . ." Ilyusha faltered in violent excitement, but apparently unable to go on, he flung his wasted arms round his father and Kolya, uniting them in one embrace, and hugging them as tightly as he could. The captain suddenly began to shake with dumb sobs, and Kolya's lips and chin twitched.

"Dad, dad! How sorry I am for you, dad!" Ilyusha moaned bitterly.

"Ilyushechka . . . darling . . . the doctor said . . . you would be all right . . . we shall be happy . . . the doctor . . ." the captain began.

"Ah, dad! I know what the new doctor said to you about me. . . . I saw!" cried Ilyusha, and again he hugged them both with all his strength, hiding his face on his father's shoulder.

"Dad don't cry, and when I die get a good boy, another one . . . choose one of them all, a good one, call him Ilyusha and love him instead of me . . ."

"Hush, old man, you'll get well," Krasotkin cried suddenly, in a voice that sounded angry.

"But don't ever forget me, dad," Ilyusha went on, "come to my grave . . . and dad, bury me by our big stone, where we used to go for our walk, and come to me there with Krasotkin in the evening . . . and Perezvon . . . I shall expect you. . . . Dad, dad!"

His voice broke. They were all three silent, still embracing. Nina was crying, quietly in her chair, and at last seeing them all crying, "mamma," too, burst into tears.

"Ilyushechka, Ilyushechka!" she exclaimed.

Krasotkin suddenly released himself from Ilyusha's embrace.

"Goodbye, old man, mother expects me back to dinner," he said quickly. "What a pity I did not tell her! She will be dreadfully anxious. . . . But after dinner I'll come back to you for the whole day, for the whole evening, and I'll tell you all sorts of things, all sorts of things. And I'll bring Perezvon, but now I will take him with me, because he will begin to howl when I am away and bother you. Goodbye!"

And he ran out into the hall. He didn't want to cry, but in the hall he burst into tears. Alyosha found him crying.

"Kolya, you must be sure to keep your word and come, or he will be terribly disappointed," Alyosha said emphatically.

"I will! Oh, how I curse myself for not having come before," muttered Kolya, crying, and no longer ashamed of it. At that moment the captain flew out of the room, and at once closed the door behind him. His face looked frenzied, his lips were trembling. He stood before the two lads and flung up his arms.

"I don't want a good boy! I don't want another boy!" he muttered in a wild whisper, clenching his teeth. "If I forget thee, Jerusalem, may my tongue . . ."

He broke off with a sob and sank on his knees before the wooden bench. Pressing his fists against his head, he began sobbing with absurd whimpering cries, doing his utmost that his cries should not be heard in the room. Kolya ran out into the street.

"Goodbye, Karamazov. Will you come yourself?" he cried sharply and angrily to Alyosha.

"I will certainly come in the evening."

"What was that he said about Jerusalem? . . . What did he mean by that?"

"It's from the Bible. 'If I forget thee, Jerusalem,' that is, if I forget all that is most precious to me, if I let anything take its place, then may . . ."

"I understand, that's enough! Mind you come! *Ici*, Perezvon!" he cried with positive ferocity to the dog, and with rapid strides he went home.

Book Eleven

BROTHER IVAN FYODOROVICH

Chapter I

At Grushenka's

Alyosha went towards the cathedral square to the widow Morozov's house to see Grushenka, who had sent Fenya to him early in the morning with an urgent message begging him to come. Questioning Fenya, Alyosha learned that her mistress had been particularly distressed since the previous day. During the two months that had passed since Mitya's arrest, Alyosha had called frequently at the widow Morozov's house, both from his own inclination and to take messages for Mitya. Three days after Mitya's arrest, Grushenka was taken very ill and was ill for nearly five weeks. For one whole week she was unconscious. She was very much changed—thinner and a little sallow, though she had for the past two weeks been well enough to go out. But to Alyosha her face was even more attractive than before, and he liked to meet her eyes when he went in to see her. A look of firmness and intelligent purpose had developed in her face. There were signs of spiritual transformation in her, and a steadfast, fine and humble determination that nothing could shake could be discerned in her. There was a small vertical line between her brows which gave her charming face a look of concentrated thought, almost austere at the first glance. There was scarcely a trace of her former frivolity. It seemed strange to Alyosha, too, that in spite of the calamity that had overtaken the poor girl, betrothed to a man who had been arrested for a terrible crime, almost at the instant of their betrothal, in spite of her illness and the almost inevitable sentence hanging over Mitya, Grushenka had yet not lost her youthful cheerfulness. There was a soft light in the once proud eyes, though ... though, at times, they gleamed with the old vindictive fire when she was visited by one disturbing thought stronger than ever in her heart. The object of that uneasiness was the same as ever—Katerina Ivanovna, of whom Grushenka had even raved when she lay in delirium. Alyosha knew that she was fearfully jealous of her. Yet Katerina Ivanovna had not once visited Mitya in his prison, though she might have done it whenever she liked. All this created a difficult problem for Alyosha, for he was the only person to whom Grushenka opened her heart and from whom she was continually asking advice. Sometimes he was incapable of telling her anything.

Full of anxiety he entered her lodging. She was at home. She had returned from seeing Mitya half an hour before, and from the rapid movement with which she leaped up from her chair to meet him he saw that she had been expecting him with great impatience. A pack of cards dealt for a game of "fools" lay on the table. A bed had been made up on the leather sofa on the other side and Maximov lay, half-reclining, on it. He wore a dressing gown and a cotton nightcap, and was evidently ill and weak, though he was smiling blissfully. When the homeless old man returned with Grushenka from Mokroe two months before, he had simply stayed on and was still staying with her. He arrived with her in rain and sleet, sat down on the sofa, drenched and scared, and gazed mutely at her with a timid, appealing smile. Grushenka, who was in terrible grief and in the first stage of fever, almost forgot his existence in all she had to do the first half hour after her arrival. Suddenly she chanced to look at him intently: he laughed a pitiful, helpless little laugh. She called Fenya and told her to give him something to eat. All that day he sat in the same place, almost without stirring. When it got dark and the shutters were closed, Fenya asked her mistress,

"Is the gentleman going to stay the night, mistress?"

"Yes; make him a bed on the sofa," answered Grushenka.

Questioning him more in detail, Grushenka learned from him that he had literally nowhere to go, and that "Mr. Kalganov, my benefactor, told me straight that he wouldn't receive me again and gave me five rubles." "Well, God bless you, you'd better stay then," Grushenka decided in her grief, smiling compassionately at him. Her smile wrung the old man's heart and his lips twitched with grateful tears. And so the destitute wanderer had stayed with her ever since. He did not leave the house even when she was ill. Fenya and her grandmother, the cook, did not turn him out, but went on serving him meals and making up his bed on the sofa. Grushenka had grown used to him, and coming back from seeing Mitya (whom she had begun to visit in prison before she was really well) she would sit down and begin talking to "Maximushka" about trifling matters, to keep her from thinking of her sorrow. The old man turned out to be a good storyteller on occasions, so that at last he became necessary to her. Grushenka saw scarcely anyone else beside Alyosha, who did not come every day and never stayed long. Her old merchant lay seriously ill at this time, "at his last gasp" as they said in the town, and he did, in fact, die a week after Mitya's trial. Three weeks before his death, feeling the end approaching, he made his sons, their wives and children, come upstairs to him at last and bade them not leave him again. From that moment he gave strict orders to his servants not to admit Grushenka and to tell her if she came, "The master wishes you long life and happiness and tells you to forget him." But Grushenka sent almost every day to inquire after him.

"You've come at last!" she cried, flinging down the cards and joyfully greeting Alyosha, "and Maximushka's been scaring me that perhaps you wouldn't come. Ah, how I need you! Sit down to the table. What will you have—coffee?"

"Yes, please," said Alyosha, sitting down at the table. "I am very hungry."

"That's right. Fenya, Fenya, coffee," cried Grushenka. "It's been made a long time ready for you. And bring some little pies, and mind they are hot. Do you know, we've had a storm over those pies today. I took them to the prison for him, and would you believe it, he threw them back to me: he would not eat them. He flung one of them on the floor and stamped on it. So I said to him: 'I will leave them with the warder; if you don't eat them before evening, it will be because your venomous spite is enough for you!' With that I went away. We quarreled again, would you believe it? Whenever I go we quarrel."

Grushenka said all this in one breath in her agitation. Maximov, feeling nervous, at once smiled and looked on the floor.

"What did you quarrel about this time?" asked Alyosha.

"I didn't expect it in the least. Only fancy, he is jealous of the Pole. 'Why are you keeping him?' he said. 'So you've begun keeping him.' He is jealous, jealous of me all the time, jealous eating and sleeping! He even took it into his head to be jealous of Kuzma last week."

"But he knew about the Pole before?"

"Yes, but there it is. He has known about him from the very beginning, but today he suddenly got up and began to curse him. I am ashamed to repeat what he said. The fool! Rakitka went in as I came out. Perhaps Rakitka is egging him on. What do you think?" she added carelessly.

"He loves you, that's what it is; he loves you so much. And now he is particularly worried."

"I should think he might be, with the trial tomorrow. And I went to him to say something about tomorrow, for I dread to think what's going to happen then. You say that he is worried, but how worried I am! And he talks about the Pole! What a fool! He is not jealous of Maximushka yet, anyway."

"My wife was dreadfully jealous over me, too, ma'am" Maximov put in his word.

"Jealous of you?" Grushenka laughed in spite of herself. "Of whom could she have been jealous?"

"Of the servant girls."

"Hold your tongue, Maximushka, I am in no laughing mood now, I feel angry. Don't ogle the pies. I won't give you any; they are not good for you, and I won't give you any vodka either. I have to look after him, too, just as though I kept an almshouse," she laughed.

"I don't deserve your kindness, ma'am. I am a worthless creature," said Maximov, with tears in his voice. "You would do better spend your kindness on people of more use than me."

"Ech, everyone is of use, Maximushka, and how can we tell who's of most use. If only that Pole didn't exist, Alyosha. He's taken it into his head to fall ill, too, today. I've been to see him also. And I shall send him some pies, too, on purpose. I hadn't sent him any, but Mitya accused me of it, so now I shall send some! Ah, here's Fenya with a letter! Yes, it's from the Poles—begging again!"

Pan Mussyalovich had indeed sent an extremely long and characteristically eloquent letter in which he begged her to lend him three rubles. In the letter was enclosed a receipt for the sum, with a promise to repay it within three months, signed by Pan Vrublevsky as well. Grushenka had received many such letters, accompanied by such receipts, from her former lover during the two weeks of her convalescence. But she knew that the two Poles had been to ask after her health during her illness. The first letter Grushenka got from them was a long one, written on large notepaper and with a big family crest on the seal. It was so obscure and rhetorical that Grushenka put it down before she had read half, unable to make head or tail of it. She could not attend to letters then. The first letter was followed next day by another in which Pan Mussyalovich begged her for a loan of two thousand rubles for a very short period. Grushenka left that letter, too, unanswered. A whole series of letters had followed—one every day—all as pompous and rhetorical, but the loan asked for, gradually diminishing, dropped to a hundred rubles, then to twenty-five, to ten, and finally Grushenka received a letter in which both the Poles begged her for only one ruble and included a receipt signed by both. Then Grushenka suddenly felt sorry for them, and at dusk she went round herself to their lodgings. She found the two Poles in great poverty, almost destitution, without food or fuel, without cigarettes, in debt to their landlady. The two hundred rubles they had carried off from Mitya at Mokroe had soon disappeared. But Grushenka was surprised at their meeting her with arrogant dignity and self-assertion, with the greatest punctilio and pompous speeches. Grushenka simply laughed, and gave her former admirer ten rubles. Then, laughing, she told Mitya of it and he was not in the least jealous. But ever since, the Poles had attached themselves to Grushenka and bombarded her daily with requests for money and she had always sent them small sums. And now that day Mitya had taken it into his head to be fearfully jealous.

"Like a fool, I went round to him just for a minute, on the way to see Mitya, for he is ill, too, my former Pole," Grushenka began again with nervous haste. "I was laughing, telling Mitya about it. 'Fancy,' I said, 'my Pole had the happy thought to sing his old songs to me to the guitar. He thought I would be touched and marry him!' Mitya leaped up swearing. . . . So, there, I'll send the pies to the Poles! Fenya, is it that little girl they've sent? Here, give her three rubles and wrap up a dozen pies, and tell her to take them. And you, Alyosha, be sure to tell Mitya that I did send them the pies."

"I wouldn't tell him for anything," said Alyosha, smiling.

"Ech! You think he is unhappy about it. Why, he's jealous on purpose. He doesn't care," said Grushenka bitterly.

"On purpose?" queried Alyosha.

"I tell you you are silly, Alyosha, that's what. You know nothing about it, with all your cleverness, that's what. I am not offended that he is jealous of a girl like me. I would be offended if he were not jealous. I am like that. I am not offended at jealousy. I have a fierce heart, too. I can be jealous myself. Only what offends me is that he doesn't love me at all. I tell you he is jealous now on *purpose*. Am I blind? Don't I see? He began talking to me just now of that woman, Katka, saying she was this and that, how she had ordered a doctor from Moscow for him, to try and save him; how she had ordered the best counsel, the most learned one, too. So he loves her, if he'll praise her to my face, more shame to him! He's treated me badly himself, so he attacked me, to make out I am in fault first and to throw it all on me. 'You were with your Pole before me, so I can't be blamed for Katka,' that's what it amounts to. He wants to throw the whole blame on me. He attacked me on purpose, on purpose, I tell you, but I'll . . ."

Grushenka could not finish saying what she would do. She hid her eyes in her handkerchief and sobbed violently.

"He doesn't love Katerina Ivanovna," said Alyosha firmly.

"Well, whether he loves her or not, I'll soon find out for myself," said Grushenka, with a menacing note in her voice, taking the handkerchief from her eyes. Her face was distorted. Alyosha saw sorrowfully that from being mild and serene, it had become sullen and spiteful.

"Enough of this foolishness," she said suddenly; "it's not for that I sent for you. Alyosha, darling, tomorrow—what will happen tomorrow? That's what worries me! And it's only me it worries! I look at everyone and no one is thinking of it. No one cares about it. Are you thinking about it even? Tomorrow he'll be tried, you know. Tell me, how will he be tried? You know it's the lackey, the lackey that killed him! Good heavens! Can they condemn him in place of the lackey and will no one stand up for him? They haven't troubled the lackey at all, have they?"

"He's been severely cross-examined," observed Alyosha thoughtfully; "but everyone came to the conclusion it was not he. Now he is lying very ill. He has been ill ever since that attack. Really ill," added Alyosha.

"Oh, dear! couldn't you go to that counsel yourself and tell him the whole thing by yourself? He's been brought from Petersburg for three thousand rubles, they say."

"We gave these three thousand together—brother Ivan, Katerina Ivanovna and I—but she paid two thousand for the doctor from Moscow herself. The counsel Fetyukovich would have charged more, but the case has become known all over Russia; it's talked of in all the papers and journals. Fetyukovich agreed to come more for the glory of the thing, because the case has become so notorious. I saw him yesterday."

"Well? Did you talk to him?" Grushenka put in eagerly.

"He listened and said nothing. He told me that he had already formed his opinion. But he promised to give my words consideration."

"Consideration! Ah, they are swindlers! They'll ruin him. And why did she send for the doctor?"

"As an expert. They want to prove that Mitya's mad and committed the murder when he didn't know what he was doing." Alyosha smiled gently, "but Mitya won't agree to that."

"Yes; but that would be the truth if he had killed him!" cried Grushenka. "He was mad then, perfectly mad, and that was my fault, wretch that I am! But, of course, he didn't do it, he didn't do it! And they are all against him, the whole town. Even Fenya's evidence went to prove he had done it. And the people at the shop, and that official, and at the tavern, too, before, people had heard him say so! They are all, all against him, all crying out against him."

"Yes, there's a fearful accumulation of evidence," Alyosha observed grimly.

"And Grigory—Grigory Vasilyevich—sticks to his story that the door was open, persists that he saw it—there's no shaking him. I went and talked to him myself. He's rude about it, too."

"Yes, that's perhaps the strongest evidence against him," said Alyosha.

"And as for Mitya's being mad, he certainly seems like it now," Grushenka began with a peculiarly anxious and mysterious air. "Do you know, Alyosha, I've been wanting to talk to you about it for a long time. I go to him every day and simply wonder at him. Tell me, now, what do you suppose he's always talking about?

talks and talks and I can make nothing of it. I fancied he was talking of something intellectual that I couldn't understand in my foolishness. Only he suddenly began talking to me about a 'babe'— that is, about some child. 'Why is the babe poor?' he said. 'It's for that babe I am going to Siberia now. I am not a murderer, but I must go to Siberia!' What that meant, what babe, I couldn't tell for the life of me. Only I cried when he said it, because he said it so nicely. He cried himself, and I cried, too. He suddenly kissed me and made the sign of the cross over me. What did it mean, Alyosha, tell me? What is this 'babe'?"

"It must be Rakitin, who's been going to see him lately," smiled Alyosha, "though . . . that's not Rakitin's doing. I didn't see Mitya yesterday. I'll see him today."

"No, it's not Rakitka; it's his brother Ivan Fyodorovich upsetting him. It's his going to see him, that's what it is," Grushenka began, and suddenly broke off. Alyosha gazed at her in amazement.

"Ivan's going? Has he been to see him? Mitya told me himself that Ivan hasn't been once."

"There . . . there! What a girl I am! Blurting things out!" exclaimed Grushenka, confused and suddenly blushing. "Wait, Alyosha, hush! Since I've said so much I'll tell the whole truth—he's been to see him twice, the first time directly he arrived. He rushed here from Moscow at once, of course, before I was taken ill; and the second time was a week ago. He told Mitya not to tell you about it, under any circumstances; and not to tell anyone, in fact. He came secretly."

Alyosha sat plunged in thought, considering something. The news evidently impressed him.

"Brother Ivan doesn't talk to me of Mitya's case," he said slowly. "He's said very little to me these last two months. And whenever I go to see him, he seems vexed at my coming, so I haven't been to see him for the last three weeks. Hm! . . . if he was there a week ago . . . there certainly has been a change in Mitya this week."

"There has been a change," Grushenka assented quickly. "They have a secret, they have a secret! Mitya told me himself there was a secret, and such a secret that Mitya can't rest. Before then, he was cheerful—and, indeed, he is cheerful now—but when he shakes his head like that, you know, and strides about the room and keeps pulling at the hair on his right temple with his right hand, I know there is something on his mind worrying him. . . . I know! He was cheerful before, though, indeed, he is cheerful today."

"But you said he was worried."

"Yes, he is worried and yet cheerful. He keeps on being irritable for a minute and then cheerful and then irritable again. And you know, Alyosha, I constantly wonder at him—with this awful thing hanging over him, he sometimes laughs at such trifles as though he were a baby himself."

"And did he really tell you not to tell me about Ivan? Did he say 'don't tell him'?"

"Yes, he told me 'don't tell him.' It's you that Mitya's most afraid of. Because it's a secret: he said himself it was a secret. Alyosha, darling, go to him and find out what their secret is and come and tell me," Grushenka besought him with sudden eagerness. "Set my mind at rest that I may know the worst that's in store for poor me. That's why I sent for you."

"You think it's something to do with you? If it were, he wouldn't have told you there was a secret."

"I don't know. Perhaps he wants to tell me, but doesn't dare to. He warns me. There is a secret, he tells me, but he won't tell me what it is."

"What do you think yourself?"

"What do I think? It's the end for me, that's what I think. They all three have been plotting my end, for Katka's in it. It's all Katka, it all comes from her. She is this and that means that I am not. He tells me that beforehand—warns me. He is planning to throw me over, that's the whole secret. They've planned it together, the three of them—Mitya, Katka, and Ivan Fyodorovich. Alyosha, I've been wanting to ask you a long time. A week ago he suddenly told me that Ivan was in love with Katka, because he often goes to see her. Did she tell me the truth or not? Tell me, on your conscience, tell me the worst."

"I won't tell you a lie. Ivan is not in love with Katerina Ivanovna, I think."

"Oh, that's what I thought! He is lying to me, shameless deceiver, that's what it is! And he was jealous of me just now, so as to put the blame on me afterwards. He is stupid, he can't disguise what he is doing; he is so open, you know. . . . But I'll give it to him, I'll give it to him! 'You believe I did it,' he said. He said that to me, to me. He reproached me with that! God forgive him! You wait, I'll make it hot for Katka at the trial! I'll just say a word then . . . I'll tell everything then!"

And again she cried bitterly.

"This I can tell you for certain, Grushenka," Alyosha said, getting up. "First, that he loves you, loves you more than anyone in the world, and you only, believe me. I know. I do know. The second thing is that I don't want to worm his secret out of him, but if he'll tell me of his own will today, I will tell him straight out that I have promised to tell you. Then I'll come to you today and tell you. Only . . . I fancy . . . Katerina Ivanovna has nothing to do with it, and that the secret is about something else. That's certain. It isn't likely it's about Katerina Ivanovna, it seems to me. Goodbye for now."

Alyosha shook hands with her. Grushenka was still crying. He saw that she put little faith in his consolation, but she was better for having had her sorrow out, for having spoken of it. He was sorry to leave her in such a state of mind, but he was in haste. He had a great many things to do still.

Chapter II

The Injured Foot

The first of these things was at the house of Madame Khokhlakov, and he hurried there to get it over as quickly as possible and not to be too late for Mitya. Madame Khokhlakov had been slightly ailing for the last three weeks: her foot had for some reason swollen up, and though she was not in bed, she lay all day half-reclining on the couch in her boudoir, in a fascinating but decorous *déshabillé*. Alyosha had once noted with innocent amusement that, in spite of her illness, Madame Khokhlakov had begun to be rather dressy—topknots, ribbons, loose wrappers, had made their appearance, and he had an inkling of the reason, though he dismissed such ideas from his mind as frivolous. During the last two months the young official, Perkhotin, had become a regular visitor at the house. Alyosha had not called for four days and he was in haste to go straight to Lisa, as it was with her he had to speak, for Lisa had sent a maid to him the previous day, specially asking him to come to her "about something very important," a request which, for certain reasons, had interest for Alyosha. But while the maid went to take his name in to Lisa, Madame Khokhlakov heard of his arrival from someone, and immediately sent to beg him to come to her "just one minute." Alyosha reflected that it was better to accede to the mamma's request, or else she would be sending down to Lisa's room every minute that he was there. Madame Khokhlakov was lying on a couch. She was particularly smartly dressed and was evidently in a state of extreme nervous excitement. She greeted Alyosha with cries of rapture.

"It's ages, ages, perfect ages since I've seen you! It's a whole week—only think of it! Ah, but you were here only four days ago, on Wednesday. You have come to see Lise. I'm sure you meant to slip into her room on tiptoe, without my hearing you. My dear, dear Alexey Fyodorovich, if you only knew how worried I am about her! But of that later, though that's the most important thing, of that later. Dear Alexey Fyodorovich, I trust you implicitly with my Lisa. Since the death of Father Zosima—God rest his soul!" (She crossed herself)"—I look upon you as a monk, though you look charming in your new suit. Where did you find such a tailor in these parts? No, no, that's not the chief thing—of that later. Forgive me for sometimes calling you Alyosha; an old woman like me may take liberties," she smiled coquettishly; "but that will do later, too. The important thing is that I shouldn't forget what is important. Please remind me of it yourself. As soon as my tongue runs away with me, you just say 'the important thing?' Ach! how do I know now what is of most importance? Ever since Lise took back her promise—her childish promise, Alexey Fyodorovich—to marry you, you've realized, of course, that it was only the playful fancy of a sick child who had been so long confined to her chair—thank God, she can walk now! . . . that new doctor Katya sent for from Moscow for your unhappy brother, who will tomorrow . . . But why speak of tomorrow? I am ready to die at the very thought of tomorrow. Ready to die of curiosity. . . . In short, that doctor was with us yesterday and saw Lise. . . . I paid him fifty rubles for the visit. But that's not the point, that's not the point again. You see, I'm mixing everything up. I am in such a hurry. Why am I in a hurry? I don't understand. It's awful how I seem growing unable to understand anything. Everything seems mixed up in a sort of tangle. I am afraid you are so bored you will jump up and run away, and that will be all I shall see of you. Goodness! Why are we sitting here and no coffee? Yulia, Glafira, coffee!"

Alyosha made haste to thank her, and said that he had only just had coffee.

"Where?"

"At Agrafena Alexandrovna's."

"At . . . at that woman's? Ah, it's she who has brought ruin on everyone. I know nothing about it though. They say she has become a saint, though it's rather late in the day. She had better have done it before. What use is it now? Hush, hush, Alexey Fyodorovich, for I have so much to say to you that I am afraid I shall tell you nothing. This awful trial . . . I shall certainly go, I am making arrangements. I shall be carried there in my chair; besides I can sit up. I shall have servants with me. And, you know, I am a witness. How shall I speak, how shall I speak? I don't know what I shall say. One has to take an oath, doesn't one?"

"Yes; but I don't think you will be able to go."

"I can sit up. Ah, you put me out; ah! this trial, this savage act, and then they are all going to Siberia, some are getting married, and all this so quickly, so quickly, everything's changing, and at last—nothing. All grow old and have death to look forward to. Well, so be it! I am weary. This Katya, *cette charmante personne*,[1] has disappointed all my hopes. Now she is going to follow one of

1. "That charming creature."

your brothers to Siberia, and your other brother is going to follow her, and will live in the nearest town, and they will all torment one another. It drives me out of my mind. Worst of all—the publicity. The story has been told a million times over in all the papers in Moscow and Petersburg. Ah! yes, would you believe it, there's a paragraph that I was a 'dear friend' of your brother's—I don't want to repeat the horrid word. Just fancy, just fancy!"

"Impossible! Where was the paragraph? What did it say?"

"I'll show you directly. I got the paper and read it yesterday. Here, in the Petersburg paper *Gossip*. The paper began coming out this year. I am awfully fond of gossip, and I subscribed to it, and now—this is what gossip comes to! to my own misfortune. Here it is, here, this passage. Read it."

And she handed Alyosha a sheet of newspaper which had been under her pillow.

It was not exactly that she was upset, she seemed overwhelmed, and perhaps everything really was mixed up in a tangle in her head. The paragraph was very typical, and must have been a great shock to her, but, fortunately perhaps, she was unable to keep her mind fixed on any one subject at that moment, and so might race off in a minute to something else and quite forget the newspaper.

Alyosha was well aware that the story of the terrible case had spread all over Russia. And, good heavens! what wild reports and despatches about his brother, about all the Karamazovs, and even about himself he had read in the course of those two months. One paper had even stated that he had gone into a monastery and become a monk, in horror at his brother's crime. Another contradicted this, and stated that he and his elder, Father Zosima, had broken into the monastery chest and "made tracks from the monastery." The present paragraph in the paper *Gossip* was under the heading, "The Karamazov Case at Skotoprigonevsk."[2] (That, alas! was the name of our little town. I had hitherto kept it concealed.) It was brief, and Madame Khokhlakov was not directly mentioned in it. No names appeared, in fact. It was merely stated that the criminal, whose approaching trial was making such a sensation—retired army captain, an idle swaggerer, and reactionary bully—was continually involved in amorous intrigues, and particularly popular with certain ladies "who were pining in solitude." One such lady, a pining widow, who tried to seem young though she had a grown-up daughter, was so fascinated by him that only two hours before the crime she offered him three thousand rubles, on condition that he would elope with her to the gold mines. But the criminal, counting on escaping punishment, had preferred to murder his father to get the three thousand, rather than go off to

2. The town name means "stockyard."

Siberia with the middle-aged charms of his pining lady. This playful paragraph finished, of course, with an outburst of generous indigination at the wickedness of parricide and at the lately abolished institution of serfdom. Reading it with curiosity, Alyosha folded up the paper and handed it back to Madame Khokhlakov.

"Well, that must be me," she hurried on again. "Of course I am meant. Scarcely more than an hour before, I suggested gold mines to him, and here they talk of 'middle-aged charms' as though that were my motive! He writes that out of spite. God Almighty forgive him for the middle-aged charms, as I forgive him! You know it's . . . do you know who it is? It's your friend Rakitin."

"Perhaps," said Alyosha, "though I've heard nothing about it."

"It's he, it's he! No 'perhaps' about it. You know I turned him out of the house. . . . You know all that story, don't you?"

"I know that you asked him not to visit you in the future, but why it was, I haven't heard . . . from you, at least."

"Ah, then you've heard it from him! He abuses me, I suppose, abuses me dreadfully?"

"Yes, he does; but then he abuses everyone. But why you've given him up I haven't heard from him either. I meet him very seldom now, indeed. We are not friends."

"Well, then, I'll tell you all about it. There's no help for it, I repent, for there is one point in which I was perhaps to blame. Only a little, little point, so little that perhaps it doesn't count. You see, my dear boy"—Madame Khokhlakov suddenly looked arch and a charming, though enigmatic, smile played about her lips—"you see, I suspect . . . You must forgive me, Alyosha. I am like a mother to you. . . . No, no; quite the contrary. I speak to you now, as though you were my father—mother's quite out of place. Well, it's as though I were confessing to Father Zosima, that's just it. I called you a monk just now. Well, that poor young man, your friend, Rakitin (Mercy on us! I can't be angry with him. I feel cross, but not very), that frivolous young man, would you believe it, seems to have taken it into his head to fall in love with me. I only noticed it later. At first—a month ago—he only began to come more often to see me, almost every day; though, of course, we were acquainted before. I knew nothing about it . . . and suddenly it dawned upon me, and I began to notice things with surprise. You know, two months ago, that modest, charming, excellent young man, Pyotr Ilyich Perkhotin, who's in the service here, began to be a regular visitor at the house. You met him here ever so many times yourself. And he is an excellent, earnest young man, isn't he? He comes once every three days, not every day (though I should be glad to see him every day), and always so well dressed. Altogether, I love young people, Alyosha, talented, modest, like you, and he has almost the mind of a statesman, he talks so charmingly, and I shall certainly, certainly try and get promotion for him. He is a future diplomat. On that awful day he almost saved me from death by coming in the night. And your friend Rakitin comes in such boots, and always stretches them out on the carpet. . . . In short, he began hinting at his feelings, in fact, and one day, as he was going, he squeezed my hand terribly hard. My foot began to swell directly after he pressed my hand like that. He had met Pyotr Ilyich here before, and would you believe it, he was constantly gibing at him, gibing at him, growling at him, for some reason. I simply looked at the way they went on together and laughed inwardly. So I was sitting here alone—no, I was laid up then. Well, I was lying here alone and suddenly Rakitin comes in, and only fancy! brought me some verses of his own composition—a short poem, on my bad foot: that is, he described my foot in a poem. Wait a minute—how did it go?

> A captivating little foot
> Started suddenly to ail,

It began somehow like that. I can never remember poetry. I've got it here. I'll show it to you later. But it's a charming thing—charming; and, you know, it's not only about the foot; it had a good moral, too, a charming idea, only I've forgotten it; in fact, it was just the thing for an album. So, of course, I thanked him, and he was evidently flattered. I'd hardly had time to thank him when in comes Pyotr Ilyich, and Mikhail Ivanovich suddenly looked as black as night. I could see that Pyotr Ilyich was in the way, for Mikhail Ivanovich certainly wanted to say something after giving me the verses. I had a presentiment of it; but Pyotr Ilyich came in. I showed Pyotr Ilyich the verses and didn't say who was the author. But I am convinced, I am convinced, that he guessed, though he won't admit it to this day, and declares he had no idea. But he says that on purpose. Pyotr Ilyich began to laugh at once, and fell to criticizing it. 'Wretched doggerel,' he said they were, 'some divinity student must have written them,' and with such vehemence, such vehemence! Then, instead of laughing, your friend flew into a rage. 'Good gracious!' I thought, 'they'll fly at each other.' 'It was I who wrote them,' said he. 'I wrote them as a joke,' he said, 'for I think it degrading to write verses. . . . But they are good poetry. They want to put a monument to your Pushkin for writing about women's feet,[3] while I wrote with a moral purpose, and you,' said he, 'are an advocate of serfdom. You have no humane ideas,' said he. 'You have no modern, enlightened feelings, you are uninfluenced by progress, you are a mere official,' he said, 'and you take bribes.' Then I began screaming and imploring them. And, you know,

3. Plans for the Pushkin monument, which was inaugurated in 1880, were begun in the 1860s, but gained momentum only in the mid-1870s. Pushkin really did seem to have a foot fetish—he writes very charmingly of feet in a number of places, including *Onegin*.

Pyotr Ilyich is anything but a coward. He at once took up the most gentlemanly tone, looked at him sarcastically, listened, and apologized. 'I'd no idea,' said he. 'I shouldn't have said it, if I had known. I should have praised it. Poets are all so irritable,' he said. In short, he laughed at him under the cover of the most gentlemanly tone. He himself explained to me afterwards that it was all sarcastic. I thought he was in earnest. Only as I lay there, just as before you now, I thought, 'would it, or would it not, be the proper thing for me to turn Mikhail Ivanovich out for shouting so rudely at a visitor in my house?' And, would you believe it, I lay here, shut my eyes, and wondered, would it be the proper thing or not. I kept worrying and worrying, and my heart began to beat, and I couldn't make up my mind whether to make an outcry or not. One voice seemed to be telling me, 'speak,' and the other 'no, don't speak.' And no sooner had the second voice said that than I cried out, and fainted. Of course, there was a fuss. I got up suddenly and said to Mikhail Ivanovich, 'It's painful for me to say it, but I don't wish to see you in my house again.' So I turned him out. Ah! Alexey Fyodorovich, I know myself I did wrong. I was putting it on. I wasn't angry with him at all really; but I suddenly fancied—that was what did it—that it would be such a fine scene. . . . And yet, believe me, it was quite natural, for I really shed tears and cried for several days afterwards, and then suddenly, one afternoon, I forgot all about it. So it's two weeks since he's been here, and I kept wondering whether he would come again. I wondered even yesterday, then suddenly last night came this *Gossip*. I read it and gasped. Who could have written it? He must have written it. He went home, sat down, wrote it on the spot, sent it, and they put it in. It was two weeks ago, you see. But, Alyosha, it's awful how I keep talking and don't say what I want to say. Ah! the words come of themselves!"

"It's very important for me to be in time to see my brother today," Alyosha faltered.

"To be sure, to be sure! You bring it all back to me. Listen, what is an aberration?"

"What aberration?" asked Alyosha, wondering.

"In the legal sense. An aberration in which everything is pardonable. Whatever you do, you will be acquitted at once."

"What do you mean?"

"I'll tell you. This Katya . . . Ah! she is a charming, charming creature, only I never can make out who it is she is in love with. She was with me some time ago and I couldn't get anything out of her. Especially as she won't talk to me except on the surface now. In short, she is always talking about my health and nothing else, and she takes up such a tone with me, too. I simply said to myself, 'Well, so be it. I don't care' . . . Oh, yes. I was talking of aberration.

This doctor has come. You know a doctor has come? Of course you know it—the one who discovers madmen. You wrote for him. No, it wasn't you, but Katya. It's all Katya's doing. Well, you see, a man may be sitting perfectly sane and suddenly have an aberration. He may be conscious and know what he is doing and yet be in a state of aberration. And there's no doubt that Dmitri Fyodorovich was suffering from aberration. They found out about aberration as soon as the law courts were reformed. It's all the good effect of the reformed law courts. The doctor has been here and questioned me about that evening, about the gold mines. 'How did he seem then?' he asked me. He must have been in a state of abberation. He came in shouting, 'Money, money, three thousand! Give me three thousand!' and then went away and immediately did the murder. 'I don't want to murder him,' he said, and he suddenly went and murdered him. That's why they'll acquit him, because he struggled against it and yet he murdered him."

"But he didn't murder him," Alyosha interrupted rather sharply. He felt more and more sick with anxiety and impatience.

"Yes, I know it was that old man Grigory murdered him."

"Grigory?" cried Alyosha.

"Yes, yes; it was Grigory. He lay as Dmitri Fyodorovich struck him down, and then got up, saw the door open, went in and killed Fyodor Pavlovich."

"But why, why?"

"Suffering from aberration. When he recovered from the blow Dmitri Fyodorovich gave him on the head, he was suffering from abberation: he went and committed the murder. As for his saying he didn't, he very likely doesn't remember. Only, you know, it'll be better, ever so much better, if Dmitri Fyodorovich murdered him. And that's how it must have been, though I say it was Grigory. It certainly was Dmitri Fyodorovich, and that's better, ever so much better! Oh! not better that a son should have killed his father, I don't defend that. Children ought to honor their parents, and yet it would be better if it were he, as you'd have nothing to cry over then, for he did it when he was unconscious or rather when he was conscious, but did not know what he was doing. Let them acquit him—that's so humane, and would show what a blessing reformed law courts are. I knew nothing about it, but they say they have been so a long time. And when I heard it yesterday, I was so struck by it that I wanted to send for you at once. And if he is acquitted, make him come straight from the law courts to dinner with me, and I'll have a party of friends, and we'll drink to the reformed law courts. I don't believe he'd be dangerous; besides, I'll invite a great many friends, so that he could always be led out if he did anything. And then he might be made a justice of the peace or something in another town, for those who have been in trouble themselves make the best judges. And, besides, who isn't suffering from aberration, nowadays?—you, I, all of us are in a state of aberration, and there are ever so many examples of it: a man sits singing a song, suddenly something annoys him, he takes a pistol and shoots the first person he comes across, and no one blames him for it. I read that lately, and all the doctors confirm it. The doctors are always confirming; they confirm anything. Why, my Lise is in a state of aberration. She made me cry again yesterday, and the day before, too, and today I suddenly realized that it's all due to aberration. Oh, Lise grieves me so! I believe she's quite mad. Why did she send for you? Did she send for you or did you come of your own accord?"

"Yes, she sent for me, and I am just going to see her." Alyosha got up resolutely.

"Oh, my dear, dear Alexey Fyodorovich, perhaps that's what's most important," Madame Khokhlakov cried, suddenly bursting into tears. "God knows I trust Lise to you with all my heart, and it's no matter her sending for you on the sly, without telling her mother. But forgive me, I can't trust my daughter so easily to your brother Ivan Fyodorovich, though I still consider him the most chivalrous young man. But only fancy, he's been to see Lise and I knew nothing about it!"

"How? What? When?" Alyosha was exceedingly surprised. He had not sat down again and listened standing.

"I will tell you, that's perhaps why I asked you to come, for I don't know now why I did ask you to come. Well, Ivan Fyodorovich has only been to see me twice, since he came back from Moscow. First time he came as a friend to call on me, and the second time, more recently, Katya was here and he came because he heard she was here. I didn't, of course, expect him to come often, knowing what a lot he has to do as it is, *vous comprenez, cette affaire et la mort terrible de votre papa.*[4] But I suddenly heard he'd been here again, not to see me but to see Lise. That's six days ago now. He came, stayed five minutes, and went away. And I didn't hear of it till three days afterwards, from Glafira, so it was a great shock to me. I sent for Lise directly. She laughed. 'He thought you were asleep,' she said, 'and came in to me to ask after your health.' Of course, that's how it happened. But Lise, Lise, mercy on us, how she distresses me! Would you believe it, one night, four days ago, just after you saw her last time, and had gone away, she suddenly had a fit, screaming, shrieking, hysterics! Why is it I never have hysterics? Then, next day another fit and the same thing on the third, and yesterday too, and then yesterday that aberration. She suddenly screamed out, 'I hate Ivan Fyodorovich. I insist on

4. "You understand, that business and the terrible death of your daddy."

your never letting him come to the house again.' I was struck dumb at these amazing words, and answered, 'On what grounds could I refuse to see such an excellent young man, a young man of such learning too, and so unfortunate," for all this business is a misfortune, isn't it? She suddenly burst out laughing at my words, and so rudely, you know. Well, I was pleased, I thought I had amused her and the fits would pass off, especially as I wanted to refuse to see Ivan Fyodorovich anyway on account of his strange visits without my knowledge, and meant to ask him for an explanation. But early this morning Lise awoke and flew into a rage with Yulia and, would you believe it, slapped her in the face. That's monstrous, I am always polite to my servants. And an hour later she was hugging Yulia's feet and kissing them. She sent a message to me, that she wasn't coming to see me at all, and would never come and see me again, and when I dragged myself down to her, she rushed to kiss me, crying, and as she kissed me, she pushed me out of the room without saying a word, so I couldn't find out what was the matter. Now, dear Alexey Fyodorovich, I rest all my hopes on you, and, of course, my whole life is in your hands. I simply beg you to go to Lise and find out everything from her, as you alone can, and come back and tell me—me, her mother, for you understand it will be the death of me, simply the death of me, if this goes on, or else I shall run away. I can stand no more. I have patience; but I may lose patience, and then . . . then something awful will happen. Ah, dear me! At last, Pyotr Ilyich!" cried Madame Khokhlakov, beaming all over as she saw Perkhotin enter the room. "You are late, you are late! Well, sit down, speak, put us out of suspense. What does the counsel say? Where are you off to, Alexey Fyodorovich?"

"To Lise."

"Oh, yes. You won't forget, you won't forget what I asked you? It's a question of life and death!"

"Of course, I won't forget, if I can . . . but I am so late," muttered Alyosha, beating a hasty retreat.

"No, be sure, be sure to come in; don't say 'if you can.' I shall die if you don't," Madame Khokhlakov called after him, but Alyosha had already left the room.

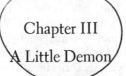

Chapter III

A Little Demon

Going in to Lisa, he found her half reclining in the invalid chair, in which she had been wheeled when she was unable to walk. She did not move to meet him, but her sharp keen eyes were simply riveted on his face. There was a feverish look in her eyes, her face was pale and yellow. Alyosha was amazed at the change that had taken place in her in three days. She was positively thinner. She did not hold out her hand to him. He touched the thin, long fingers which lay motionless on her dress, then he sat down facing her, without a word.

"I know you are in a hurry to get to the prison," Lise said curtly, "and mamma's kept you there for hours, she's just been telling you about me and Yulia."

"How do you know?" asked Alyosha.

"I've been listening. Why do you stare at me? I want to listen and I do listen, there's no harm in that. I don't apologize."

"You are upset about something?"

"On the contrary, I am very happy. I've only just been reflecting for the thirtieth time what a good thing it is I refused you and shall not be your wife. You are not fit to be a husband. If I were to marry you and give you a note to take to the man I loved after you, you'd take it and be sure to give it to him and bring an answer back, too. If you were forty, you would still go on carrying my love letters for me."

She suddenly laughed.

"There is something spiteful and yet open-hearted about you," Alyosha smiled to her.

"The open-heartedness consists in my not being ashamed of myself with you. What's more, I don't want to feel ashamed with you, just with you. Alyosha, why is it I don't respect you? I am very fond of you, but I don't respect you. If I respected you, I wouldn't talk to you without shame, would I?"

"No."

"But do you believe that I am not ashamed with you?"

"No, I don't believe it."

Lisa laughed nervously again; she spoke rapidly.

"I sent your brother, Dmitri Fyodorovich, some candy in prison. Alyosha, you know, you are quite handsome! I shall love you awfully for having so quickly allowed me not to love you."

"Why did you send for me today, Lise?"

"I wanted to tell you of a longing I have. I should like some one to torture me, marry me and then torture me, deceive me and go away. I don't want to be happy."

"You are in love with disorder?"

"Yes, I want disorder. I keep wanting to set fire to the house. I keep imagining how I'll creep up and set fire to the house on the sly, it must be on the sly. They'll try to put it out, but it'll go on burning. And I shall know and say nothing. Ah, what silliness! And how bored I am!"

She waved her hand with a look of repulsion.

"It's your luxurious life," said Alyosha, softly.

"Is it better then to be poor?"

"Yes, it is better."

"That's what your late monk taught you. That's not true. Let me be rich and all the rest poor, I'll eat candy and drink cream and not give any to anyone else. Ach, don't speak, don't say anything," she waved her hand at him, though Alyosha had not opened his mouth. "You've told me all that before, I know it all by heart. It bores me. If I am ever poor, I shall murder somebody, and even if I am rich, I may murder someone, perhaps—why do nothing! But do you know, I should like to reap, cut the rye? I'll marry you, and you shall become a peasant, a real peasant; we'll keep a colt, shall we? Do you know Kalganov?"

"Yes."

"He is always wandering about, dreaming. He says, why live in real life, it's better to dream. One can dream the most delightful things, but real life is a bore. But he'll be married soon for all that, he's declared his love to me already. Can you spin tops?"

"Yes."

"Well, he's just like a top: he wants to be wound up and set spinning and then to be lashed, lashed, lashed with a whip. If I marry him, I'll keep him spinning all his life. You are not ashamed to be with me?"

"No."

"You are awfully cross, because I don't talk about holy things. I don't want to be holy. What will they do to me in the next world for the greatest sin? You must know all about that."

"God will censure you." Alyosha was watching her steadily.

"That's just what I should like. I would go up and they would censure me and I would burst out laughing in their faces. I would dreadfully like to set fire to the house, Alyosha, to our house; you still don't believe me?"

"Why? There are children of twelve who have a longing to set fire to something and they do set things on fire too. It's a sort of disease."

"That's not true, that's not true, there may be children, but that's not what I mean."

"You take evil for good; it's a passing crisis, it's the result of your illness, perhaps."

"You do despise me though! It's simply that I don't want to do good, I want to do evil, and it has nothing to do with illness."

"Why do evil?"

"So that everything might be destroyed. Ah, how nice it would be if everything were destroyed! You know, Alyosha, I sometimes think of doing a fearful lot of harm and everything bad, and I would do it for a long while on the sly and suddenly everyone would find it out. Everyone would stand round and point their fingers at me and I would look at them all. That would be awfully nice. Why would it be so nice, Alyosha?"

"I don't know. It's a craving to destroy something good or, as you say, to set fire to something. It happens sometimes."

"I not only say it, I shall do it."

"I believe you."

"Ah, how I love you for saying you believe me. And you are not lying one little bit. But perhaps you think that I am saying all this on purpose to annoy you?"

"No, I don't think that . . . though perhaps there is a little desire to do that in it, too."

"There is a little. I never can tell lies to you," she declared, with a strange fire in her eyes.

What struck Alyosha above everything was her earnestness. There was not a trace of humor or jesting in her face now, though, in the old days, fun and gaiety never deserted her even at her most "earnest" moments.

"There are moments when people love crime," said Alyosha thoughtfully.

"Yes, yes! You have expressed my thought, they love crime, everyone loves crime, they love it always, not at some 'moments.' You know, it's as though people have made an agreement to lie about it and have lied about it ever since. They all declare that they hate evil, but secretly they all love it."

"And are you still reading nasty books?"

"Yes, I am. Mamma reads them and hides them under her pillow and I steal them."

"Aren't you ashamed to destroy yourself?"

"I want to destroy myself. There's a boy here, who lay down between the railway lines when the train was passing. Lucky fellow! Listen, your brother is being tried now for murdering his father and everyone loves his having killed his father."

"Loves his having killed his father?"

"Yes, loves it, everyone loves it! Everybody says it's so awful, but secretly they simply love it. I for one love it."

"There is some truth in what you say about everyone," said Alyosha softly.

"Oh, what ideas you have!" Lisa shrieked in delight. "And you a monk, too! You wouldn't believe how I respect you, Alyosha, for never telling lies. Oh, I must tell you a funny dream of mine. I sometimes dream of devils. It's night, I am in my room with a candle and suddenly there are devils all over the place, in all the corners, under the table, and they open the doors, there's a crowd of them behind the doors and they want to come and seize me. And they are just coming, just seizing me. But I suddenly cross myself and they all draw back, though they don't go away altogether, they stand at the doors and in the corners, waiting. And suddenly I have a frightful longing to revile God aloud, and so I begin, and then they come crowding back to me, delighted, and seize me again and I cross myself again and they all draw back. It's awful fun, it takes one's breath away."

"I've had the same dream, too," said Alyosha suddenly.

"Really?" cried Lisa, surprised. "Listen, Alyosha, don't laugh, that's awfully important. Could two different people have the same dream?"

"It seems they can."

"Alyosha, I tell you, it's awfully important," Lisa went on, with really excessive amazement. "It's not the dream that's important, but your having the same dream as me. You never lie to me, don't lie now: is it true? You are not laughing?"

"It's true."

Lisa seemed extraordinarily impressed and for half a minute she was silent.

"Aloysha, come and see me, come and see me more often," she said suddenly, in a supplicating voice.

"I'll always come to see you, all my life," answered Alyosha firmly.

"You are the only person I can talk to, you know," Lisa began again. "I talk to no one but myself and you. Only you in the whole world. And to you more readily than to myself. And I am not a bit ashamed with you, not a bit. Alyosha, why am I not ashamed with you, not a bit. Alyosha, is it true that at Easter the Jews steal a child and kill it?"

"I don't know."

"There's a book here in which I read about the trial of a Jew, who took a child of four years old and cut off the fingers from both hands, and then crucified him on the wall, hammered nails into him and crucified him, and afterwards, when he was tried, he said that the child died soon, within four hours. That was 'soon'! He said the child moaned, kept on moaning and he stood admiring it. That is nice!"

"Nice?"

"Nice, I sometimes imagine that it was I who crucified him. He would hang there moaning and I would sit opposite him eating pineapple compote. I am awfully fond of pineapple compote. Do you like it?"

Alyosha looked at her in silence. Her pale, sallow face was suddenly contorted, her eyes burned.

"You know, when I read about that Jew I shook with sobs all night. I kept fancying how the little thing cried and moaned (a child of four understands, you know) and all the while the thought of pineapple compote haunted me. In the morning I wrote a letter to a certain person, begging him *particularly* to come and see me. He came and I suddenly told him all about the child and the pineapple compote. *All* about it, *all*, and said that it was nice. He laughed and said it really was nice. Then he got up and went away. He was only here five minutes. Did he despise me? Did he despise me? Tell me, tell me, Alyosha, did he despise me or not?" She sat up on the couch, with flashing eyes.

"Tell me," Alyosha asked anxiously, "did you send for that person?"

"Yes, I did."

"Did you send him a letter?"

"Yes."

"Simply to ask about that, about that child?"

"No, not about that at all. But when he came, I asked him about that at once. He answered, laughed, got up and went away."

"That person behaved honorably," Alyosha murmured.

"And did he despise me? Did he laugh at me?"

"No, for perhaps he believes in the pineapple compote himself. He is very ill now, too, Lise."

"Yes, he does believe in it," said Lise, with flashing eyes.

"He doesn't despise anyone," Alyosha went on. "Only he does not believe anyone. If he doesn't believe in people, of course, he does despise them."

"Then he despises me, me?"

"You, too."

"That's good." Lisa seemed to grind her teeth. "When he went out laughing, I felt that it was nice to be despised. The child with fingers cut off is nice and to be despised is nice . . ."

And she laughed at Alyosha's face, a feverish malicious laugh.

"Do you know, Alyosha, do you know, I would like . . . Alyosha save me!" she suddenly jumped from the couch, rushed to him and seized him with both hands. "Save me!" she almost groaned. "Is there anyone in the world I could tell what I've told you! I've told you the truth, the truth. I shall kill myself, because I loathe everything! I don't want to live, because I loathe everything! I loathe everything, everything. Alyosha, why don't you love me in the least?" she finished in a frenzy.

"But I do love you!" answered Alyosha warmly.

"And will you weep over me, will you?"

"Yes."

"Not because I won't be your wife, but simply weep for me?"

"Yes."

"Thank you! It's only your tears I want. Everyone else may punish me and trample me under foot, everyone, everyone, not excepting *anyone*. For I don't love anyone. Do you hear, not anyone! On the contrary, I hate everybody! Go, Alyosha, it's time you went to your brother," she tore herself away from him suddenly.

"How can I leave you like this?" said Alyosha, almost in alarm.

"Go to your brother, the prison will be shut, go, here's your hat. Give my love to Mitya, go, go!"

And she almost forcibly pushed Alyosha out of the door. He looked at her with pained surprise, when he was suddenly aware of a letter in his right hand, a tiny letter folded up tight and sealed. He glanced at it and instantly read the address "to Ivan Fyodorovich Karamazov." He looked quickly at Lisa. Her face had become almost menacing.

"Give it to him, you must give it to him!" she ordered him, frenzied and trembling. "Today, at once, or I'll poison myself! That's why I sent for you."

And she slammed the door quickly. The bolt clicked. Alyosha put the note in his pocket and went straight downstairs, without going back to Madame Khokhlakov, forgetting her, in fact. As soon as Alyosha had gone, Lisa unbolted the door, opened it a little, put her finger in the crack and slammed the door with all her might, pinching her finger. Ten seconds afterwards, releasing her finger, she walked softly, slowly to her chair, sat up straight in it and looked intently at her blackened finger and at the blood that oozed from under the nail. Her lips were quivering and she kept whispering rapidly to herself:

"I am a wretch, wretch, wretch, wretch!"

Chapter IV

A Hymn and a Secret

It was quite late (days are short in November) when Alyosha rang at the prison gate. It was beginning to get dusk. But Alyosha knew that he would be admitted without difficulty. Things were managed in our little town, as everywhere else. At first, of course, on the conclusion of the preliminary inquiry, relations and a few other persons could only obtain interviews with Mitya by going through certain inevitable formalities. But later, though the formalities were not relaxed, exceptions were made for at least some of Mitya's visitors. So much so, that sometimes the interviews with the prisoner in the room set aside for the purpose were practically private. These exceptions, however, were few in number: only Grushenka, Alyosha and Rakitin were treated like this. But the captain of the police, Mikhail Mikhailovich, was very favorably disposed to Grushenka. His abuse of her at Mokroe weighed on the old man's conscience, and when he learned the whole story, he completely changed his view of her. And, strange to say, though he was firmly persuaded of his guilt, yet after Mitya was once in prison, the old man came to take a more and more lenient view of him. "He was a man of good heart, perhaps," he thought, "who, like a Swede, had come to grief from drinking and dissipation." His first horror had been succeeded by pity. As for Alyosha, the police captain was very fond of him and had known him for a long time. Rakitin, who had of late taken to coming very often to see the prisoner, was one of the most intimate acquaintances of the "police captain's young ladies," as he called them, and was always hanging about their house. He gave lessons in the house of the prison superintendent, too, who, though scrupulous in the performance of his duties, was a kind-hearted old man. Alyosha, again, had an intimate acquaintance of long standing with the superintendent, who was fond of talking to him, generally on "sacred subjects." He respected Ivan Fyodorovich, and stood in awe of his opinion, though he was a great philosopher himself: "self-taught," of course But Alyosha had an irresistible attraction for him. During the last year the old man had taken to studying the Apocryphal Gospels, and constantly talked over his impressions with his young friend. He used to come and see him in the monastery and discussed it for hours together with him and with the monks. So even if Alyosha were late at the prison, he had only to go to the superintendent and everything was made easy. Besides, everyone in the prison, down to the humblest warder, had grown used to Alyosha. The sentry, of course, did not trouble him so long as the authorities were satisfied.

When Mitya was summoned from his cell, he always went downstairs, to the place set aside for interviews. As Alyosha entered the room he came upon Rakitin, who was just taking leave of Mitya. They were both talking loudly. Mitya was laughing heartily as he saw him out, while Rakitin seemed grumbling. Rakitin did not like meeting Alyosha, especially of late. He scarcely spoke to him, and bowed to him stiffly. Seeing Alyosha enter now, he frowned and looked away, as though he was entirely absorbed in buttoning his big, warm, fur-trimmed overcoat. Then he began looking at once for his umbrella.

"I must mind not to forget my belongings," he muttered, simply to say something.

"Mind you don't forget other people's belongings," said Mitya, as a joke, and laughed at once at his own wit. Rakitin fired up instantly.

"You'd better give that advice to your own family, who've always been a slave-driving lot, and not to Rakitin," he cried, suddenly trembling with anger.

"What's the matter? I was joking," cried Mitya. "Damn it all! They are all like that," he turned to Alyosha, nodding towards Rakitin's hurriedly retreating figure. "He was sitting here, laughing and cheerful, and all at once he boils up like that. He didn't even nod to you. Have you broken with him completely? Why are you so late? I've not been simply waiting, but thirsting for you the whole morning. But never mind. We'll make up for it now."

"Why does he come here so often? Surely you are not such great friends?" asked Alyosha. He, too, nodded at the door through which Rakitin had disappeared.

"Great friends with Rakitin? No, not as much as that. Is it likely—a pig like that? He considers I am ... a blackguard. They can't understand a joke either, that's the worst of such people. They never understand a joke, and their souls are dry, dry and flat; they remind me of prison walls when I was first brought here. But he is a clever fellow, very clever. Well, Alexey, it's all over with me now."

He sat down on the bench and made Alyosha sit down beside him.

"Yes, the trial's tomorrow. Do you really have no hope, brother?" Alyosha said, with an apprehensive feeling.

"What are you talking about?" said Mitya, looking at him rather uncertainly. "Oh, you mean the trial! Damn it all! Till now we've been talking of things that don't matter, about this trial, but I haven't said a word to you about the chief thing. Yes, the trial is tomorrow; but it wasn't the trial I meant, when I said it was all over with me. Why do you look at me so critically?"

"What do you mean, Mitya?"

"Ideas, ideas, that's all! Ethics! What is ethics?"

"Ethics?" asked Alyosha, wondering.

"Yes; is it a science?"

"Yes, there is such a science ... but ... I confess I can't explain to you what sort of science it is."

"Rakitin knows. Rakitin knows a lot, damn him! He's not going to be a monk. He means to go to Petersburg. There he'll go in for criticism of an elevating tendency. Who knows, he may be of use and make his own career, too. Ough! they are first-rate, these people, at making a career! Damn ethics. I am done for, Alexey, I am, you man of God! I love you more than anyone. It rends my heart yearn to look at you, that's what. Who was Karl Bernard?"

"Karl Bernard?" Alyosha was surprised again.

"No, not Karl. Wait, I made a mistake. Claude Bernard.[5] What is that? Chemistry or what?"

"He must be a scientist," answered Alyosha; "but I must say I can't tell you much about him, either. I've heard of him as a scientist, but what sort I don't know."

"Well, damn him, then! I don't know either," swore Mitya. "A

5. Claude Bernard (1813–1878), French physiologist. A Russian translation of his *Introduction to Experimental Medi-* *cine* appeared in 1866. The first chapter of the book still merits reading.

scoundrel of some sort, most likely. They are all scoundrels. And Rakitin will make his way. Rakitin will get on anywhere; he is another Bernard. Ugh, these Bernards! They are all over the place."

"But what is the matter?" Alyosha asked insistently.

"He wants to write an article about me, about my case, and so begin his literary career. That's what he comes for; he said so himself. He wants to prove some theory. He wants to say that 'he couldn't help murdering his father, he was corrupted by his environment,' and so on. He explained it all to me. He is going to put in a tinge of Socialism, he says. But there, damn the fellow, he can put in a tinge, if he likes, I don't care. He can't bear brother Ivan, he hates him. He's not fond of you, either. But I don't turn him out, for he is a clever fellow. Awfully conceited though. I said to him just now, 'The Karamazovs are not blackguards, but philosophers; for all true Russians are philosophers, and though you've studied, you are not a philosopher—you are a low fellow.' He laughed, so maliciously. And I said to him, '*de ideabus non est disputandum.*'[6] Isn't that rather good? At least I've become a classicist, you see!" Mitya laughed suddenly.

"Why is it all over with you? You said so just now," Alyosha interposed.

"Why is it all over with me? Hmm . . . The fact of it is . . . if you take it as a whole, I am sorry to lose God—that's why it is."

"What do you mean by 'sorry to lose God'?"

"Imagine: inside, in the nerves, in the head—that is, these nerves are there in the brain . . . (damn them!) there are sort of little tails, the little tails of those nerves, and as soon as they begin quivering . . . that is, you see, I look at something with my eyes and then they begin quivering, those little tails . . . and when they quiver, then an image appears . . . it doesn't appear at once, but an instant, a second, passes . . . and then something like a moment appears; that is, not a moment—devil take the moment!—but an image; that is, an object, or an action, damn it! That's why I see and then think, because of those tails, not at all because I've got a soul, and that I am some sort of image and likeness. All that is nonsense! Mikhail explained it all to me yesterday, brother, and it simply bowled me over. It's magnificent, Alyosha, this science! A new man's arising—that I understand. . . . And yet I am sorry to lose God!"

"Well, that's a good thing, anyway," said Alyosha.

"That I am sorry to lose God! It's chemistry, brother, chemistry! There's no help for it, your reverence, you must make way for chemistry. And Rakitin does dislike God. Ough! doesn't he dislike Him! That's the sore point with all of them. But they conceal

---

6. "There is no disputing ideas." Mitya substitutes "idea" for "taste" in one of   the best known of Latin aphorisms.

it. They tell lies. They pretend. 'Will you preach this in your reviews?" I asked him. 'Oh, well, if I did it openly, they won't let it through,' he said. He laughed. 'But what will become of men then?' I asked him, 'without God and immortal life? All things are lawful then, they can do what they like?' 'Didn't you know?' he said laughing, 'a clever man can do what he likes,' he said. 'A clever man knows his way about, but you've put your foot in it, committing a murder, and now you are rotting in prison.' He says that to my face! A regular pig! I used to kick such people out, but now I listen to them. He talked a lot of sense, too. Writes well. He began reading me an article last week. I copied out three lines of it. Wait a minute. Here it is."

Mitya hurriedly pulled out a piece of paper from his pocket and read:

" 'In order to determine this question, it is above all essential to put one's personality in contradiction to one's reality.' Do you understand that?"

"No, I don't," said Alyosha. He looked at Mitya and listened to him with curiosity.

"I don't understand either. It's dark and obscure, but clever. 'Everyone writes like that now,' he says, 'it's the effect of their environment.' They are afraid of the environment. He writes poetry, too, the scoundrel. He's written in honor of Madame Khokhlakov's foot. Ha, ha, ha!"

"I've heard about it," said Alyosha.

"Have you? And have you heard the poem?"

"No."

"I've got it. Here it is. I'll read it to you. You don't know—I haven't told you—there's quite a story about it. He's a rascal! Three weeks ago he began to tease me. 'You've got yourself into a mess, like a fool, for the sake of three thousand, but I'm going to collar a hundred and fifty thousand. I am going to marry a widow and buy a house in Petersburg.' And he told me he was courting Madame Khokhlakov. She hadn't much brains in her youth, and now at forty she has lost what she had. 'But she's awfully sentimental,' he says; 'that's how I shall get hold of her. When I marry her, I shall take her to Petersburg and there I shall start a newspaper.' And his mouth was simply watering in a nasty, sensual way, the beast, watering not for the widow, but for the hundred and fifty thousand. And he made me believe it. He came to see me every day. 'She is coming round,' he declared. He was beaming with delight. And then, all of a sudden, he was turned out of the house. Perkhotin's carrying everything before him, bravo! I could kiss the silly old noodle for turning him out of the house. And he had written this doggerel. 'It's the first time I've soiled my hands with writing poetry,' he said. 'It's to win her heart, so it's in a good cause. When I get hold of the silly woman's fortune, I can be of great social utility.' They have this social justification for every nasty thing they do! 'Anyway it's better than your Pushkin's poetry,' he said, 'for I've managed to advocate civic sorrow even in that.' I understand what he means about Pushkin, I quite see that, if he really was a man of talent and only wrote about women's feet. But wasn't Rakitin stuck up about his doggerel! The vanity of these fellows! 'On the convalescence of the swollen foot of the object of my affections'—he thought of that for a title. He's a waggish fellow.

> A captivating little foot,
> Though swollen and red and tender!
> The doctors come and plasters put,
> But still they cannot mend her.
>
> Yet, 'tis not for her foot I dread—
> A theme for Pushkin's muse more fit—
> It's not her foot, it is her head:
> I tremble for her loss of wit!
>
> For as her foot swells, strange to say,
> Her intellect is on the wane—
> Oh, for some remedy I pray
> That may restore both foot and brain!

He is a pig, a regular pig, but he's very arch, the rascal! And he really has put in a progressive idea. And wasn't he angry when she kicked him out! He was gnashing his teeth!"

"He's taken his revenge already," said Alyosha. "He's written a paragraph about Madame Khokhlakov."

And Alyosha told him briefly about the paragraph in *Gossip*.

"That's his doing, that's his doing!" Mitya assented frowning. "That's him! These paragraphs ... I know ... the insulting things that have been written about Grushka, for instance. ... And about Katya, too. ... Hmm!"

He walked across the room with a harassed air.

"Brother, I cannot stay long," Alyosha said, after a pause. "To-morrow will be a great and awful day for you, the judgment of God will be accomplished ... I am amazed at you, you walk about here, talking of I don't know what ..."

"No, don't be amazed at me," Mitya broke in warmly. "Am I to talk of that stinking dog? Of the murderer? We've talked enough of him. I don't want to say more of the stinking son of Stinking Lizaveta! God will kill him, you will see. Hush!"

He went up to Alyosha excitedly and kissed him. His eyes glowed.

"Rakitin wouldn't understand it," he began in a sort of exalta-tion; "but you, you'll understand it all. That's why I was thirsting for you. You see, there's so much I've been wanting to tell you for ever so long, here, within these peeling walls, but I haven't said a word about what matters most; the moment never seems to have come. Now I can wait no longer. I must pour out my heart to you. Brother, these last two months I've found in myself a new man. A new man has risen up in me. He was hidden in me, but would never have come to the surface, if it hadn't been for this blow from heaven. I am afraid! And what do I care if I spend twenty years in the mines, breaking out ore with a hammer? I am not a bit afraid of that—it's something else I am afraid of now: that that new man may leave me. Even there, in the mines, underground, I may find a human heart in another convict and murderer by my side, and I may make friends with him, for even there one may live and love and suffer. One may resurrect and revive a frozen heart in that convict, one may wait upon him for years, and at last bring up from the dark depths a lofty soul, a feeling, suffering creature; one may bring forth an angel, resurrect a hero! There are so many of them, hundreds of them, and we are all responsible for them. Why was it I dreamed of that 'babe' at such a moment? 'Why is the babe so poor?' That was a sign to me at that moment. It's for the babe I'm going. Because we are all responsible for all. For all the 'babes,' for there are big children as well as little children. All are 'babes.' I go for all, because someone must go for all. I didn't kill father, but I've got to go. I accept it. It's all come to me here, here, within these peeling walls. There are numbers of them there, hundreds of them underground, with hammers in their hands. Oh, yes, we shall be in chains and there will be no freedom, but then, in our great sorrow, we shall rise again to joy, without which man cannot live nor God exist, for God gives joy: it's His privilege—a grand one. Ah, man should be dissolved in prayer! What would I be underground there without God? Rakitin lies! If they drive God from the earth, we shall shelter Him underground. One cannot exist in prison without God; it's even more impossible than out of prison. And then we men underground will sing from the bowels of the earth a tragic hymn to God, with Whom is joy. Hail to God and His joy! I love Him!"

Mitya was almost gasping for breath as he uttered his wild speech. He turned pale, his lips quivered, and tears rolled down his cheeks.

"Yes, life is full, there is life even underground," he began again. "You wouldn't believe, Alexey, how I want to live now, what a thirst for existence and consciousness has sprung up in me within these peeling walls. Rakitin doesn't understand that; all he cares about is building a house and letting flats. But I've been longing for you. And what is suffering? I am not afraid of it, even if it were beyond reckoning. I am not afraid of it now. I was afraid of it before. Do you know, perhaps I won't answer at the trial at all. . . . And I seem to have such strength in me now, that I think I could stand anything, any suffering, only to be able to say and to repeat to myself every moment, 'I exist.' In thousands of agonies—I exist. I'm tormented on the rack—but I exist! Though I sit alone on a post—I exist! I see the sun, and if I don't see the sun, I know it's there. And there's a whole life in that, in knowing that the sun is there. Alyosha, my cherub, all these philosophies are the death of me. Damn them! Brother Ivan . . ."

"What of brother Ivan?" interrupted Alyosha, but Mitya did not hear.

"You see, I never had any of these doubts before, but it was all hidden away in me. It was perhaps just because ideas I did not understand were surging up in me, that I used to drink and fight and rage. It was to stifle them in myself, to still them, to smother them. Brother Ivan is not Rakitin, there is an idea in him. Brother Ivan is a sphinx and is silent; he is always silent. It's God that torments me. That's the only thing that torments me. What if He doesn't exist? What if Rakitin's right—that it's an idea made up by men? Then, if He doesn't exist, man is the chief of the earth, of the universe. Magnificent! Only how is he going to be good without God? That's the question. I always come back to that. For whom is man going to love then? To whom will he be thankful? To whom will he sing the hymn? Rakitin laughs. Rakitin says that one can love humanity without God. Well, only a sniveling idiot can maintain that. I can't understand it. Life's easy for Rakitin. 'You'd better think about the extension of civic rights, or even of keeping down the price of meat. You will show your love for humanity more simply and directly by that, than by philosophy.' I answered him, 'Well, but you, without a God, are more likely to raise the price of meat, if it suits you, and make a ruble on every kopeck.' He lost his temper. But after all, what is goodness? Answer me that, Alexey. Goodness is one thing with me and another with a Chinese, so it's a relative thing. Or isn't it? Is it not relative? A treacherous question! You won't laugh if I tell you it's kept me awake two nights. I only wonder now how people can live and think nothing about it. Vanity! Ivan has no God. He has an idea. It's beyond me. But he is silent. I believe he is a freemason. I asked him, but he is silent. I wanted to drink from the springs of his soul—he was silent. But once he did drop a word."

"What did he say?" Alyosha took it up quickly.

"I said to him, 'Then everything is lawful, if it is so?' He frowned. 'Fyodor Pavlovich, our papa,' he said, 'was a pig, but his ideas were right enough.' That was what he dropped. That was all he said. That was going one better than Rakitin."

"Yes," Alyosha assented bitterly. "When was he with you?"

"Of that later, now I must speak of something else. I have said nothing about Ivan to you before. I put it off to the last. When my business here is over and the verdict has been given, then I'll tell you something. I'll tell you everything. We have something tremendous on hand. . . . And you will be my judge in it. But don't begin about that now; be silent. You talk of tomorrow, of the trial; but, would you believe it, I know nothing about it."

"Have you talked to the counsel?"

"What's the use of the counsel? I told him all about it. He's a soft, city-bred rogue—a Bernard! But he doesn't believe me—not a bit of it. Only imagine, he believes I did it. I see it. 'In that case,' I asked him, 'why have you come to defend me?' Hang them all! They've got a doctor down, too, want to prove I'm mad. I won't have that! Katerina Ivanovna wants to do her 'duty' to the end, whatever the strain!" Mitya smiled bitterly. "The cat! Hard-hearted creature! She knows that I said of her at Mokroe that she was a woman of 'great wrath.' They repeated it. Yes, the facts against me have grown numerous as the sands of the sea. Grigory sticks to his point. Grigory's honest, but a fool. Many people are honest because they are fools: that's Rakitin's idea. Grigory's my enemy. And there are some people who are better as foes than friends. I mean Katerina Ivanovna. I am afraid, oh, I am afraid she will tell how she bowed to the ground after that forty-five hundred. She'll pay it back to the last cent. I don't want her sacrifice; they'll put me to shame at the trial. I wonder how I can stand it. Go to her, Alyosha, ask her not to speak of that in the court, can't you? But damn it all, it doesn't matter! I shall get through somehow. I don't pity her. It's her own doing. She deserves what she gets. I shall have my own story to tell, Alexey." He smiled bitterly again. "Only . . . only Grusha, Grusha! Good Lord! Why should she have such suffering to bear?" he exclaimed suddenly, with tears. "Grusha's killing me; the thought of her's killing me, killing me. She was with me just now . . ."

"She told me she was very much grieved by you today."

"I know. Confound my temper! It was jealousy. I was sorry, I kissed her as she was going. I didn't ask her forgiveness."

"Why didn't you?" exclaimed Alyosha.

Suddenly Mitya laughed almost mirthfully.

"God preserve you, my dear boy, from ever asking forgiveness for a fault from a woman you love. From one you love especially, however greatly you may have been in fault. For a woman—devil only knows what to make of a woman: I know something about them, anyway. But try acknowledging you are in fault to a woman. say, 'I am sorry, forgive me,' and a shower of reproaches will follow! Nothing will make her forgive you simply and directly, she'll humble you to the dust, bring forward things that have never happened, recall everything, forget nothing, add something of her own, and only then forgive you. And even the best, the best of them do it. She'll scrape up all the scrapings and load them on your head. They are ready to flay you alive, I tell you, every one of them, all these angels without whom we cannot live! I tell you plainly and openly, dear boy, every decent man ought to be under some woman's thumb. That's my conviction—not conviction, but feeling. A man ought to be magnanimous, and it's no disgrace to a man! No disgrace to a hero, not even a Caesar! But don't ever beg her pardon all the same for anything. Remember that rule given you by your brother Mitya, who's come to ruin through women. No, I'd better make it up to Grusha somehow, without begging pardon. I worship her, Alexey, worship her. Only she doesn't see it. No, she still thinks I don't love her enough. And she tortures me, tortures me with her love. The past was nothing! In the past it was only those infernal curves of hers that tortured me, but now I've taken all her soul into my soul and through her I've become a man myself. Will they marry us? If they don't, I shall die of jealousy. I imagine something every day. . . . What did she say to you about me?"

Alyosha repeated all Grushenka had said to him that day. Mitya listened, made him repeat things, and seemed pleased.

"Then she is not angry at my being jealous?" he exclaimed. "That's a woman for you! 'I've a fierce heart myself!' Ah, I love such fierce hearts, though I can't bear anyone's being jealous of me. I can't endure it. We shall fight. But I shall love her, I shall love her infinitely. Will they marry us? Do they let convicts marry? That's the question. And without her I can't exist . . ."

Mitya walked frowning across the room. It was almost dark. He suddenly seemed terribly worried.

"So there's a secret, she says, a secret? We have got up a plot against her, and 'Katka' is mixed up in it, she thinks. No, my good Grushenka, that's not it. You are very wide of the mark, in your foolish feminine way. Alyosha, darling, well, here goes! I'll tell you our secret!"

He looked round, went close up quickly to Alyosha, who was standing before him, and whispered to him with an air of mystery, though in reality no one could hear them: the old warder was dozing in the corner, and not a word could reach the ears of the soldiers on guard.

"I will tell you all our secret," Mitya whispered hurriedly. "I meant to tell you later, for how could I decide on anything without you? You are everything to me. Though I say that Ivan is superior to us, you are my cherub. It's your decision that will decide it. Perhaps it's you that is superior and not Ivan. You see, it's a question of conscience, question of the higher conscience—the secret is so important that I can't settle it myself, and I've put it off till I could speak to you. But anyway it's too early to decide now, for we must wait for the verdict. As soon as the verdict is given, you shall decide my fate. Don't decide it now. I'll tell you now. You listen, but don't decide. Stand and keep quiet. I won't tell you everything. I'll only tell you the idea, without details, and you keep quiet. Not a question, not a movement. You agree? But, goodness, what shall I do with your eyes? I'm afraid your eyes will tell me your decision, even if you don't speak. Oo! I'm afraid! Alyosha, listen! Brother Ivan suggests my *escaping*. I won't tell you the details: it's all been thought out: it can all be arranged. Hush, don't decide, I aim to go to America with Grusha. You know I can't live without Grusha! What if they won't let her follow me to Siberia? Do they let convicts get married? Brother Ivan thinks not. And without Grusha what would I do there underground with a hammer? I would only smash my skull with the hammer! But on the other hand, my conscience? I would have run away from suffering. A sign has come, I reject the sign. I have a way of salvation and I turn my back on it. Ivan says that in America, 'with good inclinations' I can be of more use than underground. But what becomes of our hymn from underground? What's America? America is vanity again! And there's a lot of swindling in America, too, I expect. I would have run away from crucifixion! I tell you, you know, Alexey, because you are the only person who can understand this. There's no one else. It's folly, madness to others, all I've told you of the hymn. They'll say I'm out of my mind or a fool. I am not out of my mind and I am not a fool. Ivan understands about the hymn, too. He understands, only he doesn't answer—he is silent. He doesn't believe in the hymn. Don't speak, don't speak. I see how you look! You have already decided. Don't decide, spare me! I can't live without Grusha. Wait till after the trial!"

Mitya ended beside himself. He held Alyosha with both hands on his shoulders, and his yearning, feverish eyes were fixed on his brother's.

"They don't let convicts marry, do they?" he repeated for the third time in a supplicating voice.

Alyosha listened with extreme surprise and was deeply moved.

"Tell me one thing," he said, "is Ivan very keen on it, and whose idea was it?"

"His, his, and he is very keen on it. He didn't come to see me at first, then he suddenly came a week ago and he began about it right away. He is awfully keen on it. He doesn't ask me, but orders me to escape. He doesn't doubt of my obeying him, though I showed him all my heart as I have to you, and told him about the hymn, too. He told me he'd arrange it; he's found out about everything. But of that later. He's rabidly set on it. It's all a matter of money: there'll be ten thousand for the escape and twenty thousand for America. And he says we can arrange a magnificent escape for ten thousand."

"And he told you on no account to tell me?" Alyosha asked again.

"To tell no one, and especially not you; on no account to tell you. He is afraid, no doubt, that you'll stand before me as my conscience. Don't tell him I told you. Don't tell him, for anything."

"You are right," Alyosha pronounced; "it's impossible to decide anything before the trial is over. After the trial you'll decide by yourself. Then you'll find that new man in yourself and he will decide."

"A new man, or a Bernard who'll decide à la Bernard, for I believe I'm a contemptible Bernard myself," said Mitya, with a bitter grin.

"But, brother, have you no hope then of being acquitted?"

Mitya shrugged his shoulders convulsively and shook his head.

"Alyosha, darling, it's time you were going," he said, with a sudden haste. "There's the superintendent shouting in the yard. He'll be here directly. We are late; it's irregular. Embrace me quickly. Kiss me! Sign me with the cross, darling, for the cross I have to bear tomorrow."

They embraced and kissed.

"Ivan," said Mitya suddenly, "suggests my escaping; but, of course, he believes I did it."

A mournful smile came on to his lips.

"Have you asked him whether he believes it?" asked Alyosha.

"No, I haven't. I wanted to, but I couldn't. I didn't have the courage. But I saw it from his eyes. Well, goodbye!"

Once more they kissed hurriedly, and Alyosha was just going out, when Mitya suddenly called him back.

"Stand facing me! That's right!" And again he seized Alyosha, putting both hands on his shoulders. His face became suddenly quite pale, so that it was dreadfully apparent, even through the gathering darkness. His lips twitched, his eyes fastened upon Alyosha.

"Alyosha, tell me the whole truth, as you would before God. Do you believe I did it? Do you, do you in yourself, believe it? The whole truth, don't lie!" he cried desperately.

Everything seemed to heave in front of Alyosha, and he felt something like a stab at his heart.

"Hush! What do you mean?" he faltered helplessly.

"The whole truth, the whole, don't lie!" repeated Mitya.

"I've never for one instant believed that you were the murderer!" broke in a shaking voice from Alyosha's breast, and he raised his right hand in the air, as though calling God to witness his words. Mitya's whole face was lit up with bliss.

"Thank you!" he articulated slowly, as though letting a sigh escape him after fainting. "Now you have given me new life. Would you believe it, till this moment I've been afraid to ask you, you, even you. Well, go! You've given me strength for tomorrow. God bless you! Well, go along! Love Ivan!" was Mitya's last word.

Alyosha went out in tears. Such distrustfulness in Mitya, such lack of confidence even to him, to Alyosha—all this suddenly opened before Alyosha an unsuspected depth of hopeless grief and despair in the soul of his unhappy brother. Intense, infinite compassion overwhelmed him instantly. There was a poignant ache in his torn heart. "Love Ivan"—he suddenly recalled Mitya's words. And he was going to Ivan. He badly wanted to see Ivan all day. He was as much worried about Ivan as about Mitya, and more than ever now.

Chapter V

Not You, Not You!

On the way to Ivan he had to pass the house where Katerina Ivanovna was living. There was light in the windows. He suddenly stopped and resolved to go in. He had not seen Katerina Ivanovna for more than a week. But now it struck him that Ivan might be with her, especially on the eve of the terrible day. Ringing, and mounting the staircase, which was dimly lighted by a Chinese lantern, he saw a man coming down, and as they met, he recognized him as his brother. So he was just coming from Katerina Ivanovna.

"Ah, it's only you," said Ivan Fyodorovich drily. "Well, good-bye! You are going to her?"

"Yes."

"I don't advise you to; she's 'upset' and you'll upset her more."

A door was instantly flung open above, and a voice cried suddenly:

"No, no! Alexey Fyodorovich, have you come from him?"

"Yes, I have been with him."

"Has he sent me any message? Come up, Alyosha, and you, Ivan Fyodorovich, you must come back, you must. Do you hear?"

There was such a peremptory note in Katya's voice that Ivan Fyodorovich, after a moment's hesitation, made up his mind to go back with Alyosha.

"She was listening," he murmured angrily to himself, but Alyosha heard it.

"Excuse my keeping my overcoat on," said Ivan Fyodorovich, going into the drawing room. "I won't sit down. I won't stay more than a minute."

"Sit down, Alexey Fyodorovich," said Katerina Ivanovna, though she remained standing. She had changed very little during this time, but there was an ominous gleam in her dark eyes. Alyosha remembered afterwards that she had struck him as particularly handsome at that moment.

"What did he ask you to tell me?"

"Only one thing," said Alyosha, looking her straight in the face, "that you would spare yourself and say nothing at the trial of what" (he was a little confused) ". . . passed between you . . . at the time of your first acquaintance . . . in that town."

"Ah! that I bowed down to the ground for that money!" She broke in with a bitter laugh. "Why, is he afraid for me or for himself? He asks me to spare—whom? Him or myself? Tell me, Alexey Fyodorovich!"

Alyosha watched her intently, trying to understand her.

"Both yourself and him," he answered softly.

"I am glad to hear it," she snapped out maliciously, and she suddenly blushed. "You don't know me yet, Alexey Fyodorovich," she said menacingly. "And I don't know myself yet. Perhaps you'll want to trample me under foot after my examination tomorrow."

"You will give your evidence honorably," said Alyosha; "that's all that's wanted."

"Women are often dishonorable," she snarled. "Only an hour ago I was thinking I felt afraid to touch that monster . . . as though he were a reptile . . . but no, he is still a human being to me! But did he do it? Is he the murderer?" she cried, all of a sudden, hysterically, turning quickly to Ivan Fyodorovich. Alyosha saw at once that she had asked Ivan Fyodorovich that question before, perhaps only a moment before he came in, and not for the first time, but for the hundredth, and that they had ended by quarreling.

"I've been to see Smerdyakov. . . . It was you, you who persuaded me that he murdered his father. It's only you I believed!" she continued, still addressing Ivan Fyodorovich. He gave her a sort of strained smile. Alyosha started at her tone. He had not suspected such familiar intimacy between them.

"Well, that's enough, anyway," Ivan cut short the conversation. "I am going. I'll come tomorrow." And turning at once, he walked out of the room and went straight downstairs. With an imperious gesture, Katerina Ivanovna seized Alyosha by both hands.

"Follow him! Overtake him! Don't leave him alone for a minute!" she said, in a hurried whisper. "He's mad! Don't you know that he's mad? He is in a fever, nervous fever. The doctor told me so. Go, run after him. . . ."

Alyosha jumped up and ran after Ivan Fyodorovich, who was not fifty paces ahead of him.

"What do you want?" He turned quickly on Alyosha, seeing that he was running after him. "She told you to catch up to me, because I'm mad. I know it all by heart," he added irritably.

"She is mistaken, of course; but she is right, that you are ill," said Alyosha. "I was looking at your face just now. You look very ill, Ivan."

Ivan walked on without stopping. Alyosha followed him.

"And do you know, Alexey Fyodorovich, how people do go out of their mind?" Ivan asked in a voice suddenly quiet, without a trace of irritation, with a note of the simplest curiosity.

"No, I don't. I suppose there are all kinds of insanity."

"And can one observe that one's going mad oneself?"

"I imagine one can't see oneself clearly in such circumstances," Alyosha answered with surprise. Ivan paused for half a minute.

"If you want to talk to me, please change the subject," he said suddenly.

"Oh, while I think of it, I have a letter for you," said Alyosha timidly, and he took Lisa's note from his pocket and held it out to Ivan. They were just under a lamp post. Ivan recognized the handwriting at once.

"Ah, from that little demon!" he laughed maliciously, and, without opening the envelope, he tore it into bits and threw it in the air. The bits were scattered by the wind.

"She's not sixteen yet, I believe, and already offering herself," he said contemptuously, striding along the street again.

"How do you mean, offering herself?" exclaimed Alyosha.

"As wanton women offer themselves, to be sure."

"How can you, Ivan, how can you?" Alyosha cried warmly in a grieved voice. "She is a child; you are insulting a child! She is ill; she is very ill, too. She is on the verge of insanity, too, perhaps . . . I had to give you her letter . . . I had hoped to hear something from you . . . that would save her."

"You'll hear nothing from me. If she is a child I am not her nurse. Be quiet, Alexey. Don't go on about her. I am not even thinking about it."

They were silent again for a moment.

"She will be praying all night now to the Mother of God to show her how to act tomorrow at the trial," he said sharply and angrily again.

"You . . . you mean Katerina Ivanovna?"

"Yes. Whether she's to save Mitenka or ruin him. She'll pray for light from above. She can't make up her mind for herself, you see. She has not had time to decide yet. She takes me for her nurse, too. She wants me to sing lullabys to her."

"Katerina Ivanovna loves you, brother," said Alyosha sadly.

"Perhaps; but I am not very keen on her."

"She is suffering. Why do you . . . sometimes say things to her that give her hope?" Alyosha went on, with timid reproach. "I know that you've given her hope. Forgive me for speaking to you like this," he added.

"I can't behave to her as I ought—break off altogether and tell her so straight out," said Ivan, irritably. "I must wait till sentence is passed on the murderer. If I break off with her now, she will avenge herself on me by ruining that scoundrel tomorrow at the trial, for she hates him and knows she hates him. It's all a lie—lie upon lie! As long as I don't break off with her, she goes on hoping, and she won't ruin that monster, knowing how I want to get him out of trouble. If only that damned verdict would come!"

The words "murderer" and "monster" echoed painfully in Alyosha's heart.

"But how can she ruin Mitya?" he asked, pondering on Ivan's words. "What evidence can she give that would ruin Mitya?"

"You don't know that yet. She's got a document in her hands, in Mitenka's own writing, that proves conclusively that he did murder Fyodor Pavlovich."

"That's impossible!" cried Alyosha.

"Why is it impossible? I've read it myself."

"There can't be such a document!" Alyosha repeated warmly. "There can't be, because he's not the murderer. It's not he who murdered father, not he!"

Ivan Fyodorovich suddenly stopped.

"Who is the murderer then, according to you?" he asked, with apparent coldness. There was even a supercilious note in his voice.

"You know who," Alyosha pronounced in a low penetrating voice.

"Who? You mean the myth about that crazy idiot, the epileptic, Smerdyakov?"

Alyosha suddenly felt himself trembling all over.

"You know who," broke helplessly from him. He could scarcely breathe.

"Who? Who?" Ivan cried almost fiercely. All his restraint suddenly vanished.

"I only know one thing," Alyosha went on, still almost in a whisper, "*it wasn't you* who killed father."

"Not you! What do you mean by 'not you'?" Ivan was thunderstruck.

"It was not you who killed father, not you!" Alyosha repeated firmly.

The silence lasted for half a minute.

"I know I didn't. Are you raving?" said Ivan, with a pale, distorted smile. His eyes were riveted on Alyosha. They were standing again under a lamp post.

"No, Ivan. You've told yourself several times that you are the murderer."

"When did I say so? I was in Moscow. . . . When have I said so?" Ivan faltered helplessly.

"You've said so to yourself many times, when you've been alone during these two dreadful months," Alyosha went on softly and distinctly as before. Yet he was speaking now, as it were, not of himself, not of his own will, but obeying some irresistible command. "You have accused yourself and have confessed to yourself that you are the murderer and no one else. But you didn't do it: you are mistaken: you are not the murderer. Do you hear? It was not you! God has sent me to tell you so."

They were both silent. The silence lasted a whole long minute. They were both standing still, gazing into each other's eyes. They were both pale. Suddenly Ivan began trembling all over, and clutched Alyosha's shoulder.

"You've been in my room!" he whispered hoarsely. "You've been there at night, when he came. . . . Confess . . . have you seen him, have you seen him?"

"Whom do you mean—Mitya?" Alyosha asked, bewildered.

"Not him, damn the monster!" Ivan shouted, in a frenzy. "Do you know that he visits me? How did you find out? Speak!"

"Who is *he*? I don't know whom you are talking about," Alyosha faltered, beginning to be alarmed.

"Yes, you do know . . . or how could you . . . ? It's impossible that you don't know."

Suddenly he seemed to check himself. He stood still and seemed to reflect. A strange grin contorted his lips.

"Brother," Alyosha began again, in a shaking voice, "I have said this to you, because you'll believe my word, I know that. I tell you once and for all, it was *not you*. You hear, once for all! God has put it into my heart to say this to you, even though it may make you hate me from this hour."

But by now Ivan Fyodorovich had apparently regained his self-control.

"Alexey Fyodorovich," he said, with a cold smile, "I can't endure prophets and epileptics—messengers from God especially—and you know that only too well. I break off all relations with you from this moment and probably forever. I beg you to leave me at this crossing. It's the way to your lodgings, too. You'd better be particularly careful not to come to me today! Do you hear?"

He turned and walked on with a firm step, not looking back.

"Brother," Alyosha called after him, "if anything happens to you today, turn to me before anyone!"

But Ivan made no reply. Alyosha stood under the lamp post at the crossing, till Ivan had vanished into the darkness. Then he turned and walked slowly homewards. Both Alyosha and Ivan were living in lodgings; neither of them was willing to live in Fyodor Pavlovich's empty house. Alyosha had a furnished room in the house of some tradesmen. Ivan lived some distance from him. He had taken a roomy and fairly comfortable lodge attached to a fine house that belonged to a well-to-do lady, the widow of an official. But his only attendant was a deaf and rheumatic old crone who went to bed at six o'clock every evening and got up at six in the morning. Ivan Fyodorovich had become remarkably indifferent to his comforts of late, and very fond of being alone. He did everything for himself in the one room he lived in, and rarely entered any of the other rooms in his abode. He reached the gate of the house and had his hand on the bell, when he suddenly stopped. He felt that he was still trembling all over with anger. Suddenly he let go of the bell, turned back with a curse, and walked with rapid steps in the opposite direction. He walked a mile and a half to a tiny, slanting, wooden house, almost a hut, where Marya Kondratyevna, the neighbor who used to come to Fyodor Pavlovich's kitchen for soup and to whom Smerdyakov had once sung his songs and played on the guitar, was now lodging. She had sold their little house, and was now living here with her mother in what was practically a hut. Smerdyakov, who was ill—almost dying—had been with them ever since Fyodor Pavlovich's death. It was to him Ivan Fyodorovich was going now, drawn by a sudden and irresistible prompting.

Chapter VI

The First Interview with Smerdyakov

This was the third time that Ivan had been to see Smerdyakov since his return from Moscow. The first time he had seen him and talked to him after the catastrophe was on the first day of his arrival, then he had visited him once more, two weeks later. But his visits had ended with that second one, so that it was now over a month since he had seen him. And he had scarcely heard anything of him. Ivan Fyodorovich had only returned five days after his father's death, so that he was not present at the funeral, which took place the day before he came back. The cause of his delay was that Alyosha, not knowing his Moscow address, had to apply to Katerina Ivanovna to telegraph to him, and she, not knowing his address either, telegraphed to her sister and aunt, reckoning on Ivan Fyodorovich's going to see them as soon as he arrived in Moscow. But he did not go to them till four days after his arrival. When he got the telegram, he had, of course, set off posthaste to our town. The first to meet him was Alyosha, and Ivan was greatly surprised to find that in opposition to the general opinion of the town, he refused to entertain a suspicion against Mitya, and spoke openly of Smerdyakov as the murderer. Later on, after seeing the police captain and the prosecutor, and hearing the details of the charge and the arrest, he was still more surprised at Alyosha, and ascribed his opinion only to his exaggerated brotherly feeling and sympathy with Mitya, of whom Alyosha, as Ivan knew, was very fond.

By the way, let us say a word or two of Ivan's feeling towards his brother Dmitri Fyodorovich. He positively disliked him, at most, felt sometimes a compassion for him, and even that was mixed with great contempt, almost repugnance. Mitya's whole personality, even his appearance, was extremely unattractive to him. Ivan looked with indignation on Katerina Ivanovna's love for his brother. Yet he went to see Mitya on the first day of his arrival, and that interview, far from shaking Ivan's belief in his guilt, positively strengthened it. He found his brother agitated, nervously excited. Mitya had been talkative, but very absent-minded and incoherent. He used violent language, accused Smerdyakov, and was fearfully muddled. He talked principally about the three thousand rubles, which he said had been "stolen" from him by his father. "The money was mine, it was my money," Mitya kept repeating. "Even if I had stolen it, I would have had the right." He hardly contested the evidence against him, and if he tried to turn a fact to his advantage, it was in an absurd and incoherent way. He hardly seemed to wish to defend himself to Ivan or anyone else. Quite the contrary, he was angry and proudly scornful of the charges against him; he was continually firing up and abusing every one. He only laughed contemptuously at Grigory's evidence about the open door, and declared that it was "the devil that opened it." But he could not bring forward any coherent explanation of the fact. He even succeeded in insulting Ivan Fyodorovich during their first interview, telling him sharply that it was not for people who declared that "everything was lawful," to suspect and question him. Altogether he was anything but friendly with Ivan Fyodorovich on that occasion. Immediately after that interview with Mitya, Ivan Fyodorovich went for the first time to see Smerdyakov.

In the railway train on his way from Moscow, he kept thinking of Smerdyakov and of his last conversation with him on the evening before he went away. Many things seemed to him puzzling and suspicious. But when he gave his evidence to the district attorney Ivan Fyodorovich said nothing, for the time, of that conversation. He put that off till he had seen Smerdyakov, who was at that time in the hospital. Doctor Herzenstube and Varvinsky, the doctor he met in the hospital, confidently asserted in reply to Ivan Fyodorovich's persistent questions, that Smerdyakov's epileptic attack was unmistakably genuine, and were surprised indeed at his asking whether he might not have been shamming on the day of the catastrophe. They gave him to understand that the attack was an exceptional one, the fits persisting and recurring several times, so that the patient's life was positively in danger, and it was only now, after they had applied remedies, that they could assert with confidence that the patient would survive. "Though it might well be," added Doctor Herzenstube, "that his reason would be impaired for a considerable period, if not permanently." On Ivan Fyodorovich's asking impatiently whether that meant that he was now mad, they told him that this was not yet the case, in the full sense of the word, but that certain abnormalities were perceptible. Ivan Fyodorovich decided to find out for himself what those abnormalities were.

At the hospital he was at once allowed to see the patient. Smerdyakov was lying on a bunk in a separate ward. There was one other bunk in the room, and in it lay a tradesman of the town, swollen with dropsy, who was obviously almost dying; he could be no hindrance to their conversation. Smerdyakov grinned uncertainly on seeing Ivan Fyodorovich, and for the first instant seemed nervous. So at least Ivan Fyodorovich fancied. But that was only momentary. For the rest of the time he was struck, on the contrary, by Smerdyakov's composure. From the first glance Ivan Fyodorovich had no doubt that he was very ill. He was very weak; he spoke slowly, seeming to move his tongue with difficulty; he was much thinner and sallower. Throughout the interview, which lasted twenty minutes, he kept complaining of headache and of pain in all his limbs. His thin emasculate face seemed to have become so tiny; his hair was ruffled, and in place of the crest of curls in front stood up a thin tuft of hair. But in the left eye, which was screwed up and seemed to be insinuating something, Smerdyakov showed himself unchanged. "It's always worthwhile speaking to a clever man." Ivan was reminded of that at once. He sat down on the stool at his feet. Smerdyakov, with painful effort, shifted his position in bed, but he was not the first to speak. He remained dumb, and did not even look much interested.

"Can you talk to me?" asked Ivan Fyodorovich. "I won't tire you much." "Certainly I can," mumbled Smerdyakov, in a faint voice.

"Has your honor been back long?" he added patronizingly, as though encouraging a nervous visitor.

"I only arrived today. . . . To see the mess you are in here."

Smerdyakov sighed.

"Why do you sigh, you knew of it all along?" Ivan Fyodorovich blurted out.

Smerdyakov was stolidly silent for a while.

"How could I help knowing, sir? It was clear beforehand. But how could I tell it would turn out like that?"

"What would turn out? Don't prevaricate! You've foretold you'd have a fit; on the way down to the cellar, you know. You mentioned the very spot."

"Have you said so at the examination yet?" Smerdyakov queried with composure.

Ivan Fyodorovich felt suddenly angry.

"No. I haven't yet, but I certainly shall. You must explain a great deal to me, my man, and let me tell you, I am not going to let you play with me!"

"Why should I play with you, sir, when I put my whole trust in you, as in God Almighty?" said Smerdyakov, with the same composure, only for a moment closing his eyes.

"In the first place," began Ivan Fyodorovich, "I know that epileptic fits can't be foretold beforehand. I've inquired; don't try and take me in. You can't foretell the day and the hour. How was it you told me the day and the hour beforehand, and about the cellar, too? How could you tell that you would fall down the cellar stairs in a fit, if you didn't sham a fit on purpose?"

"I had to go to the cellar anyway, sir, several times a day, indeed," Smerdyakov drawled deliberately. "I fell from the garret just in the same way a year ago, sir. It's quite true you can't foretell the day and hour of a fit beforehand, but you can always have a presentiment of it."

"But you did foretell the day and the hour!"

"In regard to my epilepsy, your honor, you had much better inquire of the doctors here, sir. You can ask them whether it was a real fit or a sham; it's no use my saying any more about it."

"And the cellar? How could you know beforehand of the cellar?"

"You don't seem able to get over that cellar! As I was going down to the cellar, I was in terrible dread and doubt. What frightened me most was losing you and being left without defense in all the world. So I went down into the cellar thinking, 'Here it'll come on directly, it'll strike me down directly, shall I fall?' And it was through this fear, sir, that I suddenly felt the spasm that always comes . . . and so I went flying. All that and all my previous conversation with you at the gate the evening before, when I told you how frightened I was and spoke of the cellar, sir. I told all that to Doctor Herzenstube and Nikolay Parfenovich, the district attorney, and it's all been written down in the deposition. And the doctor here, Mr. Varvinsky, maintained to all of them that it was just the thought of it brought it on, the apprehension that I might fall. I was just then that the fit seized me. And so they've written it down, that it's just how it must have happened, simply from fear, sir."

As he finished, Smerdyakov drew a deep breath, as though exhausted.

"Then you have said all that in your evidence?" said Ivan

Fyodorovich, somewhat taken aback. He had meant to frighten him with the threat of repeating their conversation, and it appeared that Smerdyakov had already reported it all himself.

"What have I to be afraid of? Let them write down the whole truth," Smerdyakov pronounced firmly.

"And have you told them every word of our conversation at the gate?"

"No, not every word, that is, sir."

"And did you tell them that you can sham fits, as you boasted then?"

"No, I didn't tell them that either, sir."

"Tell me now, why did you send me then to Chermashnya?"

"I was afraid you'd go away to Moscow, Chermashnya is nearer, anyway, sir."

"You are lying, you suggested my going away yourself; you told me to get out of the way of misfortune."

"That was simply out of affection and my sincere devotion to you, foreseeing trouble in the house, to spare you. Only I wanted to spare myself even more, sir. That's why I told you to get out of misfortune's way, that you might understand that there would be trouble in the house, and would remain at home to protect your father."

"You might have said it more directly, you blockhead!" Ivan Fyodorovich suddenly fired up.

"How could I have said it more directly then, sir? It was simply my fear that made me speak, and you might have been angry, too. I might well have been apprehensive that Dmitri Fyodorovich would make a scene and carry away that money, for he considered it as good as his own, but who could tell that it would end in a murder like this? I thought that he would only carry off the three thousand that lay under the master's mattress, sir, in the envelope, sir, and you see, he's murdered him. How could you guess it either, your honor?"

"But if you say yourself that it couldn't be guessed, how could I have guessed and stayed at home? You contradict yourself!" said Ivan Fyodorovich pondering.

"You might have guessed from my sending you to Chermashnya and not to Moscow."

"How could I guess it from that?"

Smerdyakov seemed much exhausted, and again he was silent for a minute.

"You might have guessed, sir, from the fact of my asking you not to go to Moscow, but to Chermashnya, sir, that I wanted to have you nearer, for Moscow's a long way off, and Dmitri Fyodorovich, knowing you are not far off, would not be so bold. And if anything had happened, you might have come to protect me, too, for I warned you of Grigory Vasilyevich's illness, and that I was afraid of having a fit. And when I explained those knocks to you, by means of which one could go in to the deceased, and that Dmitri Fyodorovich knew them all through me, I thought that you would guess yourself that he would be sure to do something, and so wouldn't go to Chermashnya even, but would stay."

"He talks very coherently," thought Ivan Fyodorovich, "though he does mumble; what's the derangement of his faculties that Herzenstube talked of?"

"You are being cunning with me, damn you," he exclaimed, getting angry.

"But I thought at the time that you guessed it completely," Smerdyakov parried with the simplest air.

"If I'd guessed it, I would have stayed," cried Ivan Fyodorovich, flaring up again.

"Why, sir, I thought that it was because you guessed it that you went away in such a hurry, only to get out of misfortune, sir, only to run away and save yourself in your fright."

"You think that everyone is as great a coward as yourself?"

"Forgive me, sir, I thought you were like me."

"Of course, I ought to have guessed," Ivan said in agitation, "and I did guess there was some vileness brewing on your part . . . only you are lying, you are lying again," he cried, suddenly recollecting. "Do you remember how you went up to the carriage and said to me, 'It's always worthwhile speaking to a clever man'? So you were glad I went away, since you praised me?"

Smerdyakov sighed again and again. A trace of color came into his face.

"If I was pleased," he articulated rather breathlessly, "it was simply because you agreed not to go to Moscow, but to Chermashnya. For it was nearer, anyway. Only when I said these words to you, it was not by way of praise, but of reproach. You didn't understand it."

"What reproach?"

"Why, that foreseeing such a calamity you deserted your own father, and would not protect us, for I might have been arrested at any time for stealing that three thousand, sir."

"Damn you!" Ivan swore again. "Stay, did you tell the prosecutor and the district attorney about those knocks?"

"I told them everything just as it was, sir."

Ivan Fyodorovich was again inwardly amazed.

"If I thought of anything then," he began again, "it was solely of some vileness on your part. Dmitri might kill him, but that he would steal—I did not believe that then. . . . But I was prepared for any vileness from you. You told me yourself you could sham a fit. What did you say that for?"

"It was just through my simplicity, and I never have shammed a fit on purpose in my life. And I only said so then to boast to you. It was just foolishness. I liked you so much then, and was open-hearted with you."

"My brother directly accuses you of the murder and theft."

"What else is left for him to do?" said Smerdyakov, with a bitter grin. "And who will believe him with all the proofs against him? Grigory Vasilyevich saw the door open, sir. What can he say after that? But never mind him! He is trembling to save himself."

He slowly ceased speaking, and suddenly, as though on reflection, added:

"And look here again, sir. He wants to throw it on me and make out that it is the work of my hands—I've heard that already, sir. But as to my being clever at shamming a fit: would I have told you beforehand that I could sham one, if I really had had such a design against your father? If I had been planning such a murder could I have been such a fool as to give such evidence against myself beforehand? And to his own son, too! Upon my word, sir! Is that likely? As if that could be, such a thing has never happened. No one hears this talk of ours now, except Providence itself, sir, and if you were to tell about it to the prosecutor and Nikolay Parfenovich you might defend me completely by doing so, for who would be likely to be such a criminal, if he is openhearted beforehand? Anyone can see that."

"Well," and Ivan Fyodorovich got up to cut short the conversation, struck by Smerdyakov's last argument. "I don't suspect you at all, and I think it's absurd indeed to suspect you. On the contrary, I am grateful to you for setting my mind at rest. Now I am going, but I'll come again. Meanwhile, goodbye. Get well. Is there anything you want?"

"I am very thankful for everything, sir. Martha Ignatyevna does not forget me, and provides me anything I want, according to her kindness. Good people visit me every day."

"Goodbye. But I won't say anything of your being able to sham a fit, and I don't advise you to, either," something made Ivan say suddenly.

"I quite understand, sir. And if you don't speak of that, I shall say nothing of that conversation of ours at the gate."

Then it happened that Ivan Fyodorovich went out, and only when he had gone a dozen steps along the corridor, he suddenly felt that there was an insulting significance in Smerdyakov's last words. He was almost on the point of turning back, but it was only a passing impulse, and muttering, "nonsense!" he went out of the hospital. His chief feeling was one of relief at the fact that it was not Smerdyakov, but Mitya, who had committed the murder, though he might have been expected to feel the opposite. He did not want to analyze the reason for this feeling, and even felt a positive repugnance at prying into his sensations. He felt as though he wanted to make haste to forget something.

In the following days he became totally convinced of Mitya's guilt, as he got to know all the weight of evidence against him. There was the evidence of people of no importance, Fenya and her mother, for instance, but the effect of it was almost overpowering. As for Perkhotin, the people at the tavern, and at Plotnikov's shop, as well as the witnesses at Mokroe, their evidence seemed conclusive. It was the details that were so damning. The secret of the "knocks" impressed the prosecutor and the district attorney almost as much as Grigory's evidence as to the open door. Grigory's wife, Martha, in answer to Ivan Fyodorovich's questions, declared that Smerdyakov had been lying all night the other side of the partition wall. "He was not three paces from our bed," and that although she was a sound sleeper she waked several times and heard him moaning. "He was moaning the whole time, moaning continually."

Talking to Herzenstube, and giving it as his opinion that Smerdyakov was not mad at all but only rather weak, he only evoked from the old man a subtle smile. "Do you know how he spends his time now?" he asked, "learning lists of French words by heart. He has an exercise book under his pillow with the French words written out in Russian letters for him by someone, he, he, he!"

Ivan Fyodorovich ended by dismissing all doubts. He could not think of his brother Dmitri without repulsion. Only one thing was strange, however. Alyosha persisted that Dmitri was not the murderer, and that "in all probability" Smerdyakov was. Ivan always felt that Alyosha's opinion meant a great deal to him, and so he was astonished at it now. Another thing that was strange was that Alyosha did not make any attempt to talk about Mitya with Ivan, that he never began on the subject and only answered his questions. This, too, struck Ivan Fyodorovich particularly.

But he was very much preoccupied at that time with something quite apart from that. On his return from Moscow, he abandoned himself hopelessly to his mad and consuming passion for Katerina Ivanovna. This is not the time to begin to speak of this new passion of Ivan Fyodorovich's which left its mark on all the rest of his life: this would furnish the subject for another tale, for another novel, which I may perhaps never write. But I cannot omit to mention here that when Ivan Fyodorovich on leaving Katerina Ivanovna with Alyosha, as I've related already, told him, "I am not keen on her," it was an absolute lie: he loved her madly, though at times he hated her so that he might have murdered her. Many causes helped to bring about this feeling. Shattered by what had happened with Mitya, she rushed on Ivan Fyodorovich's return to meet him as her one salvation. She was hurt, insulted and humiliated in her feelings. And here the man had come back to her, who had loved her so ardently before (oh, she knew that very well), and whose heart and intellect she considered so superior to her own. But the sternly virtuous girl did not abandon herself altogether to the man she loved, in spite of the Karamazov recklessness of his passions and the great fascination he had for her. She was continually tormented at the same time by remorse for having betrayed Mitya, and in moments of discord and violent anger (and they were numerous) she told Ivan so plainly. This was what he had called to Alyosha "lies upon lies." There was, of course, much that was false in it, and that angered Ivan Fyodorovich more than anything. . . . But of all this later.

He did, in fact, for a time almost forget Smerdyakov's existence, and yet, two weeks after his first visit to him, he began to be haunted by the same strange thoughts as before. It's enough to say that he was continually asking himself why it was that on that last night in Fyodor Pavlovich's house he had crept out on to the stairs like a thief and listened to hear what his father was doing below. Why had he recalled that afterwards with repulsion; why, next morning, had he been suddenly so depressed on the journey; why, as he reached Moscow, had he said to himself "I am a scoundrel"? And now he almost fancied that these tormenting thoughts would make him even forget Katerina Ivanovna, so completely did they take possession of him again. It was just after fancying this, that he met Alyosha in the street. He stopped him at once, and put a question to him:

"Do you remember when Dmitri burst in after dinner and beat father, and afterwards I told you in the yard that I reserved 'the right to desire' . . . tell me, did you think then that I desired father's death or not?"

"I did think so," answered Alyosha, softly.

"It was so, too; it was not a matter of guessing. But didn't you fancy then that what I wished was just that 'one reptile should devour another'; that is, just that Dmitri should kill father, and as soon as possible . . . and that I myself was even prepared to help to bring that about?"

Alyosha turned rather pale, and looked silently into his brother's eyes.

"Speak!" cried Ivan, "I want above everything to know what you thought then. I want the truth, the truth!" He drew a deep breath, looking angrily at Alyosha before his answer came.

"Forgive me, I did think that, too, at the time," whispered Alyosha, and he did not add a single "mitigating circumstance."

"Thanks," snapped Ivan, and, leaving Alyosha, he went quickly on his way. From that time Alyosha noticed that Ivan began obviously to avoid him and seemed to have taken a dislike to him, so much so that Alyosha gave up going to see him. Immediately after that meeting with him, Ivan Fyodorovich had not gone home, but went straight to Smerdyakov again.

Chapter VII

The Second Visit to Smerdyakov

By that time Smerdyakov had been discharged from the hospital. Ivan Fyodorovich knew his new lodging, the dilapidated little wooden house, divided in two by a hall on one side of which lived Marya Kondratyevna and her mother, and on the other, Smerdyakov. No one knew on what terms he lived with them, whether as a friend or as a lodger. It was supposed afterwards that he had come to stay with them as Marya Kondratyevna's betrothed, and was living there for a time without paying for board or lodging. Both mother and daughter had the greatest respect for him and looked upon him as greatly superior to themselves.

Ivan Fyodorovich knocked, and, on the door being opened, went into the hall. By Marya Kondratyevna's directions he went straight to the better room on the left, occupied by Smerdyakov. There was a tiled stove in the room and it was extremely hot. The walls were covered with blue wallpaper, which was a good deal torn, however, and in the cracks under it cockroaches swarmed in amazing numbers, so that there was a continual rustling from them. The furniture was very scanty: two benches against each wall and two chairs by the table. The table of plain wood was covered with a cloth with pink patterns on it. There was a pot of geraniums on each of the two little windows. In the corner there was a case of icons. On the table stood a little copper samovar with many dents in it, and a tray with two cups. But Smerdyakov had finished tea and the samovar was out. He was sitting at the table on a bench. He was looking at an exercise book and slowly writing with a pen. There was a bottle of ink by him and a flat iron candlestick, but with a stearine candle. Ivan Fyodorovich saw at once from Smerdyakov's face that he had completely recovered from his illness. His face was fresher, fuller, his hair stood up jauntily in front and was plastered down at the sides. He was sitting in a motley, padded dressing gown, rather dirty and frayed, however. He had spectacles on his nose, which Ivan Fyodorovich had never seen him wearing before. This trifling circumstance suddenly redoubled Ivan Fyodorovich's anger: "A creature like that and wearing spectacles!" Smerdyakov slowly raised his head and looked intently at his visitor through his spectacles; then he slowly took them off and rose from the bench, but by no means respectfully, almost lazily, doing the least possible required by common civility. All this struck Ivan instantly, he took it all in and noted it at once—most of all the look in Smerdyakov's eyes, positively malicious, churlish and haughty. "What do you want to intrude for?" it seemed to say; "we settled everything then, why have you come again?" Ivan could scarcely control himself.

"It's hot here," he said, still standing, and unbuttoned his overcoat.

"Take off your coat, sir," Smerdyakov conceded.

Ivan took off his coat and threw it on a bench. With trembling hands, he took a chair, moved it quickly to the table and sat down. Smerdyakov managed to sit down on his bench before him.

"To begin with, are we alone?" Ivan Fyodorovich asked sternly and impulsively. "Can they overhear us in there?"

"No one can hear anything. You've seen for yourself, sir, there's a hall."

"Listen, my good fellow, what was that you babbled, as I was leaving the hospital, that if I said nothing about your faculty of shamming fits, you wouldn't tell the district attorney all our conversation at the gate. What do you mean by *all*? What could you mean by it? Were you threatening me? Have I entered into some sort of compact with you? Do you suppose I am afraid of you?"

Ivan Fyodorovich said this in a perfect fury, giving him to understand with obvious intention that he scorned any subterfuge or indirectness and meant to show his cards. Smerdyakov's eyes gleamed resentfully, his left eye winked and he at once gave his answer, with his habitual composure and deliberation: "You want to have everything above board, very well, you shall have it," he seemed to say.

"This is what I meant then, and this is why I said that, that you, knowing beforehand of this murder of your own parent, left him to his fate, and that people mightn't after that conclude any evil about your feelings and perhaps of something else, too—that's what I promised not to tell the authorities."

Though Smerdyakov spoke without haste and obviously was controlling himself, yet there was something in his voice, determined and emphatic, resentful and insolently defiant. He stared impudently at Ivan Fyodorovich, who for a moment seemed to see spots before his eyes.

"How? What? Are you out of your mind?"

"I'm perfectly in possession of all my faculties, sir."

"Do you suppose I *knew* of the murder?" Ivan Fyodorovich cried at last, and he brought his fist violently down on the table. "What do you mean by 'something else, too'? Speak, scoundrel!"

Smerdyakov was silent and still scanned Ivan Fyodorovich with the same insolent stare.

"Speak, you stinking rogue, what is that 'something else, too'?"

"The 'something else' I meant was that you probably too were very desirous of your parent's death."

Ivan Fyodorovich jumped up and struck him with all his might on the shoulder, so that he fell back against the wall. In an instant his face was bathed in tears. Saying, "It's a shame, your honor, to strike a sick man," he covered his eyes with a very dirty and used blue checked handkerchief and sank into quiet weeping. A minute passed.

"That's enough! Stop," Ivan Fyodorovich said peremptorily, sitting down again. "Don't make me lose all patience."

Smerdyakov took the rag from his eyes. Every line of his puckered face reflected the insult he had just received.

"So you thought then, you scoundrel, that together with Dmitri I meant to kill my father?"

"I didn't know what thoughts were in your mind then, sir," said Smerdyakov resentfully; "and so I stopped you then at the gate to sound you out on that very point, sir."

"To sound what, what?"

"Why, that very circumstance, whether you wanted your father to be murdered or not?"

What infuriated Ivan Fyodorovich more than anything was the aggressive, insolent tone to which Smerdyakov persistently adhered.

"It was you who murdered him!" he cried suddenly.

Smerdyakov smiled contemptuously.

"You know of yourself, for a fact, that it wasn't I who murdered him. And I should have thought that there was no need to speak of it again to a clever man."

"But why, why had you such a suspicion about me at the time?"

"As you know already, it was simply from fear, sir. For I was in such a position, shaking with fear, that I suspected everyone. I resolved to sound you out, too, for I thought if you wanted the same as your brother, then the business was as good as settled and I would be crushed like a fly, too."

"Look here, you didn't say that two weeks ago."

"I meant the same when I talked to you in the hospital, only I thought you'd understand without wasting words, and that being such a clever man you wouldn't care to talk of it openly."

"What next! Come answer, answer, I insist: what was it . . . what could I have done to put such a degrading suspicion into your mean soul?"

"As for the murder, you couldn't have done that, sir, and didn't want to, but as for wanting someone else to do it, that was just what you did want."

"And how coolly, how coolly he speaks! But why should I have wanted it, what grounds had I for wanting it?"

"What grounds had you? What about the inheritance, sir?" said

Smerdyakov sarcastically, and as it were vindictively. "Why, a
your parent's death there was at least forty thousand to come
each of you, and very likely more, but if Fyodor Pavlovich go
married then to that lady, Agrafena Alexandrovna, she would have
had all his capital made over to her directly after the wedding, for
she's plenty of sense, sir, so that your parent would not have left
you two rubles between the three of you. And were they far from a
wedding, either? Not a hairsbreadth: that lady had only to lift her
little finger and he would have run after her to church, with his
tongue out."

Ivan Fyodorovich restrained himself with painful effort.

"Very good," he commented at last, "you see, I haven't jumped
up, I haven't knocked you down, I haven't killed you. Speak on. So,
according to you, I had fixed on brother Dmitri to do it, I was
reckoning on him?"

"How could you help reckoning on him, sir? If he killed him,
then he would lose all the rights of a nobleman, his rank and
property, and would go off to exile, sir, so his share of the inheritance would come to you and your brother Alexey Fyodorovich, in
equal parts, so you'd each have not forty, but sixty thousand each.
There's not a doubt you did reckon on Dmitri Fyodorovich."

"What I put up with from you! Listen, villain, if I had reckoned
on anyone then, it would have been on you, not on Dmitri, and I
swear I did expect some vileness from you . . . at the time . . . I
remember my impression!"

"I thought, too, for a minute, at the time, that you were reckoning on me as well," said Smerdyakov, with a sarcastic grin. "So that
it was just by that more than anything you showed me what was in
your mind. For if you had a foreboding about me and yet went
away, you as good as said to me, 'You can murder my parent, I
won't hinder you!' "

"You scoundrel! So that's how you understood it!"

"It was all that going to Chermashnya. Why! You were meaning
to go to Moscow and refused all your father's entreaties to go to
Chermashnya—and simply at a foolish word from me you consented at once! What reason had you to consent to Chermashnya,
sir? Since you went to Chermashnya with no reason, simply at my
word, it shows that you must have expected something from me."

"No, I swear I didn't!" shouted Ivan, grinding his teeth.

"You didn't, sir? Then you ought, as your father's son, to have
had me taken to jail and thrashed at once for my words then . . . or
at least, to have given me a punch in the face on the spot, but you
were not a bit angry, if you please, and at once in a friendly way
acted on my foolish word and went away, sir, which was utterly
absurd, for you ought to have stayed to save your parent's life.
How could I help drawing my conclusions?"

Ivan sat scowling, both his fists convulsively pressed on his knees.

"Yes, I am sorry I didn't punch you in the face," he said with a bitter smile. "I couldn't have taken you to jail just then. Who would have believed me and what charge could I bring against you? But the punch in the face . . . oh, I'm sorry I didn't think of it. Though blows are forbidden, I should have pounded your ugly face to a jelly."

Smerdyakov looked at him almost with relish.

"In the ordinary occasions of life," he said in the same complacent and sententious tone in which he had taunted Grigory and argued with him about religion at Fyodor Pavlovich's table, "in the ordinary occasions of life, blows on the face are forbidden nowadays by law and people have given them up, but in exceptional occasions of life people still fly to blows, not only among us but all over the world, be it even the total Republic of France, just as in the time of Adam and Eve, sir, and they will never stop, but you, even in an exceptional case, did not dare, sir."

"What are you learning French words for?" Ivan nodded towards the exercise book lying on the table.

"Why shouldn't I learn them so as to improve my education, supposing that I may myself chance to go some day to those happy parts of Europe."

"Listen, monster," Ivan's eyes flashed and he trembled all over. "I am not afraid of your accusations, you can say what you like about me, and if I don't beat you to death, it's simply because I suspect you of that crime and I'll drag you to justice. I'll unmask you."

"To my thinking, you'd better keep quiet, sir, for what can you accuse me of, considering my absolute innocence; and who would believe you? Only if you begin, I shall tell everything, too, for I must defend myself."

"Do you think I am afraid of you now?"

"If the court doesn't believe all I've said to you just now, sir, the public will, and you will be ashamed."

"That's as much as to say 'It's always worthwhile speaking to a clever man,' eh?" snarled Ivan.

"You hit the mark, indeed. And you will be clever, sir."

Ivan Fyodorovich got up, shaking all over with indignation, put on his coat, and without replying further to Smerdyakov, without even looking at him, walked quickly out of the cottage. The cool evening air refreshed him. There was a bright moon in the sky. A nightmare of ideas and sensations filled his soul. "Shall I go at once and give information against Smerdyakov? But what information can I give? He is not guilty, anyway. On the contrary, he'll accuse me. And in fact why did I set off for Chermashnya then? What for? What for?" Ivan asked himself. "Yes, of course, I was expecting something and he is right . . ." And he remembered for the hundredth time how, on that last night in his father's house, he had listened on the stairs. But he remembered it now with such anguish that he stood still on the spot as though he had been stabbed. "Yes, I expected it then, that's true! I wanted the murder, I did want the murder! Did I want the murder? Did I want it? I must kill Smerdyakov! If I don't dare kill Smerdyakov now, life is not worth living!" Ivan Fyodorovich did not go home, but went straight to Katerina Ivanovna and alarmed her by his appearance. He was like a madman. He repeated all his conversation with Smerdyakov, every syllable of it. He couldn't be calmed, however much she tried to soothe him: he kept walking about the room, speaking strangely, disconnectedly. At last he sat down, put his elbows on the table, leaned his head on his hands and pronounced this strange sentence:

"If it's not Dmitri, but Smerdyakov who's the murderer, I share his guilt, for I put him up to it. Whether I did, I don't know yet. But if he is the murderer, and not Dmitri, then, of course, I am the murderer, too."

When Katerina Ivanovna heard that, she got up from her seat without a word, went to her writing table, opened a box standing on it, took out a sheet of paper and laid it before Ivan. This was the document of which Ivan Fyodorovich spoke to Alyosha later on as a "conclusive proof" that brother Dmitri had killed his father. This was the letter written by Mitya to Katerina Ivanovna when he was drunk, on the very evening he met Alyosha at the crossroads on the way to the monastery, after the scene at Katerina Ivanovna's, when Grushenka had insulted her. Then, parting from Alyosha, Mitya had rushed to Grushenka. I don't know whether he saw her, but in the evening he was at the Metropolis, where he got thoroughly drunk. Then he asked for pen and paper and wrote a document of weighty consequence to himself. It was a wordy, disconnected, frantic letter, a drunken letter in fact. It was like the talk of a drunken man, who, on his return home, begins with extraordinary heat telling his wife or one of his household how he has just been insulted, what a scoundrel had just insulted him, what a fine fellow he is on the other hand, and how he will make that scoundrel pay; and all that at great length, with great excitement and incoherence, with drunken tears and blows on the table. The letter was written on a dirty piece of ordinary paper of the cheapest kind. It had been provided by the tavern and there were figures scrawled on the back of it. There was evidently not space enough for his drunken verbosity and Mitya not only filled the margins but had written the last line right across the rest. The letter ran as follows:

Fatal Katya!

Tomorrow I will get the money and repay your three thousand and farewell, woman of great wrath, but farewell too my love! Let us make an end! Tomorrow I shall try and get it from everyone, and if I can't borrow it, I give you my word of honor I shall go to my father and break his skull and take the money from under the pillow, if only Ivan has gone. If I had to go to Siberia for it, I'll give you back your three thousand. And farewell. I bow down to the ground before you, for I've been a scoundrel to you. Forgive me! No, better not forgive me, you'll be happier and so shall I! Better Siberia than your love, for I love another woman and you got to know her too well today, so how can you forgive? I will murder the man who's robbed me! I'll leave you all and go to the East so as to see no one again. Not *her* either, for you are not my only tormentress, she is too. Farewell!

P.S.—I write my curse, but I adore you! I hear it in my heart. One string is left, and it vibrates. Better tear my heart in two! I shall kill myself, but first of all that cur. I shall tear three thousand from him and fling it to you. Though I've been a scoundrel to you, I am not a thief! You can expect three thousand. The cur keeps it under his mattress, in pink ribbon. I am not a thief, but I'll murder my thief. Katya, don't look disdainful. Dmitri is not a thief, but a murderer! He has murdered his father and ruined himself to hold his ground, rather than endure your pride. And he doesn't love you.

P.P.S.—I kiss your feet, farewell!

P.P.P.S.—Katya, pray to God that someone'll give me the money. Then I shall not be steeped in gore, and if no one does— I shall! Kill me!

Your slave and enemy,
D. KARAMAZOV.

When Ivan read this "document," he was convinced. So then it was his brother, not Smerdyakov. And if not Smerdyakov, then not he, Ivan. This letter at once assumed in his eyes the aspect of a mathematical proof. There could be no longer the slightest doubt of Mitya's guilt. The suspicion never occurred to Ivan, by the way, that Mitya might have committed the murder in conjunction with Smerdyakov, and indeed it did not fit in with the facts. Ivan was completely reassured. The next morning he only thought of Smerdyakov and his gibes with contempt. A few days later he positively wondered how he could have been so horribly distressed at his suspicions. He resolved to dismiss him with contempt and forget him. So passed a month. He made no further inquiry about Smerdyakov, but twice he happened to hear that he was very ill and out of his mind. "He'll end in madness," the young doctor, Varvinsky, observed about him and Ivan remembered this.

During the last week of that month Ivan himself began to feel very ill. He went to consult the Moscow doctor who had been sent for by Katerina Ivanovna just before the trial. And just at that time his relations with Katerina Ivanovna became acutely strained. They were like two enemies in love with one another. Katerina Ivanovna's "returns" to Mitya, that is, her brief but violent revulsions of feeling in his favor, drove Ivan to perfect frenzy. Strange to say, until that last scene described above, when Alyosha came from Mitya to Katerina Ivanovna, Ivan had never once, during that month, heard her express a doubt of Mitya's guilt, in spite of those "returns" that were so hateful to him. It is remarkable, too, that while he felt that he hated Mitya more and more every day, he realized that it was not on account of Katya's "returns" that he hated him, but just *because he was the murderer of his father!* He was conscious of this and fully recognized it to himself. Nevertheless, he went to see Mitya ten days before the trial and proposed to him a plan of escape—a plan he had obviously thought over a long time. He was partly impelled to do this by a sore place still left in his heart from a phrase of Smerdyakov, that it was to his, Ivan's, advantage that his brother should be convicted, as that would increase his inheritance and Alyosha's from forty to sixty thousand rubles. He determined to sacrifice thirty thousand on arranging Mitya's escape. On his return from seeing him, he was very mournful and dispirited, he suddenly began to feel that he was anxious for Mitya's escape, not only to heal that sore place by sacrificing thirty thousand, but for another reason. "Is it because I am as much a murderer at heart?" he asked himself. Something very deep down seemed burning and rankling in his soul. His pride above all suffred cruelly all that month. But of that later. . . .

When, after his conversation with Alyosha, Ivan Fyodorovich suddenly decided with his hand on the bell of his lodging to go to Smerdyakov, he obeyed a sudden and peculiar impulse of indignation. He suddenly remembered how Katerina Ivanovna had only just cried out to him in Alyosha's presence: "It was you, you, persuaded me of his" (that is, Mitya's) "guilt!" Ivan was thunderstruck when he recalled it. He had never once tried to persuade her that Mitya was the murderer, on the contrary, he had suspected himself in her presence, that time when he came back from Smerdyakov. It was *she*, she, who had produced that "document" and proved his brother's guilt. And now she suddenly exclaimed: "I've been at Smerdyakov's myself!" When had she been there? Ivan had known nothing of it. So she was not at all so sure of Mitya's guilt! And what could Smerdyakov have told her? What, what, had he said to her? His heart burned with violent anger. He could not understand how he could, half an hour before, have let those words pass and not have cried out at the moment. He let go of the bell and rushed off to Smerdyakov. "Perhaps I shall kill him this time," he thought on the way.

Chapter VIII

The Third and Last Interview with Smerdyakov

When he was halfway there, the keen dry wind that had been blowing early that morning rose again, and a fine, thick, dry snow began falling heavily. It did not lie on the ground, but was whirled about by the wind and soon there was a regular snowstorm. There were scarcely any lamp posts in the part of the town where Smerdyakov lived. Ivan strode alone in the darkness, unconscious of the storm, instinctively picking out his way. His head ached and there was a painful throbbing in his temples. He felt that his hands were twitching convulsively. Not far from Marya Kondratyevna's little house, Ivan Fyodorovich suddenly came upon a solitary drunken little peasant. He was wearing a coarse and patched coat, and was walking in zigzags, grumbling and swearing to himself. Then suddenly he would begin singing in a husky drunken voice:

> Ach, Vanka's gone to Petersburg,
> I won't wait till he comes back.

But he broke off every time at the second line and began swearing again; then he would begin the same song again. Ivan felt an intense hatred for him before he had thought about him at all. Suddenly he realized his presence and felt an irresistible impulse to knock him down. At that moment they met, and the peasant with a violent lurch fell full tilt against Ivan, who pushed him back furiously. The peasant went flying backwards and fell like a log on the frozen ground. He uttered one plaintive "O-oh!" and then was silent. Ivan stepped up to him. He was lying on his back, without movement or consciousness. "He will freeze," thought Ivan, and he went on his way to Smerdyakov's.

In the hall, Marya Kondratyevna, who ran out to open the door with a candle in her hand, whispered that Pavel Fyodorovich (that is, Smerdyakov) was very ill; "it's not that he's laid up, sir, but he seems not himself, and he even told us to take the tea away; he wouldn't have any."

"Why, is he making a row?" asked Ivan coarsely.

"Oh, dear, no, quite the contrary, sir, he's very quiet. Only please don't talk to him too long," Marya Kondratyevna begged him.

Ivan Fyodorovich opened the door and stepped into the room.

It was overheated as before, but there were changes in the room. One of the benches at the side had been removed, and in its place had been put a large old mahogany leather sofa, on which a bed had been made up, with fairly clean white pillows. Smerdyakov was sitting on the sofa, wearing the same dressing gown. The table had been brought out in front of the sofa, so that there was hardly room to move. On the table lay a thick book with a yellow cover, but Smerdyakov was not reading it. He seemed to be sitting doing nothing. He met Ivan with a slow silent gaze, and was apparently not at all surprised at his coming. There was a great change in his face; he was much thinner and sallower. His eyes were sunken and there were dark circles under them.

"Why, you really are ill?" Ivan Fyodorovich stopped short. "I won't keep you long, I won't even take off my coat. Where can one sit down?"

He went to the other end of the table, moved up a chair and sat down on it.

"Why do you look at me without speaking? I've only come with one question, and I swear I won't go without an answer. Has the young lady, Katerina Ivanovna, been with you?"

Smerdyakov still remained silent, looking quietly at Ivan as before. Suddenly, he waved his hand and turned his face away.

"What's the matter with you?" cried Ivan.

"Nothing."

"What do you mean by 'nothing'?"

"Yes, she has. It's no matter to you. Let me alone."

"No, I won't let you alone. Tell me, when was she here?"

"Why, I'd quite forgotten about her," said Smerdyakov, with a scornful smile, and turning his face to Ivan again, he stared at him with a look of frenzied hatred, the same look that he had fixed on him at their last interview, a month before.

"You seem very ill yourself, your face is sunken; you don't look like yourself," he said to Ivan.

"Never mind my health, tell me what I ask you."

"But why are your eyes so jaundiced? The whites are quite yellow. Are you so troubled?"

He smiled contemptuously and suddenly laughed outright.

"Listen, I've told you I won't go away without an answer!" Ivan cried, intensely irritated.

"Why do you keep pestering me? Why do you torment me?" said Smerdyakov, with a look of suffering.

"Damn it! I have nothing to do with you. Just answer my question and I'll go away."

"I have no answer to give you," said Smerdyakov, looking down again.

"You may be sure I'll make you answer!"

"Why are you so uneasy?" Smerdyakov stared at him, not simply with contempt, but almost with a revulsion. "Is this because the trial begins tomorrow? Nothing will happen to you, can't you believe that at last? Go home, go to bed and sleep in peace, don't be afraid of anything."

"I don't understand you.... What have I to be afraid of tomorrow?" Ivan articulated in astonishment, and suddenly a chill breath of fear did in fact pass over his soul. Smerdyakov measured him with his eyes.

"You don't understand?" he drawled reproachfully. "It's a strange thing a clever man should care to play such a farce!"

Ivan looked at him speechless. The startling, incredibly supercilious tone of this man who had once been his lackey was extraordinary in itself. He had not taken such a tone even at their last interview.

"I tell you, you've nothing to be afraid of. I won't say anything about you, there's no proof against you. I say, how your hands are trembling. Why are your fingers moving like that? Go home, *you* did not murder him."

Ivan started. He remembered Alyosha.

"I know it was not I," he faltered.

"Do you?" Smerdyakov caught him up again.

Ivan jumped up and seized him by the shoulder.

"Tell me everything, you viper! Tell me everything!"

Smerdyakov was not in the least scared. He only riveted his eyes on Ivan with insane hatred.

"Well, it was you who murdered him, if that's it," he whispered furiously.

Ivan sank back on his chair, as though pondering something. He laughed malignantly.

"You mean my going away. What you talked about last time?"

"You stood before me last time and understood it all, and you understand it now."

"All I understand is that you are mad."

"Aren't you tired of it? Here we are face to face; what's the use of going on keeping up a farce to each other? Are you still trying to throw it all on me, to my face? *You* murdered him; you are the real murderer, I was only your instrument, your faithful servant Licharda,[7] and it was following your words I did it."

"*Did* it? Why, did you murder him?" Ivan turned cold.

Something seemed to give way in his brain, and he shuddered all over with a cold shiver. Then Smerdyakov himself looked at him wonderingly; probably the genuineness of Ivan's horror struck him.

"You don't mean to say you really did not know?" he faltered mistrustfully, looking with a forced smile into his eyes. Ivan still gazed at him, and seemed unable to speak.

> Ach, Vanka's gone to Petersburg,
> I won't wait till he comes back,

suddenly echoed in his head.

7. See note 1, p. 249.

"Do you know, I am afraid that you are a dream, a phantom sitting before me," he muttered.

"There's no phantom here, but only us two and one other. No doubt he is here, that third, between us."

"Who is he? Who is here? What third person?" Ivan Fyodorovich cried in alarm, looking about him, his eyes hastily searching in every corner.

"That third is God Himself, sir, Providence, sir. He is the third beside us now. Only don't look for him, you won't find him."

"It's a lie that you killed him!" Ivan shouted madly. "You are mad, or teasing me again!"

Smerdyakov, as before, watched him curiously, with no sign of fear. He could still scarcely get over his incredulity; he still fancied that Ivan "knew everything" and was trying to "throw it all on him to his face."

"Wait a minute, sir," he said at last in a weak voice, and suddenly bringing up his left leg from under the table, he began turning up his trouser leg. He was wearing long white stockings and slippers. Slowly he took off his garter and fumbled to the bottom of his stocking. Ivan gazed at him, and suddenly shuddered in a paroxysm of terror.

"Madman!" he cried, and rapidly jumping up, he drew back, so that he knocked his back against the wall and stood up against it, stiff and straight. He looked with insane terror at Smerdyakov, who, entirely unaffected by his terror, continued fumbling in his stocking, as though he were making an effort to get hold of something with his fingers and pull it out. At last he got hold of it and began pulling it out, Ivan Fyodorovich saw that it was a piece of paper, or perhaps a roll of papers. Smerdyakov pulled it out and laid it on the table.

"Here," he said quietly.

"What is it?" responded Ivan, trembling.

"Kindly look at it, sir," Smerdyakov answered, still in the same low tone.

Ivan stepped up to the table, took up the roll of paper and began unfolding it, but suddenly he drew back his fingers, as though from contact with a loathsome reptile.

"Your hands keep twitching, sir," observed Smerdyakov, and he deliberately unfolded the bundle himself. Under the wrapper were three packets of hundred-ruble bills.

"They are all here, sir, all the three thousand rubles; you need not count them. Take them," Smerdyakov suggested to Ivan, nodding at the notes. Ivan sank back in his chair. He was as white as a handkerchief.

"You frightened me . . . with your stocking," he said, with a strange grin.

"Can you really, can you really not have known till now?" Smerdyakov asked once more.

"No, I did not know. I kept thinking of Dmitri. Brother, brother! Ach!" He suddenly clutched his head in both hands. "Listen. Did you kill him alone? With my brother's help or without my brother?"

"It was only with you, with your help, sir, I killed him, and Dmitri Fyodorovich is quite innocent."

"All right, all right. Talk about me later. Why do I keep on trembling? I can't speak properly."

"You were bold enough then, sir. You said 'everything was lawful,' and how frightened you are now," Smerdyakov muttered in surprise. "Won't you have some lemonade? I'll ask for some at once. It's very refreshing, sir. Only I must hide this first."

And again he motioned at the bills. He was just going to get up and call at the door to Marya Kondratyevna to make some lemonade and bring it them, but, looking for something to cover up the notes that she might not see them, he first took out his handkerchief, and as it turned out again to be very dirty and used, took up the big yellow book that Ivan had noticed at first lying on the table, and put it over the money. The book was *The Sayings of the Holy Father Isaac the Syrian*. Ivan read it mechanically.

"I won't have any lemonade," he said. "Talk of me later. Sit down and tell me how you did it. Tell me all about it."

"You'd better take off your greatcoat, sir, or you'll be too hot."

Ivan Fyodorovich, as though he'd only just thought of it, flung off his overcoat, and, without getting up from his chair, threw it on the bench.

"Speak, please, speak."

He seemed calmer. He waited, feeling sure that Smerdyakov would tell him *all* about it.

"How it was done?" sighed Smerdyakov. "It was done in a most natural way, following your very words, sir."

"Of my words later," Ivan broke in again, apparently with complete self-possession, firmly uttering his words, and not shouting as before. "Only tell me in detail how you did it. Everything, as it happened. Don't forget anything. The details, above everything, the details, I beg you."

"You'd gone away, then I fell into the cellar, sir."

"In a fit or in a sham one?"

"A sham one, naturally, sir. I shammed it all. I went quietly down the steps to the very bottom and lay down quietly, sir, and as I lay down I gave a scream, and thrashed about, till they carried me out."

"Wait! And were you shamming all along, afterwards, and in the hospital?"

"No, not at all, sir. Next day, in the morning, before they took me to the hospital, I had a real attack and a more violent one than I've had for years. For two days I was totally unconscious."

"All right, all right. Go on."

"They laid me on the bed. I knew I'd be on the other side of the partition, for whenever I was ill, Martha Ignatyevna used to put me there, near them. She's always been very kind to me from my birth up, sir. At night I moaned, but quietly, sir. I kept expecting Dmitri Fyodorovich to come."

"Expecting him? To come to you?"

"Not to me. I expected him to come into the house, for I'd no doubt that he'd come that night, for being without me and getting no news, he'd be sure to come and climb over the fence, as he used to, and do something."

"And if he hadn't come?"

"Then nothing would have happened, sir. I would never have brought myself to it without him."

"All right, all right ... speak more intelligibly, don't hurry; above all, don't leave anything out!"

"I expected him to kill Fyodor Pavlovich, sir. I thought that was certain, for I had prepared him for it ... during the last few days. . . . He knew about the knocks, that was the chief thing. With his suspiciousness and the fury which had been growing in him all those days, he was bound to get into the house by means of those taps. That was inevitable, so I was expecting him, sir."

"Wait," Ivan interrupted, "if he had killed him, he would have taken the money and carried it away; you must have considered that. What would you have got by it afterwards? I don't see."

"But he would never have found the money, sir. That was only what I told him, that the money was under the mattress. But that wasn't true. It had been lying in a box. And afterwards I suggested to Fyodor Pavlovich, as I was the only person he trusted, to hide the envelope with the money in the corner behind the icons, for no one would have guessed that place, especially if they came in a hurry. So that's where the envelope lay, in the corner behind the icons. It would have been absurd to keep it under the mattress; the box, anyway, could be locked. But all believe it was under the mattress. A stupid thing to believe, sir. So if Dmitri Fyodorovich had committed the murder, finding nothing, he would either have run away in a hurry, afraid of every sound, as always happens with murderers, or he would have been arrested, sir. So I could always have clambered up to the icons and have taken away the money next morning or even that night, and it would have all been put down to Dmitri Fyodorovich. I could reckon upon that."

"But what if he did not kill him, but only knocked him down?"

"If he did not kill him, of course, I would not have ventured to take the money, and nothing would have happened. But I calculated that he would beat him senseless, and I would have time to take it then, and then I'd make out to Fyodor Pavlovich that it was no one but Dmitri Fyodorovich who had taken the money after beating him."

"Wait . . . I am getting mixed up. Then it was Dmitri after all who killed him, you only took the money?"

"No, he didn't kill him. Well, I might as well have told you now that he was the murderer. . . . But I don't want to lie to you now, because . . . because if you really haven't understood till now, as I see for myself, and are not pretending, so as to throw your guilt on me to my very face, you are still responsible for it all, since you knew of the murder, sir, and charged me to do it, sir, and went away knowing all about it. And so I want to prove to your face this evening that you are the only real murderer in the whole affair, and sir, and I am not the real murderer, though I did kill him. You are the rightful murderer."

"Why, why, am I the murderer? Oh, God!" Ivan cried, unable to restrain himself at last, and forgetting that he had put off discussing himself till the end of the conversation. "You still mean the Chermashnya? Wait, tell me, why did you want my consent, if you really took Chermashnya for consent? How will you explain that now?"

"Assured of your consent, I would have known that you wouldn't make an outcry over those three thousand being lost, even if I'd been suspected, instead of Dmitri Fyodorovich, or as his accomplice; on the contrary, you would have protected me from others. . . . And when you got your inheritance you would have rewarded me when you were able, all the rest of your life. For you'd have received your inheritance through me, sir, seeing that if he had married Agrafena Alexandrovna, you wouldn't have had a cent."

"Ah! Then you intended to torment me all my life afterwards," snarled Ivan. "And what if I hadn't gone away then, but had informed against you?"

"What could you have informed? That I persuaded you to go to Chermashnya? That's all nonsense, sir. Besides, after our conversation you would either have gone away or have stayed. If you had stayed, nothing would have happened. I would have known that you didn't want it done, and would have attempted nothing. Since you went away, it meant you assured me that you wouldn't dare to inform against me at the trial, and that you'd overlook my having the three thousand. And, indeed, you couldn't have prosecuted me afterwards, because then I would have told it all in the court; that is, not that I had stolen the money or killed him—I would not have said that—but that you'd put me up to the theft and the murder, though I didn't consent to it. That's why I needed your consent, so that you couldn't have cornered me afterwards, sir, for what proof could you have had? I could always have cornered you, revealing your eagerness for your father's death, and I tell you the public would have believed it all, and you would have been ashamed for the rest of your life."

"Was I so eager then, was I?" Ivan snarled again.

"To be sure you were, and by your consent you silently sanctioned my doing it." Smerdyakov looked resolutely at Ivan. He was very weak and spoke slowly and wearily, but some hidden inner force urged him on. He evidently had some design. Ivan felt that.

"Go on," he said. "Tell me what happened that night."

"What more is there to tell, sir! I lay there and I thought I heard the master shout. And before that Grigory Vasilyevich had suddenly got up and came out, and he suddenly gave a scream, and then all was silence and darkness. I lay there waiting, my heart beating; I couldn't bear it. I got up at last, sir, went out. I saw the window open on the left into the garden, and I stepped to the left to listen whether he was sitting there alive, and I heard the master moving about, sighing, so I knew he was alive, sir. Ech! I thought. I went to the window and shouted to the master, 'It's I.' And he shouted to me, 'He's been here, he's been here; he's run away.' He meant Dmitri Fyodorovich had been there. 'He's killed Grigory!' 'Where?' I whispered. 'There, in the corner,' he pointed. He was whispering, too. 'Wait a bit,' I said. I went to the corner of the garden to look, and there I came upon Grigory Vasilyevich lying by the wall, covered with blood, senseless. So it's true that Dmitri Fyodorovich has been here, was the thought that came into my head, and I determined on the spot to make an end of it, as Grigory Vasilyevich, even if he were alive, would see nothing of it, as he lay there senseless. The only risk was that Martha Ignatyevna might wake up. I felt that at the moment, but the longing to get it done came over me, till I could scarcely breathe. I went back to the window to the master and said, 'She's here, she's come; Agrafena Alexandrovna has come, wants to be let in.' And he started like a baby. 'Where is she?' he fairly gasped, but couldn't believe it. 'She's standing there,' said I, 'open.' He looked out of the window at me, half believing and half distrustful, but afraid to open. 'Why he is afraid of me now,' I thought. And it was funny. I thought of knocking on the window frame those taps we'd agreed upon as a signal that Grushenka had come, in his presence, before his eyes. He didn't seem to believe my words, but as soon as he heard the taps, he ran at once to open the door. He opened it. I would have gone in, but he stood in the way to prevent me passing. 'Where is she? Where is she?' He looked at me, all of a tremble. Well, thought I, if he's so frightened of me as all that, it's a bad lookout! And my legs went weak with fright that he wouldn't let me in or would call out, or Martha Ignatyevna would run up, or something else might happen. I don't remember now, but I must have stood pale, facing him. I whispered to him, 'Why, she's there, there, under the big window, how is it you don't see her?' I said. 'Bring her then, bring her.' 'She's afraid,' said I, 'she was frightened at the noise, she's hidden in the bushes; go and call to her yourself from the study.' He ran to the window, put the candle in the window. 'Grushenka,' he cried, 'Grushenka, are you here?' Though he cried that, he didn't want to lean out of the window, he didn't want to move away from me, for he was panic-stricken; he was so frightened he didn't dare to turn his back on me. 'Why, here she is,' said I. I went up to the window and leaned right out of it. 'Here she is, she's in the bush, laughing at you, don't you see her?' He suddenly believed it; he was all of a shake—he was awfully crazy about her—and he leaned right out of the window. I snatched up that iron paperweight from his table; do you remember, weighing about three pounds. I swung it and hit him on the top of the skull with the corner of it. He didn't even cry out. He only sank down suddenly, and I hit him again and a third time. And the third time I knew I'd broken his skull. He suddenly rolled on his back, face upwards, covered with blood. I looked round. There was no blood on me, not a spot. I wiped the paperweight, put it back, went up to the icons, took the money out of the envelope, and flung the envelope on the floor and the pink ribbon beside it. I went out into the garden all of a tremble, straight to the apple tree with a hollow in it—you know that hollow. I'd marked it long before and put a rag and a piece of paper ready in it. I wrapped all the notes in the rag and stuffed it deep down in the hole. And there it stayed for over two weeks. I took it out later, when I came out of the hospital. I went back to my bed, lay down and thought, 'If Grigory Vasilyevich has been killed outright, it may be a bad job for me, but if he is not killed and recovers, it will be first rate, for then he'll bear witness that Dmitri Fyodorovich had been here, and so he must have killed him and taken the money.' Then I began groaning with suspense and impatience, so as to wake Martha Ignatyevna as soon as possible. At last she got up, and she rushed to me, but when she saw Grigory Vasilyevich was not there, she ran out, and I heard her scream in the garden. And that set it all going and set my mind at rest."

He stopped. Ivan had listened all the time in dead silence without stirring or taking his eyes off him. As he told his story Smerdyakov glanced at him from time to time, but for the most part kept his eyes averted. When he had finished he was evidently agitated and was breathing hard. Perspiration stood out on his face. But it was impossible to tell whether it was remorse he was feeling, or what.

"Wait," cried Ivan, pondering. "What about the door? If he only opened the door to you, how could Grigory have seen it open before? For Grigory saw it before you went."

It was remarkable that Ivan spoke quite amicably, in a different tone, not angry as before, so if anyone had opened the door at that moment and peeped in at them, he would certainly have concluded that they were talking peaceably about some ordinary, though interesting, subject.

"As for that door and Grigory Vasilyevich's having seen it open, that's only his fancy," said Smerdyakov, with a wry smile. "He is not a man, I assure you, but an obstinate mule. He didn't see it, but fancied he had seen it, and there's no shaking him. It's just our luck he took that notion into his head, for they can't fail to convict Dmitri Fyodorovich after that."

"Listen . . ." said Ivan Fyodorovich, beginning to seem bewildered again and making an effort to grasp something. "Listen. There are a lot of questions I want to ask you, but I forget them . . . I keep forgetting and getting mixed up. Yes! Tell me this at least, why did you open the envelope and leave it there on the floor? Why didn't you simply carry off the envelope? . . . While you were telling me, I thought you spoke about it as though it were the right thing to do . . . but why, I can't understand . . ."

"I did that for a good reason, sir. For if a man had known all about it, as I did for instance, if he'd seen that money before, and perhaps had put them in that envelope himself, and had seen the envelope sealed up and addressed, with his own eyes, if such a man had done the murder, what would have made him tear open the envelope afterwards, especially in such desperate haste, since he'd know for certain the money must be in the envelope? No, if the robber had been someone like me, he'd simply have put the envelope straight in his pocket and got away with it as fast as he could, sir. But it'd be quite different with Dmitri Fyodorovich. He only knew about the envelope by hearsay; he had never seen it, and if he'd found it, for instance, under the mattress, he'd have torn it open as quickly as possible to make sure the money was in it. And he'd have thrown the envelope down, without having time to think that it would be evidence against him. Because he was not an habitual thief, sir, and had never directly stolen anything before, for he is a gentleman born, sir, and if he did bring himself to steal, it would not be regular stealing, but simply taking what was his own, for he'd told the whole town he meant to before, and had even bragged aloud before everyone that he'd go and take his property from Fyodor Pavlovich. I didn't say that openly to the prosecutor when I was being examined, but quite the contrary, I brought him to it by a hint, as though I didn't see it myself, and as though he'd thought of it himself and I hadn't prompted him; so that Mr. Prosecutor's mouth positively watered at my suggestion, sir."

"But can you possibly have thought of all that on the spot?"

cried Ivan Fyodorovich, overcome with astonishment. He looked at Smerdyakov again with alarm.

"Mercy on us! Could anyone think of it all in such a desperate hurry? It was all thought out beforehand."

"Well . . . well, it was the devil who helped you!" Ivan Fyodorovich cried again. "No, you are not a fool, you are far cleverer than I thought . . ."

He got up, obviously intending to walk across the room. He was in terrible distress. But as the table blocked his way, and there was hardly room to pass between the table and the wall, he only turned round where he stood and sat down again. Perhaps the impossibility of moving irritated him, as he suddenly cried out almost as furiously as before.

"Listen, you miserable, contemptible creature! Don't you understand that if I haven't killed you, it's simply because I am keeping you to answer tomorrow at the trial. God sees," Ivan raised his hand, "perhaps I, too, was guilty; perhaps I really had a secret desire for my father's . . . death, but I swear I was not as guilty as you think, and perhaps I didn't urge you on at all. No, no, I didn't urge you on! But no matter, I will give evidence against myself tomorrow, at the trial. I'm determined to! I shall tell everything, everything. But we'll make our appearance together. And whatever you may say against me at the trial, whatever evidence you give, I'll face it, I am not afraid of you. I'll confirm it all myself! But you must confess, too! You must, you must, we'll go together. That's how it shall be!"

Ivan said this solemnly and resolutely, and from his flashing eyes alone it could be seen that it would be so.

"You are ill, sir, I see, you are quite ill, sir. Your eyes are yellow," Smerdyakov commented, without the least irony, with apparent sympathy in fact.

"We'll go together," Ivan repeated. "And if you won't go, no matter, I'll go alone."

Smerdyakov paused as though pondering.

"There'll be nothing of the sort, sir, and you won't go, sir," he concluded at last positively.

"You don't understand me," Ivan exclaimed reproachfully.

"You'll be too much ashamed, sir, if you confess it all. And, what's more, it will be no use at all, for I shall say straight out that I never said anything of the sort to you, and that you are either ill (and it looks like it, too), or that you're so sorry for your brother that you are sacrificing yourself to save him and have invented it all against me, for you've always thought no more of me than if I'd been a fly. And who will believe you, and what single proof have you got?"

"Listen, you showed me that money just now to convince me."

Smerdyakov lifted the book off the bills and laid it on one side.

"Take the money away with you," Smerdyakov sighed.

"Of course I shall take it. But why do you give it to me, if you committed the murder for the sake of it?" Ivan looked at him with great surprise.

"I don't want it, sir," Smerdyakov articulated in a shaking voice, with a gesture of refusal. "I did have an idea of beginning a new life with that money in Moscow or, better still, abroad. I did dream of it, chiefly because 'all things are lawful.' That was quite right what you taught me, for you talked a lot to me about that. For if there's no everlasting God, there's no such thing as virtue, and there's no need of it. You were right there. So that's how I looked at it."

"Did you come to that by yourself?" asked Ivan, with a wry smile.

"With your guidance, sir."

"And now, I suppose, you believe in God, since you are giving back the money?"

"No, sir, I don't believe," whispered Smerdyakov.

"Then why are you giving it back?"

"Stop . . . that's enough!" Smerdyakov waved his hand again. "You used to say yourself that everything was lawful, so now why are you so upset, too? You even want to go and give evidence against yourself. . . . Only there'll be nothing of the sort! You won't go to give evidence," Smerdyakov decided with conviction.

"You'll see," said Ivan.

"It isn't possible. You are very clever, sir. You are fond of money, I know that, sir. You like to be respected, too, for you're very proud; you are far too fond of female charms, too, and you care most of all about living in undisturbed comfort, without having to bow to anyone—that's what you care most about. You won't want to spoil your life forever by taking such a disgrace on yourself. You are like Fyodor Pavlovich, sir, you are more like him sir, more like him than any of his children; you've the same soul as he had."

"You are not a fool," said Ivan, seeming struck. The blood rushed to his face. "I used to think you were a fool. You are serious now!" he observed, looking suddenly at Smerdyakov with a different expression.

"It was your pride made you think I was a fool. Take the money."

Ivan took the three rolls of bills and put them in his pocket without wrapping them in anything.

"I shall show them at the court tomorrow," he said.

"Nobody will believe you, as you've plenty of money of your own now; you may simply have taken it out of your cashbox and brought it to the court."

Ivan rose from his seat.

"I repeat," he said, "the only reason I haven't killed you is that I need you for tomorrow, remember that, don't forget it!"

"Well, kill me. Kill me now, sir," Smerdyakov said, all at once looking strangely at Ivan. "You won't dare do that even!" he added, with a bitter smile. "You won't dare to do anything, you, sir, who used to be so bold!"

"Till tomorrow," cried Ivan, and moved to go out.

"Wait a moment. . . . Show them to me again."

Ivan took out the bills and showed them to him. Smerdyakov looked at them for ten seconds.

"Well, you can go," he said, with a wave of his hand. "Ivan Fyodorovich!" he called after him again.

"What do you want?" Ivan turned without stopping.

"Goodbye, sir!"

"Till tomorrow!" Ivan cried again, and he walked out of the cottage.

The snowstorm was still raging. He walked the first few steps boldly, but suddenly began staggering. "It's something physical," he thought with a grin. Something like joy was springing up in his heart. He was conscious of unbounded resolution; he would make an end of the wavering that had so tortured him of late. His mind was made up, "and now it will not be changed," he thought with relief. At that moment he stumbled against something and almost fell down; stopping short, he made out at his feet the peasant he had knocked down, still lying senseless and motionless. The snow had almost covered his face. Ivan seized him and lifted him in his arms. Seeing a light in the little house to the right he went up, knocked at the shutters, and asked the man to whom the house belonged to help him carry the peasant to the police station, promising him three rubles. The man got ready and came out. I won't describe in detail how Ivan Fyodorovich succeeded in his object, bringing the peasant to the police station and arranging for a doctor to see him at once, providing with a liberal hand for the expenses. I will only say that this business took a whole hour, but Ivan Fyodorovich was well content with it. His mind wandered and worked incessantly.

"If I had not taken my decision so firmly for tomorrow," he reflected with satisfaction, "I would not have stayed a whole hour to look after the peasant, but would have passed by, without caring about his being frozen. I am quite capable of watching myself, by the way," he thought at the same instant, with still greater satisfaction, "although they have decided that I am going out of my mind!"

Just as he reached his own house he stopped short, asking himself suddenly whether he hadn't better go at once now to the prosecutor and tell him everything. He decided the question by turning back to the house. "Everything together tomorrow!" he whispered to himself, and, strange to say, almost all his gladness and self-satisfaction passed in one instant.

As he entered his own room he felt something like a touch of ice on his heart, like a recollection or, more exactly, a reminder, of something agonizing and revolting that was in that room now, at that moment, and had been there before. He sank wearily on his sofa. The old woman brought him a samovar; he made tea, but did not touch it. He dismissed the woman for the night. He sat on the sofa and felt giddy. He felt that he was ill and helpless. He was beginning to drop asleep, but got up uneasily and walked across the room to shake off his drowsiness. At moments he fancied he was delirious, but it was not illness that he thought of most. Sitting down again, he began looking round, as though searching for something. This happened several times. At last his eyes were fastened intently on one point. Ivan smiled, but an angry flush suffused his face. He sat a long time in his place, his head propped on both arms, though he looked sideways at the same point, at the sofa that stood against the opposite wall. There was evidently something, some object, that irritated him there, worried him and tormented him.

Chapter IX

The Devil. Ivan Fyodorovich's Nightmare

I am not a doctor, but yet I feel that the moment has come when I must inevitably give the reader some account of the nature of Ivan Fyodorovich's illness. Anticipating events I can say at least one thing: he was at that moment on the very eve of an attack of brain fever. Though his health had long been affected, it had offered a stubborn resistance to the fever which in the end gained complete mastery over it. Though I know nothing of medicine, I venture to hazard the suggestion that he really had perhaps, by a terrible effort of will, succeeded in delaying the attack for a time, hoping, of course, to check it completely. He knew that he was unwell, but he loathed the thought of being ill at that fatal time, at the approaching crisis in his life, when he needed to have all his wits about him, to say what he had to say boldly and resolutely and "to justify himself to himself."

He had, however, consulted the new doctor, who had been brought from Moscow by a fantastic notion of Katerina Ivanovna's to which I have referred already. After listening to him and examining him the doctor came to the conclusion that he was actually suffering from some disorder of the brain, and was not at all surprised by an admission which Ivan had reluctantly made him.

602 • *The Brothers Karamazov*

"Hallucinations are quite likely in your condition," the doctor opined, "though it would be better to verify them . . . you must take steps at once, without a moment's delay, or things will go badly with you." But Ivan Fyodorovich did not follow this judicious advice and did not take to his bed to be nursed. "I am walking about, so I am strong enough, if I drop, it'll be different then, anyone may nurse me who likes," he decided, dismissing the subject.

And so he was sitting almost conscious himself of his delirium and, as I have said already, looking persistently at some object on the sofa against the opposite wall. Someone appeared to be sitting there, though goodness knows how he had come in, for he had not been in the room when Ivan Fyodorovich came into it, on his return from Smerdyakov. This was a person or, more accurately speaking, a Russian gentleman of a particular kind, no longer young, *qui frisait la cinquantaine*,[8] as the French say, with rather long, still thick, dark hair, slightly streaked with gray, and a small pointed beard. He was wearing a brownish reefer jacket, rather shabby, evidently made by a good tailor though, and of a fashion at least three years old, that had been discarded by smart and well-to-do people for the last two years. His linen and his long scarflike necktie were all such as are worn by people who aim at being stylish, but on closer inspection his linen was not too clean and his wide scarf was very threadbare. The visitor's checked trousers were of excellent cut, but were too light in color and too tight for the present fashion. His soft fluffy white hat was out of keeping with the season. In brief there was every appearance of gentility on straitened means. It looked as though the gentleman belonged to that class of idle landowners who used to flourish in the times of serfdom. He had unmistakably been, at some time, in good and fashionable society, had once had good connections, had possibly preserved them indeed, but, after a gay youth, becoming gradually impoverished on the abolition of serfdom, he had sunk into the position of a toady, a sponger of the best class, wandering from one good old friend to another and received by them for his companionable and accommodating disposition and as being, after all, a gentleman who could be asked to sit down with anyone, though, of course, not in a place of honor. Such gentlemen of accommodating temper and dependent position, who can tell a story, take a hand at cards, and who have a distinct aversion for any duties that may be forced upon them, are usually solitary creatures, either bachelors or widowers. Sometimes they have children, but if so, the children are always brought up at a distance, at some aunt's, to whom these gentlemen never allude in good society, seeming

8. "Approaching fifty."

ashamed of the relationship. They gradually lose sight of their children altogether, though at intervals they receive a birthday or Christmas letter from them and sometimes even answer it. The countenance of the unexpected visitor was not so much good-natured as accommodating and ready to assume any amiable expression as occasion might arise. He had no watch, but he had a tortoise shell lorgnette on a black ribbon. On the middle finger of his right hand was a massive gold ring with a cheap opal stone in it. Ivan Fyodorovich was angrily silent and would not begin the conversation. The visitor waited and sat exactly like a poor relation who had come down from his room to keep his host company at tea, and was discreetly silent, seeing that his host was frowning and preoccupied. But he was ready for any affable conversation as soon as his host should begin it. All at once his face expressed a sudden solicitude.

"I say," he began to Ivan Fyodorovich, "excuse me, I only mention it to remind you. You went to Smerdyakov's to find out about Katerina Ivanovna, but you came away without finding out anything about her, you probably forgot . . ."

"Ah, yes," broke from Ivan and his face grew gloomy with uneasiness. "Yes, I'd forgotten . . . but it doesn't matter now, never mind, till tomorrow," he muttered to himself, "and you," he added, addressing his visitor irritably, "I would have remembered that myself in a minute, for that was just what was tormenting me! Why do you interfere, as if I would believe that you prompted me, and that I didn't remember it on my own?"

"Don't believe it then," said the gentleman, smiling amicably, "what's the good of believing against your will? Besides, proofs are no help to believing, especially material proofs. Thomas believed, not because he saw Christ risen, but because he wanted to believe, before he saw. Look at the spiritualists, for instance. . . . I am very fond of them . . . only fancy, they imagine that they serve the cause of religion, because the devils show them their horns from the other world. That, they say, is a material proof, so to speak, of the existence of another world. The other world and material proofs, what next! And if you come to that, does proving there's a devil prove that there's a God? I want to join an idealist society, I'll lead the opposition in it, I'll say I am a realist, but not a materialist, he-he!"

"Listen." Ivan Fyodorovich suddenly got up from the table. "I seem to be delirious . . . I am delirious, in fact, talk any nonsense you like, I don't care! You won't drive me to fury, as you did last time. But I feel somehow ashamed . . . I want to walk about the room . . . I sometimes don't see you and don't even hear your voice as I did last time, but I always guess what you are prating, for it's I, *I myself speaking, not you.* Only I don't know whether I was dreaming last time or whether I really saw you. I'll wet a towel and put it on my head and perhaps you'll vanish into air."

Ivan Fyodorovich went into the corner, took a towel, and did as he said, and with a wet towel on his head began walking up and down the room.

"I am so glad you treat me so familiarly," the visitor began.

"Fool," laughed Ivan, "do you suppose I should stand on ceremony with you? I am in good spirits now, though I have a pain in my forehead . . . and in the top of my head . . . only please don't talk philosophy, as you did last time. If you can't take yourself off, talk of something amusing. Talk gossip, you are a sponger, you ought to talk gossip. What a nightmare to have! But I am not afraid of you. I'll get the better of you. I won't be taken to a madhouse!"

"*C'est charmant*,[9] sponger. Yes, I am in my natural shape. For what am I on earth but a sponger? By the way, I listen to you and am rather surprised to find you are actually beginning to take me for something real, not simply your fancy, as you persisted in declaring last time . . ."

"Never for one minute have I taken you for reality," Ivan cried with a sort of fury. "You are a lie, you are my illness, you are a phantom. It's only that I don't know how to destroy you and I see I must suffer for a time. You are my hallucination. You are the incarnation of myself, but only of one side of me . . . of my thoughts and feelings, but only the nastiest and stupidest of them. From that point of view you might be of interest to me, if only I had time to waste on you . . ."

"Excuse me, excuse me, I'll catch you. When you flew out at Alyosha under the lamp post this evening and shouted to him. 'You learned it from *him*! How do you know that *he* visits me?' You were thinking of me then. So for one brief moment you did believe that I really exist," the gentleman laughed blandly.

"Yes, that was a moment of weakness . . . but I couldn't believe in you. I don't know whether I was asleep or awake last time. Perhaps I was only dreaming then and didn't see you really at all . . ."

"And why were you so surly with Alyosha just now? He is a dear; I've treated him badly over Father Zosima."

"Don't talk of Alyosha! How dare you, you lackey!" Ivan laughed again.

"You scold me, but you laugh—that's a good sign. But you are ever so much more polite than you were last time and I know why: that great resolution of yours . . ."

"Don't speak of my resolution," cried Ivan, savagely.

9. "That's delightful."

"I understand, I understand, *c'est noble, c'est charmant*, you are
going to defend your brother and to sacrifice yourself . . . *C'est
chevaleresque.*"[1]

"Hold your tongue, I'll kick you!"

"I won't be altogether sorry, for then my object will be attained.
If you kick me, you must believe in my reality, for people don't
kick ghosts. Joking apart, it doesn't matter to me, scold if you like,
though it's better to be a trifle more polite even to me. 'Fool,
lackey!' My, what words!"

"Scolding you, I scold myself," Ivan laughed again, "You are
myself, myself, only with a different mug. You just say what I am
thinking . . . and are incapable of saying anything new!"

"If I am like you in my way of thinking, it's all to my credit," the
gentleman declared, with delicacy and dignity.

"You choose out only my worst thoughts, and what's more, the
stupid ones. You are stupid and vulgar. You are awfully stupid.
No, I can't put up with you! What am I to do, what am I to do!"
Ivan said through his clenched teeth.

"My dear friend, above all things I want to behave like a gentleman and to be recognized as such," the visitor began in an access of
deprecating and simple-hearted pride, typical of a sponger. "I
am poor, but . . . I won't say very honest, but . . . it's an axiom
generally accepted in society that I am a fallen angel. I certainly
can't conceive how I can ever have been an angel. If I ever was, it
must have been so long ago that there's no harm in forgetting it.
Now I only prize the reputation of being a gentlemanly person and
live as I can, trying to make myself agreeable. I love men genuinely, oh! I've been greatly calumniated! Here when I stay with
you from time to time, my life gains a kind of reality and that's
what I like most of all. You see, like you, I suffer from the fantastic
and so I love the realism of earth. Here, with you, everything is
circumscribed, here all is formulated and geometrical, while we
have nothing but indeterminate equations! I wander about here
dreaming. I like dreaming. Besides, on earth I become superstitious.
Please don't laugh, that's just what I like, to become superstitious. I
adopt all your habits here: I've grown fond of going to the public
baths, would you believe it? and I go and steam myself with merchants and priests. What I dream of is becoming incarnate once for
all and irrevocably in the form of some merchant's wife weighing
two hundred fifty pounds, and of believing all she believes. My
ideal is to go to church and offer a candle in simple-hearted faith,
upon my word it is. Then there would be an end to my sufferings. I
like being doctored too; in the spring there was an outbreak of
smallpox and I went and got vaccinated in a foundling hospital—if

---

1. "That's noble, that's delightful," "that's chivalrous."

only you knew how I enjoyed myself that day. I subscribed ten rubles to the cause of the Slavs! . . . But you are not listening. Do you know, you are not at all well this evening? I know you went yesterday to that doctor . . . well, what about your health? What did the doctor say?"

"Fool!" Ivan snapped out.

"But you are clever, anyway. You are scolding again? I didn't ask out of sympathy. You needn't answer. Now rheumatism has come in again . . ."

"Fool!" repeated Ivan.

"You keep saying the same thing; but I had such an attack of rheumatism last year that I remember it to this day."

"The devil have rheumatism!"

"Why not, if I sometimes put on fleshly form? I put on fleshly form and I take the consequences. Satan *sum et nihil humanum a me alienum puto.*"[2]

"What, what? Satan *sum et nihil humanum* . . . that's not bad for the devil!"

"I am glad I've pleased you at last."

"But you didn't get that from me," Ivan stopped suddenly, seeming struck. "That never entered my head, that's strange."

"*C'est du nouveau, n'est-ce pas?*[3] This time I'll act honestly and explain it to you. Listen, in dreams and especially in nightmares, from indigestion or anything, a man sometimes sees such artistic visions, such complex and real actuality, such events, even a whole world of events, woven into such a plot, with such unexpected details from the most exalted matters to the last button on a cuff, as I swear Leo Tolstoy could not create.[4] Yet such dreams are sometimes seen not by writers, but by the most ordinary people, officials, journalists, priests. . . . The subject is a complete enigma. A statesman confessed to me, indeed, that all his best ideas came to him when he was asleep. Well, that's how it is now, though I am your hallucination, yet just as in a nightmare, I say original things which had not entered your head before. So I don't repeat your ideas, yet I am only your nightmare, nothing more."

"You are lying, your aim is to convince me you exist apart and are not my nightmare, and now you are asserting you are a dream."

"My dear fellow, I've adopted a special method today, I'll explain it to you afterwards. Wait, where did I break off? Oh, yes! I caught cold then, only not here but yonder."

"Where is yonder? Tell me, will you be here long? Can't you go away?" Ivan exclaimed almost in despair. He ceased walking to and fro, sat down on the sofa, leaned his elbows on the table again and

---

2. "I am the devil and nothing human is foreign to me." The original quotation from Terence is "Homo sum . . ." ("I am a man . . .").

3. "That's something new, isn't it?"

4. Author of *War and Peace, Anna Karenina,* and so forth.

held his head tight in both hands. He pulled the wet towel off and flung it away in vexation. It was evidently of no use.

"Your nerves are out of order," observed the gentleman, with a carelessly easy, though perfectly polite, air. "You are angry with me even for being able to catch cold, though it happened in a most natural way. I was hurrying then to a diplomatic soirée at the house of a lady of high rank in Petersburg, who was aiming at influence in the Ministry. Well, an evening suit, white tie, gloves, though I was God knows where and had to fly through space to reach your earth. . . . Of course, it took only an instant, but you know a ray of light from the sun takes fully eight minutes, and fancy in an evening suit and open waistcoat. Spirits don't freeze, but when one's in fleshy form, well . . . in brief, I didn't think, and set off, and you know in those ethereal spaces, in the water that is above the firmament, there's such a frost . . . that is, what frost, at least one can't call it frost, you can fancy, 150° below zero! You know the game the village girls play—they invite the unwary to lick an ax at thirty degrees below zero, the tongue instantly freezes to it and the dupe tears the skin off, so the tongue bleeds. But that's only in 30°, in 150° I imagine it would be enough to put your finger on the ax and it would be the end of it . . . if only there could be an ax there."

"And can there be an ax there?" Ivan Fyodorovich interrupted, carelessly and disdainfully. He was exerting himself to the utmost not to believe in the delusion and not to sink into complete insanity.

"An ax?" the guest interrupted in surprise.

"Yes, what would become of an ax there?" Ivan Fyodorovich cried suddenly, with a sort of savage and insistent obstinacy.

"What would become of an ax in space? *Quelle idée!*[5] If it were to fall to any distance, it would begin, I think, flying round the earth without knowing why, like a satellite. The astronomers would calculate the rising and the setting of the ax, *Gatzuk*[6] would put it in his calendar, that's all."

"You are stupid, awfully stupid," said Ivan peevishly. "Fib more cleverly or I won't listen. You want to get the better of me by realism, to convince me that you exist, but I don't want to believe you exist! I won't believe it!"

"But I am not fibbing, it's all the truth; the truth is unhappily hardly ever amusing. I see you persist in expecting something big of me, and perhaps something fine. That's a great pity, for I only give what I can . . ."

"Don't talk philosophy, you ass!"

"Philosophy, indeed, when all my right side is numb and I am

5. "What an idea!"
6. An almanac published in Moscow, 1876–1890.

moaning and groaning. I've tried all the medical faculty: they can diagnose beautifully, they have the whole of your disease at their fingertips, but they've no idea how to cure you. There was an enthusiastic little student here, 'You may die,' said he, 'but you'll know perfectly what disease you are dying of!' And then what a way they have of sending people to specialists. 'We only diagnose,' they say, 'but go to such-and-such a specialist, he'll cure you.' The old doctor who used to cure all sorts of disease has completely disappeared, I assure you, now there are only specialists and they all advertise in the newspapers. If anything is wrong with your nose, they send you to Paris: there, they say, is a European specialist who cures noses. If you go to Paris, he'll look at your nose; I can only cure your right nostril, he'll tell you, for I don't cure the left nostril, that's not my specialty, but go to Vienna, there there's a specialist who will cure your left nostril. What are you to do? I fell back on popular remedies, a German doctor advised me to rub myself with honey and salt in the bathhouse. Solely to get an extra bath I went, smeared myself all over and it did me no good at all. In despair I wrote to Count Mattei in Milan. He sent me a book and some drops, bless him, and, only fancy, Hoff's malt extract cured me! I bought it by accident, drank a bottle and a half of it, and I was ready to dance, it took it away completely. I made up my mind to write to the papers to thank him, I was prompted by a feeling of gratitude, and only fancy, it led to no end of a bother: not a single paper would take my letter. 'It would be very reactionary,' they said, 'no one will believe it. *Le diable n'existe point.*[7] You'd better remain anonymous,' they advised me. What use is a letter of thanks if it's anonymous? I laughed with the men at the newspaper office. 'It's reactionary to believe in God in our days,' I said, 'but I am the devil, so I may be believed in.' 'We quite understand that,' they said. 'Who doesn't believe in the devil? Yet it won't do, it might injure our reputation. As a joke, if you like.' But I thought as a joke it wouldn't be very witty. So it wasn't printed. And do you know, I have felt sore about it to this day. My best feelings, gratitude, for instance, are literally denied me simply from my social position."

"Philosophical reflections again?" Ivan snarled malignantly.

"God preserve me from it, but one can't help complaining sometimes. I am a slandered man. You upbraid me every moment with being stupid. One can see you are young. My dear fellow, intelligence isn't the only thing! I have naturally a kind and merry heart. 'I also write vaudevilles of all sorts.'[8] You seem to take me for Khlestakov grown old, but my fate is a far more serious one. Before time was, by some decree which I could never make out, I

7. "The devil doesn't exist at all." *The Government Inspector* (1835).
8. Said by Khlestakov in Gogol's comedy

was predestined 'to deny' and yet I am genuinely good-hearted and not at all inclined to negation. 'No, you must go and deny, without denial there's no criticism and what would a journal be without a column of criticism?' Without criticism it would be nothing but one 'hosannah.' But nothing but hosannah is not enough for life, the hosannah must be tried in the crucible of doubt and so on, in the same style. But I don't meddle in that, I didn't create it, I am not answerable for it. Well, they've chosen their scapegoat, they've made me write the column of criticism and so life was made possible. We understand that comedy; I, for instance, simply and directly demand that I be annihilated. No, live, I am told, for there'd be nothing without you. If everything in the universe were sensible, nothing would happen. There would be no events without you, and there must be events. So against the grain I serve to produce events and do what's irrational because I am commanded to. For all their indisputable intelligence, men take this farce as something serious, and that is their tragedy. They suffer, of course . . . but then they live, they live a real life, not a fantastic one, for suffering is life. Without suffering what would be the pleasure of it? It would be transformed into an endless church service; it would be holy, but tedious. But what about me? I suffer, but still, I don't live. I am x in an indeterminate equation. I am a sort of phantom in life who has lost all beginning and end, and who has even forgotten his own name. You are laughing—no, you are not laughing, you are angry again. You are forever angry, all you care about is intelligence, but I repeat again that I would give away all this super-stellar life, all the ranks and honors, simply to be transformed into the soul of a merchant's wife weighing two hundred fifty pounds and set candles at God's shrine."

"Then even you don't believe in God?" said Ivan, with a smile of hatred.

"What can I say—that is, if you are in earnest . . ."

"Is there a God or not?" Ivan cried with the same savage intensity.

"Ah, then you are in earnest! My dear fellow, upon my word I don't know. There! I've said it now!"

"You don't know, but you see God? No, you are not some one apart, you are *myself*, you are *I* and nothing more! You are rubbish, you are my fancy!"

"Well, if you like, I have the same philosophy as you, that would be true. *Je pense, donc je suis*,[9] I know that for a fact, all the rest, all these worlds, God and even Satan—all that is not proved, to my mind. Does all that exist of itself, or is it only an emanation of myself, a logical development of my ego which alone has existed

---

9. "I think, therefore I am," Descartes' famous aphorism.

forever: but I make haste to stop, for I believe you will be jumping up to beat me directly."

"You'd better tell me some anecdote!" said Ivan miserably.

"There is an anecdote precisely on our subject, or rather a legend, not an anecdote. You reproach me with unbelief, you see, you say, yet you don't believe. But, my dear fellow, I am not the only one like that. We are all in a muddle over there now and all through your science. Once there used to be atoms, five senses, four elements, and then everything hung together somehow. There were atoms in the ancient world even, but since we've learned that you've discovered the chemical molecule and protoplasm and the devil knows what, we had to tuck in our tails. There's a regular muddle, and, above all, superstition, scandal; there's as much scandal among us as among you, you know; a little more in fact, and denunciations, indeed, for we have a certain department where particular 'information' is received. Well, this wild legend belongs to our middle ages—not yours, but ours—and no one believes it even among us, except the old ladies of two hundred fifty pounds, not your old ladies I mean, but ours. We have everything you have, I am revealing one of our secrets out of friendship for you; though it's forbidden. This legend is about Paradise. There was, they say, here on earth a thinker and philosopher. He rejected everything, 'laws, conscience, faith,'[1] and, above all, the future life. He died; he expected to go straight to darkness and death and he found a future life before him. He was astounded and indignant. 'This contradicts my principles!' he said. And he was punished for that . . . that is, you must excuse me, I am just repeating what I heard myself, it's only a legend . . . he was sentenced to walk a quadrillion kilometers in the dark (we've adopted the metric system, you know) and when he has finished that quadrillion, the gates of heaven would be opened to him and he'll be forgiven . . ."

"And what tortures have you in the other world besides the quadrillion kilometers?" asked Ivan, with a strange eagerness.

"What tortures? Ah, don't ask. In old days we had all sorts, but now they have taken chiefly to moral punishments—'the stings of conscience' and all that nonsense. We got that, too, from you, from the 'mellowing of your manners.'[2] And who's the better for it? Only those who have got no conscience, for how can they be tortured by conscience when they have none? But decent people who have conscience and a sense of honor suffer for it. Reforms, when the ground has not been prepared for them, especially if they are institutions copied from abroad, do nothing but mischief! The ancient fire was better. Well, this man, who was condemned to the

<hr />

1. Famusov's line from Griboedov's comedy *Woe from Wit* (1823).
2. Dostoevsky is polemicizing against Shchedrin's *Unfinished Conversations*, Chapter III—1875.

quadrillion kilometers, stood still, looked round and lay down across the road. 'I won't go, I refuse on principle!' Take the soul of an enlightened Russian atheist and mix it with the soul of the prophet Jonah, who sulked for three days and nights in the belly of the whale, and you get the character of that thinker who lay across the road."

"What did he lie on there?"

"Well, I suppose there was something to lie on. You are not laughing?"

"Bravo!" cried Ivan, still with the same strange eagerness. Now he was listening with an unexpected curiosity. "Well, is he lying there now?"

"That's the point, that he isn't. He lay there almost a thousand years and then he got up and went on."

"What an ass!" cried Ivan, laughing nervously and still seeming to be pondering something intently. "Does it make any difference whether he lies there forever or walks the quadrillion kilometers? It would take a billion years to walk it?"

"Much more than that, I haven't got a pencil and paper or I could work it out. But he got there long ago and that's where the story begins."

"What, he got there? But how did he get the billion years to do it?"

"Why, you keep thinking of our present earth! But our present earth may have been repeated a billion times. Why, it's become extinct, been frozen; cracked, broken to bits, disintegrated into its elements, again 'the water above the firmament,' then again a comet, again a sun, again from the sun it becomes earth—and the same sequence may have been repeated endlessly and exactly the same to every detail, most unseemly and insufferably tedious . . ."

"Well, well, what happened when he arrived?"

"Why, the moment the gates of Paradise were open and he walked in, before he had been there two seconds, by the clock, (though to my thinking his watch must have long dissolved into its elements on the way), he cried out that those two seconds were worth walking not a quadrillion kilometers but a quadrillion of quadrillions, raised to the quadrillionth power! In fact, he sang 'hosannah' and overdid it so, that some persons there of lofty ideas wouldn't shake hands with him at first—he'd become too rapidly reactionary, they said. The Russian temperament. I repeat, it's a legend. I give it for what it's worth. So that's the sort of ideas we have on such subjects even now."

"I've caught you!" Ivan cried, with an almost childish delight, as though he had succeeded in remembering something at last. "That anecdote about the quadrillion years, I made up myself! I was seventeen then, I was in high school. I made up that anecdote and told it to a schoolfellow called Korovkin, it was at Moscow. . . . The anecdote is so characteristic that I couldn't have taken it from anywhere. I thought I'd forgotten it . . . but I've unconsciously recalled it—I recalled it myself—it was not you telling it! Thousands of things are unconsciously remembered like that even when people are being taken to be executed . . . it's come back to me in a dream. You are that dream! You are a dream, not a living creature!"

"From the vehemence with which you deny my existence," laughed the gentleman, "I am convinced that you believe in me."

"Not in the slightest! I haven't a hundredth part of a grain of faith in you!"

"But you have the thousandth of a grain. Homeopathic doses perhaps are the strongest. Confess that you have faith even to the ten-thousandth of a grain."

"Not for one minute," cried Ivan furiously. "But I should like to believe in you," he added strangely.

"Aha! There's an admission! But I am good-natured. I'll come to your assistance again. Listen, it was I who caught you, not you me. I told you your anecdote you'd forgotten, on purpose, so as to destroy your faith in me completely."

"You are lying. The object of your visit is to convince me of your existence!"

"Just so. But hesitation, suspense, conflict between belief and disbelief—is sometimes such torture to a conscientious man, such as you are, that it's better to hang oneself at once. Knowing that you are inclined to believe in me, I administered some disbelief by telling you that anecdote. I lead you to belief and disbelief by turns, and I have my motive in it. It's the new method, sir. As soon as you disbelieve in me completely, you'll begin assuring me to my face that I am not a dream but a reality. I know you. Then I shall have attained my object, which is an honorable one. I shall sow in you only a tiny grain of faith and it will grow into an oak tree—and such an oak tree that, sitting on it, you will long to enter the ranks of 'the hermit monks and chaste women,'[3] for that is what you are secretly longing for. You'll dine on locusts, you'll wander into the wilderness to save your soul!"

"Then it's for the salvation of my soul you are working, is it, you scoundrel?"

"One must do a good deed sometimes. How ill-humored you are!"

"Fool! did you ever tempt those holy men who ate locusts and prayed seventeen years in the wilderness till they were overgrown with moss?"

"My dear fellow, I've done nothing else. One forgets the whole

3. From a poem by Pushkin.

world and all the worlds, and sticks to one such saint, because he is
a very precious diamond. One such soul, you know, is sometimes
worth a whole constellation. We have our arithmetic, you know.
The conquest is precious! And some of them, on my word, are not
inferior to you in culture, though you won't believe it. They can
contemplate such depths of belief and disbelief at the same moment
that sometimes it really seems that they are within a hairsbreadth of
being 'turned upside down,' as the actor Gorbunov says."

"Well, did you fail, did you get your nose pulled?"

"My dear fellow," observed the visitor sententiously, "it's better
to get off with your nose pulled than without a nose at all, as an
afflicted marquis observed not long ago (he must have been treated
by a specialist) in confession to his spiritual father—a Jesuit. I was
present, it was simply charming. 'Give me back my nose!' he said,
and he beat his breast. 'My son,' said the priest evasively, 'all
things are accomplished in accordance with the inscrutable decrees
of Providence, and what seems a misfortune sometimes leads to
extraordinary, though unapparent, benefits. If stern destiny has
deprived you of your nose, it's to your advantage that no one can
ever pull you by your nose. 'Holy father, that's no comfort,' cried
the despairing marquis. 'I'd be delighted to have my nose pulled
every day of my life, if it were only in its proper place.' 'My son,'
sighs the priest, 'you can't expect every blessing at once. This is
murmuring against Providence, who even in this has not forgotten
you, for if you repine as you repined just now, declaring you'd be
glad to have your nose pulled for the rest of your life, your desire
has already been fulfilled indirectly, for ·when you lost your nose,
you were led by the nose."

"Foo, how stupid!" cried Ivan.

"My dear friend, I only wanted to amuse you. But I swear that's
the genuine Jesuit casuistry and I swear that it all happened word
for word as I've told you. It happened lately and gave me a great
deal of trouble. The unhappy young man shot himself that very
night when he got home. I was by his side till the very last moment.
Those Jesuit confessionals are really my most delightful diversion
at melancholy moments. Here's another incident that happened
only the other day. A little blonde Norman girl of twenty—a
buxom, unsophisticated beauty that would make your mouth water
—comes to an old priest. She bends down and whispers her sin into
the grating. 'Why, my daughter, have you fallen again already?'
cries the priest. 'O Sancta Maria, what do I hear! Not the same
man this time, how long will this go on? Aren't you ashamed!' 'Ah,
mon père,' answers the sinner with tears of penitence, 'ça lui fait
tant de plaisir, et à moi si peu de peine!'[4] Fancy, such an answer! I
drew back. It was the cry of nature, better than innocence itself, if

4. "Ah, Father, it gives him so much pleasure and me so little trouble!"

you like. I absolved her sin on the spot and was turning to go, but I was forced to turn back. I heard the priest at the grating making an appointment with her for the evening—though he was an old man hard as flint, he fell in an instant! It was nature, the truth of nature asserted its rights! What, you are turning up your nose again? Angry again? I don't know how to please you . . ."

"Leave me alone, you are beating on my brain like a haunting nightmare," Ivan moaned miserably, helpless before his apparition. "I am bored with you, agonizingly and insufferably. I would give anything to be able to shake you off!"

"I repeat, moderate your expectations, don't demand of me 'everything great and noble' and you'll see how well we shall get on," said the gentleman impressively. "You are really angry with me for not having appeared to you in a red glow, with thunder and lightning, with scorched wings, but have shown myself in such a modest form. You are wounded, in the first place, in your aesthetic feelings, and, secondly, in your pride. How could such a vulgar devil visit such a great man as you! Yes, there is that romantic strain in you, that was so derided even by Belinsky. I can't help it, young man, as I got ready to come to you I did think as a joke of appearing in the figure of a retired general who had served in the Caucasus, with a star of the Lion and the Sun on my coat. But I was positively afraid of doing it, for you'd have thrashed me for daring to pin the Lion and the Sun on my coat, instead of, at least, the Polar Star or Sirius. And you keep on saying I am stupid, but, mercy on us! I make no claim to be equal to you in intelligence. Mephistopheles declared to Faust that he desired evil, but did only good. Well, he can say what he likes, it's quite the opposite with me. I am perhaps the one man in all creation who loves the truth and genuinely desires good. I was there when the Word, Who died on the cross, rose up into Heaven bearing on His bosom the soul of the penitent thief. I heard the joyful shrieks of the cherubim singing and screaming hosannah and the thunderous howl of the seraphim which shook heaven and all creation, and I swear to you by all that's sacred, I longed to join the choir and shout hosannah with them all. The word had almost escaped me, had almost broken from my lips . . . you know how susceptible and aesthetically impressionable I am. But common sense—oh, a most unhappy trait in my character—kept me in due bounds and I let the moment pass! For what would have happened, I reflected, what would have happened after my hosannah? Everything on earth would have been extinguished at once and no events could have occurred. And so, solely from a sense of duty and my social position, I was forced to suppress the good moment and to stick to my nasty task. Somebody takes all the credit of what's good for himself, and nothing but nastiness is left for me. But I don't envy the honor of a life of idle imposture, I am not ambitious. Why am I, of all creatures in the world, doomed to be cursed by all decent people and even to be kicked, for if I put on mortal form I am bound to take such consequences sometimes? I know, of course, there's a secret in it, but they won't tell me the secret for anything, for then perhaps, seeing the meaning of it, I might bawl hosannah, and the indispensable minus would disappear at once, and good sense would reign supreme throughout the whole world. And that, of course, would mean the end of everything, even of magazines and newspapers, for who would subscribe to them? I know that at the end of all things I shall be reconciled. I, too, shall walk my quadrillion and learn the secret. But till that happens I am sulking and fulfill my destiny though it's against the grain—that is, to ruin thousands for the sake of saving one. How many souls have had to be ruined and how many honorable reputations destroyed for the sake of that one righteous man, Job, over whom they made such a fool of me in old days. Yes, till the secret is revealed, there are two sorts of truth for me—one, their truth, yonder, which I know nothing about so far and the other my own. And there's no knowing which will turn out the better. . . . Are you asleep?"

"I might well be," Ivan groaned angrily. "All my stupid ideas—outgrown, thrashed out long ago, and flung aside like a dead carcass—you present to me as something new!"

"There's no pleasing you! And I thought I would fascinate you by my literary style. That hosannah in the skies really wasn't bad, was it? And then that ironical tone à la Heine,[5] eh?"

"No, I was never such a lackey! How then could my soul beget a lackey like you?"

"My dear fellow, I know a most charming and attractive young Russian gentleman, a young thinker and a great lover of literature and art, the author of a promising poem entitled 'The Grand Inquisitor.' I was only thinking of him!"

"I forbid you to speak of 'The Grand Inquisitor,'" cried Ivan, crimson with shame.

"And the 'Geological Cataclysm.' Do you remember? That was a poem, now!"

"Hold your tongue, or I'll kill you!"

"You'll kill me? No, excuse me, I will speak. I came to treat myself to that pleasure. Oh, I love the dreams of my ardent young friends, quivering with eagerness for life! 'There are new men,' you decided last spring, when you were meaning to come here, 'they propose to destroy everything and begin with cannibalism. Stupid fellows! they didn't ask my advice! I maintain that nothing need be destroyed, that we only need to destroy the idea of God in man, that's how we have to set to work. It's that, that we must begin with. Oh, blind race of men who have no understanding! As soon

---

5. H. Heine (1797–1856) was a German poet and essayist noted for his irony.

as men have all of them denied God—and I believe that period, analogous with geological periods, will come to pass—the old conception of the universe will fall of itself without cannibalism and what's more the old morality, and then everything will begin anew. Men will unite to take from life all it can give, but only for joy and happiness in the present world. Man will be lifted up with a spirit of divine Titanic pride and the man-god will appear. From hour to hour extending his conquest of nature infinitely by his will and his science, man will feel such lofty joy from hour to hour in doing it that it will make up for all his old dreams of the joys of heaven. Everyone will know that he is mortal and will accept death proudly and serenely like a God. His pride will teach him that it's useless for him to repine at life's being a moment, and he will love his brother without need of reward. Love will be sufficient only for a moment of life, but the very consciousness of its momentariness will intensify its fire, which now is dissipated in dreams of eternal love beyond the grave' . . . and so on and so on in the same style. Charming!"

Ivan sat with his eyes on the floor, and his hands pressed to his ears, but he began trembling all over. The voice continued.

"The question now is, my young thinker reflected, is it possible that such a period will ever come? If it does, everything is determined and humanity is settled forever. But as, owing to man's inveterate stupidity, this cannot come about for at least a thousand years, everyone who recognizes the truth even now may legitimately order his life as he pleases, on the new principles. In that sense, 'all things are lawful' for him. What's more, even if this period never comes to pass, since there is no God and no immortality anyway, the new man may well become the man-god, even if he is the only one in the whole world, and promoted to his new position, he may lightheartedly overstep all the barriers of the old morality of the old slave-man, if necessary. There is no law for God. Where God stands, the place is holy. Where I stand will be at once the foremost place . . . 'all things are lawful' and that's the end of it! That's all very charming; but if you want to swindle why do you want a moral sanction for doing it? But that's our modern Russian all over. He can't bring himself to swindle without a moral sanction. He is so in love with truth . . ."

The visitor talked, obviously carried away by his own eloquence, speaking louder and louder and looking ironically at his host. But he did not succeed in finishing; Ivan suddenly snatched a glass from the table and flung it at the orator.

"Ah, *mais c'est bête enfin*,"[6] cried the latter, jumping up from the sofa and shaking the drops of tea off himself. "He remembers

6. "Oh, but that's stupid, after all."

Luther's inkstand![7] He takes me for a dream and throws glasses at a dream! It's like a woman! I suspected you were only pretending to stop up your ears."

A loud, persistent knocking was suddenly heard at the window. Ivan Fyodorovich jumped up from the sofa.

"Do you hear? You'd better open," cried the visitor; "it's your brother Alyosha with the most interesting and surprising news, I'll be bound!"

"Be silent, deceiver, I knew it was Alyosha, I felt he was coming, and of course he has not come for nothing; of course he brings 'news,' " Ivan exclaimed frantically.

"Open, open to him. There's a snowstorm and he is your brother. *Monsieur sait-il le temps qu'il fait? C'est à pas mettre un chien dehors.*"[8]

The knocking continued. Ivan wanted to rush to the window, but something seemed to fetter his arms and legs. He strained every effort to break his chains, but in vain. The knocking at the window grew louder and louder. At last the chains were broken and Ivan Fyodorovich leapt up from the sofa. He looked round him wildly. Both candles had almost burned out, the glass he had just thrown at his visitor stood before him on the table, and there was no one on the sofa opposite. The knocking on the window frame went on persistently, but it was by no means so loud as it had seemed in his dream, on the contrary, it was quite subdued.

"It was not a dream! No, I swear it was not a dream, it all happened just now!" cried Ivan Fyodorovich. He rushed to the window and opened the movable pane.

"Alyosha, I told you not to come," he cried fiercely to his brother. "In two words, what do you want? In two words, do you hear?"

"An hour ago Smerdyakov hanged himself," Alyosha answered from the yard.

"Come round to the steps, I'll open at once," said Ivan, going to open the door to Alyosha.

Chapter X

"It Was He Who Said That"

Alyosha, coming in, told Ivan that a little over an hour ago Marya Kondratyevna had run to his rooms and informed him Smerdyakov had taken his own life. "I went in to clear away the

---

7. Luther hurled his inkstand at the devil who had come to tempt him. See Luther's "Dialogue with the Devil."

8. "Does the gentleman know what the weather is? You wouldn't put a dog out in it."

samovar and he was hanging on a nail in the wall." On Alyosha's inquiring whether she had informed the police, she answered that she had told no one, "but I flew straight to you, I've run all the way." She seemed perfectly crazy, Alyosha reported, and was shaking like a leaf. When Alyosha ran with her to the cottage, he found Smerdyakov still hanging. On the table lay a note: "I destroy my life of my own will and desire, not to blame anyone." Alyosha left the note on the table and went straight to the police captain and told him all about it. "And from him I've come straight to you," said Alyosha, in conclusion, looking intently into Ivan's face. He had not taken his eyes off him while he told his story, as though struck by something in his expression.

"Brother," he cried suddenly, "you must be terribly ill. You look and don't seem to understand what I tell you."

"It's a good thing you came," said Ivan, as though brooding, and not hearing Alyosha's exclamation. "I knew he had hanged himself."

"From whom?"

"I don't know. But I knew. Did I know? Yes, he told me. He told me so just now."

Ivan stood in the middle of the room, and still spoke in the same brooding tone, looking at the ground.

"Who is *he?*" asked Alyosha, involuntarily looking round.

"He's slipped away."

Ivan raised his head and smiled softly.

"He was afraid of you, of a dove like you. You are a 'pure cherub.' Dmitri calls you a cherub. Cherub! . . . the thunderous howl of the seraphim. What are seraphim? Perhaps a whole constellation. But perhaps that constellation is only a chemical molecule. There's a constellation of the Lion and the Sun. Don't you know it?"

"Brother, sit down," said Alyosha in alarm. "For goodness' sake, sit down on the sofa! You are delirious; put your head on the pillow, that's right. Would you like a wet towel on your head? Perhaps it will do you good."

"Give me the towel: it's here on the chair. I just threw it down there."

"It's not here. Don't worry yourself. I know where it is—here," said Alyosha, finding a clean towel folded up and unused, by Ivan's dressing table in the other corner of the room. Ivan looked strangely at the towel: recollection seemed to come back to him for an instant.

"Wait"—he got up from the sofa—"an hour ago I took that new towel from there and wetted it. I wrapped it round my head and threw it down here . . . How is it it's dry? There was no other."

"You put that towel on your head?" asked Alyosha.

"Yes, and walked up and down the room an hour ago . . . Why have the candles burned down so? What's the time?"

"Nearly twelve."

"No, no, no!" Ivan cried suddenly. "It was not a dream. He was here; he was sitting here, on that sofa. When you knocked at the window, I threw a glass at him . . . this one. Wait a minute. I was asleep last time, but this dream was not a dream. It has happened before. I have dreams now, Alyosha . . . yet they are not dreams, but reality. I walk about, talk and see . . . though I am asleep. But he was sitting here, on that sofa there. . . . He is frightfully stupid, Alyosha, frightfully stupid." Ivan laughed suddenly and began pacing about the room.

"Who is stupid? Of whom are you talking, brother?" Alyosha asked anxiously again.

"The devil! He's taken to visiting me. He's been here twice, almost three times. He taunted me with being angry at his being a simple devil and not Satan, with scorched wings, in thunder and lightning. But he is not Satan: that's a lie. He is an impostor. He is simply a devil—a paltry, trivial devil. He goes to the baths. If you undressed him, you'd be sure to find he had a tail, long and smooth like a Great Dane's, a yard long, dun color. . . . Alyosha, you are cold. You've been in the snow. Would you like some tea? What? Is it cold? Shall I tell her to bring some? *C'est à ne pas mettre un chien dehors . . .*"

Alyosha ran to the washing stand, wetted the towel, persuaded Ivan to sit down again, and put the wet towel round his head. He sat down beside him.

"What were you telling me earlier about Lisa?" Ivan began again. (He was becoming very talkative.) "I like Lisa. I said something nasty about her. It was a lie. I like her . . . I am afraid for Katya tomorrow. I am more afraid of her than of anything. On account of the future. She will cast me off tomorrow and trample me under foot. She thinks that I am ruining Mitya from jealousy on her account! Yes, she thinks that! But it's not so. Tomorrow the cross, but not the gallows. No, I won't hang myself. Do you know, I can never commit suicide, Alyosha. Is it because I am base? I am not a coward. Is it from love of life? How did I know that Smerdyakov had hanged himself? Yes, it was *he* told me so."

"And you are quite convinced that there has been someone here?" asked Alyosha.

"Yes, on that sofa in the corner. You would have driven him away. You did drive him away: he disappeared when you arrived. I love your face, Alyosha. Did you know that I loved your face? And *he* is myself, Alyosha. All that's base in me, all that's mean and contemptible. Yes, I am a romantic. He guessed it . . . though it's a libel. He is frightfully stupid; but it's to his advantage. He has cunning, animal cunning—he knew how to infuriate me. He kept taunting me with believing in him, and that was how he made me listen to him. He fooled me like a boy. He told me a great deal that was true about myself, though. I would never have owned it to myself. Do you know, Alyosha," Ivan added in an intensely earnest and confidential tone. "I should be awfully glad to think that it was *he* and not I."

"He has worn you out," said Alyosha, looking compassionately at his brother.

"He's been teasing me. And you know he does it so cleverly, so cleverly. 'Conscience! What is conscience? I make it up for myself. Why am I tormented by it? From habit. From the universal habit of mankind for seven thousand years. So let us give it up, and we shall be gods.' It was he who said that, it was he who said that!"

"And not you, not you?" Alyosha could not help shouting, looking frankly at his brother. "Never mind him, anyway; have done with him and forget him. And let him take with him all that you curse now, and never come back!"

"Yes, but he is spiteful. He laughed at me. He was impudent, Alyosha," Ivan said, with a shudder of offense. "But he was unfair to me, unfair to me about lots of things. He told lies about me to my face. 'Oh, you are going to perform an act of heroic virtue: to confess you murdered your father, that the lackey murdered him at your instigation.' "

"Brother," Alyosha interposed, "restrain yourself. It was not you who murdered him. It's not true!"

"That's what he says, he, and he knows it. 'You are going to perform an act of heroic virtue, and you don't believe in virtue; that's what tortures you and makes you angry, that's why you are so vindictive.' He said that to me about me and he knows what he says."

"It's you who say that, not he," exclaimed Alyosha mournfully, "and you say it because you are ill and delirious, tormenting yourself."

"No, he knows what he says. 'You are going out of pride,' he says. 'You'll stand up and say it was I who killed him, and why do you writhe with horror? You are lying! I despise your opinion, I despise your horror!' He said that about me. 'And do you know you are longing for their praise—"he is a criminal, a murderer, but what a generous soul; he wanted to save his brother and he confessed." ' That's a lie, Alyosha!" Ivan cried suddenly, with flashing eyes. "I don't want the low rabble to praise me, I swear I don't! That's a lie! That's why I threw the glass at him and it broke against his ugly face."

"Brother, calm yourself, stop!" Alyosha entreated him.

"Yes, he knows how to torment one. He's cruel," Ivan went on, unheeding. "I had an inkling from the first what he came for. 'Granting that you go through pride, still you had a hope that Smerdyakov might be convicted and sent to Siberia, and Mitya would be acquitted, while you would only be punished with *moral* condemnation' ('Do you hear?' he laughed then)—'and some people will praise you. But now Smerdyakov's dead, he has hanged himself, and who'll believe you alone? But yet you are going, you are going, you'll go all the same, you've decided to go. What are you going for now?' That's awful, Alyosha. I can't endure such questions. Who dare ask me such questions?"

"Brother," interposed Alyosha. His heart sank with terror, but he still seemed to hope to bring Ivan to reason, "how could he have told you of Smerdyakov's death before I came, when no one knew of it and there was no time for anyone to know of it?"

"He told me," said Ivan firmly, refusing to admit a doubt. "It was all he did talk about, if you come to that. 'And it would be all right if you believed in virtue,' he said. 'No matter if they disbelieve you, you are going for the sake of principle. But you are a little pig like Fyodor Pavlovich and what do you want with virtue? Why do you want to go meddling if your sacrifice is of no use to anyone? Because you don't know yourself why you go! Oh, you'd give a great deal to know yourself why you go! And can you have made up your mind? You've not made up your mind. You'll sit all night deliberating whether to go or not. But you will go; you know you'll go. You know that whichever way you decide, the decision does not depend on you. You'll go because you won't dare not to go. Why won't you dare? You must guess that for yourself. That's a riddle for you!' He got up and went away. You came and he went. He called me a coward, Alyosha! *Le mot de l'énigme*[9] is that I am a coward. 'It is not for such eagles to soar above the earth.' It was he who added that—he! And Smerdyakov said the same. He must be killed! Katya despises me. I've seen that for a month past. Even Lisa will begin to despise me! 'You are going in order to be praised.' That's a brutal lie! And you despise me too, Alyosha. Now I am going to hate you again! And I hate the monster, too! I hate the monster! I don't want to save the monster. Let him rot in Siberia! He's begun singing a hymn! Oh, tomorrow I'll go, stand before them, and spit in their faces!"

He jumped up in a frenzy, flung off the towel, and fell to pacing up and down the room again. Alyosha recalled what he had just said. "I seem to be sleeping awake. . . . I walk, I speak, I see, but I am asleep." It seemed to be just like that now. Alyosha did not leave him. The thought passed through his mind to run for a

9. "The answer to the riddle."

doctor, but he was afraid to leave his brother alone: there was no one to whom he could leave him. By degrees Ivan lost consciousness completely at last. He still went on talking, talking incessantly, but quite incoherently, and even articulated his words with difficulty. Suddenly he staggered violently; but Alyosha was in time to support him. Ivan let him lead him to his bed. Alyosha undressed him somehow and put him to bed. He sat watching over him for another two hours. The sick man slept soundly, without stirring, breathing softly and evenly. Alyosha took a pillow and lay down on the sofa, without undressing.

As he fell asleep he prayed for Mitya and Ivan. He began to understand Ivan's illness. "The anguish of a proud determination. A deep conscience!" God, in Whom he disbelieved, and His truth were gaining mastery over his heart, which still refused to submit. "Yes," the thought floated through Alyosha's head as it lay on the pillow, "yes, since Smerdyakov is dead, no one will believe Ivan's evidence; but he will go and give it." Alyosha smiled softly. "God will conquer!" he thought. "Either he will rise up in the light of truth, or . . . he'll perish in hate, revenging on himself and on everyone his having served the cause he does not believe in," Alyosha added bitterly, and again he prayed for Ivan.

Book Twelve

A MISCARRIAGE OF JUSTICE

Chapter I

The Fatal Day

At ten o'clock in the morning of the day following the events I have described, the trial of Dmitri Karamazov began in our district court.

I hasten to emphasize the fact that I am far from esteeming myself capable of reporting all that took place at the trial in full detail, or even in the actual order of events. I imagine that to mention everything and to explain it properly would fill a volume, even a very large one. And so I trust I may not be reproached for confining myself to what struck me personally, and what I especially remembered. I may have selected as of most interest what was of secondary importance, and may have omitted the most prominent and essential details. But I see I shall do better not to apologize. I will do my best and the reader will see for himself that I have done all I can.

And, to begin with, before entering the court, I will mention what surprised me most on that day. Indeed, as it appeared later, everyone was surprised at it, too. We all knew that the affair had aroused great interest, that everyone was burning with impatience for the trial to begin, that it had been a subject of talk, conjecture, exclamation and surmise for the last two months in local society. Everyone knew, too, that the case had become known throughout Russia, but yet we had not imagined that it had aroused such burning, such intense, interest in everyone, not only among ourselves, but all over Russia. This became evident at the trial this day. Visitors had arrived not only from the chief town of our province, but from several other Russian towns, as well as from Moscow and Petersburg. Among them were lawyers, ladies, and even several distinguished personages. Every ticket of admission had been snatched up. A special place behind the table at which the three judges sat was set apart for the most distinguished and important of the men visitors; a row of armchairs had been placed there—something exceptional, which had never been allowed before. A large proportion—not less than half of the public—were ladies, local and visiting. There was such a large number of lawyers from all parts that they did not know where to seat them, for every ticket had long since been eagerly sought, begged for, and distributed. I saw at the end of the room, behind the platform, a special partition hurriedly put up, behind which all these lawyers were admitted, and they thought themselves lucky to have standing room there, for all chairs had been removed for the sake of space, and the crowd behind the partition stood throughout the case closely packed, shoulder to shoulder.

Some of the ladies, especially those who came from a distance, made their appearance in the gallery very smartly dressed, but the majority of the ladies were oblivious even of dress. Their faces betrayed hysterical, intense, almost morbid, curiosity. A peculiar fact—established afterwards by many observations—was that almost all the ladies, or, at least the vast majority of them, were on Mitya's side and in favor of his being acquitted. This was perhaps chiefly owing to his reputation as a conqueror of female hearts. It was known that two women rivals were to appear in the case. One of them—Katerina Ivanovna—was an object of general interest. All sorts of extraordinary tales were told about her, amazing anecdotes of her passion for Mitya, in spite of his crime. Her pride and "aristocratic connections" were particularly insisted upon (she had called upon scarcely anyone in the town). People said she intended to petition the Government for leave to accompany the criminal to Siberia and to be married to him somewhere in the mines. The appearance of Grushenka in court was awaited with no less impatience, as Katerina Ivanovna's rival. The public was looking forward with anxious curiosity to the meeting of the two rivals—the proud aristocratic girl and "The hetaera." But Grushenka was a more familiar figure to the ladies of the district than Katerina Ivanovna. They had already seen "the woman who had ruined Fyodor Pavlovich and his unhappy son," and all, almost without exception, wondered how father and son could be so in love with "such a very common, ordinary Russian woman, who was not even pretty."

In brief, there was a great deal of talk. I know for a fact that there were several serious family quarrels on Mitya's account in our town. Many ladies quarreled violently with their husbands over differences of opinion about the dreadful case, and it was only natural that the husbands of these ladies, far from being favorably disposed to the prisoner, should enter the court bitterly prejudiced against him. In fact, one may say pretty certainly that the masculine, as distinguished from the feminine part of the audience were biased against the prisoner. There were numbers of severe, frowning, even vindictive, faces, and they were in the majority. Mitya, indeed, had managed to offend many people during his stay in the town. Some of the visitors were, of course, in excellent spirits and quite unconcerned as to the fate of Mitya personally. But all were interested in the trial, and the majority of the men were certainly hoping for the punishment of the criminal, except perhaps the lawyers, who were more interested in the legal than in the moral aspect of the case.

Everybody was excited at the presence of the celebrated lawyer, Fetyukovich. His talent was well known, and this was not the first time he had defended notorious criminal cases in the provinces. And if he defended them, such cases became celebrated and long remembered all over Russia. There were stories, too, about our prosecutor and about the President of the Court. It was said that Ippolit Kirillovich was in a tremor at meeting Fetyukovich, and that they had been enemies from the beginning of their careers in Petersburg, that though our sensitive prosecutor, who always considered that he had been aggrieved by someone in Petersburg because his talents had not been properly appreciated, was keenly excited over the Karamazov case, and was even dreaming of rebuilding his flagging fortunes by means of it; Fetyukovich, they said, was his one anxiety. But these rumors were not quite just. Our prosecutor was not one of those men who lose heart in the face of danger. On the contrary, his self-confidence increased with the increase of danger. It must be noted that our prosecutor was in general too hasty and morbidly impressionable. He would put his whole soul into some case and work at it as though his whole fate and his whole fortune depended on its result. This was the subject of some ridicule in the legal profession, for just by this characteristic our prosecutor had gained a wider notoriety than could have been expected from his modest position. People laughed particularly at his passion for psychology. In my opinion, they were wrong, and our prosecutor was, I believe, a man and a character of greater depths than was generally supposed. But with his delicate health he had failed to make his mark at the outset of his career and had never made up for it later.

As for the President of our Court, I can only say that he was a humane and cultured man, who had a practical knowledge of his work and progressive views. He was rather ambitious, but did not concern himself greatly about his future career. The great aim of his life was to be a man of advanced ideas. He was, too, a man of connections and property. He felt, as we learned afterwards, rather strongly about the Karamazov case, but from a social, not from a personal standpoint. He was interested in it as a social phenomenon, in its classification and its character as a product of our social conditions, as typical of the national character, and so on, and so on. His attitude to the personal aspect of the case, to its tragic significance and the persons involved in it, including the prisoner, was rather indifferent and abstract, as was perhaps fitting, indeed.

The court was packed and overflowing long before the judges made their appearance. Our court is the best hall in the town—spacious, lofty, and good for sound. On the right of the judges, who were on a raised platform, a table and two rows of chairs had been put ready for the jury. On the left was the place for the prisoner and the counsel for the defense. In the middle of the court, near the judges, was a table with the "material proofs." On it lay Fyodor Pavlovich's white silk dressing gown, stained with blood; the fatal brass pestle with which the supposed murder had been committed; Mitya's shirt, with a bloodstained sleeve; his coat, stained with blood in patches behind the pocket in which he had put his handkerchief; the handkerchief itself, stiff with blood and by now quite yellow; the pistol loaded by Mitya at Perkhotin's with a view to suicide, and taken from him on the sly at Mokroe by Trifon Borisovich; the envelope in which the three thousand rubles had been put ready for Grushenka, the narrow pink ribbon with which it had been tied, and many other articles I don't remember. In the body of the hall, at some distance, came the seats for the public. But in front of the balustrade a few chairs had been placed for witnesses who remained in the court after giving their evidence.

At ten o'clock the three judges arrived—the President, one honorary justice of the peace, and one other. The prosecutor, of course, entered immediately after. The President was a short, stout, thick-set man of fifty, with a dyspeptic complexion, dark hair turning gray and cut short, and a red ribbon, of what Order I don't remember. The prosecutor struck me and the others, too, as looking particularly pale, almost green. His face seemed to have grown suddenly thinner, perhaps in a single night, for I had seen him looking as usual only two days before. The President began by asking the court whether all the jury were present.

But I see I can't go on like this, partly because some things I did not hear, others I did not notice, and others I have forgotten, but most of all because, as I have said before, I have literally no time or space to mention everything that was said and done. I only know that neither side, that is, neither the prosecution nor the defense objected to very many of the jurymen. I remember the composition of the jury—four were petty officials of the town, two were merchants, and six peasants and artisans of the town. I remember, long before the trial, questions were continually asked with some surprise, especially by ladies, "Can such a delicate, complex and psychological case be submitted for decision to petty officials and even peasants?" And "What can an official, still more a peasant, understand in such an affair?" All the four officials in the jury were, in fact, men of no consequence and of low rank. Except one who was rather younger, they were gray-headed men, little known in society, who had vegetated on a pitiful salary, and who probably had elderly, unpresentable wives and crowds of children, perhaps even without shoes and stockings. At most, they spent their leisure over cards and, of course, had never read a single book. The two merchants looked respectable, but were strangely silent and stolid. One of them was close-shaven, and was dressed in European style; the other had a small, gray beard, and wore a red ribbon with some sort of a medal upon it around his neck. There is no need to speak of the artisans and the peasants. The artisans of Skotoprigonevsk are almost peasants, and even work on the land. Two of them also wore European dress, and perhaps for that reason, were dirtier and more uninviting looking than the others. So that one might well wonder, as I did as soon as I had looked at them, "what men like that could possibly make of such a case?" Yet their faces made a strangely imposing, almost menacing, impression; they were stern and frowning.

At last the President opened the case of the murder of the retired titular councilor, Fyodor Pavlovich Karamazov.[1] I don't quite remember how he described him. The bailiff was told to bring in the prisoner, and Mitya made his appearance. There was a hush through the court. One could have heard a fly. I don't know how it was with others, but Mitya made a most unfavorable impression on me. He looked terribly dandyish in a brand-new frock coat. I heard afterwards that he had ordered it in Moscow expressly for the occasion from his own tailor, who had his measurements. He wore immaculate black kid gloves and exquisite linen. He walked in with his yard-long strides, looking stiffly straight in front of him, and sat down in his place with a most unperturbed air. At the same moment the counsel for defense, the celebrated Fetyukovich, entered, and a sort of subdued hum passed through the court. He was a tall, spare man, with long thin legs, with extremely long, thin, pale fingers, clean-shaven face, straight brushed, rather short hair, and thin lips that were at times curved into something between a sneer and a smile. He looked about forty. His face would have been pleasant, if it had not been for his eyes, which, in themselves small and inexpressive, were set remarkably close together, with only the thin, long nose as a dividing line between them. In fact, there was something strikingly birdlike about his face. He was in evening dress and white tie.[2]

I remember the President's first questions to Mitya, about his name, his calling, and so on. Mitya answered sharply, and his voice was so unexpectedly loud that it made the President start and look at the prisoner with surprise. Then followed a list of persons who

---

1. A low rank in the civil service. It is the first indication that Fyodor Pavlovich had even a nominal position.

2. At the time, appropriate garb for a trial.

were to take part in the proceedings—that is, of the witnesses and experts. It was a long list. Four of the witnesses were not present— Miüsov, who had given evidence at the preliminary inquiry, but was now in Paris; Madame Khokhlakov and Maximov, who were absent through illness; and Smerdyakov, through his sudden death, of which an official statement from the police was presented. The news of Smerdyakov's death produced a sudden stir and whisper in the court. Many of the audience, of course, had not heard of the sudden suicide. What struck people most was Mitya's sudden outburst. As soon as the statement of Smerdyakov's death was made, he cried out aloud from his place:

"He was a dog and died like a dog!"

I remember how his counsel rushed to him, and how the President addressed him, threatening to take stern measures, if such outbursts were repeated. Mitya nodded and in a subdued voice repeated several times abruptly to his counsel, with no show of regret:

"I won't again, I won't. It escaped me. I won't do it again."

And, of course, this brief episode did him no good with the jury or the public. His character was displayed, and it spoke for itself. It was under the influence of this incident that the indictment was read.

It was rather short, but circumstantial. It only stated the chief reason why he had been arrested, why he must be tried, and so on. Yet it made a great impression on me. The clerk read it loudly and distinctly. The whole tragedy was suddenly unfolded before us, concentrated, in bold relief, in a fatal and pitiless light. I remember how immediately after it had been read, the President asked Mitya in a loud impressive voice:

"Defendant, how do you plead?"

Mitya suddenly rose from his seat.

"I plead guilty to drunkenness and dissipation," he exclaimed, again in a startling, almost frenzied, voice, "to idleness and debauchery. I meant to become an honest man for good, just at the moment when I was struck down by fate. But I am not guilty of the death of that old man, my enemy and my father. No, no, I am not guilty of robbing him! I could not be. Dmitri Karamazov is a scoundrel, but not a thief."

He sat down again, visibly trembling all over. The President again briefly but impressively admonished him to answer only what was asked, and not to go off into irrelevant exclamations. Then he ordered the case to proceed. All the witnesses were led up to take the oath. Then I saw them all together. The brothers of the prisoner were, however, allowed to give evidence without taking the oath. After an exhortation from the priest and the President, the witnesses were led away and were made to sit as far as possible apart from one another. Then they began calling them up one by one.

Chapter II

Dangerous Witnesses

I do not know whether the witnesses for the defense and for the prosecution were separated into groups by the President, and whether it was arranged to call them in a certain order. But no doubt it was so. I only know that the witnesses for the prosecution were called first. I repeat, I don't intend to describe all the questions step by step. Besides, my account would be to some extent superfluous, because in the speeches for the prosecution and for the defense the whole course of the evidence was brought together and set in a strong and significant light, and I took down parts of those two remarkable speeches in full, and will quote them in due course, together with one extraordinary and quite unexpected episode, which occurred before the final speeches, and undoubtedly influenced the sinister and fatal outcome of the trial. I will only observe that from the first moments of this "trial" one peculiar characteristic of the case was conspicuous and observed by all, that is, the overwhelming strength of the prosecution as compared with the arguments the defense had to rely upon. Everyone realized it from the first moment that the facts began to group themselves round a single point, and the whole horrible and bloody crime was gradually revealed. Everyone, perhaps, felt from the first that the case was beyond dispute, that there was no doubt about it, that there could be really no discussion, and that the defense was only a matter of form, and that the criminal was guilty, obviously and conclusively guilty. I imagine that even the ladies, who were so impatiently longing for the acquittal of the fascinating defendant, were at the same time, without exception, convinced of his guilt. What's more, I belive they would have been mortified if his guilt had not been so firmly established, as that would have lessened the effect of the closing scene of the criminal's acquittal. That he would be acquitted all the ladies, strange to say, were firmly persuaded up to the very last moment. "He is guilty, but he will be acquitted, from motives of humanity, in accordance with the new ideas, the new sentiments that had come into fashion," and so on, and so on. And that was why they had crowded into the court so impatiently. The men were more interested in the contest between the prosecutor and the famous Fetyukovich. All were wondering and asking themselves what could even a talent like Fetyukovich's make of such a desperate case; and so they followed his achievements, step by step, with concentrated attention.

But Fetyukovich remained an enigma to all up to the very end, up to his speech. Persons of experience suspected that he had some design, that he was working towards some object, but it was almost impossible to guess what it was. His confidence and self-reliance were unmistakable, however. Every one noticed with pleasure, moreover, that he, after so short a stay, not more than three days, perhaps, among us, had so wonderfully succeeded in mastering the case and "had studied it to a turn." People described with relish, afterwards, how cleverly he had "taken down" all the witnesses for the prosecution, and as far as possible perplexed them and, what's more, had aspersed their reputation and so depreciated the value of their evidence. But it was supposed that he did this rather by way of sport, so to speak, for professional glory, to show nothing had been omitted of the accepted trial methods, for all were convinced that he could do no real good by such disparagement of the witnesses, and probably was more aware of this than anyone, having some idea of his own in the background, some concealed weapon of defense, which he would suddenly reveal when the time came. But meanwhile, conscious of his strength, he seemed to be diverting himself.

So, for instance, when Grigory, Fyodor Pavlovich's old servant, who had given the most damning piece of evidence about the open door, was examined, the counsel for the defense positively fastened upon him when his turn came to question him. It must be noted that Grigory entered the hall with a composed and almost stately air, not the least disconcerted by the majesty of the court or the vast audience listening to him. He gave evidence with as much confidence as though he had been talking with his Martha, only perhaps more respectfully. It was impossible to make him contradict himself. The prosecutor questioned him first in detail about the family life of the Karamazovs. The family picture stood out in lurid colors. It was plain to ear and eye that the witness was guileless and impartial. In spite of his profound reverence for the memory of his deceased master, he yet bore witness that he had been unjust to Mitya and "hadn't brought up his children as he should. He'd have been devoured by lice when he was little, if it hadn't been for me," he added, describing Mitya's early childhood. "It wasn't fair either of the father to wrong his son over his mother's property, which was by right his."

In reply to the prosecutor's question what grounds he had for asserting that Fyodor Pavlovich had wronged his son in their money relations, Grigory, to the surprise of everyone, had no proof at all to bring forward, but he still persisted that the arrangement with the son was "unfair," and that he ought "to have paid him several thousand rubles more." I must note, by the way, that the prosecutor asked this question whether Fyodor Pavlovich had really kept back part of Mitya's inheritance with marked persistence of all the witnesses who could be asked it, not excepting Alyosha and Ivan, but he obtained no exact information from anyone; all alleged that it was so, but were unable to bring forward any distinct proof. Grigory's description of the scene at the dinner table, when Dmitri had burst in and beaten his father, threatening to come back to kill him, made a sinister impression on the court, especially as the old servant's composure in telling it, his parsimony of words and peculiar phraseology were as effective as eloquence. He observed that he was not angry with Mitya for having knocked him down and struck him on the face; he had forgiven him long ago, he said. Of the decreased Smerdyakov he observed, crossing himself, that he was a lad of ability, but stupid and afflicted, and, worse still, an infidel, and that it was Fyodor Pavlovich and his elder son who had taught him to be so. But he defended Smerdyakov's honesty almost with warmth, and related how Smerdyakov had once found the master's money in the yard, and, instead of concealing it, had taken it to his master, who had rewarded him with a "gold piece" for it, and trusted him implicitly from that time forward. He maintained obstinately that the door into the garden had been open. But he was asked so many questions that I can't recall them all.

At last the counsel for the defense began to cross-examine him, and the first question he asked was about the envelope in which Fyodor Pavlovich was supposed to have put three thousand rubles for "a certain person." "Have you ever seen it, you, who were for so many years in close attendance on your master?" Grigory answered that he had not seen it and had never heard of the money from anyone "till everybody was talking about it." This question about the envelope Fetyukovich put to everyone who could conceivably have known of it, as persistently as the prosecutor asked his question about Dmitri's inheritance, and got the same answer from all, that no one had seen the envelope, though many had heard of it. From the beginning everyone noticed Fetyukovich's persistence on this subject.

"Now, with your permission I'll ask you a question," Fetyukovich said, suddenly and unexpectedly. "Of what was that balsam, or, rather, decoction, made, which, as we learn from the preliminary inquiry, you used on that evening to rub your lumbago, in the hope of curing it?"

Grigory looked blankly at the questioner, and after a brief silence muttered "there was saffron in it."

"Nothing but saffron? Don't you remember any other ingredient?"

"There was milfoil in it, too."

"And pepper perhaps?" Fetyukovich queried.

"Yes, there was pepper, too."

"Et cetera. And all dissolved in vodka?"

"In pure alcohol."

There was a faint sound of laughter in the court.

"Well, well, in pure alcohol, even. After rubbing your back, I believe, you drank what was left in the bottle with a certain pious prayer, known only to your wife?"

"I did."

"Did you drink much? Roughly speaking, a wine glass or two?"

"It might have been a tumblerful."

"A tumblerful, even. Perhaps a tumbler and a half?"

Grigory did not answer. He seemed to see what was meant.

"A glass and a half of neat alcohol—is not at all bad, don't you think? You might see the gates of heaven open, not only the door into the garden?"

Grigory remained silent. There was another laugh in the court. The President made a movement.

"Do you know for a fact," Fetyukovich persisted, "whether you were awake or not when you saw the open door?"

"I was on my legs."

"That's not a proof that you were awake." (There was again laughter in the court.) "Could you have answered at that moment, if anyone had asked you a question—for instance, what year it is?"

"I don't know."

"And what year is it, Anno Domini, do you know?"

Grigory stood with a perplexed face, looking straight at his tormentor. Strange to say, it appeared he really did not know what year it was.

"But perhaps you can tell how many fingers you have on your hands?"

"I am a servant," Grigory said suddenly, in a loud and distinct voice. "If my betters think fit to make game of me, it is my duty to suffer it."

Fetyukovich was a little taken aback, and the President intervened, reminding him that he must ask more relevant questions. Fetyukovich bowed with dignity and said that he had no more questions to ask of the witness. The public and the jury, of course, were left with a grain of doubt in their minds as to the evidence of a man who might, while undergoing a certain cure, have seen "the gates of heaven," and who did not even know what year he was living in. But before Grigory left the box another episode occurred. The President, turning to the prisoner, asked him whether he had any comment to make on the evidence of the last witness.

"Except about the door, all he has said is true," cried Mitya, in a loud voice. "For combing the lice off me, I thank him; for forgiving my blows, I thank him. The old man has been honest all his life and as faithful to my father as seven hundred poodles."

"Prisoner, be careful in your language," the President admonished him.

"I am not a poodle," Grigory muttered.

"All right, it's I who am a poodle myself," cried Mitya. "If it's an insult, I take it to myself and I beg his pardon. I was a beast and cruel to him. I was cruel to Aesop,[3] too."

"What Aesop?" the President asked sternly again.

"Oh, Pierrot[4] . . . my father, Fyodor Pavlovich."

The President again and again warned Mitya impressively and very sternly to be more careful in his language.

"You are injuring yourself in the opinion of your judges."

The counsel for the defense was equally clever in dealing with the evidence of Rakitin. I may remark that Rakitin was one of the leading witnesses and one to whom the prosecutor attached great significance. It appeared that he knew everything; his knowledge was amazing, he had been everywhere, seen everything, talked to everybody, knew every detail of the biography of Fyodor Pavlovich and all the Karamazovs. Of the envelope, it is true, he had only heard from Mitya himself. But he described minutely Mitya's exploits in the Metropolis, all his compromising doings and sayings, and told the story of Captain Snegiryov's "wisp of tow." But even Rakitin could say nothing positive about Mitya's inheritance, and confined himself to contemptuous generalities. "Who could tell which of them was to blame, and who was in debt to the other, with their crazy Karamazov way of muddling things so that no one could make head or tail of it?" He attributed the tragic crime to the habits that had become ingrained by ages of serfdom and the distressed condition of Russia, due to the lack of appropriate institutions. He was, in fact, allowed some latitude of speech. This was the first occasion on which Rakitin showed what he could do, and he attracted notice. The prosecutor knew that the witness was preparing a magazine article on the case, and afterwards in his speech, as we shall see later, quoted some ideas from the article, showing that he had seen it already. The picture drawn by the witness was a gloomy and sinister one, and greatly strengthened the case for the prosecution. Altogether, Rakitin's discourse fascinated the public by its independence and the extraordinary nobility of his ideas. There were even two or three outbreaks of applause when he spoke of serfdom and the distressed condition of Russia. But Rakitin, in his youthful ardor, made a slight blunder, of which the counsel for the defense at once adroitly took advantage. Answering certain questions about Grushenka, and carried away by the loftiness of his own sentiments and his success, of which he was, of course, conscious, he went so far as to speak somewhat contemptuously of Agrafena Alexandrovna as "the kept mistress of Samsonov." He would have given a good deal to take back his words afterwards,

---

3. Author of the fables (sixth century B.C.).
4. The clown in traditional comedies.

for Fetyukovich tripped him up on it at once. And it was all because Rakitin had not reckoned on the lawyer having been able to become so intimately acquainted with every detail in so short a time.

"Allow me to ask," began the counsel for the defense, with the most affable and even respectful smile, "you are, of course, the same Mr. Rakitin whose pamphlet, *The Life of the Deceased Elder, Father Zosima,* published by the diocesan authorities, full of profound and religious reflections and preceded by an excellent and devout dedication to the Bishop, I have just read with such pleasure?"

"I did not write it for publication . . . it was published afterwards," muttered Rakitin, for some reason fearfully disconcerted and almost ashamed.

"Oh, that's excellent! A thinker like you can, and indeed ought to, take the widest view of every social question. Your most instructive pamphlet has been widely circulated through the patronage of the Bishop, and has been of appreciable service. . . . But this is the chief thing I would like to learn from you. You stated just now that you were very intimately acquainted with Miss Svetlov." (It must be noted that Grushenka's surname was "Svetlov." I heard it for the first time that day, during the case.)

"I cannot answer for all my acquaintances. . . . I am a young man . . . and who can answer for everyone he meets?" cried Rakitin, flushing all over.

"I understand, I quite understand," cried Fetyukovich, as though he, too, were embarrassed and in haste to excuse himself. "You, like any other, might well be interested in an acquaintance with a young and beautiful woman who would readily entertain the flower of local youth, but . . . I only wanted to know . . . it has come to my knowledge that Miss Svetlov was particularly anxious a couple of months ago to make the acquaintance of the younger Karamazov, Alexey Fyodorovich, and promised you twenty-five rubles, if you would bring him to her in his monastic dress. And that actually took place on the evening of the day on which the terrible crime, which is the subject of the present trial, was committed. You brought Alexey Karamazov to Miss Svetlov, and did you receive the twenty-five rubles from Miss Svetlov as a reward, that's what I wanted to hear from you?"

"It was a joke. . . . I don't see of what interest that can be to you. . . . I took it for a joke . . . meaning to give it back later . . ."

"Then you did take . . . But you have not given it back yet . . . or have you?"

"That's of no consequence," muttered Rakitin, "I refuse to answer such questions. . . . Of course I shall give it back."

The President intervened, but Fetyukovich declared·he had finished questioning Mr. Rakitin. Mr. Rakitin left the witness stand with something of a stain upon his character. The effect left by the lofty idealism of his speech was somewhat marred, and Fetyukovich's expression, as he watched him walk away, seemed to suggest to the public that "this is a specimen of the lofty-minded persons who accuse him." I remember that this incident, too, did not pass off without an outbreak from Mitya. Enraged by the tone in which Rakitin had referred to Grushenka, he suddenly shouted "Bernard!" When, after Rakitin's cross-examination, the President asked the prisoner if he had anything to say, Mitya cried loudly:

"Since I've been arrested, he has borrowed money from me! He is a contemptible Bernard and opportunist, and he doesn't believe in God; he took the Bishop in!"

Mitya, of course, was pulled up again for the intemperance of his language, but Rakitin was done for. Captain Snegiryov's evidence was a failure, too, but from quite a different reason. He appeared in ragged and dirty clothes, muddy boots, and in spite of the vigilance and expert observation of the police officers, he turned out to be hopelessly drunk. On being asked about Mitya's attack upon him, he refused to answer.

"God bless him. Ilyushechka told me not to. God will make it up to me yonder."

"Who told you not to tell? Of whom are you talking?"

"Ilyushechka, my little son. 'Daddy, daddy, how he insulted you!' He said that at the stone. Now he is dying . . ."

The captain suddenly began sobbing, and plumped down on his knees before the President. He was hurriedly led away amidst the laughter of the public. The effect prepared by the prosecutor did not come off at all.

Fetyukovich went on making the most of every opportunity, and amazed people more and more by his minute knowledge of the case. Thus, for example, Trifon Borisovich made a great impression, of course, very prejudicial to Mitya. He calculated almost on his fingers that on his first visit to Mokroe, Mitya must have spent three thousand rubles, "or very little less. Just think what he squandered on those gypsy girls alone! And as for our lousy peasants, it wasn't a case of flinging half a ruble in the street, he made them presents of twenty-five rubles each, at least, he didn't give them less. And what a lot of money was simply stolen from him! And if anyone did steal, he did not leave a receipt. How could one catch the thief when he was flinging his money away all the time? Our peasants are robbers, you know; they have no care for their souls. And the way he went on with the girls, our village girls! They're completely set up since then, I tell you, they used to be poor." He recalled, in fact, every item of expense and added it all up. So the theory that only fifteen hundred had been spent and the rest had been put aside in a little bag seemed inconceivable. "I saw three thousand as clear as a penny in his hands, I saw it with my own eyes; I should think I ought to know how to reckon money," cried Trifon Borisovich, doing his best to satisfy the "authorities." .

When Fetyukovich had to cross-examine him, he scarcely tried to refute his evidence, but began asking him about an incident at the first carousal at Mokroe, a month before the arrest, when Timothy and another peasant called Akim had picked up on the floor in the passage a hundred rubles dropped by Mitya when he was drunk, and had given them to Trifon Borisovich, and received a ruble each from him for doing so. "Well," asked the lawyer, "did you give that hundred rubles back to Mr. Karamazov?" Trifon Borisovich shuffled in vain. . . . He was obliged, after the peasants had been examined, to admit the finding of the hundred rubles, only adding that he had religiously returned it all to Dmitri Fyodorovich "in perfect honesty, and it's only because his honor was totally drunk, sir, at the time, he wouldn't remember it." But, as he had denied the incident of the hundred rubles till the peasants had been called to prove it, his evidence as to returning the money to Mitya, was naturally regarded with great suspicion. So one of the most dangerous witnesses brought forward by the prosecution was again discredited.

The same thing happened with the Poles. They took up an attitude of pride and independence; they vociferated loudly that they had both been in the service of the Crown, and that "Pan Mitya" had offered them three thousand "to buy their honor," and that they had seen a large sum of money in his hands. Pan Mussyalovich introduced a terrible number of Polish words into his sentences, and seeing that this only increased his consequence in the eyes of the President and the prosecutor, grew more and more pompous, and ended by speaking in Polish altogether. But Fetyukovich caught them, too, in his snares. Trifon Borisovich, recalled, was forced, in spite of his evasion, to admit that Pan Vrublevsky had substituted another pack of cards for the one he had provided, and that Pan Mussyalovich had cheated during the game. Kalganov confirmed this, and both the Poles left the witness stand with damaged reputations, even amidst laughter from the public.

Then exactly the same thing happened with almost all the most dangerous witnesses. Fetyukovich succeeded in casting a slur on all of them, and dismissing them with a certain derision. The lawyers and experts were lost in admiration, and were only at a loss to understand what good purpose could be served by it, for all, I repeat, felt that the case for the prosecution could not be refuted, but was growing more and more tragically overwhelming. But from the confidence of the "great magician" they saw that he was serene, and they waited, feeling that "such a man" had not come from Petersburg for nothing, and that he was not a man to return unsuccessful.

Chapter III

The Medical Experts and a Pound of Nuts

The evidence of the medical experts, too, was of little use to the accused. And it appeared later that Fetyukovich had not reckoned much upon it. The medical line of defense had only been taken up through the insistence of Katerina Ivanovna, who had sent for a celebrated doctor from Moscow on purpose. The case for the defense could, of course, lose nothing by it and might, with luck, gain something from it. There was, however, an element of comedy about it, through the difference of opinion of the doctors. The medical experts were the famous doctor from Moscow, our doctor, Herzenstube, and the young doctor, Varvinsky. The two latter appeared also as witnesses for the prosecution.

The first to be called in the capacity of expert was Doctor Herzenstube. He was a gray and balding old man of seventy, of middle height and sturdy build. He was much esteemed and respected by everyone in the town. He was a conscientious doctor and an excellent and pious man, a Herrnhuter or Moravian brother,[5] I am not quite sure which. He had been living amongst us for many years and behaved with wonderful dignity. He was a kind-hearted and humane man. He treated the sick poor and peasants for nothing, visited them in their slums and huts, and left money for medicine, but he was as obstinate as a mule. If once he had taken an idea into his head, there was no shaking it. Almost everyone in the town was aware, by the way, that the famous doctor had, within the first two or three days of his presence among us, uttered some extremely offensive allusions to Doctor Herzenstube's qualifications. Though the Moscow doctor asked twenty-five rubles for a visit, several people in the town were glad to take advantage of his arrival, and rushed to consult him regardless of expense. All these had, of course, been previously patients of Doctor Herzenstube, and the celebrated doctor had criticized his treatment with extreme harshness. Finally, he had asked the patients as soon as he saw them, "Well, who has been cramming you with nostrums? Herzenstube? Ha, ha!" Doctor Herzenstube, of course, heard all this, and now all the three doctors made their appearance, one after another, to be examined.

Doctor Herzenstube roundly declared that the abnormality of the

5. A Protestant denomination descended from the Bohemian Brethren in 1722.

defendant's mental faculties was self-evident. Then giving his ground for this opinion, which I omit here, he added that the abnormality was not only evident in many of the defendant's actions in the past, but was apparent even now at this very moment. When he was asked to explain how it was apparent now at this moment, the old doctor, with simple-hearted directness, pointed out that the defendant on entering the court had "an extraordinary air, remarkable in the circumstances"; that he had "marched in like a soldier, looking straight before him, though it would have been more natural for him to look to the left where, among the public, the ladies were sitting, seeing that he was a great admirer of the fair sex and must be thinking much of what the ladies are saying of him now," the old man concluded in his peculiar language.

I must add that he spoke Russian readily, but every phrase was formed in German style, which did not, however, trouble him, for it had always been a weakness of his to believe that he spoke Russian perfectly, better indeed than Russians. And he was very fond of using Russian proverbs, always declaring that the Russian proverbs were the best and most expressive sayings in the whole world. I may remark, too, that in conversation through absent-mindedness he often forgot the most ordinary words, which sometimes went out of his head, though he knew them perfectly. The same thing happened, though, when he spoke German, and at such times he always waved his hand before his face as though trying to catch the lost word, and no one could induce him to go on speaking till he had found the missing word. His remark that the prisoner ought to have looked at the ladies on entering roused a whisper of amusement in the audience. All our ladies were very fond of our old doctor; they knew, too, that having been all his life a bachelor and a religious man of exemplary conduct, he looked upon women as lofty and ideal beings. And so his unexpected observation struck everyone as very queer.

The Moscow doctor, being questioned in his turn, definitely and emphatically repeated that he considered the defendant's mental condition abnormal in "the highest degree." He talked at length and with erudition of "aberration" and "mania," and argued that, from all the facts collected, the defendant had undoubtedly been in a condition of aberration for several days before his arrest, and, if the crime had been committed by him, it must, even if he were conscious of it, have been almost involuntary, as he had not the power to control the morbid impulse that possessed him. But apart from temporary aberration, the doctor diagnosed mania, which promised, in his words, to lead to complete insanity in the future. (It must be noted that I report this in my own words; the doctor made use of very learned and professional language.) "All his actions are in contravention of common sense and logic," he continued. "Not to refer to what I have not seen, that is, the crime itself and the whole catastrophe, the day before yesterday, while he was talking to me, he had an unaccountably fixed look in his eye. He laughed unexpectedly when there was nothing to laugh at. He showed continual and inexplicable irritability, using strange words, 'Bernard!' 'Ethics!' and others equally inappropriate." But the doctor detected mania, above all, in the fact that the prisoner could not even speak of the three thousand rubles, of which he considered himself to have been cheated, without extraordinary irritation, though he could speak comparatively lightly of other misfortunes and grievances. According to all accounts, he had even in the past, whenever the subject of the three thousand rubles was touched on, flown into a perfect frenzy, and yet he was reported to be a disinterested and not grasping man.

"As to the opinion of my learned colleague," the Moscow doctor added ironically in conclusion, "that the defendant would, on entering the court, have naturally looked at the ladies and not straight before him, I will only say that, apart from the playfulness of this theory, it is radically unsound. For though I fully agree that the defendant, on entering the court where his fate will be decided, would not naturally look straight before him in that fixed way, and that that may really be a sign of his abnormal mental condition, at the same time I maintain that he would naturally not look to the left at the ladies, but, on the contrary, to the right to find his defense counsel, on whose help all his hopes rest and on whose defense all his future depends." The doctor expressed his opinion positively and emphatically.

But the unexpected pronouncement of Doctor Varvinsky gave the last touch of comedy to the difference of opinion between the experts. In his opinion the defendant was now, and had been all along, in a perfectly normal condition, and, although he certainly must have been in a nervous and exceedingly excited state before his arrest, this might have been due to several perfectly obvious causes, jealousy, anger, continual drunkenness, and so on. But this nervous condition would not involve the mental "aberration" of which mention had just been made. As to the question whether the defendant should have looked to the left or to the right on entering the court, "in his modest opinion," the defendant would naturally look straight before him on entering the court, as he had in fact done, since that was where the judges, on whom his fate depended, were sitting. So that it was just by looking straight before him that he showed his perfectly normal state of mind at the present. The young doctor concluded his "modest" testimony with some heat.

"Bravo, apothecary!" cried Mitya, from his seat, "just so!"

Mitya, of course, was checked, but the young doctor's opinion had a decisive influence on the judges and on the public, and, as appeared afterwards, everyone agreed with him. But Doctor Herzenstube, when called as a witness, was quite unexpectedly of use to Mitya. As an old resident in the town who had known the Karamazov family for years, he furnished some facts of great value for the prosecution, and suddenly, as though recalling something, he added:

"But the poor young man might have had a very different life, for he had a good heart both in childhood and after childhood, that I know. But the Russian proverb says, 'If a man has one head, it's good, but if another clever man comes to visit him, it would be better still, for then there will be two heads and not only one.' "

"One head is good, but two are better," the prosecutor put in impatiently. He knew the old man's habit of talking slowly and deliberately, regardless of the impression he was making and of the delay he was causing, and highly prizing his flat, Kraut-ish, and always gleefully complacent German wit. The old man was fond of making jokes.

"Oh, yes, that's what I say," he went on stubbornly. "A single head is good, but two are much better, but he did not meet another head with wits, and his own wits went. Where did they go? I've forgotten the word." He went on, passing his hand before his eyes, "Oh, yes, *spazieren*."

"For a walk?"

"Oh, yes, for a walk, that's what I say. Well, his wits went for a walk and fell in such a deep hole that he lost himself. And yet he was a grateful and sensitive boy. Oh, I remember him very well, a little chap so high, left neglected by his father in the backyard, when he ran about without boots on his feet, and his little breeches hanging by one button."

A note of feeling and tenderness suddenly came into the honest old man's voice. Fetyukovich positively started, as though scenting something and caught at it instantly.

"Oh, yes, I was a young man then. . . . I was . . . well, I was forty-five then, and had only just come here. And I was so sorry for the boy then; I asked myself why shouldn't I buy him a pound of . . . a pound of what? I've forgotten what it's called. A pound of what children are very fond of, what is it, what is it?" The doctor began waving his hands again. "It grows on a tree and is gathered and given to everyone . . ."

"Apples?"

"Oh, no, no. You have a dozen of apples, not a pound. . . . No, there are a lot of them, and all little. You put them in the mouth and crack."

"Nuts?"

"Quite so, nuts, that's what I say," the doctor repeated in the calmest way as though he had been at no loss for a word. "And I bought him one pound of nuts, for no one had ever bought the boy a pound of nuts before. And I lifted my finger and said to him, 'Boy, *Gott der Vater.*' He laughed and said, '*Gott der Vater.*' . . . '*Gott der Sohn.*' He laughed again and lisped '*Gott der Sohn.*' '*Gott der heilige Geist.*'[6] Then he laughed again and said as best he could: '*Gott der heilige Geist.*' I went away, and two days after I happened to be passing, and he shouted to me on his own, 'Uncle, *Gott der Vater, Gott der Sohn,*' and he had only forgotten '*Gott der heilige Geist.*' But I reminded him of it and I felt very sorry for him again. But he was taken away, and I did not see him again. Twenty-three years passed. I am sitting one morning in my study, a white-haired old man, when there walks into the room a blooming young man, whom I would never have recognized, but he held up his finger and said, laughing, '*Gott der Vater, Gott der Sohn, und Gott der heilige Geist.* I have just arrived and have come to thank you for that pound of nuts, for no one else ever bought me a pound of nuts; you are the only one that ever did.' And then I remembered my happy youth and the poor child in the yard, without boots on his feet, and my heart was touched and I said, 'You are a grateful young man, for you have remembered all your life the pound of nuts I bought you in your childhood.' And I embraced him and blessed him. And I shed tears. He laughed, but he shed tears, too . . . for the Russian often laughs when he ought to be weeping. But he did weep; I saw it. And now, alas! . . ."

"And I am weeping now, German, I am weeping now, too, you saintly man," Mitya cried suddenly from his place.

In any case the anecdote made a certain favorable impression on the public. But the chief sensation in Mitya's favor was created by the evidence of Katerina Ivanovna, which I will describe directly. Indeed, when the witnesses *à décharge,*[7] that is, called by the defense, began giving evidence, fortune seemed all at once markedly more favorable to Mitya, and what was particularly striking, this was a surprise even to the counsel for the defense. But before Katerina Ivanovna was called, Alyosha was examined, and he recalled a fact which seemed to furnish positive evidence against one important point made by the prosecution.

Chapter IV

Fortune Smiles on Mitya

It came quite as a surprise even to Alyosha himself. He was not required to take the oath, and I remember that both sides addressed him very gently and sympathetically. It was evident that his good

6. "God the Father, God the son, God the Holy Ghost."

7. A French juridical term: literally, "to lighten (the charge)."

reputation had preceded him. Alyosha gave his evidence modestly and with restraint, but his warm sympathy for his unhappy brother was unmistakable. In answer to one question, he sketched his brother's character as that of a man, violent-tempered perhaps and carried away by his passions, but at the same time honorable, proud and generous, capable of self-sacrifice, if necessary. He admitted, however, that, through his passion for Grushenka and his rivalry with his father, his brother had been of late in an intolerable position. But he repelled with indignation the suggestion that his brother might have committed a murder for the sake of gain, though he recognized that the three thousand rubles had become almost an obsession with Mitya; that he looked upon them as part of the inheritance he had been cheated of by his father, and that, indifferent as he was to money as a rule, he could not even speak of that three thousand without rage and fury. As for the rivalry of the two "persons," as the prosecutor expressed it—that is, of Grushenka and Katya—he answered evasively and was even unwilling to answer one or two questions altogether.

"Did your brother tell you, anyway, that he intended to kill your father?" asked the prosecutor. "You can refuse to answer if you think necessary," he added.

"He did not tell me so directly," answered Alyosha.

"How so? Did he indirectly?"

"He spoke to me once of his hatred for our father and his fear that at an extreme moment . . . at a moment of disgust he might perhaps murder him."

"And you believed him?"

"I am afraid to say that I did. But I never doubted that some higher feeling would always save him at the fatal moment, as it has indeed saved him, for it was *not he* who killed my father," Alyosha said firmly, in a loud voice that was heard throughout the court. The prosecutor started like a warhorse at the sound of a trumpet.

"Let me assure you that I fully believe in the complete sincerity of your conviction and do not explain it by or identify it with your affection for your unhappy brother. Your peculiar view of the whole tragic episode is known to us already from the preliminary investigation. I won't attempt to conceal from you that it is highly individual and contradicts all the other evidence collected by the prosecution. And so I think it essential to press you to tell me what facts have led you to this conviction of your brother's innocence and of the guilt of another person against whom you gave evidence at the preliminary inquiry?"

"I only answered the questions asked me at the preliminary inquiry," replied Alyosha, slowly and calmly. "I made no accusation against Smerdyakov on my own account."

"Yet you gave evidence against him?"

"I was led to do so by my brother Dmitri's words. I was told what took place at his arrest and how he had pointed to Smerdyakov before I was examined. I believe absolutely that my brother is innocent, and if he didn't commit the murder, then . . ."

"Then Smerdyakov? Why Smerdyakov? And why are you so completely persuaded of your brother's innocence?"

"I cannot help believing my brother. I know he wouldn't lie to me. I saw from his face he wasn't lying."

"Only from his face? Is that all the proof you have?"

"I have no other proof."

"And of Smerdyakov's guilt have you no proof whatever but your brother's word and the expression of his face?"

"No, I have no other proof."

The prosecutor dropped the examination at this point. The impression left by Alyosha's evidence on the public was most disappointing. There had been talk about Smerdyakov before the trial; someone had heard something, someone had pointed out something else, it was said that Alyosha had gathered together some extraordinary proofs of his brother's innocence and Smerdyakov's guilt, and after all there was nothing, no evidence except certain moral convictions so natural in a brother.

But Fetyukovich began his cross-examination. On his asking Alyosha when it was that the prisoner had told him of his hatred for his father and that he might kill him, and whether he had heard it, for instance, at their last meeting before the catastrophe, Alyosha started as he answered, as though only just recollecting and understanding something.

"I remember one circumstance now which I'd quite forgotten myself. It wasn't clear to me at the time, but now . . ."

And, obviously only now for the first time struck by an idea, he recounted eagerly how, at his last interview with Mitya that evening under the tree, on the road to the monastery, Mitya had struck himself on the breast, "the upper part of the breast," and had repeated several times that he had a means of regaining his honor, that that means was here, here on his breast. "I thought, when he struck himself on the breast, he meant that it was in his heart," Alyosha continued, "that he might find in his heart strength to save himself from some awful disgrace which was awaiting him and which he did not dare confess even to me. I must confess I did think at the time that he was speaking of our father, and that the disgrace he was shuddering at was the thought of going to our father and doing some violence to him. Yet it was just then that he pointed to something on his breast, so that I remember the idea struck me at the time that the heart is not on that part of the breast, but below, and that he struck himself much too high, just below the neck, and kept pointing to that place. My idea seemed silly to me at the time, but he was perhaps pointing then to that little bag in which he had fifteen hundred rubles!"

"Just so," Mitya cried from his place. "That's right, Alyosha, it was the little bag I struck with my fist."

Fetyukovich flew to him in haste entreating him to keep quiet, and at the same instant pounced on Alyosha. Alyosha, carried away himself by his recollection, warmly expressed his theory that this disgrace was probably just that fifteen hundred rubles on him, which he might have returned to Katerina Ivanovna as half of what he owed her, but which he had yet determined not to repay her and to use for another purpose—namely, to enable him to elope with Grushenka, if she consented.

"It is so, it must be so," exclaimed Alyosha, in sudden excitement. "My brother cried several times that half of the disgrace, half of it (he said *half* several times) he could free himself from at once, but that he was so unhappy in his weakness of will that he wouldn't do it . . . that he knew beforehand he was incapable of doing it!"

"And you clearly, confidently remember that he struck himself just on this part of the breast?" Fetyukovich asked eagerly.

"Clearly and confidently, for I thought at the time, 'Why does he strike himself up there when the heart is lower down,' and the thought seemed stupid to me at the time . . . I remember its seeming stupid . . . it flashed through my mind. That's what brought it back to me just now. How could I have forgotten it till now! It was that little bag he meant when he said he had the means but wouldn't give back that fifteen hundred. And when he was arrested at Mokroe he cried out—I know, I was told it—that he considered it the most disgraceful act of his life that when he had the means of repaying Katerina Ivanovna half (half, note!) what he owed her, he yet could not bring himself to repay the money and preferred to remain a thief in her eyes rather than part with it. And what torture, what torture that debt has been to him!" Alyosha exclaimed in conclusion.

The prosecutor, of course, intervened. He asked Alyosha to describe once more how it had all happened, and several times insisted on the question, had the prisoner seemed to point to anything. Perhaps he had simply struck himself with his fist on the breast?

"But it was not with his fist," cried Alyosha; "he pointed with his fingers and pointed here, very high up. . . . How could I have so completely forgotten it till this moment!"

The President asked Mitya what he had to say to the last witness's evidence. Mitya confirmed it, saying that he had been pointing to the fifteen hundred rubles which were on his breast, just below the neck, and that that was, of course, the disgrace, "A disgrace I cannot deny, the most shameful act of my whole life," shouted Mitya. "I might have repaid it and didn't repay it. I preferred to remain a thief in her eyes rather than give it back. And the most shameful part of it was that I knew beforehand I wouldn't give it back! You are right, Alyosha! Thanks, Alyosha!"

So Alyosha's cross-examination ended. What was important and striking about it was that one fact at least had been found, and even though this were only one tiny bit of evidence, a mere hint at evidence, it did go some little way towards proving that the amulet had existed and had contained fifteen hundred rubles and that the prisoner had not been lying at the preliminary inquiry when he alleged at Mokroe that those fifteen hundred rubles were "his own." Alyosha was glad. With a flushed face he moved away to the seat assigned to him. He kept repeating to himself: "How was it I forgot! How could I have forgotten it! And what made it come back to me now?"

Katerina Ivanovna was called to the witness stand. As she entered something extraordinary happened in the court. The ladies clutched their lorgnettes and opera glasses. There was a stir among the men: some stood up to get a better view. Everybody alleged afterwards that Mitya had turned "white as a sheet" on her entrance. All in black, she advanced modestly, almost timidly. It was impossible to tell from her face that she was agitated; but there was a resolute gleam in her dark and gloomy eyes. I may remark that many people mentioned that she looked particularly handsome at that moment. She spoke softly but clearly, so that she was heard all over the court. She expressed herself with composure, or at least tried to appear composed. The President began his examination discreetly and very respectfully, as though afraid to touch on "certain chords," and showing consideration for her great unhappiness. But in answer to one of the first questions Katerina Ivanovna replied firmly that she had been formerly betrothed to the defendant "until he left me of his own accord . . ." she added quietly. When they asked her about the three thousand she had entrusted to Mitya to post to her relations, she said firmly, "I didn't give him the money simply to send it off. I felt at the time that he was in great need of money. . . . I gave him the three thousand on the understanding that he would post it within the month if he cared to. There was no need for him to worry himself about that debt afterwards."

I will not repeat all the questions asked her and all her answers in detail. I will only give the substance of her evidence.

"I was firmly convinced that he would send off that sum as soon as he got money from his father," she went on. "I have never doubted his disinterestedness and his honesty . . . his scrupulous honesty . . . in money matters. He felt quite certain that he would receive the money from his father, and spoke to me several times about it. I knew he had a feud with his father and have always believed that he had been unfairly treated by his father. I don't remember any threat by him against his father. He certainly said nothing, made no such threat before me. If he had come to me at that time, I should have at once relieved his anxiety about those unlucky three thousand rubles, but he had given up coming to see me ... and I myself was put in such a position ... that I could not invite him. ... And I had no right, indeed, to be exacting as to that money," she added suddenly, and there was a ring of resolution in her voice. "I was once indebted to him for assistance in money for more than three thousand, and I took it, although I could not at that time foresee that I would ever be in a position to repay my debt."

There was a note of defiance in her voice. It was then Fetyukovich began his cross-examination.

"Did that take place not here, but at the beginning of your acquaintance?" Fetyukovich suggested cautiously, feeling his way, instantly scenting something favorable. I must mention in parenthesis that, though Fetyukovich had been brought from Petersburg partly at the instance of Katerina Ivanovna herself, he knew nothing about the episode of the five thousand rubles given her by Mitya, and of her "bowing to the ground to him." She concealed this from him and said nothing about it! And that was strange. It may be pretty certainly assumed that she herself did not know till the very last minute whether she would speak of that episode in the court, and waited for the inspiration of the moment.

No, I can never forget those moments. She began telling her story. She told *everything*, the whole episode that Mitya had told Alyosha, and her "bowing to the ground," and her reason. She told about her father and her going to Mitya, and did not in one word, in a single hint, suggest that Mitya had himself, through her sister, proposed they should "send him Katerina Ivanovna" to fetch the money. She generously concealed that and was not ashamed to make it appear as though she had of her own impulse run to the young officer, relying on something ... to beg him for the money. It was something tremendous! I turned cold and trembled as I listened. The hall was hushed, trying to catch each word. It was something unexampled. Even from such a self-willed and contemptuously proud girl as she was, such an extremely frank avowal, such sacrifice, such self-immolation, seemed incredible. And for what, for whom? To save the man who had deceived and insulted her and to help, in however small a degree, in saving him, by creating a strong impression in his favor. And, indeed, the figure of the young officer who, with a respectful bow to the innocent girl, handed her his last five thousand rubles—all he had in the world—was thrown into a very sympathetic and attractive light, but . . . I had a painful misgiving at heart! I felt that calumny might come of it later (and it did, in fact, it did). It was repeated all over the town afterwards with spiteful laughter that the story was perhaps not quite complete—that is, in the statement that the officer had let the young lady depart "with nothing but a respectful bow." It was hinted that something was here omitted. "And even if nothing had been omitted, if this were the whole story," the most highly respected of our ladies maintained, "even then it's very doubtful whether it was creditable for a young girl to behave in that way, even for the sake of saving her father."

And can Katerina Ivanovna, with her intelligence, her morbid sensitiveness, have failed to understand that people would talk like that? She must have understood it, yet she made up her mind to tell everything. Of course, all these nasty little suspicions as to the truth of her story only arose afterwards and at the first moment all were deeply impressed by it. As for the judges and the lawyers, they listened in reverent, almost shamefaced silence to Katerina Ivanovna. The prosecutor did not venture upon even one question on the subject. Fetyukovich made a low bow to her. Oh, he was almost triumphant! Much ground had been gained. For a man to give his last five thousand on a generous impulse and then for the same man to murder his father at night for the sake of robbing him of three thousand—the idea seemed too incongruous. Fetyukovich felt that now the charge of robbery, at least, was as good as disproved. "The case" was thrown into quite a different light. There was a wave of sympathy for Mitya. As for him . . . I was told that once or twice, while Katerina Ivanovna was giving her evidence, he started to jump up from his seat, sank back again, and hid his face in his hands. But when she had finished, he suddenly cried in a sobbing voice, stretching his hands out to her:

"Katya, why have you ruined me?"

And his sobs were audible all over the court. But he instantly restrained himself, and cried again:

"Now I am condemned!"

Then he sat rigid in his place, with his teeth clenched and his arms across his chest. Katerina Ivanovna remained in the court and sat down in her place. She was pale and sat with her eyes cast down. Those who were sitting near her declared that for a long time she shivered all over as though in a fever. Grushenka was called.

I am approaching the sudden catastrophe which was perhaps the final cause of Mitya's ruin. For I am convinced, so is everyone—all the lawyers said the same afterwards—that if the episode had not occurred, the prisoner would at least have been recommended to mercy. But of that later. A few words first about Grushenka.

She, too, was dressed entirely in black, with her magnificent black shawl on her shoulders. She walked to the witness stand with her smooth, noiseless tread, with the slightly swaying gait common in women of full figure. She looked steadily at the President, turning her eyes neither to the right nor to the left. To my thinking she looked very handsome at that moment, and not at all pale, as the ladies alleged afterwards. They declared, too, that she had a concentrated and spiteful expression. I believe that she was simply irritated and painfully conscious of the contemptuous and inquisitive eyes of our scandal-loving public. She was proud and could not stand contempt. She was one of those people who flare up, angry and eager to retaliate, at the mere suggestion of contempt. There was an element of timidity, too, of course, and inward shame at her own timidity, so it was not strange that her tone kept changing. At one moment it was angry, contemptuous and rough, and at another there was a sincere note of self-condemnation. Sometimes she spoke as though she were taking a desperate plunge; as though she felt, "I don't care what happens. I'll say it. . . ." Of her acquaintance with Fyodor Pavlovich, she remarked curtly, "That's all nonsense, and was it my fault that he would pester me?" But a minute later she added, "It was all my fault. I was laughing at them both—at the old man and at him, too—and I brought both of them to this. It was all on account of me it happened." Samsonov's name came up somehow. "That's nobody's business," she snapped at once, with a sort of insolent defiance. "He was my benefactor; he took me when I hadn't a shoe to my foot, when my family had turned me out." The President reminded her, though very politely, that she must answer the questions directly, without going off into irrelevant details. Grushenka crimsoned and her eyes flashed.

The envelope with the bills in it she had not seen, but had only heard from "that wicked wretch" that Fyodor Pavlovich had an envelope with bills for three thousand in it. "But that was all foolishness. I was only laughing. I wouldn't have gone to him for anything."

"To whom are you referring as 'that wicked wretch'?" inquired the prosecutor.

"The lackey, Smerdyakov, who murdered his master and hanged himself last night."

She was, of course, at once asked what ground she had for such a definite accusation; but it appeared that she, too, had no grounds for it.

"Dmitri Fyodorovich told me so himself; you can believe him. The woman who came between us has ruined him; she is the cause of it all, let me tell you," Grushenka added. She seemed to be quivering with hatred, and there was a vindictive note in her voice.

She was again asked to whom she was referring.

"The young lady, Katerina Ivanovna there. She sent for me,

offered me chocolate, tried to fascinate me. There's not much true shame about her, I can tell you that . . ."

At this point the President checked her sternly, begging her to moderate her language. But the jealous woman's heart was burning in her, and she did not care what she did.

"During the arrest at Mokroe," the prosecutor asked, recollecting, "everyone saw and heard you run out of the next room and cry out: 'It's all my fault. We'll go to Siberia together!' So you already believed him to have murdered his father?"

"I don't remember what I felt at the time," answered Grushenka. "Everyone was crying out that he had killed his father, and I felt that it was my fault, that it was on my account he had murdered him. But when he said he wasn't guilty, I believed him at once, and I believe him now and always shall believe him. He is not the man to tell a lie."

Fetyukovich began his cross-examination. I remember that among other things he asked about Rakitin and the twenty-five rubles "you paid him for bringing Alexey Fyodorovich Karamazov to see you."

"There was nothing strange about his taking the money," sneered Grushenka, with angry contempt. "He was always coming to me for money: he used to get thirty rubles a month at least out of me, chiefly for luxuries: he had enough to keep him without my help."

"What led you to be so liberal to Mr. Rakitin?" Fetyukovich asked, in spite of an uneasy movement on the part of the President.

"Why, he is my cousin. His mother was my mother's sister. But he's always begged me not to tell anyone here of it, he is so dreadfully ashamed of me."

This fact was a complete surprise to everyone; no one in the town nor in the monastery, not even Mitya, knew of it. I was told that Rakitin turned purple with shame where he sat. Grushenka had somehow heard before she came into the court that he had given evidence against Mitya, and so she was angry. The whole effect on the public, of Rakitin's speech, of his noble sentiments, of his attacks upon serfdom and the political disorder of Russia, was this time cancelled and destroyed. Fetyukovich was satisfied: it was another godsend. Grushenka's cross-examination did not last long and, of course, there could be nothing particularly new in her evidence. She left a very disagreeable impression on the public; hundreds of contemptuous eyes were fixed upon her, as she finished giving her evidence and sat down again in the court, at a good distance from Katerina Ivanovna. Mitya was silent throughout her evidence. He sat as though turned to stone, with his eyes fixed on the ground.

Ivan Fyodorovich was called to give evidence.

Chapter V

A Sudden Catastrophe

I may note that he had been called before Alyosha. But the usher of the court announced to the President that, owing to an attack of illness or some sort of fit, the witness could not appear at the moment, but was ready to give his evidence as soon as he recovered. But no one seemed to have heard it and it only came out later.

His entrance was for the first moment almost unnoticed. The principal witnesses, especially the two rival ladies, had already been questioned. Curiosity was satisfied for the time; the public was feeling almost fatigued. Several more witnesses were still to be heard, who probably had little information to give after all that had been given. Time was passing. Ivan Fyodorovich walked up with extraordinary slowness, looking at no one, and with his head bowed, as though plunged in gloomy thought. He was irreproachably dressed, but his face made a painful impression, on me at least: there was an earthy look in it, a look like a dying man's. His eyes were lusterless; he raised them and looked slowly round the court. Alyosha jumped up from his seat and moaned "Ah!" I remember that, but it was hardly noticed.

The President began by informing him that he was a witness not on oath, that he might answer or refuse to answer, but that, of course, he must bear witness according to his conscience, and so on and so on. Ivan Fyodorovich listened and looked at him blankly, but his face gradually relaxed into a smile, and as soon as the President, looking at him in astonishment, finished, he laughed outright.

"Well, and what else?" he asked in a loud voice.

There was a hush in the court; there was a feeling of something strange. The President showed signs of uneasiness.

"You . . . are perhaps still unwell?" he began, looking everywhere for the bailiff.

"Don't trouble yourself, your excellency, I am well enough and can tell you something interesting," Ivan Fyodorovich answered with sudden calmness and respectfulness.

"You have some special communication to make?" the President went on, still mistrustfully.

Ivan Fyodorovich looked down, waited a few seconds and, raising his head, answered, almost stammering:

"No . . . I haven't. I have nothing particular."

They began asking him questions. He answered, as it were reluctantly, with extreme brevity, with a sort of disgust which grew more and more marked, though he answered rationally. To many questions he answered that he did not know. He knew nothing of his father's money relations with Dmitri Fyodorovich. "I wasn't interested in the subject," he added. Threats to murder his father he had heard from the defendant. Of the money in the envelope he had heard from Smerdyakov.

"The same thing over and over again," he interrupted suddenly, with a look of weariness. "I have nothing particular to tell the court."

"I see you are unwell and understand your feelings," the President began.

He turned to the prosecutor and the counsel for the defense to invite them to examine the witness, if necessary, when Ivan Fyodorovich suddenly asked in an exhausted voice:

"Let me go, your excellency, I feel very ill."

And with these words, without waiting for permission, he turned to walk out of the court. But after taking four steps he stood still, as though he had reached a decision, smiled slowly, and went back.

"I am like the peasant girl, your excellency . . . you know. How does it go? 'I'll stand up if I like, and I won't if I don't.' They were trying to put on her sarafan to take her to church to be married, and she said, 'I'll stand up if I like, and I won't if I don't.' . . . It's in some book about our folklore."

"What do you mean by that?" the President asked severely.

"Why, this," Ivan Fyodorovich suddenly pulled out a roll of bills. "Here's the money . . . the bills that lay in that envelope" (he nodded towards the table on which lay the material evidence) "for the sake of which father was murdered. Where shall I put them? Mr. Bailiff, take them."

The bailiff took the whole roll and handed it to the President.

"How could this money have come into your possession if it is the same money?" the President asked wonderingly.

"I got them from Smerdyakov, from the murderer, yesterday. . . . I was with him just before he hanged himself. It was he, not my brother, who killed our father. He murdered him and I incited him to do it . . . Who doesn't desire his father's death?"

"Are you in your right mind?" broke involuntarily from the President.

"I should think I am in my right mind . . . in the same nasty mind as you . . . and as all these . . . ugly faces." He turned suddenly to the audience. "My father has been murdered and they pretend they are horrified," he snarled, with furious contempt. "They keep up the sham with one another. Liars! They all desire the death of their fathers. One reptile devours another. . . . If there hadn't been a parricide, they'd have been angry and gone home ill-humored. It's a spectacle they want! 'Bread and Circuses.'[8] Though I am one to talk! Have you any water? Give me a drink for Christ's sake!" He suddenly clutched his head.

The bailiff at once approached him. Alyosha jumped up and cried, "He is ill. Don't believe him: he has brain fever." Katerina Ivanovna rose impulsively from her seat and, rigid with horror, gazed at Ivan Fyodorovich. Mitya stood up and greedily looked at his brother and listened to him with a wild, strange smile.

"Don't disturb yourselves. I am not mad, I am only a murderer," Ivan began again. "You can't expect eloquence from a murderer," he added suddenly for some reason and laughed a queer laugh.

The prosecutor bent over to the President in obvious dismay. The two other judges communicated in agitated whispers. Fetyukovich pricked up his ears as he listened: the hall was hushed in expectation. The President seemed suddenly to recollect himself.

"Witness, your words are incomprehensible and impossible here. Calm yourself, if you can, and tell your story . . . if you really have something to tell. How can you confirm your statement . . . if indeed you are not delirious?"

"That's just it. I have no proof. That cur Smerdyakov won't send you proofs from the other world . . . in an envelope. You think of nothing but envelopes—one is enough. I have no witnesses . . . except one, perhaps," he smiled thoughtfully.

"Who is your witness?"

"He has a tail, your excellency, and that would be irregular! *Le diable n'existe point!*[9] Don't pay attention: he is a paltry, pitiful devil," he added suddenly. He ceased laughing and spoke as it were, confidentially. "He is here somewhere, no doubt—under that table with the material evidence on it, perhaps. Where should he sit if not there? You see, listen to me. I told him I don't want to keep quiet, and he talked about the geological cataclysm . . . idiocy! Come, release the monster . . . he's been singing a hymn. That's because his heart is light! It's like a drunken man in the street bawling how 'Vanka went to Petersburg,' and I would give a quadrillion quadrillions for two seconds of joy. You don't know me! Oh, how stupid all this business is! Come, take me instead of him! I didn't come for nothing. . . . Why, why is everything so stupid? . . ."

And he began slowly, and as it were reflectively, looking round him again. But the court was all excitement by now. Alyosha rushed towards him, but the bailiff had already siezed Ivan Fyodorovich by the arm.

"What are you doing?" he cried, staring into the man's face, and suddenly seizing him by the shoulders, he flung him violently to the floor. But the police were on the spot and he was seized. He

8. "Panem et circenses" were demanded by the Romans (and provided by the Caesars) to make them remain content.
9. "The devil doesn't exist at all!"

screamed furiously. And all the time he was being removed, he yelled and screamed something incoherent.

The whole court was thrown into confusion. I don't remember everything as it happened. I was excited myself and could not follow. I only know that afterwards, when everything was quiet again and everyone understood what had happened, the bailiff came in for a reprimand, though he very reasonably explained that the witness had been quite well, that the doctor had seen him an hour ago, when he had a slight attack of giddiness, but that, until he had come into the court, he had talked quite consecutively, so that nothing could have been foreseen—that he had, in fact, insisted on giving evidence. But before everyone had completely regained their composure and recovered from this scene, it was followed by another. Katerina Ivanovna had an attack of hysterics. She sobbed, shrieking loudly, but refused to leave the court, struggled, and besought them not to remove her. Suddenly she cried to the President:

"There is more evidence I must give at once . . . at once! Here is a document, a letter . . . take it, read it quickly, quickly! It's a letter from that monster . . . that man there, there!" she pointed to Mitya. "It was he who killed his father, you will see that directly. He wrote to me how he would kill his father! But the other one is ill, he is ill, he is delirious! I have seen that he is delirious for three days!" She kept crying out, beside herself.

The bailiff took the document she held out to the President, and she, dropping into her chair, hiding her face in her hands, began convulsively and noiselessly sobbing, shaking all over, and stifling every sound for fear she should be ejected from the court. The document she had handed up was that letter Mitya had written at the Metropolis tavern, which Ivan Fyodorovich had spoken of as a "mathematical proof." Alas! its mathematical conclusiveness was recognized, and had it not been for that letter, Mitya might have escaped his doom or, at least, that doom would have been less terrible. It was, I repeat, difficult to notice every detail. What followed is still confused in my mind. The President must, I suppose, have at once passed on the document to the judges, the jury, and the lawyers on both sides. I only remember how they began examining the witness. On being gently asked by the President whether she had recovered sufficiently, Katerina Ivanovna exclaimed impetuously:

"I am ready, I am ready! I am quite equal to answering you," she added, evidently still afraid that she would somehow be prevented from giving evidence. She was asked to explain in detail what this letter was and under what circumstances she received it.

"I received it the day before the crime was committed, but he wrote it the day before that, at the tavern—that is, two days before he committed the crime. Look, it is written on some sort of bill!"

she shouted breathlessly. "He hated me at the time, because he had behaved contemptibly and was running after that creature . . . and because he owed me that three thousand. . . . Oh! he was humiliated by that three thousand on account of his own meanness! This is how it happened about that three thousand. I beg you, I beseech you, to hear me. Three weeks before he murdered his father, he came to me one morning. I knew he was in need of money, and what he wanted it for. Yes, yes—to win that creature and carry her off. I knew then that he had been false to me and meant to abandon me, and it was I, I, who gave him that money, who offered it to him on the pretext of his sending it to my sister in Moscow. And as I gave it to him, I looked him in the face and said that he could send it when he liked, 'in a month's time would do.' How, how could he have failed to understand that I was practically telling him to his face, 'You want money to be false to me with your creature, so here's the money for you. I give it to you myself. Take it, if you have so little honor as to take it!' I wanted to prove what he was, and what happened? He took it, he took it, and squandered it with that creature in one night. . . . But he knew, he knew that I knew all about it. I assure you he understood, too, that I gave him that money to test him, to see whether he was so lost to all sense of honor as to take it from me. I looked into his eyes and he looked into mine, and he understood it all and he took it—he carried off my money!"

"That's true, Katya," Mitya roared suddenly, "I looked into your eyes and I knew that you were dishonoring me, and yet I took your money. Despise me as a scoundrel, despise me, all of you! I've deserved it!"

"Defendant," cried the President, "another word and I will order you to be removed."

"That money was a torment to him," Katya went on with impulsive haste. "He wanted to repay it to me. He wanted to, that's true; but he needed money for that creature, too. So he murdered his father, but he didn't repay me, and went off with her to that village where he was arrested. There, again, he squandered the money he had stolen after the murder of his father. And a day before the murder he wrote me this letter. He was drunk when he wrote it. I saw it at once, at the time. He wrote it from spite, and feeling certain, positively certain, that I would never show it to anyone, even if he did kill him, or else he wouldn't have written it. For he knew I wouldn't want to revenge myself and ruin him! But read it, read it attentively—more attentively, please—and you will see that he had described it all in his letter, all beforehand, how he would kill his father and where his money was kept. Look, please, don't overlook that, there's one phrase there, 'I shall kill him as soon as Ivan has gone away.' So he thought it all out beforehand how he would kill him," Katerina Ivanovna pointed out to the court with venomous and malignant triumph. Oh! it was clear she had studied every line of that letter and detected every meaning underlining it. "If he hadn't been drunk, he wouldn't have written to me; but, look, everything is written there beforehand, just as he committed the murder after. The whole scenario!" she exclaimed frantically.

She was reckless now of all consequences to herself, though, no doubt, she had foreseen them even a month ago, for even then, perhaps, shaking with anger, she had pondered whether to show it at the trial or not. Now she had taken the fatal plunge. I remember that the letter was read aloud by the clerk, right afterwards, I believe. It made an overwhelming impression. They asked Mitya whether he admitted having written the letter.

"It's mine, mine!" cried Mitya. "I wouldn't have written it, if I hadn't been drunk! . . . We've hated each other for many things, Katya, but I swear, I swear I loved you even while I hated you, and you didn't love me!"

He sank back on his seat, wringing his hands in despair. The prosecutor and counsel for the defense began cross-examining her, chiefly to ascertain what had induced her to conceal such a document and to give her evidence in quite a different tone and spirit just before.

"Yes, yes. I was telling lies just now. I was lying against my honor and my conscience, but I wanted to save him, for he has hated and despised me so!" Katya shouted like a madwoman. "Oh, he has despised me horribly, he has always despised me, and do you know, he has despised me from the very moment that I bowed down to him for that money. I saw that. . . . I felt it at once at the time, but for a long time I wouldn't believe it. How often I have read it in his eyes 'you came of your own will, though.' Oh, he didn't understand, he had no idea why I ran to him, he can suspect nothing but baseness, he judged me by himself, he thought everyone was like himself!" Katya hissed furiously, in a perfect frenzy. "and he only wanted to marry me because I'd inherited a fortune, because of that, because of that! I always suspected it was because of that! Oh, he is a brute! He was always convinced that I would be trembling with shame all my life before him, because I went to him then, and that he had a right to despise me forever for it, and so to be superior to me—that's why he wanted to marry me! That's so, that's all so! I tried to conquer him by my love—a love that knew no bounds. I even tried to forgive his faithlessness; but he understood nothing, nothing! How could he understand indeed? He is a monster! I only received that letter the next evening: it was brought me from the tavern—and only that morning, only that morning I wanted to forgive him everything, everything—even his treachery!"

The President and the prosecutor, of course, tried to calm her. I can't help thinking that they felt ashamed of taking advantage of her hysteria and of listening to such avowals. I remember hearing them say to her, "We understand how hard it is for you; be sure we are able to feel for you," and so on, and so on. And yet they dragged the evidence out of the raving, hysterical woman. She described at last with extraordinary clearness, which is so often seen, though only for a moment, in such overwrought states, how Ivan Fyodorovich had been nearly driven out of his mind during the last two months trying to save "the monster and murderer," his brother.

"He tortured himself," she exclaimed, "he was always trying to minimize his brother's guilt and confessing to me that he, too, had never loved his father, and perhaps desired his death himself. Oh, he has a deep, deep conscience! He tormented himself with his conscience! He told me everything, everything! He came every day and talked to me as his only friend. I have the honor to be his only friend!" she cried suddenly with a sort of defiance, and her eyes flashed. "He had been twice to see Smerdyakov. One day he came to me and said, 'If it was not my brother, but Smerdyakov committed the murder' (for the legend was circulating everywhere that Smerdyakov had done it) perhaps I too am guilty, for Smerdyakov knew I didn't like my father and perhaps believed that I desired my father's death. Then I brought out that letter and showed it him. He was entirely convinced that his brother had done it, and he was overwhelmed by it. He couldn't endure the thought that his own brother was a parricide! Only a week ago I saw that it was making him ill. During the last few days he has talked incoherently in my presence. I saw his mind was giving way. He walked about, raving; he was seen muttering in the streets. The doctor from Moscow, at my request, examined him the day before yesterday and told me that he was on the eve of brain fever—and all on his account, on account of this monster! And last night he learned that Smerdyakov was dead! It was such a shock that it drove him out of his mind . . . and all through this monster, all for the sake of saving the monster!"

Oh, of course, such an outpouring, such an avowal is only possible once in a lifetime—at the hour of death, for instance, on the way to the scaffold! But it was in Katya's character, and it was such a moment in her life. It was the same impetuous Katya who had thrown herself on the mercy of a young profligate to save her father; the same Katya who had just before, in her pride and chastity, sacrificed herself and her maidenly modesty before all these people, telling of Mitya's generous conduct, in the hope of softening his fate a little. And now, again, she sacrificed herself but this time it was for another, and perhaps only now—perhaps only at this moment—she felt and knew how dear that other was to her! She had sacrificed herself in terror for him, conceiving all of a sudden that he had ruined himself by his confession that it was he who had committed the murder, not his brother, she had sacrificed herself to save him, to save his good name, his reputation!

And yet one terrible doubt occurred to one—was she lying in her description of her former relations with Mitya?—that was the question. No, she had not intentionally slandered him when she cried that Mitya despised her for her bowing down to him! She believed it herself. She had been firmly convinced, perhaps ever since that bow, that the simple-hearted Mitya, who even then adored her, was laughing at her and despising her. She had loved him with an hysterical, lacerated love only from pride, from wounded pride, and that love was not like love, but more like revenge. Oh! perhaps that lacerated love would have grown into real love, perhaps Katya longed for nothing more than that, but Mitya's faithlessness had wounded her to the bottom of her heart, and her heart could not forgive him. The moment of revenge had come upon her suddenly, and all that had been accumulating so long and so painfully in the offended woman's breast burst out all at once and unexpectedly. She betrayed Mitya, but she betrayed herself, too. And no sooner had she given full expression to her feelings than the tension of course was over and she was overwhelmed with shame. Hysterics began again: she fell on the floor, sobbing and screaming. She was carried out. At that moment Grushenka, with a wail, rushed towards Mitya before they had time to prevent her.

"Mitya," she wailed, "your serpent has destroyed you! There, she has shown you what she is!" she shouted to the judges, shaking with anger. At a signal from the President they seized her and tried to remove her from the court. She wouldn't allow it. She fought and struggled to get back to Mitya. Mitya uttered a cry and struggled to get to her. He was overpowered.

Yes, I think the ladies who came to see the spectacle must have been satisfied—the spectacle had been a varied one. Then I remember the Moscow doctor appeared on the scene. I believe the President had previously sent the bailiff to arrange for medical aid for Ivan Fyodorovich. The doctor announced to the court that the sick man was suffering from a dangerous attack of brain fever and that he must be at once removed. In answer to questions from the prosecutor and the counsel for the defense he said that the patient had come to him of his own accord the day before yesterday and that he had warned him that he had such an attack coming on, but he had not consented to be looked after. "He was certainly not in a normal state of mind: he told me himself that he saw visions when he was awake, that he met several persons in the street, who were dead, and that Satan visited him every evening," said the doctor, in conclusion. Having given his evidence, the celebrated doctor withdrew. The letter produced by Katerina Ivanovna was added to the material proofs. After some deliberation, the judges decided to proceed with the trial and to enter both the unexpected pieces of evidence (given by Ivan Fyodorovich and Katerina Ivanovna) in the deposition.

But I will not detail the evidence of the other witnesses, who only repeated and confirmed what had been said before, though all with their characteristic peculiarities. I repeat, all was brought together in the prosecutor's speech, which I shall quote immediately. Everyone was excited, everyone was electrified by the late catastrophe, and all were awaiting the speeches for the prosecution and the defense with intense impatience. Fetyukovich was obviously shaken by Katerina Ivanovna's evidence. But the prosecutor was triumphant. When all the evidence had been taken, the court was adjourned for almost an hour. I believe it was just eight o'clock when the President returned to his seat and our prosecutor, Ippolit Kirillovich, began his speech.

Chapter VI

The Prosecutor's Speech. Sketches of Character

Ippolit Kirillovich began his speech, trembling with nervousness, with cold sweat on his forehead, feeling hot and cold all over by turns. He described this himself afterwards. He regarded this speech as his *chef d'œuvre*,[1] the *chef d'œuvre* of his whole life, as his swan song. He died, it is true, nine months later of rapid consumption, so that he had the right, as it turned out, to compare himself to a swan singing his last song if he had a premonition of his death. He had put his whole heart and all the brain he had into that speech. And poor Ippolit Kirillovich unexpectedly revealed that at least some feeling for the public welfare and "the eternal question" lay concealed in him. Where his speech really excelled was in its sincerity. He genuinely believed in the defendant's guilt; he was accusing him not as an official duty only, and in calling for vengeance he quivered with a genuine passion "for the security of society." Even the ladies in the audience, though they remained hostile to Ippolit Kirillovich, admitted that he made an extraordinary impression on them. He began in a shaky, breaking voice, but it soon gained strength and filled the court to the end of his speech. But as soon as he had finished, he almost fainted.

"Gentlemen of the jury," began the prosecutor, "this case has made a stir throughout Russia. But what is there to wonder at, what is there so peculiarly horrifying in it for us? Particularly for

1. "Masterpiece."

us? We are so accustomed to such crimes! That's what's so horrible, that such dark deeds have ceased to horrify us. What ought to horrify us is that we are so accustomed to it, and not this or that isolated crime. What are the causes of our indifference, our luke-warm attitude to such deeds, to such signs of the times, ominous of an unenviable future? Is it our cynicism, is it the premature exhaus-tion of intellect and imagination in a society that is sinking into decay, in spite of its youth? Is it that our moral principles are shattered to their foundations, or is it, perhaps, a complete lack of such principles among us? I cannot answer such questions; never-theless they are disturbing, and every citizen not only should, but must, suffer through them. Our newborn and still timid press has done good service to the public already, for without it we would never have heard in some detail, at least, of the horrors of un-bridled violence and moral degradation which are continually made known by the press, not merely to those who attend the new jury courts established in the present reign, but to everyone. And what do we read almost daily? Of things beside which the present case grows pale, and seems almost commonplace. But what is most important is that the majority of our national crimes of violence bear witness to some general, some widespread evil, now so general among us that it is difficult to contend against it.

"One day we see a brilliant young officer of high society, at the very outset of his life and career, in a cowardly underhand way, without a pang of conscience, murdering an official who had once been his benefactor, and the servant girl, to steal his own IOU and what ready money he could find on him; 'it will come in handy for my pleasures in the fashionable world and for my career in the future.' After murdering them, he puts pillows under the head of each of his victims; he goes away. Next, a young hero decorated for bravery kills the mother of his chief and benefactor, on the high-way, like a robber, and to urge his companions to join him he asserts that 'she loves him like a son, and so will follow all his directions and take no precautions.' Granted that he is a monster, yet I dare not say in these days that he is a unique monster. Another man will not commit the murder, but will feel and think just like him, and is just as dishonorable as he in soul. In silence, alone with his conscience, he asks himself perhaps: 'What is honor, and isn't the condemnation of bloodshed a prejudice?'

"Perhaps people will cry out against me that I am morbid, hys-terical, that it is a monstrous slander, that I am exaggerating, that I am delirious. Let them say so—and heavens! I would be the first to rejoice if it were so! Oh, don't believe me, think of me as morbid, but remember my words; if only a tenth, if only a twentieth part of what I say is true—even so it's awful! Look, gentlemen, look how our young people commit suicide, without asking themselves Hamlet's question what there is beyond, without a sign of such a question, as though all that relates to the soul and to what awaits us beyond the grave had long been erased in their minds and buried under the sands. Look, finally, at our vice, at our sensualists. Fyodor Pavlovich, the luckless victim in the present case, was almost an innocent babe compared with many of them. And yet we all knew him, 'he lived among us!'[2] . . .

"Yes, one day perhaps the leading intellects of Russia and of Europe will study the psychology of Russian crime, for the subject is worth it. But this study will come later, at leisure, when all the tragic topsyturvydom of today is further behind us, so that it's possible to examine it with more insight and more impartiality than people like myself, for example, can do. Now we are either horrified or pretend to be horrified, though we really gloat over the spectacle, and love strong and eccentric sensations which tickle our cynical, pampered idleness. Or, finally, like little children, we brush the dreadful ghosts away and hide our heads in the pillow so as to forget them in our sports and merriment. But yet we must one day begin life in sober earnest, we, too, must look at ourselves as a society; it's time we too tried to grasp at least something of our social position, or at least to make a beginning in that direction.

"A great writer of the last epoch, at the end of his greatest work, personifying Russia in a swift troika galloping to an unknown goal, exclaims, 'Oh, troika, birdlike troika, who invented thee!'[3] and adds, in proud ecstasy, that all the peoples of the world stand aside respectfully to make way for the recklessly galloping troika to pass. That may be, gentlemen, they may stand aside, respectfully or not, but in my poor opinion the great writer ended his book in this way either in an access of childish and naïve optimism, or simply in fear of the censorship of the day. For if the troika were drawn by his heroes, Sobakevich, Nozdryov, Chichikov, it could reach no rational goal, whoever might be driving it. And those were the heroes of an older generation, ours are worse specimens still . . ."

At this point Ippolit Kirillovich's speech was interrupted by applause. The liberal significance of this simile was appreciated. The applause was, it's true, of brief duration, so that the President did not think it necessary to caution the public, and only looked severely in the direction of the offenders. But Ippolit Kirillovich was encouraged; he had never been applauded before! He had been all his life unable to get a hearing, and now he suddenly had an opportunity of securing the ear of all Russia.

"What after all, is this Karamazov family, which has gained such an unenviable notoriety throughout Russia?" he continued. "Perhaps I am exaggerating too much, but it seems to me that certain

2. The first line of a poem by Pushkin on the Polish poet Mickiewicz.

3. Gogol, in the conclusion of *Dead Souls*.

fundamental features of our educated class of today are reflected in this family picture—oh, not all the elements, and only, of course, in miniature, 'like the sun in a drop of water,' but something is reflected nevertheless, something is expressed nevertheless. Think of that unhappy, vicious, unbridled old man, who has met with such a melancholy end, the head of a family! Beginning life of noble birth, but in a poor dependent position, through an unexpected marriage he came into a small fortune. A petty knave, a toady and buffoon, a fairly good, though undeveloped, intelligence, he was, above all, a moneylender, who grew bolder with growing prosperity. His abject and servile characteristics disappeared, his malicious and sarcastic cynicism was all that remained, and his sensuality. On the spiritual side he was undeveloped, while his vitality was excessive. He saw nothing in life but sensual pleasure, and he brought his children up to be the same. He had no feelings for his duties as a father. He ridiculed those duties. He left his little children to the servants, and was glad to be rid of them, forgot about them completely. The old man's maxim was *après moi le déluge*.[4] He was an example of everything that is opposed to civic duty, of the most complete and malignant individualism. 'The world may burn for all I care, so long as I am all right,' and he was all right; he was content, he was eager to go on living in the same way for another twenty or thirty years. He swindled his own son and spent his money, his maternal inheritance, on trying to get his own son's mistress from him. No, I don't intend to leave the defendant's defense altogether to my talented colleague from Petersburg. I will speak the truth myself, I can well understand what resentment he had heaped up in his son's heart against him.

"But enough, enough of that unhappy old man; he has paid the penalty. Let us remember, however, that he was a father, and one of the typical fathers of today. Do I insult society in saying that he is typical of many modern fathers? Alas! many modern fathers only differ in not openly professing such cynicism as his, for they are better educated, more cultured, but their philosophy is essentially the same as his. Perhaps I am a pessimist, but you have agreed to forgive me. Let us agree beforehand, you need not believe me, do not believe me but let me speak and do not believe me. Let me say what I have to say, however, and remember something of my words.

"But now for the children of this father, this head of a family. One of them is the defendant before us, all the rest of my speech will deal with him. Of the other two I will speak only cursorily. Of the other two, the elder is one of those modern young men of brilliant education and vigorous intellect, who has, however, lost all

4. "After me, the flood" (attributed to Louis XV).

faith in everything. He has denied and already rejected much, too much in life, exactly like his father. We have all heard him, he was a welcome guest in local society. He never concealed his opinions, quite the contrary in fact, which justifies me in speaking rather openly of him now, of course, not as an individual, but as a member of the Karamazov family. Another personage closely connected with the case died here by his own hand last night at the edge of the town. I mean an afflicted idiot, formerly the servant, and possibly the illegitimate son of Fyodor Pavlovich, Smerdyakov. At the preliminary inquiry, he told me with hysterical tears how that young Karamazov, Ivan Fyodorovich, had horrified him by his spiritual audacity. 'Everything in the world is lawful according to him, and nothing must be forbidden in the future—that is what he always taught me.' I believe that idiot was driven out of his mind by this theory, though, of course, the epileptic attacks from which he suffered, and this terrible catastrophe that struck their house, have helped to unhinge his faculties. But that idiot dropped one very interesting observation, which would have done credit to a more intelligent observer, and that is, indeed, why I've mentioned it, 'If there is one of the sons that is like Fyodor Pavlovich in character, it is Ivan Fyodorovich.'

"With that remark I conclude my sketch of his character, feeling it indelicate to continue further. Oh, I don't want to draw any further conclusions and croak like a raven over the young man's future. We've seen today in this court that the direct force of truth lives in his young heart, that family feeling has not been destroyed in him by lack of faith and cynicism, which has come to him rather by inheritance than by the exercise of independent thought.

"Then the third son. Oh, he is still a youth, devout and modest, in contradistinction to his elder brother's gloomy and destructive theory of life, seeking to cling, so to speak, to the 'ideas of the people,' or to what goes by that clever name in some theoretical circles of our thinking intellectual classes. He clung to the monastery, you see, and was within an ace of becoming a monk. He seems to me to have betrayed unconsciously, and so early, that timid despair which leads so many in our unhappy society, who dread cynicism and its corrupting influences, and mistakenly attribute all the mischief to European enlightenment, to return to their 'native soil,' as they say, to the bosom, so to speak, of their mother earth, like frightened children, yearning to fall asleep on the withered bosom of their decrepit mother, and to sleep there forever, only to escape the horrors that terrify them.

"For my part I wish the excellent and gifted young man every success; I trust that his youthful idealism and impulse towards the ideas of the people may never degenerate, as often happens, on the moral side into gloomy mysticism, and on the political into blind chauvinism—two elements which are even a greater menace to Russia than the premature decay, due to misunderstanding and gratuitous adoption of European enlightenment, from which his elder brother is suffering."

Two or three people started to clap at the mention of chauvinism and mysticism. Ippolit Kirillovich had been, indeed, carried away by his own eloquence. All this had little to do with the case in hand, to say nothing of the fact of its being somewhat vague, but the indignant and consumptive man was overcome by the desire to express himself once in his life. People said afterwards that he was actuated by unworthy motives in his criticism of Ivan Fyodorovich, because the latter had on one or two occasions got the better of him in argument, and Ippolit Kirillovich, remembering it, tried now to take his revenge. But I don't know whether it was true. All this was only introductory, however, and the speech passed to more direct consideration of the case.

"But to come to the eldest son of the father of a contemporary family," Ippolit Kirillovich went on. "He is the defendant before us. We have his life and his deeds and his actions, too, before us; the fatal day has come and all has been brought to the surface, all has been disclosed. In contradistinction to his brother's 'Europeanism' and 'the principles of the people,' he seems to represent Russia directly—oh, not all Russia, not all! God preserve us, if it were! Yes, here she is, our mother Russia, the very scent and smell of her. Oh, we are spontaneous, we are a marvelous mingling of good and evil, we are lovers of culture and Schiller, yet we brawl in taverns and pluck out the beards of our boon companions. Oh, we, too, can be good and noble, but only when all goes well with us. What is more, we can be carried off our feet, positively carried off our feet by noble ideals, but only if they come of themselves, if they fall from heaven for us, if they need not be paid for. We dislike paying for anything, but we are very fond of receiving, and that's so with us in everything. Oh, give us every possible good in life (we couldn't be content with less), and in particular put no obstacle in our way, and we will show that we, too, can be good and noble. We are not greedy, no, but we must have money, a great deal of money, and you will see how generously, with what scorn of filthy lucre, we will fling it all away in the reckless dissipation of one night. But if we do not get it, we will show what we are ready to do to get it when we are in great need of it. But all this later, let us take events in their chronological order.

"First, there is before us a poor abandoned child, running about the backyard 'without boots on his feet,' as our worthy and esteemed fellow citizen, of foreign origin, alas! expressed it just now. I repeat it again, I yield to no one the defense of the accused. I am here to prosecute him, but to defend him also. Yes, I, too, am human; I, too, can weigh the influence of home and childhood on the character. But the boy grows up, he becomes a youth, a young man, and becomes an officer; for a duel and other reckless conduct he is exiled to one of the remote frontier towns of our blessed Russia. There he led a wild life as an officer. And, of course, a big ship needs broad waters, he needs money, money before all things, and so after prolonged disputes he comes to a settlement with his father, and the last six thousand are sent to him. A letter is in existence in which he practically gives up his claim to the rest and settles his conflict with his father over the inheritance upon the payment of this six thousand.

"Then came his meeting with a young girl of lofty character and brilliant education. Oh, I do not venture to repeat the details; you have only just heard them. Honor, self-sacrifice were shown there, and I will be silent. The figure of the young officer, frivolous and profligate, doing homage to true nobility and to lofty ideal, was shown in a very sympathetic light before us. But the other side of the coin was unexpectedly turned to us immediately after in this very court. Again I will not venture to conjecture why it happened so, and will refrain from analysis, but there were causes. The same person, bathed in tears of long-concealed indignation, alleged that he, he of all men, had despised her for her action, which, though incautious, reckless perhaps, was still dictated by lofty and generous motives. He, he, the girl's betrothed, looked at her with that smile of mockery, which was more insufferable from him than from anyone. And knowing that he had already deceived her (he had deceived her, believing that she was bound to endure everything from him, even treachery), she intentionally offered him three thousand rubles, and clearly, too clearly, let him understand that she was offering him money to deceive her. 'Well, will you take it or not, are you so lost to shame?' was the dumb question in her scrutinizing eyes. He looked at her, saw clearly what was in her mind (he's admitted here before you that he understood it all), appropriated that three thousand unconditionally, and squandered it in two days with the new object of his affections.

"What are we to believe then? The first legend of the young officer sacrificing his last cent in a noble impulse of generosity and doing reverence to virtue, or the other side of the coin, which is so revolting? As a rule, between two extremes one has to find the mean, but in the present case this is not true. The probability is that in the first case he was genuinely noble, and in the second as genuinely base. And why? Because he was of the broad Karamazov character—that's just what I am leading up to—capable of combining the most incongruous contradictions, and simultaneously contemplating both abysses, the abyss above us, the abyss of the highest ideals, and the abyss below us, the abyss of the lowest and foulest degradation. Remember the brilliant remark made by a young observer who has observed the Karamazov family at close quarters, and profoundly—Mr. Rakitin: 'The sense of their own degradation is as essential to these reckless, unbridled natures as the sense of their lofty generosity.' And that's true, they continually and unceasingly need this unnatural mixture. Two extremes, two extremes, gentlemen, at the same moment, or they are miserable and dissatisfied and their existence is incomplete. They are wide, wide as mother Russia; they include everything and put up with everything.

"By the way, gentlemen of the jury, we've just touched upon that three thousand rubles, and I will venture to anticipate things a little. Can you conceive that a man like that, on receiving that sum and in such a way, at the price of such shame, such disgrace, such utter degradation, could have been capable that very day of setting apart half that sum, that very day, and sewing it up in a little bag, and would have had the firmness of character to carry it about with him for a whole month afterwards, in spite of every temptation and his extreme need of it! Neither in drunken debauchery in taverns, nor when he was flying into the country, trying to get from God knows whom, the money so essential to him to remove the object of his affections from being tempted by his rival, his father, did he bring himself to touch that little bag. Why, if only to avoid abandoning his mistress to the temptations of the rival of whom he was so jealous, he would have been certain to have opened that bag and to have stayed at home to keep constant watch over his beloved, and to await the moment when she would say to him at last 'I am yours,' and to fly with her far from their fatal present surroundings.

"But no, he did not touch his talisman, and what is the reason he gives for it? The chief reason, as I have just said, was that when she would say 'I am yours, take me where you will,' he might have the wherewithal to take her. But that first reason, in the defendant's own words, was of little weight beside the second. While I have that money on me, he said, I am a scoundrel, not a thief, for I can always go to my insulted betrothed, and, laying down half the sum I have fraudulently appropriated, I can always say to her, 'You see I've squandered half your money, and shown I am a weak and immoral man, and, if you like, a scoundrel' (I use the defendant's own expressions), 'but though I am a scoundrel, I am not a thief, for if I had been a thief, I wouldn't have brought you back this half of the money, but would have taken it as I did the other half!' A marvelous explanation of the fact! This frantic, but weak man, who could not resist the temptation of accepting the three thousand rubles at the price of such disgrace, this very man suddenly develops the most stoical firmness, and carries about thousands of rubles without daring to touch them. Does that fit in at all with the character we have analyzed? No, and I venture to tell you how the real Dmitri Karamazov would have behaved in such circumstances, if he really had brought himself to put away the money.

"At the first temptation—for instance, to entertain the woman with whom he had already squandered half the money—he would have unpicked his little bag and have taken out, let us say, first, one hundred rubles, for why should he have taken back precisely half the money, that is, fifteen hundred rubles; why not fourteen hundred? He could just as well have said then that he was a scoundrel and not a thief, because he brought back fourteen hundred rubles. Then another time he would have unpicked it again and taken out another hundred, and then a third, and then a fourth, and before the end of the month he would have taken the last bill but one, feeling that if he took back only a hundred it would answer the purpose, he would be a scoundrel but not a thief. I've spent twenty-nine hundred but at least I've brought one back, and a thief would have stolen it all. And finally, when he would spend the next to last bill, then he would have looked at this last bill, and have said to himself, 'It's really not worthwhile to give back one hundred; let's spend that, too!' That's how the real Dmitri Karamazov, as we know him, would have behaved. One cannot imagine anything more incongruous with the actual fact than this legend of the little bag. Nothing could be more inconceivable. But we shall return to that later."

After touching upon what had come out in the proceedings concerning the financial relations of father and son, and arguing again and again that it was utterly impossible, from the facts known, to determine who was in the wrong, Ippolit Kirillovich passed to the evidence of the medical experts in reference to Mitya's fixed idea about the three thousand owing him.

Chapter VII

An Historical Survey

"The medical experts have strived to convince us that the defendant is out of his mind and a maniac. I maintain that he is in his right mind, but that that is even worse, and that if he had not been, he might have behaved more cleverly. As for his being a maniac, that I would agree with, but only in one point, that very point the medical experts indicated, that is, his fixed idea about the three thousand rubles supposedly owed him by his father. Yet I think one might find a much simpler cause than his tendency to insanity. For my part I agree thoroughly with the young doctor who maintained that the defendant's mental faculties have always been and are normal, and that he has only been irritable and exasperated. That is just the point. The object of the defendant's continual and violent anger was not the sum itself; there was a special motive at the bottom of it. That motive is jealousy!"

Here Ippolit Kirillovich described at length the defendant's fatal passion for Grushenka. He began from the moment when the defendant went to the "young person's" lodgings "to beat her"—"I use his own expression," the prosecutor explained—"but instead of beating her, he remained there, at her feet. That was the beginning of the passion. At the same time the defendant's father, too, was captivated by the same young person—an amazing and fatal coincidence, for they both lost their hearts to her simultaneously, though both had known and met her before. And she inspired in both of them the most violent, characteristically Karamazov passion. We have her own confession: 'I was laughing at both of them.' Yes, the sudden desire to make a jest of both of them came over her, formerly she didn't want to, but now the notion suddenly came to her mind, and she conquered both of them at once. The old man, who worshipped money, at once set aside three thousand rubles as a reward for one visit from her, but soon after that he was led to such a state that he would have been happy to lay his property and his name at her feet, if only she would become his lawful wife. We have good evidence of this. As for the defendant, the tragedy of his fate is evident; it is before us. But such was the young person's 'game.' The enchantress even gave the unhappy young man no hope, for hope, true hope, was withheld until the last moment, when he knelt before her, stretching out hands that were already stained with the blood of his father and rival. It was in that position that he was arrested. 'Send me to Siberia with him, I have brought him to this, I am most to blame,' the woman herself cried, in genuine remorse at the moment of his arrest.

"The talented young man, to whom I have referred already, Mr. Rakitin, who has undertaken to describe this trial, characterized this heroine in brief and impressive terms: 'She was disillusioned early in life, deceived and ruined by a betrothed, who seduced and abandoned her. She was left in poverty, cursed by her respectable family, and taken under the protection of a wealthy old man, whom she still, however, considers as her benefactor. There was perhaps much that was good in her young heart, but it was embittered too early. She grew calculating and heaped up money. She grew sarcastic and resentful against society.' After this sketch of her character it may well be understood that she might laugh at both of them simply from mischief, from malice.

"After a month of hopeless love and moral degradation, during which he betrayed his betrothed and appropriated money entrusted to his honor, the defendant was driven almost to frenzy, almost to

madness by continual jealousy—and of whom? His father! And the
worst of it was that the crazy old man was alluring and enticing the
object of his affection by means of that very three thousand rubles,
which the son looked upon as his own property, part of his inheritance from his mother, of which his father was cheating him. Yes,
I admit it was hard to bear! It might well drive a man to madness.
It was not the money, but the fact that this money was used with
such revolting cynicism to ruin his happiness!"

Then the prosecutor went on to describe how the idea of murdering his father had entered the defendant's head, and illustrated his
theory with facts.

"At first we only talked about it in taverns—we were talking
about it all that month. Ah, we like being always surrounded with
company, and we like to tell our companions everything, even our
most diabolical and dangerous ideas; we like to share every thought
with others at once, and expect, for some reason, that those we
confide in will meet us with perfect sympathy, enter into all our
troubles and anxieties, take our part and not oppose us in anything.
If not, we fly into a rage and smash up everything in the tavern."
(Then followed the anecdote about Captain Snegiryov.) "Those
who saw and heard the defendant began to think at last that he
might mean more than shouts and threats to his father, and that
such a frenzy might turn threats into actions." (Here the prosecutor described the meeting of the family at the monastery, the conversations with Alyosha, and the horrible scene of violence when
the defendant had rushed into his father's house just after dinner.)

"I cannot positively assert," the prosecutor continued, "that the
defendant fully premeditated and intended to murder his father,
before that incident. Yet the idea had several times presented itself
to him, and he had deliberated on it—for that we have facts,
witnesses, and his own words. I confess, gentlemen of the jury," he
added, "that till today I have been uncertain whether to attribute to
the defendant conscious premeditation of the crime that occurred
to him. I was firmly convinced that he had frequently pictured the
fatal moment beforehand, but had only pictured it, contemplating it
as a possibility. He had not definitely considered when and how he
might commit the crime.

"But I was only uncertain till today, till that fatal document was
presented to the court just now by Miss Verkhovtsev. You yourselves heard that young lady's exclamation, 'it is the plan, the
scenario of the murder!' That is how she defined that miserable,
drunken letter of the unhappy defendant. And, in fact, from that
letter we see that the whole fact of the murder was premeditated. It
was written two days before, and so we know now for a fact that,
forty-eight hours before the perpetration of his terrible design, the
defendant swore that, if he could not get money next day, he would

murder his father in order to take the envelope with the money from under his pillow, 'from the envelope with the pink ribbon, as soon as Ivan had left.' 'As soon as Ivan had gone away'—you hear that; so he had thought everything out, weighing every circumstance, and he carried it all out just as he had written it. The proof of premeditation is conclusive; the crime must have been committed for the sake of the money, that is stated clearly, that is written and signed. The defendant does not deny his signature.

"I shall be told he was drunk when he wrote it. But that does not diminish the value of the letter, quite the contrary; he wrote when drunk what he had planned when sober. Had he not planned it when sober, he would not have written it when drunk. I shall be asked: Then why did he talk about it in taverns? A man who *premeditates* such a crime is silent and keeps it to himself. Yes, but he talked about it before he had formed a plan and premeditated it, when he had only the desire, only the impulse to it was ripening. Afterwards he talked less about it. On the evening he wrote that letter at the Metropolis tavern, contrary to his custom he was silent, though he had been drinking. He did not play billiards, he sat in a corner, talked to no one. He did indeed turn a local shopman out of his seat, but that was done almost unconsciously, out of habit, because he could never enter a tavern without making a disturbance. It is true that after he had made the final decision, he must have felt apprehensive that he had talked too much about his design beforehand, and that this might lead to his arrest and prosecution afterwards, when he had accomplished his design. But there was nothing for it; he could not take his words back, but his luck had served him before, it would serve him again. We believed in our lucky star, you know! I must confess, too, that he did a great deal to avoid the fatal catastrophe. 'Tomorrow I shall try and borrow the money from everyone,' as he writes in his peculiar language, 'and if they won't give it to me, there will be bloodshed.' Again written while drunk and again carried out while sober, just as it was set down."

Here Ippolit Kirillovich passed to a detailed description of all Mitya's efforts to borrow the money in order to avoid the crime. He described his visit to Samsonov, his journey to Lyagavy, all of which were attested to. "Harassed, jeered at, hungry, after selling his watch to pay for the journey (though he tells us he had fifteen hundred rubles on him—a likely story), tortured by jealousy at having left the object of his affections in the town, suspecting that she would go to Fyodor Pavlovich in his absence, he returned at last to the town, to find, to his joy, that she had not been near his father. He accompanied her himself to her protector. (Strange to say, he doesn't seem to have been jealous of Samsonov, which is psychologically interesting.) Then he hastens back to his ambush in the back gardens, and there learns that Smerdyakov is in a fit, that the other servant is ill—the coast is clear and he knows the 'signals' —what a temptation! Still he resists it; he goes off to a lady who has for some time been residing in the town, and who is highly esteemed among us, Madame Khokhlakov. That lady, who had long watched his career with compassion, gave him the most judicious advice, to give up his dissipated life, his unseemly love affair, the waste of his youth and vigor in taverns and debauchery, and to set off to Siberia to the gold mines: 'that would be an outlet for your turbulent energies, your romantic character, your thirst for adventure.' "

After describing the result of this conversation and the moment when the defendant learnt that Grushenka had not remained at Samsonov's, the sudden frenzy of the luckless man, worn out with jealousy and nervous exhaustion, at the thought that she had deceived him and was now with his father, Ippolit Kirillovich concluded by dwelling upon the fatal influence of chance. "Had the maid told him that her mistress was at Mokroe with her former lover, nothing would have happened. But she lost her head, she could only swear and protest her ignorance, and if the defendant did not kill her on the spot, it was only because he flew in pursuit of his false mistress.

"But note, frantic as he was, he took with him a brass pestle. Why that? Why not some other weapon? But since he had been contemplating his plan and preparing himself for it for a whole month, he would snatch up anything like a weapon that caught his eye. He had realized for a month past that any object of the kind would serve as a weapon, so he instantly, without hesitation, recognized that it would serve his purpose. So it was by no means unconsciously, by no means involuntarily, that he snatched up that fatal pestle. And then we find him in his father's garden—the coast is clear, there are not witnesses, darkness and jealousy. The suspicion that she was there, with him, with his rival, in his arms, and perhaps laughing at him at that moment—took his breath away. And it was not mere suspicion, why talk of suspicion—the deception was open, obvious. She must be there, in that lighted room, she must be behind the screen; and the unhappy man would have us believe that he stole up to the window, peeped respectfully in, and discreetly withdrew, for fear something terrible and immoral should happen. And he tries to persuade us of that, us, who understand his character, who know his state of mind at the moment, and that he knew the signals by which he could at once enter the house." At this point Ippolit Kirillovich temporarily interrupted his argument and found it necessary to expatiate on Smerdyakov, in order to demolish completely the suspected connection of Smerdyakov with the murder, and have done with that idea once and for all. He did this very circumstantially, and every one realized that, although he professed to despise that suspicion, he thought the subject of great importance.

Chapter VIII

A Treatise on Smerdyakov

"To begin with, what was the source of this suspicion (Ippolit Kirillovich began)? The first person who cried out that Smerdyakov had committed the murder was the defendant himself at the moment of his arrest, yet from that time to this he had not brought forward a single fact to confirm the charge, not only a single fact, but even anything that might be considered by human thought to be the faintest suggestion of a fact. The charge is confirmed by three persons only—the two brothers of the defendant and Miss Svyetlov. The elder of these brothers expressed his suspicions only today, when he was undoubtedly suffering from brain fever. But we know that for the last two months he has completely shared our conviction of his brother's guilt and did not attempt to combat that idea. But of that later. The younger brother has admitted that he has not the slightest fact to support his notion of Smerdyakov's guilt, and has only been led to that conclusion from the defendant's own words and the expression of his face. Yes, that astounding piece of evidence has been brought forward twice today by him. Miss Svyetlov was even more astounding. 'What the defendant tells you, you must believe; he is not a man to tell a lie.' That is all the evidence against Smerdyakov produced by these three persons, who are all deeply concerned in the defendant's fate. And yet the theory of Smerdyakov's guilt has been noised about, has been and is still maintained. Is it credible? Is it conceivable?"

Here Ippolit Kirillovich thought it necessary to describe briefly the personality of the late Smerdyakov, "who had cut short his life in a fit of insanity." He depicted him as a man of weak intellect, with a smattering of education, who had been thrown off his balance by philosophical ideas above his level and certain modern theories of duty and obligation which he learned in practice from the reckless life of his master, who was also perhaps his father— Fyodor Pavlovich; and, theoretically, from various strange philosophical conversations with his master's elder son, Ivan Fyodorovich, who readily indulged in this diversion, probably feeling dull or wishing to amuse himself, and finding no better target. "He spoke to me himself of his spiritual condition during the last few days at his father's house," Ippolit Kirillovich explained; "but others too have borne witness to it—the defendant himself, his brother, and the servant Grigory—that is, all who knew him well.

"Moreover, Smerdyakov, whose health was shaken by his attacks of epilepsy, had not the 'courage of a chicken.' 'He fell at my feet and kissed them,' the defendant himself has told us, before he realized how damaging such a statement was to himself. 'He is an epileptic chicken,' he declared about him in his characteristic language. And the defendant chose him for his confidant (we have his own word for it) and he frightened him into consenting at last to act as a spy and informant for him. In that capacity of domestic spy he deceived his master, revealing to the defendant the existence of the envelope with the bills in it and the signals by means of which he could get into the house. How could he help telling him, indeed? 'He would have killed me, I could see that he would have killed me,' he said at the inquiry, trembling and shaking even before us, though his tormentor was by that time arrested and could do him no harm. 'He suspected me at every instant. In fear and trembling I hastened to tell him every secret to pacify him, that he might see that I had not deceived him and let me off alive.' Those are his own words. I wrote them down and I remember them. 'When he began shouting at me, I would fall on my knees.'

"He was naturally very honest and enjoyed the complete confidence of his master, ever since he had restored him some money he had lost. So it may be supposed that the poor fellow suffered pangs of remorse at having deceived his master, whom he loved as his benefactor. Persons severely afflicted with epilepsy are, so the most skillful psychiatrists tell us, always prone to continual and morbid self-reproach. They worry over their 'guilt' about something and toward someone, they are tormented by pangs of conscience, often entirely without cause; they exaggerate and often invent all sorts of faults and crimes. And here we have a man of that type who had really been driven to wrongdoing by terror and intimidation.

"He had, besides, a strong presentiment that something bad would be the outcome of the situation that was developing before his eyes. When Fyodor Pavlovich's eldest son, Ivan Fyodorovich, was leaving for Moscow, just before the catastrophe, Smerdyakov begged him to remain, though he was too timid to tell him plainly and obviously what he feared. He confined himself to hints, but his hints were not understood. It must be observed that he looked on Ivan Fyodorovich as a protector, whose presence in the house was a guarantee that no harm would come to pass. Remember the phrase in Dmitri Karamazov's 'drunken' letter, 'I shall kill the old man, if only Ivan goes away.' So Ivan Fyodorovich's presence seemed to everyone a guarantee of peace and order in the house.

"But he went away, and within an hour of his young master's departure Smerdyakov was taken with an epileptic fit. But that's perfectly intelligible. Here I must mention that Smerdyakov, oppressed by terror and despair of a sort, had felt during those last few days that one of the fits from which he had suffered before at moments of strain might be coming upon him again. The day and hour of such an attack cannot, of course, be foreseen, but every epileptic can feel beforehand that he is likely to have one. So the doctors tell us. And so, as soon as Ivan Fyodorovich had driven out of the yard, Smerdyakov, depressed by his lonely, so to speak, and unprotected position, went to the cellar. He went down the stairs wondering if he would have a fit or not, and what if it were to come upon him at once. And that very apprehension, that very wonder, brought on the spasm in his throat that always precedes such attacks, and he fell headlong unconscious into the cellar. And in this perfectly natural occurrence people over-shrewdly try to detect a suspicion, a hint that he was shamming an attack *on purpose*. But, if it were on purpose, the question arises at once, what was his motive? What was he reckoning on? What was he aiming at? I say nothing about medicine: science, I am told, may lie, may make mistakes: the doctors were not able to discriminate between the counterfeit and the real. That may be so, that may be so, but answer me one question: what motive had he for such a counterfeit? Could he, had he been plotting the murder, have desired to attract the attention of the household by having a fit just before?

"You see, gentlemen of the jury, on the night of the murder, there were five persons in Fyodor Pavlovich's—Fyodor Pavlovich himself (but he did not kill himself, that's evident); then his servant, Grigory, but he was almost killed himself; the third person was Grigory's wife, Martha Ignatyevna, but it would be simply shameful to imagine her murdering her master. Two persons are left—the defendant and Smerdyakov. But, if we are to believe the defendant's statement that he is not the murderer, then Smerdyakov must have been, for there is no other alternative, no one else can be found. That, that is what accounts for the 'artful,' astounding accusation against the unhappy idiot who committed suicide yesterday. Precisely because, and for the sole reason that, there was no one else. Had a shadow of suspicion rested on anyone else, had there been any sixth person, I am persuaded that even the defendant would have been ashamed to accuse Smerdyakov, and would have accused that sixth person, for to charge Smerdyakov with that murder is perfectly absurd.

"Gentlemen, let us lay aside psychology, let us lay aside medicine, let us even lay aside logic, let us turn only to the facts and see what the facts tell us. If Smerdyakov killed him, how did he do it? Alone or with the assistance of the prisoner? Let us consider the first alternative—that he did it alone. If he had killed him it must have been with some object, for some advantage to himself. But not having a shadow of the motive that the defendant had for the murder—hatred, jealousy, and so on—Smerdyakov could only have murdered him for the sake of gain, in order to appropriate the three thousand rubles he had seen his master put in the envelope. And yet he tells another person—and a person most closely interested, that is, the defendant—everything about the money and the signals, where the envelope lay, what was written on it, what it was tied up with, and, above all, told him of those signals by which he could enter the house. Did he do this simply to betray himself, or to invite a rival to the same enterprise, one who would be anxious to get that envelope for himself? 'Yes,' I shall be told, 'but he betrayed it from fear.' But how do you explain this? A man who could conceive such an audacious, savage act, and carry it out, tells facts which are known to no one else in the world, and which, if he held his tongue, no one would ever have guessed!

"No, however cowardly he might be, if he had plotted such a crime, nothing would have induced him to tell anyone about the envelope and the signals, for that was as good as betraying himself beforehand. He would have invented something, he would have told some lie if he had been forced to give information, but he would have been silent about that. For, I repeat, on the other hand, if he had said nothing about the money but had committed the murder and stolen the money, no one in the world could have charged him with murder for the sake of robbery, since no one but he had seen the money, no one but he knew of its existence in the house. Even if he had been accused of the murder, it could only have been thought that he had committed it from some other motive. But since no one had observed any such motive in him beforehand, and everyone saw, on the contrary, that his master was fond of him and honored him with his confidence, he would, of course, have been the last to be suspected. People would have suspected first the man who had a motive, a man who had himself declared he had such motives, who had made no secret of it; they would, in fact, have suspected the son of the murdered man, Dmitri Fyodorovich. Had Smerdyakov killed and robbed him, and the son been accused of it, that would, of course, have suited Smerdyakov. Yet are we to believe that, though plotting the murder, he told that son, Dmitri, about the money, the envelope, and the signals? Is that logical? Is that clear?

"When the day of the murder planned by Smerdyakov came, we have him falling downstairs in a *feigned* fit—with what object? In the first place that Grigory, who had been intending to take his medicine, might put it off and remain on guard, seeing there was no one to look after the house, and, in the second place, I suppose, that his master seeing that there was no one to guard him, and in terror of a visit from his son, might redouble his vigilance and precaution. And, most of all, I suppose that he, Smerdyakov, disabled by the fit, might be carried from the kitchen, where he always slept, apart from all the rest, and where he could go in and out as he liked, to Grigory's room at the other end of the lodge, where he was always put, shut off by a screen three paces from their own bed. This was the immemorial custom established by his master and the kind-hearted Martha Ignatyevna, whenever he had a fit. There, lying behind the screen, he would most likely, to keep up the sham, have begun groaning, and so keeping them awake all night (as Grigory and his wife testified). And all this, we are to believe, that he might more conveniently get up and murder his master!

"But I shall be told that he shammed illness on purpose that he might not be suspected and that he told the defendant of the money and the signals to tempt him to commit the murder, and when he had murdered him and had gone away with the money making a noise, most likely, and waking people, Smerdyakov got up, am I to believe, and went in—what for? To murder his master a second time and carry off the money that had already been stolen? Gentlemen, are you laughing? I am ashamed to put forward such suggestions, but, incredible as it seems, that's just what the defendant alleges. When he had left the house, had knocked Grigory down and raised an alarm, he tells us Smerdyakov got up, went in and murdered his master and stole the money! I won't press the point that Smerdyakov could hardly have reckoned on this beforehand, and have foreseen that the furious and exasperated son would simply come to peep in respectfully, though he knew the signals, and beat a retreat, leaving Smerdyakov his booty. Gentlemen of the jury, I put this question to you in earnest; when was the moment when Smerdyakov could have committed his crime? Name that moment, or you can't accuse him.

"But, perhaps, the fit was a real one, the sick man suddenly recovered, heard a shout, and went out. Well—what then? He looked about him and said, 'Why not go and kill the master?' And how did he know what had happened, since he had been lying unconscious till that moment? But there's a limit to these flights of fancy.

" 'Quite so,' some astute people will tell me, 'but what if they were in agreement? What if they murdered him together and shared the money—what then?' "

A weighty question, truly! And the facts to confirm it are astounding. One commits the murder and takes all the trouble while his accomplice lies on one side shamming a fit, apparently to arouse suspicion in everyone, alarm in his master and alarm in Grigory. It would be interesting to know what motives could have induced the two accomplices to form such an insane plan.

"But perhaps it was not a case of active complicity, on Smerdyakov's part, but so to speak only of passive acquiescence; perhaps

Smerdyakov was intimidated and agreed not to prevent the murder, and foreseeing that he would be blamed for letting his master be murdered, without screaming for help or resisting, he may have obtained permission from Dmitri Karamazov to get out of the way by shamming a fit—'you may murder him as you like; it's nothing to me.' But even if it were so, since in any case this attack of Smerdyakov's was bound to throw the household into confusion, Dmitri Karamazov could never have agreed to such a plan. I will waive that point however. Supposing that he did agree, it would still follow that Dmitri Karamazov is the murderer, the direct murderer and the instigator, and Smerdyakov is only a passive accomplice, and not even an accomplice, but merely acquiesced against his will through terror, but the court would certainly be able to distinguish that, but what do we see? As soon as he is arrested the prisoner instantly throws all the blame on Smerdyakov, and accuses him *alone*, not accusing him of being his accomplice, but of being himself the murderer. 'He did it alone,' he says. 'He murdered and robbed him. It was the work of his hands.' Strange sort of accomplices who begin to accuse one another at once! It simply can't be! And think of the risk for Karamazov. After committing the murder, and he is the main murderer and the other is not the main one, while his accomplice lay in bed, he throws the blame on the invalid. But that one, the one who lay in bed, might well have resented it and in self-preservation might well have confessed the truth. 'We both participated, but I didn't murder, I only agreed and allowed it out of fear.' For he, Smerdyakov, might well have seen that the court would at once judge how far he was responsible, and so he might well have reckoned that if he were punished, it would be far less severely than the real murderer. But in that case he would have been certain to make a confession, yet he has not done so. Smerdyakov never hinted at their complicity, though the actual murderer persisted in accusing him and declaring that he had committed the crime alone.

"What's more, Smerdyakov at the inquiry volunteered the statement that it was *he* who had told the prisoner of the envelope of money and of the signals, and that, but for him, he would have known nothing about them. If he had really been a guilty accomplice, would he so readily have made this statement at the inquiry, that is, that he himself told the accused? On the contrary, he would have tried to conceal it, to distort the facts or minimize them. But he was far from distorting or minimizing them. No one but an innocent man, who had no fear of being charged with complicity, could have acted as he did. And in a fit of melancholy arising from his disease and this catastrophe he hanged himself yesterday. He left a note written in his peculiar language, 'I destroy myself of my own will and inclination, not to blame anyone.' What would it have cost him to add: 'I am the murderer, not Karamazov'? But that he did not add. Did his conscience lead him to suicide and not to avowing his guilt?

"And what followed? Notes for three thousand rubles were brought into the court just now, and we are glad that they were the same that lay in the envelope now on the table before us, and that the witness had received them from Smerdyakov the day before. But I need not recall the painful scene, though I will make one or two comments, selecting such trivial ones as might not be obvious at first sight to everyone, and so may be overlooked. In the first place, Smerdyakov must have given back the money and hanged himself yesterday from remorse. (Since he would only have hanged himself from remorse.) And he confessed his guilt to Ivan Karamazov only yesterday, as the latter informs us. If it were not so, indeed, why should Ivan Fyodorovich have kept silence till now? And so, if he has confessed, then why, I ask again, did he not avow the whole truth in the last letter he left behind, knowing that the innocent defendant had to face this terrible trial the next day?

"The money alone is no proof. A week ago, quite by chance, the fact came to the knowledge of myself and two other persons in this court that Ivan Fyodorovich had sent two five-percent coupons of five thousand each—that is, ten thousand in all—to the chief town of the province to be changed. I only mention this to point out that anyone may have money, at a particular time, and if he brings in three thousand rubles it can't be proved that these bills are the same, that is, precisely those that were in Fyodor Pavlovich's envelope.

"Finally, Ivan Karamazov, after receiving yesterday a communication of such importance from the real murderer, did not stir. Why didn't he report it at once? Why did he put it all off till morning? I think I have a right to conjecture why. His health had been giving way for a week past: he had admitted to a doctor and to his most intimate friends that he was suffering from hallucinations and seeing phantoms of the dead: he was on the eve of the attack of brain fever by which he has been stricken down today. In this condition he suddenly heard of Smerdyakov's death, and at once reflected, 'The man is dead, I can throw the blame on him and save my brother. I have money. I will take a roll of bills and say that Smerdyakov gave them to me before his death.' You will say that was dishonorable: it's dishonorable to slander even the dead, and even to save a brother. True, but what if he slandered him unconsciously? What if, finally unhinged by the sudden news of the lackey's death, he imagined it really was so? You saw the recent scene: you have seen the witness's condition. He was standing up and was speaking, but where was his mind?

"The fever-stricken man's testimony was followed by the document, the defendant's letter written two days before the crime to Miss Verkhovtsev, and containing a complete scenario of the murder. Why, then, are we looking for any other scenario and those who constructed them? The crime was committed precisely according to this scenario, and by none other than the writer of it. Yes, gentlemen of the jury, it went off without a hitch! We did not run respectfully and timidly away from our father's window, though we were firmly convinced that the object of our affections was with him. No, that is absurd and unlikely! He went in and murdered him. Most likely he killed him in anger, burning with resentment, as soon as he looked on his hated rival. But having killed him, probably with one blow of the brass pestle, and having convinced himself, after careful search, that she was not there, he did not, however, forget to put his hand under the pillow and take out the envelope with the money, the torn cover of which lies now on the table before us.

"I mention this fact that you may note one, to my thinking, very characteristic circumstance. Had he been an experienced murderer and had he committed the murder for the sake of gain only, well, would he have left the torn envelope on the floor as it was found, beside the corpse? Well, had it been Smerdyakov, for instance, murdering his master to rob him, he would have simply carried away the envelope with him, without troubling himself to open it over his victim's corpse, for he would have known for certain that the money was in the envelope—it had been put in and sealed up in his presence—and had he taken the envelope with him, no one would ever have known of the robbery. I ask you, gentlemen of the jury, would Smerdyakov have behaved in that way? Would he have left the envelope on the floor? No, this was the action of a frantic murderer, a murderer who was not a thief and had never stolen before that day, who snatched the money from under the pillow, not like a thief stealing them, but as though seizing his own property from the thief who had stolen it. For that was the idea which had become almost an insane obsession in Dmitri Karamazov in regard to that money. And pouncing upon the envelope, which he had never seen before, he tore it open to make sure whether the money was in it, and ran away with the money in his pocket, even forgetting to consider that he had left an astounding piece of evidence against himself in that torn envelope on the floor. All because it was Karamazov, not Smerdyakov, he didn't think, he didn't reflect, and how could he? He ran away; he heard behind him the servant cry out; the old man caught him, stopped him and was felled to the ground by the brass pestle.

"The defendant, moved by pity, leaped down to look at him. Would you believe it, he tells us that he leaped down out of pity, out of compassion, to see whether he could do anything for him.

Was that a moment to show compassion? No; he jumped down simply to make certain whether the only witness of his crime were dead or alive. Any other feeling, any other motive would be unnatural. Note that he took trouble over Grigory, wiped his head with his handkerchief and, convincing himself he was dead, he ran to the house of his mistress, dazed and covered with blood. How was it he never thought that he was covered with blood and would be at once detected? But the defendant himself assures us that he did not even notice that he was covered with blood. That may be believed, that is very possible, that always happens at such moments with criminals. On one point they will show diabolical cunning, while another will escape them altogether. But he was thinking at that moment of one thing only—where was *she*? He wanted to find out at once where she was, so he ran to her lodging and learned an unexpected and astounding piece of news—she had gone off to Mokroe to meet her 'first lover,' her 'rightful' one!"

Chapter IX

Psychology at Full Steam. The Galloping Troika. The End of the Prosecutor's Speech

Ippolit Kirillovich had chosen the historical method of exposition, beloved by all nervous orators, who find in its limitations a check on their own eager rhetoric. At this moment in his speech he went off into a dissertation on Grushenka's "first and rightful lover," and brought forward several interesting thoughts on this theme.

"Karamazov, who had been frantically jealous of everyone, collapsed, so to speak, and effaced himself at once before this first lover. What makes it all the more strange is that he seems to have hardly thought of this new danger to himself, looming in the person of this unexpected rival. But he had looked upon him as a remote danger, and Karamazov always lives only in the present. Possibly he regarded him as a fiction. But his wounded heart grasped instantly that the woman had been concealing this new rival and deceiving him, because he was anything but a fiction to her, because he was the one hope of her life. Grasping this instantly, he resigned himself.

"Gentlemen of the jury, I cannot help dwelling on this unexpected trait in the character of the defendant, who, it would seem, would be totally incapable of manifesting it. He suddenly evinces an irresistible desire for justice, a respect for woman and recognition of her right to love. And all this at the very moment when he had stained his hands with his father's blood for her sake! It is also true that the blood he had shed was already crying out for vengeance, for, after having ruined his soul and his life in this world, he was forced to ask himself at that same instant what he was and what he could be *now* to her, to that being, dearer to him than his own soul, in comparison with that 'former' and 'rightful' lover who had returned penitent, with new love, to the woman he had once betrayed, with honorable offers, with the promise of a reformed and happy life. And he, luckless man, what could he give her *now*, what could he offer her?

"Karamazov understood all this, understood that all ways were barred to him by his crime and that he was a criminal under sentence, and not a man with life before him! This thought crushed and destroyed him. And so he instantly flew to one frantic plan, which, to a man of Karamazov's character, must have appeared the one inevitable way out of his terrible position. That way out was suicide. He ran from the pistols he had left in pledge with his friend Perkhotin and on the way, as he ran, he pulled out of his pocket the money for the sake of which he had stained his hands with his father's blood. Oh, now he needed money more than ever. Karamazov would die, Karamazov would shoot himself and it would be remembered! To be sure, we are poets, to be sure, we have burned the candle at both ends all our life. 'To her, to her! and there, oh, there I will give a feast to the whole world, such as never was before, that will be remembered and talked of long after! In the midst of shouts of wild merriment, reckless gypsy songs and dances we shall raise the glass and drink to the woman we adore and her new-found happiness! And then, on the spot, at her feet, we shall dash out our brains before her and punish ourselves! She will remember Mitya Karamazov sometimes, she will see how Mitya loved her, she will feel for Mitya!'

"Here we see in excess a love of effect, a romantic despair and sentimentality, and the wild recklessness of the Karamazovs. Yes, but there is something else, gentlemen of the jury, something that cries out in the soul, throbs incessantly in the mind, and poisons his heart unto death—that *something* is conscience, gentlemen of the jury, its judgment, its terrible torments! The pistol will settle everything, the pistol is the only way out! But *beyond*—I don't know whether Karamazov wondered at that moment 'What lies beyond,' and whether a Karamazov could, like Hamlet, wonder 'What lies beyond.' No, gentlemen of the jury, they have their Hamlets, but we, so far, have only our Karamazovs!"

Here Ippolit Kirillovich drew a minute picture of Mitya's preparations, the scene at Perkhotin's, at the shop, with the drivers. He quoted numerous words and actions, confirmed by witnesses, and the picture made a terrible impression on the audience. The guilt of this harassed and desperate man stood out clear and convincing, when the facts were brought together.

"What need had he of precaution? Two or three times he almost confessed, hinted at it, all but spoke out." (Then followed the evidence given by witnesses.) "He even cried out to the peasant who drove him, 'Do you know, you are driving a murderer!' But it was impossible for him to speak out, he had to get to Mokroe and there to finish his romance. But what was awaiting the luckless man? Almost from the first minute at Mokroe he saw and finally understood completely that his invincible rival was perhaps by no means so invincible, that the toast to their new-found happiness was not desired and would not be acceptable. But you know the facts, gentlemen of the jury, from the preliminary inquiry. Karamazov's triumph over his rival was complete and here—oh, here his soul passed into quite a new phase, perhaps the most terrible phase through which his soul has passed or will pass.

"One may say with certainty, gentlemen of the jury," the prosecutor exclaimed, "that outraged nature and the criminal heart bring their own vengeance more completely than any earthly justice. What's more, justice and punishment on earth positively alleviate the punishment of nature and are, indeed, essential to the soul of the criminal at such moments, as its salvation from despair. For I cannot imagine the horror and moral suffering of Karamazov when he learned that she loved him, that for his sake she had rejected her 'first' and 'rightful' lover, that she was summoning him, Mitya, to a new life, that she was promising him happiness—and when? When everything was over for him and nothing was possible!

"By the way, I will note in parenthesis a point of importance for the light it throws on the defendant's position at the moment. This woman, this love of his, had been till the last moment, till the very instant of his arrest, a being unattainable, passionately desired by him but unattainable. Yet why did he not shoot himself then, why did he relinquish his design and even forget where his pistol was? It was just that passionate desire for love and the hope of satisfying it that restrained him. Throughout the heat of their revels he kept close to his adored mistress, who was reveling with him and was more charming and seductive to him than ever—he did not leave her side, abasing himself in his homage before her. His passion might well, for a moment, stifle not only the fear of arrest, but even the torments of conscience. For a moment, oh, only for a moment. I can picture the state of mind of the criminal hopelessly enslaved by three influences—first, the influence of drink, of noise and excitement, of the thud of the dance and the scream of the song, and of her, flushed with wine, singing and dancing and laughing to him! Secondly, the hope in the background that the fatal end might still be far off, that not till next morning, at least, would they come and take him. So he had a few hours and that's much, very much! In a few hours one can think of many things. I imagine that he felt something like what criminals feel when they are being taken to the scaffold. They have another long, long street to pass down and at a walking pace, past thousands of people. Then there will be a turning into another street and only at the end of that street the dread place of execution! I fancy that at the beginning of the journey the condemned man, sitting on his shameful cart, must feel that he has infinite life still before him. The houses recede, the cart moves on—oh, that's nothing, it's still far to the turning into the second street and he still looks boldly to right and to left at those thousands of callously curious people with their eyes fixed on him, and he still fancies that he is just such a man as they. But now the turning comes to the next street. Oh, that's nothing, nothing, there's still a whole street before him, and however many houses have been passed, he will still think there are many left. And so to the very end, to the very scaffold.

"This, I imagine, is how it was with Karamazov then. 'They've not had time yet,' he must have thought, 'I may still find some way out, oh, there's still time to make some plan of defense, and now, now—she is so fascinating!'

"His soul was full of confusion and dread, but he managed, however, to put aside half his money and hide it somewhere—I cannot otherwise explain the disappearance of quite half of the three thousand he had just taken from his father's pillow. He had been in Mokroe more than once before, he had caroused there for two days together already, he knew the old big house with all its passages and outbuildings. I imagine that part of the money was hidden in that house, not long before the arrest, in some crevice, under some floor, in some corner, under the roof. With what object? I shall be asked. Why, the catastrophe may take place at once, of course; he hadn't yet considered how to meet it, he hadn't the time, his head was throbbing and his heart was with *her*, but money—money was indispensable in any case! With money a man is always a man. Perhaps such foresight at such a moment may strike you as unnatural? But he assures us himself that a month before, at another critical and exciting moment, he had halved his money and sewn it up in a little bag. And though that was not true, as we shall prove directly, it shows the idea was a familiar one to Karamazov, he had contemplated it. What's more, when he declared at the inquiry that he had put fifteen hundred rubles in a bag (which never existed) he may have invented that little bag on the inspiration of the moment, because he had two hours before divided his money and hidden half of it at Mokroe till morning, in case of emergency, simply not to have it on himself. Two extremes, gentlemen of the jury, remember that Karamazov can contemplate two extremes and both at once. We have looked in the house, but we haven't found the money. It may still be there or it may have disappeared next day and be in the prisoner's hands now. In any case he was at her side, on his knees before her, she was lying on the bed, he had his hands stretched out to her and he had so entirely forgotten everything that he did not even hear the men coming to arrest him. He hadn't time to prepare any line of defense in his mind. He and his mind were caught unawares."

"And there he is, confronted with his judges, the arbiters of his destiny. Gentlemen of the jury, there are moments in the execution of our duties when it is terrible for us to face a man, terrible on his account, too! The moments of contemplating that animal fear, when the criminal sees that all is lost, but still struggles, still means to struggle, the moments when every instinct of self-preservation rises up in him at once and he looks at you with a piercing glance, with questioning and suffering eyes, studies you, your face, your thoughts, uncertain on which side you will strike, and his distracted mind frames thousands of plans in an instant, but he is still afraid to speak, afraid of giving himself away! This torment of the soul, this animal thirst for self-preservation, these humiliating moments of the human spirit, are awful, and sometimes arouse horror and compassion for the criminal even in the lawyer. And this was what we all witnessed then.

"At first he was thunderstruck and in his terror dropped some very compromising phrases. 'Blood! I've deserved it!' But he quickly restrained himself. He had not prepared what he was to say, what answer he was to make, he had nothing but a bare denial ready. 'I am not guilty of my father's death.' That was our fence for the moment and behind it we hoped to throw up a barricade of some sort. His first compromising exclamations he hastened to explain by declaring that he was responsible for the death of the servant Grigory only. 'Of that bloodshed I am guilty, but who has killed my father, gentlemen, who has killed him? Who can have killed him, *if not I?*' Do you hear, he asked us that, us, who had come to ask him that question! Do you hear that phrase uttered with such premature haste—'if not I'—the animal cunning, the naïveté, the Karamazov impatience of it? 'I didn't kill him and you mustn't think I did! I wanted to kill him, gentlemen, I wanted to kill him,' he hastens to admit (he was in a hurry, in a terrible hurry), 'but still I am not guilty, it is not I who murdered him.' He concedes to us that he wanted to murder him, as though to say, you can see for yourselves how truthful I am, so you'll believe all the sooner that I didn't murder him. Oh, in such cases the criminal is often amazingly shallow and credulous.

"At that point one of the lawyers asked him, as it were incidentally, the most simple question, 'Wasn't it Smerdyakov who killed him?' Then, as we expected, he was horribly angry at our having anticipated him and caught him unawares, before he had time to pave the way to choose and snatch the moment when it would be most natural to bring in Smerdyakov's name. He rushed at once to the other extreme, as he always does, and began to assure us that Smerdyakov could not have killed him, was not capable of it. But don't believe him, that was only his cunning; he didn't really give up the idea of Smerdyakov; on the contrary, he meant to bring him forward again; for, indeed, he had no one else to bring forward, but he would do that later, because for the moment that line was spoiled for him. He would bring him forward perhaps next day, or even a few days later, choosing an opportunity to cry out to us, 'You know I was more skeptical about Smerdyakov than you, you remember that yourselves, but now I am convinced. He killed him, he must have done it!' And for the present he falls back upon a gloomy and irritable denial. Impatience and anger prompted him, however, to the most inept and incredible explanation of how he looked into his father's window and how he respectfully withdrew. The worst of it was that he was unaware of the position of affairs, of the evidence given by Grigory.

"We proceeded to search him. The search angered, but encouraged him, the whole three thousand had not been found on him, only half of it. And no doubt only at that moment of angry silence, the fiction of the little bag first occurred to him. No doubt he was conscious himself of the improbability of the story and strove painfully to make it sound more likely, to weave it into a romance that would sound plausible. In such cases the first duty, the chief task of the investigating attorneys, is to prevent the criminal being prepared, to pounce upon him unexpectedly so that he may blurt out his cherished ideas in all their simplicity, improbability and inconsistency. The criminal can only be made to speak by the sudden and apparently incidental communication of some new fact, of some circumstance of great importance in the case, of which he had no previous idea and could not have foreseen. We had such a fact in readiness, oh, it was long ready—that was Grigory's evidence about the open door through which the defendant had run out. He had completely forgotten about that door and had not even suspected that Grigory could have seen it.

"The effect of it was amazing. He leapt up and shouted to us, 'Then Smerdyakov murdered him, it was Smerdyakov!' and so betrayed the basis of the defense he was keeping back, and betrayed it in its most improbable shape, for Smerdyakov could only have committed the murder after he had knocked Grigory down and run away. When we told him that Grigory saw the door was open before he fell down, and had heard Smerdyakov behind the screen as he came out of his bedroom—Karamazov was positively crushed. My esteemed and witty colleague, Nikolay Parfenovich, told me afterwards that he was almost moved to tears at the sight of him.

And to improve matters, the prisoner hastened to tell us about the much-talked-of little bag—so be it, you shall hear this romance!

"Gentlemen of the jury, I have told you already why I consider this romance not only an absurdity, but the most improbable invention that could have been brought forward in the circumstances. If one tried on a bet to invent the most unlikely story, one could hardly find anything more incredible. The worst of such stories is that the triumphant romancers can always be put to confusion and crushed by the very details in which real life is so rich and which these unhappy and involuntary storytellers neglect as insignificant trifles. Oh, they have no thought to spare for such details, their minds are concentrated on their grand invention as a whole and someone dares to suggest such a trifle to them! But that's how they are caught. The prisoner was asked the question, 'Where did you get the stuff for your little bag and who made it for you?' 'I made it myself.' 'And where did you get the linen?' The prisoner was positively offended, he thought it almost insulting to ask him such a trivial question, and would you believe it, his resentment was genuine, genuine! But they are all like that. 'I tore it off my shirt.' 'Then we shall find that shirt among your linen tomorrow, with a piece torn off.' And only fancy, gentlemen of the jury, if we really had found that torn shirt (and how could we have failed to find it in his chest of drawers or trunk?) that would have been a fact, a material fact in support of his statement! But he was incapable of that reflection. 'I don't remember, it may not have been off my shirt, I sewed it up in one of my landlady's caps.' 'What sort of a cap?' 'It was an old cotton rag of hers lying about.' 'And do you remember that clearly?' 'No, I don't.' And he was angry, very angry, and yet imagine not remembering it! At the most terrible moments of man's life, for instance when he is being led to execution, he remembers just such trifles. He will forget anything but some green roof that has flashed past him on the road, or a jackdaw on a cross—that he will remember. He concealed the making of that little bag from his household, he must have remembered his humiliating fear that someone might come in and find him needle in hand, how at the slightest sound he slipped behind the screen (there is a screen in his lodgings).

"But, gentlemen of the jury, why do I tell you all this, all these details, trifles?" cried Ippolit Kirillovich suddenly. "Just because the defendant still persists in these absurdities to this moment. He has not explained anything since that fatal night two months ago, he has not added one actual illuminating fact to his former fantastic statements; all those are trivialities. 'You must believe it on my honor.' Oh, we are glad to believe it, we are eager to believe it, even if only on his word of honor! Are we jackals thirsting for human blood? Show us a single fact in the defendant's favor and we shall rejoice; but let it be a substantial, real fact, and not a conclusion drawn from the defendant's expression by his own brother, or that when he beat himself on the breast he must have meant to point to the little bag, in the darkness, too. We shall rejoice at the new fact, we shall be the first to repudiate our charge, we shall hasten to repudiate it. But now justice cries out and we persist, we cannot repudiate anything."

Here Ippolit Kirillovich passed to his peroration. He looked as though he was in a fever, he spoke of the blood that cried for vengeance, the blood of the father murdered by his son, with the base motive of robbery! He pointed to the tragic and glaring consistency of the facts.

"And whatever you may hear from the talented and celebrated counsel for the defense," Ippolit Kirillovich could not resist adding, "whatever eloquent and touching appeals may be made to your sensibilities, remember that at this moment you are in a temple of justice. Remember that you are the champions of our justice, the champions of our holy Russia, of her principles, her family, everything that she holds sacred! Yes, you represent Russia here at this moment, and your verdict will be heard not in this hall only but will re-echo throughout the whole of Russia, and all Russia will hear you, as her champions and her judges, and she will be encouraged or disheartened by your verdict. Do not disappoint Russia and her expectations. Our fatal troika dashes on in her headlong flight perhaps to destruction and in all Russia for long past men have stretched out imploring hands and called a halt to its furious reckless course. And if other nations stand aside from that troika that may be, not from respect, as the poet would fain believe, but simply from horror, note that. From horror, perhaps from disgust. And well it is that they stand aside, but maybe they will cease one day to do so and will form a firm wall confronting the hurrying apparition and will check the frenzied rush of our recklessness, for the sake of their own safety, enlightenment and civilization. Already we have heard voices of alarm from Europe, they already begin to sound. Do not tempt them! Do not heap up their growing hatred by a sentence justifying the murder of a father by his son!"

In short, though Ippolit Kirillovich was genuinely moved, he wound up his speech with this rhetorical appeal—and the effect produced by him was extraordinary. When he had finished his speech, he went out hurriedly and, as I have mentioned before, almost fainted in the adjoining room. There was no applause in the court, but serious persons were pleased. The ladies were not so well satisfied, though even they were pleased with his eloquence, especially as they had no apprehensions as to the upshot of the trial and had full trust in Fetyukovich. "He will speak at last and of course carry all before him." Everyone looked at Mitya; he sat silent through the whole of the prosecutor's speech, clenching his teeth, with his hands clasped, and his head bowed. Only from time to time he raised his head and listened, especially when Grushenka was spoken of. When the prosecutor mentioned Rakitin's opinion of her, a smile of contempt and anger passed over his face and he murmured rather audibly "the Bernards!" When Ippolit Kirillovich described how he had questioned and tortured him at Mokroe, Mitya raised his head and listened with intense curiosity. At one point he seemed about to jump up and cry out, but controlled himself and only shrugged his shoulders disdainfully. People talked afterwards of the end of the speech, of the prosecutor's feat in examining the prisoner at Mokroe and jeered at Ippolit Kirillovich. "The man could not resist boasting of his cleverness," they said.

The court was adjourned, but only for a short interval, a quarter of an hour or twenty minutes at most. There was a hum of conversation and exclamations in the audience. I remember some of them.

"A solid speech," a gentleman in one group observed gravely.

"He brought in too much psychology," said another voice.

"But it was all true, the absolute truth!"

"Yes, he is first rate at it."

"He summed it all up."

"Yes, he summed us up, too," chimed in another voice. "Do you remember, at the beginning of his speech, making out we were all like Fyodor Pavlovich?"

"And at the end, too. But that was all rot."

"And obscure too."

"He was a little too much carried away."

"It's unjust, it's unjust, sir."

"No, it was smartly done, anyway. He's had long to wait, but he'd had his say, he-he!"

"What will the counsel for the defense say?"

In another group I heard:

"He had no business to make a thrust at the Petersburg man like that; 'appealing to your sensibilities'—do you remember?"

"Yes, that was awkward of him."

"He was in too great a hurry."

"He is a nervous man."

"We laugh, but what must the defendant be feeling?"

"Yes, what must it be for Mitenka?"

In a third group:

"What lady is that, the fat one, with the lorgnette, sitting at the end?"

"She is a general's wife, divorced, I know her."

"That's the one, with the lorgnette."

"She is not good for much."

"Oh, no, she is a piquant little woman."

"Two places beyond her there is a little fair woman, she is prettier."

"They caught him smartly at Mokroe, didn't they, eh?"

"Oh, it was smart enough. We've heard it before, how often he has told the story at people's houses!"

"And he couldn't resist doing it now. That's vanity."

"He is a man with a grievance, he-he!"

"Yes, and quick to take offense. And there was too much rhetoric, such long sentences."

"Yes, he tries to alarm us, he kept trying to alarm us. Do you remember about the troika? Something about 'They have Hamlets, but we have, so far, only Karamazovs!' That was cleverly said!"

"That was to propitiate the liberals. He is afraid of them."

"Yes, and he is afraid of the jurist, too."

"Yes, what will Mr. Fetyukovich say?"

"Whatever he says, he won't get round our peasants."

"Do you think so?"

A fourth group:

"What he said about the troika was good, that piece about the other nations."

"And that was true what he said about other nations not standing it."

"What do you mean?"

"Why, in the English Parliament a Member got up last week and speaking about the Nihilists asked the Ministry whether it was not high time to intervene, to educate this barbarous people. Ippolit was thinking of him, I know he was. He was talking about that last week."

"Not an easy job."

"Not an easy job? Why not?"

"Why, we'd shut up Kronstadt[5] and not let them have any wheat. Where would they get it?"

"In America. They get it from America now."

"Nonsense!"

But the bell rang, all rushed to their places. Fetyukovich mounted the tribune.

Chapter X

The Speech for the Defense. An Argument That Cuts Both Ways

All was hushed as the first words of the famous orator rang out. The eyes of the audience were fastened upon him. He began very simply and directly, with an air of conviction, but not the slightest

5. The naval base that guards the entry to St. Petersburg.

trace of conceit. He made no attempt at eloquence, at pathos, or emotional phrases. He was like a man speaking in a circle of intimate and sympathetic friends. His voice was a fine one, sonorous and attractive, and there was something genuine and simple in the very sound of it. But everyone realized at once that the speaker might suddenly rise to genuine pathos and "pierce the heart with untold power."[6] His language was perhaps more irregular than Ippolit Kirillovich's, but he spoke without long phrases, and indeed, with more precision. One thing did not please the ladies: he kept bending forward, especially at the beginning of his speech, not exactly bowing, but as though he were about to dart at his listeners, bending his long back in half, as though there were a spring in the middle of that long and narrow back that enabled him to bend at right angles.

At the beginning of his speech he spoke rather disconnectedly, without system, one may say, dealing with facts separately, though, at the end, these facts formed a whole. His speech might be divided into two parts, the first consisting of criticism in refutation of the charge, sometimes malicious and sarcastic. But in the second half he suddenly changed his tone, and even his manner, and at once rose to pathos. The audience seemed on the lookout for it, and quivered with enthusiasm.

He went straight to the point, and began by saying that although he practiced in Petersburg, he had more than once visited provincial towns as attorney for the defense, when he was convinced they were innocent or at least felt it beforehand. "That is what has happened to me in the present case," he explained. "From the very first accounts in the newspapers I was struck by something which strongly prepossessed me in the defendant's favor. Briefly, what interested me most was a fact which often occurs in legal practice, but rarely, I think, in such an extreme and peculiar form as in the present case. I ought to formulate that peculiarity only at the end of my speech, but I will do so at the very beginning, for it is my weakness to go to work directly, not keeping my effects in reserve and economizing my material. That may be imprudent on my part, but at least it's sincere. What I have in my mind is this: there is an overwhelming chain of evidence against the defendant, and at the same time not one fact that will stand criticism, if it is examined separately. As I followed the case more closely in the papers and reports my idea was more and more confirmed, and I suddenly received from the defendant's relatives a request to undertake his defense. I at once hurried here, and here I became completely convinced. It was to break down this terrible chain of facts, and to show that each piece of evidence taken separately was unproved and fantastic, that I undertook the case."

6. From Pushkin's poem "Answer to an Anonymous Correspondent."

So began counsel for the defense and then suddenly exclaimed:

"Gentlemen of the jury, I am new to this district. I have no preconceived ideas. The defendant, a man of turbulent and unbridled temper, has not insulted me. But he has insulted perhaps hundreds of persons in this town, and so prejudiced many people against him beforehand. Of course I recognize that the moral sentiment of local society is justly excited against him. The defendant is of turbulent and violent temper. Yet he was received in society here; he was even welcome in the family of my highly talented friend, the prosecutor."

(N.B. At these words there were two or three laughs in the audience, quickly suppressed, but noticed by all. All of us knew that the prosecutor received Mitya against his will, solely because he had somehow interested his wife—a lady of the highest virtue and moral worth, but fanciful, capricious, and fond of opposing her husband, especially in trifles. Mitya's visits, however, had not been frequent.)

"Nevertheless I venture to suggest," the defense attorney continued, "that in spite of his independent mind and just character, my opponent may have formed a mistaken prejudice against my unfortunate client. Oh, that is so natural; the unfortunate man has only too well deserved such prejudice. Outraged morality, and still more outraged aesthetic feeling, is often relentless. We have all heard in the highly talented prosecutor's speech a stern analysis of the defendant's character and conduct, and his severe critical attitude to the case was evident. And, what's more, he went into psychological subtleties in order to explain the essence of the matter to us, into which he could not have entered, if he had the least conscious and malicious prejudice against the defendant. But there are things which are even worse, even more fatal in such cases, than the most malicious and consciously unfair attitude. It is worse if we are carried away by a certain artistic instinct, so to speak, by the desire for artistic creation, so to speak, the composition of a novel, especially if God has endowed us with psychological insight. Before I started on my way here, I was warned in Petersburg, and was myself aware, that I should find a talented opponent whose psychological insight and subtlety had gained him peculiar renown in legal circles of recent years. But profound as psychology is, it's a knife that cuts both ways." (Laughter among the public.) "You will, of course, forgive me my comparison; I can't boast of eloquence. But I will take as an example any point in the prosecutor's speech.

"The defendant, running away in the garden in the dark, climbed over the fence, was seized by the servant, and knocked him down with a brass pestle. Then he jumped back into the garden and spent five minutes over the man, trying to discover whether he had killed him or not. And the prosecutor refuses to believe the defendant's statement that he ran to old Grigory out of pity. 'No,' he says, 'such sensibility is impossible at such a moment, that's unnatural; he ran to find out whether the only witness of his crime was dead or alive, and so showed that he had committed the murder, since he would not have run back for any other reason.' Here you have psychology; but let us take the same psychology and apply it to the case the other way round, and our result will be no less probable. The murderer, we are told, leaped down to find out, as a precaution, whether the witness was alive or not, yet he had left in his murdered father's study, as the prosecutor himself argues, an amazing piece of evidence in the shape of a torn envelope, with an inscription that there had been three thousand rubles in it. 'If he had carried that envelope away with him, no one in the world would have known of that envelope and of the money in it, and that the money had been stolen by the prisoner.' Those are the prosecutor's own words. So on one side you see a complete absence of precaution, a man who has lost his head and run away in a fright, leaving that clue on the floor, and two minutes later, when he has killed another man, we are entitled to assume the most heartless and calculating foresight in him. But even admitting this was so, it is psychological subtlety, I suppose, that discerns that under certain circumstances I become as bloodthirsty and keen-sighted as a Caucasian eagle, while at the next I am as timid and blind as a mole. But if I am so bloodthirsty and cruelly calculating that when I kill a man I only run back to find out whether he is alive to witness against me, why should I spend five minutes looking after my victim at the risk of encountering other witnesses? Why soak my handkerchief, wiping the blood off his head so that it may be evidence against me later? If he were so cold-hearted and calculating, why not hit the servant on the head again and again with the same pestle so as to kill him outright and relieve himself of all anxiety about the witness?

"Again, though he ran to see whether the witness was alive, he left another witness on the path, that brass pestle which he had taken from the two women, and which they could always recognize afterwards as theirs, and testify that he had taken it from them. And it is not as though he had forgotten it on the path, dropped it through carelessness or haste, no, we had flung away our weapon, for it was found fifteen paces from where Grigory lay. Why did we do so? Just because we were grieved at having killed a man, an old servant; and we flung away the pestle in vexation, with a curse, as a murderous weapon. That's how it must have been, what other reason could we have had for throwing it so far? And if he was capable of feeling grief and pity at having killed a man, it shows that he was innocent of his father's murder. Had he murdered him, he would never have run to another victim out of pity; then he would have felt differently; his thoughts would have been centered on self-preservation. He would have had none to spare for pity, that is beyond doubt. On the contrary, I repeat, he would have broken his skull instead of spending five minutes looking after him. There was room for pity and good feeling just because his conscience had been clear till then. Here we have a different psychology. I have purposely resorted to this method, gentlemen of the jury, to show that you can prove anything by it. It all depends on who makes use of it. Psychology lures even most serious people into romancing, and quite unconsciously. I am speaking of excessive psychology, of the abuse of psychology, gentlemen."

Sounds of approval and laughter, at the expense of the prosecutor, were again audible in the court. I will not repeat the speech for the defense in detail; I will only quote some passages from it, some leading points.

Chapter XI
There Was No Money. There Was No Robbery

There was one point that struck everyone in the defense attorney's speech. He flatly denied the existence of the fatal three thousand rubles, and consequently the possibility of their having been stolen.

"Gentlemen of the jury," he began. "Every new and unprejudiced observer must be struck by a characteristic peculiarity in the present case, namely, the charge of robbery, and the complete impossibility of proving that there was anything to be stolen. We are told that money was stolen—three thousand rubles—but whether those rubles ever existed, nobody knows. Consider, how have we heard of that sum, and who has seen it? The only person who saw it and stated that it had been put in the envelope, was the servant, Smerdyakov. He had spoken of it to the defendant and his brother, Ivan Fyodorovich, before the catastrophe. Miss Svetlov, too, had been told of it. But not one of these three persons had actually seen the money, no one but Smerdyakov had seen it.

"Here the question arises, if it's true that it did exist, and that Smerdyakov had seen it, when did he see it for the last time? What if his master had taken it from under his bed and put it back in his cash box without telling him? Note, that according to Smerdyakov's story the money was kept under the mattress; the defendant must have pulled it out, and yet the bed was absolutely unrumpled; that is carefully recorded in the deposition. How could the prisoner have found the money without disturbing the bed? How could he have helped soiling with his bloodstained hands the fine and spotless linen with which the bed had been purposely made? But I shall be asked; what about the envelope on the floor? Yes, it's worth saying a word or two about that envelope. I was somewhat surprised just now to hear the highly talented prosecutor declare of his own will—of his own will, observe—when he tried to show the absurdity of considering Smerdyakov the murderer, that but for that envelope, but for its being left on the floor, no one in the world would have known of the existence of that envelope and the money in it, and therefore of the defendant's having stolen it. And so that torn scrap of paper with its inscription is, by the prosecutor's own admission, the sole proof on which the charge of robbery rests, 'otherwise no one would have known of the robbery, nor perhaps even of the money.' But is the mere fact that that scrap of paper was lying on the floor a proof that there was money in it, and that that money had been stolen? Yet, it will be objected, Smerdyakov had seen the money in the envelope. But when, when had he seen it for the last time, I ask you that? I talked to Smerdyakov, and he told me that he had seen the money two days before the catastrophe. Then why not imagine that old Fyodor Pavlovich, locked up alone in impatient and hysterical expectation of the object of his adoration, may have whiled away the time by breaking open the envelope and taking out the money. 'What's the use of the envelope,' he may have asked himself, 'she won't believe the notes are there, but when I show her the thirty rainbow-colored bills in one roll, it will make more impression, you may be sure, it will make her mouth water.' And so he tears open the envelope, takes out the money, and flings the envelope on the floor, conscious of being the owner and untroubled by any fears of leaving evidence.

"Listen, gentlemen, could anything be more likely than this theory and such an action? Why is it out of the question? But if anything of the sort could have taken place, the charge of robbery falls to the ground; if there was no money, there was no robbery. If the envelope on the floor may be taken as evidence that there had been money in it, why may I not maintain the opposite, that the envelope was on the floor precisely because the money had been taken from it by its owner? But I shall be asked what became of the money if Fyodor Pavlovich took it out of the envelope since it was not found when the police searched the house? In the first place, part of the money was found in the cash box, and secondly, he might have taken it out that morning or the evening before to make some other use of it, to give or send it away; he may have changed his idea, his plan of action completely, without thinking it necessary to announce the fact to Smerdyakov beforehand. And if there is the barest possibility of such an explanation, how can the defendant be so positively accused of having committed murder for the sake of robbery, and of having actually carried out that robbery? This is encroaching on the domain of romance. If it is maintained that something has been stolen, the thing must be produced, or at least its existence must be proved beyond doubt. Yet no one had ever seen the money.

"Not long ago in Petersburg a young man of eighteen, hardly more than a boy, who had a small stand in the market, went in broad daylight into a moneychanger's shop with an ax, and with extraordinary, typical audacity killed the master of the shop and carried off fifteen hundred rubles. Five hours later he was arrested, and, except fifteen rubles he had already managed to spend, the whole sum was found on him. Moreover, the shopman, on his return to the shop after the murder, informed the police not only of the exact sum stolen, but even of the bills and gold coins of which that sum was made up, and those very bills and coins were found on the criminal. This was followed by a full and genuine confession on the part of the murderer that he had killed the man and had taken these very bills. That's what I call evidence, gentlemen of the jury! In that case I know, I see, I touch the money, and cannot deny its existence. Is it the same in the present case? And yet it is a question of life and death, of a man's fate.

"Yes, I shall be told, but he was carousing that night, squandering money; he was shown to have had fifteen hundred rubles—where did he get the money? But the very fact that only fifteen hundred could be found, and the other half of the sum could nowhere be discovered, shows that that money was not the same, and had never been in any envelope. By strict calculation of time it was proved at the preliminary inquiry that the prisoner ran straight from those women servants to Perkhotin's without going home, and that he had been nowhere. So he had been all the time in company and therefore could not have divided the three thousand in half and hidden half in the town. It's just this consideration that has led the prosecutor to assume that the money is hidden in some crevice at Mokroe. Why not in the dungeons of the castle of Udolpho,[7] gentlemen? Isn't this supposition really too fantastic and too much of a romance? And observe, if that supposition breaks down, the whole charge of robbery is scattered to the winds, for in that case what could have become of the other fifteen hundred rubles? By what miracle could they have disappeared, since it's proved that the prisoner went nowhere else? And we are ready to ruin a man's life with such romances!

"I shall be told that he could not explain where he got the fifteen hundred that he had, and everyone knew that he was without money before that night. Who knew it, pray? The defendant has made a clear and unflinching statement of the source of that money, and if you will have it so, gentlemen of the jury, nothing can be

7. Ann Radcliffe's gothic novel, *The Mysteries of Udolpho* (1794), was still popular in Russia.

more probable than that statement, and more consistent with the temper and spirit of the defendant. The prosecutor is charmed with his own romance. A man of weak will, who had brought himself to take the three thousand so insultingly offered by his betrothed, could not, we are told, have set aside half and sewn it up, but would, even if he had done so, have unpicked it every two days and taken out a hundred, and so would have spent it all in a month. All this, you will remember, was put forward in a tone that brooked no contradiction. But what if the thing happened quite differently? What if you've been weaving a romance, and about quite a different kind of man? That's just it, you have invented quite a different man!

"I shall be told, perhaps, there are witnesses that he spent on one day all that three thousand given him by Miss Verkhovtsev a month before the catastrophe, so he could not have divided the sum in half. But who are these witnesses? The value of their evidence has been shown in court already. Besides, in another man's hand a crust always seems larger, and not one of these witnesses counted that money; that all judged simply at sight. And the witness Maximov has testified that the defendant had twenty thousand in his hand. You see, gentlemen of the jury, psychology is a two-edged weapon. Let me turn the other edge now and see what comes of it.

"A month before the catastrophe the prisoner was entrusted by Miss Verkhovtsev with three thousand rubles to send off by mail. But the question is: is it true that they were entrusted to him in such an insulting and degrading way as was proclaimed just now? The first statement made by Miss Verkhovtsev on the subject was different, completely different. In the second statement we heard only cries of resentment and revenge, cries of long-concealed hatred. And the very fact that the witness gave her first evidence incorrectly, gives us a right to conclude that her second piece of evidence may have been incorrect also. The prosecutor will not, dare not (his own words) touch on that story. So be it. I will not touch on it either, but will only venture to observe that if a lofty and high-principled person, such as that highly respected Miss Verkhovtsev unquestionably is, if such a person, I say, allows herself suddenly in court to contradict her first statement, with the obvious motive of ruining the defendant, it is clear that this evidence has been given not impartially, not coolly. Have not we the right to assume that a revengeful woman might have exaggerated much? Yes, she may well have exaggerated, in particular, the insult and humiliation of her offering him the money. No, it was offered in such a way that it was possible to take it, especially for a man so easygoing as the defendant. Above all, he expected to receive shortly from his father the three thousand rubles that he reckoned was owing to him. It was unreflecting of him, but it was just his irresponsible want of reflection that made him so confident that his father would give him the money, that he would get it, and so could always despatch the money entrusted to him by Miss Verkhovtsev and repay the debt.

"But the prosecutor refuses to allow that he could the same day have set aside half the money and sewn it up in a little bag. That's not his character, he tells us, he couldn't have had such feelings. But yet he talked himself of the broad Karamazov nature; he cried out about the two extreme abysses which a Karamazov can contemplate at once. Karamazov is just such a two-sided nature, fluctuating between two extremes, that even when moved by the most violent craving for riotous gaiety, he can control himself, if something strikes him on the other side. And on the other side is love—that new love which had flamed up in his heart, and for that love he needed money; oh, far more than for carousing with his mistress. If she were to say to him, 'I am yours, I won't have Fyodor Pavlovich,' then he must have money to take her away. That was more important than carousing. Could a Karamazov fail to understand it? That anxiety was just what he was suffering from—what is there improbable in his laying aside that money and concealing it in case of emergency?

"But time passed, and Fyodor Pavlovich did not give the defendant the expected three thousand; on the contrary, the latter heard that he meant to use this sum to seduce the woman he, the defendant, loved. 'If Fyodor Pavlovich doesn't give the money,' he thought, 'I shall be put in the position of a thief before Katerina Ivanovna.' And then the idea presented itself to him that he would go to Miss Verkhovtsev, lay before her the fifteen hundred rubles he still carried round his neck, and say, 'I am a scoundrel, but not a thief.' So here we have already a twofold reason why he should guard that sum of money as the apple of his eye, why he shouldn't unpick the little bag, and spend it a hundred at a time. Why should you deny the defendant a sense of honor? Yes, he has a sense of honor, granted that it's misplaced, granted it's often mistaken, yet it exists and amounts to a passion, and he has proved that.

"But now the affair becomes even more complex; his jealous torments reach a climax, and those same two questions torture his fevered brain more and more: 'If I repay Katerina Ivanovna, where can I find the means to go off with Grushenka?' If he behaved wildly, drank, and made disturbances in the taverns in the course of that month, it was perhaps because he was wretched and strained beyond his powers of endurance. These two questions became so acute that they drove him at last to despair. He sent his younger brother to beg for the last time for the three thousand rubles, but without waiting for a reply, burst in himself and ended by beating the old man in the presence of witnesses. After that he had no prospect of getting it from anyone; his father would not give it him after that beating. The same evening he struck himself on the breast, just on the upper part of the breast where the little bag was, and swore to his brother that he had the means of not being a scoundrel, but that still he would remain a scoundrel, for he foresaw that he would not use that means, that he wouldn't have the character, that he wouldn't the willpower to do it. Why, why does the prosecutor refuse to believe the evidence of Alexey Karamazov, given so genuinely and sincerely, so spontaneously and convincingly? And why, on the contrary, does he force me to believe in money hidden in a crevice, in the dungeons of the castle of Udolpho?

"The same evening, after his talk with his brother, the defendant wrote that fatal letter, and that letter is the chief, the most stupendous proof of the defendant's having committed robbery! 'I shall beg from everyone, and if I don't get it I shall murder my father and shall take the envelope with the pink ribbon on it from under his mattress as soon as Ivan has gone.' A full scenario of the murder, we are told, so it must have been he. 'It has all been done as he wrote,' cries the prosecutor.

"But in the first place, it's the letter of a drunken man and written in great irritation; secondly, he writes of the envelope from what he has heard from Smerdyakov again, for he has not seen the envelope himself; and thirdly, he wrote it indeed, but how can you prove that he did it? Did the prisoner take the envelope from under the pillow, did he find the money, did that money exist indeed? And was it to get money that the prisoner ran off, if you remember? He ran off posthaste not to steal, but to find out where she was, the woman who had crushed him. He was not running to carry out a scenario, to carry out what he had written, that is, not for an act of premeditated robbery, but he ran suddenly, spontaneously, in a jealous fury. Yes! I shall be told, but when he got there and murdered him he seized the money, too. But did he murder him after all? The charge of robbery I repudiate with indignation. A man cannot be accused of robbery, if it's impossible to state accurately what he has stolen; that's an axiom. But did he murder him without robbery, did he murder him at all? Is that proved? Isn't that, too, a romance?"

Chapter XII

And There Was No Murder Either

"Allow me, gentlemen of the jury, to remind you that a man's life is at stake and that you must be very careful. We have heard the prosecutor himself admit that until today he hesitated to accuse the defendant of a full and conscious premeditation of the crime;

he hesitated till he saw that fatal drunken letter which was produced in court today. 'All was done as written.' But, I repeat again, he was running to her, to seek her, solely to find out where she was. That's a fact that can't be disputed. Had she been at home, he would not have run away, but would have remained at her side, and so would not have done what he promised in the letter. He ran unexpectedly and accidentally, and by that time very likely he did not even remember his 'drunken' letter. 'He snatched up the pestle,' they say, and you will remember how a whole edifice of psychology was built on that pestle—why he was bound to look at that pestle as a weapon, to snatch it up, and so on, and so on. A very commonplace idea occurs to me at this point: What if that pestle had not been in sight, had not been lying on the shelf from which it was snatched by the defendant, but had been put away in a cupboard? It would not have caught the defendant's eye, and he would have run away without a weapon, with empty hands, and then he would certainly not have killed anyone. How then can I look upon the pestle as a proof of his arming himself and of premeditation?

"Yes, but he talked in the taverns of murdering his father, and two days before, on the evening when he wrote his drunken letter, he was quiet and only quarreled with a shopman in the tavern, because a 'Karamazov could not help quarreling'! But my answer to that is, that, if he was planning such a murder in accordance with his letter, he certainly would not have quarreled even with a shopman, and probably would not have gone into the tavern at all, because a person plotting such a crime seeks quiet and retirement, because to efface himself, to avoid being seen and heard, that he might be forgotten about, and that not from calculation, but from instinct. Gentlemen of the jury, the psychological method is a two-edged weapon, and we, too, can use it. As for all this shouting in taverns throughout the month, don't we often hear children, or drunkards coming out of taverns shout, 'I'll kill you'? but they don't murder anyone. And that fatal letter—isn't that simply drunken irritability, too? Isn't that simply the shout of the brawler outside the tavern, 'I'll kill you! I'll kill the lot of you!' Why not, why could it not be that? What reason have we to call that letter 'fatal' rather than absurd? Because his father has been found murdered, because a witness saw the defendant running out of the garden with a weapon in his hand, and was knocked down by him: therefore, we are told, everything was done as he had planned in writing, and the letter was not 'absurd,' but 'fatal.'

"Now, thank God! we've come to the real point: 'since he was in the garden, he must have murdered him.' In those few words: 'since he *was*, then he *must*' lies the whole case for the prosecution. He was there, so he must have. And what if there is no *must* about it, even if he was there? Oh, I admit that the chain of evidence—the coincidences—are really suggestive. But examine all these facts separately, regardless of their connection. Why, for instance, does the prosecution refuse to admit the truth of the defendant's statement that he ran away from his father's window? Remember the sarcasm in which the prosecution indulged at the expense of the respectful and 'pious' sentiments which suddenly came over the murderer. But what if there were something of the sort, a feeling of religious awe, if not a filial respect? 'My mother must have been praying for me at that moment,' were the defendant's words at the preliminary inquiry, and so he ran away as soon as he convinced himself that Miss Svetlov was not in his father's house. 'But he could not convince himself by looking through the window,' the prosecution objects. But why couldn't he? Why? The window opened at the signals given by the defendant. Some word might have been uttered by Fyodor Pavlovich, some exclamation which showed the defendant that she was not there. Why should we assume everything as we imagine it, as we make up our minds to imagine it? A thousand things may happen in reality which elude the subtlest imagination.

" 'Yes, but Grigory saw the door open and so the defendant certainly was in the house, therefore he killed him.' Now about that door, gentlemen of the jury.... Observe that we have only the statement of one witness as to that door, and he was at the time in such a condition, that ... But supposing the door was open; supposing the defendant has lied in denying it, from an instinct of self-defense, natural in his position; supposing he did go into the house—well, what then? How does it follow that because he was there he committed the murder? He might have dashed in, run through the rooms; might have pushed his father away; might have struck him; but as soon as he had made sure Miss Svetlov was not there, he may have run away rejoicing that she was not there and that he had not killed his father. And it was perhaps just because he had escaped from the temptation to kill his father, because he had a clear conscience and was rejoicing at not having killed him, that he was capable of a pure feeling, the feeling of pity and compassion, and leaped off the fence a minute later to the assistance of Grigory after he had, in his excitement, knocked him down.

"With terrible eloquence the prosecutor has described to us the dreadful state of the defendant's mind at Mokroe when love again appeared before him calling him to new life, while love was impossible for him because he had his father's bloodstained corpse behind him and beyond that corpse—retribution. And yet the prosecutor allowed him love, which he explained, according to his method, talking about his drunken condition, about a criminal being taken to execution, about it being still far off, and so on and so on. But again I ask, Mr. Prosecutor, have you not invented a new personality? Is the defendant so coarse and heartless as to be able to think at that moment of love and of dodges to escape punishment, if his hands were really stained with his father's blood? No, no, no! As soon as it was made plain to him that she loved him and called him to her side, promising him new happiness, oh! then, I protest, he must have felt the impulse to suicide doubled, trebled, and must have killed himself, if he had his father's murder on his conscience. Oh, no! he would not have forgotten where his pistols lay! I know the defendant: the savage, stony heartlessness ascribed to him by the prosecution is inconsistent with his character. He would have killed himself, that's certain. He did not kill himself just because 'his mother's prayers had saved him,' and he was innocent of his father's blood. He was troubled, he was grieving that night at Mokroe only about old Grigory and praying to God that the old man would recover, that his blow had not been fatal, and that he would not have to suffer for it. Why not accept such an interpretation of the facts? What trustworthy proof have we that the defendant is lying? But we shall be told at once again, 'There is his father's corpse! If he ran away without murdering him, who did murder him?' "

"Here, I repeat, you have the whole logic of the prosecution. Who murdered him, if not he? There's no one to put in his place. Gentlemen of the jury, is that really so? Is it positively, actually true that there is no one else at all? We've heard the prosecution count on its fingers all the persons who were in that house that night. They were five in number; three of them, I agree, could not have been responsible—the murdered man himself, old Grigory, and his wife. There are left then the defendant and Smerdyakov, and the prosecutor dramatically exclaims that the defendant pointed to Smerdyakov because he had no one else to fix on, that had there been a sixth person, even a phantom of a sixth person, he would have abandoned the charge against Smerdyakov at once in shame and have accused the other. But, gentlemen of the jury, why may I not draw the very opposite conclusion? There are two persons—the defendant and Smerdyakov. Why can I not say that you accuse my client, simply because you have no one else to accuse? And you have no one else only because you have determined to exclude Smerdyakov from all suspicion. It's true, indeed, Smerdyakov is accused only by the prisoner, his two brothers, and Miss Svetlov. But there are others who accuse him: there are vague rumors of a question, of a suspicion, an obscure report, a feeling of expectation. Finally, we have the evidence of a combination of facts very suggestive, though, I admit, inconclusive. In the first place we have precisely on the day of the catastrophe that fit, for the genuineness of which the prosecutor, for some reason, has felt obliged to make a careful defense. Then Smerdyakov's sudden suicide on the eve of the trial. Then the equally startling evidence given in court today by the elder of the defendant's brothers, who had believed in his guilt, but has today produced a bundle of bills and proclaimed Smerdyakov as the murderer. Oh, I fully share the court's and the prosecution's conviction that Ivan Karamazov is suffering from brain fever, that his statement may really be a desperate effort, planned in delirium, to save his brother by throwing the guilt on the dead man. But again Smerdyakov's name is pronounced, again there is a suggestion of mystery. There is something unexplained, incomplete. And perhaps it may one day be explained. But we won't go into that now. Of that later.

"The court has resolved to go on with the trial, but, meantime, I might make a few remarks about the character sketch of Smerdyakov drawn with subtlety and talent by the prosecutor. But while I admire his talent I cannot agree with him. I have visited Smerdyakov. I have seen him and talked to him, and he made a very different impression on me. He was weak in health, it is true; but in character, in spirit, he was by no means the weak man the prosecution has made him out to be. I found in him no trace of the timidity on which the prosecutor so insisted. There was no simplicity about him at all. I found in him, on the contrary, an extreme mistrustfulness concealed under a mask of naïveté, and an intelligence of considerable range. The prosecution was too simple in taking him for weak-minded. He made a very definite impression on me: I left him with the conviction that he was a distinctly spiteful creature, excessively ambitious, vindictive, and intensely envious. I made some inquiries: he resented his parentage, was ashamed of it, and would clench his teeth when he remembered that he was the son of 'stinking Lizaveta.' He was disrespectful to the servant Grigory and his wife, who had cared for him in his childhood. He cursed and jeered at Russia. He dreamed of going to France and becoming a Frenchman. He often used to say that he hadn't the means to do so. I fancy he loved no one but himself and had a strangely high opinion of himself. His conception of culture was limited to good clothes, clean shirt fronts and polished boots. Believing himself to be the illegitimate son of Fyodor Pavlovich (there is evidence of this) he might well have resented his position, compared with that of his master's legitimate sons. They had everything, he nothing. They had all the rights, they had the inheritance, while he was only the cook. He told me himself that he had helped Fyodor Pavlovich to put the notes in the envelope. The destination of that sum—a sum which would have made his career—must have been hateful to him. Morever, he saw three thousand rubles in new rainbow-colored bills. (I asked him about that on purpose.) Oh, beware of showing an ambitious and envious man a large sum of money at once! And it was the first time he had seen so much money in the hands of one man. The sight of the rainbow-colored bundle may have made a morbid impression on his imagination, but with no immediate results.

"The highly talented prosecutor, with extraordinary subtlety, sketched for us all the arguments for and against the hypothesis of Smerdyakov's guilt, and asked us in particular what motive he had in feigning a fit. But he may not have been feigning at all, the fit may have happened quite naturally, but it may have passed off quite naturally, and the sick man may have recovered, not completely perhaps, but still regaining consciousness, as happens with epileptics.

"The prosecution asks at what moment could Smerdyakov have committed the murder. But it is very easy to point out that moment. He might have woken up from deep sleep (for he was only asleep—an epileptic fit is always followed by a deep sleep) at that moment when the old Grigory shouted at the top of his voice 'Parricide!' That extraordinary shout in the dark and stillness may have woken Smerdyakov, whose sleep may have been less sound at the moment: he might naturally have woken up an hour before. Getting out of bed, he goes almost unconsciously and with no definite motive towards the sound to see what's the matter. His head is still clouded with his attack, his faculties are half asleep; but, once in the garden, he walks to the lighted windows and he hears terrible news from his master, who would be, of course, glad to see him. His mind sets to work at once. He hears all the details from his frightened master, and gradually in his disordered brain there shapes itself an idea—terrible, but seductive and irresistibly logical. To kill the old man, take the three thousand, and throw all the blame on to his young master. Who would be accused if not the young master, how could it not be he, he was there, there is all the evidence. A terrible lust for money, for booty, might seize upon him as he realized his security from detection. Oh! these sudden and irresistible impulses come so often when there is a favorable opportunity, and especially with murderers who have had no idea of committing a murder beforehand. And Smerdyakov may have gone in and carried out his plan. With what weapon? Why, with any stone picked up in the garden. But what for, with what object? Why, the three thousand which means a career for him. Oh, I am not contradicting myself—the money may have existed. And perhaps Smerdyakov alone knew where to find it, where his master kept it. And the covering of the money—the torn envelope on the floor?

"Just now, when the prosecutor was explaining his extremely subtle theory that only an inexperienced thief like Karamazov would have left the envelope on the floor, and not one like Smerdyakov, who would never have left a piece of evidence like

that against himself, I thought as I listened that I was hearing
something very familiar, and, would you believe it, I have heard
that very argument, that very conjecture, of how Karamazov would
have behaved, precisely two days before, from Smerdyakov himself.
What's more, it struck me at the time. I fancied that there was an
artificial simplicity about him; that he was in a hurry to suggest this
idea to me that I might fancy it was my own. He insinuated it, as it
were. Did he not insinuate the same idea to the prosecution? Did he
not also suggest it to the highly talented prosecutor?

"I shall be asked, 'What about the old woman, Grigory's wife?
She heard the sick man moaning close by, all night.' Yes, she heard
it, but that evidence is extremely unreliable. I knew a lady who
complained bitterly that she had been kept awake all night by a dog
in the yard. Yet the poor beast, it appeared, had only yelped two or
three times in the night. And that's natural. If anyone is asleep and
hears a groan he wakes up, annoyed at being waked, but instantly
falls asleep again. Two hours later, again a groan, he wakes up and
falls asleep again; and the same thing again two hours later—three
times altogether in the night. Next morning the sleeper wakes up
and complains that someone has been groaning all night and keeping him awake. And it is bound to seem so to him: the intervals of
two hours of sleep he does not remember, he only remembers the
moments of waking, so he feels he has been woken up all night.

"But why, why, asks the prosecution, did not Smerdyakov confess in his last letter? 'Why did his conscience prompt him to one
step and not to both?' But, excuse me, conscience implies penitence, and the suicide may not have felt penitence, but only despair.
Despair and penitence are two very different things. Despair may
be vindictive and irreconcilable, and the suicide, laying his hands
on himself, may well have felt redoubled hatred for those whom he
had envied all his life.

"Gentlemen of the jury, beware of a miscarriage of justice! What
is there unlikely in all I have put before you just now? Find the
error in my reasoning; find the impossibility, the absurdity. And if
there is but a shade of possibility, but a shade of probability in my
propositions, do not condemn him. And is there only a shade? I
swear by all that is sacred, I fully believe in the explanation of the
murder I have just put forward. What troubles me and makes me
indignant is that of all the mass of facts heaped up by the prosecution against the defendant, there is not a single one certain and
irrefutable. And yet the unhappy man is to be ruined by the accumulation of these facts. Yes, the accumulated effort is awful: the
blood, the blood dripping from his fingers, the bloodstained shirt,
the dark night resounding with the shout 'Parricide!' and the old
man falling with a broken head. And then the mass of phrases,
statements, gestures, shouts! Oh! this has so much influence, it can

so bias the mind; but, gentlemen of the jury, can it bias your minds? Remember, you have been given absolute power, the power to bind and to loose, but the greater the power, the more terrible its responsibility. I do not draw back one iota from what I have said just now, but suppose for one moment I agreed with the prosecution that my luckless client had stained his hands with his father's blood. This is only an hypothesis, I repeat; I never for one instant doubt his innocence. But, so be it, I assume that my client is guilty of parricide. Even so, hear what I have to say. I have it in my heart to say something more to you, for I feel that there must be a great conflict in your hearts and minds. . . . Forgive my referring to your hearts and minds, gentlemen of the jury, but I want to be truthful and sincere to the end. Let us all be sincere!"

At this point the speech was interrupted by rather loud applause. The last words, indeed, were pronounced with a note of such sincerity that everyone felt that he really might have something to say, and that what he was about to say would be of the greatest consequence. But the President, hearing the applause, in a loud voice threatened to clear the court if such an incident were repeated. Every sound was hushed and Fetyukovich began in a new voice full of feeling quite unlike the tone he had used hitherto.

Chapter XIII

An Adulterer of Thought

"It's not only the accumulation of facts that threatens my client with ruin, gentlemen of the jury," he began sonorously, "no, what is really threatening my client with ruin is one fact—the dead body of his father. Had it been an ordinary case of murder you would have rejected the charge in view of the triviality, the incompleteness, and the fantastic character of the evidence, if you examine each part of it separately; or, at least, you would have hesitated to ruin a man's life simply from the prejudice against him which he has, alas! only too well deserved. But it's not an ordinary case of murder, it's a case of parricide. That impresses men's minds, and to such a degree that the very triviality and incompleteness of the evidence becomes less trivial and less incomplete even to an unprejudiced mind. How can such a defendant be acquitted? What if he committed the murder and gets off unpunished? That is what everyone, almost involuntarily, instinctively, feels at heart.

"Yes, it's a fearful thing to shed a father's blood—the father who has begotten me, loved me, not spared his life for me, grieved over my illnesses from childhood up, troubled all his life for my happiness, and has lived in my joys, in my successes. To murder such a father—that's inconceivable. Gentlemen of the jury, what is a father—a real father? What is the meaning of that great word? What is the great idea in that name? We have just indicated in part what a true father is and what he ought to be. In the case in which we are now so deeply occupied and over which our hearts are aching—in the present case, the father, Fyodor Pavlovich Karamazov, in no way corresponds to that conception of a father to which we have just referred. That's the misfortune. And indeed some fathers are like a misfortune. Let us examine this misfortune rather more closely: we must shrink from nothing, gentlemen of the jury, considering the importance of the decision you have to make. It's our particular duty not to shrink from any idea, like children or frightened women, as the highly talented prosecutor happily expresses it.

"But in the course of his heated speech my esteemed opponent (and he was my opponent before I opened my lips) exclaimed several times, 'Oh, I will not yield the defense of the defendant to the advocate who has come down from Petersburg. I am the prosecution, but I am also the counsel for the defense!' He exclaimed that several times, but forgot to mention that if this terrible defendant was for twenty-three years so grateful for a mere pound of nuts given him by the only man who had been kind to him, as a child in his father's house, might not such a man well have remembered for twenty-three years how he ran in his father's backyard, 'without boots on his feet and with his little trousers hanging by one button'—to use the expression of the humane doctor, Herzenstube?

"Oh, gentlemen of the jury, why need we look more closely at this 'misfortune,' why repeat what we all know already? What did my client meet with when he arrived here, at his father's house, and why depict my client as a heartless egoist and monster? He is uncontrolled, he is wild and unruly—we are trying him now for that—but who is responsible for his life? Who is responsible for his having received such an unseemly bringing up, in spite of his excellent disposition and his grateful and sensitive heart? Did anyone train him to be reasonable? Was he enlightened by study? Did anyone love him ever so little in his childhood? My client was left to the care of Providence like a beast of the field. He thirsted, perhaps, to see his father after long years of separation. A thousand times he may, perhaps, recalling his childhood, have driven away the loathsome phantoms that haunted his childish dreams and with all his heart he may have longed to embrace and to forgive his father! And what awaited him? He was met by cynical taunts, suspicions and wrangling about money. He heard nothing but revolting talk and vicious precepts uttered daily 'over the brandy,' and at last he saw his father enticing his mistress from him with his own money, the son's own money! Oh, gentlemen of the jury, that was cruel and revolting! And that old man was always complaining of the disrespect and cruelty of his son. He slandered him in society, injured him, calumniated him, bought up his unpaid debts to get him thrown into prison.

"Gentlemen of the jury, people like my client, who are fierce, unruly, and uncontrolled on the surface, are sometimes, most frequently indeed, exceedingly tender-hearted, only they don't express it. Don't laugh, don't laugh at my idea! The talented prosecutor laughed mercilessly just now at my client's loving Schiller—loving the 'sublime and beautiful!' I would not have laughed at that in his place, in the prosecutor's place. Yes, such natures—oh, let me speak in defense of such natures, so often and so cruelly misunderstood—these natures often thirst for tenderness, goodness, and justice, as it were, in contrast to themselves, their unruliness, their ferocity—they thirst for it unconsciously, but they do thirst for it. Passionate and fierce on the surface, they are painfully capable of loving woman, for instance, and with a spiritual and elevated love. Again do not laugh at me, this is very often the case in such natures. But they cannot hide their passions—sometimes very coarse—and that is conspicuous and is noticed, but the inner man in unseen. Their passions are quickly exhausted; but, by the side of a noble and lofty creature that seemingly coarse and rough man seeks a new life, seeks to correct himself, to be better, to become noble and honorable, 'sublime and beautiful,' however much the expression has been ridiculed.

"I said just now that I would not venture to touch upon my client's engagement to Miss Verkhovtsev. But I may say half a word. What we heard just now was not evidence, but only the scream of a frenzied and revengeful woman, and it was not for her—oh, not for her!—to reproach him with treachery, for she has betrayed him! If she had had but a little time for reflection she would not have given such evidence. Oh, do not believe her! No, my client is not a monster, as she called him! The crucified Lover of Mankind on the eve of His Crucifixion said: 'I am the Good Shepherd. The good shepherd giveth his life for his sheep, so that not of them might be lost.'[8] Let not a man's soul be lost through us!

"I asked just now what does 'father' mean, and exclaimed that it was a great word, a precious name. But one must use words honestly, gentlemen of the jury, and I venture to call things by their right names, by their proper designation: such a father as the murdered old Karamazov cannot be called a father and does not deserve to be. Filial love for an unworthy father is an absurdity, an impossibility. Love cannot be created from nothing: only God can create something from nothing.

8. *John* 10:11.

" 'Fathers, provoke not your children to wrath,' the apostle writes, from a heart glowing with love. It's not for the sake of my client that I quote these sacred words, I mention them for all fathers. Who has authorized me to preach to fathers? No one. But as a man and a citizen I make my appeal—*vivos voco!*[9] We are not long on earth, we do many evil deeds and say many evil words. So let us all catch a favorable moment when we are all together to say a good word to each other. That's what I am doing: while I am in this place I take advantage of my opportunity. Not for nothing is this tribune given to us by the highest authority—all Russia hears us! I am not speaking only for the fathers here present, I cry aloud to all fathers: 'Fathers, provoke not your children to wrath.' Yes, let us first fulfill Christ's injunction ourselves and only then venture to expect it of our children. Otherwise we are not fathers, but enemies of our children, and they are not our children, but our enemies, and we have made them our enemies ourselves. 'What measure ye mete it shall be measured unto you again'—it's not I who say that, it's the Gospel precept, measure to others according as they measure to you. How can we blame children if they measure us according to our measure?

"Not long ago a servant girl in Finland was suspected of having secretly given birth to a child. She was watched, and a box of which no one knew anything was found in the corner of the loft, behind some bricks. It was opened and inside was found the body of a newborn child which she had killed. In the same box were found the skeletons of two other babies which, according to her own confession, she had killed at the moment of their birth. Gentlemen of the jury, was she a mother to her children? She gave birth to them, indeed; but was she a mother to them? Would anyone venture to give her the sacred name of mother? Let us be bold, gentlemen of the jury, let us be audacious even; it's our duty to be so at this moment and not to be afraid of certain words and ideas like Moscow merchants' wives who are afraid of 'metal' and 'brimstone.'[1] No, let us prove that the progress of the last few years has touched even us, and let us say plainly, the father is not merely he who begets the child, but he who begets it and does his duty by it.

"Oh, of course, there is the other meaning, there is the other interpretation of the word 'father,' which insists that any father, even though he be a monster, even though he be the enemy of his children, still remains my father simply because he begot me. But this is, so to speak, the mystical meaning which I cannot comprehend with my intellect, but can only accept by faith, or, better to

<hr />

9. "I call upon the living." (Latin)
1. In Ostrovsky's play *Hard Days* (1863), "metal" and "brimstone" appear as an indication of superstition and backwardness.

say, *on faith*, like many other things which I do not understand, but which religion bids me believe. But in that case let it be kept outside the sphere of actual life. In the sphere of actual life, which has, indeed, its own rights, but also lays upon us great duties and obligations, in that sphere, if we want to be humane—Christian, in fact—we must, and ought to, act only upon convictions justified by reason and experience, which have been passed through the crucible of analysis; in a word, we must act rationally, not insanely, and not as though in dream and delirium, that we may not do harm, that we may not ill-treat and ruin a man. Then it will be real Christian work, not only mystic, but rational and philanthropic. . . ."

There was violent applause at this passage from many parts of the court, but Fetyukovich waved his hands as though imploring them to let him finish without interruption. The court relapsed into silence at once. The orator went on.

"Do you suppose, gentlemen of the jury, that our children as they grow up and begin to reason can avoid such questions? No, they cannot, and we will not impose on them an impossible restriction. The sight of an unworthy father involuntarily suggests tormenting questions to a young creature, especially when he compares him with the excellent fathers of his companions. The conventional answer to this question is: 'He begot you, and you are his flesh and blood, and therefore you are bound to love him.' The youth involuntarily reflects: 'But did he love me when he begot me?' he asks, wondering more and more. 'Was it for my sake he begot me? He did not know me, not even my sex, at that moment, at the moment of passion, inflamed by wine, perhaps, and he has only transmitted to me a propensity to drunkenness—that's all he's done for me. . . . Why am I bound to love him, simply for begetting me when he has cared nothing for me all my life after?'

"Oh, perhaps those questions strike you as coarse and cruel, but do not expect an impossible restraint from a young mind. 'Drive nature out of the door and it will fly in at the window,' and, above all, let us not be afraid of 'metal' and 'sulfur,' but decide the question according to the dictates of reason and humanity and not of mystic ideas. How shall it be decided? Why, like this. Let the son stand before his father and ask him, 'Father, tell me, why must I love you? Father, show me that I must love you,' and if that father is able to answer him and show him good reason, we have a real, normal, parental relation, not resting on mystical prejudice, but on a rational, responsible and strictly humanitarian basis. But if he does not, there's an end to the family tie. He is not a father to him, and the son has a right to look upon him as a stranger, and even an enemy. Our tribune, gentlemen of the jury, ought to be a school of true and sound ideas."

(Here the orator was interrupted by irrepressible and almost frantic applause. Of course, it was not the whole audience, but a good half of it applauded. The fathers and mothers present applauded. Shrieks and exclamations were heard from the gallery, where the ladies were sitting. Handkerchiefs were waved. The President began ringing his bell with all his might. He was obviously irritated by the behavior of the audience, but did not venture to clear the court as he had threatened. Even persons of high position, old men with stars on their breasts, sitting on specially reserved seats behind the judges, applauded the orator and waved their handkerchiefs. So that when the noise died down, the President confined himself to repeating his stern threat to clear the court, and Fetyukovich, excited and triumphant, continued his speech.)

"Gentlemen of the jury, you remember that awful night of which so much has been said today, when the son got over the fence into his father's house and stood face to face with the enemy and persecutor who had begotten him. I insist most emphatically it was not for money he ran to his father's house: the charge of robbery is an absurdity, as I proved before. And it was not to murder him he broke into the house, oh, no! If he had had that design he would, at least, have taken the precaution of arming himself beforehand. The brass pestle he caught up instinctively without knowing why he did it. Granted that he deceived his father by tapping at the window, granted that he made his way in—I've said already that I do not for a moment believe that legend, but let it be so, let us suppose it for a moment. Gentlemen, I swear to you by all that's holy, if it had not been his father, but an ordinary enemy, he would, after running through the rooms and satisfying himself that the woman was not there, have made off, posthaste, without doing any harm to his rival. He would have struck him, pushed him away perhaps, nothing more, for he had no thought and no time to spare for that. What he wanted to know was where she was. But his father, his father! The mere sight of the father who had hated him from his childhood, had been his enemy, his persecutor, and now his unnatural rival, was enough! A feeling of hatred came over him involuntarily, irresistibly, clouding his reason. It all surged up in one moment! It was an impulse of madness and insanity, but also an impulse of nature, irresistibly and unconsciously (like everything in nature) avenging the violation of its eternal laws. But even then he did not murder him—I maintain that, I cry that aloud!— no, he only brandished the pestle in a burst of indignant disgust, not meaning to kill him, not knowing that he would kill him. Had he not had this fatal pestle in his hand, he would have only knocked his father down perhaps, but would not have killed him. As he ran away, he did not know whether he had killed the old man he had knocked down. Such a murder is not a murder. Such a murder is not a parricide. No, the murder of such a father cannot be called parricide. Such a murder can only be reckoned parricide by prejudice.

"But I appeal to you again and again from the depths of my soul; did this murder actually take place? Gentlemen of the jury, if we convict and punish him, he will say to himself: 'These people have done nothing for my bringing up, for my education, nothing to improve my lot, nothing to make me better, nothing to make me a man. These people have not given me to eat and to drink, have not visited me in prison and nakedness, and here they have sent me to penal servitude. I am even, I owe them nothing now, and owe no one anything forever and ever. They are wicked and I will be wicked. They are cruel and I will be cruel!' That is what he will say, gentlemen of the jury. And I swear, by finding him guilty you will only make it easier for him: you will ease his conscience, he will curse the blood he has shed and will not regret it. At the same time you will destroy in him the possibility of becoming a new man, for he will remain in his wickedness and blindness all his life.

"But do you want to punish him fearfully, terribly, with the most awful punishment that could be imagined, and at the same time to save him and regenerate his soul? If so, overwhelm him with your mercy! You will see, you will hear how he will tremble and be horror-struck. 'How can I endure this mercy? How can I endure so much love? Am I worthy of it?' That's what he will exclaim. Oh, I know, I know that heart, that wild but grateful heart, gentlemen of the jury! It will bow before your mercy; it thirsts for a great and loving action, it will flame up and be resurrected forever. There are souls which, in their limitation, blame the whole world. But subdue such a soul with mercy, show it love, and it will curse its past, for there are many good impulses in it. Such a heart will expand and see that God is merciful and that men are good and just. He will be horror-stricken; he will be crushed by remorse and the vast obligation laid upon him henceforth. And he will not say then, 'I am even,' but will say, 'I am guilty in the sight of all men and am more unworthy than all.' With tears of penitence and poignant, tender anguish, he will exclaim: 'Others are better than I, they wanted to save me, not to ruin me!' Oh, this act of mercy is so easy for you, for in the absence of anything like real evidence it will be too awful for you to pronounce: 'Yes, he is guilty.' Better acquit ten guilty men than punish one innocent man! Do you hear, do you hear that majestic voice from the past century of our glorious history? It is not for an insignificant person like me to remind you that the Russian court does not exist for the punishment only, but also for the salvation of the fallen man! Let other nations think of retribution and the letter of the law, we will cling to the spirit and the meaning—the salvation and the reformation of the lost. If this is true, if Russia and her justice are such, she may go forward with good cheer! Do not try to scare us with your frenzied troikas from which all the nations stand aside in disgust. Not a runaway troika, but the stately chariot of Russia will move calmly and majestically to its goal. In your hands is the fate of my client, in your hands is the fate of Russian justice. You will defend it, you will save it, you will prove that there are men to watch over it, that it is in good hands!"

Chapter XIV

The Peasants Stand Firm

That was how Fetyukovich concluded, and the enthusiasm of the audience burst like an irresistible storm. It was out of the question to stop it: the women wept, many of the men wept too, even two important personages shed tears. The President submitted, and even postponed ringing his bell: "the suppression of such an enthusiasm would be the suppression of something sacred," as the ladies cried afterwards. The orator himself was genuinely touched. And it was at this moment that Ippolit Kirillovich got up to make certain objections. People looked at him with hatred. "What? What's the meaning of it? He positively dares to make objections," the ladies babbled. But if the whole world of ladies, including his wife, had protested he could not have been stopped at that moment. He was pale, he was shaking with emotion, his first words, his first phrases were even unintelligible, he gasped for breath, could hardly speak clearly, lost the thread. But he soon recovered himself. Of this closing argument of his I will quote only a few sentences.

". . . . I am reproached with having woven a romance. But what is this defense if not one romance on the top of another? All that was lacking was poetry. Fyodor Pavlovich, while waiting for his mistress, tears open the envelope and throws it on the floor. We are even told what he said while engaged in this amazing act. Is not this a flight of fancy? And what proof have we that he had taken out the money? Who heard what he said? The weak-minded idiot, Smerdyakov, transformed into a Byronic hero, avenging society for his illegitimate birth—isn't this a romance in the Byronic style? And the son who breaks into his father's house and murders him without murdering him is not even a romance—this is a sphinx setting us a riddle which he cannot solve himself. If he murdered him, he murdered him, and what's the meaning of his murdering him without having murdered him—who can make head or tail of this?

"Then we are admonished that our tribune is a tribune of true

and sound ideas and from this tribune of 'sound ideas' is heard a
solemn declaration that to call the murder of a father 'parricide' is
nothing but a prejudice! But if parricide is a prejudice, and if every
child is to ask his father why he is to love him, what will become of
us? What will become of the foundations of society? What will
become of the family? Parricide, it appears, is only a bogey of
Moscow merchants' wives. The most precious, the most sacred
guarantees for the destiny and future of Russian justice are presented to us in a perverted and frivolous form, simply to attain an
object—to obtain the justification of something which cannot be
justified. 'Oh, crush him by mercy,' cries the counsel for the defense; but that's all the criminal wants, and tomorrow it will be
seen how much he is crushed. And is not the counsel for the
defense too modest in asking only for the acquittal of the defendant? Why not found a charity in the honor of the parricide to
commemorate his exploit among future generations? Religion and
the Gospel are corrected—that's all mysticism, we are told, and
ours is the only true Christianity which has been subjected to the
analysis of reason and common sense. And so they set up before us
a false semblance of Christ! '*What measure ye mete so it shall be
meted unto you again,*' cries the counsel for the defense, and instantly deduces that Christ teaches us to measure as it is measured
to us—and this from the tribune of truth and sound sense! We peep
into the Gospel only on the eve of making speeches, in order to
dazzle the audience by our acquaintance with what is, anyway, a
rather original composition, which may be of use to produce a
certain effect—all to serve the purpose! But what Christ commands
us is something very different: He bids us beware of doing this,
because the wicked world does this, but we ought to forgive and to
turn the other cheek, and not to measure to our persecutors as they
measure to us. This is what our God has taught us and not that to
forbid children to murder their fathers is a prejudice. And we will
not from the tribune of truth and good sense correct the Gospel of
our Lord, Whom the counsel for the defense deigns to call only 'the
crucified lover of humanity,' in opposition to all orthodox Russia,
which calls to Him, 'For Thou art our God!' "

At this the President intervened and checked the over zealous
speaker, begging him not to exaggerate, not to overstep the bounds,
and so on, as presidents always do in such cases. The audience, too,
was uneasy. The public was restless: there were even exclamations
of indignation. Fetyukovich did not so much as reply; he only
mounted the tribune to lay his hand on his heart and, with an
offended voice, utter a few words full of dignity. He only touched
again, lightly and ironically, on "romancing" and "psychology,"
and in an appropriate place quoted, "Jupiter, you are angry, therefore you are wrong," which provoked a burst of approving laughter

in the audience, for Ippolit Kirillovich was by no means like Jupiter. Then, of the accusation that he was teaching the young generation to murder their fathers, Fetyukovich observed, with great dignity, that he would not even answer. As for the prosecutor's charge of uttering unorthodox opinions, and calling Christ merely 'the crucified lover of humanity' rather than 'God,' and that could not be expressed from this 'tribune of truth and good sense,' Fetyukovich noted that it was a personal insinuation and that he had expected in this court to be secure from accusations "damaging to my reputation as a citizen and a loyal subject." But at these words the President pulled him up, too, and Fetyukovich concluded his rejoinder with a bow, amid a hum of approbation in the court. And Ippolit Kirillovich was, in the opinion of our ladies, "crushed for good."

Then the defendant was allowed to speak. Mitya stood up, but said very little. He was fearfully exhausted, physically and mentally. The look of strength and independence with which he had entered in the morning had almost disappeared. He seemed as though he had passed through an experience that day, which had taught him for the rest of his life something very important he had not understood till then. His voice was weak, he did not shout as before. In his words there was a new note of humility, defeat and submission.

"What am I to say, gentlemen of the jury? The hour of judgment has come for me, I feel the hand of God upon me! The end has come to an erring man! But, before God, I repeat to you, I am innocent of my father's blood! For the last time I repeat, it wasn't I who killed him! I erred, but I loved what is good. Every instant I strove to reform, but I lived like a wild beast. I thank the prosecutor, he told me many things about myself that I did not know; but it's not true that I killed my father, the prosecutor is mistaken. I thank my counsel, too. I cried listening to him; but it's not true that I killed my father, and he needn't have supposed it. And don't believe the doctors. I am perfectly sane, only my heart is heavy. If you spare me, if you let me go, I will pray for you. I will be a better man. I give you my word before God I will! And if you will condemn me, I'll break my sword over my head myself and kiss the pieces.[2] But spare me, do not rob me of my God! I know myself, I shall rebel! My heart is heavy, gentlemen . . . spare me!"

He almost fell back in his place: his voice broke: he could hardly articulate the last phrase. Then the judges proceeded to put the questions and began to ask both sides to formulate their conclusions. But I will not describe the details. At last the jury rose to retire for consultation. The President was very tired, and so his last

2. Part of the ritual of being drummed out of the army.

charge to the jury was rather feeble. "Be impartial, don't be influenced by the eloquence of the defense, but yet weigh the arguments. Remember that there is a great responsibility laid upon you," and so on and so on.

The jury withdrew and the court adjourned. People could get up, move about, exchange their accumulated impressions, refresh themselves at the buffet. It was very late, almost one o'clock at night, but nobody went away: the strain was so great that no one could think of repose. All waited with sinking hearts; though that is, perhaps, too much to say, for the ladies were only in a state of hysterical impatience and their hearts were untroubled. An acquittal, they thought, was inevitable. They all prepared themselves for a dramatic moment or general enthusiasm. I must admit there were many among the men, too, who were convinced that an acquittal was inevitable. Some were pleased, others frowned, while some were simply dejected, not wanting him to be acquitted. Fetyukovich himself was confident of his success. He was surrounded by people congratulating him and fawning upon him.

"There are," he said to one group, as I was told afterwards, "there are invisible threads that bind the counsel for the defense with the jury. One feels during one's speech if they are being formed. I was aware of them. They exist. Our cause is won. Set your mind at rest."

"What will our peasants say now?" said one stout, cross-looking, pockmarked gentlemen, a landowner of the neighborhood, approaching a group of gentlemen engaged in conversation.

"But they are not all peasants. There are four government clerks among them."

"Yes, there are clerks," said a member of the district council, joining the group.

"And do you know that Nazaryov, the merchant with the medal, a juryman?"

"What of him?"

"He is a man with brains."

"But he never speaks."

"He is no great talker, but so much the better. There's no need for the Petersburg man to teach him: he could teach all Petersburg himself. He's the father of twelve children. Think of that!"

"But really, do you suppose they won't acquit him?" one of our young officials exclaimed in another group.

"They'll acquit him for certain," said a resolute voice.

"It would be shameful, disgraceful, not to acquit him!" cried the official. "Suppose he did murder him—there are fathers and fathers! And, besides, he was in such a frenzy. . . . He really may have done nothing but swing the pestle in the air, and so knocked the old man down. But it was a pity they dragged the lackey in.

That was simply an absurd theory! If I'd been in Fetyukovich's place, I would simply have said straight out: 'He murdered him; but he is not guilty, what the hell!' "

"That's what he did, only without saying, 'What the hell!' "

"No, Mikhail Semyonich, he almost said that, too," put in a third voice.

"Why, gentlemen, in Lent an actress was acquitted in our town who had cut the throat of her lover's lawful wife."

"Oh, but she did not finish cutting it."

"That makes no difference. She began cutting it."

"What did you think of what he said about children? Splendid, wasn't it?"

"Splendid!"

"And about mysticism, too!"

"Oh, drop mysticism, do!" cried someone else; "think of Ippolit and his fate from this day forth. His wife will scratch his eyes out tomorrow for Mitenka's sake."

"Is she here?"

"What an idea! If she'd been here she'd have scratched them out in court. She is at home with toothache. He, he, he!"

"He, he, he!"

In a third group:

"I daresay they will acquit Mitenka, after all."

"I wouldn't be surprised if he turns the Metropolis upside down tomorrow. He will be drinking for ten days!"

"Oh, the devil!"

"The devil's bound to have a hand in it. Where should he be if not here?"

"Well, gentlemen, I admit it was eloquent. But still it's not the thing to break your father's head with a pestle! Or what are we coming to?"

"The chariot! Do you remember the chariot?"

"Yes; he turned a cart into a chariot!"

"And tomorrow he will turn a chariot into a cart, just to suit his purpose."

"What clever people there are nowadays. Is there any justice to be had in Russia?"

But the bell rang. The jury deliberated for exactly an hour, neither more nor less. A profound silence reigned in the court as soon as the public had taken their seats. I remember how the jurymen walked into the court. At last! I won't repeat the questions in order, and, indeed, I have forgotten them. I remember only the answer to the President's first and chief question: "Did the accused commit the murder for the sake of robbery and with premeditation?" (I don't remember the exact words.) There was a complete hush. The foreman of the jury, the youngest of the clerks, pronounced, in a clear, loud voice, amidst the deathlike stillness of the court:

"Yes, guilty!"

And the same answer was repeated to every question: "Yes, guilty!" and without the slightest extenuating comment. This no one had expected; almost everyone had reckoned upon a recommendation for mercy, at least. The deathlike silence in the court was not broken—all seemed petrified: those who desired his conviction as well as those who had been eager for his acquittal. But that was only for the first instant, and it was followed by a fearful hubbub. Many of the men in the audience were pleased. Some were rubbing their hands with no attempt to conceal their joy. Those who disagreed with the verdict seemed crushed, shrugged their shoulders, whispered, but still seemed unable to realize this. But how shall I describe the state the ladies were in? I thought they would create a riot. At first they could scarcely believe their ears. Then suddenly the whole court rang with exclamations: "What's the meaning of it? What next?" They leaped up from their places. They seemed to fancy that it might be at once reconsidered and reversed. At that instant Mitya suddenly stood up and cried in a heartrending voice, stretching his hands out before him:

"I swear by God and the dreadful Day of Judgment I am not guilty of my father's blood! Katya, I forgive you! Brothers, friends, have pity on the other woman!"

He could not go on, and broke into a terrible sobbing wail that was heard all over the court in a voice not his own, in a new, surprising voice that suddenly emerged from God knows where. From the furthest corner at the back of the gallery came a piercing shriek—it was Grushenka. She had succeeded in begging admittance to the court again before the beginning of the attorneys' speeches. Mitya was taken away. The passing of the sentence was deferred till next day. The whole court was in a hubbub but I did not wait to hear. I only remember a few exclamations I heard on the steps as I went out.

"He'll have a twenty years' trip to the mines!"

"Not less."

"Well, our peasants have stood firm."

"And have done in our Mitenka!"

EPILOGUE

Chapter I

Plans to Save Mitya

Five days after the trial, very early in the morning, before nine o'clock, Alyosha went to Katerina Ivanovna's to make final arrangements on a matter of great importance to both of them and to give her a message. She sat and talked to him in the very room in which she had once received Grushenka. In the next room Ivan Fyodorovich lay unconscious in a high fever. Katerina Ivanovna had immediately after the scene at the trial ordered the sick and unconscious man to be carried to her house, disregarding the inevitable gossip and general disapproval of the public. One of the two relations who lived with her had departed to Moscow immediately after the scene at the court, the other remained. But even if both had gone away, Katerina Ivanovna would have adhered to her resolution, and would have gone on nursing the sick man and sitting by him day and night. Varvinsky and Herzenstube attended him. The famous doctor had gone back to Moscow, refusing to give an opinion as to the probable outcome of the illness. Though the doctors encouraged Katerina Ivanovna and Alyosha, it was evident that they could not yet give them positive hopes of recovery. Alyosha came to see his sick brother twice a day. But this time he had specially urgent business, and he foresaw how difficult it would be to approach the subject, yet he was in great haste. He had another engagement that could not be put off for that same morning, and he had to hurry. They had been talking for a quarter of an hour. Katerina Ivanovna was pale and very fatigued, yet at the same time in a state of terrible, sickly excitement. She had a presentiment of the reason why Alyosha had come to her.

"Don't worry about his decision," she said, with confident emphasis to Alyosha. "One way or another he is bound to come to it. He must escape. That unhappy man, that hero of honor and conscience—not he, not Dmitri Fyodorovich, but the man lying on the other side of that door, who has sacrificed himself for his brother," Katya added, with flashing eyes, "told me the whole plan of escape long ago. You know he has already entered into negotiations. . . . I've told you something already. . . . You see, it will probably come off at the third stopping place from here, when the party of prisoners is taken to Siberia. Oh, it's a long way off yet. Ivan Fyodorovich has already visited the superintendent of the third stop. But we don't know yet who will be in charge of the party, and it's impossible to find that out so long beforehand. Tomorrow perhaps I will show you in detail the whole plan which Ivan Fyodorovich left me on the eve of the trial in case of need. . . . That was when—do you remember?—you found us quarreling. He had just gone downstairs, but seeing you I made him come back; do you remember? Do you know what we were quarreling about then?"

"No, I don't," said Alyosha.

"Of course he did not tell you. It was about that plan of escape. He had told me the main idea three days before, and we began quarreling about it at once and quarreled for three days. We quarreled because when he told me that, if Dmitri Fyodorovich were convicted he would escape abroad with that creature, I felt furious at once—I can't tell you why, I don't know myself why. . . . Oh, of course, I was furious then about that creature, and that she, too, should go abroad with Dmitri!" Katerina Ivanovna exclaimed suddenly, her lips quivering with anger. "As soon as Ivan Fyodorovich saw that I was furious about that creature, he instantly imagined I was jealous of her and that I therefore still loved Dmitri. That is how our first quarrel began. I would not give an explanation, I could not ask forgiveness. I could not bear to think that such a man could suspect me of still loving that . . . and when I myself had told him long before that I did not love Dmitri, that I loved no one but him! It was only resentment against that creature that made me angry with him. Three days later, on the evening you came, he brought me a sealed envelope, which I was to open at once, if anything happened to him. Oh, he foresaw his illness! He told me that the envelope contained the details of the escape, and that if he died or was taken dangerously ill, I was to save Mitya alone. Then he left me money, nearly ten thousand—the very same to which the prosecutor referred in his speech, having learned from someone that he had sent them to be changed. I was suddenly tremendously impressed to find that Ivan Fyodorovich had not given up his idea of saving his brother, and was confiding this plan of escape to me, though he was still jealous of me and still convinced that I loved Mitya. Oh, that was a sacrifice! No, you cannot fully understand the greatness of such self-sacrifice, Alexey Fyodorovich. I wanted to fall at his feet in reverence, but I thought at once that he would take it only for my joy at the thought of Mitya's being saved (and he certainly would have imagined that!), and I was so exasperated at the mere possibility of such an unjust thought on his part that I lost my temper again, and instead of kissing his feet, flew into a fury again! Oh, I am unhappy! It's my character, my awful, unhappy character! Oh, you will see, I shall end by driving him, too, to abandon me for another with whom he can get on better, like Dmitri. But . . . no, I could not bear it, I would kill myself. And when you came in then, and when I called to you and told him to come back, I was so enraged by the look of contempt and hatred he turned on me that—do you remember?—I cried out to you that it was *he, he alone* who had persuaded me that his brother Dmitri was murderer! I said that malicious thing on purpose to wound him again. He had never, never persuaded me that his brother was a murderer. On the contrary, it was I who persuaded him! Oh, my vile temper was the cause of everything! I paved the way to that hideous scene at the trial. He wanted to show me that he was an honorable man, and that, even if I loved his brother, he would not ruin him for revenge or jealousy. So he came to the court . . . I am the cause of it all, I alone am to blame!"

Katya never had made such confessions to Alyosha before, and he felt that she was now at that stage of unbearable suffering when even the proudest heart painfully crushes its pride and falls vanquished by grief. Oh, Alyosha knew another terrible reason of her present misery, though she had carefully concealed it from him during those days since the trial; it would have been for some reason too painful to him if she had been brought so low as to speak to him now about that. She was suffering for her "treachery" at the trial, and Alyosha felt that her conscience was impelling her to confess it to him, to him, Alyosha, with tears and cries and hysterical writhings on the floor. But he dreaded that moment and longed to spare her. It made the commission on which he had come even more difficult. He spoke of Mitya again.

"It's all right, it's all right, don't be anxious about him!" she began again, sharply and stubbornly. "All that is only momentary, I know him, I know his heart only too well. You may be sure he will consent to escape. It's not as though it would be immediately; he will have time to make up his mind to it. Ivan Fyodorovich will be well by that time and will manage it all himself, so that I shall have nothing to do with it. Don't be anxious; he will consent to run away. He has agreed already: do you suppose he would give up that creature? And they won't let her go to him in prison, so he is bound to escape. It's you he's most afraid of, he is afraid you won't approve of his escape on moral grounds. But you must generously *allow* it, if your sanction is so necessary," Katya added viciously. She paused and smiled.

"He talks about some hymn," she went on again, "some cross he has to bear, some duty; I remember Ivan Fyodorovich told me a great deal about it, and if you knew how he talked!" Katya cried suddenly, with feeling she could not repress, "if you knew how he loved that wretched man at the moment he told me, and how he hated him, perhaps, at the same moment. And I heard his story and his tears with sneering disdain. Oh, creature! It is I who am the creature, me. It is I who am responsible for his fever. But that man in prison is he ready for suffering?" Katya concluded irritably. "And can such a man suffer? Men like him never suffer!"

There was a note of hatred and contemptuous repulsion in her words. And yet it was she who had betrayed him. "Perhaps because she feels how she's guilty towards him she hates him at moments," Alyosha thought to himself. He hoped that it was only "at moments." In Katya's last words he detected a challenging note, but he did not take it up.

"I sent for you this morning especially to make you promise to persuade him yourself. Or do you, too, consider that to escape would be dishonorable, unvalorous, or how would . . . unchristian, perhaps?" Katya added, even more defiantly.

"Oh, no. I'll tell him everything," muttered Alyosha. "He asks you to come and see him today," he blurted out suddenly, looking her steadily in the face. She started, and drew back a little from him on the sofa.

"Me? Can that be?" she faltered, turning pale.

"It can and ought to be!" Alyosha began emphatically, growing more animated. "He needs you particularly just now. I would not have opened the subject and worried you beforehand, if it were not necessary. He is ill, he is beside himself, he keeps asking for you. It is not to be reconciled with you that he wants you, but only that you would go and show yourself at his door. So much has happened to him since that day. He realizes how guilty beyond all reckoning he is towards you. He does not ask your forgiveness; 'it's impossible to forgive me,' he says himself, but only that you would show yourself in his doorway."

"You're suddenly . . ." faltered Katya. "I had a presentiment all these days that you would come with that message. I knew he would ask me to come. It's impossible!"

"Let it be impossible, but do it. Only think, he realizes for the first time how he has offended you, the first time in his life; he had never grasped it before so fully. He said, 'If she refuses to come I shall be unhappy all my life.' Do you hear? though he is condemned to penal servitude for twenty years, he is still planning to be happy—is not that piteous? Think—you must visit him; though he is ruined, he is innocent," broke like a challenge from Alyosha. "His hands are clean, there is no blood on them! For the sake of his infinite sufferings in the future visit him now. Go, lead him on his way into the darkness—stand at his door, that is all. . . . You must do it, you *must*!" Alyosha concluded, laying immense stress on the word "must."

"I must . . . but I cannot . . ." Katya moaned. "He will look at me. . . . I can't."

"Your eyes ought to meet. How will you live all your life, if you don't make up your mind to do it now?"

"Better suffer all my life."

"You must go, you *must* go," Alyosha repeated with merciless emphasis.

"But why today, why at once? . . . I can't leave the patient . . ."

"You can for a moment. It will only be a moment. If you don't come, he will be in delirium by tonight. I would not tell you a lie; have pity on him!"

"Have pity on *me!*" Katya said, with bitter reproach, and she burst into tears.

"Then you will come," said Alyosha firmly, seeing her tears. "I'll go and tell him you will come at once."

"No, don't tell him so on any account," cried Katya in alarm. "I will come, but don't tell him beforehand, for perhaps I may go, but not go in . . . I don't know yet . . ."

Her voice failed her. She gasped for breath. Alyosha got up to go.

"And what if I meet anyone?" she said suddenly, in a low voice, turning white again.

"That's just why you must go now, to avoid meeting anyone. There will be no one there, I can tell you that for certain. We will expect you," he concluded emphatically, and went out of the room.

Chapter II

For a Moment the Lie Becomes Truth

He hurried to the hospital where Mitya was lying now. The day after his fate was determined, Mitya had fallen ill with nervous fever, and was sent to the prison division of the town hospital. But at the request of several persons (Alyosha, Madame Khokhlakov, Lise, etc.), Doctor Varvinsky had put Mitya not with other prisoners, but in a separate little room, the one where Smerdyakov had been. It is true that there was a sentinel at the other end of the corridor, and there was a grating over the window, so that Varvinsky could be at ease about the indulgence he had shown, which was not quite legal; but he was a kind-hearted and compassionate young man. He knew how hard it would be for a man like Mitya to pass at once so suddenly into the society of robbers and murderers, and that he must get used to it by degrees. The visits of relations and friends were informally sanctioned by the doctor and superintendant, and even by the police captain. But only Alyosha and Grushenka had visited Mitya. Rakitin had tried to force his way in twice, but Mitya emphatically asked Varvinsky not to admit him.

Alyosha found him sitting on his bunk in a hospital dressing gown, rather feverish, with a towel, soaked in vinegar and water, on his head. He looked at Alyosha as he came in with an indefinite expression, but there was a shade of something like dread discernible in it.

He had become terribly preoccupied since the trial; sometimes he would be silent for half an hour together, and seemed to be pondering something heavily and painfully, oblivious of everything about him. If he roused himself from his brooding and began to talk, he always spoke with a kind of abruptness and never of what he really wanted to say. He looked sometimes with a face of suffering at his brother. He seemed to be more at ease with Grushenka than with Alyosha. It is true, he scarcely spoke to her at all, but as soon as she came in, his whole face lit up with joy.

Alyosha sat down beside him on the bunk in silence. This time Mitya was waiting for Alyosha in suspense, but he did not dare ask him the question. He felt it almost unthinkable that Katya would consent to come, and at the same time he felt that if she did not come, something inconceivable would happen. Alyosha understood his feelings.

"Trifon Borisich," Mitya began nervously, "has pulled his whole inn to pieces, I am told. He's taken up the flooring, pulled apart the planks, split up all the gallery, I am told. He is seeking treasure all the time—the fifteen hundred rubles which the prosecutor said I'd hidden there. He began playing these tricks, they say, as soon as he got home. Serve him right, the swindler! The guard here told me yesterday; he comes from there."

"Listen," began Alyosha. "She will come, but I don't know when. Perhaps today, perhaps in a few days, that I can't tell. But she will come, she will, that's certain."

Mitya started, would have said something, but was silent. The news had a tremendous effect on him. It was evident that he would have liked terribly to know what had been said, but he was afraid to ask. Something cruel and contemptuous from Katya would have cut him like a knife at that moment.

"This was what she said among other things; that I must be sure to set your conscience at rest about escaping. If Ivan is not well by then she will see to it all herself."

"You've spoken of that already," Mitya observed musingly.

"And you have repeated it to Grusha," observed Alyosha.

"Yes," Mitya admitted. "She won't come this morning." He looked timidly at his brother. "She won't come till the evening. While I told her yesterday that Katya was taking measures, she was silent, but she set her mouth. She only whispered, 'Let her!' She understood that it was important. I did not dare to try her further. She understands now, I think, that Katya no longer cares for me, but loves Ivan."

"Does she?" broke from Alyosha.

"Perhaps she does not. Only she is not coming this morning," Mitya hastened to explain again; "I asked her to do something for me. You know, brother Ivan is superior to all of us. He ought to live, not us. He will recover."

"Would you believe it, though Katya is alarmed about him, she scarcely doubts that he will," said Alyosha.

"That means that she is convinced he will die. It's because she is frightened she's so sure he will get well."

"Ivan has a strong constitution, and I, too, believe there's every hope that he will get well," Alyosha observed anxiously.

"Yes, he will get well. But she is convinced that he will die. She has a great deal of sorrow to bear . . ."

A silence followed. Something very important was tormenting Mitya.

"Alyosha, I love Grusha terribly," he said suddenly in a shaking voice, full of tears.

"They won't let her go out *there* to you," Alyosha put in at once.

"And there is something else I wanted to tell you," Mitya went on, with a sudden ring in his voice. "If they beat me on the way or *there*, I won't submit to it. I will kill someone, and will be shot for it. And this will be going on for twenty years! They speak to me rudely as it is. The sentinel speaks to me without ceremony. I've been lying here all night, passing judgment on myself. I am not ready! I am not able to resign myself. I wanted to sing a 'hymn'; but if a guard speaks to me, I have not the strength to bear it. For Grusha I would bear anything . . . anything except blows, that is. . . . But she won't be allowed to come *there*."

Alyosha smiled gently.

"Listen, brother, once for all," he said. "This is what I think about it. And you know that I would not tell you a lie. Listen: you are not ready, and such a cross is not for you. What's more, you don't need such a martyr's cross when you are not ready for it. If you had murdered our father, it would grieve me that you should reject your cross. But you are innocent, and such a cross is too much for you. You wanted to make yourself another man by suffering. I say, only remember that other man always, all your life and wherever you escape to; and that will be enough for you. Your refusal of that great cross will only serve to make you feel all your life an even greater duty, and that constant feeling will do more to make you a new man, perhaps, than if you went *there*. For there you would not endure it and would begin to grumble, and perhaps at last would say: 'I am even.' The advocate was right about that. Such heavy burdens are not for all men. For some they are impossible. These are my thoughts about it, if you need them. If other men would have to answer for your escape, officers or soldiers, then I would not have 'allowed' you," smiled Alyosha. "But they declare —the superintendent of that stop told Ivan himself—that if it's well managed there will be no great inquiry, and that they can get off easily. Of course, bribing is dishonest even in such a case, but I can't undertake to judge about it, because if Ivan and Katya commissioned me to act for you, I know I would go and give bribes. I must tell you the truth. And so I can't judge your own action. But let me assure you that I shall never condemn you. And it would be a strange thing if I could judge you in this. Now I think I've gone into everything."

"But I do condemn myself!" cried Mitya. "I shall escape, that was settled apart from you; could Mitka Karamazov do anything but run away? But I shall condemn myself, and I will pray for my sin forever. That's how the Jesuits talk, isn't it? Just as we are doing?"

"Yes," Alyosha smiled gently.

"I love you for always telling the whole truth and never hiding anything," cried Mitya, with a joyful laugh. "So I've caught my Alyosha being jesuitical. I must kiss you for that. Now listen to the rest; I'll open the other side of my heart to you. This is what I planned and decided. If I run away, even with money and a passport, and even to America, I would be cheered up by the thought that I am not running away for pleasure, not for happiness, but to another exile as bad, perhaps, as Siberia. It is as bad, Alyosha, it is! I hate that America, damn it, already. Even though Grusha will be with me. Just look at her; is she an American? She is Russian, Russian to the marrow of her bones; she will be homesick for the motherland, and I shall see every hour that she is suffering for my sake, that she has taken up that cross for me. And what harm has she done? And how shall I, too, put up with the rabble out there, though they may be better than I, every one of them. I hate that America already! And though they may be wonderful at machinery, every one of them, damn them, they are not my people, they are not of my soul. I love Russia, Alyosha, I love the Russian God, though I am a scoundrel myself. I'll croak there!" he exclaimed, his eyes suddenly flashing. His voice was trembling with tears.

"So this is what I've decided, Alyosha, listen," he began again, mastering his emotion. "As soon as I arrive there with Grusha, we will set to work at once on the land, in solitude, somewhere very remote, with wild bears. There must be some remote parts even there. I am told there are still Redskins there, somewhere, on the edge of the horizon. So to the country of the *Last of the Mohicans*,[1] and there we'll tackle the grammar at once, Grusha and I. Work and grammar—that's how we'll spend three years. And by that time we shall speak English like any Englishman. And as soon as we've learned it—goodbye to America! We'll run here to Russia as American citizens. Don't be uneasy—we would not come to this little town. We'd hide somewhere, a long way off, in the north or in

---

1. Novel by James Fenimore Cooper (1826) from which some Russians used to derive a notion of the United States.

the south. I will be changed by that time, and she will, too, in America. The doctors shall make me some sort of wart on my face—what's the use of their being so mechanical!—or else I'll put out one eye, let my beard grow a yard, and I will turn gray, fretting for Russia. I daresay they won't recognize us. And if they do, let them send us to Siberia—I don't care. It will show it's our fate. We'll work on the land here, too, somewhere in the wilds, and I'll make up as an American all my life. But we shall die on our own soil. That's my plan, and it won't be altered. Do you approve?"

"Yes," said Alyosha, not wanting to contradict him. Mitya paused for a minute and said suddenly:

"And how they worked it up at the trial! Didn't they work it up!"

"If they had not, you would have been convicted just the same," said Alyosha, with a sigh.

"Yes, people are sick of me here! God bless them, but it's hard," Mitya moaned miserably.

Again there was silence for a minute.

"Alyosha, put me out of my misery at once!" he exclaimed suddenly. "Tell me, is she coming now, or not? Tell me? What did she say? How did she say it?"

"She said she would come, but I don't know whether she will come today. It's hard for her, you know," Alosha looked timidly at his brother.

"I should think it is hard for her! Alyosha, it will drive me out of my mind. Grusha keeps looking at me. She understands. My God, calm my heart: what is it I want? I want Katya! Do I understand what I want? It's the headstrong, evil Karamazov spirit! No, I am not fit for suffering. I am a scoundrel, that's all one can say."

"Here she is!" cried Alyosha.

At that instant Katya appeared in the doorway. For a moment she stood still, gazing at Mitya with a dazed expression. He leaped impulsively to his feet, and a scared look came into his face. He turned pale, but a timid, pleading smile appeared on his lips at once, and with an irresistible impulse he held out both hands to Katya. Seeing it, she flew impetuously to him. She seized him by the hands, and almost by force made him sit down on the bed. She sat down beside him, and still keeping his hands pressed them violently, convulsively. Several times they both strove to speak, but stopped short and again gazed speechless with a strange smile, their eyes fastened on one another. So passed two minutes.

"Have you forgiven me?" Mitya faltered at last, and at the same moment turning to Alyosha, his face distorted with joy, he shouted to him, "Do you hear what I am asking, do you hear?"

"That's what I loved you for, that you are generous at heart!" broke suddenly from Katya. "My forgiveness is no good to you, nor yours to me; whether you forgive me or not, you will always be a sore place in my heart, and I in yours—so it must be . . ." She stopped to take breath.

"What have I come for?" she began again with nervous haste: "to embrace your feet, to press your hands like this, till it hurts— you remember how in Moscow I used to squeeze them—to tell you again that you are my god, my joy, to tell you that I love you madly," she moaned in anguish, and suddenly pressed his hand greedily to her lips. Tears streamed from her eyes.

Alyosha stood speechless and confounded; he had never expected what he was seeing.

"Love is over, Mitya!" Katya began again, "but the past is painfully dear to me. Know that will always be so. But now let what might have been come true for one minute," she faltered, with a drawn smile, looking into his face joyfully again. "You love another woman, and I love another man, and yet I shall love you forever, and you will love me; do you know that? Do you hear? Love me, love me all your life!" she cried, with a quiver almost of menace, in her voice.

"I shall love you, and . . . do you know, Katya," Mitya began, drawing a deep breath at each word, "do you know, five days ago, that same evening, I loved you. . . . When you fell down and were carried out . . . All my life! So it will be, so it will always be . . ."

So they murmured to one another frantic words, almost meaningless, perhaps not even true, but at that moment it was all true, and they both believed what they said implicitly.

"Katya," cried Mitya suddenly, "do you believe I murdered him? I know you don't believe it now, but then . . . when you gave evidence. . . . Surely, surely, you did not believe it!"

"I did not believe it even then. I've never believed it. I hated you, and for a moment I persuaded myself. While I was giving evidence I persuaded myself and believed it, but when I'd finished speaking I stopped believing it at once. Don't doubt that! I have forgotten that I came here to punish myself," she said, with a new expression in her voice, quite unlike the loving tones of a moment before.

"Woman, yours is a heavy burden," broke, as it were, involuntarily from Mitya.

"Let me go," she whispered. "I'll come again. It's more than I can bear now."

She was getting up from her place, but suddenly uttered a loud scream and staggered back. Grushenka walked suddenly and noiselessly into the room. No one had expected her. Katya moved swiftly to the door, but when she reached Grushenka, she stopped suddenly, turned as white as chalk and moaned softly, almost in a whisper:

"Forgive me!"

Grushenka stared at her and, pausing for an instant, in a vindictive, venomous voice, answered:

"We are full of hatred, my girl, you and I! We are both full of hatred! As though we could forgive one another! Save him, and I'll worship you all my life."

"You won't forgive her!" cried Mitya, with frantic reproach.

"Don't be anxious, I'll save him for you!" Katya whispered rapidly, and she ran out of the room.

"And you could refuse to forgive her when she begged your forgiveness herself?" Mitya exclaimed bitterly again.

"Mitya, don't dare to blame her; you have no right to!" Alyosha cried hotly.

"Her proud lips spoke, not her heart," Grushenka brought out in a tone of disgust. "If she saves you I'll forgive her everything . . ."

She stopped speaking, as though suppressing something. She could not yet recover herself. She had come in, as appeared afterwards, accidentally, with no suspicion of what she would meet.

"Alyosha, run after her!" Mitya cried to his brother; "tell her . . . I don't know . . . don't let her go away like this!"

"I'll come to you again at nightfall," said Alyosha, and he ran after Katya. He overtook her outside the hospital grounds. She was walking fast, but as soon as Alyosha caught her up she said quickly:

"No, before that woman I can't punish myself! I asked her forgiveness because I wanted to punish myself to the bitter end. She would not forgive me. . . . I like her for that!" she added, in an unnatural voice, and her eyes flashed with fierce anger.

"My brother did not expect this in the least," muttered Alyosha. "He was sure she would not come . . ."

"No doubt. Let us leave that," she snapped. "Listen: I can't go with you to the funeral now. I've sent them flowers for the little coffin. I think they still have money. If necessary, tell them I'll never abandon them. . . . Now leave me, leave me, please. You are late as it is—the bells are ringing for late mass. . . . Leave me, please!"

Chapter III

Ilyushechka's Funeral. The Speech at the Stone

He really was late. They had waited for him and had already decided to bear the pretty flower-decked little coffin to the church without him. It was the coffin of poor little Ilyushechka. He had died two days after Mitya was sentenced. At the gate of the house Alyosha was met by the shouts of the boys, Ilyusha's schoolfellows. They had all been impatiently expecting him and were glad that he had come at last. There were about twelve of them, they all had their schoolbags or satchels on their shoulders. "Dad will cry, be with dad," Ilyusha had told them as he lay dying, and the boys remembered it. Kolya Krasotkin was the foremost of them.

"How glad I am you've come, Karamazov!" he cried, holding out his hand to Alyosha. "It's awful here. It's really horrible to see it. Snegiryov is not drunk, we know for a fact he's had nothing to drink today, but he seems as if he were drunk ... I am always manly, but this is awful. Karamazov, if I am not keeping you, one question before you go in?"

"What is it, Kolya?" said Alyosha, stopping.

"Is your brother innocent or guilty? Was it he who killed your father or was it the lackey? As you say, so it will be. I haven't slept for the last four nights for thinking of it."

"The lackey killed him, my brother is innocent," answered Alyosha.

"That's what I said," the boy Smurov cried suddenly.

"So he will perish an innocent victim for truth!" exclaimed Kolya; "though he is ruined he is happy! I could envy him!'

"What do you mean? How can you? Why?" cried Alyosha surprised.

"Oh, if I, too, could sacrifice myself some day for truth!" said Kolya with enthusiasm.

"But not in such a cause, not with such disgrace and such horror!" said Alyosha.

"Of course ... I would like to die for all humanity, and, as for disgrace, I don't care about that—our names may perish. I respect your brother!"

"And so do I!" the boy who had once declared that he knew who had founded Troy cried suddenly and unexpectedly out of the crowd, and he blushed up to his ears like a peony as he had done on that occasion.

Alyosha went into the room. Ilyusha lay with his hands folded and his eyes closed in a blue coffin with a white frill round it. His thin face was hardly changed at all, and strange to say there was practically no smell from the corpse. The expression of his face was serious and, as it were, thoughtful. His hands, crossed over his breast, looked particularly beautiful, as though chiseled in marble. There were flowers in his hands and the coffin, inside and out, was decked with flowers, which had been sent early in the morning by Lisa Khokhlakov. But there were flowers too from Katerina Ivanovna, and when Alyosha opened the door, the captain had a bunch in his trembling hands and was strewing them again over his dear boy. He scarcely glanced at Alyosha when he came in, and he would not look at any one, even at his crazy weeping wife, "mamma," who kept trying to stand on her crippled legs to get a closer look at her dead boy. Nina had been pushed in her chair by the boys close up to the coffin. She sat with her head pressed to it and she too was no doubt quietly weeping. Snegiryov's face looked eager, yet bewildered and exasperated. There was something crazy about his gestures and the words that broke from him. "Old man, dear old man!" he exclaimed every minute, gazing at Ilyusha. It was his habit to call Ilyusha "old man," as a term of affection when he was alive.

"Dad, give me a flower, too; take that white one out of his hand and give it to me," the crazy mother begged, whimpering. Either because the little white rose in Ilyusha's hand had caught her fancy or because she wanted one from his hand to keep in memory of him, she moved restlessly, stretching out her hands for the flower.

"I won't give it to anyone, I won't give you anything," Snegiryov cried callously. "They are his flowers, not yours! Everything is his, nothing is yours!"

"Daddy, give mother a flower!" said Nina, lifting her face wet with tears.

"I won't give away anything and to her less than anyone! She didn't love Ilyusha. She took away his little cannon and he gave it to her," the captain broke into loud sobs at the thought of how Ilyusha had given up his cannon to his mother. The poor, crazy creature was bathed in noiseless tears, hiding her face in her hands. The boys, seeing that the father would not leave the coffin and that it was time to carry it out, stood around it in a close circle and began to lift it up.

"I don't want him to be buried in the churchyard," Snegiryov wailed suddenly; "I'll bury him by the stone, by our stone! Ilyusha told me to. I won't let him be carried out!"

He had been saying for the last three days that he would bury him by the stone, but Alyosha, Krasotkin, the landlady, her sister and all the boys interfered.

"What an idea, bury him by an unholy stone, as though he had hanged himself," the old landlady said sternly. "There in the churchyard the ground has been crossed. He'll be prayed for there. One can hear the singing in church and the deacon reads so plainly and verbally that it will reach him every time just as though it were read over his grave."

At last the captain made a gesture of despair as though to say, "Take him where you will." The boys raised the coffin, but as they passed the mother, they stopped for a moment and lowered it that she might say goodbye to Ilyusha. But on seeing that precious little face, which for the last three days she had only looked at from a distance, she trembled all over and her gray head began twitching spasmodically over the coffin.

"Mother, make the sign of the cross over him, give him your blessing, kiss him," Nina cried to her. But her head still twitched like an automaton and with a face contorted with bitter grief she began, without a word, beating her breast with her fist. They carried the coffin past her. Nina pressed her lips to her brother's for the last time as they bore the coffin by her. As Alyosha went out of the house he begged the landlady to look after those who were left behind, but she interrupted him before he had finished.

"To be sure, I'll stay with them, we are Christians, too." The old woman wept as she said it.

They had not far to carry the coffin to the church, not more than three hundred paces. It was a still clear day, with a slight frost. The church bells were still ringing. Snegiryov ran fussing and distracted after the coffin, in his short old summer overcoat, with his head bare and his soft, old, wide-brimmed hat in his hand. He seemed in a state of bewildered anxiety. At one minute he stretched out his hand to support the head of the coffin and only hindered the bearers, at another he ran alongside and tried to find a place for himself there. A flower fell on the snow and he rushed to pick it up as though everything in the world depended on the loss of that flower.

"And the crust of bread, we've forgotten the crust!" he cried suddenly in dismay. But the boys reminded him at once that he had taken the crust of bread already and that it was in his pocket. He instantly pulled it out and was reassured.

"Ilyushechka told me to, Ilyushechka," he explained at once to Alyosha. "I was sitting by him one night and he suddenly told me: Dad, when my grave is filled up crumble a piece of bread on it so that the sparrows may fly down, I'll hear them and it will cheer me up not to be lying alone."

"That's a good thing," said Alyosha, "we must often take some."

"Every day, every day!" said the captain quickly, seeming cheered at the thought.

They reached the church at last and set the coffin in the middle of it. The boys surrounded it and remained reverently standing so, all through the service. It was an old and rather poor church. Many of the icons were without settings but such churches are the best for praying in. During the mass Snegiryov became somewhat calmer, though at times he had outbursts of the same unconscious and, as it were, incoherent anxiety. At one moment he went up to the coffin to set straight the cover or the wreath, when a candle fell out of the candlestick he rushed to replace it and was a fearful time fumbling over it, then he subsided and stood quietly by the coffin with a look of blank uneasiness and perplexity. After the Epistle he suddenly whispered to Alyosha, who was standing beside him, that the Epistle had not been read *properly* but did not explain what he meant. During the prayer, "Like the Cherubim," he joined in the singing but did not go on to the end. Falling on his knees, he pressed his forehead to the stone floor and lay so for a long while.

At last came the funeral service itself and candles were distributed. The distracted father began fussing about again, but the touching and impressive funeral prayers moved and roused his soul. He seemed suddenly to shrink together and broke into rapid, short sobs, which he tried at first to smother, but at last he sobbed aloud. When they began taking leave of the dead and closing the coffin, he flung his arms about, as though he would not allow them to cover Ilyushechka, and began greedily and persistently kissing his dead boy on the lips. At last they succeeded in persuading him to come away from the step, but suddenly he impulsively stretched out his hand and snatched a few flowers from the coffin. He looked at them and a new idea seemed to dawn upon him, so that he apparently forgot his grief for a minute. Gradually he seemed to sink into brooding and did not resist when the coffin was lifted up and carried to the grave. It was an expensive one in the churchyard close to the church. Katerina Ivanovna had paid for it. After the customary rites the gravediggers lowered the coffin. Snegiryov with his flowers in his hands bent down so low over the open grave that the boys caught hold of his coat in alarm and pulled him back. He did not seem to understand fully what was happening. When they began filling up the grave, he suddenly pointed anxiously at the falling earth and began trying to say something, but no one could make out what he meant, and he stopped suddenly. Then he was reminded that he must crumble the bread and he was awfully excited, snatched up the bread and began pulling it to pieces and flinging the morsels on the grave. "Come, fly down, birds, fly down, little sparrows!" he muttered anxiously.

One of the boys observed that it was awkward for him to crumble the bread with the flowers in his hands and suggested he should give them to someone to hold for a time. But he would not do this and seemed indeed suddenly alarmed for his flowers, as though they wanted to take them from him altogether. And after looking at the grave and, as it were, satisfying himself that everything had been done and the bread had been crumbled, he suddenly, to the surprise of everyone, turned, quite composedly even, and made his way homewards. But his steps became more and more hurried, he almost ran. The boys and Alyosha kept up with him.

"The flowers are for mamma, the flowers are for mamma! I was unkind to mamma," he began exclaiming suddenly. Someone called to him to put on his hat as it was cold. But he flung the hat in the snow as though he were angry and kept repeating, "I won't have the hat, I won't have the hat." Smurov picked it up and carried it after him. All the boys were crying, and Kolya and the boy who discovered about Troy most of all. Though Smurov, with the captain's hat in his hand, was crying bitterly too, he managed, as he ran, to snatch up a piece of red brick that lay on the snow of the path, to fling it at the flock of sparrows that was flying by. He missed them, of course, and went on crying as he ran. Halfway, Snegiryov suddenly stopped, stood still for half a minute, as though struck by something, and suddenly turning back to the church, ran towards the deserted grave. But the boys instantly overtook him and caught hold of him on all sides. Then he fell helpless on the snow as though he had been knocked down, and struggling, sobbing, and wailing, he began crying out, "Ilyushechka, old man, dear old man!" Alyosha and Kolya tried to make him get up, soothing and persuading him.

"Captain, stop, a brave man must show fortitude," muttered Kolya.

"You'll spoil the flowers," said Alyosha, "and 'mamma' is expecting them, she is sitting crying because you would not give her any before. Ilyusha's little bed is still there . . ."

"Yes, yes, mamma!" Snegiryov suddenly recollected, "they'll take away the bed, they'll take it away," he added as though alarmed that they really would. He jumped up and ran homewards again. But it was not far off and they all arrived together. Snegiryov opened the door hurriedly and called to his wife with whom he had so cruelly quarreled just before:

"Mamma, poor crippled darling, Ilyushechka has sent you these flowers," he cried, holding out to her a little bunch of flowers that had been frozen and broken while he was struggling in the snow. But at that instant he saw in the corner, by the little bed, Ilyusha's little boots, which the landlady had put tidily side by side. Seeing the old, patched, rusty-looking, stiff boots he flung up his hands and rushed to them, fell on his knees, snatched up one boot and, pressing his lips to it, began kissing it greedily, crying, "Ilyushechka, old man, dear old man, where are your little feet?"

"Where have you taken him away? Where have you taken him?" the lunatic cried in a heartrending voice. Nina, too, broke into sobs. Kolya ran out of the room, the boys followed him. At last Alyosha too went out. "Let them weep," he said to Kolya, "it's no use trying to comfort them just now. Let us wait a minute and then go back."

"No, it's no use, it's awful," Kolya assented. "Do you know, Karamazov," he dropped his voice so that no one could hear them, "I feel dreadfully sad, and if it were only possible to bring him back, I'd give anything in the world to do it."

"Ah, so would I," said Alyosha.

"What do you think, Karamazov, had we better come back here tonight? He'll be drunk, you know."

"Perhaps he will. Let us come together, you and I, that will be enough, to spend an hour with them, with the mother and Nina. If

we all come together we shall remind them of everything again,"
Alyosha suggested.

"The landlady is laying the table for them now—there'll be a
funeral dinner or something, the priest is coming; shall we go back
to it, Karamazov?"

"Of course," said Alyosha.

"It's all so strange, Karamazov, such sorrow and then pancakes
after it, it all seems so unnatural in our religion."

"They are going to have salmon too," the boy who had discovered about Troy observed in a loud voice.

"I beg you most earnestly, Kartashov, not to interrupt again with
your idiotic remarks, especially when one is not talking to you and
doesn't care to know whether you exist or not!" Kolya snapped out
irritably. The boy flushed crimson but did not dare to reply. Meantime they were strolling slowly along the path and suddenly Smurov
exclaimed:

"There's Ilyusha's stone, under which they wanted to bury him."

They all stood still by the big stone. Alyosha looked and the
whole picture of what Snegiryov had described to him that day,
how Ilyushechka, weeping and hugging his father, had cried,
"Daddy, Daddy, how he insulted you," rose at once before his
imagination. A sudden impulse seemed to come into his soul. With
a serious and earnest expression he looked from one to another of
the bright, pleasant faces of Ilyusha's schoolfellows, and suddenly
said to them:

"I should like to say a word to you, here at this place."

The boys stood round him and at once bent attentive and expectant eyes upon him.

"Gentlemen, we shall soon part. I shall be for some time with my
two brothers, of whom one is going to Siberia and the other is
lying at death's door. But soon I shall leave this town, perhaps for a
long time, so we shall part, gentlemen. Let us make a compact,
here, at Ilyusha's stone that we will never forget first, Ilyushechka,
and second, one another. And whatever happens to us later in life,
if we don't meet for twenty years afterwards, let us always remember how we buried the poor boy at whom we once threw stones, do
you remember, by the bridge? and afterwards we all grew so fond
of him. He was a fine boy, a kind-hearted, brave boy, he felt for his
father's honor and resented the cruel insult to him and stood up for
him. And so in the first place, we will remember him, boys, all our
lives. And even if we are occupied with most important things, if
we attain to honor or fall into great misfortune—still let us always
remember how good it was once here, when we were all together,
united by a good and kind feeling which made us, for the time we
were loving that poor boy, better perhaps than we are. My little
doves—let me call you so, for you are very like them, those pretty

blue-gray birds, at this minute as I look at your good dear faces. My dear, dear children, perhaps you won't understand what I am saying to you, because I often speak very unintelligibly, but you'll remember it all the same and will agree with my words sometimes. You must know that there is nothing higher and stronger and more wholesome and good for life in the future than some good memory, especially a memory of childhood, of home. People talk to you a great deal about your education, but some good, sacred memory, preserved from childhood, is perhaps the best education. If a man carries many such memories with him into life, he is safe to the end of his days, and if one has only one good memory left in one's heart, even that may sometime be the means of saving us. Perhaps we may even grow wicked later on, may be unable to refrain from a bad action, may laugh at men's tears and at those people who say as Kolya did just now, 'I want to suffer for all men,' and may even jeer spitefully at such people. But however bad we may become— which God forbid—yet, when we recall how we buried Ilyusha, how we loved him in his last days, and how we have been talking like friends all together, at this stone, the cruelest and most mocking of us—if we do become so—will not dare to laugh inwardly at having been kind and good at this moment! What's more, perhaps, that one memory may keep him from great evil and he will reflect and say, 'Yes, I was good and brave and honest then!' Let him laugh to himself, that's no matter, a man often laughs at what's good and kind. That's only from thoughtlessness. But I assure you, boys, that as he laughs he will say at once in his heart, 'No, I do wrong to laugh, for that's not a thing to laugh at.' "

"That will certainly be so, I understand you, Karamazov!" cried Kolya, with flashing eyes. The boys were moved and they, too, wanted to say something, but they restrained themselves, looking with intentness and emotion at the speaker.

"I say this in case we become bad," Alyosha went on, "but there's no reason why we should become bad, is there, boys? Let us be, first and above all, kind, then honest and then let us never forget each other! I say that again. I give you my word for my part that I'll never forget one of you. Every face looking at me now I shall remember even for thirty years. Just now Kolya said to Kartashov that we did not care to know whether he exists or not. But I cannot forget that Kartashov exists and that he is not blushing now as he did when he discovered the founders of Troy, but is looking at me with his jolly, kind happy little eyes. Gentlemen, my dear, dear gentlemen, let us all be generous and brave like Ilyushechka, clever, brave and generous like Kolya (though he will be ever so much cleverer when he is grown up), and let us all be as bashful but also as clever and sweet as Kartashov. But why am I talking about those two! You are all dear to me, boys, from this day forth,

I have a place in my heart for you all, and I beg you to keep a place in your hearts for me! Well, and who has united us in this kind, good feeling which we shall remember and intend to remember all our lives? Who, if not Ilyushechka, the good boy, the dear boy, precious to us forever! Let us never forget him. May his memory live forever in our hearts from this time forth!"

"Yes, yes, forever, forever!" the boys cried in their ringing voices, with faces rendered soft with emotion.

"Let us remember his face and his clothes and his poor little boots, his coffin and his unhappy, sinful father, and how boldly he stood up for him alone against the whole school."

"We will remember, we will remember," cried the boys. "He was brave, he was good!"

"Ah, how I loved him!" exclaimed Kolya.

"Ah, children, ah, dear friends, don't be afraid of life! How good life is when one does something good and just!"

"Yes, yes," the boys repeated enthusiastically.

"Karamazov, we love you!" a voice, probably Kartashov's, cried impulsively.

"We love you, we love you!" they all caught it up. There were tears in the eyes of many of them.

"Hurrah for Karamazov!" Kolya shouted ecstatically.

"And may the dear boy's memory live eternally!" Alyosha added again with feeling.

"Live eternally!" the boys chimed in again.

"Karamazov," cried Kolya, "can it be true what's taught us in religion, that we shall all rise again from the dead and shall live and see each other again, all, Ilyushechka too?"

"Certainly we shall all rise again, certainly we shall see each other and shall tell each other with joy and gladness all that has happened!" Alyosha answered, half laughing, half ecstatic.

"Ah, how splendid it will be!" broke from Kolya.

"Well, now we will finish talking and go to his funeral dinner. Don't be put out at our eating pancakes—it's a very old custom and there's something nice in that!" laughed Alyosha. "Well, let us go! And now we go hand in hand."

"And always so, all our lives hand in hand! Hurrah for Karamazov!" Kolya cried once more rapturously and once more all the boys chimed in.

THE END

RALPH E. MATLAW

Afterword: On Translating *The Brothers Karamazov*

There is no more exasperating, nor perhaps rewarding, way of
confronting a text than to attempt a translation: exasperating, because one immediately becomes aware of the impossibility of the
task; rewarding, because one discovers, given a worthy text, the
immense verbal artistry that one confronts, of levels of meaning
and implication that sometimes emerge only in the laborious process of re-expression in a recalcitrant idiom that perforce distorts
the original. I had thought of translating the novel. A brief attempt
showed me the folly of that undertaking. Fortunately, the standard
translation into English, made by Mrs. Garnett more than sixty
years ago, is excellent. It is, for a variety of reasons I will detail,
deficient in certain respects (here remedied), and has frequently
been slighted both by those who read Russian and note certain
lapses, sometimes trivial, sometimes quite crucial, and by those who
do not read Russian but who clearly feel that something has been
distorted by Mrs. Garnett or, if not distorted, presented in a way
that lets one glimpse the discrepancy between her literary talents
and those of the authors she has translated, Pushkin, Gogol,
Turgenev, Dostoevsky, Tolstoy, Chekhov, and others. However, no
single person has rendered greater service to Russian literature than
Mrs. Garnett so far as the English reader is concerned and, indeed,
she thereby becomes a major figure in literary history.

In more than fifty volumes there are bound to be mistakes, and it
is in any case impossible to base a close reading of a text on a
translation. But since Mrs. Garnett's version is the basic version in
English, it has developed a critical tradition of its own, and to
change her text creates certain difficulties: chapters, characters, and
ideas are discussed in English criticism in her nomenclature, and if
that is changed an adjustment must be made so that references may
be understood. And, of course, a version that more accurately
reflects the original may well modify or even vitiate interpretations
that require a specific statement in the text. The version offered
here is a revision of Mrs. Garnett's translation. There is one dele-
tion, and there are many additions and changes. They may roughly
be grouped in three categories: first, and most important, those that
bridge the vast differences between Russian and Western cultures
and languages, in social, theological, and verbal assumptions; second, those that attempt to duplicate exactly Dostoevsky's usage of
certain words and terms, when Mrs. Garnett's eminently readable
version has modified his repetitions for the sake of a facile elegance, or when she seemed to have missed the importance of a key

word or phrase; finally, and least significant, changes necessary to accommodate the difference between genteel English at the turn of the century in England and our present idiom. The categories are not discrete. But to discuss the specific changes itself sheds some light on the novel.

I have left many things as they were, for a variety of reasons. Some could not be changed because they would be too jarring. For example, the title should read *The Karamazov Brothers*: we do not refer to "the brothers Kennedy" or "the brothers DiMaggio." But it will do. Yet the titles of individual sections can and must be corrected. Book Twelve is surely "A Miscarriage of Justice" rather than "A Judicial Error." In that book Fetyukovich is not a Victorian or Edwardian "Corrupter of Thought," but "An Adulterer of Thought," perhaps even "A Prostitutor of Thought." During the "Preliminary Investigation" Dmitri undergoes, in Mrs. Garnett's translation, "The Sufferings of a Soul, The First (Second, Third) Ordeal." Dostoevsky's term for what is given as "suffering" and "ordeal" is the same, and I have rendered it as "torment," as not only closer in meaning but quite different from "suffering," a very different concept for Dostoevsky. However, his phrase in Russian conveys a specific notion of Russian Orthodoxy, that period of forty days after death until the soul reached its destination. When Fetyukovich uses the same phrase during his peroration, Mrs. Garnett translates it as "the purgatory of a soul," which seems most felicitous. Unfortunately, Orthodoxy does not have a purgatory and the term cannot be used, not merely for that reason but also because it would obliterate a doctrinal difference from Catholicism, clearly a vital theme in *The Brothers Karamazov*.

The religious essence and overtones of the book create innumerable difficulties for the translator. We no longer have the Bible at our fingertips and find it much more difficult to achieve—and to catch—the Biblical and theological echoes that reverberate in the original, not merely in recognizing texts or references (for in his *Notebooks* and in the novel itself Dostoevsky indicates that people do not know the Gospels and even those in the monastery make mistakes), but in conveying the verbal peculiarities that constant exposure to the Bible and the speech of clerics involves. Mrs. Garnett, closer to that tradition, has been most successful precisely in conveying the religious "aura" of the book.

Even here, however, a number of comments are necessary. A Russian word may convey several meanings, only one of which is available in a single English word. The chapter title "The Breath of Corruption" points toward a less physical concept than does mine, "The Odor of Corruption." Dostoevsky was concerned with the physical as well as the spiritual, but insisted on the former in his concern that the censor pass the word "stink." There is even a kind of bonus in my version, since it may faintly suggest to some readers the "odor of sanctity" which is one of the problems the chapter examines.

The most difficult words to render consistently are those that appear in both the religious and legal aspects of the book and determine key themes: guilt, judgment, confession. They are perhaps seen quintessentially when Mitya faces, and one of the lawyers refers to, his "terrible trial." The ecclesiastic meaning of the same two words is "the Last Judgment," and every Russian reader would be aware of it. But it can only be rendered in its secular sense. "Confession" is a sacrament but also a legal concept and, in addition, an ordinary locution. In Russian the meanings are distinct, in English identical. Where the meaning is clearly one or the other, there is no problem. But when Mitya makes his "Confession of an Ardent Heart" (and it must be "ardent" rather than "passionate" to maintain Dostoevsky's imagery of fire and light) the ecclesiastic word is used, while a secular term, even a colloquial term (rendered in this case as "admission") is used by Ivan. Similarly, there are "miracles," "mysteries," and "secrets," which Dostoevsky distinguishes, but a Russian "mystery" may also be a "sacrament," and it may be a mystery in a detective sense as well as a religious one. Here, as elsewhere, Dostoevsky is always consistent in his usage, but the translator cannot be. Moreover, when a word is particularly important, Dostoevsky will repeat it several times and call attention to it to insure the reader's paying heed.

The crucial cluster is the word "guilt" along with its derivatives and attendant ideas. In the legal sense, guilt and sentencing or judgment are clear, at least linguistically. But ethically and morally their implication differs. Since the leading idea of the novel is that "we are all responsible for everyone and everything," it would not have done to translate the word "responsible" as "guilty," for that would both limit the meaning and introduce an unwarranted legal note, perhaps also a more specifically psychiatric connotation than Dostoevsky may have intended. Indeed, the same word "guilty" (*vinovat*) colloquially and most frequently means "excuse me" in Russian or, to get a closer shade of meaning, "pardon me." Dostoevsky studiously avoids this usage throughout the novel. Similarly, "to judge, condemn, blame" may be the same word in Russian but must be distinguished in English according to context, so that again certain overtones disappear. Only slightly less troublesome is the fervor, gentility, kindness, the melting of the heart in the Russian "*umilenie*," a word with strong religious overtones but also used descriptively. V. Nabokov has suggested—incorrectly— that it is the French "*attendrissement*," but that is only a partial meaning and we have no equivalent for the French word either.

There are at least two words connected with the religious vocabulary that require some explanation. The first is *"klikushka,"* the "possessed," "screaming" woman whose disease is explained in "Peasant Women Who Have Faith," a term used disparagingly by Karamazov for his second wife. It does not sound nearly so aberrant in Russian. Incidentally, the problem is not unique to Russia, nor does it necessarily require a laying on of hands by a cleric. It is worth noting in these days of equal rights that the *"couvade"* existed, and exists, among certain French peasants (and in other nationalities), wherein the woman went back to the fields after giving birth while the husband took to his bed for a week. Another accepted institution in Russia was that of the *"yurodivy,"* the "fool in Christ," the religious madman exemplified in Father Ferapont. The term is also used with various secular shades of contempt and disparagement, as madman, fool, hysterical, weak-minded, exultation (applied to Alyosha, and to his mother), with never quite the same implication in English, for the notion itself is foreign.

In other areas, too, the English sometimes overstates Dostoevsky's point. Smerdyakov is a lackey. With two exceptions he is always so designated, rather than as a servant or a footman, while Grigory never is. The word was less contemptuous in Dostoevsky's time than it is now, and could be used simply to designate a particular kind of servant, which Smerdyakov, as cook, is not. But it also contained the pejorative sense that has in effect now become the primary meaning in both languages, and by his consistency Dostoevsky emphasizes what is later called Smerdyakov's "lackey soul." The stench of his soul is implicit each time his name is given in Russian, for his name, is derived from "stink," and its physical counterpart may be felt in the pomades and lotions and dandyish dress he affects to disguise his exterior, which at the end yield to his filthy dressing-gown and snot-fouled handkerchief. The contempt for his lackey's soul may also be glimpsed in the contemptuous designation of a serf or slave in the nineteenth century as *"smerd."* Altogether it is a name with considerable implication. It may be indicated in French by mere transliteration but requires explanation in English.

Smerdyakov's peculiar abjectness, the fawning, mincing, unctuous speech, his false humility, we may sometimes get in English, as in Dickens's Uriah Heep, but hardly with the range possible in Russian. One of the obvious devices is the use of "sir" or "ma'am," done in Russian by the addition of the letter "s" to almost any word—*"nyet-s"* and *"da-s"*, both monosyllables, mean "no, sir (or ma'am)" and "yes, sir (or ma'am)." It may be done for emphasis once or twice by anyone in normal discourse but becomes the mark of a special servility when overused, and it becomes particularly annoying in Smerdyakov in conjunction with the rest of his affected speech. The effect is quite different in Captain Snegiryov, who coins a name for himself I have given as "Yessirov" ("Sigma-userov" is more exact but requires footnoting), who consciously uses it as a means of self-abasement and self-humiliation. It is used by the pretentious Marya Kondratevna (what a marvelous touch that Smerdyakov has a female admirer!), and in the pitiful Maximov, living on others' charity and speaking as a dependent is expected to. I have introduced what may strike some readers as too many "sir's" but I have by no means put in each "s" of the Russian. Again Dostoevsky is artistically consistent. In certain vital speeches both Smerdyakov and Snegiryov fail to use "sir," and that very absence alerts the reader to something important.

Maximov's speech is typical, at least in literature, of the poor relations, hangers-on, dependents that are known in Russian as *"prizhival'shchiki,"* those hangers-on who lived at the expense, and the whim, of others. When they were buffoons like Maximov or Fyodor Karamazov in his youth, assuring their keep by demeaning themselves, they may well be called "toadies," though that word probably no longer conveys a sense of an accepted institution, as Roman "parasites"—hangers-on—also were. The exemplar of a more modest form of the toady, who characterizes himself as a *"prizhival'shchik,"* is one of Dostoevsky's most stupendous creations, Ivan's devil. (Incidentally, since the father was of the same ilk of parasites, it is surprising that no one has analyzed in detail what this may mean, either for an understanding of Ivan or for the novel as a whole.) The term "toady," however, could hardly be applied in English, as it is in Russian, to Karamazov's second wife, who, before leaving her dependent's position by marrying Karamazov, had attempted to leave it by committing suicide. It was clearly a difficult and humiliating way of existing, with little comfort in the larger view expressed by a well-meaning character in Chekhov, "We are all God's *prizhival'shchiki."*

Among the varieties of speech and styles in the novel, each suited to the character, one of the most difficult to convey is that of the Prosecuting Attorney. Mrs. Garnett had eliminated so many of his repetitions, his elliptical sentence structure, his inability to state a point logically and succinctly, that he emerged a much better lawyer and thinker than Dostoevsky ever meant him to be. I have reinstated all the passages and have tried to follow Dostoevsky exactly, not an easy task, because if the attorney gets tangled up in his own rhetoric, the translator may overstate the attorney's difficiencies in another direction. Suffice it to say that Dostoevsky expended great effort and ingenuity in showing the muddled thought and obtuse psychologizing of the prosecutor in the fabric of his speech, and some of this at least is now conveyed in English. Dostoevsky himself comments in the novel on the attorney's style, modestly calling attention through the narrator to its shortcomings, as he does on that of the defense attorney's. Much as Dostoevsky despised Fetyukovich's prototype (whom he denied using as a model), he not only manages to capture the essentials of his style but perhaps makes it even more effective.

We come next to problems of diminutives, common ways of conveying affection, politeness, good humor, or deference in Russian, which may, however, also have a pejorative cast. It is quite natural to refer to "birdies" and "little this" or "little that" in Russian, but it sounds somewhat childish or silly, if not downright idiotic, in English, and I have made no attempt to indicate each time a diminutive was used. Excessive use creates a cloying sentimentality even in Russian, and totters on the annoying in the Snegiryov sections and in some of Elder Zosima's homilies. The saccharine quality may be used with deliberate effect, as Dostoevsky demonstrates in the first meeting between Grushenka and Katerina Ivanovna. The pejorative note first appears in the title of Book One. It does little good to translate *"semeyka"* as "little family" or the like, for nothing will convey the note of sarcasm and disapproval implicit in Dostoevsky's diminutive. A comparable note of faint contemptuousness is heard in references to Ivan's "little idea" or in some names, as when Grushenka refers to Rakitin as Rakitka.

Russians use a variety of diminutives in names, particularly children's names. In general, the longer the diminutive form, the greater the affection shown. Thus Ilyusha Snegiryov has a further degree of diminutive—Ilyushechka—when his father shows even greater attachment. His legal name, Il'ya, is not used at all. Alyosha in some emotive exchanges with his father and with Grushenka becomes Alyoshechka but is never quite transformed into the babyish forms Dostoevsky uses in reporting the death of his own son. Dmitri, usually Mitya, can become Mitka or Mitenka, each time with a slightly different shade of meaning, connected with his age, character, and particular circumstance. In brief, by the use of such diminutives Dostoevsky can convey both the attitude of the speaker and a particular quality of the character: his youth, something childish, something endearing, something not quite formal, or merely a degree of friendship or respect. One tends to think of Alyosha rather than of Alexey or Alexey Fyodorovich, of Grushenka (Mitya's "Grusha" betokens an even closer feeling) rather than Agrafena Alexandrovna, of Dmitri in some of his doings as Mitya, in others as Dmitri, in still others as Dmitri Karamazov, with still another level available in Russian and discussed shortly. But Ivan is only Ivan or Ivan Fyodorovich and I have had to reintroduce the two or three times he is called Vanya or Vanka by his father for an important reason: when on his way to Smerdyakov Ivan hears the peasant singing "Vanka's gone to Petersburg" the Russian reader would automatically recognize that Vanka is a diminutive of Ivan and might thus be led to consider another implication of the passage.

Diminutives are only one peculiarity of Russian names. In addition to the given name, everyone has a patronymic ("son of," "daughter of"). This permits at least one further level of formality. In the late nineteenth century the family name was rarely used in social discourse and even in certain forms of address and reference, for the name and patronymic approximate our "Mr." or "Mrs." That prefix is rare, for people would be addressed by their military or civil rank or a designation of their social status as a member of the nobility, middle class, and so on. The use of the family name alone is perfectly acceptable, for example among schoolmates, comrades, and the like, but it can convey a lesser sense of derogation than in English: when Fetyukovich refers to Grushenka at the trial he merely gives her family name. It sounds cruder in English than in Russian; the French can convey a slightly different insinuation by "la Svetlov." Russian has a form of address ("gospozha") that designates an adult female, whether single or married, for which there is unfortunately no longer a word in English (formerly "mistress" was an exact equivalent). It is used by Fetyukovich for Katerina Ivanovna, and by the prosecuting attorney for Grushenka. To maintain this hierarchy I have used "Miss" for the two rivals, have retained the original translator's "Madame" Khokhlakov, and left "Mrs." for the few instances when wives of commoners are mentioned. The family name alone for peripheral characters like Rakitin, Maximov, and Perkhotin is not merely one of convenience but also of a certain distance in attitude.

Patronymics and names in general should present problems in translation, and certain shades of attitude, for example in the difference between Trifon Borisovich and Trifon Borisich—since the "ov" is usually not pronounced anyway—cannot be conveyed in English. So, too, Barbara Nikolaevna Snegiryov occasionally is "Nikolavna." Here they are vital: It is possible to refer to a single hero as Raskolnikov, but if one were to write "Karamazov" a further distinction is necessary as four characters share the name. The patronymic offers a solution that may seem unduly cumbersome in English, where Ivan is clearly Ivan, Dmitri is Dmitri, and so on. But in Russian, certainly in the narrative portions, and frequently in direct address, they cannot be mentioned without their patronymics, and I have reintroduced them into Mrs. Garnett's translation. The reason is that Dostoevsky himself hammers away at their brotherhood and their connection with their father Fyodor, who on at least one vital occasion forgets who is a half-brother and who a full, and hints at a different alignment. Each time the two elder brothers' names appear in the narrative, and frequently in conversation, almost invariably for Ivan, Ivan is Ivan Fyodorovich and Dmitri is Dmitri Fyodorovich. Occasionally, Dostoevsky omits the patronymic. Sometimes it may be accidental, sometimes—as in Ivan's conversation with the devil—by design. I have always followed his usage, without concern for inconsistency or worries about his intentions.

When any of the brothers refer to another by his first name (not by a diminutive), without the patronymic, he frequently finds it necessary to add "brother," or perhaps to substitute it for the patronymic. I have turned it at the beginning of the novel into "my brother Ivan (Dmitri)" because in today's quaint idiom the lack of possessive pronoun may convey a different meaning. The patronymic may become annoying in English but it is necessary. The reader can gauge the effect for himself. Ivan is always Ivan Fyodorovich, but Dmitri is Mitya as well as Dmitri Fyodorovich. When Alyosha is called Alexey Fyodorovich there is a slight shock not because of the formality, but because it reminds one of the family connection. It is even more striking when Kolya and the schoolboys call him "Karamazov," which he unquestionably is.

The Karamazov brothers, however, are four. We read that old Karamazov was amused that townspeople added the patronymic Fyodorovich to Smerdyakov's Christian name, but tolerated it even though he denied paternity. The lackey is always called by the family name Fyodor devised, Smerdyakov, and it must really come as a shocking reminder that he too is a member of the family when Marya Kondratevna—the only one in the book—addresses him as "Pavel Fyodorovich." The patronymic emphasizes brotherhood, and in more than merely the legal sense. Onomastics (the study of the forms of proper names) are crucial. The family name, the given names, the names of other characters always point to something significant. Dostoevsky distributed his spiritual and intellectual strivings and shortcomings, his physical drives and his disease among the four brothers. He endowed his favorite character with the name of his recently deceased young boy, Alexey; to Dmitri he gave his sensuality, to Ivan his dialectical and rational skills, to Smerdyakov his epilepsy; and to old Karamazov, the source from which the novel turbulently flows, the father of us all, the creator of the novel assigned his own name, Fyodor—Theodore, "the gift of God"! Indeed!

I need not dwell on other difficulties. There are many. Some are touched on in the critical essays and in Dostoevsky's letters, where he is even concerned with the effects of paragraphing, though he did not bother to correct those shortcomings by the printer. I have changed some of the paragraphing in those sections according to sense, and others according to English usage. Ultimately the version must speak for itself. That it falls far short of the original, I know all too well; that it is readable, I may hope; that it is accurate, I can vouch for.

I will add a personal prejudice. *The Brothers Karamazov* hinges on the killing of a father, on patricide. For some inexplicable reason, "parricide" has taken its place in the original translation and become hallowed by the translation of Freud's article as "Dostoevsky and Parricide." I have let it stand because I have always been amused by the notion of Grigory's shouting "Parricide" at the fleeing figure who turns out to be Mitya. It is certainly Dostoevsky's intent that all should think Mitya culpable, and he emphasizes it in the shout. My amusement stems from the Russian "*ottseubiytsa*," which is perfectly colloquial but sounds like an exclamation that might more naturally issue from a Samurai or a Kamikaze pilot than from a Russian servant in the provinces. "Parricide" is bad enough, "patricide" even worse. The Germans are luckier: instead of the learned word, Grigory can rattle out the machine-gun burst: "*Vatertöter*"!

I have deleted one line of Mrs. Garnett's translation, the very last of the novel, "Hurrah for Karamazov!", an addition of her own. Dostoevsky was not modest about the book. When the prosecutor makes the invidious comparison "They have their Hamlets but we only have our Karamazovs," the reader may italicize the names, make them titles, and consider their preeminence in their respective literatures and in world literature. But the affirmative shout that ends the novel, "Hurrah for Karamazov" is only an acoustic effect, to be imagined by the reader, not a real line. The book is replete with such effects, the most notable being the silence just before the murder, which prompts Mitya to think of a verse "and only the silence whispers." Dostoevsky's conclusion is an audible chorus ("they all chimed in"), not a repetition of the shout itself. And it is clearly a more apt conclusion than a cheer for a Karamazov. The ending emphasizes unity and brotherhood, not the individual that has brought it about, not the family whose deeds have set it in motion, not the author who takes a final bow.

Backgrounds and Sources

A Brief Chronology
of Dostoevsky's Life

1821, October 30. Dostoevsky born.

1838, January. Enters Military Engineering School.

October. Informs father he must repeat first year.

1839, June. Father murdered by his peasants.

1840 (?) Begins having epileptic seizures.

1843 Finishes Military Engineering School.

1844, June & July. First published work, translation of Balzac's novel *Eugénie Grandet*.

October. Retires from military service to concentrate on literary work.

1845. Writes *Poor Folk*. Meets Belinsky, Russia's leading literary critic.

1846. Publishes *Poor Folk, The Double*. Meets Petrashevsky and later joins his discussion group on philosophy and politics.

1847–1848. Publishes several minor works.

1849, April. Arrested for political subversion (participation in the Petrashevsky circle). Sentenced to death by firing squad. Reprieved at last moment. Leaves for Siberia Christmas eve.

1850–54. In prison at Omsk.

1854–59. Serves in military disciplinary battalion, Semipalatinsk, Siberia, first as private, then as non-com (1855), ensign (1856).

1857, February. Marries a widow, M. D. Isaev. Resumes publishing.

1859, August. Permitted to move to Tver (120 miles N.W. of Moscow).

December. Permitted to move to Petersburg.

1860–63. Issues (under the nominal editorship of his brother Michael) the successful journal *Time*.

1860. Begins publishing *Notes from a Dead House*.

1862–63. Liaison with Polina Suslov.

1862. First trip to Europe. *Winter Notes on Summer Impression* published 1863.

1863. *Time* closed by censorship. Travels to Italy with Polina Suslov.

1864. Publishes periodical *The Epoch* (folds at end of year). First issue contains beginning of *Notes from Underground*. Works on *Crime and Punishment*. April, wife dies. July, brother Michael dies. Assumes personal and business debts of both. Contracts for an advance of 3,000 rubles, for an edition of his work including a new work. Will forfeit all literary rights if work is not produced by deadline.

1866. Finishes *Crime and Punishment* and simultaneously dictates *The Gambler* to fulfill contract.

1867. February. Marries Anna Grigorevna Snitkin, 18-year-old stenographer to whom he dictated *The Gambler* and epilogue of *Crime and Punishment*. Goes abroad to escape creditors.

1867–1871. Lives in Europe. Writes and publishes *The Idiot, The Eternal Husband*, starts work on *The Possessed*.

1871. July. Returns to Russia. Begins publishing *The Possessed*.

1873. Editor of *The Citizen*.

1874. Leaves *The Citizen* to write *The Adolescent*.

1875. Publication and conclusion of *The Adolescent*.

1876. Beginning of monthly publication, *A Writer's Diary*.

1878, May, Death of son Alexey. Journey to Optina Monastery with Vladimir Solovyov (June) during which he tells him details of *The Brothers Karamazov*. Ceases publication of the *Diary* (December) to work on the novel.

1879. Begins to publish *The Brothers Karamazov*.

1880. June, "Pushkin Day Speech," published in single issue of the *Diary*.

November, finishes *The Brothers Karamazov*.

1881, January 28. Dies.

L. M. REYNUS

Prototypes and Heroes of *The Brothers Karamazov*†
(Staraya Russa, *Notes from the Dead House, Notebooks*)

Various impressions and episodes of the writer's life in Staraya Russa can be traced through many pages of the novel. The scenery of Staraya Russa became the setting against which the action of Dostoevsky's last novel develops. It was here, too, that its subject arose.

† L. M. Reynus, *Dostoevsky v Staroy Russe* (Leningrad, 1971), pp. 43–46. Translated by Ralph E. Matlaw. Dostoevsky first stayed in Staraya Russa (Old Rus), a sizable town and spa about 125 miles south of St. Petersburg, in 1872. He spent every summer but one thereafter in the town, remaining well into the autumn and sometimes later, and wrote most of *The Brothers Karamazov* there.

It is possible that an insignificant but interesting circumstance affected its gestation. When the writer decided to spend the winter of 1874 in Staraya Russa, he moved to Ilinsky Street. Ilinsky . . . Ilinsky . . . The name of the street, impinging on him every day and every hour, apparently resurrected in Dostoevsky's mind an episode from the most difficult period of his life, the Omsk prison:

> Only in prison have I heard stories of the most terrible, the most unnatural crimes, the most monstrous murders, told with the most irrepressible, most childishly merry laughter. I particularly cannot forget one parricide. He was a nobleman, had served [in the army], and was something like a prodigal son to his sixty-year-old father. He was completely dissolute in character and had run heavily into debt. His father tried to restrain him, to bring him to his senses. But the father had a house and a farm, was thought to have money—and the son killed him, eager to get his inheritance. The crime was not discovered for a month. The murderer himself informed the police that his father had disappeared without a trace. He spent the entire month in wild carousing. Finally, in his absence, the police found the body. Along the entire length of the yard ran a sewage ditch covered with boards. The body lay in that ditch. It was fully dressed and decorated, the grey head had been cut off and replaced on the trunk, and beneath the head the murderer had placed a pillow. He did not confess. He was deprived of his nobility and rank and sent to hard labor for twenty years. During the entire period I lived with him he was in the best and happiest frame of mind. He was flighty, thoughtless, irresponsible to an extraordinary degree, but he was no fool. I never noticed any particular cruelty in him. The other prisoners despised him not for the crime, which was never mentioned, but for his foolishness, his inability to behave properly. He never mentioned his father in conversation. Once, talking to me about the healthy constitution hereditary in the family, he added, "My *parent* now, never complained of any illness to his very end." Such brutal insensitivity is of course inconceivable. It is a phenomenon; there is some sort of constitutional defect here, some physical and moral abnormality not yet known to science, and not simply a crime. Of course I did not believe in that crime. But people from his town who knew all the details of his story told me all about his case. The facts were so clear that it was impossible to doubt them.
>
> The prisoners heard him cry in his sleep one night "Hold him, hold him! Cut off his head, his head, his head!"

* * *

The publisher of *Notes from the Dead House* has recently received information from Siberia that the criminal was indeed innocent and underwent ten years' penal servitude in vain; that his innocence was officially proclaimed by the court. That the real criminals were found and have confessed and that he has already been released from prison. The publisher cannot doubt the authenticity of this report.[1]

The dramatic quality of this story stirred Dostoevsky's creative imagination. On September 13, 1874 he wrote in his *Notebook*:

> Plot. In Tobolsk, twenty years ago, like Ilinsky's case. Two brothers, an old father, one is engaged to a girl with whom the second is secretly and enviously in love. But she loves the older. But the older, a young lieutenant, carouses and plays the fool, quarrels with the father. The father disappears. For several days neither hide nor hair of him. The brothers discuss the inheritance. And suddenly the authorities: the body is dug out of the cellar. Evidence against the older (the younger doesn't live with him). The older is tried and sentenced to penal servitude. (NB. Quarreled with his father, bragged of his inheritance from his late mother and other follies. When he entered the room and even his fiancé turns away, he somewhat drunk, said, "Do you really believe it too?" The evidence splendidly falsified by the younger). The public does not know for sure who killed him.
>
> *Scene* in prison. They want to kill *him*.
>
> Administration. He doesn't betray. The convicts swear fraternity to him. The Administrator reproves him for killing his father.
>
> Twelve years later the brother comes to see him. Scene, where *silently* they understand each other.
>
> Another seven years later, the younger brother has attained rank and station, but is tormented, splenetic, discloses to his wife that he killed him. "Why did you tell me?" He goes to his brother. The wife also runs to him.
>
> On her knees the wife asks the convict to remain silent, to save her husband. The convict says: "I've gotten used to it." They are reconciled. "You're punished even without that," the older says.
>
> The younger brother's birthday. Guests are gathered. He comes in: "I killed him." They think he has had a stroke.
>
> Ending: the other returns. The first at a transport point. He is being sent away. [the Slanderer asks] The younger asks the older to be a father to his children.
>
> "You have gone on the right path."[2]

At that time the writer was occupied with his work on *The Adolescent,* but he did not forget the idea that had germinated. Imperceptibly and involuntarily it began to develop, ripening for transformation into a new work.

Another event that took place in Staraya Russa in 1875, on the Cathedral side, not far from the former salt factory, also did not escape his attention.

Peter Nazarov who lived there killed his father. Dostoevsky ques-

1. The excerpt is given in full from *Notes from the Dead House,* (1862), Part I, Chapter 1, and Part II, Chapter 7. F. M. Dostoevsky, *Sobranie sochineniy* (Moscow, 1956–58), III, 403–4, 650–51 [*Editor*].
2. Quoted in full from *Literaturnoe nasledstvo,* 83 (Moscow, 1971), 356 [*Editor*].

tioned his Staraya Russa acquaintances at length about the event and looked into all details of this extraordinary occurrence. The *Novgorod News* announced that the trial would take place September 20. Toward that time the Dostoevsky's left for St. Petersburg. But knowing the writer's interest in the case, A. P. Orlova informed his wife "They tried the parricide, you remember, who killed his blind father. Despite Andrushkevich's exhortations the jury said "Yes, guilty" and condemned him to life imprisonment."

Now the important motive of parricide in the future *Brothers Karamazov* seemed even more closely connected with the district town where the writer himself lived. * * *

Certain traits of the father of the family, Fyodor Pavlovich Karamazov, were prompted by the von Sohn story, which the writer had heard several years before starting work on the novel:

> "Your reverence, do you know who von Sohn was?" Fyodor Karamazov himself asks in the novel. "It was a famous murder case. He was killed in a house of harlotry. I believe that is what such places are called among you—he was killed and robbed, and in spite of his venerable age, he was nailed up in a box and sent from Petersburg to Moscow in the luggage van."

Dostoevsky had already mentioned that von Sohn in *The Adolescent*.

Staraya Russa apparently reminded the writer of von Sohn every day, as it did of Ilinsky. Dostoevsky then lived in Leontev's house. A few steps from there, on the corner to the right, began Sohn Lane, consisting of houses that belonged, by a strange coincidence of names, to the von Sohns of Staraya Russa. Beyond the lane, on peaceful Silin Street, where number 33 now is, stood the two-story house, partly in stone, that belonged to the head of the family, Major General K. K. von Sohn, who at one time was director of the spa in Staraya Russa. From his wife's correspondence Dostoevsky unquestionably knew about the owner of the house, who had died in 1870. It was well known that von Sohn was a rapacious man, trying in every possible way to make money. Our contemporary writer, V. M. Glinka, who was born in Staraya Russa, heard from the older inhabitants in his youth that von Sohn was just such an old profligate as his more famous namesake, who was killed in Moscow.

The inhabitants of Staraya Russa were struck while reading Dostoevsky's novel by the resemblance of Fyodor Karamazov to the von Sohn who had lived among them. They could not fail to notice that one of Karamazov's sons was a carouser while the other was distinguished by his piety—just like the sons of the Major General.

In Dostoevsky's day town gossip persistently connected von Sohn and his sons with the novel's heroes. It is interesting to note that among the inhabitants of Staraya Russa that conviction still exists.

* * *

F. M. DOSTOEVSKY

Letters†

No. 318. To A. N. Maykov.[1] Florence, December 11, 1868

* * * Now I have in mind a huge novel entitled *Atheism* (for God's sake, that's strictly between us), but before I can start on it I have to read practically a whole library of atheists, Catholics, and Orthodox. Even with complete freedom for work it would take at least two years. I have a [central] character: a Russian, one of our society, *getting on in years*, not very educated but also not uneducated, with a certain distinction in rank,—*suddenly*, in his later years, loses faith in God. All his life he had devoted himself to work completely, never went astray, and to the age of forty-five didn't distinguish himself in any way. (A psychological riddle: deep feelings, a man, and a Russian man.) Loss of faith in God has a colossal effect on him. (The action of the novel, the background, is very extensive.) He scuttles among the younger generation, the atheists, the Slavophiles and Westerners, among Russian fanatics and hermits, among the clergy; he happens to fall into the clutches of a Jesuit, a propagator of the faith, a Pole, moves on from him into the depths of the flagellant sectants—and toward the end discovers Christ and the Russian earth, the Russian Christ and the Russian God. For God's sake, don't tell anyone; but as far as I'm concerned, I'd die happy if I could finish this final novel, for I would have expressed myself completely. Ah, my friend! I have a completely different notion of actuality and realism than our realists and critics. My idealism is more real than theirs. God! If one were to relate meaningfully what we Russians have gone through in the last ten years of our spiritual development, wouldn't the realists exclaim that it was a fantasy! But that is the fundamental, basic realism. That's just what realism is, only deeper, while theirs merely skims the surface. Isn't Lyubim Tortsov[2] really insignificant—and

† From F. M. Dostoevsky, *Pis'ma (Letters)* ed. A. S. Dolinin, vols. II–IV (Moscow, 1930, 1934, 1959). Translated by Ralph E. Matlaw. All dates are Old Style (Julian Calendar) then in use in Russia. Twelve days should be added for the corresponding date in the West.

Footnotes are by the present editor.
1. A. N. Maykov (1821–97), poet, critic, one of Dostoevsky's closest friends.
2. Character in A. N. Ostrovsky's play *Poverty Is No Crime* (1854), particularly exalted by Apollon Grigoryev for his humility.

that's the only ideal thing that their realism has allowed them. Realism is a profound thing—no question about it! You won't explain a hundredth part of real, actual facts through their realism. While we, with our idealism, have even predicted facts. It has happened.

No. 345. To A. N. Maykov. Dresden, March 25, 1870

* * * I promised *The Dawn*[3] something good and I want to do it well. That piece for *The Dawn* has matured in my mind for two years. It is the same idea I have already written to you about. It will be my last novel, about the size of *War and Peace*, and with an idea you would approve, at least judging by our previous conversations. That novel will consist of five large parts (each about 250 pages— the plan has matured in my mind for two years). The stories are completely separate from each other, so they might even be sold separately. The first novel I have earmarked for Kashpirev[4]: its action takes place in the 1840's. The general title for the novel is *The Life of a Great Sinner*, but each novel will have a separate title. The main question, which will run through all the parts—is the very one I have struggled with consciously and unconsciously all my life—the existence of God. Through the course of his life my hero is at times an atheist, then a believer, then a fanatic and a sectant, then again an atheist. The second part will take place entirely in a monastery. I have put all my hopes in this second tale. Perhaps it will finally be said that I have not merely written trifles. (I confess it to you alone, Apollon Nikolaevich—I want to make the main figure of the second tale Tikhon Zadonsky,[5] under a different name, of course, but yet the bishop will live peacefully in the monastery. A thirteen-year-old boy, who participated in a criminal act, mature and corrupted—don't worry—I know the type— (of our educated circle), the future hero of the whole novel is placed in the monastery for instruction. The little wolf and child-nihilist meets Tikhon (You know the character and the whole figure of Tikhon). I'll put Chaadaev[6] in the same monastery (also under a different name, of course). Why shouldn't Chaadaev be confined to a monastery for a year? Imagine that Chaadaev, who had to be certified by doctors every week after his first essay, couldn't hold out and published a pamphlet, let's say abroad, in French—it is very possible that he might have been confined to a monastery for a year for that. Others could come to visit Chaadaev,

3. Dostoevsky had accepted an advance from the periodical and had sent it *The Eternal Husband* as part of his obligation.
4. Editor of *The Dawn*.
5. (1724–83) canonized in 1861, prototype, with others, for Elder Zosima.

6. P. Chaadaev (1794–1856), published the first of his *Philosophical Letters* in 1836, rejecting Russia and Orthodoxy for Catholicism and Western civilization. This brilliant thinker was declared by Nicholas I to be insane and was confined to house arrest.

Belinsky, for example, Granovsky, even Pushkin.[7] (After all it's not Chaadaev, I am just using that type in my novel. Pavel Prussky is also in the monastery, and Golubov and the monk Parfeny[8] (I am an expert in that field and I know the Russian monastery since childhood). But Tikhon and the child are the main thing. For God's sake don't tell anyone the contents of that second volume. (I never tell anyone my plans in advance, I'm somehow ashamed. But I confess myself to you.) Let others consider it worthless, but for me it is a treasure. Do not tell anyone about Tikhon. I wrote Strakhov[9] about the monastery, but didn't mention Tikhon. Perhaps I will create a grandiose, *positive*, holy figure. That's no longer a Konstanzhoglo[1] or the German (I forget his name) in *Oblomov*.[2] How do we know, perhaps it is precisely Tikhon who is our *positive* Russian type our literature is seeking and not Lavretsky, not Chichikov, not Rakhmetov and the others, and not the Lopukhovs, not the Rakhmetovs.[3] Actually I won't create anything, I will merely present the real Tikhon, whom I long ago took into my heart with rapture. But I consider even that an important achievement if I am successful. Don't tell anyone. But I have to be in Russia for the second novel, for the monastery. Oh, if it were to turn out successfully! The first novel is the hero's childhood. Of course it isn't about children; there is a romance.* * *

No. 550. To V. A. Alekseev.[4] Petersburg, June 7, 1876

You raise a shrewd question, particularly as it must be answered at length. In itself the matter is clear. The devil's temptation contains three colossal, eternal questions, and after eighteen centuries there are no more difficult, that is, shrewd, ideas than these, and they still cannot be resolved.

"Stones and bread" signify the contemporary social question, *environment*. It isn't prophecy, it has always existed. "How should one approach the ruined poor, who out of hunger and oppression

7. V. G. Belinsky (1811–48), most famous and influential of Russian critics; T. N. Granovsky (1813–55), professor of history, a leader of the idealists of the 1840's and a prototype for Stepan Verkhovensky in *The Possessed*; A. S. Pushkin (1799–1837), Russia's greatest poet.
8. Pavel Prussky (1821–95) an active sectant, later Orthodox, well known religious writer; Golubov, pupil and follower of Pavel, publicist on religious, philosophical, and political questions. Parfeny (died 1868) author of *Tale of Pilgrimage Through Russia, Moldavia, Turkey, and the Holy Land*.
9. N. N. Strakhov (1828–1896) Critic, philosopher, collaborator on Dostoevsky's journals *Time* and *Epoch*.

1. A "good" (but flat) character in Gogol's *Dead Souls*, II.
2. Novel by I. A. Goncharov (1861).
3. Characters respectively in Turgenev's *A Nest of Noblemen*, Gogol's *Dead Souls*, and Chernyshevsky's *What Is to Be Done?*
4. V. A. Alekseev, a singer at the Mariinsky Opera, had asked Dostoevsky what he meant by calling the concern of Pisareva, a recent suicide, with the small amount of money she left "the final expression of the greatest prejudice of contemporary youth, who value material means above everything, dream of stones turned into bread." Alekseev points out that in the *Gospels* the stones were not turned to bread.

resemble beasts rather than humans—go to them and preach to the starving the avoidance of sin, humility, chastity—would it not be better to *feed* them first? It would be more humane. They come to preach to you too, but then you are the Son of God, the whole world awaited you eagerly; then act as the foremost in mind and fairness, give all of them food, give them *security*, give them a social structure that will guarantee them bread and order forever, and only then ask them not to sin. If they then sin they would be ungrateful, whereas now they sin out of hunger. It is sinful even to ask them to refrain.

You are the Son of God, consequently you can do anything. Here are stones, look, how many. All You need do is command, and the stones will be turned to bread.

Command also that the earth will bear without labor, teach people a science or teach them a procedure that will secure their lives henceforth. Do you really not believe that man's greatest vices and misfortunes arose from hunger, cold, poverty, and the impossible struggle for survival?"

That is the first idea the evil spirit proposed to Christ. Admit that it is difficult to deal with it. Contemporary *socialism* in Europe, and here, constantly dismisses Christ, and concerns itself first of all with *bread*, calls upon science and maintains that the only reasons for all man's miseries are *poverty*, the struggle for survival, "the environment ruined him."

To that Christ replied, "Man does not live by bread alone," that is, he stated as well the axiom of man's spiritual origin. The devil's idea could only apply to the beast in man, while Christ knew that by bread alone you cannot animate man. If there were no spiritual life, no ideal of Beauty, man would pine away, die, go mad, kill himself or give himself to pagan fantasies. And as Christ, the ideal of Beauty in Himself and his Word, he decided it was better to implant the ideal of Beauty in the soul. If it exists in the soul, each would be the brother of everyone else and then, of course, working for each other, all would also be rich. Whereas if you gave them bread, they might become enemies to each other out of boredom.

But suppose you gave them Beauty and Bread at the same time? Then you would deprive man of *work, individuality, self-sacrifice and the sacrifice of one's goods for one's neighbor*, in short, all life, the ideal of life would be taken away. And therefore it is better to proclaim only the spiritual ideal.

The proof that this brief excerpt from the *New Testament* concerns precisely this idea and not merely Christ's being hungry and the devil's advising him to take *stone* and command it to become bread, the proof lies precisely in that Christ answered by disclosing the secret of man's nature "Man does not live by bread alone" (that is, like the animals).

If the matter merely concerned assuaging Christ's hunger, why speak of the spiritual nature of man in general? And for that matter, had He wished, He could have obtained bread earlier, without the devil's counsel. Incidentally, consider current ideas by Darwin and others on man's descent from the monkey. Without going into any theories Christ proclaimed outright that there is a spiritual realm in man apart from the animal. So what does it matter—let man descend from wherever you like (the Bible doesn't explain how God fashioned man from clay or made him from stone) but on the contrary that God *breathed into his nostrils the breath of life* (but badly, that man might turn into a beast again through his sins).

Your obedient servant, F. Dostoevsky.

P.S. Pisareva studied with, and frequented, contemporary youth, where there is no question of religion, but where they dream of socialism, that is, of a structure of the world where there will first of all be bread and bread will be divided equally and there will be no property. According to my observations these socialists, while waiting for the future structure of society without individual responsibility, are in the meantime terribly fond of money and even value it immoderately, but precisely for the significance they attach to it.

No. 617. To V. V. Mikhaylov.[5] Petersburg, March 16, 1878

* * * You indicated in your last letter that you would have no objection to writing me again. I value that highly, and *I count on you*. What interests me particularly in your letter is that you love children, have lived among children a great deal, and do so even now. Here, then, is my request, dear Vladimir Vasilyevich: I have conceived and will soon start writing a large novel where, among other things, children, particularly youngsters aged approximately seven to fifteen, will play a great role. Many children will be introduced. I am studying them and have studied them all my life, and love them dearly, and have children myself. But the observations of a man like yourself would be very valuable to me (I understand that). So write me *about children*—everything you know. Both about Petersburg children who call you "uncle" and Elizavetgrad children, and *about whatever you know*. (Incidents, habits, answers, sayings and puns, traits, relation to the family, misdeeds and innocence; their nature and the teacher, Latin, etc., etc.,—in short what you know.) You will help me greatly, I shall be very grateful and will await your correspondence eagerly. * * *

5. A teacher, educator, and supervisor.

No. 632 to N. M. Dostoevsky, Petersburg, Tuesday, May 16, 1878

My very dear brother Nikolay Mikhaylovich, today our Alyosha died from a sudden attack of epilepsy, which he had never had before. Yesterday he was still merry, sang, ran around, and today he is laid out for burial. The attack started at 9:30 in the morning, and at 2:30 Lyoshechka died. He will be buried Thursday the 18th in the Great Okhtensky Cemetery. Goodbye, Kolya, pity Lyosha, you petted him frequently (remember how he imitated a drunk, "Vanka the foo' "?). I have never felt so sad. We all grieve.

Your brother, F. Dostoevsky

No. 652. To N. A. Lyubimov.[6] *Petersburg, January 30, 1879*

Tomorrow, that is, January 31, I will send you the continuation of my novel (*The Karamazovs*), the third book (*all of it*). That third book concludes the entire *first part* of the novel. Thus the first part will consist of three books.

There will be three parts altogether and each Part will correspondingly be divided into *books* and the books into *chapters*.

This third book contains *eighty-eight* of my sheets, which I think will make up exactly eighty-eight pages of the *Russian Herald*.

Thus the whole first part of the novel will contain between 210 and 225 pages of the *Russian Herald*.

At the same time, esteemed Nikolay Alexeevich, I hasten to forewarn you that I will not be able to send anything for the March issue (I haven't the strength), so that the publication of Part two will begin with the fourth, that is, the April issue of the *Russian Herald*, and I would like to publish this *second part*, too, without interruption, to its very end.

I will *await the proofs of part two from the office*, with the greatest impatience. I will now forward all proofs by registered mail.

(N.B. I am sending the third part of the novel by registered parcel post, too, as I am this letter.)

Am I addressing mail correctly, and does it help to add detailed notations, "Strastnoy Boulevard," etc., to the address as I do?

I am still extremely disturbed, did you receive *all* the packages of proof for Part One? I only sent the last one registered, after your telegram. The first *three* I sent by ordinary mail. It disturbs me greatly: there weren't many corrections, but they were significant.

And so I await the proofs for this *third* Book, which I am sending now, impatiently. Incidentally: I most earnestly beg you to

6. Editor of the *Russian Herald*, pub-   novel appeared.
lished by M. N. Katkov, where the

publish the *entire third* book (88 pages) in the February issue of the *Russian Herald,* without interruption, not splitting it up *for March* when I cannot send you material. It would completely destroy its harmony and artistic proportion.

I consider *this third book* I am now sending off *not bad at all,* on the contrary, *well done* (Be magnanimous enough to forgive my praising myself. Remember the Apostle Paul "I am not praised, therefore I start praising myself".)[7]

No. 660. To N. A. Lyubimov. Staraya Russa, May 10, 1879

Today I sent off to you at the *Russian Herald* forty pages (minimum) of the text of *The Brothers Karamazov* for the forthcoming May issue of the *Russian Herald.*[8]

That is the fifth book, entitled *Pro and Contra,* but not all of it, only half. The second half of that fifth book will be sent (in time) for the June issue, and will consist of fifty pages. I had to divide this fifth book of my novel into two issues of the *Russian Herald* because in the first place, even if I put all my efforts into it I would hardly be able to finish it before the end of May (it took too long to get everything together and to move to Staraya Russa)—and therefore I would not have time to see the proofs, which is the most important thing of all for me, and in the second place, this fifth book is in my view the culminating point of the novel and must be finished with particular care. Its meaning, as you will see from the text I sent, is the depiction of extreme blasphemy and the kernel of the idea of destruction of our time, in Russia, among our youth who have broken away from reality, and together with the blasphemy and anarchy, their refutation in the last words of the Elder Zosima, a character in the novel, which I am preparing at the moment. Since the difficulty of the task I have undertaken is obvious, you will of course understand, esteemed Nikolay Alexeevich, and will forgive my preferring to stretch it over two issues rather than to spoil the culminating chapter by my rushing it. The whole chapter will be full of movement. In the text I sent you I merely depict the character of one of the leading figures in the novel who expresses his fundamental convictions. These convictions are precisely what I consider the *synthesis* of contemporary Russian anarchism. The rejection not of God but of the sense of His creation. All of socialism emerged and began with the rejection of sense in historical reality and developed into a program of destruction and anarchism. The

7. A jocular paraphrase, apparently of II *Corinthians,* 11, 16 ". . . that I may boast myself a little."
8. Dostoevsky uses the term "sheets" (signatures), the unit used for serial rights. A "printed sheet" consisted of sixteen pages, more specifically, 40,000 typographical characters. The figures have been rounded off to end in 5 or 0. Dostoevsky received 300 rubles a sheet for his last novel.

original anarchists were, in many instances, people of sincere convictions. My hero chooses a theme I consider irrefutable: the senselessness of children's suffering, and develops from it the absurdity of all historical reality. I don't know whether I executed it well but I know that the figure of my hero is a real one to the utmost degree. (I was reproached for many figures in *The Possessed* as being fantastic but later, would you believe it, they were justified by reality, so they must have been apprehended correctly. K. P. Pobedonostsev,[9] for example, told me of two or three incidents about imprisoned anarchists which strikingly resembled what I depicted in *The Possessed*.) Everything my hero says in the text I sent you is based on reality. All the anecdotes about children took place, existed, were published in the press, and I can cite the places, I invented nothing. The general who ran down the child with his hunting dogs and that whole incident is a real fact and was published last year, I think in the *Archive*, and was reprinted in many newspapers. My hero's blasphemy will be triumphantly refuted in the next (June) issue, on which I am now working with fear, trembling, and veneration, since I consider my task (the destruction of anarchism) a civic deed. Wish me success, esteemed Nikolay Alexeevich.

I await the proofs with great impatience. Address: F. M. Dostoevsky, Staraya Russa.

In the text I sent there does not seem to be a single *indecent* word. There is only the bit about the tormentors who were raising a five-year-old child and smeared *it with its feces* because she didn't ask to be taken up during the night. But I ask you, I beg you not to strike that. It comes from a current criminal trial. The word "feces" was retained in all the newspapers (only two months ago in the *Voice*). It can't be toned down, Nikolay Alexeevich, that would be too, too sad! After all, we're not writing for ten-year-old children. But I am sure you would have stuck to my text even without my request.

And one more trifle. The lackey Smerdyakov sings a lackey's song, and it contains a couplet:

> What do I care for splendid wealth
> If but my dear one be in health?

I did not write the song, but set it down in Moscow. I had heard it forty years ago. It was composed by merchant clerks of the Third Guild and was then taken up by lackeys, but it was never set down by any of the song collectors and appears here for the first time.

But the real text of the couplet is:

---

9. (1827–1907). Prosecutor of the Holy Synod, an extreme reactionary with great influence on Alexander III. Dostoevsky valued his comments and advice on the novel highly.

What do I care for royal wealth
If but my dear one be in health?

Therefore, if you find it convenient, for God's sake keep the word *royal* instead of *splendid*, to which I changed it just in case (The censor will of course pass *splendid*). * * *

P.S. Can you insert an announcement on the last page "The conclusion of the fifth book "Pro and Contra" will appear in the next issue, number six"?

I will send the text for the June issue toward June tenth (at the very latest) and possibly earlier. That way I'll get on schedule and will send material even earlier than the tenth of each month. I will publish each month without interruption.

No. 664. To N. A. Lyubimov. Staraya Russa, June 11, 1879

Two days ago I sent to the office of the *Russian Herald* the continuation of the *Karamazovs* for the June issue (the ending of the fifth book, *Pro and Contra*). In it is concluded what is said by "a mouth speaking great things and blasphemies."[1] A contemporary *nay-sayer*, one of the most vehement, openly declares himself in favor of the devil's counsel and maintains that it insures mankind's happiness more than Christ. It is an *omen*, and a striking one for Russian, stupid socialism (but terrible, because our youth is in it): bread, the tower of Babel (that is, the future reign of socialism) and the total enslavement of the freedom of conscience —that is what the desperate nay-sayer and atheist comes to. The difference lies in that our socialists (and you know very well that it is not merely the underground nihilists) are conscious Jesuits and liars who do not admit that their ideal is the ideal of coercing human consciousness and reducing humanity to a herd of cattle, while my socialist (Ivan Karamazov) is a sincere man, who admits openly that he agrees with the "Grand Inquisitor's" view of humanity and that Christ's faith (seemingly) raised man much higher than he in fact is. The question is brought to a head: "Do you despise humanity or respect it, you, its future saviors?"

And they give the impression of doing all this in the name of love for humanity. "Christ's law is difficult and abstract, unbearable for weak men," and in place of the law of Freedom and Enlightenment, they bring them the law of chains and enslavement by bread.

The next book will cover the Elder Zosima's death and his conversations with friends before he dies. It is not a sermon but rather a story, the tale of his own life. If it succeeds I shall have done a good deed: *I shall compel them to recognize* that a pure, ideal

1. *Revelation* xiii.5.

Christian is not something abstract but is graphically real, possible, obviously present, and that Christianity is the sole refuge for the Russian land from all its woes. I pray God it may succeed, it will be a moving thing, if I only have enough inspiration. And the main theme is one that could not even occur to any of today's writers and poets, therefore something completely *original*. The whole novel is written for its sake, if it will only come off, that's what worries me now! I will unfailingly send it for the *July* issue, and also no later than July tenth. I'll try my very best. * * *

No. 685. To N. A. Lyubimov. Ems, Germany, August 7, 1879

I rush to enclose *the sixth book of the Karamazovs, all of it,* for publication in the eighth (August) issue of the *Russian Herald.* I have entitled this sixth book *"The Russian Monk"*—a daring and challenging title, since all our hostile critics will cry out: "Is this what the Russian monk is like, how dare he to place him on such a pedestal?" But it's all the better if they cry out, isn't it? (And I'm sure they won't refrain.) But I reckon that I did not transgress against reality: it is true not only as an ideal but also as the reality.

Only I don't know whether I succeeded. I reckon myself that I wasn't able to express one tenth of what I wanted. Nevertheless, I look upon this *sixth* book as the culminating point of the novel. Of course, many of Elder Zosima's exhortations (or one might better say the manner of their expression) belong to him, that is, to the way he is depicted artistically. Though I completely share the thoughts he expresses, if I had expressed them as coming *from me* personally, I would have expressed them in a different form and in different style. But he *could not* express himself either in a different style *or in a different spirit* than that which I gave him. Otherwise there would have been no artistic character. Such, for example, are the Elder's reflections on *The Russian Monk, Of Masters and Servants, Can a Man Judge His Fellow Creatures,* and so on. I took a character and a figure out of ancient Russian monks and saints: for all their profound humility, they have infinite, naive hopes for the future of Russia, for its moral and even political predestination. Didn't Saint Sergius, the Metropolitans Peter and Alexey[2] always have Russia in mind in that sense?

I ask you in particular (I *beg* you), esteemed Nikolay Alexeevich, to give the proofs to a dependable proofreader, as I will not be able to correct them in my absence. I especially ask you to pay close attention to the proofs for pages ten to seventeen inclusive (the chapter entitled *Of the Holy Scriptures in the Life of Father*

---

2. Fourteenth-century ecclesiastics.

Zosima). It is an enraptured and poetic chapter, the prototype is taken from several exhortations of Tikhon Zadonsky, while the naiveté of the exposition is taken from the *Pilgrimages* of the monk Parfeny. Correct them yourself, esteemed Nikolay Alexeevich, do me that great favor!—When the proof is done for the whole book, show it to M. N. Katkov. I would like him to read it and give me his opinion, for I value his opinion highly.

I trust you will find nothing, as editor, to delete or correct in this book, not the slightest word, I guarantee it.

I also ask you particularly to keep all the divisions into chapters and *subchapters* as I have them. At this point there is introduced into the novel what is someone else's manuscript (The Notes of Alexey Karamazov) and of course Alexey Karamazov divides his manuscript according to his own notions. Here I add a *Nota bene* of complaint: in the June issue, in the chapter "The Grand Inquisitor," all my rubrics were omitted, and even more, the whole thing was published without a break, ten pages in a row, without even *paragraph indentations*. That distressed me greatly, and I make this bitter complaint to you.

I will infallibly send the following, seventh book, entitled "Grushenka," with which the second part of the Karamazovs will end this year, from Staraya Russa around the tenth of September. I plan this book for two issues of the *Russian Herald*, September and October. There will only be 65 pages altogether in the seventh book, so that for September there will be only 32 pages, not more, but nothing can be done: there are two separate episodes in this seventh book, two separate stories, as it were. However, with the completion of the second part the *spirit and idea* of the novel will be completely *filled out*. If it doesn't come off, it will be my fault as an artist. I will postpone the third part of the novel (no larger than the first) until next year, as I already wrote you. My health interfered, my health! So the second part somehow comes out disproportionately long. But nothing could be done, that's how it turned out.

No. 694. To K. P. Pobedonostsev. Ems, August 24, 1879

* * * Your opinion of what you have read in the Karamazovs (so far as the force and vividness of the published material is concerned) gratified me greatly. But at the same time you raise the *most crucial* question: my reply to all these atheistic propositions has not yet appeared, and it must be made. That's precisely it and my worry now and all my disquiet lies in that. For I proposed to make the sixth book, *the Russian Monk*, which will appear August 31, the answer to that whole *negative side*. And for that reason I tremble for it in this sense: will it be answer *enough*? The more so as it is not a direct point for point answer to the propositions previously expressed (in the Grand Inquisitor and earlier) but an oblique one. Something completely opposite to the world view expressed earlier appears in this part, but again it appears not point by point but so to speak in artistic form. And that is what worries me, that is, will I be understood and will I achieve anything of my aim? In addition there were the demands of art: it was necessary to present a modest and majestic figure, but life is full of the comic and is only majestic in its external sense, so that I was necessarily forced, for artistic reasons, to touch also on the most banal aspects of the monk's biography, in order to maintain artistic realism. Then there are several exhortations of the monk that will be thought absurd because they are too exalted. Of course they are absurd in the ordinary sense, but in another, inner sense they are just. In any case, I am very uneasy and would greatly appreciate your opinion, for I value your opinion highly. I wrote it with a great deal of love. * * *

No. 697. To N. A. Lyubimov. Staraya Russa, September 16, 1879

With this I am sending to the *Russian Herald* the *seventh book* of the Karamazovs for the September issue, forty-one pages. This *book* contains four chapters: I am sending three, and will send the fourth in three days, it will arrive at the office on the twentieth. The fourth chapter will only consist of four pages, but it is the crucial and the concluding chapter. I would have sent them together, but an attack of epilepsy forced me to postpone work for two days. But at least I am sending 41 pages and they can be set up immediately (they will arrive on the eighteenth), the remaining three pages (that is, the fourth chapter) which I delayed two days, is very little and will not detain you, if only you decide to print everything despite the late posting. I would very much like it not to be split now. All my hopes rest on you, esteemed Nikolay Alexeevich.

Toward September 25th I am moving back to Petersburg (same address). And therefore again I cannot wait for the proofs. I think it is copied clearly. Please convey my humble plea, esteemed Nikolay Alexeevich, to the proofreader, that he not let me down this time either. For the last issue, many thanks to him.

I beg you, Nikolay Alexeevich, not to delete anything in this Book. And there is no reason to: *everything is in order*. There is only one little word (about the dead body): *he stank*. But it is said by Father Ferapont, and he can't speak differently, and even if he could say *smelled* he would not, but would say *stank*. Leave it, *for God's sake*. There is nothing else. Except perhaps about the purgative. But that is well written and moreover it is significant as an important accusation. The last chapter (which I'll send later),

Cana of Galilee, is the most significant in the whole book, perhaps even in the whole novel. With this posting I am finished with the monastery. There will be nothing more about the monastery. The following Book (for October) will end that Part, and then there will be a break, as I have already informed you.

* * * One small *nota bene* in any case: for heaven's sake don't imagine that I could permit myself, in my work, even the slightest doubt in the miraculous efficacy of reliques. The matter concerns only the reliques of the defunct monk Zosima, but that is something completely different. A commotion similar to the one I described once occurred on Mt. Athos and is briefly related with touching naiveté in the "Pilgrimages" of Monk Parfeny.

P.S. Esteemed Nikolay Alexeevich, I particularly beg you to proofread the legend of *the little onion* carefully. That is a gem, taken down by me from a peasant woman, and of course published *for the first time.* At least I have never heard it until now.

No. 701. *To E. N. Lebedev.*[3] *Petersburg, November 8, 1879*

Dear Madame:

The servant Smerdyakov killed old Karamazov. All the details will become clear as the novel progresses. Ivan Fyodorovich participated in the murder only obliquely and remotely, only by failing (intentionally) to inform Smerdyakov during their conversation before his departure for Moscow and clearly and categorically expressing his repugnance for the crime Smerdyakov conceived (which Ivan Fyodorovich clearly saw and had a presentiment of) and thus *seemed to permit* Smerdyakov to commit that crime. Smerdyakov had to have that *permission,* the reason for which will again become clear in the rest of the novel. Dmitri Fyodorovich is completely innocent of his father's murder.

When Dmitri Karamazov jumped down from the fence and started to wipe the blood from the head of the old servant he had wounded, by that very act and his words: "You've come to grief old man," etc., he already seems to indicate to the reader that he is *not* the parricide. Had he killed the father and then ten minutes later Grigory, he wouldn't have jumped off the fence to go to the servant he had knocked down, except possibly to convince himself that a vital witness of his crime had been destroyed. But besides that, he seems to feel compassion for him, says: "You've come to grief, old man," etc. Had he killed the father, he would not have stood over the servant's body with words of pity. The plot is not the only important thing for the reader, but also some knowledge of the

---

3. Apparently confused by the row of dots after "Dmitri took the pestle out of his pocket," this incarnation of Madame Kokhlakov could not bear the suspense, and wrote to Dostoevsky.

human soul (psychology), which every author is entitled to expect from the reader.

In any case, I am flattered by your interest in my work.

No. 702. To N. A. Lyubimov. *Petersburg, November 16, 1879*

Yesterday I sent off the end of the eighth book of the *Karamazovs*, and you have probably already received it at the office. Once again I apologize profusely for the delay. Suddenly many completely new characters appeared in that eighth book, though fleetingly, but each had to be sketched as fully as possible, and therefore the book turned out longer than I had originally anticipated and also took longer, so that this time my delay came as a surprise even to me. I particularly ask you to look at the proofreading, esteemed Nikolay Alexeevich, so that it may be done just as splendidly as it has been up to now.

I wrote you that I would finish in November and stop until nert year, but meantime circumstances have changed since I *will send yet a new ninth book for the December issue* and therewith conclude that Part. The fact is that I originally wanted to limit myself to a *judicial inquiry*, at the trial. But discussing the matter with a certain prosecutor (who has wide experience), I suddenly noticed that a whole part of our criminal trials, an extremely curious and extremely hobbling part (a sore spot of our criminal trials) would thereby disappear completely, without a trace, from the novel. That part of the trial is called a *Preliminary Investigation*, with its old-fashioned routine and new abstraction in the figures of our young advocates, district attorneys, etc. And therefore, in order to complete the Part, I am writing a different ninth book, entitled "A *Preliminary Investigation*," which I will get to you in December, as early as possible. Moreover, I will mark Mitya Karamazov's character even more strongly: he purifies his heart and conscience under the threat of misfortune and false accusation. He accepts punishment in his heart not for what he has done, but for being so dissipated that he could have, and wanted to commit the crime for which he will be falsely found guilty by a miscarriage of justice. A thoroughly Russian character: unless there's thunder, the peasant won't cross himself. His spiritual purification begins during the several hours of the preliminary investigation, to which this ninth book is devoted. It is very important to me as the author. There is one inconvenience: the whole book will probably occupy only 25 pages. But it will turn out whole and well finished.

And so I will present that ninth book in December, and at the same time an apology[4] to the periodical (for publication), about

---

4. Since the novel had been promised for 1879, Dostoevsky felt he had placed the periodical in an uncomfortable posi- tion, for readers would have to subscribe for another year if they wanted the balance of the novel.

carrying over the completion of the novel to next year, about which (letter) I already wrote you last summer. I definitely want to publish that letter, it weighs on my conscience.

But there will be a little postscript to that letter, to wit: So far only the second Part of the novel stretches on and has expanded to 320 pages. I originally really wanted to write it in three Parts. But as I write *book by book*, I forgot (or neglected) to correct what I had planned out long ago. And therefore I will also send the postscript to the letter to the periodical, that this second Part should be considered as two parts, that is, the second and third, and that next year, therefore, only the concluding *Fourth Part* will appear. Thus Books four, five, and six constitute *Part Two* of the novel, Books seven, eight, and nine Part Three. Each of the three Parts will therefore have *three* Books, and will be almost the same length. Part Four will be the same, that is, in three Books and approximately 160–175 pages. I find it necessary to inform you all about this now, esteemed Nikolay Alexeevich, that is, beforehand. In case you find any objections, there is still time to decide beforehand. But I hope you won't find any objections, the matter is unimportant.

In the material I sent you two Poles are introduced, who speak either in Polish (to each other), or in a broken mixture of Russian and Polish. The purely Polish phrases are correct, but in the mixed speeches the Polish words may have come out a little strange, but I think also correct. I would very much appreciate it if the proofreading of those Polish parts be done as carefully as possible. I think everything is copied clearly.

An anecdote is introduced about Pan Podvysotsky—a legendary anecdote among all small-time Polish gamblers-card cheats. I have heard that anecdote three times in my life, at various times and from different Poles. They can't even sit down to "a little game" without telling it. The legend goes back to the 1820's. But Podvysotsky is mentioned, a name that seems well known (there are also Podvysotskys in the Chernigov Province). But as *nothing insulting, shameful, or even comic* is said about Podvysotsky in that anecdote, I have used the real name. I don't think anyone, anywhere, could ever be insulted or have cause for taking offense. * * *

P.S. If not Podvysotsky, you can print "Podvisotsky," which is quite different in Polish, but it would be better to print "Podvysotsky" as I have it.

N.B. The song the chorus sings was copied down by me and is a real example of contemporary compositions.

No. 705. To N. A. Lyubimov. Petersburg, December 8, 1879

Again I am terribly at fault toward you and the *Russian Herald*: the ninth Book of the *Karamazovs* that I so positively promised for December—I cannot send in December. The reason is—I have worked so hard I have become ill, that the theme of the book (A Preliminary Investigation) has stretched out and become more complex, and mainly, mainly—that this book has turned out for me to be one of the most important in the novel and demands (I can see it) such careful polishing that if I shortened it or messed it up I would harm myself as a writer now and forever. And even the idea of my novel would suffer, and it is dear to me. Everyone is reading my novel, I receive letters about it, the young are reading it, high society reads it, critics praise or abuse it, and I have never had such a success, to judge by the effect it has made. That is why I want to finish it well.

And therefore, please forgive me, if you can. I will send this ninth book to you for the January issue. It will have a *minimum* of 50 pages, maybe 60 (the same number as in the November issue). That book will conclude three parts of the Karamazovs. I will publish the fourth part next year, beginning with the March issue (that is, omitting February). That break is an absolute necessity for me. But then I will finish it without interruption. * * *

No. 725. To N. A. Lyubimov. Petersburg, April 9, 1880

* * * There is one other minor circumstance that troubles me a bit: that is, that in the book "Little Boys," middle-school is mentioned. Suddenly, after I sent you the manuscript, it occurred to me that all those boys of mine are dressed in their ordinary clothes. I asked those around here who know about these things, and they told me that 13 years ago (when my novel takes place), students had some kind of uniform, though not the one they have now. The preparatory classes (particularly when the parents were poor) could also attend in their regular clothes. Overcoats, and caps, could be of any sort. But is that really true? And won't it be necessary to correct something about the clothes in proof? *If it is*, drop me a line at the top of the first galley, and I will change what I can. *If it isn't very necessary*, it'll do as it is.

N. A. Lyubimov to Dostoevsky. Moscow, April 12, 1880

Two copies of *Karamazov* will be sent to you in sheets. So far as the uniforms go, no one I have spoken to remembers. But I think there is no definite indication in your story. There is mention of outer garments and the children weren't in school. That part was splendidly done (you love children very much). I am sure it will produce a strong effect. As a reader, I take the liberty of making only one remark about Kolya Krasotkin. It seems to me that you have presented Kolya as he was between 12 and 16 in a foreshortened way. What he might have thought and said during those years you assigned to age 13. You remark that a comparable degree of development may be observed in nature. But I think poetry must be truer than nature. It seems to me that at least one year should be added to his age. At any rate, that's how I feel. Fourteen would be more appropriate if not 15 (they play robbers even at 15). I leave the matter to your judgment. * * *

No. 727. To N. A. Lyubimov. Petersburg, April 13, 1880

I thank you for your letter, which I received today. I thank you for sending the proofs you promised, and mainly, for your opinion of that ninth book. I am glad you liked my boys. *I am quite ready to agree* with your opinion of Kolya Krasotkin. But here's the problem: I didn't change it in the proofs, and I already sent them off today. Will it therefore be possible to correct my slight error, and would there be enough time if you yourself, esteemed Nikolay Alexeevich, would undertake the corrections? And wouldn't it be troublesome for you (even if there were time) as in that case it would be necessary to change the number, that is, to add a year to Kolya Krasotkin's age, in many places in the book. [There follows a list of a half dozen instances.] I think that suffices. In short, I completely agree to add *one year* (but only one), but only in the sense that he is 13 but *almost* 14, that is, he will be 14 in *two weeks.* * * * My wife made exactly the same observation to me before you did. * * *

No. 761. To N. A. Lyubimov. Staraya Russa, August 10, 1880

* * * I consider the 6th, 7th, and 8th chapters of Book 11 successful. But I don't know how you will regard the 9th chapter, esteemed Nikolay Alexeevich. Perhaps you'll call it too characteristic! But I really did not want to be eccentric. I am duty bound to tell you that I have gotten opinions from doctors (more than one) long ago. They confirm that not only similar nightmares but even hallucinations are possible before "brain fever." My hero, of course, also sees hallucinations, but he confuses them with his nightmares. This is not only a physical (diseased) trait, when a man begins at times to stop differentiating between reality and the imagined (which has happened to everyone at least once a lifetime), but it is also a spiritual trait, corresponding to the hero's character: denying the reality of the phantom, he insists on its reality when the phantom disappears. *Tormented by disbelief, he (unconsciously) at the same time wishes that the phantom were something real and not a fantasy.*

Though why do I bother to explain? You will see everything for yourself when you read it, highly esteemed Nikolay Alexeevich. But forgive my *Devil*: it's only a devil, a petty devil, and not Satan with "fallen wings." I don't think the chapter will be too boring, though it is longish. I also don't think the censor could object to anything, except perhaps two tiny words: "the cherubim's *hysterical shrieks*." I beg you to leave it that way. After all, it's the *devil* who says it, and he can't speak otherwise. If it can't be done, substitute *joyful shouts* for *hysterical shrieks*. But is *shrieks* impossible? Otherwise it would be very prosaic and out of character.

I don't think anything else my devil prattles would raise objections from the censor. Though the two stories about the *confessionals* are indiscreet, they don't seem at all obscene. Doesn't Mephistopheles babble the same sort of thing in both parts of *Faust*?

I think Ivan's spiritual state is adequately explained in the tenth and last chapter, and therefore the nightmare in the ninth is, too. I again repeat that I checked the medical condition with doctors.

Brain fever strikes my hero with a virulent attack precisely at the moment he gives his testimony in court (that will be in the following, twelfth, book). * * *

No. 770. To N. A. Lyubimov. Staraya Russa, September 8, 1880

No matter how I tried to finish and send you all of the *twelfth* and last book of the Karamazovs so that it might be printed at one time, I finally saw that I couldn't do it. I broke it off at a place where the narrative could present something complete (though perhaps not as effective), and the action breaks off for a while anyway. That is "The Trial." I don't think I made any *technical* mistakes in the story. I consulted two prosecutors before hand. I stopped the story at the recess before the "Closing Arguments." There remain the speeches of the prosecutor and the counsel for the defense—and these must be done as well as possible, the more so as both the lawyer and prosecutor are presented by me in part as types of our contemporary court (though not based on anyone specifically), with their morality, liberalism, and view of their task. I am occupied with those two speeches now, and they, together with the "Verdict," will conclude the twelfth and *last* part of the novel. There remains an Epilogue of 25 pages. But I have the firm intention and desire to publish the end of Part Four *together with the Epilogue*.

No. 781. To N. A. Lyubimov. Petersburg, November 8, 1880

I am sending off to the *Russian Herald* the concluding *Epilogue* of the Karamazovs, which ends the novel. Altogether 31 sheets and probably not more than 28 pages of the journal. * * *

Well, and now the novel is finished! I worked on it for three years, published it for two—a great moment for me. Toward Christmas I want to issue a separate edition. It is in great demand, both here and by other book dealers in Russia. They've even sent money.

You will permit me not to bid you farewell. After all, I intend to live and write for another 20 years. Think kindly of me. * * *[5]

F. M. DOSTOEVSKY

From *The Notebooks*†

KATERINA IVANOVNA. SELF-INVENTION. A person fails to live throughout his life but invents himself.

KARAMAZOVS. Those villains have mocked me for an *uneducated* and retrograde faith in God. Those blockheads have never even conceived so powerful a rejection of God as exists in the Inquisitor and the preceding chapter, to which *the whole book* will serve as answer. After all, I do not believe in God like a fool (a fanatic). And they wanted to teach me, and mocked my backwardness! Their stupid sort never even conceived a rejection as powerful as the one I overcame. And they are going to teach me!

THE DEVIL. (A psychological and *detailed* critical explanation of Ivan Fyodorovich and the devil's appearing.) Ivan Fyodorovich is profound, he isn't one of the contemporary atheists who merely show the narrowness of their world-view and the dullness of their dull little capacities in their disbelief.

ALL ARE NIHILISTS. Nihilism has appeared among us because we *are all nihilists*. Only the new, original form of its appearance has scared us. (We are all, to the last man, Fyodor Pavloviches.)

TO KAVELIN.[1] * * * I cannot consider someone who burns heretics a moral man, for I do not admit your thesis that morality means accord with one's inner convictions. My moral image and ideal is Christ. I ask you—did he burn heretics? No. Therefore burning heretics is an immoral action.

The Inquisitor is immoral by the very fact that the idea of burning heretics could dwell in his heart, in his conscience. * * *

* * * the tenacious and constant belief of mankind in *contact with other worlds* is also highly significant. It cannot be dismissed

---

5. Dostoevsky died January 28, 1881.
† From F. M. Dostoevsky, *Biografiya, pis'ma, i zametki iz zapisnoy knizhki* (Petersburg, 1883), pp. 359, 368–75, and *Literaturnoe nasledstvo*, 83 (Moscow, 1971), p. 671. Translated by Ralph E.

Matlaw.
1. A projected reply to K. D. Kavelin, who had attacked Dostoevsky's view in an "Open Letter" in the *Russian Herald*, November, 1880 [*Editor*].

by a stroke of the pen, by the same means you used to dismiss the question of Russia. * * *

The Inquisitor and the chapter on children. In view of these chapters you might still have treated me in a scholarly fashion, but not with such condescension so far as philosophy is concerned, though philosophy is not my specialty. And throughout Europe there *has not been* and does not exist so powerful an *expression* [of these ideas] from the aesthetic point of view as mine. It is clear that I do not believe in Christ and preach Him like a child, but my *hosannah* has passed through a great *furnace of doubt*, as my devil says in the same book. But perhaps you didn't read *The Karamazovs*—that's something else, and then I beg your pardon.

F. M. DOSTOEVSKY

The Kroneberg Case†

I think everyone has heard of the Kroneberg case that was tried in the circuit court in Petersburg last month, and that everyone has read the newspaper reports and commentaries. It was an extremely interesting case, and the newspaper accounts were remarkably spirited. * * * I will recapitulate the facts: according to the indictment, a father flogged a child, his seven-year-old daughter, too cruelly, and he had treated her cruelly before. A stranger, a common woman, could not stand the cries of the daughter who (according to the indictment) had cried "daddy! daddy!" for a quarter of an hour while she was being flogged. The flogging, according to the testimony of one expert, turned out to be with "Spitzruten" (rods) rather than switches, that is, something completely unsuitable for a seven-year-old. They lay in court among the material exhibits and could be seen by everyone, even by Mr. Spasovich[1] himself. Incidentally, the indictment mentioned that when the father was asked to remove at least a certain twig before the flogging he replied, "No, that will add vigor to it." It is also known that after the punishment the father almost fainted himself. * * *

† From *The Writer's Diary*, February, 1876. F. M. Dostoevsky, *Dnevnik Pisatelya* (Paris, YMCA Press, 1951), II, 66–101. Translated by Ralph E. Matlaw. The *Writer's Diary* was published monthly in 1876 and 1877 (and one issue each in 1873, 1880, and 1881). It was an enormously successful commentary on events, ideas, history, and literature, and is in many ways a workshop for *The Brothers Karamazov*, to write which Dostoevsky stopped publishing the *Diary*.
1. V. D. Spasovich (Spasowicz), (1829–

1906), Polish jurist, literary historian, liberal, professor of law at the University of St. Petersburg, author of a standard legal text, one of the most brilliant and renowned lawyers in Russia, prototype (despite Dostoevsky's denials) for Fetyukovich (Blockhead). The three volumes of his *Collected Works* devoted to arguments for the defense omit the Kroneberg case. He rarely mentions Dostoevsky at all in his many critical works, except one written in collaboration [*Editor*].

The counsel for the defense was Mr. Spasovich. He is a man of talent. Whenever anyone speaks of him, they universally say "That is a man of talent." I am very glad of that. I will note that Mr. Spasovich was appointed by the court to conduct the defense, and therefore he conducted the defense under some coercion, so to speak. * * *

It is well known that Mr. Spasovich is also a remarkably gifted lawyer. His speech in this case is, in my estimation, the height of art; nevertheless, it left an almost disgusting impression on me. You see, I begin with complete sincerity. But the problem lay in that falseness of all the circumstances of the case that grouped themselves around Mr. Spasovich, and from which he could in no way extricate himself by the very force of things; that is my view, and therefore everything that was strained and tormenting in his position as defense counsel necessarily was also reflected in his speech. The case was so set up that a verdict of guilty would have exposed his client to a heavy, incommensurate penalty. And a misfortune would have occurred: a family destroyed, everyone left unprotected, and everyone unhappy. His client was charged with "torture," and that was the charge that was dreadful. Mr. Spasovich started right off by rejecting any notion of torture. "There was no torture, there was no harm whatsoever done to the child!" He denied everything: the rods, the bruises, the blows, the blood, the integrity of the witnesses for the prosecution, everything, everything, a very bold stratagem, an onslaught, so to speak, on the jurors' conscience, but Mr. Spasovich knows his strength. He even rejected the child, its infancy, he even destroyed and tore up by its roots the pity for it in the hearts of his auditors. The cries that continued for a quarter of an hour during the flogging "daddy! daddy!" (even if it had been five minutes)—everything disappeared, and in its place appeared a "mischievous little girl, with a rosy face, smiling, cunning, spoiled, and with secret vices." Listeners practically forgot that she was seven years old; Mr. Spasovich artfully confiscated her age as the single thing most dangerous to him. When he had destroyed all that, he naturally obtained a verdict of acquittal, but what could he do, "what if the jury had found his client guilty"? So that of course he could not worry about the means or use genteel methods. "A lofty end justifies any means." But let us examine that remarkable speech in detail, you will see that it is well worth it.

From the first words you feel that you are in contact with an extraordinary talent, with a force. Mr. Spasovich reveals himself from the beginning, is the first to point out to the jury the weakness of the defense he has undertaken, reveals its weakest part, that which he fears most of all. * * *

"Gentlemen of the jury," Mr. Spasovich began, "I do not fear the decision of the tribunal or the prosecutor's charges. I fear an abstract idea, a phantom, I fear that the crime, as it has been called, has as its object a weak defenseless creature. The very words 'torturing a child' arouse, in the first place, a feeling of great compassion for the child, and in the second, just as great a feeling of indignation against him who tortured it."

Very clever. Extraordinary sincerity. The auditor, who is bristling, prepared beforehand to hear something that inevitably would be very tricky, devious, deceptive, who had just said to himself, "Well, friend, let's see how you're going to deceive me," is suddenly struck by the man's practically being totally defenseless. The supposed trickster needs defense himself and, moreover, from you, from those he was prepared to deceive! Thus Mr. Spasovich immediately breaks the ice of mistrust and percolates into your heart, even though it may be just a single drop. True, he spoke about a "phantom," said that he was only afraid of a phantom, that is to say, practically a prejudice; you haven't heard anything else, but already you are ashamed that you may be thought to be a man with prejudices. Isn't that right? Very clever.

"Gentlemen of the jury," Mr. Spasovich continued, "I am not a partisan of flogging. I can quite understand that *a system of education may be introduced* (don't worry, these are all new expressions and are taken verbatim from various pedagogical papers), from which flogging will be barred. Nevertheless, I have as little expectation of the complete and unconditional eradication of physical punishment as I have of the expectation that you will have no further function in trials because there will be a cessation of punishable crimes and the destruction of that law which must exist in the family as in the state."

Thus the whole trial seems to concern only a flogging, not a bundle of switches, not rods. You look carefully, you listen—no, the man is speaking seriously, he is not joking. In other words, this whole Sodom has been raised about the question whether a little twig should or should not be used at a certain age. Is it worthwhile to have been convened for that? True, he is not a partisan of flogging; he proclaims it himself, but yet—

"In the normal course of things normal methods are used. In the present case, abnormal means were unquestionably used. But if you look into the circumstances that brought about those means, if you take into account the nature of the child, the temperament of the father, the goal that guided him during the punishment, you will understand a great deal in this case, and once you have understood, you will exonerate him, because a *profound* understanding of the case inevitably leads to much being explained and seeming natural, not requiring criminal prosecution. That is my task: to explain the incident."

That is, don't you see, "punishment," not "torture," he himself says that a father is being tried only because he whipped his child too painfully. Oh, what a state of things we've come to! But if you look more deeply. * * * That's just it, neither the tribunal nor the prosecutor was able to look deeper. But as soon as we, the jury, look into it, we will acquit him, because he himself says "a profound understanding will lead to acquittal," and that *profound understanding* of course exists only among us on the jury bench. * * * In short, "flatter, flatter," an old, commonplace trick, but then the most dependable one.

After that, Mr. Spasovich turned directly to the presentation of the history of the case and began *ab ovo*.[2] * * * of course, we will not repeat it word for word. * * * But the pillars, the real Pillars of Hercules, begin where Mr. Spasovich reaches the "father's righteous anger."

"When this nasty habit had been discovered in the girl," Mr. Spasovich said (that is, the habit of lying), "in addition to all her other faults, when the father found out that she *stole*, he really became very angry. I believe that *each one of you would become just as angry*, and I think that to prosecute a father because he punished his child painfully *but for good reason*—is to render a disservice to the family, is to render a disservice to the state, for the state can only be solid when it is supported by the solidity of the family. If the father became indignant, he was completely within his rights. * * *"

* * * In conclusion Mr. Spasovich said something very shrewd: "In conclusion, I take the liberty of stating that in my opinion the whole charge against Kroneberg is framed entirely incorrectly, that is to say in such a way, that the questions that will be put to you cannot be answered at all."

That is really clever; that is the essence of the case and from it stems all its falseness. But Mr. Spasovich adds even a few more quite solemn words on the subject: "I take it that all of you will admit that the family exists, that parental authority exists."

On that point I will take the liberty of introducing one very small point, and that only in passing.

We Russians are a young nation. We are only beginning to live, though we have already lived a thousand years, but a large ship needs broad horizons. We are a fresh nation and we have no sacred things *quand-même*.[3] We love our sacred things but only because they are really holy. We do not merely insist on them in order to defend *l'Ordre*.[4] Our sacred things remain so by our faith, not by their utility. We would not even defend such sacred things if we stopped having faith in them, like the ancient priests who, at the

2. "From the egg," i.e., from the very beginning [*Editor*].

3. "Notwithstanding" [*Editor*].

4. "The system" [*Editor*].

end of paganism, defended their idols, whom they had long since stopped considering gods. Not a single one of our sacred things needs fear free investigation, precisely because it is solid in reality. We love the sanctity of the family when it is really sacred, and not because the solidity of the state is founded on it. * * * But there must be measure and limits in everything, and we are ready to understand that. I am not a jurist, but I cannot fail to note a profound falseness in the Kroneberg case. Something was wrong here, something must have been different, regardless of who was actually guilty. Mr. Spasovich is profoundly correct when he spoke of the framing of the question. However, that solves nothing. Perhaps we need a profound and *independent* review of our laws on that point, in order to fill gaps and to fit the character of our society.

Essays in Criticism

KONSTANTIN MOCHULSKY

The Brothers Karamazov†

* * * The architectonics of *Karamazov* are distinguished by their unusual rigidity: the law of balance, of symmetry, of proportionality is observed by the author systematically. It is possible to conjecture that Vladimir Solovyov's harmonious philosophical schema influenced the technique of the novel's structure. This is the most "constructed" and ideologically complete of all Dostoevsky's works. The human world of the novel is disposed in a symbolic order: at the center of the plot appears Dmitri—he is the promoter of the action and the source of dramatic energy. His passion for Grushenka, rivalry with his father, his romance with Katerina Ivanovna, the apparent crime, the trial and exile constitute the external content of the novel. On both sides of him stand Ivan and Alyosha; the first prepares the parricide by his ideas and by this influences Dmitri's fate: he is his ideational adversary and spiritual antipode, but is joined to him by blood, by their common hatred for their father and their common guilt. Alyosha sets his "quietness" in opposition to Dmitri's violence, his purity—to his sensuousness; but even in his modesty chastity lives the "Karamazov element," he also knows the gnawing of sensuality. They are different and alike: the ecstatic sense of life mysteriously unites them. Therefore, Dmitri's sin is Alyosha's sin.

Behind the group of legitimate sons, set on the first plane in the distance, in half-illumination, stands the figure of the illegitimate brother, the lackey Smerdyakov. He is separated from them by origin, descent, social position, character; the spiritual unity of the family is rent by his wanton isolation. But nonetheless how mysteriously profound is his tie with his brothers: as a medium, he executes their subconscious suggestion; Ivan determines Smerdyakov's destiny by his ideas, Dmitri by his passions, Alyosha by his squeamish indifference. The theme of "children" in its four ideational aspects is developed by the four brothers; the theme of "fathers" is represented only by Fyodor Pavlovich. It is unique and simple: the impersonal, innate element of life, the terrible force of the earth and sex.

A tragic struggle takes place between the father and his children. Only the men contend, masculine ideas clash together. Dostoevsky's women do not have their own personal history—they enter the heroes' biography, constitute part of their fate. Each of the brothers Karamazov has his own complement in a female image:

† From Konstantin Mochulsky, *Dostoevsky, His Life and Work*, translated by Michael A. Minihan (Copyright © 1967 by Princeton University Press; Princeton Paperback, 1971), pp. 601, 608–17, 621–36. Reprinted by permission of Princeton University Press.

beside Ivan stands Katerina Ivanovna, beside Dmitri—Grushenka, by Alyosha—Liza Khokhlakov; even Smerdyakov has his own "lady of his heart"—the maidservant Marya Kondratyevna. The brothers' indivisible unity comes forward on the "amorous" plane with special precision. The threads, uniting them with their loves, cross and intertwine. Ivan loves Katerina Ivanovna, Dmitri's fiancée; Alyosha for an instant becomes his rival, feeling himself stung with passion for Grushenka; Katerina Ivanovna is a fatal woman both for Ivan and for Dmitri; Grushenka unites in her love Dmitri and Alyosha. Finally, the unity of the Karamazov family is symbolically shown in Fyodor Pavlovich's and Dmitri's passion for one woman—Grushenka. The remaining dramatis personae are disposed around this central group. Fyodor Pavlovich is surrounded by his own "world" of boon-companions and dissolute women; Grushenka brings with her her admirers and a company of Poles; Mitya bursts in with gypsies, chance friends, and creditors. Richest of all is Alyosha's world: the "young lover of mankind" introduces two aspects of human communality into the novel: the monastic communal life and the "brotherhood of children." He connects the dark Karamazov kingdom with the world of the Elder Zosima and Ilyusha Snegiryov. Only Ivan does not have his own world: he does not accept God's creation, that which is human is alien to him, he is disembodied. His sole companion is a phantom, the spirit of nonbeing, the devil.

The story of the Karamazov brothers' collective personality is depicted in a *novel-tragedy*. Everything is tragic in this artistic myth about man, both the enmity of the children toward the father, and the brothers' struggle among themselves, and the inner strife of each brother individually. The disclosure of the metaphysical significance of human fate belongs to Dmitri. In his experience of the passions he came to understand that "the devil struggles with God, and the field of battle is the human heart." Before him are revealed two abysses—above and below. But he is powerless to make a choice and in this lies his personal tragedy. Among the brothers he occupies a middle, neutral position. Ivan and Alyosha, standing on his left and on his right side, already have made this choice. Ivan is irresistibly drawn to the lower abyss, Alyosha reaches for the higher. The one says "no," the other "yes." Fyodor Pavlovich, sitting over his "little cognac," asks Ivan: "Is there a God or not?" He appeals to Alyosha: "Alyosha, does God exist?" Alyosha answers: "God does exist." Ivan's personal tragedy is in that "his mind is not in harmony with his heart": with his feelings he loves God's world, although with his reason he cannot accept it.

Of the three brothers the most in harmony is Alyosha, but even in his integral nature there is a split: he knows the temptations of Karamazov sensuality and his faith passes through a "furnace of doubt." The religious idea of the novel—the struggle of faith with disbelief—emerges beyond the limits of the Karamazov household. Ivan's negation begets the ominous figure of the inquisitor; Alyosha's affirmation is mystically deepened in the Elder Zosima's image. Human hearts are only the field of battle, and God and the devil struggle. Under the psychological exterior of the personality, Dostoevsky unveils its ontology and metaphysics. The history of the Karamazov family is an artistic myth which encompasses a *religious mystery*: here is why the *Legend of the Grand Inquisitor* stands at its center.

* * * We turn now to the third side of Dostoevsky's art—to the artistic embodiment. His heroes are not allegorical figures, but men endowed with the powerful force of life. It seems that they breathe not air, but pure oxygen, do not live, but burn themselves up. The whole Karamazov family possesses an intense vitality.

Fyodor Pavlovich is a fifty-five-year-old man who has grown flabby. He has long, fleshy bags under his eyes, little, impudent, suspicious, and mocking eyes, a great number of wrinkles on his little fat face, a sharp chin with a great and fleshy Adam's apple, a long mouth with thick-set lips. He spatters himself with saliva when he speaks; he has a "repulsive-sensual appearance." The old man prides himself on his large, thin, aquiline nose. "A real Roman one," he used to say, "together with my Adam's apple the genuine physiognomy of an ancient Roman patrician of the decadent period." Fyodor Pavlovich indistinctly senses his relationship: in him, in fact, lives the soul of the ancient pagan world, a cosmic force, the irresistible element of sex.

There is in his nature something of the faun and the satyr. His lust is insatiable, since it passes into infinity. This is by no means physical sensuousness, seeking and finding satisfaction, this is a spiritual passion, thirst, an eternal excitement, sensuality. The "earthly Karamazov force" in Fyodor Pavlovich is elementary and impersonal. He loves not women, but *woman*, his lasciviousness still does not rise to eros. *Over a little Cognac* the father talks intimately with his sons. Something ancient and painful breathes from his confessions. "To my thinking in my whole life I have never found an unseemly woman, here has been my rule! Can you understand me? . . . According to my rule one can find in every woman something, damn it, extraordinarily interesting, which you won't find in any other; only one must know how to find it, here's where the trick is! This is a talent! For me ugly women have not existed: the very fact that she is a woman already is half everything. Even in *vieilles filles*,[1] even in them, you sometimes will discover a thing that makes you simply wonder at the rest of fools, how they allowed her to grow old and up till now did not notice

1. "Old maids" [*Editor*].

her! With a barefooted girl or an ugly one you must take her by surprise right from the start; here's how one should go after them."

But ancient paganism has ended. Great Pan is dead and the fauns have turned into demons. Fyodor Pavlovich is not only a sensualist, but also a wicked buffoon, cynic, and blasphemer. The innocent shamelessness of the natural demigod passes into delight in one's personal ignominy and fall. The faun is no longer innocent; he knows that his lust is sinful and protects himself by buffoonery and cynicism. His shamelessness is a perversion of the feeling of shame. After the "sensualist's" indecent sallies in the monastery, the Elder Zosima says to him: *"Don't be so ashamed of yourself,* for this alone is the cause of everthing." And Fyodor Pavlovich exclaims that by this remark the elder's perspicacity "pierced right through him." "Precisely, I always feel just like that," he adds, "when I meet people, that I'm lower than everyone and that they take me for a buffoon. . . . Here's why I am a buffoon, *a buffoon from shame.* . . . It's simply from over-anxiety that I am rowdy." Shame, over-anxiety, wounded dignity, vindictiveness, and rapture in his personal shame—such is the complex composition of old Karamazov's buffoonery. Absorption in the sexual element makes a man weak and timid. Fyodor Pavlovich does not believe in God, but is afraid of hell. He "intends to remain on the earth as long as possible," wants "to belong to the line of man for about twenty years yet," and therefore he amasses money; the sensualist is naturally greedy. Money allows him to devote himself without concern to his "filth," but does not save him from the fear of death. He knows his sin and for his tranquility he must be convinced that there is no God, no life beyond the grave. . . . "Do you see," he confesses to Alyosha, "however stupid I am about this, yet I keep thinking, keep thinking, now and then, of course, not all the time. Why, it's impossible, I think, for the devils to forget to drag me down by them with their hooks, when I die. . . . And if there are no hooks, everything just falls apart, which again is not very likely: for then who will drag me down with hooks, because, if they don't drag me down, what will there be then, where will justice be in the world?" This unexpected confession sheds a new light on the cynic and blasphemer. The enormous "Karamazov" force of life has in Fyodor Pavlovich passed into lust and debauchery; but, however stifled it is by this base element, its nature remains spiritual and creative. The sensualist condemns himself and *thirsts for justice.* More than that: sitting up to his neck in "filth," he is, at moments, capable of perceiving beauty and loving good: his second wife, the "orphan" Sofya Ivanovna he married without any calculation, for her beauty alone. " 'Those innocent little eyes slashed my soul then, like a razor,' he used to say afterward."

He loves Alyosha sincerely and tenderly and trusts in him "as in the last thing": he does not offend his religious feelings and even asks him to say a prayer for him. Alyosha sadly reflects upon his family: "Here there is the 'earthly Karamazov force,' earthly and raging, unfashioned.... I don't even know if the Spirit of God hovers over this force."... But Dosteovsky believed in the great and saving force of Mother Earth: the father Karamazov's "impetuosity" is the chaotic ebullition of creative powers, which are predestined to transfigure the world.

This transfiguration already begins in Karamazov's oldest son, Dmitri. His youth was spent in wild passions: "He did not finish his studies in the gymnasium, got then into a certain military school, then turned up in the Caucasus, rose in the service, fought a duel, was demoted to the ranks, again was promoted, caroused a lot and, comparatively, squandered a significant amount of money.' Mitya is twenty-eight years old; he is of medium height and a pleasant face, is muscular and strong.... "His face was thin, his cheeks were sunken in; their color was distinguished by an unhealthy sallowness. His rather large, prominent dark eyes, had apparently an expression of firm determination, yet somehow there was a vague look in them." Fyodor Pavlovich's sensuality is expressed by two "exterior marks": his Roman nose and great Adam's apple. Dmitri's all-engulfing passion is indicated by his sunken cheeks and the vague expression of his dark eyes. Of the three sons the oldest most resembles the father. He is also a sensualist, also knows the shameful sweetness of debauchery. "I have always loved little side-streets," he confesses to Alyosha, "deserted and dark blind alleys, behind the public square; there one finds adventures and surprises, virgin nuggets in the dirt.... I loved debauch, loved even the ignominy of debauch. I loved cruelty. Really am I not a bug, not an evil insect? In fact, it is said—a Karamazov!" Rakitin characterizes Dmitri: "He may even be an honest man, your Mitenka, but he's a sensualist. Here is his definition and whole inner essence. It's your father who transmitted his own base sensuality to him.... Why, in your family sensuality is carried to an infection." But the materialist Rakitin knows only half the ruth about Mitya: sensuality is by no means "his whole inner essence." The dark earthly element is in Mitya's "ardent heart" transfigured into the blinding flame of Eros. He perceives it as a great birth-giving and creative force. Nature reveals itself to him as the "ancient Mother Earth," as the divine fire, which gives life and joy to all God's creation. Mitya's cosmic sense finds its expression in Schiller's *Hymn to Joy.* Trembling with ecstasy, [he] declaims these verses and weeps: to him, a rough and uneducated officer, is sent this revelation of the Mother Earth, he, a sensuous insect, is accorded a knowledge of cosmic rapture! Where does his mystical ecstasy come from? In his life there took place an event, which decided his fate forever. Mitya saw Grushenka. "The storm thundered," he says, "The plague struck, I was infected and am infected till now and I know that everything is now over, there'll never be anything else. The cycle of the times is fulfilled." Dmitri has become the victim of the terrible and merciless god— Eros. In his passion the fiery heart of the world was disclosed to him; his cosmic inspiration is a gift of Eros. But Mitya knows also another, dark countenance of the god "the sensuality of the insects." This enigmatic ambiguity, this contradiction between the chaotic element of sex and Eros' "creation in beauty" strikes him with superstitious horror. "I go on and don't know whether I've fallen into a mire and shame, or into light and joy? Here's just the trouble, for everything in the world is a riddle! And whenever I've happened to sink into the most, into the most profound shame of debauchery (and it's always been happening), then I always read that poem about Ceres and about man. Has it reformed me? Never! Because I am a Karamazov. . . . And here in this very shame I would suddenly begin a hymn. Let me be damned, let me be base and vile, but let me too kiss the hem of that garment in which my God is clothed; let me go at the same time right after the devil, yet all the same I am Your son, O Lord, and I love You and feel the joy without which the world cannot stand or be."

The fatal discord between sex and Eros is the first enigma which Mitya encounters. The second and even more terrible is ahead of him. Sex is motion about a circle, continual and without any issue; Eros is an ascension, a ladder, leading to a height. Eros has an *aim* and an ideal—Beauty. It creates Beauty and worships it. And here is the second enigma. "Beauty—this is a terrible and awful thing," says Mitya, "terrible because it is indefinite, and to define is impossible, for God has posed only enigmas. Here the shores meet, here all contradictions live side by side. . . . Beauty! I cannot, besides, endure the thought that a man with a lofty heart and with a lofty mind begins from the ideal of the Madonna, and ends with the ideal of Sodom. . . . What is presented to the mind as shameful, to the heart is uninterrupted beauty. . . . What's awful is that beauty is not only a terrible, but also a mysterious thing. *Here the devil struggles with God, and the field of battle is the human heart. . . .*"

This is one of the most brilliant pages in Dostoevsky. The mystery of beauty, the tragic duality of the aesthetic consciousness is expressed with astounding force. Dmitri knows only one way to God—through Eros. In his amorous inspiration he longs to press himself "to the garment of the Divinity" and recoils with horror: his divinity is two-faced, Beauty comprises the ideal of the Madonna and the ideal of Sodom. "Is there beauty in Sodom?" asks Mitya and answers: "Believe me that for the vast multitude of people it is found in Sodom; did you know this secret, or not?"

Beauty is from God; Beauty is the breath of the Holy Spirit. But in this fallen world its face has been darkened and distorted. It is not Beauty which will save, but it itself must be saved. In the aesthetic consciousness there are most subtle temptations: Beauty can be an evil demonic attraction. Mitya does not see the way out of these tragic contradictions. He has to pass through the purification of suffering, through the torment of conscience and the spiritual death of penal servitude in order that the flame of Eros, which has caught fire in him might become a spiritual force that transfigures the world. As an epigraph to his novel Dostoevsky took the words from the Gospel of John: "Except a corn of wheat fall into the ground and die, it abideth alone: but if it die, it bringeth forth much fruit."

Fyodor Pavlovich's second son, Ivan, is four years younger than Dmitri. He grew up in a family of strangers as a sullen boy and early manifested brilliant talents. He studied natural sciences at the University, supported himself by giving penny lessons and journal work, wrote an article about the ecclesiastical courts, which attracted universal attention. His arrival at his father's is surrounded by mystery. Alyosha does not understand how his brother, so proud and isolated, can get on with the unseemly Fyodor Pavlovich. In the scene in the tavern he confesses to Ivan: "Brother Dmitri says about you: Ivan is a tomb. I say about you: Ivan is an enigma. Even now you are an enigma to me." Alyosha feels that Ivan is occupied with something interior and important, is striving for some goal, perhaps, a very difficult one. "He knew perfectly well that his brother was an atheist." In this enigmatic fashion the author introduces the figure of the "learned brother." His behavior is incomprehensible and ambiguous: why, being an atheist, does he write about a theocratic organization of society? Why does he suggest to his father that he appeal to Zosima's mediation and arrange a family council at the monastery? Why does he "firmly and seriously" receive the Elder's blessing and kiss his hand?

The clear-sighted Zosima at once guesses the young philosopher's secret. "God frets" Ivan; his consciousness is torn between faith and disbelief. The Elder says to him: "This idea is still not resolved in your heart and frets you.... In this lies your great grief, for it urgently demands a solution.... But thank the Creator that He gave you a loftier heart, capable of suffering such torture, of 'thinking exalted thoughts and seeking exalted things, for our dwelling is in the heavens.'"

Ivan is not a self-satisfied atheist, but a lofty mind, a "loftier heart," the martyr of an idea, who experiences lack of faith as a personal tragedy. Zosima concludes with the wish: "God grant you that your heart may attain the answer while you are still on earth, and may God bless your path." The just man blesses the sinner's "incessant striving" and predicts that he will fall and rise up. The author of *The Legend of the Grand Inquisitor* will not perish like Stavrogin,[2] whose heart was frozen. In the epilogue, Mitya prophesies: "Listen, our brother Ivan will surpass everyone. He ought to live and not us. He will recover."

Ivan will be saved by the "earthly Karamazov force" which he inherits from his father. His blood also overflows with the poison of sensuality; as Dmitri, he too knows the inspirations of Eros and cosmic raptures. In him there is "such strength, that it will endure everything."

Alyosha asks: "What strength?" Ivan answers: "The Karamazov . . . strength of baseness." "That is to sink in debauchery, to stifle your soul with corruption, yes, yes?" "I daresay even that. . . ."

But the "sensuality of insects" is for Ivan only a *possibility*, a remote threat in old age. He is still young and pure, human passionate love is accessible to him. Upon becoming acquainted with Katerina Ivanovna, "wholly and irrevocably" he surrendered to his flaming and mad passion for her. His love for the world is just as ecstatic as Dmitri's. Ivan confesses to Alyosha: "But I still would want to live and now that I've touched upon this cup, so I would not tear myself away from it until I have drained it. . . . I've asked myself many times: is there in the world such despair that might overcome *this enraptured and, perhaps indecent, thirst for life* in me and have decided that, apparently there is not. . . . I have a longing for life and I go on living even contrary to logic. I may not believe in the order of things, but the sticky, little leaves, as they open in spring, are dear to me; the blue sky is dear, another man is dear. . . ." Ivan inwardly is linked to the hero of *The Adolescent*, Versilov: he also would like to travel to Europe, to bow down before the holy graves. He, a logician and rationalist, makes a surprising confession: "I know beforehand," he says, "that I shall fall on the ground and kiss the stones and weep over them. . . . *I shall get drunk on my own emotion*." Tears of rapture and emotion are accessible to the atheist Ivan! And he, like Alyosha, is capable of falling onto the ground and watering it with his tears. But the Karamazov force—the love for life—conflicts in his soul with another force—atheistic reason, which breaks it down and kills it. With his mind he rejects that which he loves with his heart, considers his love senseless and indecent. Really is it worthy of man to love "with his inners, and his bowels" that which presents itself to his reasonable consciousness as "a disorderly, accursed and, perhaps, diabolic chaos?"

In Ivan we find completed the age-old development of the *philosophy of reason* from Plato to Kant. . . . "Man is a rational

2. In *The Possessed* [*Editor*].

being"—this axiom has entered his flesh and blood. Ivan is proud of his reason and for him it is easier to renounce God's world than reason. If the world is not justified by reason, it is impossible to accept it. The rationalist does not want to be reconciled with a kind of "nonsense." Here begins the tragedy: rational consciousness finds no meaning in the world-order. In the world there is an irrational principle, evil and suffering, which is impervious to reason. Ivan builds his own ingenious argumentation on the most pure form of evil—the suffering of children. It is in no way possible either to explain or to justify the tears of a five-year-old girl, tortured by her sadist-parents, the torments of a boy, hunted down by wolf-hounds, the whines of infants, massacred by the Turks in Bulgaria. If world harmony is *necessarily* founded on tears and blood, then away with such harmony! "It isn't worth the little tear, though it be only of that one tormented child who beat itself on the breast with its little fists and prayed in its stinking hole, with its unexpiated tears, to 'dear, kind God,' " declares Ivan and derisively concludes: "Too high a price has been set on harmony, and it's not at all within our means to pay so much to enter it. And therefore I hasten to return my admission ticket. . . . It's not God that I don't accept, Alyosha, only I most respectfully return my ticket to Him."

The "learned brother" disdains mockery à la Voltaire and banal refutations of God's existence. His tactics are more cunning and dangerous. Disputing with an imaginary opponent, he begins by conceding to him the main and, it would seem, most important thing: *he admits the existence of God.* By this crafty device he only reinforces the import of his basic argument. "It's not God I don't accept, understand this, I do not accept the world, that He created, this world of God's, and cannot agree to accept it." God he does accept, but only so as to lay upon Him the responsibility for the "accursed chaos," created by Him, so as to blaspheme His holy Name and with murderous "respect" return his ticket to Him. Ivan's "revolt" is more terrible than the naive farces of the atheists of the 18th century. Ivan is not an atheist, but struggles with God. His argumentation seems completely irrefutable. He appeals to the Christian Alyosha and *forces* him to accept his atheistic way out. "Tell me yourself frankly," he says, "I challenge you—answer me: imagine that you yourself are raising up the structure of man's destiny with the aim of making men happy in the end, of giving them, at last, peace and rest; but it was necessary and unavoidable for this to torture only one tiny creature to death, that child who was beating itself on the breast with its fist—and to found this edifice on its unrevenged tears, would you consent to be the architect on these conditions, tell me and don't lie!"

And Alyosha, believing and ardently loving God, is forced to answer this question: "No, I would not consent." This means: I do not accept the architect, Who has created the world on the tears of children; I cannot believe in such a God. Ivan triumphs: he has caught the "monk" in the snare of his logical syllogisms and drawn him into his "revolt." In fact, Alyosha could not have answered differently: if he had agreed to purchase the happiness of mankind at the price of "a child's little tear," at that very moment he would have lost his image of God and ceased to be a man. The keenness of Ivan's reasoning lies in that he renounces God *out of love for mankind*, comes forward against the Creator in the role of the advocate of all suffering creation. In this imposture is hidden a diabolic deceit. The atheist appeals to the noble human sentiments of compassion, magnanimity, love, but on his lips this is pure rhetoric. Alyosha could have reminded his brother of his favorite idea: "There is decidedly nothing on the whole earth which could force men to love others as themselves . . . if there is love on the earth and has been till now, then it's not from any natural law, but solely because men have believed in their immortality. . . ." Ivan does not believe in immortality and cannot love others. He himself dons the mask of love for mankind in order to raise himself to the place of the lover of mankind—God. He is, he says, more kind and more compassionate than God; he would have created a more just order. Lucifer's arrogant pretension is ancient as the world. If one were to remove its deceitful humane veil from the God-struggler's "revolt," it would emerge as a sole thesis: the existence of evil in the world shows that there is no God. Christianity acknowledges the Fall from grace and believes in the coming of the Final Judgment; Ivan denies the first and contemptuously rejects the second: he does not want any reward for innocent sufferings. To the Christian all mankind is only Adam; in him all have sinned, all are "conceived in iniquity and born in sins." Ivan declares that there is no original sin, that man is born without guilt. Consequently, the sufferings of children are *unjust* and the Final Judgment is *senseless*. Denying original sin, he absolves man of any responsibility for evil and fixes it upon God. *But an evil God is not God*—which is the proof he required. All the force of Christianity is in the personality of Christ, who overcame sin and death. But if there is no sin, then redemption is not needed. The dialectics of his ideas unavoidably lead the atheist to an encounter with the most shining Face of the God-man. Alyosha, crushed by Ivan's arguments and forced to share his "revolt," suddenly becomes aware: he remembers that "in the world there is a Being, Who can forgive everything, everyone, and all, and *for everything*, because He Himself gave His innocent blood for everyone and for everything. . . ." Alyosha naively thinks that Ivan "has forgotten about Him." But the latter has for a long time been waiting for this objection; he knows that all his proofs will appear impotent, if he does not succeed in subverting the *Work of Christ*.

Having destroyed the idea of the *fall* and *reward*, the atheist must do away with the idea of *redemption*. His task involves titanic daring. How is one to struggle with the Living God? Of what can one accuse the "One Without Sin"? How can one raise up one's hand against the "everlasting ideal of Beauty"? The God-struggler understands the infinite difficulty of the conflict. He sharply changes his tactics. In place of logical proofs there is set a religious myth, in place of facts from contemporary reality—a legend whose action takes place in Spain of the 16th century. *The Legend of the Grand Inquisitor* is Dostoevsky's greatest creation. Here is the culmination of his work, the crowning of his religious philosophy.

* * *

Ivan has finished. Alyosha asks about the Inquisitor's subsequent fate. "This kiss burns in his heart," answers Ivan, "but the old man adheres to his former idea." " 'And you along with him, you too?' exclaimed Alyosha sadly. *Ivan burst out laughing*."

Yes, Ivan is with the Inquisitor, with the "terrible and wise spirit" against Christ. He must follow the road of apostasy and struggle with God to the end. His idea "everything is permitted" is realized in Smerdyakov's parricide, the "spirit of self-destruction and nonbeing" is embodied in his "devil." The celebrated scene of Ivan's nightmare is a brilliant creation of the artist and philosopher. In the beginning of the novel the Elder Zosima says to the "learned brother" that the question of God is "still not resolved in his heart and frets him." The dichotomy of his consciousness between faith and disbelief is shown in the hero's dialogue with the devil. The derisive guest does everything in his power to compel the atheist to accept his reality: he has only to believe in the supernatural, and his positive concept of the world is destroyed, his "Euclidean mind" is demolished. Ivan struggles desperately with the "nightmare"; in rage he shouts at the devil: "Not for one minute have I taken you for real truth. You are a lie, you are my illness, you're a phantom. You are the incarnation of myself, only, however, of one side of me . . . of my thoughts and feelings, only the most nasty and stupid of them." Nonetheless, he jumps up so as to thrash his "hanger-on," to shower him with blows; he hurls a glass at him, and after his disappearance says to Alyosha: "No, no, no, this wasn't a dream! He was here, he was sitting here, right on that divan. . . ." So the question of the enigmatic visit will remain unresolved in Ivan's heart. He believes, when he does not believe, denying, he affirms. Reality escapes the man who has lost the highest reality— God; fact merges with delirium, nothing exists, everything only seems. With extraordinary art the author reproduces this confusion of the fantastic and real. The devil is an hallucination; Ivan is on the eve of falling ill with cerebral fever, but the devil is also a reality: he says that which Ivan could not have said, relates facts which the latter did not know.

In the scene of the "nightmare" Dostoevsky treats the theme of apparitions, which was noted in the novel *The Possessed*. To Stavrogin appears a "nasty little scrofulous imp with a cold in his head, one of those who have miscarried"; he has the "self-content-ment of the sixties, is a lackey in thought and a lackey in soul." Ivan Karamazov's visitor, a Russian gentleman-hanger-on is also "simply a devil, a wretched petty devil." With hatred the hero says of him: "Undress him and, be sure, you'll find a tail, long, smooth, like a dachshund's, it'll be two feet long. . . ." What concreteness there is in this description of the fantastic, with what mean trivial-ity the supernatural is arrayed! Stavrogin in his fate is linked with Karamazov: he prided himself on his demonic grandeur and was humiliated by the appearance of the nasty imp "with a cold." The same humiliation also befalls Ivan. The devil provokes him: "You're angry at me because I didn't appear to you somehow in a red light, 'thundering and flashing' with singed wings, but have appeared in such an unassuming form. You're offended, in the first place, in your aesthetic feelings, and, secondly, in your pride: how, you say, could such a banal devil have come to such a great man?" Stavrogin's demon and Karamazov's devil are two variations of one theme: both in the one and the other the falsehood of satanic beauty is unmasked. In his *Legend* Ivan represented the devil in the majestic image of a terrible and wise spirit, and here he has proved to be a vulgar hanger-on with a dark chestnut tail, like a dachs-hund's. . . . The spirit of nonbeing is an impostor: this is not Lucifer with singed wings, but an imp, "one of those who have mis-carried," the incarnation of world boredom and world vulgarity.

However, Ivan Karamazov has not one double, but two: along-side the "hanger-on" stands the lackey, next to the devil—Smerdya-kov. The face of the "learned brother" is distorted in the reflection of two mirrors. The devil repeats his thoughts, but only "the most nasty and stupid." Smerdyakov reduces his "idea" to a hideous capital crime. In the lackey's base soul Ivan's theory, "everything is permitted," is turned into his design of murder in order to commit theft. Ivan thinks abstractly, Smerdyakov accomplishes the practi-cal conclusion. "You killed him," he declares to his "teacher," "it's you who are the main murderer, and I was only your helper, your faithful servant Licharda[3] and even committed this deed with your

3. Smerdyakov is here alluding to the *Tale of Bova, the King's Son*, a Russian adaptation of the Italian romance *Buova d'Antona*, dating back to the late 16th century. In the story Licharda, servant of King Gvidon, is sent by Queen Mili-trisa to King Dodon with a message that she has decided to kill her husband. In this way, the faithful Licharda becomes a tool in the murder of his master.

words in mind." Smerdyakov follows Ivan as the "executor": this same way Pyotr Verkhovensky follows Stavrogin. Son of the libertine Fyodor Pavlovich and the idiot-girl Stinking Lizaveta, Smerdyakov, the lackey-murderer is a sickly and strange man. He suffers from epilepsy, talks self-contentedly, in a doctrinaire tone and profoundly despises everyone. "In his childhood he was very fond of hanging cats and then burying them with ceremony." This little trait alone sketches the character of the malicious and pompous degenerate. Smerdyakov is an egoistic, arrogant, and suspicious nonentity. He is an innate skeptic and atheist. The servant Grigory was teaching the twelve-year-old boy sacred history. The latter mockingly and haughtily taught him: "The Lord God created light on the first day, and the sun, the moon and stars on the fourth day. Where then did the light shine from on the first day?"

For a few years he lived in Moscow and there studied the art of cooking. He returned, aged, "had grown wrinkled, yellow, had begun to resemble a eunuch." He adopted culture in the manner of a lackey, as foppishness; twice a day he carefully brushed his clothes and liked terribly to shine his boots with a special English polish. But as before he was sullen, unsociable, and haughty. Ironically the author calls him a "contemplator." Smerdyakov is by no means a fool; he has a base mind, but clever and resourceful. Fyodor Pavlovich calls him a "Jesuit" and "casuist."

And into this deformed soul falls the kernel of Ivan's teaching. The lackey accepts it with rapture; "God frets Ivan"—for him, the question of immortality is not resolved. In Smerdyakov's heart, God never existed; he is an atheist by nature, a *natural atheist*; and the principle, "everything is permitted," fully corresponds to his inner law. Ivan only desires the death of his father; Smerdyakov kills him.

In the accomplices' three meetings there is unfolded the tragic struggle between the moral murderer and the actual murderer. Smerdyakov simply cannot understand Ivan's horror and torment; he feels that the other is pretending, is "playing a farce." In order to prove that Dmitri did not kill their father, but that it was he, the lackey shows him the bundle of money that he stole after the murder. Dostoevsky finds details that give this scene a character of unutterable horror. " 'Just wait, sir,' said Smerdyakov in a weak voice and suddenly, drawing his left leg out from under the table, began to turn up his trouser leg. He had on *a long white stocking* and a slipper. Without hurrying, he took off the garter and reached

---

King Dodon is the real murderer (as is Ivan Karamazov in the novel). By the late 19th century this tale had become a favorite of uncultured readers of the Russian lower middle class. Thus Smerdyakov's words (his identification with Licharda) acquire a deeper meaning in the novel. Smerdyakov is not only an instrument in the murder of his master and father; the books which he reads also disclose his aesthetic interests, divulge his banality and vulgarity.

his fingers deeply into the stocking. Ivan Fyodorovich looked at him and suddenly trembled in convulsive alarm.... Smerdyakov drew out the packet and laid it on the table." One further detail. The murderer wants to call the landlady and have her bring some lemonade and searches for something with which to cover the money; finally, he covers it with a thick yellow book: *The Sayings of Our Holy Father Isaac The Syrian.*

The "long white stocking," which conceals the packet of rainbow-colored notes, and the *Sayings of Isaac The Syrian*—the expressiveness of these artistic symbols can be only shown, but not explained.

Smerdyakov gives the money to Ivan: "I have really no need for it," he says. He thought that he had committed the murder for the money, but now has understood that this was a "dream." He has proven to himself that "everything is permitted"; for him this is enough. Ivan asks: "And now, therefore, you have come to believe in God, since you are giving back the money?" " 'No, I do not believe, sir,' whispered Smerdyakov."

Like Raskolnikov, he had only to assure himself that he could "step beyond." Also like the student-murderer, the stolen goods do not interest him. "Everything is permitted" means "it's all, all the same." Once having transgressed God's law, the parricide surrenders to the "spirit of nonbeing." Smerdyakov ends with suicide and leaves the note: "I am doing away with my own life *by my own personal will* and inclination so as not to throw blame on anyone." Thus he performs his final act of demonic *self-will.*

The youngest of the Karamazov brothers, Alyosha, is drawn more palely than the others. His personal theme is suppressed by Dmitri's passionate pathos and Ivan's ideational dialectics. Like his spiritual predecessor Prince Myshkin,[4] Alyosha shares in the feelings and experiences of the others, but the action of the novel is not determined by him and his "idea" is only noted. But meanwhile *Karamazov* was conceived by its author as Alyosha's biography and in the preface he is directly named the *hero* of the novel. Dostoevsky attempted to explain this discrepancy between the design and its execution: Alyosha does not resemble a hero because "his acts are vague, unexplained." His image was to be disclosed in the future. "The main novel is the second," wrote the author; "this is my hero's activity now in our time, namely in our present current moment. The first novel took place thirteen years ago and is almost not even a novel, but only one moment out of my hero's early youth." But the second novel was not written and Alyosha has been left just as "incomplete" as Prince Myshkin. Working on *The Idiot,* the author confessed: "depicting the *positively beautiful* is an im-

4. In Dostoevsky's *The Idiot* [*Editor*].

measurable task." In *Karamazov* the ideal image of man is only a presentiment and prevision.

Alyosha was born to the same mother as Ivan. His mother, the humble, "meek" Sofya Ivanovna, was epileptic. From her he inherited the religious formation of his soul. One memory of early childhood has determined his fate. "Alyosha recalled one evening, summer, peaceful, an open window, the slanting rays of the setting sun, in the room, in the corner, a holy icon, before it a lighted lamp and on her knees before the icon, sobbing hysterically, with moans and shrieks, his mother, who grasped him in both arms, clasped him violently, till it hurt, and praying for him to the Mother of God, held him out in both arms toward the image, as though to put him under the Mother's protection." Sofya Ivanovna, the martyr-mother, is as mystically joined with the most Holy Mother of God, as the Mother in *The Adolescent*—Sofya Andreyevna. Alyosha was placed by her under the Mother's veil; he was consecrated, and from his childhood years grace would rest on him. He was brought up in another family, did not finish his course in the gymnasium and suddenly returned to his father. The old Karamazov was astonished by the reason for his return: Alyosha had come to seek out his mother's grave. Shortly after he entered the monastery as a novice to the famous Elder and healer Zosima. The author is afraid that his young hero will seem an exultant eccentric and fanatic to the reader. He insists on his hero's physical and moral health. . . . "Alyosha was at that time a well-built, clear-eyed, *red-cheeked*, nineteen-year-old lad, *radiant with health*. He was at that time even very handsome, slender, moderately tall in height, dark-haired, with a regular, although somewhat long oval-shaped face, with brilliant wide-set dark grey eyes; he was very pensive and, apparently, very serene." He has the special gift of inspiring universal love; he loves everyone, does not remember injuries, never is troubled on whose resources he is living; is steady and clear; he has an extravagant, enraptured modesty and chastity.

The first attempt to portray a "positively beautiful individual"—Prince Myshkin—did not satisfy the writer; in *Karamazov* once again he reworks his draft. Prince Myshkin is a holy fool, epileptic, is "not fully embodied"; Alyosha "radiates with health," is red-cheeked, stands firmly on the ground and is full of Karamazov elemental vitality. But why did this youth, so full of life, become a novice? The writer explains: his hero is "not even a mystic at all"—he is a realist. "In the realist faith does not arise from a miracle, but the miracle from faith."

In Alyosha's image a new type of Christian spirituality is projected—*a monk serving in the world*: he passes through the monastic ascesis, but does not remain in the monastery; before his death the Elder Zosima says to his favorite: "I think of you in this way—you will go forth from these walls, but you will live like a monk in the world. . . . Life will bring you many misfortunes, but it is in them that you will attain happiness and will bless life and will cause others to bless it—which is most important of all. . . ." Such was Dostoevsky's plan regarding Alyosha; the Elder's predictions were to have been realized in the second novel.

The "youthful lover of mankind" clashes with his brother, the atheist; Alyosha believes in God and lovingly admits God's world; he says to Ivan: "I think that everyone should come to love life above all else in the world. . . . Love it before logic—and only then will I understand its meaning." Ivan does not believe in God and before loving the world, wants to understand its meaning. Christian love is opposed by atheistic reason. *Pro and Contra* enters into Alyosha's very soul, becomes his inner struggle, temptation, and victory over temptation. The Elder dies; his disciple expected that his teacher would be glorified, but instead of this, he is present at his disgrace: from the esteemed just-man's coffin a "decaying smell" emanates prematurely; the "temptation" seizes both the monks and the pilgrims; even the "realist" Alyosha, "firm in his faith," is scandalized. Where now is the spiritual transfiguration of nature, about which the Elder used to preach? And if it does not exist, then Ivan is right. Alyosha's "revolt" is an echo of Ivan's revolt. He also rises up against Providence and demands "justice" of it. "It was not miracles he needed," explains the author, "but only the 'higher justice,' which had, in his belief, been violated by the blow that had wounded his heart so cruelly and unexpectedly. . . . And what if there had been no miracles at all, if nothing marvelous had been proclaimed and what was expected had not been realized at once— but then why has the disgrace been proclaimed, why had this humiliation been permitted, why this sudden decay, which even anticipated nature? . . . Where is Providence and its Finger? Why did it hide its Finger at the most critical moment (so Alyosha thought), and as though voluntarily submit to the blind, dumb, pitiless laws of nature." These questions about "justice," about Providence, about world evil, which Alyosha experiences so tragically, are Ivan's questions. At this fatal moment the novice suddenly feels his spiritual proximity to his brother, the atheist. Incessantly he calls to mind his conversation with Ivan. "A certain vague, but tormenting and evil impression from the memory of yesterday's conversation with his brother Ivan now suddenly began to stir in his soul and more and more urged to break onto its surface." But Ivan's "revolt" ends in his struggle with God and negation of God's world; Alyosha's "revolt" is completed by his mystical vision of the resurrection; he is saved by a feat of personal love. Alyosha goes out of the monastery, falls into the power of his Mephistopheles—Rakitin— and the latter takes him to Grushenka. In the chaste youth awakens the Karamazov sensuality. The "infernal woman" sits on his lap, entertains him with champagne. But, upon learning about the death of the Elder Zosima, she piously blesses herself and "as in alarm" springs from his knees. "Loudly and firmly" Alyosha says to Rakitin: "Did you see how she has had pity on me? I came here to find a wicked soul—I felt myself drawn to it, because I was base and evil, but I've found a true sister, have found a treasure—a loving soul. Agrafena Alexandrovna, I'm speaking of you, you have just now restored my soul."

Grushenka relates a fable about an onion. A wicked, very wicked old woman has during her whole life done nothing good; only once she had given a beggar woman an onion and after her death this onion helped her to get out of the fiery lake. For Alyosha, Grushenka's pity was the "onion," Alyosha's compassion proved also to be an "onion" for her wronged heart. " 'He has turned my heart upside down. . . . He's the first, the only one who's shown me pity, that's what! Why didn't you come before, you cherub'—she suddenly fell before him on her knees, as though in a frenzy. 'I've been waiting my whole life for someone like you, knew that such a one would come and forgive me. I believed that someone would love even me, nasty as I am, not only with a shameful love.' "

Alyosha's meeting with Grushenka is the bridegroom's mystical betrothal with his fiancée—earth; in *The Possessed* we find the same nuptial symbolism (Stavrogin—the cripple). The law of death (sensuality) is overcome by resurrecting love. The souls understand their relationship and mystical unity. Alyosha bears Grushenka's guilt, Grushenka, Alyosha's guilt. "All men are guilty for everyone." In their common guilt they are loving brother and sister. The spiritual regeneration has been accomplished: Grushenka is ready to sacrificially share "Mitya's redemptive feat." Alyosha is open for the mystical vision of "Cana of Galilee."

The novice returns to the monastery and prays at the Elder's coffin. In a state of drowsiness he hears Father Paisy read the Gospel story about the wedding in Cana of Galilee. And now the walls spread apart—the coffin is no longer there; he sees guests, a wedding chamber. The Elder Zosima "joyful and gently laughing" says to him: "We are rejoicing, we are drinking the new wine, the wine of the new, great joy; you see how many guests? Here are both the bridegroom and bride, here is the all-wise Governor of the Feast; he is tasting the new wine. . . . And do you see our Sun, do you see Him? Do not fear Him. He is dreadful in His majesty before us, terrible in His sublimity, but infinitely merciful. . . ." Alyosha's vision is a symbol of the resurrection, the joy of the Kingdom of God.

He leaves the cell; like one mown down, falls onto the earth, embraces and kisses it. "He was weeping in his rapture even over those stars that were shining to him from the abyss, and 'was not

ashamed of this ecstasy.' As it were, threads from all these innumerable worlds of God had joined together at once in his soul
and it was trembling all over, 'touching other worlds.' He longed to
forgive everyone and for everything and to beg forgiveness, oh! not
for himself, but for all men, for all and for everything. . . ."

After the light of the resurrection comes cosmic rapture and a
vision of the transfigured world. This is that second of "world
harmony" of which Dostoevsky's heroes have a presentiment and
for which they are oppressed. Man's heart is the mystical center of
the universe, threads from all the worlds join together in it and the
new Adam, reestablished in his original glory, "weeping, sobbing,
and shedding tears," kisses the earth, the holy Mother, whom once
before he had profaned by his fall from grace.

The Karamazov "earthly" force is turned into a transfiguring
force. Alyosha's ecstasy answers Ivan's confession. Ivan does not
understand how the mother of a child tormented to death can
forgive. Alyosha has understood: in the new world one forgives
"for all men, for everything and for all."

The novice's mystical experience becomes the source of his spiritual energy. It empties onto the world, enlightening it from within.
In the novel only the beginning of this service is shown. Inheriting
from Prince Myshkin his children's theme, Alyosha enters into the
life of the schoolboys, makes friends with them, reconciles them
with Ilyusha, who is dying of consumption, and on his grave lays
the foundation of a "completely universal brotherhood of mankind." The new community, in opposition to the socialistic anthill,
is built on *personality and love*. This is a free society of friends of
the late Ilyusha: the personal love for one becomes the common love
of all. "All you, lads, are dear to me from this day on," Alyosha
says to the boys, "I will gather you all into my heart, and beg you
to gather me also in your hearts! Well, and who has united us in
this kind, good feeling. . . . Who, if not Ilyushechka, the good boy,
the dear boy, the boy precious to us for ever and ever."

Ilyusha is not dead: he will live in the love of friends whom he
has united "for ever and ever."

Kolya Krasotkin makes the "youthful lover of mankind" explain
his thought completely

" 'Karamazov!' cried Kolya, 'Is it really true now what religion
says that we all will rise from the dead and come to life and see
each other and everyone again, even Ilyushechka?'

" 'Certainly we will rise, certainly we will see and gladly, joyfully
tell each other all that has passed,' answered Alyosha, half-laugh-
ing, half in ecstasy."

The novel concludes with a triumphal confession of faith in the
resurrection.

*   *   *

DMITRY TSCHIŽEWSKIJ

Schiller and *The Brothers Karamazov*†

3

* * * In *The Brothers Karamazov* Dostoevsky frequently applies a special, so to speak "orchestral," concept of art, in order to underscore ideas that are important to him in some way. An idea is proposed by one character, picked up by another, then by a third, a fourth, and so passes through all the voices of the polyphonic orchestra of the characters.

A brief example that will be helpful later. There is something unearthly, superhumanly pure and transparent in Alyosha's being; Alyosha is an "angel," a "cherub." This theme is woven into the extremely complex development of the novel, placed in the mouth of the highly variegated characters, one after the other. "Like an angel, nothing touches you," Fyodor Pavlovich has to acknowledge between his great and small blasphemies; "You are a pure cherub," Ivan, too, affirms; "You are the earthly angel," "you, my cherub," Dmitri says to him;—"Even if I believe that Ivan is the higher man, yet you are my cherub . . . perhaps, though, it is just precisely you who are the higher man and not Ivan"; "Alyosha, my cherub. . . . He was the first and only one to have compassion for me. Why did you not come to me earlier, my cherub?" Grushenka says sobbingly, while kneeling before Alyosha; and Mrs. Khokhlakov "whispers to him in excited enthusiasm" after the scene "Laceration in the Drawing Room," "You have behaved like an angel." "You have behaved like an angel, an angel, I am ready to repeat it to you a hundred thousand times." And in order not to let this enthusiastic outburst of the eccentric lady get lost in her incoherent and senseless prattle, Dostoevsky emphasizes it through Liza Khokhlakov's double question from the adjoining room, where she had eavesdropped on the whole conversation, "Mama, why did he behave like a angel?" and to Alyosha "For what deed have you been promoted to an angel?"

Dostoevsky develops other themes vital to him in a similar way, shifting them from one character to the next and reshaping and changing them to conform to the personality of each character. Thus the theme of the double nature of the beautiful, the theme of innocent suffering (the suffering children in Ivan's and Liza's

† D. Tschižewskij, "Schiller und *Die Brüder Karamazov*," *Zeitschrift für slavishe Philologie*, IV (1929), 1–42. Reprinted by the kind permission of the author. Translated by Ralph E. Matlaw. (Most footnotes omitted.)

speeches, the "babe" in Mitya's dream, Ilyushechka, Fyodor Pavlovich's abandoned children, etc.), the theme of Rebellion, the
revolt against God (Fyodor Pavlovich rebels through blasphemy;
Smerdyakov through casuistry; not only Ivan, but also Dmitri and
even Alyosha rebel); the theme of "guilt for others" (cf. Zosima's.
exhortations): Dmitri bears the guilt for Smerdyakov's deed before
others, Ivan before himself.

Among the orchestrated themes is that of Schiller. We suddenly
hear of Schiller from Fyodor Pavlovich, when he presents his sons
to the Elder Zosima: "Most pious and holy elder," he cried, pointing to Ivan Fyodorovich "that is my son, flesh of my flesh, the
dearest of my flesh! He is my most dutiful Karl Moor, so to speak,
while this son who has just come in, Dmitri Fyodorovich, against
whom I am seeking justice from you, is the undutiful Franz Moor
—they are both out of Schiller's *The Robbers*, and so I am the
reigning Count von Moor! Judge and save us!" Dostoevsky does
not want the reader to forget these words that seem to fall accidentally from Fyodor Pavlovich. Fyodor Pavlovich reminds us of them
again as he leaves the monastery: "Ivan Fyodorovich, my most
respectful Karl von Moor," and repeats Schiller's name: " 'A kiss
on the lips and a dagger in the heart,' as in Schiller's *The Robbers*."

We hear Schiller's name again at a seemingly totally inappropriate moment: Schiller's verses flow from the lips of the half-drunk
Dmitri: first the "Eleusinian Festival" (strophes 2–4 and the beginning of 6), then the "Ode to Joy" (strophes 4 and 3). At the
end of the novel Dostoevsky shows through the prosecuting attorney that the citing of Schiller by the Karamazovs is no accident:
"And now the third son of this contemporary family. . . . We are
admirers of Schiller and of education," and through the counsel for
the defense: "the distinguished prosecutor has tried to mock my
client in an unmerciful way in that he has indicated in a very
special way that Dmitri Karamazov loved Schiller, loved everything
'beautiful and exalted.' If I were in his place, I would not have
mocked that." Even Ivan cannot do without a quotation from
Schiller, moreover, in German: " 'Den Dank, Dame, begehr' ich
nicht [This reward, my lady, I do not crave],' he suddenly let out,
and thereby showed quite unexpectedly that he, too, had read
Schiller to the extent that he knew him by heart, which Alyosha
would not have believed earlier." And we are again reminded of
that citation—by Mrs. Khokhlakov—"and when he then cited that
German verse." That citation from "The Glove" is so neutral in its
content that it could only be significant for Dostoevsky as instrumentation, that is, as a way of emphasizing that all the Karamazovs
stand in some sort of relation to Schiller, that they have reflected
on Schiller's ideas and problems. Later, too, at the beginning of his
"Legend of the Grand Inquisitor," there is yet another citation

from Schiller, through which Ivan testifies to his earlier enthusiasm for Schiller:

> Du musst glauben, du musst wagen,
> Denn die Götter leihn kein Pfand,[1]

a citation which is clearly somewhat more closely connected with the development of the central notions, but nevertheless is probably designed primarily to serve the instrumentation of the Schiller theme.

* * *

5

But let us leave aside purely external allusions, references, and reminiscences. If we turn now to the ideational content of *The Brothers Karamazov* itself, we are immediately confronted by a whole series of problems that also tormented Schiller. Dostoevsky gives new answers to the questions posed by Schiller, different from those that he had earlier found in Schiller, and that he perhaps also shared earlier. The answers are now different, and thereby the posing of the questions is also slightly changed. But in many instances we find clear traces of reflections on Schiller and occasionally differences from him, that is, attempts to overcome that former "Schillerism" through which Dostoevsky had at one time passed and, which still, as he thought, afflicted a part of current Russian society.

One of the novel's leading ideas is that of the "higher man." Dostoevsky expresses this idea in Dmitri's words: "Even if I say that Ivan stands higher than we, you are still my cherub. . . . perhaps it is precisely you who are the higher man and not Ivan." And the whole structure of the novel, with its varieties of human types, with their "revolts" and collisions, the whole hierarchy of types, which rises to a really higher—and genuinely human—form of human individuality in Alyosha and Zosima, the whole thematics of the novel leads us in many ways to the basic theme, the theme of the "higher man." The theme is touched on in *The Adolescent* (note Versilov and Makar Ivanovich), in *The Possessed*, in *Crime and Punishment*, and that very same theme was the main theme Schiller introduced into the development of German Idealism.

Kant's ethics split the unity of personality, since for Kant morality consists of the struggle between duty and inclination, between reason and sensuality. Schiller finds the main task of his Ethics

---

1. "You must believe, you must dare,/As the gods give no pledge." "Die Sehnsucht" ("Longing"), stanza 4. Dostoevsky quotes Zhukovsky's translation [which differs slightly]. All . . . translations of the novel retranslate from the Russian.

(*Moraltheorie*) in overcoming Kant's dualism. For Schiller, the ethical ideal is a personality in which the two forces that struggle in the human soul are reconciled, united, brought into harmony with each other. The triumph of either one of those forces, whether duty or inclination, would lead to a degeneration, to a decay of individuality, to the creation of a type that is only one-sided. Beyond these two possibilities—one-sided types of man—extant in reality, above the man of intellect, the "cold," and the sensual man, the "narrow" (egoistic), between the "barbarian" (in whose soul "uniformity" rules) and the "wild" (who lives in "confusion")—beyond them stands the "aesthetic" type, since the union of intellect and sensuality, of duty and spontaneous experience, is possible only in art and in the Beautiful.

It is obvious that the same problem lies at the core of *The Brothers Karamazov*. The men of intellect, the "cold," are Ivan, Smerdyakov, Rakitin, and Fetyukovich; the sensualists, the "narrow," are Fyodor Pavlovich and Dmitri. Both sons mentioned (and Alyosha, too) stem from Fyodor Pavlovich, since the sexual instinct is probably at the base of all higher forms of life. But intellect and sensuality belong to every man. Dostoevsky would hardly entertain the possibility of a "one-sided" type carried out completely. Therefore he also lets Dmitri reflect on the highest problems of human life, lets Fyodor Pavlovich enjoy the dialectics of Smerdyakov's subtleties and have a certain inclination toward Ivan; nor does he raise in vain the notion that in one sense Ivan is the son who most resembles Fyodor Pavlovich. Ivan himself notes that he has "the mad, raging, and perhaps indecent thirst for life," and admits that he is a Karamazov. And Alyosha is slightly akin to the "cold" and the "narrow," he understands both, for he, too, "is a Karamazov."

The idea of the higher man had for Dostoevsky the closest ties with Schiller's world of ideas, and all objections to it may be seen as objections directed against Schiller. But Dostoevsky rejected this idea only insofar as it failed to achieve a religious significance, insofar as it was not transfigured and purified by religion. Dostoevsky sees certain dangers in this idea in the form Schiller presented it, that is, in the possibility of its culminating in a direction against the moral world order and against God. That danger really exists, yet in Dostoevsky's time perhaps no one had drawn all the conclusions from the idea of the higher man that Dostoevsky did. Only a few years later did Nietzsche come to approximately the same conclusions. While they served Nietzsche as the basis of his *Transvaluation of Values*,[2] they served Dostoevsky as the starting point for his criticism of the idea of higher man.

2. Friedrich Nietzsche (1844–1900), German philosopher, began *The Transvaluation of Values* in 1887 [*Editor*].

The first danger Dostoevsky points out in the idea of the higher man is the possibility of the transformation of the self-consciousness of a "higher man" into "satanic pride" (it is precisely this danger that became real in Nietzsche's "New Table of Commandments"). This pride, hubris, or willfulness (*svoevolie*) seizes the soul of a man who considers himself a "higher man" if his consciousness does not contain inner forces that control him. This "willfulness" necessarily leads to crime, to a transgression of the commandments, as it seduces Raskolnikov to murder the old woman.[3] Or it at least leads to participating in a crime, if not in an empirical, physical sense, then in moral participation. Thus Dmitri comes to participate in the murder of his father since he *condemned* the father, placed himself above him and felt justified in denying the sense of his existence: "Why is such a man alive! No, tell me, can one permit him to shame the world with his existence any longer?" Ivan, too, later feels himself a participant, since he, too, had come to an unconditional condemnation of his father, and at the same time of his brother Dmitri: "One reptile will devour the other, and it will serve them both right." Ivan and Dmitri consider themselves "higher men," or rather, "higher" than Fyodor Pavlovich, feel themselves justified in judging and condemning him. But to place oneself higher than another in itself already constitutes a sin! A truly higher man does not condemn or scorn anyone. Dostoevsky sees the key to ethical consciousness in "the refusal to judge" even a deeply sinful man, a man egoistic to the highest degree, concerned to the highest degree with himself. That is how Alyosha finds the way to Fyodor Pavlovich's heart. Dostoevsky lets Fyodor Pavlovich repeat frequently: "yet I feel that you are the only person in the world that has not condemned me, you, my dear boy, I feel it, how can I help feeling it. . . . Alyosha cuts me to the heart, since he lived, saw everything, and condemned nothing. . . . Alyosha looks at one and his eyes sparkle; Alyosha does not despise me." Dmitri feels the same thing: "You will hear about it, you will consider it, and you will forgive. . . . that is just what I need, that a higher man forgive me." But Alyosha does not consider himself a higher man at all. His "refusal to condemn" "touches the heart." Even Grushenka, who had expected contempt from him, but whom "he had called his sister," "he was the first and only person to have compassion for me—that's what it is!" Alyosha himself recognizes this refusal to condemn as the basic concept of ethics: "There was something in him that told and suggested to everyone that he was not the judge of man, that he did not wish to take condemnation upon himself and would under no circumstances do so. It even seemed that he permitted everything and condemned nothing, even

3. In *Crime and Punishment* [*Editor*].

if it often came hard to him." And Alyosha himself says to Ivan: "Does man really have the right when looking at others to decide who is worthy of living and who no longer is so?" He applies the same norm to himself in comparison to Dmitri, whom he tries to convince that "I am the same as you. It is one and the same ladder. I am on the lowest rung, while you are high up, let us say on the thirteenth rung, but it is one and the same, completely equal." And in the discussions with the Captain (Snegiryov), "one must above all convince him that he is on an equal footing with all of us, and not only on equal footing but even above us." And so, too, to Grushenka, when he himself admits to her "I haven't spoken to you as a judge, but as the first who must be judged." Zosima has a similar conception of mankind: "avoid feeling disgust for yourself and for others"; a monk needs the consciousness "that he is worse than everyone and anyone on earth," "as I am the worst of the worst myself," "love man even in his sin," "above all do not forget that you cannot be anyone's judge."

Clearly, Dostoevsky could also find the notion of the danger in judging others in Schiller. We will return to this point later. Dostoevsky particularly wants to emphasize that each and everyone participates in the lowest, "satanic" aspect of nature, in that nature which is characterized by Dostoevsky (as by Schiller) as "insect-like." Thus Fyodor Pavlovich is "depraved and in his voluptuousness gruesome like an evil insect." Dmitri is an "insect"—"I loved cruelty, am I not a roach, an evil insect?" "Voluptuousness was given to the worm (In Russian, 'to the insect')—do you know, I am that insect, and it is said especially of me"; and he repeats again and again: "I am a roach," "an evil tarantula," "a stinking insect," "a worm, a useless worm"; the dark forces in Dmitri's soul are "a cruel insect in the soul," "a phalange (a sort of poisonous spider) stung me in the heart." Dmitri notes in himself what Fyodor Pavlovich was incapable of noting and which is not so easy to note in others. But even Ivan feels the same insect quality in himself and Dmitri sees the same "satanic nature" even in Alyosha: "And in you, too, in the angel, the insect lives and raises storms in your blood." Cruel sensuality gushes from Ivan's tales of tortured children and from similar tales by Liza Khokhlakov. But there is something common to all mankind in this voluptuous cruelty: "Everyone is glad that Dmitri murdered his father," Liza says, and Alyosha confirms it: "there is some truth in your words." Ivan says the same thing before the court: "Who does not desire his father's death? Everyone wishes his father's death." Nevertheless, the norm of refusal to judge remains in force, *despite* the fact that the satanic nature is present in everyone, or perhaps *precisely for that reason.* Because the "insect quality" lives in everyone, and therefore everyone "is guilty for each and all," since all are sinful, even the "higher man."

And the third type (Alyosha, Zosima) stands above the two "one-sided" characters, for Dostoevsky as for Schiller. And both characterize this third type similarly, as more creative, more efficacious, more active.

Zosima teaches: "Work unceasingly. If you wake up during that night and have to say to yourself 'I have not done what I should have done,' get up immediately and do it," and Alyosha fulfills his commandment. What are his cares about Dmitri, his talks with the Boys and with Ivan, with Liza and Grushenka, even his keeping silent company with his father, but constant, untiring action? In these actions are united in a singular way activity and passivity (talking and listening), concern for others and calm acceptance of others' concern for himself, aid to others and the consciousness of his own need for aid, active love for others and becoming loved by others, the union of seriousness with joking and play. Formally, this corresponds exactly to the characteristics Schiller assigns his aesthetic type: "If we have given ourselves to the enjoyment of real beauty, at that point we become masters of our sufferings and active forces to an equal degree, and we turn with equal ease to the serious and to play, to calm and to movement, to abstract thought and to contemplation. . . . The mood in which a genuine work of art may issue from us is one in which calm and freedom of the spirit is connected with strength and vigor."[4] Formally, the characteristics of the type of the "higher man" are similar, indeed identical, in Schiller and in Dostoevsky. But the basis for this particular attitude must be sought in entirely different spheres.

Dostoevsky turns his assault on Schiller's conception of the "higher man" as one higher in beauty, as an "aesthetic" man. For Dostoevsky, as for Schiller, beauty has a double existence—it participates in two worlds, on the border of which it stands. But in contrast to Schiller, Dostoevsky does not believe that beauty can create, secure, and preserve a stable equilibrium between the two forces battling each other in man's soul. In Dmitri's often cited ecstatic monologue, the dual nature of beauty—in agreement with Schiller—is recognized, but at the same time its inner weakness, its inability to become the guide for human existence is disclosed. "Beauty is a terrible and fearful thing! Here the abysses approach each other, here contradictions coexist!" The ideal of the Madonna and the ideal of Sodom are aesthetically close and approach each other. "What seems vile to the mind, seems total beauty to the heart. Is there beauty in Sodom? Believe me, for the immense mass of mankind it lies precisely in Sodom. . . . It is terrible that beauty

---

4. *Letters on Aesthetic Education*, XII, 2, 3.

is not only something terrible but also something mysterious. God and the devil are fighting there, and the battlefield is the heart of man." And if for Schiller there is no other way to make sensual man rational than to make him aesthetic,[5] Dostoevsky cannot see man redeemed and saved by beauty. The "breadth" of beauty is closely related to the "breath of character" of the Karamazov nature, "which is capable of uniting all possible contradictions in itself and of looking simultaneously into both abysses, the abyss above us, the abyss of the highest ideal, and the abyss below us, the abyss of the most shameful degradation. . . . A Karamazov dares to look at both abysses, and at the same time! . . ." "[They] constantly need precisely this unnatural mixture, two abysses at all times, two abysses at one and the same moment—without that they are unhappy and dissatisfied, their existence is incomplete. They are broad natures—they include everything, and put up with everything."

Precisely for that reason does Dmitri feel that beauty is more of a danger than a support for him: "For when I do leap into the abyss, I go headlong with my heels up, and am pleased to be falling into that degrading attitude, and consider it beauty. And in the very depths of that degradation I begin a hymn of praise." Dmitri thinks it is the same for others: "I can't endure the thought that a man of lofty mind and heart begins with the ideal of the Madonna and ends with the ideal of Sodom. What is still more awful is that a man with the ideal of Sodom in his soul does not renounce the ideal of the Madonna, and his heart may be on fire with that ideal, genuinely on fire, just as in the days of his youth and innocence. Yes, man is broad, too broad, indeed. I'd have him narrower." The only real support, the only possible starting point for the really "higher" man, he who does not view and consider himself high but is so, is religion. Only religious consciousness, which does not deny him the possibility of viewing both abysses nor deny his sensitivity to the beautiful, gives man the firmness and the power to protect himself from the decline into disgrace and shame, and at the same time to guard him from a divorce from reality, from the concrete, from the earth. Here, however, Dostoevsky can no longer proceed from Schiller, here a different and higher sphere of ideas begins, which for Dostoevsky is connected with the characteristics of Russian Orthodox religious consciousness. Here, too, is the end of this part of our analysis.

6

Dostoesvky did not have to remind himself of Schiller in presenting the sensual emotional type—Dmitri, and Fyodor Pavlovich,

5. Ibid., **XXIII**, 2.

who stands close to him—since a great deal that is purely Russian and lies close to Dostoevsky himself lies in the breadth of the Karamazov nature, in their recklessness and impetuosity. The matter stands quite differently with Ivan. In that theorizing ideologue Dostoevsky naturally had to reflect the ideological conflicts he himself underwent, in which Schiller's ideas play a significant role. And in fact we find two indictments of Schiller's ideas, in the problem of Theodicy and the problem of "refusing to judge."

That whole marvelous conversation of Ivan's with Alyosha is dedicated to the problem of theodicy, a problem that may perhaps have become foreign and inappropriate to the nineteenth and twentieth centuries, but which was so characteristic for the eighteenth century, which in particular greatly tormented Schiller and played a major role in the formation of his views. Ivan, who by no means represents Dostoevsky's own thought at the time the novel was written, develops the main thoughts of Schiller's (or better, Schiller-Kant's) theodicy in his conversation with Alyosha: "Why must this rigmarole (*akhineya*) be and be permitted? Without it, I am told, man could not have existed on earth, for he could not have known good and evil. Why should he know that diabolical good and evil when it costs so much. Why, the whole world of knowledge is not worth [these children's tears]. . . . the world rests on an absurdity —I cannot conceive why everything is so constructed." And the "Legend of the Grand Inquisitor" serves to disclose the only possible sense of this absurdity, the *akhineya*, the senselessness of existence, the inappropriate sense of the sufferings of the innocent and the just. Man has an option and he must choose one of the two—either "freedom" or "bread," either "heavenly light" (*ogon' s nebesi*) or "fodder." In other words, man must accept evil into the bargain *if he wishes to be free*. Since evil is unavoidable where there is an *ungodly* existence. Where freedom does not exist, there is also no sin or evil. Man must purchase freedom as the *highest good* through the cost of suffering and sin, he must leave thought to chance, choose freedom consciously, that he may thereby also choose the possibility of bringing evil and "absurdity" into the world. The divine order of the world is justified through this choice, that order through which evil and sin are redeemed and indemnified by the possession of freedom. The main paradox of the "Legend of the Grand Inquisitor" consists in the Inquisitor's not considering freedom the *highest* good and not believing that man can prize freedom above happiness or can ever do so. On the contrary, the Inquisitor believes that men "will lay their freedom at his feet and will say 'enslave us but give us bread,'" since man can never be free because "nothing is more certain than bread." But Christ, "instead of rejecting man's freedom, even increased it."

And if Ivan doubts the justness of the solution offered by Christ and Christianity (in the version sketched above) to a certain extent, the question whether "weak man" can "bear" freedom in no way invalidates for Dostoevsky the theodicy developed by him, that theodicy which we earlier find in Schiller (which on this point anticipates Kant's thought) and which was familiar to Dostoevsky in the speeches of the Marquis Posa, of which he was so fond in his youth:

> . . . Look about you
> At this splendid nature! On freedom
> Is it based—and how rich it is
> Through freedom!—He, the great Creator—
> — — — — He, freedom's
> Enchanting appearance not to disturb—
> He rather leaves the dreadful host of evil
> To rage in his universe—Him,
> The artist, one will not perceive.[6]

Schiller's verses cited by Ivan at the beginning of the conversation with Alyosha have the same sense:

> You must believe, you must dare,
> For the gods give no pledge.

Man is left to his own freedom by the gods (in the Russian translation "heavens"—*nebesa*)—to his own choice, decision, daring (to his own "heart," as Zhukovsky rendered it in Russian). His destiny is not assured and is not guaranteed from above, "for the gods give no pledge." Therein lies the sense of human freedom.

Indeed, Dostoevsky could hardly know that Schiller's conception of Christianity was also built on the idea of freedom, and that Schiller was also close to the notion that the "weak man" does not need the so-called ideal social organization of the Grand Inquisitor, since Schiller believed that consciousness finds sufficient support in God to bear the whole burden of the freedom offered to it.[7] Dostoevsky was also in total agreement with the negative characterization Schiller gave such social organization, as when the Marquis Posa says of Phillip II's state:

> your creation
> How narrow and poor!

Like Dostoevsky's Grand Inquisitor, however, Phillip himself thought that he knew mankind and its inability to live in freedom. And behind Phillip also stands the Grand Inquisitor—a sinister figure drawn by Schiller in a way similar to Ivan's Inquisitor. But Schiller poses the problem singly and only Phillip himself is placed

---

6. *Don Carlos*, III, 10 [*Editor*].
7. Schiller's letter to Goethe, August 17, 1795. To be sure, in a letter to his brother, January 1, 1840, Dostoevsky refers to Schiller as the "Christian poet."

in the dilemma between freedom and sin (in the Grand Inquisitor's view, Philip has embarked on this road) or, alternatively, the Inquisition will assume the sin if Phillip in return will give up all personal freedom, a posing of the problem whose sense is identical with Dostoevsky's Legend.

* * * To be sure, [Schiller] only contains the outlines of ideas that Dostoevsky fleshed out in persons and pictures of extraordinary vitality, plasticity, and profundity.

7

We have already noted that Schiller, too, occupied himself with the problem of "the refusal to judge." To be sure, his statement of the problem differed from that in Dostoevsky. But the problem leads Schiller to a motif that is also used in *The Brothers Karamazov*, that of the double. . . .

Naturally, the theme of the double was terribly and enticingly meaningful to Dostoevsky, whose whole work is an ecstatic, rapturous battle for securing the *individual, personal being* of man. He wrote the short novel *The Double* (1846), touches on the related theme of imposture (*samozvanstvo*) in *The Possessed*, and he finally uses this theme for the presentation of his basic ethical thoughts in *The Brothers Karamazov*.

Ivan Karamazov is a representative of Intellectualism in ethics. His spiritual endowments, his interest in theories, and his unique "pride of the intellect" mark him as such. Even Ivan's ethical views are intellectualized. The consciousness of his guilt "for everything and everyone," which is an expression of love for one's neighbor, is utterly inaccessible to him. But for Dostoevsky, such consciousness is a necessary basis for all morality. Ivan, however, understands "love from afar," love for "man in general," the abstract concept of man, rather than love for one's neighbor. And if the chief axiom of moral consciousness, "each is responsible for everyone and for everything," is accessible to Alyosha directly through his active *love* for the concrete neighbor, and if Dmitri is led to the recognition of the same axiom through his own and others' *suffering* (the babe), Ivan, the intellectual and "enlightener," has only one possible road to ethical rebirth—which Dostoevsky does not follow to its conclusion in that part of the novel he finished—that road is through mental derangement, through the splitting of the personality.

Ivan cannot feel guilty for all, but he at least feels guilty for one—for Smerdyakov, and does so precisely because Smerdyakov is his double.

The parallel Smerdyakov-Ivan is carried through the novel with extraordinary persistence and importance. We encounter both together or in adjoining chapters. The characterization of Smerdyakov is built on the following motifs: enlightenment, "critical" sophistry, arrogance and contemptuousness for all ("aversion"— *brezglivost'*), and, finally, total self-sufficiency (*samodavlenie*), the lack of need for any kind of society. Yet these are Ivan's main characteristics, too, though we see them in Smerdyakov in an absurd and "mean" way. And no matter how large the discrepancy may be between Ivan's powerful intellect and Smerdyakov's "little intellect," and, most important, the difference between their vivid personalities, yet we hear certain ideas expressed which they hold in common: from Smerdyakov, the justification of mortal sin; from Ivan, "all is permitted"; in Smerdyakov's second appearance, his judgment of Europe corresponds in some ways to the views expressed by Ivan a few pages earlier. And even Ivan's consciousness that his intellect has its limits, that it is "Euclidian," has its counterpart in Smerdyakov's avowal that perhaps "two hermits" exist whose relationship to God is not subject to the laws of Smerdyakov's spiritual being (or, rather, nonbeing). Ivan immediately notices and admits his similarity to Smerdyakov on *this* point. And Smerdyakov, who feels Ivan's spiritual force, does not remain indifferent to him, "begins to respect him (*zauvazhal*)." Fyodor Pavlovich notices it, too: "Ivan, he's doing all that for your sake, he wants you to praise him. . . . You are the one who interests him so. How did you manage to do that?" And this respect remains no secret from Ivan: "He's taken it into his head to respect me"; Smerdyakov himself admits it to Marya Kondratevna, who reminds him of it later: "You yourself said that you esteem Ivan Fyodorovich so." The prosecuting attorney also comes to speak of the impression that Ivan made on Smerdyakov.

Yet Ivan and Smerdyakov are connected much more deeply than by mere similarity. They participate in each other ontologically, intrinsically, to an uncanny degree. Their ontological interdependence expresses itself in all their contacts. They are brought together against Ivan's will in the conversation in the courtyard. Throughout that episode Ivan seems to be driven by an outer force which seems peculiar to him. He sees Smerdyakov sitting by the gate and "remains standing, and precisely the fact that he suddenly remained still and did not pass through, as he had intended to do a moment before, made him shake with anger." Further, "unexpectedly for himself," he says something "completely different" than he had wanted to say, and "then, just as unexpectedly for himself," he sits down on the bench next to Smerdyakov, and after hearing everything Smerdyakov wanted to say to him, explains to him "loudly and clearly" that he will leave for Moscow the next day, which is what Smerdyakov wanted to hear, and "wondered himself afterwards what need there was then to say this to Smerdyakov." Ivan leaves, "moving and walking as though his limbs were cramped," but the following day, too, at his departure, he again says it to Smerdyakov, without wishing to: "Suddenly, like yesterday, it came out by itself and with a peculiar nervous laugh. He remembered it long afterwards." Thus is his ontological connection with Smerdyakov expressed in the psychopathological sphere.

The details of this conversation come into Ivan's consciousness only later, after his three visits to Smerdyakov before the trial. Only then does he understand that even if he has no empirical connection with the murder of his father, even if Smerdyakov erred in counting on Ivan's interest in his father's death, he nevertheless also shares guilt in the murder, guilt in a special sense of the word, guilt for another, for Smerdyakov, and guilt because "the lackey Smerdyakov sat in his soul." Ivan is ashamed of Smerdyakov because he recognizes his similarity to and kinship with him, and feels responsible for him, since the consonance of their souls becomes clear to him, a consonance the whole evolution of their relationship attests.

Like Karl Moor, Ivan considers himself above others, despises them, prefers the "abstract man," the distant one, to the concrete, living "neighbor," and that is the punishment—like Karl Moor he is united in evil with the worst, the most despicable of all men. And this most despicable of creatures (Spiegelberg, Smerdyakov) leaves his mark on the "existence" of the "higher man," breaks into the spheres of his individual existence. For Dostoevsky and his pathos of individuality, the loss of independence of individual existence is the worst thing that can befall man. However, Smerdyakov's death does not signal the death of Ivan (as the destruction of his double brought about that of Moor). Ivan raises himself to a new moral consciousness through shame and mental illness. We see only the beginning of this road in the parts of the novel Dostoevsky completed. It is crucial that Ivan's illness, his "nightmare," is again an appearance of the double, of the "devil," in which Ivan sees "an embodiment of my own self, though only a part of myself, my thoughts and feelings, but only the lowest and stupidest. . . . You are me, me myself, only with a different mug . . . only you always take only my worst ideas, and above all, the stupidest. . . . You are stupid and mean. . . . All my stupid ideas—outgrown, thrashed out long ago and flung aside like a dead carcass, you present to me as something new. . . . No, I was never such a lackey! How, then, could my soul beget a lackey like you. . . . That is *me*, my own self. Everything mean and nasty and despicable in myself." Smerdyakov dies. But shame for him, the consciousness of guilt for another remains in Ivan's soul. Where Schiller has destruction at the end, Dostoevsky sees the beginning of a rebirth, the beginning of a "new novel" that unfortunately was not written.

We may conjecture that the only way out remaining to Ivan in

Dostoevsky's mind is humility ("Humble yourself, proud man!")[8] and faith. For faith alone can give man the strength that will help him bear freedom and the consciousness of being "guilty for everything and everyone."

ROBERT L. BELKNAP

The Structure of Inherent Relationships: The Buffoon, The *Nadryv* (Laceration) †

The Buffoon

Clusters of associations generate three other presences which touch upon the Karamazovan and the diabolic, but which lack the focus these two concepts gain from the figures of the Devil and of Fyodor's family. The first of these new presences grows partly out of the association between Fyodor and Maximov. These two figures are attracted to one another for no visible reason and Ivan uses Maximov as a butt for his filial hatred when he sends him flying from his father's carriage. Maximov and Fyodor are slapped, whipped, or beaten on several occasions. Maximov, like Fyodor, had married both an unfaithful wife and a handicapped one. Maximov is associated with Von Sohn by Fyodor's fiat, while Fyodor is associated with Von Sohn by their common lust, disreputable murder, and trial. Above all, Maximov and Fyodor blather.[1]

Compare, for example, the stories Fyodor tells in Zosima's cell with those Maximov tells at Mokroe. Maximov tells the following five:

1. The Polish girls jump upon the Uhlan's knees after a mazurka, and are proposed to the next day.

2. I married a lame woman. She concealed the fact from me by hopping. I thought she hopped for joy.

3. My second wife ran off with a m'sieu, with all I owned.

4. I'm the Maximov whom Nozdryov whipped in *Dead Souls*.

5. I was whipped for being educated enough to quote an epigram about Piron.

Fyodor has also mentioned Piron, and has told a group of anecdotes at Zosima's so like these of Maximov's that the latter seems to

8. A line from Pushkin's narrative poem "The Gypsies," used as the key to Russian salvation (Dostoevsky's interpretation in the "Pushkin Day Speech," 1880) [*Editor*].
† From *The Structure of The Brothers Karamazov* (The Hague: Mouton & Co., 1967), pp. 41–47. Reprinted by permission of Edicom N.V., Laren, The Netherlands.
1. Book I, Chapter 2; Book IX, Chapter 1.

be Fyodor himself resurrected, rather than Von Sohn. Here is Fyodor's group of anecdotes. The first cannot be summarized:

1. I go straight up to [the constable] and with the nonchalance of a man of the world, "Constable," I say, "You be, as one might say, our Dunstable."

"How's that," says he, "Dunstable?"

So I see from the first half-second that it's a fizzle; he got serious and held back; "I," say I, "wanted to joke, for the general pleasure, since Mr. Dunstable is our well-known Russian conductor, and for the harmony of our undertaking, we need some one like a conductor. . . ."

"Excuse me," he says, "I am a Constable and permit no puns to be made upon my calling."[2]

2. The second anecdote is also a shaggy dog story about calling a man's wife a "touchy (or ticklish) woman," and being asked "Have you been touching (or tickling) her?"

3. Diderot denied God and was miraculously converted at the court of Catherine the Great.

4. A saint beheaded for his faith picked up his head and " 'fondly kissed it,' and walked a long time, carrying it in his hands, and 'fondly kissed it'."

The parallels are plain; the self-dramatization, the aggressive shame, the almost deliberate faux pas, the famous Frenchman in a ridiculous Russian setting, and above all, a joyful disregard for impossibility. Fyodor explains that this propensity to blather dates to "my youth, as I was a toady to the gentry and toadied for my bread. I am a buffoon at bottom, from my birth." At Mokroe, Maximov gives a demonstration of just such toadying:

[Grushenka] especially delighted in the "old goat," as she called Maximov. He kept running up to kiss her hand "and each little finger," and towards the end danced one more dance to one old song, which he sang himself. He danced with ardor at the refrain especially:

> "Piggy wiggy Hru, Hru, Hru,
> Calfy Waffy, moo, moo, moo,
> Ducky wucky, quack, quack, quack,
> Goosie gander, gak, gak, gak.
> Chicky chick through the straw kept strutting
> Tu ru, ru, ru, she kept on clucking
> Ai, ai, she kept on clucking."

"Give him something, Mitya," said Grushenka, "Make him a gift—He's so poor."

This poverty represents an earlier stage of Fyodor's buffoonery:

Fyodor Pavlovich, for example, began with almost nothing; he was

---

2. The Russian word for constable is *"ispravnik"*; the conductor's name, Napravnik.

the smallest of landowners, ran to dine at others' tables, took to toadying, and yet at his death was found to have a hundred thousand rubles in hard cash. And at the same time, all his life he was still one of the most irrational madmen in our whole district.

This irrationality is another name for the fine disregard for impossibility which characterized the stories told by Maximov and Fyodor. It is impossible for Maximov to be Von Sohn, but Fyodor's assertion that he is involves both Fyodor and Maximov in this absurdity. Fyodor's shrewdness lies in his ability to see through common sense down to the level of functioning absurdity where there are sermons in moving beards, names which are not names, and nonsense in everything. Fyodor describes another buffoon as follows:

> He's a liar, that's the hitch. He sometimes lies so hard you just wonder why. A couple of years ago, he made up the yarn that his wife had died and he'd already married another, and none of this was so; imagine; his wife never had died; she's living to this day, and she beats him once every three days. . . . You must watch his goatee. . . . When his goatee wiggles, he may be talking and getting mad, but it means, O.K., he's telling the truth and wants to make a deal; but if he smoothes his beard with his left hand and chuckles, that means he wants to pull a fast one. He's on the make. . . . He's Gorstkin—only he's not Gorstkin, but Lyagavy, so don't you tell him he's Lyagavy, or he'll get sore.

In this passage, Fyodor's irrationality is revealed as the practical mastery of the non sequitur.

Such abnormal reactions will be discussed further under the heading of causality. Here, the non sequitur must merely take its place beside the blathering, the self-dramatization, the aggressive shame, and the other elements which make the buffoon one of the foci of the inherent structure of the novel. After Fyodor, the chief exponent of the non sequitur is Madame Khokhlakov, who like Fyodor falls into an ecstasy of self-abasement before Zosima, and like Fyodor is urged to solve her problems by not lying. (Book II, chaps. 1 and 2) When Mitya rushes to beg a loan of her, she greets him:

> I know it's a most crucial matter, Dmitri Fyodorovich; these are no sort of forebodings, no reactionary hankering after miracles (did you hear about the elder Zosima?) This, this is mathematics; you could not help but come after all this happened with Katerina Ivanovna. You couldn't. That's mathematics.

This command of the non sequitur is coupled in this passage with the self-dramatization which is as characteristic of Madame Khokhlakov as it is of Fyodor.

"Dear Alexey Fyodorovich," [she moans earlier] "It is not particular things that are killing me, not some stray Herzenstube, but everything together, as a whole, there is what I can't endure."

When she learns of Mitya's odd behavior, she exclaims to Perkhotin in fine defiance of chronology, "God gracious. That means he's killed his old father! . . . I gave him no money, none at all. Oh run, run! Don't talk, not a word more. Save the old man. Run to his father, run! . . ." After this speech, she keeps Perkhotin waiting while she blathers:

Come to tell me what you see and learn there . . . and what transpires, and how they decide and where they sentence him to. Tell me, we haven't capital punishment, have we? But come, for certain, even if it's at three o'clock at night, or even at four, or at half-past four. Have them wake me and give me a shake if I don't get up. Oh, Lord, I won't even get to sleep.

The Dostoevskian buffoon is characterized by this stream of consciousness, with thought leading to thought through the structure of associations rather than causally. Madame Khokhlakov describes the scene with Perkhotin later,

On that terrible day, [Perkhotin] almost saved me from death, coming to me by night. Now, your friend Rakitin always came in such boots and stuck them out on the carpet. In a word, he began to even make insinuations to me, and suddenly, once, on his way out squeezed my hand awfully hard. No sooner had he squeezed my hand than my foot began to hurt.

This monologue, worthy of Fyodor or Maximov, contains the hidden connections which characterize the mind of the buffoon, and the proper locus for sensuality takes over from the hand, for no rational cause.

Kolya Krasotkin likes to blather, to dramatize himself, to entertain people. But underlying his outrageousness is a desperation and a shame akin to Madame Khokhlakov's, Fyodor's or Maximov's:

"Oh, Karamazov," [he says,] ". . . I am deeply unhappy. I sometimes imagine Lord knows what, that everyone is laughing at me, the whole world, and then I am ready simply to annihilate the whole order of things."

Alyosha underlines this aspect of buffoonery when Kolya asks him whether Snegiryov, who dramatizes himself and sometimes blathers, is a mere buffoon:

No, there are deeply sensitive people who are somehow crushed. Their buffoonery is sort of a bitter irony at those to whose face they dare not tell the truth because of long, degrading bashfulness before them. Believe me, Krasotkin, such buffoonery is sometimes extraordinarily tragic.

This tragic aspect of buffoonery can be connected with its irrationality by considering Ivan's statement, when Alyosha claims to have spoken absurdly in favor of shooting a vicious general:

> Know, novice, that absurdities are too necessary on earth. On absurdities the whole world stands, and without them, perhaps nothing in it would have happened at all. We know what we know! . . .
> I understand nothing . . . and I don't want to understand anything now. I want to remain with the fact. I long ago resolved not to understand. (Book V, Chap. 4)

This necessary absurdity resembles the Devil, the "indispensable minus," without whom nothing might have existed. His is the metaphysical rejection of God's world, and its order, while buffoonery is the practical, everyday rejection of it, in the name of the self, ordering the world according to one's own patterns, but rejecting the reasonable, the socially acceptable, the religiously acceptable externals, and lapsing into the self-perpetuating shame caught in its self-dramatization.

The nadryv

This tragic sense of the absurd does not properly belong to the buffoons like Fyodor or Maximov, but to a second group, including Ivan, Katerina Ivanovna, Lise, Grushenka, Mitya, and Snegiryov. Like buffoonery, this concept is emphasized by chapter headings, and unlike buffoonery, it is brought into existence primarily by fiat. *Nadryv*, the central word in this cluster, is hard to translate. It has been rendered as "laceration," and is derived from *rvat'*, to "rend," "tear," "burst," "split," as is shown in the translations "heartbreak" or "hysterics." Yet it also implies a heightening at the beginning, middle, or end of the process which can justify "exacerbation," "paroxysm," or "anguish" as occasional translations. The adjective derived from it can almost always be translated "heartrending."

Madame Khokhlakov introduces the term, although the reader has been alerted for it by the title of Book Four, just as he was alerted for the word "buffoon" by the title of Book I, Chapter 2. Madame Khokhlakov says, "This is awful, I tell you, it's a *nadryv*, an awful story, beyond all conceivable belief; they're both ruining themselves for goodness knows what, knowing this, and relishing it themselves." (Book 4, chap. 4) This definition of the *nadryv* shows its boundary with the diabolic, along the line of self-annihilation, as well as with the buffoonery, along the line of irrationality. Lise Khokhlakov is immediately linked to the *nadryv*, for a few lines later, her voice is *nadryvčatyj* [strained].

Dostoevsky's narrator underlines the word still more strongly when Alyosha goes to meet Ivan and Katerina Ivanovna.

The word *nadryv* just pronounced by Madame Khokhlakov had almost made him jump, because just that night, half waking at dawn, he had suddenly said "*nadryv, nadryv*" probably responding to a dream of his. He had dreamed that whole night about the scene at Katerina Ivanovna's the day before. Now, suddenly, the direct and persistent assertion of Madame Khokhlakov's that Katerina Ivanovna loved his brother Ivan and was intentionally, in some sort of play, "out of *nadryv* deceiving and torturing her own self with her faked love for Dmitri for some so-called gratitude. . . ."

In this passage Dostoevsky not only fixes the *nadryv* in the reader's mind as the center of an important cluster of associations, but connects it with gratitude. Gratitude implies benefits received, and just as buffoonery was a twisted response to poverty and blows received, so the *nadryv* is a twisted response to wealth and benefits received, or at least offered. Katerina Ivanovna's love for Mitya is connected with the money he lent her, and reaches the level of the *nadryv* when her affluence lets her return the money and entrust further money to Mitya. In the same way, the *nadryv* at Snegiryov's occurs when Alyosha comes to offer money, and centers upon the gratitude for the money, which necessitates its abrupt refusal. In this sense, the *nadryv* is the exact opposite of buffoonery, involving pride, riches, dignity, and a pressing fear of being base while the buffoon embodies humiliation, poverty, shame, and pursuit of baseness. The buffoon makes himself laughable in order to make others so. The *nadryv* causes a person to hurt himself in order to hurt others, or, perversely, to hurt others in order to hurt himself.

These oppositions do not obscure the fact that *nadryv* and buffoonery have much in common. Both embody perversity, willfulness, self-consciousness, self-dramatization, and absurdity. From such connections, a pattern of foci begins to form in the inherent structure of the novel. Buffoonery and the *nadryv* may be said to lie on one axis of the novel, the axis which has done most to make Dostoevsky the old testament of the existentialists today, but they lie at opposite ends of this axis, and various characters may be ranked hierarchically along it, with Katerina Ivanovna near one end and Maximov near the other. Snegiryov would fall somewhere near the middle, since he is a hysterical buffoon. Figures like Ivan and Fyodor would lie near to this axis, one being involved with *nadryv*, and the other with buffoonery, but they would be removed from this axis into a second dimension, since they are equally involved in Karamazovism.

* * *

EDWARD WASIOLEK

The Brothers Karamazov: Idea and Technique†

After the preliminary exposition *The Brothers Karamazov* begins
with one of Dostoevsky's great scenes. Ostensibly a gathering in the
Elder's cell to settle the grievance between Dmitri and Fyodor, the
scene captures in image and dramatic gesture the polarities and
dialectical oppositions of the novel. It is a magnificent introduction
to the entire novel. Near the end of the scene, Dmitri Karamazov
springs at his father and cries out in agonized rage, "Why does a
man such as he live?" As Fyodor raises the cry of "father-killer,"
and the cell fills with commotion and disorder, the Elder rises from
his seat and, supported by Alyosha, shakily walks up to Dmitri,
where he falls to the ground and asks for forgiveness. The scene
ends, and the novel begins with the hand of the child raised against
the father. But only raised. For his cry of hate is muted into
silence, and his gesture of violence is stayed by the long bow of
expiation by the Elder. Like a camera click, the oppositions that
Dostoevsky will dramatize in the novel are caught and stilled in the
gestures of the father, son, and Elder: child against father; humility
against hate; monastery against the world; expiation against threat.
Only the novel itself will resolve the oppositions. When the scene
ends, we do not know whether the son will destroy the father, or
whether the act of humility will destroy the hate for him.

What is at stake is important: the right of the child to raise his
hand against his father is for Dostoevsky the right of man to raise
his hand against God. Later, Ivan will base his rebellion against
God on the rights of children against the fathers who mistreat
them, and by analogy the rights of men against the God who has
mistreated them; the defense attorney at Dmitri's trial will argue
that a child has the right to demand that a father prove his love,
and that a child has the right to look upon a bad father as an
enemy; and Dmitri will feel the stirrings of a new man within him
when he accepts the suffering of children in his dream of the burnt-
out huts. Finally, Alyosha will see in children the first signs of
corruption and the first impulses of faith. Children are the moral
touchstone of the novel.

In the same opening scene Ivan gives us the law by which a child
is set against his father, and the law by which man humbles himself

† Reprinted from *Dostoevsky: The Major
Fiction,* by Edward Wasiolek (Cambridge, Mass.: M.I.T. Press, 1964), pp.
144–60. By permission of the M.I.T.
Press, Cambridge, Massachusetts. Copyright © 1964 by The Massachusetts Institute of Technology; all rights reserved.

before man. *The law, in short, that propels Dmitri's spring and the law by which the Elder bows before the murderer are both given by Ivan.* The oppositions that are caught in the gestures of Dmitri and the Elder are both carried in the breast of Ivan. The external drama is Ivan's internal drama. In the ecclesiastical article Ivan had written, he maintains that the church cannot logically come to terms with the state and occupy a clearly defined but limited place in the state, as his ecclesiastical opponent had argued. According to him, the church must, to fulfill its true purpose, contain the whole state. The logic is impeccable, for the church, as the true representative of God, can no more give power to a temporal authority than God can. But while seemingly insisting on a theocracy of the most absolute kind, Ivan is also saying, as Miüsov gleefully and quickly points out, that there is no natural law to compel man to love his fellow man. According to Ivan, if men have loved others, it is only because they have believed in immortality; and if you were to destroy the idea of immortality, you would destroy virtue and the love of others. If there is no immortality, all is permitted—and not only permitted, but enjoined. Every "right"-thinking and honest man will be obligated to express his self-interest, even to the point of crime. Miüsov, who has been miffed by the attention Ivan's ecclesiastical article has provoked, gives the group this résumé so as to expose what he believes are contradictory views as well as Ivan's insincerity. The Elder Zosima knows that Ivan's views are not contradictory. He looks into Ivan's eyes and says, "If you so believe, you are blessed or most unhappy." With this statement, the Elder has drawn the logical consequences from Ivan's views. He sees that Ivan has logically drawn conclusions from two different premises, the most important and the most irreconcilable in Dostoevsky's whole work. If God exists, then what Ivan has written in his article about the church follows; if God and the attendant idea of immortality do not exist, then indeed there is only the law of self-interest, and man is obliged—if he is to live without deception—to express this law even to the point of crime. There is no contradiction in Ivan's views, but there is dreadful indecision, and this, too, the Elder sees. As the novel begins, the reader waits to see not only whether Dmitri's leap will reach his father or whether it will be stayed by the law of Zosima, but also whether Ivan, who carries both laws in his breast, will choose one or the other. *What is objectified in Dmitri against his father and in Zosima against both is internalized in Ivan against Ivan.*

Dmitri and Katerina

In the confession of an ardent heart, Dmitri tells Alyosha—he is our ears—what Katya means to him. But he tells only what he knows, and she means more to him than he knows. The relations between them bristle with paradoxes. A high-minded, well-educated, rich girl insists on an engagement with an impoverished, dissolute army officer. When Dmitri basely repays her generosity by stealing her money and spending it on a wild orgy with another girl, Katerina rises nobly to forgiveness. Throughout the novel she stands ready to bear everything for his sake: vice, theft, unfaithfulness, insult, and even marriage to Grushenka. Despite all this, Dmitri not only is incorrigibly ungrateful but unaccountably sees her love and sacrifice as oppressive burdens. Katerina's "goodness" drives him to murder. The incriminating letter he writes Katya threatening his father's life makes this clear. In that letter he states that only by paying her back the money he had stolen from her could he preserve his honor, and if he could not get the money any other way, he would kill his father to get it. If the Elder's bow stays Dmitri's hand against his father, Katya's had originally moved it and continues to move it throughout the novel. The first meeting with Katerina begins with a bow, as low and as long as the Elder's bow of expiation. It is characteristic of Dostoevsky that he uses the same gesture for opposite meanings, as if to emphasize that the act remains without significance until we ourselves choose the significance.

On the simplest level it would appear that Katerina is sacrificing herself out of gratitude for Dmitri's noble gesture in saving her father and sparing her. This is the way that Alyosha understands her motives and her relations with Dmitri. As he goes to see Katya at her request early in the novel, he tells himself: "The girl's aims were of the noblest, he knew that. She was trying to save his brother Dmitri simply through generosity (*velikodushie*), though he had already behaved badly to her." And this is the way he understands it in his conversation with Dmitri, when his brother tells him about his first meeting with Katya: he assures Dmitri that Katerina loves him, and not Ivan. When Dmitri tells him about the 3,000 rubles that he had stolen from Katerina, Alyosha says:

> "Katerina Ivanovna will understand it all," Alyosha said solemnly. "She'll understand how great this trouble is and will forgive. She has a lofty mind, and no one could be more unhappy than you. She'll see that for herself."

Yet even while Alyosha is convinced that Katerina's motives are lofty, pure, and sincere, he has moments of uneasiness. From the very beginning, something about her troubles him. On his way to his first meeting with her, even while paying justice to her fine qualities, "a shiver began to run down his back as soon as he drew near her house." When he sees her, he sees pride, self-confidence, and strong will in her face. Her black burning eyes are set beautifully in a thin, pale, almost yellow face, and he sees why Dmitri could easily fall in love with her. But he also sees unclearly something that makes it unlikely for Dmitri to love her for a long time. He tells his brother: "Perhaps you will always love her, but perhaps you will not always be happy with her." But he no sooner says this than he feels ashamed of himself. Later, when he goes to her with Dmitri's farewell message, he feels that his first impression must have been wrong. As she comes out to meet him, he sees in her face only simplicity, goodness, and sincerity.

Again and again Alyosha tries to take her as she sees herself, but each time he is stopped by a feeling he cannot understand. He swings from facing up to his doubt about Katerina's motives to feeling ashamed of having that doubt. Alyosha is our ears and our eyes, and the difficulty he has in understanding Katerina is our difficulty. And the difficulty is great. Engaged to Dmitri, Katerina regards him as a repugnant monster; determined to save him, she plots his ruin; frantic to keep him faithful, she provokes his betrayal of her. It is she who almost saves him at the trial, and it is she who most irrevocably ruins him legally by the letter she produces in which he had uttered threats against his father's life. Throughout her relations with Dmitri, her fitful character sweeps her from love to hate, generosity to spite, arrogance to submissiveness. She is all contradiction, flailing each action with its opposite. There is something in her relations with Dmitri that she cannot forgive, something that drives her to pursue him with an unrelenting, self-punishing love. She herself best expresses it in Mrs. Khokhlakov's drawing room before Ivan and Alyosha, when after a night of shame and rage at Grushenka's insult, she triumphantly announces that she will bear that too out of love for Dmitri:

"I've already decided, even if he marries that—creature" (she began solemnly), "whom I never, never can forgive, *even then I will not abandon him*. Henceforward I will never, never abandon him!" she cried, breaking into a sort of pale, hysterical ecstasy. "Not that I would run after him continually, get in his way and worry him. Oh, no! I will go away to another town—where you like—but I will watch over him all my life—I will watch over him all my life unceasingly. When he becames unhappy with that woman, and that is bound to happen quite soon, let him come to me and he will find a friend, a sister. . . . Only a sister, of course, and so forever; but he will learn at least that that sister is really his sister, who loves him and has sacrificed all her life to him. I will gain my point. I will insist on his knowing me and confiding entirely in me, without reserve," she cried, in a sort of frenzy. "I will be a god to whom he can pray—and that, at least, he owes me for his treachery and for what I suffered yesterday through him. And let him see that all my life I will be true to him and the promise I gave him, in spite of his being untrue and betraying me."

It is this something that Alyosha finally understands as he listens to Katerina's final decision, even though he had been firmly convinced up to the previous night that she loved Dmitri: "Alyosha had till the evening before implicitly believed that Katerina Ivanovna had a steadfast and passionate love for Dmitri; but he had only believed it till the evening before." When he had awakened that morning—after dreaming of Grushenka all night—the word *nadryv* is on his lips. It is this word that startles him when it is used by Mrs. Khokhlakov about Katerina's love for Dmitri, and which—while listening to Katerina—sparks his illumination. For as he excitedly expresses it to the startled Katerina, her love for Dmitri is a love from *nadryv*, that is, a self-punishing love, delighting in its self-hurt, needing the hurt, and only masquerading as love. Ivan proves a further illumination: "Believe me, Katerina Ivanovna, you love only him. And the more he insults you, the more you love him—that's your 'laceration.' You love him just as he is; you love him for insulting you. If he reformed, you'd give him up at once and cease to love him. But you need him so as to contemplate continually your heroic fidelity and to reproach him for infidelity. And it all comes from your pride."

Alyosha and Ivan tell us what Katerina's love is, but they do not tell us why it is so. We can begin to understand why by going back—as indeed Katerina and Dmitri keep going back—to that first fateful meeting. The scene had ended with Dmitri's heroic and successful struggle to overcome the noxious Karamazov insect of passion within him. The tragic relations between them have their seeds in that success, or rather in the gesture that accompanies the "triumph" of Dmitri: Dmitri's long bow of respect, and Katerina's low bow of respectful gratitude. They know it, and the fateful bow is insisted upon by both of them in their conversations.

Katerina Ivanovna is convinced that Dmitri hates her, and he hates her because he had compelled her to bow to him. She explains the reason for "his hatred" for her in this way:

> Oh, he has despised me horribly, he has always despised me, and do you know, he has despised me from the very moment that I bowed down to him for that money. I saw that. I felt it at once at the time, but for a long time I wouldn't believe it. How often have I read in his eyes. "You came of yourself, though."

Forgetting that it was she, not Dmitri, who had insisted on marriage, Katerina adds: "He was always convinced that I should be trembling with shame all my life before him, because I went to him then, and that he had a right to despise me forever for it, and so to be superior to me—that's why he wanted to marry me." Despite his contempt and monstrous ingratitude, "I tried to conquer him by my love, a love that knew no bounds. I even tried to forgive his faithlessness; but he understood nothing, nothing! How could he understand indeed? He is a monster!"

But the truth is that the hate and contempt that she ascribes to Dmitri is the hate and contempt she herself feels for him. This is, I think, clear to the reader who can pierce the rather transparent attempt to hide her own hate by giving the hate and all base qualities to Dmitri and all noble qualities to herself. In the notebooks to *The Brothers Karamazov* Dostoevsky makes the hatred she feels explicit. He writes of her in the first sketch of the scene: "Oh, he laughed at me because of that long, low bow. I hated him." It is his bow, out of respect to her, that hurts. For with the bow Dmitri changes from one who abases and humiliates to one who respects and forgives. And she hates the long low bow she must return, for it acknowledges his triumph over her.

We can now understand Katerina's paradoxical and contradictory motives, for once we perceive the subtle deceptions she has drawn over her feelings, perhaps without knowing it, we can see that her motives and actions have followed consistently from what the bowing scene meant to her. Katerina wishes only to hurt because her meeting with Dmitri is compounded of nothing but hurt. She is humiliated in having to appeal for help to the repugnant sensualist, and she is humiliated in having to receive the respectful bow from him. The heroic sacrifice of Dmitri in overcoming the noxious Karamazov insect within him by his deep bow of respect is not an act of sacrifice executed in selflessness and taken in gratitude, but an act of sacrifice given and taken as a subtle and exquisite insult. It is sacrifice used as insult; and ravishment, by comparison, would have been kind. After Dmitri's respectful bow, Katerina carries away in her heart the intolerable burden of an act of sacrifice and the desire to repay it with an equally intolerable act of sacrifice. Is it any wonder, then, that she is obsessed, from this point on, with only one idea: to save Dmitri, to sacrifice herself wholly and fully, to repay the burning insult of sacrifice with the burning insult of sacrifice. The oscillations between arrogance and submissiveness, love and hate, and unselfishness and spitefulness are not the struggle of a proud nature between its good intentions and, as has been usually suggested, the selfish impulses of its spirit. The love no less than the hate, and the submissiveness no less than the arrogance, are needed to bring to her feet a Dmitri ruined and ashamed before all, but contrite and nobly forgiven by her. As a consequence, she courts his betrayal, provokes his humiliations of her, works for his shame, and plots her own injury. The more sunken Dmitri is, the stronger her spirit is in lifting him; the deeper the injury to herself, the more lofty her forgiveness; and the more lofty her forgiveness, the sweeter her repayment of the insult of Dmitri's respectful bow.

Dmitri understands this. He understands why she gives him the 3,000 rubles when she knows that he will use it to carry Grushenka away. He knows that she gives him the money to destroy his honor and to provoke his humiliations of her. And he understands that she wants to be dishonored, so that her forgiveness will be all the nobler. How else is one to explain his agonized cry, "Katya, why have you destroyed me!" when at the trial he hears with dismay her generous account of their first meeting. As Katerina tells Alyosha, she is ready to bear all for his sake. Referring to the 3,000 rubles Dmitri had "stolen" from her, Katerina says: "Let him be ashamed of himself, let him be ashamed of other people's knowing, but not of my knowing. He can tell God everything without shame. Why is it he still does not understand how much I am ready to bear for his sake? . . . I want to save him forever."

What Katerina cannot bear is the possibility of a Dmitri who does not want to be forgiven. This is why, for instance, she becomes hysterical when Alyosha, after a meeting with Dmitri in the garden adjoining the Karamazov house, comes to convey to her Dmitri's "good-bye." Katerina is startled by the word "good-bye" and insists that Alyosha must have made a mistake in giving her the message. In the face of Alyosha's assurances that there has been no mistake, since Dmitri has asked him three times not to forget it, Katerina flushes and insists that Dmitri must not have said it deliberately but in a moment of reckless indecision. "He's merely in despair, and I can still save him," she infers exultantly.

It is at this point in the narration that translations blur this intention to trace back the drama of insult and repayment to Dmitri's respectful bow. The word "good-bye" (Magarshack has "good-bye" and Garnett "give his compliments") is in Russian the verb *klanyat'sya*, that is, "good-bye" by bowing. The Russian word expresses at once the sense of parting and recalls to Katerina the insulting respectful bow of the first meeting, when the same verb was used in a different aspect. The blurring in translation of Dostoevsky's intention is unfortunate since a phrase like "to bow out" would have caught, as does the Russian, both the sense of parting and a reminder of the fateful bow. Is it any wonder, then, that Katerina clings almost hysterically to the possibility of some mistake in Alyosha's message, which doubles the intolerable insult by recalling the first sacrifice and severing the possibility of repayment.

Dmitri, as the dissolute officer who struggled against the Karamazov sensuality within him, seemed unconscious of the enormity of the insult he had offered the proud girl, although in the ecstasy of self-satisfaction after she leaves, when he almost stabs himself with his sword, Dostoevsky hints that Dmitri has shared in the intention to insult. The Dmitri who reminds Katerina that she is rich and he but a poor rake, when she writes her letter of declaration of love for him, is also conscious of Katerina's motives. At times his awareness comes out sharply, though involuntarily, as when he retorts to Alyosha's assurance that Katerina loves him, and not Ivan: "She loves her virtue, and not me." He is always sorry for statements of this kind, ashamed of his base nature that erupts in criticism of Katerina, when morally he considers himself infinitely below her. Yet, despite his conscious intentions, he insists again and again in reminding her of the bow. In his last incriminating letter to her, he returns once again to the bow: "Farewell, I bow down to the ground before you, for I've been a scoundrel to you. Forgive me! No, better not forgive me, you'll be happier, and so shall I! Better Siberia than your love." Better murder and prison than such love! Such love and sacrifice, and the bow that symbolizes them, are not purifying and uplifting but abasing and persecuting. They are not Zosima's love, nor is Katerina's bow Zosima's bow. Zosima's bow stays the hand of the murderer; Katerina's raises it. What is wrong with such a love?

Katerina loves Dmitri from *nadryv*, and in this word Dostoevsky catches the vortex of her emotions and motives; with this word he points to one of his most penetrating insights into human motives. Dostoevsky devotes all of Book Four of Part Two to examples of *nadryv*, pointing to something that Ferapont, Captain Snegiryov, Katerina, and little Ilyusha have in common. Magarshack has ineptly translated the word as "heartache," Garnett less ineptly as "laceration." It is impossible to think of a translation more misleading than Magarshack's. It is romantic and trivial in connotation, and wholly inappropriate to what sears Katerina's breast. Garnett's translation is not much more helpful, but it is not the positive hindrance Magarshack's translation is.

The word comes from the verb *nadryvat'*, which means—apart from its literal meaning of tearing things apart, like paper—"to strain or hurt oneself by lifting something beyond one's strength." To this must be added Dostoevsky's special use of the word to mean a *purposeful* hurting of oneself, and to this, an explanation of the purpose. *Nadryv* is for Dostoevsky a purposeful and pleasurable self-hurt. Father Ferapont's ascetic deprivations are a self-denial from *nadryv*. He "hurts" himself, so that he can hurt the other monks; he needs the "indulgent" monks (which his exercises in asceticism create) as much as Katerina needs a fallen Dmitri. Father Ferapont's ascetic deprivations are weapons of humiliation of others and exaltation of self. Captain Snegiryov's *nadryv* is more pathetic and less violent than Father Ferapont's, but it shares some of the same quality. He deliberately hurts himself—when he stamps on the money Alyosha offers him and which he needs so desperately—because of the beautiful and noble image he has of himself at that moment.

Nadryv is for Dostoevsky a primal psychological fact. It is the impulse in the hearts of men that separates one man from another, the impulse we all have to make the world over into the image of our wills. Katerina *loves* from *nadryv*; Father Ferapont *fasts* from *nadryv*; Captain Snegiryov *loves honor* from *nadryv*. Dostoevsky shows this basic psychological characteristic working to corrupt what seem to be good motives. From the Underground Man on, one of the premises of Dostoevsky's mature dialectic has been that the Will will subvert the best and highest motives to its own purposes. *Nadryv* is Dostoevsky's mature pointing to the psychological impulse that works to corrupt everything to its own purposes.

Ivan has his *nadryv* also, for his hurt is his bruised sense of justice. He raises *nadryv* to a level of universal revolt against God.

* * *

HARRY SLOCHOWER

Incest in *The Brothers Karamazov*†

In *The Brothers Karamazov*, Mitya publicly competes with his father for Grushenka. And Dostoevsky criticism has accepted Grushenka as the incest figure in the novel. However, the main plot of the story and Mitya's major inner dilemma center, not in Grushenka, but in another woman: Katerina or Katya. And this essay will attempt to show that Katya is the deeper of Mitya's incest burdens. The paper would also suggest that although Freud's study of Dostoevsky never mentions Katya, she appears there in a veiled form.[1]

Freud names *The Brothers Karamazov*, *Hamlet*, and *Oedipus Rex* three literary masterpieces, dealing with patricide, motivated by sexual rivalry. He regards three of Fyodor Karamazov's sons guilty of patricide, and sees Grushenka as the object of the sexual contest between Fyodor and Mitya.

Now, *The Brothers Karamazov* is a later, more complex form of the Oedipal situation than are *Oedipus Rex* and *Hamlet*. In Sophocles, Oedipus actually commits incest and patricide. Shakespeare's modern, sophisticated scene presents more tangled relations. There is a scene in Hamlet's mind between his father and Claudius, between his mother and Ophelia, and between himself, as the son, and Gonzago "the nephew" (in the play between the play). In Dostoevsky, the pattern becomes still more intricate. We have three

† From *American Imago*, XVI (1959), pp. 127–45. Reprinted by permission of the author. A somewhat revised version is contained in the author's book, *Mythopoesis: Mythic Patterns in the Literary Classics* (Detroit: Wayne State University Press, 1970), pp. 267–273. (Footnotes omitted.)
1. That concluding section, *"Freud's Analysis of a Katya Figure in Zweig's Story,"* is omitted here.

father figures: Fyodor Karamazov, Grigory (who brings up Mitya and Smerdyakov), and Father Zosima; three or four sons: Mitya, Ivan, Alyosha, and Smerdyakov, who divide the patricidal guilt. But most complex of all is the problem of incest. Grushenka is the manifest object of Mitya's desire. The hidden and more troublesome incest figure is Katya.

Katya is pivotal not only for the plot. She is also the source of Mitya's obsessive feeling of his "debt" to her. His inability to return the money he took from Katya is the chief ground of his emotional disturbance. This is the reason, Mitya says, "why I fought in the tavern, that is why I attacked my father." Here, Mitya associates his patricidal impulse with his "debt" to Katya. What tortures him when he is arrested is not the false charge that he murdered his father, nor so much the thought that he killed Grigory, but "the damned consciousness" that he had not repaid Katya and had become "a downright thief." (In passing, we might note that Mitya recalls that as a boy he stole twenty kopeks from his mother which he returned three days later).[2] Why does Mitya feel that this is "the most shameful act of my whole life," that his very *"life"* depends on his returning the 3,000 rubles to Katya?

Katya as Mother Image

Dostoevsky gives Katya features which he also assigns to Mitya's mother, Adelaida. Both belong to a fairly rich and distinguished family and become heiresses. Both possess an imperious beauty and are described as strong, vigorous, and intelligent. Mitya's mother was "a hot-tempered, bold, dark-browed, impatient woman," and according to rumor used to beat her husband. She left Fyodor, running away with a divinity student. Katya strikes Mitya as proud, reckless, defiant, self-willed. She too defies convention: She comes to Mitya alone, impulsively offers to become his wife.

From the outset, Katya appears to Mitya as "a person of character." Indeed, he speaks of her as a kind of goddess. At the meeting in Father Zosima's cell, he is particularly outraged by his father's aspersions of Katya's good and honorable name for whom Mitya feels "such reverence that I dare not take her name in vain." (We are told that there were everlasting scenes between Fyodor and Mitya's mother and that after Adelaida left her husband, "Fyodor Pavlovich introduced a regular harem into the house.") And just as the question is raised how Adelaida could have married "such a worthless puny weakling" as Fyodor, so Mitya cannot understand that Katya should choose "a bug" like himself.

Mitya comes to Katya's attention by his wild exploits which set

2. Mitya jokingly repeats a confession of Perkhotin's (Book 8, chap. 5) [*Editor*].

the whole town talking. He felt that this made him "a hero." But, he complains, Katya "didn't seem to feel it." When she first saw him, she "scarcely looked at me, and compressed her lips scornfully." (Mitya's mother abandoned him when he was three years old and apparently never "looked" at him afterward.) Thereupon, Mitya plans revenge on Katya by humiliating her. The opportunity comes when disgrace threatens Katya's father (a lieutenant-colonel), who is suspected of irregularities in connection with an apparent deficit of 4,500 rubles of government money which is held in his account. Katya, desperately trying to save her father from dishonor, gets word from Mitya that he will give her the money if she comes to him alone, Mitya promising "to keep the secret religiously."

When Katya came to him, Mitya's first thought "was a—Karamazov one," to treat this "beauty" as a prostitute. But she also appeared to him beautiful "in another way . . . because she was noble . . . in all the grandeur of her generosity and sacrifice for her father." In contrast, Mitya thought of himself as a little animal, "a bug . . . a venomous spider." His feelings toward her comprised a mixture of hatred and love. His hatred for Katya, he tells Alyosha, was such as he never felt for any other woman. But it is the kind "which is only a hair's-breadth from love, the maddest love."

Katya's visit aroused a powerful sexual desire in Mitya. He was so excited by the "venomous thought" of possessing her that he nearly swooned "with suspense." Although Mitya gained mastery over his demon, his deep guilt begins at this point. It is as though by offering herself to him, Katya divined his hidden wish to enter into an impermissible relation with her. But Mitya curbed his desire, gave Katya the money (we should bear in mind that it is the money left him by his mother). After she leaves, Mitya drew his sword, nearly stabbing himself—"why, I don't know," he adds. Mitya's ability to control his Karamazov sensualism in this scene is a major test of his manhood, and *foreshadows that he will resist the other temptation, that of killing his father*. He was held back from taking Katya by—perhaps also despite—the thought that she was ready to surrender herself for the sake of her father.

However, soon afterward, Mitya yielded to another enticement. He took the 3,000 rubles which Katya asked him to post and spent half of the sum on his mistress figure, Grushenka (repeating his father's act in which Fyodor attempted to keep the dowry of Mitya's mother). At about the same time, he agreed to Katya's proposal or demand that they become engaged. (How this comes about, Dostoevsky-Mitya does not make clear).

The engagement takes place shortly after the incident in Mitya's room and immediately following the death of Katya's father. She offers to become Mitya's wife to save him from himself:

"I love you madly," she writes him, "even if you don't love me, never mind. Be my husband. Don't be afraid. I won't hamper you in any way. I will be your chattel. I will be the carpet under you feet. I want to love you for ever. I want to save you from yourself."

Mitya makes a form of resistance, writing Katya that she is now rich (having become an heiress on her father's death), whereas he was "only a stuck-up beggar." For some unexplained reason, Mitya sends his brother Ivan to her who thereupon falls in love with Katya. This "one stupid thing," he says later to Alyosha, "may be the saving of us all now."

Katya as the Possessive Mother

The identification of Katya with Mitya's mother lies above all in their attempt to dominate their men. Katya's authoritative character is suggested first by her outward appearance. Alyosha is struck "by the imperiousness, proud ease, and self-confidence of the haughty girl." Her love for Mitya is that of a commanding or pitying mother for a wayward son. She would be Mitya's "God," as she says. When Alyosha tells her that Mitya sends her his "compliments" (his manner of letting Katya know that her betrothal is off), she retorts:

"No, he won't recognize that I am his truest friend; he won't know me, and looks on me merely as a woman. . . . Let him feel ashamed of himself, let him be ashamed of other people's knowing [that he had not returned the money he owed her], but not of my knowing. He can tell God everything without shame . . . I want to save him for ever. Let him forget me as his betrothed."

The Pan-Slavic Mother Goddess is worshipped for her fruitbearing and yielding qualities, not for her beauty. She is generally identified with the good Russian earth and its earthy peasant folk. Katya, with her aristocratic pride, stern virtue, and possessiveness is a distortion of this Eastern Mother Goddess. She cannot produce because she cannot yield.

At one point, Katya seems almost ready to accept the role of Mitya's "friend" and "sister." When told that Mitya has gone to Grushenka, she exclaims:

"I've already decided, even if he marries that—creature . . . *even then I will not abandon him*. . . . I will watch over him all my life unceasingly. When he becomes unhappy with that woman, and that is bound to happen quite soon, let him come to me and he will find a friend, a sister. . . . Only a sister, of course, and so for ever; but he will learn at least that that sister is really his sister, who loves him and has sacrificed all her life to him."

Yet, in the same breath, she reverts to the tyrannical nature of her love:

> "I will gain my point. I will insist on his knowing me and con-
> fiding entirely in me, without reserve," she cried, in a sort of
> frenzy, "I will be a god to whom he can pray!"

at the trial, she relates the humiliating errand on which she came to Mitya. And the author comments that such self-immolation seemed incredible even "from such a self-willed and contemptuously proud girl, as she was." She herself confesses at the trial: "I tried to conquer him by my love. . . ."

Katya offers to sacrifice herself for Mitya. But she would *impose* her sacrifice on him, *would be his Mother-Savior by command.* Mitya senses this. He calls Katya "a woman of great wrath . . . Hard-headed creature," realizes that "she loves her own *virtue,* not me," that she wants "to sacrifice her life and destiny out of grati- tude," that her love for him is "more like revenge." The revenge consists in Katya's attempt to reform him, that is, to deprive him of the "bug" in himself which he enjoys. It is the threat of the mother engulfing the son by her all-possessive love.

Mitya keeps speaking of his "debt" to Katya and of his "dis- grace." On the manifest level, he is referring to the fact that he had squandered 1,500 of Katya's 3,000 rubles on a spree with Gru- shenka. At first, he heatedly resists revealing this fact:

> "I won't speak of that gentleman," he says at the trial, "because
> it would be a stain on my honour. The answer to the question
> where I got the money would expose me to far greater disgrace
> than the murder and robbing of my father, if I had murdered
> him."

When pressed, he reveals his "shame," stating that he stole the money, not from his father, "but from her . . . a noble creature, noblest of the noble." But "she has hated me ever so long, oh, ever so long . . . and hated me with good reason, good reason!" The "good reason" is that he asked her to come alone knowing that she was aware of and despised his debaucheries. Even after his en- gagement to her, Mitya was unable to curb his dissipations, indeed, carried them on "before the very eyes of his betrothed!" The "trag- edy" of it, he adds, is that "these lofty sentiments of hers are as sincere as a heavenly angel's." But Mitya did not want to reform. He would rather vanish into "his filthy back-alley, where he is at home and where he will sink in filth and stench at his own free will and with enjoyment."

Mitya makes desperate efforts to free himself from the "debt" to his surrogate "God"-mother. This, although Katya herself does not press him for the money, indeed, acts as if she did not care what he did with it. Furthermore, Mitya *could* get the money: Alyosha offers him 2,000 rubles and says that Ivan would give him another 1,000. Moreover, he could borrow from Grusha. But no! Mitya is obsessed with the feeling that *he can be rid of his "debt" to Katya only by giving her the money which he has inherited from his mother and which his father is withholding from him.* (Mitya's attempts to get the money from Samsonov, Lyagavy, Madame Khokhlakov are a wild-goose chase which invite failure.) And he wants no more than 3,000 rubles, although by his reckoning, his mother left him 28,000 rubles. If his father would give him 3,000 rubles, Mitya tells Alyosha, he would draw his soul "out of hell":

> "Let him give me back only three out of the twenty-eight thousand . . . For that three thousand—I give you my solemn word—I'll make an end of everything, and he shall hear nothing more of me. For the last time, I give him the chance to be a father."

Grushenka: The Hetaira-Magdalene

From this perspective, Grushenka is the lighter of Mitya's burdens. The conflict with his father over her is open and somewhat literal. Mitya is ready to accept all his rivals, except Fyodor. He is not jealous of the old merchant Samsonov, or of the Pole who, Mitya declares, has priority because he was her "first lover." It is of some significance that Mitya's attitude toward Grushenka is a transference of Katya's to him. As Katya was willing to accept any conditions if Mitya would agree to be her husband, so he declares:

> "I'll be her [Grusha's] husband if she deigns to have me, and when lovers come, I'll go into the next room. I'll clean her friends' goloshes, blow up their samovar, run their errands."

However, Mitya does not want to force his love on Grusha. And, it is his hope that she may be the means by which he can free himself from Katya. Her soft, voluptuous, noiseless movements contrast with Katya's bold and vigorous step, her simple "child-like good nature" with Katya's complex ironic consciousness.

Mitya speaks of Grusha's "infernal curves." Yet, the story does not have a single erotic scene between them. Even at his "wedding" with Grusha at Mokroe, Mitya does not go beyond kissing his beloved. Dostoevsky himself remarks that Grusha is Russian in that her beauty is only of the moment. Russian literature, as Berdyaev notes, does not know the erotic motifs of the West. It has no stories comparable to Tristan and Isolde or Romeo and Juliet. The attraction of Russian women (as of the Russian Mother Goddess) lies not in their seductiveness but in their earthy productivity.

Mitya's meeting with Grushenka at Mokroe is the poem of *The Brothers Karamazov*, the lovers' Dionysian song to life. For the

first and only time, the two are united, at one with "the people," the
Russian peasants, over whom they reign as King and Queen. It is
their Eden where all is love, kindness, forgiveness, and generosity.
To the rhythm of children's songs, Mitya, and his bride themselves
act like children. Everything—down to the language and mood—is
simple, elemental, and earthy. Here, all are equal (except for the
"foreigners," the Poles, who leave before the high point of the revel
is reached).

But it is a Karamazov-Eden, and the celebration takes on the
character of a delirious orgy. Mokroe is the scene of Mitya's and
Grushenka's "wedding." It takes place at about the same time when
the father is murdered and after Mitya thought he may have killed
his surrogate father Grigory. At this point, "society" steps in and
arrests Mitya.

Like many of Dostoevsky's women, Grushenka turns from the
hetaira to the madonna. Her transformation begins during Alyosha's
visit when his kindness frees her for a generous, overflowing love of
the "soul," becoming "more loving than we," as Alyosha puts it.
The change takes on a stable form after Mitya's arrest. Now, there
were

> signs of a spiritual transformation in her, and a steadfast, fine and
> humble determination that nothing could shake. . . . There was
> scarcely a trace of her former frivolity.

Through Grusha's love, Mitya declares, he has "become a man
himself."

Mitya's Need of the Two Women

Although Mitya states that Grusha has made "a man" of him, it
appears that she does not completely fulfill his needs. She is the
permissive figure who *accepts Mitya as he is*. But Mitya also needs
the authoritative, censorious conscience, especially since his father
lacks this quality altogether. Fyodor is a satyr figure, embodies an
amorphous, chaotic sensualism intent solely on the pursuit of pleasure. And Mitya has only a distant relation to Father Zosima,
Alyosha, and Ivan, the religious and rational superegos in the
novel.

This may explain why Mitya cannot and does not want to free
himself from Katya, why he kneels and prays "to Katya's image" in
Grusha's presence. When she produces the letter which virtually
condemns him, Mitya cries out:

> "We've hated each other for many things, Katya, but I swear, I
> swear I loved you even while I hated you, and you didn't love
> me!"

When, at the trial, Katya tells of her visit to Mitya and her bow to him, Mitya sobs: "Katya, why have you ruined me? . . . Now, I am condemned." Does her recital reactivate his incestuous desire for her? Does her attempt to save him again put him in her "debt"?

Even as Mitya turns towards Grushenka, he remains bound to Katya. Following the trial, he seems concerned only about seeing Katya. Alyosha tells her:

> "He needs you particularly just now . . . he keeps asking for you.
> . . . He realizes that he has injured you beyond reckoning. . . .
> He said, if she refuses to come, I shall be unhappy all my life."

When Katya appears in the doorway of his prison cell,

> a scared look came into his face. He turned pale, but a timid, pleading smile appeared on his lips at once, and with an irresistible impulse he held out both hands to Katya.

And now, the two confess their mutual tie. Katya tells him:

> "Love is over, Mitya! but the past is painfully dear to me. . . . I shall love you for ever, and you will love me; do you know that? Do you hear? Love me, love me all your life!" she cried, with a quiver almost of menace in her voice.

Mitya replies:

> "I shall love you . . . All my life! So it will be, so it will always be . . ."

He pleads with her that she forgive him for having wanted to humiliate her, for his desire to have "the proud aristocratic girl" appear as "the hetaira." His plea is met in Katya's final resignation, in her words to the rival Grushenka: "Forgive me . . . Don't be anxious, I'll save him for you."

In his book *Hamlet and Oedipus*, Ernest Jones gives examples of the mythic process of decomposition in which the tyrannical figure is broken up into several characters, some of whom may be veiled as beneficent. Applying this strategy, one may say that Dostoevsky-Mitya divide the mother figure into Katya and Grushenka. The decomposition may be due to Mitya's repressed feelings about his own mother who was apparently unconcerned about abandoning him when she left Fyodor. Mitya moves from the commanding goddess-mother to the yielding mistress-mother. In the end, he needs both: "the proud aristocratic girl and the hetaira." Grusha can only follow, but not guide. He needs both, moreover, for the mixture of elements in each. Grusha is submissive. Yet, in the scene with Katya, Mitya recognizes in her "the queen of all she-devils." Katya is defiant, haughty, and domineering. Yet, Alyosha notes that her face can beam "with spontaneous good-natured kindliness, and direct warmhearted sincerity." She would be Mitya's "God," but is also ready to sacrifice herself to help him. In the end, the two women figures tend to merge.

Mitya almost marries Katya and nearly kills Fyodor. Like Hamlet, he wrestles with the demon driving him to violate the primary taboos. Mitya too shows no hesitation to "act," except where it concerns Katya and Fyodor. His promise lies in his gradual awareness of the nature of his "debt" and guilt, awareness that his involvement with Katya was injurious to her and himself.

* * *

D. H. LAWRENCE

The Grand Inquisitor†

It is a strange experience, to examine one's reaction to a book over a period of years. I remember when I first read *The Brothers Karamazov*, in 1913, how fascinated yet unconvinced it left me. And I remember Middleton Murry saying to me: "Of course the whole clue to Dostoevsky is in that Grand Inquisitor story." And I remember saying: "Why? It seems to me just rubbish."

And it was true. The story seemed to me just a piece of showing off: a display of cynical-satanical pose which was simply irritating. The cynical-satanical pose always irritated me, and I could see nothing else in that black-a-vised Grand Inquisitor talking at Jesus at such length. I just felt it was all pose; he didn't really mean what he said; he was just showing off in blasphemy.

Since then I have read *The Brothers Karamazov* twice, and each time found it more depressing because, alas, more drearily true to life. At first it had been lurid romance. Now I read *The Grand Inquisitor* once more, and my heart sinks right through my shoes. I still see a trifle of cynical-satanical showing off. But under that I hear the final and unanswerable criticism of Christ. And it is a deadly, devastating summing up, unanswerable because borne out by the long experience of humanity. It is reality versus illusion, and the illusion was Jesus', while time itself retorts with the reality.

If there is any question: Who is the Grand Inquisitor?—then surely we must say it is Ivan himself. And Ivan is the thinking mind

† From D. H. Lawrence, *Selected Literary Criticism*, ed. by Anthony Beal (New York: Viking, 1961), pp. 233–41. Copyright 1936 by Frieda Lawrence; 1964 by the Estate of the late Frieda Lawrence Ravagli. All rights reserved. Reprinted by permission of The Viking Press, Inc., and by Laurence Pollinger Ltd. Originally published as the preface to *The Grand Inquisitor*, trans. S. S. Koteliansky, London, 1930.

of the human being in rebellion, thinking the whole thing out to the bitter end. As such he is, of course, identical with the Russian revolutionary of the thinking type. He is also, of course, Dostoevsky himself, in his thoughtful, as apart from his passional and inspirational self. Dostoevsky half hated Ivan. Yet, after all, Ivan is the greatest of the three brothers, pivotal. The passionate Dmitri and the inspired Alyosha are, at last, only offsets to Ivan.

And we cannot doubt that the Inquisitor speaks Dostoevsky's own final opinion about Jesus. The opinion is, baldly, this: Jesus, you are inadequate. Men must correct you. And Jesus in the end gives the kiss of acquiescence to the Inquisitor, as Alyosha does to Ivan. The two inspired ones recognize the inadequacy of their inspiration: the thoughtful one has to accept the responsibility of a complete adjustment.

We may agree with Dostoevsky or not, but we have to admit that his criticism of Jesus is the final criticism, based on the experience of two thousand years (he says fifteen hundred) and on a profound insight into the nature of mankind. Man can but be true to his own nature. No inspiration whatsoever will ever get him permanently beyond his limits.

And what are the limits? It is Dostoevsky's first profound question. What are the limits to the nature, not of Man in the abstract, but of men, mere men, everyday men?

The limits are, says the Grand Inquisitor, three. Mankind in the bulk can never be "free," because man on the whole makes three grand demands on life, and cannot endure unless these demands are satisfied.

1. He demands bread, and not merely as foodstuff, but as a miracle, given from the hand of God.
2. He demands mystery, the sense of the miraculous in life.
3. He demands somebody to bow down to, and somebody before whom all men shall bow down.

These three demands, for miracle, mystery and authority, prevent men from being "free." They are man's "weakness." Only a few men, the elect, are capable of abstaining from the absolute demand for bread, for miracle, mystery, and authority. These are the strong, and they must be as gods, to be able to be Christians fulfilling all the Christ-demand. The rest, the millions and millions of men throughout time, they are as babes or children or geese, they are too weak, "impotent, vicious, worthless and rebellious" even to be able to share out the earthly bread, if it is left to them.

This, then, is the Grand Inquisitor's summing up of the nature of mankind. The inadequacy of Jesus lies in the fact that Christianity is too difficult for men, the vast mass of men. It could only be realized by the few "saints" or heroes. For the rest, man is like a horse harnessed to a load he cannot possibly pull. "Hadst Thou respected him less, Thou wouldst have demanded less of him, and that would be nearer to love, for his burden would be lighter."

Christianity, then, is the ideal, but it is impossible. It is impossible because it makes demands greater than the nature of man can bear. And therefore, to get a livable, working scheme, some of the elect, such as the Grand Inquisitor himself, have turned round to "him," that other great Spirit, Satan, and have established Church and State on "him." For the Grand Inquisitor finds that to be able to live at all, mankind must be loved more tolerantly and more contemptuously than Jesus loved it, loved, for all that, more truly, since it is loved for itself, for what it is, and not for what it ought to be. Jesus loved mankind for what it ought to be, free and limitless. The Grand Inquisitor loves it for what it is, with all its limitations. And he contends his is the kinder love. And yet he says it is Satan. And Satan, he says at the beginning, means annihilation, and not-being.

As always in Dostoevsky, the amazing perspicacity is mixed with ugly perversity. Nothing is pure. His wild love for Jesus is mixed with perverse and poisonous hate of Jesus: his moral hostility to the devil is mixed with secret worship of the devil. Dostoevsky is always perverse, always impure, always an evil thinker and a marvelous seer.

Is it true that mankind demands, and will always demand, miracle, mystery, and authority? Surely it is true. Today, man gets his sense of the miraculous from science and machinery, radio, airplanes, vast ships, zeppelins, poison gas, artificial silk: these things nourish man's sense of the miraculous as magic did in the past. But now, man is master of the mystery, there are no occult powers. The same with mystery: medicine, biological experiment, strange feats of the psychic people, spiritualists, Christian scientists—it is all mystery. And as for authority, Russia destroyed the Tsar to have Lenin and the present mechanical despotism, Italy has the rationalized despotism of Mussolini, and England is longing for a despot.

Dostoevsky's diagnosis of human nature is simple and unanswerable. We have to submit, and agree that men are like that. Even over the question of sharing the bread, we have to agree that man is too weak, or vicious, or something, to be able to do it. He has to hand the common bread over to some absolute authority. Tsar or Lenin, to be shared out. And yet the mass of men are *incapable* of looking on bread as a mere means of sustenance, by which man sustains himself for the purpose of true living, true life being the "heavenly bread." It seems a strange thing that men, the mass of men, cannot understand that *life* is the great reality, that true living fills us with vivid life, "the heavenly bread," and earthly bread merely supports this. No, men cannot understand, never have understood that simple fact. They cannot see the distinction between bread, or property, money, and vivid life. They think that property and money are the same thing as vivid life. Only the few, the potential heroes or the "elect," can see the simple distinction. The mass *cannot* see it, and will never see it.

Dostoevsky was perhaps the first to realize this devastating truth, which Christ had not seen. A truth it is, none the less, and once recognized it will change the course of history. All that remains is for the elect to take charge of the bread—the property, the money —and then give it back to the masses as if it were really the gift of life. In this way, mankind might live happily, as the Inquisitor suggests. Otherwise, with the masses making the terrible mad mistake that money is life, and that therefore no one shall control the money, men shall be "free" to get what they can, we are brought to a condition of competitive insanity and ultimate suicide.

So far, well and good, Dostoevsky's diagnosis stands. But is it then to betray Christ and turn over to Satan if the elect should at last realize that instead of refusing Satan's three offers, the heroic Christian must now accept them? Jesus refused the three offers out of pride and fear: he wanted to be greater than these, and "above" them. But we now realize, no man, not even Jesus, is really "above" miracle, mystery, and authority. The one thing that Jesus is truly above, is the confusion between money and life. Money is not life, says Jesus, therefore you can ignore it and leave it to the devil.

Money is not life, it is true. But ignoring money and leaving it to the devil means handing over the great mass of men to the devil, for the mass of men *cannot* distinguish between money and life. It is hard to believe: certainly Jesus didn't believe it: and yet, as Dostoevsky and the Inquisitor point out, it is so.

Well, and what then? Must we therefore go over to the devil? After all, the whole of Christianity is not contained in the rejection of the three temptations. The essence of Christianity is a love of mankind. If a love of mankind entails accepting the bitter limitation of the mass of men, their inability to distinguish between money and life, then accept the limitation, and have done with it. Then take over from the devil the money (or bread), the miracle, and the sword of Caesar, and, for the love of mankind, give back to men the bread, with its wonder, and give them the miracle, the marvellous, and give them, in a hierarchy, someone, some men, in higher and higher degrees, to bow down to. Let them bow down, let them bow down *en masse*, for the mass, who do not understand the difference between money and life, should always bow down to the elect, who do.

And is that serving the devil? It is certainly not serving the spirit of annihilation and not-being. It is serving the great wholeness of mankind, and in that respect, it is Christianity. Anyhow, it is the service of Almighty God, who made men what they are, limited and unlimited.

Where Dostoevsky is perverse is in his making the old, old, wise governor of men a Grand Inquisitor. The recognition of the weakness of man has been a common trait in all great, wise rulers of people, from the Pharaohs and Darius through the great patient Popes of the early Church right down to the present day. They have known the weakness of men, and felt a certain tenderness. This is the spirit of all great government. But it was not the spirit of the Spanish Inquisition. The Spanish Inquisition in 1500 was a newfangled thing, peculiar to Spain, with her curious death-lust and her bullying, and, strictly, a Spanish-political instrument, not Catholic at all, but rabidly national. The Spanish Inquisition actually was diabolic. It could not have produced a Grand Inquisitor who put Dostoevsky's sad questions to Jesus. And the man who put those sad questions to Jesus could not possibly have been a Spanish Inquisitor. He could not possibly have burnt a hundred people in an *auto-da-fé*. He would have been too wise and far-seeing.

So that, in this respect, Dostoevsky showed his epileptic and slightly criminal perversity. The man who feels a certain tenderness for mankind in its weakness or limitation is not therefore diabolic. The man who realizes that Jesus asked too much of the mass of men, in asking them to choose between earthly and heavenly bread, and to judge between good and evil, is not therefore satanic. Think how difficult it is to know the difference between good and evil! Why, sometimes it is evil to be good. And how is the ordinary man to understand that? He can't. The extraordinary men have to understand it for him. And is that going over to the devil? Or think of the difficulty in choosing between the earthly and heavenly bread. Lenin, surely a pure soul, rose to great power simply to give men—what? The earthly bread. And what was the result? Not only did they lose the heavenly bread, but even the earthly bread disappeared out of wheat-producing Russia. It is most strange. And all the socialists and the generous thinkers of today, what are they striving for? The same: to share out more evenly the earthly bread. Even *they*, who are practicing Christianity *par excellence*, cannot properly choose between the heavenly and earthly bread. For the poor, they choose the earthly bread, and once more the heavenly bread is lost: and once more, as soon as it is really chosen, the earthly bread begins to disappear. It is a great mystery. But today, the most passionate believers in Christ believe that all you have to do is to struggle to give earthly bread (good houses, good sanitation, etc.) to the poor, and that is in itself the heavenly bread. But it isn't. Especially for the poor, it isn't. It is for them the loss of heavenly bread. And the poor are the vast majority. Poor things, how everybody hates them today! For benevolence is a form of hate.

What then is the heavenly bread? Every generation must answer for itself. But the heavenly bread is life, is living. Whatever makes life vivid and delightful is the heavenly bread. And the earthly bread must come as a by-product of the heavenly bread. The vast mass will never understand this. Yet it is the essential truth of Christianity, and of life itself. The few will understand. Let them take the responsibility.

Again, the Inquisitor says that it is a weakness in men, that they must have miracle, mystery and authority. But is it? Are they not bound up in our emotions, always and for ever, these three demands of miracle, mystery and authority? If Jesus cast aside miracle in the Temptation, still there is miracle again in the Gospels. And if Jesus refused the earthly bread, still he said: "In my Father's house are many mansions." And for authority: "Why call ye me Lord, Lord, and do not the things which I say?"

The thing Jesus was trying to do was to supplant physical emotion by moral emotion. So that earthly bread becomes, in a sense, immoral, as it is to many refined people today. The Inquisitor sees that this is the mistake. The earthly bread must in itself be the miracle, and be bound up with the miracle.

And here, surely, he is right. Since man began to think and to feel vividly, seed-time and harvest have been the two great sacred periods of miracle, rebirth, and rejoicing. Easter and harvest-home are festivals of the earthly bread, and they are festivals which go to the roots of the soul. For it is the earthly bread as a miracle, a yearly miracle. All the old religions saw it: the Catholic still sees it, by the Mediterranean. And this is not weakness. This is *truth*. The rapture of the Easter kiss, in old Russia, is intimately bound up with the springing of the seed and the first footstep of the new earthly bread. It is the rapture of the Easter kiss which makes the bread worth eating. It is the absence of the Easter kiss which makes the Bolshevist bread barren, dead. They eat dead bread, now.

The earthly bread is leavened with the heavenly bread. The heavenly bread is life, is contact, and is consciousness. In sowing the seed man has his contact with earth, with sun and rain: and he *must not* break the contact. In the awareness of the springing of the corn he has his ever-renewed consciousness of miracle, wonder, and mystery: the wonder of creation, procreation, and re-creation, following the mystery of death and the cold grave. It is the grief of Holy Week and the delight of Easter Sunday. And man must not, must not lose this supreme state of consciousness out of himself, or he has lost the best part of him. Again, the reaping and the harvest are another contact, with earth and sun, a rich touch of the cosmos, a living stream of activity, and then the contact with harvesters, and the joy of harvest-home. All this is life, life, it is the heavenly bread which we eat in the course of getting the earthly bread. Work is, or should be, our heavenly bread of activity, contact and consciousness. All work that is not this, is anathema. True, the work is hard; there is the sweat of the brow. But what of it? In decent proportion, this is life. The sweat of the brow is the heavenly butter.

I think the older Egyptians understood this, in the course of their long and marvelous history. I think that probably, for thousands of years, the masses of the Egyptians were happy, in the hierarchy of the State.

Miracle and mystery run together, they merge. Then there is the third thing, authority. The word is bad: a policeman has authority, and no one bows down to him. The Inquisitor means: "that which men bow down to." Well, they bowed down to Caesar, and they bowed down to Jesus. They will bow down, first, as the Inquisitor saw, to the one who has the power to control the bread.

The bread, the earthly bread, while it is being reaped and grown, it is life. But once it is harvested and stored, it becomes a commodity, it becomes riches. And then it becomes a danger. For men think, if they only possessed the hoard, they need not work; which means, really, they need not live. And that is the real blasphemy. For while we live we must live, we must not wither or rot inert.

So that ultimately men bow down to the man, or group of men, who can and dare take over the hoard, the store of bread, the riches, to distribute it among the people again. The lords, the givers of bread. How profound Dostoevsky is when he says that the people will forget that it is their own bread which is being given back to them. While they keep their own bread, it is not much better than stone to them—inert possessions. But given back to them from the great Giver, it is divine once more, it has the quality of miracle to make it taste well in the mouth and in the belly.

Men bow down to the lord of bread, first and foremost. For, by knowing the difference between earthly and heavenly bread, he is able calmly to distribute the earthly bread, and to give it, for the commonalty, the heavenly taste which they can never give it. That is why, in a democracy, the earthly bread loses its taste, the salt loses its savour, and there is no one to bow down to.

It is not man's weakness that he needs someone to bow down to. It is his nature, and his strength, for it puts him into touch with far, far greater life than if he stood alone. All life bows to the sun. But the sun is very far away to the common man. It needs someone to bring it to him. It needs a lord: what the Christians call one of the elect, to bring the sun to the common man, and put the sun in his heart. The sight of a true lord, a noble, a nature-hero puts the sun into the heart of the ordinary man, who is no hero, and therefore cannot know the sun direct.

This is one of the real mysteries. As the Inquisitor says, the mystery of the elect is one of the inexplicable mysteries of Christianity, just as the lord, the natural lord among men, is one of the inexplicable mysteries of humanity throughout time. We must accept the mystery, that's all.

But to do so is not diabolic.

And Ivan need not have been so tragic and satanic. He had made a discovery about men, which was due to be made. It was the rediscovery of a fact which was known universally almost till the end of the eighteenth century, when the illusion of the perfectibility of men, of all men, took hold of the imagination of the civilized nations. It was an illusion. And Ivan has to make a restatement of the old truth, that most men *cannot* choose between good and evil, because it is so extremely difficult to know which is which, especially in crucial cases: and that most men *cannot* see the difference between life-values and money-values: they can only see money-values; even nice simple people who *live* by the life-values, kind and natural, yet can only estimate value in terms of money. So let the specially gifted few make the decision between good and evil, and establish the life-values against the money-values. And let the many accept the decision, with gratitude, and bow down to the few, in the hierarchy. What is there diabolical or satanic in that? Jesus kisses the Inquisitor: Thank you, you are right, wise old man! Alyosha kisses Ivan: Thank you, brother, you are right, you take a burden off me! So why should Dostoevsky drag in Inquisitors and *autos-da-fé* and Ivan wind up so morbidly suicidal? Let them be glad they've found the truth again.

ALBERT CAMUS

The Rejection of Salvation†

If the romantic rebel extols evil and the individual, this does not mean that he sides with mankind, but merely with himself. Dandyism, of whatever kind, is always dandyism in relation to God. The individual, in so far as he is a created being, can oppose himself only to the Creator. He has need of God, with whom he carries on a kind of gloomy flirtation. Armand Hoog[1] rightly says that, despite its Nietzschean atmosphere, God is not yet dead even in romantic literature. Damnation, so clamorously demanded, is only a clever trick played on God. But with Dostoevsky the description

† From *The Rebel* by Albert Camus, trans. by Anthony Bower (New York: Knopf, 1956), pp. 55–61. Copyright © 1953 by Albert Camus, and 1956 by Alfred A. Knopf, Inc. Reprinted by permission of the publisher, and of Hamish Hamilton Ltd.
1. *Les Petits Romantiques.*

of rebellion goes a step farther. Ivan Karamazov sides with mankind and stresses human innocence. He affirms that the death sentence which hangs over them is unjust. Far from making a plea for evil, his first impulse, at least, is to plead for justice, which he ranks above the divinity. Thus he does not absolutely deny the existence of God. He refutes Him in the name of a moral value. The romantic rebel's ambition was to talk to God as one equal to another. Evil was the answer to evil, pride the answer to cruelty. Vigny's ideal, for example, is to answer silence with silence. Obviously, the point is to raise oneself to the level of God, which already is blasphemy. But there is no thought of disputing the power or position of the deity. The blasphemy is reverent, since every blasphemy is, ultimately, a participation in holiness.

With Ivan, however, the tone changes. God, in His turn, is put on trial. If evil is essential to divine creation, then creation is unacceptable. Ivan will no longer have recourse to this mysterious God, but to a higher principle—namely, justice. He launches the essential undertaking of rebellion, which is that of replacing the reign of grace by the reign of justice. He simultaneously begins the attack on Christianity. The romantic rebels broke with God Himself, on the principle of hatred. Ivan explicitly rejects the mystery and, consequently, God, on the principle of love. Only love can make us consent to the injustice done to Martha, to the exploitation of workers, and, finally, to the death of innocent children.

"If the suffering of children," says Ivan, "serves to complete the sum of suffering necessary for the acquisition of truth, I affirm from now onward that truth is not worth such a price." Ivan rejects the basic interdependence, introduced by Christianity, between suffering and truth. Ivan's most profound utterance, the one which opens the deepest chasms beneath the rebel's feet, is his *even if*: "I would persist in my indignation even if I were wrong." Which means that even if God existed, even if the mystery cloaked a truth, even if the starets Zosima were right, Ivan would not admit that truth should be paid for by evil, suffering, and the death of innocents. Ivan incarnates the refusal of salvation. Faith leads to immortal life. But faith presumes the acceptance of the mystery and of evil, and resignation to injustice. The man who is prevented by the suffering of children from accepting faith will certainly not accept eternal life. Under these conditions, even if eternal life existed, Ivan would refuse it. He rejects this bargain. He would accept grace only unconditionaally, and that is why he makes his own conditions. Rebellion wants all or nothing. "All the knowledge in the world is not worth a child's tears." Ivan does not say that there is no truth. He says that if truth does exist, it can only be unacceptable. Why? Because it is unjust. The struggle between truth and justice is begun here for the first time; and it will never end. Ivan, by nature a solitary and therefore a moralist, will satisfy himself with a kind of metaphysical Don Quixotism. But a few decades more and an immense political conspiracy will attempt to prove that justice is truth.

In addition, Ivan is the incarnation of the refusal to be the only one saved. He throws in his lot with the damned and, for their sake, rejects eternity. If he had faith, he could, in fact, be saved, but others would be damned and suffering would continue. There is no possible salvation for the man who feels real compassion. Ivan will continue to put God in the wrong by doubly rejecting faith as he would reject injustice and privilege. One step more and from *All or Nothing* we arrive at *Everyone or No One*.

This extreme determination, and the attitude that it implies, would have sufficed for the romantics. But Ivan,[2] even though he also gives way to dandyism, really lives his problems, torn between the negative and the affirmative. From this moment onward, he accepts the consequences. If he rejects immortality, what remains for him? Life in its most elementary form. When the meaning of life has been suppressed, there still remains life. "I live," says Ivan, "in spite of logic." And again: "If I no longer had any faith in life, if I doubted a woman I loved, or the universal order of things, if I were persuaded, on the contrary, that everything was only an infernal and accursed chaos—even then I would want to live." Ivan will live, then, and will love as well "without knowing why." But to live is also to act. To act in the name of what? If there is no immortality, then there is neither reward nor punishment. "I believe that there is no virtue without immortality." And also: "I only know that suffering exists, that no one is guilty, that everything is connected, that everything passes away and equals out." But if there is no virtue, there is no law: "Everything is permitted."

With this "everything is permitted" the history of contemporary nihilism really begins. The romantic rebellion did not go so far. It limited itself to saying, in short, that everything was not permitted, but that, through insolence, it allowed itself to do what was forbidden. With the Karamazovs, on the contrary, the logic of indignation turned rebellion against itself and confronted it with a desperate contradiction. The essential difference is that the romantics allowed themselves moments of complacence, while Ivan compelled himself to do evil so as to be coherent. He would not allow himself to be good. Nihilism is not only despair and negation but, above all, the desire to despair and to negate. The same man who so violently took the part of innocence, who trembled at the suffering of a child, who wanted to see "with his own eyes" the lamb lie down with the lion, the victim embrace his murderer, from the moment that he rejects divine coherence and tries to discover his own rule

---

2. It is worth noting that Ivan is, in a certain way, Dostoevsky, who is more at ease in this role than in the role of Alyosha.

of life, recognizes the legitimacy of murder. Ivan rebels against a murderous God; but from the moment that he begins to rationalize his rebellion, he deduces the law of murder. If all is permitted, he can kill his father or at least allow him to be killed. Long reflection on the condition of mankind as people sentenced to death only leads to the justification of crime. Ivan simultaneously hates the death penalty (describing an execution, he says furiously: "His head fell, in the name of divine grace") and condones crime, in principle. Every indulgence is allowed the murderer, none is allowed the executioner. This contradiction, which Sade swallowed with ease, chokes Ivan Karamazov.

He pretends to reason, in fact, as though immortality did not exist, while he only goes so far as to say that he would refuse it even if it did exist. In order to protest against evil and death, he deliberately chooses to say that virtue exists no more than does immortality and to allow his father to be killed. He consciously accepts his dilemma; to be virtuous and illogical, or logical and criminal. His prototype, the devil, is right when he whispers: "You are going to commit a virtuous act and yet you do not believe in virtue; that is what angers and torments you." The question that Ivan finally poses, the question that constitutes the real progress achieved by Dostoevsky in the history of rebellion, is the only one in which we are interested here: can one live and stand one's ground in a state of rebellion?

Ivan allows us to guess his answer: one can live in a state of rebellion only by pursuing it to the bitter end. What is the bitter end of metaphysical rebellion? Metaphysical revolution. The master of the world, after his legitimacy has been contested, must be overthrown. Man must occupy his place. "As God and immortality do not exist, the new man is permitted to become God." But what does becoming God mean? It means, in fact, recognizing that everything is permitted and refusing to recognize any other law but one's own. Without it being necessary to develop the intervening arguments, we can see that to become God is to accept crime (a favorite idea of Dostoevsky's intellectuals). Ivan's personal problem is, then, to know if he will be faithful to his logic and if, on the grounds of an indignant protest against innocent suffering, he will accept the murder of his father with the indifference of a man-god. We know his solution: Ivan allows his father to be killed. Too profound to be satisfied with appearances, too sensitive to perform the deed himself, he is content to allow it to be done. But he goes mad. The man who could not understand how one could love one's neighbor cannot understand either how one can kill him. Caught between unjustifiable virtue and unacceptable crime, consumed with pity and incapable of love, a recluse deprived of the benefits of cynicism, this man of supreme intelligence is killed by contradiction. "My mind is of this world," he said; "what good is it to try to understand what is not of this world?" But he lived only for what is not of this world, and his proud search for the absolute is precisely what removed him from the world of which he loved no part.

The fact that Ivan was defeated does not obviate the fact that once the problem is posed, the consequence must follow: rebellion is henceforth on the march toward action. This has already been demonstrated by Dostoevsky, with prophetic intensity, in his legend of the Grand Inquisitor. Ivan, finally, does not distinguish the creator from his creation. "It is not God whom I reject," he says, "it is creation." In other words, it is God the father, indistinguishable from what He has created.[3] His plot to usurp the throne, therefore, remains completely moral. He does not want to reform anything in creation. But creation being what it is, he claims the right to free himself morally and to free all the rest of mankind with him. On the other hand, from the moment when the spirit of rebellion, having accepted the concept of "everything is permitted" and "everyone or no one," aims at reconstructing creation in order to assert the sovereignty and divinity of man, and from the moment when metaphysical rebellion extends itself from ethics to politics, a new undertaking, of incalculable import, begins, which also springs, we must note, from the same nihilism. Dostoevsky, the prophet of the new religion, had foreseen and announced it: "If Alyosha had come to the conclusion that neither God nor immorality existed, he would immediately have become an atheist and a socialist. For socialism is not only a question of the working classes; it is above all, in its contemporary incarnation, a question of atheism, a question of the tower of Babel, which is constructed without God's help, not to reach to the heavens, but to bring the heavens down to earth."[4]

After that, Alyosha can, in fact, treat Ivan with compassion as a "real simpleton." The latter only made an attempt at self-control and failed. Others will appear, with more serious intentions, who, on the basis of the same despairing nihilism, will insist on ruling the world. These are the Grand Inquisitors who imprison Christ and come to tell Him that His method is not correct, that universal happiness cannot be achieved by the immediate freedom of choosing between good and evil, but by the domination and unification of the world. The first step is to conquer and rule. The kingdom of heaven will, in fact, appear on earth, but it will be ruled over by men—a mere handful to begin with, who will be the Caesars, because they were the first to understand—and later, with time, by all men. The unity of all creation will be achieved by every possible means, since everything is permitted. The Grand Inquisitor is old

3. Ivan allows his father to be killed and thus chooses a direct attack against nature for procreation. Moreover, this particular father is infamous. The repugnant figure of old Karamazov is con- tinually coming between Ivan and the God of Alyosha.

4. These questions (God and immortality) are the same questions that socialism poses, but seen from another angle.

and tired, for the knowledge he possesses is bitter. He knows that men are lazy rather than cowardly and that they prefer peace and death to the liberty of discerning between good and evil. He has pity, a cold pity, for the silent prisoner whom history endlessly deceives. He urges him to speak, to recognize his misdeeds, and, in one sense, to approve the actions of the Inquisitors and of the Caesars. But the prisoner does not speak. The enterprise will continue, therefore, without him; he will be killed. Legitimacy will come at the end of time, when the kingdom of men is assured. "The affair has only just begun, it is far from being terminated, and the world has many other things to suffer, but we shall achieve our aim, we shall be Caesar, and then we shall begin to think about universal happiness."

By then the prisoner has been executed; the Grand Inquisitors reign alone, listening to "the profound spirit, the spirit of destruction and death." The Grand Inquisitors proudly refuse freedom and the bread of heaven and offer the bread of this earth without freedom. "Come down from the cross and we will believe in you," their police agents are already crying on Golgotha. But He did not come down and, even, at the most tortured moment of His agony, He protested to God at having been forsaken. There are, thus, no longer any proofs, but faith and the mystery that the rebels reject and at which the Grand Inquisitors scoff. Everything is permitted and centuries of crime are prepared in that cataclysmic moment. From Paul to Stalin, the popes who have chosen Caesar have prepared the way for Caesars who quickly learn to despise popes. The unity of the world, which was not achieved with God, will henceforth be attempted in defiance of God.

But we have not yet reached that point. For the moment, Ivan offers us only the tortured face of the rebel plunged in the abyss, incapable of action, torn between the idea of his own innocence and the desire to kill. He hates the death penalty because it is the image of the human condition, and, at the same time, he is drawn to crime. Because he has taken the side of mankind, solitude is his lot. With him the rebellion of reason culminates in madness.

NATHAN ROSEN

Style and Structure in *The Brothers Karamazov* (The Grand Inquisitor and the Russian Monk) †

The two crucial sections of *The Brothers Karamazov*, according to Dostoevsky, are Books V and VI, centering on the Grand Inquisitor and the Russian monk respectively. Both these sections,

† From *Russian Literature Triquarterly*, I (1971), 1, 352–65. Reprinted by permission of *Russian Literature Triquarterly* and Ardis. (Footnotes omitted.)

which Dostoevsky characterized in his letters as "culminating points," occur one-third of the way through the novel, so they do not culminate in anything except the main action of the novel. They are "culminating points" only as the *pro* and *contra* of an ideological debate, crystallizing the main issues in the novel. Such ideological debates can also be found at the beginning of the Book of Job and Goethe's *Faust*, works specifically mentioned in *The Brothers Karamazov*. Dostoevsky's ideological debate differs sharply in certain respects.

First, the debate takes place on earth, and God and Satan are replaced by mortals; we are in the modern world in which heaven and hell are within us. Second, the two protagonists do not confront each other but appear in successive books; they do not really "talk" to one another. (Alyosha Karamazov is the more or less passive listener in each case.) Third, the debate is, according to all critics, one-sided, with the victory clearly won by the Grand Inquisitor. And finally, critical attention has been concentrated almost entirely on the Grand Inquisitor; "The Russian Monk" section has been ignored except by the theologically minded. This is all the more remarkable and unjust since Dostoevsky declares that *both* are "culminating points" in the novel. His statement should be respected and given the attention it deserves. How strange that Dostoevsky should compose a debate in which Satan wins so obviously! Why include the debate at all? When critics like Rozanov, Camus, D. H. Lawrence, and Rahv ignore this question, they not only misunderstand the Grand Inquisitor and the Russian Monk, but the whole novel as well.

The misinterpretation began with Rozanov's celebrated book, *The Legend of the Grand Inquisitor*, first published in 1894, with a third edition in 1906. Rozanov explained that although "The Grand Inquisitor" is "only an episode . . . its connection with the plot of this novel is so weak that one can study it as a separate work." To make up for this structural weakness in the novel, however, "there is an inner connection: The Legend constitutes the essence of the whole work, which is merely grouped around it like variations on its theme." Philip Rahv, writing sixty years later, does not even trouble to mention the novel: "The Legend," he says, "lends itself to analysis, quite apart from its local narrative setting, as a unique essay in the philosophy of history." It is therefore not surprising to find "The Grand Inquisitor" published separately as a modern "relevant" classic whose life and meaning are independent of the novel. For such readers "The Grand Inquisitor" becomes identical with *The Brothers Karamazov*, the very essence of it—precisely what Rozanov maintains. And the very opposite of what Dostoevsky sought to achieve in writing the novel: a defense of Christianity as the only true way of life in our time.

Let us examine two implications in Rozanov's argument. If, as he says, "The Legend" is the essence of the whole novel, one must conclude that it could have been inserted anywhere in the novel without suffering any important change in meaning. As a matter of fact, Rozanov fails to notice just where "The Legend" is placed. It occurs immediately after Ivan Karamazov shows his strength of will by breaking off with Katerina Ivanovna, who wishes to be his "grand inquisitor"; and he is about to order champagne "to celebrate my first hour of freedom." He is therefore one of the elect, capable of free choice, and unlike the submissive majority. Nor does Rozanov note what follows "The Legend": the meeting with Smerdyakov in which Ivan tacitly authorizes the murder of the father. After Ivan's noble obsession with the suffering of mankind it is surprising that he should add to that suffering by killing his father. This becomes a damaging commentary on the meaning of "The Grand Inquisitor." And Ivan's personal vindictiveness about his father is doubled or reinforced by Smerdyakov's. Thus the context of "The Grand Inquisitor"—what precedes and what follows it—adds to its meaning.

A second implication of Rozanov's argument: if "The Legend" is the essence of the novel, then the author of "The Legend"—Ivan Karamazov—must be the central character in the novel. Rozanov says this without any qualification. Yet the novel is entitled *The Brothers Karamazov*; Zosima bows before Mitya, not Ivan; and indeed Mitya is the major figure in the action of the novel. Ivan is only one element. To concentrate upon him means to disregard the major part of the novel.

Rozanov and other critics could have regained their perspective if they had reminded themselves that the novel has *two* "culminating points" and one of them is "The Russian Monk." But they have unanimously chosen to disregard this section, dismissing it as mawkish and unctuous, a sentimental lyrical effusion, pallid, abstract, lacking in drama. The most charitable evaluation was made by E. H. Carr: "Ivan's denunciation of God remains more powerful and cogent than the defense which is put into the mouths of Zosima and Alyosha." Other critics, like Mochulsky and Wasiolek, silently pass over the artistic weaknesses of "The Russian Monk" but draw upon it as a reservoir of Dostoevsky's favorite ideas on religion. Religious commentators have, of course, worked thoroughly over this section, treating its ideas with veneration but ignoring its relation to the novel.

Could Dostoevsky have known so much less than his critics? Could he have supposed that "The Russian Monk" was an adequate, i.e., artistically persuasive refutation of the views of the Grand Inquisitor? And if it was not an adequate refutation, why did he retain it? These questions can best be answered by examining "The Russian Monk" and "The Grand Inquisitor" from an artistic standpoint rather than as intellectual debating propositions.

Ivan's arraignment of God is found in the three chapters "The Brothers Make Friends," "Rebellion," and "The Grand Inquisitor." These chapters are overwhelming in their intellectual and artistic power, and Dostoevsky was justly proud of what he had achieved. "My hero," he remarked, "takes a theme which *in my opinion* [Dostoevsky's emphasis] is irrefutable: the senselessness of the suffering of children, and draws from it the absurdity of the whole of historical actuality." Ivan's indictment is therefore irrefutable as an intellectual position. As to the artistic merit of these chapters Dostoevsky was also proud: "In all Europe," he exulted, "there have been no expressions of atheism, past or present, as powerful as mine."

Not only is the intellectual argument irrefutable, but it is vividly dramatized with the aid of actual newspaper reports on Turkish atrocities and horror stories of every kind. When Ivan relates how a Russian general orders a serf boy to be torn to pieces by hunting dogs while the boy's mother is forced to watch, Alyosha has a traumatic experience; the meek apostle of Zosima cries out that the general should be shot! The journalistic reports are followed by a vivid and startling drama: the confrontation between Christ and the Grand Inquisitor in the dungeons of the Inquisition. The confrontation reaches a climax when Christ silently kisses the Inquisitor and departs; Christ's mission on earth—to correct the work of the Grand Inquisitor—is left unfinished, and the Inquisitor is free to carry on his diabolic work of stamping out freedom in the world. What could be more crushing to Father Zosima's (and Dostoevsky's) philosophy? Pobedonostsev, the head of the Russian church, was so disturbed by the power of the Grand Inquisitor's arguments that he anxiously wrote Dostoevsky to find out what refutation was possible. (*The Brothers Karamazov* was being published serially in a conservative magazine.) Dostoevsky replied that the refutation would appear that very month (August, 1879) under the title "The Russian Monk."

Although Dostoevsky had worked longer on this section than any other (more than three months) he was worried about its success. "Will it be adequate as a refutation?" he wrote Pobedonostsev. "Especially as the answer is not direct, not a point-by-point refutation of what had been said previously in "The Grand Inquisitor" and before, but only indirectly . . . so to say, in an artistic picture." There was also the problem of the "absurdity" of Zosima's views for the modern reader. And there were "artistic obligations: I had to present a modest and august figure, whereas life is full of the comic and is only august when looked at from within, so that willy-nilly, due to the demands of art, I had to deal in the biography of my monk with the most vulgar and common-place aspects so as not to weaken artistic realism."

Nevertheless there is little that is realistic in "The Russian Monk." On the level of intellectual argument there is, as Dostoevsky admitted, no attempt at a refutation since no intellectual refutation was possible. The refutation is indirect, "an artistic picture." It consisted originally of a series of three narratives entitled "From the Life (*Zhitie*) of the Deceased Monk and Priest, the Elder Zosima." Dostoevsky later added a second part, "Conversations and Teachings of the Elder Zosima."

"The Russian Monk" is indeed a saint's life (*zhitie*), that is, it is not a reliable factual biography, but a sort of dramatized sermon, the most popular genre in old Russian literature. The *zhitie* depicted the life and teachings of a holy person, usually idealized, with standardized and selected details to make the moral lesson as striking as possible. Events in the holy person's life that diverged from the didactic goal were omitted. If necessary elements in his life were lacking, they would be added. Legends and miracles were associated with the saint, testifying to his spiritual power. The life was usually written by disciples of the saint. When Zosima's biography, set down by his disciple Alyosha, is described as a *zhitie*, we must be prepared (as Alyosha himself was) for the introduction of the miraculous.

The second half of "The Russian Monk," a sermon, was also in keeping with the *zhitie* since it presented the *teachings* of the saint.

Let us examine the three narratives related by Zosima about his life before his conversion.

The first story is about Markel, Zosima's elder brother, an atheist who underwent a death-bed conversion at Easter. Nothing is said about his character or his past that could supply the basis for the sudden conversion. It remains a mystery.

The second story has to do with a duel contrived by Zosima before his conversion. He wishes to revenge himself on an innocent young man. The night before the duel Zosima savagely beats up his own orderly. On the morning of the duel he recalls the beating with shame, recalls Markel's conversion, and refuses to duel. There is no explanation of the change in his behavior between night and morning. It remains a mystery.

The last story is a confession made to Zosima by a mysterious stranger. Rebuffed by a girl he loved, the stranger had killed the girl and had managed to plant incriminating evidence on a servant who died soon after. The murderer then married, had children, and lived an irreproachable life as father, husband, and citizen. "And after that the punishment began." He began to suffer an intolerable isolation, walled off even from members of his family. This isolation reminds the reader of Raskolnikov after the murder of the pawnbroker,[1] but there is an important difference. Raskolnikov's reaction can be understood from the strength of his religious background, his close ties with his mother and sister, his obsession with the suffering of the poor. But nothing of this sort—nothing about the past or nature of the mysterious stranger—is introduced to make plausible his growing isolation. It remains a mystery.

In all three stories what could have made the conversions persuasive—psychological motivation—is missing. We are given not so much an artistic picture as a frame without a picture. And it is equally clear that this omission was deliberate. It is as if Dostoevsky wished to emphasize mystery as a dimension of human experience, even if this had to be done at the expense of the "artistic realism" which had so preoccupied him in his letter to Pobedonostsev. Yet, given the genre of the *zhitie*, the lack of realism could be expected.

Between the first and second of these stories is a short essay entitled "Of the Holy Scriptures in the Life of Father Zosima." This essay deals principally with the influence on the young Zosima of the Old Testament stories, especially the Book of Job. Two things are noteworthy in his account of the Book of Job: he retells the story in great detail, and he leaves much out. What is left out is revealing: Job's vehement insistence on his own innocence, his demand for a personal encounter with God to plead his innocence, and God's reply as the Voice in the Whirlwind. That is to say, Job's integrity and independence, his intellectual and spiritual energy—which in the end win God's favor—these are left out. Zosima's own emphasis is quite different, and rather surprising. He discusses Job's children, whom Satan destroyed as part of the testing of Job, and then the new children that Job received at the end:

> What mysteries are solved and revealed; God raises Job again, gives him wealth again. Many years pass by, and he has other children and loves them. But how could he love those new ones when those first children are no more, when he has lost them. Remembering them, how could he be fully happy with those new ones, however dear the new ones might be? But he could, he could. It's the great mystery of human life that old grief passes gradually into quiet tender joy.

The emphasis throughout is on children, perhaps as an indirect answer to Ivan's obsession with the suffering of children, but note how Zosima has shifted the emphasis: from the theological question of why Job must suffer and why must his children die (to vindicate God before Satan), Zosima shifts to a psychological question: how can Job recover from the loss of his first children and love the new children which God has provided for him? It turns out

---

1. In *Crime and Punishment* [*Editor*].

that this too is a mystery, the mystery of the healing power of time upon sorrow, but this mystery is at any rate psychologically valid, attested to by experience.

Thus Zosima offers as a sacred remembrance from his childhood a version of the Book of Job carefully pruned of Job's defiance and intellectual challenge of God, and also of God's reaction to this challenge, which involves the power of coercion. There is also the mystery of human nature whereby Job manages to forget his first children and love the new children. This essay easily blends into the three stories that emphasize the mystery of conversion, the enigma of human nature.

The second half of "The Russian Monk" consists of the teachings of Zosima: a long abstract series of exhortations, a rapturous, poetic, and at times sentimental sermon. Since it is abstract, it has even less artistic effect than the three stories related by Zosima. By adding this sermon, did Dostoevsky intend to strengthen the refutation he had made in the three stories?

At first glance the answer would seem to be no. I have mentioned, however, that Dostoevsky worked longer on "The Russian Monk" than on any other section of the novel. In exasperation he wrote his wife: "For a long time this Elder has been sitting on my neck, from the very beginning of the summer he has tormented me." The difficulty does not seem to be in theme or construction but in style. In creating Zosima's life and teachings Dostoevsky labored to reproduce the style of the *zhitie*. "This chapter is rapturous and poetical," wrote Dostoevsky to his editor. "The prototype [for Zosima] was in some teachings of Tikhon Zadonsky, and the naiveté of the exposition was taken from the book on the wanderings of Father Parfeny." Dostoevsky's concern with style is also clear in another part of his letter:

> Even though I am in full agreement with the ideas that he [Zosima] expresses, if I had to express them personally with my own voice, I would have done so in a different form and in different words. He *couldn't* have used other words or spoken in a *different spirit* than what I have given him. Otherwise he would not have been an artistically created person. . . . I have taken this person and figure from old Russian monks and saints: in deep humility he holds limitless, naive hopes for the future of Russia.

We are indebted to two scholars, Pletnev and Komarovich, for intensive studies of Dostoevsky's sources for the style of "The Russian Monk." In addition to Zadonsky and Parfeny, Dostoevsky made use of Biblical texts, recollections of his visit to the saintly elder Amvrosy at the Optina Pustin monastery, various lives of the saints, etc. In short, a mosaic of old Russian literary style. Even Parfeny's memoirs, although written in the nineteenth century, fol-

low the traditions of old Russian literature. Yet the question must
be raised: if Dostoevsky wishes to refute the views of the Grand
Inquisitor, and indirectly by an artistic picture, why choose a
consciously archaic style which would seem to set the refutation
even more distantly into the past?

This question can be resolved by examining the style. The prose
is rhythmic, sounds and words are repeated, especially *umilenie*
(tender emotion) as noun, verb, adjective, and adverb. *Umilenie*:
the cult of tears and of the heart, which is so characteristic of
Zosima. The effect of *umilenie*, according to Pletnev, "is to melt sin
away and in the joyous tears of the repentant sinner arises the new
man." The sinner's tears are joyous because he knows he is being
forgiven. Much of this came from Parfeny's book, but the studied
repetition of tears, heart, tender emotion in "The Russian Monk"
seems to me to have a special function. The reader is being acted
on to open his heart as well. There are other stylistic examples that
produce the same effect. Zosima often uses caressing diminutives,
which are not characteristic of old Russian literature but do rein-
force the impression of a warm-hearted open person who lives by
his heart. Sentences often begin with verbs followed by noun-
subjects, building up parallel structures as, for example, in Zosima's
account of how he later met his orderly Afanasy or Zosima's version of the Book of Job:

> *Byla u menia togda kniga, sviashchennaia istoriia . . .*
> *Posetilo menia nekotoroe proniknovenie dukhovnoe . . .*
> *Povela matushka menia odnogo . . . vo khram Gospoden' . . .*
> *Smotrel ia umilenno . . .*
> *Vyshel na sredinu khrama otrok s bol'shoiu knigoi . . .*
> *Byl muzh v zemle Un . . .*[1]

Such parallel verb-subject structures recall the word order in lives
of saints or Russian folklore. Also common is the practice of beginning each sentence with "and"—reminiscent of the Bible. Modern Russian and Church Slavic unobtrusively blend as in: "*Na
vsiak den' i chas, na vsiakuiu minutu . . .*" [Every day and hour,
every minute . . ."]. *Vsiak den'* is Church Slavic, *vsiakuiu minutu* is
Russian. The Russian reader may vaguely recall that the phrase *na
vsiak den'* parallels the structure of "*Izhe na vsiakoe vremia i na
vsiakii chas . . .*" ["Who at any time and at any hour . . ."], and is
part of an important daily prayer, the Great Doxology (*Velikoe
Slavoslovie*). The whole chapter consists of such deft reminders.

---

1. There was a book in my hands then, Scripture history . . .
There afflicted me a certain spiritual penetration . . .
There led my mother myself alone . . . into God's temple . . .
Looked I tenderly . . .
Emerged a youth into the center of the church with a large book . . .
There was a man in the land of Uz . . .

[*Editor's translation*]

And associated with these recollected words and sounds is an esthetic picture. Zosima remembers that as an eight-year-old boy he heard the story of Job read in church for the first time, while "the incense rose from the censer and softly floated upwards and, overhead in the cupola, mingled in rising waves with the sunlight that streamed in the little window."

The function of Zosima's style is not only to assure its "realism" —a style that authenticates his profession—but by verbal legerdemain it works on the Russian reader's *unconscious*, making him recall his own childhood. Bits and pieces of sermons, Biblical stories, esthetic images, sonorous words, incense, rhythmical prose— all these stir the imagination of a child and are linked to innocence, goodness, Christianity. As Zosima says, "There are no memories more precious than those of early childhood in one's first home." And these unconscious memories of childhood, the period when one is most impressionable, can exert a powerful influence in later life precisely because they are unconscious. Thus Mitya Karamazov may have been saved from killing his father by the unconscious memory of that pound of nuts once given him by a pious kindly German doctor who, at the same time, made the little Mitya repeat: "*Gott der Vater, Gott der Sohn, und Gott der heilige Geist.*" Father and son are divinely linked. And the good doctor testifies in court that twenty-three years later Mitya remembered those words. Alyosha emphasizes the importance of good childhood impressions to his twelve disciples at the end of the novel.

Thus the indirect refutation of the Grand Inquisitor is contained not only in the subject matter of Zosima's speech and the veneration of the mystery of man's nature but also in something very practical: in the cunning mosaic of Church Slavic and modern Russian in which Zosima's words are inlaid, so that the Russian reader unconsciously responds with what is best in his own childhood, with the most potent memories of religious and esthetic experience. "The Russian Monk" is the literary equivalent of a precious, hallowed old church icon.

This refutation of the Grand Inquisitor is so indirect, however, that Dostoevsky had good reason to worry whether his "artistic picture would be understood" and whether he "had reached even an inch of his goal." He wrote in his notebook a scathing attack on his critics: "The villians teased me for my *uneducated* and reactionary faith in God. These blockheads did not even dream of such a powerful negation of God as was put into the Inquisitor and in the preceding chapter, to which *the whole novel* serves as an answer."

"*The whole novel* serves as an answer." The italics are Dostoevsky's. Here we have the true refutation of the Grand Inquisitor: in the movements made successively by Alyosha, by Mitya, and by Ivan. Christ's silence before the Grand Inquisitor, deepened by

Zosima's non-logical "artistic picture," is now to be made psychologically plausible. The frame of "The Russian Monk," with the pale sketch of Zosima erased or to be covered over as in a palimpsest, is now to be filled with a vivid picture: the destinies of the Karamazov brothers.

Let us glance briefly at those destinies.

Zosima's recollections end with his death, a painless and graceful death in which he sinks to the earth and thanks God: the traditional ending in a saint's life. His death releases Alyosha from tutelage. Alyosha now faces in freedom his first crisis. Zosima's body stinks; the miracle has not come to pass. The Karamazov sensuality breaks out in the despairing Alyosha; he goes to Grushenka to be tempted and seduced. But she too faces a crisis. Should she forget her five years of laceration and return to the Polish officer who had ruined her but who now promised to make amends and marry her—or should she revenge herself upon him for her miseries? A mysterious interaction takes place. Learning of the death of Zosima, Grushenka forgets her own problem, her own ego, and feels acutely Alyosha's agony and bewilderment. This is her "onion." And Alyosha gratefully offers her an onion too: he appeals to her higher nature (which no one hitherto had thought she possessed, hence she too had not thought she possessed it): he tells her she will not yield to her egoistic dream of revenge for humiliation. Grushenka has already taken the first step of suppressing her ego in feeling for Alyosha; she now goes further, suppresses her evil longings, and goes in a forgiving mood to her Polish officer. This episode climaxes in the "Cana of Galilee" scene in which Alyosha kisses the earth in acknowledgment of the true miracle—not the false miracle of coercive power, of Zosima's bones not stinking—but the true miracle that arises each day in each person when he freely follows the verdict of his heart and prefers doing good to doing evil. This movement, powerful and plausible, is the first answer to the Grand Inquisitor.

The second answer is provided by Mitya Karamazov. Despite his passionate nature, his deep hatred of his father, his need of money, his vow to kill his father; even given the opportunity and the weapon to commit the murder with, he finds within himself sufficient strength to run away from the temptation of parricide. Psychologically, regarded theoretically, this "self-denial" on his part would seem improbable. Yet no critic has ever questioned the power and plausibility of Mitya's self-denial. It is psychologically plausible and effective: men enslaved by passion—the presumed subjects of the kingdom of the Grand Inquisitor—are shown to have the inner strength to overcome their passion. This is the second answer to the Grand Inquisitor.

The third answer is provided by Ivan Karamazov. From his

rational standpoint he did not kill his father. Even if he had killed him there should be no regret, for how can one regret killing a *reptile* (as he called Fyodor)? Nor should he have conscience stings like Raskolnikov since he is an atheist and there is nothing in his background suggesting a religious upbringing or the importance of his mother (which is stressed as motivation for his brother Alyosha). Nevertheless he is mysteriously driven to confess publicly his role in the murder. If Smerdyakov had murdered his father, then Ivan had tacitly approved it. Still more humiliating for a proud person like Ivan is the realization that even when confessing, he will not be believed: he has no evidence, and Smerdyakov has hanged himself. Confessing in such circumstances is an utterly irrational act, senseless and ridiculous. And yet something drives him to confess. It is not surprising that he goes insane. This is the third answer to the Grand Inquisitor.

These three movements of Alyosha, Mitya, and Ivan are just as powerful and persuasive as—or even more powerful than—the intellectual arguments advanced by Ivan to Alyosha in the chapters on "Rebellion" and "The Grand Inquisitor." These "arguments" of all the brothers—their movements—have one common feature: they are not intellectual but are made with the whole of man's being. And for that reason they are all the more powerful and convincing. We may forget the complicated threads of Ivan's arguments but we cannot forget the destinies of the three brothers.

We see now that the two "culminating points" in the novel, the ideological debate between the Grand Inquisitor and the Russian Monk, are not placed haphazardly but just where they would be most effective: as a prelude that ushers in the main action.

We have also seen that the defects of "The Russian Monk" are both deliberate and unavoidable, arising from the very problem of an "indirect" refutation of the Grand Inquisitor. To make "The Russian Monk" as imaginatively powerful as "The Grand Inquisitor" Dostoevsky would have had to make the conversions of Markel, Zosima, and the Mysterious Stranger psychologically plausible. This would have been to duplicate what he would do so effectively in tracing the destinies of the three Karamazov brothers. It would also have destroyed the point of the debate as an ideological *prelude* to the action. "The Russian Monk" is best understood as a two-dimensional icon that has its fourth dimension in the reader's unconscious memories of childhood.

Finally, by transferring our attention from the Grand Inquisitor to the novel as a whole we have restored a necessary balance. No longer is Ivan seen as the hero of the novel (Rozanov, Camus, Rahv). The hero is the spirit of God acting through all the Karamazovs. This is the refutation contained in Christ's silence before the Grand Inquisitor.

LEONID GROSSMAN

Dostoevsky as Artist†

1. *Dostoevsky's Genre*

* * * The figure of one of his favorite heroes, Dmitri Karamazov, is taken from life. The author had described him in the so-called "parricide" of the Omsk prison, Lieutenant Ilinsky. Mitenka, like his prototype, is an ex-lieutenant who had served at home. These details from old military orders and criminal justice are transported by the author into the Karamazovs' family chronicle. The author's personal reminiscences of that man who was condemned though innocent, complete the striking liveliness of the novelistic figure.

Dmitri's destiny is profoundly tragic. A man of high spiritual impulses, he is incapable of extricating himself from the slough of vices that ensnares him. Falsely accused of parricide, he must expiate someone else's crime by twenty years' penal servitude!

But at the moment of catastrophe his whole being undergoes an inner illumination. In his dream he sees a burnt out village, charred stumps, emaciated women bearing in their arms infants crying from hunger. He wants to know "why is it those poor mothers stand there? Why are people poor? Why is the babe poor? Why is the steppe barren? Why don't they hug and kiss each other? Why don't they sing songs of joy? Why are they so dark from black misery? Why don't they feed the babe?" And he wants to do battle with that evil, "so that no one should shed tears again from that moment."

Such is one of Dostoevsky's last pages on the sufferings of his people. Dmitri Karamazov is penetrated by a feeling of grief for the poverty and torment of peasant folk. He strives to be the defender of the dying inhabitants of the village, the creator of their happiness, the compassionate benefactor of their general sorrow.

The most important section of *The Brothers Karamazov* is also constructed on the same principle. The action of the central chapters in the fifth book takes place in a local tavern. Ivan sits in a private room. The artist limits himself to depicting the wretched tavern by sounds alone: the shouts of the customers, the popping of corks from bottles, the clicking of billiard balls, the drone of the organ. But soon the brothers' conversation turns to eternal ques-

† L. P. Grossman, "*Dostoevsky kak khudozhnik*," from *Tvorchestvo Dosto-* *evskogo*, (Moscow, 1959), pp. 333–48. Translated by Ralph E. Matlaw.

tions. "I accept God simply and directly," but "I do not accept that world of God's," the young thinker hurls out his challenge.

Ivan Karamazov's famous thesis ascends into the realm of current politics and reports of crimes. The young thinker argues his arraignment of "the Creator of the world" from a collection of "little facts" and "little anecdotes" taken from newspapers, brochures, historical journals, and trial reports. War atrocities, punishments, the torture of children, all based on actual published material, disclose the entire "devil's vaudeville" of contemporary reality. In order to broaden the inquiry that has been started, the narration is transposed to the historico-philosophical plane, and Ivan relates the poem he has constructed. Fundamentally it is a criticism of Christianity. But the Inquisitor's speech is preceded by an historical novella.

This is really the only attempt to reconstruct the past in Dostoevsky's work. In Ivan Karamazov's poem the novelist proves himself an outstanding painter of the historical past who possesses a genuine talent for recreating great men of the past in their full stature, against a background of ancient epochs, in the brilliance of their rank and power, in all the individuality of their decorum and array.

Dostoevsky chooses Seville in the sixteenth century as the locale of his legend. The ancient Catholic city is created in brief and concentrated strokes. In its squares a hundred heretics had been burned in the presence of the king and the most beautiful ladies only the night before. The ancient inquisitor in his purple cardinal's raiments had directed this "splendid *auto da fé*." His gloomy and dreadful portrait, reminiscent of the pitiless features of ancient Spanish rulers in El Greco's paintings, is splendid: "tall and erect, with a withered face and sunken eyes, in which there was still a gleam of light." He has the bloodless lips of a ninety-year-old man. His features present not only the characterization and biography of the figure but also the entire ideological atmosphere of the epoch, with its exalted mottoes and its burning pyres.

The ending of the tale is carried out in the spirit of the Romantic Drama. At night, the ancient cardinal, in coarse monk's garb, enters the subterranean cell of his prisoner with a candlestick in his hands. His terrifying decrepitude and bloodthirsty vengefulness are momentarily contrasted to the world's beauty, Spain's warm twilight, in Pushkin's verse—"The night is fragrant with laurel and lemon." The Primate's accusatory speech sounds forth and develops into a monologue on man's fate. Eternal questions are posed. Dostoevsky's sacred theme of mankind's suffering and happiness rises above the Karamazovs' family chronicle like a triumphant chorale, oratorio, or *Dies irae*—the day of the Last Judgment. Everything is transformed. A critique of the Gospels, reminiscent of an historical tragedy, resounds from an impoverished tavern in the gloomy provinciality of Russia.

The novelist's artistic method is unique. He does not turn to the numerous historical sources of his theme, and apparently limits himself to a single monograph on the Inquisition, the *History of the Reign of Phillip II, King of Spain* by William Prescott, author of the popular *Conquests of Peru* and *Mexico* which Dostoevsky valued highly.

That book, with its extensive materials on the tribunals and punishments of militant Catholicism, was in Dostoevsky's library. It provided him a great deal of information for reconstructing the historical background of the meeting between the dreadful investigator of the "Holy Inquisition" and the founder of Christianity.

But the novelist strives to give a more generalized criticism of old Spain, which he needs as background for the philosophical monologue on man's fate. He is concerned only with recreating it in a poetically true sense, rather than being attracted by a detailed description of the epoch. To that purpose he intentionally introduced into his exposition (as he always liked to do) certain literary keys to his thought, imperceptible analogies and correspondences from folklore and lyric poetry. He is not interested in a concrete historical approach, in the accuracy of detail in describing life, but in poets' large formulations of man's great feelings and thoughts, his achievements and sufferings, his striving for universal happiness. Therefore he purposely introduces Victor Hugo's *Notre Dame de Paris*, miracle plays of the Middle Ages, Russian Apocrypha, verse by Zhukovsky, Tyutchev, and Schiller, a character from *Faust* into the introduction to the poem and to its afterword. Dostoevsky illuminates and shades his huge tragic conception through these themes and artistic incarnations. In his visits to the world's museum he came to know thoroughly the men of the Renaissance painted by such masters as Velasquez, Dürer, Cranach, Holbein, Titian, Rubens, Ribera, Van Dyck, and many others. This experience in museums conveyed to him a knowledge of the characteristic traits of the epoch and a delicate creative method for recreating its types. Even apart from the idea of the poem, the figure of the Grand Inquisitor is an outstanding example of historical portraiture. He rises above the Karamazov world of suffocating sins and criminal desires as a huge generalization of another cruel era.

Ivan's monologue, which occupies three chapters of the novel, exhibits Dostoevsky's genre especially fully. So far as the plot is concerned, it is merely the "getting acquainted" or first rapprochement of the younger Karamazovs, who have come to their Skotoprigonevsk to settle a family quarrel. But the grandiose problems of religion and socialism unexpectedly burst into the monstrous "history of a certain family" with its financial wrangling and sensual rivalry. Like a skilled orator, Ivan bases his theme on current political material and develops it on the most contemporary reflections of Russia's inner life. But under his penetrating glance war correspondence and chronicles of trials grow into a universal picture of the hopeless suffering of innocent beings: he is shaken by the fate of perishing children. And above the collection of events reported in newspapers and that weave this tragedy of the present, there rise legendary figures who by their meeting conclude the philosophical discussion of two "Russian children" about the aims and bases of the creation of the world. The great writer reveals himself a thinker and a writer of tragedy. Landscape, portrait, and description of life dissolve into drama and lyric verse of immortal figures and universal ideas.

That is what Dostoevsky's unique genre was in its highest form. The universal visions pass by, and Ivan and Alyosha finish the last words of their unexpected discussion on the steps of a tavern with a sign "Metropolis." From there they go off in different directions, with parting expressions of brotherly love, but, in the author's view, irreconcilably and forever.

2. Scandal Scenes

Crowded and stormy scenes which seem to shake the whole structure of the novel are characteristic of Dostoevsky's construction—gatherings, arguments, scandals, hysterics, slaps in the face, fits.

In criticism and critical theory such assemblies have been called "conclaves." That Latin term designates a plenary council of cardinals in the Vatican, gathered to elect a new Pope. In Dostoevsky's novels and tales these are exceptional meetings with important purposes and unforeseen complications.

* * * In his last work—*The Brothers Karamazov*—Dostoevsky presents the sum of all his compositional devices, but with the utmost intensity and maximal expressiveness, a real *fortissimo*. The novel is built on the sharp juxtaposition of characters and events: at one extreme, moral monsters—Fyodor Pavlovich and Smerdyakov, at the other, "angels"—Alyosha and Zosima. The monastery is juxtaposed to Skotoprigonevsk, the Russian monk to the sensualist, the elder's exhortations to the conversation over the cognac, the Reverend Father, that is, *Pater seraphicus*, to the monster-monk. One of the most important books of the novel is even called "Pro and Contra." To the very end, antithesis remained Dostoevsky's primary architectonic principle.

The novelist's favorite device—the meeting of all the characters—here acquires new scope. The gathering of the Karamazovs, father and sons, in the monastery for the friendly settlement of their disagreements soon turns into an unprecedented scandal, first in the Elder's cell, then at the Father Superior's dinner. Fyodor Pavlovich's clash with Dmitri, his challenging him to a duel, the insult to the monastery, all this strains the atmosphere of the meeting to the limit. But at that point a sudden break occurs. Elder Zosima sinks to his knees before Dmitri and bows down to the earth before him. That is the transition of the quarrel into drama.

Similar "gatherings" also control the central books of the novel. Such is the bout of revelry in Mokroe. In contrast to the monastery, this is an out-of-town tavern-den with a bed in each room. A card game with unmasked cheats, the humiliation of Grushenka by Vrublyovsky, the expulsion of the Poles, an orgy—a feast for the entire world: cynical songs, cymbalon players, drunkenness, dancing. Out of this debauchery and fumes Grushenka's confession of her love for Mitya rises and sounds like a pure and thrilling song. Life is broken in two. The hero's moral rebirth glimmers to him from afar. But at that moment of illumination and spiritual arousal, a catastrophic disruption occurs:

> —Ex-Lieutenant Karamazov, it is my duty to inform you that you are charged with the murder of your father, Fyodor Pavlovich Karamazov, perpetrated this night.

This is a peculiar variation of Gogol's ending [in *The Government Inspector*] but completely bereft of all comedy. Mitya's new life, which had just begun, is broken off by the merciless intervention of the authorities. Before him stand his friend the prosecutor, the district attorney, the Captain of Police, the policeman. A grave accusation is made. Throughout the whole house deathly silence suddenly takes the place of songs and drunken hubbub. Thus the gendarme's announcement in Gogol caused the petrification of the whole company assembled in the mayor's rooms.

The coming together of all the personages for the final catastrophe is mounted with a daring new turn near the end of the novel. As in a chorus, it is a *tutti*, that is, all the voices join in. At the trial the three brothers, the two female rivals, Captain Snegiryov, Rakitin, the servant Grigory, the innkeeper Trifon Borisovich, Mitya's fellow carousers from Mokroe all meet; renowned jurists, elderly dignitaries, ladies in their finery, correspondents from the capitals, the town's inhabitants, the peasant-jurors are all present. A truly unprecedented conclave. All Russia follows the course of the trial. An ordinary domestic brawl is matched by an orderly investigation, decorous disputes, and the brilliant debate of the antagonists.

But even the examination of witnesses is interrupted by a "sudden catastrophe" (as the turning point of that trial chronicle is called). Ivan proclaims to all that Smerdyakov killed the old man "and I

taught him to kill." The witness is carried from the hall in an attack
of raging madness. Katerina Ivanovna, shaken, considering that her
beloved Ivan Fyodorovich has ruined himself by his testimony,
decides to save him by sacrificing Dmitri. She discloses to the court
the accused's letter, which incriminates him in parricide. That outburst of the enraged woman is poured out in an accusatory speech
of exceptional force and sounds like a genuine inculpation of the
accused. "Mitya, your serpent has destroyed you!" Grushenka
shouts through the entire hall, shaking with anger. Katerina
Ivanovna is carried out in hysterics. "Yes, I think the ladies who
came to see the spectacle must have been satisfied—the show had
been a varied one," the author notes. All the components of [Dos-
toevsky's earlier] conclaves are maintained, but on a scale of
Russia-wide resonance, genuinely tragic peripeties, and psychological conflicts of a Shakespearean breadth.

Thus Dostoevsky organizes the materials of his novel in different
variations and combinations according to the basic principles of his
compositional system.

* * *

Ya. E. GOLOSOVKER

The Words "Secret" and "Mystery"†

Among the words of particular significance in Dostoevsky's
novel there is one word which is a *specificum*, continually teasing
the reader with its direct meaning and its ambiguity, penetrating
into his conscience in some particularly poisonous and ironic way,
to his very blood, so to speak, like the tiniest filament of some plant
that nevertheless thereby shimmers like a rotted stump in the
darkness—that word is "secret." And though its synonyms "riddle"
and "mystery" coexist with it, the sense of "riddle" is neutral, while
that of "mystery" is normally the opposite of the word "secret,"
that is to say its sense is positive, profound, affirmative, while the
word "secret" seems to contain something negative, cautionary,
something cunning, plotting, insidious. The word "secret" creeps
into every possible situation, being used both by the heroes of the
novel and the author-narrator himself, but it is used most of all by
Mitya. The reader goes through dozens and even hundreds of the
novel's tormenting pages before he reaches the last secret, the secret
that, as it were, crown the other secrets—"the devil's secret," which

† From Ya. E. Golosovker, *Dostoevsky*   Translated by Ralph E. Matlaw.
i Kant, (Moscow, 1963), pp. 24–30.

remains secret even from the devil himself. It is here that the whole *specificum* of the word "secret" is disclosed to the reader.

Mitya sits in the neighboring garden attached to Fyodor Pavlovich's garden, sits "in secret" and "guards a secret": "I am here in secret and guard a secret. The explanation will come later, but since I understood that it was secret I suddenly started to speak in secret, too," the excited Mitya says.

He is on guard for Grushenka, in order to intercept her if she should come to his father, to old man Karamazov, who indulges the hope that she will come for the envelope with the 3,000 rubles. The circumstance that Mitya sits there is a *secret*—the owners of the garden and house know nothing about it. Mitya tells that to Alyosha *secretly*, in a whisper. And the existence of the fateful envelope with the 3,000 is also a secret, even "*the greatest secret*," known only to Smerdyakov and him, Mitya, in addition to Grushenka.

Let me remind the reader that Mitya had also "secretly" suggested to Agatha Ivanovna, the niece of the lieutenant colonel who had embezzled four and half thousand rubles of government funds, that she send him the Institute student, the colonel's daughter, the proud Katerina Ivanovna, for a sum equal to the embezzled funds, moreover, objuring her to guard Katya's visit as "a sacred and inviolable" secret. In answer, Agatha Ivanovna calls him "a scoundrel."

Katerina Ivanovna hands Mitya 3,000 rubles in great *secret*, in the first place pretending that Mitya was to send them by mail to that same Agatha Ivanovna in Moscow, in the second, in order to test Mitya's nobility, third, with the aim of helping Mitya, her betrothed, to provide him with money so that he might run off with her rival Grushenka. That is, Katerina Ivanovna hands Mitya 3,000 rubles which he "basely" squandered on Grushenka in Mokroe in two bouts, money he somehow both stole and didn't steal. In short, the secret handing over of the money was completely ambiguous, as was also shown at the trial in Katerina Ivanovna's two rounds of testimony, which refute each other.

Half of that sum, which Mitya had originally sewn into a bag and had told no one about, is also a *secret*—and at the same time also a *mystery*. It is a "secret" because Mitya had separated it with the intention of running off with Grushenka on Katya's money and all Mitya's shame lies in his appropriating that half. But it is also a "mystery," because Mitya acknowledges his shame, because he sewed up that money in order to return it to Katerina Ivanovna. Had he returned it, he would have been "a scoundrel but not a thief," in his own opinion, but now he is a thief. *The secret has vanquished the mystery*.

The little demon Liza Khokhlakov writes a love letter to Alyosha "in secret from everyone," and from her mother, knowing how improper it is. Now Alyosha has her "secret" in his possession. But even Alyosha has a special, *secret* sort of sorrow: because Elder Zosima began to smell, Alyosha begins to think that perhaps he, too, does not believe in God. Through that *secret* sorrow he, the novice, is ready meantime even "to eat sausage, and drink vodka, and go to Grushenka."

Treacherously, "in great secret," Smerdyakov informed Mitya of the signs—the taps on old Karamazov's window. The reader knows that the whole project of murdering Fyodor Pavlovich was connected with this secret, with these taps.

Incidentally, the mysterious visitor whose story is related by the Elder Zosima also has his *secret*. That secret also turned out be murder, to wit, the murder of a widow, committed by him in an attack of rage and spite.[1]

Grigory was rubbed with vodka that had some *secret* strong herbs on the night of the murder. Grigory drank the rest of the medicine with "a certain prayer" and went to bed, and later gave false testimony that was ruinous to Mitya, about the open gate from the house to the garden. But the gate into the garden was not open at all: the *secret* concoction misled the witness. Grigory gave false testimony without realizing it himself.

There are still further secrets in the novel. But even if the conclusion were drawn now, it is clear that the word "secret" is connected with murder, baseness, theft, treachery, false testimony, intrigue, jealousy, and a confusion of thoughts and feelings. Basically, however, the "secret" turns about the murder of old Karamazov, around that "devil's deed."

And if both words "secret" and "mystery" are used in relation to a single fact, it ordinarily indicates that there is some ambiguity about it: both something positive and something negative.

But in order to reach the "devil's secret," two further chapters of the novel must be looked at closely, chapters where "secret" barely emerges, like a turtle's head out of its shell.

There is first of all a certain *secret* of Mitya's—it is a *mystery* as well—but it is not only his personal secret, it is also a "common secret," a secret of three people, Mitya, Ivan, and Katerina Ivanovna, a secret which "he" (we'll find out later who the "he" is) forbade telling Alyosha, a secret that is also withheld from Grushenka, a secret which torments, troubles, and disconcerts Mitya, and which Mitya discloses to Alyosha with terror in his heart, discloses it to him as to a cherub, perhaps as to a higher man. That *secret*, a matter of the highest conscience and therefore also a *mystery*, is so important that Mitya cannot deal with it himself.

---

1. That "mysterious visitor-murderer" seems to me to be Zosima himself (before he became an Elder). His story is Zosima's confession.

That secret is nothing else than the proposal made by Ivan to Mitya to *escape* with Grushenka after the sentence, and, moreover, *escape to America.*

Why is that a secret? Why must it be withheld from Alyosha? Because such an escape is for Mitya an escape from suffering, from his cross, because such an escape is a rejection of a higher indication, of the voice of conscience, of purification, of the underground hymn of the prisoner to God, God driven from the earth: in short, to escape means to reject immortality and God.

And escape where? *To America,* in other words, to swindlery.

For Mitya himself defines America as a land of swindlers and "wonderful machinists."

Of course that treacherous project could not be disclosed to Alyosha the cherub, because Alyosha is for the "hymn," for suffering, for purification, for immortality and God, for Alyosha is conscience which may interfere with the proposal for escape.

Who was it that conceived this project and who ordered Alyosha not to be told about it?

"*He, he* conceived it, *he* insists! He hadn't visited me at all, and suddenly he came last week and started right in with that," Mitya informs Alyosha.

This time "he" does not seem to be that "he" who visited Ivan, not the devil but Ivan himself. The reader and Mitya do not doubt it at all, but for some reason the author doubts it to some extent, and, apparently, so does Alyosha. The author doubts it, therefore the very style of Mitya's relating to Alyosha how "he" (Ivan) suddenly appeared is remarkably similar to Ivan's telling Alyosha beneath the streetlamp how "he" (the devil) came to Ivan. Alyosha is in doubt. And therefore Alyosha then questions Mitya: "Tell me one thing, does Ivan very much insist on it [escape], and who *first* conceived it?"

Yes, reader, who first conceived it? Who suggested to Mitya the idea of escaping to America? Who is he, the author of this secret?

. . . Let us repeat an excerpt from the conversation beneath the streetlamp:

"You were at my place at night when *he* came. Admit it. You saw *him,* you saw? Do you know that *he* visits me?" Ivan questions Alyosha.

"Who is *he*? Whom are you talking about?" Alyosha asks in amazement, just as in his conversation with Mitya he asks in amazement, "Who first conceived this?"

A little later, in the chapter "It was *He* who said it," Alyosha again asks Ivan, "Who is *he*?"—the "he" who told Ivan that Smerdyakov had hanged himself even before Alyosha arrived. It seems that "he" slinked off, that "he" was afraid of Alyosha, that "he" had sat there on the couch, that "he" is terribly stupid, that "he"—is the devil. And the devil, that *he*, was chased away by the mere appearance of the "cherub" Alyosha.

It also turns out that "he," that is, the devil, dissuaded Ivan from performing a virtuous deed, from purifying himself, from admitting at the trial the next day that he, Ivan, killed the father, that is, that Smerdyakov killed him at Ivan's instigation.

"It is *he* who says it—*he*, and *he* knows it," Ivan complains in despair to Alyosha, losing all his senses. And although Alyosha again repeats to Ivan, "You did not kill him," it does not convince Ivan.

What has happened, reader? This is what: Ivan, who so proudly rejected the "hosannah" to the end, suddenly, just like Mitya, also decided to sing a "hymn" with the cherubim, to suffer, to purify himself through repentance, and now the devil laughs at it, that is, he seems to propose to Ivan to remain in his iniquity rather than sing the hymn, or, to speak allegorically, to escape morally to that same America to which Ivan proposed Mitya escape. That is the he, the *first*, who conceived the project of escape to America: *the devil conceived it*. Therefore Alyosha could not believe that Ivan conceived the escape to America.

In both instances there is a single secret. It means that the devil has again taken a hand: the devil prompted Ivan and later Ivan transmitted the secret to Mitya. And if a duel has taken place here, it has taken place between the devil and the cherub Alyosha, and the cherub Alyosha has emerged victorious.

Even the verbal formulations of both brothers' confessions to Alyosha, with the repetition of "he," are quite similar:

"*He, he* thought it up, *he* insists," Mitya says to Alyosha about Ivan.

"It was *he* who said it, *he*, and *he* knows it," Ivan says to Alyosha about the devil.

The common secret of the three—Mitya, Ivan, and Katerina Ivanovna, or more accurately, the secret of both, Mitya and Ivan— the secret of escape to America, that is, the decision to renounce suffering, purification, the hymn, immortality, God—turns out to be the invention of the devil, the "devil's secret."

RALPH E. MATLAW

Myth and Symbol†

A larger unit of Dostoevsky's technique is the myth and the mythical construct. Myth is an immediate intuition of reality, and it

† From Ralph E. Matlaw, *The Brothers Karamazov: Novelistic Technique* (The Hague, Mouton & Co., 1957), pp. 20– 33. Reprinted by permission of Edicom N. V., Laren, Netherlands.

is primarily ritualistic or religious in character, but it may, like Ivan's Legend, be purely literary. We must distinguish between the reality apprehended and the poetic function the myth may have. Many of the myths in the book are simple in nature and occur in single scenes. Like literary references, however, they eventually coalesce into mythic constructs, so that realization may arise through a succession of related episodes.

The central myth, of course, concerns regeneration, whether expressed in religious terms or considered as psychological rehabilitation. It is stated in several forms in the two chapters "Women of Faith" and "A Lady of little Faith" during Father Zosima's ministrations to physical and mental illnesses, and affects in turn the leading characters in the narrative. Grushenka is the first to undergo a transformation, occasioned by Alyosha's presence and having a reciprocal effect on him. The scene takes place under the most propitious circumstances: Alyosha's temporary loss of faith has lead him to Grushenka, but in place of a temptress he finds a creature mollified by the imminent reunion with her first seducer, the man who can make complete amends to her. Grushenka in any case is a profound believer, and her reaction to the news of Zosima's death need not depend on immediate circumstances. By her consideration for Alyosha's feelings and her respect for Zosima's position, she restores belief to Alyosha. And he, in turn, verbalizes his estimate of her goodness and moral stature. At this point we are given the folk legend of "the little onion," mythologically representing the charitable act that leads to redemption, but simultaneously emphasizing that it is the spirit of the act, rather than the gift itself, that leads to the desirable theological conclusion. The same myth is echoed in the trial, but represents simply human recognition of kindness, when Dr. Herzenstube estimates Mitya's character solely on Mitya's remembering the gift of a pound of nuts. The turning point in Mitya's career, the beginning of his regeneration, occurs during his dream of "the babe" in Book IX. His dream intensifies the feeling involved in the myths of onions and nuts into an overwhelming compassion for suffering humanity. Alyosha's spiritual resurrection naturally assumes an explicitly religious statement of the same myth, Cana of Galilee. Ivan performs a similar deed when he rescues a peasant in the snow, and himself comments that he would not have done so had he not decided to confess his guilt during the trial (contrition). Negative involvement in this mythic construct relates to Fyodor Pavlovich, whose vacillations between a sensual perversion of love and a certain anxiety about the nether regions of a possible after-life are terminated by his murder; to Smerdyakov, whose inability to accept either Ivan's moral anarchy or orthodox religion leads to his suicide; and Rakitin, whose identity with Judas is obvious in promising to convey Alyosha to Grushenka for twenty-five rubles.

Another level of myth appears in connection with parricide, the pivot of the plot. It is impossible to account satisfactorily for Smerdyakov's act if only psychological or material motivations are considered. The prosecutor and Fetyukovich each has a different "character analysis" of Smerdyakov, but neither completely accounts for the murder. Similarly Mitya and Ivan have their views, the first dismissing (with some uncertainty) the possibility of Smerdyakov as murderer, the second, after different doubts, finally being confronted with irrefutable proofs of his guilt. But in Smerdyakov's confession to Ivan extenuations appear. Circumstances were extremely favorable and the idea had only occurred to Smerdyakov after Grigory was struck down. That is, in part chance guides the action. It may further be added that other motivations are possible: Smerdyakov's bastardy, the taunting by Fyodor Pavlovich, the desire to please Ivan, the possibility of financial gain. Whatever else may be involved in parricide, and echoed in Ivan's shattering remark at the trial "Who does not desire his father's death?" can only be adumbrated, hinted in a novel, not stated or solved. Smerdyakov's role in the murder, then, can never be justified on purely rational grounds. But another literary level is possible:

> But is it not a sculpturesque and simple theme, worthy of the most classical art, a frieze interrupted and resumed on which the tale of vegeance and expiation is unfolded, the crime of old Karamazov getting the poor idiot with child, the mysterious, animal, unexplained impulse by which the mother, herself unconsciously the instrument of an avenging destiny, obeying also obscurely her maternal instinct, feeling perhaps a combination of physical resentment and gratitude towards her seducer, comes to bear her child on old Karamazov's ground. That is the first episode, mysterious, grand, august as a Creation of Woman among the sculptures at Orvieto. And as counterpart, the second episode more than twenty years later, the murder of old Karamazov, the disgrace brought upon the Karamazov family by this son of the idiot, Smerdyakov, followed shortly afterwards by another action, as mysteriously sculpturesque and unexplained, of a beauty as obscure and natural as that of the childbirth in old Karamazov's garden, Smerdyakov hanging himself, his crime accomplished.[1]

Cultural anthropologists provide a less imaginative but more specific interpretation. Particularly in earlier and more primitive myths, parricide is an integral and vital stage in the development of the mythic figure, and under various guises is intimately connected with the concepts of maturity, fertility, and rebirth. While tapping the profound primitive significance of parricide, Dostoevsky treats it in the *Brothers Karamazov* primarily in psychological and ethical

1. Marcel Proust, *The Captive*, translated by C. K. Scott Moncrieff (New York: Random House, 1929) pp. 518–19.

terms. Thus the murder involves not only the actual culprit, but all the brothers—Ivan, who provides the theory; Dmitri, who creates the opportunity in the turmoil during the sexual rivalry of father and son; and Alyosha, who foresees a crime but remains passive. Beyond the immediate family, the myth involves Fetyukovich, "An Adulterer of Thought," the townspeople who desire to see Mitya convicted and, by extension, all of Russia and humanity, since the trial becomes a *cause célèbre*, creating interest throughout the land.

Another method of creating a literary myth consists of dramatizing ideas (without specific mythological statements) and repeating or varying these ideas, in applying them to various personages. A significant example exists in the problem of immortality or the afterlife. In addition to such discussions as were here treated under other headings, Dostoevsky treats the problem as one of resurrection. Thus in the peasant mother's description of her son Alexey her very reminiscence recaptures the image of her son and reintroduces him into the actual world.[2] A more sophisticated approach, that of Mrs. Khokhlakov, presents the possibility of an afterworld as a constant source of torment and a deterrent to belief. Among the clerics Miïusov again raises the question, as the fundamental tenet of Ivan's system (and hence one of the causes of the murder), that man need have no moral compunctions if he believes neither in God nor in the afterlife. A "return" from the other world is implied in the life-long memory Alyosha retains of his mother and even receives verbal, though vague, mention from Mitya's "I don't know whether my mother prayed to God . . . at that moment." The secret of Ivan's ethics is disclosed by the Inquisitor when he denies the possibility of an afterlife. Afterlife is a fundamental article of belief in Ferapont, the devil crusher, and is derided specifically by Ivan's devil, who calls Ferapont's ilk "spiritualist." In a slightly different sense, there is a resurrection in Kolya after his escapade with the train. But the most dramatic implementation of the concept occurs in that extraordinary final chapter of the epilogue, the summation, resolution, and promised amelioration in the future of the deepest conflicts presented in the book, when the influence of Ilyusha from beyond the grave becomes an ethical imperative.

This theme and others like it could be traced in still greater detail. However, another equally important device must first be noted, that of the symbol.[3] It is frequently difficult to determine whether something is only symbolic or whether it assumes a still larger mythic meaning, particularly since Dostoevsky's symbolic

2. K. Mochulsky, *Dostoevskij* (Paris, 1947), p. 471.
3. Many myths and symbols are noted in Vjačeslav Ivanov's book. George Gibian,

"Traditional Symbolism in *Crime and Punishment*," PMLA, LXX (1955), 979–996, demonstrates the extent and consistency of Dostoevsky's symbols.

procedure depends upon large symbolic scenes as much as on the specific, limited symbol. There are scenes and even symbols, usually echoed elsewhere in the book, that achieve almost mythic stature. Moreover, they are analogous to the interrelation between myth and rational statement in combining real (natural) phenomena with a metaphysical ambiguity that is solvable only in terms of the whole structure. In general, the first scene is long, stated in considerable detail, while the second is at times only a passing remark. Our first example concerns the corruption of Zosima's body.[4]

Natural conditions point toward the fact that rapid decomposition is unavoidable and is hastened by the expectation of a miracle. The day is described as clear, the season is late summer, consequently the temperature is high. Zosima's partisans await the odor of sanctity and therefore keep the window shut; they refuse to place flowers in the room, in order to notice at once the slightest smell. There is a constant throng around the bier, composed of those paying their last homage and the merely curious (whatever their motives they all breathe and thereby raise the room temperature). The aged elder had been moribund for some time. In other words, chemically and biologically it would be rather sanguine to expect anything other than the actual result. Under different conditions Zosima's sparse frame might indeed have been helpful in slowing the process of decomposition, but the point here is that such miracles are not to be predicted, expected, and abetted by human volition. When man predicts a miracle, which theologically he cannot do, he may also hinder the miracle physically. The matter might have rested here except that error continues in both camps. Those of "little faith" accept the smell as God's judgment on Zosima's perversion of his office and those who still believe in him anticipate another miracle as the justification of their trust. This new sign, however, entails another argument, on the merits or correctness of innovations introduced at Mt. Athos, and both factions again lose sight of the real issue.[5]

Much later, another set of circumstances precedes Ilyusha's funeral. Although the boy has been ill, his body is young. The season is winter, and while his body lies inside, Snegiryov's room is badly heated. There are fewer visitors; Katerina Ivanovna sends flowers. Thus while a certain ambiguity exists in the physical conditions, the absence of odors is quite logical. Dostoevsky reintroduces the metaphysical note: "Strangely, there was hardly any smell from the body." Zosima's decomposition is presented in eleven pages and its repercussions extend to the end of the book; Ilyusha's is treated in a paragraph. The comment on the boy's odor

4. Cf. Renato Poggioli, "Dostoevsky and Western Realism," *Kenyon Review*, XIII (1951).
5. This is the second time the monastery at Mt. Athos is maligned in the *Brothers*. Fyodor Pavlovich attributes specific sexual connotations to the absence of female animals and fowl from that monastery.

reports a fact which may be variously interpreted, but Dostoevsky clearly wishes something to be made of it. It is certainly not for the reader to judge whether a miracle has taken place, or to adduce proper biblical texts on the innocence and purity of children, or to postulate ethical or religious redemption through love and suffering, despite the fact that all are suggested. They are suggested not in the particular scene, but in the larger complex of the book, where the ramifications of suffering, redemption, corruption, and love occur.

Another example of scenic echo is seen in Kolya Krasotkin's mirroring Ivan's thought and behavior. The impingence of reason on belief, or, in Dostoevsky's formulation, the corrupting effect of Roman Catholicism, western socialism, and utopian theories, shakes Ivan's belief. Disbelief assumes many forms, ranging from the tortured doubts of Ivan, through the complacent Rakitin and shallow Fetyukovich, to the precocious but inexperienced Kolya. It is a widespread phenomenon, propagated less easily by the involved compositions of Ivan than by the superficial, "popularized" views of Rakitin. Each has his followers, Ivan in Smerdyakov, Rakitin in Kolya, who is receptive to a proselytizer of liberal views. The central fact of disbelief finds expression in deeds attuned to the respective characters. Mitya and others note, and Smerdyakov ultimately acts, on Ivan's rational hypothesis "all is permitted if there is no God." The problem of Ivan's guilt is enormously complex and provides the subject for much of the book. Yet the same problem appears in its simplest form in the killing of the goose (Book X, Chapter 5), where the issue is perfectly clear, the guilt and moral consequences (if any) obvious. Like Ivan, Kolya states a scheme; the peasant, putting the scheme into operation, pulls the horse, thereby killing the goose. The episode also points ahead to the trial, for the amused judge condemns the peasant (the instrument) to pay, while he dismisses Kolya (the instigator) with a warning to stop projecting such schemes.

Disbelief may also stem from psychological causes, but here again Kolya resembles Ivan. The chapters devoted to Kolya's background and his behavior among his schoolmates graphically illustrate that he tries to stifle all demonstrative, "emotional" behavior, to seem aloof and indifferent. The same psychological mechanism, developed and petrified, produces Ivan's incapacity for love. Each has had an overdemonstrative mother or female relative; each suffers from the absence of a father. But Kolya is still sufficiently young to permit Alyosha's consideration and good nature to provide a remedy that Ivan would only be able to attain after a grave crisis.

* * *

An explicitly stated concept may be dramatically illustrated by objects which become symbolic. I take the ethical center of the book to lie in Mitya's conclusion in the first part of his confession. . . . The possibility of good and evil constantly coexist in Mitya. He may kill his father, he may not. He may reform, or he may wind up in a slum. At one point they exist in physical objects side by side: as Khokhlakov sends Mitya off to the gold mines, she hangs a medallion of St. Barbara around his neck. The reader of course remembers the other object around Mitya's neck.

Such symbolism pervades the *Brothers Karamazov,* as it does Dostoevsky's other works. In his notes to the novel there is an indication that this is a conscious method. A *nota bene* for the meeting in Book VII between Alyosha and Grushenka admonishes "*Don't forget*—candles,"[6] clearly a symbolic counterpart to the spiritual illumination Grushenka undergoes. Symbols like these can be conveniently grouped. Although physical details are comparatively few in Dostoevsky's works, a description may contain a symbolic detail. Thus Fyodor Pavlovich's fleshy, oblong Adam's apple, the fleshy bags under his eyes, accentuate his propensity for physical debauchery. Ivan's sagging right shoulder, Alyosha's downcast eyes, and Mitya's gesture toward his heart also emphasize characteristic traits. Perhaps the most striking descriptive detail concerns Fetyukovich: as he rises to speak "he constantly bent his back in a peculiar way, particularly at the beginning of the speech, not quite bowing, but as if he were rushing or flying toward his listeners, bending, as it were, just with half of his long back, as though a spring had been placed in the middle of that long, thin back which would enable him to bend almost at a right angle." The mechanical device and bending at unnatural angles perfectly symbolize Fetyukovich's mind.

In addition to those object-symbols previously mentioned, note should be taken of the rock in the epilogue (and the stone casting among the schoolboys), the "dozen" schoolboys who come to Ilyusha's funeral, the envelope Fyodor Pavlovich prepares for Grushenka, the pestle Mitya picks up, the pillow Mitya finds under his head when he wakes from his dream about "the babe"—symbolic proof that his feelings are shared by someone among those surrounding him, Mitya's dirty socks and Smerdyakov's long white sock that contains the 3,000 rubles. . . .

Even colors, though by no means all of them, form a symbolic scheme, in an interplay of red, black and white. A plethora of red colors appears during and after Mitya's vigil under Fyodor Pavlovich's window, and is clearly designed to emphasize blood spilling.

6. F. M. Dostoevskij, *Materiali i issledovanija pod red. A. S. Dolinina* (Leningrad, 1935), p. 177.

The dominating color of the book, however, metaphorically and literally, is black. When it is not merely descriptive, as in Grushenka's dress (though there is something funereal about her reunion with the Pole), it is associated with the elemental force (or black "humor") of the Karamazovs, a corruption of earth's life giving force. Both elements are present in the name: Karamazov is derived from a Turkish root (kará) meaning black, and a Russian one (maz') signifying tar or grease.[13] To emphasize the blackness, Dostoevsky purposely distorts the name in the mouth of Snegiryov's wife, when she substitutes Russian for Turkish and refers to Alyosha as Chernomazov. (Similarly, Dostoevsky emphasizes the significance of the dog's name "Perezvon" ["a chiming of bells"] through Kolya's remark to the Moscow doctor, just in case the reader missed the implication.) Probably the two most important uses of the color black occur during Mitya's dream of the black, charred earth, and in the chapter title "In the Dark" while Mitya is in his own Gethsemane. Black's symbolic counterpart appears most strikingly during Ilyusha's funeral, when the snow is not only a harbinger of winter but of spiritual purification as well, and in Ivan's rescue of the peasant.

Other names, too, form a kind of symbolic shorthand, while remaining perfectly common cognomens.[14] They are sometimes revealed at critical junctures, as during the trial: Grushenka's —Svetlov (light, bright) or Katerina Ivanovna's—Verkhovtsev (upper, supreme—i.e., proud). Dmitri's name is derived from Demeter (earth), Khokhlakov's, like the person, a risible appellation, Fetyukovich (blockhead), Snegiryov (bullfinch, also snow), Rakitin, who is supple like a willow, Smerdyakov (stink), Dr. Herzenstube. Place names are significant—Chermashnya (the name of an estate owned by Dostoevsky's father!) stems from the Slavonic "vermilion" and thus works into the symbolism of red; Mokroe (wet), comparable to the wetting of the earth with tears; Sukhoy Posyolok (dry hamlet), where Mitya rushes to salvage his fortunes through Lyagavy; and, most important, the town of the action, Skotoprigonevsk (stockyard), aptly characterizes the inhabitants, but is not disclosed until the full symbolic meaning can be felt (Book XI, chapter 2).

More traditional symbolism of the four elements, particularly earth and fire, is naturally widespread in the novel. I shall merely note here their main occurrences and functions. The earth as regenerative substance appears first in the epigraph from St. John the Evangelist (later quoted again by Zosima and in a different form by

---

13. W. L. Komarowitsch, *Die Urgestalt der Brüder Karamasoff* (Munich, 1928), p. 93. It is very striking that the Russian *kára* (punishment, retribution) is studiously avoided. It is used only twice, first

by Zosima (Book II, chapter 5), then by Fetyukovich in his peroration.
14. See Ivanov, op. cit., and L. A. Zander, *Dostoïevsky, Le Problème du Bien* (Paris, 1946).

the devil), and is most extensively applied to Mitya: his name, his lengthy exposition of the earth's blessings in the Schiller quotations, the scorched barren earth in his dream at Mokroe, expiation through hard labor underground in Siberia, his project to till the soil in America, his ardent desire to return to Russian soil; even, in comic relief, Khokhlakov's advice to extract gold from the mines. This flighty commercial venture has a double echo in Smerdyakov's returning the money he picks off the ground to Fyodor Pavlovich, and in Snegiryov's trampling money into the ground. Mitya is also the recipient of the symbolic bow to the ground, from Katerina Ivanovna and Zosima. It is Zosima and Alyosha who are most specifically involved in this symbol, so much so that the earth almost discloses its symbolic function: Zosima in his many pronouncements and in his remarkable death (embracing and kissing the earth) and Alyosha whose faith is restored when he repeats his mentor's prostrations. We must also note, and pass over quickly, references to Russian soil and the Russian troika in the trial speeches.

The images of fire in the *Brothers Karamazov* operate primarily as symbols for spiritual ardor and, strikingly, frequently misdirected or excessive ardor. Thus Mitya is physically and symbolically in the dark while he waits in his father's yard, but his is the "Confession of an Ardent Heart."[15] When he is illuminated by (artificial) lights he is at his impulsive worst: he rushes in to beat Fyodor Pavlovich, he receives Katerina Ivanovna, he hails the lights at Mokroe before his final fling. Grushenka uses the image in concealing her presence before departing to the officer: "Draw the curtains . . . otherwise he'll fly directly into the fire." Similarly, Ivan's Legend is permeated with burning and fire; Smerdyakov's indifference occurs in an over-heated room; artificially induced heat by use of liquor or wine leads to excesses in Mitya, Fyodor Pavlovich, and even Grigory, while Lyagavy and Mitya almost die of asphyxiation waiting for the former to sober up. On the other hand, all the moments of regeneration involve not fire but cold: Mitya's dream of the cold babe, Ivan's rescuing the present from freezing, Alyosha's prostration onto the earth on a cold, clear night, the schoolboys during the winter funeral. Dostoevsky almost states his meaning directly. When Katerina Ivanovna comes to Mitya for the money, Mitya reports "I looked at her then for three or four seconds with terrible hatred, that very hatred that only hair separates from love, from the maddest love! I went up to the window, placed my head against the frozen window-pane, and I remember that my head started to burn from that ice as if it were fire". At the farthest extreme from Ivan's burning heretics, his devil recounts his

15. The title is poorly translated in English versions. *Gorjacij* should be ren- dered either by "burning" or "ardent."

sufferings from the excessive cold between planets.

Water in the novel is conspicuous by its absence. Ditches inter-
sect the town, but fresh water is only available outside the town.
When water is mentioned, it becomes significant: dew, redeeming
tears, snow. It appears in each of the regeneration scenes: Ivan's
snow, Alyosha's dew, Mitya's vision of the babe's frozen clothes. . . .

R. P. BLACKMUR

The Brothers Karamazov: III. The Peasants Stand Firm and the Tragedy of the Saint†

With the arrest and examination of Dmitri for the murder of his
father, Dostoevsky changes the phase of his story from something
predominantly outside society and erupting into society, to something within society, acted upon by society, and reacting to society.
At the center is Dmitri passing through ordeal after ordeal. In each
ordeal he attempts to contribute himself *to* society, and in each he
is rejected. Society will have none of what he is, in any sense that
he can give himself. As Alyosha, at the death of his Elder, wanted
justice, and got only the image of justice in his dream of the
miracle at Cana, so here, Dmitri wanted justice at the hands of his
inquisitors but received from them only the deformity of law; as if
in the higher order which he knew he lacked, society could only
express in the individual the injustice wreaked by institutions. It
does him no good that he wishes to be punished for *his* guilt, *his*
baseness, *his* disgrace; and he is in furious rebellion—burning indignation, but not like Swift—against the notion of general guilt or
the worse notion of averaged guilt. It is that fury, that burning,
which compel his confessions to be so insistently individual. This is
why, when the preliminary examination is over, the officials cannot
shake his hand, and this why the young Kalganov does shake his
hand, believing him almost certainly guilty, and sits weeping when
Dmitri is taken away, with no desire to live, asking, Is it worth it?
For the officials, Dmitri has not made himself one of them. For the
youth Kalganov, he has made it plain that there is a point in the
foulest crime where there is no guilt in the criminal, the point
where crime is the natural responsive act against the evil of God's
creation. In the officials and in the youth there is an irretrievable
kind of innocence, which keeps them from direct life. For Dmitri
himself, as for Alyosha, there is the dream in which life is green

† Reprinted from *Eleven Essays in the
European Novel* (New York: Harcourt,
Brace, Jovanovich, 1964), pp. 222–43.

again. Dmitri's dream of the peasants and the weeping babe is a lower version—perhaps a more fundamental version—of Alyosha's dream of his Elder. It will perhaps turn out to be about as far as he can go: the dream of the babe and the embrace of Grushenka. Dmitri is one of those for whom rebirth is not permanent, but only a deeper form of a New Year's resolution; and it would be only to contemn the gods to expect it to last or be complete. It is the straw to catch at, an onion for the moment. It is what men are like. His own words "I have had a good dream, gentlemen," are as much as can be said for it, and it is a great deal, for such dreams happen again. The dreams of Alyosha and the Elder, and of Ivan, are fierce theoretic creations of the ideal which the flesh abuses and which abuse the flesh. In the abuse is the very *plot* of man's created agony.

If Dmitri's ordeals and his dream have a further meaning, it may be that the dream suggests how he may come on himself and rid himself of the institutionalized society which the officials represent. To Dostoevsky, this is no society at all—these forms for judgment and toleration and indifference. True society, for him, is Christian society, full of compassion and intolerance and the sense of identification; based on the lives of those who know, and who are themselves, insult, injury, and humiliation: those who sin like children: elders and peasants and children themselves.

It should be observed that there is a great deal of comedy in the ordeals and examination of Dmitri. This is partly Dostoevsky's way of criticizing the operation of society. More important, it is his recognition that there is always comedy when an individual is confronted without perspective by institutions which wish to take him over; but it is a comedy which constantly edges into the unseemly, at least in Dostoevsky: into the unseemly, the shabby, the scream of degradation. Man is funniest seen against the immediate backdrop of his institutions, always most unseemly when he acts as if he were himself his institutions. If we think of Dmitri naked with his feet sticking out under his quilt, we see it is the three officials, not Dmitri, who have become unseemly. It is they who soil, sully, and rummage in Dmitri's heart. But it is the comedy and unseemliness of real forces: forces to which, for example, Dmitri speaks the truth, because of which he wishes to die honest, with which he must deal: forces which are in the conditions of life. What Dmitri stands for here is the plea that conditions are not ends, nor beginnings, nor meanings. A man does not need positive aspirations or ideals to be revolted at the conditions in which he finds himself; he will respond by tragic gestures and comfort himself by crying out in the most revolting conditions of all. Perhaps the young Kalganov in his own tears sees Dmitri, carried away in his cart, as such a tragic gesture both for Dmitri and for the life he himself has not yet lived.

It is at such points that the comic passes through the tragic into the lyric.

It is as if Dostoevsky had some notion of enforcing such a pattern when he places at the beginning of Part IV and between the book of "The Preliminary Investigation" and the book of "Ivan," the comic, tragic, and lyric book of "The Boys," which has very little directly to do with the story of the murder and indeed provides Alyosha (and Dostoevsky) the opportunity to escape from that murder in the close of the novel. The story of the boys is of course woven into the story of the murder, and once we have read it we are tempted to see deeper parallels than the intention of the author could have commanded merely because it was going on at the same time—namely, the two autumn months between the murder and the trial. If we see different things at the same time it gives us a different vision, while if we see only one thing at a time we sometimes see nothing. In the novel the episode of the boys is what is happening to Alyosha at the same time; it is Alyosha among the nestlings: the other half of his entry into the world at his Elder's command. With the affair and the arrangements and the amenities of the murder as one form of initiation, he must combine the affair of Kolya Krasotkin the mastermind of possibility at thirteen, and Ilyusha Snegiryov, master of nothing but his furious anger—that furious indignation which, in the early teens and even before, is our earliest and first lesson as to what life might and cannot be if only there were no need for arrangements and no deceit in amenities beyond the need and the deceit of transforming the shaggy dog Perezvon—the peal of bells—into the even shaggier dog Zhuchka, whose presence comforts death—a chime of bells to come. Alyosha is the young Scout Master or the Camp Counsellor or the social service worker among the underprivileged or the potentially delinquent boys: Kolya Krasotkin's gang; but he is so in the Russian or Dostoevsky style and to the comedy of Kolya and the tragedy of Ilyusha supplies the lyric at the end.

It is good in itself, this narrative of the *enfant terrible* Kolya and his dog Perezvon, good like something from a more ferocious Dickens or a more "possessed" Cervantes; but let us think what it turns out to be doing here. It is an example of the straight look transforming itself into a deep mimesis. It is the naïve rather than the innocent view of the whole affair of the Karamazovs: baseness, vitality, recklessness, pride, humiliation, humility and all. The naïve is the direct and unimpeded, the innocent is the ignorant and untainted. It ends not with a dream but with Kolya's declaration of love for Alyosha: a declaration not at all innocent. Dostoevsky's babes are innocent but not his young boys. Here we have the special naïvety of the precocious, which with regard to experience and maturity means what is forced and not earned. It is the *jump* to

kingdom come, and it is a wrenching, distorting jump: what gets
there is not all that ought to have got there. The precocious is like
the *cliché* with too little of the original experience animating it.
There is the language without its underpinning; like eunuchs on
Love. Kolya in his precocity is obedient to the attraction of two
forces, one the vanity and ridiculousness of intellectual man which
he thinks he is, and second the spiritual goodness of Alyosha to
which he gradually submits. In a way—the precocious, naïve way
—he responds to everything that confronts him; and he suffers
everywhere from the anguish of not being more than he is. He
suffers what he has not yet become. He has the great advantage of
precocity and naïvety of not knowing to *accommodate* himself
to the quarrel of the forces that infect him. He has no incentive
either to action or to the compromise of action except the incen-
tives of possibility and recklessness as these represent the conditions, not of life, but of his own nature—though his own nature is
a parody of life—life in general and his own specific life to come.
Dostoevsky exposes his secret almost immediately: he is nowhere
equal to his role, is always either excessive or minimal, when he
looks either for words or for actions to correspond to his feelings.
Not that he lacks a full life of feeling; but that life is not organized,
and its parts complete: which must happen in the precocious mind.
Its real life is disorganized and its superficial life is mechanical, and
the mechanics work wonderfully on the organic, wonderfully right
and wonderfully wrong. Thus he has an ascendancy over the other
boys that is a parody of the ascendancy of Alyosha or Zosima. He
is a "desperate character" because it is only by assuming that role
that he can express his feelings. He is not so very different from
Ivan, and his pranks represent the same sort of imagination as that
which produced the Grand Inquisitor: he is a primitive and ferocious form of Ivan—and he feels the same need for Alyosha as
Ivan does.

If we think of Kolya in this way, we see why Alyosha's words on
buffoonery are rightly addressed to him. In his precocity and
naïvety the boy is himself a kind of buffoon *manqué*.[1] His pranks
and vanity and recklessness, his fear of ridicule, his very ascendancy itself, come out in expression a very near thing to buffoonery:
—"a form of resentful irony against those to whom [he] daren't
speak the truth." A near thing but not the same thing.

What is different is why Alyosha could speak these words to him,
and the quality of the difference is plain in what Kolya says to
Ilyusha in his effort to prove that the new dog Perezvon is "really"
the little boy's old dog Zhuchka. " 'You see, old man, he couldn't
have swallowed what you gave him [a pin in a piece of bread on

1. "Failed," "failure" [*Editor*].

Smerdyakov's suggestion]. If he had, he must have died, he must have! So he must have spat it out, since he is still alive. You did not see him do it. But the pin pricked his tongue, that is why he squealed. He ran away squealing and you thought he'd swallowed it. He might well squeal, because the skin of dogs' mouths is so tender . . . tenderer than in men, much tenderer!' Kolya cried impetuously, his face glowing and radiant with delight." Kolya Krasotkin has a power of understanding by mimesis—by dramatic imitation—extraordinarily superior to any mere mechanical precocity. He is brother in precocity to the Karamazovs, especially to Ivan.

The book of "Ivan," like that of "The Boys," covers the two months between the murder and the trial, and the two months reach as far back or forward as you will. It is another mirror held up to the mighty effort of the novel to show how the stress of life is between the harsh and dreadful thing of active love and that beauty which for the immense mass of mankind is found in Sodom. This time the stress is shown in a single soul and is in the end neither resolved nor transcended but is rather tautened to the breaking point of pride. We leave Ivan unconscious, incapable of bearing the burden which he has yet taken up; which he may come to deny or come to affirm: the final version of his tragic gesture that all things are lawful. It is that lawfulness which has reduced him.

But the book is not simply Ivan's, nor his fate simply his own fate. It is the book in which the guilt for the murder is factualized in Smerdyakov, specialized in Ivan, and, so to speak, generalized all round, but not yet realized. But Ivan is only reached after he has been "grown on" a little in the general muddle of guilt and awareness and the consequent atmosphere of mutual self-distrust and plain conspiratorial mistrust that spreads among them all. He is at first only an embittered and half-withdrawn comment upon the others—on Grushenka and Katerina in their raging jealousy of each other; on Mme. Khokhlakov, that woman of little faith, with her swollen foot; on Lise who would eat a pineapple compôte at a crucifixion and who smashes her finger in the door after having said so; on Dmitri, turbulent and wayward in prison, bursting with new life and despairing of God: he will both sing a hymn from underground and will escape to America. It is Alyosha who is the agent of all this as he goes from one to the other, and it is Alyosha who precipitates us into the marmalade of illness in which Ivan struggles for the identity of his own mind as that mind splits: in which dreams become reality and reality evaporates like a dream, and in which the coming of the man who makes himself God is prophesied. Ivan struggles with a devil who does not exist as a means of wrestling with the God in whom he does not believe. He is like Jacob at the stream's edge, but without the treasure of blessings to support him. He would wrestle like a Karamazov, who would give rather than receive blessings. He has lived little, he has hardly begun to love; his mind thus falls apart, reptiles devouring each other. It is the gift of Alyosha to see this: that God was mastering Ivan's unbelieving heart: "He will either rise up in the light of truth, or . . . he'll perish in hate, revenging on himself and on everyone his having served the cause he does not believe in." It is at the end of Ivan's book that Alyosha sees this. We are at the beginning.

Let us see again how the approaches to that end are made. Each is an approach through emotion, the emotion which is at large and quite beyond grasping, and also the emotion which we look to create, though we know it will be inadequate, for the circumstances at hand. At the beginning, Ivan is in the air; something is working him up and he is at the edge of working something up. Dmitri has a secret he cannot fathom. His relations with Katerina are imperfect, as Katerina's with Dmitri are mutilated. Yet all three are clearly bound together, after a fashion which will be the end of Grushenka, as it is at present the source of her jealousy; and out of this relation there is engendered a vast unusable, unchannelable emotion which can vent itself only in quarrels and jealousy and new profundities of distrust. That other proud man, Rakitin the intellectual, sees no less than Grushenka that the emotion is there; a buffoon of pride, he eggs the emotion on by gossip and spite, by the undifferentiated caprice of the underground intellect, until love itself is an early form of jealousy and jealousy the only certain form of love.

Mme. Khokhlakov, on the other hand, is looking for emotion. Her foot swells when Rakitin presses her hand, and she throws him out because to do so makes such a fine scene. For her, aberration is the explanation of everything, and from the point of view of little faith she is right: she says that Dmitri and Katerina and Ivan will all go to Siberia "and they will all torment each other." In her daughter Lise, we find put together both unusable emotion and looked-for emotion worked up together into the great theme of pride as destruction and crime. Ivan is right when, after tearing up unread her letter to him, he says of her that this girl of sixteen offers herself for sale. Lise is parallel to the boy Kolya in precocity, but she is a true phase; she speaks not distortions as Kolya did but base and basic truths. She has a longing to revile God aloud, which is awful fun and takes the breath away. Kalganov, the boy of twenty who shook Dmitri's hand and wept, has made love to her. Lise says of him that he spins like a top and wants to be lashe' Lashed, lashed with a whip. She loves disorder and wants to set to the house, to do evil of all sorts so that everything may destroyed. And so on. The moments when everyone loves c are every moment; everybody secretly loves Dmitri's killing his father. To all this Alyosha assents; it is part of his lesson. But it was Ivan whom she had sent for; and no wonder—she was the pure expressive form of that of which Ivan was only the critical form. She *imagines* the crime and the sweetness of the crime of which she has read: the Jews who crucify the four-year-old boy who dies "soon" in four hours: it was like eating a pineapple compôte. She rejoices in what Ivan found intolerable. She believes where Ivan cannot believe. She has learned the harshness of love and the beauty of Sodom in exactly the sense represented when after she crushes her finger in the door she cries "Wretch wretch wretch," and watches the finger end blacken.

She has learned in little and for the moment what Dmitri has learned in big and uncertainly. Dmitri in prison is in full rebellion against society. Papa was a pig, he quotes Ivan, but his ideas were right enough. His rebellion has three clear forms, and for each there is a corresponding assent and image. There is Rakitin, who has the power of creating the blackguard in you by his bite. Rakitin has a dry, flat soul like a bedbug or a tick which has not eaten for a long time: he is one of those full of rhetoric and pus. He is man the reformer without the idea of God, one of those who make a "social justification for every nasty thing they do." Again, Dmitri rebels at losing God: "One cannot exist in prison without God; it's even more impossible than out of prison. And then we men underground will sing from the bowels of the earth a glorious hymn to God." And third, there is Grushenka's love, which is a kind of conscience he abuses as he abuses his own, by asking forgiveness for an offense which is repeated in the asking: "They are ready to flay you alive, I tell you, all these angels without whom we cannot live." But of Grushenka he also says, "I love such fierce hearts." By that love, by that suffering, he *uses* the unusable emotion. Yet he is tempted between singing the hymn from underground and the idea of escape to America. He wants his guilt and also to be free of it in the world because he was not guilty in the world. In prison he can be the guiltless new man—but outside, who knows? That is why he has to wrench unwilling out of Alyosha a declaration of faith in his innocence.

It is fresh from that declaration, and the accompanying perception of unsuspected depths of hopeless grief in imprisoned innocence, that Alyosha charges Ivan with his general guilt by absolving him, in God's name, of particular guilt. *It was not you.* He spoke by irresistible command; and it leads Ivan at once to assume into himself the nature, if not the mystery, of things: as they have been imaged out by God's spies, Alyosha, Smerdyakov, and his own other self.

This is the preparation for Ivan's three visits to Smerdyakov and his crushing self-communion. The three visits are in parallel to the lacerations of Alyosha and to the ordeals of Dmitri. Each ends in a dream—Alyosha's of his Elder, Dmitri's of the Babe, Ivan's of the devil. Ivan's dream is the most human of the three from—for us, at any rate—the pressure into it of the dream of humility in miracle and the dream of innocence in mystery. It is the dream of pride in authority, the last of the Inquisitor's three terms for the temptations of Christ. Unlike the others, which were additions in stature of soul, his third dream is an exorcism or purgation. Perhaps the three dreams represent the vision of the whole novel and suggest that the culmination is in this dream of lacerated, exacerbated pride; but it may be that the three dreams represent only parallel intimations of another structure: which will emerge in the trial.

But let us look at the three visits. We see at once that the intimacy and cruelty of Ivan's relations to Smerdyakov come about from Ivan's overwhelming knowledge that Smerdyakov is his own other self. This at first he denies, though he wears its burden in the image of himself the night before the murder listening in the dark at the top of the stairs to his father's movements below. That was the crossing point between the two selves, and to remember it now, after Smerdyakov has said, "Forgive me, I thought you were like me," is the laceration of self-suspicion, the awakening of the self to suspecting the self.

When in the second visit, Smerdyakov supplies him with a motive good for both his selves, he finds that he must kill his other self. Then the image of the stairs becomes not the crossing point but the merging point of the two selves. He had not only helped the murder along by awareness, he had partly created it and shared the guilt of Smerdyakov by being a murderer at heart. That—that recognition—was why he and Katerina had become like two enemies in love. This is the laceration of created motive, when the creation has been done without conscience.

The third visit completes this part of the movement of Ivan's soul. It begins with the peasant, drunk and freezing in the snow by Ivan's doing as it ends with Ivan reviving him, sobering him for the judgment to come. This is Ivan's wretched rejoicing—the sweet excitement of the pineapple compôte; he is approaching a mature form of the precocity of Lise and, in his own way, the fierce hearts of Dmitri and Grushenka. On this visit the night before the trial Ivan falters when he says "I knew it was not I"—as if he knew he could never save himself from the real by retreat upon the mere actual. But he learns most by understanding that Smerdyakov was not a fool, that he had enacted "all things are lawful," and that he, too, had dreamed of a new life. How wonderful it is, that as Ivan is about to go, leaving Smerdyakov to hang himself among the crackling cockroaches, Smerdyakov cries "Stay a moment. . . . Show me those notes again," and looks at the money for ten seconds. Perhaps the money burned Ivan, too. When he goes, though he helps the freezing peasant who on the morrow will come to judgment upon them all, he is not himself ready to act on his own resolution. The irritating monster of his other self is still within him, the monster of the truth refused; which is the worst laceration of all, and altogether the right last preparation for his dream of the devil —that poor relation [sponger—ed.] of the best class who lives within us. The dream needs no comment. It is with the poor relations within us we see where we ourselves are shabby.

One has an odd feeling in the book of "Ivan" that the guilt of Ivan, or Smerdyakov, or of the others, is not adult guilt but childish guilt. Think of any of them and you think of Lise and her smashed finger. Perhaps Dostoevsky thought that for guilt, as for redemption, at the crisis the thing is to become a child. Just the same, Dostoevsky does not show us so much the relapse to the child as the breakdown of the mature. It is the mature that is precarious— with one moment of ripeness—not the childish that is safe. Maturity, if ever we had had it, would haunt us like the Muse. The old innocence cannot be recovered—though a new one may be achieved, whether along Alyosha's exemplary path or Ivan's wrestling fling, if it does not kill him. One wonders whether Alyosha was old enough to follow. There is a curse on us about children, which is the baggage we carry and which we think they do not. But *we* know that the children know, and so does Dostoevsky's novel. That is why the trial of Dmitri is a "Miscarriage of Justice"—any child would know that!—and why is it essentially, as any trial may seem to the individual tried, trial by ordeal and laceration and calumny: by injury, insult, humiliation: fire, water, whips. That is why, in defense, the prisoner tries—as any child would—tantrums, hysterias, stigmata. Perhaps it is in the nature of guilt to be childish; perhaps guilt does not mature well; perhaps that is why so many of us don't want to grow up: we cling to our guilt as the only thing that is ours.

Before going into the trial of Dmitri, it is worth considering once again how after Dmitri's arrest everything takes a different direction, which is the direction of society—the very society *within which* the Elder and the Karamazovs had been operating all along. What we get is a series of smudges from the dirty thumb of society without loss of the sense of what is smudged. When Dmitri breaks down, it is into society—both in his confession about the three thousand rubles and in his dream of the babe. He is at once sent into Coventry by "official" society and is ever afterwards left there without being "understood" and without the possibility of being understood. Official society is not meant to understand; it absorbs or expels; and leaves the job of understanding to the individual to whom society happens. All along, here, the author is working on those instincts which prophesy society and make it necessary, but which differ sharply in object from any society which has ever existed. That is why when we see Dmitri on the verge of going to trial, he is torn by the motive of escape to America and also by the motive of the hymn from underground or submission. This is not just a contrivance of the novelist, not motive (or the conflict of motives) at the level of plot; it is the created motive which is the positive achievement of literary art; it rises from way under the social routines in which it is engaged. One way of defining the "form" of the novel is as the sum of stresses upon character by which such motive is elicited—is elucidated—is created. It was *in order* to create such a motive that in the beginning the Karamazovs were given as without motives but as with conflicts; that there was a murder posited; that the figures of Zosima and the Grand Inquisitor were furnished *outside* the brothers and the murder, though tied to them; and—still *in order* to create motive—that Dmitri is precipitated by his act, and by his dream, into "society" both official and other. Only in society could the motive show as moving anything worth moving, for it is only in society that all of us partly live.

But Dmitri alone would not have been enough. We need all the brothers and all their women. They must all break down into society—and so they do in the fellowship of jealousy and suspicion and devils. We need also Smerdyakov and the death of Smerdyakov: to provide the foil of a full breakdown of the man without a motive—but with possibilities of only the routine sort of nastiness (the epileptic half of the saint). We need also the Boys, the affair of Kolya and Ilyusha, to provide another foil of plain unseemliness, of original evil, where those who are not yet ready or ripe for motive are broken down into a society stripped of routine to a bare piety which has no place to lodge. We need all this—at this point in this novel—as provision and bedding for Dmitri's motive and Dmitri's innocent guilt or guilty innocence. It seems thus in the natural order to introduce Dmitri's motive with Lise slamming the door on her finger after her epiphany, not of guilt but of crime or positive evil; and equally natural to follow it with the affair of Ivan and the freezing peasant. What are peasants for—even to Dostoevsky—but to strike down and, after an indecent interval in hell, to rise up? It is the peasant in us who can stand both the act of murder and the act of creation; he is the fellow who can take up the slack of both kinds of unseemliness, both kinds of faith, both kinds of motive: the social and the rebellious; and he gets back at us, when the line is taut, by collectively standing firm. The peasant is under society, or used to be, and is ready to receive it when it is played out; yet he needs society to fulfill his rôle—in that respect only resembling the proletariat, his political successor, for otherwise he is the proletariat's deadly enemy. Neither the peasant nor the proletarian needs to understand himself; the function of either is to judge those who presume to understand him. Should one say that the proletariat—those who are in but not of the society—is what an urban society does to the peasantry? Can the imagination turn for succor to the proletariat as it has so long turned (when is apparent foundations were shaken) to the peasantry? Does the proletariat represent the extreme of that "mighty movement against nature" (Bergson's phrase) which we call democracy? Dostoevsky would have refused these questions. We cannot.

Dostoevsky had the earlier question. At the trial the paradigm of Society and the Peasants is at once set up and never dropped till the verdict is brought in. Society is the audience, the jury without a vote, and divides by sex in its sympathies. The presiding judge is interested in crime as a product of society. The prosecutor is interested in the security of society. The defending attorney is interested in psychology in the "scientific" or explanatory sense (rather than in the penetrating, identifying sense). In short, we have society in an hysterico-official form. The prisoner wears a new frock coat, black kid gloves, fine linen: a dandy; and pleads guilty to dissipation and debauchery, innocent to the crime as charged. Beyond the prisoner is the jury, composed of two stolid and silent merchants, four petty officials almost peasants who never read books, the rest artisans and peasants. The whole jury was thus potentially peasant and half of it actually so. Could such a jury try such a case? Dostoevsky says of them: "Their faces made a strangely imposing, almost menacing, impression; they were stern and frowning." This jury would try the case it saw—which is what juries commonly do when provoked or cheated or implicated.

What Dostoevsky is showing is that in law—in society—Dmitri is guilty and ought to be acquitted, and that in fact—in the peasants—Dmitri is innocent and must be convicted. It does not matter in the least that to secure either of these imperatives the reading of the facts must be mistaken. A false reading may be nearer the creative heart, and to Dostoevsky it is Dmitri's new-created motive that must be judged and judged through the medium of judicial error. We see the error happen.

The prosecution with cross-examination takes three forms. The Dangerous Witnesses establish motive and opportunity with much sound circumstantial evidence. But the witnesses themselves are also on trial and are subjected to the ordeal of humiliation. Old Grigory was drunk enough to have seen the gates of heaven, let alone a garden gate. Rakitin is making money and prestige out of the trial and is smirched by his relations with Grushenka—the twenty-five rubles received for bringing Alyosha to her in his monk's clothes. Trifon Borisovich, the innkeeper, has evidently mulcted Dmitri. The Poles had cheated at cards. The evidence is sound but the witnesses are shown unsound. The Medical Experts, who make the next stage of the prosecution, no doubt fuddled the jury as much as they annoyed Dostoevsky and outraged the prisoner. In the third stage, called "Fortune Smiles on Mitya," we have the unsupported goodness of Alyosha stating his conviction of Dmitri's innocence and remembering how Dmitri had struck his breast meaning he had the money before the murder. He is followed by Katerina, all in black. She says she had given Dmitri the three thousand rubles not only to post but to use if he wanted. He had a right. She tells her story how Dmitri had saved her father from arrest for embezzlement with his own five thousand rubles and how he had bowed down to her. When she has done humiliating herself, everybody thinks she has helped Dmitri. The prisoner knows better and cries out that she has ruined him and that now he is condemned; and he was right. Grushenka, also all in black and shawled, adds nothing not harmful: how she had played with the father and the son and Katerina. She accuses Katerina of general guilt and Smerdyakov of particular guilt. All this stirs up fresh emotion and hysteria and leaves her in contempt.

It is now Ivan's turn to present the Sudden Catastrophe: his assumption of guilt and Katerina's consequent reversal of her first testimony. Ivan enters, irreproachable, but with an earthy look, like a dying man's look. He struggles within himself, hesitates—like the peasant girl, as he says, who will stand up if she likes and won't if she doesn't. He then produces the three thousand rubles for the sake of which "our father was murdered." He then states that Smerdyakov did it but that he incited him. Here, from an upward urge, is the visible conversion downwards. In some sense he does not believe the cause which he is serving and therefore revenges it on himself and everyone else. Even so, within the intention, he is honest. Perhaps it is the honesty of the sick soul: of the soul which discovers itself to be sick; a universal possibility.

"Who doesn't desire his father's death?" he cries and looks at the "ugly faces" in the courtroom. "They all desire the death of their fathers. One reptile devours another. . . . If there hadn't been a murder, they'd have been angry and gone home ill-humored." Here is the fruition of Lise who, when she hears the story of a murdered child, thinks of a pineapple compôte. Here is Ivan, like Lise, slamming his finger in the door. It is a whole school of insight: whether or not there is guilt, and especially if there is no guilt, there must be a crime. One would not doubt that Ivan is speaking for the official society which the court—all but the jury—represents. Thus he goes on that the devil who does not exist is his only witness—that bad half of himself—and urges that *that* monster, Dmitri, singing a hymn, should be released. . . . But society is never sure enough of itself to accept any one hysteria except in the form of another hysteria, only superficially more healthy, such as crime or love. Katerina is good in both cases. When she is confronted by Ivan's vision of "that monster," she gives in evidence his letter of desperation and murderous intent and tells the "other" truth (for doubtless both accounts were true enough) about the three thousand rubles. She had given them to tempt and humiliate Dmitri: to dishonor him. They had hated each other in their love, which had risen on a point of honor, and each strove to dishonor the other, since neither trusted the other's love and each was injured by his own. At the height of her hysteria, Katerina turns to Ivan and sees "how Ivan had been driven nearly out of his mind during the last two months trying to save 'the monster and murderer,' his brother." What then was the true nature of Katerina's love, or Ivan's love, or Dmitri's: pride, revenge, honor, the ignominy which is attached to all these, at any rate a laceration? Like the money—and whichever three thousand rubles you like—the love, any of these loves, was convertible.—At any rate, the evidence ends in the coil and recoil of contentious hysterias. It is at least true that everybody has been stripped of his finery, whether of simple crime or active love.

Forthwith, in the two speeches for the Prosecution and for the Defense, Dostoevsky puts the finery right back but with the thing stripped naked more than ever there: the beauty and the horror of seeing people naked under their clothes. The Prosecution, the Defense, and the Jury all look at the Karamazovs as characteristic, as representative Russian criminals, Russian heroes, Russian Christs. We have a triptych on an altar, with the Jury of Peasants in the center. We have also a trial at law.

The prosecutor argues for the security of society and he uses the language of a liberal sociology. The criminal must be socially punished to alleviate the sting of his conscience and as part of an effort to halt the furious course of the Galloping Troika which was Russia on her wild and irrational way. To this Dmitri listened and looked on, and at one time, when Rakitin's opinion of Grushenka is mentioned, he murmured: "The Bernards!"—as if the evils of this sort of thinking were children of Claude Bernard, of the new physiology and the new medicine.

The speech for the defense must have been nearly as unwelcome to Dmitri as the prosecutor's. The first part merely upset the chain of evidence; and the second part, though technically claiming innocence, assumed factual guilt but so reconstructed the crime that mercy was the only possible punishment for it. It was again liberal sociology, but this time on the psychological side. The very reasons the prosecution had advanced to give Dmitri motive for the murder, now become palliatives and even justification for his having done it. The argument in short is that Dmitri is guilty but his father was not a father, the money did not exist, and so on. It is not Dmitri who is guilty in any justiciable sense, but society. To the Elder Zosima's belief that all are guilty of all sin; to the Grand Inquisitor's or Ivan's belief that none are guilty, all is lawful; —to either of these, counsel for defense argues: Society is guilty of my sin.

Zosima's peasants—the "krest'yánye," as the word goes in Russian—those who were there first, will have neither the sociology nor the psychology nor any facts not pertinent to their own rôle. The peasants stand firm and find Dmitri guilty of a crime he did not commit: which they might even know ever so well and still find irrelevant. From their point of view, and I think from ours, as the old Karamazov was the proper man for murder, so Dmitri was the proper man for guilt. If it is thought about at all, it ought surely to be held that the jury, in its own way, was possessed of our superior knowledge. But it is better not to think about it that way at all. The peasants may or may not have seen a crime; they certainly saw guilt: hysteria, upset, hubbub, the creature of the dark; and in their verdict they only said what they saw. Granted the story, granted the characters, and granted the pitch or level at which the characters take over the story, no less a mystery—and no more of a mystification—would have been possible. The blank space had to be left in the darkness:[2] to be filled partly by the momentum of the novel, partly by the needs of the brothers Karamazov, and partly by the needs of the readers. The one thing certain is that society had to convict the wrong man; and the one prophecy certain is that the wrong man of society should be—no matter who he was—the right man for the peasants.

There is always a deeper justice done to the whole of society in the conviction of a wrong man than there can ever be in the conviction of the right man. The wrong man is guilty regardless; the right man only incidentally. The wrong man is guilty of ourselves, if not of ourselves individually, then of our ideals or of our institutions. The right man is gulty only of—some paltry crime like another.... This would be seemingly true with or without Dostoevsky's anterior convictions, for it has to do with an incontrovertible actuality: that the determination of guilt is a very human process forced upon us equally by our ideals and the failure of our ideals in action. That is why we have scapegoats, and why we have so often conceived scapegoats as innocent. The innocence of the scapegoat is sometimes a terrible enlargement of our individual experience of guilt. Naturally we are tempted to let him off, to let

2. In the preceding part of the essay, Blackmur writes: "the murder is committed 'In the Dark'—in a gap of white paper in the black print of the book. We see why we are not given the mere deed. There was no 'mere' deed" [*Editor*].

him escape, if we could. After all we are not peasants; we only resort to them; we know all along that they are an impossible ideal of which our best knowledge, like our other knowledge, is what is seen in the mirror of the possible. We resort to the impossible and enact it dramatically or symbolically in art or religion, as Dostoevsky does, because we have no satisfying measure of the possible. Yet it is our grace to revert to the possible when we are not fanatic.

So, in the "Epilogue," when the sense of the possible returns to her, Katerina is desperate because of her treachery at the trial. So, too, Alyosha can tell Dmitri that *because he is innocent* he cannot take up the cross of Siberia: "Such heavy burdens are not for all men. For some they are impossible." And so again, between Dmitri and Katerina, each will always be a sore place in the other's heart because each had tried to make a scapegoat of the other. But Dostoevsky cannot let it go at that; he must reverse the insight and give it pristine form. Just before Ilyusha's funeral, Kolya the teenager, hearing from Alyosha that Dmitri is innocent, Smerdyakov guilty, of the murder, cries out: "So he will perish an innocent victim! though he is ruined he is happy! I could envy him!" When asked why, he answers: "Oh, if I, too, could sacrifice myself someday for truth!" As if this were not enough, we have the funeral, the crumbling of the bread on the grave so the sparrows will come, and the breakdown of the "wisp of tow," the dead boy's father. Sorrow and then pancakes, says Kolya. But before the pancakes Alyosha makes it plain at the stone that Ilyusha "at whom we threw stones," is a scapegoat willy-nilly and must be remembered come evil or come good. They go in to eat pancakes, and the boys cry to Alyosha, "Hurrah for Karamazov!"

Before we repeat that cheer, let us go back once again to the trial. Those who longed for acquittal were convinced of guilt: the guilt of their own humanity, sentiments, and new ideas. Many of those who testified against Dmitri—Grigory a servant, Rakitin a sneak, Snegiryov a drunkard, Trifon Borisovich a thief, the Poles who were cheats—are all discredited forms of truth. The two doctors are impertinent forms of truth. Alyosha shows the goodness of truth incredibly. Katerina shows first incredible immolation, then incredible hysterias of truth. Grushenka in the flaring revenge she takes at the contempt shown to her belittles the truth. Only Ivan tries to tell the truth straight and is compelled to act like a buffoon; he, like Katerina, is taken as hysterical. He is right when he says he is not mad, only a murderer. He remembers his last night in his father's house.

The speeches of counsel reach the same conclusion by a different route; each is after a scapegoat, one to stop the Troika, the other to find a means in mercy to ignore—or accept—it: one masculine, the other feminine. The prosecutor insists on the credible truth—the creditable "social" truth—all but the "truth" itself. The defense discredits all the credible truth, any version of it, insisting that no one is up to his own actions; he too wants a creditable "social" truth: that you can punish only by mercy. In either case, Dmitri is not a murderer but mad: mad by the pressure of society. When the peasants stand firm, it seems to me they stand opposed to all the forms and versions of the facts to which they have been exposed. They take what is there and react. Like the underground man,[3] when given an instant of power, they react by caprice, by a goatish act of their own inner natures—an act, that is, both goatish and the result of contemplation, long digested in long silence. I do not say Dostoevsky would have admitted this; but the underground was nearer the steady surface of him than he thought, a part of every balance, however brief, however recurring, that his nature struck. The idea of the scapegoat and the idea of caprice are as close as the words.

There is a trick of the mind, a caprice of our own, to which we can here resort in looking at this tale of parricide. Is there not something capricious—however recurring, no less capricious— about the notions of both guilt and innocence whenever we see them stripped of their conventions and their sanctions in institutions? This is one of the possibilities to which Dostoevsky's extraordinary powers of mimesis led him. This is what is intermittently envisaged in the baseness of the Karamazovs; and it makes a magnificent example of the inevitable irresponsibility—that is, the absolute responsiveness—of the aesthetic imagination to any *instance* of life once seen and felt as possible. The imagination itself, what apprehends the instance, and what survives it, is something else again; perhaps inevitably responsible, perhaps at some point, by a great act of will, capable of uniting in a single responsive act the two forms of responsibility—to the possibilities and to the everlasting necessities of life. Some believe that such acts took place at certain moments of history when tradition united with experience: Sophocles, Dante, and the later Shakespeare. (Thus we speak of *The Tempest* as the prophetic image of the modern mind; a prophecy unfulfilled.) This is a convenient belief. I wonder if it is not the better part of tradition to believe that on the evidence such imaginative acts are so rare as to escape particular instants of history; they yield rather to the rigors and simplicities of aesthetic form by some even rarer contingency of miracle, mystery, and authority and not always—certainly not in *The Brothers Karamazov*—in the conclusion of the work. I think Dostoevsky knew that, and the title to his next to last chapter—"For a Moment the Lie Becomes the Truth"—is his acknowledgement. There the lacerated

3. The narrator in Dostoevsky's *Notes from Underground* [Editor].

love of the two elder brothers and the two women becomes, in the midst of vindictiveness and inadequacy, at once a mutual sore spot and something like a full motivation, not only for them all together but for each in his or her independence.

Again, lastly, the final chapter is by way of a sermon, a prayer, and an invocation. The last thing Dostoevsky can find to say is about the good memory of a dead boy: of a great evil and a greater good without innocence without guilt without sin, but under the images of all these: about what happened before life had begun to be fully lived and what, so to speak, could not happen in full life at all. It is almost as if Dostoevsky was compelled to say that as a regular thing the truth will at most for a moment become a lie. I suggest that in the last words of the novel—"Hurrah for Karamazov!"—[4] Dostoevsky is making for his whole novel one of those tragic phrases which comfort the heart beyond possibility and denying necessity, and which must be forgiven, for "without them, sorrow would be too heavy for men to bear." The whole novel? Let us say that "Hurrah for Karamazov!" covers and includes the tragic phrases of the three dreams: the wine of new gladness, the babe, and the devil of the other self, and does so under the triple aegis of Zosima's harsh and dreadful thing which is active love, of Dmitri's beauty of Sodom, and of Ivan's wise and dread spirit of destruction. This is how it is that in *The Brothers Karamazov* the plain and overwhelming story of a murder is lifted into the condition of miracle, mystery, and authority. Hurrah for all the Karamazovs! for here is the condition where all are guilty and none are guilty. To live in that condition, and to love life, is to endure the tragedy of the saint. In his novel the saint is migratory among the three brothers, nowhere at home.

---

4. The phrase itself does not conclude the original, but its echo does. It was added by the translator, Mrs. Garnett, and has been excised from this edition. See "Afterword: On translating *The Brothers Karamazov*" [*Editor*].

Selected Bibliography

The books from which the essays in this volume were derived are not listed. A bibliography of works in English appears in *Modern Fiction Studies*, IV, iii (Autumn, 1958).

Dostoevsky, F. M., *The Notebooks for* The Brothers Karamazov, edited and translated by Edward Wasiolek. Chicago, 1971.
———, *The Diary of a Writer*, translated by Boris Brasol. New York, 1949.
Berdiaev, N. A., *Dostoevsky*, translated by D. Attwater. New York, 1957.
Carr, E. H., *Dostoevsky*. New York, 1973.
Coulson, J., *Dostoevsky: A Self-Portrait*. London, 1962.
Curle, R., *Characters of Dostoevsky: Studies from Four Novels*. London, 1950.
Eng, J. van der & J. M. Meijer, The Brothers Karamazov *by F. M. Dostoevskij*, The Hague, 1971.
Freud, S., "Dostoevsky and Parricide," Collected Works, XXI (New York, 1976).
Holquist, M., *Dostoevsky and the Novel*. Princeton, 1977.
Gide, A., *Dostoevsky*. London, 1952.
Hemmings, F. W. J., *The Russian Novel in France, 1884–1914*. London, 1950.
Ivanov, V., *Freedom and the Tragic Life: A Study in Dostoevsky*. New York, 1957.
Magarshack, D., *Dostoevsky*. New York, 1961.
Rahv, P., "The Legend of the Grand Inquisitor," *Partisan Review*, XXI (1954).
———, "The Other Dostoevsky," *New York Review of Books*, April 20, 1972.
Rozanov, V. V., *Dostoevsky and the Legend of the Grand Inquisitor*, translated by Spencer E. Roberts. Ithaca, N. Y., 1972.
Sandoz, E., *Political Apocalypse: A Study of Dostoevsky's Grand Inquisitor*. Baton Rouge, 1971.
Seduro, V., *Dostoevsky in Russian Literary Criticism*. New York, 1957.
Sewall, R. B., "The Tragic World of the Karamazovs," in *Tragic Themes in Modern Literature*, edited by C. Brooks. New York, 1955.
Shestov, L., *Dostoevsky, Tolstoy and Nietzsche*. Columbus, Ohio, 1969.
Simmons, E. J., *Dostoevsky, the Making of a Novelist*. London, 1950.
Terras, V., *A Karamazov Companion: Commentary on the Genesis, Language, and Style of Dostoevsky's Novel*. Madison, WI, 1981.
Vivas, E., "Two Dimensions of Reality in *The Brothers Karamazov*," *Sewanee Review*, LIX (1951).
Wasiolek, E. (ed.), The Brothers Karamazov *and the Critics*. Belmont, California, 1967.
Wellek, R. (ed.), *Dostoevsky: A Collection of Critical Essays*. Englewood Cliffs, N.J., 1962.
Yarmolinsky, A., *Dostoevsky, His Life and Art*. New York, 1957.
Zander, L., *Dostoevsky*, translated by N. Duddington. London, 1948.

NORTON CRITICAL EDITIONS

ANDERSON *Winesburg, Ohio* edited by Charles E. Modlin and Ray Lewis White
AQUINAS *St. Thomas Aquinas on Politics and Ethics* translated and edited by
Paul E. Sigmund
AUSTEN *Emma* edited by Stephen M. Parrish *Third Edition*
AUSTEN *Mansfield Park* edited by Claudia L. Johnson
AUSTEN *Persuasion* edited by Patricia Meyer Spacks
AUSTEN *Pride and Prejudice* edited by Donald Gray *Second Edition*
BALZAC *Père Goriot* translated by Burton Raffel, edited by Peter Brooks
BEHN *Oroonoko* edited by Joanna Lipking
Beowulf (the Donaldson translation) edited by Joseph F. Tuso
BLAKE *Blake's Poetry and Designs* selected and edited by Mary Lynn Johnson and
John E. Grant
BOCCACCIO *The Decameron* selected, translated, and edited by Mark Musa and
Peter E. Bondanella
BRONTË, CHARLOTTE *Jane Eyre* edited by Richard J. Dunn *Second Edition*
BRONTË, EMILY *Wuthering Heights* edited by William M. Sale, Jr., and Richard Dunn
Third Edition
BROWNING, ELIZABETH BARRETT *Aurora Leigh* edited by Margaret Reynolds
BROWNING, ROBERT *Browning's Poetry* selected and edited by James F. Loucks
BURNEY *Evelina* edited by Stewart J. Cooke
BYRON *Byron's Poetry* selected and edited by Frank D. McConnell
CARROLL *Alice in Wonderland* edited by Donald J. Gray *Second Edition*
CERVANTES *Don Quijote* translated by Burton Raffel, edited by Diana de Armas Wilson
CHAUCER *The Canterbury Tales: Nine Tales and the General Prologue* edited by
V. A. Kolve and Glending Olson
CHEKHOV *Anton Chekhov's Plays* translated and edited by Eugene K. Bristow
CHEKHOV *Anton Chekhov's Short Stories* selected and edited by Ralph E. Matlaw
CHOPIN *The Awakening* edited by Margo Culley *Second Edition*
The Classic Fairy Tales edited by Maria Tatar
CONRAD *Heart of Darkness* edited by Robert Kimbrough *Third Edition*
CONRAD *Lord Jim* edited by Thomas C. Moser *Second Edition*
CONRAD *The Nigger of the "Narcissus"* edited by Robert Kimbrough
CRANE *Maggie: A Girl of the Streets* edited by Thomas A. Gullason
CRANE *The Red Badge of Courage* edited by Donald Pizer *Third Edition*
DARWIN *Darwin* selected and edited by Philip Appleman *Second Edition*
DEFOE *A Journal of the Plague Year* edited by Paula R. Backscheider
DEFOE *Moll Flanders* edited by Edward Kelly
DEFOE *Robinson Crusoe* edited by Michael Shinagel *Second Edition*
DE PIZAN *The Selected Writings of Christine de Pizan* translated by Renate
Blumenfeld-Kosinski and Kevin Brownlee, edited by Renate Blumenfeld-Kosinski
DICKENS *Bleak House* edited by George Ford and Sylvère Monod
DICKENS *David Copperfield* edited by Jerome H. Buckley
DICKENS *Great Expectations* edited by Edgar Rosenberg
DICKENS *Hard Times* edited by George Ford and Sylvère Monod *Second Edition*
DICKENS *Oliver Twist* edited by Fred Kaplan
DONNE *John Donne's Poetry* selected and edited by Arthur L. Clements *Second Edition*
DOSTOEVSKY *The Brothers Karamazov* (the Garnett translation) edited by Ralph E. Matlaw
DOSTOEVSKY *Crime and Punishment* (the Coulson translation) edited by George Gibian
Third Edition
DOSTOEVSKY *Notes from Underground* translated and edited by Michael R. Katz

MILTON *Paradise Lost* edited by Scott Elledge *Second Edition*
Modern Irish Drama edited by John P. Harrington
MORE *Utopia* translated and edited by Robert M. Adams *Second Edition*
NEWMAN *Apologia Pro Vita Sua* edited by David J. DeLaura
NEWTON *Newton* edited by I. Bernard Cohen and Richard S. Westfall
NORRIS *McTeague* edited by Donald Pizer *Second Edition*
Restoration and Eighteenth-Century Comedy edited by Scott McMillin *Second Edition*
RHYS *Wide Sargasso Sea* edited by Judith L. Raiskin
RICH *Adrienne Rich's Poetry and Prose* edited by Barbara Charlesworth Gelpi and
Albert Gelpi
ROUSSEAU *Rousseau's Political Writings* edited by Alan Ritter, translated by
Julia Conaway Bondanella
ST. PAUL *The Writings of St. Paul* edited by Wayne A. Meeks
SHAKESPEARE *Hamlet* edited by Cyrus Hoy *Second Edition*
SHAKESPEARE *Henry IV, Part I* edited by James L. Sanderson *Second Edition*
SHAW *Bernard Shaw's Plays* edited by Warren Sylvester Smith
SHELLEY, MARY *Frankenstein* edited by J. Paul Hunter
SHELLEY, PERCY BYSSHE *Shelley's Poetry and Prose* selected and edited by
Donald H. Reiman and Sharon B. Powers
SMOLLETT *Humphry Clinker* edited by James L. Thorson
SOPHOCLES *Oedipus Tyrannus* translated and edited by Luci Berkowitz and
Theodore F. Brunner
SPENSER *Edmund Spenser's Poetry* selected and edited by Hugh Maclean and
Anne Lake Prescott *Third Edition*
STENDHAL *Red and Black* translated and edited by Robert M. Adams
STERNE *Tristram Shandy* edited by Howard Anderson
STOKER *Dracula* edited by Nina Auerbach and David Skal
STOWE *Uncle Tom's Cabin* edited by Elizabeth Ammons
SWIFT *Gulliver's Travels* edited by Robert A. Greenberg *Second Edition*
SWIFT *The Writings of Jonathan Swift* edited by Robert A. Greenberg and William B. Piper
TENNYSON *In Memoriam* edited by Robert H. Ross
TENNYSON *Tennyson's Poetry* selected and edited by Robert W. Hill, Jr. *Second Edition*
THACKERAY *Vanity Fair* edited by Peter Shillingsburg
THOREAU *Walden and Resistance to Civil Government* edited by William Rossi *Second Edition*
THUCYDIDES *The Peloponnesian War* translated by Walter Blanco, edited by Walter Blanco
and Jennifer Tolbert Roberts
TOLSTOY *Anna Karenina* edited and with a revised translation by George Gibian *Second Edition*
TOLSTOY *Tolstoy's Short Fiction* edited and with revised translations by Michael R. Katz
TOLSTOY *War and Peace* (the Maude translation) edited by George Gibian *Second Edition*
TOOMER *Cane* edited by Darwin T. Turner
TURGENEV *Fathers and Sons* translated and edited by Michael R. Katz
TWAIN *Adventures of Huckleberry Finn* edited by Thomas Cooley *Third Edition*
TWAIN *A Connecticut Yankee in King Arthur's Court* edited by Allison R. Ensor
TWAIN *Pudd'nhead Wilson and Those Extraordinary Twins* edited by Sidney E. Berger
VOLTAIRE *Candide* translated and edited by Robert M. Adams *Second Edition*
WASHINGTON *Up From Slavery* edited by William L. Andrews
WATSON *The Double Helix: A Personal Account of the Discovery of the Structure of DNA*
edited by Gunther S. Stent
WHARTON *Ethan Frome* edited by Kristin O. Lauer and Cynthia Griffin Wolff
WHARTON *The House of Mirth* edited by Elizabeth Ammons
WHITMAN *Leaves of Grass* edited by Sculley Bradley and Harold W. Blodgett
WILDE *The Picture of Dorian Gray* edited by Donald L. Lawler
WOLLSTONECRAFT *A Vindication of the Rights of Woman* edited by Carol H. Poston
Second Edition
WORDSWORTH *The Prelude: 1799, 1805, 1850* edited by Jonathan Wordsworth,
M. H. Abrams, and Stephen Gill

DOUGLASS *Narrative of the Life of Frederick Douglass, an American Slave, Written by Himself* edited by William L. Andrews and William S. McFeely

DREISER *Sister Carrie* edited by Donald Pizer *Second Edition*

Eight Modern Plays edited by Anthony Caputi

DU BOIS *The Souls of Black Folk* edited by Henry Louis Gates Jr. and Terri Oliver

ELIOT *Middlemarch* edited by Bert G. Hornback

ELIOT *The Mill on the Floss* edited by Carol T. Christ

ERASMUS *The Praise of Folly and Other Writings* translated and edited by Robert M. Adams

FAULKNER *The Sound and the Fury* edited by David Minter *Second Edition*

FIELDING *Joseph Andrews with Shamela and Related Writings* edited by Homer Goldberg

FIELDING *Tom Jones* edited by Sheridan Baker *Second Edition*

FLAUBERT *Madame Bovary* edited with a substantially new translation by Paul de Man

FORD *The Good Soldier* edited by Martin Stannard

FORSTER *Howards End* edited by Paul B. Armstrong

FRANKLIN *Benjamin Franklin's Autobiography* edited by J. A. Leo Lemay and P. M. Zall

FULLER *Woman in the Nineteenth Century* edited by Larry J. Reynolds

GOETHE *Faust* translated by Walter Arndt, edited by Cyrus Hamlin

GOGOL *Dead Souls* (the Reavey translation) edited by George Gibian

HARDY *Far from the Madding Crowd* edited by Robert C. Schweik

HARDY *Jude the Obscure* edited by Norman Page *Second Edition*

HARDY *The Mayor of Casterbridge* edited by James K. Robinson

HARDY *The Return of the Native* edited by James Gindin

HARDY *Tess of the d'Urbervilles* edited by Scott Elledge *Third Edition*

HAWTHORNE *The Blithedale Romance* edited by Seymour Gross and Rosalie Murphy

HAWTHORNE *The House of the Seven Gables* edited by Seymour Gross

HAWTHORNE *Nathaniel Hawthorne's Tales* edited by James McIntosh

HAWTHORNE *The Scarlet Letter* edited by Seymour Gross, Sculley Bradley, Richmond Croom Beatty, and E. Hudson Long *Third Edition*

HERBERT *George Herbert and the Seventeenth-Century Religious Poets* selected and edited by Mario A. DiCesare

HERODOTUS *The Histories* translated and selected by Walter E. Blanco, edited by Walter E. Blanco and Jennifer Roberts

HOBBES *Leviathan* edited by Richard E. Flathman and David Johnston

HOMER *The Odyssey* translated and edited by Albert Cook *Second Edition*

HOWELLS *The Rise of Silas Lapham* edited by Don L. Cook

IBSEN *The Wild Duck* translated and edited by Dounia B. Christiani

JAMES *The Ambassadors* edited by S. P. Rosenbaum *Second Edition*

JAMES *The American* edited by James W. Tuttleton

JAMES *The Portrait of a Lady* edited by Robert D. Bamberg *Second Edition*

JAMES *Tales of Henry James* edited by Christof Wegelin

JAMES *The Turn of the Screw* edited by Deborah Esch and Jonathan Warren *Second Edition*

JAMES *The Wings of the Dove* edited by J. Donald Crowley and Richard A. Hocks

JONSON *Ben Jonson and the Cavalier Poets* selected and edited by Hugh Maclean

JONSON *Ben Jonson's Plays and Masques* selected and edited by Robert M. Adams

KAFKA *The Metamorphosis* translated and edited by Stanley Corngold

LAFAYETTE *The Princess of Clèves* edited and with a revised translation by John D. Lyons

MACHIAVELLI *The Prince* translated and edited by Robert M. Adams *Second Edition*

MALTHUS *An Essay on the Principle of Population* edited by Philip Appleman

MANN *Death in Venice* translated and edited by Clayton Koelb

MARX *The Communist Manifesto* edited by Frederic L. Bender

MELVILLE *The Confidence-Man* edited by Hershel Parker

MELVILLE *Moby-Dick* edited by Harrison Hayford and Hershel Parker

MEREDITH *The Egoist* edited by Robert M. Adams

Middle English Lyrics selected and edited by Maxwell S. Luria and Richard L. Hoffman

Middle English Romances selected and edited by Stephen H. A. Shepherd

MILL *Mill: The Spirit of the Age, On Liberty, The Subjection of Women* selected and edited by Alan Ryan